Jeremiah 2

A Commentary on the
Book of the Prophet Jeremiah
Chapters 26—52

by William L. Holladay

Edited by
Paul D. Hanson

**Fortress
Press**   Minneapolis

© 1989 by Augsburg Fortress

Library of Congress Catalog Card Number 88-45437
ISBN 0-8006-6022-6

Printed in the United States of America
Design by Kenneth Hiebert
Type set on an Ibycus System at Polebridge Press
3463K88   20-6022

MEMORIAE
LITTERATISSIMORUM
DEVOTISSIMORUMQUE
SANCTI HIERONYMI
ET JACOBI MUILENBURG
QUORUM NEUTER
COMMENTARIUM SUUM
DE LIBRO HIEREMIAE
ABSOLVERE POTUIT
AMBAE PARTES
HUIUS OPERIS
DEDICATAE SUNT

Contents
Jeremiah 2

The name *Hermeneia*, Greek ἑρμηνεία, has been chosen as the title of the commentary series to which this volume belongs. The word *Hermeneia* has a rich background in the history of biblical interpretation as a term used in the ancient Greek-speaking world for the detailed, systematic exposition of a scriptural work. It is hoped that the series, like its name, will carry forward this old and venerable tradition. A second, entirely practical reason for selecting the name lies in the desire to avoid a long descriptive title and its inevitable acronym, or worse, an unpronounceable abbreviation.

The series is designed to be a critical and historical commentary to the Bible without arbitrary limits in size or scope. It will utilize the full range of philological and historical tools, including textual criticism (often slighted in modern commentaries), the methods of the history of tradition (including genre and prosodic analysis), and the history of religion.

Hermeneia is designed for the serious student of the Bible. It will make full use of ancient Semitic and classical languages; at the same time, English translations of all comparative materials—Greek, Latin, Canaanite, or Akkadian—will be supplied alongside the citation of the source in its original language. Insofar as possible, the aim is to provide the student or scholar with full critical discussion of each problem of interpretation and with the primary data upon which the discussion is based.

Hermeneia is designed to be international and interconfessional in the selection of authors; its editorial boards were formed with this end in view. Occasionally the series will offer translations of distinguished commentaries which originally appeared in languages other than English. Published volumes of the series will be revised continually, and eventually, new commentaries will replace older works in order to preserve the currency of the series. Commentaries are also being assigned for important literary works in the categories of apocryphal and pseudepigraphical works relating to the Old and New Testaments, including some of Essene or Gnostic authorship.

The editors of *Hermeneia* impose no systematic-theological perspective upon the series (directly, or indirectly by selection of authors). It is expected that authors will struggle to lay bare the ancient meaning of a biblical work or pericope. In this way the text's human relevance should become transparent, as is always the case in competent historical discourse. However, the series eschews for itself homiletical translation of the Bible.

The editors are heavily indebted to Augsburg Fortress for its energy and courage in taking up an expensive, long-term project, the rewards of which will accrue chiefly to the field of biblical scholarship.

Frank Moore Cross	*Helmut Koester*
For the Old Testament	For the New Testament
Editorial Board	Editorial Board

The present volume completes my study of the book of Jeremiah begun in *Jeremiah 1*. That volume likewise contained an Author's Foreword (pp. xi–xiii); much of what is said there is relevant for the present volume as well and hardly needs reiteration —the distinction between the abbreviations Jer (for the book) and Jrm (for the prophet), the use in the translation of single diagonal brackets ⟨ ⟩ for words gained from a revocalization of the consonantal text and of double brackets ⟪ ⟫ for words gained by an emendation of the consonantal text, and the like.

But a further word must be said about the citation of Ugaritic texts. These are cited as in Richard E. Whitaker, *A Concordance of the Ugaritic Literature* (Cambridge: Harvard University, 1972). That is, texts contained in Andrée Herdner, *Corpus des tablettes en cunéiformes alphabétiques* (Paris: Imprimerie Nationale, 1963), are listed by the Herdner numbers; texts published in Charles Virolleaud, *Le Palais royal d'Ugarit* II and V (Paris: Imprimerie Nationale, 1957, 1965) are listed by numbers in the 1000s and 2000s respectively (as in Cyrus H. Gordon, *Ugaritic Textbook* [Rome: Pontifical Biblical Institute, 1965]); texts published in Jean Nougayrol et al., *Ugaritica* V (Paris: Imprimerie Nationale, 1968), are listed as UG5.

The present volume contains an exegesis of chapters 26—52, a general introduction, a general bibliography (which has a brief explanation at its head), and indices covering both volumes (explanation for which is likewise found at their head).

I should like to express my appreciation to Professor Nahman Avigad of the Institute of Archaeology of the Hebrew University of Jerusalem for permission to use a photograph of the bulla of Baruch for the endpapers of this volume. And once more I should like to express appreciation to my son David F. Holladay for the word-processing program he designed for my use and for his processing of the data disks to render them useful for publication. Without the aid of such a word processor I should doubtless still be typing drafts of my treatment of some early chapter of Jer.

The dedication of my work is to the memories of Saint Jerome and of James Muilenburg. Inasmuch as Jerome did not know English, it seemed appropriate to draft a Latin dedication.

February 1988   *William L. Holladay*

1. Sources and Abbreviations

The abbreviations used for biblical books are in common use. The abbreviations of names of Dead Sea Scrolls and related texts conform to the sigla in Joseph A. Fitzmyer, *The Dead Sea Scrolls: Major Publications and Tools for Study* (SBLSBS 8; Missoula, MT: Scholars, 1975) 3–53. Note also the form for rabbinic literaure: *m. Ta'an.* refers to the Mishna, tractate Ta'anit; *b. Šabb.* refers to the Babylonian Talmud, tractate Šabbat; *Midr. Cant.* refers to the Midrash on Canticles.

a'	Aquila
AASOR	Annual of the American Schools of Oriental Research
AB	Anchor Bible
AHR	*American Historical Review*
AJBA	*Australian Journal of Biblical Archaeology*
AJSL	*American Journal of Semitic Languages and Literature*
AJT	*American Journal of Theology*
ALUOS	Annual of Leeds University Oriental Society
AnBib	Analecta biblica
ANEP	*Ancient Near East in Pictures* (ed. J. B. Pritchard)
ANET	*Ancient Near Eastern Texts* (ed. J. B. Pritchard)
AnOr	Analecta orientalia
ANQ	*Andover Newton Quarterly*
Anton	*Antonianum*
AOAT	Alter Orient und Altes Testament
ARW	*Archiv für Religionswissenschaft*
ASTI	*Annual of the Swedish Theological Institute*
ATANT	Abhandlungen zur Theologie des Alten und Neuen Testaments
ATD	Das Alte Testament Deutsch
AusBR	*Australian Biblical Review*
AUSS	*Andrews University Seminary Studies*
BA	*Biblical Archaeologist*
BAG	W. Bauer, W. F. Arndt, and F. W. Gingrich, *Greek-English Lexicon of the New Testament*
BAR	*Biblical Archaeologist Reader*
BASOR	*Bulletin of the American Schools of Oriental Research*
BASP	*Bulletin of the American Society of Papyrologists*
BBB	Bonner biblische Beiträge
BDB	F. Brown, S. R. Driver, and C. A. Briggs, *Hebrew and English Lexicon of the Old Testament*
BeO	*Bibbia e oriente*
BETL	Bibliotheca ephemeridum theologicarum lovaniensium

BFCT	Beiträge zur Förderung christlicher Theologie
BHH	*Biblisch-Historisches Handwörterbuch* (ed. B. Reicke and L. Rost)
BHK	R. Kittel, *Biblia hebraica*
BHS	*Biblia hebraica stuttgartensia*
Bib	*Biblica*
BibLeb	*Bibel und Leben*
BibOr	Biblica et orientalia
BibS(N)	Biblische Studien (Neukirchen, 1951–)
BJRL	*Bulletin of the John Rylands University Library of Manchester*
BK	*Bibel und Kirche*
BKAT	Biblischer Kommentar: Altes Testament
BLit	*Bibel und Liturgie*
BN	*Biblische Notizen*
BO	*Bibliotheca orientalis*
BR	*Biblical Research*
BT	*The Bible Translator*
BTB	*Biblical Theology Bulletin*
BVC	*Bible et vie chrétienne*
BWANT	*Beiträge zur Wissenschaft vom Alten und Neuen Testament*
BZ	*Biblische Zeitschrift*
BZAW	Beihefte zur *ZAW*
ca.	*circa*, approximately
CAH	*Cambridge Ancient History*
CBQ	*Catholic Biblical Quarterly*
CBQMS	*CBQ* Monograph Series
CChr	Corpus Christianorum
CJT	*Canadian Journal of Theology*
ConB	Coniectanea biblica
CTM	*Concordia Theological Monthly*
DBSup	*Dictionnaire de la Bible, Supplement*
DISO	C.-F. Jean and J. Hoftijzer, *Dictionnaire des inscriptions sémitiques de l'ouest*
DJD	Discoveries in the Judaean Desert
DTC	*Dictionnaire de théologique catholique*
EBib	Etudes bibliques
ed(s).	editor(s), edited by, edition
EncJud	*Encyclopaedia judaica* (1971)
EstBib	*Estudios bíblicos*
ETL	*Ephemerides theologicae lovanienses*
ETR	*Etudes théologiques et religieuses*
EvQ	*Evangelical Quarterly*
EvT	*Evangelische Theologie*
ExpTim	*Expository Times*
FRLANT	Forschungen zur Religion und Literatur des Alten und Neuen Testaments
G	Septuagint; note also G^B = codex Vaticanus, etc.
GKC	*Gesenius' Hebrew Grammar* (ed. E. Kautzsch, tr. A. E. Cowley)
Greg	*Gregorianum*

HALAT	W. Baumgartner et al., *Hebräisches und aramäisches Lexikon zum Alten Testament*		*NRT*	*La nouvelle revue théologique*
HAT	Handbuch zum Alten Testament		NS	new series
HDR	Harvard Dissertations in Religion		NT	New Testament
Hermeneia	Hermeneia—A Critical and Historical Commentary on the Bible		NTD	Das Neue Testament Deutsch
HKAT	Handkommentar zum Alten Testament		OBO	Orbis Biblicus et Orientalis
HSM	Harvard Semitic Monographs		*OrAnt*	*Oriens antiquus*
HTR	*Harvard Theological Review*		OT	Old Testament
HUCA	*Hebrew Union College Annual*		*OTS*	*Oudtestamentische Studiën*
IB	*Interpreter's Bible*		*PEFQS*	*Palestine Exploration Fund, Quarterly Statement*
ICC	International Critical Commentary		*PEQ*	*Palestine Exploration Quarterly*
IDB	*Interpreter's Dictionary of the Bible* (ed. G. A. Buttrick)		*PJ*	*Palästina-Jahrbuch*
IDBSup	Supplementary volume to *IDB*		PL	J. Migne, *Patrologia latina*
IEJ	*Israel Exploration Journal*		*PRU*	*Le Palais royal d'Ugarit*
Int	*Interpretation*		*RB*	*Revue biblique*
JA	*Journal asiatique*		rep.	reprinted
JAAR	*Journal of the American Academy of Religion*		*RevExp*	*Review and Expositor*
JAOS	*Journal of the American Oriental Society*		*RevQ*	*Revue de Qumran*
JB	*Jerusalem Bible* (ed. A. Jones)		*RevScRel*	*Revue des sciences religieuses*
JBL	*Journal of Biblical Literature*		*RGG*	*Religion in Geschichte und Gegenwart*
JBR	*Journal of Bible and Religion*		*RHPR*	*Revue d'histoire et de philosophie religieuses*
JJS	*Journal of Jewish Studies*		*RHR*	*Revue de l'histoire des religions*
JNES	*Journal of Near Eastern Studies*		*RivB*	*Rivista biblica*
JQR	*Jewish Quarterly Review*		*RSO*	*Rivista degli studi orientali*
JR	*Journal of Religion*		*RSPT*	*Revue des sciences philosophiques et théologiques*
JSOT	*Journal for the Study of the Old Testament*		*RSR*	*Recherches de science religieuse*
JSS	*Journal of Semitic Studies*		*RSV*	*Revised Standard Version*
JTS	*Journal of Theological Studies*		*RTL*	*Revue théologique de Louvain*
KAI	H. Donner and W. Röllig, *Kanaanäische und aramäische Inschriften*		*RTP*	*Revue de théologie et de philosophie*
KAT	Kommentar zum A. T. (ed. E. Sellin)		S	Syriac version (Peshiṭta)
KB	L. Koehler and W. Baumgartner, *Lexicon in Veteris Testamenti libros*		s'	Symmachus
KD	*Kerygma und Dogma*		SBLDS	SBL Dissertation Series
KJV	*King James Version*		SBLMS	SBL Monograph Series
LCL	Loeb Classical Library		SBLSBS	SBL Sources for Bible Study
LD	Lectio divina		SBLSCS	SBL Septuagint and Cognate Studies
LSJ	Liddell-Scott-Jones, *Greek-English Lexicon*		SBLTT	SBL Texts and Translations
M	Masoretic Text		SBS	Stuttgarter Bibelstudien
McCQ	*McCormick Quarterly*		SBT	Studies in Biblical Theology
MS(S).	manuscript(s)		*ScEs*	*Science et Esprit*
MUSJ	*Mélanges de l'université Saint-Joseph*		*SEÅ*	*Svensk exegetisk Årsbok*
NAB	*New American Bible*		sec(s).	section(s)
NEB	*New English Bible*		*Sem*	*Semitica*
NF	Neue Folge, new series		SOTSMS	Society for Old Testament Study Monograph Series
NICOT	New International Commentary on the Old Testament		SSS	Semitic Study Series
NJV	*New Jewish Version* (The Jewish Publication Society of America)		*ST*	*Studia theologica*
NKZ	*Neue kirchliche Zeitschrift*		Str-B	[H. Strack and] P. Billerbeck, *Kommentar zum Neuen Testament*
NorTT	*Norsk Teologisk Tidsskrift*		*s.v.*	*sub verbo* or *sub voce*, under the word (entry)
NovT	*Novum Testamentum*		*T*	Targum
NovTSup	*Novum Testamentum*, Supplements		*θ'*	Theodotion
			TBl	*Theologische Blätter*
			TBT	*The Bible Today*
			TBü	Theologische Bücherei
			TDNT	*Theological Dictionary of the New*

	Testament (ed. G. Kittel and G. Friedrich)
TDOT	*Theological Dictionary of the Old Testament* (ed. G. J. Botterweck and H. Ringgren)
TGl	*Theologie und Glaube*
TLZ	*Theologische Literaturzeitung*
TPQ	*Theologisch-Pratische Quartalschrift*
TQ	*Theologische Quartalschrift*
tr.	translation, translated by
TRu	*Theologische Rundschau*
TSK	*Theologische Studien und Kritiken*
TToday	*Theology Today*
TU	Texte und Untersuchungen zur Geschichte der altchristlichen Literatur
TWAT	*Theologisches Wörterbuch zum Alten Testament* (ed. G. J. Botterweck and H. Ringgren)
TZ	*Theologische Zeitschrift*
UF	*Ugarit Forschungen*
Ug.	Ugaritic texts, Herdner numbers (see Author's Foreword)
USQR	*Union Seminary Quarterly Review*
UT	C. H. Gordon, *Ugaritic Textbook*
V	Vulgate
VCaro	*Verbum Caro*
VD	*Verbum domini*
VSpir	*Vie spirituelle*
VT	*Vetus Testamentum*
VTSup	*Vetus Testamentum*, Supplements
WMANT	Wissenschaftliche Monographien zum Alten und Neuen Testament
WO	*Die Welt des Orients*
ZAW	*Zeitschrift für die alttestamentliche Wissenschaft*
ZDMG	*Zeitschrift der deutschen morgenländischen Gesellschaft*
ZDPV	*Zeitschrift des deutschen Palästina-Vereins*
ZKT	*Zeitschrift für katholische Theologie*
ZTK	*Zeitschrift für Theologie und Kirche*

2. Short Titles of Commentaries, Studies, and Articles Often Cited

Aharoni, *Land of the Bible*
Yohanan Aharoni, *The Land of the Bible, A Historical Geography* (Philadelphia: Westminster, 1967).

Alonso Schökel, "Esperanza"
Luis Alonso Schökel, "'Tú eres la esperanza de Israel' (Jer 17,5–13)," *Künder des Wortes, Beiträge zur Theologie der Propheten* (ed. Lothar Ruppert et al.; Würzburg: Echter, 1982) 95–104.

Alonso Schökel, "Jeremías como anti-Moisés"
Luis Alonso Schökel, "Jeremías como anti-Moisés," *De la Tôrah au Messie, Mélanges Henri Cazelles* (ed. M. Carrez, J. Doré, and P. Grelot; Paris: Desclée, 1981) 245–54.

American Translation
J. M. Powis Smith et al., and Edgar J. Goodspeed, *The Complete Bible, An American Translation* (Chicago: University of Chicago, 1939).

Amiran, *Ancient Pottery*
Ruth Amiran, *Ancient Pottery of the Holy Land* (New Brunswick, NJ: Rutgers University, 1970).

Avigad, "Baruch the Scribe and Jerahmeel the King's son"
Nahman Avigad, "Baruch the Scribe and Jerahmeel the King's Son," *IEJ* 28 (1978) 52–56.

Avigad, "Jerahmeel and Baruch"
Nahman Avigad, "Jerahmeel & Baruch, King's Son and Scribe," *BA* 42 (1979) 114–18.

Bach, *Flucht*
Robert Bach, *Die Aufforderungen zur Flucht und zum Kampf im alttestamentlichen Prophetenspruch* (WMANT 9; Neukirchen: Neukirchener, 1962).

Bailey-Holladay
Kenneth E. Bailey and William L. Holladay, "The 'Young Camel' and 'Wild Ass' in Jeremiah ii 23–25," *VT* 18 (1968) 256–60.

Baldwin, "Ṣemaḥ"
Joyce G. Baldwin, "Ṣemaḥ as a Technical Term in the Prophets," *VT* 16 (1964) 93–97.

Baltzer, *Covenant Formulary*
Klaus Baltzer, *The Covenant Formulary in Old Testament, Jewish, and Early Christian Writings* (Philadelphia: Fortress, 1971).

Baly, *Geography*
Denis Baly, *The Geography of the Bible* (New York: Harper, 1974).

Bardtke, "Fremdvölkerprophet"
Hans Bardtke, "Jeremia der Fremdvölkerprophet," *ZAW* 53 (1935) 209–39; 54 (1936) 240–62.

Barnett, *Nimrud Ivories*
Richard D. Barnett, *A Catalogue of the Nimrud Ivories, with other examples of Ancient Near Eastern Ivories in the British Museum* (London: Trustees of the British Museum, 1957).

Barrois, *Manuel*
Augustin-Georges Barrois, *Manuel d'archéologie biblique* I (Paris: Picard, 1939).

Bauer-Leander
Hans Bauer and Pontus Leander, *Historische Grammatik der hebräischen Sprache des Alten Testaments* (Halle: Niemeyer, 1922; rep. Hildesheim: Olms, 1965).

Baumgartner, *Klagegedichte*
Walter Baumgartner, *Die Klagegedichte des Jeremia* (BZAW 32; Giessen: Töpelmann, 1917).

Bennett, "Edom"
Crystal-Margaret Bennett, "Edom," *IDBSup* 251–52.

Berridge
John M. Berridge, *Prophet, People, and the Word of Yahweh, An Examination of Form and Content in the Proclamation of the Prophet Jeremiah* (Basel Studies of Theology 4; Zürich: EVZ, 1970).

Berridge, "Jeremia und die Prophetie des Amos"
John M. Berridge, "Jeremia und die Prophetie des Amos," *TZ* 35 (1979) 321–41.

Beuken and van Grol
W. A. M. Beuken and H. W. M. van Grol, "Jeremiah 14,1—15,9: A Situation of Distress and Its Hermeneutics, Unity and Diversity of Form—Dramatic Development," *Le Livre de Jérémie, le prophète et son milieu, les oracles et leur transmission* (ed. Pierre-Maurice Bogaert; BETL 54; Leuven: Leuven University, 1981) 297–342.

Bodenheimer, "Fauna"
Friedrich S. Bodenheimer, "Fauna," *IDB* 2:246–56.

Boecker, *Redeformen*
Hans Jochen Boecker, *Redeformen des Rechtslebens im Alten Testament* (WMANT 14; Neukirchen: Neukirchener, 1964).

Boling and Wright, *Joshua*
Robert G. Boling and G. Ernest Wright, *Joshua* (AB 6; Garden City, NY: Doubleday, 1982).

Brenner, *Colour Terms*
Athalya Brenner, *Colour Terms in the Old Testament* (JSOT Supplement Series 21; Sheffield: JSOT, 1982).

Bright
John Bright, *Jeremiah* (AB 21; Garden City, NY: Doubleday, 1965).

Bright, "Apodictic Prohibition"
John Bright, "The Apodictic Prohibition: Some Observations," *JBL* 92 (1973) 185–204.

Bright, *History*
John Bright, *A History of Israel* (Philadelphia: Westminster, 1981).

Bright, "Jeremiah's Complaints"
John Bright, "Jeremiah's Complaints—Liturgy or Expressions of Personal Distress?" *Proclamation and Presence, Old Testament Essays in Honour of Gwynne Henton Davies* (ed. John I. Durham and J. Roy Porter; Richmond: Knox, 1970), 189–214.

Brongers, "Zornesbecher"
Hendrik A. Brongers, "Der Zornesbecher," *OTS* 15 (Leiden: Brill, 1969) 177–92.

Brueggemann, "Crisis"
Walter A. Brueggemann, "The Epistemological Crisis of Israel's Two Histories (Jer 9:22–23)," *Israelite Wisdom, Theological and Literary Essays in Honor of Samuel Terrien* (ed. John G. Gammie et al.; Missoula, MT: Scholars, 1978) 85–105.

Budde, "Erste Kapitel"
Karl Budde, "Über das erste Kapitel des Buches Jeremia," *JBL* 40 (1921) 23–37.

Burrows, "Jerusalem"
Millar Burrows, "Jerusalem," *IDB* 2:843–66.

Calvin
John Calvin, *Commentaries on the Book of the Prophet Jeremiah and the Lamentations* (Calvin Translation Society, 1850–55, rep. Grand Rapids: Eerdmans, 1950).

Carroll
Robert P. Carroll, *Jeremiah, A Commentary* (Philadelphia: Westminster, 1986).

Castellino, "Observations"
Giorgio R. Castellino, "Observations on the Literary Structure of Some Passages in Jeremiah," *VT* 30 (1980) 398–408.

Charlesworth, *OTP*
The Old Testament Pseudepigrapha (ed. James H. Charlesworth; Garden City, NY: Doubleday, 1983, 1985).

Childs, *Exodus*
Brevard S. Childs, *The Book of Exodus, A Critical, Exegetical Commentary* (Philadelphia: Westminster, 1974).

Childs, *Isaiah and the Assyrian Crisis*
Brevard S. Childs, *Isaiah and the Assyrian Crisis* (SBT 2d Series 3; Naperville, IL: Allenson, 1967).

Christensen, "Terror"
Duane L. Christensen, "'Terror on Every Side' in Jeremiah," *JBL* 92 (1973) 498–502.

Christensen, *Transformations*
Duane L. Christensen, *Transformations of the War Oracle in Old Testament Prophecy* (HDR 3; Missoula, MT: Scholars, 1975).

Clark, "Wine on the Lees"
David J. Clark, "Wine on the Lees (Zeph 1.12 and Jer 48.11)," *BT* 32 (1981) 241–43.

Cogan, "Sentencing"
Morton Cogan, "Sentencing at the Gate in Jeremiah 1:15–16," *Gratz College Annual* 1 (1972) 3–6.

Cohen, "Edom"
Simon Cohen, "Edom," *IDB* 2:24–26.

Condamin
Albert Condamin, *Le Livre de Jérémie* (EBib; Paris: Gabalda, 1936).

Cooke, *Ezekiel*
George A. Cooke, *A Critical and Exegetical Commentary on the Book of Ezekiel* (ICC; New York: Scribner's, 1936).

Cooke, *Inscriptions*
George A. Cooke, *A Textbook of North-Semitic Inscriptions* (Oxford: Clarendon, 1903).

Cornill
Carl H. Cornill, *Das Buch Jeremia* (Leipzig: Tauchnitz, 1905).

Cross, *CMHE*
Frank M. Cross, *Canaanite Myth and Hebrew Epic* (Cambridge: Harvard University, 1973).

Cross, "Scripts"
Frank M. Cross, "The Development of the Jewish Scripts" (ed. G. Ernest Wright), *The Bible and the Ancient Near East* (New York: Doubleday, 1961) 133–202.

Curtis and Madsen, *Chronicles*
Edward L. Curtis and Albert A. Madsen, *A Critical and Exegetical Commentary on the Books of Chronicles* (ICC; New York: Scribner's, 1910).

Dahood, "'ākal//kālāh"
Mitchell Dahood, "The Word-Pair 'ākal//kālāh in Jeremiah xxx 16," *VT* 27 (1977) 482.

Dahood, "Hebrew-Ugaritic Lexicography II"
Mitchell Dahood, "Hebrew-Ugaritic Lexicography II," *Bib* 45 (1964) 393–412.

Dahood, "Jeremiah 17,13"
Mitchell Dahood, "The Metaphor in Jeremiah 17,13," *Bib* 48 (1967) 109–10.

Dahood, "Jer 18,14–15"
Mitchell Dahood, "Philological Notes on Jer 18,14–15," *ZAW* 74 (1962) 207–9.

Dahood, *Psalms I, II, III*
Mitchell Dahood, *Psalms 1—50*, AB 16; *Psalms 51—100*, AB 17; *Psalms 101—150*, AB 17A (Garden City, NY: Doubleday, 1966, 1968, 1970).

Dahood, "Two Textual Notes"
Mitchell Dahood, "Two Textual Notes on Jeremiah," *CBQ* 23 (1961) 462–64.

De Roche, "Contra Creation"
Michael De Roche, "Contra Creation, Covenant and Conquest (Jer. viii 13)," *VT* 30 (1980) 280–90.

Driver, "Jeremiah"
Godfrey R. Driver, "Linguistic and Textual Problems: Jeremiah," *JQR* 28 (1937/38) 97–129.

Duhm
Bernhard Duhm, *Das Buch Jeremia* (Kurzer Hand-Commentar zum Alten Testament 11; Tübingen and Leipzig: Mohr [Siebeck], 1901).

Ehrlich, *Randglossen*
Arnold B. Ehrlich, *Randglossen zur hebräischen Bibel* 4 (Leipzig: Hinrichs, 1912).

Eichrodt, *Theology 1, 2*
Walther Eichrodt, *Theology of the Old Testament* (Philadelphia: Westminster, 1961, 1967).

Eissfeldt, "Drohorakel"
Otto Eissfeldt, "Jeremias Drohorakel gegen Ägypten und gegen Babel," *Verbannung und*

Heimkehr, Beiträge zur Geschichte und Theologie Israels im 6. und 5. Jahrhundert v. Chr., Wilhelm Rudolph zum 70. Geburtstage (Tübingen: Mohr [Siebeck], 1961) 31–37 = *Kleine Schriften* 4 (Tübingen: Mohr [Siebeck], 1968) 32–38.

Eissfeldt, *Introduction*
Otto Eissfeldt, *The Old Testament, An Introduction* (Oxford: Blackwell, 1965).

Elliger, *Deuterojesaja*
Karl Elliger, *Deuterojesaja* (BKAT 11/1; Neukirchen: Neukirchener, 1978).

Emerton, "Jeremiah vi. 23 and l. 42"
John A. Emerton, "A Problem in the Hebrew Text of Jeremiah vi. 23 and l. 42," *JTS* NS 23 (1972) 106–13.

Fishbane, "Revelation and Tradition"
Michael A. Fishbane, "Revelation and Tradition: Aspects of Inner-Biblical Exegesis," *JBL* 99 (1980) 343–61.

Fohrer, "Gattung der Berichte über symbolische Handlungen"
Georg Fohrer, "Die Gattung der Berichte über symbolische Handlungen der Propheten," *ZAW* 64 (1952) 101–20 = *Studien zur alttestamentlichen Prophetie (1949–1965)* (BZAW 99; Berlin: Töpelmann, 1967) 92–112.

Fontaine, *Traditional Sayings*
Carole R. Fontaine, *Traditional Sayings in the Old Testament* (Bible and Literature Series 5; Sheffield: Almond, 1982).

Forbes, "Chemical, Culinary, and Cosmetic Arts"
Robert J. Forbes, "Chemical, Culinary, and Cosmetic Arts," *A History of Technology* I (ed. Charles Singer, E. J. Holmyard, and A. R. Hall; Oxford: Oxford University, 1954) 238–98.

Forbes, "Extracting, Smelting, and Alloying"
Robert J. Forbes, "Extracting, Smelting, and Alloying," *A History of Technology* I (ed. Charles Singer, E. J. Holmyard, and A. R. Hall; Oxford: Oxford University, 1954) 572–99.

Forbes, *Metallurgy*
Robert J. Forbes, *Metallurgy in Antiquity* (Leiden: Brill, 1950).

Forbes, *Studies 8*
Robert J. Forbes, *Studies in Ancient Technology* VIII (Leiden: Brill, 1964).

Freedman
Harry Freedman, *Jeremiah* (Soncino Books of the Bible; London: Soncino, 1949).

Frick, "The Rechabites Reconsidered"
Frank S. Frick, "The Rechabites Reconsidered," *JBL* 90 (1971) 279–87.

Gemser
Berend Gemser, "The *rîb-* or Controversy-Pattern in Hebrew Mentality," *Wisdom in Israel and in the Ancient Near East, Presented to Professor Harold Henry Rowley by the Society for Old Testament Study in Association with the Editorial Board of Vetus Testamentum in Celebration of His Sixty-fifth Birthday, 24*

March 1955 (ed. Martin Noth and D. Winton Thomas; VTSup 3; Leiden: Brill, 1955) 120–37.

Giesebrecht
Friedrich Giesebrecht, *Das Buch Jeremia* (HKAT 3,2; Göttingen: Vandenhoeck & Ruprecht, 1907).

Ginsburg, *Introduction*
Christian D. Ginsburg, *Introduction to the Massoretico-Critical Edition of the Hebrew Bible* (London: Trinitarian Bible Society, 1897; rep. New York: Ktav, 1966).

Glueck, *Explorations, III*
Nelson Glueck, *Explorations in Eastern Palestine, III* (AASOR 18–19; New Haven, CT: American Schools of Oriental Research, 1939).

Gray, "Bel"
John Gray, "Bel," *IDB* 1:376.

Gray, *Kings*
John Gray, *I & II Kings* (Philadelphia: Westminster, 1970).

Guillaume, *Prophecy and Divination*
Alfred Guillaume, *Prophecy and Divination Among the Hebrews and Other Semites* (London: Hodder & Stoughton, 1938).

Habel, "Call Narratives"
Norman Habel, "The Form and Significance of the Call Narratives," *ZAW* 77 (1965) 297–323.

Hanson, *Dawn of Apocalyptic*
Paul D. Hanson, *The Dawn of Apocalyptic* (Philadelphia: Fortress, 1975).

Harper, *Amos and Hosea*
William R. Harper, *A Critical and Exegetical Commentary on Amos and Hosea* (ICC; New York: Scribner's, 1905).

Harris, "Linguistic Structure"
Zellig S. Harris, "Linguistic Structure of Hebrew," *JAOS* 61 (1941) 143–67.

Hatch-Redpath
Edwin Hatch and Henry A. Redpath, *A Concordance to the Septuagint and the Other Greek Versions of the Old Testament* (Oxford: Clarendon, 1897).

Heider
George C. Heider, *The Cult of Molek, A Reassessment* (JSOT Supplement Series 43; Sheffield: University of Sheffield, 1985).

Held, "Action-Result"
Moshe Held, "The Action-Result (Factitive-Passive) Sequence of Identical Verbs in Biblical Hebrew and Ugaritic," *JBL* 84 (1965) 272–82.

Herr, *Scripts*
Larry G. Herr, *The Scripts of Ancient Northwest Semitic Seals* (HSM 18; Missoula, MT: Scholars, 1978).

J. Herrmann, "Jer 22,29; 7,4"
Johannes Herrmann, "Zu Jer 22,29; 7,4," *ZAW* 62 (1949–50) 321–22.

Heschel, *The Prophets*
Abraham J. Heschel, *The Prophets* (New York and Evanston: Harper, 1962).

Hillers, *Micah*
  Delbert R. Hillers, *Micah* (Hermeneia; Philadelphia: Fortress, 1984).

Hillers, *Treaty-Curses*
  Delbert R. Hillers, *Treaty-Curses and the Old
  Testament Prophets* (BibOr 26; Rome: Pontifical
  Biblical Institute, 1964).

Hoffmeier, "Apries"
  James K. Hoffmeier, "A New Insight on Pharaoh
  Apries from Herodotus, Diodorus and Jeremiah
  46:17," *Journal of the Society for the Study of Egyptian
  Antiquities* 11 (1981) 165–70.

Holladay, *Architecture*
  William L. Holladay, *The Architecture of Jeremiah
  1—20* (Lewisburg, PA: Bucknell University,
  1976).

Holladay, "Background"
  William L. Holladay, "The Background of
  Jeremiah's Self-Understanding: Moses, Samuel,
  and Psalm 22," *JBL* 83 (1964) 153–64.

Holladay, "Coherent Chronology"
  William L. Holladay, "A Coherent Chronology of
  Jeremiah's Early Career," *Le Livre de Jérémie, le
  prophète et son milieu, les oracles et leur transmission*
  (ed. Pierre-Maurice Bogaert; BETL 54; Leuven:
  Leuven University, 1981) 58–73.

Holladay, "Deuteronomic Gloss"
  William L. Holladay, "The So-Called 'Deuteronomic Gloss' in Jer. viii 19b," *VT* 12 (1962) 494–
  98.

Holladay, "Identification"
  William L. Holladay, "The Identification of the
  Two Scrolls of Jeremiah," *VT* 30 (1980) 452–67.

Holladay, "Jer 20:1–6"
  William L. Holladay, "The Covenant with the
  Patriarchs Overturned: Jeremiah's Intention in
  'Terror on Every Side' (Jer 20:1–6)," *JBL* 91
  (1972) 305–20.

Holladay, *Jeremiah 1*
  William L. Holladay, *Jeremiah 1* (Hermeneia;
  Philadelphia: Fortress, 1986).

Holladay, "Jeremiah and Moses: Further Observa-
tions"
  William L. Holladay, "Jeremiah and Moses:
  Further Observations," *JBL* 85 (1966) 17–27.

Holladay, "Lawsuit"
  William L. Holladay, "Jeremiah's Lawsuit with
  God," *Int* 17 (1963) 280–87.

Holladay, "On Every High Hill"
  William L. Holladay, "'On Every High Hill and
  Under Every Green Tree,'" *VT* 11 (1961) 170–
  76.

Holladay, "Prototype"
  William L. Holladay, "Prototype and Copies: A
  New Approach to the Poetry-Prose Problem in
  the Book of Jeremiah," *JBL* 79 (1960) 351–67.

Holladay, "Recovery"
  William L. Holladay, "The Recovery of Poetic
  Passages of Jeremiah," *JBL* 85 (1966) 401–35.

Holladay, *Spokesman*
  William L. Holladay, *Jeremiah, Spokesman Out of
  Time* (New York: Pilgrim, 1974).

Holladay, "Style"
  William L. Holladay, "Style, Irony and Authenticity in Jeremiah," *JBL* 81 (1962) 44–54.

Holladay, *Šûbh*
  William L. Holladay, *The Root Šûbh in the Old
  Testament, With Particular Reference to Its Usages in
  Covenantal Contexts* (Leiden: Brill, 1958).

Holm-Nielsen, "Shiloh"
  Svend Holm-Nielsen, "Shiloh (City)," *IDBSup*,
  322–23.

Hubmann, *Untersuchungen*
  Franz D. Hubmann, *Untersuchungen zu den Konfessionen, Jer 11,18—12,6 und Jer 15,10–21* (Forschung zur Bibel 30; Würzburg: Echter, 1978).

Hyatt
  J. Philip Hyatt, "Introduction and Exegesis,
  Jeremiah," *IB* 5:775–1142.

Jacob, "Mourning"
  Edmond Jacob, "Mourning," *IDB* 3:452–54.

Jacobsen, "Babylon"
  Thorkild Jacobsen, "Babylon (OT)," *IDB* 1:334–
  38.

Janzen
  J. Gerald Janzen, *Studies in the Text of Jeremiah*
  (HSM 6; Cambridge: Harvard University, 1973).

Jastrow
  Marcus Jastrow, *A Dictionary of the Targumim, the
  Talmud Babli and Yerushalmi, and the Midrashic
  Literature* (New York: Putnam, 1903).

Jerome
  (S.) *Hieronymi Presbyteri in Hieremiam Prophetam,
  Libri Sex* (ed. Siegfried Reiter; CChr, Series Latina
  74; Turnhout: Brepols, 1960).

Johnson, *Cultic Prophet*
  Aubrey R. Johnson, *The Cultic Prophet in Ancient
  Israel* (Cardiff: University of Wales, 1962).

Johnson, *Vitality of the Individual*
  Aubrey R. Johnson, *The Vitality of the Individual in
  the Thought of Ancient Israel* (Cardiff: University of
  Wales, 1949).

Joüon, *Gramm.*
  Paul Joüon, *Grammaire de l'Hébreu Biblique* (Rome:
  Pontifical Biblical Institute, 1947).

Kelso, "Pottery"
  James L. Kelso, "Pottery," *IDB* 3:846–53.

Knox
  Ronald Knox, *The Holy Bible, A Translation from the
  Latin Vulgate in the Light of the Hebrew and Greek
  Originals* (New York: Sheed & Ward, 1954).

Koch, *Growth*
  Klaus Koch, *The Growth of the Biblical Tradition, The
  Form-Critical Method* (New York: Scribner's, 1969).

König, *Syntax*
  Eduard König, *Historisch-Comparative Syntax der
  hebräischen Sprache* (Leipzig: Hinrichs, 1897).

Kraus, *Psalmen*
Hans-Joachim Kraus, *Psalmen* (BKAT 15; Neukirchen: Neukirchener, 1961).

Kraus, *Worship*
Hans-Joachim Kraus, *Worship in Israel* (Richmond: Knox, 1966).

Kugel, *Poetry*
James F. Kugel, *The Idea of Biblical Poetry* (New Haven and London: Yale University, 1981).

Kumaki
F. Kenro Kumaki, "A New Look at Jer 4,19–22 and 10,19–21," *Annual of the Japanese Biblical Institute* 8 (1982) 113–22.

Kuschke, "Jeremia 48,1–8"
Arnulf Kuschke, "Jeremia 48,1–8. Zugleich ein Beitrag zur historischen Topographie Moabs," *Verbannung und Heimkehr, Beiträge zur Geschichte und Theologie Israels im 6. und 5. Jahrhundert v. Chr., Wilhelm Rudolph zum 60. Geburtstage* (ed. Arnulf Kuschke; Tübingen: Mohr [Siebeck], 1961) 181–96.

Landes, "Jazer"
George M. Landes, "The Fountain at Jazer," *BASOR* 144 (December 1956) 30–37.

Lemaire, "*bn hmlk*"
André Lemaire, "Note sur le titre *bn hmlk* dans l'ancien Israël," *Sem* 29 (1979) 59–65.

Lemke, "Nebuchadrezzar"
Werner E. Lemke, "'Nebuchadrezzar, my Servant,'" *CBQ* 28 (1966) 45–50.

Lévi
Israel Lévi, *The Hebrew Text of the Book of Ecclesiasticus, Edited with Brief Notes and a Selected Glossary* (SSS 3; Leiden: Brill, 1904).

Limburg
James Limburg, "The Root ריב and the Prophetic Lawsuit Speeches," *JBL* 88 (1969) 291–304.

Lindblom, *Prophecy*
Johannes Lindblom, *Prophecy in Ancient Israel* (Oxford: Blackwell, 1963).

Lindblom, "Wisdom in the OT Prophets"
Johannes Lindblom, "Wisdom in the Old Testament Prophets," *Wisdom in Israel and in the Ancient Near East, Presented to Professor Harold Henry Rowley by the Society for Old Testament Study in Association with the Editorial Board of Vetus Testamentum in Celebration of His Sixty-fifth Birthday, 24 March 1955* (ed. Martin Noth and D. Winton Thomas; VTSup 3; Leiden: Brill, 1955) 192–204.

Lipiński, "אחרית הימים"
Edouard Lipiński, "אחרית הימים dans les textes préexiliques," *VT* 20 (1970) 445–50.

Lohfink, "Der junge Jeremia"
Norbert Lohfink, "Der junge Jeremia als Propagandist und Poet, Zum Grundstock von Jer 30—31," *Le Livre de Jérémie, le prophète et son milieu, les oracles et leur transmission* (ed. Pierre-Maurice Bogaert; BETL 54; Leuven: Leuven University, 1981) 351–68.

Lohfink, "Kurzgeschichte"
Norbert Lohfink, "Die Gattung der 'Historischen Kurzgeschichte' in den letzten Jahren von Juda und in der Zeit des babylonischen Exils," *ZAW* 90 (1978) 319–47.

Long, "Reports of Visions"
Burke O. Long, "Reports of Visions Among the Prophets," *JBL* 95 (1976), 353–65.

Long, "Schemata"
Burke O. Long, "Two Question and Answer Schemata in the Prophets," *JBL* 90 (1971) 129–39.

Luckenbill, *ARAB*
Daniel D. Luckenbill, *Ancient Records of Assyria and Babylonia* (2 vols.; Chicago: University of Chicago, 1927; rep. New York: Greenwood, 1968).

Lundbom, *Jeremiah*
Jack R. Lundbom, *Jeremiah, A Study in Ancient Hebrew Rhetoric* (SBLDS 18; Missoula, MT: Scholars, 1975).

Malamat, "Twilight of Judah"
Abraham Malamat, "The Twilight of Judah," *Congress Volume, Edinburgh 1974* (VTSup 28; Leiden: Brill, 1975) 123–45.

March, "Prophecy"
W. Eugene March, "Prophecy," *Old Testament Form Criticism* (ed. John H. Hayes; San Antonio: Trinity University, 1974) 141–77.

May, *Oxford Bible Atlas*
Herbert G. May, ed., *Oxford Bible Atlas* (London/New York: Oxford University, 1974).

Mayes, *Deuteronomy*
Arthur D. H. Mayes, *Deuteronomy* (The New Century Bible Commentary; Grand Rapids: Eerdmans, 1979).

Mays, *Micah*
James L. Mays, *Micah* (Philadelphia: Westminster, 1976).

McKane, "Jeremiah 13:12–14"
William McKane, "Jeremiah 13:12–14: A Problematic Proverb," *Israelite Wisdom, Theological and Literary Essays in Honor of Samuel Terrien* (ed. John Gammie et al.; Missoula, MT: Scholars, 1978) 107–20.

McKane, "משא"
William McKane, "משא in Jeremiah 23 $_{33-40}$," *Prophecy, Essays Presented to Georg Fohrer on His Sixty-fifth Birthday, 6 September 1980* (ed. John A. Emerton; BZAW 150; Berlin: de Gruyter, 1980) 35–54.

McKane, "Poison"
William McKane, "Poison, trial by ordeal and the cup of wrath," *VT* 30 (1980) 474–92.

McKane, *Prophets and Wise Men*
William McKane, *Prophets and Wise Men* (SBT 44; Naperville, IL: Allenson, 1965).

McKane, *Proverbs*
William McKane, *Proverbs, A New Approach* (Philadelphia: Westminster, 1970).

Mendenhall, *Tenth Generation*
George E. Mendenhall, *The Tenth Generation, The Origins of the Biblical Tradition* (Baltimore: Johns Hopkins, 1973).

Meyer, *Jeremia*
Ivo Meyer, *Jeremia und die falsche Propheten* (Göttingen: Vandenhoeck & Ruprecht, 1977).

Michaelis
Johann D. Michaelis, *Observationes Philologicae et Criticae in Jeremiae Vaticinia et Threnos* (Göttingen: Vandenhoeck & Ruprecht, 1793).

Migsch, *Das Ende Jerusalems*
Herbert Migsch, *Gottes Wort über das Ende Jerusalems, Eine literar-, stil- und gattungskritische Untersuchung des Berichtes Jeremia 34,1–7; 32,2–5; 37,3—38,28* (Österreichische Biblische Studien 2; Klosterneuburg: Österreichisches Katholisches Bibelwerk, 1981).

Moffatt
James Moffatt, *A New Translation of the Bible, Containing the Old and New Testaments* (New York: Harper, 1934).

Montgomery, *Kings*
James A. Montgomery, *A Critical and Exegetical Commentary on the Books of Kings* (ICC; New York: Scribner's, 1951).

Moore, *Judges*
George F. Moore, *A Critical and Exegetical Commentary on Judges* (ICC; Edinburgh: Clark, 1895).

Mowinckel, "Drive and/or Ride"
Sigmund Mowinckel, "Drive and/or Ride in O.T.," *VT* 12 (1962) 278–99.

Mowinckel, *Komposition*
Sigmund Mowinckel, *Zur Komposition des Buches Jeremia* (Kristiania [= Oslo]: Dybwad, 1914).

Muilenburg, "Baruch"
James Muilenburg, "Baruch the Scribe," *Proclamation and Presence, Old Testament Essays in Honour of Gwynne Henton Davies* (ed. John I. Durham and J. Roy Porter; Richmond: Knox, 1970) 215–38.

Muilenburg, "Covenantal Formulations"
James Muilenburg, "The Form and Structure of the Covenantal Formulations," *VT* 9 (1959) 347–65.

Myers, *Ezra, Nehemiah*
Jacob M. Myers, *Ezra, Nehemiah* (AB 14; Garden City, NY: Doubleday, 1965).

Naegelsbach
C. W. Eduard Naegelsbach, *The Book of the Prophet Jeremiah, Theologically and Homiletically Expounded* (New York: Scribner's, 1886).

Nicholson, *Jer. 1—25, Jer. 26—52*
Ernest W. Nicholson, *The Book of the Prophet Jeremiah Chapters 1—25; The Book of the Prophet Jeremiah Chapters 26—52* (The Cambridge Bible Commentary on the New English Bible; Cambridge: Cambridge University, 1973, 1975).

Nicholson, *Preaching*
Ernest W. Nicholson, *Preaching to the Exiles, A Study of the Prose Tradition in the Book of Jeremiah* (Oxford: Blackwell, 1970).

Niditch, *Symbolic Vision*
Susan Niditch, *The Symbolic Vision in Biblical Tradition* (HSM 30; Chico, CA: Scholars, 1983).

Nielsen, *Oral Tradition*
Eduard Nielsen, *Oral Tradition* (SBT 11; Chicago: Allenson, 1954).

Noth, *Exodus*
Martin Noth, *Exodus* (Philadelphia: Westminster, 1962).

Noth, *Könige*
Martin Noth, *Könige I. 1–16* (BKAT 9/1; Neukirchen: Neukirchener, 1968).

Noth, *Leviticus*
Martin Noth, *Leviticus* (Philadelphia: Westminster, 1965).

Nötscher
Friedrich Nötscher, *Das Buch Jeremias* (Die Heilige Schrift des Alten Testaments 7,2; Bonn: Hanstein, 1934).

Nötscher, "Zum emphatischen Lamed"
Friedrich Nötscher, "Zum emphatischen Lamed," *VT* 3 (1953) 372–80.

O'Connor, *Structure*
Michael Patrick O'Connor, *Hebrew Verse Structure* (Winona Lake, IN: Eisenbrauns, 1980).

Oosterhoff, "Detail"
Berend J. Oosterhoff, "Ein Detail aus der Weisheitslehre (Jer. 9,11ff.)," *Travels in the World of the Old Testament, Studies Presented to Professor M. A. Beek on the Occasion of His 65th Birthday* (ed. M. S. H. G. Heerma von Voss et al.; Assen: Van Gorcum, 1974) 197–203.

Oppenheim, *Ancient Mesopotamia*
A. Leo Oppenheim, *Ancient Mesopotamia, Portrait of a Dead Civilization* (Chicago: University of Chicago, 1964).

Ottosson, *Gilead*
Magnus Ottosson, *Gilead, Tradition and History* (ConB, OT Series 3; Lund: Gleerup, 1969).

Overholt, *Falsehood*
Thomas W. Overholt, *The Threat of Falsehood, A Study in the Theology of the Book of Jeremiah* (SBT 2d Series 16; Naperville, IL: Allenson, 1970).

Overholt, "Idolatry"
Thomas W. Overholt, "The Falsehood of Idolatry: An Interpretation of Jer. x. 1–16," *JTS* NS 16 (1965) 1–12.

Pardee, "Epistolography"
Dennis Pardee, "An Overview of Ancient Hebrew Epistolography," *JBL* 97 (1978) 321–46.

Pardee, *Letters*
Dennis Pardee, *Handbook of Ancient Hebrew Letters* (SBLSBS 15; Chico, CA: Scholars, 1982).

Paton, "'Two Walls'"
　Lewis B. Paton, "The Meaning of the Expression
　'Between the Two Walls,'" *JBL* 25 (1906) 1–13.

Pedersen
　Johannes Pedersen, *Israel, Its Life and Culture*
　(Copenhagen: Branner; London: Oxford Univer-
　sity, 1926, 1940).

Percy, *Lead*
　John Percy, *The Metallurgy of Lead, Including
　Desilverization and Cupellation* (London: Murray,
　1870).

Percy, *Silver and Gold*
　John Percy, *Metallurgy: The Art of Extracting Metals
　from Their Ores, Silver and Gold, Part I* (London:
　Murray, 1880).

Petersen, *Haggai and Zechariah 1—8*
　David L. Petersen, *Haggai and Zechariah 1—8*
　(Philadelphia: Westminster, 1984).

Petersen, *Late Prophecy*
　David L. Petersen, *Late Israelite Prophecy: Studies in
　Deutero-Prophetic Literature and in Chronicles*
　(SBLMS 23; Missoula, MT: Scholars, 1977).

Phillips, "Nebalah"
　Anthony Phillips, "Nebalah," *VT* 25 (1975) 237–
　42.

Pohlmann, *Studien*
　Karl-Friedrich Pohlmann, *Studien zum Jeremiabuch,
　Ein Beitrag zur Frage nach der Entstehung des
　Jeremiabuches* (FRLANT 118; Göttingen: Vanden-
　hoeck & Ruprecht, 1978).

Pope, *Song of Songs*
　Marvin H. Pope, *Song of Songs* (AB 7C; Garden
　City, NY: Doubleday, 1977).

Porten, *Elephantine*
　Bezalel Porten, *Archives from Elephantine, The Life
　of an Ancient Jewish Military Colony* (Berkeley/Los
　Angeles: University of California, 1968).

Post, *Flora*
　George E. Post, *Flora of Syria, Palestine and Sinai*
　(Beirut: American, 1932–33).

Preuss, *Verspottung*
　Horst Dietrich Preuss, *Verspottung fremder
　Religionen im Alten Testament* (BWANT 92;
　Stuttgart: Kohlhammer, 1971).

von Rad, *Deuteronomy*
　Gerhard von Rad, *Deuteronomy* (Philadelphia:
　Westminster, 1966).

von Rad, *OT Theology 1, 2*
　Gerhard von Rad, *Old Testament Theology 1, 2*
　(New York: Harper, 1962, 1965).

von Rad, *Studies in Deuteronomy*
　Gerhard von Rad, *Studies in Deuteronomy* (SBT 9;
　Naperville, IL: Allenson, 1953).

von Rad, *Wisdom*
　Gerhard von Rad, *Wisdom in Israel* (Nashville:
　Abingdon, 1972).

Raitt, "Summons to Repentance"
　Thomas M. Raitt, "The Prophetic Summons to
　Repentance," *ZAW* 83 (1971) 30–49.

Ramsey, "Speech-Forms"
　George W. Ramsey, "Speech-Forms in Hebrew
　Law and Prophetic Oracles," *JBL* 96 (1977) 45–
　58.

Reed, "Burial"
　William L. Reed, "Burial," *IDB* 1:474–76.

Reventlow, *Liturgie*
　Henning Graf von Reventlow, *Liturgie und
　prophetisches Ich bei Jeremia* (Gütersloh: Gütersloher
　[Mohn], 1963).

Rietzschel, *Urrolle*
　Claus Rietzschel, *Das Problem der Urrolle, Ein
　Beitrag zur Redaktionsgeschichte des Jeremiabuches*
　(Gütersloh: Gütersloher [Mohn], 1966).

Roberts, "Athbash"
　Bleddyn J. Roberts, "Athbash," *IDB* 1:306–7.

Roberts, *Text and Versions*
　Bleddyn J. Roberts, *The Old Testament Text and
　Versions* (Cardiff: University of Wales, 1951).

Rudolph
　Wilhelm Rudolph, *Jeremia* (HAT 12; Tübingen:
　Mohr [Siebeck], 1968).

Sakenfeld
　Katherine D. Sakenfeld, *The Meaning of Ḥesed in
　the Hebrew Bible* (HSM 17; Missoula, MT: Scholars,
　1978).

Sauer, "Transjordan"
　James A. Sauer, "Transjordan in the Bronze and
　Iron Ages: A Critique of Glueck's Synthesis,"
　BASOR 263 (August 1986) 1–26.

Sawyer, "Partridge"
　John F. A. Sawyer, "A Note on the Brooding
　Partridge in Jeremiah xvii 11," *VT* 28 (1978) 324–
　29.

Scharbert, "ארר"
　Josef Scharbert, "ארר," *TDOT* 1:405–18.

Sebastian Schmidt
　Sebastian Schmidt, *Commentarii in Librum Prophe-
　tiarum Jeremiae* (Frankfurt am Main, 1706).

Schmidt, *Exodus*
　Werner H. Schmidt, *Exodus* (BKAT 2; Neu-
　kirchen: Neukirchener, 1974–).

Schottroff, "Horonaim"
　Willi Schottroff, "Horonaim, Nimrim, Luhith und
　der Westrand des 'Landes Ataroth,' Ein Beitrag
　zur historischen Topographie des Landes Moab,"
　ZDPV 82 (1966) 163–208.

Seidl, *Texte und Einheiten*
　Theodor Seidl, *Texte und Einheiten in Jeremia 27—
　29* (Arbeiten zu Text und Sprache im Alten
　Testament 2; St. Ottilien: EOS, 1977).

Seitz, *Studien*
　Gottfried Seitz, *Redaktionsgeschichtliche Studien zum
　Deuteronomium* (BWANT 93; Stuttgart: Kohl-
　hammer, 1971).

Sellin-Fohrer
　Ernst Sellin and Georg Fohrer, *Introduction to the
　Old Testament* (New York and Nashville: Abing-
　don, 1965).

van Selms, "Motivated Interrogative Sentences"
  Adriaan van Selms, "Motivated Interrogative
  Sentences in Biblical Hebrew," *Semitics* 2
  (1971/72) 143–49.
Shiloh and Tarler, "Bullae"
  Yigal Shiloh and David Tarler, "Bullae from the
  City of David: A Hoard of Seal Impressions from
  the Israelite Period," *BA* 49 (1986) 196–209.
Skinner
  John Skinner, *Prophecy and Religion, Studies in the
  Life of Jeremiah* (Cambridge: Cambridge Univer-
  sity, 1922).
Skweres, "Strafgrunderfragung"
  Dieter E. Skweres, "Das Motiv der Strafgrunder-
  fragung in biblischen und neuassyrischen
  Texten," *BZ* NF 14 (1970) 181–97.
Smith, *Historical Geography*
  George A. Smith, *The Historical Geography of the
  Holy Land* (London: Hodder & Stoughton, 1931;
  rep. Collins, 1966).
Snaith, "Jeremiah XLVI"
  John G. Snaith, "Literary Criticism and Historical
  Investigation in Jeremiah Chapter XLVI," *JSS* 16
  (1971) 15–32.
Soggin, *Joshua*
  J. Alberto Soggin, *Joshua* (Philadelphia: West-
  minster, 1972).
Speiser, *Genesis*
  Ephraim A. Speiser, *Genesis* (AB 1; Garden City,
  NY: Doubleday, 1964).
Stoebe, "Seelsorge"
  Hans Joachim Stoebe, "Seelsorge und Mitleiden
  bei Jeremia, Ein exegetischer Versuch," *Wort und
  Dienst* NF 4 (1955) 116–34.
Stulman, *Prose Sermons*
  Louis Stulman, *The Prose Sermons of the Book of
  Jeremiah, A Redescription of the Correspondences with
  the Deuteronomistic Literature in the Light of Recent
  Text-critical Research* (SBLDS 83; Atlanta: Scholars,
  1986).
Tawil, "Lexicographical Note"
  Hayim Tawil, "Hebrew צלח/הצלח, Akkadian
  ešēru/šūšuru: A Lexicographical Note," *JBL* 95
  (1976) 405–13.
Thiel, *Jer 1—25*
  Winfried Thiel, *Die deuteronomistische Redaktion von
  Jer 1—25* (WMANT 41; Neukirchen: Neu-
  kirchener, 1973).
Thiel, *Jer 26—45*
  Winfried Thiel, *Die deuteronomistische Redaktion von
  Jer 26—45* (WMANT 52; Neukirchen: Neu-
  kirchener, 1981).
Thomas, "מלאו"
  D. Winton Thomas, "מלאו in Jeremiah IV.5: A
  Military Term," *JJS* 3 (1952) 47–52.
Thompson
  John Arthur Thompson, *The Book of Jeremiah*
  (NICOT; Grand Rapids: Eerdmans, 1980).

Tov, *Jeremiah and Baruch*
  Emanuel Tov, *The Septuagint Translation of
  Jeremiah and Baruch, A Discussion of an Early
  Revision of the LXX of Jeremiah 29—52 and Baruch
  1:1—3:8* (HSM 8; Missoula, MT: Scholars, 1976).
Tov, "Textual and Literary History"
  Emanuel Tov, "Some Aspects of the Textual and
  Literary History of the Book of Jeremiah," *Le
  Livre de Jérémie, le prophète et son milieu, les oracles et
  leur transmission* (ed. Pierre-Maurice Bogaert;
  BETL 54; Leuven: Leuven University, 1981)
  145–67.
Toy, *Proverbs*
  Crawford H. Toy, *A Critical and Exegetical Com-
  mentary on the Book of Proverbs* (ICC; New York:
  Scribner's, 1899).
Trible, "God, nature of"
  Phyllis Trible, "God, nature of, in the OT,"
  IDBSup 368–69.
Trible, *Rhetoric*
  Phyllis Trible, *God and the Rhetoric of Sexuality*
  (Overtures to Biblical Theology; Philadelphia:
  Fortress, 1978).
Turkowski, "Peasant Agriculture"
  Lucian Turkowski, "Peasant Agriculture in the
  Judaean Hills," *PEQ* 202 (1969) 21–33, 101–12.
Vaggione, "Over All Asia?"
  Richard P. Vaggione, "Over All Asia? The Extent
  of the Scythian Domination in Herodotus," *JBL* 92
  (1973) 523–30.
Vaggione, "Scythians"
  Richard P. Vaggione, "Scythians," *IDBSup* 797–
  98.
Van Beek, "Tabor"
  Gus W. Van Beek, "Tabor, Mount," *IDB* 4:508–9.
Van Zyl, *Moabites*
  A. H. Van Zyl, *The Moabites* (Leiden: Brill, 1960).
de Vaux, *Ancient Israel*
  Roland de Vaux, *Ancient Israel, Its Life and Insti-
  tutions* (New York: McGraw-Hill, 1961).
Vawter, "Levitical Messianism"
  Bruce Vawter, "Levitical Messianism and the New
  Testament," *The Bible in Current Catholic Thought*
  (ed. John L. McKenzie; New York: Herder, 1962)
  83–99.
Vogel, *Bibliography I*
  Eleanor K. Vogel, *Bibliography of Holy Land Sites*,
  offprint from *HUCA* 42 (1971).
Vogel and Holtzclaw, *Bibliography II*
  Eleanor K. Vogel and Brooks Holtzclaw, *Bibliog-
  raphy of Holy Land Sites, Part II (1970–81)*, offprint
  from *HUCA* 52 (1981).
Volz
  Paul Volz, *Der Prophet Jeremia* (KAT 10; Leipzig:
  Deichert, 1928).
Wanke, *Baruchschrift*
  Gunther Wanke, *Untersuchungen zur sogenannten
  Baruchschrift* (BZAW 122; Berlin: de Gruyter,
  1971).

Weinfeld, "בְּרִית"
    Moshe Weinfeld, "בְּרִית," *TDOT* 2:253–79.
Weinfeld, *Deuteronomy*
    Moshe Weinfeld, *Deuteronomy and the Deuteronomic School* (Oxford: Clarendon, 1972).
Weinfeld, "Metamorphosis"
    Moshe Weinfeld, "Jeremiah and the Spiritual Metamorphosis of Israel," *ZAW* 88 (1976) 17–55.
Weippert, *Prosareden*
    Helga Weippert, *Die Prosareden des Jeremiabuches* (BZAW 132; Berlin: de Gruyter, 1973).
Weiser
    Artur Weiser, *Das Buch Jeremia* (ATD 20/21; Göttingen: Vandenhoeck & Ruprecht, 1969).
Westermann, *Basic Forms*
    Claus Westermann, *Basic Forms of Prophetic Speech* (Philadelphia: Westminster, 1967).
Westermann, *Genesis*
    Claus Westermann, *Genesis* (BKAT 1; Neukirchen: Neukirchener, 1974–82).
Westermann, *Isaiah 40—66*
    Claus Westermann, *Isaiah 40—66* (Philadelphia: Westminster, 1969).
Whybray, *Intellectual Tradition*
    Roger N. Whybray, *The Intellectual Tradition in the Old Testament* (BZAW 135; Berlin: de Gruyter, 1974).
Wildberger, *Jesaja*
    Hans Wildberger, *Jesaja* (BKAT 10; Neukirchen: Neukirchener, 1972–82).
Wilson, "Prophecy and Ecstasy"
    Robert R. Wilson, "Prophecy and Ecstasy: A Reexamination," *JBL* 98 (1979) 321–37.
Wilson, *Prophecy and Society*
    Robert R. Wilson, *Prophecy and Society in Ancient Israel* (Philadelphia: Fortress, 1980).
Wiseman, *Chronicles*
    Donald J. Wiseman, *Chronicles of Chaldaean Kings (626–556 B.C.)* (London: British Museum, 1956).
Wisser
    Laurent Wisser, *Jérémie, Critique de la vie sociale, Justice sociale et connaissance de Dieu dans le livre de Jérémie* (Le monde de la Bible; Geneva: Labor et Fides, 1982).
Wolff, *Anthropology*
    Hans Walter Wolff, *Anthropology of the Old Testament* (Philadelphia: Westminster, 1974).
Wolff, *Hosea*
    Hans Walter Wolff, *Hosea* (Hermeneia; Philadelphia: Fortress, 1974).
Wolff, *Joel and Amos*
    Hans Walter Wolff, *Joel and Amos* (Hermeneia; Philadelphia: Fortress, 1977).
Wolff, *Micha*
    Hans Walter Wolff, *Micha* (BKAT 14/4; Neukirchen: Neukirchener, 1982).
Wolff, *Obadja und Jona*
    Hans Walter Wolff, *Obadja und Jona* (BKAT 14/3; Neukirchen: Neukirchener, 1977).

van der Woude, *Micha*
    A. S. van der Woude, *Micha* (De Prediking van het Oude Testament; Nijkerk: Callenbach, 1976).
Yadin, *Warfare*
    Yigael Yadin, *The Art of Warfare in Biblical Lands* (New York: McGraw-Hill, 1963).
Zimmerli, *Ezekiel 1, 2*
    Walther Zimmerli, *Ezekiel 1, 2* (Hermeneia; Philadelphia: Fortress, 1979, 1983).
Zimmerli, *Hope*
    Walther Zimmerli, *Man and His Hope in the Old Testament* (SBT 2d Series 20; Naperville, IL: Allenson, 1971).
Zimmerli, "παῖς θεοῦ"
    Walther Zimmerli, "παῖς θεοῦ," *TDNT* 5:656–77.
Zorell
    Franz Zorell, *Lexicon Hebraicum et Aramaicum Veteris Testamenti* (Rome: Pontifical Biblical Institute, 1962).

The translation of Jeremiah 26—52 presented by Professor Holladay in this volume is new, and is based on a thorough study of the ancient texts. Words of the translation enclosed within parentheses ( ) amplify the sense of the literal Hebrew, while angle brackets ⟨ ⟩ or ⟪ ⟫ indicate emendations of *M* discussed in the textual notes (see Author's Foreword, p. xvii). Words of the biblical text enclosed by square brackets [ ] are regarded by the author as secondary interpolations or redactional supplements to the book of Jer; within these supplements, braces { } enclose segments of text considered to be even later interpolations. Reverse angle brackets ⟩ ⟨ are occasionally used to set off material less certainly deemed to be secondary.

Pictured on the endpapers is a Hebrew bulla with an inscribed seal impression that reads: *lbrkyhw bn nryhw hspr*, "Belonging to Berechiah son of Neriah the scribe." This person is most likely to be identified with Baruch, the trusted secretary of the prophet Jeremiah, who is better known by the hypocoristic form of his name found in the Bible (e.g. Jer 32:12). Now in the Israel Museum, the bulla belongs to a large group of inscribed bullae of unknown provenance in Judah (cf. Avigad, *BA* 42/2 [1979], pp. 114–118.). The script belongs to the classical Hebrew formal tradition, showing the influence of cursive features typical for the mid- to late-seventh century B.C.E.

1. Preliminary Remarks

"Prophetism taken as a whole constitutes a sort of backbone of the Old Testament. . . . Now the prophet par excellence, the one who can allow us to surmise to some degree the experience lived by those men and their role in history, is indisputably Jeremiah"—so a French scholar has recently written.[1]

And indeed the reader finds in the Book of Jer a combination of words attributed to that prophet and of narratives of alleged events in his career that is unparalleled in the Old Testament. We have more biographical narrative regarding King David and we have more recorded words from the apostle Paul in the New Testament: but with respect to both recorded words and biographical narrative in the Bible, Jer would be difficult to match.[2] And it is not only in extent of words and narrative that Jrm stands out for us, but in the range of his experience. He spoke out during the closing years of the Judean monarchy and saw that monarchy fall to Babylon, he found himself isolated from his fellow citizens and more than once under threat of death at the hand of the authorities, and in all of this he continued to proclaim the word of Yahweh. It is no coincidence, then, that in time of peril those who are nourished on the Bible rediscover Jer. Thus Dietrich Bonhoeffer, in his *Letters and Papers from Prison*, refers four times to Jer 45:4–5— no other biblical passage is referred to there more than twice. "There are two passages in the Bible which always seem to me to sum the thing up. One is from Jeremiah 45: 'Behold, what I have built I am breaking down, and what I have planted I am plucking up. . . . And do you seek great things for yourself? Seek them not . . . but I will give your life as a prize of war . . .'; and the other is from Psalm 60: 'Thou hast made the land to quake, thou hast rent it open; repair its breaches, for it totters.'"[3] And one could make a collection of articles, pamphlets, and booklets on Jer written by Christians in occupied lands during World War II and in Germany just after the end of the war.[4]

Nevertheless, from a critical point of view the book offers daunting problems and uncertainties. Establishment of a dependable text is a difficulty. As is well known, the Greek Version (the Septuagint, hereinafter *G*) differs markedly from the traditional Hebrew text (the Masoretic text, hereinafter *M*): the oracles against foreign nations (chaps. 46—51) as a group are to be found in *G* after 25:13, and there in an altogether different sequence from that in *M*. And more generally in the prose passages of the book the text of *G* often does not exhibit phrases and sequences present in *M*; most of these omissions are short, but a few are extensive—the longest being 33:14–26. The question then arises regarding the textual history of the book, and what text can be used as the basis for literary analysis and exegetical work.

Behind questions of text history lie intricate questions of literary history, answers to which bear on the most basic question of all: To what degree, if at all, can one reconstruct a historical Jrm from the material of the book, and, if one can reconstruct him, what are the details of that reconstruction? On the one hand one has the impression from the book of a distinctive personality,

1   "Le prophétisme, pris dans son ensemble, constitue comme l'épine dorsale de l'Ancien Testament. . . . Or, le prophète par excellence, celui qui va nous permettre de deviner quelque peu l'expérience vécue par ces hommes et leur rôle dans l'histoire, c'est, sans conteste possible, Jérémie": André Ridouard, *Jérémie, l'épreuve de la foi* (Paris: Cerf, 1983) 7.

2   Compare Holladay, *Spokesman*, 11.

3   Dietrich Bonhoeffer, *Letters and Papers from Prison* (New York: Macmillan, 1971) 105.

4   See Aage Bentzen, *Helgen eller Højforraeder? Jeremias og hans folk* [Hero or Traitor? Jeremiah and His People] (Copenhagen: Gad, 1943); Leonard E. Elliott-Binns, *Jeremiah, A Prophet for a Time of War* (London: SCM, 1941); Krijn Strijd, *Jeremia: De Roep Gods in deze Tijd* [Jeremiah: The Call of God in These Times] (Lochem, The Netherlands: "De Tijd-

stroom," [1941]); Karl Thieme, "Jeremias, Opportunist oder Utopist?" [Jeremiah, Opportunist or Utopian?], *Judaica* 2 (1946) 106–27, particularly on the question of the Babylonian invasion of Judah as a just war; Josef Weiger, "Jeremias, Der Prophet, seine Person und sein Wirken in schicksalsschwerer Zeit" [Jeremiah, The Prophet, His Person and His Activity in Catastrophic Times], *BK* 1 (1946) 1–15, particularly on the special vocation of the Jews.

and of specific details of the words and actions of that personality, an impression that has produced scores of studies for both the specialist and the nonspecialist, of Jrm's view, or Jrm's role, in one respect or another (see the Bibliography). On the other hand a variety of considerations emerging out of the material of the book suggests that that naive view is untenable. I offer three such considerations here.

(1) There is the general awareness that biblical material is gathered by a community, and that more often than not there is a period of oral tradition between whatever events lie behind the tradition and the fixing of the tradition in writing. Thus for the student of the New Testament it is clear that forty to seventy years passed from the time of the events in Jesus' career to the time when those events were fixed in writing, so that an immense effort has been expended to discern the process by which oral tradition was reshaped into the form accessible to us. The books of the eighth-century prophets give evidence of having been compiled by disciples and of being expanded by secondary additions; one assumes therefore a similar process at work in the Book of Jer.

(2) The narrative in chapter 36 is enticing, indicating that Jrm dictated a scroll to his scribe Baruch in 605, during the reign of Jehoiakim, and then, after its destruction by the king, dictated another scroll, this time with additions; scholars are impelled to search within the present book for the contents of the original scroll, or scrolls. On the other hand, there are, roughly speaking, three distinctive kinds of material in the book: (a) poetry, which exhibits the heightened language, compact diction, and parallelism found in the poetry of other preexilic prophets; (b) biographical material about Jrm, especially in 19:1—20:6; chapters 26—29; 36—45 (except for 44:1–14); and 51:59–64; and (c) sermonic prose, notably in 7:1—8:3; 11:1–17; 18:1–12; 21:1–10; 25:1–11; 32:1–2, 6–16, 24–44; 34:1–7, 8–22; 35:1–19; 44:1–14. This analysis was given classic expression by Sigmund Mowinckel, who designated these materials as "A," "B," and "C," respectively, and, on the analogy of the hypothesis of sources in the Pentateuch, called them not only literary types but sources.[5] And inasmuch as there is a close resemblance between the "C" material

and both Deuteronomy and the Deuteronomistic redaction of Kings, many scholars have assumed an analogous Deuteronomistic redaction of Jer, presumably well into the exilic period, after Jrm's death.

(3) There is the awareness of many scholars that ancient Israel did not have our own biographical interests and that what has come down to us of Jrm has been shaped by the religious needs, more particularly the liturgical needs, of his contemporaries and of those who followed him. Especially would this be the case with first-person testimony within the book, notably with the call of Jrm in chapter 1 and the so-called Confessions. An extreme expression of this view is that of Henning Reventlow,[6] and though his assertion has been vigorously contended, it is a useful caution. All three of these considerations, then—the process of oral tradition, the contrastive nature of the various kinds of literary material within the book, and the religious needs of the community—complicate one's attempt to reconstruct a historical Jrm.

The three problems interlock—the relation between *M* and *G* in the attempt to establish a text for analysis, an analysis of the literary development of the Book of Jer, and a reconstruction of the life and work and proclamation of Jrm. Each is to some degree dependent on the others, so that one could begin with any one of them: Wilhelm Rudolph, in the introduction in his commentary, begins with the life of Jrm and then continues with his activity and his theology, before he turns to consider the Book of Jer. I choose to deal first with the question of text, then with an analysis of the literary development of the book, and then with the prophet Jrm himself. (Beyond the major divisions and subdivisions, I have chosen to number the individual sections in a single sequence for simplicity of cross-references.)

I. The Text of the Book of Jeremiah

2. The Relation of *M* and *G*; The Nature of *G*: Preliminary Remarks

The disparity between *M* and *G* in Jer is well known: Jer is comparable to the Books of Samuel in the contrasting texts of *M* and *G*. But whereas in Samuel *M* is often shorter and defective in comparison with *G*, in Jer *M* is

---

5   Sigmund Mowinckel, *Zur Komposition des Buches Jeremia* (Kristiania [=Oslo]: Dybwad, 1914).
6   Reventlow, *Liturgie*.

longer: Friedrich Giesebrecht estimated that about twenty-seven hundred words of *M* are lacking in *G*, while *G* contains about one hundred words lacking in *M*;[7] the result is that *G* is about one-eighth shorter than *M*. The question of the relation between *G* and *M* has been discussed for a century and a half,[8] but until the recovery of the Qumran material it was possible to slight the importance of *G*: one could assume that its omissions had arisen secondarily within the Greek tradition, whether by design or accidentally.

A few fragments of Hebrew texts of Jer from Qumran Cave 4, however, have altered our understanding of the issue. There are, to be sure, twelve fragments of 4QJer[a], dated by Frank Cross to about 200 B.C.E.,[9] that reflect the text of *M*. But there are on the other hand three fragments of 4QJer[b], two large and one small, from the Hasmonean period (last century and a half B.C.E.);[10] the two large ones (covering 9:22—10:18[11] and 43:3–9) offer samples of the type of text reflected in *G*, while the small one (covering 50:4–6) sides with *M* against *G*.[12] *G* thus emerges as a version in Greek of a valid Hebrew text tradition of Jer.[13]

The question becomes: In the main is *G* a shortened form of *M*, or is *M* an expanded form of *G*? Or is the question unanswerable? Is the ideal of a "more original" text form unattainable?

Gerald Janzen has examined the question freshly in the light of the existence of 4QJer[b]. His conclusions follow.

The text of *M* has undergone much secondary expansion. Names are filled out frequently to their full form, and titles and epithets are added to them, while pronoun objects and subjects of verbs are made explicit. The text is heavily interpolated from parallel, related, or nearby passages. Many of these interpolations are innocuous, but many others are of such size and character as to reflect conscious scribal notation and harmonization. Particularly striking are the large doublets, and the interpolations from O.T. passages outside Jeremiah.

The high incidence of conflation, together with the rarity of haplography, indicates that *M* is a revised text. . . .

The text of *G* contains only a very small amount of secondary expansion, In the great majority of its zero variants, it preserves a text superior to that of *M*. The evidence does not support the commonly held theory that the translator abridged his *Vorlage*, so that, except where scribal lapse is patent or must be assumed, *G* may be taken as a substantially faithful witness to the Hebrew text at home in Alexandria. This conclusion, if correct, closes one long-standing debate about the text of Jeremiah.[14]

The propensity of *M* to offer expansions over *G*, it must be stressed, is a characteristic of the prose sections, not the poetic ones.

An analysis of chapter 28 will illustrate the matter. A typical example is vv 8–9. *G* presupposes a text that reads, "The prophets who were before me and you from early times—they prophesied to many lands and great kingdoms war. The prophet who shall prophesy peace—when the word of the prophet comes, then the prophet shall be recognized as one whom Yahweh has really sent." Though the contrast is clearly between "war" and "peace," *M* in v 8 has inserted after "war" the words "and disaster and pestilence," though some MSS. read "and

---

7 Giesebrecht, xxv.

8 A convenient summary of the discussion may be found in Janzen, pp. 2–7.

9 Frank M. Cross, "The Evolution of a Theory of Local Texts," *Qumran and the History of the Biblical Text* (ed. Frank M. Cross and Shemaryahu Talmon; Cambridge: Harvard University, 1975) 308 and n. 8.

10 Ibid., 308.

11 This fragment is reproduced on the endpapers of *Jeremiah 1*.

12 Until the full publication of these texts, the best treatment is Janzen, pp. 173–84 (Appendix D).

13 For a full survey of recent literature on the matter see conveniently Louis Stulman, *The Other Text of Jeremiah, A Reconstruction of the Hebrew Text Underlying the Greek Version of the Prose Sections of Jeremiah With English Translation* (Lanham, MD, New York, and London: University Press of America, 1985) 3–5, n. 12–27.

14 Janzen, pp. 127, 128.

famine and pestilence," approaching the triad "sword, famine and pestilence" that occurs repeatedly in the book (14:12 and about a dozen more times).[15] Both Jrm and Hananiah are repeatedly identified as "the prophet" in *M* (Jrm: vv 5, 6, 10, 15; Hananiah: vv 5, 10, 12, 15); these gratuitous identifications are lacking in *G*. In both vv 2 and 14 "Yahweh" (*G*) has been expanded in *M* to "Yahweh of hosts, the God of Israel." In *M* the word "all" has been inserted before "the vessels" (v 3), "the exiles" (v 4), and "the people" (v 11); "all" is lacking at these points in *G*. The "vessels of the house of Yahweh" in v 3 are identified in *M* as those "which Nebuchadnezzar king of Babylon took from this place and brought to Babylon"; again this identification, which is perhaps derived from chapter 27, is lacking in *G*. "Jeconiah" (v 4) is identified as "son of Jehoiakim, king of Judah" in *M*, and in the same verse "the exiles of Judah" are identified as those "who have come to Babylon," and are made the object of an extra verb phrase, "I am returning to this place, oracle of Yahweh"; none of this is in *G*. In both vv 11 and 14 "the king of Babylon" is identified as "Nebuchadnezzar"; again these identifications are not in *G*. In v 16 Jrm's oracle against Hananiah is explained as "because you have uttered rebellion against Yahweh": this clause, not in *G*, is evidently derived from Deut 13:6. And there are several more instances in which identifying nouns are introduced in *M* where *G* does not offer them. Furthermore, at the beginning of v 1 *G* offers a straightforward and trustworthy text, "And in the fourth year of Zedekiah king of Judah, in the fifth month . . . ," while *M* offers a conflate text contaminated erroneously with material from the beginning of chapters 26 and 27: "In that year, in the accession year of Zedekiah king of Judah, in the fourth year, in the fifth month. . . ." To read this chapter as *M* offers it, or as *M* is rendered in any current translation, is to experience, at least unconsciously, a fussy and cluttered text; to read *G*, or a translation of it, is to experience a clean and straightforward narrative. Given the conclusion that *M* is an expansionist text, the necessity to base one's exegesis in the first instance on a text unencumbered by expansions is clear. (For the expansions in *M* see sec. 8.)

But one must stress that each textual variation must be assessed in its own right. Thus some omissions of *G* are clearly the result of haplography; Janzen offers his own compilation,[16] but my own judgment differs at points from his, and other scholars may come to still other conclusions.

On the other hand, pluses in *G* over *M* are not necessarily due to a conflate text: indeed examples of a conflate text are rare in the *G* of Jer. Two examples from the poetic sections must stand for many. In 2:28b *M* reads, "Yes, as many as your cities are your gods, O Judah"; to this *G* adds, "and as many as the streets of Jerusalem have they sacrificed to Baal," an addition that, one may surmise, is a development of an antecedent Hebrew "and as many as your streets, O Jerusalem, have they sacrificed to Baal." Carl H. Cornill, and then Rudolph and Janzen, accept this plus in *G* as part of the original text; but William McKane[17] rejects the plus as the reflection of a secondary expansion in 11:13. I judge the plus to be original: I assume that 11:13 is a prose form of the poetic original in the verse under discussion, that the parallelism of the verse needs the balancing line, and that *M* is defective, probably by a haplography with a twice-occurring מִסְפַּר. Again in 4:29 while *M* reads "They have gone in(to) the thickets, and into the rocks have gone up," *G* reads, "They have gone into the caves, and have hidden in the thickets, and into the rocks have gone up." There are other textual questions in the verse, but the striking reading in *G* commends itself, as Paul Volz and Janzen agree: Volz points out the possibility that a haplography of the consonants באו produced the present text of *M*.

In the discussion that follows, *M* and *G* will be used in their ordinary sense, the presently existing Masoretic Text on the one hand, and the presently existing text of the Septuagint, represented by the major uncials, on the other. By the "Proto-Masoretic text" I mean the text antecedent to *M*, as it existed at the time of its differentiation from the Proto-Septuagintal text. By the "Proto-Septuagintal text" I mean the Hebrew antecedent from which the Greek translation was initially made: it is represented by 4QJer[b]. By the "Old Greek" I mean the initial translation of Jer made into Greek from the Proto-Septuagintal text before any revisions in that translation could be made.

---

15 For a thorough treatment of the triad see Weippert, *Prosareden*, 149–80.

16 Janzen, pp. 117–19.

17 William McKane, *A Critical and Exegetical Commentary on Jeremiah*, volume 1 (ICC; Edinburgh: Clark, 1986) 47.

3. The Contrastive Sequence of Chapters in *G* and *M*

It has already been noted that the oracles against foreign nations (chaps. 46—51 in *M*) are to be found in *G* after 25:13. These oracles thus make up 25:14—31:44 within the Greek numeration, and then, following these oracles, *G* continues the material designated in *M* as 25:15—45:5, but of course with its own numeration (*G* 32:1—51:5). Furthermore, the sequence of the individual oracles against foreign nations is altogether different in *G* than in *M*. This disparity between *G* and *M* in the sequence of material of the book calls out for explanation. Because the disparity concerns specifically the oracles against foreign nations, in the present study the matter is discussed in detail in the general article on those oracles before the treatment of 46:1–12 and will only be summarized here.

G associates the oracles with 25:15–29, the listing of various nations who will drink the cup of wrath; the association is undoubtedly the original one, so that it follows that the oracles were moved secondarily to their position in *M*, after chapter 45; that shift may have taken place in the Maccabean period, when the defeat of Babylon (that is, the Seleucid Empire) would be seen as the ultimate event of history (compare the Book of Daniel). But it is to be assumed that the sequence of oracles in *M* is the original one, since it seems to have a chronological basis: the first oracle against Egypt, the oracle against Philistia, and the earliest section of the material against Moab were probably delivered at the time of the battle of Carchemish; oracles against the Transjordanian states follow, together with other peoples farther away (Damascus, the Arabs, Elam); and the oracles against Babylon, whose fall would be delayed, come last. On the other hand, though the oracles are in their original position in *G*, their sequence has been rearranged, evidently in the Maccabean period: Elam seems to be understood as the Parthian Empire, followed then by Egypt and Babylon (the Seleucid Empire); the

others follow geographically, closing with the longest, Moab.

4. The Contrast in Translation of the Two Halves of *G*

Though unsystematic observations had been made for many years, it was Henry St. John Thackeray in 1902 who proposed that the translation of *G* is the work of more than one translator and that the two sections are *G* Jer 1—28 (= *M* 1:1—25:13; 49:34–39; 46:1–28; 50:1—51:64) and *G* Jer 29—51 (= *M* 47:1–7; 49:7–22; 49:1–5, 28–33, 23–27; 48:1–44; 25:15–38; 26:1—45:5)—the nature of chapter 52 remained problematic.[18] He offered twenty-eight examples of contrasting translation between the two sections, which he designated Jeremiah *a* and Jeremiah *β* respectively: for example, כֹּה אָמַר יהוה is rendered τάδε λέγει Κύριος in Jeremiah *a* and οὕτως εἶπεν Κύριος in Jeremiah *β*; עֵת is rendered καιρός in Jeremiah *a* and χρόνος in Jeremiah *β*; שׁכן is rendered κατασκηνόω in Jeremiah *a* and καταλύω in Jeremiah *β*. Though Thackeray went on to offer a tentative theory for this contrast—that the two parts had at one time circulated independently, this theory is to be rejected: for one thing there is evidence of more than one translator in *G* for several individual books of the OT.[19]

The question has received renewed attention in recent years by Emanuel Tov:[20] it is his contention that it is not a matter of two translators at all, but of a reviser of Jeremiah *β* (which, in his understanding, includes Jer 52 and the first portion of Baruch).[21] He offers a whole series of striking Greek words or phrases common to both Jeremiah *a* and Jeremiah *β* whose antecedent Hebrew is rendered differently in the rest of the OT; and he offers ten instances in which a striking Greek word renders different Hebrew antecedents within Jer.[22] Tov concludes that the hypothesis of two translators cannot be maintained. As to which of the two, Jeremiah

18 Henry St. John Thackeray, "The Greek Translators of Jeremiah," *JTS* 4 (1902/1903) 245–66.

19 For bibliography on proposals for more than one translator in *G* for specific books see Harry Orlinsky, "The Septuagint as Holy Writ and the Philosophy of the Translators," *HUCA* 46 (1975) 89–90, n. 2.

20 Emanuel Tov, *The Septuagint Translation of Jeremiah and Baruch, A Discussion of an Early Revision of the LXX*

of Jeremiah 29—52 and Baruch 1:1—3:8 (HSM 8; Missoula, MT: Scholars, 1976).

21 Ibid., 79.

22 Ibid., 19–40.

α or β, underwent revision, Tov puts the evidence to careful analysis and concludes that it was Jeremiah β that underwent the revision, in the direction of more precise renditions, of the replacement of nonstereotyped (free) renditions by stereotyped (literal) ones, and of more exact renderings:[23] for example, זְרֹעַ "arm" is translated by βραχίων in Jeremiah α and generally in the OT but by ἐπίχειρον in Jeremiah β and nowhere else in Greek literature (the word may have been coined by the reviser);[24] again דבר pi'el is normally rendered λαλέω in Jeremiah α, and in Jeremiah β that verb is retained when the subject is a human being, but when the subject is God or a prophet it is χρηματίζω: this verb occurs in G only in Jeremiah β.[25] Tov thus concludes that it was Jeremiah β that underwent revision. But there would be no reason to leave α unrevised; he therefore concludes that both halves of G were revised, but that the text (in both the unrevised and the revised forms) stretched over two scrolls and that accidentally the unrevised form (that is, the Old Greek) of the first half (Jeremiah α) and the revised form of the second half (Jeremiah β) became the archetype of the present preserved text.[26] He tentatively assigns the revision to a date between 116 B.C.E. and about 50 C.E.[27] His analysis appears cogent.

5. The Translation Technique of the Old Greek

Little need be said about the specific translation technique of the Old Greek for Jer. It is a relatively literal rendering: whatever may be the given translation of a Hebrew word or phrase, it is usually possible to see a one-to-one correspondence between the Hebrew and the Greek in such a way that a back-translation can be done with fair certainty. There is little evidence in Jer of the avoidance of anthropomorphisms and anthropopathisms in expressions involving God.[28] Nevertheless, there are points where the Old Greek departs from M in ways that suggest secondary adaptation, notably in the confessions; one assumes that this adaptation took place at a point antecedent to the translation of the Old Greek, though there is no way to be sure, given our lack of the full Hebrew text antecedent to the Old Greek (see below, sec. 7).

6. The Date of the Old Greek Translation

If there was a revision in the Old Greek about the time of the turn of the common era (evidence for which is found in Jeremiah β), when would the initial translation from Hebrew into Greek have been made? Sirach's grandson testifies that he knew the prophets in Greek (Sirach, Prologue), so that it may be presumed that Jer was translated before 116 B.C.E.[29] There is no evidence for an absolute date for the translation of Jer; the generally accepted date for the prophets is about 200 B.C.E.[30]—the date is that of Thackeray, based on the style of the translation.[31]

7. The Origin of the Proto-Septuagintal and Proto-Masoretic Texts; The Nature of the Proto-Septuagintal Text

The presence at Qumran of a Hebrew text representing the text tradition of G (4QJer[b]) dating from the Hasmonean period alongside a Proto-Masoretic text from the beginning of the second century B.C.E. (4QJer[a]) immediately raises the question of the origin of these two text types. It is hardly possible to imagine two radically different text types evolving side by side in Palestine: their existence would rapidly have produced a mixed text. Since the examplar of the Proto-Masoretic text at Qumran (4QJer[a]) is to be dated very near the time of the translation of the Old Greek, one must conclude that the Proto-Septuagintal text must have been preserved in isolation. The natural conclusion is that the shorter text had been preserved in Egypt. On the other hand the longer Proto-Masoretic text exhibits harmonistic tendencies also found in the Samaritan Pentateuch (obviously a Palestinian text type—on this matter see sec. 8): the Proto-Masoretic text thus became the standard one in Palestine.[32] The two text traditions branched off from

23 Ibid., 41–91.
24 Ibid., 48–49.
25 Ibid., 71.
26 Ibid., 162.
27 Ibid., 167.
28 Bernard M. Zlotowitz, *The Septuagint Translation of the Hebrew Terms in Relation to God in the Book of Jeremiah* (New York: Ktav, 1981); compare Emanuel Tov, "Septuagint, Contribution to OT Scholarship," *IDBSup*, 810a.
29 Compare Tov, *Jeremiah and Baruch*, 165.
30 Bleddyn J. Roberts, *The Old Testament Text and Versions* (Cardiff: University of Wales, 1951) 116.
31 Henry St. John Thackeray, *A Grammar of the Old Testament in Greek according to the Septuagint* I (Cambridge: Cambridge University, 1909) 12–15.

each other during the period when expansions were being made in the text: one pair of doublets appears in both texts (10:12–16 = 51:15–19) while others are found only in *M* (see below).

It is worth noting that although the Proto-Masoretic text is the longer text, particularly in the prose, there are evidences of recensional activity in the Proto-Septuagintal text as well. A. R. Diamond has recently pointed out that in Jrm's confessions *G* minimizes the specificities of some passages, so that the material becomes more a generic lament. Thus in a sequence in 15:15–16, where *M* reads, "Know how I have borne disgrace on your account; your words were found, and I ate them," *G* reads, "Know that I have borne disgrace on your account from those who set aside your words; consume them." Again in 15:18 the text in *M* reads, "Why has my pain become endless, my wound incurable, refusing to be healed? You really are becoming for me, as it were, a deception, untrustworthy waters!" In *G*, however, the last half continues to describe the wound, not God: "Why do those who grieve me prevail against me? My wound is severe, whence shall I be healed? It has indeed become to me like false water, not having faithfulness."[33]

If the Proto-Septuagintal text evolved in Egypt, it is striking that an examplar found its way to Qumran. One wonders, did the Qumran community derive from the authorities in Jerusalem an interest in a variety of text traditions of Scripture, or was this an interest confined to Qumran itself? One can at least conclude that manuscripts were carried long distances and that the Qumran community was hospitable to variant text traditions, at least for Jer.

8. The Nature and Date of the Proto-Masoretic Text

Tov has summarized the nature of the expansions that produced *M*.[34] Tov assumes that all changes in the Proto-Masoretic text are the product of the same editor, including the rearrangement of the oracles against foreign nations,[35] but I would question on methodological grounds whether that is necessary—the rearrangement of a text is a different sort of change than an expansion, and in the present instance such rearrangements may have been due to later editorial work. As to the expansions, it is impossible to determine whether they were the product of one editor or more than one, but it is more economical to assume one editor whose activity carried the prestige to win acceptance.

The editor has added headings to prophecies (2:1–2; 7:1–2; 16:1; 27:1). He has created doublets by repeating sections from elsewhere in the book (8:10b–12 = 6:13–15; 46:27–28 = 30:10–11; 48:40b, 41b = 49:22).[36] He has added material, such as the synchronisms in 25:1 and 32:1 (which, by the reckoning of the present study, are in error by one year), the "athbash" codes of 25:25 and 26 and 51:41, the remarks on the vessels taken by Nebuchadnezzar (27:19–22), and the identification of Baruch as "the scribe" (36:26, 32). He has made an effort to clarify the damaged text of 29:24–25, he has expanded the diction in 35:18–19 and recast the third-person affirmation there into a second-person address, he has shifted the phraseology of 36:32, he has softened the diction of Ebed-melech in his address to Zedekiah (38:9) so that it is not the king but the courtiers who have tried to kill Jrm, and in his expansion of 44:12 he has forgotten that Jrm's audience is already in Egypt. Many of his expansions indeed disturb the flow of the Hebrew (36:6; 41:2; and often) or even add contradictions (28:1). The editor has added personal names and full patronymics in order to make the text as fully clear as possible: thus "king of Babylon" becomes "Nebuchadnezzar king of Babylon" (21:2 and often), "Jeconiah" becomes "Jeconiah son of Jehoiakim king of Judah" (28:4 and often), and "Jeremiah said to Hananiah" becomes "Jeremiah the

---

32 For these conclusions see Cross, "The Evolution of a Theory of Local Texts," 308–9; Tov, "Septuagint, Contribution to OT Scholarship," 809a; idem, "Some Aspects of the Textual and Literary History of the Book of Jeremiah," *Le Livre de Jérémie, le prophète et son milieu, les oracles et leur transmission* (ed. Pierre-Maurice Bogaert; BETL 54; Leuven: Leuven University, 1981) 161.

33 A. R. Diamond, "Jeremiah's Confessions in LXX and MT: A Witness to Developing Canonical Function?" *VT* (forthcoming).

34 Tov, "Textual and Literary," 150–67.

35 Ibid., 152.

36 But I propose, against Tov, (1) that 17:3–4 is not a repetition of 15:13–14 and that *G* is deficient in 17:1–4 by haplography, and (2) that it is 30:10–11

prophet said to Hananiah the prophet" (28:5: see above, sec. 2).[37] It is worth noting also that he has three times identified Nebuchadnezzar as "my [= Yahweh's] servant" (25:9; 27:6; 43:10).

Louis Stulman has assessed the theological interests of the editor: the incessant disobedience of the people, and the Babylonian exile as a part of the program of Yahweh at that point in history.[38]

One may ask, When did the Proto-Septuagintal and Proto-Masoretic texts branch off from each other? Or, put another way, When may we assume that the expansions were made in the Proto-Septuagintal text to produce the Proto-Masoretic text? There are passages in Jer found in *G* (and therefore in *M* as well) that appear to be from Nehemiah's time (445 B.C.E. or soon thereafter). Two examples are 17:19–27 and 31:38–40: the phraseology of the former passage is close to that of Neh 13:15–22, and the geographical landmarks named in the latter passage match those of Nehemiah's time. On the other hand 33:14–26 is a major section added in the Proto-Masoretic text, and that passage, with its twin concerns of a future for Levitical priests and Davidic kingship, appears to emerge out of the same milieu as that of Zechariah 10—14 and of the Chronicler (compare 1 Chronicles 23). (Tov, taking a clue from Cross, has noticed that the harmonistic additions in the *M* of Jer are analogous to similar harmonistic additions in the Samaritan Pentateuch; but this observation does not help in locating a precise date.) A date toward the end of the fifth century B.C.E. will serve for the expanded edition.[39] I disagree with Tov's contention that the editor had access to genuine tradition of Jrm not theretofore included in the book;[40] his examples within the poetry are mostly examples of haplography within *G*.[41] Independent traditions about Jrm had faded before the

editor did his work. (Compare the remarks about the references to Jrm in Chronicles, sec. 83.)

9. The Later Greek Versions

As is well known, there are three later Greek versions, those of Aquila (*a'*), Symmachus (*s'*) and Theodotion (*θ'*). These versions, all evidently produced in the second century C.E.,[42] were separate efforts to produce translations in Greek of the Proto-Masoretic text, and their efforts were therefore separate from that of the earlier reviser responsible for Jeremiah *β*, though their efforts often coincided. Thus Tov points out that the Old Greek rendition of שׁדד was ταλαιπωρέω; it was revised in Jeremiah *β* to (ἀπ)όλλυμι; *a'* usually translated the verb with προνομεύω (or προνομή), *s'* used mainly διαφθείρω, and *θ'* reverted to the Old Greek ταλαιπωρέω (or ταλαίπωρος). On the other hand, the rendering of נְאֻם יהוה in the Old Greek is λέγει Κύριος; it was changed by the reviser in Jeremiah *β* to φησὶ Κύριος (a rendering occurring only three times outside Jeremiah *β*), and this is the standard rendition of *a'*, *s'*, and *θ'*. Tov offers three other examples that suggest that the work of *a'*, *s'*, and *θ'* are in continuity with that of the reviser of Jeremiah *β*.[43] Unfortunately, there are no remains of these three translations of Jer outside the fragments of the Hexapla collected by Frederick Field.[44]

10. The Vulgate (*V*)

The Latin Vulgate (*V*), translated by Jerome at the end of the fourth century, is based, as one might expect, on a Hebrew consonantal text almost always identical with that preserved in *M*. (But it is to be noted that Jerome is very much aware of *G* and of *a'*, *s'*, and *θ'*: he cites all of them in the course of his commentary on Jer.) There are occasional noteworthy readings; thus *V* sides with *a'*

37   See Janzen, pp. 139–55 (Appendix A).
38   Louis Stulman, *The Prose Sermons of the Book of Jeremiah, A Redescription of the Correspondences with the Deuteronomistic Literature in the Light of Recent Text-critical Research* (SBLDS 83; Atlanta: Scholars, 1986) 142–44.
39   So also ibid., 2.
40   Tov, "Textual and Literary History," 157.
41   Thus 5:15 (compare Janzen, p. 117); probably also 13:17 (compare my text note on the plus in *M*) and 14:3 (compare *Jeremiah 1*, 423).

42   Roberts, *Text and Versions*, 120–27.
43   Tov, *Jeremiah and Baruch*, 161.
44   Frederick Field, *Origenis Hexaplorum quae Supersunt, Sive Veterum Interpretum Graecorum in Totum V. T. Fragmenta* II (Oxford: Oxford University, 1875) 573–740, and idem, "Auctarium ad Origenis Hexapla," 36–54.

that is original, not 46:27–28.

against both *M* and *G* in the vocalization of the consonantal text of 7:3, reading וְאֶשְׁכְּנָה אִתְּכֶם "I may dwell with you" instead of the reading of *M* and *G*, וַאֲשַׁכְּנָה אֶתְכֶם "I may let you dwell."

There are no features in the translation of Jer to distinguish it from Jerome's rendering of other books of the OT.

11. The Peshiṭta (S)

A critical edition of the Syriac Peshiṭta (*S*) to Jer is forthcoming; until its appearance one has to be content with the Codex Ambrosianus (probably from the sixth century c.e.). Generally *S* follows *M*, but there are many points at which it sides with *G* against *M*. For example, *S* along with *G* omits וְהִתְבּוֹנְנוּ in 9:16; *S* and *G* read יהוה at the beginning of 10:12, a word missing in *M*; in 11:18 *S* and *G* read "O Yahweh, inform me" instead of the *M* reading "Yahweh informed me."

In chapter 28 *S* has all the pluses of *M* over *G*, but like *G* (and *T*) identifies Hananiah in v 1 as "the false prophet." The result is that in vv 5, 10, 12, and 17, where *M* identifies Hananiah as "the prophet" (and *G* does not), *S* (like *T*) has "the false prophet." And strikingly *S* has two more pluses that even *M* does not have (nor do any of the other Versions), namely, "the prophet" after "Jeremiah" in v 12a and "the false prophet" after "Hananiah" in v 13. Again, in v 7, where both *M* and *G* have "in your ears and in the ears of all the people," *S* (along with *T*) softens the rendering to "in your presence and in the presence of all the people."

The impression one gets, therefore, is that of an eclectic text: it is surmised that some at least of the Syriac OT was based on Jewish Aramaic Targums (one notes that the ruling house of Adiabene, east of the Tigris, became converted to Judaism in the first century c.e.); and *G* would have become available to Syriac-speaking areas after they became Christianized in the fourth century c.e.[45]

Since there is as yet no concordance to *S*, there is no way to analyze the translation technique or recognize the presence of more than one translator within a book.[46] But for what it is worth I became aware in my study of שוב that the rendering of that verb in *S* is contrastive in the two halves of Jer: through chapter 31 *hĕpak* is used for concrete contexts (such as "return to a place") and *tāb* is used in covenantal contexts (such as "return to God" = "repent"), whereas in chapter 32 and thereafter *tāb* is abandoned (except for one isolated instance in 35:15) and *hĕpak* is employed for both usages.[47]

Only occasionally does *S* stand alone and appear to offer help to a textual difficulty. One such instance may be 29:24–25: *S* there has "And Shemaiah the Nehelamite said, 'Thus Yahweh the God of Israel has said. . . .'" The oracle of that prophet is missing, but form-critically that reading is superior to either *M* or *G* and does not appear to be a secondary remedy to a damaged text.

12. The Aramaic Targum (T)

In contrast to *G*, *M*, *V*, and *S*, Targum Jonathan (*T*) to the Prophets is notably periphrastic: in that regard the rendering of Jer is no different from the rendering of other books of that collection. Anthropomorphic expressions are regularly softened: where Jrm prays to God, "remember me" (15:15), *T* says "let my memorial come up before you." When the language about God is offensive to piety, *T* simply shifts the language. Thus in 14:8–9 *M* reads, "O hope of Israel, O Yahweh, her savior in time of distress, why are you like a stranger in the land, and like a traveler stopping for the night? Why are you like a helpless man, like a champion who cannot save? You are indeed in our midst, Yahweh, and we bear your name: do not leave us!" In this instance *T* renders, "O hope of Israel, his Redeemer in the time of trouble, why does your anger hover over us, when we are like settlers in the land, and like travelers on the road who turn aside to lodge for the night? Why does your anger hover over us when we are taken into exile and forsaken? You, O mighty One, are able to redeem, and as for you, your

---

45 See the discussion in Roberts, *Text and Versions*, 217–23; Arthur Vööbus, "Syriac Versions," *IDBSup*, 848–49.

46 Tov refers to an unpublished dissertation of F. Freifelder, "An Introduction to a Hebrew-Syriac and Syriac-Index to the Book of Jeremiah": see Tov, "Textual and Literary History," 147, n. 14.

47 Holladay, *Šûbh*, 38–39.

Shekinah is among us, O Lord, and your Name has been called over us: you will not forsake us." Where Jrm accuses God, "You have deceived me [or, seduced me], Yahweh" (20:7) *T* has, "You have confounded me, O Lord": the Aramaic verb שׁבשׁ means "send forth branches" (like a grapevine), therefore "entangle." Jrm's wholesale condemnations of Israel are nuanced. Thus in 5:3 Jrm says, "Your eyes look for honesty, Yahweh, do they not? You struck them, but they did not feel pain . . .," but *T* says, "O Lord, is it not revealed before you to do good to those who perform faithfulness? As for the wicked, you punished them, but they did not repent. . . ." Metaphors and poetic images are explained, often in a pedestrian way: the common expression "daughter Zion" (in this study "fair Zion") is rendered by "the assembly of Zion" (4:31); "A lion has come up from his thicket," a figure for the foe from the north (4:7), has become "A king has gone away from his fortified city." Sometimes a metaphor becomes a simile: in *T* Jrm is set "as strong as a fortified city, and like a pillar of iron, and like a bronze wall" (1:18). Titles of public officials are sometimes modernized: "Hilkiah, of the priestly family at Anathoth" (1:1) becomes "Hilkiah, one of the leaders of the course of the priests of the Amarkelin [temple treasury officials?] who were in Jerusalem, the man who received his inheritance at Anathoth." And foreign names are updated: "I am punishing Amon from No' [that is, Thebes]" (46:25) becomes "I am punishing the noise of Alexandria."[48]

As one might expect, it is *M* that stands behind *T*— rarely does the Targum follow another text tradition; when it does diverge from *M*, it usually does so in concert with one or more other Versions when *M* has suffered an error through carelessness.

By a careful sifting of citations of *T* of Jer in other early literature Robert Hayward adduces evidence suggesting that *T* for Jer originated sometime before 300 C.E.[49] He has also collected evidence that at many points Jerome in his commentary on Jer drew on the Jewish exegesis that has survived in *T* of Jer.[50] For example, for 5:12, "They have denied Yahweh and have said, 'He is nothing!' 'Disaster shall not come upon us!' and 'We shall not see sword and famine!'" *T* renders, "They have lied against the Word of the Lord, and have said, Not from before Him do good things come upon us. Moreover, evil will not come upon us, nor shall we see those who kill with the word, and the famine." That is to say, *T* shifts a pragmatic denial that Yahweh will bring disaster to a general denial of God's providence. Jerome offers the same interpretation: "Because 'they have denied the Lord and said, it is not He' by whose justice everything shall come about, but all these things happen by chance; nor shall the things with which the voices of the prophets threaten us come to pass . . . this is the oracle. Let the Church hear this, as she neglects and denies God's providence."[51]

II. Analysis of the Literary Development of the Book of Jeremiah

13. Preliminary Remarks

An enormous amount of energy has been expended in attempts to determine the literary evolution of the Book of Jer. There are many enticing details that appear to offer clues: thus chapters 27—29 offer spellings of "Nebuchadnezzar" and "Jeremiah" different from those in the rest of the book; there are clearly subcollections within the book (oracles against foreign nations in chaps. 46—51, the "little book of hope" that begins in chap. 30); there are contrasts in types of literature (oracular poetry, repetitive sermonic prose); there are many disjunctions that suggest the processes of accretion in the literary material. But no one theory of literary development has commended itself to scholars.

There are two interrelated questions at issue here: the process by which the Book of Jer evolved, and the extent to which it is appropriate to reconstruct the words and deeds of the prophet Jrm from the various portions of the book.

---

48 On translation technique see C. T. Robert Hayward, *The Aramaic Bible (The Targums)* 12 (Wilmington, DE: Glazier, 1987) 21–26.

49 Ibid., 11–12.

50 C. T. Robert Hayward, "Jewish Traditions in Jerome's Commentary on Jeremiah and the Targum of Jeremiah," *Proceedings of the Irish Biblical Association* 9 (1985) 100–120.

51 Ibid., 103–5.

14. History of Discussion

It would not be useful to offer a complete history of work on these questions, but one must review the suggestions that still influence current discussions of the matter.[52]

Bernhard Duhm (1901) drew a strong line between the poetic oracles of Jrm, Baruch's book, and expansions of the poetic oracles and of Baruch's book. As to Jrm's oracles, Duhm was convinced that the only genuine oracles were those made up of a series of two bicola, each bicolon consisting of three stresses plus two (the so-called qinah-meter).[53] He judged then that 2:2b–3 was followed originally by 2:14–28, since 2:4–13 did not offer the "Jeremianic meter."[54] He judged much material to be late on grounds of contents and theology, for example, the description of the drought (14:2–10) and descriptions of catastrophe such as 15:5–9.[55] Baruch's biography, according to Duhm, is to be found in chapters 26—29 and 32—45; it, too, has been subject to expansions. Duhm calculated that approximately 280 verses of poetry were genuine to Jrm, and approximately 220 verses were genuine to Baruch's biography; roughly 850 verses then are due to later expansions (notably chaps. 30—31, 46—51, and 52).[56] The redactors have added the stereotypical prose, and the added material shows the influence of Deuteronomy, Ezekiel, Deutero-Isaiah, and Trito-Isaiah.[57] Though research in this century has moved beyond Duhm, his suggestions on the details of the wording of Jer are often acute, so that his perception of larger literary questions has also been influential. Thus Robert Carroll appreciates Duhm's judgment: "Although modern scholarship has moved considerably from the time of Duhm and would hardly now regard the book of Jeremiah as the product of three kinds of material, it seems to me that much of what Duhm has to say about the supplements and their relation to later

literature is quite sound."[58]

Mowinckel (1914) moved the discussion beyond Duhm. Mowinckel proposed three written sources ("A," "B," and "C"). Source "A" is a collection of poetic oracles loosely attached to one another: it is difficult to separate the sections from one another. The collection is found within chapters 1—25. This collection is a compilation of as complete an assemblage of Jrm's oracles as possible. The poems give the impression of an individual personality of sharply defined character. Unauthentic additions to these poems are the work of a redactor.[59] Source "B" is the work not of a compiler but of an author who has created a personal-historical work (not really a biography in our sense); beyond portions of 19:1—20:6 "B" is found in parts of chapters 26, 28, 29, and 36—44. The purpose of the author is to narrate the experiences of the prophet that are the occasion of memorable words. The narratives are gathered together in chronological order by the author (though 36:1—37:2 and 19:1—20:6 are out of chronological order).[60] Mowinckel rejects Baruch's authorship of "B."[61] Source "C" is a set of monotonous long speeches with strong affinities with Deuteronomy and the Deuteronomic sections of the historical books. The speeches offer invectives and threats; there is an appeal to repentance, a statement of the unwillingness of the people to repent, and the inevitable punishment. Source "C" includes 7:1—8:3; 11:1–5, 9–14; 18:1–12; 21:1–10; 25:1–11a; 32:1–2, 6–16, 24–44; 34:1–7, 8–22; 35:1–19; 44:1–14.[62] There are parallels between "B" and "C," for example, 7:1—8:3 ("C") and 26:1–6 ("B"), and between "A" and "C," for example, 1:10 ("A") and 18:7, 9 ("C").[63] Source "C" had no chronological interest, but using the superscriptions of individual units, a redactor worked the units into the order of "B."[64] The original scroll of the fourth year of

---

52 The most thorough recent review of the history of literary analysis of the book in this century, with particular reference to the origin and nature of the prose sermons of the book, is to be found in Louis Stulman, *Prose Sermons*, 7–31; see also in general Robert P. Carroll, *Jeremiah, A Commentary* (Philadelphia: Westminster, 1986) 38–50.

53 Duhm, pp. xii–xiii.

54 Ibid., 17.

55 Ibid., xiv.

56 Ibid., xvi.

57 Ibid., xx.

58 Carroll, p. 39.

59 Mowinckel, *Komposition*, 17–24.

60 Ibid., 24–27.

61 Ibid., 30.

62 Ibid., 31–34.

63 Ibid., 40.

64 Ibid., 45.

Jehoiakim (see chap. 36) contained "A" material only, but we cannot determine more closely the actual contents of the scroll.[65] Mowinckel suggests that "A" and "B," as separate works, are early, and came out of an Egyptian milieu; both could have been edited between 580 and 480.[66] It is impossible to date "C," but it has the stamp of legalistic Judaism, and Mowinckel suggests a *terminus a quo* of 400.[67] Then there was a completely independent collection of oracles of salvation (chaps. 30—31) that the redactor placed before chapter 32 (salvation material of "B").[68] Still later a collection of foreign-nations oracles, attributed to Jrm, was added.[69] The placement of chapters 46—51 after 25:13 in *G* is a secondary shift for unknown reasons.[70] In a later book (1946) Mowinckel stated that he prefers the term "tradition complexes" rather than "sources": this allows for greater flexibility in analysis.[71]

As Carroll remarks, "Much of recent research on Jeremiah consists of the development or modification of views of Duhm and Mowinckel."[72] Four basic questions need to be answered. (1) What is the extent and nature of Mowinckel's "Source C," that is, the sermonic prose? Is it a product of Deuteronomistic editorial work as Kings is, or, on the contrary, does it reflect Jrm's own diction, and if so, to what degree? Again, is there any literary relation between the poetic oracles and this sermonic prose? (2) What is the nature of Mowinckel's "Source B," that is, the historical narrative? May one attribute it to Baruch? Is the narrative trustworthy? (3) Is the narrative of chapter 36 trustworthy? Can the narrative of the dictated scroll (or of the two dictated scrolls) provide a basis for our reconstruction of the literary history of the book? Indeed (4) what is a plausible scenario for the growth of the book, given the impression of disorder it now presents?

The distinctiveness of the repetitive sermonic prose of Jer and its resemblance to Deuteronomy and the Deuteronomistic additions in Kings has long been noted. Following Duhm and Mowinckel, J. Philip Hyatt developed the theory of a Deuteronomic edition of Jer.[73] Moshe Weinfeld subsumes the sermonic prose in Jer within "the Deuteronomic school."[74] This approach is affirmed by Siegfried Herrmann[75] and pressed by Winfried Thiel.[76] Thiel and Ernest Nicholson, in the English-speaking world, see in these sermonic passages little that can be traced to Jrm and much that reflects the preaching offered to the exiles in the sixth century.[77] Hyatt is less extreme, allowing a place for genuine Jeremianic material within this prose material: "D sometimes preserves genuine prophecies of Jeremiah in the prophet's words; sometimes he gives the gist of Jeremiah's prophecies in his own words; and sometimes he composes freely and departs from Jeremiah's thoughts."[78] John Bright is similar; he points out that the prose is "a characteristic rhetorical prose of the seventh/sixth century."[79] He continues, "These discourses scarely provide us— certainly not as a rule—with Jeremiah's *ipsissima verba*. Though the prose tradition of Jeremiah doubtless had its origin in his preaching, it does not record that preaching verbatim, but rather as it was remembered, understood, and repeated in the circle of his followers."[80]

I proposed in 1960 that more often than not the

65 Ibid., 48.
66 Ibid., 56.
67 Ibid., 57.
68 Ibid., 46–47.
69 Ibid., 55.
70 Ibid., 14.
71 Sigmund Mowinckel, *Prophecy and Tradition: The Prophetic Books in the Light of the Study of the Growth and History of the Tradition* (Avhandlinger utgitt av Det Norske Videnskaps-Akademi i Oslo II, Hist.-Filos. Klasse 1946, 3; Oslo: Dybwad, 1946) 21–23, 28, 49.
72 Carroll, p. 40.
73 J. Philip Hyatt, "The Deuteronomic Edition of Jeremiah," *Vanderbilt Studies in the Humanities* 1 (Nashville: Vanderbilt University, 1951) 71–95; Hyatt, pp. 788–90.
74 Weinfeld, *Deuteronomy*, 27–32.
75 Siegfried Herrmann, *Die prophetischen Heilserwartungen im Alten Testament: Ursprung und Gestaltwandel* (BWANT 85; Stuttgart: Kohlhammer, 1965) 159–241.
76 Thiel, *Jer 1—25*; Winfried Thiel, *Die deuteronomistiche Redaktion von Jer 26–45* (WMANT 52; Neukirchen: Neukirchener, 1981).
77 Nicholson, *Preaching.*
78 Hyatt, p. 789.
79 Bright, p. lxxi; so already William O. E. Oesterley and Theodore H. Robinson, *An Introduction to the Books of the Old Testament* (New York: Macmillan, 1934) 304.
80 Bright, p. lxxii.

phrases of the prose sermons were generated by proto-typical phrases in the poetic oracles, usually those of Jrm, but sometimes of other prophets as well.[81] This suggestion dealt simply with the origin of the prose and not with the question whether or not it embodies valid tradition about Jrm. Then in 1973 Helga Weippert made both an intensive and an extensive study of the phraseology of the sermonic prose passages.[82] She notes particularly the points at which presumed Deuteronomistic phrases are found in fresh contexts. Thus "with all one's heart and with all one's soul" appears eight times in Deuteronomy and four times in the Deuteronomistic historical work; it also appears in Jer 32:41, but in that passage, in contrast to all twelve others, it refers to God, not to human beings.[83] Weippert concludes that the prose addresses represent a tradition that stands nearer to Jrm than do the biographical narratives (Mowinckel's "Source B"), near enough to call them a Jeremianic tradition.[84] Detailed investigation of specific phrases indicates that the ties to Deuteronomic-Deuteronomistic speech are weak: only in a few cases (like "walk after other gods") do we have a direct line to Deuteronomistic phraseology, and in most of such cases the material in Jer gives a distinctive turn to the phrases. Indeed at some points the Deuteronomists seem themselves to be dependent on Jeremiah rather than the reverse (see sec. 76). These observations then raise the question whether there is a literary "source" at all. Finally, it should be noted that Stulman has recently done a thorough review of the repeated "Deuteronomistic" phrases in the prose sermons, but on the basis of a retrojected Old Greek text tradition rather than from the expansionist M text;[85] he fails, however, to deal, in the way Weippert has done, with the fresh contexts in which the various stereotyped phrases appear.

In regard to "Source B," the biographical material, even though Mowinckel did not follow Duhm in attributing it to Baruch, most scholars have assumed the attribution (Giesebrecht, Volz, Rudolph, Hyatt, Bright).

Gunther Wanke has made the most thorough recent study of that material.[86] He concludes that the so-called Source B is made up of three different "cycles," each with a different origin, none of which can be attributed with any confidence to Baruch. His first "cycle" is made up of chapters 37—44; in his analysis of these chapters he depends on a prior work of Heinz Kremers and finds a convincing structure to that sequence.[87] The purpose of this sequence, he maintains, is "the reality of what it is for Jeremiah to be a prophet"—here, for the first time in the OT, we find a connection between the life of faith and suffering.[88] His second "cycle," he is convinced, is made up of 19:1—20:6 plus chapters 26—29 and 36. The purpose of this cycle is "the truth of the proclamation of the prophet Jeremiah."[89] Then he discusses briefly what he believes to be a third "cycle," consisting of 45:1–5 plus 51:59–64. Finally, he makes a tentative proposal as to how these collections of material were fitted together with the remainder of the material of the Book of Jer.[90]

The existence of the narrative in chapter 36, that of Jrm's dictation of a scroll to Baruch in the fourth year of Jehoiakim (36:1–4), has seemed to be an attractive clue in the reconstruction of the process by which the Book of Jer came to be: it is plausible to assume that the scroll was the first stage in that process—or rather that the second expanded scroll (36:32) was, the first having been burned by the king. But there are three interrelated difficulties. The first is that the sequence of material in the book as it stands at present is immensely complex, so that any reconstruction of the stages by which the book came to be must necessarily be subjective. The second difficulty arises from the assumption of most scholars (on the basis of 1:2) that Jrm began his proclamations in the thirteenth year of Josiah (627); if the first scroll was dictated in the fourth year of Jehoiakim (605), the assumption implies that the scroll contained oracles from a period of twenty-two years, arranged no one knows

81 Holladay, "Prototype."
82 Weippert, *Prosareden*; see also William L. Holladay, "A Fresh Look at 'Source B' and 'Source C' in Jeremiah," *VT* 25 (1975) 402–8.
83 Weippert, *Prosareden*, 23, n. 108.
84 Ibid., 228–29.
85 Stulman, *Prose Sermons*.
86 Wanke, *Baruchschrift*.

87 Ibid., 94–95; since in the main I accept his analysis, I discuss the matter in detail under 37:1—44:30, Form and Structure.
88 Wanke, *Baruchschrift*, 155–56.
89 Ibid., 156.
90 Ibid., 133, 140, 150.

how. And since the poetic oracles that are now found in the first part of the book lack firm historical settings, it is clear that here as well there is much room for subjective judgment. The third difficulty is that the narrative of Jrm's dictation of the scroll in chapter 36 is modeled closely on the narrative of the discovery of the scroll read to Josiah (2 Kings 22): some scholars have therefore concluded that the narrative in chapter 36 is a late and unhistorical construct.[91]

The result is that the attempts to reconstruct the original scroll or scrolls have varied enormously.[92] Duhm, as we have seen, assumed that Jrm dictated only poetry of a specific meter and that those poems were in the original scroll.[93] Cornill wondered why the scroll could not include prose: he suggested including, among other passages, 7:1—8:3.[94] Mowinckel is certain that it is impossible to reconstruct the original scroll, but Theodore H. Robinson, in 1924, suggested that since Mowinckel's "Source C" was specifically literary, it was that material that was contained in the scroll.[95] This suggestion was taken up and elaborated by Otto Eissfeldt: he concluded that since the scroll contained primarily threats, the prose sermons meet this description.[96] In the meantime Hyatt conjectured that the scroll contained essentially the poetry within 1:4—9:1;[97] Rudolph likewise concluded that it contained poetry, but Rudolph's proposed list was far more extensive than Hyatt's.[98] More recently, scholars have expressed the judgment that certainty in specifying the contents of the scrolls is impossible (so James Muilenburg,[99] Bright,[100] Georg Fohrer,[101] Artur Weiser[102]).

Then a fresh attempt was made by Claus Rietzschel in 1966 to identify the steps by which the Book of Jer came to be.[103] He rejects the idea that Mowinckel's "A," "B," and "C" were handed down separately; he suggests that in the "tradition complexes" that went to make up the book prose and poetry existed side by side.[104] He approaches the book as it now is and tries to identify the major components in the order in which they were added to the growing tradition. He identifies four main "tradition blocks": (1) predictions of doom against Judah and Jerusalem, chapters 1—24; (2) predictions of doom against foreign nations, 25:1–13 + 46:1—51:58 + 25:15–38; (3) predictions of salvation for Israel and Judah, chapters 26—35; and (4) narrative of the prophet, chapters 36—44.[105] The original scroll, he is convinced, must lie within chapters 1—24, which contains six "tradition complexes"; he suggests that the original scroll is to be found in the first of these, chapters 1—6, and that the "other words added" (36:32) must lie within the following four "tradition complexes," namely, chapters 7—10, 11—13, 14—17, and 18—20.[106] He is puzzled by the problem of dating: most commentators have assumed that chapters 2—6 contain early oracles, that is, 627–621, while Rietzschel accepts the identification of "foe from the north" as the Babylonians, so that whether the oracles of 2:1—4:4 are early or not, the oracles of 4:5—6:30 must come from 605.[107]

With many of Rietzschel's conclusions the present study is in agreement; but my own suspicion is that the book grew in a less orderly and schematic fashion than Rietzschel set forth.

---

91 See Charles D. Isbell, "II Kings 22:3—23:24 and Jeremiah 36: A Stylistic Comparison," *JSOT* 8 (1978) 33–45; Robert P. Carroll, *From Chaos to Covenant, Prophecy in the Book of Jeremiah* (New York: Crossroad, 1981) 15–16; Carroll, 663–66.

92 For a survey of the history of the question from Duhm to about 1965 see Rietzschel, *Urrolle*, 10–19; for a survey of more recent opinion see Thompson, pp. 56–59.

93 Duhm, pp. xiii–xiv.

94 Cornill, p. 93.

95 Theodore H. Robinson, "Baruch's Roll," *ZAW* 42 (1924) 209–21.

96 Eissfeldt, *Introduction*, 350–52.

97 Hyatt, 787.

98 Rudolph, pp. xviii–xix.

99 James Muilenburg, "Jeremiah the Prophet," *IDB*

2:833.

100 Bright, p. lxi.

101 Ernst Sellin and Georg Fohrer, *Introduction to the Old Testament* (New York and Nashville: Abingdon, 1968) 393.

102 Weiser, p. xxxix.

103 Rietzschel, *Urrolle*.

104 Ibid., 19–24.

105 Ibid., 122–25.

106 Ibid., 125, 130–31.

107 Ibid., 136.

15. A Plausible Theory for the Growth of the Book of Jeremiah: Preliminary Remarks

In my judgment Mowinckel's idea of "sources" is not valid; there are obviously form-critical contrasts between the prophetic oracles and the parenetic sermonic prose, but this contrast does not imply the existence of literary sources. There are several general considerations that lead me to this conclusion.

The first is that vocabulary distinctive to Jrm is found across the "sources." Two examples must suffice. Both the prophetic oracles and the sermonic prose use the verb שׁוב "(re)turn" in what I have called "covenantal contexts,"[108] that is, to express a change of loyalty on the part of Israel (or another nation) or God, each for the other. About 15 percent of the occurrences of שׁוב in the OT are in covenantal contexts, and of these, about 30 percent are in the Book of Jer: forty-eight occurrences. Of these forty-eight occurrences twenty-eight are in Jer's prophetic oracles[109] and eleven are in sermonic prose.[110] (There are an additional nine occurrences in the book: six are in 3:6–11, a late passage; two are in miscellaneous expansions [24:7 and 32:40]; and one is evidently a scribal error [49:4].)[111] Of the four occurrences of covenantal שׁוב in Deuteronomy, three are late and evidently dependent on the diction in Jer (Deut 4:30; 30:2, 10); only Deut 23:15 is evidently early. Of the eight occurrences of covenantal שׁוב in Kings, seven are clearly exilic and evidently dependent on Jrm (1 Kgs 8:33, 35, 47, 48; 9:6; 13:33; 2 Kgs 17:13); only 2 Kgs 23:25 is likely to be from the early Deuteronomistic edition. That is to say, the usage is overwhelmingly distinctive to Jrm, both in the prophetic oracles and in the sermonic prose. Any contrasts of usage between the oracles and the sermonic prose may be attributed to the form-critical difference between the two types of material; those contrasts are not "striking," as I maintained in my study of שׁוב.[112] The second example is the use of שֶׁקֶר "falsehood"; though the noun is fairly frequent within the OT (111 occurrences), "there is such a sudden burst of occurrences in the book of Jeremiah that one immediately suspects that the concept of falsehood had a special significance in the message of that prophet."[113] There are 36 occurrences of the noun in Jer. These occurrences, and their theological angle of vision, are found in all of Mowinckel's "sources": Jrm's oracles against the "false prophets" (6:13–15; 23:9–32) and material in prose recording such polemic (chaps. 27—29), sermonic prose in which Jrm speaks out against the people's false sense of security in the temple (7:1–12).[114]

More substantial even than common vocabulary across the presumed "sources" is the identification of what I may call the "authentic voice" of Jrm in all the "sources." This "voice" is not easy to specify in the abstract. Its characteristics include surprise, freshness, imagination, and irony. Words are often exploited for multiple meanings; conventional views are often reversed.[115] I shall discuss Jrm's style more thoroughly in sec. 70, but the matter needs to be stressed here. These characteristics are clearly to be found in the prophetic oracles, but they are to be found in the other "sources" as well. Thus I have proposed the shift in 7:2b–12 from "so that I may dwell with you in this place" (7:3) to "then I shall let you dwell in this place" (7:7), a shift undetectable in the consonantal text; the same passage also offers highly unusual syntax—the interrogative particle followed by a series of infinitive absolutes (7:9), the sequence גַּם plus the subject pronoun plus הִנֵּה plus a perfect verb (7:11). By contrast the style of Deuteronomy is solemn, passionate, and didactic, and the style of the Deuteronomistic redactional passages of Kings is pious and repetitive. It is of primary importance, therefore, to be alert to the distinctive "voice" of Jrm beyond the prophetic oracles. Of course one may propose that the prophetic oracles are Jrm's *ipsissima verba* while the sermonic prose is the "gist" of a message of Jrm preserved by Baruch in the prose style of his day;[116] still, all I am proposing here is that the sermonic prose may preserve Jrm's "voice" and that it is not to be taken as a literary source.

---

108 Holladay, *Šûbh*, 116.
109 Jer 2:19; 3:1, 12 (twice), 14 (twice), 19, 22 (three times); 4:1 (twice); 5:3, 6; 8:4 (twice), 5 (three times), 6; 14:7; 15:7, 19 (twice); 23:14, 22; 31:19, 22.
110 Jer 11:10; 18:8, 11; 25:5; 26:3; 34:15, 16; 35:15; 36:3, 7; 44:5.
111 All these tabulations differ from those in Holladay, *Šûbh*, 137–38, and are based on the judgments of the present study.

112 Holladay, *Šûbh*, 138–39.
113 Overholt, *Falsehood*, 1.
114 Thomas W. Overholt, "Remarks on the Continuity of the Jeremiah Tradition," *JBL* 91 (1972) 457–62.
115 For a brief attempt to explore the matter of style see Holladay, "Style."
116 See Holladay, "A Fresh Look at 'Source B' and 'Source C' in Jeremiah," 411–12.

In the analysis of the relationship between *M* and *G* (secs. 2–8) I essentially work backward in time from what now lies before us to the earlier traditions behind the present forms of text; and for methodological consistency it might be appropriate to continue that process (it is the procedure of Rietzschel: see above). But instead, for the sake of clarity, I shall begin with the earliest literary deposit and move forward in time.

16. The First Two Scrolls, and the Identification of the First Scroll: Chapters 1—6

I assume *ex hypothesi* that Jrm's first scroll (36:4), and then his second scroll (36:32), became the core of the present Book of Jer. One can, of course, question the historicity of the narrative in chapter 36, but although it may be a stylized account, it would seem prudent to accept the basic data offered: that Jrm dictated a first scroll to Baruch in 605 (vv 1–8) and, after the king burned that scroll (in December 601, by the date in v 9 according to *G*: see Interpretation on 36:9–11), Jrm dictated a second scroll to Baruch with additions. We are told that Baruch was with Jrm when he bought the field at Anathoth, presumably in 588, and accompanied him to Egypt, probably in the autumn of 587 or winter of 587/586: thus there was opportunity for Baruch to enlarge upon the second scroll at least until that period of time.

Of course it is clear that any reconstruction of either the first or the second scroll is to some degree conjectural: there are no obvious rhetorical marks to delimit the material dictated in the earliest written form from material added later. It is nevertheless worth an attempt, conjectural though it may be: if a proposal is at least plausible, it may sharpen our awareness of both the setting of the early oracles and of the ordering of these oracles in Jrm's mind before he dictated them.

At the outset I assume the lower chronology for Jrm, by which the thirteenth year of Josiah (627/626) marks the prophet's birth, not the acceptance of his prophetic call (for this, see the argumentation in sec. 27). By this chronology there are no oracles from the period 627–622 (this chronology solves the difficulty Rietzschel faced in dealing with the material in chaps. 2—6: see sec. 14). I assume that Jrm as a very young man supported Josiah's campaign to reunify north and south (the early core of chaps. 30—31), and that the death of Josiah (609)

brought the prophet into mature and independent proclamation of Yahweh's word, beginning with the temple sermon (609/608, probably the late summer or early autumn of 609), a sermon that put his life at risk (chap. 26).

Chapter 36 offers several important data in regard to the nature of the first two scrolls. The first, most obviously, is that the first scroll was dictated in the fourth year of Jehoiakim (36:1), the same year as the battle of Carchemish (46:2). Jrm states that the reason he is dictating the scroll is that he is "restricted" from going to the temple area personally, but the reason he is "restricted" is not given; one may guess, however, that he is *persona non grata* for having announced, directly after the battle of Carchemish, that the foe from the north is coming. The second datum is that the purpose of the scroll, which contained oracles "against [or about, עַל] Israel and Jerusalem and all the nations" (v 2), was to warn Judah so that she might repent and Yahweh might forgive her (vv 3, 7). By contrast the purpose of the second scroll is Yahweh's declaration of irrevocable punishment (vv 28–31). Material involving appeals to repentance will therefore have been part of the first scroll.

In the first few chapters of the present book, where one would expect to find material contained in the first two scrolls, one encounters the following. Most of 2:1—4:4 offers accusations, but in the midst of these are several verses offering Yahweh's call for repentance: 3:12–14, 22a; 4:1–4; furthermore 3:22b–25 appears to imply the people's repentance. Most of the material beginning with 4:5, however, offers scenarios of punishment, usually battle scenes; in this portion of the book there are only three passages that imply the possibility of repentance: 4:14 ("Wash from evil your heart, O Jerusalem, that you may be rescued!"), 6:8 ("Take warning, Jerusalem, or my heart will wrench away from you, and I will make you a desolation, a land uninhabited"), and the temple sermon, 7:2b–12 ("Make good your ways and your doings, so that I may dwell with you in this place . . ."). There are similar scenarios of punishment in 8:4—10:25, but within them no further words regarding repentance. One could then well imagine the first scroll to contain at least some of the material included in 2:1—7:12 and the second scroll to have added some of the material up to 10:25.

Any suggestions of greater specificity with regard to the contents of the first two scrolls must be based on two kinds of evidence: similarity in vocabulary or phraseology that might suggest contemporaneity, and patterns appropriate to Jrm's retention and presentation of the material he dictated, such as symmetries, catchword associations, and other devices appropriate to material committed to memory. But obviously there are several difficulties with such evidence. First, with regard to similarity in vocabulary or phraseology, such similarity merely suggests contemporaneity, it does not demand it. Second, with regard to any patterning appropriate to retention in memory, there is a double difficulty: for one thing, in examining the material today it is always possible to perceive pseudo-patterns—one may propose organizing schemes that played no part in Jrm's thinking and that mask whatever scheme he did have. For another, even a valid pattern is rarely open to proof—only occasionally can one propose an organizing principle that is utterly persuasive. Nevertheless, I offer my present suggestions regarding the content of the first two scrolls, suggestions that appear to me at least plausible.

Two more preliminary points need to be made. First, it is clear that the second scroll will include two sorts of material: (1) that which Jrm had delivered orally from the time after the first scroll was dictated (605) until the burning of that scroll (December 601), a period of time during which Jrm presumably still hoped for repentance, and (2) that which Jrm delivered orally after the king burned the scroll. Second, it is not stated how long it was after the king burned the first scroll that Jrm dictated his second scroll—it could have been an extended period of time—and in any case the second scroll is "open-ended," so that one cannot expect any signs of a "cut-off," since one might assume Baruch could continue to add fresh material as time went on.

It is convenient to begin with 4:5–31, a unit of discourse that is set apart from what precedes and what follows.[117] Three sequences within this unit (vv 5–8, 13–18, 29–31) are comparable in offering shifts of speaker including a brief lament of the people (vv 8, 13b, 31b); in

respect to speaker I propose that vv 5–8 and 29–31 are completely parallel, a speech of Yahweh (vv 5–7 and 29–30) followed by a speech of Jrm (vv 8, 31) that is closed by a citation of the people's lament; the middle sequence (vv 13–18) offers a more complex shift of speakers. Since these three sequences include Yahweh's call to Jerusalem to repent (v 14), I propose that they were included in the first scroll.

The two intervening sequences, vv 9–12 and 19–28, are parallel in a different way: the first half of each pair (vv 9–10, 19–20) offers לֵב "heart" twice (vv 9, 19) followed by נֶפֶשׁ "throat, soul" once (v 10, 19), and the second half of each pair offers the word-play מִדְבָּר "wilderness" (vv 11, 26) followed by דבר pi'el "pronounce, speak" (vv 12, 28). Though both the three sequences here assigned to the first scroll (vv 5–8, 13–18, 29–31) and the intervening two sequences (vv 9–12, 19–28) offer scenarios of destruction, v 28 implies the irrevocability of Yahweh's judgment, appropriate to the second scroll. I therefore propose that in the second scroll vv 5–8, 13–18, 29–31 were expanded by vv 9–12 and 19–28.

It is convenient now to consider chapter 5. Both 5:1–9 and 5:20–29 end with an identical refrain, and so does another sequence in chapter 9 (see 9:8). The fact that material beyond chapter 7 shares a refrain with material in chapter 5 and the fact that there is nothing in either 5:1–9 or 5:20–29 that suggests repentance suggest in turn that these sequences in chapter 5 do not belong to the first scroll; the exasperation implied in the refrain suggests a time when Jrm's expectation of repentance was waning. One wonders, too, whether behind the wording of 5:5 stands the attention gained by Jrm's scroll in the king's court (36:20–26). As to 5:10–17, the implication of that passage is of irrevocable destruction (for the negative in v 10, see Text): Jrm's role is not to warn the people but to destroy them by the fire of his words (v 14b). One may conclude therefore that 5:1–9, 10–17, and 20–29 were part of the second scroll. (Verses 18–19 and 30–31 are short pieces that appear to have been added secondarily.)

With regard to chapter 6, it has already been noted

---

117 So also Volz, Rudolph, Bright.

that 6:8 contains the implication of repentance; I propose then that 6:1–8 stood after 4:5–8 + 13–18 + 29–31 in the first scroll. In this regard one may note (1) the likeness of 6:1 to 4:5–6, (2) the fact that בַּת־צִיּוֹן (literally "daughter Zion," here "fair Zion") could link 4:31 and 6:2, (3) the shifts of speaker in 6:4–5 similar to those in the three sequences of chapter 4 assigned here to the first scroll, and (4) the possible link between "woe to us" in 6:4b and in 4:13b.

The material in 6:9–15 is similar to that in 5:10–17 in associating Jrm's word to the destruction of the vineyard Israel (one notes particularly 6:11); this sequence is doubtless part of the second scroll. The same would be true of 6:16–26: the diction in v 21 is similar to that in vv 11–12 and 15, and the expression "terror is all around!" in v 25 is evidently a generalization of Jrm's use of it with Passhur (20:1–6) after Jrm broke the earthenware flask (chap. 19), itself a gesture indicating Yahweh's irrevocable punishment. In short, 6:16–26 must have been added in the second scroll. And in vv 27–30 Jrm pronounces the people "reject silver," again a judgment appropriate in the second scroll.

As I have already noted, the temple sermon, 7:2b–12, is also an appeal to repentance. It is also to be observed that 6:8, though the end of a unit, would appear to be an abrupt ending for the first scroll. The temple sermon, 7:2b–12, would make (and, I propose, did make) an admirable closing to the first scroll: 6:8 says, "Be warned," and 7:2b–12 embodies that warning; here, then, would be an instance in which both the sermonic prose of the book and Jrm's prophetic oracles entered into the first literary deposit side by side. There are no other references to repentance in chapters 7—10; I am satisfied that in 2:1—10:25 nothing after 7:12 was to be found in the first scroll. (For 7:13—10:25 see sec. 17.)

To sum up so far: of the material contained in 4:5—6:30, the first scroll contained 4:5–8, 13–18, 29–31; 6:1–8; 7:2b–12. In the second scroll the following were added: 4:9–12, 19–28; 5:1–9, 10–17, 20–29; 6:9–15, 16–26, 27–30.

I now turn to 2:1—4:4. Here the task is far more difficult: most of the material, as already noted, consists of accusations, and these would have been appropriate either for the first scroll or for any additions in the second. There are, to be sure, evidences in 2:1—4:4 of literary discontinuity, but to work from these to specific assignments to one or the other of the scrolls is risky. And there is a further difficulty. It appears that before any of the material in 2:1—4:4 was addressed to Judah and Jerusalem, some of it had been addressed to the north (this, I have concluded, is the implication of 3:12). One must therefore make allowance for the possibility of an early recension to the north and a later, expanded recension to the south, and that recension to the south was the one Jrm dictated in his first scroll.

The details of my analysis are laid out in Preliminary Observations and Setting for that section of the book and will only be summarized here: the first scroll contained all of 2:1—4:4 except three poetic additions, 2:26–28; 3:3 and 20, and two prose additions, 3:6–11 and 16–18bα. The latter are redactional and were probably added in the Persian period. As for the poetic additions (2:26–28; 3:3 and 20), all three break the continuity of their context. As for 2:26–28, it is the only sequence in chapter 2 with an address in the masculine singular: all the others are either feminine singular (vv 2–3, 14–25, 33–37) or masculine plural (vv 4–13, 29–32). Similarly, 3:20 has an address in the masculine plural, whereas 3:19 has an address in the feminine singular. Again 3:3 suddenly speaks of a drought, appearing to interrupt the continuity of 3:2 and 4. In syntax also 2:26–28 and 3:20 are parallel: both have similes with כְּ "like, as" and כֵּן "so"; there are no other similes in 2:1—4:4. In vocabulary it may be noted that the drought (3:3) is associated in the present study with the fast called by Jehoiakim in the context of which the first scroll was burned (36:9); and the operative verb in 3:20 ("betray," בגד) is also the operative verb in 5:11, already assigned to the second scroll. On the other hand, 2:26–28 appears to have been added in 594: on this matter see the discussion below.

Was the first scroll opened with any part of the call in chapter 1? In seeking an answer to this question one must examine not only chapter 1 but 25:1–7: the present study has reconstructed a first-scroll recension in those verses. But this recension reads like an introduction to the scroll: "The word which came to Jeremiah concerning all the people of Judah in the fourth year of Jehoiakim son of Josiah, king of Judah, as follows: From the thirteenth year of Josiah son of Amon, king of Judah, to this day, I have spoken to you as follows: Return each from his evil way and from the evil of your doings, and remain on the soil which I have given to you and to your fathers, from of old, for ever, and do not walk after other gods to your own hurt, oracle of Yahweh." Volz and Sheldon Blank (among others) have proposed that 25:1–14 was the introduction to the scroll;[118] John Skinner, on the other hand, saw it as the closing of the scroll.[119] In its present position the passage closes off a collection, but a closing summary is not normal in the prophetic literature.

I propose therefore that the first-scroll recension of 25:1–7 was the introduction to that scroll, and that in the second scroll this introduction was shifted to the end (and expanded), and portions of chapter 1 became the new introduction. We are accustomed to assume that the call of the prophet is the normal beginning for prophetic discourse, but most of the prophetic collections do not include a call narrative, and the call of Isaiah, though evidently the beginning of a small collection dealing with the Syro-Ephraimite War, Isa 6:1—9:6, has been inserted in the midst of what is evidently a primary collection.[120] I have proposed that Jrm's earliest confessions emerged in the crisis at the time Jehoiakim burned his first scroll, a crisis in which Jrm's status as a true prophet was challenged by the optimistic prophets. I could imagine, therefore, that it was the second scroll that began with the call narrative as an attempt at self-legitimation.[121] The second scroll would then have begun with an earlier form of 1:1 or 1:2 and continued with 1:4–16.

To sum up regarding the first scroll: it consisted of the first-scroll recension of 25:1–7, followed by 2:1–25, 29–37; 3:1–2, 4–5, 12, 14–15, 18bβ–19, 21–23, the poetic core of 24–25; 4:1–4, 5–8, 13–18, 29–31; 6:1–8; 7:2b–12.

17. Further Discussion of the Initial Form of the Second Scroll: Chapters 7—10

The rest of the material in chapters 7—10 is easily dealt with. Verses 13–15 of chapter 7, usually considered the end of the original form of the temple sermon, are by the argumentation of the present study an appendix to the sermon added by Jrm to the second scroll. There follow in chapter 7 three prose units, vv 16–20, 21–28, and 29–34. These three are not unified—vv 16–20 are Yahweh's personal address to Jrm; while vv 21–28 are an address by Yahweh to the people, first a parody of priestly torah and then an accusation report; and vv 29–34 (if I have correctly reconstructed the passage, opening with the clause "and you shall say to them" now displaced in v 28) are evidently the content of what Yahweh tells Jrm to tell the people, namely, a lament for the people followed by a grounding for that lament. The setting for both vv 16–20 and 29–34 appears to be the time of the burning of the first scroll, but the setting of vv 21–28 is evidently later, in 594 (see below). I could then imagine that the prose ending of the first scroll (7:2b–12) would first be extended by the appendix (vv 13–15) and then by the personal addresses to Jrm, vv 16–20 and 29–34 (it is clear that 8:1–3 is a redactional addition from later times).

The setting I propose for 8:4–10a + 13 is the autumn of 601. As for 8:14–23, the diction of v 14 is deliberately reminiscent of that of 4:5–6 in the light of Yahweh's irrevocable judgment and is therefore likely to have been pronounced soon after Jehoiakim burned the first scroll; and 9:1–8, closing with the refrain also found in 5:9 and 29, suggests a time close to that for 5:1–9 and 20–29.

Settings for 9:9–10 and 16–21 are impossible to discover precisely, but I would tentatively propose that these passages, too, were included in the immediate dictation of the second scroll: if the second scroll was concluded by the second-scroll recension of 25:1–13, then the funeral diction in 9:16–21 could well be rounded off by the reference to the extinguishing of wedding sounds in 25:10. (The setting for 9:11–15 is late; 9:22–23 and 24–25, though Jeremianic, seem to have been inserted in the corpus at a later date.)

---

118 Volz, p. 252; Sheldon H. Blank, *Jeremiah, Man and Prophet* (Cincinnati: Hebrew Union College, 1961) 31; see further Rudolph, p. 161.

119 Skinner, *Prophecy and Religion*, 240.

120 Wildberger, *Jesaja*, 234; Sellin-Fohrer, 371.

121 This conclusion amends my conclusion in *Jeremiah 1*, 32, that the call narrative was the beginning of the first scroll. See further sec. 69, and see Jon L.

Berquist, "Prophetic Legitimation in Jeremiah," *VT* 39 (1989).

A discussion of 10:1–16 is offered in sec. 21. The setting of 10:17–25 seems to be just before the siege of Jerusalem in December 598; at this point, then, one moves beyond the presumed contents of the initial form of the second scroll.

To sum up regarding the second scroll: it expanded 25:1–7 to 25:1–13 and shifted it to the end of the scroll; it began with a form of 1:1 or 1:2 and continued with 1:4–16, and continued with the contents of the first scroll with the added insertions of 3:3, 20; 4:9–12, 19–28; 5:1–9, 10–17, 20–29; 6:9–15, 16–26, 27–30, and with additions past 7:12; the result then was an early form of 1:1 or 1:2; 1:4–16; 2:1–25, 29–37; 3:1–5, 12–15, 18bβ, 19–23, the poetic core of 24–25; 4:1–4, 5–31; 5:1–17, 20–29; 6:1–8, 9–15, 16–26, 27–30; 7:1–15, 16–20, 29–34; 8:4–10a, 13, 14–23; 9:1–8, 9–10, 16–21; the scroll was then rounded off with the second-scroll recension of 25:1–13 and possibly with chapter 45 as well—the four verbs in 45:4 would make a nice inclusio with those verbs in 1:10.

As I have already mentioned, the second scroll would have been "open-ended." Since the setting of 10:17–25 presupposes a siege (v 17), doubtless the first siege of Jerusalem, which began in December 598, one must envisage the recording of that passage during that period. One must also assume that 25:1–13 and 45:1–5 were "unattached," since they continued to be last after that addition.

18. A Fresh Scroll in 594?

There are a whole series of passages that appear to have their setting in the crisis in Jrm's life in 594, when he challenged Zedekiah's Jerusalem conference (chap. 27) and confronted Hananiah (chap. 28). One could continue to imagine an open-ended scroll, except that there are at least three passages seemingly from this period that are embedded in chapters 1—10, namely, 1:17–19; 2:26–28; and 7:21–28. (One might imagine 10:1–16 to be one of these as well: I suggest that that passage is authentic to Jrm, but I believe it was a later insertion; see sec. 21.) There are two data suggesting that Jrm himself dictated a fresh scroll in 594. First, as I have already noted, 1:17–19; 2:26–28; and 7:21–28 are not simply added after 10:25 but are inserted appropriately: 1:17–19 closes off the call narrative; 2:26–28, a poetic accusation of religious disloyalty, is embedded within similar accusations; and 7:21–28 is embedded within similar prose passages. Second, Jrm's confessions and the counter-liturgy of drought and battle (14:1—15:9) appear to offer a shape appropriate to memory and oral dictation. I propose, then, that the whole corpus was dictated anew in 594—this fresh dictation then would be a replacement for the earlier second scroll. I have proposed in the present study that Jrm proclaimed his confessions to the public after the death of Hananiah in order to publish his vindication as a true prophet; if this is the case, then the purpose of this fresh scroll, like the purpose of the earlier two, would be the proclamation of Yahweh's words to the public. One wonders whether Jrm was once more *persona non grata* in the temple area; one thinks of 28:11—after Hananiah broke the yoke-pegs on Jrm's neck, "Jeremiah went his way." But of course this is all speculation.

The new material, evidently dictated in 594, that is now found after chapter 10 appears to embody the core of chapters 11—20, and the skeleton of that core is evidently the confessions. The confessions, like the accusations of chapter 2, evidently had a prehistory: there is evidence for some of them of earlier settings before they were recorded in writing, but it is the process of recording that is at issue here.

I have proposed that the setting of 11:1–17 is the festival of booths in the autumn of 594, when the septennial reading of Deuteronomy would have taken place: the extension of the new scroll would then begin with this sequence.

The month of the festival of booths in 594 was the month in which Hananiah died (28:1, 17). The new scroll then contained the sequence of confessions; indeed there may be a connection in Jrm's mind between 11:1–17 (especially the key word "conspiracy," v 9) and 11:18–23 (on this matter see 11:18—12:6, Structure, *Position of Unit*). Two sequences of confessions surround the counter-liturgy for drought and battle, 14:1—15:9: 11:18—12:6 (consisting of lament, Yahweh's answer, lament, and Yahweh's answer) precedes the counter-liturgy, and 15:10–21 (again lament, Yahweh's answer, lament, and Yahweh's answer), follows the counter-liturgy. In this symmetry one senses both the link of "your father" in 12:6 with "my mother" in 15:10, and the link of 15:8–9 ("mother," ילד "give birth") with 15:10. Though it is possible that 16:1–9 was also included at the earliest dictation (one notes "fathers" and "mothers" in 16:3), the fact that this sequence is in prose suggests that it was inserted at a later stage (see sec. 19).

There is less "shape" to the sequences that follow, but I suggest that more material was included in the initial dictation of this scroll beyond what is now in chapter 15. With hesitation I propose that 17:1–4 and 5–8 were added on the basis of the parallel with 15:13–14 and 15:18–19, respectively. There is no way to determine whether 17:9–10 was part of the series at this time. There follow three sequences of confessions, none of which offers an answer from Yahweh (17:14–18; 18:18–23; 20:7–12; these doubtless were part of that initial dictation); 20:12 repeats 11:20, and these two verses make a good inclusio. And the curious verse 20:13 may well have closed the dictation, if, as I have suggested, this verse marks Jrm's prayer of thanksgiving to Yahweh on the death of Hananiah and thus Jrm's vindication as a true prophet. (Other passages within chapters 11—20 with an early setting appear to have been added to the corpus later; see below.)

To sum up: I propose that to the second scroll, extended by 10:17–25 in 598, the following passages were added in a fresh dictation in 594: the insertions 1:17–19; 2:26–28; 7:21–28; and then 11:1–17; 11:18—12:6; 14:1—15:9; 15:10–21; 16:1–9; 17:1–4, 5–8 (+ 9–10?), 14–18; 18:18–23; 20:7–12, 13. That scroll will have been closed by the "unattached" endings 25:1–13 and 45:1–5.

This scroll, like the second, was evidently open-ended, since 20:14–18 was added sometime after 20:13; this passage, too, makes an inclusio, this time with 1:5.

19. The Inclusion of Four Prose Passages

There is evidently some patterning to the extended prose passages 13:1–12aα; 16:1–9; 18:1–12; and 19:1—20:6. Thus both 13:1–12aα and 18:1–12 narrate events that took place before Jehoiakim burned the first scroll, the sign of the linen loincloth and the visit to the potter's workshop, respectively, and they are united by the word שחת nip'al "be ruined, spoiled" (13:7, compare 10; 18:4). And as for 16:1–9 and 19:1—20:6, both these passages are Yahweh's commands to Jrm to demonstrate by overt action the irrevocability of Yahweh's punishment of the people, the call to celibacy, and the smashing of the earthenware flask, respectively. Except for the possible

link between "father" and "mother" in the confessional material (12:6; 15:10) and "fathers" and "mothers" in 16:3, there is no obvious connection between these prose passages and the confessional material around them; it is likely then that if there was a fresh scroll in 594 that had the shape already suggested, that scroll was enlarged sometime later by the insertion of these four prose passages that each offer a "sign" in some fashion, and the patterning of their position suggests the memory devices appropriate to Jrm.

20. Three Small Sequences Now Found within Chapters 21—24

There are two small collections of material now found within chapters 21—23, namely 21:11—23:8, a collection centering on Jerusalem and the royal house (so also Rudolph and Weiser), and 23:9–33, a collection on the false prophets. The oracles in 21:11—23:8 have settings during the reign of Jehoiakim (or just before, in the case of 22:10 + 11–12); the setting of the units in 23:9–33 is evidently in the conflict with the false prophets in 601/600. Both collections have superscriptions (21:11; 23:9), though these are probably secondary additions.

The core of the first collection is a sequence on the kings of Judah—Josiah and Jehoahaz (22:10 + 11–12) and Jehoiakim (22:13–19). This core is surrounded by material involving "Lebanon" and "cedars" (22:6–7; 22:20–23); the whole is preceded by an oracle against the royal house (21:12) containing the catchword "fire," two more oracles containing "fire," the first being 21:13–14 and the second being 22:6–7, the first "Lebanon-cedars" oracle. In short, one has here a typical sequence ordered by symmetries and a chain of catchwords, an ordering process suggesting the memory process of Jrm.

The second small collection is a simple sequence on the false prophets. There is no discernible ordering process of the units, and since they were all evidently delivered within a short space of time, the order may be simply chronological.

It is more than possible that these two small collections were attached to chapter 20 at Jrm's behest: "morning" in 21:12 could be linked to that word in 20:16, and "my heart" and "my bones" in 23:9 to those expressions in 20:9. These two collections could then have been added at Jrm's dictation any time after that addition of 20:14–18, that is, in 594 or soon thereafter.

The setting proposed in the present study for chapter 24 is likewise in 594; that material could therefore have been appended to the two small collections at that time.

21. The Preservation of Other Early Material Now Found in Chapters 10—20

Other units of material authentic to Jrm are now to be found scattered at various points within what is now chapters 10—20. Unlike the four prose passages already discussed (13:1–12aα; 16:1–9; 18:1–12; 19:1—20:6), the array of these units seems to offer no pattern: they appear to be inserted one by one on the basis of association with preexistent adjoining material. Thus 10:1–16, if authentic to Jrm (as I suggest it is), is evidently placed after 9:16–21 on the basis of the verb למד (9:19; 10:2). Again 18:13–17 evidently follows 18:1–12 because "Lebanon" in Isa 29:17 follows "potter" in Isa 29:16. I suggest that such memory devices are more appropriate to the "filing" mentality of a scribe than to the memory of Jrm, in which prophetic material had a total "shape." The purpose of these insertions is then not proclamation, as was the case of the earlier dictated scrolls, but rather preservation (and indeed this is the purpose of further expansions in the corpus to be made by Baruch). It is as if Jrm said to Baruch, "Here are further words from Yahweh: record them as best you can." And again it is speculation what circumstances would have given rise to the concern to preserve, but one recalls that Jrm was confined in the court of the guard during the final siege of Jerusalem (588–587: 32:2), that Baruch had access to him, and that after he negotiated the purchase of the field at Anathoth, he told Baruch to take the double deed of purchase and place it in an earthen vessel "so that it may remain a long time" (32:14): preservation, then, was on his mind during those months, and this setting would be an appropriate one for the preservation of these miscellaneous units of Yahweh's word within the scope of the scroll at hand. These units are: 10:1–16; 12:7–13, 14–17; 13:12aβb–14, 15–17, 18–19, 20–27; 16:10–13, 16–18, 19–21; 17:11, 12–13; 18:13–17.

22. A Separate, Hopeful Scroll; The Development of Chapters 26—36

There is direct evidence within the book of one other document prepared by Jrm, containing words of hope:

Jrm is told to write in a document words that Yahweh has vouchsafed, "for the days are surely coming . . . when I shall restore the fortunes [שׁוּב שְׁבוּת] of my people Israel" (30:1–3). Though the instructions do not directly state that Jrm dictated the material to Baruch, the setting of this scroll is doubtless the period just after Jrm purchased the field at Anathoth, when Jrm was confined to the court of the guard (32:2; 37:15); Baruch had access to him (32:12), so one must assume again that Jrm dictated the material to Baruch. This document, it must be stressed, was not a replacement of the scroll dictated (by my proposal) in 594, but a fresh collection.

Like some of the material in chapters 2—3 and some of the confessions, some of what Jrm committed to writing in this scroll seems to have had an earlier context (early hopeful material addressed to the north), but this will be the occasion for its being recorded. I propose in the present study that this scroll in the earliest form contained the introductions now in 30:1–3 and 30:4, that the prophetic material proper was 30:5–7, 10–21; 31:1aβγb, 2–9, and 15–22, and that the scroll closed with 31:27–28. The prophetic material offers in 30:18 the operative phrase of the introduction, "I shall restore the fortunes [שׁוּב שְׁבוּת] of my people Israel."

This brief collection was evidently expanded by 31:31–34 after its delivery (by my proposal, at the festival of booths in September/October 587).

Then at some point Baruch made two additions to the collection: he added the original form of chapter 32, the narrative of the word from Yahweh that evidently first released Jrm to proclaim hope, the command to buy the field at Anathoth, a narrative closing with the words, "I shall restore their fortunes" (אָשִׁיב אֶת־שְׁבוּתָם, 32:44); and he added the original form of 33:1–11, a passage closing with the words, "I shall restore the fortunes of the land [אָשִׁיב שְׁבוּת־הָאָרֶץ] as before." These two units are thus prose additions affirming the restoration of fields and the restoration of houses, respectively.

Then to this material in chapters 30—33 were prefixed 29:1–23 and 24–32. These two units are narratives of events in 594 that first speak of restoration after a long exile: 29:14 has "I shall restore your fortunes" (וְשַׁבְתִּי אֶת־שְׁבוּתְכֶם), and I speculate in the present study that the missing oracle in 29:25 may originally have included the same phrase, though no trace of it now remains. As to the addition of the units of chapter 29, there is no reason why it could not have been made at the behest of Jrm.

Perhaps at the time when the units of chapter 29 were prefixed to the collection, chapter 35 was appended: both 29:5 and 28 say, "Build houses and live in them, plant gardens and eat their fruit," and in 35:7 we hear the command to the Rechabites, "No house shall you build, . . . nor vineyard shall you plant." It is to be noted that chapter 35 is not in chronological order: the setting of the incident is evidently in 599 or 598; the symmetry of chapter 29 with chapter 35 strikes one as being the kind of organizing principle appropriate to Jrm.

On the other hand, the addition of chapters 27 and 28 and of 34:1–7 and 8–22 is likely to be at the initiative of Baruch. As to chapters 27 and 28, they offer narratives of events taking place earlier in 594 than those of chapter 29 but likewise dealing with false hope (שֶׁקֶר "falsehood" occurs in 27:10, 14, 15, 16; 28:15; 29:9, 31). The material in 34:1–7 and 8–22 adds two divine words, one to Zedekiah and one to the leading citizens, that took shape during the last siege of Jerusalem: their association may simply be due to the fact that they were very near in time. But one wonders if there is a further association between 34:1–7 and chapter 33: if עֲתֶרֶת in 33:6 means "fragrance" (see Interpretation there), a reference to purification after the defilement caused by unburied corpses, then it is possible that the use of "burn" in 34:5, evidently of spices in connection with the king's corpse, is the operative link between these two passages.

As to chapters 26 and 36, it is clear that these two narratives have much in common: in both of them Jrm expresses hope for the repentance of the people ("perhaps," "hear," "turn each from his evil way," 26:3; 36:3, 7), and in both narratives Jrm is in danger (26:8; 36:26). The two chapters, the first concerning the consequences of Jrm's temple sermon in 609, the second concerning the consequences of the reading of Jrm's first scroll, must have been drafted side by side; but their present position is puzzling. Rudolph assumes that each chapter begins its respective large section of the book (thus chaps. 26—35 and chaps. 36—45, respectively), but this seems doubtful: chapters 37—44 give a continuous narrative of the events in Jrm's life during the final siege of Jerusalem in 588–587, and the narrative of the first scroll and its burning, from 605–601, has no immediate connection with it. One could imagine at least two scenarios. Thus

both chapters could have been drafted soon after the dictating of the second scroll, and added directly after 25:1–13; in that case chapters 27—35 would have been inserted between the two chapters. But it would seem more likely that Baruch drafted chapters 26 and 36 at the time when the hopeful scroll was being developed, when Jrm was imprisoned in the court of the guard: the two chapters, by offering narratives of two occasions when Jrm was in danger, could serve as the envelope about chapters 27—35, which were becoming a collection of memoirs of Jrm. If that is the case, then chapters 26—36 could be perceived as fitting easily within 25:1–13 and chapter 45, the two "loose" passages referred to earlier: 25:5 is reminiscent of the diction of the temple sermon, and chapter 26 of course gives a narrative of the delivery of the temple sermon; chapters 36 and 45 both record incidents from the fourth year of Jehoiakim (36:1; 45:1).

23. The Oracles against Foreign Nations; The Addition of 25:15–29 and 30–38

At some point the oracles against foreign nations were added after 25:13 (so in *G*; for the sequence of these oracles, see "The Oracles against Foreign Nations" before 46:1–12, and for the shift of these oracles to a position after chapter 45, see sec. 3 above). One must make a distinction between a shorter collection without the oracles against Babylon, and the full collection that includes the oracles against Babylon: the analysis of the present study indicates that the material against Babylon must have been proclaimed by Jrm during the final siege of Jerusalem, that is, 588–587, but that he had delivered some of the other oracles against foreign nations as early as the time of the battle of Carchemish (605); the individual oracles of the shorter collection were all delivered by 594. The motive for the collection and preservation of the oracles in the shorter collection must be sought in Jrm's conviction that the yoke of Nebuchadnezzar will inevitably be imposed on the whole world (27:5–7); Yahweh's words concerning the defeat by Babylon of the various nations around Judah will demonstrate that conviction. The collecting of the oracles in the shorter collection then could also have been begun in 594. If the shorter collection was appended to 25:13 at this time, then at the same time 21:11—25:13 could have been prefixed by 21:1–10, a prose narrative that likewise depicts the hopelessness of resistance to Babylon; and during that period Baruch may well have inserted 25:15–17, 27–29, and 30–38 after the shorter collection of oracles against foreign nations.

Then the shorter collection of oracles against foreign nations could have been expanded by the oracles against Babylon during the months preceding the final fall of Jerusalem, words that would give hope to the people.

Sometime in this whole process the scroll containing chapters 26—36 was appended to the scroll of Jrm's preaching (containing the body of chapters 1—25), but there is no way to determine when that took place.

24. The Narrative of the Final Months of Jeremiah's Career, Chapters 37—44

I assume it was Baruch that prepared the long narrative of the final months of Jrm's career, chapters 37—44. If the analysis of the structure of the narrative offered in the present study is correct, the narrative was constructed in two stages; the first stage would begin with 37:1 (or 3) and end with 43:1–3 + 42:19–21 + 18 + 22 (there are evident dislocations of text at the end of chap. 42 and the beginning of chap. 43); the second stage would be 43:3—44:30. By this analysis the larger portion of the narrative tells the story from the time the Egyptians pushed north into Judah in the summer of 588 until the event of Jrm's argument with Johanan and his officers at the caravansary near Bethlehem: one could imagine Baruch, setting down the narrative, extending the scroll embodying chapters 26—36, perhaps during the stopover at Tahpanhes (43:7). The second stage, recording the move of the group into Egypt, would then have been added after Jrm and Baruch had settled there.

25. Later Additions to the Collection

After the collection passed out of Baruch's hands various expansions are made. It is often impossible to date these with any precision: many of the additions are too short to offer clues, and the sixth and fifth centuries do not offer us much comparable dated material. In the exilic period I would place: 5:18; 8:1–3; 9:11–13; 22:8–9; and the borrowing from 2 Kings of the material in chapter 52 (with the exception of vv 28–30, from a contemporary record). At the end of the sixth century I would place: 9:14–15; 31:10–14, 23, 24–25, and 26. In the fifth century I would place: 3:6–11, 16–18bα; 17:19–27; 23:7–8, 34–40; 30:8–9; 31:29–30, 35–36, 37, and 38–40. I do not detect any pattern among the additions for a given period, except that there are three passages involving a "change of speech pattern" assigned to the fifth century, namely, 3:16–18bα; 23:7–8; and 31:29–30: these may be from a single hand.

III. The Prophet Jeremiah

26. Preliminary Remarks

For our knowledge of Jrm we are confined to the data within the Book of Jer; thus the prophet is not mentioned, for example, in 2 Kings, as Isaiah is. (For the references to him in Ezra and 2 Chronicles, see secs. 72, 83.) The discovery in recent years of the bullae of Baruch the son of Neriah the scribe (32:12) and of Jerahmeel the king's son (36:26) reinforces the historicity of these men mentioned in the course of the record of Jrm, but for Jrm himself we must gain what we can from the book called by his name.

As I have already indicated, commentators have come to very different conclusions in regard to the historical value of the data within the book. For example, Bright affirms, "A general reconstruction of the prophet's career is possible and may be attempted with some confidence,"[122] while Carroll asserts, "To the question 'what is the relation of the book of Jeremiah to the historical Jeremiah?' no answer can be given. . . . It is not clear that 'historical' prophets can be reconstructed from books associated with their names, nor is it established that such 'historical' figures are *not* the products or even the epiphenomena of the traditions in which they appear!"[123] The conclusions of the present study are that most of the poetry preserved in the book exhibits a distinctive vocabulary, style, and theology that one may attribute to Jrm, that the narrative portions of the book are trustworthy in the events they record, and that the book is largely the work of the scribe Baruch (see the discussion above). To put it another way, I have concluded that the picture of Jrm that emerges from the

---

122 Bright, pp. lxxxvii.
123 Carroll, pp. 62–63.

book is that of a highly distinctive and innovative person: it is not the kind of figure that later generations would be likely to create. The fact that both Ezekiel and Deutero-Isaiah seem to be dependent on his phrases points in the same direction. I submit, then, that the data of the book can be used to build up a credible portrayal of the prophet, a portrayal against which there are no opposing data.

But even if the data are credible, it is no easy task to fit them together; there are too few of them, and those that we have offer too many variables (for example, the controverted question of a higher or lower chronology). All one can hope to do is to produce a reconstruction that is plausible.

As with the interrelationship of questions regarding the reconstruction of the text of the book, of the literary history of the book, and of the life and proclamation of Jrm, so with the reconstruction of the life and proclamation of Jrm itself: several questions are interrelated, and they all beg to be examined at once. I shall begin with my reconstruction of the life and times of Jrm, setting the events of his life chronologically in the context of the history of the period. That reconstruction is a more extended form of "A Chronology of Jeremiah's Career" in *Jeremiah 1*. I shall then examine the sources from which Jrm drew his material. This analysis is straightforward in the discussion of parallels with the early traditions of Israel and with the eighth-century prophets, but it becomes complex in dealing with two bodies of material, Deuteronomy and the Psalms: the analysis of parallels with Deuteronomy is complex because it becomes clear that Jrm drew from an early form of Deuteronomy and that later additions to Deuteronomy drew from Jrm, so there is no way to avoid a thoroughgoing discussion of the relation between Deuteronomy and Jer at that point; and the analysis of parallels with the Psalms is complex because few psalms offer any secure dating, so again the matter of the direction of dependence must be dealt with case by case.

I shall then treat the person and proclamation of Jrm, setting forth his theology, the forms he used in his proclamation, his style and poetic technique. Finally I shall assess the impact of Jrm on his own and later generations.

A. The Life and Times of Jeremiah

27. Birth of Jeremiah (627/626); Josiah's Reform (622)

Josiah had come to the throne of Judah in 640 B.C.E. when a child of eight years (2 Kgs 22:1). Judah had been a vassal of Assyria for decades, but by roughly 630 the hold of Assyria on the west was beginning to weaken, and in 627/626 Ashurbanipal died; sometime during those years Josiah began withholding tribute from Assyria with impunity. At the same time, given the inability of Assyria to maintain control over the old northern kingdom of Israel, Josiah made attempts to exert his authority over that area.[124]

It is in the year 627/626 that I place the birth of Jrm: this is the "thirteenth year of Josiah," when "the word of Yahweh came to him" (1:2). This view was first set forth by Friedrich Horst,[125] and has been pressed by Hyatt[126] and myself, among others.[127] It is true, the majority of commentators take the thirteenth year of Josiah, if a historical datum and not artificial, to be the beginning of Jrm's acceptance of his vocation as a prophet, when he began to proclaim Yahweh's word. But I see seven arguments in favor of the lower chronology, some more substantial than others. I shall list the arguments from silence first: separately they are not strong, but together they bring at least unease to a reconstruction of Jrm's career that has him beginning his prophetic speaking in 627/626.

(1) No oracles of Jrm can confidently be dated to the period between 627 and 622, the date of Josiah's reform. Commentators do assume that the accusations of Baal worship in chapters 2—3 stem from this period, but there is nothing in the oracles that cannot be attributed

124   Bright, *History*, 316–17.
125   Friedrich Horst, "Die Anfänge des Propheten Jeremia," ZAW 41 (1923) pp. 94–153.
126   Hyatt, pp. 779, 798.
127   For a full bibliography on the suggestion and analogous ones until 1968 see Berridge, p. 74, nn. 5, 6, 7.

as well to the early years of Jehoiakim's reign. (Of course, the occurrence of "Assyria" in 2:18, 36 would seem to indicate a time of Assyrian hegemony, but I submit that this term in those verses simply refers to the current power in Mesopotamia, that is, Babylon; see sec. 30.) If the oracles of chapters 2—3 are to be attributed to the period 627–622, then one is moved to assume a "silent period" for Jrm until 609; though recent commentators do not embrace the notion of a "silent period," the seeming hiatus in Jrm's life remains troubling.[128]

(2) Related to the seeming silence of Jrm after Josiah's reform in 622 is the fact that there is no clear indication of Jrm's attitude toward the reform itself: indeed commentators have proposed both that he supported the reform and that he opposed it. It is true, 11:1–17 is often cited to demonstrate the prophet's support of the reform, but that passage speaks only of "this covenant" (11:3), a covenant identified as that from Sinai (11:4). If the reform is as important an event as the Deuteronomic historian indicates—the greater part of 2 Kings 22—23 is given over to it—then Jrm's silence is surprising.[129]

(3) The earliest dated event in Jrm's career, aside from the thirteenth year of Josiah itself, is the temple sermon, delivered during the accession year of Jehoiakim (609/608, probably the autumn of 609: 26:1). Again this is not a strong argument, but it is unsettling nevertheless.

(4) The identity of the "foe from the north" (1:15; 4:6; 6:1, 22; 10:22; compare 4:15, 16; 5:15) is puzzling. On the assumption that the foe from the north is part of the call narrative in 1:15, as certainly appears to be the case, commentators had to resort to the assumption that Jrm was referring to the Scythians. When a closer examination of the Scythian hypothesis resulted in its overturn, scholars suggested a mythic background for the northerners. But the matter has continued to trouble those who hold to a higher chronology.[130]

(5) The call to celibacy (16:1–4) is the sign par excellence of Yahweh's irrevocable decision to punish the people; it must therefore have been declared after Jehoiakim burned the first scroll (in December 601, by the datum in 36:9 G: see Interpretation of vv 9–11 there). If 627 is the date when Jrm accepted his call, by which he would have been at least twelve years old (compare sec. 29), he would have been at least thirty-eight years old, perhaps older, by the time he declared his celibacy. Rudolph is puzzled by this chronological issue, wondering why Jrm did not marry "in the quiet years between 622 and 609."[131]

(6) Positively, "Your [= Yahweh's] words were found, and I ate them" (15:16) suggests that the discovery of the scroll in the temple, the stimulus to Josiah's reform ("your words were found"), predates Jrm's acceptance of his call ("and I ate them," compare 1:9). The expression "your words were found" is, as Giesebrecht described it, "a somewhat drastic expression," but it makes sense as a description of the finding of the scroll in the temple.

(7) Theologically the words of 1:5 suggest that the thirteenth year of Josiah, when "the word of Yahweh came to Jrm," was the time of his birth.

If 627 is the year of his birth, then there are no oracles from 627–622, his silence regarding Josiah's reform is understandable, there is no "silent period," the foe from the north was Babylon, and he declared his celibacy when he was twenty-six years old.

Jrm was born in Anathoth, four kilometers northeast of Jerusalem (that is to say, of its center on Mt. Zion), the son of the priest Hilkiah. His priestly family may have preserved the religious tradition of Shiloh associated with Samuel (see Interpretation on 1:1). By the lower chronology he would have been five years old at the time of the reform of Josiah. That reform, as already noted, was based upon the discovery of a scroll in the Jerusalem temple containing an early form of Deuteronomy (see secs. 53–58, 60). The reform, of course, meant a resurgence of orthodox Yahwism, but for Jrm's father, Hilkiah, its most crucial shift was that he could no longer function as a priest in Anathoth—one could imagine Jrm's boyish fascination with the details of this shift.

---

128 See Bright, p. lxxxiii; and for a recent assessment of the issue see Joseph Blenkinsopp, *A History of Prophecy in Israel, From the Settlement in the Land to the Hellenistic Period* (Philadelphia: Westminster, 1983) 160–61.

129 For a discussion of Jrm's silence on Josiah's reform see again Bright, p. lxxxii, and Blenkinsopp, *A History of Prophecy in Israel*, 161.

130 See in detail Excursus: The Problem of the Identity of the Foe from the North, *Jeremiah 1*, 42–43.

131 Rudolph, pp. 111–12.

28. The Septennial Reading of Deuteronomy

Now I assume that the injunction of Deut 31:9–13 was carried out seriously, that an early form of Deuteronomy was recited every seven years at the feast of booths (tabernacles), thus at the end of September or the beginning of October. If the proclamation of Deuteronomy was initially in 622, then subsequent readings would have taken place in the autumn of 615, 608, 601, 594, and 587. It is my proposal that these occasions offer a chronological structure for the career of Jrm, and more specifically that several of the parade examples of Deuteronomistic prose in the book are Jrm's various counterproclamations at those times when Deuteronomy was recited. This proposal, as I shall show, is most convincing for 594 and is plausible for 587; beyond those dates I have suggestions for Jrm's proclamations in 608 and 601[132] (as well as at times other than those occasions when Deuteronomy was read, of course).

29. A Propagandist for Josiah (615–609); The Battle of Megiddo (609)

As I have already indicated, Deuteronomy would have been recited again in the autumn of 615; by my reckoning Jrm would have been twelve years old. With hesitation I suggest the possibility that this was the occasion for his responding to his call (1:4–10): vv 7 and 9 are very similar to Deut 18:18, the word to Moses about a prophet like Moses in time to come. Is this not a likely occasion? Jrm himself protests that he is "only a youth [נַעַר]" (v 6). I have elsewhere proposed that Jrm's perception of his call was shaped by traditions regarding Moses and Samuel.[133] As for Samuel, there is the tradition, doubtless known to Jrm, of Yahweh's speaking to the boy Samuel: 1 Sam 2:18, 21, 26; 3:1, 8 all refer to him as a "boy" (נַעַר). (And one may recall that Jesus is recorded as discussing matters with the teachers in the temple when he was twelve years old, Luke 2:41–47.) In any event during a period of time before Josiah was

killed on the battlefield of Megiddo in the spring of 609, the youthful Jrm acted to support the king's program of cultic and political reunion between the north and south (2 Kgs 23:15–18).

Some of the evidence for this activity of the young Jrm is laid out in a recent study by Norbert Lohfink.[134] It has long been recognized that some at least of chapters 30—31 may have been directed to the north.[135] Lohfink has subjected these chapters to careful analysis and isolates 30:5–7, 12–15, 18–21; 31:2–6 and 15–22 as having that setting; I agree, only adding 31:1aαb and 9b to this material. Lohfink suggests that the young Jrm proclaimed Yahweh's initiative in Josiah's effort to win the north ("Ephraim") back to political and religious union with Jerusalem.[136]

I would only add that there is a trace of an early form of Jrm's call narrative, namely, 1:4–14, in which the vision of the pot implies that Yahweh will summon the northern tribes (that is, Israel) for judgment, and there are traces of the prophet's words to the north in chapters 2—3, specifically in 2:4–9 ("families" in v 4 is really "tribes," a word that he uses more than once for the northern tribes); 3:1–2, 4–5, 12, 14–15 (one notes "north" in v 12 and "family" [= tribe] in v 15), portions of 18, 19, 21a, 22–23, the core of 24–25, and 4:1–2. Of course the material in chapters 1—3 and 30—31 directed to the north was incorporated later by the prophet in the context of addresses to the south.

In the year 609 events moved quickly. Nineveh, the capital of Assyria, had been taken by Babylonia in 612, and Assyria had only the remnant of an army left in the field. Egypt, recognizing Babylon to be the new enemy, marched north through Palestine in the spring of 609 to bolster the fading Assyrian force. Josiah tried to interpose his own army at Megiddo to prevent the passage of the Egyptians and in the ensuing battle was killed, at the age of thirty-nine. His death was felt so keenly that he was mourned for generations (2 Chr 35:25). His second son, Jehoahaz, was put on the throne by the country

---

132 See now William L. Holladay, "A Proposal for Reflections in the Book of Jeremiah of the Seven-Year Recitation of the Law in Deuteronomy (Deut 31, 10–13)," *Deuteronomium, Entstehung, Gestalt und Botschaft* (ed. Norbert Lohfink; BETL 68; Leuven: Leuven University, 1985) 326–28.

133 Holladay, "Background"; "Jeremiah and Moses: Further Observations."

134 Lohfink, "Der junge Jeremia."

135 See, for example, Bright, pp. 284–85.

136 Compare Bright, *History*, 322.

gentry but ruled for only three months (2 Kgs 23:30–31); the victorious Egyptian army deposed him and took him to Egypt where he disappeared from history (2 Kgs 23:33–34; compare 22:10–12). His older brother, Jehoiakim, was placed on the throne as an Egyptian vassal, and the Egyptians imposed heavy tribute on the nation (2 Kgs 23:33, 35). By the end of that September, then, Judah had seen three kings on the throne in the year.[137]

30. From the Temple Sermon (609) to the Battle of Carchemish (605); The First Scroll

It was in the swirl of these events that Jrm stood out against the priests and prophets attached to the temple in Jerusalem, delivering the so-called temple sermon (7:2b–12). The date given is the accession year of Jehoiakim (26:1), probably at the feast of booths in the autumn of 609; by the reckoning adopted here Jrm would have been eighteen years old. The sermon is a call to repentance: "make good your ways and your doings" (7:3, 5); if the people do make their ways good, then Yahweh will let them dwell in the land (7:7); if, however, the people persist in making their ways evil, then Yahweh, it is indicated, will make the Jerusalem temple like Shiloh of old and will destroy the city (7:12; 26:6). The religious officials responded to the sermon by putting Jrm on trial before the king's officials, accusing him of prophesying against the temple and the city; the officials exonerated him, at least partly because of the precedent of the prophet Micah in the eighth century (26:7–19). Nevertheless, Jrm's view evidently brought on the enmity of Jehoiakim; we are told that a prophet named Uriah, whose words resembled those of Jrm, fled to Egypt but was brought back and executed by Jehoiakim (26:20–23). Jrm did not suffer the fate of Uriah at least partly because he had friends at court (26:24). The prophet, who earlier was a youthful supporter of Josiah, is now a mature antagonist of Josiah's son.

The king manifested none of the religious and ethical concerns of his father: he embarked upon an ambitious building program, either rebuilding the palace he inherited or building a new one, and he drafted free citizens to do the building. Jrm delivered a scathing oracle of judgment against the king for this building project (22:13–19), an oracle that must have hardened the hostility of the king toward the prophet. Jehoiakim evidently allowed the reform of Josiah to lapse; there must have been many who judged the early death of Josiah to be a signal that the ways of fertility-cult worship had divine approval instead (compare 44:16–18).

The autumn of 608 was the occasion again to hear the reading of the Book of Deuteronomy, and Jrm doubtless took advantage of the gathering of pilgrims to proclaim once more his perception of Yahweh's word. There is reason to believe that 2:1–3 introduced his proclamation on that occasion: the poem in vv 2–3 carries overtones of the feast of booths—thus both Lev 23:39 and Deut 16:13–15, which make provision for that festival, use the term "harvest" (תְּבוּאָה) that occurs in 2:3. The introductory words, literally "Go call out in the ears of" (2:2), suggest an audience at a festival: the instructions for reciting Deuteronomy use the same phrase (Deut 31:11). Doubtless much (if not all) of 2:1—4:4 was delivered on that occasion—one notes the likeness of 4:4 to Deut 10:16.

It must have been a pinched time for Judah. Its king was a small-minded tyrant, the boundaries of the nation had probably contracted to their extent before Josiah's efforts, and the tribute demanded by Egypt doubtless angered the country gentry, who in any case tended to be anti-Egyptian (compare 2 Kgs 23:30, 35).[138] Jrm must have continued to level criticism at the king: it is plausible to date in this period 17:11; 21:11–12; 22:1–5.

The world was turned upside-down once more as news filtered back to Jerusalem of the outcome of another battle: in May or June of 605 the Egyptian army was dealt a stunning defeat by the Babylonian army under the command of Nebuchadnezzar, who was still crown prince, at the city of Carchemish, in northern Syria; and later in the same year the remnant of the Egyptian army was defeated in central Syria. If the leadership of Judah had been convinced after Megiddo (609) that Egypt was invincible, it was no longer possible to hold to that belief.

It was in this period that Jrm reassessed the meaning of the vision of the pot: it now indicated the foe from the north (1:15–16). To his fellow citizens he proclaimed

---

137 Bright, pp. 324–25.
138 See Bright, *History*, 325.

28

Yahweh's word of the fickleness of Judah's loyalty, 2:14–19 and 33–37, and of the possible invasion of the foe from the north, 4:5–8, 13–18, 29–31; 6:1–8. This also may be the period when Jrm executed the symbolic action of the burial of the linen loincloth (13:1–12aα) and perceived the symbolic meaning of a visit to the potter's workshop (18:1–12). The meaning of the former is that the pride of Judah will be spoiled, and of the latter that Yahweh can suddenly change his mind regarding the destiny he has in mind for one nation or another. And though there is no way to be sure, one may hazard the guess that the following were also proclaimed in this period: 12:7–12; 13:12aβ–13; and 16:16–18. Jrm also evidently proclaimed oracles against foreign nations at this time, against Egypt (46:3–12), and, it is likely, against Philistia (47:1–7) and Moab (48:1–4, 6–9, 11–12) as well.

During that same year, possibly at the time of the feast of booths in the autumn, Jrm was "restricted" from going to the temple (36:5). The reason is not given, but could well have been because of his preaching the word regarding the foe from the north in the summer of that year. His stratagem then was to call in the scribe Baruch and dictate to him a scroll containing words of accusation and warning, perhaps prefixing these oracles with an early form of 25:1–7. Baruch then read out the words on the scroll on "a day of fasting" (36:6), doubtless the Day of Atonement. (For what may have been included in that scroll, see sec. 16.)

31. The Babylonian Invasion of Philistia (604); The Drought Begins; The King Burns the Scroll (601)

There is a delay in Babylon's exertion of power in the west, because in August of 605 Nebuchadnezzar had to return to Babylon to take the throne. But in the next year (604) he turned his attention to the west once more, and in November/December his army marched west to the Mediterranean Sea and south along the Palestinian coastal plain, sacking the Philistine city of Ashkelon;[139] it was the end of independence for the Philistines. And it was probably some time in that same year that Jehoiakim gave way to the inevitable and became a vassal of Baby-

lon (2 Kgs 24:1).[140] (In spite of the *M* reading of 36:9, it was not evidently in that year that Jehoiakim burned Jrm's scroll, but three years later, in 601—so *G*; see Interpretation of 36:9–11.)

Jrm would have continued during the next two or three years to proclaim words of warning to Judah: among these may be the addition of 13:14 to 13:12aβ–13; 13:20–27; 18:13–17; and 22:20–23.

The drought (14:1—15:9) cannot be dated directly, but a number of considerations combine to suggest that it began in the spring of 601. (1) The fast called by Jehoiakim in November/December 601 (36:9 *G*) could well have been because of the drought. (2) The oracle of 8:4–10a + 13 combines phraseology about the "law of Yahweh" (v 8) with a description of drought (v 13), and by the proposal of the present study the feast of booths of 601 was an occasion on which the law of Deuteronomy was to be read once more. (3) The earliest deposit of Jrm's confessions contains a reference to the drought (12:4), and those confessions seem to be a reaction to the opposition to Jrm that set in after Jehoiakim burned the scroll (see sec. 32).

One must assume then that the spring of 601 had been dry, and that the rains of autumn did not come either; perhaps there had been days when the desert wind (Arabic *ḥamsīn*) blew dust in from the south. Cisterns became dry (14:3), fruit trees withered (8:13), and the animals of the field began to die (14:5–6). In this autumn of growing drought the feast of booths was celebrated: Jrm's words were biting as always, both against the pretension of the scribes who recited the Deuteronomic law (8:4–10a + 13) and against the conduct of Judah in general—one can imagine 5:1–9, 20–29, and 8:14—9:8 on this occasion as well, and perhaps 13:15–17 and 17:12–13.

During that autumn the Babylonian army pressed south along the coast and in November/December fought the army of Pharaoh Neco in the Egyptian delta; both sides suffered heavily,[141] but the army of Babylon was far from home and needed to retreat in order to regroup, while the Egyptian army was fighting on home ground. Jehoiakim interpreted the result of the battle as a defeat for Nebuchadnezzar, and he rebelled against his

---

139 Ibid., 326.
140 Ibid., 327.
141 Ibid.

Babylonian overlord (2 Kgs 24:1). From Jrm's point of view Yahweh was sending mixed signals: the drought suggested to him that Yahweh's judgment had come upon the nation, but the ability of the king to rebel against Nebuchadnezzar suggested that that threat from the north was not so much a threat as Jrm had proclaimed.

The drought evidently continued into the autumn, and as a consequence Jehoiakim declared a fast in Jerusalem in November/December. Whether Jrm was again (or still) *persona non grata* at the temple area is impossible to say, but Baruch read the scroll in the temple area (36:10). When some of the courtiers heard the reading, they reported it to other courtiers, and it was read a second time (v 15); and then it was read a third time in the presence of the king. Though he was urged not to, Jehoiakim saw to the burning of the scroll, piece by piece (vv 21–25)—whether out of contempt or superstitious fear it would be impossible to say—and ordered the arrest of Baruch and Jrm; they were both able, however, to avoid being seized.

32. The Word of Irrevocable Judgment; The Second Scroll; The Counter-Liturgy of Drought and Battle; The Declaration of Celibacy and the Smashing of the Flask; The Opposition of the Optimistic Prophets and the First Confessions (601–600)

The king's burning of the scroll had several immediate consequences within the same period of time. First of all, chapter 36 indicates that Jrm perceived two words from Yahweh, a command to dictate a second scroll, and a judgment to be leveled against the king, his courtiers, and the people in general.

The judgment first. If the king burned the scroll, it was the utter rejection of Yahweh's word by the head of the nation: Yahweh then had no choice but to set in motion an irrevocable judgment against his covenant people (36:31; compare 4:28). Yahweh would no longer accept Jrm's intercessions on behalf of the people (7:16; 14:11–12; 15:1). If Jrm had felt called upon to be the prophet like Moses, his shift in perception of Yahweh's will at this time in his career shifted his own self-understanding: he was now to be an anti-Moses figure (see again 15:1).

Then Jrm obtained a second scroll and dictated to Baruch the contents of the scroll of 605, with additions (36:32): those additions would be both the oracles that he had delivered between 605 and the time when the king burned the scroll and the oracles that had come to him thereafter (for my suggestion of the contents of that second scroll, see secs. 16–17). Though Jrm was not altogether hindered from proclaiming Yahweh's word, the fact that the king tried to arrest him and the fact that he would soon be placed in the stocks in the temple area overnight (see below) suggest that the scroll would continue to be a resource for proclamation when the prophet himself could not exercise his vocation personally.

Jrm was convinced that Yahweh's judgment would come in the twin punishments of the drought and the foe from the north, and this conviction was embodied in the cycle now found in 14:1—15:9: this is evidently his own counter-liturgy, his own perception of what the public necessities should have been instead of what they were under the king's sponsorship at the time of the fast.

Jrm embarked on two symbolic acts at this time to signal Yahweh's irrevocable judgment, one more private, one public. The first was his declaration of celibacy (16:1–4): he was not to marry and have children, for both children and parents were to die of deadly diseases. He would, by my reckoning, be twenty-six years old at this point. And the second symbolic act was the smashing of the earthenware flask (בַּקְבֻּק) at the Potsherd Gate in Jerusalem (chap. 19), for, Yahweh says, "I shall annul [וּבַקֹּתִי] the plans of Judah and Jerusalem" (v 7). This act, executed at a spot near the temple, evidently earned him a night in the temple stocks (20:1–6).

And Jrm continued to speak as well as to act; during this period he evidently proclaimed 4:9–12, 19–28; 5:10–17; 6:9–15, 16–26, 27–30; 7:29–34; 8:14–23; 9:9–10, 16–21, and perhaps also 21:13–14 and 22:6–7, and he may have added 12:13 to 12:7–12.

But if Jrm maintained in public his confidence in his own perception of Yahweh's word, he was evidently puzzled in private. There were optimistic prophets, cult prophets in Jerusalem and the like, who continued to maintain that all would be well and that Babylon was a "paper tiger" (14:13–15); the series of oracles against the optimistic prophets in 23:9–33 was proclaimed by Jrm at this time (one notes a word about the drought in 23:10). For their part they were convinced that Jrm was a false prophet, and it was they who plotted to kill Jrm (compare

23:12 with 11:23). This plot in turn was evidently what prompted the first set of confessions. That collection, I propose, consisted of 11:18–23, minus "the men of Anathoth" in v 21 and "upon the men of Anathoth" in v 23; 12:1–5; 15:15–19; 17:5–8 [+ 9–10?]; and 18:18–23. This analysis is based upon the intensive analysis of Franz Hubmann, which I largely follow;[142] thus "the men of Anathoth" are evidently a secondary addition to 11:18–23: I believe that the words are genuine to Jrm but were added during the crisis in 594 (see sec. 34). In the words of these confessions Jrm pours out to Yahweh his sense of abandonment over against his persecutors: rather than being destined for slaughter himself (11:19), he affirms that it is his persecutors who should be slaughtered (12:3). He is puzzled why his circumstances turn the norms of Psalm 1 upside down (12:1b) so that it is the "wicked" (or "guilty") who thrive. His opponents he calls "merrymakers" (15:17), another clue that they are optimistic in their view of the nation's future. He describes Yahweh in terms appropriate to an outer drought as well as an inner one (15:18). Yahweh calls him to repent (15:19), and, by my analysis, he affirms his repentance (17:5–8), again in a variation of Psalm 1, but using words appropriate to a period of drought.

33. Babylon Renews the Pressure on Judah; The First Siege of Jerusalem (599–597)

In the meantime Nebuchadnezzar, preoccupied elsewhere, was unable for the moment to punish Jehoiakim for his rebellion, but he did dispatch various bands of Chaldeans, Arameans, Ammonites, and Moabites to harass Judah (2 Kgs 24:2), probably in 599.[143] These raids may be the setting for 12:14; and the raids were evidently what forced the band of Rechabites into Jerusalem (chap. 35): in Jrm's estimation they stood as an example of fidelity to Yahweh's will. This also may have been the circumstance in which Jrm pronounced oracles against various foreign nations—Moab once more (perhaps 48:14–20, 25, 28, 38b), the Ammonites (49:1–5),

the Arameans (49:23–26). Nebuchadnezzar also made raids among the Arab tribes in November/December 599, and news of those depredations may have aroused Jrm to proclaim 49:28–32.

Jrm's persistent conviction that Babylon would return to execute Yahweh's judgment was justified a year later: in December 598 the Babylonian army marched. In that same month Jehoiakim died—perhaps he was assassinated as the one responsible for the anticipated disaster.[144] His son Jehoiachin came to the throne while Nebuchadnezzar was besieging Jerusalem. Jrm's word to the besieged city is 10:17–22. The city fell to the Babylonians in March 597; the young king, members of the royal family, and other leading citizens were led off to exile in Babylon. Jrm had proclaimed words on the fate of Jehoiachin, 13:18–19 and 22:24–30. The prophet's teaching on the meaning of the event is found in 16:19–21.

34. The Jerusalem Conference and Its Consequences (594)

The Babylonians placed a brother of Jehoiakim, Zedekiah, on the throne, and there is nothing datable from Jrm for the next three years, although 17:1–4 may have been proclaimed at this time. Then a chain of incidents took place that brought Jrm into another crisis in his prophetic vocation.

There was an uprising against Nebuchadnezzar from within his own army in December 595 or January 594: he boasts of killing the ringleader with his own hands.[145] The attempted coup d'état must have excited the Jewish exiles in Babylon into a hope that Nebuchadnezzar could fall, and the reception of the news in Jerusalem stimulated Zedekiah to call a conference of ambassadors from Edom, Moab, Ammon, Tyre, and Sidon in the late spring or early summer of 594;[146] that meeting is presupposed by chapter 27.[147]

Jrm was convinced that the optimism of the conference was misplaced; he not only wore a collar of

142 Hubmann, *Untersuchungen.*
143 Bright, *History,* 327.
144 Ibid.
145 Compare Bright, *History,* 392. For Nebuchadnezzar's boast see Wiseman, *Chronicles,* 72–73, lines 21–22.
146 Bright, *History,* 329.
147 The date in 27:1 is erroneous; see Interpretation.

thongs and yoke-pegs[148] but gave similar collars to all the ambassadors—everyone must be ready to submit to the yoke of Nebuchadnezzar. The conference came to nothing, and Zedekiah later sent a delegation to Babylon, doubtless to assure Nebuchadnezzar of his loyalty (29:3).[149]

In this period we may tentatively place 7:21–28; 12:15–17; chapter 24; and (if it is authentic) 10:1–16, a word to the exiles in Babylon. It may also have been at this time that further oracles against foreign nations were delivered: this is a possible setting for an oracle against Moab, 48:39–40aα, 41a, 42–44a, 45b, 44b; an oracle against Edom, 49:7aβ–8, 10–11, 18–22; and an oracle against Elam, 49:34–38.

Jrm sent a letter to the exiles in Babylon instructing them to submit and be prepared for a long stay there (29:1–23). Then in late July or early August 594 he was confronted by the optimistic prophet Hananiah in the temple area (chap. 28); Jrm was still wearing his collar. Hananiah proclaimed good news: the exile would be over within two years (28:3). Jrm expressed his doubts (28:5–9). Then Hananiah broke the pegs of Jrm's collar in a symbolic act, and Jrm, dejected, could only go his way (28:10–11). Later Jrm heard Yahweh say that the wooden pegs would be replaced by iron ones, since Nebuchadnezzar's yoke would also be one of iron (28:12–14). And Jrm's final word to Hananiah was that the latter was an illegitimate prophet and would die within one year. This was not simply Jrm's personal curse; the prophet who prophesies falsely was to die (Deut 18:20).

This opposition from Hananiah was reinforced by opposition from other quarters which we may discern or surmise. Thus there was opposition from optimistic prophets among the exiles in Babylon who objected to Jrm's word that the exile would be long: they sent a letter back to the priest in charge of the temple police asking him to lock Jrm up in the stocks (29:24–32) as he had been locked up years before (20:1–6). Though the priest did not accede to the request, it is clear that Jrm's word aroused enmity.

The opposition to Jrm elicited from him the prayers of the earlier confessions and more besides: in this crisis I would find the setting for the addition of 1:17–19 to the call narrative, and for the rest of the confessions, specifically the addition of "men of Anathoth" in 11:21 and 23, the addition of 12:6, the passage 15:10–14, the addition of 15:20–21, then 17:14–18 and 20:7–12. The warrant for this setting for the passages is indirect but suggestive. I believe that the addition of "men of Anathoth" in 11:21 and 23 and the addition of 12:6 come from Jrm himself: these additions (particularly 12:6) are not likely to have been devised by someone unacquainted with his circumstances. If there was opposition by his fellow villagers and his family, and if it did not take place in the crisis of 601–600, and further if opposition by his family is unlikely when he bought the field at Anathoth (32:1–15), evidently in the summer of 588, then this is the most likely time. Hananiah was from Gibeon (28:1), eight kilometers west of Anathoth; was there some reason why the folk in these villages thought Jrm was too extreme? (For further hints of opposition from his family, see below.)

I have dated the call to abstain from marriage (16:1–4) in the crisis of 601–600 (see sec. 32). But the associated command to abstain from attending funerals and weddings (16:5–9), more extreme even than the abstention from marriage, doubtless dishonored Jrm's family and brought opposition against him from that quarter.

It appears, in any event, that the confessions of 601–600 were the vehicles for Jrm's lamentation to Yahweh once more, and the material that seems to have been added in 594 has overtones that link them to the encounter with Hananiah. Thus with regard to the puzzling שְׁרוּתֶךָ in 15:11, I accept the vocalization of the qere', שֵׁרִיתִךָ, as a denominative piʻel (שׁרה) from שִׁרְיוֹן "armor"; the phrase would then be rendered "I swear I have armored you well." Verse 12 I would render "Can he break iron, iron from the north, and bronze?": that is, the subject of the verb is not the indefinite "one" but "he," that is, Hananiah; the three terms are the "iron" of the hypothetical iron yoke-pegs (28:13), the "iron from the north" of Nebuchadnezzar's yoke (28:14), and the "bronze" wall into which Yahweh would make Jrm (1:18; 15:20); and the vocabulary of metals is anticipated by the "armored" of v 11. Jrm's complaint in v 10 is an apos-

---

148 On "yoke-pegs" see Interpretation on 27:2.
149 Bright, *History*, 329.

trophe to his mother; is this evidence of family opposition? Yahweh's answer to Jrm's complaint in v 10 is that the prophet has been satisfactorily armored for the crisis, and that Hananiah is bound to fail when he tries to break the iron and bronze.

I thus date 15:20–21 to this period as well, as 20:7–12 likewise, for reasons that will become clear in a moment.

The autumn of 594 is the occasion once more to hear the recitation of Deuteronomy. I propose that 11:1–17 is Jrm's counterproclamation on that occasion. The resemblance of "cursed is" in 11:3 and "so be it" (= "Amen") in 11:5 to the "curses" and "Amens" of Deut 27:15–26 has long been noted;[150] see the discussion in sec. 58. And Jrm has "iron" on his mind (11:4). But most crucially he says (v 9) that "there is revolt among the men of Judah and inhabitants of Jerusalem." The word "revolt" (or "conspiracy," שֶׁקֶר) does not otherwise appear in Jer (or Deuteronomy); it is typically used of an attempted revolt by a vassal against his overlord (as Hoshea against the king of Assyria, 2 Kgs 17:4). And this word precisely fits the situation of 594: a conference to revolt against Nebuchadnezzar. But, says Yahweh, Nebuchadnezzar's yoke is my will, so that the revolt is against me: so Jrm at the feast of booths in late September or early October 594. Was Jrm prevented again from going personally to the temple area? There are indications that Jrm dictated a fresh scroll at this time (see sec. 18), and 28:11 at least indicates that Jrm came out the worse from the confrontation with Hananiah two months before.

But something else happened that month, perhaps even during the festival: Hananiah dropped dead (28:17). What a stunning validation of Jrm's prophetic word (Deut 18:20)! The event must have made a great impression on everyone: the month is carefully identified. I suggest that the event of Hananiah's death explains two puzzles. The first is the meaning of 20:13, a verse otherwise so out of the emotional context; I propose that it is Jrm's praise to Yahweh that the conspiracy against him has been broken and that in effect his prophetic standing has been validated. The second is why the confessions are part of the public record at all. They are after all private transactions between Jrm and

Yahweh; no one in those days was interested in the "psychology of prophetism." But these prayers and answers were made public by Jrm to affirm his validity as a true prophet of Yahweh. Yahweh had answered his prayers. Note well: one has 10:17–22 dated to 598, then 11:1–17 from the autumn of 594, followed immediately by the whole confessional collection from 11:18 through chapter 20: Hananiah dropped dead. The material was thus collected in chronological order and became a part of the growing corpus of Jeremianic material.

But if 20:13 marks Jrm's response to the death of Hananiah, 20:14–18 suggests that the prophet's depression continued, and the diction suggests that it was family opposition that continued. One may surmise that a struggle between the optimistic prophets and a pessimistic prophet in Jerusalem meant less to his family in Anathoth than his actions, which continued to dishonor them.

35. The Second Siege of Jerusalem (588–587)

The events of the prophet's career in 588 and 587 are better known (though some details remain obscure), since we have the biographical material of chapters 37—44.

By about 589 Judah was in open revolt against Nebuchadnezzar once more; the revolt was doubtless stimulated by the advent in that year of a new pharaoh on the throne of Egypt, Hophra, who in his interest in intervention in Asia must have assured Judah of his support.[151] In January 588 Nebuchadnezzar began a second siege of Jerusalem; it may have been at that point that Jrm was arrested and confined in the court of the guard (32:2). It was perhaps in that early stage of the siege that we must place 21:1–7, 8–10, a word from Yahweh to Zedekiah, and 23:1–4, 5–6.

Then during the spring or early summer the Egyptian army forced the Babylonians temporarily to withdraw, but Jrm proclaimed the weakness of Egypt in a fresh oracle against her, 46:13–24.

It was probably during that respite in the siege that Jrm was approached by a cousin to purchase his field at Anathoth (32:1–15): the puzzling wording of 37:12 suggests that context for the event. Such a gesture by the

---

150 For example, Rudolph, p. 77.
151 Bright, *History*, 329; Malamat, "Twilight of Judah," 142.

prophet would at least have helped to heal the breach with his family. In the details of the drawing up of the deed Jrm's scribe Baruch reappears (32:12).

But the siege was renewed, and Jrm was in and out of the custody of the authorities. Two or three times Zedekiah asked Jrm to intervene with Yahweh or to give news of any change of heart on Yahweh's part (21:1–10; 37:1–21; 38:14–28), but the prophet continued to insist that resistance to Babylon was futile; he was imprisoned in the house of Jonathan the scribe (37:15), moved at the intervention of the king to the court of the guard (37:21), thrown into a muddy cistern by the courtiers (38:6), and then again at the intervention of the king sent back to the court of the guard (38:13). The king is depicted as a pathetic figure (38:19), a victim really of the forces swirling around him. From scattered indications one may gather how grim the siege was. Food ran low (37:21), and Jews began deserting the city (38:19). Houses that had been built on the outer walls were demolished to become defense installations (33:4), and there was no place to bury the corpses within the city (33:5). In the midst of these awful events Jrm, doubtless stimulated by the buying of the field at Anathoth, perceived Yahweh to call him to prepare a new scroll with optimistic words for the future (30:2–4). That scroll evidently contained the old words which in his youth he had directed to the north (see sec. 29), now redirected to the south, and to these he added fresh words for the south (I believe 30:10–11, 16–17, and 31:7–9a). I further propose that that scroll, whose last word of poetry was 31:21–22, was rounded off by 31:27–28. That scroll would have been read out during the months before the fall of the city, and to that scroll was ultimately appended a hopeful word of the future about fields that would again be bought (32:15) and about the houses of Jerusalem that would be rebuilt (33:7). Yet there was still the necessity to pronounce Yahweh's judgment: slaveowners had freed their slaves when the siege began (with all sorts of mixed motives, no doubt) but had then taken them back when the Egyptian army approached; Jrm condemned this new instance of the faithlessness of the covenant people.

It was in July 587 that the city fell; Zedekiah tried to escape capture by the Babylonians but was overtaken near Jericho, taken to Nebuchadnezzar's headquarters in central Syria, and sentenced (39:1–7): his sons and his courtiers were executed in his presence, the king himself was blinded and taken in shackles to Babylon (39:6–7), where he seems to have been put to grinding grain until his death (52:11 G).

In the meantime, in August of that year the Babylonian general burned the palace and temple in Jerusalem, broke down the walls of the city, and deported to Babylon the leaders that were left in the city. He appointed Gedaliah, who had been an officer in the court in Jerusalem, to be governor over the Babylonian province, administering it from Mizpah, just north of Jerusalem (40:7–12).

Jrm was released from the court of the guard, but in the chaos of events was evidently seized and held with others at Ramah, north of Jerusalem, in preparation for deportation; a Babylonian officer charged with looking after him found him manacled there (40:1). The officer gave him his freedom, and Jrm chose to put himself under the protection of Gedaliah at Mizpah.

Sometime during these months Jrm must have delivered the oracles against Babylon now collected in chapters 50—51: Israel would be a means for the fall of Babylon, and Israel would return to Jerusalem.

Gedaliah tried to reassure the scattered Jewish officers and refugees that it was safe to come out of hiding and return to their homes, but one officer, named Ishmael, perceived Gedaliah to be a traitor and gathered a group of soldiers around him under the protection of the king of the Ammonites across the Jordan. An officer loyal to Gedaliah, named Johanan, tried to warn Gedaliah that Ishmael intended to assassinate him, but Gedaliah did not take the warning (40:8–16).

36. The New Covenant; The Flight into Egypt (587)

In September/October 587 it was time to recite Deuteronomy once more. Could one imagine the priests embarking on this ritual at the appointed time, when the temple itself had been burned a scant six weeks before? I submit that they did. I suggest that this was the goal of the eighty pilgrims from the north, from Shechem, Shiloh, and Samaria, who were coming to present their offerings at the temple "in the seventh month" (41:1, 5): the year of that pilgrimage is not mentioned, but if these pilgrims had remained loyal to Josiah's program of cultic and political reunion between north and south, as their action indicates, then the occasion of the recitation of Deuteronomy was an appropriate one.

During that month Ishmael and ten of his men paid a call on Gedaliah at Mizpah. As they were at table, Ishmael and his soldiers assassinated Gedaliah and his retainers and the Babylonian soldiers stationed there (41:1–3). Ishmael then caught sight of the eighty pilgrims passing on their way south to Jerusalem, urged them to pay a call on Gedaliah, and then began to kill them: ten bribed their way out, but the rest were slaughtered. Ishmael's band then attempted to take hostage all the civilians who had been entrusted to Gedaliah and to make their way back across the Jordan to the Ammonites. Johanan and his forces caught up with them at Gibeon and freed the civilians; Ishmael, however, escaped with eight of his men. Among the civilians was Jrm (compare 42:2) and, evidently, Baruch as well (compare 43:3)—the extent to which he had stayed by Jrm during these months is not known. Johanan gathered his group to move south, intending to go to Egypt, away from Judah and out of harm's way; they made a stop at a caravansary near Bethlehem (41:17–18).

Did they stop in Jerusalem for the feast of booths? I propose that the recitation of Deuteronomy at that festival in 587 was the occasion for Jrm's proclamation of the new covenant (31:31–34). That passage is now placed after what I take to be the end of the hopeful scroll (31:27–28); its diction is strongly reminiscent of Deuteronomy, and it states that the old covenant is obsolete. If this is its setting, then its vision of the shape of a new initiative by Yahweh is astonishing.

It was to be Jrm's last word in Jerusalem. Johanan and his group soon moved off from the Bethlehem area and into the delta area of Egypt, where there were already Jews living; Jrm and Baruch were taken with them, not altogether willingly (chaps. 42—43), and there Jrm continued to preach against disloyalty to Yahweh (44:1–25). It must have been horrid for Jrm to see himself going into Egypt, whence Moses had led the people out; if he were an anti-Moses figure (see sec. 32), then this is the crowning deed of an anti-Moses! No wonder his last recorded word to his fellow Jews is, "Look, I have sworn by my great name, Yahweh has said, that my name will

no more be invoked in the mouth of all Judah who says, 'By the life of Yahweh'" (44:26). If Yahweh had taught Moses the divine name and enjoined him to teach the name to his people, then Jrm would announce the extinguishing of the divine name in Egypt. At any rate the hope for the future of the people lay in Babylon, not in Egypt (29:7).

It is the last we hear of the prophet; by my reckoning he would have been about forty years old. Perhaps Baruch died first, since we have no notice of the prophet's death.

37. Conclusion

If this is a valid reconstruction of the prophet's life, it exposes the shifts of his perception of Yahweh's will through several decades: a prophetic career which we can come to know in unparalleled detail.

Some years ago Stanley Brice Frost suggested that the Book of Jer is a memorial to a childless man.[152] It is ironic that some of the wealth of detail which we have of Jrm's career may thus be due to Yahweh's command that he not marry and have children. Though a book may be a poor substitute for sons to carry on one's name, Jrm's sacrifice is our gain.

B. The Sources on Which Jeremiah Drew: The Data

38. Preliminary Remarks

The corpus of material attributable to Jrm is large enough that one can sketch a reasonably accurate picture of the sources from which Jrm drew.

Parallels by which one may establish this dependence are of two sorts. There are first the occasional deliberate citations, or allusions to earlier narratives, that Jrm intended to be recognized as such: among these are his citation in 4:3 of Hos 10:12, and his allusions in 4:23–24 to Genesis 1 and 2. Then there is his less deliberate use of distinctive phrases found in earlier material: sometimes this use may be unconscious—he might simply be drawing on appropriate phraseology, particularly from previous prophets. Of course, it is usually not possible to distinguish between the more deliberate and the less deliberate use of earlier phraseology, nor is it really

---

152 Stanley Brice Frost, "The Memorial of a Childless Man, A Study in Hebrew Thought on Immortality," *Int* 26 (1972) 446–47.

necessary. And it should also be said that though parallel phrases are not the only way earlier material shaped Jrm, it is the only secure evidence we now have at hand.

Though there is no way to quantify the certain, the probable, and the possible parallels to earlier corpora, which themselves are of varying lengths, it will be useful before dealing with the details to offer a very rough tally that will at least suggest the shape of Jrm's heritage.

There are a scattering of reminiscences of material in Genesis: five of the creation narratives, three of the flood and of the Tower of Babel narratives, and twelve of the patriarchal narratives. There are fifteen reminiscences of the story of Moses and of the exodus from Egypt, seven from the Covenant Code, and three from Leviticus and Numbers. There is one reminiscence from Judges (Judges 11). There are three reminiscences of the narrative of the boyhood of Samuel and one of Samuel as intercessor. There is nothing of the ark narrative, the story of Saul, or of David's rise to power. The only reminiscences of David's and Solomon's reigns are two regarding the episode of David and Bathsheba and his mourning over the dead child, a possible one regarding the violence at the altar in Jerusalem (if Jer 17:1–4 ever contained that reference), and a possible one regarding Solomon's modesty at the beginning of his kingship. There are two or three reminiscences of Elijah and Elisha, one of Micaiah ben Imlah (1 Kings 22), two of the narrative of the lepers at the gate of Samaria (2 Kings 7), and two of the eighth-century siege of Jerusalem (2 Kings 18—19).

There are, as one might expect, a large number of reminiscences to the writing prophets: fifteen to Amos, fifty-five to Hosea, fifty-eight to Isaiah of Jerusalem, fourteen to Micah (drawn almost entirely from Micah 1—3), sixteen to Zephaniah (drawn entirely from Zeph 1:1–13), six to Nahum, and two to Habakkuk.

Jrm evidently drew heavily on Proto-Deuteronomy: there are eighteen reminiscences to Deuteronomy 32, and at least sixteen reminiscences to the prose of Deuteronomy.

There are a cluster of reminiscences of Huldah's oracle (2 Kings 22).

Jrm drew on seventeen separate psalms for thirty-three reminiscences. There are at least two reminiscences of Proverbs, perhaps a few more.

39. Jeremiah's Reminiscences of the Traditions in Genesis

There is a surprising number of reminiscences by Jrm of the narratives of Genesis, both of primeval history and of the patriarchs, and these reminiscences come from both J and P, and evidently from E as well.

The creation narratives are presupposed by Jer 4:23–26—indeed both the P account and the J account side by side: v 23, "I looked at the earth, to see a formless waste [תֹהוּ וָבֹהוּ], and to the heavens, and their light was no more," reflects the beginning of the P account, Gen 1:2–3, where "formless waste" (תֹהוּ וָבֹהוּ) occurs in v 2 and "light" in v 3; and v 25, "I looked, to see no man [וְאֵין אָדָם]," reflects a statement at the beginning of the J account, "and there was no man [וְאָדָם אַיִן] to till the ground," Gen 2:5—strikingly there is no other collocation of אָדָם and אַיִן or אֵין in the OT, as far as I know.[153] And 33:2 collocates "make" (עשׂה) and "shape" (יצר) in a hymnic passage on creation, so again vocabulary of P ("make," Gen 1:7 and ten more times through 2:4, as well as three times of Yahweh in the J material of 2:18—3:21) and J ("shape," Gen 2:7, 8, 19) are placed side by side. The collocation of reminiscences of the two accounts of creation immediately raises the issue of the status of these two accounts in Jrm's day, whether they were separate accounts but both well known, or whether they were already joined into a single narrative. The verb עשׂה "make" also appears in 4:28 in a context that suggests the reversal of creation (compare the remarks on 4:23–26 above); and יצר "shape" occurs in the context of creation in a hymnic passage, 10:16 (if 10:1–16 is genuine to Jrm). And in a passage that resembles 10:1–16 in some ways, 16:20, the rhetorical question is asked, "Can a human being make himself God/a god/gods?"—an ironic reversal of Gen 1:26, in which God makes the human being.

God's command to the human beings in the primeval history, to "be fruitful and increase" (Gen 1:28; 9:1, 7), is repeated with respect to the patriarchs Abraham and Jacob; Jrm offers several reminiscences of these words,

---

153 Holladay, "Recovery," 406.

but he doubtless had the promise to the patriarchs in mind, so the parallels will be dealt with below.

In 17:9 Jrm remarks that the "heart" is devious above all else; he may have had in mind Gen 6:5, "Yahweh saw that the wickedness of man was great in the earth, and that every imagination of the thoughts of his heart was only evil continually"—at least Jerome cites the Genesis passage in his commentary on 17:9.

In Jer 9:9 the birds of the heavens and the beasts have gone: does Jrm intend this to be an abrogation of the covenant with Noah, Gen 9:9?

It is the conclusion of the present study that most of the material in the oracles against Babylon (chaps. 50—51) is genuine to Jrm, and I suggest that in this sequence there are two reminiscences of the narrative of the Tower of Babel (Gen 11:1–9). The first is a difficult verse, 51:25: I suggest that the last phrase, הַר שְׂרֵפָה, is to be understood as "mountain of burnt bricks," שְׂרֵפָה occurring with the meaning "burnt bricks" in Gen 11:3: Yahweh will make Babylon into a mound of burnt bricks resembling the Tower of Babel of old. (And it may be noted that there may be an assonantal link between "lest we be scattered [נָפוּץ]," Gen 11:4, and "and I shall smash [וְנִפַּצְתִּי]" in Jer 51:20–23.) And 51:53 again seems to reflect the narrative of the Tower of Babel: that verse reads, "Though Babylon should go up to the heavens, and though she should put her strong height out of reach [בצר pi'el], from me devastators shall come upon her," while Gen 11:4 states that the top of the tower will be "in the heavens," and in v 6 Yahweh's judgment on the builders of the tower is that "nothing that they may presume to do will be out of their reach [בצר nip'al]."

There is a series of reminiscences of the patriarchal narratives. I begin with God's promise (in the P tradition) at the time of his renaming of Abram and of Jacob that he would "make them fruitful," or that they were to "be fruitful and increase" (Gen 17:5–6; 35:10–11). These positive words doubtless lie behind Jrm's word to the exiles in Babylon, "increase [רבה], do not decrease [מעט]" (29:6). Negatively, the command "be fruitful" appears to lie behind Jrm's renaming of Pashhur (20:3–6): I have proposed that Jrm distorted the name into the Aramaic paš sĕḥôr "fruitful around," which he

reversed to the Hebrew "terror on every side."[154] Again 10:24 says, "Correct me, but in moderation, not in your anger, or you decrease me [מעט hip'il]": here again is the threat of the reversal of the blessing to Abraham and Jacob. And the words of 15:8, "Their widows have become for me more than the sand of the seas," is a terrible reversal of the word to Abraham and Jacob that the number of their offspring should be more in number than the sand of the sea, Gen 22:17 and 32:13. The first of these verses is assigned to E, the second to J. The verse from E, Gen 22:17, is followed (v 18) by the assurance of God to Abraham, "And all the nations of the earth shall bless themselves in your offspring"; this assurance is repeated in Gen 26:4 (J) in a word to Isaac, and this promise evidently stands behind Jer 4:2, "If . . . you swear 'By the life of Yahweh' truly, justly and rightly, then nations will bless themselves in him"—it is to be noted that both occurrences of this assurance to the patriarchs are associated with the verb "swear" (Gen 22:16; 26:3).

Gen 18:4, Yahweh's word to Abraham, "Is anything too hard for me?" is repeated in his word to Jrm in Jer 32:27, but there the question picks up Jrm's affirmation to Yahweh in 32:17, "Nothing is too hard for you."

And Abraham's bargaining with Yahweh over the number of righteous men in Sodom that might save the city (Gen 18:23–32) is presupposed by Jer 5:1, "Search through the streets of Jerusalem, . . . whether you find a man, whether there is anyone doing justice, anyone seeking honesty, so that I can pardon her": again the parallel was already noted by Jerome.

The citation of the overthrow of Sodom and Gomorrah (Gen 19:21, 25, 29) is a commonplace in the prophets (Amos 4:11; Isa 1:9, 10; 3:9; Zeph 2:9); Jrm cites it in 20:16.

The identification of Edom with Esau (by implication in Gen 25:25, explicitly in Gen 25:30) is presupposed by Jer 49:8.

Jer 9:3–5 offers a tissue of reminiscences of Jacob's dealings with Esau and Laban. As Hosea offered a word-play on the name "Jacob" in regard to Jacob's dealings with Esau (Hos 12:3–5), so Jrm does in v 3, in the indictment against Israel, "every brother does deceive"

---

154 Holladay, "Jer 20:1–6," 316.

(עָקֹב יַעְקֹב, heard also as יַעֲקֹב "Jacob"); in this way the expression is similar to the word-plays in Gen 25:26a and 27:36 (J). Then in v 4 we have "each cheats [תלל] his neighbor": one is reminded that Laban cheated (תלל) Jacob (Gen 31:7). And in v 5 we have "fraud" [מִרְמָה] upon fraud," a reminder that Isaac reported to Esau that Jacob had taken his brother's blessing "deceitfully [בְּמִרְמָה]" (Gen 27:35), to which Esau answers with one of the word-plays on "Jacob" (Gen 27:36); and again that the sons of Jacob answered Shechem and his father "deceitfully" (בְּמִרְמָה), because Shechem had defiled Dinah (Gen 34:13).

Though there is no certainty, it is possible that Jer 50:5 offers a word-play on "Levi": the verse says, "And they shall come [to Zion] and join themselves [לוה nip'al] to Yahweh"—this verb is the same one used in the folk-etymology at the birth of Levi, Gen 29:34. Jrm may thus be suggesting a renewal of the cult on Zion.

Finally there is the possibility that Jer 17:1–4 suggests Judah's sexuality and that in such a way it reflects Gen 49:10 (see the discussion on 17:1–4).

40. Jeremiah's Reminiscences of Moses and to Material in Exodus

Jrm evidently understood his vocation to be the prophet like Moses set forth in Deut 18:18. And though the figure of Moses was certainly mediated to Jrm through Deuteronomy (for which see the treatment of Deuteronomy below), it was evidently mediated to him through material in Exodus as well. Jrm's words reflect the infancy narrative of Moses, his call by Yahweh, his dealings with Pharaoh, the great event at the sea, his effort to lead the Israelites, and his task of intercession, and (just as with the material in Genesis) Jrm appears to have drawn on both JE and P material.

Jrm perceived Yahweh's call to him to be from the womb (1:5); that notion suggests royal models, but the infancy narrative of Moses (Exodus 2), doubtless reinforced by the diction of Ps 22:10–11, probably shaped his perception. In particular it is to be noted that he calls himself a נַעַר (here "youth," 1:6), a designation also of the baby Moses in the basket (Exod 2:19[J]).

Form-critically Jer 1:5–9 closely resembles the call of Moses narrated in Exod 3:10–12, and there is a bit of verbal similarity as well ("I will be with you," Jer 1:8; Exod 3:12, evidently E).

The time will come when Jrm perceives Yahweh to exclude from the prophet's vocation any intercession to the people, so that in a way Jrm becomes an anti-Moses figure (see below); and that identity as an anti-Moses figure is reinforced at the end of his life as the Jews take him to Egypt: there through Jrm Yahweh swears that his name will no longer be invoked in Egypt (44:26–30), thus reversing the *Heilsgeschichte* by which Yahweh had revealed his name to Moses in Egypt (Exod 3:14, again evidently E).

At the time of his call Jrm objects to Yahweh, "I do not know how to speak" (1:6); in Exod 4:10 (J) Moses objected to Yahweh, "Oh, my Lord, I am not eloquent, either heretofore or since thou hast spoken to thy servant; but I am slow of speech and of tongue," and in Exod 6:12 and 30 (P) Moses objected to Yahweh that he was a "man of uncircumcised lips."

The phrase "let my people go" (שַׁלַּח אֶת־עַמִּי) occurs again and again in Exodus in Moses' addresses to Pharaoh (Exod 5:1 [JE]; 7:16, 26; 8:16; 9:1, 13; 10:3 [all J]); Jrm perceives Yahweh to use the verb ironically when Yahweh rejects the possibility of intercession: "I have no heart for this people; send them out [שלח pi'el], that they may go away" (15:1). Again, the phrase "refuse to let them go" appears more than once in Exodus (Exod 4:23 [JE]; 7:14, 27; 9:2 [all J]); Jrm uses the phrase in Jer 50:33 in a fresh context: it is the Babylonians who "refuse to let them go."

Though it would be difficult to prove, the fact that "speak in his [Yahweh's] name" occurs in Exod 5:23 and Deut 18:19–22 (four times) of Moses suggests that Jrm's using the term for himself (Jer 20:9) again reflects his self-understanding as the prophet like Moses.

There are no unequivocal references to the Song of the Sea and the Song of Miriam (Exod 15:1–21), but some phrases may be reminiscent. Thus the boast of Egypt, "I will cover the earth" (Jer 46:8), may be an ironic echo of the waters that covered the Egyptian chariots (Exod 15:5, 10); and I suggest that the original text of Jer 46:18 indicated that "like Carmel he [Egypt] shall be brought into the sea," just as Pharaoh and his horsemen went into the sea (Exod 15:19). And the mention of "timbrels" in Jer 31:4 recalls past victories when the women celebrated with timbrels, notably that celebrated by Miriam and the other women (Exod 15:20), but those celebrated by other women as well (see 1 Sam 18:6).

For reminiscences of the Covenant Code (Exodus 20—23) see below.

The phrase "stiffen the neck" (Jer 7:26; 19:15) is an adaptation of the description of Moses' generation as a "stiff-necked people"; the latter phrase appears four times in the JE tradition of Exodus 32—34 (e.g., Exod 32:9) and twice in Deuteronomy (Deut 9:6, 13).

And Moses' role as intercessor (Exod 32:11–13, 20–34) was crucial to Jrm. He mentions Moses and Samuel as intercessors (15:1), so that Jrm's struggle with the question whether or not he is to intercede for his people (7:16; 14:11; 15:1; compare 42:1–6) is shaped by the tradition of Moses' call to intercede.

When Moses broke the tables of the law, Yahweh said to him, "Cut two tables of stone like the first; and I will write upon the tables the words that were on the first tables, which you broke" (Exod 34:1). The narrative in Jer 36:27–28 is undoubtedly modeled on this: "Now the word of Yahweh came to Jeremiah after the king had burned the scroll, the words which Baruch had written at the dictation of Jeremiah, as follows: again, get yourself another scroll and write all the former words which were on the scroll which Jehoiakim burned." This is not to say that the event did not take place as stated, but simply that Jrm and Baruch must have joked wryly that even in this way he is the prophet like Moses.

There are a couple of reminiscences of the creed in Exod 34:6–7, "Yahweh, Yahweh, a God merciful and gracious, slow to anger, and abounding in steadfast love and faithfulness, keeping steadfast love to the thousandth generation, forgiving iniquity and transgression and sin, but who will certainly not leave the guilty unpunished, visiting the iniquity of the fathers upon the children and the children's children, to the third and the fourth generation." In Jer 15:15 Jrm ironically adapts one of the phrases to pray that Yahweh not be too gracious: "Do not, because of your slowness of anger, take me away." In Jer 30:11 there is an adaptation into the first person of another of its phrases, "though I will certainly not leave you unpunished" (though it is to be noted that the antecedent phrase is also found in Nah 1:3).

Jrm cites the Decalogue (7:9); this fact, of course, does not determine whether he heard it in the form recorded in Exodus 20, in the form recorded in Deuteronomy 5, in both, or in neither. But there is certainly evidence

beyond the Decalogue itself to indicate that he drew on Deuteronomy 5 (see sec. 57).

Thus there are two passages that appear to presuppose the laws in Exod 21:8–10 regarding the disposition of an Israelite slave-girl as a concubine. Jer 3:20 reads, "As a woman betrays [בגד] her lover, so you [Israel] have betrayed [בגד] me [Yahweh]"; the immediate background of the passage is likely to be Hos 5:7 and 6:7, but behind them stands Exod 21:8, the only passage in the legal material containing "betray": "If she [the slave-girl] does not please her master who has designated her for himself, then he shall let her be redeemed; he [the master] shall have no right to sell her to a foreign people, since he has betrayed her [בגד]." And Jer 13:27 seems to offer the verb יעד "designate," likewise found in Exod 21:8 (and 9)—that is to say, it does if the consonantal text is revocalized as I suggest in the present study; if so, the phrase in Jrm will be "other partners you designate," that is, the female (Jerusalem) makes disposition of her sexual partners as the male is wont to do in the legal formulation.

Then both 2:26 and 2:34 presuppose the law on burglary in Exod 22:1, "If a thief is caught in burglary, and is struck so that he dies, there shall be no bloodguilt for him": 2:26 has "like the shame of a thief when caught," and 2:34 has "not in burglary did you catch them."

Jer 20:7, "You have deceived/seduced me, Yahweh, and I let myself be deceived/seduced [both verbs פתה pi'il]," is evidently a reminiscence of both Exod 22:15, "If a man deceives/seduces [פתה pi'el] a virgin . . . ," and 1 Kgs 22:20 (for which see below, on the ninth-century prophets).

Finally the feast of booths is called "Ingathering" (אָסִיף) in Exod 23:16 (and again in 34:22); Jrm doubtless had that term in mind in the multiple word-plays of Jer 8:13.

41. Possible Parallels in Leviticus and Numbers

There is little in Leviticus or Numbers that offers itself as material from which Jrm drew. One possibility in Leviticus is Lev 13:46, the law regarding anyone suffering from "leprosy": "he shall dwell alone [בָּדָד יֵשֵׁב] outside the camp"; in one of his confessions Jrm states that he did not sit in the circle of the merrymakers, but that he "sat alone" (בָּדָד יָשַׁבְתִּי, Jer 15:17), and it is difficult to escape the conclusion that Jrm intended to indicate that he was a social "leper." But of course the use of the phrase need not imply that Jrm was drawing on a law within the corpus of the P-code; the usage was undoubtedly traditional.

There are a few usages that suggest the Holiness Code: in Jer 2:7 we read, "my heritage you made loathsome" (נַחֲלָתִי שַׂמְתֶּם לְתוֹעֵבָה); one recalls the repetition of תּוֹעֵבָה in Lev 18:22–30. Again Jer 6:9 contradicts the law on gleaning in Lev 19:9–10, but it is more likely to reflect the form of the law in Deut 24:21 (see below, in the discussion of Deuteronomy). Jer 9:3 may well have the sequence of laws in Lev 19:16–18 in mind: the verse in Jer associates "neighbor," "brother," and "slanderer," offering a picture of the breakdown of covenant solidarity; Lev 19:16 forbids going around as a slanderer and mentions "neighbor," and vv 17–18 state that one should not hate one's brother and should love one's neighbor as oneself. Finally, "your burnt offerings are not acceptable, nor are your sacrifices pleasing to me" (Jer 6:20) suggests an antecedent Lev 22:20, "You shall not offer anything that has a blemish, for it will not be acceptable for you." My conclusion is that it is possible, though not proven, that phrases of Jrm's reflect the Holiness Code. In addition, there are phrases at the end of Leviticus 26 that imply the experience of the fall of Jerusalem in 587 and the consequent exile,[155] and some of these phrases appear to be borrowed from Jrm: the striking image of the corpses of idols (Lev 26:30) is doubtless drawn from Jer 16:18, and the image of the uncircumcised heart (Lev 26:41) may be dependent on that in Jer 4:4.

There are a few instances in which phrases of Jrm may be dependent on material in Numbers, but none for certain. Rudolph suggests that the expression "poisoned water" in Jer 8:14 is dependent on the ordeal set forth in Num 5:16–28; it is less likely that the image of Yahweh's filling all the inhabitants of the land with drunkenness (Jer 13:13) or the notion of the "cup of wrath" (Jer 25:15) have the same origin. The command to "shear your hair and throw it away" (Jer 7:29) may presuppose the Nazirite vow (Num 6:1–21). The expression "God of all flesh" (32:27) may be an adaptation of "God of the

spirits of all flesh" in Num 16:22 and 27:16. The only possible reminiscence of Balaam's oracles is Num 24:8, "He shall eat up the nations his foes," an expression that seems to be reflected in Jer 30:16, "For you all who eat of you shall be eaten, and all your foes are consumed," and compare the similar use of "eat" in Jer 2:3 and 5:17. (Parallels of Balaam's oracles in Jer 48 are late redactional additions.) Finally Yahweh's address to Israel as a woman, "So I gave you a lovely land, the most glorious inheritance of the nations," might be a reminder of the decision regarding inheritance for the daughters of Zelophehad (Num 27:1–11). But it is clear that if Jrm drew on the material of Numbers at all, it was not heavily.

42. Possible Parallels in Joshua and Judges

There seem to be two parallels to Jrm's words in Joshua, but in both instances the material in Joshua is evidently dependent on Jer. The first is Josh 9:25, the words of the Gibeonites to Joshua, "So now, look, we are in your hand: as is good and proper in your eyes to do to us, do," parallel to Jer 26:14, the words of Jrm to the officials and people gathered to put him to trial, "But as for me, look, I am in your hand: treat me as is good and proper in your eyes." These two verses virtually duplicate each other; Robert Boling assigns Josh 9:15b–27 to "Dtr 2," that is, to an exilic Deuteronomist.[156] Again Josh 23:15, "But just as all the good things which Yahweh your God promised concerning you have been fulfilled for you, so Yahweh will bring upon you all the evil things, until he has destroyed you from off this good land which Yahweh your God has given you," is parallel to Jer 32:42, "Just as I have brought in upon this people all this great evil, so I am bringing in upon them all the good which I am speaking over them." It is clear that there is a literary dependence between these two verses: the findings of the present study indicate that Jer 32:42 is authentic to Jrm and that Josh 23:15 is dependent upon it.[157]

There is one surprising parallel between Jrm's words and the Book of Judges: in Jer 49:1–2, the beginning of the oracle against the Ammonites, we read, "Has Israel no sons? Has he no heir [ירש qal participle]? Why then has Milcom dispossessed [ירש qal] Gad, and his people

---

155 See Martin Noth, *Leviticus* (Philadelphia: Westminster, 1965), 197–99; compare Eissfeldt, *Introduction*, 237–38.

156 Robert G. Boling and G. Ernest Wright, *Joshua* (AB 6; Garden City, NY: Doubleday, 1982), 272.

157 So also Weippert, *Prosareden*, 206–8; compare the

settled in its cities? So I shall let the blast of battle be heard against Rabbah, and it will become a desolate ruin, her daughter-villages will burn with fire, and Israel shall dispossess [ירש qal] his dispossessors [ירש qal participle]." This verse is clearly dependent on Judg 11:24, the climax of Jephthah's message to the Ammonite king, suggesting that the Ammonites stay in their allotted territory and not invade Gilead, "Is it not right that whatever your god Chemosh expropriates for you [ירש hip'il], you should possess [ירש qal]; and that everything that Yahweh our God expropriates [ירש hip'il] for us, we should possess [ירש qal]?" The latter passage gives no indication of late redaction; Boling attributes it to a "pragmatic compiler," whom he dates to the eighth century;[158] one must conclude therefore that Jrm drew on that narrative. Then in Jer 22:20 Jrm perceives Yahweh to be addressing Jerusalem in the feminine singular, "Climb Lebanon and cry out, and in Bashan raise your voice, and wail from Abarim: for all your lovers have been broken." The appeal to a woman to wail on the mountains must surely be a reminiscence of the narrative of Jephthah's daughter bewailing her virginity on the mountains (Judg 11:37–38), though the verbs are different. It is curious that the narrative of Jephthah appears to be the only one in Judges from which Jrm drew.

43. Jeremiah's Reminiscences of Events in the Time of Samuel

Jrm's reference to the destruction of the sanctuary at Shiloh (7:12, 14; 26:6) is presumably to the destruction by the Philistines (compare 1 Samuel 4), though certitude is lacking.

There are several points at which Jrm does draw on material now in 1 Samuel, and all of these are specific to the narrative of Samuel himself. One notes that Jrm names Moses and Samuel as the two great intercessors of the past (Jer 15:1). The parallels in Jrm's words are particularly to the narrative of Samuel's infancy and

boyhood (1 Samuel 1—3). That narrative is surely traditional; Kyle McCarter concludes that it was compiled by a prophetic writer of the eighth century,[159] so that it would have been accessible to Jrm.

In particular the motifs of Samuel's being called from birth (1 Sam 1:22) and his being referred to as a "youth" (נַעַר, 1 Sam 2:18, 21, 26; 3:1, 8) clearly formed part of the backdrop for Jrm's call narrative.[160]

Jer 15:9 offers, "She [the mother of warriors] languishes [אֻמְלְלָה] who has borne seven": this is a reversal of a phrase in Hannah's Song, 1 Sam 2:5, "The barren has borne seven, but she who has many children languishes [אֻמְלָלָה]." The date of the song has been controverted, but most opinion now dates it early: David N. Freedman has assigned it to the eleventh-tenth century,[161] and McCarter provisionally dates it to the tenth-ninth century.[162]

The expression "ears tingle" (with the verb צלל) occurs only three times in the OT—1 Sam 3:11; 2 Kgs 21:12; Jer 19:3. The verse in 2 Kgs 21:12 is part of a late Deuteronomistic insertion (vv 8–15).[163] McCarter assumes that both 1 Sam 3:11 and Jer 19:3 exhibit Deuteronomistic supplements.[164] To the contrary, the conclusion of the present study is that 19:3, and the material in chapter 19 in general, are authentic to Jrm. The expression in 2 Kgs 21:12 is evidently dependent on Jer 19:3 (Yahweh's judgment over Jerusalem and Judah); by contrast 1 Sam 3:11 is Yahweh's judgment, announced through the boy Samuel, on the fate of the house of Eli. I see no reason to deny the expression to the original prophetic writer and to conclude that Jrm is drawing on the diction he understood to be that of Samuel.

Mention has already been made of Samuel as intercessor: a narrative depicting his intercession for Israel is

assessment of the literary history of Joshua 23 in Boling and Wright, *Joshua*, 526.

158 Robert G. Boling, *Judges* (AB 6A; Garden City, NY: Doubleday, 1975) 31, 35–36, 205.

159 P. Kyle McCarter, *I Samuel* (AB 8; Garden City, NY: Doubleday, 1980) 19, 22.

160 Holladay, "Background."

161 David Noel Freedman, "Divine Names and Titles in

Early Hebrew Poetry," *Magnalia Dei, The Mighty Acts of God, Essays on the Bible and Archaeology in Memory of G. Ernest Wright* (ed. Frank M. Cross, Werner E. Lemke, and Patrick D. Miller, Jr.; Garden City, NY: Doubleday, 1976) 71–72, 96.

162 McCarter, *I Samuel*, 75–76.

163 Gray, *Kings*, 705.

164 McCarter, *I Samuel*, 98.

1 Sam 7:9, again part of the narrative of the early prophetic writer.[165]

Finally, there may be hints in Jer 15:5–9 (beyond the reminiscence already mentioned of Hannah's Song, Jer 15:9 and 1 Sam 2:5) of Samuel's activity. The verb "make childless" (שכל pi'el) occurs in Jer 15:7—Yahweh will make his people childless—in the context of "mother of young men" (v 8) and "sword" (v 9); in 1 Sam 15:33 Samuel says to Agag, "As your sword has made women childless, so your mother shall be childless among women." And Jer 15:5 is one of a number of verses in 14:1—15:9 that hints of Sheol—"Who will turn aside to ask about your well-being?" could also be heard as "Who will turn aside to Sheol about your well-being?" and one thinks of Saul's seeking to summon the spirit of Samuel from Sheol—"Why then do you ask me, since Yahweh has turned aside from you?" (1 Sam 28:16).

It is to be noted that Jrm offers no reminiscences of the ark narrative, or of the Saul cycle, or of the history of David's rise.[166]

44. Jeremiah's Reminiscences of Events during the Kingship of David and Solomon

There is only one clear reminiscence in Jrm's words to material from David's kingship (that is, from 2 Samuel), and that is the incident of David's statement to his servants when weeping over his dead child (2 Sam 12:22–23): "While the child was still alive, I fasted and wept; for I said, 'Who knows whether Yahweh will be gracious to me, that the child may live?' But now he is dead; why should I fast? Can I bring him back again? I shall go to him, but he will not return to me." Jrm, in his word over Jehoahaz (Jer 22:10), shifts David's irony: "Do not weep for him who is dead [Josiah], nor grieve for him: do weep for him who is gone [Jehoahaz, Josiah's son], for he shall not return again."

Just before that point in the narrative the prophet Nathan had told David the parable of the poor man and his ewe lamb: I suggest in the present study that Jer 13:21 (as reconstructed) may offer an allusion to that parable, but given the difficulties of the text, that is only a suggestion.

Finally, Jrm's description of Judah's humiliation at the hands of Egypt or Assyria, when she will go out with her hands on her head (Jer 2:36–37), may reflect the description of Tamar's fleeing after her rape by Amnon (2 Sam 13:16, 19). McCarter suggests that the material in 2 Sam 11:27b—12:25 is to be attributed to the same prophetic writer responsible for many of the narratives in 1 Samuel, that is, someone from the eighth century,[167] and that 2 Samuel 13 is part of material that probably derived from the time of David.[168] By this analysis, then, such material would have been available to Jrm. What is surprising is the paucity of reminiscences from the time of David's kingship. It was prophetic material (thus Nathan) and injustice (the rape of Tamar) that caught Jrm's ear.

There remains no clear-cut reminiscence from the tradition of Solomon's kingship. I have revocalized "at the horns of your altars" in Jer 17:1 to "at the horns of the altar is their oppression"; if this reconstruction is correct, one is reminded of Benaiah's killing of both Adonijah and Joab at the horns of the altar in Jerusalem (1 Kgs 1:50; 2:19–25, 28–35), and I have gone on to suggest that the defective text of Jer 17:1–2 is the result of a haplography and that "the son of Jehoiada" (that is, Benaiah) might have originally appeared in that sequence. If these suspicions are correct, then that passage would originally have been a reminiscence of the violence at the altar as kingship passed from David to Solomon.

The protestation of Jrm at the time of his call, "I am only a youth" (Jer 1:6), reminds one of the similar protestation of Solomon when he entered into kingship, "I am a mere youth" (1 Kgs 3:7). Deuteronomistic editing is evident in Solomon's prayer (1 Kgs 3:1–14), but it is editing of pre-Deuteronomic material;[169] so that it is possible that Jrm had this tradition in mind.

45. Jeremiah's Reminiscences of the Ninth-Century Prophets

There is little in Jrm's words that is reminiscent of the narratives of the kings in the century after the death of Solomon; there are several echoes, however, of material about the ninth-century prophets Elijah, Elisha and Micaiah ben Imlah.

165 Ibid., 19.
166 Compare ibid., 23–30.
167 P. Kyle McCarter, *II Samuel* (AB 9; Garden City, NY: Doubleday, 1984) 290.
168 Ibid., 9.
169 Noth, *Könige*, 44–46.

The clearest example of Jrm's use of Elijah's words is his use of the judgment about Jezebel, cited by Jehu (2 Kgs 9:37), that "the corpse of Jezebel shall be as dung upon the face of the field": this word is universalized by Jrm (Jer 9:21), that "the corpses of humanity shall fall like dung on the face of the field."[170] This reference to Jezebel may be reinforced by the reference to "windows" in Jer 9:20, since Jezebel looked out of the window at her assassin-to-be, and she was thrown out the window to her death (2 Kgs 9:30, 32). There may be another suggestion that all the people have become like Jezebel in Jer 4:30, where Yahweh accuses the people, personified as a whore, of "enlarging her eyes" with eye shadow; Jezebel is said to have done this just before her death (2 Kgs 9:30 once more). And (to stay with Jer 9:16–21) it is possible that the summons there to the women to practice their dirges may be a mockery of women devoted to Baal who mourn his death (one thinks of Elijah's mockery of the prophets of Baal in 1 Kgs 18:27).

Jrm offers two references to the "running" of prophets (Jer 12:5; 23:21); one is not certain whether this was a standard term for ecstasy or other prophetic behavior, but the fact that Elijah was said to have "run" before Ahab's chariot (1 Kgs 18:46) may have reinforced his use of the verb.

At that time it is said that the "hand of Yahweh" was upon Elijah, and the same thing is said of Elisha (2 Kgs 3:15). Jrm said it of himself (Jer 15:17); though it is a traditional term, again the fact that it is said of Elijah and Elisha may have reinforced Jrm's use of the phrase. (It is to be noted that a similar expression occurs in Isa 8:11.)

Elijah escaped from Jezebel and "lodged" (לִין, 1 Kgs 19:9) in the wilderness; one wonders whether Jrm's mediating of Yahweh's word, "O that I had in the wilderness a wayfarers' lodging [מָלוֹן]!" (Jer 9:1), does not ironically reflect that narrative about Elijah; and one may further wonder whether Elijah's word to Yahweh in the next verse, "I, even I only, am left" (1 Kgs 19:10), did not help stimulate Jrm's confessions, particularly the statement, "I have sat alone" (Jer 15:17).

As to Micaiah ben Imlah, in that narrative in 1 Kings 22 it is said that a lying spirit from the heavenly court would be in the mouth of the king's prophets, and in this way the prophets will "deceive" (פתה pi'el) the king (1 Kgs 22:20, 22); in the same way Jrm complained to Yahweh that he deceived him (פתה pi'el, Jer 20:7). The problem of false prophecy was always severe, but the use of this verb may well indicate a dependence on the old narrative.

Though not directly a narrative of Elisha, the story of the lepers at the gate of Samaria during the Syrian siege (2 Kgs 7:3–10) is part of the Elisha cycle. The lepers say (2 Kgs 7:3–4), "Why do we sit here till we die? If we say, 'Let us enter the city,' the famine is in the city, and we shall die there; and if we sit here, we die also. Come, let us go over to the camp of the Syrians; if they spare our lives we shall live, and if they kill us we shall but die." This sequence is very close to the word of the people threatened by the foe from the north, "Why are we sitting? Gather and let us get in to the fortified cities" (Jer 8:14), so that it is at least possible that Jrm had the narrative in mind. Is he suggesting that the people are no better than lepers? And again, in the divine word to the people (Jer 21:8–9), we seem to have another echo of the lepers' word: "He who stays in this city shall die by sword and famine, but he who goes out to the Chaldeans besieging you shall live."

46. Jeremiah's Reminiscences of the Eighth-Century Siege of Jerusalem

There appear to be recollections in Jrm's words of the eighth-century siege of Jerusalem, especially of the Rabshakeh's speeches (2 Kgs 18:19–35). The Assyrian officer mocks Judah for being ignorant of the skills of chariots and their horsemen and dependent on Egypt for them (vv 23–24); I propose in the present study that Yahweh's battle orders addressed to Egypt (Jer 46:3–4) mock them for being ignorant of the skills of cavalry. The Rabshakeh urges the defenders of Jerusalem not to let Hezekiah "deceive" them (נשא II) with regard to their safety (v 29; compare 19:10); Jrm in his day accuses Yahweh of "deceiving" (נשא II) the people and Jerusalem with regard to their safety (Jer 4:10). And I suggest that Jer 10:1–16 is Jrm's witty reconception of the incident with the Rabshakeh: the Assyrian officer belittles the power of the gods of the nations (2 Kgs 18:33–35), and

---

170 Holladay, "Prototype," 359.

Hezekiah complains that the Rabshakeh has come to mock the living God (2 Kgs 19:4), and according to the narrative, Hezekiah prayed to Yahweh, noting that the kings of Assyria had laid waste the nations and had "cast their gods into the fire; for they were no gods, but the work of men's hands, wood and stone; therefore they were destroyed" (2 Kgs 19:18); these are the notes, of course, that are struck in Jer 10:1–16. And above all the confrontation over the walls of Jerusalem involves the Hebrew and Aramaic languages: the Rabshakeh addresses the officers of Jerusalem in Hebrew, while the officers urge him to speak Aramaic, which they understand, in order not to lower the morale of those manning the defense walls (2 Kgs 18:27); Jer 10:1–16 includes a verse (v 11) mocking the Babylonian idols in the language that the Babylonians and their gods can understand, namely, Aramaic.

47. Jeremiah's Dependence on the Eighth- and Seventh-Century Prophets: Preliminary Remarks

As one might expect, Jrm drew heavily on the prophets immediately preceding him whose oracles have been preserved in the tradition, particularly on Hosea, but on the others as well. It would be interesting to discern the value that shared phraseology had for Jrm. It is clear that at some points Jrm is deliberately citing earlier material and assumed that his audience would recognize the citations (Jer 4:3–4; 10:23–25). In other instances he adapted earlier material, again evidently with the intent of startling his audience: the shift from "hear, O heavens" (Isa 1:2) to "be horrified, O heavens" (Jer 2:12) might well be in that category. In other instances the phrases were doubtless used because they were congenial; Jrm may not even have been conscious of their source.

48. Jeremiah's Dependence on Amos

Jrm drew at many points on Amos.[171] There are striking form-critical parallels—for example, the use of nonsense questions for rhetorical effect (Jer 18:14; 30:6; Amos 6:12), or of the parody of priestly torah regarding sacrifices (Jer 7:21–23; Amos 4:4–5). But there are verbal parallels as well. The most extended perhaps is Amos 3:6–11, expanded on in Jer 6:1–8. Amos 3:6 has "Is a horn blown in a city?" and Jer 6:1 has "In Tekoa sound the horn," Tekoa being of course Amos's village. Amos 3:9 has "[See] those extorted in her midst," while Jer 6:6 has "There is nothing but extortion in her midst." Amos 3:10 has "Those who store up violence and destruction in their strongholds," while Jer 6:7, slightly emended, has "Violence and destruction are heard in her, before me she measures them out."

The other parallels are most conveniently listed in the order in which they appear in Amos. The opening verse of Amos's oracles, Amos 1:2, is clearly imitated in Jer 25:30; Jrm has taken Amos's word over Israel and extended it to cover the earth.

Amos's description of the collapse of the soldiers of Israel, "Flight shall perish from the swift, . . . nor shall the warrior escape with his life" (Amos 2:14), is applied by Jrm to the Egyptians in an early prophecy against them, "The swift cannot flee, nor the warrior escape" (Jer 46:6).

The words of Jer 31:4–5, "Again I shall build you so that you may be built, maiden Israel; . . . again you shall plant vineyards in the mountains of Samaria," seem to reverse the curse-judgment expressed in Amos 5:11, "You have built houses of hewn stone, but you shall not dwell in them; you have planted pleasant vineyards, but you shall not drink their wine"; but such a "futility curse" may simply be a traditional one.[172]

Amos 5:12, "I know how many are your transgressions, how great are your sins," is imitated in Jer 5:6, "How many are their transgressions, how numerous their turnings," and 30:15, "Because of the greatness of your guilt, because your sins are so numerous."

Jer 17:16, "Now have I longed for the day of collapse," appears to be a variation on Amos 5:18, "Woe to those who long for the day of Yahweh."

Amos 6:2, "Cross to Calneh and see, and thence go to Hamath the great, then go down to Gath of the Philistines," is imitated in Jer 2:10, "Cross to the shores of the Cypriots and see, and to Kedar send and make careful inquiry": Jrm has expanded Amos's geographical horizons.

171 See particularly Berridge, "Jeremia und die Prophetie des Amos."

172 Hillers, *Treaty-Curses*, 29.

It is possible that Amaziah's prohibition to Amos, "Never again prophesy at Bethel" (Amos 7:13), is reflected in the words of Jrm's opponents, "Never prophesy in the name of Yahweh" (Jer 11:21).

Amos's description of the rise and fall of the Nile (Amos 8:8) is used by Jrm in his early prophecy against Egypt, 46:7 (compare the discussion above of his use of Amos 2:14 in Jer 46:6).

The expression "mourning for an only son" (Amos 8:10) is repeated in Jer 6:26, though again it may be a proverbial expression.[173]

Amos's description of people's inability to escape the punishing hand of Yahweh (Amos 9:2–3), itself doubtless a reflection of Ps 139:7–12, is perhaps in Jrm's mind in Jer 23:23–24 (see the extended discussion on Psalm 139 below, sec. 63).

And "I will set my eyes upon them for evil and not for good" (Amos 9:4) is deliberately reversed in Jer 24:6, "I shall set my eyes upon them [the exiles of Judah] for good."[174]

Though Jrm did not draw on Amos so massively as he did on Hosea and Zephaniah 1, it is clear that the words of Amos were a part of the prophetic tradition to which he was indebted.

49. Jeremiah's Dependence on Hosea

That Jrm is deeply dependent on Hosea has long been recognized.[175] Jrm inherited from Hosea the ruling metaphor of Israel as the unfaithful wife of Yahweh and thus vocabulary referring to Baal worship and to sexual relations in a religious context: the diction of Hosea 2 evidently presupposes the legal situation described in Deut 24:1–4 (see esp. Hos 2:9); Jrm draws on both Hosea and Deuteronomy in Jer 3:1–5; and in general Hosea's use of שוב "return" in chapters 11 and 14 stimulated Jrm's wide use of the verb. And—to name one detail— the designation of the northern kingdom in Hosea, "Ephraim" (thirty-six times), appears four times in Jer 31. Alfons Deissler has recently analyzed the theological

parallels between Jrm and Hosea.[176] But the likenesses extend beyond theology to phraseology: there are in the words of Jrm two or three times as many reminiscences for each chapter of Hosea as for each chapter of Amos.

I begin with two instances that are evidently deliberate quotations. Jer 14:10 cites Hos 8:13aβb word for word, "Yahweh has not approved them: now he shall remember their iniquity and deal with their sin," taking Hosea's word against Ephraim and applying it to Judah. And Jer 4:3 cites Hos 10:12, "Plow yourselves unplowed ground," in the context of a citation from Deuteronomy in Jer 4:4.

The easiest listing of parallels is in the order of the Book of Hosea. Jrm drew on Hosea 2 not only in the metaphor of marriage (see above) but also in phrasing. In Hos 2:4–5 Yahweh will make "your mother" (i.e., Israel) "like a wilderness, and set her like a land of drought"; in Jer 2:31 Yahweh accuses Israel of treating Yahweh like "a wilderness or a land of deep darkness," and again in Jer 50:12, Yahweh addresses the Babylonians, saying that "your mother" shall be "a wilderness, a drought and waste."

Again Jer 2:6 piles up the synonyms for wilderness, after the phrase "walk after a nothing [= Baal]," 2:5; Hos 2:7 portrays Gomer/Israel as saying, "let me walk after my lovers" (and compare Jer 2:25, where Israel says, "I have loved strangers, and after them I will walk").

"Days of her youth" (Hos 2:17) may be echoed in Jer 2:2, "I have recalled in your favor the loyalty of your youth."

And Hos 2:20–25 may be reflected in Jer 31:27–28 + 31–34: in Hos 2:20 Yahweh says, "I will make for them a covenant on that day with the beasts of the field, the birds of the air, and the creeping things of the ground," and in v 25 he says, "And I will sow her for myself in the land"; Jer 31:27 has "Behold the days are coming, says Yahweh, when I will sow the house of Israel and the house of Judah with the seed of man and the seed of

173 So also Berridge, p. 101.

174 Holladay, "Prototype," 364.

175 See, for example, Skinner, *Prophecy and Religion*, 21–22, 33, 60 n. 2, 64–65, 84, 86; von Rad, *OT Theology 2*, 192; and, from the point of view of the sociology of prophetic traditions, Wilson, *Prophecy and Society*, 225–52.

176 Alfons Deissler, "Das 'Echo' der Hosea-Verkün-

digung im Jeremiabuch," *Künder des Wortes, Beiträge zur Theologie der Propheten, Josef Schreiner zum 60. Geburtstag* (ed. Lothar Ruppert, Peter Weimar, and Erich Zenger; Würzburg: Echter, 1982) 61–75.

beast," and of course 31:31–34 describes the new covenant.

Jer 25:31, "For Yahweh has a lawsuit with the nations," seems to reflect Hos 4:1, "For Yahweh has a lawsuit with the inhabitants of the land."

Jrm's citing of some of the Ten Commandments with infinitive absolutes in Jer 7:9 is evidently modeled on Hos 4:2, where again some of the Ten Commandments are listed with infinitive absolutes.

Hos 4:3 is reflected in three passages: Jer 4:28, "On this account the land/earth shall mourn"; 8:13, an expression of the reversal of creation; and 14:2, with the parallel of "mourn" (אבל) and "languish" (אמל pu'al).

The association of "eat" and "commit harlotry" in Hos 4:10 may be reflected in the same association in Jer 5:7.

Hos 4:13 describes Baal worship on mountains and hills and under trees; this expression was evidently the basis of the formulation in Deut 12:2, and that formulation in turn evidently lies behind Jrm's "on every high hill and under every green tree," Jer 2:20, a phrase later replicated.[177]

In Jer 31:18 Ephraim is compared to a "calf untrained"; this expression seems to be based on Hos 4:16, "Like a stubborn heifer, Israel is stubborn," and 10:11, "Ephraim was a trained heifer," and one notes that Egypt is called a heifer in Jer 46:20 (for another use in Jer of Hos 10:11 see below).

Twice Hosea states that Israel betrayed (בגד בְּ) Yahweh (Hos 5:7; 6:7); Jrm uses the expression in 3:20.

Though the expression "sound the trumpet" is not overly distinctive, Jrm uses it in Jer 4:5 and 6:1 in the ambiguous context of a call to both battle and lament (compare 4:6–8 and 6:1b–8) just as Hosea does in Hos 5:8.

In Hos 5:10 Yahweh states, "I will pour out my wrath upon them [the princes of Judah] like water"; in Jer 6:11 Jrm states, "of the wrath of Yahweh I am full," and Yahweh says, "Pour it out on the children in the streets."

Jrm adapts Hos 6:10, "In the house of Israel I have seen something horrible," making the target more specific: "In the prophets of Jerusalem I have seen something horrible" (Jer 23:14).

And Hos 6:11 contains the expression שׁוב שְׁבוּת

"restore the fortunes"—it is evidently the stimulus for the use of that expression five times in Jer, beginning in 29:14 (see there).

In Hos 7:4 one hears that "they [the inhabitants of Ephraim] are all adulterers," and the same phrase occurs in Jer 9:1.

In Hos 7:11 it is affirmed, "Ephraim is like a dove, silly, without heart [= sense], to Egypt they have called, to Assyria they have walked"; Jrm pairs Egypt and Assyria as twin goals for Israel in seeking aid (Jer 2:18; compare 2:36) and addresses Israel as a "people foolish and without heart [= sense]."

It is possible that the expression "They have sown wheat and reaped thorns" (Jer 12:13) is based on Hos 8:7, "They sow the wind, and they shall reap the whirlwind," though both appear to be wisdom sayings.

The expression כְּלִי אֵין־חֵפֶץ בּוֹ "useless vessel," "vessel no one cares for," is used in Hos 8:8 of Israel and then in Jer 22:28 of Jehoiachin and 48:38 of Moab.

Hos 8:9 offers the metaphor of Israel as a wild ass; Jrm uses it in Jer 2:24.

The sarcasm of Hos 8:13aα with regard to Israel's love of eating the meat of sacrifices is reflected in Jer 7:21 with the same vocabulary. (For Hos 8:13aβb, cited by Jrm in another context, see above.)

Hos 9:4 says, "They shall not please him with their sacrifices"; in Jer 6:20 Yahweh says, "Nor are your sacrifices pleasing to me."

Jer 5:31, "What will you do at her end [i.e., the end of the land]?" is an expression that seems to be based on Hos 9:5, "What will you do on the day of meeting?" and Isa 10:3, "What will you do on the day of punishment?"

In Hos 9:8 the prophet is called "the watchman of Ephraim"; Jrm reflects that designation (Jer 6:17) when Yahweh says, "I set watchmen over you."

Hos 9:10 stimulated several verses in Jer. The verse in Hosea reads, "Like grapes in the wilderness, I found Israel. Like the first fruit on the fig tree, in its first season [בְּרֵאשִׁיתָה], I saw your father. But they came to Baal-peor, and consecrated themselves to Shame, and became detestable like the thing they loved." Jer 31:2–3a states (with slight emendations), "He [Yahweh] found him [Israel] in the wilderness"; Jer 2:2–3 portrays Israel in

177 Holladay, "On Every High Hill."

the wilderness, the "first fruits of his [Yahweh's] harvest [רֵאשִׁית תְּבוּאָתֹה]," and 2:5 states that "Israel walked after a nothing and shared in nothingness"; and finally Jeremiah 24 compares Israel to figs.

Hos 9:15 has "evil of your/their doings" (as does Isa 1:16), and that phrase occurs in Jer 4:4. Hos 9:15 also has "all their princes are rebels"—the latter phrase, along with Isa 1:23, "Your princes are rebels," evidently stimulated Jer 6:28, "They are all princely rebels."

Hos 10:1a and Isa 5:1–7, offering the metaphor of Israel as a vine, lie behind Jer 2:21; and Hos 10:1b, "The more his fruit increased, the more altars he built," must have stimulated Jer 2:28 (restored with G), "As many as your cities are your gods, O Judah, and as many as your streets, O Jerusalem, have they sacrificed to Baal."

"Double iniquity" in Hos 10:10 may lie behind "double crime" in Jer 2:13.

"Trained heifer" in Hos 10:11 has already been mentioned in connection with Hos 4:16; but a later phrase, "I will put Ephraim to the yoke," evidently is the source of Jer 2:20, "Look, long ago you broke your yoke."

Hos 11:1–9 is a rich source for Jrm, especially in 31:9b, 18–20, Yahweh's words over Ephraim: it is noteworthy that Jerome in his commentary on Jer 31:20 refers to Hos 11:8–9. "My son" in Hos 11:1 surely stimulated Jer 31:9b and 20aα. In Hos 11:5b the prophet plays with the verb שׁוב: they will return to Egypt, because "they refused to return [to me]"; this phrase is picked up in Jer 5:3 and occurs again in 8:5, where it likewise partakes in word-play on the variety of meanings of the verb.

In Hosea 12 the prophet offers two word-plays on proper names: in vv 3–5 he plays on the name "Jacob," as Jrm does in Jer 9:3; and in v 8 he plays on Canaan, as Jrm does in Jer 10:17.

It is possible that the word in Hos 12:13 that attributes prophetic status to Moses reinforced Jrm's self-understanding as a prophet in the line of Moses (compare Deut 18:18).

In Hos 13:14 there is a personification of Death, as there is also in Jer 9:20. The description of the dry desert wind in Hos 13:15 may have stimulated a similar description Jer 4:11–12.

"For she has defied [מרה] her God" (Hos 14:1) may have stimulated "For it is I she has defied [מרה]" (Jer 4:17).

Clearly "return, Israel" (שׁוּבָה יִשְׂרָאֵל) in Hos 14:2, "return to Yahweh" (שׁוּבוּ אֶל־יהוה) in Hos 14:3, and "I will heal your turnings" (אֶרְפָּא מְשׁוּבָתָם) in Hos 14:5 are adapted in "turn a turning, Israel" (שׁוּבָה מְשֻׁבָה יִשְׂרָאֵל) in Jer 3:12, "[re]turn, turnable children" (שׁוּבוּ בָנִים שׁוֹבָבִים) in 3:14, 22, and "I will heal your turnings" (אֶרְפָּה מְשׁוּבֹתֵיכֶם) in Jer 3:22.

Finally, Israel in Hos 14:7 is compared to a fair olive-tree, and Yahweh calls Israel a lovely olive-tree in Jer 11:16.

Here, then, are at least fifty points at which Jrm draws on the diction of Hosea, and it is to be noted that the relevant passages in Hosea are drawn from every part of the book and that the parallels in Jer are mostly to material in chapters 2—10 and 30—31, proclaimed early in his career.

50. Jeremiah's Dependence on Isaiah

Isaiah is not usually thought of as a source for Jrm, but it is clear that Jrm did draw on Isaiah, themes and occasionally phrases as well.

Thus the theme of Israel as a vine (Jer 2:21) is found in both Hos 10:1 and Isa 5:1–7; if Jrm drew on Hos 10:1 (see above), he also drew on Isa 5:1–7: Isa 5:2 reads, "he planted it as śōrēq grapes," and Jer 2:21 reads, "I planted you as śōrēq grapes." Further the text in Jer 2:21 may conceal a rare word for "putrid," synonymous with the word in Isa 5:2, 4. And Isa 5:7 offers two more possible expressions that Jrm may have drawn on: outside Psalms and Proverbs the word שַׁעֲשׁוּעִים "darling" appears only in Isa 5:7 and Jer 31:20—in Isa 5:7 the men of Judah are his "dear planting," while in Jer 31:20 Ephraim is his "darling child"; and the expression "long for X, and behold, Y" occurs in Isa 5:7 and also in Jer 8:15 (compare 4:23–26).

The imperative "hear" (שִׁמְעוּ) is normal for the call to the witnesses in the cosmic lawsuit (Isa 1:2; Mic 1:2; 6:2), so the variation of Isa 1:2, "hear, O heavens [שִׁמְעוּ שָׁמַיִם]," to "be horrified, O heavens [שֹׁמּוּ שָׁמַיִם]" (Jer 2:12) is surely deliberate.

One wonders whether the designation in Isa 1:4 of the nation as בָּנִים מַשְׁחִיתִים, "destructive children," is not reflected in the judgment of Jer 6:28, כֻּלָּם מַשְׁחִיתִים הֵמָּה, "All of them are destructive."

The theme in Isa 1:5, that Yahweh struck the people in discipline but they did not notice, is picked up in Jer

5:3; and beyond the shared theme the passages share the verb נכה hipʻil "strike." And it is possible that the description in Isa 1:5–6 of the people's sores and wounds that do not heal lies behind a similar description in Jer 30:12–15.

Isa 1:7a, "Your land is desolate, your cities burned with fire," may have helped stimulate Jrm to employ such phrases (Jer 2:15; 4:27), and a further phrase in that verse of Isaiah, "aliens devour it [your land]," may have given rise to the elaborate description in Jer 5:17 of the eating by the foe from the north of the produce and population of the land.

The text of Jer 11:15 needs serious emendation; if my reconstruction of the first colon is sound, "What have your kettles to do with me?" then a similar rhetorical question in Isa 1:11, "What to me is the multitude of your sacrifices?" may lie behind the verse, but this is speculation.

It is clear, however, that both Isa 1:15–20 and Psalm 51 lie behind Jer 2:22; Isa 1:15 describes Israel's bloody hands, and both passages have synonymous imperatives for "wash" (Isa 1:16; Ps 51:4). Again, Isa 1:15 states that though the people make many prayers, Yahweh will not listen to them: this affirmation may have stimulated Jer 7:16 and 11:11, 14.

And Isa 1:16 (and Hos 9:15) share the phrase "evil of your/their doings" with Jer 4:4.

Isa 1:21 states, "Righteousness lodged [לין] in her, but now murderers," and Yahweh says in Jer 4:14, "How long shall your baneful schemes lodge in your inner self?"

Then Isa 1:22–25 is the model for Jer 6:27–30, not only the vocabulary of refining silver but also in the phrase "your princes are rebels" (Isa 1:23): that phrase, along with a similar expression in Hos 9:15, stimulated the variation in Jer 6:28, "They are all princely rebels."

And the expression at the end of the chapter, Isa 1:31, "with none to quench," is the model for the same phrase in Jer 4:4.

Isa 2:6–22—and 7:18–19 and 8:7–8—seem to lie behind the narrative of Jrm's symbolic action in burying the linen loincloth, Jer 13:1–12aα: the passages share the words "rock" (סֶלַע, Isa 2:21) or "cleft of the rock" (נְקִיק הַסֶּלַע, plural Isa 7:19; singular Jer 13:4), and "pride"

(גָּאוֹן, Isa 2:10; Jer 13:9); Jrm's act seems to be a symbolic fulfillment of Isaiah's prophecy in Isa 8:7–8 that the Euphrates will inundate Judah.

Further, the word that Yahweh "forsakes" (נטש) his people is found in both Isa 2:6 and Jer 7:29. The phrase "the work of their hands" (for idols), Isa 2:8 (and in Huldah's oracle, 2 Kgs 22:17), occurs in Jer 1:16.

The expression "fruit of one's deeds" (Jer 17:10) seems to be derived from Isa 3:10.[178]

The description in Jer 5:27–28 of the houses of the rich, full of the possessions of the poor, is evidently stimulated both by Isa 3:14, "Goods stolen from the poor are in your houses," and by Zeph 1:9, "And I will punish . . . those who fill their master's house with violence and fraud."

The striking phrase in Isa 3:26, "Her [Jerusalem's] entrances shall lament and mourn," is the model for Jer 14:2, "She [Judah] mourns, and her gates languish."

The stimulus of Isa 5:1–7 has already been dealt with at the head of this section.

Isa 5:19 sets forth the word of scoffers, "Let him [Yahweh] make haste, let him speed his work that we may see it, let the purpose of the Holy One of Israel draw near, and let it come, that we may know it!"; this is doubtless the model for Jer 17:15, "Look, they keep saying to me, 'Where is the word of Yahweh?—let it come!'"

Isa 5:24 has "They have rejected [מאס] the law of Yahweh of hosts, they have despised [נאץ piʻel] the word of the Holy One of Israel"; Jer 6:19 reflects the first half, "And my law, they rejected it," and Jer 23:17 the second half, offering "those despising the word of Yahweh."

Though form-critically Jrm's call is not modeled closely on that of Isaiah, nevertheless one notes that in Isa 6:6–7 the seraph touched Isaiah's lips with the glowing coal from the altar to purify them, while in Jer 1:9 Yahweh put forth his hand and touched Jrm's mouth; it is likely then that Jrm knew the tradition of Isaiah's call. And is it a coincidence that Isa 6:10 speaks of Isaiah's call to dull the heart, the ears, and the eyes of the people, while in Jer 5:21 the people are addressed as "a people stupid and without heart, eyes they have but do not see, ears they have but do not hear"?

---

178 Holladay, "Prototype," 355–56.

In Isa 7:2 and 13 Ahaz is referred to as "house of David," doubtless ironically; the same irony may lie behind that phrase in Jer 21:12. And an analogous depreciation of Jehoiakim, in comparison with Ahaz, may lie behind Jer 22:15, though that is evident only when the text is emended. Then later in Isa 7:2 it is said that the heart of Ahaz and the heart of his people shook as the trees of the forest shake; in Jer 4:9 Yahweh says that "On that day the heart of the king will fail, and the heart of the officials": Jrm evidently sensed that the situation would grow worse in his own day.

In Isa 7:11 and 13 Isaiah's interchange with Ahaz offers a notable shift of pronouns in reference to God: Isaiah first challenges Ahaz to "ask a sign of Yahweh your [second-person singular] God," and a moment later asks, "Is it too little for you to weary men, that you weary my God also?" Jrm does the same thing in his interchange with Johanan and his group (Jer 42:2–6): the group asks Jrm to pray to Yahweh "your [second-person singular] God," Jrm in turn assures the group that he will pray to "Yahweh your [second-person plural] God," and the group then agrees to obey the voice of "Yahweh our God."

Again in Isa 7:11 there is evidently a word-play on "ask" and "to Sheol" (see the contrast between *M* and the Versions there), a word-play that may have stimulated a similar double meaning between "to ask" and "to Sheol" in Jer 15:5.

Does the name of the child prophesied by Isaiah, *'immānû-'ēl* (Isa 7:14), a theophoric name with a first-person plural suffix, help to stimulate Jrm to prophesy of a coming king with the name *Yahweh-ṣidqēnû* (Jer 23:6)?

I have already mentioned the stimulus that Isa 8:7–8 gave to the narrative of Jrm's hiding of the linen loincloth (Jer 13:1–12aα: see above on Isa 2:6–21). Isa 8:5–8 says that because Judah refuses the waters of Shiloah, "The Lord is bringing up against them the waters of the River [the Euphrates], mighty and many, . . . and it will rise over all its channels and go over all its banks; and it will sweep on into Judah, it will overflow and pass on . . . and its outspread wings will fill the breadth of your land." This passage evidently gave rise to several passages of Jrm's. Thus in Jer 2:13 the people abandoned the spring of running water and have dug broken cisterns instead; and in Jer 2:18 they go to Egypt to drink the water of the Nile, or to Assyria to drink the water of the Euphrates. And the motif recurs in the oracles against foreign nations: in Jer 46:7–8 Egypt rises like the Nile and says, "Let me arise, let me cover the earth, let me destroy its inhabitants!"; in 47:2, "Waters are coming up from the north, to become an overflowing stream, to overflow the land and what fills it, a city and its inhabitants"; and in 51:13 Babylon is addressed, "You who dwell by many waters, great in treasures, your end has come." There is one instance in which Jrm referred to Yahweh's hand to express prophetic experience; that expression occurs in earlier material only with respect to Elijah (1 Kgs 18:46), Elisha (2 Kgs 3:15), and Isaiah (Isa 8:11).

The affirmation that the people will "be broken" (שבר nip'al), Isa 8:15, may stand behind Jrm's statement to Jerusalem that "all your lovers are broken," Jer 22:20.

Jer 21:12, "Render [דין] each morning justice [מִשְׁפָּט], and save him who is robbed [גָּזוּל] from the hand of the oppressor," seems to be based on Isa 10:2, "[Woe to those who decree iniquitous decrees,] to turn aside from a verdict [דִּין] the needy, and to rob [גזל] the justice [מִשְׁפָּט] of the poor of my people."

A phrase in the next verse in Isaiah, Isa 10:3, "What will you do on the day of punishment?" along with Hos 9:5 ("What will you on the day of meeting?"), is evidently the basis for Jer 5:31, "What will you do at her end [i.e., the end of the land]?"

A phrase in Isa 10:6, "the people of my [Yahweh's] rage [עֶבְרָתִי]," evidently stands behind the phrase in Jer 7:29, "the community of his [Yahweh's] rage [עֶבְרָתוֹ]."

The theme of gleaning as judgment is common to Isa 17:4–6 and Jer 6:9; Jrm may have derived the image from Isaiah.

The expression "incurable pain [כְּאֵב אָנוּשׁ]" in Isa 17:11 may be the source for "Why has . . . my wound been incurable [מַכָּתִי אֲנוּשָׁה]?" in Jer 15:18 and "your pain is incurable [אָנוּשׁ מַכְאֹבֵךְ]" in Jer 30:15.

Isa 18:5, "The shoots he takes away, he breaks off," is evidently the source of Jer 5:10, "Take away her [Jerusalem's] shoots" (the noun "shoots" [נְטִישׁוֹת] appears in the OT, beyond these two passages, only in Jer 48:32, in a different context).

Isa 19:2, "And I will stir up Egyptians against Egyptians, and they will fight, every man against his brother and every man against his neighbor, city against city, kingdom against kingdom," is evidently a source for

Jer 9:3, "Let each of you watch out for his neighbor, and put no trust in any brother."

Isa 19:11, "How can you [the wise counselors] say to Pharaoh, 'I am a son of the wise, a son of ancient kings'?" is evidently the source of Jer 8:8, "How can you say, 'We are wise, and the law of Yahweh is with us'?"

I have suggested that the strange expression "Valley of Vision" (Isa 22:1, 5) may be an ironic denomination of the Valley of Ben-Hinnom and may have stimulated Jrm to announce a change of name of that place (Jer 7:32), but the suggestion cannot be proved.

The sarcastic command in Isa 29:1 in regard to festivals, "Add [סְפוּ] year to year," must have stimulated Jrm's similarly sarcastic "your burnt offerings add [סְפוּ] to your sacrifices" in Jer 7:21.

I have suggested that the phraseology of Jer 14:2 implies Sheol; if so, the expression "the outcry of Jerusalem rises" may have as its background the description in Isa 29:2 of the voice of Ariel rising from Sheol.

The description on insincerity in Isa 29:13, "This people draw near with their mouth and honor me with their lips, while their hearts are far from me," is reflected in Jrm's confession (Jer 12:2), "'You are near' is in their mouth but is far from their mind [literally kidneys]."

And the image of the potter for Yahweh in Isa 29:16 must lie behind Jrm's visit to the potter's workshop in 18:1–12.

Isa 30:5–6 lies behind Jer 2:6–8: Isa 30:5 has "Every one [i.e., in Judah] comes to shame through a people [Egypt] that cannot profit [לֹא־יוֹעִילוּ]," and Jer 2:8 has "after profitless things [לֹא־יוֹעִלוּ, the Baals] they have walked"; and Isa 30:6 describes the land of the southern desert as a "land of trouble and anguish [אֶרֶץ צָרָה וְצוּקָה]," a phrase that gave rise to the extended description of the wilderness in Jer 2:6, "land of drought and utter darkness [אֶרֶץ צִיָּה וְצַלְמָוֶת]" and the rest.

The mocking name given by Isaiah to Egypt that includes the designation "Rahab" (Isa 30:7) may be reflected in Jer 46:16, if that text is to be restored to include "Rahab," and in 46:17, where the Pharaoh is given a new name.

Isa 30:13–17 lies behind Jer 4:6: in Isa 30:13–14 the root שׁבר "break, smash" occurs three times, and in 30:17 there is נֵס "signal"; in Jer 4:6 one has "raise a signal in Zion" and "for disaster I am bringing from the north,

and great collapse [שֶׁבֶר גָּדוֹל]." In the meantime Isa 30:15, "In returning [שׁוּב] and rest you shall be saved [ישׁע], in quietness [שׁקט] and in trust shall be your strength," stimulated Jer 30:10, "I am going to save you [ישׁע] from afar, . . . Jacob shall return [שׁוּב] and rest [שׁקט]."

The declaration in Isa 31:3a, "The Egyptians are men [אָדָם] and not God," along with Ps 118:9, may lie behind the contrast between God and man [אָדָם] in Jer 17:5–8. And the expression in Isa 31:3b, "When Yahweh stretches out his hand, the helper [Egypt] will stumble, and he who is helped [Judah] will fall," probably lies behind Jer 6:12 and 15—the first verse has, "I shall stretch out my hand against the inhabitants of the land," and the second, "Therefore they shall fall among the fallen: at the time I deal with them they shall stumble."

Again the imagery in Isa 31:4–5, in which Yahweh will come down to fight on Mount Zion, like a bird hovering, may lie behind the diction of Jer 21:13, where Jrm ironically cites Jerusalem, "enthroned over the valley," to be saying, "Who can come down against us, who can enter our habitations?"

Finally, Jer 49:4 may have been stimulated by Isa 32:9, though the argumentation is circular, because I (with Duhm, Cornill, and Rudolph) emend Jer 49:4, "faithless daughter [הַבַּת הַשּׁוֹבֵבָה]" to "complacent daughter [הַבַּת הַשַּׁאֲנַנָּה]" on the basis of the very phrase in Isa 32:9, "complacent women [נָשִׁים שַׁאֲנַנּוֹת]." Nevertheless, the possibility is worth recording.

This list of parallels is surprisingly extensive. Phrases antecedent to Jrm are found in almost every section of material attributable to Isaiah of Jerusalem. One may note that the two passages about the ideal ruler, Isa 9:1–8 and 11:1–9, are not represented, but this lack may be nothing more than accidental; on the other hand, if those passages are authentic to Isaiah, and if Jrm knew them, then it may be Jrm's marginal interest in Davidic kingship that led him to pass them by.

51. Jeremiah's Dependence on Micah

There are many striking form-critical parallels between Jrm's words and those of Micah. Thus the summons of the witnesses to the cosmic lawsuit (Jer 2:12; 6:18–19) is very much the same as those in Mic 1:2 and 6:1–2 (and Isa 1:2), and the use of a series of names of cities and villages in a lament (Jer 48:1–4) is likewise found in Mic

1:10–15. But there are few if any phrases of Jrm's that echo those in Micah 1—2: the only possibilities might be "incurable wound" (Jer 15:18; Mic 1:9) and "we are ruined" and similar expressions with שדד (Jer 4:13; Mic 2:4). Jrm draws heavily, however, on Mic 3:5–8, the oracle against the false prophets, and 3:9–12, the oracle against Jerusalem. Thus "(prophets who) lead astray [תעה hip'il] my people" (Mic 3:5) is found in Jer 23:13, and the discussion with Hananiah about the prophets who prophesy peace or war (Jer 28:7–9) may also have this verse from Micah in mind ("who cry 'Peace' when they have something to eat, but declare war against him who puts nothing into their mouths"). Jrm prays to Yahweh that his opponents be ashamed (Jer 20:11); if his opponents are the false prophets, this may be a reflection of Mic 3:7 ("the seers shall be disgraced, and the diviners put to shame"). Micah affirms that he is filled with power (Mic 3:8); Jrm affirms that he is filled with the wrath of Yahweh (Jer 6:11). Then Mic 3:9–11 is a gold mine for Jrm. Jrm may have had Mic 3:9–10 in mind ("heads of the house of Jacob and rulers of the house of Israel, who abhor justice and pervert all equity, who build Zion with blood and Jerusalem with wrong") in his accusation against Jehoiakim ("who builds his house with unrighteousness and his roof-chambers with injustice," Jer 22:13). Micah's accusation that rulers, priests, and prophets take bribes (Mic 3:11a) is reflected in Jer 22:17 and 6:13. And the complacent remarks of the leaders in Micah's time (Mic 3:11b) are cited by Jrm: for "Is not Yahweh in our midst?" compare Jer 8:19, "Is Yahweh not in Zion? Is her King not in her?" and 14:9, "You are indeed in our midst, Yahweh"; and for "disaster will not come upon us" compare Jer 5:12 and 23:17—Jrm affirms the opposite in Jer 2:3. And of course Mic 3:12 is cited by the elders of the land in defense of Jrm after his temple sermon (Jer 26:17–19).

The only material in Micah 4—7 that might suggest itself as a source for Jrm is Mic 5:4–5: there Assyria comes in to "tread down" (דרך) the land of Israel, an expression that may lie behind Jer 4:11 (revocalized), where it is said that the desert wind "has trodden down" (דרך) Yahweh's people, the wind evidently being a metaphor for the foe from the north; again Mic 5:5

affirms that "the shepherds" who subjugate Assyria "will graze the land of Assyria with the sword," and in Jer 6:3 the "shepherds" (again, the foe from the north) "will graze" fair Zion by battle. But critical opinion assumes a late date for the passage,[179] and one could imagine a redactor of the Book of Micah drawing on Jrm's words.

This survey reinforces the impression of critics that the words of Micah are to be located largely, if not entirely, within Micah 1—3.

52. Jeremiah's Dependence on the Seventh-Century Prophets: Zephaniah, Nahum, Habakkuk

Jrm drew heavily from the opening verses of Zephaniah, Zeph 1:2–13a. The word of Yahweh in Zeph 1:2–3, that he will sweep away everything, is given a variation in Jer 8:13, where there is a word-play on "sweeping" and "gathering," and the diction of Zeph 1:3 appears again in Jer 12:4, "You have swept away beast and bird." (Two parenthetical remarks are necessary: first, that the repeated use by Jrm of the phrase "man and beast," found in both J and P, may have been encouraged by its appearance in Zeph 1:3, and second, that Jer 8:13 and 12:4 are dependent not only on Zeph 1:2–3 but on Hos 4:3 as well—see the discussion on the latter passage.)

The phrase "all the houses upon whose roofs they have sacrificed to all the host of heaven" (Jer 19:13) is doubtless stimulated by Zeph 1:5a, "those who bow down on the roofs to the host of heaven."

The depiction of Yahweh's punishment of a nation as his offering of a sacrifice (Zeph 1:7) is evidently reflected in Jer 46:10 in reference to Egypt.

The phrase "their houses are filled with fraud" (Jer 5:27) is dependent on Zeph 1:9, "And I will punish . . . those who fill their master's house with violence and fraud" (and that passage in Jer is also dependent on Isa 3:14, "Goods stolen from the poor are in your houses").

The phrase שֶׁבֶר גָּדוֹל ("great collapse" or "great fracture") occurs in six passages authentic to Jrm (4:6; 6:1; 14:17; 48:3; 50:22; 51:54), and beyond these only in Zeph 1:10: one assumes, therefore, that that is the source from which Jrm drew the phrase.

In Zeph 1:11 there is evidently a play on the name

---

179 Mays, *Micah*, 119; Wolff, *Micha*, 107–10.

"Canaan," as there is also in Hos 12:8 and Jer 10:17; both prior passages doubtless had their effect on Jrm.

The phrase "resting on one's lees" in Jer 48:11 and "thickening on one's lees" in Zeph 1:12 may both be based on a proverbial expression, but Jrm's expression may have been stimulated by the antecedent in Zephaniah.

But the following sequence in Zeph 1:12, "those who say in their hearts, 'Yahweh will not do good, nor will he do evil,'" surely stimulated Jer 5:12, "They have denied Yahweh and have said, 'He is nothing,'" and, more closely, 10:5, "They [the idols] cannot do evil, though doing good is not in them either," if 10:1–16 is authentic to Jrm, as here argued.

The matter of Zeph 1:13b is difficult. It has widely been thought to be a gloss,[180] but Rudolph has recently argued for its authenticity.[181] If the half-verse is original to Zephaniah, then it is perhaps dependent on Amos 5:11; Jrm may have both in mind in his reversal in Jer 30:5 (see the discussion in sec. 48).

This dependence of Jrm on his elder contemporary is impressive, but, strikingly, the sequence of parallels with Jer ends at this point. In particular, there are no parallels to the "day of wrath" section (Zeph 1:14–18). There is one more possibility in Zephaniah that may be mentioned, Zeph 3:17, "Yahweh, your God, is in your midst, a warrior who gives victory," may lie behind Jer 14:9, "Why are you like a helpless man, like a warrior who cannot save? You are indeed in our midst, Yahweh . . . ," but this is the only parallel beyond Zeph 1:13 that I have noted. An argument from silence is precarious, but from a literary- and form-critical point of view one could separate Zeph 1:2–13a from what follows.[182]

Nahum and Habakkuk were both evidently contemporaries of Jrm, both perhaps Jerusalem cult prophets;[183] there are a handful of instances in which Jrm seems to be dependent on the words of these prophets.

Elements of Nah 1:5–6 stand behind several passages in Jer. Nah 1:5a offers הָרִים רָעֲשׁוּ מִמֶּנּוּ וְהַגְּבָעוֹת הִתְמֹגָגוּ,

"Mountains quake before him, and the hills melt," and Jer 4:24 has רָאִיתִי הֶהָרִים וְהִנֵּה רֹעֲשִׁים וְכָל־הַגְּבָעוֹת הִתְקַלְקָלוּ, "I looked at the mountains, to see them quaking, and all the hills rocked to and fro."

Then Nah 1:6 reads, "Who can stand before his indignation? Who can endure the heat of his anger? His wrath is poured out like fire, and the rocks are broken asunder by him." This sequence appears to be taken up by Jer 7:20, "My anger and my wrath are going to be poured out on this place . . . and it shall burn and not go out," and it also appears to be reflected in the linking of burning fire and the smashing of rocks in Jer 23:29, "Scorching is my word like fire, oracle of Yahweh, and like a sledgehammer that smashes a rock."

And though the vocabulary is different, Nah 2:11, "Anguish is on all loins, all faces grow pale," may lie behind Jer 30:6–7, "Why have I seen every hero his hands on his loins, and every face changed, into pallor turned?"

Nah 3:1 appears to stand behind Jer 6:6b, but the latter text must be emended; following clues in *G*, I have read הוֹי עִיר הַפֶּקֶר כֻּלָּהּ עֹשֶׁק בְּקִרְבָּהּ "Woe, licentious city! It is all extortion in her midst," a word over Jerusalem that appears to be an ironic variation on Nahum's word over Nineveh (Nah 3:1), הוֹי עִיר דָּמִים כֻּלָּהּ כַּחַשׁ פֶּרֶק מְלֵאָה "Woe, bloody city! It is all lies, full of plunder."

And again Nahum's word against Nineveh, "I will lift up your skirts over your face, and I will let nations look on your nakedness and kingdoms on your shame" (Nah 3:5), has been applied by Jrm to Jerusalem, "I too have pulled off your skirts, and your shame is to be seen" (Jer 13:26).

It is to be noted that these antecedent verses in Nahum are drawn from the two major sections of the book, the (truncated) acrostic poem and the poem over Nineveh; if the links with Jrm are sound, then we have an indication that Jrm at least knew both poems, whether they were combined in his day or not.

The description in Habakkuk of the terrible Chal-

---

180 So first Ernst Sellin, *Das Zwölfprophetenbuch* (KAT 12; Leipzig: Deichert, 1930) 420, 424; see recently Karl Elliger, *Das Buch der zwölf Kleinen Propheten*, II (ATD 25; Göttingen: Vandenhoeck & Ruprecht, 1975) 59, 65, and see *BHS*.

181 Wilhelm Rudolph, *Micha—Nahum—Habakuk—Zephanja* (KAT 13/3; Gütersloh: Gütersloher

[Mohn], 1975) 269 n. 19.

182 Elliger, *Das Buch der zwölf Kleinen Propheten*, 60; Rudolph, *Micha—Nahum—Habakuk—Zephanja*, 264.

183 Wilson, *Prophecy and Society*, 276–79.

deans (Hab 1:6–11)—as well as a similar description in Isa 5:26–29—offers a likeness to Jrm's descriptions of the foe from the north in 4:13; 5:15–17; and 6:22–23, but it is certainly not possible to show any indebtedness in either direction.

There are only two secure points of contact between Jrm's words and Habakkuk. Hab 1:8 would appear to lie behind Jer 4:13aγ, "His horses are swifter than eagles": in the half-verse Jrm offers an intricate tricolon; by contrast the verse of Habakkuk (even when allowance is made for textual difficulties) is more diffuse, so it seems more likely that Jrm is dependent on Habakkuk.

Again Jer 51:58b is identical with Hab 2:13b (with exchange of "fire" and "nought"). But Hab 2:13 is integrated with 2:12 ("build," "found," "labor," "weary oneself") while Jer 51:58b is united with the preceding half-verse by "fire," and the collocation is ironic. Since Jrm has elsewhere ended discourses with quotations (4:3–4; 10:23–25), it is likely that he is here quoting Habakkuk's curse of the bloody city of the Chaldeans (Hab 2:12 may itself be a reference to Nah 3:1). But if Nahum and Habakkuk were cultic prophets in Jerusalem, it is not surprising that there are so few instances of Jrm's dependence on them.

53. Relations between Jeremiah and Deuteronomy: Preliminary Remarks

The question of the relation between Jer and Deuteronomy has always been a troublesome one. Attempts to list common phraseology are misleading, because such lists lump together phrases that may be original to Deuteronomy and were borrowed by Jrm, phrases that appear to be original to Jrm and were borrowed by later strata in Deuteronomy, and common phrases of the day.[184] Most such compilations have led to the conclusion that Jer is a book heavily edited by Deuteronomists (see sec. 14). The listing of parallels in Weinfeld, *Deuteronomy*, 359–61, makes no attempt to separate pre-Jeremianic from post-Jeremianic portions of Deuter-

onomy, nor poetry from prose in Jer, nor is his judgment on what is authentic or nonauthentic to Jrm always identical with that of the present study. Recently there have been scattered attempts to analyze specific instances in which Jrm drew on material in Deuteronomy. Thus Robert Davidson has suggested that Jrm responded to Deut 13:1–6 and 18:22,[185] and Michael Fishbane analyzes how Jrm in Jer 3:1 drew on Deut 24:1–4.[186]

Conclusions on the direction of borrowing can hardly be made from phraseological parallels that occur often; it is best to concentrate on restricted or unusual diction, ideally when such diction occurs one or twice in Deuteronomy and once or twice in Jer. The best evidence for Jrm's borrowing from Deuteronomy is found when the passage in Jer evidences a distortion or an ironic reuse of the material in Deuteronomy, but obviously these conditions cannot always be met. One must therefore have recourse both to the conclusions on authenticity or nonauthenticity of a given passage to Jrm, on the one hand, and to the general critical work done on the redaction history of Deuteronomy on the other. I shall announce my conclusion at the beginning: Jrm drew on Proto-Deuteronomy, and exilic redactors of Deuteronomy sometimes drew on Jrm's words.

54. Relations between Jeremiah and Deuteronomy 32 and 33

Before the matter of the parallels between material authentic to Jrm and the prose of Deuteronomy is examined, however, it is appropriate to deal with parallels in the poetry of Deuteronomy. Deuteronomy 33 offers only one possible parallel with material authentic to Jrm: "dwell in safety" (שָׁכַן לָבֶטַח) appears in Jer 23:6 (and in a secondary reflection in 33:16), and in Deut 33:12, said of Benjamin, and in v 28 (with preposition omitted), of Israel. But the phrase also appears in Ps 16:9 and Prov 1:33 in descriptions of individuals, and the parallel is certainly not evidence of any dependence.

In contrast there are many parallels with Deuter-

184 One of the most extensive lists, but by no means complete or altogether accurate, is found in Gustav Hölscher, *Die Profeten, Untersuchungen zur Religionsgeschichte Israels* (Leipzig: Hinrichs, 1914) 382, n. 2.

185 Robert Davidson, "Orthodoxy and the Prophetic Word, A Study in the Relationship Between Jeremiah and Deuteronomy," *VT* 14 (1964) 407–16.

186 Michael A. Fishbane, "Torah and Tradition,"

Tradition and Theology in the Old Testament (ed. Douglas A. Knight; Philadelphia: Fortress, 1977) 284–86.

onomy 32. In this instance the immediate difficulty is to establish a date for the poem before or after Jrm. Current proposals range from the eleventh century (Eissfeldt,[187] W. F. Albright,[188] George Mendenhall[189]) to the sixth (Fohrer,[190] Sten Hidal,[191] A. D. H. Mayes[192]). In general it may be said that the poem offers many *hapax legomena* and archaic usages; that fact by itself need not indicate an early date, because a late poem may offer deliberate archaisms. David Robertson has recently subjected the poem to minute analysis from the linguistic point of view, and he struggles with the question whether the evidence argues for an early date or for the presence of deliberate archaisms; his tentative conclusion is that the poem is early, but not so early as Exodus 15—very tentatively he places the poem in the eleventh-tenth century;[193] Freedman, working with divine names and titles, dates it in the tenth-ninth century.[194] The poem certainly does not give the same impression of late date that Lamentations or the poetry of Ezekiel does.

Before I cite the parallels between Deuteronomy 32 and Jer, I shall state my own conclusion: the poem clearly antedates Jrm. The parallels with Jrm's words offer substantial data for this conclusion. Not all of the parallels are of equal weight—some are persuasive and some only suggestive; I shall list them in order of their appearance in Deuteronomy 32 and then assess them.

Deut 32:4 declares that Yahweh is אֵין עָוֶל, "without wrong," and Jrm hears Yahweh ask Israel, "What did your fathers find wrong [עָוֶל] with me?" (Jer 2:5); it is likely that it is the verse in Deuteronomy that is antecedent.

Both Deut 32:5 and 20 offer the parallelism of "children" (בָּנִים) and "generation" or "community" (דּוֹר): "they are no longer his children [בָּנִים] because of their blemish; they are a perverse and crooked generation

[דּוֹר]" (v 5), and "They are a perverse generation [דּוֹר], children [בָּנִים] in whom is no faithfulness" (v 20); though Jer 2:30–31 offers text difficulties, it is clear that v 30 has בָּנִים "children," and v 31 דּוֹר (usually "generation," in the present study "community"), so that the parallelism in Deuteronomy 32 is likely to have been the trigger for the two verses in Jer.

Jer 10:16 (if genuine to Jrm, a conclusion pressed in the present study) appears to be an adaptation of Deut 32:9: the latter says, "For Yahweh's portion is his people, Jacob the allotment of his possession," while 10:16 says, "Not like these is the portion of Jacob, . . . and Israel is the tribe of his possession."

Deut 32:10 and Hos 9:10 offer similar phraseology, and the two verses together appear to have stimulated Jer 31:2. Deut 32:10 reads, "He [Yahweh] found him [Israel] in the land of the wilderness [אֶרֶץ מִדְבָּר]," and Hos 9:10 reads, "Like grapes in the wilderness, I found Israel." Jer 31:2 for its part reads, "He found him . . . in the wilderness."

The expression אֵל נֵכָר "alien god" in Deut 32:12 probably lies behind the phrase אֱלֹהֵי נֵכָר "alien gods" in Jer 5:19.

The verb שׁמן qal appears only twice in the OT, in Deut 32:15a and Jer 5:28, and the general wording is so close as to suggest a relationship: the former reads, "But Jeshurun grew fat [שׁמן] and kicked, you grew fat [שׁמן], grew thick, became sleek," and the latter reads, "They have grown fat [שׁמן], grown sleek"; it is likely then that Jer 5:28 is dependent on Deut 32:15a.

Then there are three verbs occurring in two separate verses of Jer that seem to have been stimulated by their occurrence in two separate verses of Deuteronomy 32. Two of the verbs are in Deut 32:15b: there it is said that Jeshurun (= Israel) "forsook [נטשׁ] God who made him

187 Eissfeldt, *Introduction*, 227.

188 William F. Albright, "Some Remarks on the Song of Moses in Deuteronomy xxxii," *VT* 9 (1959) 339–46.

189 George E. Mendenhall, "Samuel's 'Broken *Rîb*,' Deuteronomy 32," *No Famine in the Land, Studies in Honor of John L. McKenzie* (ed. James W. Flanagan and Anita W. Robinson; Missoula, MT: Scholars, 1975) 63–74.

190 Sellin-Fohrer, pp. 189–90.

191 Sten Hidal, "Some Reflections on Deuteronomy 32," *ASTI* 11 (1977/78) 19.

192 Mayes, *Deuteronomy*, 382.

193 David A. Robertson, *Linguistic Evidence in Dating Hebrew Poetry* (SBLDS 3; Society of Biblical Literature, 1972) 153–56.

194 Freedman, "Divine Names and Titles in Early Hebrew Poetry," 79.

and disdained [נבל pi'el] the Rock of his salvation"; and one is in Deut 32:19, "Yahweh saw and spurned [נאץ] (them)." Two of these verbs are in Jer 14:21: there the people pray, "Do not spurn [נאץ], for your name's sake, do not disdain [נבל pi'el] your glorious throne," and one is in 15:6, where Yahweh replies, "It is you who have rejected [נטש] me." That is to say, Jrm seems to drawn on specific vocabulary having to do with rejection of Yahweh for Israel, or of Israel for Yahweh.

Deut 32:16 uses זָרִים "strangers" for alien gods; Jer 2:25 uses the same term to imply both alien gods and foreigners (the word is used with the latter implication in Isa 1:7; Hos 7:9 and often).

In Deut 32:17a occurs the expression לֹא אֱלֹהַּ "non-god": Jrm evidently imitates this with לֹא אֱלֹהִים "non-gods" in Jer 2:11; 5:7; in Deut 32:17b is the verb שׂער "dread"—"(non-gods) whom your fathers did not dread," and Jer 2:12 offers the same verb (here translated "stand aghast"): the sequence of the two parallels in Deut 32:17 and in Jer 2:11 and 12 suggests that Jrm is offering his variation here on the verse in Deuteronomy.

Deut 32:18 uses the metaphor of Yahweh's giving birth to Israel, "You were unmindful of the Rock that bore you [ילד], and you forgot [שׁכח] the God who was in birth-pangs with you"; Jrm accuses the people of using this metaphor for idols of wood and stone (Jer 2:27)—"[who] keep saying to the tree, 'You are my father,' and to the stone, 'It is you (who) bore me [ילד]!'" And again Jer 2:32 may have been stimulated by the same verse of Deuteronomy, "Can a virgin forget [שׁכח] her ornaments? . . . But my people have forgotten me [שׁכח] days without number."

In Deut 32:20 Yahweh says, "I will see what their [Israel's] end (will be)," and in Jer 12:4 Jrm has Israel's doubters say, "He will not see our end"; again Jrm seems to have adapted the old phrase for a new purpose.

In Deut 32:21 we have "They offended me [כעס pi'el] with their nothings [הֲבָלִים, that is, idols]," and in Jer 8:19 Yahweh interrupts with "Why have they offended me [כעס pi'el] with their idols, with alien nothings [הֲבָלִים]?"

Deut 32:22 and Jer 15:14 have the identical colon, "For a fire is kindled by my anger" (כִּי־אֵשׁ קָדְחָה בְאַפִּי), and in both instances the following colon begins with a form of יקד "burn"; Deut 32:22 describes the punishing fire in cosmic terms, while the passage in Jer appears to have reused the phrase in the immediate historical context (and compare Jer 17:4, a freer adaptation).

The background of Jrm's triad "sword, famine, pestilence" (which appears for the first time in Jer 14:12) is difficult to establish, but one source may have been Deut 32:23–25: v 23 offers "arrows," a substitute for "sword," and v 24 offers expressions for pestilence, followed by רָעָב "hunger," and then v 25a summarizes, using "sword."[195]

In Deut 32:25b there is an inclusive listing of categories of the population to be destroyed, "both young man and virgin, the sucking child with the man of gray hair"; such an inclusive listing could easily lie behind Jer 6:11, "Pour it out on the children in the street, and on the circle of youths as well; yes, both husband and wife shall be caught, the elder with him who is aged."

The depiction in Deut 32:32–33 of the vine of Israel, "For their vine comes from the vine of Sodom, and from the fields of Gomorrah, their grapes are grapes of poison, their clusters are bitter; their wine is the poison of serpents, and the cruel venom of asps," along with Isa 5:1–7, may be the antecedents for Jer 2:21, "But it was I who planted you choice grapes, wholly sound stock, so how could you turn putrid?"

"Retribution [נקם] and recompense [שׁלם] is mine" (Deut 32:35) may have stimulated the association of those two roots in Jer 20:10 (though see the exegesis of that verse: I have suggested the revocalization of the word referred to שׁלם).

Finally, Deut 32:35 mentions the "day of their calamity" (יוֹם אֵידָם), in the context of which "he [Yahweh] will say, 'Where are their gods, the rock in which they took refuge, who ate the fat of their sacrifices, and drank the wine of their drink offering? Let them arise and help you, let them be your protection!'" (Deut 32:37–38); Jrm uses the material ironically, perceiving Yahweh to put some of this in the mouth of Judah, "But in the time of their disaster [בְּעֵת רָעָתָם] they will say, 'Arise and save us!' Where are your gods which you made for yourself? Let them arise if they can save you in the time of your disaster!" (Jer 2:27b–28a).

---

195 Weippert, *Prosareden*, 150, 153.

My own conclusion is that nine parallels are persuasive (Deut 32:4 and Jer 2:5; Deut 32:5, 20 and Jer 2:30–31; Deut 32:15a and Jer 5:28; Deut 32:17 and Jer 2:11–12; 5:7; Deut 32:20 and Jer 12:4; Deut 32:21 and Jer 8:19; Deut 32:22 and Jer 15:14; 17:4; Deut 32:25a and Jer 6:11; Deut 32:35, 37–38 and Jer 2:27b–28a) and that eight are at least suggestive (Deut 32:10 and Jer 31:2; Deut 32:12 and Jer 5:19; Deut 32:15b, 19 and Jer 14:21; 15:6; Deut 32:16 and Jer 2:25; Deut 32:18 and Jer 2:27, 32; Deut 32:23–25a and Jer 14:12 [and other passages]; Deut 32:32–33 and Jer 2:21; Deut 32:35 and Jer 20:10). And in three of the parallels I have called "persuasive" an affirmation about or by Yahweh in Deuteronomy 32 has been given an ironic turn by Jrm. The first is Deut 32:4, "[Yahweh is a God] without wrong," third person, affirmation; Jer 2:5, "What wrong did your fathers find in me?" first person, question. The second is Deut 32:20, "I will see their end," first person, affirmation; Jer 12:4, "he will not see our end," third person, denial. The third is Deut 32:38, "Let them [the idols] arise and help you," where Jrm replicates the challenge, "Let them arise if they can save you" (Jer 2:28) but adds an adaptation of the challenge, the people's prayer to the idols, "Arise and save us!" (Jer 2:27). These three parallels make it clear that Deuteronomy 32 is prior to Jrm.[196] In passing it may be noted that these three parallels, from Deut 32:4, 20, and 37–38, are drawn from the whole span of the poem, and that in general the seventeen parallels are drawn from every section of the poem from vv 4–38.

The fact that there are so many parallels from vv 4–38 and none from vv 39–43 raises the question whether for Jrm the poem ended with v 38. Verse 38 closes a portion of the poem in which the poet/prophet speaks; v 39 begins a section in which Yahweh speaks. It is certainly striking that v 39 finds its major parallels with Deutero-Isaiah (see esp. Isa 44:6, but also 41:4; 43:10, 13; 45:6–7, 22; 48:12) and with Deut 4:35, 39 (Deut 4:1–40 is doubtless a late addition to the book), and that the vocabulary of Yahweh as a warrior (vv 41–42) has parallels with Isa 34:5–6; 63:1–4; and with secondary material in Jer 46:10.[197] An argument from silence is weak, but the fact that Jrm does not seem to have drawn from vv 39–43 might at least encourage scholars to ask

whether the old poem was not extended by these verses at the end of the exilic period or the early postexilic period.

Two questions arise at this point. First, why might Jrm have drawn so heavily from Deuteronomy 32 and so little, if at all, from Deuteronomy 33? Of course no answer is possible: Deuteronomy 33, though old, may not have become associated with the tradition of Deuteronomy by Jrm's day, or else the form of Deuteronomy 33, a collection of sayings on the individual tribes presented as the deathbed blessing of Moses, may have been unsuitable for Jrm's purposes. But it is clear that Deuteronomy 32 was congruent with Jrm's task. Its *rîb*-form was likewise employed by the eighth-century prophets (compare Hos 4:1; Isa 1:2; Mic 1:2; 6:1–2). That is to say, it was understood by Jrm as a prophetic discourse ascribed to Moses, so that Jrm, who understood himself to be a prophet like Moses, would have heard it as the poetic oracle of Moses the prophet.

The second question is at what point Deuteronomy 32 joined the remainder of the form of Deuteronomy known to Jrm. I shall defer that question until I deal with the prose of Deuteronomy.

55. Deuteronomy 12—26 as Background for Jeremiah's Poetry

In an analysis of the parallels between Jrm and the prose of Deuteronomy it is best to begin with the parallels between the poetry of Jrm on the one hand and the core of Deuteronomy, namely, the law-code in chapters 12—26, on the other; though there may be passages within Deuteronomy 12—26 that are later insertions, such passages will be discussed case by case. Again, it is generally acknowledged that the form of Deuteronomy known to Jrm included introductory chapters before Deuteronomy 12 and closing material after Deuteronomy 26, but the extent of the introductory chapters and the closing chapters is a matter of debate, and I shall defer a discussion of parallels with these chapters until secs. 57 and 58.[198]

Most scholars assume that there is a relation between Jer 3:1 and Deut 24:1–4, but they differ on the nature of the parallel: Bright assumes that Jrm quotes the law in

196 Against Rudolph, p. 79 n. 1, who suggests dependence could just as well go in the other direction.
197 Compare Mayes, *Deuteronomy*, 392.

198 For a current discussion on "Proto-Deuteronomy" see Sellin-Fohrer, pp. 169–72.

Deuteronomy,[199] while Trevor Hobbs maintains that both are dependent on an earlier form of the law.[200] Raymond Westbrook has recently expressed his doubt that the law has any connection with Jer 3:1,[201] but Fishbane affirms, I believe correctly,[202] that Jrm reuses the law in Deuteronomy in a radically new way. The passage in Deuteronomy states the law that applies when a husband divorces his wife and she marries a second husband who then either divorces her or dies: the first husband is not free to remarry her. In Jer 3:1 Yahweh himself raises a question about law; metaphorically the husband is Yahweh, and the wife is Israel. Deut 24:4 says, "Her first husband . . . cannot turn [שׁוב] to take her [= cannot again take her] to be a wife to him," while Jer 3:1 says, "Would he (re)turn to her again?" In shifting the verb שׁוב from its meaning of "again" to "return," and using עוֹד for "again," Jrm has subtly implied a humbling action on Yahweh's part. And the connection with Deut 24:4 is sealed by the fifth colon of Jer 3:1, "Would that land not be greatly profaned?" which reflects Deut 24:4, "For that is an abomination before Yahweh, and you shall not bring guilt upon the land which Yahweh your God gives you for an inheritance." Yahweh affirms, in Jrm's proclamation, that Israel is worse than the wife in the case cited in Deut 24:1–4, because she has "whored" with "many partners."

The wording of Jer 2:20, "on every high hill and under every leafy tree" (עַל־כָּל־גִּבְעָה גְּבֹהָה וְתַחַת כָּל־עֵץ רַעֲנָן), suggests that it is a tightening of Deut 12:2, "upon the high mountains and upon the hills and under every leafy tree" (עַל־הֶהָרִים הָרָמִים וְעַל־הַגְּבָעוֹת וְתַחַת כָּל־עֵץ רַעֲנָן), and that wording in turn suggests a summary of Hos 4:13, "They sacrifice on the tops of the mountains, and make offerings upon the hills, under oak, poplar, and terebinth" (עַל־רָאשֵׁי הֶהָרִים יְזַבֵּחוּ וְעַל־הַגְּבָעוֹת יְקַטֵּרוּ תַּחַת אַלּוֹן וְלִבְנֶה וְאֵלָה). Josiah could not have destroyed the sanctuaries outside Jerusalem (2 Kgs 23:15–19) without legal warrant; that warrant is found in Deut 12:2–3, a law that therefore must have existed in the form of

Deuteronomy known to Jrm.[203] Then the phrase in Jer was repeated several times in later material—in expansions in Jer (Jer 3:6, 13; 17:2) and in Deuteronomistic additions in Kings (1 Kgs 14:23; 2 Kgs 17:10).[204] In regard to Deuteronomy 12 Mayes takes vv 13–19 as the original law on the central sanctuary and vv 1–7 as part of a late editorial addition.[205] But one must surely argue that Deut 12:2 is not from the same epoch as 1 Kgs 14:23 and 2 Kgs 17:10: the redactor(s) responsible for the Kings passages knew the wording of Jer, wording that would have fit just as well in Deut 12:2 as the wording that it actually offers. My conclusion, already suggested above, is that the writer responsible for Deut 12:2 drew on Hos 4:13 but that writer predates Jrm, and thus Jrm drew on Deut 12:2.

There are one or two other possible links between Jrm's poetry and the prose of Deuteronomy that might be mentioned here.

The phraseology of 50:6, "Perishing sheep were my people" (צֹאן אֹבְדוֹת הָיָה עַמִּי), is strongly reminiscent of the old confession at the presentation of first fruits at the central sanctuary, "A perishing Aramean was my father" (אֲרַמִּי אֹבֵד אָבִי), Deut 26:5. (There are no other comparable passages using the participle of אבד: other occurrences refer to individuals or are in later passages.) The confession is old,[206] and the conclusion of the present study is that the material in Jer 50—51 in general is genuine to Jrm (including the verse under discussion). Jrm has added the perfect verb (הָיָה) to the phrase to underline the temporary nature of the description: the time will come when the sheep of Israel will no longer be perishing.

In his confession in Jer 20:7 Jrm uses language with sexual overtones, complaining of having been violated by Yahweh (פתה pi'el and nip'al). He then says "you are stronger than I [חזק]," and then in v 8 he speaks of "crying out" (זעק). The background of his expression may well be Deut 22:25, 27; v 25 speaks of a man in the field "seizing" (חזק hip'il) a young woman, and v 27 speaks of

---

199 Bright, p. 23.
200 Trevor R. Hobbs, "Jeremiah 3:1–5 and Deuteronomy 24:1–4," *ZAW* 86 (1974) 23–29.
201 Raymond Westbrook, "The Prohibition on Restoration of Marriage in Deuteronomy 24:1–4," *Studies in Bible, 1986* (ed. Sara Japhet; Scripta Hierosolymitana 31; Jerusalem: Magnes, 1986) 405, n. 66.
202 Fishbane, "Torah and Tradition."
203 Norbert Lohfink, by personal correspondence.
204 See Gray, *Kings*, 340, 638. For a full analysis of the phrase see Holladay, "On Every High Hill."
205 Mayes, *Deuteronomy*, 221–22; compare von Rad, *Deuteronomy*, 93.
206 Mayes, *Deuteronomy*, 333.

her "crying out" (צעק, evidently a by-form of זעק).[207]

It is conceivable that a couple of passages in Jrm's poetry reflect the law against cutting down (כרת) and destroying (שחת hip'il) one's enemy's fruit trees during a siege of his city, a formulation unique to Deuteronomy (Deut 20:19–20). Jer 6:6 portrays Yahweh as commanding the enemy to cut down [כרת] the trees of Jerusalem to construct a siege mound; though the latter passage does not specify fruit trees, it is possible that Yahweh is countermanding the law in order to dramatize the special horror of the siege of Jerusalem. Again in Jer 11:19 the words "let us destroy [שחת hip'il] the tree, . . . and let us cut him off [כרת] . . . ," words of Jrm's enemies regarding him, may presuppose Jrm's having this law in mind: the law poses the rhetorical question, "Are the trees in the field men that they should be besieged by you?" Jrm then may be reversing the metaphor: he is a man, a soldier for Yahweh, and his enemies are trying to cut him down in a way they are forbidden to do with fruit trees.

There is an instance in which material in Jrm's poetry reflects both Deuteronomy and the Holiness Code. Thus 6:9 seems to suggest that Yahweh is countermanding his own law in an address to Jrm. Deut 24:21 reads, "When you harvest your vineyard, you shall not glean it [עלל] after you; it shall be for the sojourner, the orphan and the widow." In the metaphor of Jer 6:9 on the other hand Yahweh commands Jrm, "Glean, glean [or, do glean] like a vine the remnant of Israel." Particularly if the second verb is construed as an infinitive absolute, the wording implies, "In your case do glean; even though it has been forbidden, do it anyway." But the prohibition against gleaning appears also in the Holiness Code ("and your vineyard you shall not glean [עלל], and the droppings of your vineyard you shall not gather up; for the poor and the sojourner you shall leave them: I am Yahweh your God," Lev 19:10), so one cannot be certain that Jrm drew specifically on Deuteronomy.

56. Deuteronomy 12—26 as Background for Jeremiah's Prose

It is appropriate now to deal with the parallels between the prose of Jer attributable to the prophet Jrm and the material within Deuteronomy 12—26. There are a good number of these; the difficulty that arises, of course, is that the prose passages of Jer are attributed by many scholars to a Deuteronomistic editor. I shall not attempt to reargue the genuineness of these prose passages in Jer: for this see the respective passages in the exegesis. Instead I shall simply discuss them briefly, beginning with those passages in which the wording in Jer appears to be an ironic variation or reversal of that in Deuteronomy.

In Jer 21:5 Yahweh addresses Israel, saying, "I myself will fight against you with outstretched hand and mighty arm." This is a unique expression with reversed adjectives: the conventional wording, "with mighty hand and outstretched arm," appears in Deut 26:8 (and four times in Deuteronomy 1—11, and in a Deuteronomistic passage, 1 Kgs 8:42). It is clear that Jrm has reversed the expression to underline the fact that Yahweh will fight against his own people.[208]

In Deut 26:19 occurs the triplet "for praise, and name, and honor" (לִתְהִלָּה וּלְשֵׁם וּלְתִפְאָרֶת). The same triplet (with the order of the first two elements reversed) appears in Jer 13:11. Deut 26:17–19 is evidently part of the framework of Deut 5—28;[209] it is likely then that it is the source for Jrm's use of the phrase.

The sequence of 7:21–28 and 29–34 evidently presupposes Deut 12:5–6. Jer 7:21–28 mocks and rejects the bringing of burnt offerings and sacrifices (vv 21–22), while Deut 12:6 speaks of the bringing of burnt offerings and sacrifices to the central sanctuary; Jer 7:29–34 states that the evil of child sacrifice will bring a terrible judgment, that "they shall bury at a fire-pit, without a 'place' [מָקוֹם]" (v 32), while Deut 12:5 states that "you shall seek the 'place' [מָקוֹם] that Yahweh your God will choose. . . ." The word "place" is evidently ambiguous in 7:32, but one meaning evidently is that Jerusalem will no longer be the sacral place indicated in Deuteronomy. I have already argued the availability of Deut 12:2 (with regard to Jer 2:20, "on every high hill and under every leafy tree"), and Deut 12:5–6 is surely part of the same layer of tradition.[210] It is the association of the two reversals in Jer 7:21–28 and 29–34 with the two verses in Deuteronomy 12 that attracts attention; it is likely that

---

207 Compare Berridge, pp. 153–54, who notes the parallel of Jer 20:8 and Deut 22:27.
208 Berridge, pp. 117–18; Weippert, *Prosareden*, 82,

n. 241.
209 See Norbert Lohfink, "Dtn 26,17–19 und die 'Bundesformel,'" *ZKT* 91 (1969) 517–53.

Deuteronomy 12 is in the background of Jrm's rhetoric.

The triad "stranger, orphan, widow" in 7:6 and 22:3 is specifically dependent on the usage in Deuteronomy; the term appears nine times in Deuteronomy 12—26, beginning in 14:29.[211] The triad appears in the Covenant Code, Exod 22:20–21, but there the order is "stranger, widow, orphan," so that one looks to Deuteronomy for the source of Jrm's usage.

57. Material in the Prose of Deuteronomy outside Chapters 12—26 as Background for Jeremiah's Poetry and Prose

One may now turn to parallels between Jer and the prose of Deuteronomy outside Deuteronomy 12—26, and in that category one may deal first with expressions in Jrm's poetry that appear to be dependent on such prose.

There is a clear relation between Jer 4:4 and Deut 10:16: 4:4 reads הִמֹּלוּ לַיהוה וְהָסִרוּ עָרְלֹת לְבַבְכֶם, "Be circumcised [or, circumcise yourselves] for [or, by] Yahweh, remove the foreskin of your heart," and Deut 10:16 reads וּמַלְתֶּם אֵת עָרְלַת לְבַבְכֶם, "Circumcise the foreskin of your heart" (and adds the parallel "and your neck do not stiffen any longer"). (One notes in passing two comparable passages in Jrm: the imitative 9:25, כָּל־בֵּית יִשְׂרָאֵל עַרְלֵי־לֵב, literally "All the house of Israel is foreskinned of heart," that is, "uncircumcised in heart"; and 6:10, הִנֵּה עֲרֵלָה אָזְנָם, literally "Behold foreskinned is their ear," that is, "Their ear is uncircumcised." One may also cite Deut 30:6, "And Yahweh your God will circumcise your heart and the heart of your offspring"; but that passage may be laid aside: there Yahweh is the subject of the verb, while in Deut 10:16 and Jer 4:4 the people are the subject; further, Deut 30:1–10 is late.[212] Three further passages in the OT with comparable phraseology are also late: Lev 26:41; Ezek 44:7, 9.) Scholars are uncertain whether Deut 10:12—11:17 is early or late; Mayes concludes that the section is late,[213] but I suggest to the contrary that Jrm has borrowed the expression in 4:4 from Deuteronomy. One datum is the contrastive usage

in Deuteronomy and Jer of the by-forms לֵב and לֵבָב "heart."[214] In Deuteronomy there are forty-seven instances of לֵבָב and four of לֵב (Deut 4:11; 28:65; 29:3, 18); it is to be noted that Deut 4:11 offers לֵבָב in the Samaritan Pentateuch, that Deut 29:3 may be dependent on Jer 24:7 and Deut 29:18 on Jeremianic diction, and in any event all four exceptions are a part of late additions to the book. On the other hand Jer offers fifty-seven instances of לֵב and only eight of לֵבָב (4:4; 5:24; 13:22; 15:16; 29:13; 32:40; 51:46, 50). These eight exceptions in Jer appear to have various explanations. Thus two of them, 32:40 and 51:46, are clearly late; 51:50 is not late, but it is possible that a copyist at that point carelessly replicated the form of 51:46 (לִבְבְכֶם); and 29:13 is probably late. Both 5:24 and 13:22 offer a specific idiom ("say in one's heart" [אמר בּלֵבָב] = "think"), and it may be that for some reason in that idiom Jrm used לֵבָב—the usage in Hosea is analogous, since there are nine instances of לֵב and only one of לֵבָב, and that in the expression "say to one's heart" (אמר לְלֵבָב). This leaves 4:4 and 15:16. I suggest that both passages use לֵבָב because Deuteronomy lies in the background. In 15:16 I have proposed that "your words were found" refers to the finding of the scroll of Deuteronomy in the temple (2 Kings 22); it is possible therefore that the form of "heart" in the phrase "your word became for me a joy and the delight of my heart" is deliberately Deuteronomic. The use of לֵבָב in 4:4 is striking, given the use of לֵב in 4:9 and 14. I propose then that the form of "heart" in 4:4 suggests that it is understood as a citation of Deuteronomy. (This argument is weakened if the suffixed form לִבְבְכֶם was not part of Jrm's speech: it appears only three times in the OT—Gen 18:5; Isa 66:14; Ps 48:14; thus not in Jer.) It is clear that 4:3 contains a citation of Hosea; Jrm, then, I submit, offers two citations here, one from Hosea and one from Deu-

---

210 Mayes, *Deuteronomy*, 221.

211 See Weinfeld, *Deuteronomy*, 356, 6, and Weippert, *Prosareden*, 42.

212 See Gottfried Vanoni, "Der Geist und der Buchstabe: Überlegungen zum Verhältnis der Testamente und Beobachtungen zu Dtn 30,1–10," *BN* 14 (1981) 65–98.

213 Mayes, *Deuteronomy*, 207–8.

214 See Charles A. Briggs, "A Study of the Use of לֵב and לֵבָב in the Old Testament," *Semitic Studies in Memory of Rev. Dr. Alexander Kohut* (ed. George A. Kohut; Berlin: Calvary, 1897) 94–105.

teronomy, to sum up Yahweh's appeal to his people in 2:1—4:4. (Compare his citations in 10:23–25.) If this conclusion is correct, it obviously helps to give a *terminus ad quem* for the Deuteronomy passage.

It is possible that Jer 9:19 is Jrm's reversal of Deut 11:19: the latter says, "You shall teach them [these words of Yahweh] to your children/sons [בָּנִים]," while Jer 9:19 is an address to the women (evidently the dirge-women, v 16), "Hear, you women, the word of Yahweh, and let your ear take up the word of his mouth, and teach your daughters [בָּנוֹת] a wailing, and each her neighbor a dirge." Jrm has elsewhere shifted masculine to feminine language in reversing an oracle (31:8–9a reverses 6:21–22).

The instruction in Deut 11:18–21 (and 6:6–9) to teach Yahweh's words to one's children also reminds one of the new covenant passage, Jer 31:31–34; if the latter passage likewise has Deut 6:6–9 and 11:18–21 in mind, then it offers another reversal: "And no longer shall they teach one another, or each other, saying, 'Know Yahweh!' for they shall all know me, from the least of them to the greatest." Now scholars disagree on whether Jer 31:31–34 is authentic to Jrm, and whether it is poetry; the conclusion of the present study is that it is indeed authentic, and that while the first half is to be heard as prose, the second half is to be heard as poetry. It is clear that the passage is deliberately framed to reflect the assumptions and idiom of Deuteronomy; the question then arises what passage or passages in Deuteronomy are presupposed by Jrm? I propose that beyond Deut 11:19 it is chapter 5, indeed 4:45—5:33. Deut 4:45 has "when they came out of Egypt," as Jer 31:32 has "to bring them out of the land of Egypt." Deut 5:2, 3 are the only occurrences of "make a covenant" (כָּרַת בְּרִית, Jer 31:31, 32, 33) until chapter 29, surely a late addition to the book. The diction of Deut 5:3 is curiously like that of Jer 31:32: the former says, "Not with our fathers did Yahweh make this covenant [לֹא אֶת־אֲבֹתֵינוּ כָּרַת יהוה אֶת־הַבְּרִית הַזֹּאת], but with us, who are all of us here alive this day"; the latter says, "Not like the covenant which I made with their fathers [לֹא כַבְּרִית אֲשֶׁר כָּרַתִּי אֶת־אֲבוֹתָם] on the day I took them by the hand. . . ." And Deut 5:22 states that Yahweh wrote the commandments on two tablets of stone, while in Jer 31:33 Yahweh says, "I shall put my law within them, and on their heart shall write it." If this

analysis is sound, then Deut 4:45—5:33 (in some form) was known to Jrm; and if the setting of the new covenant passage suggested in the present study is correct (the time of the recitation of the Deuteronomic law in the autumn of 587, see sec. 36), then one must reckon with the probability that Deut 4:45—5:33 (at least in the form known at that time) was part of the recitation of Deuteronomy on that occasion. (For the Decalogue itself, see sec. 59.)

There is a relation between Deut 5:33 and Jer 7:23: the latter reads, "Walk in exactly the way [בְּכָל־הַדֶּרֶךְ] I command you, so that it may go well [לְמַעַן יִיטַב] with you," and the former reads, "In exactly the way [בְּכָל־הַדֶּרֶךְ] Yahweh your God has commanded you you shall walk, so that you may live and it may be well [לְמַעַן תִּחְיוּן וְטוֹב] with you." The expression כָּל־הַדֶּרֶךְ is found twice otherwise in Deuteronomy (1:31; 8:2), but not otherwise in Jer. Given that 7:21–28 is a parody of Deuteronomy, it is likely that Jrm drew on 5:33.

58. Jeremiah's Dependence on the Decalogue and on the Curses: Were These Parts of Proto-Deuteronomy?

A consideration of the parallels with Deuteronomy 5 is a good bridge to a consideration of two instances in the authentic prose of Jrm where he seems to depend on material now found in the prose of Deuteronomy outside chapters 12—26, namely, the Decalogue and the curses in 27:15–26. This is difficult terrain: on the side of Jrm, the parallels are in prose generally thought to be "Deuteronomistic," as already affirmed; and on the side of Deuteronomy, it is by no means clear, if Jrm took the Decalogue and the curses as models, that he heard the Decalogue as it now appears in Deuteronomy 5 *as part of Deuteronomy 5*, nor the curses as part of Deuteronomy.

The series of forbidden actions in the parenesis of 7:9 is surely a citation of some of the prohibitions in the Decalogue. There is a similar series in Hos 4:2, so that two obvious conclusions may be drawn—the fact that both prophets offer a similar partial list is strong evidence that they were both drawing on the Decalogue, and the fact that Hosea did it encouraged Jrm to do it as well. But it is not possible to know the form of the Decalogue known to Jrm; it may not have been heard by him in the form now found in Deuteronomy 5, nor even as part of Deuteronomy 5.[215] The question must therefore remain open.

The rhetoric of 11:3–5 appears to be a deliberate variation on the pattern represented by Deut 27:15–26, where a series of verses begins with "cursed" (אָרוּר) and ends with "so be it" (אָמֵן, "Amen"). Evidence offered in the present study suggests that 11:1–14 is authentic to Jrm, and one must conclude therefore that the pattern offered in Deut 27:15–26 was the antecedent stimulus for the three verses in question.[216]

But again it is not clear whether Deut 27:15–26 was a part of the Deuteronomy known to Jrm: it might have been a cultic form known to Jrm independently from Deuteronomy, only later to be incorporated into Deuteronomy.

On both these parallels then the question must remain open.

59. Two Instances of Dependence between Jeremiah and Deuteronomy: In Which Direction?

The uncertainty just mentioned is matched by another kind of uncertainty: there is clearly a parallel between 30:21 and Deut 17:15, and there is clearly a parallel between 1:7 and 9 and Deut 18:15–18, and both these parallels strongly suggest dependence in one direction or the other; but in which direction does the dependence lie?

These two instances must be discussed together, because they are linked. The parallels in Deuteronomy are both from the section containing the laws for officials, Deut 17:15 in the laws for the king and Deut 18:15–18 in the laws for the prophet. Deut 17:15 states, "You shall set over yourself a king whom Yahweh your God shall choose: from the midst of your brothers [מִקֶּרֶב

אָחֶיךָ] you shall place over yourself a king, you cannot appoint over yourself a foreigner, one who is not your brother." Deut 18:18 states, "A prophet I will raise up for them from the midst of their brothers [אֲחֵיהֶם מִקֶּרֶב] like you; and I will put my words in his mouth, and he shall speak to them all that I command him." From the side of the analysis of Deuteronomy, then, these two laws are parallel and are clearly part of the same literary stratum.

From Jrm's side, 30:21 speaks of an ideal king: "and his [Israel's] ruler from his midst [מִקִּרְבּוֹ] shall go forth" (that is, in contrast to a foreign ruler). The passage is part of the hopeful scroll, but it is evidently in the first instance a word of hope to the north, referring to Josiah as ruler over a restored united monarchy (in contrast to an Assyrian ruler).

The parallel on the side of Jrm with the law about the prophet is in his call narrative, 1:7, 9; 1:7 reads "everything I command you you shall speak," and 1:9 "I have put my words in your mouth."[217] The conclusion of the present study is that 1:4–10 is authentic to Jrm and has not been subject to the redaction of a Deuteronomic editor.[218]

The general consensus today is that the laws concerning king, priest, and prophet in 17:14—18:22 were not part of Proto-Deuteronomy, at least as they now stand.[219] But scholars differ on the details of the strata. I shall confine myself to remarks on Deut 17:15 and 18:18.

As far as Deut 17:15 is concerned, Lohfink points out that vv 16–17 clearly presuppose the experience of Solomon's kingship, but there is nothing in the Books of Kings to suggest a background for the prohibition in

215 On this question see Norbert Lohfink, "Zur Dekalogfassung von Dt 5," *BZ* 9 (1965) 17–32.
216 Albrecht Alt proposed the antiquity of Deut 27:15–26, "The Origins of Israelite Law," *Essays on Old Testament History and Religion* (Oxford: Blackwell, 1966) 114–15, 125–26 and so also von Rad, *Deuteronomy*, 167.
217 For some recent literature on the relation of 1:7, 9 to Deut 18:18 see Berridge, p. 50, n. 139.
218 Against Nicholson, *Jer. 1—25*, 25–26.
219 See Sellin-Fohrer, pp. 170–71; Norbert Lohfink, "Die Sicherung der Wirksamkeit des Gotteswortes durch das Prinzip der Schriftlichkeit der Tora und durch das Prinzip der Gewaltenteilung nach den Ämtgesetzen des Buches Deuteronomium (Dt 16,18—18,22)," *Testimonium Veritati, Philosophische und theologische Studien zu kirchlichen Fragen der Gegenwart* (ed. Hans Wolter; Frankfurter Theologische Studien 7; Frankfurt: Knecht, 1971) 143–55.

17:15; on the other hand, Jer 30:21 clearly has in mind Josiah rather than an Assyrian ruler—all of which suggests the priority of 30:21 over Deut 17:15.[220] But Mayes offers two suggestions for an early background for Deut 17:15.[221] (1) Omri has a foreign name, and the name of his father is not given, so it is possible then that he was a non-Israelite.[222] (2) Rezin of Damascus and Pekah of Samaria attempted to put "the son of Tabeel" on the throne of Judah (Isa 7:6): there was a Tub'il who was king of Tyre in 738, and it is likely that it was his son who is referred to here:[223] if so, it was a move to put a foreigner on the throne. And I would add that I am troubled by the expression מִקִּרְבּוֹ in 30:21: this form appears only once otherwise in the OT, in Num 14:13, where it is used of the people coming out "from his midst," that is, from the midst of Egypt. But in 30:21 it is used of the ruler coming out "from the midst of himself," which seems rather harsh unless heard as a poetic equivalent of the expression "from the midst of your brothers," that is to say, of a preexistent Deut 17:15.

As for Deut 18:18, if Jer 1:7, 9 are original to Jrm, as the structural analysis of the present study indicates, and if there is a relation of dependence between these verses and Deut 18:18, and if at the same time Deut 18:18 is exilic, then we have the scenario of a law being drafted on the basis of Yahweh's word to one prophet, presumably to underline a conviction of the Deuteronomist that Jrm is the prophet like Moses. But I find this unlikely. I can conceive of Deut 18:19–22 being drafted in exilic times on the basis of the experience of Jrm with the false prophets;[224] after all, it was a problem for Ezekiel as well (Ezekiel 13). But it is the specificity to the call of Jrm that I find unlikely in the scenario of the late drafting of Deut 18:18. I therefore prefer to see Deut 18:18, like 17:15, as part of Proto-Deuteronomy, drawn on by Jrm to shape his own understanding of his role as the prophet like Moses.

But the question of these two parallels must remain open.

60. Instances in Which Late Deuteronomy Appears to Be Dependent on Jeremiah

It is appropriate now to consider passages in Deuteronomy that are late and appear to be dependent on genuine phrases of Jrm. Deut 28:49, 51–52 is evidently dependent on Jer 5:15, 17, portions of a sequence of Jrm's poetry. Jer 5:15 reads, "I am going to bring upon you a nation from afar, . . . it is a perennial nation, it is a nation from long ago, a nation whose tongue you do not know, whose speech you do not understand"; Deut 28:49 reads, "Yahweh shall lift against you a nation from afar, from the end of the earth, as swift as the eagle flies, a nation whose tongue you do not understand." Similarly Deut 28:51–52 expands on Jer 5:17, both the themes of the enemy's eating all the produce of the land and of the bringing down of the fortified cities in which the people trusted. The redactional history of Deuteronomy 28 is a complicated one, but it is in any event clear that vv 47–69 represent one or more layers added after the fall of Jerusalem.[225]

It then becomes clear that Deut 28:48, "and he will put an iron yoke on your neck," is dependent upon Jer 28:14, and in general upon that whole encounter between Jrm and Hananiah.

There are indeed a whole series of phrases in Deuteronomy 28 that are dependent on words of Jrm. Thus in v 25b there occurs the sequence "I shall make you a terror to all the kingdoms of the earth"; it also occurs four times in Jer—15:4; 24:9; 29:18; 34:17—all four instances, by the conclusions of the present study, authentic to Jrm. And in v 26 there occurs the sequence "the corpses of X shall be food for the birds of the heavens and the beasts of the earth"; this sequence too (or its variant "I shall give the corpses of X for food . . .") occurs four times in Jer—16:4; 7:33; 19:7; 34:20—all again, by present findings, authentic to Jrm. The sequence Deut 28:25b–26 interrupts the continuity of vv 25a + 27,[226] and it is altogether likely, then, that Deut 28:25b–26 is drawn from Jer.

220 Norbert Lohfink, by personal correspondence.
221 Mayes, *Deuteronomy*, 272.
222 For discussions of this possibility see Gray, *Kings*, 364; Hugh B. MacLean, "Omri," *IDB* 3:601.
223 Antoine Vanel, "Ṭâbe'él en Is. vii 6 et le roi Tubail de Tyr," *Studies on Prophecy* (VTSup 26; Leiden: Brill, 1974) 17–24.
224 Compare Lohfink, "Die Sicherung der Wirksam-

keit," 149.
225 For other discussions of the redactional history of Deuteronomy 28 and/or the relation with Jer 5:15, 17 see von Rad, *Deuteronomy*, 173–76; Rudolph, p. 39; Gottfried Seitz, *Redaktionsgeschichtliche Studien zum Deuteronomium* (BWANT 93; Stuttgart: Kohlhammer, 1971) 293–94, 298; Mayes, *Deuteronomy*, 348–51.

Verse 53 reads, "You shall eat [אכל qal] the fruit of your belly, the flesh of your sons and your daughters which Yahweh your God has given you, in the siege and hardship which your enemy shall inflict upon you," and the pair "siege" and "hardship," a word-play (מָצוֹר and מָצוֹק) occurs also in vv 55 and 57; Jer 19:9 has "and I shall feed them [אכל hip'il] the flesh of their sons and the flesh of their daughters, and they shall eat each other's flesh, in the siege and hardship which their enemies shall inflict upon them." In this instance again there is no doubt of the priority: the word-play in particular suggests the originality of Jrm; and vv 47–57 are a late addition to Deut 28.[227]

In Deut 28:63 there appears a phrase, said of Yahweh, that appears twice more—Deut 30:9 and Jer 32:41: "rejoice [שיש] over you/them to do you/them good." By the analysis of the present study the verse in Jer 32 is authentic to Jrm. Deut 28:58–68 is a very late addition to the chapter,[228] and again Deut 30:9 is part of an exilic addition to the book.[229]

There are three sequences in Deuteronomy 1—11 that are evidently dependent on phrases of Jrm. Two of them appear to be dependent on Jer 11:4–5. The first is the expression "iron furnace," a description of Egypt; it is found only three times in the OT—Deut 4:20; 1 Kgs 8:51; Jer 11:4. It is recognized that 1 Kgs 8:44–53 is from an exilic redactor;[230] and Deuteronomy 4, for its part, is also late.[231] The analysis of the present study is that the expression is original to Jrm, a development of his imagery of the "iron yoke" of Babylon, and that 1 Kgs 8:51 and Deut 4:20 alike are dependent on Jrm.

The triplet "in wrath, anger and great rage" occurs three times in the OT: in Deut 29:27 and Jer 21:5 and 32:37. Jer 21:5 is the verse in which is to be found the unique form of the stereotyped phrase with exchange of adjectives, "with outstretched hand and mighty arm" (see above); and in Jer 32:37 the three nouns carry personal suffixes. In short, both expressions in Jer appear to be original.[232] Deut 29:21–27 is an explanation of the basis

for punishment;[233] the passage is clearly from the exilic period.[234] It is likely then that Deut 29:27 drew on the phraseology of Jrm.

61. The Shape of Proto-Deuteronomy

There are no surprises here: that is to say, I have drawn on the general consensus concerning the development of the Book of Deuteronomy. Nevertheless, it is important to establish the shape of the Book of Deuteronomy at the time of Jrm, for that produces an absolute date.

If the parallels adduced here have been properly dealt with, Jrm knew Deuteronomy 5—26, for there are parallels to Deuteronomy 5 in general, and specifically to 5:33; 10:16; 11:19; 12:2, 5–9; 14:29; 20:19–20; 22:25, 27; 24:1–4, 21; and 26:5, 8, and 19. I leave open, however, the question whether Jrm knew the laws regarding officials in 16:18—18:22. I have concluded that there is no evidence that Jrm drew from Deuteronomy 1—3, or from Deuteronomy 4. I have concluded that Jrm knew Deut 27:15–26 in some form, but whether it was a part of Proto-Deuteronomy I leave uncertain. There is no direct evidence that he drew on any of the blessings and curses in Deuteronomy 28. It is clear that he knew Deuteronomy 32 (or at least Deut 32:1–38). One might raise the question whether Jrm heard Deuteronomy 32 as part of Proto-Deuteronomy or whether it was heard as a separate work (compare the discussion on Huldah's oracle, below). There is no way, of course, to answer this question definitively, but the fact that Jrm drew from both the prose of Proto-Deuteronomy and from Deuteronomy 32 and the fact that they were associated at least by the postexilic period suggests that they were likely to have been associated for Jrm. Indeed the fact that (by the conclusions of the present study) Jrm, the prophet like Moses, offered both poetic oracles and parenetic prose suggests that he had as a model what he considered to be Moses' poetry (Deuteronomy 32) and Moses' parenetic prose.

---

226 Seitz, *Studien*, 279–80; compare von Rad, p. 175.

227 Von Rad, *Deuteronomy*, 175–76; Mayes, *Deuteronomy*, 350–51.

228 Von Rad, *Deuteronomy*, 176; Mayes, *Deuteronomy*, 349.

229 Von Rad, *Deuteronomy*, 183; Mayes, *Deuteronomy*, 367.

230 Noth, *Könige*, 173–74; Gray, *Kings*, 226; Montgomery, *Kings*, 194, with references to other analyses.

231 Mayes, *Deuteronomy*, 148; compare von Rad, *Deuter-*

onomy, 50, on vv 25–28.

232 See further Weippert, *Prosareden*, 82.

233 Skweres, "Strafgrunderfragung."

234 Compare Norbert Lohfink, "Der Bundesschluss im Land Moab, Redaktionsgeschichtliches zu Dt. 28,69—32,47," *BZ* NF 6 (1962) 40–41; Mayes, *Deuteronomy*, 358–59.

62. The Question of Huldah's Oracle

In 2 Kgs 22:14–20 one reads the narrative of the delegation from Josiah's court to Huldah the prophetess to inquire about the scroll found in the temple. Verses 16–17 contain what purports to be her oracle regarding the scroll, and there is evidently some kind of relation between that oracle and Jrm's words. John Gray offers the conventional view: 2 Kgs 22:16–20 "is so developed by the Deuteronomistic redactor that the original oracle is no longer distinguishable."[235] But Jack R. Lundbom has pointed out[236] that the oracle in 2 Kgs 22:17 can be understood as a summary of Deut 32:15–22 in the diction of the seventh century: "they have abandoned me" reflects 32:15, "he forsook [a different verb] the God who made him"; "they have sacrificed to other gods" reflects 32:17, "they sacrificed [a different verb] to demons which were no gods, to gods they have never known, to new gods that had come in of late, whom your fathers had never dreaded"; "that they might offend me with all the work of their hands" reflects 32:16, "they stirred him to jealousy with strangers, with abominable practices they offended him [same verb]"; and "my wrath will be kindled against this place, and it will not be quenched" reflects 32:22, "for a fire is kindled [different verb] in my anger [different noun], and it burns to the depths of Sheol, devours the earth and its increase, and sets on fire the foundations of the mountains." The individual phrases in 2 Kgs 22:17 are in some cases traditional ones: for example "abandon (Yahweh)" is found in Hos 4:10 and Isa 1:4, 28. But if the vocabulary in that verse is appropriate to a seventh-century prophet, the association of expressions is identical with that in Deut 32:15–22 and occurs in almost the same order; and this association of expressions is not found elsewhere in the OT. Lundbom proposes then that the diction of 2 Kgs 22:16–17 is not Deuteronomistic but that Huldah drew on Deut 32:15–22 in her indictment against Israel, and in this I believe he is correct. Since such diction is not found in Deut 5—26 (+ 28), Lundbom goes on to propose (I believe incorrectly) that Deuteronomy 32, but not Deuteronomy 5—26 (+ 28), was the content of the scroll discovered in the temple during the kingship of Josiah. (Jrm's references to material in those chapters of Deuteronomy would speak against the proposal; see above.)

One can go on to discuss the repetition of the phrases in 2 Kgs 22:16–17 in Jer. Jer 1:16 reads, "And I shall pronounce my judgments on them for all their crime in abandoning me, in sacrificing to other gods, and in worshiping the work of their hands": that sequence, I have concluded, is not a Deuteronomistic addition but is poetry integrated into its context, embodying the words of Jrm himself, added to the call narrative at the time of the battle of Carchemish (spring of 605), and is deliberately reminiscent of Huldah's oracle. Similarly the expostulation of Yahweh in Jer 8:19 "Why have they offended me with their idols, with alien nothings?" not only reflects Deut 32:16 but Huldah's oracle as well. And "My wrath will be kindled against this place, and it will not be quenched" is replicated almost word-for-word in Jer 7:20, "My anger and my wrath are going to be poured out on this place, on man and beast, on the tree of the field and fruit of the ground, and it shall burn and not go out," and again the conclusion of the present study is that the passage in Jer is authentic to the prophet. Other passages in Jer that employ these phrases, notably 19:3–4 and 44:2–6, likewise give evidence of Jrm's intention to reflect Huldah's oracle.[237]

63. Relations between Jeremiah and the Psalms: Preliminary Remarks

It has long been recognized that there is a close relation between passages in Jer and passages in the Psalms, notably between Jrm's confessions and the psalms of individual lament. It was long assumed that Jrm had used such psalms for his model.[238] Then when critical opinion assigned most of the psalms to the postexilic period, it was assumed that psalmists drew on Jrm. Thus in 1960 Pierre Bonnard proposed that thirty-three psalms were written under the stimulus of Jrm,[239] but Bright in his review of that work wondered whether the dependence did not in some cases run the other way.[240] Now that critical opinion has swung back to dating most of the psalms in the preexilic period, the question is again open. The conclusions of the present study allow more precision on the matter.

---

235 Gray, *Kings*, 727.
236 Jack R. Lundbom, "The Lawbook of the Josianic Reform," *CBQ* 38 (1976) 295–99.
237 Compare Berridge, p. 99.
238 For a survey of older opinion see Baumgartner, *Klagegedichte*, 1–5.

I conclude that Jrm drew on the following: Psalms 1; 79; 2; 78; 122; 22; 9—10; 63; 64; 6 and 38; 35; 7; 83; 84; 139; that in the case of Psalm 107 there may have been mutual borrowing; and that the following are dependent on Jrm: Psalms 31; 135; 148; 40:1–12; 51; 55; 69; 74. It will be convenient to discuss them in that order.

64. Psalms on Which Jeremiah Drew: Cases of Fair Certitude

It is clear that Jrm drew phraseology from psalms he knew. The most striking example is perhaps Psalm 1: Jrm evidently offered two contrasting variations (12:1b–2 and 17:5–8) on this psalm.[241] This is a surprise, because almost all critics have assumed that the psalm is late and dependent on Jer 17:5–8.[242] But the data of the present study indicate not only that 17:5–8 is authentic to Jrm, but that both 12:1b–2 and 17:5–8 have shifted the psalm in different ways: 12:1b–2, obviously, by identifying the guilty rather than the innocent as the ones who prosper, and 17:5–8, more subtly, by portraying not only the juniper in the desert but also the tree planted by the canal as being without water, the contrast then not being the absence or presence of water but the depth of rootage that allows the tree to produce fruit even in a year of drought. The fact that 12:4 also mentions a drought also brings these passages together. If this analysis is sound, the conclusion is inescapable that Psalm 1 is prior. And one can go on to note two other word-plays: that Jer 17:8 offers יוּבָל "stream," a play on a verb in Ps 1:3, where it is affirmed that the leaves of the tree do not "wither" (יִבּוֹל), and then that Jer 11:19 again plays on Ps 1:3, offering "tree" and יוּבָל "is led."

If Jrm deformed Psalm 1, he evidently used Ps 79:6–7 in 10:25 as a deliberate quotation. Again, 10:25 is widely thought to be a secondary citation of 79:6–7, but 10:23 is an expansion of Prov 16:9 and 20:24, and 10:24 is an expansion of Pss 6:2 or 38:2. I have proposed that this catena of quotations is a deliberate attempt on Jrm's part to cite those passages that portray the unwillingness of the people to accept covenant responsibility, and I have also suggested that these quotations at a certain stage in the compilation of Jrm's oracles may balance the quotations in 4:3–4. These considerations strongly suggest that Jrm drew on Psalm 79. It is also of interest that the diction of 2:27b–28a appears to draw on Ps 79:9–10 (synonyms for "save us," the question pattern "where is/are your/their God/gods?"—the question also appears in Pss 42:4, 11; 115:2, but not associated with "save me/us"), so that it is possible that Jrm drew on these verses of the psalm as well.

Psalm 2 is obviously preexilic.[243] The curious sequence Jer 15:10–12 is surely dependent on that psalm. Ps 2:9 has "break" (רעע II) and "iron," and "iron" is accompanied by what is evidently the same verb in Jer 15:12; and Ps 2:7 has "I have given birth to you," while Jer 15:10 has "You have given birth to me." It is possible that Jrm's perception of a call from birth contains a royal motif; so here by the same token he appears to have taken a royal psalm over for himself. There may also be an echo of Ps 2:9 ("like a potter's vessel smash them") in Jer 22:28 ("smashed . . . a vessel no one cares for").

Psalm 78 is a didactic recitation of the history of Israel, evidently used at one of the major festivals.[244] Ps 78:60 is the only mention of the fall of Shiloh outside Jer (for the latter see 7:12, 14; 26:6 [and 9]). It may be worth noting that in the same summary of Jrm's temple sermon 26:4 presents Yahweh as speaking of Israel's obligation "to walk in my law," a phrase occurring also in Ps 78:10 (as well as elsewhere in early tradition); but it is certainly

239 Pierre E. Bonnard, *Le psautier selon Jérémie, Influence littéraire et spirituelle de Jérémie sur trente-trois Psaumes* (LD 26; Paris: Cerf, 1960); he cites the following: Psalms 1, 6, 7, 16, 17, 22, 26, 31, 35, 36, 38, 40, 41, 44, 51, 55, 69, 71, 73, 74, 75, 76, 78, 79, 81, 83, 86, 89, 106, 109, 119, 135, 139.

240 John Bright, review of Pierre E. Bonnard, *Le Psautier selon Jérémie, JBL* 80 (1961) 299, and see further John Bright's "Jeremiah's Complaints—Liturgie or Expressions of Personal Distress?" *Proclamation and Presence, Old Testament Essays in Honour of Givynne Henton Davies* (ed. John I. Durham and J. Roy Porter;

Richmond: Knox, 1970) 189–214.

241 See Holladay, *Spokesman*, 93, 99.

242 See *Jeremiah 1*, 17:5–8, n. 1.

243 Kraus, *Psalmen*, 14.

244 Ibid., 540.

significant that Jer 20:11, part of one of the confessions, appears to draw on Ps 78:65–66: both passages describe Yahweh as "like a warrior" (כְּגִבּוֹר) and speak in synonymous terms of "the everlasting disgrace/shame" of the adversaries. Eissfeldt first pointed out the resemblance between Psalm 78 and Deuteronomy 32,[245] a song from which Jrm drew deeply. Robertson has recently dated the psalm to the divided monarchy,[246] and Antony Campbell to the tenth century;[247] the psalm is clearly antecedent to Jrm.

The phraseology of Jer 15:5 (concern for the "peace [well-being, šālôm] of Jerusalem") undoubtedly has Ps 122:6–8 as a background, as John M. Berridge suggested a number of years ago.[248] Whether the walls of Jerusalem described in this psalm are preexilic or postexilic has been a matter of debate,[249] but if the foregoing conclusion is sound, then the psalm is preexilic.

I argued in 1964 that the imagery of Ps 22:10–11 would have been heard by Jrm as a description of the narrative of the infancy of Moses, and since Jrm understands the prediction of the prophet like Moses in Deut 18:18 to refer to himself, and since Jrm understands himself to be called from his mother's womb (1:5) and refers more than once in his confessions to his mother's bearing him (15:10; 20:14) and to his mother's womb (20:18), Psalm 22 must have been known and used by him.[250] I may add that there are other verses of the psalm that appear to have stimulated phrases in 20:7–12, one of the confessions, notably the accusation of Yahweh's dereliction (20:7a; Ps 22:2), perhaps the mode of mockery of the adversaries (20:7b–10; Ps 22:8–9), and doubtless the collocation of "heart" and "bones" as the seat of pain (20:9; Ps 22:15).

Psalms 9—10 were originally a single acrostic psalm.[251] This psalm provided phrases for Jrm's words during the drought. Thus though the expression לְעִתּוֹת בַּצָּרָה (Pss 9:10; 10:1) is often understood as "in times of trouble," either by emending בַּצָּרָה to הַצָּרָה[252] or by assuming the בְּ as a preposition within a construct chain,[253] one can just as well read the phrase as "in times of drought."[254] In any event the mention of "the gates of death" and of "the gates of daughter Zion" in Ps 9:14–15 seems to lie behind the identification of the gates of Judah with the gates of Sheol in Jer 14:2. Furthermore, the general diction of Ps 10:1–4 appears to lie in the background of Jer 12:1b–4, part of a confession voiced by Jrm at the time of the drought (12:4): beyond the fact that both passages share the form-critical likeness of laments, Yahweh is "far" (רָחוֹק) from the mind of the guilty in 12:2 and "far" from the psalmist in Ps 10:1, and the guilty say "he will not see where we end" in 12:4 and "there is no God" in Ps 10:4. And there are other reflections of this psalm elsewhere in Jrm: Ps 10:7a offers "oppression and fraud" (מִרְמָה וָתֹךְ), as does Jer 9:5 (with a generally agreed-upon emendation), and Ps 10:8 offers the root "ambush" (ארב), as does 9:7. The psalm then is not late, as many critics have assumed, nor does the acrostic suggest the sixth century.[255]

The idiom in Ps 63:11, "deliver them into the hands of the sword," is curious and appears to be the antecedent for Jer 18:21. Likewise the combination in Ps 63:12 of "swear (by Yahweh)" and "bless oneself (in Yahweh)" seems to be one of the antecedents for these phrases in Jer 4:2 (compare Gen 22:18; 26:4). One may thus establish a preexilic date for the psalm (compare the mention of the "king" in v 12).[256]

There is evidently a relation between Ps 64:7 and Jer 17:9. Both, of course, could be dependent on antecedent wisdom sayings,[257] but Jrm evidently put an ironic twist on the description of the "heart" in the psalm: the psalm

245 Otto Eissfeldt, *Das Lied Moses Deuteronomium 32 1–43 und das Lehrgedicht Asaphs Psalm 78 samt einer Analyse der Umgebung des Moses-Liedes* (Berichte über die Verhandlungen der sächsischen Akademie der Wissenschaften zu Leipzig, Philologisch-historische Klasse 104/5; Berlin: Akademie, 1958); see further Kraus, *Psalmen*, 541.

246 Robertson, *Linguistic Evidence in Dating Early Hebrew Poetry* (SBLDS 3; Society of Biblical Literature, 1972) 150–52.

247 Antony F. Campbell, "Psalm 78: A Contribution to the Theology of Tenth Century Israel," *CBQ* 41

(1979) 51–79.

248 Berridge, p. 178.

249 Kraus, *Psalmen*, 839.

250 Holladay, "Background," 156–59.

251 Kraus, *Psalmen*, 77; Dahood, *Psalms I*, 54. G and V reckon a single psalm.

252 Kraus, *Psalmen*, 76; Hans Bardtke in *BHS*.

253 Dahood, *Psalms I*, 52, 57; G reads two prepositional phrases.

254 So Zorell, p. 123b; *HALAT*, p. 143a.

255 Compare Kraus, *Psalmen*, 79.

256 Compare ibid., 441.

states that the heart is עָמֹק, "deep," and this is evidently the reading of *G* in Jer 17:9, but *M* reads an assonantal variant עָקֹב, "devious" or the like, probably to bring the word into the orbit of יַעֲקֹב "Jacob (compare the word-play on Jacob's name in 9:3). If that is the case, the psalm must be preexilic (Hans-Joachim Kraus can find no evidence by which to date the psalm).[258]

Jer 10:24, as already noted, is a citation of either Ps 6:2 or 38:2 (it must be reiterated that Jer 10:23–25 is a catena of citations: see above); the wording of Jer 10:24 is closer to that of Ps 6:2 than of 38:2. And both these psalms, which are psalms of personal lament, appear to have been drawn on by Jrm for one of his confessions, 15:15–18. Thus "do not, because of the slowness of your anger, take me away" in Jer 15:15 is evidently a witty variation on "do not in your anger rebuke me" in Ps 6:2. (On the other hand, the likeness of the next phrase, "for on your account I have borne disgrace," to the same phrase in Ps 69:8, with slight variation in word order and verb-form, is evidently the result of borrowing in the reverse direction: see sec. 66.) Then the psalmist of Psalm 38 states that Yahweh's hand is upon him (Ps 38:3–4), and Jrm affirms the same about himself in Jer 15:17: J. J. M. Roberts has noted the resemblance of Jer 15:17 to Ps 38:3 with regard to this phrase.[259] And there may be another relation between Psalm 38 and Jer 15:15–17: Ps 38:2–11 is likely to be the self-description of a leper,[260] and the phrase in Jer 15:17, "I have sat alone," is reminiscent of Lev 13:46, the situation of the leper. Neither Psalm 6 nor Psalm 38 offers any clue as to date, but nothing suggests that the preexilic period is wrong. I conclude that Jrm drew on the diction of Psalms 6 and 38 for 10:24 and 15:15–18.

Psalm 38 shares the expression "render evil for good" (רָעָה תַּחַת טוֹבָה + שׁלם) with Psalm 35 (Ps 38:21; Ps 35:12). Either psalm verse could lie behind 18:20, "Is evil a recompense for good?" Since Psalm 35 offers several parallels to expressions of Jrm's, both in his confessions and outside them, I turn now to that psalm. The most striking parallel lies outside the confessions, 23:12 with Ps 35:5–6. The latter passage reads, "Let them be like chaff before the wind, and the angel of Yahweh driving (them) [דחה]! Let their way be Darkness [חֹשֶׁךְ] and

Perdition [חֲלַקְלַקּוֹת], and the angel of Yahweh pursuing them!" and 23:12 reads, "Their way shall be to them like Perdition [חֲלַקְלַקּוֹת], into Darkness [אֲפֵלָה] they shall be driven [דחה, though see Interpretation], and they shall fall into it." Jrm used the word for "Darkness" found in Prov 4:19, but the parallel is otherwise close to Psalm 35. Given the conclusion of the present study that the false prophets (described in 23:9–12) were the opponents described by Jrm in his confessions, it is not surprising that Psalm 35 shares diction both with Jer 23:12 and the confessions. Thus there is the parallel יְרִיבַי "my adversaries" and לֹחֲמָי "my opponents" in Ps 35:1, while 18:19 has יְרִיבָי "my adversaries," and from that parallel in Ps 35:1 I have suggested the revocalization of the troublesome לַחְמוֹ "his bread" to לֹחֲמוֹ "his opponent" in 11:19 and the emendation of רִיבִי "my legal case" to יְרִיבָי "my adversaries" in 11:20 = 20:12 (see Text and Interpretation for 11:19 and 20). And the expression "my stumbling" (בְּצַלְעִי), Ps 35:15, is also found in 20:10, where it may be translated either "my stumbling" or "my rib" (see there). It is not likely that the psalmist drew his phrases from Jrm's. Though there are no direct clues for dating the psalm, it must be said that neither יָרִיב "adversary" nor לֹחֵם "opponent" is common vocabulary in the OT: the former, outside 18:19 and my proposal for 11:20 = 20:12, is found only in Ps 35:1 and Isa 49:25, and the latter, outside my proposal for 11:19, is found only in Ps 35:1; 56:2, 3. One concludes then that the terms are archaic and that Jrm drew on Psalm 35.

The sequence Ps 7:10–12 appears to stand behind Jer 11:20 = 20:12 and 17:10a; in literal translation Ps 7:10 has "(you) who assay hearts and kidneys," and v 12 has שׁוֹפֵט צַדִּיק "[God is a] righteous judge [or, judge of the righteous (man)]"; Jer 11:20 has "[O Yahweh of hosts,] judge of righteousness [שֹׁפֵט צֶדֶק], (you) who assay kidneys and heart," while Jer 20:12 has "[O Yahweh of hosts,] who assay the righteous (man), who see kidneys and heart"; Jer 17:10a has "[I am Yahweh,] who search heart and assay kidneys." (It should be noted that Ps 17:3 has "you have tried my heart" but no more of this cluster of expressions.) Though there can be no certainty, one

257 Compare ibid., 447.
258 Ibid., 446.
259 J. J. M. Roberts, "The Hand of Yahweh," *VT* 21

(1971) 250–51.
260 Kraus, *Psalmen*, 294.

may assume that Jrm was in these passages deliberately citing Psalm 7; certainly Ps 7:10–12 appears to be making traditional affirmations in the context of the prayer of someone who is persecuted and takes refuge in the sanctuary: it is likely to be a preexilic psalm.[261]

There is a resemblance between Jer 11:19bδ and Ps 83:5b: Jrm quotes his enemies, who conspire against him so that "his name shall be remembered no more," while in Ps 83:5 the national enemies are quoted, conspiring against the nation so that "the name of Israel shall be remembered no more." Psalm 83 is thus a communal lament, while Jrm's is of course that of an individual. Assyria is named in the psalm as a national enemy (Ps 83:9); there is no reason to doubt that the psalm is preexilic[262] and that Jrm drew on it.

It is possible that "From evil to evil they have advanced" (Jer 9:2) is a parody of Ps 84:8, "They go from strength to strength": Psalm 84 is surely preexilic.[263]

Finally I turn to Psalm 139. This psalm offers a complicated problem: first, there are in this psalm, as is the case in most psalms, no direct clues for dating; second, the psalm shows a likeness to the Book of Job, the dating for which is also controverted; and third, likenesses elsewhere could go in either direction. The closest resemblance in Jer is in 23:23–24, a passage similar to Ps 139:7–12. Now there is a close resemblance between Ps 139:7–12 and Amos 9:2–3.[264] But if Ps 139:7–12 affirms that there is no hiding place from Yahweh's awareness, Amos 9:2–3 affirms that there is no hiding place from Yahweh's punishing reach; it is difficult to avoid the conclusion that Amos has deliberately given a dark twist to the words of Psalm 139. If Psalm 139 is prior to Amos, then the passage in Jer is doubtless dependent on both Psalm 139 and Amos. If one argues that the psalm is postexilic and the passage in Jer is simply dependent on Amos, one must imagine that the psalmist, with the two prophetic passages at hand, both of which evoke a fear of Yahweh, drafted his words of confidence in Yahweh: but there is no evidence that the

words of the psalmist are a corrective. Further, there may be a further instance in Jrm's words of the pattern of two alternative destinations that drew on Ps 139:7–12 and Amos 9:2–3, namely, Jer 14:18. On balance it is better to conclude that both Amos and Jrm drew on the psalm.

Other parallels between the Psalms and Jrm's words might be adduced, and beyond the phraseological parallels are form-critical ones, but they are not strong enough to demonstrate dependency.

65. Mutual Borrowing?—Psalm 107

The contents of Ps 107:1–7 resemble that of Jer 31:8–9a, material authentic to Jrm. The phrase "straight path" (דֶּרֶךְ יְשָׁרָה or דֶּרֶךְ יָשָׁר) is found in Ps 107:7 and Jer 31:9, and otherwise only in Isa 26:7 and Ezra 8:21, late passages. Both passages have pairs of adjectives describing those in difficulty (Ps 107:5, "hungry and thirsty"; Jer 31:8, "blind and lame"). The mood of the two passages is certainly similar. Kraus suggests that Ps 107:1 + 4–9 may be the first stanza of a preexilic liturgy of thanksgiving:[265] this stanza is a description of Yahweh's care for the people in the exodus from Egypt. Jrm certainly employed the motif of a second exodus when he proclaimed 31:8–9a, and he may have drawn on these verses of the psalm. On the other hand vv 2–3 of the psalm appear to be an exilic or postexilic addition ("redeemed of Yahweh"; the four compass points—compare Isa 43:5–6);[266] since Jrm mentions "the land of the north" in 31:8, the diction of Ps 107:3 may be dependent on the passage in Jrm. There is no way to be sure.

66. Psalms Dependent on Jeremiah

There are some instances in which passages in the Psalms are dependent on Jrm. One is Ps 31:14aαβ, phrases identical with Jer 20:10aαβ. The phrase "terror on every side" (māgôr-missābîb) appears in the OT six times: five in Jer (6:25; 20:3, 10; 46:5; 49:29) and once in Ps 31:14. The second element (missābîb) appears to be a gloss in

---

261 So also ibid., 56.

262 Kraus, *Psalmen*, 577; Dahood, *Psalms II*, 273.

263 Kraus, *Psalmen*, 583; compare the discussion in Dahood, *Psalms II*, 279.

264 Compare James L. Mays, *Amos* (Philadelphia: Westminster, 1969) 154.

265 Kraus, *Psalmen*, 737–38.

266 Ibid., 737–38.

46:5. The initial occurrence of the expression in Jrm's career appears to be that in 20:1–6, where it figures in a word-play on the name of Pashhur: I suggest that Jrm meant it to express, among other meanings, "*māgôr* from every point of view," given that *māgôr* may be open to three meanings. The occurrence in 49:29 may be open to the same multiple meanings, this time when addressed to the nomadic Arabs. The occurrence in 6:25 appears to be a generalization of its application to Pashhur, and its occurrence in 20:10 is evidently intended as the ironic quotation of the crowd, throwing Jrm's expression back to him. And one may add the phrase *paḥad . . . mikkol-sĕbîbāyik* in 49:5. Given these variations in the expression, it is hard to imagine the six words in Ps 31:14aaβ as anything but a later citation of Jer 20:10aaβ.

Again, Ps 135:7 duplicates (with minor variations) the last three cola of Jer 10:13. One difficulty here of course is that 10:1–16 is widely thought to be unoriginal to Jrm, a late addition to the book. The present study cautiously concludes that it is after all original to him. Verse 13 is part of the poem included in the recension of *G*. On the other hand, beyond the verse in question Psalm 135 is in large part a tissue of quotations from other psalms, from Exodus and Deuteronomy, so that a late date seems likely.[267] One may conclude that the verse is borrowed from Jrm.

A third instance is Ps 148:6b, which bears a relation to Jer 5:22b. In 5:22 the verb עבר is clearly ambiguous—Yahweh established the sand as a bound for the sea, a limit forever; and (1) it (the sea) shall not surpass it, and (2) it (the sand) shall not pass away for it (the sea): and the repetition of the verb in the meaning of "surpass" under-lines the ambiguity. In Ps 148:6 the subject is not the sand but the sun, moon, stars, and waters above the heavens, so that the meaning of "pass away" is stressed (although the use of חָק "limit" allows the possibility that the meaning "surpass" lies in the background—compare *RSV*). The ambiguity has thus faded; and since Ps 148 appears to have a close relation to the Song of the Three Young Men (Dan 3:52–90 *G*), it is undoubtedly post-exilic; the psalmist is thus dependent on Jrm.[268]

A difficult question to decide is the relation between Jer 17:5–8 and Ps 40:1–12. It is a conclusion of the present study that 17:5–8 is genuine to Jrm, and I have indicated (see sec. 64) that Jrm drew on Psalm 1 for that passage. I have assumed that he also drew on Ps 40:4–5,[269] but further thought suggests rather that Ps 40:1–12 is dependent on Jer 17:5–8. Ps 40:5a of course closely resembles Jer 17:7. Both passages share the word-play of "see" and "fear," but where the two verbs appear within the same colon in Ps 40:4, the two verbs appear in the two parallel halves of the Jer passage, 17:6 and 17:8 (ketib). The psalm passage then seems to have sum-marized Jrm's words. Furthermore, the rejection of the necessity of sacrifice in Ps 40:7 appears to be a kind of low-key summary of prophetic teaching, in contrast for example with the striking wording of Ps 50:7–15. Kraus points to the possibility that Ps 40:8–11 is evidence of Torah-piety appropriate to the postexilic period.[270] The likelihood, then, is that the psalmist drew on Jrm.

A similarly difficult question is the priority of Psalm 51 and Jrm: both Ps 51:4, 9 and Jer 2:22 and 4:14 use the verb כבס pi'el "wash, scrub" for purification from sin. Again I assumed in the present study that the psalm lies behind 2:22,[271] but I now believe that the psalm is post-exilic. Jrm drew on Isa 5:1–7 for 2:21, and Isa 1:15–20 lies behind the parallel 2:22. In Isa 1:16 the verb רחץ is used, but, as in the Jrm passages, it is the people who are addressed. In the psalm, by contrast, God is addressed, to accomplish what Jrm has implied in 2:22 the people themselves cannot do. In addition Ps 51:12 suggests a dependence on Jer 31:33, and in that verse the verb "create" (ברא) suggests the diction of P and Deutero-Isaiah.[272] It may be further noted that Ps 51:18–19 strongly resembles Ps 40:7, likewise judged to be post-exilic in the discussion above. (Verses 20–21 may have been added still later.)

There is a relation between Ps 55:7–12 and Jer 9:1–7, for both passages offer a striking chain of expressions in almost the same order: מִי־יִתֵּן, literally "who will give" = "O that I had," the verb with preposition and suffix in Ps 55:7 (יִתֶּן־לִי) and with dative suffix in Jer 9:1 (יִתְּנֵנִי); the root לין "lodge" and בַּמִּדְבָּר "in the wilderness" (Ps 55:8; Jer 9:1); the reference to "their tongue" (לְשׁוֹנָם: Ps 55:10; Jer 9:2, 7); the reference to "oppression and fraud" (תֹּךְ וּמִרְמָה) "in her/his midst" (בְּקִרְבּוֹ/בְּקִרְבָּהּ: Ps 55:12;

267 Ibid., 895–96.
268 Ibid., 961.
269 *Jeremiah 1*, 490.

270 Kraus, *Psalmen*, 307.
271 *Jeremiah 1*, 99.
272 Kraus, *Psalmen*, 384; Dahood, *Psalms II*, 2.

Jer 9:6–7). Of the two, the psalmist's lines appear to be an expansion, almost a midrash, of Jrm's, and of course the image of the psalmist's wishing to fly from his difficulties is theologically less threatening than that of Yahweh's wishing to flee his people. Further Jrm describes the fraternal warfare within the covenant community, while the psalmist says, "It is not simply my enemies—this I could manage; no, it is you, my bosom friend" (Ps 55:13–15), phraseology that suggests a heightening or correcting of Jrm's words. I conclude that Psalm 55 is dependent on Jrm.[273] (For another instance in a psalm of "oppression and fraud," where the psalm [Psalms 9—10] seems to be antecedent to Jrm, see above).

Ps 69:8a is almost identical with Jer 15:15b, "For on your account I have borne disgrace." In the treatment of 15:15 in the present study I assumed that Jrm had drawn on Ps 69:8,[274] but now I feel sure that the psalm is postexilic[275] and thus that the psalmist drew on Jrm's words here.

Finally it is possible that Jrm's description in 22:6–7 of the destruction of the palace in Jerusalem may have stimulated the description in Ps 74:4–8 of the destruction of the temple: there is little overlap of vocabulary, but there is a similar approach and attention to detail—most authorities assume that this psalm portrays the destruction in 587.[276] And the diction of Ps 74:9 is curious: the question could at least be raised whether it does not reflect the passing of Jrm from the scene.

67. Jeremiah's Dependence on the Wisdom Tradition, Especially Proverbs

Jrm is dependent upon the wisdom tradition at many points, but there are few points where one can be sure that Jrm is citing or paraphrasing specific proverbs. One such instance is 10:23: it will be recalled that vv 23–25 of that chapter are united in being citations or expansions of known Scripture (compare the discussion above of the use in these verses of Psalms 6 and 79). Verse 23 paraphrases Prov 16:9 and 20:24. Verse 23 reads, "I know, Yahweh that a person's way is not his, nor is it for a man to walk and make firm [הָכִין] his step"; Prov 16:9 reads, "The heart of a person plans his way, but Yahweh makes

firm [יָכִין] his step," and 20:24 reads, "A man's steps are from Yahweh, and a person, how can he understand [יָבִין] his way?" (Since there is a double reading in ketib/qere' and the Versions in Prov 21:29 between יָבִין and יָכִין, it is likely, given the readings in Jer 10:23 and Prov 16:9, that Prov 20:24 should also read יָכִין.)

Again, 5:3, "You struck them, but they did not feel pain, you destroyed them, they refused to take correction," is reminiscent of Prov 23:35, "They struck me, but I did not feel pain, they beat me, I did not know (it)."

But most of the passages of Jrm's words that suggest antecedents in Proverbs are less than definitive. I have suggested Ps 35:5–6 as background for Jer 23:12 (see above), but Prov 4:19 has similar vocabulary, "The way of the wicked is like the darkness [אֲפֵלָה]; they do not know into what they stumble."

The expression "bearers of scandal" (הֹלְכֵי רָכִיל) in 6:28 may reflect the singular "bearer of scandal" (הוֹלֵךְ רָכִיל) in Prov 11:13 and 20:19.

I suggest in my exegesis of 49:7 that בָּנִים there may involve a word-play, suggesting both "sons" and "perceptive ones"; the same word-play is possible in Prov 4:1.

Six parallels in Proverbs are too few for a firm conclusion, but for what it is worth one may note that these parallels are not confined to any one section of the book.

And one must add that there are other words of Jrm in which he employs wisdom vocabulary (4:22) or wisdom themes—lessons from creation (the sand dunes, 5:22; the regularity of birds, 8:7), and the nature of the human heart (17:9); or in which he suggests where boasting is not appropriate (9:22–23); or in which he sets forth a mocking wisdom statement evidently directed at Jehoiakim (17:11). And he speaks of those who claim wisdom but do not have it (8:8–9).

C. The Person and Proclamation of Jeremiah

68. Preliminary Remarks

Though it might be thought useful to separate a discussion of Jrm's self-understanding, of his understanding of God, and his message to his people, there is in fact no way to separate these three. For Jrm, as for the other prophets in Israel, Yahweh is preeminently the God who

---

273 Compare Kraus, *Psalmen*, 403, against Dahood, *Psalms II*, 30.
274 *Jeremiah 1*, 457.
275 See Kraus, *Psalmen*, 481; Dahood, *Psalms II*, 155–56.
276 See Kraus, *Psalmen*, 514–15; Dahood, *Psalms I*, 199.

had covenanted with Israel and thereupon had guided and maintained Israel through the years, and Yahweh had called Jrm to speak on his behalf to Israel: Jrm can hardly be seen in any other way than in his task to proclaim Yahweh's word, and Yahweh's will for Israel is at the center of Jrm's attention. The covenant relation between Yahweh and Israel is a central concern for the whole OT, and most emphatically for the prophets; but the three-way relation among Yahweh, Jrm, and the people is especially well depicted in what has been preserved for us. In regard to Jrm's relation to Yahweh, we have not only the call narrative but the rich collection of confessions, in which Jrm sometimes quotes his opponents (11:19, 21; 20:10); in regard to Yahweh's relation to the people, we have the covenant-lawsuit material in chapters 2 and 3 that not only depicts Yahweh's accusations directed to the people but the people's response to his accusations, or in any event Jrm's perception of Yahweh's citations of the people's answers to him (or mock citations: 2:23, 25, 35; 3:22); we have several passages in which Yahweh forbids Jrm to pursue one of the tasks of the prophet, namely, to pray for the people (7:16–20; 14:11; 15:1). Thus Jrm's understanding of his role and his understanding of Yahweh and Yahweh's expectation for the people are all interrelated.

And in Jrm's perception these relations were open to change as circumstances changed. If I have read the evidence rightly, Jrm began his career with appeals to the north to come to terms with Yahweh and rejoin the south; during the period from the death of Josiah (609) until Jehoiakim burned the scroll (601) Jrm spoke out Yahweh's appeals to the people in the south to repent; after 601 Jrm perceived repentance no longer to be possible and declared Yahweh's decision to destroy the people, but in the context of the final siege of Jerusalem (588), after he bought the field at Anathoth, he once more spoke of hope, after "a long time," for the fall of Babylon and for the restoration of the people (29:28).

A personal word may be appropriate at this point regarding the whole question of the establishment of authenticity to Jrm of various passages within the book. I have of course offered a judgment as to the authenticity or nonauthenticity of each passage in the book, and these judgments sometimes differ from that of other scholars. Each judgment is based on the extent to which the vocabulary, point of view, and rhetorical technique of the passage in question seems congruent with that of passages taken by common consent to be authentic. It should be said, however, that as I was establishing my own understanding of Jrm's voice I was paying no attention to the oracles against foreign nations. Thus when I began working on these, I had formed no judgment for or against authenticity: these passages became fresh material on which to bring to bear my mode of analysis. I was therefore struck by passages that by my judgment were congruent with Jrm's voice, but passages with which I had not been theretofore familiar; and this was particularly the case with chapters 50—51, material that many scholars has dismissed as late redactional additions to the corpus. I have even dared to try to assign the authentic portions of chapters 46—51 to the various periods of Jrm's career, and these decisions of setting have struck me not only as plausible but as a pleasing "test case" of my approach to questions of authenticity.

69. The Prophet Jeremiah: His Tradition and His Role

There had been prophetic figures in Israel and Judah for many centuries, men and women who were believed to mediate the divine word. Sometimes they were found near the center of power (Nathan in the court of David, Isaiah in the court of Hezekiah), sometimes they were peripheral to the center of power (Elijah, Amos);[277] sometimes they were attached to cult centers (26:7),[278] sometimes they were independent of cult centers; there were prophets who functioned on behalf of Baal (23:13) as well as those who spoke for Yahweh; some prophets doubtless depended on ecstatic states while some did not, and some were doubtless more sincere than others (compare Mic 3:5). The term "prophet" then covers so wide a range that the term itself hardly defines Jrm's understanding of his role.[279]

On the other hand our information about Jrm is so comparatively full and Jrm appears as such a signal figure during the last few decades of the monarchy (as the record has survived for us) that it is easy to take our

---

277 See Wilson, *Prophecy and Society*.
278 Aubrey R. Johnson, *The Cultic Prophet in Ancient Israel* (Cardiff: University of Wales, 1962).

279 The literature on prophetic experience is enormous; two classic studies in English are Guillaume, *Prophecy and Divination*, and Lindblom, *Prophecy*. For a recent

conception of the prophet from him.[280] It is important then to examine what from his tradition Jrm took over for himself, what his role was in his years of proclamation.

One may assume that Jrm's access to his tradition was through his father, Hilkiah, a priest in Anathoth (1:1); Anathoth may have been the center that preserved the northern tradition from Shiloh (see the discussion on this matter in the Interpretation of 1:1). He took over from the northern prophet Hosea the ruling metaphor of Israel as the bride of Yahweh (2:2–3) and that prophet's critique of Baalism, and, if the origin of Deuteronomy lay in the covenant theology of northern prophetic or Levitical circles,[281] then Jrm's interest in Deuteronomy may well have been due in part to its mediation of northern traditions.

On the other hand Anathoth was only four kilometers from Jerusalem, and, particularly after 622, when Hilkiah would have been absorbed into the roster of priests serving in Jerusalem, Jrm would have had access to traditions current there as well. It is true, he manifested little interest in the ideology of Zion or of the Davidic monarchy (compare 26:11!): in his mind Zion and king can be the centers of the cultic and political unity of the people (30:18–21; 31:6), but he was scathing in his judgments on the temple of his day (6:20; 7:21–22), and his views of the kings of his day depended simply on their faithfulness to Yahweh's will, so that he supported Josiah and was contemptuous of Jehoiakim (22:13–19). And his prediction of a king to come whose name would reverse the name of Zedekiah (23:5–6) was only one small facet of his message. But it is clear that he drew on the prophetic traditions of the south (Amos and Isaiah) as freely as he did those of the north.[282]

By the same token Jrm stands ambiguously between the role of peripheral prophet and the role of prophet at the center of power (at least as far as our record indicates). There is no way clearly to discern his status before 609, when, by the conclusion of the present study,

he supported Josiah's program of political and cultic reunion with the north. When Jrm preached the temple sermon in 609, he was peripheral, and yet in contrast to Uriah he had supporters in the Jerusalem establishment who could protect him (26:20–24). His scribe Baruch entered his service in 605; since Baruch had doubtless been schooled at the court, Jrm's use of him again suggests ties with the court. In 601 there were courtiers who tried to persuade the king not to burn Jrm's scroll (36:25), but the fact that the king did burn the scroll suggests that Jrm continued to play a peripheral role. Then in 594, during Zedekiah's conference with the ambassadors from neighboring kingdoms, Jrm had become central enough to be able to walk into the conference seemingly without being challenged and to address the ambassadors and Zedekiah (chap. 27). And by the time of the last siege of Jerusalem the king consulted Jrm as if he was a central prophet, but one gains the impression that by then there was no longer any real center of power: the king was a pathetic, demoralized figure working at cross-purposes with his courtiers (chaps. 37—38). After the fall of Jerusalem the Babylonian officer treated Jrm as a central figure (39:11–12), and after the assassination of Gedaliah Jrm was central to the only center remaining within our purview, Johanan and his band (chap. 42). (Compare further sec. 73.)

For understandable reasons what his community preserved and thus what has come down to us in the Book of Jer is almost entirely restricted to proclamation to the people of Judah; though there are oracles against foreign nations, those oracles are surely proclaimed in the context of an audience of Judahite citizens, and some of the oracles directed at specific kings, like 13:18–19 and 22:13–19, may well have been only formally destined for the kings and actually, again, delivered in the context of the whole community. It is true, we have from time to time instances in which specific individuals or groups came to him for divine guidance—Baruch (chap. 45), Zedekiah (37:3–10, 17; 38:14–23), Johanan and his

study of the experience of prophecy, with bibliography, see Benjamin Uffenheimer, "Prophecy, Ecstasy, and Sympathy," *Congress Volume, Jerusalem, 1986* (VTSup 40; ed. John A. Emerton; Leiden: Brill, 1988) 257–69.

280 See the quotation in n. 1.
281 See the discussion in Mayes, *Deuteronomy*, 103–8.
282 Robert Wilson is therefore too one-sided in his classi-

fication of Jrm as a prophet in the Ephraimite tradition: Wilson, *Prophecy and Society*, 231–51.

group (chap. 42)—or in which Jrm was bidden to deliver a divine word to an individual privately, such as Ebed-melech (39:15–18) and perhaps Pashhur (20:1–6), but we hear of these instances only accidentally in the transmission of the tradition. And again it is only by accident that we have an instance in which Jrm directed Yahweh's word in Jerusalem to an audience composed of foreign ambassadors (27:4–11).

Jrm senses the overwhelming certainty of being called by Yahweh, of having been called from birth, of having a special relationship with Yahweh (1:5), of being prom-ised the protection of Yahweh to overcome any fear he may have of opposition (1:8, 17–19). In the course of one of his confessions he affirms that Yahweh is a "ter-rifying warrior" fighting on his behalf (20:11).

Still the fact that the narrative of his call is a part of his proclamation to his people suggests the importance for him of legitimating his calling by Yahweh: indeed the wording of 1:5–6, in which Jrm objects to his call, suggests not only that Yahweh is responsible but that Jrm's embarking on prophetic proclamation is not his own idea.[283]

Nevertheless he struggles with his relation to Yahweh: the confessions are the vehicle for his prayerful laments to Yahweh. Indeed Jrm is set apart from other prophets of whom we have knowledge in the preservation of his confessions: no other prophetic book offers such a series of laments, which appear to lay bare his struggle with his vocation. (For an extended discussion of this matter see *Jeremiah 1*, "The Confessions of Jeremiah," before the discussion of 11:18—12:6.) These confessions appear to be bound up inextricably with Jrm's struggle with the optimistic prophets: Jrm's faith in the validity of his call to proclaim Yahweh's word sometimes gives way to doubt when the signs of Yahweh's action seem absent, or when the opposing optimistic prophets seem to prosper (see, for example, the language of deception in 4:10 and 20:7, and the impression of defeat he underwent in 28:11). The struggle with false prophets is not unique

(compare Ezekiel 13), but the prophet's giving voice to doubt about which word is operative is unique in the prophetic literature.

The confessions allow us to glimpse Jrm's feelings toward Yahweh, at least in a stylized way. But only rarely are we afforded any hint of Jrm's emotions as a simple human being, apart from his office, when he is threat-ened by pain and death. At one point, when Zedekiah has sent for him, he begs the king not to send him back to the place of detention, "that I might not die there" (37:20). And at a later point, when Zedekiah asks for a fresh word from Yahweh, Jrm says, "If I tell you, you will kill me, will you not? and if I advise you, you will not listen to me" (38:15): Jrm's reaction is—what? suspicious? cross? At least he is reacting understandably in a situation that appears to him insupportable.

The confessions suggest a person with a profound sense of social isolation: he said, "I have sat alone" (15:17). He perceived himself called not to marry and have children and to abstain from funerals and weddings (16:1–9). This isolation, in a culture that took com-munity for granted,[284] must have been an enormous burden.

Jrm mentions his mother several times, indirectly in his call (1:5) and directly in his confessions (15:10; 20:14, 17); such references are unique in the prophets. Since Jrm identified himself with Moses and Samuel (15:1), and since tradition recalls the crucial role of the mothers of both those figures, this identification may have en-couraged Jrm to make reference to his mother. His references to his mother and his abstention from mar-riage might suggest the possibility of an Oedipal fixation, but our data are far too slim even for the most deter-mined devotee of psychohistory. (Compare the dis-cussion of Jrm's use of imagery of women in sec. 70.)

Like all OT prophets, Jrm understood himself called to mediate the דְּבַר־יהוה, not only the "word of Yahweh" but the "action of Yahweh" as well: דָּבָר means both (see Interpretation on 1:1). Jrm therefore not only pro-

283 See Jon L. Berquist, "Prophetic Legitimation in Jeremiah," *VT* 39 (1989) [forthcoming].

284 See H. Wheeler Robinson, *Corporate Personality in Ancient Israel* (originally "The Hebrew Conception of Corporate Personality," *Werden und Wesen des Alten Testaments: Vorträge gehalten auf der Internationalen Tagung Alttestamentlicher Forscher zu Göttingen von 4.– 10. September 1935*, [ed. Paul Volz, Friedrich Stum-mer, and Johannes Hempel; BZAW 66; Berlin: Töpelmann, 1936, 49–62; rep. and expanded: Facet Books, Biblical Series 11; Philadelphia: Fortress, 1964; see there esp. 28–29]).

claimed through his own voice and through a written scroll Yahweh's words of appeal and judgment and hope, but he communicated Yahweh's will through symbolic actions as well, actions like the burying of the linen loincloth (13:1–12aα) and the breaking of the flask (19:1–15), prolonged signs like the wearing of the thongs and yoke-pegs (27:2; 28:10), abstentions like the abstention from marriage and from attending funerals and weddings (16:1–9). (One may compare the symbolic actions of other prophets: Hosea's marriage to a prostitute, Hos 1:2–3; Isaiah's going naked and barefoot for three years, Isa 20:3; Ezekiel's abstention from funeral rites for his wife, Ezek 24:15–18. See further the excursus "The Theology of Symbolic Actions" in Interpretation of 13:1–12aα.) In this way the prophet becomes himself a sign of Yahweh's revelation.

Jrm expresses in a couple of passages the understanding that Yahweh's word proclaimed by Jrm itself has destructive power: in 5:14b Yahweh tells Jrm, "I am going to make my words in your mouth into fire, and this people into sticks, and it will eat them" (compare 6:10–11); and in 23:29, "Scorching is my word like fire, and like a sledgehammer which smashes a rock!"

The question is often posed in our own day how the prophet received the divine word, by what channel or in what psychological state the prophet gained the revelation. For Jrm (as for the other prophets) there are almost no data to answer the question. He, like others, uses the conventional expression וַיְהִי דְבַר־יהוה אֵלַי "The word of Yahweh came [more literally, happened] to me" (1:4 and often; compare Ezek 3:16; Zech 7:4), but such wording does not tell us what we want to know. Dreams were doubtless the medium for many prophets, but the word from Jrm is that those who dream dreams are not in the same category as those who have Yahweh's word (23:28). Jrm states that true prophets "stand in Yahweh's council" (23:22), and Yahweh promises Jrm, "in my presence you will stand" (15:19); Jrm affirms that he is who he is because of "Yahweh's hand" (15:17). But what sort of experience these phrases imply, or indeed whether they are not simply idiomatic ways of referring to the reception of Yahweh's revelation, there is no way to determine. Jrm never speaks of "seeing" (ראה) Yahweh as

Isaiah does (Isa 6:1), nor of "hearing" (שמע) a decree of destruction from Yahweh (Isa 28:22). The coming of Yahweh's word, like a poem coming into shape in the mind of a poet, or a piece of music in the mind of a composer, doubtless originates in the creative insight of the prophet in the context of the expectations of his culture, but this is of course to explain nothing. And it must be stressed that in contrast to all theories of creativity and insight that center in the self, the process of receiving Yahweh's word was perceived by the prophet to be at the initiative of Yahweh, rather than originating with the prophet. Thus it was a process that could not be forced: we learn almost by accident that when Jrm sought a word from Yahweh in response to the request of Johanan and his officers, it took ten days to receive an answer (42:7). By the same token, when the word of Yahweh is upon him, Jrm cannot abstain from speaking but feels compelled to speak out (6:11; 20:9).

This perception of the "otherness" of the voice of Yahweh in contrast to his own voice is expressed not only in the confessions but even in the proclamation of scenarios of judgment to the people, where Yahweh and Jrm take different roles. Thus Yahweh announces the coming of the foe from the north, while Jrm appeals to the people to change their ways before it is too late (4:13a, 14). Indeed on at least one occasion, if I have identified the speakers correctly, Jrm substitutes a more tender metaphor for Yahweh's harsh one (4:30, 31).

Since the eighth-century prophets on which Jrm drew, Amos and Hosea, Isaiah and Micah in their various ways, spoke again and again of social injustice and Yahweh's concern for justice, it is striking that Jrm spoke little of it.[285] Why the paucity of texts? Did Jrm assume that the words of the eighth-century prophets were available to his people, and he did not need to repeat them? Did he have so little expectation, from the time of his temple sermon until the king burned his scroll, of the people's ability or willingness to repent that the words of divine accusation did not include the details of the people's injustices?[286] (See further sec. 71.)

If the prophet is to proclaim Yahweh's word and action, he is also to intercede with Yahweh on behalf of the people. Only occasionally is this task alluded to in the

---

285 For a recent study of the texts of Jer dealing with social justice see Wisser.

286 Compare Weippert, *Prosareden*, 61–62.

prophets (see, for example, Amos 7:2–3, 5–6). In Jrm's case one hears of his call to intercede mostly by the negative, when Yahweh forbids him to intercede, evidently when Jrm is convinced Yahweh is determined to punish the people (7:16–20; 14:11–12; 15:1). But still the king could expect Jrm to pray for the people (37:3), and Johanan asks him to pray for the little group he is leading (42:2).

70. Jeremiah's Use of Language

There are limitations on our ability to assess Jrm's use of language: we have no native speakers with whom to check our impressions; the texts we have are limited, and in any event they have been preserved for us by copyists who may not always have understood them fully. But we may at any rate set down some impressions.

I shall first make some observations on grammar. There has been an attempt in recent years to examine the poetry of the OT in the light of grammatical features brought to light in the Ugaritic material.[287] Bright suggests more than once the possibility of explaining an expression by assuming an enclitic mem,[288] but I see no reason in any passage to resort to this explanation.[289] Nor do I explain 4:27 or 9:2 by the assumption of an emphatic lamed.

On the other hand the paralleling of suffixed verbs (perfect) and prefixed verbs (imperfect) in Ugaritic for rhetorical effect[290] is found also in Jrm: indeed in one tricolon the paralleling of perfect and imperfect is completed by a participle (5:6).

By the same token there are many instances of double-duty particles:[291] double-duty prepositions (for example, 2:22, 24; 3:23; 5:14), suffixes (22:18, perhaps 30:21), the double-duty negative לֹא (5:2; 15:13), a double-duty interrogative (30:15), the double-duty conjunction כִּי (4:20).[292]

Occasional dative suffixes have been acknowledged by the grammarians: GKC acknowledges a dative suffix in 31:3,[293] but there are more than the grammarians have

noted,[294] including 9:1; 10:20; and ambiguous contexts may yield a few more (5:22; 8:13; 51:34).

The use of the infinitive absolute is not always easy to determine; two or three usages in Jer need discussion. When an infinitive absolute reinforces the corresponding finite verb it often expresses the contradiction of a denial: thus in 6:9 the expression means not "glean thoroughly" (*RSV*) but "do glean (in spite of a previous prohibition in the law)"; other examples of the device are 4:10; 13:12; 22:10. An infinitive absolute unattached to a corresponding finite verb often suggests a distance of the action from the speaker; I have translated it by "to think that . . ." in the present study (3:1; 4:18; 8:15). Twice Jrm seems to use the infinitive absolute of one verb with the finite form of a second verb resembling the first in assonance: in 8:13 one has אָסֹף אֲסִיפֵם, evidently the infinitive absolute of אסף qal with the imperfect of סוף hip'il (compare Zeph 1:2), and in 42:10 one has שׁוֹב תֵּשְׁבוּ, the infinitive absolute of שׁוב with the imperfect of ישׁב. GKC, sec. 113w, note 3, discusses 8:13 and Zeph 1:2 (and, in addition, Isa 28:28, where the same phenomenon seems to occur) and rejects the possibility; but (even though copyists' errors are always possible) one should not exclude the possibility of a witty near-miss on expected diction.

In addition it may be mentioned that, by the analysis offered here, the conjunction אָכֵן cannot be asseverative but is always contrastive (see the extended discussion in the Interpretation of 3:23 and compare 4:10).

Several uses of the conjunction כִּי merit attention. (1) It sometimes introduces a quotation or marks a shift of speaker (4:8, 15, 22, 31; 8:22). (2) In a lament before a verb like "we are ruined" it seems best translated by "Oh!" (4:13). (3) Before a verb like "we have sinned" it seems best translated by "how" (3:25; 8:14; 14:7, 20). (4) Before an adjective it seems best translated by "how" (2:19; 4:18; 6:26).

There are several points at which one may suspect that Jrm moved out beyond being an unreflective user of

---

287 For an attempt to reconceive the poetry of Jrm in this manner see Robert Althann, *A Philological Analysis of Jeremiah 4—6 in the Light of Northwest Semitic* (BibOr 38; Rome: Pontifical Biblical Institute, 1983).

288 See Bright on 3:23 and 4:16.

289 For a discussion of several passages see the index under "enclitic mem."

290 See Dahood, *Psalms III*, 420–23.

291 See ibid., 435–39.

292 For a complete listing of the device see the index under "double-duty particle."

293 GKC, sec. 117x.

294 Compare Dahood, *Psalms III*, 377–78.

Hebrew. He evidently could use Aramaic. Thus I have proposed that 10:11, a verse in Aramaic, is the center-piece of 10:1–16, employing a pun that works only in Aramaic (עבד and אבד) and offering ambiguity until the last word; if, then, 10:1–16 is authentic to Jrm, it is a witty bit of mockery in that tongue. Again the expression *māgôr missābîb* "terror all around" is evidently a reshaping of the name Pashhur (*pašḥûr*) heard as the Aramaic *pāš sĕḥôr* "fruitful around" (20:3). But I suggest there is more: that the new name means not simply "terror all around" but "*māgôr* from every point of view," that is, that the word of judgment to Pashhur explicates the three possible meanings of *māgôr* (20:4–6).

Allied with this awareness of language is the phenomenon that is now called "Janus parallelism." I have located three possible examples in Jer, although unfortunately none of them is beyond question. In 17:1 the reconstructed word תֻּכָּם means both "their midst" and "their oppression"; in 31:2 the revocalized word חֹרֶב may mean both "Horeb" and "sword-wielder"; and in 49:30 נְדוּ may mean both "wander" and "bemoan"—in each passage the two meanings parallel words elsewhere in the vicinity. And beyond Janus parallelism are other instances when an expression trembles between two homonyms, either one possible in the context. Thus in 14:8 Yahweh is called מִקְוֵה יִשְׂרָאֵל, either "hope of Israel" or "pool of Israel." And again in 15:5 לִשְׁאֹל can be understood either as "to ask" or "to Sheol": both fit the context.

These examples move one to ponder the range of ambiguities with which Jrm's poetry is studded, ambiguities that devolve around single lexemes open to multiple meanings. There are about a hundred citations in the index of this study under the entry "ambiguity"; several of these are multiple entries to the same ambiguity, doubtless some of the suggested ambiguities are false leads, but doubtless also some inherent ambiguities in the present text have passed unnoticed. Sometimes the ambiguities are elaborate: thus the (seemingly) impenetrable last colon of 8:13, "And I have given them (what) they pass over for them," can be resolved in four different ways: (1) "And I have given to them that [the commandments] which they [Israel] have been passing over

[= transgressing] for themselves"; (2) "And I have given to them that [the land, its fruits] which will pass over [in ownership] to them [the enemy]"; (3) "And I have given to them those [the enemy] who shall pass over [= overrun] them [Israel]"; (4) "And I have given to them that [the land, its fruits] which will pass away [= disappear] for themselves [= in their regard]": all of these interpretations are implicit in the formulation. Indeed the verb עבר, the second verb in this colon, is open to ambiguity elsewhere: in 5:22 the sand is "a limit forever, and it shall not pass away for it"; one can construe the second clause to mean both that the limit shall not pass away (that is, it is permanent) and that the sand is a limit that the sea shall not pass over (that is, cross) (a similar ambiguity with this verb occurs in Ps 148:6).

In 10:17 Jerusalem is addressed as a woman, "Gather up from the land your bundle, (you who are) dwelling under siege." But the participle יֹשֶׁבֶת not only means "dwelling" but also "sitting." She may be "dwelling" under siege, but she is also "sitting" on the ground, ready to pick up a refugee's bundle. But she is also "enthroned," another implication of "sitting": enthroned both on Zion above the surrounding valleys (compare 21:13), and enthroned in a way that suggests self-divinization, since Yahweh is the one who is properly "enthroned" in the heavens, or on the cherubim. The address thus manages to run the gamut from abasement to self-exaltation with a single participle. And there are other possibilities in the other words of the address: אסף "gather up" may also imply "get rid of," and the word translated "bundle" sounds like a pun on "peddling" and "Canaan," as if "get rid of your life style of profit" is one of the implications of the passage; and "from the land" could well imply "from Sheol," as if the life style of peddling leads only to the tomb. All of this suggests the excitement of words vibrating in a variety of directions and with a variety of implications.

A consideration of ambiguity leads to a consideration of irony,[295] the spirit of humor, mockery, incongruity which appears everywhere in Jrm's words:[296] there are over 135 references in the index of this volume to irony and sarcasm. It is ironic that the covenant people have abandoned their only real source of water, namely

---

295 For a general consideration of irony in the OT, without reference to Jrm, see Edwin M. Good, *Irony in the Old Testament* (London: SPCK, 1965).

296 For an unsystematic treatment of Jrm's use of irony see Holladay, "Style."

Yahweh, and then, because they must have water, they go after false sources of fertility, namely the Baals, digging cisterns that do not produce water but can only hold water: but in this case the cisterns leak (2:13). The Baals thus are not positive sources of fertility; they are negative, drawing off fertility. It is ironic that that Jrm, having been "consecrated" to Yahweh in his call (1:5), should be treated like a lamb "consecrated" for sacrifice, that is, destined for death (12:3). It is ironic that Jrm could imagine the people in the midst of the drought asking Yahweh, the God of creation and covenant, why he seems like a helpless stranger traveling through the land, looking for a place to spend the night (14:8–9), when all the time Jrm is convinced that the drought is evidence of the judgment of Yahweh upon an erring people (14:12).

Jrm produces irony by citation: he portrays the people as quoting a proverb to exculpate themselves from responsibility for their actions, as quoting a psalm to direct Yahweh's wrath upon the enemy (10:23–25).

He produces irony also by incongruous collocation. Jrm in the height of emotion describes his panic as he envisages the coming invasion by the foe from the north, in a speech that begins "My bowels, my bowels!" (מֵעַי מֵעַי, 4:19); Yahweh replies quietly, unemotionally, laying out in six synonymous cola the stupidity of the people, in a speech beginning with "my people" (עַמִּי, 4:22), thus reversing the first two consonants of "my bowels." Indeed the sudden shifts of speaker in the material on the foe from the north in 4:5—10:25 are masterstrokes of rhetoric: for example, the sudden voice of the enemy in 6:4–5 is altogether unexpected (for a discussion of shifts of speaker see Preliminary Observations on 4:5—10:25, *Identification of Speakers*).

Jrm likewise parodies existing forms: priestly torah (7:21–22), perhaps the women's mourning of the dead Baal (9:20–21), the liturgy for the drought (14:1—15:9).[297]

There are many instances of word-play and assonance in the poetry and prose of Jrm, but since this is a feature of other prophetic material as well,[298] there is no need to stress it unduly. The word-play on "my bowels" and "my people" has already been cited. In 3:14 and 22 we have *šûbû bānîm šôbābîm* "(re)turn, turnable children," an expression that not only offers two forms of the root שוב, thus with the repeated *š* + *b*, but with the repeated *bā* and the repeated *îm*, and with a succession of seven long vowels without short vowels. Assonance and word-play are the very texture of poetry, and Jrm's use of them is striking.[299]

I deal with more hesitation with what might be called the lyricism of Jrm's poetry. Our cultural distance from him and from his age, from his language and the conventions of his speech, is so great that one can make only very tentative esthetic judgments. But a few observations may be made that contribute to at least the impression of lyricism.

In the matter of the metaphor of the covenant people as the wife of Yahweh Jrm stands in contrast to both Hosea before him and Ezekiel after him, with whom the metaphor is shared. In Hosea 2 there is one tender passage, it is true (vv 16–18), but the major portion of the chapter is shaped by ugly, judgmental language describing harlotry (vv 3–15). Ezekiel employs the metaphor twice (chaps. 16 and 23) in extended passages that are again ugly and judgmental, with only passing tenderness (Ezek 16:4–14). By contrast Jrm uses the imagery of a bride (2:2–3, 32); when harlotry is mentioned, the judgmental language is either passed over quickly (2:20b; 3:3, 13, 20; 13:26–27) or heard as Yahweh's words in contrast to Jrm's words (4:30, 31). Indeed Jrm speaks tenderly of women in general: he describes with pathos the pangs of a woman giving birth to her first child (4:31), he mentions pregnant women and women in birthpangs among those coming home to Zion (31:8), he portrays more than once the mourning of mothers for their lost children (10:20; 31:15; compare 14:8–9), he uses "virgin Israel," "daughter Zion [here:

---

297 For a complete listing see the index in this volume under "parody."

298 For a full analysis of these features in Isaiah 1—35 see Luis Alonso Schökel, *Estudios de Poética Hebrea* (Barcelona: Flors, 1963).

299 For full citations see the index in this volume under "assonance, word-play."

fair Zion]" and the like repeatedly to refer to the people and proposes that Yahweh can bring a new power to virgin Israel (31:21–22). (Compare the remarks on his references to his own mother, sec. 69.) Even in irony he has an eye for women, portraying the funeral women practicing their songs (9:16–21). Yahweh is portrayed as relating to his people as a father to children, using words of affection in speaking of his people (3:19; 31:20). The vocabulary of weeping occurs often, both of the people (22:10; 31:9, 16) and of Jrm (8:18–23; 13:17; 14:17), and perhaps even of Yahweh himself (3:21; 9:9). Then Jrm has a keen eye for animals: for war horses (5:8; 8:6), migratory birds (8:7), birds of prey and hyenas (12:9), the young camel (2:23), the doe in the underbrush (14:5), the wild ass (2:24; 14:6), the lion in the thicket (4:7; 5:6), the wolf and the leopard (5:6). Jrm's evocative language is evident even in his descriptions of desolation (4:23–26; 13:16; 18:15–16).

71. The Content of Jeremiah's Proclamation

Central to Jrm's proclamation is the covenant established by Yahweh with Israel. It is true, the word "covenant" (בְּרִית) appears only intermittently in the words of Jrm: it refers to the covenant at Sinai in 11:2, 3, 6, 8, 10; 14:21; 22:9; 50:5; and it is used both for the old covenant and the new in 31:31, 32, 33. The occurrences in both 11:1–17 and 31:31–34 appear to be deliberately modeled on Deut 5:2–3, where the word also occurs. (The term is also used in 34:8, 10, 13, 15, and 18 to refer to the specific covenant made before the final fall of Jerusalem to release slaves.) And the paucity of occurrences of the word "covenant" is a characteristic Jrm shares with other preexilic prophets.[300]

But the covenantal relation is the constant basis of Yahweh's words to Israel (as again it is in the other preexilic prophets). A whole array of expressions presuppose the covenant: metaphors and idioms whose semantic fields reach out in various directions. Israel is the wife of Yahweh, faithful in the early days, unfaithful now (2:2–3, 5; 3:1), and that unfaithfulness is described as harlotry (2:20; 3:2–3, 13; 4:30) or betrayal (3:20; 5:11). Israel "walked after" Yahweh in the early days (2:2), an expression suggesting not only marriage but religious

devotion; now Israel "walks after" the Baals (2:23), and the same expression is used with synonyms for Baal, "a nothing" (2:5) or "profitless things" (2:8). Again Yahweh is portrayed as a father to Israel (3:14, 19, 22; 31:20). Yahweh "has loved" (אהב) Israel "with an everlasting love" (31:3); Israel "loved" Yahweh in the beginning (2:2). Israel is קֹדֶשׁ to Yahweh (2:3): not so much "holy" (RSV) as Yahweh's own possession, at his disposal. And other metaphors are used: Yahweh is the spring of running water, always available to sustain Israel (2:13), and again he is the potter "shaping" Israel (18:1–12); Israel is a refractory farm animal that refuses to work (2:20a), or a vine planted by Yahweh that has gone bad (2:21).

It is striking that Jrm never says that Yahweh "knows" Israel, as Amos and Hosea do (Amos 3:2; Hos 5:3), for this is a word that carries not only sexual but covenantal implications.

Jrm rarely offers an adjective to describe Yahweh, but in 3:12 he is חָסִיד—"faithful, dependable," doubtless also "compassionate" (NJV).

Occasionally the covenant stipulations allow one to glimpse Jrm's perception of Yahweh's obligations to Israel in the covenant: if the people obey the covenant stipulations, then Yahweh will "dwell" with them, and indeed will allow them to dwell in the land (7:3, 7). But these verbs assume a whole texture of assumptions, of Yahweh as creator of the people, and sustainer, as guarantor of their safety and health and prosperity, as guide in right living and judge in wrong living, assumptions that must be discerned from the metaphors that have already been mentioned.

On the other hand Israel's obligation to Yahweh is clear. Israel is to continue to act with Yahweh as she acted at the beginning—to be loyal and loving to him, to "walk after him" (2:2), stay "in his presence" (4:1), "know him" (9:2), "fear him" (5:22, 24), and "obey his voice" (7:23). This obligation is often spelled out, though not systematically. Thus when Israel swears "by the life of Yahweh," it is to be with sincerity (4:2). Israel's circumcision must be more than skin deep (4:3). Israel must keep torah (5:4–5; 8:7)—the Decalogue is basic (7:9); but beyond these dos and don'ts the life of the community

---

300 See the discussion in Lindblom, *Prophecy*, 329–30.

must be based on truth-telling (9:4) and justice (5:28; 22:13), mutuality (9:3), and concern for the poor and the orphan (5:27–28).

Beyond the covenant with Israel Jrm proclaims Yahweh to be the creator and sustainer of the earth, of human beings in general and of animals and birds (4:24–25; 5:22; 9:9; 27:6), who brings the rain (14:22). He stands most emphatically against the Baals and the idols of the nations, who are affirmed as being made by human beings (16:20; compare 2:13), as unable to bring rain (2:13; 14:22), as nothings (2:5; 16:19), as things that do not profit (2:8, 11; 16:19), as a lie (16:19; compare 5:31; 13:25; 23:14). (It is to be noted that the contrast between the idols and Yahweh is portrayed extensively in 10:1–16, if that passage is authentic to Jrm.)

However, the references to Yahweh's work of creation are usually set as a backdrop to proclamation about the covenant with Israel. As for Yahweh's governance of human beings outside of Israel, the latter usually appear as specific nations of the world in the context of Yahweh's will for the covenant people: thus Yahweh decrees that Babylon will come to punish Judah, that Egypt is useless as a resource against Babylon, that the various small nations of the Levant will likewise come into the hand of Babylon, and that Babylon ultimately will go down to defeat as well.

One is thus turned back to a consideration of the covenant with Israel, and again that covenant is almost always presented in the context of historical events: it is the succession of those events in history, and the discernment of Israel's decisions in most of those events, that the covenant is proclaimed.

Yahweh had made a promise to Abraham and Jacob (by implication in the pun of 20:1–3, explicitly in 11:5). To fulfill that promise, he made a covenant with Israel when he brought her out of Egypt (11:3–4; 31:32).

Jrm is not consistent about when Israel broke the covenant. In an early word he affirms that Israel was faithful during the time in the wilderness (2:2–3), but in a later, darker word he states that Moses' generation broke the covenant (7:24–26; compare Ezek 20:13). In any event, their breaking it was in the context of Israel's coming into Canaan (2:5–7). "Israel" was of course a single nation until the death of Solomon, when it split into two kingdoms. The northern kingdom, with its capital at Samaria, had disappeared from history a century before Jrm's time, but Jrm could still refer to the inhabitants of the northern kingdom as "brothers" (7:15). The covenant people have broken the covenant, but in particular its religious leaders have not fulfilled their responsibilities (2:8; 5:31; 6:13; 10:21; 14:18), nor have the people paid any attention to the prophets whom Yahweh has sent to warn the nation (6:17; 7:25). The prophets of both Samaria and Jerusalem have been unfaithful, but those of Jerusalem have been worse (23:13–14). Yahweh had sent Ephraim into exile as punishment (7:15), though Jrm held out a hope in his early days that they could come back from exile (3:12), repent and be restored (31:18–20). That hope Jrm saw as mediated by Josiah, who was a righteous king (22:15): north and south would then be reunited politically and cultically (3:14; 30:18–21; 31:4–6).

During the kingship of Jehoiakim there are signs on every hand of unfaithfulness to the covenant: the worship of Baal (2:23–25), misuse of sacrifice (6:20), the seeking of support from Egypt or Mesopotamia (2:18), exploitation of the helpless (5:27–28), indeed the neglect of torah (7:9). In fact, the present generation is more unfaithful than the generation of Moses' time (7:26). False prophets abound, who claim to have been sent by Yahweh (27:16; 28:2), who claim their dreams are valid (23:25): Jrm at first seems to conclude that Yahweh has sent them to deceive his people (so, evidently, 4:10) but finally that Yahweh has not sent them at all (14:14; 23:16, 21; 28:15). And if there are false prophets among the covenant people, the various seers in pagan nations are all the more false (27:9–10).

By contrast Jrm obviously proclaims himself as a prophet sent by Yahweh (1:4–5), though there were points at which the prophet gave way to doubt about Yahweh's intention in calling him (20:7, 14–15).

Yahweh appeals to the people to repent (4:1–2, 14; 6:8; 7:3, 5); but unfaithfulness to the covenant is characteristic of everyone in the nation, both low and high (5:1–5). Why is it so easy to turn from Yahweh and so hard to turn back (8:4–5)?

Jrm perceives Yahweh not only to level accusations against the people for breaking the covenant, but to warn her of the consequences if she does not repent. In the early years those warnings are general depictions of humiliation (2:36–37), but after the battle of Carchemish (605), when Babylon gained the upper hand over Egypt, Jrm perceived the threat of Babylon to be the prime means through which Yahweh was warning his people (4:5–8, 13–18; 5:15–17; 6:1–8, 22–26). Indeed it would appear that the hope for repentance began to fade in Jrm's mind; more and more he became convinced that Yahweh would punish his people (5:9, 29; 9:8). This conviction grew stronger as the great drought increased its grip over the land (8:6, 13); drought and battle became Yahweh's twin scourges (14:1—15:9).

When Jehoiakim burned Jrm's scroll, Jrm became convinced that Yahweh's warnings had been in vain, that there could be no repentance, and that the punishment of the people was irrevocably decreed (4:28; 36:31). If the people had broken the covenant with Yahweh (11:10; 31:32), then Yahweh has no choice but to break the covenant with them (compare 14:21). Yahweh might weep over the destruction of his people (9:9–10), but he is determined on his course.

Within a few years (598/597) the city of Jerusalem was besieged by Babylon (10:17). Yet the city survived, and kingship survived, and Zedekiah's subjects doubtless felt relieved. But Jrm was convinced that the future of the covenant people lay with the exiles (24:1–10; 29:1–23), who must submit to the power of Babylon for a long time (29:28), indeed that all nations must submit to the power of Babylon (27:6).

Babylon besieged Jerusalem once more (588), and Jrm continued to proclaim Yahweh's will in the fall of the city (32:24; 37:10; 40:3 as restored). Yet paradoxically, in the midst of the collapse of the city, Jrm was moved to proclaim hope beyond the fall of Jerusalem: its houses will be rebuilt (33:7) and fields bought once more (32:15). Astonishingly, Israel in exile will be the means for the downfall of Babylon (chaps. 50—51), they will return from exile (31:8–9; 50:5) to be restored to vigor (31:22), and Yahweh will make a fresh covenant with the people, a renewal of the intimacy of Yahweh with his people without any further occasion for unfaithfulness toward him (31:31–34). Indeed ultimately all nations will acknowledge the sovereignty of Yahweh (16:19–21).

Thus at every point and with every nation Yahweh's will is sovereign: he can suddenly change his mind, and his plans take everyone by surprise (18:6–10; 31:22, 31–34; 32:27).

D. The Impact of Jeremiah on His Own and Later Generations

72. Preliminary Remarks

Jrm's proclamation was crucial in the development of a theology adequate to the disaster that his people were undergoing.[301] But the data for assessing in detail Jrm's impact on his own and later generations are of course far less than we could wish.

His impact on his own generation we can guess from the material in the Book of Jer itself, especially the narratives.

We can discern his impact in the next century best through the use by others of his distinctive emphases or phrases. As one might expect, the various bodies of material pick up different emphases of Jrm. Thus among other motifs Ezekiel picked up Jrm's image of "eating" the word of Yahweh (Ezek 2:8—3:3; see Jer 15:16); Deutero-Isaiah and the poet of the Book of Job picked up themes from Jrm's confessions. It is also to be noted that various sixth-century writings employ Jrm's material in contrasting ways. Thus the exilic Deuteronomists take over distinctive phrases; the poet of the Book of Job takes over not phrases but the motif of the innocent man struggling with disasters sent by God; and at several points Deutero- and Trito-Isaiah create a kind of poetic midrash of specific turns of phrase in Jrm.

By the end of the sixth century, at least in prophetic circles, Jrm was evidently considered a true prophet: this is the impression one gains from Zech 1:4, which cites an appeal to repentance close to 25:5. Later OT literature continues to draw on Jrm's phrases, sometimes in distinctive ways: thus in Jonah 3:8–9 the king of Nineveh uses phrases for repentance reminiscent of Jrm's. The first personal references to Jrm appear during the period when Jer was gaining canonicity (2 Chr 35:25; 36:21, 22); one may doubt that these references contain any valid historical memory—they appear to be legends. So with 1 Esdr 1:26, so with the superscription of Lamentations in G, and so with the Epistle of Jeremiah. Sir 49:6–7

---

301 For a theological survey see conveniently Peter R. Ackroyd, *Exile and Restoration, A Study of Hebrew Thought of the Sixth Century* B.C. (Philadelphia: Westminster, 1968) 50–61.

mentions him among the canonical prophets, and both the Qumran literature and the NT make reference to him and draw on his phrases.

The evidence for Jrm's impact on the later redaction of Deuteronomy and on later Psalms has already been discussed (see secs. 60, 65–66). Other bodies of material will be examined below for parallel phrases. (It must be noted, however, that the survey of later imitations of Jrm's diction is by no means complete: such a task would be far beyond the reach of the present study.)

73. Jeremiah's Impact on His Own Generation

It is not easy to assess Jrm's impact on his own generation: this is not a question to which either the data of the Book of Jer or contemporary witnesses give full information (compare sec. 69). The first full glimpse we have of Jrm is as a peripheral prophet from Anathoth proclaiming Yahweh's word in the temple area in 609 (26:1–4, 6). It was a word that inspired immediate opposition from the religious authorities and the general citizenry and the threat of death (26:7–19); nevertheless he had a sponsor at court, Ahikam, who saw to it that he was not executed (26:24). One cannot say, of course, why Ahikam protected him—whether he was a family friend or whether it was the impact of his preaching that led to Ahikam's help.

Jrm continued to be controversial for the rest of his career: the last glimpse we have of him is his controversy with the Jews who were resident in Egypt (chap. 44).

In 605 Jrm availed himself of Baruch, a scribe who again must have had friends at court, since his training had doubtless been in that circle. Baruch's relationship with Jrm was more than a professional one, since in that same year Baruch asked for guidance from Yahweh for his own distress (45:1–5). And Baruch stayed with him: we hear of Baruch when Jrm's scroll came to the attention of the king, evidently in 601 (36:10–32), again when Jrm bought the field at Anathoth, probably in 588 (32:12–15), and when Jrm was a part of the group of refugees going to Egypt, probably late in 587 or early in 586 (43:3, 6).

When the king heard the scroll being read in 601, he had the scroll burned and ordered Jrm and Baruch arrested, and yet there were courtiers that advised against its destruction (36:23–25), so again Jrm was the object of both opposition and support; but it was the opposition of his persecutors that called forth his bitter prayers to Yahweh (11:18–20; 15:10, 15; 20:10–12).

The evidence adduced in sec. 74 suggests that in 601/600 Ezekiel, as a young priest in Jerusalem, was struck by Jrm's preaching and may have known him personally.

In 594 Jrm was able to walk into Zedekiah's conference with the ambassadors of the other Levantine states and speak out as if he had some authority (chap. 27), and in that same year he could arrange to send a letter to the exiles in Babylon (29:1–23) and a symbolic document to be sunk in the Euphrates (51:59–64); but in consequence he was the subject of a hostile letter from a prophet in Babylon to the temple police in Jerusalem (29:24–32).

Chapters 37—44 offer a particularly clear picture of both the opposition and the support that Jrm drew from those around him in high and low places. Zedekiah consulted him on several occasions before the final fall of the city in 587 in the context of his imprisonment by pro-Egyptian courtiers, and the slave Ebed-melech was able at one point to persuade the king to release Jrm (chaps. 37—38). Jrm was known enough in Jerusalem after the fall of the city in 587 that the Babylonian officer was told to protect him (39:11), and he was important enough to be taken to Egypt along with the group under the officer Johanan (chaps. 42—43), where, as already noted, he continued to appeal to the Jews residing in Egypt for fidelity to Yahweh's will (chap. 44). Baruch's preservation of the words and actions of Jrm in the document or documents that became the Book of Jer, and the preservation and copying of that material after Baruch's death, is evidence that there were circles who looked to the material as valid revelation from Yahweh.

74. Jeremiah's Impact on Ezekiel

There have been scattered efforts to assess Ezekiel's borrowing from Jrm's phrases. An early list that is still useful is that of Rudolph Smend.[302] John W. Miller's study[303] is of limited usefulness from the point of view of the present study because he believes that only the prose

---

302 Rudolf Smend, *Der Prophet Ezechiel* (Leipzig: Hirzel, 1880) xxiv–xxv.

303 John W. Miller, *Das Verhältnis Jeremias und Hesekiels sprachlich und theologisch untersucht* (Assen: Van Gorcum, 1955).

of Jer was part of Jrm's scroll, and that such prose passages as 3:6–11 were part of that scroll.

I would offer the following instances in which Ezekiel was dependent on Jrm.

It is clear that the imagery of Ezek 2:8—3:3, the scroll that Ezekiel was given to eat, is a development of Jer 1:9 and 15:16. I have suggested that "your words were found" in 15:16 is a reference to the scroll of Deuteronomy found in the temple: if Ezekiel took it so, then this verse may have been the specific stimulus for the vision of the scroll; and the verse in Jer continues, "And I ate them"—so in his vision Ezekiel tastes the scroll.

Again the "iron griddle" that Ezekiel is to set against his clay city-plan of Jerusalem (Ezek 4:3) is a visual manifestation of what had been metaphorical for Jrm, that Yahweh had made Jrm into "a fortified city, an iron bolt and a bronze wall" (Jer 1:18).

Ezek 6:13, "upon every high hill . . . and under every green tree," is an adaptation of the phraseology of Hos 4:13, Deut 12:2, and Jer 2:20.[304]

The form of Ezek 7:26a, "Ruin upon ruin comes," may be derived from Jer 4:20, "'Crash upon crash!' is shouted"; and certainly the expression in Ezek 7:26b, "The law fails from the priest, and counsel from the elders," is derived from Jer 18:18, "The law will not fail from the priest, nor counsel from the wise man, nor the word from the prophet."

In Ezek 11:15 the inhabitants of Jerusalem say of the exiles, "They have gone far from Yahweh" (vocalizing with most רָחֲקוּ מֵעַל יהוה): it is an ambiguous statement, implying both "far from Yahweh's ways" and "far from Canaan," and is surely derived from Jer 2:5, "They went far from me [= Yahweh]," which carries only the former implication.

The statement in Ezek 11:19, "I will give them one heart [probably: a new heart; see the commentaries], and put a new spirit within them [corrected text בְּקִרְבָּם: see the commentaries], and remove the heart of stone out of their flesh and give them a heart of flesh," presupposes

Jer 31:33, "Then I shall put my law within them [בְּקִרְבָּם], and on their heart shall write it."

In Ezek 12:3 the prophet hears the command, "Prepare for yourself baggage for exile" (עֲשֵׂה לְךָ כְּלֵי גוֹלָה): this is evidently an adaptation of Jer 46:19, where the command is given to Egypt, "Baggage for exile prepare for yourself" (כְּלֵי גוֹלָה עֲשִׂי לָךְ).

The text in Ezek 12:10 is difficult: as it stands, it reads, "The prince is this burden [or oracle]" (הַנָּשִׂיא הַמַּשָּׂא הַזֶּה). Several commentators favor the view that there is a connection between this expression and Jer 23:33,[305] and that is surely correct: whatever the original text of the verse, מַשָּׂא is not used in the sense of "oracle" anywhere else in Ezekiel. Jrm says, "You [plural] are the burden," while Ezekiel says, "The prince is the burden" —doubtless Zedekiah, and using נָשִׂיא for the word-play on מַשָּׂא.

Ezek 13:1–16, a passage on the false prophets, is clearly based on Jer 23:16–32, and, beyond that passage, Ezek 13:10 and 16 are based on Jer 6:14 ("'Peace, peace,' when there is no peace"). The parallels with Jer 23:16–32 are as follows: the false prophets prophesy "out of their own minds [מִלִּבָּם]," Ezek 13:2, compare Jer 23:16 (and 14:14, 15; 28:15); Yahweh did not send the false prophets, Ezek 13:6, compare Jer 23:21, 32; "who say, 'oracle of Yahweh,'" Ezek 13:6, 7, compare Jer 23:31; "I am against you [the false prophets]," Ezek 13:8, compare Jer 23:32. The passage in Ezekiel continues with 13:17–23, against female prophets; in Ezek 13:22 the phrase לְבִלְתִּי־שׁוּב מִדַּרְכּוֹ הָרָע, "(with the result) that he does not turn from his wicked way," an expression derived from Jer 23:14, לְבִלְתִּי־שָׁבוּ אִישׁ מֵרָעָתוֹ (reading the infinitive שׁוּב with G), "so that no one turns from his evil" (these are the only two instances of שׁוּב + לְבִלְתִּי qal in the OT).

In Ezek 14:21 Yahweh says, "I have sent my four evil judgments, sword, famine, wild beasts and pestilence"; this is likely to be dependent on Jer 15:3, where there are again four kinds of destroyers, though with differences:

---

304 Holladay, "On Every High Hill," 175.
305 Smend, *Der Prophet Ezechiel*, xxv; Volkmar Herntrich, *Ezekielprobleme* (BZAW 61; Giessen, Töpelmann, 1932) 123; Moshe Greenberg, *Ezekiel 1—20* (AB 22; Garden City, NY: Doubleday, 1983) 211–12. The suggestion is mentioned by Zimmerli, but he hesitates to accept it: *Ezekiel 1*, 266, 273.

"I shall appoint over them four sorts (of destroyers)—the sword to slay, the dogs to drag off, and the birds of the air and the beasts of the earth to devour and destroy."

Ezek 16:1–43 sets forth an allegory of Jerusalem, the unfaithful wife of Yahweh; this sequence is dependent on the themes of Jer 2:1—4:4. Ezek 16:44–52 elaborates on the previous section by insisting that Jerusalem in her harlotry has acted worse than her "elder sister" Samaria (and worse than her younger sister Sodom!), and Ezek 23:1–27 is another allegory with a similar message; both these sections are dependent not only on Jer 2:1—4:4 but on 23:13–14, where the same comparison of the two cities is made.

In Ezek 20:6 and 15 the promised land is called not only the land flowing with milk and honey, but also "the most glorious of all lands" (צְבִי הִיא לְכָל־הָאֲרָצוֹת); this expression is evidently derived from Jer 3:19, "I gave you a lovely land, the most glorious inheritance of the nations" (נַחֲלַת צְבִי צִבְאוֹת גּוֹיִם).

The association of בֶּצַע "cut, bribe," עֹשֶׁק "extortion," and שָׁפַךְ דָּם "shed blood" in Ezek 22:12–13, in the indictment of Jerusalem, the "bloody city," is reminiscent of Jer 22:17, in the indictment of Jehoiakim.

In the description of the house of Israel as "dross" (סִיג) in Ezek 22:18–22, Ezekiel seems to have drawn on both Isa 1:23 and Jer 6:28–30, though it appears that Ezekiel has listed the various metals without a realistic sense of the refining process.

The use of נֶפֶשׁ "self" as subject of the verb יקע "wrench away" is confined to Jer 6:8 and Ezek 23:17, 18. Conceivably these verses simply use an idiom, but one suspects that Jrm coined the phrase and that Ezekiel imitated it.

Ezek 23:29–30 has "your lewdness and your harlotry have done these things to you," and Jer 4:18 has "your way and your deeds have done these things to you"; though the parallel may seem unremarkable, one may suspect that both passages offered an infinitive absolute (עָשׂוֹ or עָשׂה): compare the text variations in both passages.

In the present study I have used Ezek 24:10b–11 to explain Jer 1:13–14: I suggest that the image is the same. It is plausible then to suggest that Ezekiel has used Jrm's vision in his extended image.

Ezekiel is told that his wife is to die but that he is not to mourn for her (Ezek 24:15–17) as a sign that Yahweh is taking away all normal life from the people; in this he is surely stimulated by Jrm's abstention from funerals (Jer 16:5–7).

Ezek 26:15, יִרְעֲשׁוּ הָאִיִּים . . . מִקּוֹל מַפַּלְתֵּךְ "at the sound of your falling . . . the coastlands quake," seems to imitate Jer 49:21, מִקּוֹל נִפְלָם רָעֲשָׁה הָאָרֶץ "at the sound of their fall the earth has quaked."

Ezek 26:19 has "when I make you a city laid waste, like the cities that are not inhabited [עָרִים אֲשֶׁר לֹא־נוֹשָׁבוּ]," a prose expansion of Jer 22:6 qere', "I swear I shall make you a wilderness, uninhabited cities [עָרִים לֹא נוֹשָׁבוּ]": these are the only passages with נוֹשָׁבוּ in the OT, and the only other passage with similar diction is Jer 6:8.

In Ezek 27:30 one has "they roll in dust [בָּאֵפֶר יִתְפַּלָּשׁוּ]," and in the following verse "and they gird on sackcloth"; Jer 6:26 has "My poor people, gird on sackcloth and roll in the dust." Only in these two passages is פלשׁ hitpa'el linked with בָּאֵפֶר, and one must conclude that the Ezekiel passage is dependent on the Jer one.

The diction of Ezek 29:5, "You shall fall upon the face of the field, and not be gathered or buried; to the beasts of the earth and to the birds of the heavens I have given you as food," is a variation of several sequences in Jer, notably Jer 16:4, "They shall not be lamented, nor shall they be buried; they shall become dung on the face of the ground; by sword and famine they shall perish, and their corpses shall become food for the birds of the heavens and the beasts of the earth," and 9:21, "so that corpses of people fall like dung on the face of the field, and like grain-stalks behind the reaper, and no one gathering."

Ezek 34:1–16, an oracle against the shepherds of Israel, is evidently an expansion of Jer 23:1–4; and conceivably the oracle on David in Ezek 34:23–24 was added by Ezekiel because of Jer 23:5–8.

The idiom "deliver (someone) into the hands of the sword" appears only in Jer 18:21, in Ezek 35:5, and in Ps 63:11. I have concluded that Jrm drew on Ps 63:11 for his use of the phrase. The fact that Ezek 35:5 ends with "at the time of their final punishment" and that the last colon of Jer 18:23 has "at the time of your anger" suggests that it was the passage in Jer that stimulated Ezekiel.

These parallels are not all of equal cogency, and there are doubtless a few more of which I am unaware, but the parallels I have listed, roughly twenty-five in number, offer a striking pattern. Of these twenty-five, there are only five whose antecedents in Jer are dated in the present study after the year 600: they are Ezek 4:3 (Jer 1:18: 594); Ezek 11:19 (Jer 31:33: 587); Ezek 12:3 (Jer 46:19: 588); Ezek 26:15 (Jer 49:21: 594?); and Ezek 34:1–16 (Jer 23:1–4: 588). The remaining twenty parallels are to material in Jer which I have dated to 600 or before, and of these, thirteen are to material in Jer which I have dated to the time immediately after Jehoiakim burned the scroll, that is, December 601, into the first months of 600. These thirteen are the following: Ezek 2:8—3:3 (Jer 15:16); Ezek 7:26 (Jer 4:20; 18:18); Ezek 12:10 (Jer 23:33); Ezek 13:1–23 (Jer 23:16–32); Ezek 13:10, 16 (Jer 6:14); Ezek 14:21 (Jer 15:3); Ezek 16:44–52; 23:1–27 (Jer 23:13–14); Ezek 22:18–22 (Jer 6:28–30); Ezek 24:15–17 (Jer 16:5–7); Ezek 26:19 (Jer 22:6); Ezek 27:30 (Jer 6:26); Ezek 29:5 (Jer 9:21; 16:4); and Ezek 35:5 (Jer 18:21). The remaining seven are as follows: Ezek 11:15 (Jer 2:5: collected in the first scroll, 605); Ezek 16:1–43 (Jer 2:1—4:4: in general, collected in the first scroll, 605); Ezek 20:6, 15 (Jer 3:19: collected in the first scroll, 605); Ezek 22:12–13 (Jer 22:17: early in Jehoiakim's reign); 23:17, 18 (Jer 6:8: 605); 23:29–30 (4:18: 605); and 24:10–11 (Jer 1:13–14: vision in the context of Jrm's call).

The seemingly high incidence of parallels with material that, by my proposals, Jrm proclaimed in 601/600 could be specious in several ways: the dates assigned here to the passages in Jrm may be altogether wrong, and I may have been too rigorous in assigning to one period passages whose settings were actually less restricted.

But it does not seem so: the passages dated to 601/600 represent a wide variety of material: not only the oracles against false prophets (Jer 23:13–33) but judgments against Judah (Jer 6:14, 26, 28–30) and even a couple of early confessions (Jer 15:16; 18:18, 21). Conceivably Ezekiel could have gained his knowledge of Jrm's material through a copy of the latter's scroll either in Jerusalem before 598, in Babylon after 598, or both. But it seems to me more plausible to explain the cluster of parallels with the material from 601/600 as a consequence of Ezekiel's personal hearing of Jrm's preaching in Jerusalem at just this period. By the

proposal of the present study Jrm became convinced, after Jehoiakim burned his scroll in December 601, that the repentance of the people was no longer possible, that the optimistic prophets were false, that doom was certain. This message appears to have caught the attention of the young priest Ezekiel. He did hear Jrm's earlier material, but when that earlier material was more hopeful he turned it to a darker point of view (compare Jer 6:8 with Ezek 23:18). But Jrm's fresh oracles from 601/600 seem to have made a greater impression on the young priest. What is surprising is resonances with Jrm's confessions dated to this period (Jer 15:16; 18:18, 21). The proposal of the present study is that none of the confessions were "published" until after Hananiah's death in 594; if that proposal is correct, then Ezekiel's knowledge of the confessions voiced in 601/600 suggests a personal acquaintance with the prophet.

Ezekiel was evidently among those deported to Babylon in 597. Jrm's letter to the exiles in 594 and the attempt of the prophet Shemaiah in Babylon later that year to have Jrm arrested in Jerusalem (29:24–32) would have been known to Ezekiel, and these events may have helped to trigger the call that Ezekiel received in 593 (Ezek 1:2) to prophesy. At the time of the fall of Jerusalem in 587 Jrm and Baruch must have seen to it that copies of his scroll(s) would come to Babylon; Ezekiel would then have drawn on the notion of Yahweh's judgment on the shepherds (Jer 23:1–4) and the new covenant (Jer 31:31–34).

75. Jeremiah's Impact on Lamentations
Though the tradition had grown up by the third century B.C.E. that Jrm had written Lamentations (so the prologue to Lamentations in *G*: "And it came to pass, after Israel was taken captive, and Jerusalem made desolate, Jeremiah sat weeping, and lamented this lamentation over Jerusalem and said"), the conclusion of critical scholars is that the attribution is false. Beyond phrases that would be hard to credit to Jrm (such as Lam 2:9, "her [Jerusalem's] prophets obtain no vision from Yahweh"), the question arises, if Jrm composed laments over Jerusalem, why were they not included in the Book of Jer?[306] Nevertheless, the author or authors drew on

---

306 For recent treatments see Hans-Joachim Kraus, *Threni* (BKAT 20; Neukirchen: Neukirchener, 1960) 13–15; Delbert Hillers, *Lamentations* (AB 7A; Garden City: Doubleday, 1972) xix–xxiii.

phrases of Jrm; the best list of phrases of which I am aware is that of S. R. Driver.[307]

It is striking that the greatest number of parallels is in Lamentations 2.

Thus Lam 2:8b–9a, "He [Yahweh] caused rampart and wall to lament, they languish together; her gates have sunk into the ground, he has ruined and broken her bars," is an expansion of 14:2.

Lam 2:11a, "My eyes are spent with weeping, my bowels are in tumult, my liver is poured out to the earth because of the shattering of my fair people," is a variation of 8:21, 23: it is to be noted that the only occurrences of the phrase שֶׁבֶר בַּת־עַמִּי are in Jer (8:21; 6:14 omits בַּת, and 8:11 is a secondary reuse of 6:14 with בַּת) and in Lam (2:11; 3:48; 4:10).

In Lam 2:14a the description of the false prophets of Jerusalem resembles Jrm's description of the prophets of Samaria in 23:13—the striking word תָּפֵל "fatuous" occurs in both passages—and to a lesser degree his description of the prophets of Jerusalem in 23:16.

The description of passers-by who hiss and shake their heads at Jerusalem (Lam 2:15–16) appears to be dependent on 18:16.

Lam 2:18, like 2:11, mentions weeping over Jerusalem; this passage resembles 8:23 even more closely with the use of "day and night."

And Lam 2:22 offers a variation on Jrm's phrase "terror is all around" (מָגוֹר מִסָּבִיב: 6:25; 20:3, 10): "You [Yahweh] invited as to the day of an appointed feast my terrors all around."

The only other parallel in Lamentations that is convincingly a reflection of Jrm is Lam 3:47, where the phrase פַּחַד וָפַחַת imitates the longer phrase פַּחַד וָפַחַת וָפָח in 48:43.

Beyond this parallel one could ask whether the use of the phrase "sit alone" in Lam 1:1 and 3:28 is dependent on Jer 15:17, and whether Lam 3:14, "I have become a laughingstock of all peoples," is dependent on Jer 20:7, "I have become a laughingstock the whole day."

One may conclude that Lamentations 2 is a poem deeply shaped by the rhetoric of Jrm, though not a poem to be attributed to him (Lam 2:9!), that the other poems are hardly shaped by his rhetoric (in the case of Lamentations 3, it is perhaps as much shaped by the rhetoric of Lamentations 2 as by Jrm's rhetoric directly). These observations make it more likely that the five poems of Lamentations are not the product of a single poet.

76. Jeremiah's Impact on the Exilic Deuteronomists

In their expansion of Deuteronomy, the exilic Deuteronomists drew on Jrm's diction; for a discussion of this material, see section 60. It remains to present the use made by the Deuteronomists of Jrm in the Deuteronomistic historical work. The most useful listing of such phrases is that of Weinfeld,[308] though my conclusions on the direction of borrowing at specific points differ from his. It is clear that to distinguish phrases distinctive to Jrm from other phrases current in Deuteronomic circles in the period is exceedingly difficult.

I begin with the phrases that are surely dependent on Jrm.

In 1 Kgs 8:51 the phrase "iron furnace" appears; this is derived from Jer 11:4 (see the discussion of the same phrase in Deut 4:20, sec. 60).

In 1 Kgs 14:23 and 2 Kgs 17:10 appears the phrase "on every high hill and under every leafy tree"; the phrase is dependent on Jer 2:20.[309]

In 2 Kgs 17:15 appears "they walked after a nothing and shared in nothingness"; this expression is dependent on Jer 2:5.[310]

In 2 Kgs 21:12 appears the phrase "such that the ears of everyone who hears it will ring"; in the context of the destruction of Jerusalem this phrase is evidently dependent on Jer 19:3, though the occurrence in Jer seems in turn to be dependent on 1 Sam 3:11 (see the discussion in sec. 43).

---

307 Samuel R. Driver, *An Introduction to the Old Testament* (6th ed.; rep. New York: Meridian, 1956) 462. The study of Max Löhr, "Der Sprachgebrauch des Buches der Klagelieder," *ZAW* 14 (1894) 31–50, deals not with phrases but with isolated nouns and verbs and is thus unhelpful for this question.

308 Weinfeld, *Deuteronomy*, 320–59.

309 Holladay, "On Every High Hill," 173–74, 176.

310 So also Weinfeld, *Deuteronomy*, 323, n. 5.

Beyond these are several more expressions that are likely either to be dependent on Jrm's diction or stimulated by it.

In 1 Kgs 9:8–9 we have the form of question, "Why has Yahweh done thus to this land and to this house?" Such sequences appear in Jer 5:19; 9:11–12; 16:10–11; and 22:8–9. There is an Assyrian form like this,[311] but Jrm's usage certainly encouraged this sequence (and that in Deut 29:23–24).

Likewise 1 Kgs 9:8 has "everyone who passes it is horrified at it and will hiss": this phrase is derived from Jer 18:16, though the existence of the similar phrase "become a horror, a byword," etc., in Deut 28:37 and a similar phrase in Huldah's prophecy (2 Kgs 22:19) and the combination of the verbal and nominal phrases in Jer 19:8 renders the precise dependence difficult.

In 2 Kgs 17:13 occurs the command, "Turn from your evil way"; this phrase is at least stimulated by Jer 18:11. But the same phrase in the indicative evidently predates Jrm (1 Kgs 13:33).

In 2 Kgs 17:14 one has, "But they did not listen but stiffened their neck"; this phraseology is evidently stimulated by Jer 7:26, "But they did not listen to me nor turn their ear, and they stiffened their neck." But Deut 10:16b has "your neck do not stiffen again"; Jrm cites Deut 10:16a in Jer 4:4, so the dependence is complex.

In 2 Kgs 17:20 and 24:20 there appears the phrase "fling (someone) away from before the presence of Yahweh"; as I have noted,[312] the phrase may have been an old one current in the north (2 Kgs 13:23) and in the temple cult (Ps 51:13), but the use in 2 Kgs 17:20 and 24:20 is probably stimulated by its use in Jer 7:15.

It is clear that the tradition of Jrm, and doubtless his scroll, fed the impulses of the exilic redactors of both Deuteronomy and the Deuteronomic historical work; and it is also clear that these Deuteronomists were responsible for some expansions in the Book of Jer, such as 32:28–35, 38–40—though for by no means so much expansion as some commentators have assumed (see the

discussion in sec. 15). The mutual literary influence of Deuteronomy and the Deuteronomistic corpus on the one hand and Jer on the other is one of the central literary phenomena of the OT. One can only speculate upon what lay behind this mutual literary work: perhaps it was Baruch's status in the scribal circles of Jerusalem.

77. Jeremiah's Impact on Job

The poet of the Book of Job drew on the poetry of Jrm. The most striking evidence for this conclusion is that Job 3:3–10 uses both Jer 20:14–18 and Genesis 1 in its structure, Jer 20:14–18 in Job 3:3 and 10, and Genesis 1 in Job 3:4–9.[313] Furthermore the rhetoric of Jer 20:18 is continued in the "why's" of Job 3:11–23.

In a way the forensic language of Job's struggle with God, especially in Job 9:14–22; 13; 23, offers variations on Jer 12:1. Thus Job's wish to confront God in court (Job 9:14–22) is a variation on Jer 12:1a, and the question in Jer 12:1b, "Why has the way of the guilty succeeded?" is expanded in Job 21:7–26.[314] Jrm's confessions then were a prime stimulus for the poetry of the Book of Job.

It is noteworthy, however, that I can find no specific phrases in the poetry of the Book of Job that are dependent on phrases of Jrm; at most one can find here and there a thematic resemblance, such as Elihu's declaration that he is full of words, ready to burst (Job 32:18–20), phraseology that resembles Jer 6:11. Rather it is the presentation of the plight of the sufferer before God, in Jrm's confessions, on which the poet of Job drew.

78. Jeremiah's Impact on Deutero-Isaiah

A list of parallels between Isaiah 40—66 and Jer was drawn up by Umberto Cassuto,[315] though many of his presumed parallels are not convincing.

There are two parallels in which critical opinion has usually judged the dependence to be in the other direction—that is, that secondary additions in Jer are dependent on the diction of Deutero-Isaiah; in both

311 See *Jeremiah 1*, 585.
312 See *Jeremiah 1*, 249.
313 Norman C. Habel, *The Book of Job* (Philadelphia: Westminster, 1985) 41, 103–4.
314 Holladay, "Lawsuit."
315 Umberto Cassuto, "On the Formal and Stylistic Relationship between Deutero-Isaiah and Other Biblical Writers," *Biblical and Oriental Studies, I, Bible*

(Jerusalem: Magnes, 1973) 149–60; the Italian original appeared in *Rivista Israelitica* 8 (1911) 191–214.

these instances I have offered evidence that in fact it is Deutero-Isaiah that is dependent on Jrm.

The first of these is Isa 41:8–10, which is closely related to Jer 30:10–11a. By the conclusions of the present study, 30:10–11 offers Jrm's diction and is authentic to him, part of his expansion for Judah in 588/587 of his hopeful words to the north. If it was antecedent to Deutero-Isaiah, then clearly the latter found the phrasing congenial.

The second is Isa 44:6–22, a sequence in which a self-asseveration of Yahweh and an oracle of salvation (vv 6–8, 21–22) enclose a mockery of idols (vv 9–20); this passage appears to be dependent on Jer 10:1–16, where mockery of idols alternates with hymnic passages about Yahweh. The authenticity of 10:1–16 is widely doubted, but it resembles 16:19–21, a passage that shares diction with material elsewhere authentic to Jrm, and the wit of the Aramaic climax of the poem (10:11) is worthy of the prophet. As for the parallels with Deutero-Isaiah, the only two occurrences in the OT of "adze" (מַעֲצָד) are found in Isa 44:12 and Jer 10:3, and the contexts are much the same; again בער "burn" occurs in Isa 44:15, 16, 19 and is suggested (along with the homonymous בער "be stupid") in Jer 10:8. Beyond these immediate resemblances the tone of both passages is close.

Isa 47:1, "Descend and sit in the dust, virgin daughter Babylon; sit on the ground without a throne, daughter of the Chaldeans," is evidently a gentler adaptation of Jer 48:18, "Descend from glory and sit in dung, enthroned daughter Dibon."

Isa 49:1 and 5 are closely related: v 1 says, "Yahweh called me from the womb, from the body of my mother he named my name," and v 5 says, "[Yahweh,] who formed me from the womb to be his servant." I propose that the two verbs "call" (קרא) and "form" (יצר) represent the two verbs suggested in the first verb of Jer 1:5, יצר "form" and צור "summon" (see there).

In the same way Isa 49:15 and 18 appear to be a midrash on Jer 2:32: Isa 49:15 reads, "Can a woman forget her sucking child, that she should have no compassion on the son of her womb? Even these may forget, yet I will not forget you," and v 18 reads, "Lift up your eyes round about and see; they all gather, they come to you. As I live, says Yahweh, you shall put them all on as an ornament, you shall bind them on as a bride does"; Jer 2:32 reads, "Can a virgin forget her ornaments, a bride her breast-band? But my people have forgotten me days beyond number."

Isa 49:19–20 appears to be a commentary on Jer 10:18. The verb צרר "be narrow," with the land as subject, appears in both passages, but where in Jer 10:18 it expresses judgment, in Isa 49:19–20 it expresses salvation. One notes too the occurrence of "children" in reference to the population in contexts of bereavement in both Isa 49:20 and Jer 10:20.

In Isa 51:19 מִי יָנוּד לָךְ "Who will grieve for you?" is evidently taken from the same phrase in Jer 15:5 (though it should be noted that "Who will grieve for her?" occurs in Nah 3:7).

The description of the suffering servant in Isa 53:6–8 is drawn from Jrm's confessions, both 11:19 and 15:11 and 15. Thus the difficult verb פגע hip'il is used with Yahweh as subject with respect to both the servant in Isa 53:6 and Jrm in Jer 15:11. The servant in Isa 53:7 is described as being like a lamb led to the slaughter: this resembles Jrm's complaint in 11:19, though the words for "lamb" are different; the servant is "cut off from the land of the living" (Isa 53:8), and Jrm cites his enemies, who say, "let us cut him off from the land of the living" (Jer 11:19), though again the verbs for "cut off" are different. And the servant "is taken away" (Isa 53:8), while Jrm prays to Yahweh, "do not take me away" (Jer 15:15).

Isa 54:1–3 appears to be a variation on Jer 10:20–25: the reference to the restoration of children in Isa 54:1 reverses Jer 10:20; "enlarge the place of your tent, and let the curtains of your habitations be stretched out" (Isa 54:2) is reminiscent of the parallel between "tent" and "curtains" in the same verse of Jer; finally Isa 54:3, "you will spread abroad to the right and to the left, and your descendants will possess the nations and will people the desolate cities," reflects the promise to Jacob in Gen 28:14, the reverse of which is implied in Jer 10:24, and reinforces the diction of Jer 10:25, which Jrm himself rejected.

There are in addition several parallels that are plausible, if not certain. The affirmation in Isa 40:2 that Jerusalem has received "double for all her sins" may be a reflection of Jer 16:18, "So I shall recompense them double for their iniquity and their sin," though the words for "double" are different in the two passages.

In Isa 40:5 and 6 the word בָּשָׂר "flesh" appears, and in

v 9 מְבַשֶּׂרֶת "bearer of (good) news" is a word-play on the earlier word; the same word-play appears in Jer 17:5 (בָּשָׂר) and 20:15 (M בִּשַּׂר, by my revocalization בְּשַׂר): I propose that in the structure of the confessions these two passages may form an inclusio (see on 17:5–8, Preliminary Observations).

The simile of Isa 40:11, in which Yahweh is likened to a shepherd, probably has its origin in Jer 23:1–4.

Isa 42:17, "They shall be turned back and utterly put to shame, who trust in graven images, who say to molten images, 'You are our gods,'" looks like a variation of 2:26–27.

Isa 43:19, "Behold, I am doing a new thing [חֲדָשָׁה],", following the affirmation of v 15 that Yahweh is the Creator of Israel, probably reflects Jer 31:22, "Yahweh has created a new thing [חֲדָשָׁה] on the earth," and the "new covenant" (בְּרִית חֲדָשָׁה) in 31:31. Given that probable link, the phrase in Isa 43:25, "I will not remember your sins," could well pick up "I will remember their sin no more" in 31:34.

"Why . . . when I called, was there no answer?" in Isa 50:2 is reminiscent of 7:13 and 27 (but in Isa 65:12 there is a fuller reflection of 7:13).

Again in Isa 50:3, "I clothe the heavens with blackness, and make sackcloth their covering," there seems to be a reflection of 4:28, "On this account the earth shall mourn, and the heavens be dark above."

It is striking, then, that what Deutero-Isaiah did with the poetic images and sequences of Jrm's was to reconceive them in fresh ways.

79. Jeremiah's Impact on Trito-Isaiah

There are a few secure parallels between Isaiah 56—66 and Jrm. Thus Isa 57:5 has the phrase "under every green tree," and v 7 has "on a high and lofty mountain," both in reference to fertility worship; these phrases are derived from Jer 2:20, "on every high hill and under every green tree."[316]

Isa 57:16–19 seems to be a development of phrases in Jer 3:5 + 12–14 + 22: one has "I will not contend for ever" in Isa 57:16 and "I will not bear a grudge for ever" in Jer 3:12 (different verbs); "nor will I be angry endlessly" in Isa 57:16 and "will he [Yahweh] keep watch

endlessly?" in Jer 3:5; the adjective שׁוֹבָב "turnable, backsliding" appears in Isa 57:17 and Jer 3:14 and 22; "I will heal him" occurs in Isa 57:18, 19; and "I will heal your turnings" in Jer 3:22.

Isa 63:11–13 is a sequence that appears to be modeled on Jer 2:6–8: in both passages one has "Where is?" followed by a sequence of hip'il participles depicting Yahweh's rescue of Israel from Egypt, including מוֹלִיךְ.

And Isa 65:12, 24; 66:4 have the same sequence of four verbs: Isa 65:12 reads "When I called, you did not answer; when I spoke, you did not listen": this sequence imitates Jer 7:13, "Though I have spoken to you you have not listened, and though I have called you you have not answered." Since Isa 65:19, "No more shall be heard in her [Jerusalem] the voice of weeping and the voice of distress," resembles Jer 7:34, "And I shall silence from the cities of Judah and from the streets of Jerusalem the voice of joy and the voice of gladness, the voice of the bridegroom and the voice of the bride," one wonders if Isaiah 65 is not shaped in part by the diction of Jer 7.

The fact that in several instances Trito-Isaiah uses the diction of Jrm just as Deutero-Isaiah does—that is to say, the poetic material of Jrm is reshaped in fresh ways—raises once more the suspicion that "Trito-Isaiah" is the same Deutero-Isaiah at work a generation later.[317]

A few further possible parallels may be mentioned. The summons to the wild beasts to devour (Isa 56:9) may be derived from a similar summons in Jer 12:9. "You did not say, נוֹאָשׁ" (Isa 57:10) may be dependent on Jer 2:25, "So you said, נוֹאָשׁ." "They shall build houses and inhabit them, they shall plant vineyards and eat their fruit" (Isa 65:21) may be dependent on Jer 29:5, "Build houses and live (in them), plant gardens and eat their fruit." And the phrase "and like the whirlwind are his chariots" in Isa 66:15 may be derived from that phrase in Jer 4:13.

80. Jeremiah's Impact on the Remainder of the Isaianic Corpus

There are some parallels between Isa 34—35 and Jrm. Isa 34:2 and Jer 25:9 are the only two passages in the OT where Yahweh is the subject of חרם hip'il "devote to destruction," and it is therefore possible that the passage of Jrm was the stimulus for the one in Isaiah.

---

316 Holladay, "On Every High Hill," 174.
317 For a useful recent survey of critical opinion on the nature of Trito-Isaiah see Paul D. Hanson, *The Dawn of Apocalyptic* (Philadelphia: Fortress, 1975) 32–46.

Then Isa 34:6, "For Yahweh has a sacrifice in Bozrah, a great slaughter in the land of Edom," is modeled on Jer 46:10, "For Yahweh has a sacrifice in the land of the north by the river Euphrates."

And Isa 35:5–6, a passage describing the joy of the handicapped, the blind, deaf, lame, and dumb beside the water in the wilderness, is surely modeled on Jer 31:8–9, a passage that describes the joy of the blind and lame, the pregnant woman and the woman giving birth as they walk beside brooks of water.

The only significant parallel between Jrm and the late material within Isaiah 13—23 is Isa 16:11, עַל־כֵּן מֵעַי לְמוֹאָב כַּכִּנּוֹר יֶהֱמוּ, "That is why my very heart for Moab like a lyre trembles," which is dependent on Jer 31:20, עַל־כֵּן הָמוּ מֵעַי לוֹ, "That is why my very heart trembles for him."[318]

And the only parallel in Isaiah 24—27 is Isa 24:17–18a, which replicates Jer 48:43–44: Isa 24:13–23 is a pastiche of prophetic quotations.

81. Jeremiah's Impact on Zechariah 1—8

There are several points at which Zechariah 1—8 picks up phrases from Jrm (there is no similar evidence of such dependence in Haggai).

In Zech 1:2–6 there is an extended sequence on "fathers" and "repentance": the "fathers" evidently refers to those of Jrm's generation (see below). In Zech 1:3 we have the formulation "Thus says Yahweh of hosts, Return to me . . . and I will return to you." It is Jrm of course who plays on the forms of "(re)turn" (שׁוּב). There is nothing quite like this formulation in Jrm, though Jer 15:19, "If you return and I [Yahweh] let you return," is close. It is clear then from the context that Jrm is the stimulus. In both Zech 1:4 and 8:14 there is reference to Yahweh's word to the fathers; in Zech 1:4 one has, "Be not like your fathers, to whom the former prophets cried out, 'Thus says Yahweh of hosts, Return from your evil ways and your evil deeds,'" phraseology that is close to Jer 25:5 (and compare 18:11), and in Zech 8:14 one

reads, "As I purposed [זָמַמְתִּי] to do evil to you, when your fathers provoked me to wrath, and I did not retract [לֹא נִחָמְתִּי] . . . ," phraseology that is close to Jer 4:28, "I have not retracted [לֹא נִחַמְתִּי], I have decided [זַמֹּתִי]. . . ." Both passages imply that Zechariah counts Jrm as a true prophet.[319]

Again the use of "seventy years" in Zech 1:12 and 7:5 suggests a reuse of the mention of that span of time in Jer 25:11 and 29:10.[320]

Finally the use of צֶמַח "Branch" in Jer 23:5 as a designation of the future king stimulated its use in Zech 3:8 and 6:12, evident applied by Zechariah to Zerubbabel.[321]

82. Jeremiah's Impact on the Remainder of the Prophetic Corpora

Reminiscences of Jrm in the remainder of the prophetic corpora are spotty.

The phrase of the king of Nineveh in Jonah 3:8, "Let everyone turn from his evil way" (וְיָשֻׁבוּ אִישׁ מִדַּרְכּוֹ הָרָעָה), with אִישׁ, is derived from Jrm (18:11; 25:5; 26:3; 35:5; 36:3, 7).[322] The expression in Jonah 3:9, "Who knows, God may yet retract and turn from his fierce anger," with נחם nip'al and שׁוּב in parallel, appears to reflect Jer 4:28, "I have spoken and have not retracted, I have decided and will not turn back from it": these are the only two passages in the OT where these two verbs are in parallelism (Jer 31:19 evidently offers a corrupt text). And Jonah 3:10 continues similar diction. The book thus uses Jrm's words in an ironic context: Jrm had suggested that the people of Israel have not repented; now one hears that the king of Nineveh did!

The Book of Joel appears to be without echoes of Jrm, except possibly for the late gloss in Joel 4:21a: the text there is difficult, but since it is a first-person formulation, it may be dependent on Jer 30:11 as well as on Exod 34:7 and Num 14:18.

Neither is there evidence of any dependence by Zechariah 9—14 on Jrm.

---

318 On this dependence see further Wildberger, *Jesaja*, 629.

319 Compare David L. Petersen, *Haggai and Zechariah 1—8* (Philadelphia: Westminster, 1984) 132, 309.

320 Ibid., 150.

321 Ibid., 210.

322 Holladay, "Prototype," 355; Weinfeld, *Deuteronomy*, 351, n. 7.

Mal 3:7 cites Zech 1:3, "Return to me, and I will return to you," and Zech 1:3 in turn was stimulated by Jrm (see the discussion in sec. 81).

83. Jeremiah's Impact on Ezra-Nehemiah and Chronicles

Jrm is cited by name in Ezra 1:1; 2 Chr 35:25; 36:12, 21–22. Ezra 1:1 and 2 Chr 36:22 both offer the same reference: Cyrus moved to liberate the people in exile "to fulfill the word of the Lord by the mouth of Jeremiah." Jrm offered no such prophecy: the narrator is evidently citing Isa 41:2–3; 44:28; 45:1. In 2 Chr 35:25 it is stated that "Jeremiah also uttered a lament for Josiah; and all the singing men and singing women have spoken of Josiah in their laments to this day. They made these an ordinance in Israel; behold, they are written in the Lamentations." Again, there is no recorded lament by Jrm for Josiah, and such a lament is not preserved in Lamentations. In 2 Chr 36:12 it is stated that Zedekiah "did what was evil in the sight of the Lord his God. He did not humble himself before Jeremiah the prophet, who spoke from the mouth of the Lord." Finally 2 Chr 36:21 states that Nebuchadnezzar brought the exiles to Babylon "to fulfill the word of the Lord by the mouth of Jeremiah, until the land had enjoyed its sabbaths. All the days that it lay desolate it kept sabbath, to fulfill seventy years." The reference to seventy years is valid Jeremianic tradition (compare sec. 81), but the rest of these references are evidence that the Chronicler wished to make good the silence of 2 Kings on Jrm without being able to offer first-hand data about him.

There is little in this corpus of material that reflects the phraseology of Jrm. Neh 3:37a, "Do not cover their iniquity, and their sin do not blot out from your presence," is, with minor variations, taken from Jer 18:23aβ. And the sequence on Hezekiah's reform in 2 Chr 29:8–10 reflects Jrm's diction—in v 8 there, "He [Yahweh] has made them an object of horror, a desolation, and a hissing," reflects the diction of passages like Jer 29:18,

and in v 10 there, "in order that his fierce anger may turn away from us," reflects Jer 4:8, but one suspects that such diction had by then become general in the community (compare the discussion on "hissing" in sec. 76).

84. Jeremiah's Impact on Daniel and on the Deuterocanonical Books

The Book of Daniel draws directly on Jrm only for the phrase "seventy years" in Jer 25:11 (Dan 9:2), which Dan 9:24 then explains as "seventy weeks of years."[323] But it is also possible that the story of the three young men, sent by Nebuchadnezzar into the fiery furnace (Daniel 3), was stimulated by the mention of "Zedekiah and Ahab, whom the king of Babylon roasted in the fire" (Jer 29:22).

The references to Jrm in 2 Chronicles 35—36 are replicated in 1 Esdras 1—2:[324] thus 1 Esdr 1:30 (Greek numeration; English 32) replicates 2 Chr 35:25; 1 Esdr 1:45 replicates 2 Chr 36:12; 1 Esdr 1:54 replicates 2 Chr 36:21; 1 Esdr 2:1 replicates 2 Chr 36:22. Beyond these parallels, 1 Esdr 1:26 (English 28) has shifted 2 Chr 35:22: the latter reads, "Josiah would not turn away from him [Neco], but disguised himself in order to fight with him. He did not listen to the words of Neco from the mouth of God, but joined battle in the plain of Megiddo," but 1 Esdr 1:26 has substituted "Jeremiah the prophet" for "Neco."[325]

In 2 Esdr 2:18 God addresses a mother, a figure for Jerusalem, and reassures her, "I will send you helpers in the person of my servants Isaiah and Jeremiah." Beyond this mention of Jrm, 2 Esdras has many reminiscences of prophetic diction, including diction ultimately derived from Jer. This is particularly true of the so-called Sixth Ezra (2 Esdras 15—16): for example, one finds "famine, sword and pestilence" (2 Esdr 15:49, compare Jer 14:12 and often) and "the dead will be cast off like dung with none to mourn them" (2 Esdr 16:24; compare Jer 9:22).[326]

There are two deuterocanonical works that purport to

---

323 See Lester L. Grabbe, "'The End of the Desolations of Jerusalem': From Jeremiah's 70 Years to Daniel's 70 Weeks of Years," *Early Jewish and Christian Exegesis, Studies in Memory of William Hugh Brownlee* (ed. Craig A. Evans and William F. Stinespring; Atlanta: Scholars, 1987) 67–72.

324 The verse citations here are to the Greek text; the numeration differs in English translations.

325 Curtis and Madsen likewise assume that 2 Chronicles is the original reading: Curtis and Madsen, *Chronicles*, 518.

326 For the details see Jacob M. Myers, *I & II Esdras* (AB 42; Garden City, NY: Doubleday, 1974).

carry on the Jer tradition, namely Baruch (or 1 Baruch) and the Epistle of Jeremiah. The attribution of authorship of both these books is clearly false,[327] though, as one might imagine, there are reminiscences of the Book of Jer in both. In the case of the Book of Baruch, there are reminiscences particularly in Bar 1:15—2:5, a confession for the Palestinian remnant ("he [God] handed them over to all the neighboring kingdoms to be an object of reproach and horror to all the neighboring peoples among whom the Lord had scattered them," Bar 2:4; compare Jer 29:18); and Bar 2:6—3:8, prayers for the exiled community ("since only a few of us [some texts here add "of many"] are left," Bar 2:13; compare Jer 42:2). As for the Epistle of Jeremiah, it is an expansion of Jer 10:1–16.[328]

In 2 Macc 2:1–12 it is said that Jrm was told to go up to Mount Nebo and take there the tent, the ark, and the altar of incense and seal them in a cave; this is clearly a later legend dependent on Jer 3:16–17.[329] The story of the martyrdom of seven brothers and their mother in 2 Maccabees 7 was doubtless stimulated by Jer 15:8–9, "I have brought in on the mother of young men the devastator at noon, . . . she languishes who has borne seven."[330] And in 2 Macc 15:14–16 Judas relates a dream or vision in which he saw the high priest Onias (III) and Jrm praying encouragement for the Jews in their battle with Nicanor.

Finally, Sir 49:6–7 lists Jrm among the godly people of the past.

85. Jeremiah's Impact on the Pseudepigrapha

Several pseudepigraphical works continue to elaborate legends regarding Jrm.

As would be expected, there are references to Jrm in the (Second) Apocalypse of Baruch (also known as Syriac Apocalypse of Baruch and 2 Baruch; it was written after 70 C.E.), namely, 2:1; 5:5; 9:1; 10:2, 4; and 33:1. Most of these references are casual ("and I went away and took with me Jeremiah and Adu and Seraiah . . . ," 2 Apoc. Bar. 5:5), though in 2 Apoc. Bar. 33:1 it is indicated that Jrm went to Babylon (in contradiction to Jer 43:6–7). The diction of the work offers many reminiscences of Jrm: for example, in 2 Apoc. Bar. 6:8 the Lord Most High said to the earth, "Earth, earth, earth, hear the word of the mighty God," a reminiscence of Jer 22:29; in 2 Apoc. Bar. 35:2 Baruch wept and said, "O that my eyes were springs, and my eyelids, that they were a fountain of tears," a reminiscence of Jer 8:23.[331]

Though Third Apocalypse of Baruch (also known as Greek Apocalypse of Baruch; it was written in the first to third century C.E.) carries the name of Baruch, it is an apocalyptic reworking of material from Genesis.

There is also a book called in Greek Paraleipomena Ieremiou and in Ethiopic 4 Baruch (first to second centuries C.E.).[332] As in 2 Macc 2:1–12, Jrm is told to guard the vessels of the temple (Paraleipomena Ieremiou 3:9–12, 18), and as in 2 Apoc. Bar. 33:1 Jrm and Baruch are exiled to Babylon (Paraleipomena Ieremiou 4:6); the two lead the exiles back from Babylon (Paraleipomena Ieremiou 8:1–2). Though the work has many reminiscences of the Book of Jer, it is full of unhistorical details; for example, Baruch dictates a letter to Jrm! (Paraleipomena Ieremiou 6:15–18).[333]

The Lives of the Prophets (first century C.E.) comes out of Jewish circles that treated the prophets as national heroes; chapter 2 of the work is devoted to Jrm. It states that he was stoned to death by his people in Egypt and was buried in the environs of pharaoh's palace, "because the Egyptians held him in high esteem" (vv 1–2). There

327 For the details see Carey A. Moore, Daniel, Esther and Jeremiah, The Additions (AB 44; Garden City, NY: Doubleday, 1977) 256, 318–19.

328 See particularly ibid., 357–58.

329 See in detail Jonathan A. Goldstein, II Maccabees (AB 41A; Garden City, NY: Doubleday, 1983) 182–83.

330 Ibid., 295–96.

331 See in detail A. F. J. Klijn, "2 (Syriac Apocalypse of) Baruch," The Old Testament Pseudepigrapha (ed. James H. Charlesworth; Garden City, NY: Doubleday, 1983, 1985) 1:615–52.

332 See Paraleipomena Ieremiou (ed. and tr. Robert A.

Kraft and Ann-Elizabeth Purintun; SBLTT 1, Pseudepigrapha Series 1; Missoula, MT: Society of Biblical Literature, 1972); Stephen E. Robinson, "4 Baruch," Charlesworth, OTP 2:413–25.

333 See Jean Riaud, "La figure de Jérémie dans les Paralipomena Jeremiae," Mélanges bibliques et orientaux en l'honneur de M. Henri Cazelles (ed. André Caquot and Matthias Delcor; AOAT 212; Neukirchen: Neukirchener, 1981) 373–85.

follows a paragraph about the efficacy of his prayers to heal the bite of asps (vv 3–7). After a Christian interpolation (vv 8–10) the narrative describes Jrm's burial of the ark of the law before the capture of the temple (v 11); Jrm explains that the ark will reappear in the age to come (vv 14–15), and the narrative concludes with the affirmation that Jrm has become a partner of Moses (v 19).[334]

There is a work called *History of the Rechabites* that emerged in the early centuries C.E.; it evidently had a Jewish nucleus and Christian expansions. Especially in its middle chapters (chaps. 8—10) it is a midrash on Jer 35; Jrm is mentioned in 1:2; 8:2; 9:6.[335]

A work now called *Pseudo-Philo* was produced in the first century C.E.; it is a retelling of the history of Israel from Adam to David. In *Pseudo-Philo* 56:6 Saul remonstrates to Samuel on being named king in words taken from Jer 1:6: "Who am I and what is the house of my father that my lord should say to me this word? For I do not understand what you are saying, because I am young." Samuel said to Saul, "Who will grant that your word be accomplished of itself to the end that you should have a long life? Nevertheless, consider this, that your words will be compared to the words of the prophet whose name will be Jeremiah."[336]

In a Christian interpolation in *Sibylline Oracles* 2:249–50 it is stated that Christ in the last judgment "will destroy all the Hebrews after Jeremiah."

Beyond the use made in the pseudepigraphical literature of the figure of Jrm, there are, as one might expect, reminiscences of specific phrases of Jrm: for example, in *Jubilees*, which draws freely on OT material, one finds rhetoric against idols drawn from Jer 10:1–16, "Why do you worship those who have no spirit in them? Because they are the works of the hands, and you are carrying them upon your shoulder, and there is no help from them for you, except great shame for those who made them and the misleading of the heart for those who worship them" (*Jub.* 12:5), and the expression "so that

you might not make our name a curse, and all your life a hissing" (*Jub.* 20:6; compare Jer 29:18).[337]

Passages from Jrm also contributed to the development of fresh doctrine. Thus the idea of the two ways or inclinations, the good way and the evil way (*T. Asher* 1:3—5:4), is drawn from Deut 30:15 but is reinforced by Jer 21:8. And there developed a belief that the antichrist would come from Dan (see *T. Dan* 5:6, evidently part of a Christian interpolation); this belief was derived from Gen 49:17, but would be reinforced by Deut 33:22; Judg 18:11–31; and Jer 8:16–17—it is to be noted that Dan is missing from the list in Rev 7:5–8 (Joseph and Manasseh are both listed, to make twelve) and that Irenaeus interprets Jer 8:16 of the antichrist.[338]

86. Jeremiah's Impact on the Qumran Literature

For a description of the small scraps of MSS. of the Book of Jer at Qumran, see sec. 2.

In the sectarian literature of Qumran Jrm is mentioned once, in CD 8.20; it is the beginning of a section that evidently concerns those excommunicated from the community of the new covenant: "This is the word that Jeremiah said to Baruch, the son of Neriah, and Elisha to Gehazi his servant: 'All the men who enter into the new covenant in the land of Damascus. . . .'"

The Qumran community drew deeply on themes of Jrm's. Thus they understood themselves to be the people of the "new covenant"; the term occurs not only in CD 8.21, just cited, but also in CD 6.19 and 20.12. Furthermore in 1QpHab 2.3 there is a phrase with a lacuna, "in the matter of those who betray the new . . ."; it is presumed that the missing word is covenant. In this respect Jer 31:31–34 was central for the community.[339]

By the same token the phraseology in 1QS 5.5, "to circumcise in the community the foreskin of the inclination and the stiff neck," is drawn from both Jrm and Deuteronomy.

CD 6.1 reads, "They prophesied a lie so as to turn

334 Douglas R. A. Hare, "The Lives of the Prophets," Charlesworth, *OTP* 2:379–99.

335 See James H. Charlesworth, "History of the Rechabites," Charlesworth, *OTP* 2:443–61.

336 Daniel J. Harrington, "Pseudo-Philo," Charlesworth, *OTP* 2:297–377.

337 See Orval S. Wintermute, "Jubilees," Charlesworth, *OTP* 2:35–142.

338 *Adv. Haer.* 5.30.2.

339 See conveniently William L. Holladay, "New covenant, the," *IDBSup*, 624–25.

Israel from God"; "prophesy a lie" drawn from Jer 14:14 and similar passages.

The high frequency of the verb שׁוב "(re)turn" in a theological sense in Jer is reflected also in the Qumran literature, where one finds "return from evil, from sin," and the like, and "return to the law, to truth," and the like. Typical are: "This is the rule for the men of the community, who volunteer to turn from all evil and to hold fast to all that he has commanded according to his will" (1QS 5.1); "They shall enroll him with the oath of the covenant that Moses made with Israel, the covenant to return to the law of Moses with all one's heart and with all one's soul" (CD 15.8–10).[340] Interestingly enough, however, there is no citation of an imperative of the verb, that is, no appeal to repent, in contrast to the OT prophets (and to John the Baptist—Matt 3:2—who, it is speculated, might have been reared in the Qumran community).[341] But if there is no appeal to repent, it is clear that the Qumran community took with deep seriousness the prior repentance of its members.[342]

The hymns of the community (1QH) are particularly rich with reminiscences of the OT, phrases from Jrm among them. Thus "the life of the poor" (נפש אביון) appears in 1QH 2.32 and 3.25, and "you have saved the life of the wretched" (ותצל נפש עני) in 1QH 5.13; these phrases are dependent on "he has saved the life of the poor" (הִצִּיל אֶת־נֶפֶשׁ אֶבְיוֹן) in Jer 20:13. The poet declares, "And I have become a man of lawsuit" (אִישׁ רִיב), 1QH 2.14, a phrase taken from Jer 15:10. He says, "Your chastisement has become for me a joy and delight," 1QH 9.24, an adaptation of Jer 15:16.

But other works of the community are also heavy with citations from the OT, including Jrm. Thus 4QDibHam ("Words of the Luminaries"), a collection of liturgical texts, offers, "They abandoned the spring of living water

and served a strange god on their land" (4QDibHam 5.1–3): these words combine Jer 2:13 and 5:19.

One has the impression then of a community that drew deeply from the entire OT and adapted a wide variety of texts for its use.[343]

87. Jeremiah's Impact on the New Testament

Jrm is mentioned three times in the NT: all the occurrences are in Matthew. The most striking is in Matt 16:14: when Jesus asks his disciples, "Who do men say that the Son of man is?" they said, "Some say John the Baptist, others say Elijah, and others Jeremiah or one of the prophets"—"Jeremiah or" is a plus in Matthew over the parallels in Mark 8:27 and Luke 9:19. The expectation of the return of Elijah is well known (Mal 3:23–24; Sir 48:10), but it is difficult to know what to make of the mention of Jrm here. Is it a valid memory of perceptions of people in Jesus' day, or is it an addition to the tradition by Matthew for reasons of his own? Traditionally commentators have suggested either that Jrm was understood to be a forerunner of the Messiah (in the light of 2 Macc 15:14–16: see sec. 84), or that Jrm was in some way a "figure" of Jesus. It is more likely that Jesus, like Jrm, was seen to be a prophet of doom who was rejected by many. Jean Carmignac points out that Jesus foresaw the destruction of Jerusalem and in this respect was like Jrm. Furthermore, in the developing Christology of the church Jesus was seen to be, like Jrm, a prophet to the nations.[344] But obviously there are other possibilities. Jrm was to be a "prophet to the nations" (1:10)—compare Matt 28:19. Again, Howard Clark Kee suggests that it was Jrm's word on the new covenant (31:31–34) that was the stimulus for the occurrence of the prophet's name here.[345]

The two other occasions where Jrm is mentioned are

340 See in detail Heinz-Josef Fabry, *Die Wurzel Šûb in der Qumran Literatur, Zur Semantik eines Grundbegriffes* (BBB 46; Cologne and Bonn: Hanstein, 1975).

341 William L. Holladay, review of Fabry, *Die Wurzel Šûb*, in *VT* 29 (1979) 368.

342 Heinz-Josef Fabry, "Umkehr und Metanoia als monastisches Ideal in der 'Mönchsgemeinde' von Qumran," *Erbe und Auftrag, Benediktinische Monatsschrift* 53 (1977), Sonderdruck Heft 3 (Beuron) 163–80.

343 For references see Jean Carmignac and Pierre Guilbert, *Les Textes de Qumran* (Paris: Letouzey et

Ané, 1961, 1963).

344 See Eduard Schweizer, *Das Evangelium nach Mattäus* (NTD 2; Göttingen: Vandenhoeck & Ruprecht, 1973) 221; Jean Carmignac, "Pourquoi Jérémie est-il mentionné en Mattieu 16,14?" *Tradition und Glaube, Das frühe Christentum in seiner Umwelt, Festgabe für Karl Georg Kuhn zum 65. Geburtstag* (ed. Gert Jeremias, Heinz-Wolfgang Kuhn, and Hartmut Stegemann; Göttingen: Vandenhoeck & Ruprecht, 1971) 283–98.

345 Howard Clark Kee, lecture at the 23rd Biblical Institute, Trinity College, Burlington, VT,

Matt 2:17 and 27:9; both of these are citations of prophetic words in Jer. Matt 2:17–18 cites Jer 31:15, "A voice was heard in Ramah wailing and loud lamentation, Rachel weeping for her children; she refused to be consoled, because they were no more," to explain Herod's slaughter of the innocents. Matt 27:9–10, in citing an OT reference to Judas's end, offers a difficulty: "Then was fulfilled what had been spoken by the prophet Jeremiah, saying, 'And they took the thirty pieces of silver, the price of him on whom a price had been set by some of the sons of Israel, and they gave them for the potter's field, as the Lord directed me." The "quotation" is actually a pastiche from Zech 11:12–13 ("thirty pieces of silver"), Jer 18:1–3 ("potter"), and Jer 32:6–15 (the purchase of a field); the attribution to Jrm is a famous problem for NT readers. It has been suggested that Matthew is citing an apocryphal Jer text,[346] but it is to be noted that Matthew was not the only one who combined OT citations (in Mark 1:2–3 the evangelist attributes to Isaiah a combination of Mal 3:1 and Isa 40:3, and in 2 Cor 6:16–18 Paul cites as a continuous quotation loose citations of Lev 26:12; Ezek 37:27; Isa 52:11; and 2 Sam 7:14). It is more likely that it is a simple matter of incompleteness of attribution.[347] The matter of Matthew's extensive use of OT quotations is too complex to enter into here.[348]

By far the most important debt of the NT to Jrm is its adoption of the notion of the "new covenant" (Jer 31:31–34), an adoption that it shares with the Qumran community (see sec. 86). According to the tradition, this usage began with Jesus himself. The earliest citation is in one of Paul's letters, 1 Cor 11:25 (dated to 55 C.E.); Paul gives the words of Jesus at the last supper on the basis of careful oral tradition (1 Cor 11:23): his version of the words over the cup are, "This cup is the new covenant in my blood. Do this, as often as you drink it, in remembrance of me." The wording in Mark (dated not long after 65 C.E.) is slightly different: "This is my blood of the covenant, which is poured out for many. Truly, I say to you, I shall not drink again of the fruit of the vine until that day when I drink it new in the kingdom of God" (Mark 14:24–25). Matthew (26:27–29) enlarges on this phrase slightly, but neither Mark nor Matthew, in the earliest and best MSS., uses "new" with "covenant" (though later MSS. do offer "new" at that point). Luke (22:17–20) offers two text traditions, a shorter one which does not mention "covenant" at all, and a longer one which mentions "the new covenant" (compare the *RSV* footnote to v 19). It is altogether likely that the traditions in Paul and in Mark rest on reliable historical information. If Jesus said "new covenant," he had Jrm's passage in mind; if he said "covenant" without "new," he had Exod 24:8 in mind, a covenant secured by shedding blood; but he might also have had the Jer passage in mind, as the earliest Christian church certainly did in handing down the tradition.

Paul mentions the "new covenant" once more, in 2 Cor 3:5–6: "Our sufficiency is from God, who has qualified us to be ministers of a new covenant, not in a written code but in the Spirit." This passage reflects the basic dichotomy in Paul's thinking between "law" and "faith" and affirms that all those in the church serve to mediate the new covenant. The work in the NT which reflects Jer 31:31–34 in the greatest detail, however, is Hebrews: Heb 8:8–12 quotes the complete passage, and Heb 10:16–17 quotes parts of Jer 31:33 and 34 once more; the book applies the passage to the sacrifice of Jesus Christ.[349]

The NT emphasis on repentance is solidly based on appeals to repentance made by the OT prophets, among

---

22 June 1988.

346 Georg Strecker, *Der Weg der Gerechtigkeit, Untersuchung zur Theologie des Matthäus* (FRLANT 82; Göttingen: Vandenhoeck & Ruprecht, 1962) 76–82, esp. 80–81.

347 Schweizer, *Das Evangelium nach Mattäus,* 329.

348 See recently Robert H. Gundry, *The Use of the Old Testament in St. Matthew's Gospel* (NovTSup 18; Leiden: Brill, 1967); Michael D. Goulder, *Midrash and Lection in Matthew* (London: SPCK, 1974) 124–29; O. Lamar Cope, *Matthew, A Scribe Trained for the Kingdom of Heaven* (CBQMS 5; Washington, DC:

Catholic Biblical Association, 1976).

349 These two paragraphs are taken from William L. Holladay, "New covenant, the," *IDBSup* (Nashville: Abingdon, 1976) 625, used by permission. For further discussion of the matter see Joachim Jeremias, *The Eucharistic Words of Jesus* (New York: Scribner's, 1966) 171, 185, 194–95; Werner Georg Kümmel, *The Theology of the New Testament* (Nashville: Abingdon, 1973) 91–92, 94, 129, 133, 252.

whom of course Jrm was prominent. The basic note in the message of John the Baptist was repentance (Mark 1:4; Matt 3:7–10 = Luke 3:7–9). Repentance was central to Jesus' teaching: there it is bound up with his understanding of the inbreaking of the kingship of God in his own person (thus his first preaching, Mark 1:14–15 = Matt 4:12–17; Luke 4:14–15). And this emphasis continued in Paul's letters (for example, Rom 2:4).[350]

Jesus is remembered as expressing the distinction between true and false prophets in the same kind of way that Jrm did (Luke 6:23, 26) and as suspecting that many of those who claim to prophesy in God's name do not in fact do so (Matt 7:22; compare Jer 14:14).

Tradition attributes further use of words of Jrm by Jesus. Thus when Jesus drove out the money-changers from the temple, he is reported in his speech to have cited Isa 56:7, "My house shall be called a house of prayer," and Jer 7:11, "a robbers' cave" (Mark 11:17 = Matt 21:13; Luke 19:46). And phrases of Jrm's enter into Jesus' own diction: "rest for your souls" (Jer 6:16) appears in Jesus' words in Matt 11:29.

In both 1 Cor 1:31 and 2 Cor 10:17 Paul paraphrases Jer 9:22–23: "Let him who boasts boast of the Lord."

In Rom 9:19–21 Paul draws on the common OT metaphor of potter and clay: in the notion of the clay arguing with the potter the antecedent is Isa 45:9 (compare Isa 29:15), but in the notion that the potter shapes one part of the lump of clay one way and another part another way he finds his motif in Jer 18:6–10.

And in Gal 1:15 Paul uses the words of Jrm's call (Jer 1:5) to apply to himself: "But when he who had set me apart before I was born, and had called me through his grace. . . ."

Finally Revelation is heavy with citations and reminiscences of the OT, Jrm included.[351] Thus Rev 7:17

has "springs of living water" (Jer 2:13); Rev 13:9–10 has, "If any one has an ear, let him hear: 'If any one is to be taken captive, to captivity he goes; if any one slays with the sword, with the sword must he be slain," a paraphrase of Jer 15:2.

There are several echoes of Jrm in Revelation 18, a dirge over the great city, called Babylon (v 2) but understood as Rome, and the echoes are particularly from Jer 50—51, the oracles against Babylon. Thus the reference in Rev 18:3 to the nations having "drunk the wine of her impure passion" is reminiscent of Jer 51:7. Rev 18:4, "Come out of her, my people," is taken from Jer 51:45. In Rev 18:21, "Then a mighty angel took up a stone like a great millstone and threw it into the sea, saying, 'So shall Babylon the great city be thrown down with violence, and shall be found no more,'" the writer had Jer 51:63–64 in mind, Jrm's command to Seraiah to sink into the Euphrates the document on which was written the words of destruction of Babylon.

And in Rev 18:22–23 there is a recasting of Jer 25:10: "And the sound of the millstone shall be heard in you no more, and the light of a lamp shall shine in you no more, and the voice of bridegroom and bride shall be heard in you no more."

The fresh literatures of the Pseudepigrapha, of the Qumran community, and of the NT, therefore, drew deeply on the canonical scriptures for resources, among them Jer, now canonical.

350 Johannes Behm, in Johannes Behm and Ernst Würthwein, "νοέω, κτλ.," *TDNT* 4:1000–1006.
351 A convenient listing is found in Robert H. Charles, *A Critical and Exegetical Commentary on the Revelation of St. John* (ICC; New York: Scribner's, 1920) 1:lxviii–lxxxii.

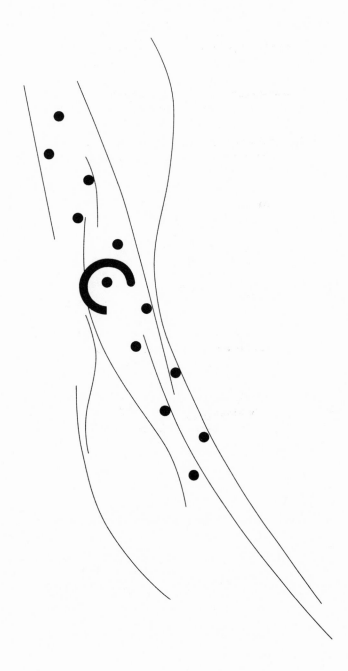

The Temple Sermon
and Its Consequences

Bibliography

On 26:1—45:5:
Kessler, Martin
 "Jeremiah 26—45 Reconsidered," *JNES* 27 (1968)
 81–88.
Thiel
 Jer 26—45.

On 26:1—35:19:
Rietzschel
 Urrolle, 110–22.

On 26:1–24 (see also 7:1–15):
Carroll, Robert P.
 "Prophecy, Dissonance, and Jeremiah xxvi," *Trans-actions of the Glasgow University Oriental Society* 25
 (1976) 12–23, rep. *A Prophet to the Nations, Essays in
 Jeremiah Studies* (ed. Leo G. Perdue and Brian W.
 Kovacs; Winona Lake, IN: Eisenbrauns, 1984)
 381–91.
Driver, Godfrey R.
 "Jeremiah xxvi 6," *VT* 1 (1951) 244–45.
Hadey, Jean
 "Jérémie et le temple, le conflit de la parole
 prophétique et de la tradition religieuse, Jer. 7/1–
 15, 26/1–19," *ETR* 54 (1979) 438–43.
Holt, Else K.
 "Jeremiah's Temple Sermon and the Deutero-nomists: An Investigation of the Redactional Rela-tionship Between Jeremiah 7 and 26," *JSOT* 36
 (1986) 73–87.
Hossfeld, Frank-Lothar, and Ivo Meyer
 "Der Prophet vor dem Tribunal, Neuer Aus-legungsversuch von Jer 26," *ZAW* 86 (1974) 30–
 50.
Jirku, Anton
 "Neues keilinschriftliches Material zum Alten
 Testament, 3: Jer 26$_{22f.}$—die Folge eines Ver-trages?" *ZAW* 39 (1921) 148.
Kegler, Jürgen
 "The Prophetic Discourse and Political Praxis of
 Jeremiah: Observations on Jeremiah 26 and 36,"
 *God of the Lowly, Socio-Historical Interpretations of the
 Bible* (ed. Willy Schottroff and Wolfgang Stege-mann; Maryknoll, NY: Orbis, 1984) 47–56 =
 "Prophetisches Reden und politische Praxis
 Jeremias, Beobachtungen zu Jer. 26 und 36," *Der
 Gott der kleine Leute, Sozialgeschichtliche Bibelaus-legungen* (Munich: Kaiser, 1979) 67–79.
Lohfink, Norbert
 "Die Gattung der 'Historischen Kurzgeschichte' in
 den letzten Jahren von Juda und in der Zeit des
 babylonischen Exils," *ZAW* 90 (1978) 319–47.
Meyer
 Jeremia, 15–45.

Reventlow, Henning Graf
"Gattung und Überlieferung in der 'Tempelrede Jeremias,' Jer 7 und 26," *ZAW* 81 (1969) 315–52.
Schreiner, Josef
"Sicherheit oder Umkehr? Aus der Verkündigung des Propheten Jeremias, Jer 7,1–15; 26,1–6 (II. Teil)," *BibLeb* 7 (1966) 98–111.

Schulz, Hermann
Das Todesrecht im Alten Testament (BZAW 114; Berlin: de Gruyter, 1969) 118–23.
Wanke
Baruchschrift, 77–91.

26

1 In the accession year of Jehoiakim son of Josiah king of Judah this word came from Yahweh, as follows: 2/ Thus Yahweh has said: Stand in the court of the house of Yahweh and speak to all [the cities of]ᵃ Judah who enter to worship at the house of Yahweh all the words which I have commanded you to speak to them; do not subtract a thing. 3/ Perhaps each of them will listen and turn from his evil way, and I may retract the evil which I am planning to do to them because of the evil of their doings. 4/ And you shall say to them, Thus Yahweh has said: If you do not listen to me, to walk in my law which I have set before you, [5/ to listen to the words of my servants the prophets, whom I have sent to you earlyᵇ and constantly—but you have not listened—]ᵃ 6/ then I shall make this house like Shiloh, and the [*M*: this]ᵃ city I shall make an object of contempt for all the nations of the earth.

7 And the priests and prophets and all the people listened to Jeremiah speaking these words in the house of Yahweh. 8/ And when Jeremiah had finished speaking all that Yahweh ⟪had commanded him⟫ᵃ to speak to all the people, the priests and prophets and all the people seized him, saying, "You must die!— 9/ why have you prophesied in the name of Yahweh saying, 'Like Shiloh this house shall be, and this city shall lie in ruins without an inhabitant'?" And all the people thronged around Jeremiah in the house of Yahweh.

10 When the officials of Judah heard these words, they went up from the house of the king to the house of Yahweh and sat at the entrance of the new gate of ᵃthe house ofᵃ Yahweh. 11/ And the priests and the prophets said to the officials and all the people, "This man deserves the death sentence, for he has prophesied against this city, as you have heard with your own ears!"

12 Then Jeremiah said to [all]ᵃ the officials and all the people, "It is Yahweh who sent me to prophesy to this house and this city all the words which you have heard. 13/ So now, make good your ways and your doings and listen to the voice of Yahweh your God, so that Yahweh may retract the evil which he has spoken against you. 14/ But as for me, look, I am in your hand: treat me as is good and proper in your eyes. 15/ Note well, however: if you are going to put me to death, then you will be bringing innocent

Text

2a *G* lacks this expression, which is doubtless a secondary insertion (from 11:6?); compare 7:2.

5a This verse is a secondary addition (so also Rudolph) which breaks the syntax of vv 4 and 6; see further Interpretation.

b Omit וֹ before הַשְׁכֵּם with many MSS. and with the Versions.

6a Read "the city" with *G*. Note that the qere' of *M* reads "this city," but the curious ketib reading הוֹאֹתה suggests an intrusion from a MS. tradition in which this spelling was normal (see Janzen, p. 45, and compare Godfrey R. Driver, "Jeremiah xxvi 6," *VT* 1 [1951] 244–45).

8a Reading צִוָּהוּ with *G*, *V*, and *S* for *M* צִוָּה.

10a—a Reading the expression with many MSS., with some MSS. of *G*, with *V*, *S*, and *T*; *M* lacks it.

12a Delete with *G* (compare Janzen, pp. 65–67); it is dittographic from the next "all."

blood upon yourselves and this city and its inhabitants, for Yahweh really has sent me to you to speak in your ears all these words."

16 Then the officials and all the people said to the priests and the prophets, "This man does not deserve the death sentence, for it is in the name of Yahweh our God that he has spoken to us." 17/ And some of the elders of the land arose and said to all the crowd of people, 18/ "Micah[a] the Morashtite used to prophesy in the days of Hezekiah king of Judah, and he said to all the people of Judah, Thus Yahweh [of hosts][b] has said, 'Zion to a field shall be plowed, and Jerusalem rubble shall be, and the mount of the house for beasts[c] of the forest.' 19/ Did Hezekiah king of Judah—or anyone else in Judah—actually put him to death? Did he not fear Yahweh and entreat the favor of Yahweh, and did Yahweh not retract the evil which he had spoken against them? But we would be doing great evil to our own undoing."

20 But there was also a man prophesying in the name of Yahweh, Uriah the son of Shemaiah from Kiriath-jearim, and he prophesied [a][against this city and] against this land[a] in words like all those of Jeremiah. 21/ When King Jehoiakim [a][and all his warriors] and all the officials[a] heard his words, the king sought to put him to death; Uriah [b][heard and] was afraid and fled [and went][b] to Egypt. 22/ So King Jehoiakim sent [a][men to Egypt,] Elnathan son of Achbor and men with him to Egypt,[a] 23/ and they brought out Uriah from Egypt and brought him in to King Jehoiakim, and he struck him down with the sword and dumped his corpse into the commoners' burial place.

24 However the hand of Ahikam son of Shaphan protected Jeremiah to prevent his being handed over to the people to be put to death.

18a The qere' is מִיכָה "Micah"; the ketib is the fuller form מִיכָיָה. Compare the citations of the two names in the articles in *IDB* 3:369–72.

b Delete with *G* (compare Janzen, pp. 79–80).

c Reading *M* במות as a variant of בָּהֲמוֹת both here and in Mic 3:12. The suggestion was first made for Mic 3:12 by Ehrlich, *Randglossen*, 280, and is accepted by van der Woude, *Micha*, 122, and Delbert R. Hillers, *Micah* (Hermeneia; Philadelphia: Fortress, 1984) 47; Wolff, *Micha*, 62, calls it "quite probable." It is accepted for Jer by Rudolph. *M* is traditionally read as בָּמוֹת "high places" (of the forest), a dubious expression in this context, and *G* ("a grove of woods") suggests a correction to a singular. See the commentaries.

20a—a *G* lacks "against this city and." Either *G* has suffered haplography, or *M* is a conflate text combining the readings "against this city" and "against this land." See Janzen, pp. 21, 199.

21a—a *G* lacks "and all his warriors." The words are evidently a variant of "and all the officials": the inconcinnity of "his (warriors)" and "the (officials)" renders the text suspect (so Janzen, p. 21).

b—b *G* lacks "and was afraid and fled," and again one may have either haplography in *G* or a conflate text in *M* ("heard"/"feared"; "fled"/"went") (so Janzen, p. 21), doubtless the latter.

22a—a *G* lacks "Elnathan . . . Egypt." Here *M* is clearly conflate (Bright; Janzen, pp. 14, 100–101).

Preliminary Observations

This chapter has always attracted attention, and for many reasons. It gives the fullest account of a trial to be found in the OT (see Form), and it narrates what is clearly a crucial encounter between Jrm and the authorities. From the point of literary criticism of the book, the chapter offers a narrative of the temple sermon and its consequences, while 7:1–12 offers in parenetic prose a fuller version of that sermon, without accompanying narrative, and this duplication of material inevitably gives rise to the question how this double tradition could have come to be.

There is another such instance in the book: the narrative in 19:1—20:6 alongside 7:30–34, and long ago

Abraham Kuenen suggested a common literary process for both pairs (see 19:1—20:6, and n. 1 there). Beyond the form-critical resemblance between the two pairs there is resemblance in a small detail that has been overlooked: in the introductory words of each narrative a personal reference to Jrm is missing, and in each instance one or more Versions have felt the lack and supplied the reference—in 19:1 *M* reads "Thus Yahweh said," and *G* and *S* have added "to me," while in 26:1 *M* reads ". . . this word came from Yahweh . . ." and Vetus Latina and *S* have added "to Jeremiah" after "came." The lack of personal reference in each passage is awkward enough that several commentators have accepted the Versional addition(s): in the case of 19:1, Cornill, Albert

Condamin, and Bright; and in the case of 26:1, Giesebrecht, Volz, Rudolph, and Bright. But the fact that *M* has the lack in each case suggests a common origin for both 19:1—20:6 and chapter 26; and the fact that a personal reference was not considered necessary points for both passages toward Baruch, who was personally associated with the prophet, tending to confirm the conclusion to which many commentators had already come.[1]

If Baruch wrote both narratives, then they can fruitfully be compared. Since the present passage narrates Jrm's signal appeal for repentance, the purpose of the first scroll (36:2–3), the narration in chapter 19 just as clearly represents Jrm's public declaration of Yahweh's irrevocable punishment, the purpose of the second scroll (36:30–32). According to the present passage Jrm's temple sermon brought him into conflict with the authorities; 20:1–6 is an analogous narrative of the reaction of the authorities to Jrm's public declaration (compare the analysis in 19:1—20:6, Preliminary Observations).

Structure

The present chapter begins a collection of material which ends in chapter 36: for the organizing principle see Introduction, sec. 22.

Internal Structure of the Unit. Verses 20–23, the story of Uriah, have been judged by most commentators to be an addition to the text, a kind of appendix of Baruch's (see, for example, Volz, Condamin, Hyatt, Weiser); the assumption is that the narrator must stay only with Jrm and cannot have given a dramatic parallel story. But v 19 leaves the narrative "up in the air," and v 24 is scarcely a conclusion for v 19. On the other hand, the diction of v 20a is like that of v 18a (היה plus a participle from a stem of נבא), and v 21 is parallel to v 19 (the subject is the king; "put to death" [מות hip‘il]; "fear"). It would appear that Micah is a parallel to Jrm in a previous generation, and that Uriah is a parallel to Jrm in his own generation;

the narrative of Uriah is thus integrated into the larger narrative.

The narrative is likewise held together by "hand": Jrm states in his defense that he is in the "hand" of his accusers (v 14), and the narrator concludes by noting that the "hand" of Ahikam protected Jrm (v 24). There seems to be no need to analyze the passage in more detail.[2]

Form

One has here a unit of prophetic biography,[3] the purpose of which is to set forth the truth of the proclamation of Jrm.[4] This narrative is the most detailed description of a trial in the OT: we have a pretrial accusation (vv 8–9), then the trial proper (vv 10–16) including a speech by the prosecution (v 11), a speech by the defense (vv 12–15), and a formulation of the verdict (v 16), which in this case is for exoneration.[5]

The trial, evidently for blasphemy, is the consequence of Jrm's temple sermon, a summary of which is given in vv 4 and 6, parenesis based on covenant formulations (for which see 7:1–15, Form); and the sermon is in turn the prophet's response to Yahweh's summons (*Anruf*) to the prophet to appeal to the people in the uncertain hope they might repent (vv 2–3). The parenesis is repeated in Jrm's defense (v 13).

The speech of the elders (vv 17–19) might seem to have been a speech of witnesses for the defense, more appropriate before the sentence is pronounced (compare Volz); one must either conclude that the narrator wished to place the case of Micah and Uriah side by side (see Structure, Interpretation) and thus gave the material out of logical order, or else that the order of events is correct and the speech of the elders is in the nature of confirmation of the verdict. (John Calvin as usual is sensible: "It is uncertain whether what is here recited was spoken before the acquittal of Jeremiah or not; for the Scripture does not always exactly preserve order in narrating things," but he goes on to point out that the elders

1 Compare the conclusion in Wanke, *Baruchschrift*, 144, and the bibliography in that study.
2 But see the analysis of Wanke, *Baruchschrift*, 82–90.
3 See March, "Prophecy," 174–75, and further Klaus Koch, *The Growth of the Biblical Tradition, The Form-Critical Method* (New York: Scribner's 1969) 203–5.
4 Wanke, *Baruchschrift*, 156.
5 Hans Jochen Boecker, *Law and the Administration of Justice in the Old Testament and Ancient East* (Minneapolis: Augsburg, 1980) 44.

attemped to calm the fickle crowd.)

The elders cite the precedent of Micah, and the narrator of the present chapter cites the parallel of Uriah, so that vv 20–23 represent a small unit of biography of another prophet which gives dramatic perspective to Jrm's ordeal; v 24 closes the chapter, linking it to material elsewhere concerned with later events in the prophet's career.

Setting

There is no need to resort to the idea that this chapter comes from a Deuteronomistic editor; the phrases presumed to be Deuteronomic can be better explained otherwise. Thus "make good your ways and your doings" (v 13) is found in the temple sermon itself (7:3, 5; compare 18:11); "turn (each) from his evil way" is likewise found in 18:11. The conventional phrases here are not arbitrarily set forth as part of a particular editorial work of a later generation but give every evidence of offering authentic historical narrative.

There are several resemblances in specific detail between this chapter and chapter 36, beyond those already cited (see Introduction, sec. 22). Thus there is the simplification by omission of the protasis in both 26:9 and 36:29, and the possible parallel between the fate of Uriah in 26:23 and the curse on Jehoiakim in 36:30 (for the details see Interpretation on the respective verses of the present chapter). These resemblances lead to the conclusion that the same narrator is responsible for both chapters, and it is altogether likely that the narrator is Baruch himself (as commentators have assumed: so Volz and Rudolph, and so my own proposal,[6] against Wanke).[7] Baruch participated in the events of chapter 36 and could well have heard from Jrm the details of that earlier occasion when the prophet was threatened by royal power. And one small detail: in both v 9 here and in 43:2 opponents of Jrm misquote a divine word delivered by him, by omitting the protasis (see both passages); and since Baruch is by most commentators

understood to be responsible for chapters 37—44, it is likely that one finds the hand of that scribe here in the same narrative technique. There is therefore no reason to question the essential historicity of the narrative, however much it may have been shaped by the skill of the narrator and by his specific purpose (see Form).

If one understands the first phrase of v 1 correctly, the event of Jrm's trial took place as a consequence of his preaching the temple sermon in the accession-year of Jehoiakim, by the reckoning adopted here sometime between August/September 609 and March/April 608 (see Interpretation on v 1), most likely at the feast of Booths in September/October 609. The likelihood is that the execution of Uriah took place not too much later: it is suggested in the present study that the phrasing of the curse of Jehoiakim (22:18–19) is due to his treatment of Uriah's corpse, and that curse is associated with the king's building program, which doubtless got under way within the first year or two of his reign (compare Setting for 22:13–19).

Interpretation

■ **1** The suggestion of Joachim Begrich[8] is accepted by commentators as a virtual certainty, that the phrase רֵאשִׁית מַמְלְכוּת here (literally "beginning of the kingship") is used in the technical sense of "accession-year," corresponding precisely to the Akkadian rēš šarrūti. By this understanding the reference is to the period in a king's reign before his first New Year's Day, at which point his first regnal year is reckoned.[9] This is evidently the mode of reckoning regnal years used in Judah at this period.[10] If the New Year at that time was reckoned in the spring, then the period falls between August/September 609 and March/April 608.[11] Aside from the "thirteenth year of Josiah" itself (1:2), this is the earliest dated event of Jrm's career; the reference here is to the delivery of the so-called temple sermon (7:3–12), as vv 4 and 6 make clear. This is the only occurrence in Jer of the particular form of the word "kingship" (מַמְלְכוּת); the other two

---

6   William L. Holladay, "A Fresh Look at 'Source B' and 'Source C' in Jeremiah," *VT* 25 (1975) 402.

7   Wanke, *Baruchschrift*, 147.

8   Joachim Begrich, *Die Chronologie der Könige von Israel und Juda und die Quellen des Rahmens der Königsbücher* (Tübingen: Mohr [Siebeck], 1929) 91, 93.

9   Simon J. De Vries, "Chronology of the OT," *IDB* 1:586a.

10   Ibid., 587a.

11   Compare Malamat, "Twilight of Judah," 127, note 9, who assumes an autumn New Year.

occurrences of the phrase in question offer מַמְלֶכֶת
(though in those passages, namely, 27:1 and 28:1, the
chronological data are in error: see there).

■ **2** For "court of the house of Yahweh" see 19:14. The
parallel in 7:2 (where the text is secondary) uses "gate"
for "court." The assumed shorter phrase "all (those of)
Judah" matches "all (you of) Judah" in 7:2. The expansion "all the cities of Judah" suggests "all the citizens of
Judah": this meaning of "city" is cited elsewere,[12] but not
otherwise in the plural. "Enter to worship" is found in
the secondary text of 7:2; for "worship" see 1:16. "All the
words which I have commanded you to speak" is an
expansion of the phrase in 1:7.

The one fresh phrase in the verse is "do not subtract a
thing," a phrase found also in Deut 4:2 and 13:1:[13] it is a
formula found generally in ancient Near Eastern legal
and wisdom texts.[14] But in Deuteronomy Moses instructs
the Israelites not to subtract anything from what Moses
commands them, while here Yahweh instructs Jrm not to
subtract anything from what Yahweh has commanded
him to say. The implication is that the prophet would
mitigate the word out of fear of consequences (compare
1:17): in this way the narrator prepares for the opposition depicted in vv 7–9. The verb (גרע) means "diminish"
or "reduce"; the same notion, that the prophet is not to
withhold any word, no matter how unwelcome, is
rendered elsewhere by the synonyms כחד pi'el (38:14,
25) and מנע (42:4).

■ **3** This verse states Yahweh's purpose in Jrm's temple
sermon: it is warning, so that the people will repent and
Yahweh will not have to carry out the punishment he has
in mind (the same point of view is implied in 7:3, 5–7).
Similar phrasing is found in 36:3, the purpose of the
dictation of the first scroll (see Introduction, sec. 22, and
Setting on the present chapter).

The particle "perhaps" (אוּלַי) attracts the sequence of
imperfect followed by simple ו and the imperfect, as in
21:2:[15] "listen" and "turn" are thus virtually synonymous.
The phraseology of this verse is similar to that in 18:8,

11: see the discussion there. For "retract" (נחם) see 18:8,
10; for this verb with a negative see 4:28.

■ **4–6** Verses 4 and 6 summarize the sermon itself; in
particular, "then I shall make this house like Shiloh" is
close to the references in 7:12 and 14. The phrase "walk
in my law which I set before you" has its closest previous
analogy in the book in 9:12 (see there); the component
"walk in (Yahweh's) law" is found both within Deutero-
omistic phraseology (2 Kgs 10:31) and outside it (Ps
78:10). It is conceivable that the use of the phrase here is
intended to give resonance to the reference to Shiloh,
since the same Psalm 78 that makes use of the phrase
mentions the fall of Shiloh later on (v 60) as a punishment for Ephraim's unwillingness to walk in Yahweh's
law. It is to be noted that there is no reference to "this
city" in 7:1–15, but rather to "this place" (7:7, 14); a
recent study suggests that "house" and "city" are a parallel word pair.[16] For "object of contempt" (קְלָלָה) see
24:9. One notes also the chiastic structure of the apodosis in v 6.

Verse 5 interrupts the flow between vv 4 and 6: (1) the
infinitive phrase is an odd continuation of the protasis in
v 4, and the twofold use of "listen" (שמע) in v 5 hardly fits
after the occurrence of the same verb in v 4—indeed the
closing clause "but you have not listened" really contradicts the protasis; and (2) the diction of the verse is that
of material associated with the second scroll, dictated
when Jrm was convinced there was no hope (compare
7:25 and 25:4, especially the treatment of the Setting of
the passages containing those verses). For the specific
phrases see Interpretation of 7:25. (The same conclusion
is reached by Rudolph, and by Franz-Lothar Hossfeld
and Ivo Meyer.[17])

■ **7–19** There is need to clarify the meaning of the
expression "all the people," which occurs in vv 7, 8
(twice), 9, 11, 12, and 16 (in v 18 the reference is to
those in Micah's time). The problem is that in vv 11, 12,
and 16 the "people" are bracketed with the "officials"
who defend Jrm, while in vv 7, 8, and 9 the "people" are

---

12 *HALAT*, 777a, n. 3.
13 So also Weinfeld, *Deuteronomy*, 360, n. 14.
14 Similar phraseology is found in Prov 30:6; Eccl 3:14;
    Sir 18:6; 42:21; and Rev 22:18–19; see further
    Oswald Loretz, *Qohelet und der Alte Orient, Unter-
    suchungen zu Stil und theologischer Thematik des Buches
    Qohelet* (Freiburg: Herder, 1964) 66–69.
15 See König, *Syntax*, sec. 367p.

16 Daniel E. Fleming, "'House'/'City': An Unrecog-
    nized Parallel Word Pair," *JBL* 105 (1986) 689–93.
17 Frank-Lothar Hossfeld and Ivo Meyer, "Der Prophet
    vor dem Tribunal, Neuer Auslegungsversuch von Jer
    26," *ZAW* 86 (1974) 35.

bracketed with the "priests" and "prophets" who wish to execute him. The usage is particularly difficult in v 8b, and the majority of commentators have excised "and all the people" at that point as a gloss from v 7 (so first Ferdinand Hitzig; Duhm, Cornill, Condamin, Rudolph, Bright).[18] Beyond the seeming contradiction between vv 7–9 and vv 11–16 is the fact that "all the people" would hardly "seize" Jrm, and in any event the phrase in v 8b hardly fits the statement in v 9, where all the people "throng around" Jrm. Wanke accepts that excision[19] but still struggles with the reference of the phrase in its other occurrences.

It may be admitted that the solution of the problem, by the excision of the phrase in v 8b, is conceivable, but it should be said that there is no textual warrant for it, and not all commentators accept it (notably Volz). The implication of vv 11, 12, and 16 is that "the officials and all the people" sit as a kind of judicial body (Volz, followed by Rudolph and Nicholson[20]) and are therefore distinct from "all the people" in v 7. Why then can "all the people" in vv 8 and 9 not be still different segments of the crowd? (The same nuance is evidently intended in the different circumstance of 36:9.) It is doubtless a festival season (compare v 2), there is always a crowd on the city streets of a Near Eastern city waiting for excitement, the general tone of a festival crowd in the temple area would be optimistic (7:10): any crowd would be aroused by these words of the prophet. Calvin may not be far wrong, furthermore, when he stresses the fickleness of crowds: "But there is another thing to be noticed, —that the common people suffer themselves to be drawn in all directions; but they may also be easily restored, as it has been said, to a right mind" (on v 11). It follows further that there is no real need to struggle, as Wanke does, with the nuance of "thronged around" (קהל nip'al + אֶל) at the end of v 9, whether the crowd is hostile ("gathered together against") or neutral ("gathered together for judgment").[21] Thompson may be allowed a summary word on the matter; he notes that "all the

people" in v 8b must be understood as "some of the people."

■ **7–9** The common cause of "prophets" with "priests" here is clear evidence that prophets as well as priests were officially connected with the temple cultus:[22] both groups together arrest Jrm. (It is noteworthy that both *G* and *S* use "false prophets" [ψευδοπροφῆται, *nby' dgl'*] consistently for "prophets" from here through v 16 [as they do also in 6:13].) The cultic prophets' opposition to Jrm is the reason for his frequent parallelism of "prophet" and "priest" (4:9; 5:31; 6:13; 14:18; 23:11; compare 2:8); the same opposition elicited the same parallelism in earlier prophetic oracles (Isa 28:7; Mic 3:11).[23]

■ **8** The verb תפש carries the general meaning of "grasp, seize" (compare the discussion on the only previous occurrence in the book, 2:8); here "seize" implies "arrest" (as it does also in 37:13, 14).

"You must die" is the nuance of the phrase מוֹת תָּמוּת. The phrase occurs otherwise twelve times in the OT.[24] The context of 1 Sam 14:44 and 1 Kgs 2:37, 42 makes it clear that it is the formula by which a death sentence is pronounced against the accused;[25] compare 20:6, where the verb תָּמוּת occurs without the infinitive absolute in a poetic context. But here the formula is not used in the official judicial sense, since the trial proper is not narrated until v 10; rather the crowd uses the formula with the connotation "you should be sentenced to death" (*NEB* paraphrases the last of the verse, "seized him and threatened him with death"). For the nature of Jrm's offense which would merit such a sentence, see below on v 9.

■ **9** Jrm's opponents paraphrase his message. The rhetoric of the paraphrase is noteworthy in two respects. First, the protasis is omitted ("if you do not listen to me," v 4); the divine message is thereby transformed from a covenant speech—in which the people are reminded that if they break their covenant obligations, Yahweh will punish them—to an announcement of divine punishment (by

18   So further Janzen, p. 133.

19   Wanke, *Baruchschrift*, 87.

20   Ernest W. Nicholson, *The Book of the Prophet Jeremiah Chapters 26—52* (The Cambridge Bible Commentary on the New English Bible; Cambridge: Cambridge University, 1975) 23.

21   Wanke, *Baruchschrift*, 88.

22   Johnson, *Cultic Prophet*, 60–61.

23   The matter is explored at length in Johnson's study (see n. 22) and more recently in Wilson, *Prophecy and Society*.

24   Gen 2:17; 20:7; 1 Sam 14:44; 22:16; 1 Kgs 2:37, 42; 2 Kgs 1:4, 6, 16; Ezek 3:18; 33:8, 14.

25   Gerhard Liedke, *Gestalt und Bezeichnung alttestamentlichen Rechtssätze* (WMANT 39; Neukirchen: Neukirchener, 1971) 127–28.

implication, an irrevocable one). This omission is specifically noted by Sebastian Schmidt (1706): he assumes it is deliberate, since the prophet's opponents could not claim they had heard the word of God.

This is the easiest assumption, but it must be said that there is a parallel omission in v 11 (where the declaration about "this house" is missing); and one may note a similar omission of the implied protasis in Jehoiakim's question after he burns Jrm's scroll (36:29, compare vv 3 and 7 there). It is proposed that the present chapter and chapter 36 come from the same narrator (see Setting), so that even though it is human nature in polemical exchange to omit or distort the words of one's opponent, what one has here is doubtless the result of the narrator's intention as much as it is a reflection of the words of the crowd.

This conclusion is strengthened by examination of the second noteworthy characteristic of the rhetoric of the paraphrase. The apodosis in v 6, as already pointed out, is in the form of a chiasmus; the paraphrase here is likewise a chiasmus, but one that reverses the form of v 6, since there "this house" and "this city" were objects of occurrences of the verb "make" (נתן), while here they are subjects of their respective verbs. In this regard one sees the art of the narrator, and thus the omission of the protasis of Jrm's speech (and the further omission of "this house" in v 11) must in its present shape likewise be the work of the narrator.

The omission of the protasis clears the way for an understanding why the crowd should be moved to threaten Jrm with death: they heard him predicting Yahweh's destruction of the temple and the city with it. In the form of the temple sermon in 7:1–12 the people's trust in the inviolability of the temple is made clear (7:4; compare 7:14, "the house . . . in which you trust"). Calvin, in his remarks on the present verse, says, "God seemed in appearance to be inconsistent with himself, 'This is my rest for ever' [Ps 132:14], 'this shall be a desert' [his paraphrase of the phrase in the present verse]. We hence see that the priests and the prophets were not without some specious pretext for condemning Jeremiah." That is to say, the crowd felt the contradiction between such unconditional affirmations as "this

is my rest for ever" and the covenantal condition "if you do not listen to me, I will destroy the temple," so that one could even say that the simplification of Jrm's speech, in the omission of the protasis, was justifiable. Calvin goes on to say, "God had not promised that the Temple should be perpetual in order to give license to the people to indulge in all manner of wickedness." Calvin suggests, in other words, that Jrm announces the covenantal condition with such an affirmation as "this is my rest for ever"; and indeed this is precisely what is recorded in 7:3 and 7:5–7 (see Interpretation there).

Since, however, by the people's understanding of Jrm's contradiction of Yahweh's promises regarding the temple, he must be a false prophet, he is to be sentenced to death (Deut 18:20). What one sees here then is not so much mob hysteria as a theological judgment anchored in the tradition.

The paraphrase "this city shall lie in ruins without an inhabitant" is rather far from the wording of v 6, "the city I shall make an object of contempt for all the nations of the earth." The verb חרב means both "become dry" (see 2:12) and "lie in ruins" (as here); these are the only two occurrences of the qal stem of this verb in Jer. For "without inhabitant," with a parallel verbal expression, see 4:7.

This is the only occurrence in Jer of קהל nip'al, translated here "thronged (around)." The verb simply means "assemble," whether for conflict (2 Sam 20:14) or for a religious festival (1 Kgs 8:2) or whatever: nothing is implied about the mood or discipline of the crowd, and the nuance must be gathered from the context. "Thronged" is Bright's rendering; *NJV* translated "crowded about Jeremiah."

■ 10 The trial proper begins; the "officials" (שָׂרִים) may in different contexts be either military or civil functionaries (compare 1:17–19)—here they obviously serve as judges. "These words" may just as well be translated "these things" (so Sebastian Schmidt, and so Weiser), since it is not a matter of a direct hearing of Jrm's words. The officials went up from the palace to the temple area, which was located on the summit of Zion. The gate, having a plaza in front, was the location where judicial proceedings could take place (Amos 5:10, 12, 15).[26] The

---

26   See further Chester C. McCown, "Gate," *IDB* 2:355.

"new gate" is also mentioned in 36:10, where it is described as "in the upper court," but its location is not more precisely known. Traditionally commentators have identified it with the "upper gate" built by Jotham (2 Kgs 15:35)—so first Abrabanel,[27] and so recently Louis Hugues Vincent;[28] similarly there is an identification with the "Upper Benjamin Gate" mentioned in 20:2.[29]

■ **11** The priests and prophets (vv 7–8) bring their accusation to the officials who sit as judges; "all the people" is an expression for the general crowd who stand around listening (see above, vv 7–19). They say, literally, "A judgment of death to this man"; for the idiom compare the variants in Deut 21:22 and 2 Sam 12:5.

As was noted above (on v 9), the accusation oversimplifies in mentioning "this city" but not "this house"; it is a further simplification after v 9 and concentrates on the item that could be understood to have political consequences ("city") rather than mentioning with it the item that would have cultic consequences ("temple"). But it is only a matter of accent, for the city as a whole was both a political and cultic center (compare again the observations on v 9). The effect of the accusation then is to suggest that Jrm is subverting the state and at the same time to suggest that to speak against the city is to blaspheme against Yahweh, who makes his name dwell there; and the punishment for blasphemy is death (Exod 22:27; Lev 24:10–16). It is a perfect instance of the Israelite union of "secular" and "religious" perceptions in the image of covenant.

The last phrase, "as you have heard with your own ears," is doubtless directed to "all the people," who had heard Jrm's speech, not to the officials who were sitting in judgment, who had not.

■ **12–15** Jrm in his defense restores "this house" along with "this city" (v 12) and insists that, far from subverting the political order or blaspheming, he is simply carrying out his mission to speak the word from Yahweh. He begins and ends his speech by insisting that he is speaking at Yahweh's initiative—in v 12, where the subject is emphatic, before the verb, and in v 15, where the same verb with the same subject is this time in normal order but the emphatic word before the verb is "really" (בֶּאֱמֶת). For Yahweh's "sending" Jrm to "speak," see in detail 1:7. Verse 13 offers the phrase "make good your ways and your doings," which is not found in vv 4 and 6 but is repetition from 7:3 (compare 7:5). For "retract" see v 3; the verb does not appear in 7:3–12.

In vv 12–13 the emphasis is on Yahweh's initiative and the people's response to it; in v 14, by contrast, Jrm refers to his own situation—the initial phrase means really "as far as I am concerned." He is passive about his own fate: the phraseology of the verse is precisely parallel to Josh 9:25, the end of the Gibeonites' speech to Joshua. Jrm deliberately puts himself in the power of the court, a power that obviously includes the possibility of the death penalty (v 15). He reminds them quietly, however, that if they execute him, they will be "bringing [נתן] innocent blood upon themselves," that is, bringing bloodguilt upon themselves, shedding innocent blood (compare 2:34; 22:17). Bloodguilt involves the whole community (Deut 19:10–13), a notion Jrm underlines ("yourselves and this city and its inhabitants").[30] If Jrm's accusers imply that he is guilty of blasphemy, Jrm says explicitly that his executioners would bring bloodguilt on the whole community. Where does Yahweh's will lie?

■ **16** Faced with a theological argument, the officials appear to turn to the accusers and say, "This is not in our jurisdiction," but such a conclusion doubtless modernizes the text. What is clear is that Jrm convinced the judges, who declared for acquittal, as did "all the people." Are we to assume the people are fickle (compare again vv 8 and 9)? The acquittal is pronounced before the precedent of Micah is cited (vv 17–19).

■ **17–19** The elders' citing of the precedent from Micah suggests that the bystanders approved the declaration of acquittal, but the elders' speech may not be given here in narrative sequence (see Form). The subject is literally "men from the elders of the land." The "elders" were

---

27   So Sebastian Schmidt.

28   Louis Hugues Vincent, *Jérusalem de l'Ancien Testament, Recherches d'archéologie et d'histoire* (Paris: Gabalda, 1954) 603.

29   Freedman, p. 175; Thompson, p. 526.

30   See Moshe Greenberg, "Bloodguilt," *IDB* 1:449–50; Pedersen, I/II, 420–25.

always an important group within society, but it is not possible to state with precision what group of people comes forward in the designation "elders of the land";[31] Weiser suggests a connection with elders from various cities who had there judicial functions similar to those of the "officials" in Jerusalem. These elders were doubtless in Jerusalem for the festival occasion when Jrm preached the temple sermon. "Crowd" (קָהָל) is literally "assembly": it was those assembled for the trial, but they could well have been an unruly assemblage, given the use of the cognate verb ("thronged") in v 9 (for the rendering compare Bright).

The elders cite what is now Mic 3:12 to reinforce the judgment of the officials: there is precedent a hundred years earlier for a prophet's speaking against Jerusalem without being executed. The details of exegesis of v 18 may be found fully in commentaries on Micah:[32] "the Morashtite" is one from Moresheth, doubtless identical with Moresheth-gath (Mic 1:14); it is identified with the modern *tall el-judeideh* (Atlas of Israel grid 141–115), about forty kilometers southwest of Jerusalem on the edge of the Shephelah. The verbal phrase translated "used to prophesy" (the perfect of היה followed by the participle nip'al of נבא) is striking, though not without parallel (GKC, sec. 116r, where the present passage is not cited; Joüon, *Gramm.*, sec. 121f, where it is). The wording of the quotation from Micah is word-for-word what appears in Mic 3:12 (the only contrast is the Aramaic plural of "rubble" in Micah: the text here has the expected Hebrew plural).

In the first (interrogative) clause in v 19 both the verb and the subject carry emotional nuances. The verb is reinforced by an infinitive absolute. The subject is literally "Hezekiah king of Judah, and all Judah," but "all" in negative and hypothetical clauses is best translated "any" (compare Gen 3:1, "than any other beast"),[33] so that the compound subject means "Hezekiah . . . or anyone else in Judah." The finite verb may be vocalized either as a singular (as G, V, and S have it) or as a plural (as M has it), and the likelihood of a singular here in turn suggests that "and all Judah" is rhetorically intended as an afterthought. The infinitive absolute, by the context, does not mean "really" but emphasizes the extremeness

of the meaning of the verb; one may paraphrase, "Did Hezekiah, king of Judah, or anyone else in Judah for that matter, go so far as to put him to death?" (compare Bright). The first clause, implying a negative answer, is followed by two clauses implying a positive answer, one of them Hezekiah's attitude toward Yahweh, the other Yahweh's reaction. For "fear Yahweh" see 5:22. The phrase "entreat the favor of Yahweh" (חלה pi'el + פְּנֵי־ יהוה) is a curious idiom which is evidently rooted in the ideology and ceremony of the court, but the concrete notion behind it ("soften the monarch's face"?) is unclear.[34] The idiom is not otherwise used of Hezekiah, but 2 Kgs 13:4 uses it of King Jehoahaz of Israel. "Retract" of course echoes that verb in v 13—the intention is to parallel Jrm's diction; and the narrator uses both occurrences to reinforce the occurrence of the verb in v 3. The speech ends with a contrast between Hezekiah's action and what "we," the court in session, have considered doing; the participial clause (literally "but we are doing great evil against ourselves"), by the context, must be understood as future potential (here translated "but we would be doing"; Bright, "we are on the point of doing," and so similarly other recent translations). The noun רָעָה, literally "evil," occurs twice in the last two clauses. In the next-to-last it is the common usage by which Yahweh brings "disaster" on the people (so in v 13; compare the first instance in 1:14). But the last occurrence may have more than one implication; it may be that "we" are about to match or trigger the disaster that Yahweh intends upon the people (so *NEB*, "disaster"; so Bright and *NJV*, "injury"); but it also may be that "we" are about to "commit a crime" (*JB*; compare 2:13) or a moral "evil" "to our own undoing" (*NAB*). The closing expression of the verse reinforces the ambiguity: עַל־נַפְשׁוֹתֵינוּ can be a periphrasis for "upon/against ourselves" (compare נַפְשֹׁתֵיכֶם in 37:9) or else carry the meaning "upon/against our lives" (compare 17:21). Doubtless both implications are intended. The same expression, one notes, occurs in 44:7.

■ **20–24** Verses 20–23 sketch quickly the story of the prophet Uriah, whose message was similar to that of Jrm, and how Jehoiakim executed him (for the relation of these verses to the rest of the chapter see Structure).

---

31   Compare Joachim Conrad, "זָקֵן," *TDOT* 4:128.
32   Wolff, *Micha*, 79–80; Mays, *Micah*, 92.
33   See BDB 482a, entry e.

34   For a discussion, with a bibliography of various suggestions, see Klaus Seybold, "חָלָה," *TDOT* 4:407–9.

Since Jehoiakim's posse had the freedom to enter Egypt to extradite Uriah, the event must have taken place early in Jehoiakim's reign when he was still an Egyptian vassal (see the discussion in Setting).

This Uriah is otherwise unknown; it is tantalizing to have the mention of another prophet of doom contemporary with Jrm.

Kiriath-jearim is to be identified with *tall al-ʿazar*, near *qaryat el-ʿinab*, also known as *abū ġawš* (Atlas of Israel grid 160–135), about thirteen kilometers west-northwest of Jerusalem.[35]

Though one's first impression is that the narrative of Uriah is intended as a counterfoil to that of Jrm (and v 24 confirms that impression), the phraseological parallels of the Uriah narrative are with the references to Micah immediately preceding. Thus the king sought to "put him to death" (מות hipʿil; v 21, compare v 19); and Hezekiah had "feared" Yahweh, but Uriah was "afraid" of Jehoiakim.

These parallels are reinforced when one notes the close parallel between the beginning of v 20 and that of v 18 (the subject preceding the verb, the verb היה, and a participle of the root נבא "prophesy"), and the parallel is reinforced by the particle גם at the beginning of v 20. The phrase does not then quite mean "there was another man," as most translations have it (it is not איש אחר, as one finds in 1 Kgs 20:37), but "there was also a man" (implication: "like Micah"). The question then arises, given this parallel, is there an intended distinction between the nipʿal participle (נִבָּא) in v 18 and the hitpaʿel participle (מִתְנַבֵּא) found in v 20?—both are commonly translated "prophesying" without differentiation. The hitpaʿel stem of this verb is used by Jrm of the false prophets (14:14; 23:13), but here it is used of someone whose message is similar to Jrm's. It is used in a derogatory fashion by Shemaiah about Jrm's message ("every madman who acts like a prophet," 29:26). Clearly, then, the verb implies nothing about the content of the message but is concerned rather with the form in

which it is presented. In this way the hitpaʿel of the verb seems to conform to the meaning of some other examples of the hitpaʿel, "act like X," "pretend to be X," if one is to press a contrast between this stem and the nipʿal of this verb.[36] One might paraphrase the opening clause, then, "But there was someone claiming to prophesy in the name of Yahweh." If there is a distinction intended by the narrator, then Micah is presented as a true prophet by common consent, while Uriah, a contemporary of the narrator, made prophetic claims, and nothing at this point is implied about the rightness or wrongness of his message.

If there is a parallel between Uriah and Micah, is there any significance to the fact that both Moresheth and Kiriath-jearim are in the Shephelah? Does the narrator thus intend the hearer to think of two prophets from the same region?

Achbor the father of Elnathan (v 22), and both Shaphan the father of Ahikam (v 24) and Ahikam himself, had been advisors to Josiah, part of the delegation he sent to Huldah the prophetess to validate the newly found scroll (2 Kgs 22:12, 14). And in the present generation Elnathan and Gemariah, a brother of Ahikam, would be part of the circle around Jehoiakim when Jrm's scroll is brought to the attention of the king (36:12) and would caution him against burning it (36:25). Yet Elnathan in the present passage is in charge of the group that the king sent to Egypt to fetch Uriah. It is to be noted that in 2 Kgs 24:8 an "Elnathan of Jerusalem" is stated to have been the father of Nehushta, the mother of Jehoiachin; Rudolph doubts the identification with Elnathan the son of Achbor mentioned in the present passage, but it is altogether likely.[37] If the

---

35   For the identification of the site see Francis T. Cooke, "The Site of Kirjath-jearim," AASOR 5 (1923–24) (New Haven: American Schools of Oriental Research, 1925) 105–20; for bibliography on excavations of the site see "Abu Ghosh" in Eleanor K. Vogel, *Bibliography of Holy Land Sites*, offprint of *HUCA* 42 (1971) 3, and Eleanor K. Vogel and Brooks Holtzclaw, *Bibliography of Holy Land Sites,*

Part II (1970–81), offprint from *HUCA* 52 (1981) 4.

36   On the whole question see Robert R. Wilson, "Prophecy and Ecstasy: A Reexamination," *JBL* 98 (1979) 321–37, esp. 335–36.

37   The name also occurs on a seal from the last half of the eighth century and on two from the late sixth or early fifth century: see Herr, *Scripts*, 25, n. 36; 28, n. 45; and 51, n. 110. For the identification of the

identification is correct, then it is his father-in-law whom Jehoiakim sends to Egypt to fetch Uriah; how much pressure there must have been on this courtier—what a dilemma the prophets of doom must have presented to the king's advisors!

No details are given of any inquiry or trial for Uriah; the narrator intends by his concision to underline the contempt the king held for that prophet, a contempt made explicit in the last clause of v 23, "dumped his corpse into the commoners' burial place" (literally "to the graves of the children of the people"; for a discussion of "sons/children of the people" see 17:19). The phraseology of Jrm's curse on Jehoiakim in 36:30 is close enough to the narrative here ("dump his corpse," and compare "dump" in the poetic form of the curse on the king in 22:19) to warrant the suspicion that that curse was specifically called forth by the king's treatment of Uriah (see Setting, and see the comments in the Setting of 22:13–19 and Interpretation of 22:19). One may surmise, therefore, that while the king's treatment of Uriah was expected to serve as a warning to Jrm, it only stiffened his resolve.

The word "hand" appears twice in v 24: the "hand" of Ahikam was with Jrm, literally "so as not to put him into the hand of the people": in this way the conclusion of the chapter harks back to v 14, where Jrm says to the officials and the people, "I am in your hand." And "put to death" at the end of the verse resonates with v 21, in which the king sought to put Uriah to death; with v 19, in which the elders' rhetorical question indicates that Hezekiah did not put Micah to death; and ultimately with v 15, in which Jrm states to the court the possibility, "if you are going to put me to death." The last verse serves then in several ways to round off the chapter.

Ahikam is not mentioned again in the book. He had been old enough in 622 to have served with his father in the circle of advisors to Josiah (2 Kgs 22:12, 14); it is now thirteen years later. It is his brother Gemariah who would be a part of the circle of advisors around Jehoiakim when the scroll was burned (36:12, 25), and it will be his son Gedaliah to whom the Babylonians will entrust Jrm in 587 and whom the Babylonians will appoint to be governor over the province (39:14; 40:7). The impres-

sion with which one is left, then, is that Ahikam, though not part of the king's group of advisors, was a person of standing and influence.[38]

Aim

On the aim of Jrm himself in the temple sermon see 7:1–15.

The narrator here sets forth a crucial event in the beginning of Jrm's career in which the prophet proclaims the word of Yahweh, is then challenged by his opponents, and is finally confirmed in his activity.

Jrm is threatened with death at the beginning of his career, but it will not be the last time he is threatened: Jehoiakim tried to seize him when the prophet's scroll was read (36:26), the optimistic prophets plotted to have him put to death, evidently soon thereafter (11:19; 18:20), his life was probably threatened by them again in the summer of 594 (20:10, 13), and he is imprisoned during the final siege of Jerusalem (37:14–21; 38:4–28).

Opposition to the prophetic word is a commonplace in the OT—one thinks of the stories of Elijah and of many other prophets, but two themes are outstanding here, the judicial trial of Jrm and the execution of Uriah. To take the second theme first: 2 Chr 24:20–22 records the martyrdom of Jehoiada during the reign of Joash of Judah late in the ninth century, and there is a memory of those martyred by Jezebel (1 Kgs 18:4, 13; 19:10). Then Jewish legend added Isaiah to the list (*Mart. Isa.*).[39] Rabbinic literature preserves a tradition of a prayer of Jrm's: "I cannot prophesy against them [the Israelites]; what prophet has arisen for them whom they have not tried to kill?"[40] And Christian tradition likewise held on to such a memory: Jesus is remembered as speaking of it (Matt 23:37 = Luke 13:34), Stephen mentions it (Acts 7:52), and the writer of Hebrews seems to allude to it (Heb 11:37).

The judicial trial of Jrm inevitably was viewed by the Christians of the NT as of a piece with the trials of Jesus, of Stephen (Acts 6:8—8:1a), and on several occasions of Paul (at Philippi, Acts 16:20–24; at Jerusalem, Caesarea, and beyond, Acts 21:27—28:31). It is a company of men and women whose ranks have continued to swell.

Elnathan of this passage with the father-in-law of Jehoiakim see James M. Ward, "Elnathan," *IDB* 2:94.

38   Compare Wilson, *Prophecy and Society*, 247–48.

39   *Mart. Isa.* 5; see Michael A. Knibb, "Martyrdom and Ascension of Isaiah," Charlesworth, *OTP* 2:151.

40   *Pesiq. R.* 26 (129a); see Str-B 1:943.

**The Yoke of the
King of Babylon**

Bibliography

On chapters 27–29:

Overholt
Falsehood, 24–48

Overholt, Thomas W.
"Jeremiah 27—29: The Question of False Prophecy," *JAAR* 35 (1967) 241–49.

Sarna, Nahum M.
"The Abortive Insurrection in Zedekiah's Day (Jer. 27—29)," *Eretz-Israel* 14 (1978) 89*–97*.

Seidl, Theodor
Formen und Formeln in Jeremia 27—29, Literaturwissenschaftliche Studie, 2 Teil (Arbeiten zu Text und Sprache im Alten Testament, 5; St. Ottilien: EOS, 1978).

Seidl, Theodor
Texte und Einheiten in Jeremiah 27—29 (Arbeiten zu Text und Sprache im Alten Testament, 2; St. Ottilien: EOS, 1977).

Wilson, Robert R.
Sociological Approaches to the Old Testament (Guides to Biblical Scholarship; Philadelphia: Fortress, 1984) 67–80.

On chapters 27–28:

Schmidt, Hans
"Das Datum der Ereignisse von Jer 27 und 28," *ZAW* 39 (1921) 138–44.

Schreiner, Josef
"Tempeltheologie im Streit der Propheten, Zu Jer 27 und 28," *BZ* 31 (1987), 1–14.

Seebass, Horst
"Jeremias Konflikt mit Chananja, Bemerkungen zu Jer 27 und 28," *ZAW* 82 (1970) 449–52.

Wanke
Baruchschrift, 19–36, 74–77.

On 27:1–22:

Lang, Bernhard
"Ein babylonisches Motiv in Israels Schöpfungsmythologie (Jer 27,5–6)," *BZ* 27 (1983) 236–37.

Lemke, Werner E.
"'Nebuchadnezzar, my Servant,'" *CBQ* 28 (1966) 45–50.

Reventlow
Liturgie, 188–89.

Seidl, Theodor
"Datierung und Wortereignis, Beobachtungen zum Horizont von Jer 27,1," *BZ* 21 (1977) 23–44, 184–99.

Seidl, Theodor
"Die Wortereignisformel in Jeremia: Beobachtungen zu den Formen der Redeeröffnung in

Jeremia, in Anschluss an Jer 27,1.2," *BZ* 23 (1979) 20–47.

Tov, Emanuel
"Exegetical Notes on the Hebrew Vorlage of the LXX of Jeremiah 27 (34)," *ZAW* 91 (1979) 73–93.

Weippert
Prosareden, 107–21.

27

1 ᵃᵇ ⟪In the fourth year⟫ of the reign ofᵇ Zedekiahᶜ son of Josiah king of Judah, this word came to Jeremiahᵈ from Yahweh as follows:ᵃ 2/ Thus Yahweh has said [to me:]ᵃ "Prepare for yourself cords and yoke-pegs, and put them on your neck; 3/ and you shall send them off to the king of Edom, the king of Moab, the king of the Ammonites, the king of Tyre and the king of Sidon, by the hand of ⟪their ambassadors⟫ᵃ coming to Jerusalem to Zedekiah king of Judah; 4/ and you shall give them the following charge to their masters: Thus Yahweh [of hosts,]ᵃ the God of Israel, has said, Thus shall you say to your masters: 5/ 'I have made the earth, [man and beast which are on the surface of the earth,]ᵃ by my great power and my outstretched arm, and I can give it to whomever I please. 6/ So now I am the one who has given all ⟪the earth⟫ [*M* these lands]ᵃ into the hand of Nebuchadnezzarᵇ king of Babylon ⟪to serve him;⟫ᶜ even the animals of the field I have given to him to serve him. [7/ And all nations shall serve him and his son and his grandson, until the time comes for his land in turn, and many nations and great kings shall make a slave of him.]ᵃ 8/ And the nation or kingdom which will not serve him, [Nebuchadnezzar the king of Babylon]ᵃ and which will not put its neck

Text

1a—a   The whole of v 1 is missing in *G*; *M*, by contrast, is clearly mistaken (see b–b and c). Given the literary unity between chapters 27 and 28, the present chapter must have had a date-formula, and that formula must have been something like what is reconstructed here. For the whole problem see Janzen, p. 14; Theodor Seidl, *Texte und Einheiten in Jeremiah 27–29* (Arbeiten zu Texte und Sprache im Alten Testament 2; St. Ottilen: EOS, 1977) 34–37, with bibliography.

b—b   *M* has "in the beginning of the reign of," which suggests "in the accession-year of" (see 26:1); the wording is erroneously duplicated from 26:1. The restoration here is supplied from 28:1, where an immediately subsequent incident is narrated; so most scholars (see Preliminary Observations, Setting).

c   So a few MSS. and *S* (compare vv 3 and 12); *M* "Jehoiakim."

d   The spelling of the prophet's name here and in subsequent occurrences through 29:3 lacks the usual final waw (see Peculiarities of Spelling, 27:1—29:3, below).

2a   Omit with *G* (compare Structure and Form); the words are evidently a secondary accommodation to the first-person diction of vv 12 and 16.

3a   So read with *G*; *M* reads simply "ambassadors" but irregularly lacks the definite article which one would expect (thus מלאכים instead of המלאכים): a restoration of מלאכיהם is easy.

4a   Omit with *G*.

5a   Omit with *G* (against Janzen, 118, who believes that *G* is deficient by haplography); the object pronoun in the expression "I can give it" is feminine and refers to "the earth."

6a   Reading *G* (הָאָרֶץ) for *M* הָאֲרָצוֹת הָאֵלֶּה; see Interpretation, and compare Janzen, 66, n. 5.

b   The spelling of the name with nun instead of reš is found here and in subsequent occurrences of the name in *M* through 29:3 (see Peculiarities of Spelling, 27:1—29:3, below).

c   Reading *G* לְעָבְדוֹ for *M* עַבְדִּי (compare "to serve him" at the end of the verse). For a thorough review of the matter see Rudolph; Werner E. Lemke, "'Nebuchadnezzar, my Servant,'" *CBQ* 28 (1966) 45–50; and Janzen, pp. 54–57.

7a   Omit the verse with *G*; it is a secondary expansion from popular piety (see Interpretation, and compare Janzen, pp. 101–03).

8a   *M* evidently offers a conflate text, "serve him" and

under the yoke of the king of Babylon, with sword and famine [and pestilence][b] I shall visit[c] «them» [M that nation,][c] oracle of Yahweh, until I have finished «giving»[d] them into his hand. 9/ As for you, do not listen to your prophets or your diviners or ⟨your dream-interpreters⟩[a] or your sooth-sayers or your sorcerers who say [to you, as follows:][b] "You will not serve the king of Babylon." 10/ For it is a lie they are prophe-sying to you, so as to remove you far from your soil [and I will drive you out and you will perish.][a] 11/ But the nation which will bring its neck under the yoke of the king of Babylon and serve him I shall leave on their soil, oracle of Yahweh, and they shall till it and shall dwell on it.'"

12   And to Zedekiah king of Judah I have spoken with similar words, as follows: "Bring your necks under the yoke of the king of Babylon and serve him and his people and live. 13/ Why should you die, you and your people, by sword, famine and pestilence, as Yahweh spoke concerning the nation which will not serve the king of Babylon? 14/ Do not listen to the words of the prophets who say to you, 'You will not serve the king of Babylon,' for it is a lie they are prophesying to you. 15/ For I did not send them, oracle of Yahweh, and they are prophesying in my name falsely, «so as to chase you off»[a] and you perish, you and the prophets prophesying to you."

16   And to the priests and to all this people I have spoken as follows: Thus Yahweh has said, "Do not listen to the words of your prophets who prophesy to you, 'The vessels of the house of Yahweh are going to be brought

"serve (Nebuchadnezzar) the king of Babylon," whether "Nebuchadnezzar" was an original part of the second alternative or not. See Janzen, 14.

b   *G* omits. Conceivably *M* is correct (with the full triad) and *G* is defective by haplography, but the occurrence of "sword" and "famine" without "pesti-lence" elsewhere (for example, 14:13, 15, 16, 18) encourages the view that *G* here offers the original reading and that *M* is expansionist (so also Cornill). Compare d.

c—c   Reading *G*; *M* seems to represent an unnecessary specificity.

d   *M* reads "until I have finished them in/by his hand," a reading which makes little sense. *G* reads "until they are consumed by his hand"; *V* "until I consume them in his hand"; *T* "until I have given them into his hand." *S* (*'ašlem*) could mean either "I have finished (them)" or "I have given (them)." The use of "give" (נתן) at the end of v 6, and the ren-dering of *T*, suggests strongly that "give" is part of the phrase here, but it is hard to imagine *M* תֻּמִּי to be a corruption from תִּתִּי, the standard solution of the commentators. I propose that the original text read תמי תתי (that is, תֻּמִּי תִתִּי): תמם occurs with a parallel verb in Josh 3:6. *M* will then have originated by haplography (the omission of תתי), and *T* contrariwise by the omission of תמי. The suspicion that תֻּמִּי belongs here is slightly increased by its occurrence in 14:15 alongside "sword" and "famine" (compare b above).

9a   *M* reads "your dreams" (חֲלֹמֹתֵיכֶם); *G*, *V*, and *S* read "your dreamers." Clearly one needs a reference to a person here to conform to the others in the list; the spelling is evidently not a mistake, since the word occurs again in 29:8. Ehrlich, *Randglossen*, 312–33, revocalizes to חַלָּמֹתֵיכֶם, comparing the word to the Mishnaic דָּרוֹכוֹת, "grape-treaders," a masculine plural word in spite of its suffix, and this is the emendation adopted here (*S* assumes the noun to be masculine, while the expressions in *G* and *V* are not defined for gender). Alternatively one could vocalize חֹלְמוֹתֵיכֶם, a feminine participle, literally "dreaming women": this is evidently the solution of *NEB*. Ordinarily *M* is emended to חֹלְמֵיכֶם "your dreamers" (masculine), but this entails deleting the taw. See further Interpretation.

b   Omit with *G*; the words are perhaps an expansion from v 14 (so Janzen, p. 45).

10a   Omit with *G*; the words are an expansion from v 15 (see Janzen, p. 45).

15a   Omitting the suffix on the infinitive and reading לְמַעַן הַדִּיחַ for *M* לְמַעַן הַדִּיחִי "so that I chase you off." The reading of *G* ("so as to destroy you") and the parallel with v 10 suggests the emendation (so Cornill). *V* reads *ut eiciant vos* "so that they throw you out," the subject thus being the prophets; Jerome's commentary, by contrast, follows *M* (*ut eiciam vos*)—with textual diversity on the verb, however.

back from Babylon [quite soon now':]ᵃ for it is a lie they are prophesying to you. 17/ Do not listen to them; serve the king of Babylon and live. Why should this city be ᵃa ruin?ᵃ 18/ If they were prophets, and if the word of Yahweh were with them, then they would be interceding ᵃ《with me》 [M with Yahweh of hosts]ᵃ [that the vessels which are left in the house of Yahweh, and in the house of the king of Judah, and in Jerusalem, ᶜmight not goᶜ to Babylon."]ᵇ 19/ For thus Yahweh [of hosts]ᵃ has said concerning [the pillars and the sea and the stands and]ᵇ the rest of the vessels [which remain in this city,]ᶜ 20/ which [Nebuchadnezzar]ᵃ the king of Babylon did not take when he exiled Jeconiah [son of Jehoiakim king of Judah]ᵃ from Jerusalem [to Babylon, and all the nobles of Judah and Jerusalem— 21/ for thus Yahweh of hosts, the God of Israel, has said concerning the vessels left in the house of Yahweh and the house of the king of Judah and Jerusalem—]ᵇ 22/ "To Babylon they shall be taken, [and there they shall be until the day of my attending to them,]ᵃ oracle of Yahweh; [then I shall bring them up and return them to this place."]ᵃ

16a   Omit with G. The addition was evidently made to clarify the disagreement between Jrm and the false prophets after the additions were made to v 22; see Janzen, p. 45.

17a—a   For M חָרְבָּה a few MSS. vocalize חֲרֵבָה "desolate."

18a—a   Reading G; M has been influenced by the preceding "Yahweh." See Janzen, p. 74.

b   Omit with G; the words are an expansion from vv 21–22. So Janzen, p. 46.

c—c   Reading the infinitive בֹא with a few MSS. for the anomalous M perfect בָּאוּ.

19a   Omit with G (Janzen, p. 76).

b   Omit with G; the list is an expansion from 52:17 and 2 Kgs 25:13 (so Rudolph; compare Janzen, p. 46).

c   Omit with G. Janzen, p. 46, suggests it may be a summarizing gloss based on v 21.

20a   Omit these expansions with G; see Janzen, p. 46, 69–75, esp. 72.

20–21b   Omit the whole sequence with G. The anacoluthon in v 21 is particularly awkward: see the discussion in Rudolph, and in Janzen, pp. 46–47. (For bibliography on the matter see also Seidl, *Texte und Einheiten*, 33–34 n. 29.)

22a   Omit these expansions with G; they indicate an interest in return from exile alien to Jrm's concerns at this time (compare Ezra 1:7–11): so Rudolph, and Janzen, p. 47.

Peculiarities of Spelling in 27:1—29:3

Chapters 27—29 are united by their subject matter (see Preliminary Observations, Structure). They are also united by two peculiarities of spelling that are found in *M* from 27:1 through 29:3. This first is the spelling of the prophet's name, which is uniformly יִרְמְיָהוּ in the rest of the book: it is spelled יִרְמְיָה, without final waw, in 27:1; 28:5, 6, 10, 11, 12, 15; 29:1. The shorter spelling is also found, with reference to the prophet, in Ezra 1:1 and Dan 9:2. The normal spelling returns in Jer in 29:29. The second is the name of the king of Babylon, which is uniformly (and more correctly) נְבוּכַדְרֶאצַּר (with minor variations, such as בֻ) in the rest of the book; it is נְבוּכַדְנֶאצַּר (or with בֻ) in 27:6, 8, 20; 28:3, 11, 14; 29:1, 3. The spelling with reš occurs in Ezekiel; that with nun occurs in 2 Kings, Chronicles, Ezra, Nehemiah, Esther, and Daniel. The spelling with reš recurs in Jer in 29:21. With regard to the name of the king of Babylon, however, it must be said that its occurrence in chapters 27—

29 is secondary in every instance but 27:6 (see Text). Given the distribution of the variant spellings of both names outside Jer, one may assume that they are both later spellings: in the case of the king of Babylon the spelling of the name with nun developed either by dissimilation or by a scurrilous deformation of the name.[1] These characteristics have led most commentators in the twentieth century to assume an independent literary existence of the three chapters,[2] but one cannot gain specificity on the matter simply from these spellings.

Preliminary Observations

Chapters 27—29 form a literary unit with characteristics of its own and deal with matters connected with the renewal of hope aroused in those subject to Nebuchadnezzar during the year 594 (see Introduction, sec. 22; and see below, Structure and Form, and further Setting for each of the three chapters). These chapters, like other prose chapters in the book, are characterized by

---

1   See Interpretation of 21:2, and n. 17 there.

2   For a full survey of opinion see Seidl, *Texte und Einheiten*, 21–22, n. 5, and further Tov, "Textual

and Literary History," 161, n. 30.

expansions in *M*.

Chapter 27 presents exceptional difficulties in text criticism, however: the plusses in *M* over *G* are large indeed. Since v 21 (present in *M*, lacking in *G*) clearly interrupts the connection between vv 19–20 and v 22, and since *G* jumps from v 12 to v 14, reading there "Bring your neck and be subject to the king of Babylon, for it is a lie they are preaching to you," a clearly defective reading which needs at least the missing v 14a to bring sense, it is clear that to restore an original text one cannot simply delete the plusses of *M* in favor of *G*; if *M* has secondary expansions, *G* also suffers by haplography. A certain subjectivity therefore cannot be avoided in the establishment of a text, and commentators differ in their judgments. Each passage must be dealt with on its own merits. The text offered here is conservative: there may be a few phrases which are secondary beyond those which are bracketed (for the details see Interpretation).

The text difficulty of v 1 has direct bearing on the setting of the incident. The reading of *M*, "In the beginning of the reign [= in the accession-year?—see 26:1] of Jehoiakim" is impossible, given the mention of Zedekiah in vv 3 and 12; these words must have been copied erroneously from 26:1. A few MSS., and *S*, read the king's name correctly as Zedekiah, but "in the beginning of the reign" still remains. Since 28:1 begins "in that year," and defines it as "the fourth year," and since that fourth year of Zedekiah (594) is appropriate for the event narrated in 27:3, that datum must have stood here instead of "in the beginning of the reign." On the other hand, v 1 is missing altogether in *G*, leading one to wonder whether the introductory words appropriate to v 1 had not been lost early in the transmission of the text (so *G*) and secondarily (and wrongly) restored by an editor. In any event something like the text offered here must have stood at this point originally.[3]

The text of v 2 has a bearing on Form. In 28:1 we find "to me" (in both *M* and *G*), but the style reverts to third-person references to "Jeremiah" beginning in v 5 there (five times in the chapter), so that the text of 28:1 must be restored to "to Jeremiah." Here in 27:2 *M* has "to me," an expression lacking in *G*. There are no further clues in the remainder of the chapter by which to clarify the reference. Given the unity of chapters 27 and 28 (see Setting), it is better to conclude that the expression "to me" in v 2 is an erroneous secondary addition, and that 28:1 has "to me" by attraction.

In v 5 "man and beast which are on the surface of the earth" must be taken as an expansionist gloss reflecting the thought of v 6: the phrase is lacking in *G*, the pronoun object referent in "I shall give it" is feminine singular and is to be understood as referring to "the earth" (against Rudolph[4] and Janzen,[5] who assume that *G* is deficient by homoioteleuton).

In v 6 the *G* reading "the earth" is preferable to *M* "these lands" (against Rudolph): "the earth" includes the animals of the field. *M* reflects the concern of (the secondary) v 7, which focuses on various nations, and of 28:14 (so Janzen).[6] The designation of Nebuchadnezzar in *M* of this verse as "my [Yahweh's] servant" has called forth much discussion; the expression occurs also in *M* for 25:9 and 43:10, in both of which passages it is lacking in *G*. In the present passage its place in *G*[B] is taken by "to serve him." It is clear that these contrasting expressions here have had a complicated prehistory, but the parallelism with "to serve him" at the end of the verse renders *G* preferable;[7] *M* of 25:9 and 43:10 will thus be imitative of the expression here. Werner E. Lemke speculates that *M* here may have been influenced by the tradition represented in Dan 2:47; 3:28–29; 4:34–37 (and compare on v 7).

Verse 7 is lacking altogether in *G*; commentators divide as to whether *G* deliberately omitted the verse because the prediction was not fulfilled literally (Rudolph) or whether the verse is a later product of popular piety (Cornill, Friedrich Nötscher). The duration of the Babylonian Empire is elsewhere expressed by the term "seventy years" (25:12; 29:10); the unusual

---

3   See Seidl, *Texte und Einheiten*, 34–38, with bibliography.

4   *BHS*.

5   Janzen, p. 118.

6   Ibid., 66, n. 5.

7   So Lemke, "Nebuchadnezzar," and so Janzen, with a long discussion, pp. 54–57; against Walther Zimmerli, "παῖς θεοῦ," *TDNT* 5:656–77, esp. 664, n. 48, and Rudolph.

phraseology "him and his son and his grandson" could mean simply "him and those who follow him," but Janzen suggests[8] that it is an expression of popular piety from late in the Persian period which had in mind the succession Nebuchadnezzar, Nabonidus, and Belshazzar.[9] The analysis of Janzen is accepted here; the verse interrupts the continuity between vv 6 and 8—the interest of the passage in the chapter is not in the punishment of Nebuchadnezzar but in the yoke which he is imposing on the kings of the earth.

The question of vv 13 and 17 is more difficult. G has clearly suffered haplography from vv 12 to 14 (see above), so that one cannot make a judgment about the originality of v 13 from the present text of G. Giesebrecht and Rudolph conclude that the verse is a secondary expansion, interrupting the imperatives in v 12 and the corresponding prohibition in v 14. Form-critically the verse is comparable to v 17—both verses contain rhetorical questions, and the latter verse is omitted in G (Giesebrecht and others thus judge it to be secondary). The easy conclusion then would be to follow Giesebrecht and judge both verses to be secondary. On the other hand rhetorical questions are not likely to have been framed secondarily: there is no parallel instance of such a secondary addition with "why" (לָמָּה) elsewhere in the book. Furthermore one could maintain that vv 12–14 and vv 16–17 have a chiastic structure with respect to each other: (A) "serve the king of Babylon" (v 12), "why should you die?" (v 13); (B) "do not listen to the prophets" (v 14); (B′) "do not listen to the prophets" (vv 16, 17); (A′) "serve the king of Babylon," "why should this city be a desolation?" (v 17). If this structure is not fortuitous, it suggests the rhetoric of original material. It is safer, then, to judge both vv 13 and 17 to be original (against Giesebrecht); one then assumes that G has either accidentally omitted v 17 or omitted it deliberately for the sake of concision (both v 16 and v 17 begin with "do not listen").[10]

Verses 16–22 otherwise contain a whole array of secondary expansions in M, the identification of which does not cause particular difficulty.

Structure and Form
Chapters 27—29 all deal with the prophet's words and actions in the reign of Zedekiah in reaction to hopes for rebellion against Nebuchadnezzar; in the case of chapters 27 and 28 at least, there is a unity of historical setting, the events in chapter 28 presupposing the actions and words of chapter 27. But the chapter divisions correspond with the divisions of the literary units, so that each chapter can be dealt with individually.

The internal structure of chapter 27 is peculiar. It begins with instruction to Jrm to perform one or more symbolic actions (v 2, and v 3 as well if M is followed rather than the reading of the Lucianic recension followed by most commentators and translations—see Interpretation) directed to various foreign kings and with parallel instruction to send word to those kings (vv 4–11). By contrast vv 12–15 and vv 16–22 represent parallel first-person reports from the prophet as to divine words he has spoken (evidently by commission from Yahweh, though this is not stated), first to the king, and second to the priests and "all this people": the subject of "I have spoken" in vv 12 and 16 is surely Jrm, given "Thus Yahweh has said" in v 16. Admittedly the issue is clouded; thus Rudolph follows M in v 18, where the reference to "Yahweh of hosts" is third person, and he therefore deletes "Thus Yahweh has said" in v 16 as an erroneous secondary intrusion, and if this were correct, the clue in v 16 for the identity of the speaker for "I have spoken" would be lacking. But the phraseology of "with words like all these" in v 12 surely presupposes that the speaker is Jrm. If this analysis if correct, then form-critically vv 12–15 and vv 16–22 are left unrelated to anything in vv 1–11, a consideration that suggests in turn that vv 12–15 and vv 16–22 are additions to vv 1–11 on the basis of the similarity of the theme of putting one's neck under the yoke of the king of Babylon and

---

8   Janzen, pp. 101–3.

9   Compare the discussion by David N. Freedman, "The Prayer of Nabonidus," *BASOR* 145 (February 1957) 32.

10   Against Rudolph, and against Janzen, p. 43; for bibliography see Seidl, *Texte und Einheiten*, 32–33, n. 28.

serving him (vv 8, 12) and of the theme of not listening to optimistic prophets (vv 9, 14, 16). Given the assumption that Jrm did in fact express himself both in action and in word to the foreign kings, one may assume a corresponding expression to Zedekiah and perhaps to the priesthood in Jerusalem, but it is curious that there is no clear evidence in the chapter that Jrm gave cords and yoke-pegs to Zedekiah. The present literary condition of the chapter is not good, and one can only guess at what carelessness of recording or transmission has left the material in its present shape.

Mention has already been made of the parallel between vv 12–15 and vv 16–22 (see Preliminary Observations on the discussion of vv 13 and 17, and more particularly below on the form of the passages).

Verses 12–15 are in turn parallel to the words to the foreign kings which precede them, though it is difficult to know with how much of that earlier speech to match vv 12–15. The speech extends from v 5 to v 11. Verses 5–6 are a general statement about the identity of Yahweh and his action with Nebuchadnezzar. Verses 8 and 11 are parallel with each other, the first a negative, the second a positive statement—the nation that will not serve Nebuchadnezzar Yahweh will visit with death, while the nation that will serve him Yahweh will let live. In the parallel speech to Zedekiah there is only the positive statement (v 12). Then vv 9–10, in the speech to the foreign kings, closely parallel vv 14–15: "Do not listen to the prophets who say, 'You will not serve the king of Babylon,' for it is a lie they are prophesying to you, so as to remove you/drive you off. . . ."[11]

Form-critically the situation in vv 1–11 is complicated by the descending series of quotations (that is, quotations within quotations). Given the text here presented, what one has is as follows. Verse 1 introduces a third-person report of revelation to the prophet analogous to what is found in 18:1; 26:1; and elsewhere. Verses 2–3, introduced by the messenger formula, contain Yahweh's command to the prophet to perform symbolic actions (compare 13:1; 18:2; 19:1–2). There is, however, no report of the prophet's carrying out the command (as there is, for example, in 13:1–12aα—see Structure and Form there; such a report is also lacking in 19:1–3); but

the narrative in 28:10 implies the carrying out at least of the command in 27:2. Verse 4 contains a parallel command from Yahweh to send a message through the kings' envoys to the kings themselves; the prophetic word to the envoys is introduced by the messenger formula, then by the rubric of instruction to the envoys, "Thus shall you say to your masters." Verses 5–11, finally, embody the message itself which the kings are to hear. That message is partly in the third person ("the nation which," vv 8, 11) and partly in the second-person plural (vv 9–10). That second-person plural is doubtless influenced partly by the fact that the message is to be delivered to several kings, but inasmuch as the parallel to Zedekiah is also in the second-person plural (vv 12–15), the narrator may have had in mind each king and his people (so v 13). Oracles against foreign nations are a commonplace in the prophetic books, but such oracles function within the context of Israel and Judah as words of warning or reassurance;[12] here, by contrast, one has a rare look into the mode of discourse of a Yahwistic prophet delivering an oracle to pagan kings who must be expected to hear the words outside the norms of the covenant people: the argumentation is thus of Yahweh as the omnipotent creator. Verse 5 is a self-predication by Yahweh of his identity as creator of all that is (compare Isa 44:24 and 45:12, where similar discourse is in the context of Yahweh's address to Cyrus). Verse 6 is the announcement by Yahweh of his assignment (*Anweisung*) of the earth for the present time to Nebuchadnezzar; for a similar assignment compare Gen 1:29. Verses 8 and 11 are Yahweh's statement of the alternatives that lead to death and to life; such third-person statements may have had their origin in priestly instruction but are here completely accommodated to prophetic discourse (as are similar declarations in 18:7–11: see Form there); Yahweh himself states the divine decrees that lead to woe and weal. Verses 9–10 contain a prohibition couched in the form of parenetic appeal (compare 23:16): the kings are urged to pay no attention to any of their various sorts of prophets who speak reassuringly about the future; this prohibition is followed by Yahweh's assessment of those false prophets (compare 14:14).

In vv 12a and 16a, on the other hand, we have the

---

11   On the structural parallels of the three sections of the chapter see Wanke, *Baruchschrift*, 26.

12   Compare, for example, the remarks on Amos 1:3—

2:3 in Wolff, *Joel and Amos*, 147–49.

introduction, rather mysteriously, of two first-person reports by Jrm of his performance of implied commands by Yahweh to speak to Zedekiah and to the priests and people; form-critically such first-person reports are unique here to Jer. The words spoken to Zedekiah extend from v 12b through v 15. Again, as in vv 10–11, the words of vv 12b–14 are couched in the form of parenetic appeal. There are commands (v 12b) to submit to Nebuchadnezzar; these are followed by a rhetorical question (v 13): compare the rhetorical question in 7:9–10 in the midst of parenetic appeal. The question is in turn followed by a prohibition (parallel to the commands in v 12b) against paying attention to prophets who preach good news, followed by Yahweh's assessment of these prophets (v 14, like vv 9–10). And if the phrase "it is a lie they are prophesying to you" in v 14 is like 14:14, as it is, then the opening phrase in v 15 continues the rhetoric found in 14:14, "for I did not send them," Yahweh's declaration of nonresponsibility (see there).

Verse 16, like v 14, is a prohibition against paying attention to prophets who preach good news, and Yahweh's assessment of those prophets; the prohibition is repeated in v 17, followed by positive parenetic appeals, followed in turn by a rhetorical question comparable to that in v 13. Now if the prohibition against listening to the prophets, and Yahweh's assessment of those prophets, are followed in the case of v 14 by Yahweh's declaration of nonresponsibility in v 15, then that prohibition and Yahweh's assessment are followed here by a contrary-to-fact conditional sentence (v 18: see Interpretation), which says in effect, "They are no prophets: if they were, then their behavior would have been altogether different." It is striking that the little poetic unit 23:21–22, against false prophets, embodies the form of both 27:15 (compare 23:21) and 27:18 (compare 23:22), strong indication that the sequence of material here is sound (see Setting). The original material in vv 19–22 comprises a supplementary oracle from Yahweh correcting the statement of the false prophets in v 16: the first shipment of vessels will not come back from Babylon —to the contrary, a second shipment will be taken to Babylon.

The expansions of the original text which are found in M are either small additions that are form-critically insignificant or are large additions on the analogy of the original, in some cases reflecting the interests of the community late in the exilic period or beyond.

Setting

This chapter has been widely attributed to a Deuteronomistic editor (see below). But whatever the source of the narrative, the historicity of the situation presupposed in vv 1–11, and therefore by implication the rest of the chapter, cannot be questioned. For the dating of the incident in 594 see Text, Interpretation.

The meeting in Jerusalem of envoys from Edom, Moab, Ammon, Tyre, and Sidon to conspire with Zedekiah to revolt against Nebuchadnezzar is a direct consequence of a rebellion against the king in Babylon itself in December 595 and January 594. The rebellion is referred to in the Babylonian Chronicle: "In the tenth year the king of Akkad was in his own land; from the month of Kislev to the month of Tebet there was rebellion in Akkad . . . with arms he slew many of his own army. His own hand captured his enemy."[13] News of the rebellion must have reached the West and precipitated the Jerusalem meeting, to be dated in late spring or early summer. The response of these Western kings, and Jrm's own response during the conference, is completely believable.

The recurrence of the verb "prophesy" (נבא nip'al) with the noun "lie" (שֶׁקֶר) four times in vv 10 and 14–16 led Mowinckel to attribute the chapter to his "Source C," and more recently commentators like Nicholson have reaffirmed the judgment that the chapter is to be attributed to a Deuteronomistic editor; Hyatt assumes it is part of Baruch's memoirs as revised by the Deuteronomistic editor,[14] but Rudolph denies that there is here any characteristic of such an editor other than the phrase "by my great power and my outstretched arm" in v 5.[15]

Weippert has subjected the use of "prophesy" with "lie," "prophets who prophesy," and "I did not send them," characteristics of vv 10 and 14–16, to minute scrutiny[16] and concludes that these phrases are reminiscent of 14:14, that there is no connection with Deuteronomistic language, and that the repetition is part

---

13 British Museum 21946, rev. 21–22: see Wiseman, *Chronicles*, 72–73, and compare 36; and see further Bright, *History*, 329, and Malamat, "Twilight of Judah," 136–37.

14 Hyatt, p. 1010.

15 Rudolph, p. 173.

of the rhetorical purpose of the prophet. (It must be added that the existence of expansions in *M* has encouraged the assumption of the origin of the chapter in a presumed source characterized by repetition.)

The argument to the foreign kings of the basis of the power of the creator is conceivable in the mind of someone within the exilic period (compare the rhetoric of Deutero-Isaiah), but it is completely appropriate for Jrm himself in such a context (compare in this regard the phrasing of v 5 with 10:12).

It is of course true that the phrase "by my great power and my outstretched arm" is reminiscent of a Deuteronomic phrase descriptive of the exodus ("with mighty hand and outstretched arm"),[17] but the phrase appears in that form only once in Jer, there in reference to the exodus (32:21). It appears with adjectives reversed in an address to Zedekiah (21:5), suggesting that Yahweh is reversing the direction of his military activity (see there). It appears twice with "great power" (כֹּחַ גָּדוֹל) substituted for "mighty hand" (יָד חֲזָקָה), in both instances of Yahweh's power in creation (here and in 32:17). Comparable also is "my hand and my power" (יָדִי וּגְבוּרָתִי) in Yahweh's self-declaration regarding the nations in 16:21. The conclusion must be that there Jrm employed a variation of the exodus formula for the divine warrior in expressing Yahweh's power in creation.[18]

The phrase "to whomever I think right" (לַאֲשֶׁר יָשַׁר בְּעֵינַי) resembles closely "as seemed right in the eyes of the potter" (כַּאֲשֶׁר יָשַׁר בְּעֵינֵי הַיּוֹצֵר) in 18:4 (though the verb there should be revocalized יָשֵׁר); there, too, Jrm speaks of the arbitrariness of the potter as an image of the arbitrariness of Yahweh: note "hand of the potter" in 18:4 and "a nation or a kingdom" in 18:7. The two passages offer different expressions of the same semantic field.

The reference to "even the animals of the field" in v 6 reinforces the expression of the omnipotence of Yahweh in v 5: the implication is double—(1) if Yahweh gives even the wild animals to Nebuchadnezzar, then domestic animals who are yoked have no chance of freedom, and (2) if the kings of the earth resent being compared to domestic animals, they are surely more under control than are wild animals, so that in either case they have no

choice. This kind of reasoning bespeaks the irony of Jrm, not the routine statement of an editor.

The listing of the variety of prophetic figures available to the foreign kings which is found in v 9 does not correspond exactly to any other such list: the longer listing in Deut 18:10–11 has different participial forms in several instances, and the list of Manasseh's acts in 2 Chr 33:6 offers finite verbs; the agent noun "sorcerers" (כַּשָּׁף, here plural) occurs only here in the OT. Again, then, this list is not something routinely found elsewhere.

One notices finally in the speech to the foreign kings the play on the meanings of "serve" in v 11: "serve" Nebuchadnezzar and thus stay on your land to "till" (literally "serve") your soil.

The phraseology in the speeches to Zedekiah and to the priests resembles diction elsewhere in the book, as already noted, but the resemblance is not to Deuteronomistic diction but to Jrm's enunciation of Yahweh's judgment against the optimistic prophets which is found in 14:14; 23:9–32; and elsewhere. And one must note the mordant irony in the genuine word of Yahweh about the vessels still in Jerusalem (vv 19–22) over against the false word from the prophets about the vessels taken to Babylon (v 16).

The conclusion is inescapable: the material here derives from Jrm's own diction, though one must allow for the vicissitudes of transmission between Baruch's record and the text before us.

Interpretation

■ **1** For the text difficulties of this verse see Text, Preliminary Observations.

■ **2** The words here translated "cords" (מוֹסֵרוֹת) and "yoke-pegs" (מֹטוֹת) require explanation. The meaning "cords" or "straps" is itself not in doubt: all the Versions translate the word in this fashion, but the function of the cords is not clear, nor the meaning and function of the second term, nor the odd order of the two terms.

The Versions differ greatly in their rendering of the second term: *V* gives "chains" (*catenas*), *T* "yokes" (נִירִין),

---

16 Weippert, *Prosareden*, 107–21.

17 Weinfeld, *Deuteronomy*, 329, n. 14.

18 Compare Helga Weippert, *Schöpfer des Himmels und* *der Erde* (SBS 102; Stuttgart: Katholisches Bibelwerk, 1981) 65–68.

and S "yoke," singular (*nîrā'*), and S reverses the order of the two terms. G translates "collars" (κλοιούς), a rendering which turns out to be the most helpful; the Greek word refers to the large wooden collar put on the neck of a dog that tends to bite. This is the translation in G for all occurrences of the Hebrew word in these chapters (here and in 28:10, 12, and 13 twice).

Gottlieb Schumacher has supplied a clear description, with illustrations, of the plow and yoke used by the Palestinian Arab peasant at the end of the nineteenth century, and the yoke is evidently identical with that presupposed in the present passage.[19] The yoke rests on the back of the neck of the pair of oxen; four holes have been bored through the yoke, placed longitudinally along the yoke, on both sides of the spot where the yoke touches the neck of either ox. Through each hole a wooden peg or rod is driven which thus extends downward from the yoke (the pegs thus appearing much like the tines of a wooden hay-rake), and each pair of pegs fits around the neck of one of the oxen. Cords secure the bottom of the pegs to each other on the underside of the neck, so that the wooden pegs and the cords together make up a collar.[20]

Jrm evidently wore this "collar" consisting of a pair of pegs and the cords to tie them, thus suggesting that the people (and all peoples) must submit to the yoke of Nebuchadnezzar. At no point in the narrative of chapters 27—28 is it said that Jrm bore a "yoke" (that is, עֹל) (against KJV and JB), only that the collar he wore made him fit to bear a yoke. If the second term signified the yoke itself, then surely this term would have been named before the "cords" (thus the misunderstanding of S). But there may have been a simpler arrangement for oxen in some instances, in which there are no yoke-pegs but a simple "noose" of cords around the neck of the

oxen, attached directly to the yoke,[21] and this alternative may have misled translators into understanding the second term as "yoke." Note that the interpretation given here meets the phraseology of Isa 58:6 as well.

■ 3 If Jrm was told to fashion "cords" and "pegs" and put them on his neck (v 2), then one may understand the text in M "and you shall send them" in this verse to refer to further "collars" to be sent by the envoys to each of the kings named. Thus the emendation "and you shall send word" of RSV and JB, under the assumption that Jrm would not send whole yokes to each king, becomes unnecessary.[22] Jrm matched an action to the word he was sending to the kings (vv 4–11).

It was envoys of the Transjordanian states and of the Phoenician coastal cities who attended the meeting in Jerusalem (see Setting). Tyre, Edom, the Ammonites, and Moab are mentioned in the oracles against foreign nations a century and a half earlier in Amos 1:9—2:3— of the five mentioned in the present passage, only Sidon is missing. Conspicuously absent here is any mention of Philistine cities (compare 25:20–22), which were by now Babylonian territory: Nebuchadnezzar had sacked Ashkelon in December 604.[23] For the expression "Ammonites" (בְּנֵי עַמּוֹן) see 9:24–25.

■ 4 The verb ordinarily translated "command" (צוה pi'el) here carries a meaning not otherwise found in Jer, "give a charge to messengers to transmit [to others]"; for this meaning see Deut 1:3 and elsewhere.

■ 5 The argument which Jrm perceives Yahweh to be using with the foreign kings is that of the arbitrary power of God in creation (see Setting). The form of the relative "to whomever" (לַאֲשֶׁר instead of אֲשֶׁר + לוֹ) is unusual but not rare.[24] The phraseology is much like 18:4 (see again Setting). The expansion in M ("man and beast which are on the surface of the earth") simply anticipates what will

19 Gottlieb Schumacher, "Der arabische Pflug," ZDPV 12 (1889) 157–66; see also Lucian Turkowski, "Peasant Agriculture in the Judaean Hills," PEQ 202 (1969) 21–33, 101–12, esp. 30, and the illustration, 29, figure 2b.

20 See also, more briefly, Kurt Galling and Dorothy Irvin, "Pflug," Biblisches Reallexikon (ed. Kurt Galling; HAT, Erste Reihe, 1; Tübingen: Mohr [Siebeck], 1977) 255b; Augustin-Georges Barrois, Manuel d'archéologie biblique I (Paris: Picard, 1939) 311, and figure 114.

21 Compare C. Umhau Wolf, "Yoke," IDB 4:924b.

22 For debate about the soundness of the text of M here see Seidl, Texte und Einheiten, 42–43, with bibliography.

23 Compare Malamat, "Twilight of Judah," 135.

24 GKC, sec. 138e; see Solomon Mandelkern, Veteris Testamenti Concordantiae Hebraicae atque Chaldaicae (rep. Graz: Akademische Druck- und Verlagsanstalt, 1955) 1311.

be affirmed in v 6.

■ **6** Yahweh then identifies himself as the one who is responsible for Nebuchadnezzar's steady taking over of one kingdom after another: to rebel against Nebuchadnezzar would be to rebel against God.

The "animals of the field" are wild animals (Exod 23:11; Hos 2:14); if even the wild animals will be subject to Nebuchadnezzar, then kings have no chance, even if those kings by wearing the collars of oxen are no better than domestic animals (see again Setting).

The reading "the earth" is preferable to the *M* reading "these lands"; the reference is to the omnipotence of Nebuchadnezzar over everything on the earth, including wild animals, not to specific nations. And the *M* reading "my servant" as a designation for Nebuchadnezzar instead of the infinitive expression "to serve him" is a surprising variation which has occasioned much comment (see Bibliography); it is evidently the fruit of later theological speculation which exalted the station of Nebuchadnezzar (as a negative figure alongside of Cyrus, "his anointed," Isa 45:1—a positive figure?).

■ **7** This entire verse is a secondary expansion in *M*, reflecting the interest of later generations in the reversal which will come when Babylon in turn will submit to surrounding nations. It is the same impulse which gave rise to 25:12 and 14; indeed the diction of the latter part of the present verse is close to that in 25:14a.

■ **8** This verse states the fate of any nation which will not submit. This is the only instance in Jer in which "sword" and "famine" (with or without "pestilence," see Text) are stated to apply to pagan nations; for a discussion of the triad see 14:12. The phraseology with "finished giving them," if correctly reconstructed (see Text) is striking; the suffixed infinitive of תמם ("finish") likewise appears after "until" in 24:10, and the verb appears, in association with "sword" and "famine," of the false prophets in 14:15, but the only other occurrence of the verb with a parallel verb is in Josh 3:6. One is left with the impression that Jrm envisages an extended process for Nebuchadnezzar's seizure of all the nations.

■ **9** The message in this verse and v 10 shifts to second person, here plural (for which see the discussion in Structure and Form, Setting). For the advice against paying attention to one's prophets see 23:16. In the parallel word to Zedekiah (v 14) only "prophets" are mentioned; here by contrast we have an array of five sorts of pagan soothsayers—one has the impression that Jrm delighted to list these various types of experts whom Yahweh declares to be wrong (is it something like the repeated list of musical instruments in Dan 3:5, 7, 10, 15?).

Whether the word "prophet" (נָבִיא) was current in the other Levantine states is unclear, but the analogous word "seer" (חֹזֶה) was.[25]

The "diviner" (קֹסֵם) typically read omens. He is mentioned in association with the prophet in many texts (thus Balaam is called a "diviner" in Josh 13:22, and in Mic 3:6 "divination" is mentioned as part of the activity of the prophets). Ezek 21:16 describes the activities of a Babylonian diviner: "He shakes the arrow, he consults the teraphim, he looks at the liver."[26]

The association of "dreaming" with prophesying is set forth in 23:23–32 and in Deut 13:2–4; dream interpretation was of course widespread in the ancient Near East.[27]

There is no description of the activities of the "soothsayer" (עֹנֵן or מְעֹנֵן) in the OT that would help distinguish them from those of the diviner or sorcerer: the term is simply found in lists of forbidden activities (Lev 19:26; Deut 18:10, 14) or in other negative contexts (for

---

25 So the inscription of Zakir of Hamat (eighth century B.C.E.), 1.12: see conveniently *KAI*, 37, 205, 208, or John C. L. Gibson, *Textbook of Syrian Semitic Inscriptions* 2 (Oxford: Clarendon, 1975) 8, 9; and so the Deir 'Alla inscriptions (eighth century), which describe Balaam son of Beor as "seer of the gods" (Text 1, Combination 1): see Jacob Hoftijzer and G. van der Kooij, *Aramaic Texts from Deir 'Alla* (Documenta et Monumenta Orientis Antiqui 19; Leiden: Brill, 1976) 173, 179. For a recent survey of prophetic activity in the ancient Near East see Herbert B. Huffmon, "Prophecy in the ANE,"

IDBSup 697–700, with bibliography.

26 See in general Isaac Mendelsohn, "Divination," 1:856–58.

27 For a general survey of dreams and dream-revelations in Israel and in the ancient Near East see Jan Bergman, Magnus Ottosson, and G. Johannes Botterweck, "חָלַם," *TDOT* 4:421–32.

example, Isa 57:3; Mic 5:11) which offer no clues. Further the etymological link of the word is uncertain: suggestions include a connection with the Arabic ǧanna "hum" (of augurs?), with the Arabic ʿanna "present oneself" (thus "cause [spirits] to appear"?), and with עַיִן "eye" (thus "inspect [omens]"?).[28]

The word "sorcerer" (כַּשָּׁף) is connected with Akkadian verb forms for "practice magic" (kašāpu, kuššupu), but though specific magical practices were doubtless involved, it is not possible to identify them; the root in the OT is often used simply as a negative term (for example, 2 Kgs 9:22).[29]

For the participial phrase "who say," followed by reassuring words, compare 14:15; Jrm equates the optimistic words of these foreign "experts" with the false prophets in Judah—they simply mislead.

■ **10** As v 9 resembles 14:15, so this verse resembles 14:14: it is a lie (שֶׁקֶר) they are prophesying. The word לְמַעַן, which before an infinitive ordinarily expresses purpose ("in order to"), here (as occasionally elsewhere) expresses result ("so as to"), as it does in the parallel in v 15.[30] This is the only occurrence of "remove far" (רחק hip'il) in the book. For "off one's soil" compare 24:10.

■ **11** Here is the positive alternative to v 8: the nation which does submit to Nebuchadnezzar Yahweh will allow to stay on their soil. The verb "leave" (נוח hip'il II) is used here in a nuance different from that in 14:9, the only previous occurrence—there it is "abandon," here it is "leave untouched." The double meaning of עבד here, already noted by Calvin, is untranslatable—"serve" (the king of Babylon) and "till" (the soil).

■ **12–15** The speaker of "I have spoken" is Jrm himself (see Structure and Form). "With similar words" is literally "like all these words": "these" refers to the words delivered to the foreign kings (vv 5–11), not to what follows (as NEB assumes). The diction of the speech is inconsistent: in v 13 "Yahweh" is in the third person, while in v 15 "I" is Yahweh. Is the listener to understand that Jrm is the speaker at the beginning of the speech (v

12) but that he is quoting Yahweh in v 15 ("oracle of Yahweh")?—or is it a matter of shifting reference such as occurs in 2:2–3?

The second-person pronouns and verbs are plural; this plural is expanded in v 13 to "you (singular) and your (singular) people," the latter expression suggesting that the speaker (whether Yahweh or Jrm) has no involvement with the people. The only parallel is 22:2, where "your people" suggests "those having business in the palace"; so here, the expression may imply "your court" (contrast "all this people," v 16).

The expansion into "you and your people" in v 13 is paralleled by "him and his people" in v 12 and by "you (plural) and the prophets prophesying to you" in v 15. The phrase in v 15 is conceivably redactional, but it appears in *G* and there is no warrant to omit it. (Note that "and his people" in v 12 is omitted in *G* but that that omission is part of haplography within *G*: see Preliminary Observations.)

The phraseology of the speech stays close to that of vv 8–11; the infinitive in v 15, however, is different ("chase off," נדח hip'il).

■ **16–17** For "I have spoken" see v 12.

The fate of the vessels taken from the temple was a particular concern of the priests, and optimistic prophets like Hananiah raised their hopes (28:3). The vessels are specified in 2 Kgs 24:13 to be "of gold." There is disagreement about the historical value of 2 Kgs 24:13–14; Gray takes it to be an anachronistic insertion,[31] while James A. Montgomery concludes that though v 13 is out of place, the verse possesses a basis of real fact.[32] It is clear from Jer 28:3 that Nebuchadnezzar did take vessels from the temple, but of the type and quantity of these we know nothing.

■ **18** Commentators and translations differ as to whether this verse is to be construed as a condition capable of fulfillment ("If they are prophets, and if the word of Yahweh is with them, then let them intercede . . ."), as the particle נָא with the verb of the apodosis implies[33] (so

28   See Zorell; *HALAT*; Isaac Mendelsohn, "Divination," *IDB* 1:857b.
29   See Isaac Mendelsohn, "Magic," *IDB* 3:224–25.
30   See Joüon, *Gramm.*, sec. 169g.
31   Gray, *Kings*, 760–61.
32   Montgomery, *Kings*, 556.
33   So König, *Syntax*, sec. 184b.

most commentators, and so *RSV, NEB, NJV*), or whether it is to be construed as a contrary-to-fact condition ("If they were prophets . . ."), as the parallel in 23:22 and the general attitude of Jrm toward these prophets suggests (so Rudolph, and so *JB, NAB*). The latter is adopted here, but the presence of נָא is nevertheless striking; perhaps in the verb "they would be interceding with me" there is just a hint of "Why do they not try it?" For "intercede" (פגע) see 7:16. If the text as reconstructed here is correct, Jrm does not specify the burden of their hypothetical intercession: what is implied is that they are to pray that things get no worse, because Yahweh has decreed they will get worse. The specifics of what will get worse is the loss of the rest of the cultic vessels (vv 19–22), and the expansion in *M* at the end of v 18 is a transition to the following verses which makes those specifics clear.

■ **19–22** Volz rejects the originality of any of this material, but the divine word at the beginning of v 22, "to Babylon they shall be taken," resembles the word to Pashhur in 20:6, "to Babylon you shall go"; there is no reason not to follow the guidance of *G* here (see Text). Jrm's word that Nebuchadnezzar will take even more vessels to Babylon than he took in 597 was intended to contradict the optimistic prophets (see on vv 16–17). For details on the "pillars," "sea," and "stands" see commentaries on 1 Kgs 7:15–37 and general reference works.[34] It was during the exilic period that the interest shifted from the fulfillment of the prophecy to the recovery of those vessels; hence the expansions in *M* (see Text).

Aim

Jrm's action in wearing a collar appropriate for an ox-yoke as a sign that all nations must submit to the yoke of Nebuchadnezzar closely resembles Isaiah's action in going naked and barefoot for three years as a sign that the Ethiopian dynasty of Egypt would submit to Assyria and the Egyptians would be led away as naked captives (Isa 20:1–6). And if one understands v 3 correctly, Jrm extended his sign by sending similar collars to all the kings whose envoys had gathered in Jerusalem to plan rebellion against Nebuchadnezzar: in this the prophet matched symbolic action to symbolic word,[35] and in this action fulfilled his calling to be a prophet "over nations and over kingdoms" (1:10). And unlike other symbolic actions of Jrm which were intended to touch other nations (against Egypt, 43:8–13; against Babylon, 51:59–64), there was a chance this action would come to the attention of the kings in question.

Yet Calvin acutely senses that the central actor in the chapter is Zedekiah: it is he around whom the ambassadors have come, and it is the word of Jrm the prophet against the word of the ambassadors in Zedekiah's ears. Calvin furthermore points out what might be overlooked by readers unmindful of the etiquette of a court: that the ambassadors were dishonored, that they might have complained that they were treated with indignity. The reaction of Zedekiah and the people would then have been great anger against the prophet. One must marvel all the more then at Jrm's sense of statesmanship to seize the moment for communication to all the independent Syro-Palestinian states, his sense of mockery, his courage.[36]

There must have been many in Judah who wished to believe that the fall of Jerusalem in 597 was the limit of Yahweh's punishment (compare 10:24). For them to learn from Jrm that worse was yet to come, to learn from him of the loot that Nebuchadnezzar would take the next time, must have been bitter indeed.

34   For 1 Kings 7 see not only Montgomery, *Kings*, 160–84, and Gray, *Kings*, 176–204, but also Noth, *Könige*, 130–67; see further conveniently Georges A. Barrois, "Pillar," *IDB* 3:815–16, and Joseph L. Mihelic, "Sea, molten," *IDB* 4:253.

35   Compare Lindblom, *Prophecy*, 170.

36   Compare Stanley R. Hopper, "Exposition of Jeremiah," *IB* 5:1009–13, and T. Crouther Gordon,

The Rebel Prophet (New York: Harper, 1932) 67 and n. 1 there, which Hopper cites.

Jeremiah's Confrontation
with Hananiah

Bibliography

Goldenberg, Robert
"The Problem of False Prophecy: Talmudic Interpretations of Jeremiah 28 and 1 Kings 22," *The Biblical Mosaic, Changing Perspectives* (ed. Robert M. Polzin and Eugene Rothman; Philadelphia: Fortress; and Chico, CA: Scholars, 1982) 87–103.

Koch
Growth, 200–210.

Lys, Daniel
"Jérémie 28 et le problème du faux prophète ou la circulation du sens dans la diagnostic prophétique," *Prophètes, poètes et sages d'Israël, Hommages à Edmond Jacob à l'occasion de son 70ème anniversaire par ses amis, ses collègues et ses élèves, RHPR* 59 (1979) 453–83.

Sawyer, John F. A.
"The Meaning of 'barzel' in the Biblical Expressions of 'Chariots of Iron,' 'Yokes of Iron,' etc.," *Midian, Moab and Edom: The History and Archaeology of Late Bronze and Iron Age Jordan and North-West Arabia* (ed. John F. A. Sawyer and David J. A. Clines; *JSOT* Supplement Series 24; Sheffield: *JSOT*, 1983) 129–34.

28

1 And [in the same year]ᵃ ᵈ[in the accession-year]ᵇ [. . .] in the fourth yearᶜ of 《Zedekiah king of Judah,》ᵈ in the fifth month, Hananiah son of Azzur, the prophet from Gibeon, spoke [to me]ᵉ in the house of Yahweh in

Text

1a Omit with *G*; these words, present along with "in the fourth year" in *M*, evidently represent a conflate text (Janzen, pp. 14–15).

b Omit with *G*; this expression is a harmonizing gloss from 27:1, where it is likewise erroneous, having come into the text from 26:1: see Text on 27:1 (Janzen, pp. 14–15).

c For the double reading, ketib בִּשְׁנַת, qere' בַּשָּׁנָה, see GKC, sec. 134p (compare Text on 32:1).

d—d Reading "in the fourth year of Zedekiah king of Judah" with *G*; *M* has "in the accession-year of Zedekiah king of Judah, in the fourth year" (!). See Janzen, pp. 14–15.

e Though both *M* and all the Versions have this expression, it is either to be omitted (compare the diction of v 11) or to be read as "to Jeremiah" (assuming that אֶל + a yod that was intended as an abbreviation for "Jeremiah" was misread as אֵלִי), given the third-person references to Jeremiah in vv 5–15. The second solution is preferred by most commentators (so, for example, Rudolph and Bright), but as Volz points out, Hebrew word order will hardly allow "to Jeremiah" in the position in which "to me" now stands. Conceivably "to Jeremiah" might have stood originally after "from Gibeon" and the word-order subsequently shifted

the presence of the priests and all the people, as follows: 2/ Thus Yahweh [of hosts, the God of Israel]ª has said, I have broken the yoke of the king of Babylon. 3/ Within two years' time I am returning to this place [all]ª the vessels of the house of Yahweh [which Nebuchadnezzar king of Babylon took from this place and brought to Babylon,]ᵇ 4/ and Jeconiah [son of Jehoiakim, king of Judah,]ª and [all]ᵇ the exiles of Judah [who have come to Babylon I am returning to this place, oracle of Yahweh,]ᶜ for I shall break the yoke of the king of Babylon.

5   Then Jeremiah [the prophet]ª spoke to Hananiah [the prophet]ª in the presence of the priests and in the presence of all the people standing in the house of Yahweh, 6/ and Jeremiah [the prophet]ª said, "So be it! May Yahweh do so. May he [M: Yahweh]ᵇ perform ᶜyour wordsᶜ which you have prophesied, to return the vessels of the house of Yahweh and all the exiles from Babylon to this place! 7/ Nevertheless just hear this word which I am speaking in your ears and in the ears of all the people: 8/ The prophets who were before me and you from early times—they prophesied to many lands and great kingdoms war [and disasterᵇ and pestilence.]ª 9/ The prophet who shall prophesy peace—when the word of the prophet comes (true), then the prophet shall be recognized (as one) whom Yahweh has really sent."

10   Then Hananiah [the prophet]ª took 《the yoke-pegs》ᵇ off the neck of Jeremiah [the prophet]ª and 《broke them.》ᶜ 11/ And Hananiah said in the presence of [all]ª the people, Thus Yahweh has said, So shall I break the yoke of [Nebuchadnezzar]ᵇ the king of Babylon [in two more years]ᶜ off the neck of all the nations; and Jeremiah [the prophet]ᵈ went his way.

12   Then the word of Yahweh came to Jeremiah after Hananiah [the prophet]ª had broken 《the yoke-pegs》ᵇ off 《his neck》 [M: the neck of Jeremiah]ᶜ [the prophet:]ª 13/ Go and say to Hananiah, Thus Yahweh has said, Yoke-pegs of wood you have broken, but you shall make in their place yoke-pegs of iron. 14/ For thus Yahweh [of hosts, the God of Israel]ª has said, An iron yoke I have put on the neck of all the nations [M: these nations]ᵇ to serve [Nebuchadnezzar]ᶜ the king of Babylon, [and they shall serve him, and even the animals of the field I have given to him.]ᵈ 15/ And Jeremiah [the prophet]ª said

(compare the evident shift of the words "of Zedekiah king of Judah" from the word-order represented by G to that in M).

2a   Omit with G (Janzen, pp. 75–76); compare v 14.

3a   Omit with G (Janzen, pp. 65–67); compare vv 4 and 11.

b   Omit with G; this expansionist gloss was developed from chapter 27, especially v 20 there (Janzen, p. 48).

4a   Omit with G (Janzen, pp. 69–71).

b   Omit with G (Janzen 65–67); compare vv 3, 11.

c   Omit with G; this expansionist gloss was developed from both the original text and the expanded text of v 3 (Janzen, p. 48).

5a   Omit both occurrences of "the prophet" with G (compare Janzen, pp. 69–70); compare vv 6, 10, 11, 12, 15.

6a   Omit with G; compare v 5.

b   Omit the repeated noun subject with G.

c—c   Some MSS., G, and T read "your word"; either reading is appropriate, but there is no need to reject M.

8a   Omit with G; the contrast is with "peace" (v 9).

b   Many MSS. read "famine," doubtless stimulated by the threefold pattern "sword, famine, pestilence": but the first item here is "war," not "sword."

10a   Omit both occurrences of "the prophet" with G; compare vv 5, 6, 11, 12, 15 (see Janzen, pp. 69–70).

b   M reads the singular "the yoke-peg" (הַמּוֹטָה) in both v 10 and v 12; but the plural occurs in v 13 (and in 27:2), and the plural in G in both verses of the present chapter likewise encourages reading the plural הַמֹּטוֹת.

c   M most curiously reads a masculine singular suffix (וַיִּשְׁבְּרֵהוּ), though the antecedent in M is feminine singular (see b). I propose reading וַיִּשְׁבְּרֵיהֶן (compare "in their place," תַחְתֵּיהֶן, in v 13): the confusion of nun and waw is easy.

11a   Omit with G; compare vv 3, 4 (Janzen, pp. 65–67).

b   Omit with G; compare v 14, and 27:20 and often.

c   Omit with G; this gloss is from v 3, where the phrase has a different function (Janzen, p. 48).

d   Omit with G; compare vv 5, 6, 10, 12, 15 (Janzen, pp. 69–70).

12a   Omit both occurrences of "the prophet" with G; compare vv 5, 6, 10, 11, 15 (Janzen, pp. 69–70).

b   Read the singular הַמּוֹטָה for M plural הַמֹּטוֹת; see 10b.

c   The reading of G is preferable to the repetition of "Jeremiah." It is conceivable that the expansion with "the prophet" after "Jeremiah" was added at the same time (compare 17a).

14a   Omit with G; compare v 2 (Janzen, pp. 75–76).

b   "These" is an addition analogous to the phraseology of 25:9, 11, and compare 27:6 (see Janzen, p. 48).

c   Omit with G; compare v 11.

d   Omit with G; the words are an expansion from

to Hananiah [the prophet:]ᵃ Just hear, Hananiah—Yahweh has not sent you, and you have been leading this people to trust in a lie. 16/ Therefore thus Yahweh has said, I am going to send you off the surface of the ground; this year you will die, [because you have uttered rebellion against Yahweh.]ᵃ 17/ And he [*M*: Hananiah the prophet]ᵃ died [that year]ᵇ in the seventh month.

27:6 (Janzen, p. 48).

15a   Omit both occurrences of "the prophet" with *G*; compare vv 5, 6, 10, 11, 12.

16a   Omit with *G*; Janzen, p. 48, describes it as a "scholarly" gloss derived from Deut 13:6.

17a   Omit the repeated subject and apposition of office with *G*; compare v 12.

  b   Omit with *G*; the words are derived from v 16 (Janzen, p. 48).

Preliminary Observations

The text of *M* for this chapter has undergone as much expansion as that of chapter 27 has, and evidently by the same or similar agency: one finds here the addition of "all," of "Nebuchadnezzar," and of other phrases that clutter up the diction, as well as longer phrases and clauses that indicate either a fussy urge to expand and explain or the impulse to express the concerns of a later generation.

The chapter, though the narrative follows that of chapter 27 (note 28:10 after 27:2), has a unity and interest of its own. The confrontation between Hananiah the optimistic prophet and Jrm, with the direct quotation of the words of both, gives the narrative a unique immediacy and interest, and the chapter has received close attention in studies of the "false prophets."[1] It is noteworthy that Hananiah is designated by the same title ("prophet," v 1) as Jeremiah is (1:5); it remained for *G*, *S*, and *T* to expand his designation to "false prophet." Further, the form of Hananiah's oracles is identical with those of Jrm ("Thus Yahweh has said," vv 2, 11); Jeremiah's symbolic action (27:2; 28:10) is matched by Hananiah's symbolic action (28:10); and the predictive word that Hananiah offers to accompany his symbolic action, "So shall I break . . ." (כָּכָה אֶשְׁבֹּר, v 11), exactly matches Jrm's words accompanying similar actions (19:11; 51:64; compare 13:9). In fact, as has often been pointed out, Hananiah's word is not dissimilar from that of Isaiah slightly more than a century before.[2] Because of these resemblances, Israel urgently needed to establish means by which to distinguish "true" from "false" prophets (see particularly Deut 18:21).[3]

Structure and Form

This chapter offers a self-contained narrative closely associated with chapter 27; in 27:2 Jrm is told to "put on" (נתן, literally "give") the yoke-pegs, and in 28:10 Hananiah "takes" them (לקח) off Jrm's neck. For the position of chapters 27—28 within chapters 26—36, see Introduction, sec. 22.

Verses 1–16 break easily into four sections as the two prophets alternate in initiating action: Hananiah (vv 1–4), Jrm (vv 5–9), Hananiah (vv 10–11), and Jrm (vv 12–16). Verse 17 is a concluding announcement of the fulfillment of the prophecy of Jrm announced in v 16. The chapter turns on the verb "send" (שׁלח)—whether Hananiah has really been "sent" by Yahweh or not (vv 9, 15, 16).

The narrative is a brief unit of prophetic biography depicting a dispute between Jrm and the opposing prophet Hananiah, the purpose of which is to affirm the truth of Jrm's proclamation.[4]

After the historical notices in v 1, vv 2–4 present Hananiah's salvation oracle; it has been prepared for, in the present organization of text, by 27:16, in which Yahweh warns the listeners not to pay attention to the hopeful message of the return of the temple vessels: now in vv 2–4 one has precisely such a message from the mouth of a particular prophet. For the diction of "I have broken the yoke of the king of Babylon," compare Ezek 30:21, "I have broken the arm of Pharaoh king of Egypt."

1   For example, Overholt, *Falsehood*, 37–45; Simon J. De Vries, *Prophet Against Prophet* (Grand Rapids: Eerdmans, 1978) 142–47; and see further James L. Crenshaw, "Prophecy, false," *IDBSup* 701–2 and the bibliography there, and the bibliography at the end of the present volume, sec. 13b.

2   See Overholt, *Falsehood*, 40 and n. 30.

3   See the extensive treatment of the issue in Eva Osswald, *Falsche Prophetie im Alten Testament* (Sammlung gemeinverständlicher Vorträge und Schriften aus dem Gebiet der Theologie und Religionsgeschichte, 237; Tübingen: Mohr [Siebeck], 1962).

4   Wanke, *Baruchschrift*, 156.

Jrm's reply (vv 6–9) begins with optative imperfects expressing the wish that Hananiah's salvation oracle might come true (v 6). This wish appears to be poised between a real hope and a contrary-to-fact expression ("Would that it might be true!"), just as 27:18 does (see Interpretation on that verse). It is possible that the expressions of this verse function as does Micaiah's first insincere word to the king of Israel (1 Kgs 22:15), which was intended to ridicule.[5] The remainder of the word to Hananiah (vv 7–9) is not couched as a divine word—that word was presumably delivered previously (27:16). It is rather a word of prudent caution, an appeal to precedent (v 8) and an attitude of wait-and-see for optimistic oracles probably based on Deut 18:22 ("come [true]," בוא).

There follows the report of Hananiah's symbolic action and accompanying predictive word (vv 10–11); for the resemblance to analogous symbolic actions and accompanying words of Jrm see Preliminary Observations.

Verses 12–17 offer some form-critical confusion: vv 12–13 report a command of Yahweh to speak a divine word of judgment against an individual (here Hananiah); v 14 appears to be a supplementary word couched as a divine word of judgment against the nations, but whether this supplementary word is intended to be understood as Jrm's supplementary word to Hananiah on that occasion, or is simply evidence offered by the narrator that Jrm had spoken the general word elsewhere, is unclear. There is no report of the execution of the command in vv 12–13; this is assumed, as often elsewhere (compare 27:2–11). Verse 15 is then a personal word from Jrm to Hananiah, not a divine word: it is a rejection of Hananiah's claim to be a prophet. Jrm's word to Hananiah is completed by the divine word of judgment against Hananiah (v 16), a prophecy of his death; and (as already noted) v 17 reports the fulfillment of the word of judgment. The form-critical variety in these last six verses suggests that the patterns of form here are at the service of a vivid narrative.

Setting

If the reconstruction of the text of v 1 offered here, which is the consensus of scholars, is correct, the narra-

tive reports an incident occurring in the fifth month of Zedekiah's fourth year, that is July/August 594. The encounter with Hananiah is a plausible consequence of Zedekiah's conference in Jerusalem to plan a rebellion against Nebuchadnezzar, which is presupposed in chapter 27, and that conference is in turn a plausible consequence of the aborted rebellion against Nebuchadnezzar in Babylon in December 595/January 594 (see Setting for chapter 27). The specificity of the notice of Hananiah's death in September/October 594 (v 17) likewise speaks for its historicity.

One may furthermore detect the mind of Jrm at work in the description of the encounter, notably in the play on the meanings of "send" in vv 15 and 16. There are two parallels between the diction of Deuteronomy and *M* in the present chapter, "an iron yoke I have put on the neck" (v 14, compare Deut 28:48), and "you will die, because you have spoken rebellion against Yahweh" (v 16, compare Deut 13:6); but there is evidence that Deut 28:48 is part of a secondary addition stimulated by phrases in Jer (compare the remarks on 5:15 and 17, and on 19:9),[6] and the phrase in v 16 is secondary (see Text). The conclusion that the present chapter is the product of Deuteronomistic authors (compare Nicholson) is therefore inappropriate.

Interpretation

■ **1** For the date see Text, Setting. For the curious occurrence of וַיְהִי (literally "and it happened," here left untranslated), followed by the perfect "spoke," see König, *Syntax*, sec. 370b.

The name "Hananiah" was a common one (for reference to two others in Jer, see 36:12 and 37:13); the name "Azzur" is borne by two others in the OT (Ezek 11:1; Neh 10:18). The prophet Hananiah is not mentioned in the OT outside the present chapter, but the definite article ("the prophet from Gibeon") suggests someone well known at the time (compare the diction of 1 Kgs 13:11, "there dwelt an old prophet in Bethel"). His place of origin, Gibeon, was located, like that of Jrm (Anathoth), in Benjamin; indeed Gibeon (the present-day *el-jib*) is only five and a half kilometers northwest of Anathoth (Atlas of Israel grid 167–139),[7] so that the propin-

5   Montgomery, *Kings*, 338.
6   See further Mayes, *Deuteronomy*, 350, 351, 356.
7   For a summary of the excavations at Gibeon through

1960 see conveniently James B. Pritchard, "Gibeon," *IDB* 2:391–93, with bibliography, and the more popular account, James B. Pritchard, *Gibeon, Where*

quity of the origins of the two prophets might have sharpened the tension of their exchange (compare "me and you" in v 8).

■ **2–4** For the parallels with the oracles of Isaiah and Jrm see Preliminary Observations, Setting, and see further Aim.

The naming of the vessels of the temple before the exiled king and the rest of those deported is curious. The simplest solution is that Hananiah really thought more of the temple vessels than of the exiled king, or that the narrator wished to portray him so, but such an explanation is doubtless too simple. It may be that the narrator wished to link this episode closely with 27:16–22, where the topic is the vessels. There is another possibility. Calvin points out acutely that when Hananiah predicts the return of Jeconiah (=Jehoiachin, compare 24:1) he implies the abdication of Zedekiah. This being the case, one could imagine Hananiah's hesitation to mention the king first. It is also possible that the words of v 4 (that is, those here unbracketed), though present in *G*, may have been added somewhat later by someone concerned for the welfare of those in the first deportation (compare 29:2).

For the expression "exiles of Judah" (גָּלוּת יְהוּדָה) see 24:5; for the plural participle ("who have come") modifying the collective singular see König, *Syntax*, sec. 334i.

■ **6** The only other occurrence of "So be it!" (אָמֵן) in Jer is 11:5: there it serves to confirm a curse perceived to be valid, while here it expresses an optative of dubious validity (see below).

The imperfect יַעֲשֶׂה clearly must be construed as a jussive ("May Yahweh do so"), given the jussive "May Yahweh perform" (יָקֵם). (Curiously the expected jussive יַעַשׂ appears in the OT only twice, 2 Sam 2:6 and Ruth 1:8 qere'.)[8]

The context indicates that Jrm had little or no hope that the optimistic prediction of Hananiah would come true; indeed the model of Micaiah's speech in 1 Kgs 22:15 suggests that Jrm might be mocking Hananiah (on this see Form). Calvin puts forth another suggestion, namely that Jrm's sympathy for his people was what moved him; Calvin paraphrases the prophet's mood, "'Amen,' he said, 'may it thus happen, I wish I were a

false prophet; I would willingly retract, and that with shame, all that I have hitherto predicted, so great is my care and anxiety for the safety of the public; for I would prefer the welfare of the whole people to my own reputation.'"

Jrm uses the alternative collective term for the exiles, גּוֹלָה (compare Hananiah's גָּלוּת in v 4). This is the first appearance of the word in Jer, but the terms are interchangeable.

■ **7–9** The sharp adversative conjunction "nevertheless" (אַךְ) functions with the same imperative in 34:4 and begins a new verse in three other passages of the book (3:13; 26:15, 24). Jrm suggests that Hananiah's word is invalid because it does not fit the precedents; he evidently maintains that prophets have delivered judgment oracles, never oracles of salvation. This is a sobering contention in view of oracles or announcements of salvation in such books as Isaiah and Hosea that give evidence of being part of the authentic expression of the prophets in question (for example Isa 7:4–9; Hos 14:2–9), but it is clear that the overwhelming proportion of prophetic utterances from the canonical prophets of the eighth and seventh centuries are of judgment, and it is equally clear that it is easy to give voice to cheap optimism, so that any optimistic words should be examined with care. Note that Jrm uses the imperfect ("the prophet who shall prophesy peace"), not the participle (which would be "the prophet who prophesies peace," compare 14:15; 23:15, 16, 25; 27:15), suggesting that he is talking not in general but about particular instances in that historical context. He is using the principle set forth in Deut 18:21–22 (see Structure and Form).

"Before me and you": in Hebrew (as in Arabic) the first-person pronoun must precede a coordinate second- or third-person pronoun, or third-person noun (compare Gen 31:44 and often).[9] "From early times" is a translation of מִן־הָעוֹלָם; though עוֹלָם is ordinarily translated "eternity" or "for ever" (3:5), the present instance excellently illustrates the fact that the word means "an indefinitely long period of time extended into the past and/or the future"—one might translate "the prophets . . . have always prophesied." The waw-consecutive imperfect "they prophesied" in v 8 after the noun phrase

the Sun Stood Still (Princeton: Princeton University, 1962).

8   For the phenomenon see GKC, sec. 107n; Joüon,

Gramm., sec. 79m; König, *Syntax*, sec. 183b.

9   For Arabic see Maurice Gaudefroy-Demombynes and Régis Blachère, *Grammaire de l'Arabe Classique*

has been interpreted as a *casus pendens* (compare 6:19; 33:24);[10] but whatever the analysis, vv 8 and 9 in their parallel way contrast "the prophets who were before me and you" and "the prophet who shall prophesy peace" by giving the phrases independent status at the beginning of their respective verses. The terms "war" and "peace" clearly represent more than the presence or absence of strife: שָׁלוֹם ("peace") here denotes good news of the survival and continued well-being of the people (German *Heil*), whereas מִלְחָמָה ("war") is the contrary (compare the discussion in 6:14). Question: Do Jrm's words here have as their background Micah's judgment against prophets who, if paid, preach peace, and if not paid, preach war (Mic 3:5)? For "really sent" (שְׁלָחוֹ בֶּאֱמֶת, v 9) compare Jrm's own claim in 26:15 (and see the discussion of this verbal link in Introduction, sec. 22).

■ **10–11** For "yoke-pegs" see 27:2. Hananiah resorted to a symbolic action alongside his word (see Preliminary Observations, Structure and Form): here is a unique narrative of symbolic action that is the intended annulling of the symbolic action of an opposing prophet. For a culture that saw power residing in both godly word and godly action, the event must have been awesome. Calvin compared the cords and yoke-pegs on Jrm's neck to a sacrament; Hananiah's breaking of the yoke-pegs thus partakes of blasphemy. Jrm's response was simply to "go his way," whether out of prudence, knowing that the optimistic word of Hananiah was popular with the crowd, or out of the conviction that he had already said and done all he could, or out of dread that perhaps Hananiah's action was at the instigation of Yahweh (see the Interpretation of 20:7), one cannot say.

■ **12–14** According to the narrative, Yahweh took fresh initiative with Jrm after the encounter. If the yoke-pegs resembled wooden spikes (see again 27:2), then the analogy of iron spikes is plausible. *G* reads "I shall make" for "you shall make" in v 13, and that reading has been adopted by some (*RSV*, *JB*), but *M* is the *lectio difficilior* and clearly to be preferred: Yahweh holds Hananiah

responsible for his action and sets forth the prospect of a far worse situation that Hananiah himself is to shape (*NAB* is succinct: "By breaking a wooden yoke, you forge an iron yoke," though by the analysis presented here "yoke" is wrong).

Evidence has been given that the image of the "iron yoke" is original to Jrm and secondarily entered Deuteronomy (Deut 28:48: see Setting); the origin of that grotesque image will then be found in the incident with Hananiah. One notes the association with that other image of "iron," the "iron furnace" of the exile in Egypt in 11:4, a passage that by the analysis of the present study has its setting two months later than that of the present passage (see Setting there). John F. A. Sawyer has recently pointed out the pejorative, ugly associations of "iron" in the OT: the word in Hebrew (בַּרְזֶל) is a foreign word, and the technology was a recent and uncanny one in people's minds.[11]

■ **15–16** If Jrm had "gone his way" (v 11), then these verses narrate a second encounter with Hananiah; one must assume, therefore, that the command narrated in vv 13–14 was carried out before the words recorded here (compare Structure and Form). Verse 15 is the climax of Jrm's words to Hananiah; Jrm insists that Hananiah was not sent by Yahweh: Jrm could not wait to see if the optimism of Hananiah was justified, as he had suggested one should (v 9) (for the link of "send" in vv 9 and 15–16 see Structure and Form). There follows the play on words between "send" (שלח qal) and "send off, dismiss" (שלח pi'el) (compare Setting): if Yahweh did not send Hananiah, he will surely send him off—to death. For "trust in a lie" see 13:25; this is one of two passages where the verb is causative ("lead someone to trust in a lie": the other instance in 29:31). Jrm's announcement of the coming death of Hananiah is not foreknowledge, but a death sentence based on Deut 18:20 (compare vv 7–9, and Structure and Form); a false prophet must die.[12]

(Paris: Maisonneuve, 1952), secs. 248c, 253.

10 See the discussions in GKC, sec. 143d, and König, *Syntax*, sec. 366r.

11 John F. A. Sawyer, "The Meaning of 'barzel' in the Biblical Expressions of 'Chariots of Iron,' 'Yokes of Iron,' etc.," *Midian, Moab and Edom: The History of Archaeology of Late Bronze and Iron Age Jordan and North-West Arabia* (ed. John F. A. Sawyer and David J.

A. Clines; *JSOT* Supplement Series 24; Sheffield: JSOT, 1983) 129–34.

12 Compare Lindblom, *Prophecy*, 200.

■ 17 There is no reason to doubt the sober note of the death of Hananiah; the seventh month is September/October, near the time of the festival of Booths (see Setting of 11:1–17).

Aim

It would be easy to reduce this encounter between Jrm and Hananiah to questions of the sociology of prophetism, to two different opinions struggling for support in the marketplace (or, in this case, in the temple precincts). Whose understanding of the word and will of Yahweh will win out? But this is not the perspective of those who recorded the tradition and incorporated it into the corpus of material that would become scripture; for them the question is how it can be that Yahweh's word can be countered by someone who claims to speak for Yahweh, how a symbolic action effective for Yahweh can be countered by another symbolic action in the name of Yahweh intending to nullify it. It is awesome. More than once in the course of exegesis on this chapter there has been occasion to refer to Calvin, but that is only because he so well senses the awesomeness of the encounter. So let him have the last word: "The people saw that God's name was become a subject of contest; there was a dreadful conflict, 'God has spoken to me'; 'Nay, rather to me.' Jeremiah and Hananiah were opposed, the one to the other; each of them claimed to be a prophet. Such was the conflict; the name of God seemed to have been assumed at pleasure, and flung forth by the devil as in sport."

A Letter to the Exiles

Bibliography

On 29:1–32:
Schreiner, Josef
 "'Durch die Propheten gelehrt, das Heil zu er-
 warten'; Erwägungen in Anschluss an Jeremia 29,"
 *Praesentia Christi, Festschrift Johannes Betz zum 70.
 Geburtstag* (ed. Lothar Lies; Düsseldorf: Patmos,
 1984) 25–36.
Wanke
 Baruchschrift, 36–59, 74–77.

On 29:1–23:
Berlin, Adele
 "Jeremiah 29:5–7: A Deuteronomic Allusion,"
 Hebrew Annual Review 8 (1984) 3–11.
Dahood, Mitchell
 "Word and Witness: A Note on Jeremiah xxix 23,"
 VT 27 (1977) 483.
Gunneweg, Antonius H. J.
 "Heil im Gericht, Zur Interpretation von Jeremias
 später Verkündigung," *Traditio, Krisis, Renovatio,
 Festschrift Winfried Zeller zum 65. Geburtstag* (ed.
 Bernd Jaspert and Rudolf Mohr; Marburg: Elwert,
 1976) 1–9.
Holladay, William L.
 "Enigmatic Bible Passages: God Writes a Rude
 Letter (Jeremiah 29:1–23)," *BA* 46 (1983) 145–46.
Pardee, Dennis
 Handbook of Ancient Hebrew Letters (SBLSBS 15;
 Chico, CA: Scholars, 1982), esp. 175–77.
Pardee, Dennis
 "An Overview of Ancient Hebrew Episto-
 lography," *JBL* 97 (1978) 321–46.
Rubinger, Naphtali J.
 "Jeremiah's Epistle to the Exiles and the Field in
 Anathoth," *Judaism* 26 (1977) 84–91.
Soggin, J. Alberto
 "Jeremiah 29,8b," *Old Testament and Oriental
 Studies* (BibOr 29; Rome: Pontifical Biblical
 Institute, 1975) 238–40 = "Geremia 29,8b," *BeO*
 16 (1974) 33–34.
Welch, Adam C.
 "Jeremiah's Letter to the Exiles in Babylon,"
 Expositor, 8th Series, 22 (1921) 358–72.

29

1 These are the words of the letter which
 Jeremiah [the prophet]ᵃ sent from Jerusalem to the preeminentᵇ elders among the
 exiles, and to the priests and prophets and
 all the people [whom Nebuchadnezzar

Text

1a Omit with *G* (compare 28:5, 6, 10, 11, 12, 15).
b *G* omits this word, but given the fact that its
meaning is somewhat uncertain (see Interpretation),
it is hardly the kind of expansion that would be
added secondarily to the text. It is better to conclude that *G* omitted it because of uncertainty
regarding its meaning (against Giesebrecht, with

131

exiled from Jerusalem to Babylon—]ᶜ [2/ after Jeconiah the king, and the queen-mother, and the eunuchs and officials of Judah and Jerusalem and the craftsmen and smiths left Jerusalem—]ᵃ 3/ by the hand of Elasar son of Shaphan, and Gemariah son of Hilkiah, whom Zedekiah king of Judah sent to [Nebuchadnezzar]ᵃ the king of Babylon, to Babylon, as follows: 4/ Thus Yahweh [of hosts]ᵃ the God of Israel has said: To all the exiles ᵇwhom I have exiledᵇ from Jerusalem [to Babylon:]ᶜ 5/ Build houses and live (in them), plant gardens and eat their fruit; 6/ take wives and have sons and daughters, and take for your sons wives and your daughters give to husbands ᵃand let them bear sons and daughters;ᵃ increase there, do not decrease, 7/ and seek the welfare of the cityᵃ to which I have exiled you: pray for it to Yahweh, for in its welfare you will have welfare. 8/ For thus Yahweh [of hosts, the God of Israel,]ᵃ has said: Let not your prophets who are in your midst, or your diviners, deceive you; do not listen to ⟨your dream-interpreters⟩ᵇ whom you ᶜ set to dream,ᶜ 9/ for falsely they prophesy to you in my name; I did not send them, [oracle of Yahweh.]ᵃ

10   For thus Yahweh has said: Only when Babylon's seventy years are completed shall I deal with you and perform my [good]ᵃ wordᵇ to bring you back to this place. 11/ For I [surely know the plans which I]ᵃ am making concerning you, [oracle of Yahweh,]ᵇ plans of welfare and not of

Duhm, Cornill, and others).

c   Omit with *G*; it is a gloss similar to material in 24:1 and 52:28–30 (see Janzen, p. 48).

2a   Though *G* includes this verse, it interrupts the continuity of vv 1 and 3; it is material derived, like a portion of 24:1, from 2 Kgs 24:14–16 (so Volz, Rudolph).

3a   Omit with *G* (compare 27:20; 28:11, 14; 29:21).

4a   Omit with *G* (compare 28:2, 14).

b—b   This is the text of *M* (אֲשֶׁר הִגְלֵיתִי). If one reads "Thus Yahweh . . . has said to all the exiles whom I have exiled," then there is an inconcinnity between third and first persons, which *S* has remedied by reading "who have been exiled" (אֲשֶׁר הָגְלְתָה). The latter reading is adopted by Volz and Rudolph, but *M* is the *lectio difficilior*, it is matched by *G*, and the punctuation offered here (a colon after "has said," so *NEB*) solves the problem. See further Form.

c   Omit with *G* (so Janzen, p. 48).

6a—a   This sequence is omitted by *G*; it is possible therefore either to assume expansion in *M* or an omission, perhaps by haplography, in *G*. For a discussion of the problem see Janzen, pp. 103–4.

7a   *G* reads "land," which is preferred by Duhm, Giesebrecht, Cornill, Volz, Rudolph, Bright. But surely *M* is the *lectio difficilior*. The argument that not all the exiles were in one city but were distributed around the country misses the force of the word, which is a synecdoche: compare the argument in Isa 7:8–9, and see further Interpretation.

8a   Omit with *G* (compare 28:2, 14; 29:21).

b   Vocalizing חֲלֹמֹתֵיכֶם for *M* חֲלֹמֹתֵיכֶם "your dreams"; for the vocalization see 27:9. This reading is supported by the causative interpretation of the following participle (see c—c, and further Interpretation).

c—c   The consonantal text of the participle suggests a hip'il or pi'el, suggesting in turn a causative meaning; this is the interpretation adopted here (see J. Alberto Soggin, "Jeremiah 29,8b," *Old Testament and Oriental Studies*, BibOr 29 [Rome: Pontifical Biblical Institute, 1975] 238–40, and see further Interpretation). For more traditional explanations, which suggest a non-causative interpretation, see GKC, sec. 53o.

9a   Omit with *G* (see Janzen, p. 83 [c]).

10a   Omit with *G*.

b   *G* reads "my words," plural, which may be correct: compare 28:6, where the same verb appears and *G* has the singular and *M* the plural.

11a   Omit with *G*. The commentators accept *M*, and Janzen, p. 118, assumes that *G* is defective by haplography (two occurrences of אָנֹכִי). But the simple idiom of "make plans" (חֹשֵׁב מַחֲשָׁבוֹת) is stable in Jer (for example, 11:19; 18:11) and should be retained. Doubtless the inserted words represent the conflation of a variant text. The inserted words seem more plausible after the intrusion of "oracle of Yahweh" just after.

disaster, to give you a future [and a hope.]ᶜ
12/ [And you will call me]ᵃ [and come,]ᵇ and
you will pray to me, [and I shall hear you,
13/ and you will search for me and find
(me),]ᶜ ⟨ᵈ ⟩if you seek me with all your heart,⟨ ᵈ
14/ 《I shall appear》ᵉ to you, ᶠ[oracle of
Yahweh;] and I shall restore your fortunesᵍ
[and shall gather you from all the nations
and from all the places where I have driven
you,] oracle of Yahweh, [and I shall bring
you back to the place from which I exiled
you.]ᶠ [15/ . . . .]ᵃ

16   For thus Yahweh has said concerning the king
who sits on the throne of David, and
concerning all the people who live in this
city, your brothers who have not gone out
with you into exile: 17/ [Thus Yahweh of
hosts has said:]ᵃ I am going to send against

b   Omit with *G* (compare v 9).

c   The commentators take the two nouns as a
hendiadys, "a hopeful future." But the curious *G*
reading that covers both nouns, ταῦτα, simply
"these," suggests that a single noun stood here. *Gᴸ*
reads (τὰ) μετὰ ταῦτα, "(things) thereafter," a
translation of "future" (אַחֲרִית)—compare 5:31. The
majority *G* reading will then have arisen by haplography of -τα-. The expression "and a hope" is either
a gloss or an evidence of conflation of a variant text;
the two nouns are often in parallel (Prov 23:18;
24:14; compare Jer 31:17).

12–14a Omit with *G*; the phrase may be an early
variant of "and you will pray to me" in a conflate
text.

b   Omit "and come" with *G* and *S*; it may be a
careless dittography of "and you will pray."

c   Omit the whole sequence with *S*; though one
might suspect haplography, the whole sequence
appears prolix. "And I shall hear you" duplicates the
meaning of "and I shall be found by you/appear to
you" in v 14, and "and you will search for me and
find (me)" reflects the diction of Deut 4:29 (compare
Rudolph).

d   Though this sequence is found in *M* and all the
Versions, I suggest that it is probably a secondary
addition, again based on Deut 4:29. The form of
"heart" (לֵבָב) is not that preferred by Jrm (which is
לֵב).

e   Reading with *G* וְנִרְאֵיתִי for the *M* reading וְנִמְצֵאתִי
"I will be found (by you)" (so Cornill, Rudolph,
compare Volz). For the phrase *S* has "you will find
me," a reading that appears to be a simplification of
that of *M*.

f—f *G* omits this long sequence. The easy solution is to
view the whole passage as an expansion by *M* from
16:15; 23:3; 32:37; and elsewhere (so Janzen, pp.
48–49). Some of the material is clearly secondary:
for "and will gather you from all the nations and
from all the places where I have driven you,"
compare the expansion in v 18. The last sequence,
"and I will bring you back to the place from which I
exiled you," is similar to the sequence at the end of v
10 and is surely extraneous here. But the phrase
"and I will restore your fortunes" is an idiom that
appears in Hos 6:11, and the phrase makes a good
parallel to "I will appear to you"; furthermore the
use of שׁוּב qal here would form an inclusio with שׁוּב
hip'il in v 10 (see further Interpretation). The
phrase "oracle of Yahweh" may or may not be
original here (compare its use at the end of v 23).
The present *G*, by this analysis, will have suffered
haplography with the repeated suffix כֶם-.

g   The two readings, ketib שְׁבִיתְכֶם, qere' שְׁבוּתְכֶם,
are identical in meaning. For bibliography on the
problem see Interpretation, nn. 27 and 28.

15a   For v 15 see after v 20.

17a   Omit: the clause is unnecessary repetition of v 16
(compare the same secondary repetition in 27:19–

them sword, famine[b] and pestilence, and I shall make them like putrid figs so bad they cannot be eaten. 18/ And I shall pursue them with sword, famine[a] and pestilence, and I shall make them a terror[b] to all the kingdoms of the earth, a curse and a desolation, a hissing[c] and a reproach [to all the nations to which I have driven them,][d] 19/ inasmuch as they did not listen to my words, oracle of Yahweh, to whom I sent my servants the prophets early and constantly, [but you did not hear, oracle of Yahweh.][a]

20 As for you, hear the word of Yahweh, all (you) exiles whom I sent from Jerusalem to Babylon: 《15/ Because you have said, "Yahweh has raised up for us prophets in Babylon!"》[a] 21/ thus Yahweh [of hosts the God of Israel][a] has said concerning Ahab [b]son of Kolaiah[b] and Zedekiah [b]son of Maaseiah,[b] [who prophesy to you in my name a lie:][c] I am going to give them into the hand of [Nebuchadnezzar][d] the king of Babylon and strike them down before your eyes; 22/ and because of them the following curse shall be used by all the exiles of Judah in Babylon: "May Yahweh make you like Zedekiah and Ahab,[a] whom the king of Babylon roasted in the fire!" — 23/ because they have committed an outrage in Israel, and committed adultery with the wives of their neighbors and spoken a word in my name, [a falsehood,][a] which I did not command them; and I am [the one who knows and][b] witness, oracle of Yahweh.

21, and see Form).

b   Many MSS. of the Hebrew, G^L, some MSS. of T, V, and S read "and famine."

18a   The data for "famine" in v 17 apply here as well.

b   The data for "terror" in 15:4 apply here as well.

c   A few MSS. read וְלִקְלָלָה "and an object of contempt" (compare 24:9).

d   Omit for the same reason the phrase is to be omitted in 24:9 (see there).

19a   A secondary addition: the personal reference has shifted, and the verb repeats שמע at the beginning of the verse; the clause is a conflation from 25:4. Note that some MSS. of the Hebrew read "you to whom" in the middle of the verse, and that G^L and S conversely read "but they did not hear, oracle of Yahweh" here.

15a   For the restoration of v 15 after v 20 see the discussion in Preliminary Observations.

21a   Omit with G; compare v 2.

b—b G omits the patronymics of both prophets; commentators have divided over the question whether G has omitted authentic phrases (Volz, Rudolph) or whether M has artificially expanded the text (Cornill). Janzen, p. 71, points out the fact that Neh 11:7 mentions ". . . son of Kolaiah son of Maaseiah" as a possible source for artificial patronymics. One may suspect that there is a word-play in the passage between the patronymic קוֹלָיָה here and קְלָלָה "curse" and קָלָם "roasted them" in v 22, but if the names are genuine, why would G have omitted them? Out of an urge for symmetry with v 22? See the discussion in Janzen, pp. 71–72, 104.

c   Omit with G; the sequence is an expansion from v 9 and other parallels (Janzen, p. 49).

d   Omit with G; compare v 3.

22a M has mistakenly spelled the prophet's name here אחב, so vocalized אֲחָב, for אַחְאָב (v 21).

23a   Omit with G (see Janzen, p. 49).

b   Omit with G. The qere' of the substantive is הַיּוֹדֵעַ; if the ketib is not a *lapsus calami*, it must be read as הוּא יָדַע (הוּ for הוּא). The similarity between the substantive and the word "witness" suggests that one has here either an early error or a variant reading, M being a conflate text (see Janzen, p. 22).

Preliminary Observations

Chapter 29, like chapter 27 (which see), presents severe difficulties in the establishment of a text. Here, as in chapters 27 and 28, M has many plusses over G. In most instances M has been expanded in ways that are easy to locate, but in a few instances one is left uncertain whether M has expanded the text secondarily or whether G has compressed it deliberately or inadvertently by haplography, for example, in the matter of the patronymic phrases in v 21. In three instances, however,

textual questions carry larger consequences: these occur in vv 12–14, 16–20 and 24–25, and these call for discussion at the outset.

M is verbose from v 12 to the beginning of v 14, and both G and S are shorter in different ways. Though certainty is impossible, I propose that the sequence was originally simply "and you will pray to me and I shall appear to you," the rest being various expansions and conflate readings. As for v 14 itself, only "I shall appear to you" occurs in G: the balance of the verse is lacking.

Some of the *M* plus is clearly expansionist,[1] but I propose that "and I will restore your fortunes" dropped out of the proto-*G* tradition by haplography. This small detail has consequences for the process by which vv 24–32 were added to vv 1–23, and by which chapters 30—31 were added to chapters 27—29, since I would propose that "restore one's fortunes" (שׁוּב + שְׁבוּת or שְׁבִית) is a catchword in that process; it is thus a pity that the text traditions are ambiguous on the question (see further Text, and see Introduction, sec. 22).

The question of vv 16–20 is that of v 14 on a large scale: these verses are lacking altogether in *G*, and their position in *M* appears to interrupt the continuity of vv 15 and 21. Thus most critical commentators conclude that vv 16–20 are a secondary interpolation adding nothing to one's understanding of Jrm (Duhm, Cornill, Volz, Rudolph); those who hold to the view of large-scale Deuteronomistic revision of the book see the hand of that editor here, as they see it in the related chapter 24.[2] Volz points out the practical problem: How could Jrm send a negative judgment about Zedekiah by the hand of a royal courtier (v 3)? But there is another possibility: that though some phrases within *M* in vv 16–20 are secondary, *G* has also suffered haplography in the omission of these verses.

Thus there are several instances of striking phraseology in vv 16–19 that should give one pause. There is a play of ישׁב ("sits," "live") in v 16, picking up "live" in v 5. The only parallel in Jer to "your brothers" in v 16, a reference to the inhabitants of Jerusalem in an address to the exiles, is 7:15, a reference to the inhabitants of Ephraim in an address to Jerusalem. The adjective modifying "figs" in v 17 (שֹׁעָר, presumably "putrid") is found only here in the OT. "Pursue" (רדף, v 18) with Yahweh as subject is found only here in Jer (and only four times otherwise in the OT).[3] The conjunction "inasmuch as" (תַּחַת אֲשֶׁר, v 19) is rare in the OT (eleven times with this meaning, once otherwise in Jer, 50:7).[4] One may then cautiously conclude that the verses

contain genuine material.

If vv 16–20 contain genuine material, it is possible that they were inserted here secondarily where they do not originally belong (so Bright).

A third possibility is that the five verses have belonged in the context of this chapter but that the order of verses has been disturbed. Several suggestions have been made. (1) Verses 16–20 belong between vv 9 and 10 (so Condamin, who cites Houbigant). (2) Verses 8–9 belong after v 15 even if one believes vv 16–20 to be secondary (Rudolph). (3) Verses 16–20 belong between vv 14 and 15 (Giesebrecht): this is actually the order of the Lucianic recension of *G*[5] (though one might argue that that order is a secondary shift that only accidentally coincides with a plausible solution). The last is the order given in some translations earlier in this century (James Moffatt, *A New Translation of the Bible, Containing the Old and New Testaments* [New York: Harper, 1934], and J. M. Powis Smith, et al, *The Complete Bible, An American Translation* [Chicago: University of Chicago, 1939]) and is the solution reached by Janzen.[6] It is the solution adopted here, having the advantage of explaining the omission of vv 16–20 in *G* and fitting the form-critical analysis of the chapter.

Both vv 15 and 20 end with "Babylon" (בָּבֶלָה). One may assume that the text anterior to *G* allowed vv 16–20 to drop out by homoioteleuton, and that the text anterior to *M* corrected such a gap by a marginal insertion of the missing verses, which were then restored to the body of the text at the wrong spot. The reference to those in exile (vv 4–14) and to those in Jerusalem (vv 16–20) would then parallel the same references in 24:4–7 and 8–10, respectively.[7] It is altogether likely that Jrm wished to deal with the status of those in Jerusalem when he wrote to the exiles just as much as he wished to deal with the status of the exiles when he communicated with those in Jerusalem (the implicit purpose of chapter 24).

This is not to say that the text of *M* for vv 16–19 does not have secondary additions in it: but there is no way to

---

1   So Janzen, pp. 48–49, who takes all of it as secondary.
2   So, for example, Nicholson, *Jer. 26—52*, 46–47.
3   Ps 83:16; Job 13:25; Lam 3:43, 66.
4   See BDB, 1066a, II, 3.
5   Joseph Ziegler, ed., *Ieremias, Baruch, Threni, Epistula Ieremiae* (Septuaginta, Vetus Testamentum Graecum Auctoritate Societatis Litterarum Gottingensis editum 15; Göttingen: Vandenhoeck & Ruprecht,

1957) 347.
6   Janzen, p. 118.
7   On both points see ibid., p. 118.

"control" these by reference to *G*. One may locate with fair confidence expansions at the beginning of v 17, at the end of v 18, and at the end of v 19; these are here bracketed (see in detail Text). One may suspect that what remains after the removal of bracketed material in vv 17 and 18 represents a conflate text: surely "sword, famine and pestilence" is not original here twice over, but it is difficult to be sure: see the detailed discussion in Interpretation.

The mention of the "king" in v 16 cannot be secondary: it involves the play on ישׁב ("sits," "live"—see above, and compare further 24:8); the problem posed by Volz (see above) must therefore be solved in some other way. It may be noted that Elasah, one of the envoys, was probably the brother of Ahikam who protected Jrm at the time of the trial after his temple sermon (26:24; see Interpretation on v 3 in the present passage), and it is conceivable that Hilkiah, the father of the other envoy, Gemariah, was the Hilkiah who was high priest under Josiah (2 Kings 22); in this event the envoys were likely to have been supportive of Jrm's message. (For Zedekiah's motives in sending the envoys see again Interpretation on v 3.) Zedekiah need not have known the contents of Jrm's letter (Thompson: "The letter went in the diplomatic mailbag!").

The problem posed by the text of vv 24–25 is just as severe. Rarely does *S* differ from both *M* and *G* when the latter two differ (usually *S* follows either *M* or *G*), but it does here; it will therefore be convenient to offer the three texts side by side.

M: 24/ And to Shemaiah the Nehelamite you [singular] shall say as follows: 25/ Thus Yahweh of hosts the God of Israel has said, as follows: Because you yourself sent in your (own) name a letter to all the people who are in Jerusalem and to Zephaniah son of Maaseiah the priest and to all the priests, as follows. (*T* =; *V* = except for the evident omission of "as follows" in the first two instances.)

G: 24/ And to Samaeas the Aelamite you [singular] shall say, 25/ I did not send you in my name, and to Sophonias the son of Maasaeas the priest, as follows.

S: 24/ And Shemaiah the Nehelamite said, 25/ Thus Yahweh the God of Israel has said; and he sent in his name a letter to all the people who are in Jerusalem and to Zephaniah son of Maaseiah the priest and to the priests.

The contrast between the end of v 25 in *M* and *G*

allows one to bracket as secondary the phrases "to all the people who are in Jerusalem and" and "and to all the priests"; they represent the generalizing of the passage typical of *M*.

The "because" clause in *M* of v 25 has no apodosis in the vicinity. The "you [singular] shall say" in *M* and *G* is inadmissible; as it stands, it appears to be addressed to Jrm, but form-critically this is impossible: the only other second-person address to Jrm is in v 31, where it is subordinate to "And the word of Yahweh came to Jeremiah as follows" (v 30), but in v 24 there is no such context in which to understand the address. The quite different syntax of *S* in v 24 thus attracts attention. If one assumes the correctness of that text and that of the first clause of v 25, and if one further assumes that originally an optimistic oracle stood after "Thus Yahweh God of Israel has said," then not only does *S* make perfect sense, but it offers a form-critical parallel to 28:2–4: Shemaiah does in Babylon what Hananiah does in Jerusalem—both announce an optimistic oracle and deliver it. Shemaiah then writes a letter to Zephaniah the priest in Jerusalem asking him to annul Jrm's prophetic activity, just as Hananiah broke the yoke-pegs (28:10), and the narrative closes with a divine word to Jrm of judgment against Shemaiah (v 32) corresponding to the divine word to Jrm of judgment against Hananiah (28:16). There is of course no way to reconstruct Shemaiah's optimistic oracle; doubtless it began with a word for "soon" (compare v 28, by contrast, "It will be a long time!" and compare 28:3, "within two years' time"), and it could well have ended with "Israel," leading to the haplographic omission of the oracle (given the previous "Israel")—one could imagine "Soon I will restore the fortunes of my people Israel" (compare 29:14; 30:3). Such an omission of the optimistic oracle must have taken place at a very early stage of text transmission, since there is no trace of it remaining.

Once the oracle was lost, the text was patched up in various ways. (1) The opening was shifted to "to Shemaiah the Nehelamite you [singular] shall say," since nothing remained of the specifics of what he said, and since "thus Yahweh the God of Israel has said" did not seem to the tradents to be appropriate on the lips of an opponent of Jrm (so *M* and *G*). (2) The personal reference of the "send" clause was shifted in two different ways: (a) the person was shifted to the second to match the second person of v 24, and "because" (יַעַן אֲשֶׁר) was supplied as a parallel to that conjunction in v 31 (*M*); (b) the person was shifted to the first as an appropriate divine word after "Thus Yahweh the God of Israel has said," and the "send" clause altered to "I did not send you in my name" on the analogy of "I did not send him" in v 31 (proto-*G*). There were two further steps in the tradition of *G*: (i) the clause "Thus Yahweh the God of Israel has said" was omitted (haplography of forms of "say" [לֵאמֹר, אמר]?), and (ii) the expression "as follows" (לֵאמֹר) at the end of v 25 was left syntactically unattached, so the word was reinterpreted as an imperative singular "say" (אֱמֹר) (so *G*[B, S]) or other adjustments were made.

This solution, depending upon an existing text tradition, appears to be safer than that of Volz and Rudolph, who assume that "to Shemaiah the Nehelamite" is original but must be understood as an unattached title ("concerning Shemaiah the Nehelamite") and reconstruct the text subjectively.

With the understanding of vv 24–25 offered here, vv 24–32 become as separate from vv 1–23 as chapter 28 is from chapter 27; the present study will accordingly consider them separately (so, for example, Volz and Nicholson). That judgment is reinforced by a form-critical examination of vv 4–23, which suggests the marks of the opening of a letter in v 4 and the closing of that letter in v 23 (see Form).

Structure

For the separation of vv 1–23 from vv 24–32 see Preliminary Observations, and see below on Form; for the placement of these passages within chapters 26—36, see Introduction, sec. 22.

Though vv 1–3 label v 4 as the beginning of a letter that Jrm sent to the exiles in Babylon, and though the present form of text suggests that the latter portions of vv 4–23 are also a part of that letter, some commentators have judged those portions to be secondary additions: thus Rietzschel argues that the original letter is confined

to vv 4–7 and that vv 8–23 embody later additions.[8] Others assume without question that the original letter continues through v 23 (so, for example, Rudolph), though it must be borne in mind that several solutions to the problem of vv 16–20 have presented themselves (for which see Preliminary Observations). The latter judgment is sustained by the analysis given in Form.

The passage offers repeated occurrences of the messenger-formula "Thus Yahweh has said." Though the formula could easily have been added secondarily at one point or another in the text,[9] if the text offered here is sound, then the passage is broken up into sections marked by its occurrences in vv 4, 8, 10, 16, and 21. It seems best to see vv 4–9 embodying the basic theme of the letter: settle down and "live" in Babylon and pray for Babylon (vv 4–7), and do not listen to optimistic prophets who falsely excite your hopes (vv 8–9). Then vv 10–23 offer three sections that expand on that basic theme: your hope must be deferred to seventy years, but your hope is a real hope based upon my plans at that time (vv 10–14); he who "sits" on the throne and those who "live" in Jerusalem must abandon hope (vv 16–19), and as for you, you will live to see your optimistic prophets Ahab and Zedekiah become the vehicles for a curse (vv 20 + 15 + 21–23). There is no reason then to assume that any of the non-bracketed material in vv 8–23 is secondarily added: the self-understanding of the exiles that Jrm is trying to engender is based upon the divine assessment of their falsely optimistic prophets, on the nature of true hope, and on the status of those who were still in Jerusalem; just as in chapter 24 Jrm sets forth an understanding both of those in Jerusalem and of those in exile (see there). For further remarks on the authenticity of this material see Setting.

Form

As v 1 itself states, vv 4–23 embody a letter.[10] Verses 1 and 3 are therefore a superscription (*Überschrift*) offered

---

8   Rietzschel, *Urrolle*, 116–18.
9   On this matter see Janzen, pp. 82–86.
10 For the form of OT letters see Eissfeldt, *Introduction*, 22–24, with bibliography; Oscar J. F. Seitz, "Letter," *IDB* 3:113–15, and Nils A. Dahl, "Letter," *IDBSup* 538–41, each with bibliography; Dennis Pardee, "Epistolography"; and idem, *Letters*.

by an editor (Baruch?) who preserved a copy of the letter.

Letters of the period begin with an address (*Anrede*) followed by a greeting (*Grüssformel*). The address is typically "To X": compare Lachish Letter 2, אל אדני יאוש "To my lord Yaosh",[11] and Aramaic letters are comparable (Ezra 4:17; 5:7). The address is evidently found in the last part of v 4 (so the punctuation here, and so *NEB*), though the fact that the letter is at the same time a prophetic oracle means that the messenger formula of v 4a can carry v 4b along with it (so the punctuation of most translations). That the epistolary convention of an address is to be found here is substantiated to some degree by two data: (1) the occurrences of שָׁלוֹם in v 7 (here "welfare") seems to be a deferred greeting substitute (see below), and (2) v 23b may be interpreted as a signature (or counter-signature) (see again below).

The greeting (*Grüssformel*) in letters of the period normally make use of (the Hebrew) שָׁלוֹם or (the Aramaic) שְׁלָם; Lachish Letter 2, cited above, continues, אשמע יהוה את אדני שמעת שלם "May Yahweh cause my lord to hear tidings of peace,"[12] and again Aramaic letters are comparable (once again Ezra 4:17; 5:7).[13] As already indicated, the greeting is missing in vv 4 and 5 and a greeting substitute appears in v 7 (see below).

The imperatives in vv 5–6 are expansions of the command in the P tradition of Genesis, "increase" (רְבוּ, v 6, compare Gen 1:22, 28; 9:1, 7), and as such they are an affirmation of Yahweh's promise;[14] but because the context, which challenges the assumption that Yahweh's blessing on them is focused on their presence in the land of Canaan (see Interpretation), these imperatives resemble parenetic appeal (compare the diction and form of 7:3–7). Thus understood, "Build houses and live in them . . ." implies not only "Yahweh will bless you (in your strange surroundings)" but also "accept your strange surroundings (and thus allow Yahweh to bless you there)." These two emphases become explicit in v 7, which deals with שָׁלוֹם (here "welfare"), since שָׁלוֹם is very

much a manifestation of Yahweh's blessing (see Interpretation on 4:10). Verse 7 relieves the tension caused by the absence of a greeting in vv 4 or 5. The greeting one would have expected would be שָׁלוֹם לָכֶם ("peace to you," Gen 43:23) or its equivalent; instead one has בִּשְׁלוֹמָהּ יִהְיֶה לָכֶם שָׁלוֹם, literally "in its [Babylon's] peace shall there be peace to you"—if you obey my word and do that highly unexpected thing, that is, to pray for Babylon. One notes also that שָׁלוֹם appears again in v 11, "plans of welfare," like "tidings of peace" in Lachish Letter 2 already cited.

Verses 8–9 embody a prohibition couched in parenetic appeal (compare 23:16; 27:9–10, 16); the exiles are instructed not to trust their prophets.

Verses 10–14 are a proclamation of salvation (*Heilsankündigung*). This form differs from the more common oracle of salvation (*Heilsorakel*) in that there is no reassurance for the present (such as "fear not") but rather a statement oriented toward the future.[15] But the verb "complete" in v 10, especially when preceded by an expression implying "only when" (see Interpretation), suggests that ultimate good news is held distant from the hearers, and that the present news is bad (so already Calvin). Isaiah seems to have offered utterances that could be taken as either good news or bad news (Isa 7:17; the name Shear-jashub? Isa 7:3); here, however, Jrm seems to have schematically woven together an expression that presents bad news followed by good news after the lapse of a stated interval of time. The mood of caution which the beginning of v 10 implies appears to be appropriate to the world of wisdom; one thinks of Jesus' parables of the rash builder and the rash king (Luke 14:28–33). Verses 12–14 embody within the proclamation of salvation an assurance of divine answer (compare Isa 30:19; 58:9; 65:24). Verses 16–19 cite a prophetic oracle of judgment: vv 17–18 make up the announcement of judgment proper, while v 19 is the accusation, giving the reason for the judgment ("inasmuch as," תַּחַת אֲשֶׁר, compare 2 Kgs 22:17).

---

11 See further Pardee, "Epistolography," 332–33, and idem, *Letters*, 145–48.

12 See futher Pardee, "Epistolography," 332–33, and *Letters*, 148–49.

13 See the great variety of such expressions in *DISO*, 304, under definition 1.

14 Compare GKC, sec. 110c, which notes that an

imperative may express a distinct assurance or promise.

15 Claus Westermann, *Isaiah 40—66* (Philadelphia: Westminster, 1966) 79, on Isa 41:17–20; compare March, "Prophecy," 163–64.

Verse 20 is what Hans Walter Wolff has termed a "summons to receive instruction" (*Lehreröffnungsformel*),[16] also called a "call to attention" (*Aufmerksamkeitsruf*).[17] Verse 15, which in the reconstruction offered here intervenes between vv 20 and 21, introduces an oracle of judgment. The oracle of judgment is ostensibly one against the prophets Ahab and Zedekiah, but the implication of v 15 is that what follows is essentially an oracle against the exiles for trusting in these prophets; v 15 is thus the accusation against the exiles ("because," כִּי). Verses 21–23 embody that judgment oracle proper against Ahab and Zedekiah; vv 21–22 state the judgment against those prophets and v 23 offers a reason for the judgment (just as v 19 closed vv 16–18 with a reason for the judgment): v 23 begins with "because," יַעַן אֲשֶׁר. Verse 15 expresses its accusation against the exiles by quoting their triumphant word regarding the prophets; that word appears to be a glad affirmation, perhaps an acclamation (compare Interpretation)—the form of vv 20 + 15 is very close to that of Isa 28:14–15, and there, too, the quoted word appears to be a word of triumph; it has been characterized as a parody of a communiqué from Judah's state department.[18] (Accusations by quotation or pseudo-quotation are frequent in Jer: see for example 2:20, 23, 25, 27; 3:4; 14:13.) One aspect of the judgment on Ahab and Zedekiah is the curse that will employ their names (vv 22b); this curse is in jussive form ("May Yahweh make you like . . . ," יְשִׂמְךָ יהוה כְּ), but exactly the same form occurs for a blessing (Gen 48:20, "May God make you like Ephraim and Manasseh," יְשִׂמְךָ אֱלֹהִים כְּ). Curses frequently arise out of the people's disobedience of covenant law (see 11:1–17, Form), but the curse cited here appears to reflect a setting in the private sphere.[19]

Verse 23b, "I am witness [עֵד]," functions in two ways. First, since this document is a "letter" (v 1), "witness" denotes a counter-signatory for the letter; this is the form in the Muraba'at letters, for example papMur 42,[20] where witnesses other than the sender are recorded as

שָׁאוּל בֶּן אֶלְעָזָר עֵד "Saul son of Elazar, witness," and יהוסף בֶּן יהוסף עֵד "Yehosef son of Yehosef, witness",[21] and compare (for an item contemporaneous with Jrm) the use of "witnesses" (עֵדִים) in the drawing up of the deed of sale (סֵפֶר) in 32:12. The letter in the present passage is a letter from Jrm to the exiles (v 1), but it also sets itself forth as a message from Yahweh (see above on v 4), so this phrase is the equivalent of "countersigned, Yahweh." Second and more obviously, the phrase functions as a reminder that Yahweh is a witness to covenants (Gen 31:50) and oaths (Jer 42:5; 1 Sam 12:5); here the divine self-assertion is affirmation that this word to the exiles through his prophet is genuine. The double function of v 23b thus corresponds to the double nature of the letter as both from Jrm and from Yahweh (v 4 once more).

Setting

There is no reason to doubt the assertion that these verses contain a letter from Jrm to the exiles in Babylon; neither Elasar nor Gemariah, who are named as carriers of the letter, is known elsewhere, but their patronymics suggest well-known Jerusalem families (see Interpretation on v 3). There is no reason either to confine the authentic words of the letter to vv 4–7 (see Structure): v 23b is an expression suggesting the signatory of a letter (see Form), vv 20 + 15 + 21–23 mention the specific prophets Ahab and Zedekiah and their specific fate in Babylon, including a word-play on the name of Ahab's father (see Interpretation on v 21), and vv 16–19 offer some quite distinctive language (on which see Preliminary Observations). Verses 10–14 appear open to the suspicion of Deuteronomistic provenience: thus the expression "seventy years" (v 10) here serves a positive purpose, not a negative one as the expression does in 25:11. But the expression here is couched with caution ("only when Babylon's seventy years are completed," compare Form), and it is clear that Jrm saw a positive role for the exiles to play (the "good figs" of 24:5–7: see Setting on that chapter). If the "seventy years" in 25:11 is

16 Hans Walter Wolff, *Hosea* (Hermeneia; Philadelphia: Fortress, 1974) 96.
17 Wolff, *Joel and Amos*, 231.
18 Edwin M. Good, *Irony in the Old Testament* (London: SPCK, 1965) 120, 147.
19 Compare the observations on this phenomenon in Scharbert, "ארר," 417.
20 Roland de Vaux, "Quelques textes hébreux de Muraba'at," *RB* 60 (1953) 268–75; Pardee, *Letters*, 122–28.
21 On the form see Pardee, "Epistolography," 341, and idem, *Letters*, 152; on the formula in the present verse see Pardee, *Letters*, 177.

part of the conclusion to the second scroll (thus to be dated early in 600?—see Setting there) and if the letter set forth in the present passage is to be dated to 594 (see below), then it is possible to see the shift from a negative to a positive value for the "seventy years" to be catalyzed by the fall of Jerusalem in 597. One notes further that the word "welfare" (שָׁלוֹם) appears in v 11 as it does in v 7. Much of the judgment for an exilic setting for vv 10–14 is based on the secondary additions to the text, which are indeed exilic or postexilic; but the basic text one may accept as part of the original letter.

The letter is not dated, but its presence after chapters 27 and 28, and the similar setting it presumes (optimistic prophets in Babylon), suggests the excitement aroused by the attempted revolt against Nebuchadnezzar in December 595/January 594, a revolt which did not succeed (see Setting on chapter 27); the royal delegation to Babylon that carried the letter (v 3) may well have been sent to reassure Nebuchadnezzar of Zedekiah's loyalty (see Interpretation). The date 594 is thus doubtless correct.

Interpretation

■ **1** The word סֵפֶר is a general word for any kind of document; it is used in 3:8 for a "bill (of divorce)" and in 25:13 for the (second) scroll of Jrm. Here (and in vv 25 and 29) it refers to a "letter."

The meaning of יֶתֶר (here translated "preeminent") is puzzling. The word ordinarily means "remnant (of), rest (of)" with reference to things (27:19) or people (39:9; 52:15), but its usage in these passages for people is restricted to common people, not leaders; one would expect שְׁאֵרִית with reference to leaders (compare 39:3). If "the rest of" is the meaning here, then one must conclude that some of the elders were no longer present: were they in prison, or executed, for siding with those revolting against Nebuchadnezzar (compare Rudolph, Bright, Thompson)? But it has a strikingly different meaning in its double occurrence in Gen 49:3, "pre-

eminence (of)," and Bernard N. Wambacq has suggested that that may be the meaning here.[22] Perhaps Jrm ironically intended a little of both: the "rest" of the vessels are in Jerusalem, the "rest" of the elders are in Babylon, doubtless "preeminent" in their way. All is scattered.

The letter is a general one to the leaders and the followers among the exiles.

■ **2** This verse offers two items more than 24:1 does, "the queen-mother" (הַגְּבִירָה) and "the eunuchs" (הַסָּרִיסִים). For the former see 13:18. Since "eunuchs" could hold high office, it is often uncertain whether the term is used in the physical sense or whether it is simply one more term for "officers."[23] For "craftsmen" see 10:3; for the uncertain word translated "smiths" see 24:1.

■ **3** The Elasar cited here is mentioned only once in the OT. There is no way to be sure that his father was the same Shaphan who was an officer under Josiah when the book of the law was found (2 Kgs 22:3–13), nor can one be sure that the Ahikam who protected Jrm after the trial subsequent to the temple sermon (26:24) was his brother, nor that the Gemariah who figured in the incident of the reading of Jrm's scroll (36:10, 12, 25) was another brother, but it is virtually certain that all these were members of a single family.[24]

One is less certain with regard to Gemariah son of Hilkiah, who is likewise unmentioned elsewhere. The "Hilkiah" in question is hardly Jrm's father (1:1), for the notation would otherwise have been phrased differently. It is conceivable that this Hilkiah was the chief priest under Josiah (2 Kgs 22:4—23:4)—at least Shaphan and Hilkiah are closely associated in that narrative (2 Kgs 24:12, 14), so that it is altogether likely.[25]

There is no way to discern the purpose of the royal delegation. The question is connected with that of the relation between this delegation and the one mentioned in 51:59. There were evidently two royal delegations from Jerusalem to Babylon that year! Was it simply carrying annual tribute? Was it making peace with

22 Bernard N. Wambacq, *Jeremias, Klaagliederen, Baruch, Brief van Jeremias* (De Boeken van het Oude Testament 10; Roermond and Maaseik: Romen, 1957) 187.

23 See de Vaux, *Ancient Israel, Its Life and Institutions* (New York: McGraw-Hill, 1961) 121.

24 On the matter see James M. Ward, "Shaphan," *IDB* 4:307–08.

25 James M. Ward, "Gemariah," *IDB* 2:362, thinks the identification unlikely; some commentators think it more probable—it is standard speculation.

Nebuchadnezzar after the Jerusalem conference mentioned in 27:3? These are possibilities mentioned by commentators (compare Rudolph, Bright, Thompson). One can be sure that relations between Zedekiah and Nebuchadnezzar were delicate after the conference had discussed revolt (so again Thompson).

For the problem posed by the negative judgment on Zedekiah (vv 16–20) contained in a letter sent by a royal delegation see Preliminary Observations.

■ **5–7** Here is a fresh application of the call to Jrm to "build" and to "plant" (1:10). Jrm's message to the exiles is not simply that they will not come home soon (compare 28:6–14). Inevitably those who were exiled from their homeland would find themselves counting the days till they return, marking the time meanwhile. No, their stay in Babylon must not simply be negative, it must be positive; their home for the indefinite future must be in Babylon, and it is there that they must build their lives. It has recently been suggested[26] that Jrm is here citing Deut 20:5–10: the initiating of activities that exempt one from military service. Thus Jrm is here subtly counseling against revolt. Indeed the exiles are not simply to abstain from revolt, certainly not to live lives nurtured by private satisfactions, walled off from the society around them; they are positively to pray for the welfare (שָׁלוֹם), the prosperity of Babylon, for only as Babylon thrives will they thrive. Note that "live" (ישׁב) in v 5 will be picked up by "sits" and "live" (both ישׁב) in v 26.

"Have sons and daughters" in v 6 is literally "beget sons and daughters"; the verb is the causative of "bear" which follows it. The words "increase, do not decrease" are covenantal words, found both in Deut 26:5 and in P (thus "be fruitful and increase," Gen 1:22; see Form). These words are to be heard here in conjunction with 20:1–6, the incident with Pashhur, where Jrm indicates that the promise of fruitfulness to Abraham and Jacob is to be annulled, and with 10:24, in which the people fatuously express the fear that their population will shrink rather than expand. The command to increase is now valid again, but away from the land promised to Abraham and Jacob!

For the irony of the deferred greeting implied by the use of "welfare" (שָׁלוֹם), see Form.

"Pray for it to Yahweh" implies the obligation to see to some kind of community liturgy while in exile. Jrm had been told not to pray for the people (7:16; 11:14; 14:11). Now the people are told to pray for Babylon, thereby gaining welfare for themselves. (See further vv 12–14 below.)

■ **8–9** For "deceive" (נשׁה hipʻil) see 4:10. For "diviners" and "dream-interpreters" see 27:9. The three categories of soothsayers here are identical with the first three in the list of foreign soothsayers in 27:9; is the likeness of the first three in the list a hint that the Jewish exiles are in danger of becoming paganized?—compare the suggested context of 10:1–16.

Given the vocalization "your dreams" in *M* (rather than the vocalization adopted here, "your dream-interpreters"), the tendency through the centuries has been to assume that the participle which follows, though intended as a causative (see Text), is to be translated as a non-causative, that is, "which you dream" (so already *G*, *V*, *S*). Commentators have tended to emend the phrase either to "the dreams which they dream" or to "their dreams which they dream" (Duhm with hesitation, Cornill, Condamin, Rudolph, Bright; *RSV*, *JB*, *NJV*). But the correction becomes unnecessary with the vocalization "your dream-interpreters" (compare *NEB*).

For v 9 compare 27:15.

■ **10** The expression לְפִי with the infinitive here implies "only when" (so Rudolph, Bright; *JB*: see Form); the only other instance of the expression, Num 9:17, usually translated "whenever," may carry the same nuance. For "seventy years" see 25:11. For "deal with" (פקד) in a positive meaning ("reward") see 15:15.

■ **11** The "welfare" of the exiles is tied to the "welfare" of Babylon during the exile (v 7), but at the end of the exile the "welfare" of the people will be based on a new set of "plans" that will give the people a (hopeful) "future." "Future" (אַחֲרִית) has had a negative connotation in Jrm's utterances (5:31; 23:20); now it will be positive.

■ **12–14** There is a close link between the wording in v 7 and here: v 7 and v 12 are the only two passages in Jer in which the people are the subject of "pray," and in both passages the context is positive, in contrast to 7:16; 11:14; 14:11, in which Jrm is prohibited from praying

---

26   Adele Berlin, "Jeremiah 29:5–7: A Deuteronomic
      Allusion," *Hebrew Annual Review* 8 (1984) 3–4.

for the people. In this chapter, by contrast, the exiles are told to pray to Yahweh for Babylon (v 7), and then at the end of the exile they shall pray to Yahweh for their own sakes.

I propose that the phrase "and I will restore your fortunes" in v 14 is original to the passage and has dropped out of the text antecedent to G by haplography (see Text). Though the expression was a favorite of the exilic period, it occurs in Hos 6:11, and there is no reason why Jrm cannot have used it here (compare its use in 30:3, 18). Some kind of phrase denoting an action of Yahweh seems necessary after "I will appear to you" to close the sequence. The phrase itself (שוב qal or hip'il + שְׁבוּת or שְׁבִית) offers difficulties both in etymology and in denotation. It appears twenty-seven times in the OT, eleven of these in Jer; the most satisfactory treatment remains that of Ernst Dietrich,[27] who proposed that the expression is a cognate accusative, "render a restoration," and that the vocalization of the noun in its occurrences, and the semantic range of the phrase, has undergone some development.[28] The occurrence of the corresponding Aramaic phrase השב שיבת in Sefire 3.24 indicates that the phrase means "render a restoration" (of property taken by someone else).[29]

■ 15 See after v 20.

■ 16–19 Remarks have already been made at several points in regard to these problematic verses: for the matter of the authenticity of the core of the verses, their placement, and questions of literary history see Preliminary Observations, and see further Structure, Form.

Verses 17 and 18 give a strong impression of being variants of each other. Thus rhetorically it is odd to have the double occurrence of "sword, famine and pestilence" in the two verses (compare the single occurrence in chapter 24—it is in v 10 there), and the double occurrence of "and I shall make them" (וְנָתַתִּים or וְנָתַתִּי אוֹתָם) in the two verses is equally suspicious. But neither verse strikes one as more "original" than the other. The הִנְנִי מְשַׁלֵּחַ is the normal form for the beginning of such an oracle (compare 28:16; the only other occurrence in Jer of the expression with this verb is 8:17). But, as already noted, the parallel in v 18, with וְרָדַפְתִּי, is the only passage in Jer in which Yahweh serves as the subject of "pursue." Again, in the last half of v 17, the imagery of the figs (v 17) is found in 24:3 and 8, and the expression "I shall make them a terror to all the kingdoms of the earth, a curse and a desolation, a hissing and a reproach" is found in 24:9, with a different selection of the last four nouns: indeed this particular selection of four nouns is found in no parallel passage in which this "listing" diction appears.[30] In sum, neither v 17 nor v 18 can be judged to be an expansion from some other passage, and neither gives the impression of having been devised secondarily; but together the two verses give the impression of parallel tradition, each with a claim to authenticity. The solution of the puzzle lies beyond one's grasp. As for vv 16 and 19, the core of these verses appears again to be authentic (see Preliminary Observations).

■ 16 The expression "king who sits on the throne of David" has occurred once before for a given king, for Jehoiakim in 22:2 (see Setting on that passage). The contrast in phraseology between that passage and the present one is striking. There the address is to Jehoiakim and his fellow courtiers in the palace; here it is to Zedekiah and to his fellow citizens in the city who are called "your brothers," that is, the brothers of those in Babylon (compare the use of the same expression in a different reference in 7:15; on this see Preliminary Observations), the impression being that everyone in Jerusalem from king to laborer is at the mercy of Nebuchadnezzar—none of them has remained in Jerusalem through any merit, they are "brothers."

■ 17 For the first clause see 24:10, and for the second see 24:3, 8. The word here translated "putrid" (שֹׁעָר) appears only here in the OT. It is obviously a synonym for "bad" (24:3, 8), but its derivation and meaning are uncertain: it might mean "horrible," related to שַׁעֲרוּרָה ("horrible thing," 5:30—so Rashi, and so BDB), or it might mean

27 Ernst L. Dietrich, שוב שבות, *Die endzeitliche Wiederherstellung bei den Propheten* (BZAW 40; Giessen: Töpelmann, 1925) 36–37; and see recently John M. Bracke, "Šûb Šebût: A Reappraisal," *ZAW* 97 (1985) 233–44, with bibliography.

28 See also Holladay, *Šûbh*, 110–14.

29 See Joseph A. Fitzmyer, "The Aramaic Suzerainty Treaty from Sefire in the Museum of Beirut," *CBQ*

20 (1958) 463–64; Ernst Vogt, "Nova Inscriptio Aramaica Saec. 8 A.C.," *Bib* 39 (1958) 274; Jonas C. Greenfield, "Aramaic Studies and the Bible," *Congress Volume, Vienna 1980* (ed. John A. Emerton; VTSup 32; Leiden: Brill, 1981) 112.

30 See the chart in Weippert, *Prosareden*, 188.

"split," related to שַׁעַר ("gate," a split in a wall—so KB: since figs that are split turn bad).

■ **18** For "pursue" compare Preliminary Observations. For "terror to all the kingdoms of the earth" see 15:4; for the unique selection of the four succeeding terms, "curse, desolation, hissing and reproach" see again Preliminary Observations. "Curse" (אָלָה) has appeared in the text of M in the book (23:10) with the implication of "drought," and is reconstructed in 2:34; 4:12; 5:25; 14:22; 18:13. For "desolation" and "hissing" see 18:16 and 19:8; for "reproach" see 6:10.

■ **19** For the diction see 7:25–26.

■ **20** For Yahweh's "sending" the exiles to Babylon see 24:5.

■ **15** "Yahweh raised up" (קוּם hip'il): the only other occurrence of this verb with "prophet(s)" is Deut 18:15, 18; it is used with "scion," the king to come, in 23:5, as it is used of "judges" or "a savior" in Judg 2:16; 3:9, 15. One has the impression here then that Jrm is quoting the exiles' glad affirmation of the legitimacy of their prophets, perhaps even voicing an acclamation. Is there a hint here that the exiles were implying, "Even in Babylon Yahweh raises up prophets"? Since "in Babylon" is more properly בְּבָבֶל (v 22), and since the expression here, בָּבֶלָה, more properly means "to Babylon," is the implication here that Yahweh's power reaches all the way to Babylon (so Naegelsbach)?

■ **21–23** The prophets Ahab and Zedekiah are otherwise unmentioned in the OT. "Give into the hand of the king of Babylon" became a conventional phrase in the book, figuring often in editorial expansions (such as 20:4 and 21:7). But it was clearly used by Jrm himself: he predicted in 598/597 that Yahweh would give Jehoiachin into the hand of the Chaldeans (22:25), and indeed that Yahweh had given the whole earth into the hand of Nebuchadnezzar (27:6). It is ironic that Jrm should predict that Yahweh would give two prophets into the hand of the king of Babylon when they were exiles in Babylon already, but "strike them down before your eyes" indicates that "give into the hand" means here more than "put under political control"; it means "place under arrest."

The two prophets had not yet been arrested and

executed when Jrm wrote, so that John Arthur Thompson's statement that "Nebuchadnezzar had them executed by roasting in the fire" is too simple a reading of the passage. The curse (קְלָלָה) is that Nebuchadnezzar shall have roasted them (קְלָם) in the fire: the wording appears to be based on a play on the name of Ahab's father Kolaiah (קוֹלָיָה) and on the fact that the Code of Hammurabi prescribes execution by burning for certain offenses[31]—Dan 3:6 preserves the memory of such executions. The verb "roast" (קלה) appears as a finite verb only here in the OT, but the passive participle is used for "parched" grain.

There is no way to determine why Nebuchadnezzar could be expected to execute the two prophets; the offenses named in v 23 are within the Israelite community ("in Israel"). If they proclaim the hopeful word proclaimed by Hananiah (28:2–4, compare 27:16), then Nebuchadnezzar could well perceive them to be part of those supporting the uprising against him (see Setting); the Babylonian Chronicle preserves his statement that he executed those within his army who led the revolt (see 27:1–22, Setting).

"Curse" (קְלָלָה) has been used in Jer for "object of cursing" (24:9); here, of course, it is "formula of cursing." If one may assume the correctness of the placement of v 15 in the present sequence, one may conclude that Jrm intends a stark contrast: those who acclaim Ahab and Zedekiah as prophets will soon be using their names for cursing; Yahweh's action in them is to give them into the hand of Nebuchadnezzar for execution, not to raise them up as prophets (v 15).

The preposition לְ occasionally, as here, introduces the agent of a passive verb ("by," v 22).[32]

The expression "commit an outrage [נְבָלָה] in Israel" is evidently a technical legal term (Deut 22:21), and it has stimulated several studies in recent years.[33] Anthony Phillips states that the expression is reserved for extreme acts of disorder or unruliness that themselves result in a dangerous breakdown in order and the end of an

---

31   Laws 25, 110, 157; see conveniently *ANET*, 167, 170, 172.

32   König, *Syntax*, sec. 103.

33   See Martin Noth, *Das System der zwölf Stämme Israels* (BWANT 4/1; Stuttgart: Kohlhammer, 1930) 104–6; Wolfgang M. W. Roth, "Nbl," *VT* 10 (1960) 404–

existing relationship;[34] it sometimes refers to sexual atrocities—the rape of Dinah (Gen 34:7), the Benjaminites' rape of the Levite's concubine at Gibeah (Judg 19:23–24; 20:6, 10), and Amnon's rape of Tamar (2 Sam 13:12)—but is also applied to such nonsexual offenses as Achan's breach of the ban on Jericho (Josh 7:15). The expression then refers to acts perceived as utterly opposed to the solidarity of a covenant community, so that "committed folly" (*RSV*), though true to the etymology of the noun in question, is an inadequate translation; compare "perpetrate infamies" (*JB*), "their conduct was an outrage" (*NEB*), "did vile things" (*NJV*).

What in the conduct of the two prophets calls forth such a judgment? Is one to understand that the two following clauses in v 23 specify the outrage they committed—that is, that one is to translate "in committing adultery . . . and in speaking . . ."? This is the most natural flow of thought (so already Calvin; so Cornill and Bright; so Phillips;[35] so *JB, NEB, NAB, NJV*). But questions remain. Were Ahab and Zedekiah literally guilty of committing adultery, or is this hyperbolic language?—Paul D. Hanson suggests that Trito-Isaiah indulges in such hyperbole in Isa 57:5–8 and 65:3–4a.[36] One could well imagine that the news of the words of optimistic prophets in the exiled community, coming to the ears of Jrm (after the incident with Hananiah?), might have called forth such excesses of language (compare 5:7–8). The basic issue, as always, would be that they "have spoken a word in my name which I did not command them"; that deed, in that context, could well have been the commission of an outrage in Israel.

The nature of the offense of Ahab and Zedekiah is sufficiently puzzling to have given rise to a Talmudic tale,[37] cited by Rashi, regarding the two prophets. "What did they do? They went to Nebuchadnezzar's daughter: Ahab said to her, 'Thus saith God, "Give thyself unto Zedekiah"'; whilst Zedekiah said to her, 'Thus saith God, "Surrender to Ahab."'" She reported them to her father, and when they next approached her, she referred them

to him. The two told Nebuchadnezzar that God had so commanded, but the king told them that he had inquired of Hananiah, Mishael, and Azariah (these being, of course, Shadrach, Meshach, and Abednego!—Dan 1:6–7; 3:16–18), who informed him that it was forbidden. The prophets were ultimately put into the fiery furnace, having chosen Joshua the High Priest as their companion; the prophets were burned (Jer 29:22), while Joshua's garments were merely singed, for the Lord said of Joshua, "Is not this a brand plucked from the fire?" (Zech 3:2). Here is an explanation for the wording of vv 21, 22, and 23!

For "I am witness," a statement implying that Yahweh is a signatory (or counter-signatory) to the letter, see Form.

Aim

Jrm here displays unlimited confidence in the power of the word of Yahweh to work through him across space and time. Divine words are entrusted to a royal delegation, to be brought to fellow countrymen in Babylon, and those words are expected to do their work (see also in 51:59–64). And the divine words will not do their work in general, but specifically, through judgment on the prophets Ahab and Zedekiah. And the words are words of judgment on the exiles for now, but words of salvation after a lapse of seventy years. Here is an illustration of Isa 55:10–11, in which Yahweh's word is compared to the effectiveness of rain and snow, which bring forth seed and bread: the word "shall not return to me empty, but it shall accomplish that which I purpose, and prosper in the thing for which I sent [שלח] it"—compare "sent" (שלח) in v 1 of the present passage. A letter to the exiles is a fresh way for Jrm to exercise his vocation "over nations and over kingdoms, to pluck up and break down, to build and to plant" (1:10), just as was his sending of yoke-collars through the ambassadors to the foreign kings (27:3).

7; Hans Jochen Boecker, *Redeformen des Rechtslebens im Alten Testament* WMANT 14; Neukirchen: Neukirchener, 1964) 18–19, 141–42; Anthony Phillips, "Nebalah," *VT* 25 (1975) 237–42.

34   Phillips, "Nebalah," 238.
35   Ibid., 239.
36   Hanson, *Dawn of Apocalyptic,* 147.
37   *b. Sanh.* 93a.

**Shemaiah Opposes
the Message of Jeremiah**

Bibliography

Dijkstra, Meindert
  "Prophecy by Letter (Jeremiah xxix 24–32)," *VT*
  33 (1983) 319–22.
Pardee, Dennis
  Letters, 177–78.
Yaure, L.
  "Elymas—Nehelamite—Pethor," *JBL* 79 (1960)
  297–314.

29

24 《Shemaiah the Nehelamite said:》[a] 25/ [a] Thus
Yahweh of hosts, the God of Israel, has
said:[a] 《 . . . .》[b] 《And he sent in his (own)
name》[c] [d]a letter[d] [to all the people who are
in Jerusalem and][e] to Zephaniah son of
Maaseiah the priest [and to all the priests,][e]
as follows: 26/ Yahweh himself made you
priest instead of Jehoiada the priest, to be
《overseer》[a] of the house of Yahweh for any
madman who plays the prophet, by putting
him into the stocks and collar. 27/ So now,
why have you not reprimanded Jeremiah
the Anathothite,[a] who is playing the
prophet among you?— 28/ inasmuch as he
has sent (a message) to us in Babylon, as
follows: It will be (a) long (time)!—build
houses and live (in them), plant gardens and
eat their fruit.

29 And Zephaniah [the priest][a] read the [*M:*
this][b] letter in the hearing of Jeremiah [the
prophet].[a] 30/ And the word of Yahweh
came to Jeremiah as follows: 31/ Send (a
message) to [all][a] the exiles as follows: Thus
Yahweh has said concerning Shemaiah the
Nehelamite: Because Shemaiah has prophesied to you, though I did not send him, and
has led you to trust in a lie, 32/ therefore
thus Yahweh has said, I am going to punish
Shemaiah [the Nehelamite][a] and his
offspring; he shall have no one dwelling [b]《in
your midst》 [*M:* in the midst of this people,][b]
to enjoy seeing the good which I am going to
do [b]《for you》 [*M:* for my people,][b] [oracle of

Text

24a So read with *S*. *M* and *G* read "To Shemaiah the
Nehelamite you [masculine singular] shall say." For a
defense of the reading see 29:1–23, Preliminary
Observations.

25a—a For the omission of the whole clause in *G* see
29:1–23, Preliminary Observations. Note that
Rudolph and Janzen, p. 85, judge *G* to offer the
correct text.

b By the reconstruction proposed here, an optimistic oracle has dropped out, perhaps by haplography if the oracle closed with the word "Israel": see
29:1–23, Preliminary Observations, and see Interpretation.

c So read with *S*. *M* reads "because you yourself
sent in your (own) name" (so also *V, T*), and *G* reads
"I did not send you in my name." See 29:1–23,
Preliminary Observations.

d—d *M* has the plural סְפָרִים; this form denotes a single
"letter" in 2 Kgs 10:1; 19:14. Compare v 29; see
GKC, sec. 124b, n. 2; and see Interpretation.

e Omit the two phrases with *G*: note the second
singular address in v 26.

26a Read the singular פָּקִיד with *G, V, S* (and compare
T) for the *M* plural פְּקִדִים, a reading that may have
arisen, in spite of the second singular reference,
because of implied plurality in v 25 with the
expansions there.

27a The MSS. vocalize this word variously (הָעֲנָתֹתִי [!],
הָעֲנָתֹתִי) in spite of the spelling of the name of the
village itself (עֲנָתוֹת, 1:1 and elsewhere).

29a Omit the bracketed words "the priest" and "the
prophet" with *G* (compare 28:5, 6, 10, 11, 12, 15,
where "the prophet" has been added).

b Omit הַזֶּה with *G* (compare similar expansions in
chapters 27 and 28).

31a Omit with *G* (compare 28:3, 4, 11).

32a Omit with *G*; the gentilic already appears in v 31
(compare 29a above).

b—b Reading בְּתוֹכְכֶם and לָכֶם with *G*; *M* has moved
away from the specificity of *G* (note that *M* has

Yahweh, for he has uttered rebellion against Yahweh.][c]

retained לָכֶם in v 31); so Janzen, p. 74.

c   Omit with *G*; for the closing clause see 28:16, where the same clause has been added.

Structure

For the relation of this passage to vv 1–23, see 29:1–23, Preliminary Observations; and for the relation of both vv 1–23 and vv 24–32 to chapters 27 and 28, see Introduction, sec. 22.

The present passage falls easily into two halves: vv 24–28, Shemaiah's word and action in Babylon; and vv 29–32, the reaction in Jerusalem.

Form

In the text of *M* vv 24–25 indicate that the material is a divine word addressed to Jrm ("To Shemaiah the Nehelamite you [singular] shall say"); this literary form is not congruent with anything else in the context, so that one is led to understand the text in the light of *S* (see Text, and see 29:1–23, Preliminary Observations). By this understanding vv 24–25a are the report of an optimistic prophetic oracle (an oracle unfortunately now missing), and vv 25b–28 are the report of the associated letter that Shemaiah wrote in response to Jrm's letter to the exiles; after the statement of the sending of the letter (v 25b) vv 26–28 give the contents of Shemaiah's letter, closing at the end of v 28 with a summary of Jrm's letter. The center of Shemaiah's letter is his expression of fault-finding (*Tadel*),[1] a form elsewhere called a "formula of disappointment" (*Enttäuschungsformel*)[2]—other examples in the OT are Gen 12:18–19;[3] 20:9; 29:25; Num 23:11. Though the present purpose of vv 24–28 is to defend Jrm in the contest between Jrm and Shemaiah, the passage is remarkable in offering a fairly full account of word and action of a "false" (optimistic) prophet.

Verses 29–32 are an associated prophetic narrative: v 29 narrates the priest's reading of Shemaiah's letter to Jrm, and vv 30–32 record a divine word to Jrm to oppose that letter, a command to send a return letter to the exiles (v 31a*a*), and the contents of that letter (vv 31a*β*–32), an oracle of judgment against Shemaiah consisting of the accusation (v 31b) and the announcement of punishment (v 32). There is no declaration of performance of the command in v 31.

The whole passage has close resemblances to chapter 28, Jrm's confrontation with an optimistic prophet in Jerusalem.

Setting

Shemaiah quotes Jrm's letter (v 28 = v 5, and by implication v 10), so that the events narrated here are just subsequent to those in vv 1–23 (see there), again in the course of 594.

Interpretation

■ **24** From the context one concludes that this Shemaiah is another optimistic prophet in Babylon alongside Ahab and Zedekiah (vv 21–22); he is otherwise unknown. The attempt to explain "the Nehelamite" (הַנֶּחֱלָמִי) as "the dreamer" (חלם), so Qimḥi and recently L. Yaure,[4] founders on the fact that the form here is a gentilic, analogous to "Jeremiah the Anathothite" in v 27.

■ **25** If the text of vv 24–25 is reconstructed here correctly, then Shemaiah's optimistic oracle has dropped out of the text: any reconstruction of it is purely hypothetical. But the one suggested in 29:1–23, Preliminary Observations, namely, "Soon I will restore the fortunes of my people Israel," at least allows for several plausibilities. (1) An oracle ending in "Israel" allows for the subsequent loss of the oracle by haplography with the expression "God of Israel" just preceding. (2) If "I will restore your fortunes" was an original part of Jrm's letter to the exiles in Babylon (v 14: see Interpretation there), then Shemaiah understands himself and Jrm to differ

1   Compare Wanke, *Baruchschrift*, 55: "Why have you not reprimanded Jeremiah?" v 27.

2   Rudolf Pesch, "'Kind, warum hast du so an uns getan?' (Lk 2,48)," *BZ* NF 12 (1968) 247.

3   Claus Westermann, *Genesis* (BKAT 1; Neukirchen: Neukirchener, 1974–82) 2:194.

4   L. Yaure, "Elymas—Nehelamite—Pethor," *JBL* 79 (1960) 307–9.

only on when the deliverance will take place; Jrm has said "only when Babylon's seventy years are completed" (v 10), while Shemaiah must have been convinced the deliverance would take place soon (compare his summary of Jrm's message, "a long time," v 28). The fact that there is no verbal clause with "a long time" in that verse suggests that the clause in the missing oracle in the present verse is identical with the operant clause of Jrm's letter. (3) The shape of the oracle is likely to be similar to that of Hananiah in 28:3, suggesting again an expression for "soon" and a clause of deliverance. (4) If the oracle included "I will restore the fortunes of my people Israel," the tie of chapters 30—31 with chapter 29 would be strengthened: "And I will restore the fortunes of my people Israel" occurs in 30:3 (see Introduction, sec. 22).

Verse 29 uses the singular for "letter," and since the plural which occurs here (סְפָרִים) may mean a single letter (see Text), there need be no inconsistency; but the addition of further recipients in Jerusalem (see again Text) may have encouraged the plural form with a plural meaning.

Zephaniah the son of Maaseiah has already been mentioned in 21:1; at the beginning of the second siege of Jerusalem he will be one of the delegation sent by King Zedekiah to Jrm to ask for his intercession to Yahweh for the people (37:3).

■ **26** Zephaniah's predecessor Jehoiada is otherwise unknown. For "overseer" (פָּקִיד) see the discussion in 20:1; Zephaniah holds the position that Pashhur held on that occasion. The word "madman" (מְשֻׁגָּע) had been applied to other prophets in earlier times (2 Kgs 9:11; Hos 9:7); the related verb in Arabic means "coo" (of pigeons), and so refers to babbling. Though the hitpaʿel of נבא may be used of legitimate prophesying (26:20), here clearly it is used contemptuously of someone making prophetic claims, one who "acts like a prophet."[5] The terms translated "stocks" and "collar" are of uncertain meaning: see the discussion in 20:2.

■ **27** This is the only occurrence of the verb "reprimand" (גער) in the book (this is the translation of *NEB*, for the more usual "rebuke"). It implies more than a casual tongue-lashing: it is often used with Yahweh as subject in the context of his battle with the forces of chaos;[6]

Thompson translates "disciplined."

■ **28** If the text is correct at the beginning of the verse, כִּי עַל־כֵּן must mean something like "inasmuch as" (compare Gen 19:8).[7] Traditions of *G* have the attractive reading "during this month" (διὰ τοῦ μηνὸς τούτου, $G^{V, C}$), but there is no convincing way to propose this as the original text.

Shemaiah summarizes Jrm's letter: "It will be a long time" paraphrases v 10, and the rest is a quotation from v 5. The adjective "long" (אֲרֻכָּה) is used in exactly the same context in 2 Sam 3:1, "The war was long between the house of Saul and the house of David."

■ **29** Zephaniah carried out Shemaiah's commission only to the extent of reading the letter to Jrm; there is no hint of a reprimand, and it is altogether possible that the priest was more sympathetic to Jrm than Shemaiah could have wished (compare 37:3).

■ **31–32** For the phraseology of v 31 see 28:15. For "punish" (פקד) in this context compare 23:2. The reference to the "offspring" of Shemaiah and to "dwelling" (ישׁב) appears to be a nice variation on Jrm's word over Jehoiachin (22:30), none of whose offspring would succeed in "sitting" (ישׁב) on the throne of David.

"Enjoy seeing" is the nuance of רָאָה בְּ.[8] The subject of the verb is "(no) one" (אִישׁ), not "Shemaiah," as *G* correctly understood.

Aim

This narrative is analogous to that of chapter 28; the remarks offered there with regard to Jrm's confrontation with Hananiah are relevant here as well in regard to his contest with Shemaiah. But now a striking thing emerges: Jrm and Shemaiah are both optimistic prophets. Shemaiah, however, evidently said that the people will return from exile soon (see on v 25), while Jrm said it will happen only after "seventy years" (v 28, compare v 10). In that contrast comes the necessity of an oracle of judgment on Shemaiah (v 32). "The Prophet declares that Shemaiah would die childless, and be precluded from enjoying the favour which God had resolved and even promised to bestow on his people" (Calvin).

5   Wilson, "Prophecy and Ecstasy," 336.
6   Wildberger, *Jesaja*, 673.
7   König, *Syntax*, sec. 373e.

8   *HALAT*, 1080b, 7 (a).

The Book of Comfort

Bibliography

On 30:1—31:40:

Böhmer, Siegmund
  Heimkehr und neuer Bund, Studien zu Jeremia 30—31
  (Göttinger Theologische Arbeiten 5; Göttingen:
  Vandenhoeck & Ruprecht, 1976).

Fohrer, Georg
  "Der Israel-Prophet in Jeremia 30—31," *Mélanges
  bibliques et orientaux en l'honneur de M. Henri Cazelles*
  (ed. André Cacquot and Matthias Delcor; AOAT
  212; Neukirchen: Neukirchener, 1981) 135–48.

Lohfink
  "Der junge Jeremia."

Lohfink, Norbert
  "Die Gotteswortverschachtelung in Jer 30—31,"
  *Künder des Wortes, Beiträge zur Theologie der Pro-
  pheten; Josef Schreiner zum 60. Geburtstag* (ed. Lothar
  Ruppert, Peter Weimar, and Erich Zenger;
  Würzburg: Echter, 1982) 105–19.

Ludwig, Theodore M.
  "The Shape of Hope: Jeremiah's Book of Consolation," *CTM* 39 (1968) 526–41.

Schröter, Ulrich
  "Jeremias Botschaft für das Nordreich, zu N.
  Lohfinks Überlegungen zum Grundbestand von
  Jeremia xxx—xxxi," *VT* 35 (1985) 312–29.

On details in 30:1–24:

Berridge
  pp. 187–98.

Brueggemann, Walter
  "The 'Uncared For' Now Cared For (Jer 30:12–
  17): A Methodological Consideration," *JBL* 104
  (1985) 419–28.

Conrad, Edgar W.
  *Fear Not Warrior, A Study of 'al tîrā' Pericopes in the
  Hebrew Scriptures* (Brown Judaic Studies 75; Chico,
  CA: Scholars, 1985) 108–15.

Dahood, Mitchell
  "The Word-Pair *'ākal//kālāh* in Jeremiah xxx 16,"
  VT 27 (1977) 482.

Gerlach, Monica
  "Zur chronologischen Struktur von Jer 30,12–17,
  Reflexion auf die involvierten grammatischen
  Ebenen," *BN* 33 (1986) 34–52.

Jeannotte, Henri
  "תְּעָלָה תֻּעָלָה Jér 30,13; 46,11; (48 = 31,2)," *BZ* 9
  (1911) 142–43.

**On 31:1–40 in general, or on two or more
  sections of chapter 31:**

Fackenheim, Emil L.
  "New Hearts and the Old Covenant: On Some
  Possibilities of a Fraternal Jewish-Christian
  Reading of the Jewish Bible Today," *The Divine*

Helmsman, Studies on God's Control of Human Events, Studies Presented to Lou H. Silberman (ed. James L. Crenshaw and Samuel Sandmel; New York: Ktav, 1980) 191–205.

Hertzberg, Hans W.
"Jeremia und das Nordreich Israel," *TLZ* 77 (1952) columns 595–602.

Schreiner, Josef
"Ein neuer Bund unverbrüchlichen Heils, Aus der Verkündigung des Propheten Jeremias: Jer 31,1–6. 31–37," *BibLeb* 7 (1966) 242–55.

On 31:2–6:

Feuillet, André
"Note sur la traduction de Jér. xxxi 3c," *VT* 12 (1962) 122–24.

On 31:15–22:

Anderson, Bernhard W.
"'The Lord Has Created Something New'—A Stylistic Study of Jer 31:15–22," *CBQ* 40 (1978) 463–78; rep. *A Prophet to the Nations, Essays in Jeremiah Studies* (ed. Leo G. Perdue and Brian W. Kovacs; Winona Lake, IN: Eisenbrauns, 1984) 367–80.

Lindars, Barnabas
"Rachel Weeping for Her Children, Jeremiah 31, 15–22," *JSOT* 12 (1979) 47–62.

Trible, Phyllis
"God, nature of, in the OT," *IDBSup* 368a.

Trible, Phyllis
God and the Rhetoric of Sexuality (Overtures to Biblical Theology; Philadelphia: Fortress, 1978) 40–50.

On 31:15–20:

Bartlett, David L.
"Jeremiah 31:15–20 (Exposition)," *Int* 32 (1978) 73–78.

On 31:15–17:

Burrows, Eric
"Cuneiform and Old Testament: Three Notes. III *Bakītu mušēniktu* (C.T. 16, 10, 26)," *JTS* 28 (1926/27) 185.

On 31:18–20:

Lipiński, Edouard
"'Se battre la cuisse,'" *VT* 20 (1970) 495.

Schildenberger, Johannes
"'Drum schlägt ihm mein Herz, Ich muss mich seiner erbarmen,' Vom Innenleben Gottes im Licht des Alten Testaments," *Geist und Leben* 36 (1963) 163–78.

On 31:21–22:

Holladay, William L.
"Jer. xxxi 22b reconsidered: 'The Woman Encompasses the Man,'" *VT* 16 (1966) 236–39.

Jacob, Edmond
"Féminisme ou Messianisme? A propos de Jérémie 31,22," *Beiträge zur alttestamentlichen Theologie, Festschrift für Walther Zimmerli zum 70. Geburtstag* (ed. Herbert Donner, Robert Hanhart, and Rudolf Smend; Göttingen: Vandenhoeck & Ruprecht, 1977) 179–84.

Nestle, Eberhard
"Miscellen—14. Jeremia 31,22," *ZAW* 25 (1905) 220–21.

Schedl, Claus
"'Femina circumdabit virum' oder 'via salutis'? Textkritische Untersuchungen zu Jer 31,22," *ZKT* 83 (1961) 431–42.

Ziener, Georg
"'Femina circumdabit virum' (Jer 31,22), eine Dittographie?" *BZ* NF 1 (1957) 282–83.

On 31:29–30:

Harvey, Julien
"Collectivisme et individualisme, Ez. 18,1–32 et Jér. 31,29," *Sciences Ecclésiastiques* 10 (1958) 167–202.

May, Herbert G.
"Individual Responsibility and Retribution," *HUCA* 32 (1961) 107–20.

Schoneveld, Jacobus
"Jeremia xxxi 29, 30," *VT* 13 (1963) 339–41.

On 31:31–34 (see also the bibliography on covenant under 11:1–17):

Anderson, Bernhard W.
"The New Covenant and the Old," *The Old Testament and Christian Faith, A Theological Discussion* (ed. Bernhard W. Anderson; New York: Harper, 1963) 225–42, with bibliography.

Bright, John
"An Exercise in Hermeneutics: Jeremiah 31:31–34," *Int* 20 (1966) 188–210.

Buis, Pierre
"La Nouvelle Alliance," *VT* 18 (1968) 1–15.

Coppens, Joseph
"La Nouvelle Alliance en Jér 31,31–34," *CBQ* 25 (1963) 12–21.

Devescovi, Urbano
"Annotazione sulla dottrina di Geremia circa la nuova alleanza," *RivB* 8 (1960) 108–28.

Hillers, Delbert R.
Covenant, The History of a Biblical Idea (Baltimore: Johns Hopkins, 1969) 167–68.

Holladay, William L.
"New covenant, the," *IDBSup*, 623–25.

Lemke, Werner E.
"Jeremiah 31:31–34," *Int* 37 (1983) 183–87.

Lempp, Walter
"Bund und Bundeserneuerung bei Jeremia," *TLZ* 80 (1955) columns 238–39.

Levin, Christoph
Die Verheissung des neuen Bundes in ihrem theologie-

geschichtlichen Zusammenhang ausgelegt (FRLANT
137; Göttingen: Vandenhoeck & Ruprecht, 1985).

Martin-Achard, Robert
  "La nouvelle alliance, selon Jérémie," *RTP* 12
  (1962) 81–92.

Martin-Achard, Robert
  "Quelques remarques sur la nouvelle alliance chez
  Jérémie (Jérémie 31,31–34)," *Questions disputées
  d'Ancien Testament, Méthode et Théologie* (ed.
  Christian Brekelmans; BETL 33; Leuven: Leuven
  University, 1974) 141–64.

Mejía, Jorje
  "La Problématique de l'Ancienne et de la Nouvelle
  Alliance dans Jérémie xxxi 31–34 et quelques
  autres Textes," *Congress Volume, Vienna 1980* (ed.
  John A. Emerton; VTSup 32; Leiden: Brill, 1981)
  263–77.

Potter, H. D.
  "The New Covenant in Jeremiah xxxi 31–34," *VT*
  33 (1983) 347–57.

Renaud, Bernard
  "L'alliance éternelle d'Ez 16,59–63 et l'alliance
  nouvelle de Jér 31,31–34," *Ezekiel and His Book:
  Textual and Literary Criticism and their Interrelation*
  (ed. Johan Lust; BETL 74; Leuven: Leuven
  University, 1986) 335–39.

Swetnam, James
  "Why Was Jeremiah's Covenant New?" *Studies in
  Prophecy* (VTSup 26; Leiden: Brill, 1974) 111–15.

Weinfeld, Moshe
  "Jeremiah and the Spiritual Metamorphosis of
  Israel," *ZAW* 88 (1976) 17–55, esp. 26–35.

Weippert, Helga
  "Das Wort vom neuen Bund in Jeremia xxxi 31–
  34," *VT* 29 (1979) 336–51.

On 31:38–40:
Birch, W. F.
  "The Valley of Hinnom and Zion, Notes on
  Jeremiah xxxi 38–40," *PEFQS* (1882) 58–59.

30

1 The word which came to Jeremiah from
Yahweh: 2/ Thus Yahweh the God of Israel
has said: Write for yourself in a document all
the words which I have spoken to you; 3/ for
the days are surely coming, oracle of
Yahweh, when I shall restore the fortunes of
my people Israel and Judah, says Yahweh;
and I shall bring them back to the land
which I gave to their fathers, and they shall
inherit it.

4 These are the words which Yahweh spoke to
Israel and to Judah:

5 For thus Yahweh has said:
A voice of panic we have heard,
  "Terror!" and "No peace!"

6 Just ask and see
  if a male gives birth!
Why have I seen every hero
  his hands on his loins [like one giving
    birth,]ᵃ
and every face changed,
  into pallor 7/ 《turned?》ᵃ
"How great is that day!"
  "Whence any like it?"
It is a time of distress for Jacob,
  and out of it shall he be saved?
  [8/ And it shall happen on that day, oracle
of Yahweh of hosts, that I shall break his
yoke off your neck, and your cords I shall
tear up, and strangers shall no longer
enslave him. 9/ And they shall serve
Yahweh their God, and David their king,
whom I shall appoint for them.]ᵃ

10 And you, do not fear, my servant Jacob,
          [- - - -]ᵃ
  and do not be dismayed, Israel,
for I am going to save you from afar,

Text

30:6a The expression is lacking in *G*; omit as a gloss (so
  Duhm, Cornill, Volz, Rudolph, Bright), which was
  doubtless influenced by 6:24.

7a Reading *M* הוֹי as the verb הָיָה with *G* (so Volz,
  Rudolph).

8–9a These verses are an expansionist gloss interrupting the continuity of vv 7 + 10; see Preliminary
  Observations.

10–11a After "my servant Jacob" in v 10 *M* reads
  "oracle of Yahweh"; the phrase is missing in 46:27.
  M for v 11a reads, "For I am with you, oracle of
  Yahweh, to save you." The first colon of v 11 is
  restored from 46:28 (so also Volz and Rudolph). In
  any event, the expression "oracle of Yahweh" may
  have been added later.

your offspring from the land of their
captivity;
Jacob shall return and rest,
be relaxed with none to frighten him.

11 《You, do not fear, my servant Jacob—oracle
of Yahweh,》ᵃ
for I am with you [. . .]ᵃ to save you;
for I shall make an end of all the nations
[where I have scattered you,]ᵇ
but of you I will not make an end,
and I will chastise you moderately,
though I will certainly not leave you
unpunished.

- - - -

12 For thus Yahweh has said,
Incurable 《for you is your fracture,》ᵃ
unhealable your wound;

13 《You》ᵃ have no 《softener》ᵃ for a sore,
healing of new skin none for you;

14 all your lovers have forgotten you,
for you they do not care,
for the wound of an enemy I have dealt you,
ᵃthe punishment of someone cruel,ᵃ
[because of the greatness of your guilt,
(because) your sins are so numerous.]ᵇ

15 Why do you cry out over your fracture,
(why is) your pain unhealable?
Because of the greatness of your guilt,
(because) your sins are so numerous,
I have done these things to you.

16 《For you》ᵃ all who eat of you shall be eaten,
and all your foes ⟨are consumed⟩—ᵇ
they shall march into captivity;
those despoiling you shall become spoil,
and all those plundering you I shall give for
plunder.

17 For I shall bring out new flesh for you,
and of your wounds I shall heal you,
oracle of Yahweh,
for they have called you an outcast,
"She is 《our prey,》ᵃ
no one cares for her."

- - - -

18 Thus Yahweh has said:
I am going to restore the fortunes of the
tents of Jacob,
and on his dwellings I will show compassion;
(every) city shall be rebuilt on its ruin,
and citadel inhabited on its rightful site;

19 there shall go forth 《he who brings》ᵃ a
thank-offering
and the sound of merrymakers;
I shall make them many, and they shall not
be few,
I shall make them impressive, and they
shall not be beneath notice.

20 His sons shall be as of old,
and his congregation established before
me,
and I shall punish [all]ᵃ his oppressors.

21 His mighty one shall be from him,
and his ruler shall go forth from his midst,
and I shall bring him near, to approach
me.

b   A gloss from 9:15 (so also Cornill); see further
Interpretation.

12a   Reading לָךְ שִׁבְרֵךְ for M לְשִׁבְרֵךְ (so also Rudolph).
Nötscher suggests that M offers an emphatic lamed
(Friedrich Nötscher, "Zum emphatischen Lamed,"
VT 3 [1953] 380), and Bright cautiously accepts this,
but the appearance of לָךְ in the last colon of v 15
suggests that Rudolph is correct.

13a   The M reading דָּן דִּינֵךְ, literally "anyone to judge
your cause," or even "he judged your cause," makes
no sense in the context. Volz judged it to be the
pious exclamation of a reader; Bright likewise omits
it (so also Janzen, p. 133). I propose that Rudolph is
on the right track: on the analogy of Isa 1:6, he
proposes רֻכְּכִים "softening." But that noun is cited in
postbiblical Hebrew only in the meaning "deli-
cacies"; I would propose a reduplicated noun with
pronominal suffix, רככך, which, with confusion of
dalet for reš and nun for kap, could be antecedent
to the present M text. (For such reduplicated nouns,
see GKC, sec. 84ᵇo; Hans Bauer and Pontus
Leander, *Historische Grammatik der hebräischen
Sprache des Alten Testaments* (Halle: Niemeyer, 1922;
rep. Hildesheim: Olms, 1965), sec. 61dδ.)

14a—a   If the vocalization of מוסר is altered to מוּסַר, the
phrase would mean "cruel punishment" (so Rudolph,
Bright).

b   Delete with G as dittographic from v 15.

16a   For the curious M לָכֵן "therefore" read לָכִי
(compare ketib in 2 Kgs 4:2 and Cant 2:13), an
archaic form of לָךְ, which was then misread as the
present text. See further Interpretation.

b   Vocalizing כָּלֵם (plural participle of כלה) with
Mitchell Dahood, "'ākal//kālāh," for the meaning-
less M כֻּלָּם "all of them." See further Interpretation.

17a   Reading צִידֵנוּ with G for M צִיּוֹן "Zion"; this
reading fits the imagery better (see in detail Interpretation).

19a   Reading מָבָא for the weak M מֵהֶם "from them";
see in detail Interpretation.

20a   Omit with G; see Janzen, pp. 65–67, esp. 66.

For [who then has risked his life to approach me?

oracle of Yahweh.][a]

22 [And you shall be a people to me,
and I shall be God to you.][a]

23 [Look—the gale of Yahweh,
(his) wrath has gone forth,
a gale is whirling,
on the head of the wicked it shall
whirl.

24 The {fierce}[b] anger of Yahweh shall not
return,
until he performs and carries out the
decisions of his heart.
In time to come
you will give it attention.][a]

31

1 [At that time, oracle of Yahweh,][a]
I shall be God to [all][b] the tribes of Israel
and they shall be to me a people.

- - - - -

2aα Thus Yahweh has said,
3a 《Long ago Yahweh appeared 《to him,》[b] 》[a]
2aβγb he found (him) 《encamped》[c] in the
wilderness,
a people remnant ⟨from Horeb,⟩[d]
《bringing》[e] to its rest Israel.
3a [. . .][a]
3b [And][f] (with) an everlasting love I have
loved you,
that is how I have prolonged kindness to
you;
4 again I shall build you so that you may be
built,
maiden Israel;
again you shall adorn your timbrels
and go forth in the dance of merrymakers;
5 again you shall plant vineyards
in the mountains of Samaria,
[a]⟨they are planted⟩ [planters] ⟨and
enjoyed;⟩[a]
6 For there is a day when watchmen have
called
on Mount Ephraim,
"Arise, let us go up to Zion,
to Yahweh our God."
7 For thus Yahweh has said,
Sing joyfully for Jacob,
and shout over the chief of the nations,
proclaim, praise and say,
"Yahweh [a]⟨has saved⟩ 《his people,》[a]
the remnant of Israel."
8 I am going to bring them from the land of the
north,
and gather them from the ends of the
earth,
among them the blind and the lame,
those pregnant and those in labor
together,
a great company they shall return hither.
9 With weeping they shall come,
and 《with consolations》[a] I shall lead
them,
I shall bring them to streams of water,

21a   Omit as a pious gloss (Volz); the interrogative
expression does not fit the general style of the
passage (see further Interpretation). "For" introduces 31:1.

22a   Omit with *G*; the diction of second-person plural
address does not fit the passage. The appropriate
covenantal formula is in 31:1.

23–24a   These two verses repeat 23:19–20 with minor
variations; they fit the context in chapter 23 but not
here (Bright).

b   Omit חָרוֹן with 23:20 as an expansion (Rudolph).

31:1a   Transitional gloss inserted after the original cola
of v 1 were separated from כִּי in 30:21. The phrase
"at that time" introduces secondary material in 3:17
and 8:1; it is (evidently) authentic in 4:11.

b   Omit with *G*; compare 30:20a.

2–3a   Removing v 3a to a position before v 2aβ; see in
detail Interpretation.

b   Reading לוֹ with *G* for *M* לִי "to me" (so Duhm,
Cornill, Condamin, Rudolph); see Interpretation.

c   Reading חֹנֶה for *M* חֵן "grace, favor": see in detail
Interpretation.

d   Reading חֹרֵב, ambiguous for both "from Horeb"
and "from the sword-wielder," for *M* חֶרֶב "(of) the
sword": see in detail Interpretation.

e   Reading הֹלִיךְ (hip'il participle) for הָלוֹךְ (qal
infinitive absolute): see Interpretation.

f   Omit "and" with some MSS. of the Hebrew and
with *G*.

5a—a   Revocalizing the consonantal text presupposed
by *G* to נִטְעוּ וְחִלֵּלוּ. *G* reads φυτεύσατε καὶ αἰνέσατε
"plant and praise" (imperative plural), which
retranslates to נִטְעוּ וְהַלְלוּ (he, not ḥet). *M* reads
נָטְעוּ נֹטְעִים וְחִלֵּלוּ "the planters shall plant and enjoy."
The second word appears to be a gloss inserted
when the passive verb was wrongly vocalized as
active. See in detail Interpretation.

7a—a   Read with *G* and *T* הוֹשַׁע עַמּוֹ for *M* הוֹשַׁע עַמְּךָ
"save [imperative singular] your people" (so all
commentators).

9a   Reading וּבְתַחֲנוּנִים with *G* for *M* וּבְתַחֲנוּנִים "with
supplications" (so Duhm, Cornill, Volz, Rudolph,
Bright). *M* is evidently influenced by 3:21. See
Interpretation.

10   in a straight path in which they shall not
        stumble;
    for to Israel I have been a father,
      and Ephraim is my first-born.

10   [Hear the word of Yahweh, O nations,
      and announce to the coastlands afar {and
        say:}b
    He who scattered Israel will gather him,
      and will keep him as a shepherd his flock.

11   For Yahweh has ransomed Jacob
      and redeemed him from the hand of one
        stronger than he.

12   And they shall come and sing on the height
        of Zion,
      and be radiant over the bounty of Yahweh,
      {over the grain, the wine and the oil,
      the young of flock and herd;}c
    their life shall be like a watered garden,
      and never again shall they languish.

13   Then shall virgins rejoice in the dance,
      young men and elders ⟨be merry,⟩d
    and I shall turn their mourning to gladness,
      {and I shall comfort them}e and give them
        joy for sorrow.

14   I will slake the thirst of the priests with
        fatness,
      and my people shall eat their fill of my
        bounty,
                          oracle of Yahweh.]a

                  - - - -

15   Thus Yahweh has said,
    A voice on the height may be heard,
      lamenting and bitter weeping,
        Rachel bewailing her children,
        she refuses to be consoled:
          《My babes!》a ⟨My children!
          Is there⟩b none left?"

16   Thus Yahweh has said,
    Keep your voice from weeping,
      your eyes from tears,
    for there is reward for your effort,
                 [oracle of Yahweh,]a

    [. . .]b
17   and there is hope for your future,
                 oracle of Yahweh:
    (your) children shall return to their (own)
        border,
      《and they shall return from the land of the
        enemy.》b
                 - - - -

18   ⟨A sound⟩a I have heard,
      Ephraim rocking with grief:
    "You punished me, and I took the punish-
        ment,
      like a calf untrained.
    Bring me back, and let me come back,
      for you are Yahweh my God.

19   For after 《my captivity》a I was sorry 《once
        more,》b
      and after I was brought to know, I slapped
        my thigh.
        I was ashamed, even humiliated,
          for I bore the disgrace of my youth."

10–14a   These five verses are evidently from the Persian period: see Preliminary Observations.

b   Omit as an excessive addition (compare 4:5) (so Rudolph).

c   Delete as a prosaic gloss (so Volz).

d   Revocalize with G, reading יַחְדּוּ (חדה) for M יַחְדָּו "together."

e   Omit with G (Duhm, Cornill); the bracketed verb may be a variant of the verb that follows, so that the text is conflate.

15a   Reading עָלַי for M עַל "for (her children)" (see note b and see Interpretation).

b   Reading בָּנֶיהָ הֲכִי for M בָּנֶיהָ כִּי "her children, for there (is not one)"; see Interpretation.

16–17a   Omit with G (compare the same expression in v 17a).

b   Reinsert the last colon of v 16 after v 17 (see Interpretation).

18a   Revocalizing שָׁמֵעַ (or reading שְׁמֹעָה) for the infinitive absolute שָׁמוֹעַ (see Interpretation).

19a   Reading G שְׁבִיִי for M שׁוּבִי "my turning" (returning? turning away?) (so Rudolph); see Interpretation.

b   Inserting שַׁבְתִּי with Rudolph; one assumes that the verb dropped out by haplography (see Interpretation).

20

Is Ephraim a dear son to me,
  a darling child?
For every time I speak of him,
  in fact remember him again,
    that is when my very heart trembles for
      him,
      when in fact I show compassion on
        him,
           oracle of Yahweh.

- - - -

21

Set up for yourself road-markers,
  put up for yourself signposts;
set your mind on the highway,
  the road ᵃyou went on.ᵃ
Return, maiden Israel,
  return to your cities 《with mastery!》ᵇ

22

How long dilly-dally, turnable daughter?
  For Yahweh has created something new
    on earth,
    a female shall encompass a hero.

- - - -

[23

Thus Yahweh of hosts, the God of Israel,
has said: Again they shall say this word in
the land of Judah and in its cities when I
restore their fortunes:
  "May Yahweh bless you,
    O righteous home,
      O holy hill!"

24

And they shall dwell in it {Judah and all its
  cities}ᵇ together,
  farmhands 《and those who journey》ᶜ with
    flocks.

25

For I will slake the thirst of (every) faint one,
  and the appetite of every weary one I will
    fill.]ᵃ

[26

On this account I awoke and looked: and
my sleep was pleasant to me.]ᵃ

27

The days are surely coming, oracle of
Yahweh, when I shall sow the house of
Israel and the house of Judah with the seed
of man and the seed of beast. 28/ And just
as I have watched over them to uproot and
demolish, [to overthrow, destroy and bring
evil,]ᵃ so I shall watch over them to build
and to plant, oracle of Yahweh.

- - - -

[29

In those days it shall no longer be said,
"The parents have eaten sour grapes,
  but it is the children's teeth that become
    numb."

30

But everyone shall die for his (own) sin; every
person who eats sour grapes, his teeth shall
become numb.]ᵃ

31

The days are surely coming, oracle of
Yahweh, when I shall make with the house
of Israel and the house of Judah a new
covenant, 32/ not like the covenant which I
made with their fathers on the day I took
them by the hand to bring them out of the
land of Egypt: it was they who broke that
covenant of mine, while I was master over
them, oracle of Yahweh; 33/ but this is the
covenant which I shall make with the house
of Israel after those days, oracle of Yahweh:
ᵃthen I shall putᵃ my law within them,
  and on their heart shall write it,

154

21a—a The ketib הלכתי is archaic spelling for the perfect second-person singular feminine (qere' הָלָכְתְּ); compare 2:20, 33; 3:4, 5.

b For the dubious *M* אֵלֶּה "these" read בֹּעֲלָה (feminine participle of בעל): for justification see Interpretation.

23–25a These verses represent an expansion (or two expansions, v 23 and vv 24–25) on v 21, probably originating at the close of the sixth century (see Preliminary Observations).

b These words give evidence of being a gloss to explain "in it," being borrowed from v 23. *G* gives a slightly different text, "dwellers in the cities of Judah and in all her land. . . ." Cornill excises "and all its cities together" as a gloss.

c Reading וְנֹסְעֵי with Volz and Rudolph (compare Bright) for *M* וְנָסְעוּ "and they shall journey." For the use of a construct before a preposition see GKC, sec. 130a.

26a This short gloss again seems to have originated at the close of the sixth century (see Preliminary Observations).

28a Omitting these three verbs as a prosaicizing reinforcement, compare the two additional verbs in the gloss of 1:10. Note that for "uproot and demolish" *G* has "destroy and bring evil."

29–30a This short passage appears to be modeled on Ezekiel 18, an attempt (by priestly circles?) to correct the implication of vv 31–34; it perhaps originated in the fifth century (see Preliminary Observations).

33a—a Reading וְנָתַתִּי with many MSS. for *M* נָתַתִּי "I have put."

34

and I shall be to them God,
 and they shall be to me a people;
and no longer shall they teach one another,
 or each other, saying,
 "Know Yahweh!"
for they shall all know me,
 from the least of them to the greatest,
 oracle of Yahweh,
for I will forgive their iniquity,
 and their sin remember no more.

[35
Thus Yahweh has said—he who gives the sun for light by day, the {statutes of the}[b] moon and stars for light by night, who stirs up the sea so that its waves roar, Yahweh of hosts is his name— 36/ if these statutes should vanish from my presence, oracle of Yahweh, then the offspring of Israel would also cease to be a nation before me for all time.

37
[c]Thus Yahweh has said,[c] If the heavens above could be measured, and the foundations of the earth below be explored, then I would also reject {all}[d] the offspring of Israel because of all they have done, oracle of Yahweh.][a]

38
[b]The days are surely coming,[b] oracle of Yahweh, when the city shall be rebuilt for Yahweh from the Tower of Hananel [c]to the Corner Gate;[c] 39/ and the measuring-line[d] shall go out again opposite it on Gareb Hill and go around to Goah; 40/ [e] {and the whole valley, the corpses and the ashes,} and all the terraces[fe] 《over》[g] the brook Kidron, as far as the corner of the Horse Gate eastwards, shall be holy to Yahweh; it shall not be uprooted or overthrown again for ever.][a]

35–37a   These verses represent a sequence (or two sequences, vv 35–36, and v 37) added probably in the fifth century (see Preliminary Observations).

b   Omit with *G*; the word is intrusive from v 36 and overloads the phrase (Janzen, p. 49).

c—c   It is uncertain whether these words are primary or secondary here. *G* omits them, but then *G* offers v 37 before vv 35–36. The presence or absence of the words would help to determine whether v 37 is to be understood as a separate unit or taken with vv 35–36 (see Form).

d   Omit with *G* (compare 30:20 and 31:1).

38–40a   This sequence was added probably during the fifth century (see Preliminary Observations).

b—b   This expression, literally "behold days are coming," follows the qere', many MSS., and the Versions; the ketib omits בָּאִים ("are coming"), evidently by haplography with the following נְאֻם ("oracle of").

c—c   Conceivably the Hebrew text without a preposition can mean this; but *G* reads "as far as [ἕως] the Corner Gate," a reading that (if not periphrastic) suggests that לְ has dropped out by haplography.

d   The first word of the construct phrase ("line of") offers the ketib קְוֵה, the qere' קָו. The same double reading is found in 1 Kgs 7:23 and (with the absolute state) in Zech 1:16; the meaning is unaffected.

e—e   The text here either is conflate or offers glosses, or both. *G* omits "and the whole valley, the corpses and the ashes"; since the word translated "terraces" is difficult (see note f and Interpretation), one could imagine that the words omitted by *G* represent a conflate text. But these omitted words themselves are either a conflate text or offer a gloss: the words cannot mean "and all the valley of corpses and ashes" (as Condamin has it) because of the article on "valley." The most likely solution is that "and all the corpses and ashes" was originally a gloss (or alternative reading) for "and all the terraces," and that "the valley" is a further gloss. It is unlikely that "the corpses and ashes" is a stopgap for "of the sons of Hinnom" (as Volz has it).

f   The ketib הַשְּׁרֵמוֹת (so also the transliteration of *G*) is a mistake; qere' הַשְּׁדֵמוֹת, see further Interpretation.

g   The Hebrew עַד "as far as" should doubtless be corrected to עַל: the presumed mistake would have been under the influence of the following "as far as."

Preliminary Observations, Structure, Setting

For the role played by these chapters in the growth of the collection in chapters 26—36 see Introduction, sec. 22.

The poetic material in these two chapters marks them off as separate from surrounding material. At the same time, the nature of several prose passages within the chapters suggests what one might expect, namely, that hopeful poetry has had its share of prose expansions from later periods (one notes particularly 30:8–9 and 31:38–40 in this regard).

But the poetry itself is mixed. It is clear, for example,

that 30:12–15 is a self-contained unit, moving from "hurt" and "pain" to "guilt" and "sins," from Yahweh's assessment of the hurt of the people to his statement of what its origin is. Then vv 16–17 build on the diction of vv 12–15 but affirm the opposite, not that the wound is incurable and that Yahweh intends it so, but that he will heal the wound. The easy solution is that of Duhm, that vv 12–15 are genuine and vv 16–17 are an addition by an editor (so also Hyatt). But this is surely arbitrary: Jrm liked expressions with the permutation of verb stems such as one finds in v 16 (compare 17:14; 20:7; 22:22), so that verse is surely authentic, and thus v 17 as well.

The problem is deepened by the fact that some of the poetry shows a resemblance to that of Deutero-Isaiah (compare 30:10–11a with Isa 41:8–10, or 31:8–9a with Isa 43:5–7). One may argue, of course, that the diction of Deutero-Isaiah was influenced by genuine poetic material of Jrm's, but the argument has usually gone the other way (see Cornill and again Duhm).

The solution to which the present study has come with regard to portions of chapters 1, 2, and 3 commends itself here as well, namely that Jrm at the earliest stage of his career—reflecting Josiah's program of political and cultic reunion between the north and the south—directed the core of this material to the north (31:6!), reshaping it for Judah at the end of his career, in the context of the fall of Jerusalem and consequent exile. The repetition of "Ephraim" (31:6, 9, 18, 20) suggests the former stage; the present position of chapters 30—31 within the context of material from 594 (chapters 27—29) and of the buying of the field at Anathoth, doubtless in 588 (see chapter 32), and (again) the analogy of chapters 1—3, suggests the latter stage. But it is a difficult matter to sort the material out: by the solution proposed here, "Jacob" belongs both in the early recension (to the north) and in the late recension (to the south)—note 30:7 and 10—and "Zion" is not only the cultic center of the south but in Jrm's mind the goal of the north as well (31:6 once more, compare 3:14).

Fortunately, textual questions are minimal in these chapters (in contrast to the puzzles presented by chapters 27 and 29, for example).

A full survey of critical discussion of the question is given by Sigmund Böhmer,[1] and a shorter one is given by Lohfink.[2] It is clear that the basic issue of the nature of the chapters involves the relation between setting and structure, so that both questions are dealt with in the present section. When the units (strophes) of the early recension to the north are isolated, does one have a series arranged by Jrm himself? Lohfink deals with the question, and the present study depends heavily on his analysis. For convenience I shall present my conclusions first and then analyze the data.

The Early Recension to the North. This recension consists of seven strophes: (1) 30:5–7; (2) 30:12–15; (3) 30:18–21 + 31:1αβγb; (4) 31:2–6 + 9b; (5) 31:15–17; (6) 31:18–20; and (7) 31:21–22. The arrangement of the sequence suggests that the series has an architectural unity. The first two are negative, dealing with the crisis of the people; the last five are positive, proclaiming hope for restoration. There is a symmetry in second-person or third-person reference to the people, and in masculine and feminine reference (see *Symmetry of the Seven Strophes to the North*). The sequence is bound together by the words "male" and "warrior" in the first and "female" and "warrior" in the last strophe (see below, and in detail in Interpretation).

Justification for the Assignment of Strophes to the Early Recension. One begins obviously with the occurrences of "Ephraim" (31:6, 9b, 18, 20) and "Samaria" (31:5). The reference to "Rachel" (31:15) likewise needs to be included (for the relation of Rachel to the north see Interpretation on 31:15). There is rhetorical unity within 31:15–17 and 31:18–20 but a break between these two (the shift from Rachel to Ephraim).

A variety of considerations suggest that 31:21–22 completes 31:15–17 and 18–20, and several scholars have analyzed the connection;[3] Phyllis Trible points to a

1   Siegmund Böhmer, *Heimkehr und neuer Bund, Studien zu Jeremia 30—31* (Göttinger Theologische Arbeiten 5; Göttingen: Vandenhoeck & Ruprecht, 1976) 11–20.

2   Lohfink, "Der junge Jeremia," 352–53.

3   Trible, *Rhetoric*, 40–50; Bernhard W. Anderson, "'The Lord Has Created Something New'—A

Stylistic Study of Jer 31:15–22," *CBQ* 40 (1978) 463–78.

unity in feminine imagery in the sequence (but see in detail my remarks in Interpretation for 31:20), and Bernhard W. Anderson points to the unity of the sequence in speaker and message. Negatively it must be affirmed that vv 21–22 are hardly a gloss on anything; that if isolated they are hardly self-explanatory; and that they serve admirably as a climax to something larger.[4] It may also be noted that the diction of "return . . . turnable daughter" is closely reminiscent of "turn, turnable children" in 3:14, 22, part of an early recension to the north.

The congruence of "female" and "warrior" in 31:22 with "male" and "warrior" in 30:5–7 turns one's attention to that sequence. Of course 31:21–22 could be associated secondarily with 30:5–7 by a redactor, but the striking sexual imagery of both passages (for which see in detail Interpretation on each) suggests a parity, and the proposal made here that 30:10–11 is Jrm's extension of vv 5–7 for the late recension to Jerusalem, analogous to his extension by 31:8–9a to the northern strophe in 31:2–6 (for which see below), renders plausible the hypothesis that 30:5–7 is the first strophe directed to the north.

The relation between 30:12–15 and 16–17 is analogous to that between 30:5–7 and 10–11. Verses 12–15 give every evidence of being a rhetorical unit (medical diction in v 15a rounds off that diction in vv 12–13 and the third colon of v 14); it offers judgment while vv 16–17 suddenly offer hope. Both vv 12–15 and vv 5–7 express traditional curses, the warriors turned to women and the incurable wound, respectively (for the details see Form). One has no difficulty, then, in positing vv 12–15 as one strophe in the series.

The mention of "Samaria" and "Ephraim" in 31:3b–6 leads one to include these verses in a strophe: there is rhetorical unity within this sequence (an address to the people in the feminine singular). Unfortunately there are severe text problems in vv 2–3a (see Interpretation); if they are correctly solved here, then one has Yahweh's third-person references to "Israel" and to "him" (the latter the reading of *G*) that fit awkwardly at the beginning of vv 3–6 with its feminine address. To this difficulty three observations are appropriate. First, "Israel"

is after all masculine, and the companion strophe to this one (30:18–21), proposed below, likewise mentions "Israel" in the third-person masculine. Second, the shift to feminine is of course due to the address "virgin Israel" in v 4. Third, v 9b makes an appropriate closing to the strophe, and there "Israel" and "Ephraim" are mentioned.

As to v 9b, the mention of "Ephraim" moves one to include it in the early recension to the north; it is a striking adaptation of the covenantal formula (see Form). Its position, closing vv 2–6 (so also Volz, Bright), would be matched by 31:1aβγb, proposed below for the closing of the strophe that includes 30:18–21. On the other hand, 31:7–9a does not belong in the early recension to the north: the diction of these lines is close to that of 30:10–11 ("Jacob shall return," 30:10; "they shall return," 31:8). I propose thus that one of the strophes to the north is composed of 31:2–6 + 9b.

Finally, there is 30:18–21. If 31:2–6 suggests cultic unity between north and south (31:6), 30:18–21 suggests not only cultic concerns ("his congregation," v 20, and perhaps "tents," v 18, and "thanksgiving" [= "thank-offering"?—see Interpretation], v 19) but also right monarchy ("his mighty one shall be from him, and his ruler shall go forth from his midst," v 21, doubtless an indication that the ruler will no longer be the Assyrian governor). The theme of rebuilding (v 18) matches that in 31:2–6 (see v 4). And to this sequence one is moved to add the conclusion of 31:1 (less the gloss "at that time, oracle of Yahweh"): the two cola match v 9b in the next strophe (see above), and "tribes of Israel" not only suggests the northern tribes (compare 1:15; 2:4; 3:14, and see further Interpretation) but also forms a nice inclusio with "tents of Jacob" in v 18.

Symmetry of the Seven Strophes to the North. If the analysis of 31:2–6 + 9b is correct, then the seven strophes are precisely symmetrical with respect to the person and gender references to the people: (1) 30:5–7, about him; (2) 30:12–15, to you (feminine); (3) 30:18–21 + 31:1aβγb, about him; (4) the central strophe, 31:2–6 + 9b: vv 2–3a and 9b, about him, enclosing vv 3–6, to you (feminine); (5) 31:15–17, to you (feminine); (6) 31:18–20, about him; (7) 31:21–22, to you (feminine). This

---

4   Compare Lohfink, "Der junge Jeremia," 359.

symmetry is reinforced by the inclusio of "male" and "warrior" in 30:6 and "female" and "warrior" in 31:22. The sequence of the strophes essentially moves in pairs. The first two are negative, centering about two traditional curses (see Form). The second two contain Yahweh's promises in the first person ("I am going to restore," 30:18; "I shall rebuild you," 31:4) and end with variations of the covenantal formula (31:1, 9b). Both stress the political and cultic reunion between north and south (see above). Both center around the verbs "build" (30:18; 31:4) and "plant" (31:5)—for these verbs compare 1:10; indeed the matching of these two verbs in the central strophe may be the key to the symmetry of the sequence. The third pair centers on quotations of Rachel and Ephraim and Yahweh's responses to them. The last strophe contains the only imperatives addressed to the people in the whole sequence (though formally those commands perhaps round off the vague imperatives "ask" and "see" in 30:6); they are commands to action, given the promises and reassurances of Yahweh in the preceding material. (For additional evidence of the arrangement in pairs see *Internal Structure of the Seven Strophes to the North*.) Formally also the questions in 31:20a and 22a may balance those in 30:7 and 15.

Setting of the Seven Strophes to the North. Commentators have in general been in agreement on the authenticity of 31:2–6 and 15–22 to Jrm, and Volz and Rudolph in particular have pressed for the authenticity of 30:5–7, 12–15, and 18–21. Considerations of structural symmetry already offered here render the conclusion of authenticity secure. And the period of Jrm's career in which these strophes were articulated, and their audience, has already been set forth in the designation "early recension to the north." The strophes reflect Josiah's program for reunion between north and south: this is particularly apparent in 31:5–6 but is to be seen in 30:20–21 as well (see above). There is no way to specify more narrowly a period of time for this material. If Jrm was born in 627, as maintained in this study, then he

would have been roughly eighteen years old when Josiah was killed at Megiddo in 609. It is at least possible that the twelve-year-old Jrm heard a recitation of Deuteronomy in Jerusalem in 615, and that it was on that occasion that he perceived his call ("I am only a youth"). Lohfink sees the young Jrm as a propagandist and poet for Josiah,[5] so that I would propose the span of 615–609 as the setting for this sequence. There is an account of an expedition to the north by Josiah in 2 Kgs 23:15–22, summarized in 2 Chr 34:6–7, and that account mentions Samaria (2 Kgs 23:19). The passage in Kings has been judged to be a late midrash drafted by a Deuteronomist,[6] but recently uncovered inscriptional material has made it clear that Josiah did regain control of many northern areas,[7] so that an expedition to Samaria is altogether likely. If such an expedition were mounted within the period proposed for the sequence, it would make an admirable setting, but there is no way to be sure.

Internal Structure of the Seven Strophes to the North. The first strophe, 30:5–7, consists of six bicola. The general structure is of three groups of two cola each; the first pair of cola is marked by "we have heard" (v 5) and the second by "have I seen" (v 6). But this structure is in some tension with another: the opening two cola, the second of which is a quotation, balancing the last four cola, the first two of which are a quotation (if the analysis of quotations here is correct: see Interpretation). These surround the central six cola—the description of the symptom of panic, males who appear to be in labor.

The second strophe, 30:12–15, consists of thirteen cola: a series of bicola is closed by a climactic tricolon in which the reason for the incurable wound is explained. And the structure is analogous to that of vv 5–7: four cola (vv 12–13), "your wound is incurable"; four cola (v 14), the wounding done by Yahweh through the "lovers"; and five cola (v 15), two cola of a rhetorical question and three cola of Yahweh's answer. The rhetorical question in v 15a is then parallel to the rhetorical exclamation and question in the same position in v 7a.

5   Ibid.
6   Montgomery, *Kings*, 534–35; Gray, *Kings*, 738–39.
7   Joseph Naveh, "A Hebrew Letter from the Seventh Century B.C.," *IEJ* 10 (1960) 129–39; Frank M. Cross, "Epigraphic Notes on Hebrew Documents of the Eighth–Sixth Centuries B.C.: II. The Murabba'ât Papyrus and the Letter Found Near Yavneh-yam," *BASOR* 165 (February 1962) 42–46; see the dis-

cussion in Bustenay Oded, "Judah and the Exile," *Israelite and Judaean History* (ed. John H. Hayes and J. Maxwell Anderson; Philadelphia: Westminster, 1977) 463–64.

The third strophe, 30:18–21 + 31:1αβγb, has a different form: four cola plus four in vv 18–19; three cola plus three in vv 20–21 (v 21b is a gloss); and two cola in 31:1 (if that formula belongs to the strophe). There is symmetry in arrangement of verbs of the first and third persons. Essentially the arrangement is chiastic in vv 18–19: v 18a has two verbs in the first-person singular (though strictly speaking the first is הִנְנִי with the first-person singular suffix plus participle), and v 19b has two hip'il perfect first-person singular verbs with strong assonance (וְהִכְבַּדְתִּים, וְהִרְבִּתִים). The cola with those verbs enclose cola with verbs in the third-person singular, two verbs in v 18b, and one verb governing two parallel cola in v 19a. The two hip'il first-person singular verbs in v 19b have associated with them two negated third-person plural verbs synonymous with the first-person singular verbs, and they too have strong assonance (יִצְעָרוּ, יִמְעָטוּ). The arrangement in vv 20–21 (three cola plus three) is parallel: in each verse two verbs in the third person are in closely parallel cola, followed by one verb in the first-person singular in a less closely parallel colon. It is also noteworthy that the verb in the first colon both of v 20 and of v 21 is "be" (היה). These occurrences of "be" pave the way for the two occurrences of "be" in the closing covenantal formula (31:1), first-person singular and then third-person plural.

The fourth strophe, 31:2–6 + 9b, is commensurate in length with the third (nineteen cola against sixteen), but its arrangement is different. The central core is vv 4–5, with "again" (עוֹד) at the beginning of vv 4a, 4b, and 5; v 4 has four cola and v 5 three cola, and v 4 begins with "build" and v 5 with "plant." Though v 5 is one colon shorter than v 4, their structure is similar: two occurrences of "build" in the first colon of v 4 matching two occurrences of "plant," one in the first, and one in the last colon, of v 5 (if the text is reconstructed correctly). The second colon of v 4 is verbless (a construct chain functioning adverbially). And as if to reflect the two verbs in the first colon of v 4 and the single parallel verbs in the third and fourth cola of v 4, the last colon of v 5 has two verbs. Yet out from the core of vv 4–5 are extended both the two cola of v 3 and the four cola of v 6. Verse 6 moves out directly from v 5 in that the second

cola of each are parallel ("in the mountains of Samaria," "on Mount Ephraim"), and the third colon of v 6 has two verbs like the third colon of v 5 (and the first of v 4). Verse 3 is just as closely involved with vv 4–5, however, in beginning the address in the feminine singular. But v 3 is in contrast to vv 4–5 in offering perfect verbs rather than imperfect ones (and is the perfect "called" in v 6 in symmetry with the verbs in v 3?): v 3 therefore summarizes the past as v 2 reviews events in the past in which the covenant came into being: v 2 then matches v 9b (if that half-verb belongs in the strophe) with its formulation of the covenant. If vv 4–5 form the core of the strophe, then it is possible that the four cola plus two of vv 2–3 match the four cola plus two of vv 6 + 9b.

The fifth strophe, 31:15–17, consists of twelve cola in a simple arrangement: v 15—the first four cola are a description of Rachel, the last two cola (if correctly reconstructed) are Rachel's lament; vv 16–17 offer six cola of Yahweh's speech, consisting of v 16a, two cola of reassurance, followed by four cola (vv 16b–17) introduced by כִּי predicting grounds for hope.

The sixth strophe, 31:18–20, consists of sixteen cola (if v 19a is divided correctly).[8] The passage divides unequally: Yahweh's report of Ephraim's lamenting, two cola, v 18aα; Ephraim's lament, eight cola, v 18aβb with the focus on "you" (= Yahweh), and v 19 with the verbs and other references all first-person singular; and Yahweh's meditation, six cola, v 20. Yet v 20 divides into two cola (the rhetorical questions about Ephraim) plus four (Yahweh's reaction to Ephraim), and the first two cola in v 20 correspond in a way to the two cola at the beginning of v 18—both pairs of cola offer parallelisms mentioning "Ephraim"—so that in a way there is symmetry here as well.

The seventh strophe, 31:21–22, is irregular, but in its shrinking form (four cola about the road, three cola involving "return" and "virgin"/"daughter," the final two cola introduced by כִּי) it resembles that same shrinking form in the longer third strophe. One wonders: do the two occurrences of "for yourself" (לָךְ) in the first two cola of v 21 match the two occurrences of "return" (שׁוּבִי) in the last two cola of that verse?

---

8   One notes that Michael Patrick O'Connor, *Hebrew Verse Structure* (Winona Lake, IN: Eisenbrauns, 1980) 305–6, does not count "particles," including prepositions, in the constituents of a colon.

The Three Extensions by Jrm for the Recension to the South.
I propose here that Jrm reused the recension to the
north just before the fall of Jerusalem in 587 by the
addition of three sequences of material: 30:10–11;
30:16–17; and 31:7–9a.

It is best to deal first with 30:16–17. There is no
denying the style of Jrm here: the reversal of the action
of verbs in v 16 (compare 11:18; 17:14; 20:7; 22:22,
among many such passages), the use of a specific idiom
for the growth of healthy flesh in v 17 (compare 8:22).
But there is more than identity in style and vocabulary.
The passage specifically proclaims an action counter-
balancing that of 5:17: in that passage the foe from the
north will eat up everything in sight; now those who eat
you shall themselves be eaten (v 16). Indeed the logic of
linking "eating" and "looting" in v 16 is the logic of the
double meaning of "our prey" in the last colon of v 17 (if
the *G* reading there is the correct one: see in detail
Interpretation) and the logic of the association between
2:3 and 2:14. In 2:3 "all who ate of him" (כָּל־אֹכְלָיו), that
is, of Israel, were held guilty, were punished, whereas in
2:14 the question is, "Why has he become a victim
[לָבַז]?"—here "all who eat of you" (כָּל־אֹכְלַיִךְ) will be
eaten, and all those plundering you I will give "for
plunder" (לָבַז) (for the association of 2:14 with 2:3 see
Interpretation on 2:14). The sequence then cannot be
denied to Jrm; he affirms that though the punishment of
Judah will take place, as he has affirmed in 2:14 and
5:17, the punishing nation will itself be punished in turn.
The two verses then reverse vv 12–15: v 17a speaks of
restoring health, and v 17b picks up the theme of those
who do not "care" (דרש) for the people.

The other two sequences, 30:10–11 and 31:7–9a,
must be dealt with together, since both offer a style
closely resembling that of Deutero-Isaiah (compare the
opening remarks at the beginning of these Preliminary
Observations). Thus 30:10–11a is very close to Isa 41:8–
10, and 31:7–9a has resemblances to such passages as Isa
42:15–16 and 43:5–7. The question whether Deutero-
Isaiah imitated hopeful material from Jrm or whether
someone influenced by Deutero-Isaiah added later
material to the Book of Jer therefore becomes a crucial
one. Opinion has differed: already Karl H. Graf insisted

that 30:10–11 is authentic, and form-critics have pointed
out that v 10 begins in a way typical of the priestly
salvation oracle (see Form),[9] so that some have felt that
the matter of priority is hardly an issue.[10] Yet it becomes
urgent to seek a setting or settings for the two sequences.

As for 30:10–11, it is clear that it serves as a continuation to v 7 (occurrences of the verb "save," and perhaps
"frighten" [חרד], compare "panic" [חֲרָדָה] in vv 5 and 10).
It is also the case that one's perception of the diction
shifts from vv 10–11a to v 11b: the former resembles
Deutero-Isaiah, while the latter draws on motifs common
to Jrm, motifs in fact specifically found in the material
added in Jrm's second scroll. Thus, to stay with v 11b, "I
will make a full end of all the nations . . . , but of you I
will not make a full end," reverses 5:10a (if one deletes
the negative there with most commentators: see Text
there) and the general import of 4:27 (see Text and
Interpretation there). "I will chastise you moderately"
(וְיִסַּרְתִּיךָ לַמִּשְׁפָּט) reflects 10:24, where the people are
quoted as saying, "Chastise me . . . but moderately"
(יַסְּרֵנִי . . . אַךְ־בְּמִשְׁפָּט), and it may reflect the use of the
same verb in 6:8 as well; the verb does not occur in
Deutero-Isaiah. But one cannot assume a setting for vv
10–11a different from that of v 11b: v 11b supplies the
substantiation for the words "fear not" in vv 10–11a (v
11b is introduced by כִּי; see further Form). And it may
be affirmed that the phrases of vv 10–11a may be
considered part of Jrm's vocabulary: for "fear not" see
1:8; for "do not be dismayed" see 1:17; for "none to
make him afraid" see 7:33; for "for I am with you to save
you" see 1:8 and 15:20—these phrases are characteristic
of the salvation oracle (see Form). One must conclude
that these two verses are authentic to Jrm and are
intended to extend or reshape vv 5–7; this conclusion
implies that Jrm laid the groundwork in this form for
Deutero-Isaiah (see Interpretation). (These two verses, it
may here be remarked, are duplicated in 46:27–28, but
there they are not integrated in their context. The
curious circumstance that *G* omits them in the present
passage and includes them in chapter 46 is to be
explained by the fact that in the ordering of chapters in
G the material of chapter 46 precedes the material of
chapter 30: *G* has thus included the material in their first

---

9   Rudolph, p. 191, offers bibliography.
10   Compare Bright, pp. 285–86.

occurrence and omitted them in their second.)

With 31:7–9a one faces similar issues, since this passage also is reminiscent of Deutero-Isaiah. But the parallel of "land of the north" and "ends of the earth" (v 8) is found in 6:22; neither phrase in found in Isaiah 40—66. One is led then to see the parallelism in v 8 as a reminder that exiles will come back from Babylon, since that is the reference in 6:22, so again this passage is a "corrective" to vv 2–6: the latter describes specifically the return of Ephraim to Zion, so that the present passage extends the word to apply to exiles from Judah returning from Babylon. Then it may be observed that "shall not stumble" (v 9) reverses 6:21, and that the listing in 6:21, "fathers and sons together, neighbor and friend," is reflected in the listing here in v 8, "the blind and the lame, those with child and those in labor together." The present listing offers "together" (יַחְדָּו) after two feminine words; the earlier listing offers it after two masculine words. The passage is then a reversal of 6:21–22, and one must conclude that it is authentic to Jrm.

These three sequences then—30:10–11; 30:16–17; and 31:7–9a—all in some way reverse or offer compensation for the words of disaster spoken over the south in passages added in the second scroll that are now to be found in chapters 5 and 6, and all of them in some way correct or offer compensation for the words in the first, second, and fourth strophes of the early recension to the north. A reassurance of the correctness of these conclusions is afforded by 50:4–7, dated in the present study to the same period as these extensions: 50:4 offers a parallel to 31:9, and 50:7 offers a parallel to 30:16.

One concludes, then, that the early recension to the north, along with these enlargements, forms a later recension to the south.

Setting of the Recension to the South. It is difficult to determine a *terminus a quo* for the recension. In 594 Jrm was evidently stressing a double message—on the one hand that the exiles would have to remain in Babylon "a long time" (29:28) and that during this period any "building" and "planting" would have to be in Babylon (29:5, 28); on the other hand that Babylon would finally fall (50:1—51:58). In the passages under discussion the stress is on "building" and "planting" in Canaan (the implication of 31:4–5 in this recension). This was his message in buying the field at Anathoth (32:15), an event that took place in the tenth year of Zedekiah (32:1), that

is, March/April 588 to March/April 587. If that event took place during the Egyptian military move north that evidently took place in the spring and summer of 588, a synchronism that is altogether likely (it identifies the reference in 37:11–12 to the buying of the field), and if the buying of the field was the occasion for the first proclamation of "building" and "planting" in Canaan, then this is the most likely *terminus a quo*. And if the proclamation of the new covenant (31:31–34) took place after the proclamation of this recension to the south, a setting that is likely if 30:1–3 and 31:27–28 are the frame around this recension, and if the new covenant was proclaimed on the occasion of the septennial recitation of Deuteronomy in September/October 587 (on both matters see below), then this is the *terminus ad quem*. It is likely then that the recension was offered between summer 588 and summer 587. During this period Jrm was evidently under detention (32:2; 37:21), under which circumstances a written scroll would be necessary (compare the reason for the first scroll, 36:5, and see below on the setting for 30:1–3).

Structure of the Three Extensions in the Recension to the South. The internal structure of each of these three extensions appears to offer no mutual relationship, one to another, nor does there appear to be any relationship between a given extension and the strophe of the recension to the north immediately preceding it. Each of these three brief passages appears to be independent structurally (though there are of course form-critical resemblances to one another and thematic resemblances both to one another and to their respective preceding northern strophes—see above—and a congruence of personal reference to the preceding northern strophes).

The two verses of 30:10–11 form the two halves of this simple sequence: v 10 contains three bicola, and v 11 three more; the first colon of each verse contains "do not fear" (אַל־תִּירָא). This analysis is in tension with an alternative analysis: four bicola, the first and last of which begin with "do not fear," forming an inclusio (vv 10–11a); the last two bicola (v 11b) will then offer the motive for not fearing, introduced by כִּי (a motive anticipated by the כִּי clause in the second colon of v 11!), v 11b offering a comparison between the punishment of "all the nations" and of "you."

The two verses of 30:16–17 likewise form the two halves of that sequence: v 16 sets forth Yahweh's reversal

—Israel's enemies will be punished; v 17 speaks of Yahweh's healing (compare the diction of vv 12–15). Each verse has five cola, and the tricola enclose the bicola (Dahood assumes that the third colon of v 16 belongs with the fourth and fifth of that verse, but the assonance of v 16a and the play of verb stems in v 16b are against this analysis).[11]

The structure of 31:7–9a is more complex. Each verse contains five cola. One might suggest that v 7 has three cola plus two (three of imperatives, two of the quotation), while v 8 has two cola plus three (two in close parallelism with the first-person singular participle or verb, three summarizing the "great company" who will return). Verse 9 manages to be both two plus three and three plus two: the first three cola are closely parallel ("with weeping" and "with supplications" in the first two cola, first-person singular hip'il verbs in the second and third cola—with assonance—אוֹלִיכֵם, אוֹבִילֵם), but just as clearly the verb in the third colon governs all that follows.

The Nature of 31:10–14: Setting, Internal Structure. It is appropriate at this point to examine 31:10–14, since that passage gives the same impression of sharing the diction of Deutero-Isaiah as do 30:10–11 and 31:7–9a.

But this passage gives evidence of being from a later period. One notes first the parallelism of "priests" and "my people" in v 14 as an expression of the totality of the population. The pairing of "priests" and "people" occurs in the narrative portions of the book (27:16; 28:1, 5), but these are in descriptions of actual circumstances. The pairing also occurs in Hos 4:9a, but there it is in the context of a judgment on the priests, not a summary of the population. It occurs in a context more like the present one in Isa 24:2, at the beginning of the apocalyptic section on that book. It is not a parallelism that would occur to Jrm, for whom "priests" and "prophets" are the natural pair (5:31; 23:11).

The finite verb "redeem" (גאל, v 11) does not appear otherwise in Jer, though the participle גֹּאֵל, "redeemer," does appear in a verse that seems authentic (50:34); and the parallel verb "ransom" (פדה) appears only once otherwise, where the object is Jrm (15:21). The two verbs appear in parallelism elsewhere only in Isa 35:9–

10; 51:10–11; Hos 13:14; and Ps 69:19. The phrase "like a watered garden" (v 12) is found otherwise in Isa 58:11. In general the concern for water and fertility in the restored land was likewise a concern in Trito-Isaiah (not only Isa 58:11 but 61:11; 66:12) and other late passages in Isaiah (notably chapter 35, but also 29:17–21). For further details of vocabulary which fit the early postexilic period see Interpretation.

Form-critically also the passage is a prophecy of salvation (*Heilsweissagung*) rather than an oracle of salvation (*Heilsorakel*) as 30:10–11, 16–17; and 31:7–9a are; that form is common in late passages added to Isaiah 1—39, notably Isaiah 35.[12]

The passage then seems to have been added to make more specific the joy to be experienced by the returning exiles: is there a catchword link with what precedes, "sing" (רנן, vv 7, 12)? A setting in the later decades of the sixth century or even in the fifth (like Isaiah 35?)[13] is appropriate.

With the assumption that v 12aβ is a gloss, the passage breaks easily into eight bicola: the opening invitation to the nations (v 10a), two bicola describing the action of Yahweh in the third person (vv 10b–11), two bicola declaring what returning Israel will do (third person, v 12), a bicolon specifying the joy in segments of the population (v 13a), a bicolon in which Yahweh suddenly speaks in the first person of creating joy among the people (v 13b), and a closing bicolon in which a first-person verb (subject Yahweh) is balanced by a third-person verb (subject "my people").

The Frame of the Recension for the South: 30:1–3 and 31:27–28. These two passages have not been associated by the commentators: 31:27–28 has been assumed to be a gloss (Volz) or a short sequence along with others in this section (vv 23–30, Rudolph; vv 27–30, 31–34, 38–40, Bright); 30:1–3 is of course assumed to be introductory, but Rudolph deletes "and Judah" in vv 3 and 4 (as he does in 31:31) in assuming that the introductory words are intended as words to the north.[14] Rudolph states that Jrm needed to write down words to the north because they could not hear him, but 3:12a belies this notion. It is far more likely that this scroll would have supplemented previous scrolls (compare chapter 36),

---

11 Dahood, "'ākal//kālāh."
12 See Wildberger, *Jesaja*, 1355.
13 Ibid., 1359.

14 Rudolph, pp. 188–89.

which contained words of judgment; it would be difficult to perceive inevitable judgment to be modified or extended in some way by the words of hope contained in chapters 30 and 31—it is plausible to understand a fresh start to be necessary. Further, a scroll would be necessary if Jrm was in detention at the time (see above). Because of the way in which words to the north were supplemented to become valid for the south, it is altogether likely that the words "Israel" and "Judah" are both original in 30:3 and 4. Verse 4 will then immediately introduce the words of the recension to the south; v 3 will be a more general introduction, a proclamation of salvation (see Form); and v 2 will be the instructions to prepare such a scroll of hopeful words for the south.

If 31:27–28 is the closing of that scroll to the south in the original intention of 30:2, as the present study proposes, then it is united with 30:1–3 by the words "the time is surely coming" (more literally, "behold, the days are coming," הִנֵּה יָמִים בָּאִים), a phrase that appears in these two chapters only in the two passages under discussion and in 31:31 and 38 (for which see below), and by the mention once more of "Israel" and "Judah." Because of the occurrence in v 28 of the verb "watch" (שקד) found in 1:12 and of the verbs of destruction and construction found in the call in 1:10, it is commonly assumed that the passage is a late gloss (Rudolph) or at least that v 28 is (Volz). But beyond 1:10 this set of verbs may appear in authentic passages with a variety of immediate meanings (18:7–9; 24:6; 45:5), and the fact that they can appear in what are doubtless later passages (12:17; 31:40) does not mean that the present passage is unauthentic; indeed the meaning of 24:6 is very close to that of the present passage. The phrase "sow . . . with the seed of man and the seed of beast" is more striking. There is no parallel elsewhere in Jer for "sow" with Yahweh as subject, but it appears in Hos 2:25 (an authentic passage), and the parallel of "man" (אָדָם) and "beast" (בְּהֵמָה) is found in Jer 7:20; 21:6; and 27:5, all authentic passages; and indeed the present passage appears to reverse the message of 7:20 and 21:6 (the parallelism is a traditional one, being found in both J and P in the Pentateuch).[15] One notes also that "seed" (translated "offspring," זֶרַע) occurs in 30:10, part of the added

material in the recension to the south. Given the symbolism of the purchase of the field at Anathoth (chapter 32), the expression is a plausible one.

These two passages thus serve to open and close the recension to the south.

"Sour Grapes" (31:29–30) and the New Covenant (31:31–34). These two passages carry distinctive theological weight, the first on individual responsibility and the second on a new covenant. Most commentators assume that vv 31–34 are authentic, a judgment in which the present study concurs (see below). Verses 29–30 are a different matter; these will be discussed first.

There is obviously a close relation between vv 29–30 and Ezek 18:2, indeed all of Ezekiel 18. Since Ezekiel elsewhere seems to expand on themes in Jer (thus Ezek 2:8—3:3 from Jer 15:16), it has seemed possible to believe that this little passage is authentic to Jrm (so Giesebrecht and Condamin; compare Bright's cautious comment with regard to vv 27–30 and 38–40: "One ought not too hastily to declare that the prophet could not have expressed such sentiments").[16] But the judgment of most scholars is against authenticity (Duhm, Cornill, Volz, Rudolph), correctly, it would seem from the data available.

In contrast to vv 31–34, there is no close link in catchword or theme between these two verses and authentic material that precedes them (that is, vv 21–22 or 27–28): "days" (vv 29 and 27) and "man" (vv 30 and 27) are hardly sufficient. Again, the notion of individual responsibility appears to some degree to contradict the corporate restoration set forth in vv 33–34; indeed the passage seems to be intended as a corrective to the message of corporate restitution (Rudolph). The phrase "die for one's (own) sin" is not appropriate to Jrm but is found elsewhere in Ezekiel (Ezek 3:18, 19). The form of the passage (a change of speech pattern: see Form) is identical with that of 3:16 and 23:7–8; both those passages, on other grounds, are judged to stem from Nehemiah's time (fifth century: see Setting for both). One concludes that the passage is secondary to Ezekiel 18 and is the attempt (by priestly circles?) to correct the implication of the "new covenant" passage ("his sin," v 30; "their sin," v 34), perhaps in the fifth century.

15 See BDB, 9a, sec. 2.
16 Bright, p. 287.

As for 31:31–34, it was Duhm who most vigorously opposed its authenticity: "I find in it only the effusion of a scribe who holds as the highest ideal that everyone among the Jewish people shall know by heart and understand the Law, that all Jews shall be scribes."[17] Cornill, on the other hand, defended its authenticity vigorously and with detailed argumentation.[18] Recent criticism has centered around the prolixity of the first part and the occurrence of "I shall be to them God, and they shall be to me a people" in v 33. For example Hyatt has written, "It is entirely possible that the wording of vss. 31–34 is not Jeremiah's. The style is more prolix than his, and in some places is a bit awkward, especially in vs. 32. Nevertheless the thought is essentially his. We cannot now identify with precision the disciple or editor who may be responsible for the present form. He may have been Baruch. He probably was not the Deuteronomic editor, in spite of the presence of some Deuteronomic phrases."[19] Nicholson maintains, "The passage is composed in the characteristic style of the prose in the book of Jeremiah and very probably comes from a Deuteronomic author."[20]

The question of authenticity cannot be answered on the basis of specific phrases only, but also on what can be discerned of its placement within chapters 30—31 and on its theological content.

As to its placement, it stands outside the framework of the recension to the south (see above) but is tied to it by several catchwords or phrases. (1) "The time is surely coming" (הִנֵּה יָמִים בָּאִים) marks the frame of the recension (30:3; 31:27) and the beginning of the present passage (v 31) and does not occur in intervening material (for v 38 see below); and "house of Israel and house of Judah" (v 31) is likewise tied to v 27. (2) The covenant formula in v 33 reflects variations of that formula in 31:1 and 9b. (3) Most substantially the word "new," feminine (חֲדָשָׁה, v 31) picks up that same word in v 22; the adjective appears nowhere else in Jer except in the proper name "New Gate" in 26:10 and 36:10. It is also possible (4) that the

theme of "writing" the law on the heart of the people (v 33) reflects the command to "write" the words of Yahweh in 30:2. And it is conceivable, if the reconstruction "with mastery" in v 21 is correct (see Interpretation), that (5) the verb "be master" (בעל) reflects that verb there: indeed this would be a most noteworthy link if true. The passage is then strongly integrated with the recension to the south and appears to be a substantial supplement to that recension, offering themes related to it.

It is important to stress that theologically the striking message of the passage is not typical of anything else in the exilic or postexilic period, when the passage would need to have had its origin if unauthentic to Jrm (against Duhm). It is not referred to again until the intertestamental literature, that of Qumran, and the NT,[21] and it appears to be bracketed by material unauthentic to Jrm (vv 29–30, for which see above, and vv 35–37, for which see below), which has the effect of modifying to some degree the implication of the passage. It can be argued, then, that it is not material likely to have been drafted in later decades to supplement the genuine words of Jrm.

The internal structure of the passage is noteworthy: it is best to analyze it here, since it has at least an indirect bearing on the question of authenticity. The first half (vv 31–33aα) is prose and the second (vv 33aβ–34) poetry, but both halves are carefully organized. Though the first half is strongly reminiscent of Deuteronomy (see below), it is arranged chiastically. Thus it begins and ends with "the days" (translated here "the time") and "those days." Within those expressions are the references to the new covenant, "I shall make with the house of Israel . . . a new covenant" and "this is the covenant which I shall make with the house of Israel." Within these in turn are references to the old covenant, "not like the covenant which I made with their fathers" and "it was they who broke my covenant, of whom I was master." Finally the centerpiece is the word of salvation history, "on the day I took them by the hand to bring them out of the land of Egypt"; so that if the prose section is framed by "the

17   Duhm, p. 255: "Ich finde darin nur den Erguss eines Schriftgelehrten, der er für das höchste Ideal hält, dass jedermann im jüdischen Volke das Gesetz auswendig kennt und versteht, dass alle Juden Schriftgelehrte sind."
18   Cornill, pp. 348–53.
19   Hyatt, p. 1038.
20   Nicholson, Jer. 26—52, 71.

21   William L. Holladay, "New covenant, the," *IDBSup*, 623–25.

days" to come, then the center is "the day" of the original exodus. The poetic portion, for its part, begins and ends with two bicola, each of which contains a pair of first-person singular verbs; each of these bicola offers a chiasmus with respect to verbs and prepositional complements. Then the opening bicolon is extended by the second bicolon, the covenantal formula (the last cola of v 33), which of course contains one first-person singular verb and one third-person plural verb. The middle section of the poem thus consists of five cola (v 34abα), the operative verbs of which are "they teach" and "they know"; the middle colon is the command "Know Yahweh!" It would appear, then, that the passage is something other than an "effusion." If the passage is authentic to Jrm, as is here maintained, then the contrast between prose and poetry is part of the intentional effect of the passage, manifesting in the mode of presentation the contrast between the old covenant and the new.

With regard to diction, a basic question that calls for solution is the contrast between the idea of a new covenant and the last colon in 50:5, בְּרִית עוֹלָם לֹא תִשָּׁכֵחַ, "The everlasting covenant will never be forgotten," part of material judged in the present study to be authentic. Of course one can say that "the everlasting covenant" in 50:5 is the new covenant (so, by implication, Thompson on that passage), but there is no hint in 50:5 of a fresh covenant (see Interpretation on that verse). It is thus likely that 50:5 is part of material proclaimed some time before the final fall of Jerusalem (see 50:1—51:58, Structure, Form, Setting, *Setting*), and that the fall moved Jrm to speak more explicitly of Yahweh's inaugurating a new covenant (for a setting for the passage see below).

There are other words and phrases within the passage that recollect or reverse earlier passages of Jrm. Thus the association of "their fathers" with the rescue from Egypt (v 32) is reminiscent of that association in 2:5–6; 7:22 and 25; and 11:4 and 7. The occurrence of the verb "be master" (בעל, v 32) to express Yahweh's relation to the fathers matches an occurrence of the same verb to express his relationship to "sons/children" (בָּנִים) in 3:14. The theme of Yahweh's putting his law "within them" (בְּקִרְבָּם) is reminiscent of the violence and oppression that has been "within" the city (4:14; 6:6), and the theme of Yahweh's writing the law on their heart is reminiscent of the sin of Judah written on the tablet of his heart (17:1). The question of "knowing" Yahweh is a steady

preoccupation of Jrm: see particularly 4:22; 9:2; 22:16; and 24:7. The phrase "from the least of them to the greatest" is fairly common in the OT, but the phrase in v 34 appears to resonate with 6:13, an expression of the sinfulness of the total population, and perhaps 16:6; and with 5:4–5 as well (though the word for "least" is different there) in view of the occurrence of "forgive" (צלח) in 5:1 and 7 (and nowhere else in Jrm's poetry). The use of the parallel "remember" in connection with "sin" is reminiscent of the use of that verb with "iniquity" in 14:10 and with "the loyalty of your youth" in 2:2. These links help to confirm the authenticity of the passage.

The association of "fathers" with covenant is of course found in Deuteronomy: note there 5:3; 7:12; 8:18; likewise the phrase "bring out of Egypt by (Yahweh's) hand," Deut 5:15; 6:21; 7:8; 9:26; 26:8. The "writing" of the law on the heart of the people is in strong contrast to the "writing" of the law on stone tablets in Deut 5:22; 10:2, 4.

The setting that commends itself from these data is Jrm's counter-proclamation to the recitation of Deuteronomy in Jerusalem at the festival of booths in September/October 587 (compare Setting for 11:1–17, where the proposal is made that the setting for that passage is the analogous occasion in 594). Such a recitation would then be approximately two months after the fall of the city in July (39:2) and a month after the temple was burned (2 Kgs 25:8–9). It is not at all unlikely that such an observance would have taken place; indeed it is likely that this was the destination of the pilgrims from the north (41:1, 4–5) who were intercepted at the time of the assassination of Gedaliah (see Interpretation on that passage). The destruction of the main buildings of the city and the associated deportation of the leading citizens would have been for Jrm evidence for the end of the reality of the covenant mediated by Moses; it makes appropriate an announcement of Yahweh's fresh work for his people in time to come.

The Remainder of the Unauthentic Passages: 30:8–9; 31:23–25, 26, 35–37, 38–40. The remaining passages can be dealt with less elaborately.

Verses 8–9 of chapter 30 interrupt the continuity between the first strophe addressed to the north and its extension to the south; they are united by the verb "serve" (עבד). Verse 9 belongs in the orbit of messianic eschatology (compare the expression "and David their king" in Hos 3:5).[22] The diction of v 8 is of course dependent on chapters 27 and 28 (see particularly 27:2 and 28:11), but the general phraseology reminds one of Isa 10:27a ("his yoke from your neck"), which Hans Wildberger dates from the later Persian period,[23] and of Ezek 34:27 ("break the pegs of their yoke . . . those who enslaved them"), part of a passage which Zimmerli assigns to the disciples of Ezekiel at the time of Haggai and Zechariah.[24] A guess for the closing decades of the sixth century would be plausible.

As to 31:23–25, they are united by the words "Judah and its cities," but form-critically v 23 seems to be distinct from vv 24–25 (see Form); there may then be here two short additions by different hands. Nevertheless they come from the same period. Thus the saying in v 23 comes out of the orbit of Trito-Isaiah ("holy hill": compare "my holy hill" in Isa 56:7; 65:26; 66:20). One may note also that the phrase "righteous home" (נְוֵה־צֶדֶק) refers in Deutero-Isaiah to Yahweh (Isa 50:7), not to the temple. The verb "bless" (ברך pi'el) does not otherwise appear in Jer. The diction of v 25 is close to that of v 14, so that a similar setting is suggested, the end of the sixth century (or sometime in the fifth?). The verses are evidently intended to supplement v 21 ("Israel," "your cities" calling forth "Judah" and "its cities").

Verse 26 is puzzling as it stands, but its diction is close to that in Zechariah 1—8 ("I saw in the night," Zech 1:8; "the angel . . . waked me like a man that is wakened out of his sleep. And he said to me, 'What do you see?'" Zech 4:1–2), so that a setting in the closing decades of the sixth century is again appropriate. (On this verse see further Form, Interpretation.)

Verses 35–36 and 37 are two related sayings in which Yahweh guarantees his salvation to the "offspring of Israel" by reference to the stability of the cosmos; both also have the same protasis-apodosis structure (see Form). The words go considerably beyond the establishment of a new covenant by the initiative of Yahweh in the forgiveness of sins in assuring Israel of the inviola-bility of his relation to them. Though Jrm spoke of regularities in nature (5:22, 24; 8:7), the regularities of the sun and moon are themes at home in the P tradition (Gen 1:14–16) and in Deutero- and Trito-Isaiah (Isa 40:26; 60:19). The origin of vv 35–37 must be viewed together with that of 33:14–26: there is the same preoccupation with the regularity of day and night (33:20, 25), the same protasis-apodosis form for reassurance (33:20–21, 25–26), the term "statutes" (חֻקִּים, 33:25). But 33:14–26 is missing in G and is evidently modeled on the present passage; it is best dated to the second half of the fifth century (see on that passage). The use of the verb "vanish" (מוש) in the present passage is similar to its use in Isa 59:21, a late addition to Trito-Isaiah.[25] The expression "offspring [literally 'seed'] of Israel" occurs in one other passage in Jer, 23:8, and outside the book in Ps 22:24; Neh 9:2; and 1 Chr 16:13; on the basis both of this phrase and of other evidence, 23:7–8 is assigned a setting in the fifth century, and that setting is appropriate for the present passage as well (compare the setting of vv 38–40 below). It should be noted in passing that v 35b is identical with Isa 51:15aβb; the present passage is then drawing on that earlier material.

Verses 38–40 speak of the rebuilding of Jerusalem with geographical landmarks known from the time of Nehemiah (for the details see Interpretation); a period in the middle of the fifth century is thus fitting.[26]

Verses 35–37 and 38–40 are in their present position evidently because the catchwords "plant" and "build" are still operative, and vv 35–37 deal with "offspring" (= "seed") and vv 38–40 with "building." It may then have been perceived that vv 31–34 were not sufficiently specific and that vv 27–28 needed to be reinforced by these two sections. If both sections were added to the chapter at the same time, the setting of vv 38–40 in the time of Nehemiah argues for the same setting for vv 35–37.

Summary. From the evidence there seems to have been recensional work on the recension to the south plus

---

22 See the remarks on that expression in Wolff, *Hosea*, 63.

23 Wildberger, *Jesaja*, 419.

24 Zimmerli, *Ezekiel 2*, 222.

25 Westermann, *Isaiah 40—66*, 352, 427–28, dates the verse to a time similar to that of Zechariah 14.

26 Compare Guy P. Couturier, "Jeremiah," *The Jerome Biblical Commentary* (ed. Raymond E. Brown, Joseph A. Fitzmyer, and Donald E. Murphy; Englewood Cliffs, NJ: Prentice-Hall, 1968) 1:328.

31:31–34 both at the time of the return from exile (30:8–9; 31:23–25 and 26) and in the following century (31:29–30, 35–37, and 38–40). The setting of 31:10–14 is uncertain—by the data available the passage could fit either period.

Form

It is easiest to deal first with the forms employed in the sequence of strophes that made up the early recension to the north (see Preliminary Observations), then with the material added in the recension for the south, and then with still later material.

The Northern Recension: 30:5–7. It is altogether likely that Yahweh speaks in this passage (against Volz and Rudolph, who assume Jrm speaks: see Interpretation). The two cola of v 5 are a report of panic analogous to 4:19–21 and 6:24: the former passage, like this one, contains quotations expressing panic. Verse 6a is a command to search for precedents, like 2:10, but whereas 2:10 offers a command to look for something unlikely, this is a command to look for something absurd (compare Amos 6:12a). The mood of mockery continues in the rest of the verse with the "why?" question.

There are two interrelated themes here, that of panic engendered in the victims of holy war, and that of the curse of warriors turned into women. For the former, compare not only 6:24 but also Deut 2:25 and 11:25.[27] The panic is conventionally localized in the "loins": one notes the phrasing of Isa 21:3.[28] "Loins" of course suggests also the theme of childbirth (see again 4:31; 6:24), and this leads to the theme of warriors turned into women, a standard curse against the enemy (compare the curse on Babylon in 50:37 and 51:30).[29] (That this curse is still operative in the Middle East is indicated by an incident reported in September 1970, when the tank corps of King Hussein of Jordan wished to be unleashed against the Palestinians in their midst but were prevented by the king; an armored commander at Zarqa flew a brassiere from the antenna of his tank because, he said,

"We have all become women.")[30] The point here, of course, is that if Israel is the victim of panic, if her warriors are turned to women, then they are victims of a holy war launched by Yahweh; and this fact, and the atmosphere of taunting, suggests that the passage as a whole embodies a judgment oracle (but see below). The same tone of taunting seems to be found in 30:12–15 (see there).

The first two cola of v 7 are again quotations of the panic of the people, as in v 5 (if the rhetoric of the passage is understood correctly: see Interpretation). The third colon is an affirmation of the situation, what Brevard S. Childs calls the "summary appraisal" form,[31] like 10:19. The last colon is here construed as a question (see Interpretation), a rhetorical question suggesting a negative answer, but with the possibility that it could be construed as an oracle of salvation (*Heilsorakel*) in the later recension to the south, given the addition of vv 10–11 (see below on that recension).

30:12–15. Verses 12–13 on the surface are a medical report, the words of a physician to the patient; since Yahweh is understood to "heal" (v 17, and see likewise 3:22), it is appropriate that a diagnosis from Yahweh be mediated through the prophet (see similarly Isaiah's words to Hezekiah, 2 Kgs 20:1 = Isa 38:1). But there is clearly no way to know the emotional tone behind the words; is Yahweh presumed to be announcing a diagnosis not theretofore known, or is he only repeating news already known, with the aim of humiliation or mockery (compare v 6)? The incurable wound is a traditional curse.[32] Verse 14a moves out from medical terminology to a word about "all your lovers": similar wording in 4:30b is in the context of taunting (see there), so that these words (and therefore vv 12–13 as well) may move in that orbit (compare the remarks about vv 5–7 above). Verse 14aα is ambiguous: "for the wound of an enemy I have dealt you, the punishment of the pitiless" may reinforce the report on the state of the nation which Yahweh gives (if the "enemy" is to be identified with the

27 See Gerhard von Rad, *Studies in Deuteronomy* (SBT 9; Naperville, IL: Allenson, 1953) 47–48.

28 On this see Aubrey R. Johnson, *The Vitality of the Individual in the Thought of Ancient Israel* (Cardiff: University of Wales, 1949) 75.

29 For more instances see Hillers, *Treaty-Curses*, 66–68.

30 *Time*, September 28, 1970, 17.

31 Brevard S. Childs, *Isaiah and the Assyrian Crisis* (SBT

2d Series 3; Naperville, IL: Allenson, 1967) 128–36.

32 Hillers, *Treaty-Curses*, 64–66.

"lovers"), or it may move on to state the reason for the state of the nation (if the "enemy" is Yahweh): for the ambiguity see Interpretation. Verse 15a consists of parallel rhetorical questions posed by Yahweh (see Interpretation), and v 15b is his answer. The form comes out of a didactic context—compare 1 Sam 16:1,[33] and more generally Job 38—39:[34] the questioner raises the question in order to be able to deliver the answer. This form presupposes the derived form of didactic question and answer explored by Burke O. Long[35]—see, for example, 13:22. But whereas Long analyzes the form when people ask the rhetorical question, here the question is posed by Yahweh himself. The answer in v 15b (and therefore by implication the rhetorical question as well) is an explanation for the current situation: it is Yahweh's punishment for sin, and is analogous to the summary-appraisal form (see above on v 7).

30:18–21 + 31:1aβb. This strophe has the general form of a proclamation of salvation (*Heilsankündigung*): Yahweh announces the restoration of his people in every aspect of their lives. Behind the positive words stand some negative ones ("city"/"ruin"; "make many"/"be few"; "make impressive"/"be beneath notice"); the negative ones refer glancingly to Yahweh's prior judgment, that judgment which was the focus of the first two strophes. In particular there will be a restoration of kingship over Jacob, a kingship according to Yahweh's will (v 21), and the covenantal promises made to the patriarchs ("I shall make them many," v 19—compare Gen 17:2 and often) will be fulfilled. (Compare Jrm's word of the annulment of those promises, 10:24 and 20:1–6.) Finally (if the cola of 31:1 close this strophe: see Preliminary Observations) one has a variation on the traditional covenantal formula, "I will be to you God and you will be to me a people";[36] given the fact that a variation of that formula appears in Gen 17:7 and 8 ("to be to you God"), one wonders whether Jrm did not intend the whole passage to be a reaffirmation of the covenant with Abraham. (Compare the diction of 31:33, added in the recension to the south.)

31:2–6 + 9b. If the text is correctly reconstructed, the strophe begins with v 3a and continues with the three poetic cola of v 2; these four cola embody an account of Yahweh's saving acts in times past (*Erzählung der Heilsgeschichte*), for which compare Amos 2:9–10; Hos 12:4–5. Verses 3b–6 shift the discourse: Yahweh in the first person addresses Israel, personified as feminine. Verse 3b is a declaration of eternal love (compare Judg 16:15; Isa 43:4): thematically it continues the recitation of the saving acts (compare the same association in Hos 11:1, in reverse order). Verses 3–6 are a proclamation of salvation (*Heilsankündigung*) with themes closely paralleling those of 30:18–21—the restoration of the people, building and planting, the hint of success in war (v 4b), and the promise that the people of Samaria will participate in the Zion cult, indeed the quotation of the eager cry of pilgrims (compare Ps 122:1; Isa 2:3 = Mic 4:2). If v 9b closes the strophe (see Preliminary Observations), then one has here a shift to second singular masculine; it is a striking variation of the covenant formula (compare v 1aβb, which appears to close the previous strophe). The "father/son" formulation closely resembles 2 Sam 7:14a; there the formulation is part of the royal ideology of adoption, but the concept appears to be part of the theology of covenant from the beginning (see Interpretation).

31:15–17. Even aside from the rubric at the beginning of v 15, economy leads to the conclusion that Yahweh speaks: he surely speaks in vv 16–17 (it can hardly be Jrm who reassures the weeping Rachel). Other reports of the

---

33 On this see Ashley S. Rose, "The 'Principles' of Divine Election, Wisdom in 1 Samuel 16," *Rhetorical Criticism, Essays in Honor of James Muilenburg* (ed. Jared J. Jackson and Martin Kessler; Pittsburgh: Pickwick, 1974) 45.

34 Gerhard von Rad, "Job xxxviii and Egyptian Wisdom," in *The Problem of the Hexateuch and Other Essays* (New York: McGraw-Hill, 1966) 288–90 = "Hiob xxxviii und die altägyptische Weisheit," *Wisdom in Israel and in the Ancient Near East, Presented to Professor Harold Henry Rowley* (ed. Martin Noth and D. Winton Thomas; VTSup 3; Leiden: Brill, 1955)

299–301 = *Gesammelte Studien zum Alten Testament* (TBü 8; Munich: Kaiser, 1958) 269–70.

35 Burke O. Long, "Two Question and Answer Schemata in the Prophets," *JBL* 90 (1971) 129–39.

36 For literature on this formula see 7:21–28, nn. 13, 14.

sound of lamentation using קוֹל, נִשְׁמָע, or both seem also to be spoken by Yahweh (see for example 3:21; 8:19). The report of wailing closes at the end of v 15 with the quotation of the words of her wailing, if the analysis given here is correct (see Interpretation). The image of a mother weeping for her lost children is surely a traditional one; Samuel N. Kramer cites a Sumerian prototype, the goddess Ninhursag weeping for her lost son.[37] Then in vv 16–17 one has the response of Yahweh: in v 16a, his reassurance (*Beruhigung*) to Rachel, in vv 16b–17 a proclamation of salvation (*Heilsankündigung*) promising restoration: here, as in vv 3–6, in the form of direct address.

31:18–20. Verses 18–19 are a report by Yahweh of what he has heard, parallel to v 15. The first two cola are a statement that he has heard Ephraim, and the balance of the verses are a citation of the words of Ephraim. Verse 18aβ is an acknowledgment of Yahweh's punishment (*Bekenntnis der Strafe Jahwes*), implying an acknowledgment of guilt (*Schuldbekenntnis*); compare Ps 51:5. This is followed (v 18ba) by a plea for help (*Hilfeschrei*) and (v 18bβ) by an affirmation of confidence (*Vertrauenserkenntnis*). Verse 19 continues the mood by an affirmation of remorse (*Reugefühlerkenntnis*), reaffirming the reality of guilt in the last colon. These expressions are thus most closely allied with motifs in the individual laments of the psalms.[38]

Verse 20 embodies Yahweh's response, but in his meditation on his affection for Ephraim he refers to him in the third person, in contrast to his second-person address to Rachel in vv 16–17. In theme and mood this verse is close to the themes and moods in Hos 11:1–9: the sonship of Ephraim and the affection for him, Yahweh's affirmation of the affection for Ephraim reflected in his inner parts. But the passage in Hosea shifts from third person to second person; in the present passage the reference remains in the third person. The verse here begins with parallel rhetorical questions that affirm parental affection for Ephraim (compare Interpre-

tation), and the final four cola are an affirmation of sympathy (*Zuneigungserkenntnis*) congruent with Ephraim's affirmation of remorse in v 19.

31:21–22. Verses 21–22a are an appeal to virgin Israel to return from exile; the cola of v 21 are couched as commands to road-builders (see on this Interpretation), for which compare Isa 40:3; 62:10. Verse 22b gives the motive (*Begründung*), introduced by כִּי, for the commands: it is a proclamation (*Verkündigung*) by Yahweh of his reversal of the order of creation (compare Isa 41:17–20).

Summary: The Recension to the North. The two opening strophes are oracles of judgment, centering on traditional curses, and in both there is evidence of the summary-appraisal form. The last five strophes make up in general a collection of proclamations of salvation (*Heilsankündigungen*). For further data on the symmetries in the recension see Preliminary Observations.

Additions for the Recension to the South: The Frame (30:1–3; 31:27–28). After the opening rubrics in 30:1–2a one has in v 2b a divine command (*Befehl*) to write a scroll; the motive (v 3) is a proclamation of salvation (*Heilsankündigung*), and the recension is closed off by a matching proclamation of salvation in 31:27–28 which offers a comparison between Yahweh's activity in destruction in the past and his activity in restoration in the future (for a similar matching of these verbs see 24:6 and 45:4).

30:10–11. These verses are a double oracle of salvation (*Heilsorakel*); for the form see 1:17–19. (1) Address (*Anrede*)—"and you" (vv 10–11); (2) exhortation of salvation (*Heilszuspruch*)—"do not fear . . . do not be dismayed" (vv 10, 11); (3) substantiation (*Begründung*)—"I am going to save you" (v 10), "I am with you to save you" (v 11); (4) result (*Folge*)—"Jacob shall return" (v 10). There will be a profound reversal of the defeat of Jacob-Israel, and the nations shall suffer defeat in turn: for the whole pattern compare Isa 41:8–13. For the innovativeness of Jrm with this form see Interpretation.

30:16–17. The phrases of v 16 resume those in the

37   Samuel N. Kramer, "BM 98396: A Sumerian Prototype of the *Mater Dolorosa*," *Eretz-Israel* 16 (1982) 141*–46*.

38   See conveniently Erhard Gerstenberger, "Psalms," *Old Testament Form Criticism* (ed. John H. Hayes; San Antonio: Trinity University, 1974) 200, and Kraus, *Psalmen*, xlvi.

"result" section (*Folge*) of the oracle of salvation in v 11b; it would almost appear, then, that these two verses must be heard in the context of vv 10–11 as well as in the content of vv 12–15, since one seems to have a truncated oracle of salvation. The description in the third person of the results of Yahweh's action shift back to the first person in v 17a, and v 17b closes the oracle with a motive for Yahweh's action, a description of the mockery of Jerusalem by her enemies (compare the mocking word to Jrm in 12:6).

31:7–9a. It is not at all clear who the hearers are to whom the commands in v 7 are directed. In form the imperatives are a summons to heralds (*Beauftragung von Gesandten*), for which compare 4:5.[39] Rudolph assumes it is addressed to the other nations. In any event one has here a summons to rejoice (*Aufforderung zum Jubel*), a summons to affirm Yahweh's salvation of his people. Verses 8–9a are portions of an oracle of salvation, characteristics of the substantiation by Yahweh and the results of his activity being intermixed.

The New Covenant, 31:31–34. This passage is a proclamation of salvation (*Heilsankündigung*) matching the form of the framework for the recension to the south (see above); for the shift within the passage from prose to poetry, and for its reflection of Deuteronomy, see Preliminary Observations.

Unauthentic Additions: 30:8–9. These two verses begin with the connection formula (*Anschlussformel*) "and it shall happen on that day" (וְהָיָה בַיּוֹם הַהוּא, compare 4:11); there follows a proclamation of salvation (*Heilsankündigung*).

31:10–14. Unlike the oracles of salvation in the extensions in the recension to the south, or the proclamations of salvation in the frame of the recension and in the "new covenant" passage, this passage is a prophecy of salvation (*Heilsweissagung*); such prophecies are often met with in the secondary additions in the first part of the Book of Isaiah as well.[40] It begins, typically for such a prophecy, with an appeal for attention (*Aufforderung zum Hören*), here to foreign nations, to witness the saving acts of God. These acts are the ransoming of Israel, who will come singing (compare Isa 51:11), filled with food and drink. The shift of reference to Yahweh from third

person (vv 10b–11) to first person (vv 13–14a) is curious.

31:23–26. Verse 23 is a proclamation of salvation (*Heilsankündigung*) in the form of the prediction of a new speech pattern; it resembles the change in speech pattern exemplified in vv 29–30 (see below). For the poem compare Ps 128:5. Verses 24 and 25 appear to share characteristics with vv 10–14, a prophecy of salvation (*Heilsweissagung*). Verse 26 seems to be a fragment of a vision report (*Visionsschilderung*), characterized by the verb "I looked" (see further Interpretation). These verses are thus form-critical fragments that may have been added by several hands (see Preliminary Observations).

31:29–30. The origin of this sequence is Ezekiel 18 (see Preliminary Observations), which in form is a disputation saying (*Disputationswort*).[41] Here, however, one has a brief proclamation of salvation (*Heilsankündigung*) in the form of a change of speech pattern (see on this 3:16 and 23:7–8): no longer shall a conventional proverb be used. But it must be admitted that salvation here is only implied by the form: the content is not clear on the matter, and its juxtaposition with vv 31–34 suggests not salvation so much as a limitation on unlimited salvation such as might come out of priestly legal disputation (compare again Ezekiel 18). See further Interpretation.

31:35–37. Form-critically there are two units here, vv 35–36 and v 37. Verse 35 opens with the messenger formula appropriate to a prophetic unit, but then identifies Yahweh with hymnic (participial) phrases such as are found in the hymnic passages of Amos (Amos 4:13; 5:8–9; 9:5–6): for "Yahweh of hosts is his name" compare the variations of that closing phrase in Amos 4:13 and 9:6. Yahweh is thus he who sets the heavenly bodies in their places.[42] But the messenger formula at the beginning is odd with the hymn form: the hymn form has been subsumed in a prophetic oracle, the body of which is to be found in v 36 (one notes also the rubric "oracle of Yahweh" in that verse). The text of *M* opens v 37 with a fresh messenger formula, "Thus Yahweh has said," suggesting that v 37 is a parallel prophetic oracle; in *G* v 37 precedes vv 35–36, without the messenger formula, but the verbs in v 37a in *G* are different. The contrast between *M* and *G* in any event suggests that v 37 is a

39   See Wolff, *Joel and Amos*, 191, n. 3.
40   See Wildberger, *Jesaja*, 1355, on Isa 35:1–10.
41   Zimmerli, *Ezekiel 1*, 374.

42   For an analysis of the hymnic form see Hermann Gunkel, *Einleitung in die Psalmen* (Göttingen: Vandenhoeck & Ruprecht, 1933, 1966) 44–45.

separate unit. Both vv 36 and 37 embody divine reassurances (*Beruhigungen*) that the nation Israel will endure under Yahweh; both use a protasis-apodosis sequence in which an impossible (or inconceivable) circumstance negatively reinforces the assurance: "if [אִם] . . . (then) also [גַּם]."[43] The general assurance (v 36) that Israel will not cease is comparable to Yahweh's reflection at the end of the Yahwistic flood narrative (Gen 8:21–22) that the natural order on earth will not cease. The protasis in v 37 implying the impossibility of measuring the heavens or exploring the foundations of the earth is comparable to the protasis in Gen 13:16 implying the impossibility of counting the dust of the earth, and that passage has the same sort of protasis-apodosis sequence (one notes also Jer 13:23b, which varies the form with a question instead of a protasis).

31:38–40. This passage has the general form of a proclamation of salvation (*Heilsankündigung*) like vv 31–34 or the framework around the recension to the south; it seems to embody a surveyor's report (vv 38bβ–40aα) in its depiction of the sections of Jerusalem to be rebuilt.

Interpretation

■ **30:1-3** For v 1 compare 7:1; 11:1.

The divine command comes to Jrm to write a document (סֵפֶר) with words of hope. The fuller narrative of 36:2–8 offers the analogy here. The setting proposed for the carrying out of this command is the period just before the final fall of Jerusalem (588–587), when Jrm was confined in the court of the guard (32:2; 37:15: see Preliminary Observations); his scribe Baruch had access to him (32:12), so that it was doubtless to him that Jrm dictated the material on a scroll.

Rudolph proposes to excise the words "and Judah" in v 3 as a gloss; but if these words form the opening of a recension of words of hope to the south, as is here proposed (Preliminary Observations), then the words are appropriate: "Israel and Judah" suggests the presence in this recension to the south of the earlier recension to the north. For the phrase "restore the fortunes" see 29:14. For "the land which I gave to their fathers" see 7:7. This is the first occurrence of the verb "inherit" (ירש) in the book. It is a crucial verb in Deuteronomy;[44] given the

fact that Jrm perceives the purchase of the field at Anathoth to lie behind the words of hope in this recension, a field that was his "inheritance" (32:8), the use of the verb is appropriate here.

■ **30:5-7** The identification of the speaker in the poem is difficult, and there are interlocking considerations. *M* has "we have heard" (v 5) in evident parity with "I have seen" (v 6); *G* has a second-person plural verb in v 6, matching the plural imperatives at the beginning of v 6. Volz and Rudolph emend "we have heard" in v 5 to "I have heard," though there is no Versional support for this. Volz and Rudolph further assume that Jrm is the speaker in the passage and therefore that the introductory rubric in v 5 is redactional (so also Janzen).[45] But it must be said: first-person references elsewhere in the early recension to the north (30:14–15, 18–21; 31:18–20) are all to Yahweh—unless one honors the dubious "to me" in the first colon of 31:3, which would refer to Israel. If Jrm is not heard to speak elsewhere in this recension, then given the rubric at the beginning of v 5, it would be prudent to assume that Yahweh speaks here as well. And the first plural in v 5 is not a problem if the text of Isa 6:8 is sound: "Whom shall I send, and who will go for us?"

The use of "voice" (קוֹל) in v 5 suggests the presence of one or more quotations (compare 4:15, 29, 31, and often). Lohfink assumes that the second colon means that one hears "Terror!" and not "Peace!"; he is undoubtedly correct in locating quotational material here, but the negative surely would be וְלֹא if that were the meaning. It is better to construe the negative as part of the quotation, as translated here: "'Terror!' and 'No peace!'" The presence of quotations in the second colon raises the question whether there is balancing quotational material later in the strophe. I construe כִּי at the beginning of v 7 to introduce an exclamation of lament, "How great is that day!" (see below; compare 2:19; 4:13, 20, and often): here then is a matching quotation. The meaning of the first expression in the second colon of v 7, מֵאַיִן, is uncertain; if it is "whence?"[46] as accepted here (like 10:6, 7: see below), then one has a rhetorical question, perhaps indeed a second quotation rather than a continuation of the quotation in the first colon.

If the second colon embodies a question, then there is

43   For such clauses in general see König, *Syntax*, sec. 415γ.

44   Weinfeld, *Deuteronomy*, 313–16.

45   Janzen, p. 134.

46   So BDB, 32a.

perhaps justification for viewing the last colon likewise as a question: this understanding leads to better congruence between the third and the fourth cola (see below).

Verse 5 offers the only occurrence in the book of חֲרָדָה "fright, panic," but the related word "frighten" occurs in v 10 (and in 7:33). The first word in the second colon, פַּחַד, "dread, terror," is not different in meaning. Normally the word is taken here as the equivalent of "panic" in the first colon (*RSV*: "We have heard a cry of panic, of terror and no peace"), but the word may denote not only the emotion of terror but the object of terror (so 48:44); if the word is a quotation here (see above), then it is an exclamation on the confrontation with an object of terror. "No peace" is the phrase found in 6:14 ("there is no peace").

Verse 6a offers two imperatives, "ask" and "see," followed by the indirect question "if a male gives birth"; for similar diction see 2:10; 5:1; 6:16; 13:20; 18:13. The question is absurd (see Form). The word "male" is that found in Gen 1:26 (and in Jer 20:15); its counterpart, "female" (31:22), binds together the total sequence of strophes in the early recension to the north (see Preliminary Observations). The question leads into the direct question that follows, "Why have I seen every hero, his hands on his loins?" The word translated "hero" (גֶּבֶר) is sometimes a parallel for "man" (17:5), but it has implications of military prowess (Isa 22:17); note that it too appears in 31:22. This is the only occurrence in the book of this word for "loins" (חֲלָצִים) instead of the more common word (מָתְנַיִם, 1:17; 13:1–11). The immediate reference is to the gesture of a woman in labor (hence the gloss); for the intertwined themes of panic in holy war and the curse of warriors turned to women see Form.

The condition described in the color of the face (יֵרָקוֹן) appears as a human condition only here in the OT; the word refers otherwise to a disease of plants ("rust" or "mildew"). The Hebrew root gives rise also to words for verdure or greens (יֶרֶק, יָרָק), but in this passage G and V

translate by words for "jaundice"; one must assume that the range of reference is to "yellow-green,"[47] and that one has here a description of pallor, when the blood "leaves" the face.[48]

For the translation "how great!" in v 7 for כִּי גָדוֹל compare "how bad and bitter!" in 2:19 and "how suddenly!" in 6:26.[49]

The alternative to the translation "Whence any like it?" is to vocalize the first word as מֵאַיִן, "without (any like it)" (so most translations); compare מֵאֵין יוֹשֵׁב, "without inhabitant," in 4:7 and elsewhere. But the preserved vocalization is preferable. The "day" is a "time of distress": for that phrase see 14:8, and for "distress" see 4:31.

The reference to "Jacob" is not specific; it is proposed here that the reference is originally to the northern kingdom (so also the proposal below for 30:18), as is the proposal in the present study for 2:4, but that it is later enlarged to refer to the southern kingdom as well (see Preliminary Observations).

The import of the last colon of v 7 is much discussed. On the face of it the clause is an expression of hope: Rudolph titles the passage "Through Night to the Light." There is hope in other strophes of the recension to the north (vv 18–21 and those that follow), and in the context of the addition to the poem in the recension to the south (vv 10–11) there is hope, but in the context simply of vv 5–7 hope is questionable. The form of these verses suggests panic in the context of holy war—panic and lamentation (see above, and Form); parallelism with the third colon of the verse suggests here another statement of desolation. If the first colon is closely parallel to the third ("day" and "time"), and if the second colon is construed as a question, then the last colon may likewise be construed as a question. The word order of the colon itself points in the same direction; if a strongly adversative statement were to be made, one might have expected the verb "shall be saved" to come first, perhaps even an adversative conjunction like אַךְ if the verb is to

47   Compare the discussion in Athalya Brenner, *Colour Terms in the Old Testament* (JSOT Supplement Series 21; Sheffield: JSOT, 1982) 100–102.

48   See Johnson, *Vitality of the Individual*, 43.

49   See the literature in 2:1—4:4, n. 153, and see further the remarks by Dahood on the meaning of the same expression כִּי גָדוֹל in Ps 138:5, *Psalms III*, 278–79.

come last (see v 11!). Further, the material that immediately followed this verse in the recension to the north (vv 12–15) is equally hopeless and plays upon a parallel curse, the incurable wound (see there). All these considerations lead to the conclusion that an ironic rhetorical question is intended here.

■ **30:8–9** The continuity between vv 7 and 10 in the recension to the south (see Preliminary Observations) is broken by these two inserted verses. The personal references in *M* are muddled: in v 8 "I" (Yahweh) shall break "his" (the oppressor's) yoke off "your" (Jacob's, masculine singular) neck . . . and strangers (plural) shall no long enslave "him" (Jacob). *G* has regularized the sequence to conform to v 9: "I shall break the yoke of their neck . . . and they shall no longer serve strangers." In the text of *M* (and of *G*) in v 9 Jacob/Israel is now third-person plural, but the reference to Yahweh shifts from third-person to first-person singular.

For "and it shall happen on that day" compare 4:9. Though the context of the earlier recension suggests that the yoke is that of the oppressor(s) of the preexilic and exilic period, the setting of the verses indicates that the postexilic redactor had in mind any oppressor who imposes a yoke; the image originates with Jrm's word about the yoke of Nebuchadnezzar (27:12), but it had become a commonplace (compare Isa 10:27a, a late redactional insertion). For the association of "enslave/serve" (עבד) with "strangers" see 5:19.

The phrase "serve Yahweh" is not found in Jrm's poetry but is a commonplace of legal (Exod 23:25; Deut 10:12) and liturgical (Ps 2:12) diction. For the linking of "Yahweh their God" and "David their king" see Hos 3:5 (and compare Preliminary Observations); here is the thought world of those in postexilic times, dreaming of the restoration of the Davidic monarchy.

■ **30:10–11** All the phraseology of reassurance in vv 10a and 11b is also found in Yahweh's reassurances to Jrm himself: for "do not fear" see 1:8; for "do not be dismayed" see 1:17; for "for I am with you to save you" see 15:20. Commentators are accustomed to seeing in Deutero-Isaiah an innovativeness in developing the salvation oracle for the nation;[50] but if the conclusion of the present study, that these verses are authentic to Jrm, is correct, then one must conclude that it is Jrm who was innovative, and that such examples in Deutero-Isaiah of the salvation oracle as Isa 41:8–13 must be viewed as variations on these themes in Jrm.[51] The word of contempt to Jacob (vv 5–7), closing with an ambiguous line about Jacob's being saved, has been transformed into the emboldening promises. Question: Is the designation of Jacob as "my servant" a way to dignify the mocking word of 2:14?

For "from afar" (מֵרָחוֹק) compare the word that the foe comes "from afar" (מִמֶּרְחָק, 5:15) and the word to the nations that they will be "removed far" from their own land (רחק hip'il, 27:10); for "captivity" (שְׁבִי) compare 15:2 and 20:6. The verb "rest" (שׁקט) appears here for the first time in the book; it means "be quiet, undisturbed" and is used by the Deuteronomistic editor of Joshua and Judges to speak of respite from war (Josh 11:23; 14:15; Judg 3:11, 30; 5:31; 8:28). Isaiah used it with "return" (Isa 30:15); is there a reminiscence of that passage here? The parallel verb "be at ease" (שׁאן pa'lal) means "be secure"; a related adjective occurs in Amos 6:1 of leaders who are complacent in Samaria. For the phrase "none to frighten" see the discussion in 7:33. What a future!—without any threat to a peaceful and prosperous life on the land.

Verse 11b has five clauses as it stands. It is of course possible to leave this half-verse in five cola, as Rudolph does (see *BHS*), but the parallelism of the two occurrences of "make an end" (עשׂה כָלָה) and the plausibility of the matching parallelism of the last two cola of the verse lead to the conclusion that "where I have scattered you" is a gloss (so also Cornill). The expression "the nations" is used occasionally for Babylon in Jrm's diction (4:16, compare 25:11), and this is evidently the meaning here, but in later decades it would certainly need to be glossed,

50   See originally Joachim Begrich, "Das priesterliche Heilsorakel," *ZAW* 52 (1934) 81–92 = *Gesammelte Studien zum Alten Testament* (Theologische Bücherei 21; Munich: Kaiser, 1964) 217–31; *Studien zu Deutero-Jesaja* (BWANT IV, 25; Stuttgart: Kohlhammer, 1938) 6–19 = TBü 20 (Alte Testament) (Munich: Kaiser, 1963) 14–26; see more recently Westermann, *Isaiah 40—66*, 67–69, and Karl Elliger,

Deuterojesaja (BKAT 11/1; Neukirchen: Neukirchener, 1978) 133–36.
51   See further Holladay, *Spokesman*, 108.

since God would not have destroyed "all the nations" in general. The affirmation here, that Yahweh will not make a full end of Israel, stands as a correction to 5:10 (with the gloss אַל deleted there: see Text on that passage) and to the implication of 4:27 (if, as is here maintained, that passage has a word-play on "full end"); 5:18 is then in conformity with the present passage, and the gloss in 5:10 and the present vocalization in 4:27 (if the understanding of that passage here is correct) are efforts to square those passages with the present one. It must have come as wonderful news indeed that total destruction will be visited upon Babylon rather than upon Israel (compare the verb כלה in 10:25).

The phrase "I will chastise you moderately" is modeled on 10:24 (see Preliminary Observations); if 10:24 was an ironic word for Jrm, wherein Yahweh quotes the people's fatuous request that Yahweh punish them, if at all, with moderation (see Interpretation on that passage), then it is doubly ironic that Yahweh should at this point accede to the people's request.

The last colon, "though I will certainly not leave you unpunished" (וְנַקֵּה לֹא אֲנַקֶּךָ) is an adaptation by Jrm of the credal affirmation in Exod 34:7 and Num 14:18, "but he will by no means leave unpunished (the guilty)" (וְנַקֵּה לֹא יְנַקֶּה), an affirmation employed without adaptation in Nah 1:3. Jrm here affirms the continuity of Yahweh's character for Israel with the tradition associated with Moses.[52] The people will not go scot-free, but the total destruction Yahweh intends will be visited upon Babylon. (Jrm's first-person formulation of the credal formula appears once more, in a late gloss in Joel 4:21.)

■ **30:12–15** All four verses contain synonyms for "wound" and "pain": the strophe centers on the traditional curse of the incurable wound, just as vv 5–7 center on the traditional curse of the warriors turned to women (see there). This vocabulary has occurred earlier in the book, notably in 6:7; 8:21–22; 10:19; 14:17, 19; 15:18.[53] The people are addressed with feminine references (so similarly the diction in 8:21–22 and 10:19–20).

For "fracture" (שֶׁבֶר, vv 12, 15) see 6:14; the word is used widely for the "collapse" of a people (see 4:6). For "incurable" (אָנוּשׁ, vv 12, 15) and "wound" (מַכָּה, vv 12, 14) see 15:18; for "unhealable" (נַחְלָה, v 12) see 10:19. The word "sore" (מָזוֹר, v 13) appears in the OT only here and twice in Hos 5:13, where it is parallel to "sickness" (חֳלִי, for which see Jer 6:7); one cannot therefore determine its precise denotation. Various proposals have been made for its root: מזר "be foul" (BDB, *HALAT*); זור or זרר "press out" or זרר "tie up" (suggestions in Zorell based on Isa 1:6);[54] זור "flow" (Dahood)[55]—the matter is uncertain. The word "new skin" (תְּעָלָה) appears in the OT only here and in the similar sequence of 46:11, but compare the use of the related verb "arise" (עלה) in 8:22. "Pain" (מַכְאֹב, v 15) is found otherwise in the book in 45:3 and 51:8, but the cognate כְּאֵב occurs in 15:18.

Into the avalanche of words for pain and hurt the words דָּן דִּינֵךְ enter (in the first colon of v 13), but they are baffling in the context. G translates them, so they have been in the text from an early stage. If taken out of context, the verb can be taken as a perfect, thus "he has judged your cause": by this understanding it is the pious exclamation of a reader which has crept into the text (so Volz). Or in the context the verb can be taken as a participle, thus "(There is not) anyone judging your cause, (for a sore, healing)." I adapt the suggestion of Rudolph, derived from Isa 1:6, and read רַכְּרֵךְ (or similar vocalization), "your softener": a confusion of dalet for reš and nun for kap could give rise to the text at hand (see Text); for the reduplicated form compare Jrm's use of שַׁעֲשֻׁעִים in 31:20.

The diction of the wound is open to extension to the "wound" of a whole people; the people is here personified as a female (compare שֶׁבֶר בַּת־עַמִּי in 8:21, translated in the present study "the shattering of my fair people") in telling contrast to the masculine reference to "Jacob" in vv 5–7.

The metaphorical structure is continued in the use of "your lovers" in v 14; for this expression see 22:20. Are

---

52 For the further association of "leave unpunished" (נקה pi'el) with the wisdom milieu see Robert C. Dentan, "The Literary Affinities of Exodus xxxiv 6f," *VT* 13 (1963) 46.

53 See n. 32.

54 Compare Wildberger, *Jesaja*, 19.

55 Mitchell Dahood, "Philological Notes on Jer 18,14–15," *ZAW* 74 (1962) 208.

the "lovers" presumed to avoid her because she is repellent with a festering wound? Here the primary reference is to foreign nations from which Israel has expected aid: they have "forgotten" Israel, they do not "care" (דרש) for her. These words resonate widely in the poetry of Jeremiah: in the next-to-last strophe of the recension to the north Yahweh affirms that he continues to "remember" Ephraim (31:20), by contrast to these "lovers" who "forget"; the people should have been "seeking" (דרש) Yahweh (10:21), so now the alien partners do not "seek" (= "care," דרש) for Israel.

The third colon of v 14 is crucial (by the text offered here, the center colon of fifteen): כִּי מַכַּת אוֹיֵב הִכִּיתִיךְ. There are two accusatives: the outer object is a cognate accusative (literally "for I have wounded you the wound of an enemy"), and the presence of the cognate accusative reinforces with the second *kk-* the assonance of two occurrences of *kî-* and of *-îk*. The word "enemy" is poised between "your lovers" in the first colon and the first-person reference of the verb; is Yahweh the enemy, or does Yahweh direct the human enemy? The last colon of the verse continues the ambiguity: the "someone cruel" (אַכְזָרִי) is used of military enemies (6:23; 50:42), though it could conceivably refer to Yahweh (a related word is so used in Job 30:21). The companion word "punishment" (מוּסָר) covers also "discipline" and "training," and in Jer almost always suggests Yahweh's "correction" of the people (2:30; 5:3; 7:28; 17:23). The two cola then suggest the intimate way in which Yahweh is involved in the damage the enemy has done to the people. There is no further reference to military enemies, and the reference to Yahweh here is quietly reinforced by the first-person singular verb in the last colon of v 15.

There is some kind of text difficulty in *M* at the end of v 14 and all of v 15, since the words "because of the greatness of your iniquity, (because) your sins are so numerous" appear twice. All of v 15 is missing in *G*; one assumes a haplography in *G* and dittography in *M*. Given the logic of the sequence (see Form), it is best to omit the duplication in v 14 (so Volz, Rudolph, Bright), though one cannot be altogether sure that the resulting text is sound.

The interrogative at the beginning of v 15 clearly

means "why?"—given the meaning "because" in the second half of the verse. That interrogative would normally be עַל־מָה (8:14), but the preposition is doubtless omitted because it occurs later in the colon. The second colon is not likely to stand alone, as various translations have assumed (*RSV*: "Why do you cry out over your hurt? Your pain is incurable"—and *JB* and *NAB* are similar). Such a translation suggests that Israel is unjustified in crying over her hurt. Given the close parallelism of the last two cola in the verse, one is led to hear the first two cola as parallel. But it is not necessary to assume that a כִּי has dropped out (as proposed by Volz and Rudolph); the interrogative מָה can do double duty for both cola (so by implication Bright).[56] The preposition עַל likewise doubtless "governs" both the third and the fourth cola, though strictly speaking the expression needs to be heard as עַל־אֲשֶׁר before the finite verb of the fourth colon (compare 16:11).[57] For "greatness of your guilt" (רֹב עֲוֺנֵךְ) compare 13:22; for "be numerous" (עצם) with a word for "sins" see 5:6.

The closing colon gives the action of Yahweh in response to the guilt and sins of the people: "I have done these things to you" (compare once more the diction of 13:22). If the setting of this poem presupposes an early word to the north, then it is unlikely that "these things" (אֵלֶּה) should be revocalized to "a curse" (אָלָה); but compare the diction of 14:22 on this matter.

■ **30:16–17** *M* begins v 16 with "therefore" (לָכֵן). Typically this word introduces the divine announcement of judgment after an accusation (6:15; 8:10; Isa 30:13; Hos 2:8; Mic 3:12), especially in the messenger formula ("therefore thus Yahweh has said," 5:14 and often). Johannes Pedersen has pointed out that this conjunction often has only a very loose connection with what precedes, so that it should be translated "under these circumstances,"[58] but I find no parallel in Jer for the use of the conjunction to introduce a stark reversal. The frequent occurrence of the prepositional expression לָךְ "to/for you" at the end of vv 13 and 15 and twice in v 17, along with "to her" (לָה) at the end of v 17, makes plausible an emendation of לָכֵן to לָכִי here: this is an archaic form.[59] The restoration would make a remark-

---

56   For the double-duty מָה see Dahood, *Psalms III*, 438.

57   For double-duty עַל see Dahood, *Psalms III*, 437.

58   Pedersen, I/II, 115–17: note his citation of Jer

16:21 in this regard.

59   GKC, sec. 91e.

able assonance with "shall march" (יֵלֵכוּ) in the second colon of v 16. Indeed the permutations of *k* and *l* in the two verses, especially in v 16a, are striking (whether one emends "therefore" or not).

The association of "eat" (אכל) and "plunder" (בזז) is somewhat unexpected but reflects a preexistent association in Jrm's diction—see 2:2–3, 14; 5:17. In 2:2–3 Yahweh reminds the people of their pristine loyalty to him; the consequence of that loyalty was that "all who ate of him [Israel]" (כָּל־אֹכְלָיו) were visited with disaster. Then Yahweh raises the question how it has come about that Israel has become a "victim" (לָבַז, 2:14): what a reversal of roles! And in a terrible passage he describes how the foe from the north will "eat" everything in sight that belongs to Israel. Now in this passage there will be a reversal once more, when "all who eat of you" (כָּל־אֹכְלַיִךְ) will in turn be eaten, and all who "plunder you" shall be designated as "plunder" (לָבַז).

The two themes of "eating" and "plundering" are likewise associated in the restored text of the last colon of v 17, צֵידֵנוּ, which means both "our prey" and "our food": BDB and *HALAT* both list two homonymous lexemes, צַיִד I, "hunting, game" and צַיִד II, "food(-supply)"—it is not at all certain that one has to do here with homonyms (Zorell lists only a single lexeme), but in any event there are two semantic centers. The linking of the two themes in v 16 thus lends cogency to the restoration of the text in v 17, which is based on *G*.

The restoration of the participle "are consumed" in the third colon of v 16 instead of the useless *M* reading "all of them" is an instance of the parallelism of "eat" and "consume" found also in 10:25.[60]

The use of parallel stems of verb roots and the like ("eat," "shall be eaten"; "despoil," "spoil" [noun]; "plunder" [verb], "plunder" [noun]) is frequent in Jrm (see Preliminary Observations). This is the first appearance of the particular word for "foe" (צָר) in Jer, but it is an old word, occurring for instance in Deut 32:27. It is likewise the first occurrence in the book of the verb and related noun for "spoil" (root שסה/שסס), but it is a standard parallel to "loot" (בזז), for example, in Zeph 1:13.

The assurance of healing in v 17a is a reversal not only of the words in vv 12–15 but of similar declarations elsewhere (8:21–22); specifically for the expression "new flesh" (אֲרֻכָה) see 8:22.

"Outcast" is a nip'al participle of the verb נדח "scatter"; the hip'il stem is common both in the mouth of Jrm (27:15) and in later additions in the book. "She is our prey/food" is a mocking word of triumph over the prostrate people: compare the mood of 4:16 and 6:3. "No one cares for her" picks up "for you they do not care" in v 14.

■ **30:18** The verse is remarkable for the assonance of *š-b* (three times) and *miš-* (twice).

For the phrase "restore the fortunes" see 29:12–14. *G* omits "the tents of," but even though it might seem to overload the colon, it should be retained. The word is a standard parallel to "dwellings" (מִשְׁכָּנוֹת): note Isa 54:4, and particularly Num 24:5, about which see below; and both words function here in parallelism with "city" and "citadel." The diction of "house of Jacob" in 2:4 and "tribes of (the house of) Israel" in 2:4 and at the end of the present strophe, 31:1, likewise urges the retention of the word. The verb "show compassion" (רחם pi'el) here clearly denotes more than warm emotion; it is action as well (see the further discussion in 31:20); it contrasts strikingly with affirmations elsewhere that Yahweh will show no compassion (for example, 21:7).

What is the implication of the "tents" and "dwellings" to which Yahweh's mercy will be directed? It is proposed in the present study that "tent(s)" and "curtains" in 4:20 and 10:20 are a reference to the temple in Jerusalem, and although that reference would be possible in the present passage in the recension to the south, it can hardly suggest northern sanctuaries in the setting to the north: it is the assumption here that that recension reflects Josiah's program of cultic reunion between the north and the south (3:14; 31:6). Balaam addressed Jacob-Israel in Num 24:5 with the same parallelism: in that instance he was referring to real "tents" and "encampments." But "dwellings" (מִשְׁכָּנוֹת), when not referring to Yahweh's sanctuary in Jerusalem, refers in poetry to permanent buildings. One must therefore assume that diction like that found in 2 Sam 20:1 and 1 Kgs 12:16 reinforces for these words notions of decentralized traditional tribal life in the north, the old "homes" of

---

60   And Lam 4:11 and Ugaritic: for the parallels and the
      emendation here see Dahood, "'ākal//kālāh."

Israel, with pastoral and rural connotations; the terms are then linked with the two urban words "city" and "citadel."

The singularity of "city" and "citadel" is remarkable. In the recension to the south the words would be understood to refer to Jerusalem, but if the understanding offered here of the recension to the north is sound, the words could scarcely have referred to Samaria specifically; since Graf[61] the words have been taken in a collective sense (see, for example, Cornill and Rudolph). "Ruin" (תֵּל) appears also in 49:2 and in three other instances in the OT: like the cognate Arabic *tall* (Anglicized as "tell") it is the mound-heap of a ruined city, examples of which are found all across the Near East, the object today of archeologists' excavations. On "citadel" (אַרְמוֹן) see 6:5. The parallel in the last colon to "on its ruin" is curious: עַל־מִשְׁפָּטוֹ, literally "on (or according to) its justice (or norm)." The noun normally means "justice" or "judgment," but is used occasionally for "legitimate procedure," therefore "custom" (in Gen 40:13 כַּמִּשְׁפָּט הָרִאשׁוֹן means literally "like the former custom"),[62] so that *NJV* here translates "in its proper place." But in Exod 26:30 and 1 Kgs 6:38 the word means the specific "plan" of a building, so that "on (or according to) its plan" is a possibility here (so BDB). There is still another possibility, which depends on the nuance of the verb in the colon. The verb, literally "shall sit" (ישׁב), may carry the connotation of "abide inhabited," therefore "be inhabited" (so the idiom of 17:6), and that is the meaning usually understood here. But the verb may also mean "sit" (of a judge or king, Exod 18:14; Ps 61:8), and that nuance is proposed here for 21:13 and 22:23, in which Jerusalem is portrayed as being "enthroned," doubtless because of the palace and temple buildings (compare the reference to "Lebanon" and "cedars" in 22:23), so the nuance of "enthroned" here for "citadel" would not be unexpected. Further, מִשְׁפָּט may mean "legitimate claim": it means the "(priest's) due (from the people in the sacrifice)" in Deut 18:3 and 1 Sam 2:13, so that the colon may imply "a citadel shall be enthroned on (the basis of) its legitimacy."

In any event the verse suggests a restoration of Jacob and his habitations to their primal glory.

■ **30:19** Something is wrong with the text of the first colon of the verse: *M* is translated "there shall go forth from them thanksgiving," but the gender of "thanksgiving" (תּוֹדָה, feminine) does not match the masculine verb, and one would expect a reference to persons to match "merrymakers" in the second colon (Rudolph and Bright translate the second colon "and the sound of laughter" to match the first). I propose that "from them" (מֵהֶם) was originally a masculine singular participle and that תּוֹדָה depends on the participle. The phraseology of 33:11 gives the clue: the required form is מֵבָא "he who brings (a thank-offering)." That parallel passage links the sounds of joy with the mention of those who bring thank-offerings to the house of Yahweh: indeed that verse might be considered a midrash on the present passage. If the reconstruction is correct, the image is of worshipers "going forth" (יצא) from the cities of the north to "bring in" thank-offerings to Zion. The word "merrymakers" (מְשַׂחֲקִים) appears not only here but in 31:3: by the reconstruction offered here the diction of v 19a is very close to that of 31:4–6. For the broad range of meaning for "merrymakers" see 15:17; the context there, Jrm's detractors, is in great contrast to the present one. Elsewhere Jrm speaks of the absence of the sound of joy (7:34; 16:9; 25:10); here, by contrast, the sound of joy will be restored, and in the context of the cult.

The diction of v 19b suggests a second meaning for קוֹל, "voice," here, and that is קֹל, "frivolity" (for which see 3:9). Note that in Isa 8:23 "make glorious" (כבד hip'il) is in contrast to "bring into contempt" (קלל hip'il); the presence of כבד hip'il here (translated "make impressive") then suggests a contrast with the "lightness, frivolity" (קוֹל) of the merrymakers.

The diction of the parallel cola in v 19b is much more concise in Hebrew than in English: each colon sounds something like "I'll expand them and they'll not shrink." For the form of "this and not that" compare 4:28b (as reconstructed); 5:21; and 17:11. The last colon of the verse is usually translated "I will make them honored, and they shall not be small" (*RSV*; other translations similarly), but it has recently been shown that the verbs רבב and כבד are a fixed pair,[63] so that though it is true

61   Karl H. Graf, *Der Prophet Jeremia erklärt* (Leipzig: Weigel, 1862) 376.

62   Ephraim A. Speiser, *Genesis* (AB 1; Garden City, NY:

Doubleday, 1964) 306, translates "as was your former practice."

63   John S. Kselman, "*rb//kbd*: a new Hebrew-Akkadian

that Yahweh will honor them, the parallel suggests that he will do so by "making them vast." The translation here, "make them impressive," should cover the range of "make heavy, numerous, honored." The correlative expression means "be(come) small," but clearly must be the opposite of "make impressive." The translation of Bright, "I'll exalt them—they'll not be menials," seems too specific; "they shall not be disdained" (*JB*), "despised" (*NEB*), and "humbled" (*NJV*) make no implication about the size of population, which seems to be at issue (see above). "They shall not be beneath notice," though periphrastic, covers the field.

One notes that the verbs of the third colon are part of Jrm's instructions to the exiles (29:6) and more generally are traditional words of Yahweh's blessing to the covenant people (see the remarks on 10:24).

■ **30:20–21a** The six cola of this sequence are at first blush easy to understand and translate, but the sequence of thought and the implication of the words are not at all clear. The six cola must evidently be grouped in tricola (see Preliminary Observations): the third and sixth cola each begin with a waw-consecutive first-person singular perfect verb, and the first and fourth cola begin with a waw-consecutive third-person perfect form of "be" (היה) (for this reason the rendering in *G* of the verb of the first colon, which suggests וּבָאוּ—so Rudolph—must be viewed as periphrastic). The general parallelism of the cola, however, appears to be heard not only as two tricola but as three bicola, in that there is the possibility of ambiguity in the third and fourth cola (see below). That possible ambiguity seems to have been to some degree effaced by small expansions in the text during transmission in an attempt to overcome the ambiguity. The details follow.

"His children" and "his congregation" refer to the children and congregation of Jacob (v 18): "his children" are also Rachel's children in 31:15, 17. The parallelism between the two cola is thematic rather than exact: thus the two prepositional phrases "as of old" (מִקֶּדֶם) and "before me" (לְפָנַי) are formally comparable, and קֶדֶם elsewhere may carry the meaning "front, forward," but here the meaning is clearly temporal, while "before me" is, metaphorically speaking, spatial. The first two cola

then affirm Yahweh's restoration of Jacob's children (the north, in that recension) with an emphasis on those children as a worshiping assemblage: this motif then matches the implication of "tents" in v 18 and "he who brings a thank-offering" in v 19, if that reconstruction is correct.

The third colon in *M* reads "and I shall punish all his oppressors"; this colon is not impossible here, but the seeming lack of any parallel to "all his oppressors" is surprising. "His oppressors" (לֹחֲצָיו) is in form an active participle, and "his ruler" (מֹשְׁלוֹ) in the fifth colon, similarly a suffixed participle, may be a formal parallel. But פקד (here "appoint") has another range of meaning: could it mean here "and I shall appoint (him) over all his oppressors"?—in this way the colon would go well with "be established" in the second colon, since both verbs can be used, for example, of the king (כון nip'al in 1 Sam 20:31) or governor (פקד hip'il in 2 Kgs 25:22). Can such a meaning be perceived here without the suffix "him" on the verb? Can the presence of third-person singular masculine references in the first two cola carry over here, or can the presence of such a suffix on the verb in the sixth colon do double duty here?[64] It is at least plausible.

The word "oppressors" is plural not only in *M* but in all the Versions, but given the possibility of understanding מִמֶּנּוּ in the fourth colon to refer to "oppressor(s)" (see below), and the possibility that "his rule" (מֹשְׁלוֹ) in the fifth colon is in some way analogous to "his oppressor(s)," I would propose to omit the yod and to read "his oppressor" (לֹחֲצוֹ) here. By this reading Jrm would have intended Assyria for the first recension. The verb occurs in Amos 6:14, and that expression, if known to Jrm, could only be understood as Assyria. In the second recension, of course, the expression would refer to Babylon as well, and the pluralization of the participle would serve to broaden the application of the colon in the decades after Jrm, a process that continued with the addition of "all" in *M*.

M in the fourth colon (the first colon of v 21) reads "and his prince shall be from him." On the face of it this colon offers good parallelism with "and his ruler shall come forth from his midst." Now Volz emends the text, reading אַדִּיר for אַדִּירוֹ with one MS. (K 227) and מֵהֶם for

formulaic pair," *VT* 29 (1979) 110–13, esp. 111.

64   Compare the list of double-duty suffixes with a verb when the suffix is omitted in the first colon, Dahood,

Psalms III, 431.

מִמֶּנּוּ with S and T, translating "he shall be mightier than they." Volz's suggestion is interesting, though the textual evidence he cites cannot bear the weight of it: S and T both have a plural suffix on אַדִּיר ("their king shall be [T: shall be anointed] from them"), and the single Hebrew MS. may only coincidentally have read the substantive without suffix. But a reading of אַדִּיר without the suffix would allow a double meaning here, both "and the prince (= prince of Jacob) shall be from him (that is, from his own ranks)"—a rather insipid colon which is reinforced by the synonymity of the fifth colon—and at the same time "and he (= Jacob) shall be mightier than he (= Jacob's oppressor)." The word אַדִּיר not only serves as a noun that by implication (the parallel with "ruler" in the fifth colon) is a poetic reference to the king (compare 25:34) but also may be an adjective ("majestic, mighty") modifying "king" (Ps 136:18, where it is parallel to "great"). This possibility of a parallel with the third colon, and a second reference to "his oppressor," is convincing enough that the proposal to delete the suffix on אַדִּיר is justified. If מִמֶּנּוּ may mean "than he" and refer to the oppressor, then the singular "oppressor" is justified. On the other hand, the meaning of the colon "and his prince shall be from him" can be derived from the emended text (אַדִּיר without suffix) on the basis of a double-duty suffix.[65] By this hypothesis the suffix would have been added onto אַדִּיר secondarily for clarity's sake to avoid the ambiguity.

For "ruler" (מֹשֵׁל) compare the participle of the verb in the last colon of 22:30. The implication of the fourth and fifth cola, taken together, is of course that "Jacob" will be ruled by a king from his own ranks. For the recension to the north the implication is that the north will no longer be under the rule of Assyria but will have Josiah instead: although Josiah is a southerner, he is "one of them" as the Assyrian king is not, and this represents an effective way to further Josiah's program. For the recension to the south it suggests a time when kingship will be reestablished once more in Jerusalem. The expression מִקִּרְבּוֹ, "from his midst," sounds very much like Deut 17:15, "from the midst of your brothers you shall set up over yourself a king": here Jrm follows the Deuteronomic prescription for kingship. But the verb יצא, "come forth,"

also has royal associations in prophetic material (2 Sam 7:12; Isa 11:1).

Yahweh's initiative makes possible the king's initiative in the sixth colon: "I shall bring him near so that he may approach me." The verb "bring near" (קרב hip'il) offers a nice play on "from his midst" in the fifth colon (מִקִּרְבּוֹ). The connotation of "bring near" is cultic: other than the present passage the only context in which the verb appears in the hip'il stem with Yahweh as subject is Num 16:5 and 10, where Yahweh brings the priests near (to himself at the altar), and the only passage where the qal stem appears with the king as subject is 2 Kgs 16:12, where the king draws near to the altar in Jerusalem which was made on the pattern of the one in Damascus.

With the word "congregation" in the second colon, then one has the image of the king as cultic leader: if the strophe in the recension to the north reflects the ideology of Josiah, then one has here the image of Josiah the cultic leader of a reunited people. The image is then transferred to the future king in the recension to the south.

■ **30:21b—31:1** If in the recension to the north 31:2–6 was closed by 31:9b (see Preliminary Observations, and see Interpretation on that passage), a fresh formulation of the covenant formula introduced by כִּי, then I propose that vv 18–21a were closed by the similar covenant formula in 31:1 (less "at that time, oracle of Yahweh") introduced by the כִּי which stands at the head of v 21b. Verse 22 is missing in G and the second-person plural address does not fit the context (so also Volz, Rudolph, Janzen).[66] Verses 23–24 repeat with minor variations 23:19–20; they fit the context of 23:16–20 and do not fit here (see for example Bright). Verse 21b is not poetry; it is a pious comment that no one would on his own risk his life to approach God: it can only be at God's initiative. It is thus a reinforcement of that last colon of v 21a.

The expression "who, then?" (מִי הוּא־זֶה) appears in this form only otherwise in Ps 24:10 and Esth 7:5, but the less intense form מִי־זֶה is fairly frequent (in Jer see 49:19 = 50:44).[67] The expression "risk his life" is literally "pledge his heart" (עָרַב לִבּוֹ) and is found only here in the OT.

For the covenantal formula in the same order as that

---

65 For such double-duty suffixes on a noun where the suffix is omitted in the first colon see Dahood, *Psalms III*, 429–30.

66 Janzen, p. 49.

67 See further BDB, 261a, 4, and Dahood, *Psalms I*, 153.

in v 22 see 11:4; for the reverse order of terms see 7:23 and the bibliography cited there.

For vv 23–24 in general see 23:19–20. There are two trivial contrasts between the text of the two passages and one more notable one. The trivial ones are the addition of חָרוֹן after אַף in v 24a to expand the expression "wrath," and the absence of "with understanding" at the end of v 24—the latter expression is judged in 23:20 to be a gloss. The more notable contrast is מִתְגּוֹרֵר here in v 23 ("continuing") for מִתְחוֹלֵל in 23:19 ("whirling"); most commentators assume that the reading here is erroneous, but it is quite possibly a deliberate change.[68]

"At that time" in 31:1 appears to be a gloss appropriate to the postexilic period (compare the same expression in 3:17).

The remaining phrases of 31:1 embody the covenant formula in a fresh format.[69] The word "all," missing in G, is surely a gloss (so most), but the reading in G of the singular "tribe, family" is scarcely correct given the plural in 1:15; 2:4; 3:14 (as well as the plural "tents of Jacob" in 30:18, which probably balances the expression here).[70]

■ **31:2–3a** With v 3b the text is sound ("with an everlasting love I have loved you"), but with the four cola that comprise vv 2–3a things are amiss. Verse 2a is customarily translated "the people who survived the sword found grace in the wilderness" (RSV; compare NEB, NAB), but it is impossible to accept a bicolon in which the subject makes up the second colon and the predicate the first. JB and NJV solve the problem by reversing in effect the two cola (NJV: "the people escaped from the sword, found favor in the wilderness"), but it is not evident that the translations suggest that the original text had the cola in reverse order, only that they are offering a translation into smooth English. G offers a different rendering of the four cola; at some points clearly it is offering its own "second guess" to a difficult text, but its rendering of the first colon, "I/they found (him?) hot in the wilderness," suggests that G did not read or recognize חֵן but חַם or the like, so that the common phrase "find grace/favor" (מצא

חֵן) is suspect. The other major difficulty is that whatever the last colon of v 2 means (literally "going to give/find his repose, Israel"), it fits ill with v 3a ("from afar/long ago Yahweh appeared to me [G: to him]"), so that RSV paraphrases "When Israel sought for rest, the LORD appeared to him from afar" (so similarly NAB, NJV), and JB and NEB do not connect the cola at all. When the commentators do not accept M, their reconceptions are unconvincing: thus Cornill emends "in the wilderness" (בַּמִּדְבָּר) to "in prison" (בַּמַּסְגֵּר). Volz follows G in the first verb ("I found") and emends "grace" to "encamped" (חֹנֶה); this is on the right track, as will be suggested here, but the solution that I propose cuts more deeply.

It is the action of Yahweh that is celebrated throughout (v 3a, "Yahweh appeared"; the verbs in vv 3b–4a). I propose then that v 3b had fallen out of the text at an early stage and was reinserted at the wrong spot—that this colon belongs at the head of the strophe. The poem is about time: everlastingness (v 3) and future time ("again" three times, vv 4–5; "there shall be a day," v 6) and therefore the expression מֵרָחוֹק in v 3a means "long ago" (NEB, NJV), not "from afar" (RSV, NEB margin, JB, NAB). Aside from the expression "long ago," which sets the stage, the rest of the colon is a quotation from Exod 3:16: these are the words that Yahweh bids Moses to repeat to the elders of Israel. If this colon begins the strophe, then "Yahweh" is at the head of the four cola, and "Israel" closes them (whatever the colon means that contains the name); these two names are balanced by "Ephraim" and "Yahweh our God" in v 6, framing the poem (compare v 9b!). But one must read G "to him" for M "to me" in v 3a; the first person in the recension to the north is otherwise only Yahweh (compare 30:5–7 on this matter), and the reference should probably match "his rest" in the last colon of v 2. M may here offer a slip of the pen or an adaptation to Exod 3:16.

If the colon with "Yahweh" is placed at the head, economy suggests that the subject of "found" is Yahweh, not the people, and one's attention is directed to the

---

68 So Godfrey R. Driver, in WO 1 (1950) 413, according to Rudolph, p. 192; I have not seen the reference.

69 For the judgment that the diction here is unstereotypical see Lohfink, "Der junge Jeremia," 355, n. 21. For the formula in general see 7:21–28, nn. 13, 14.

70 Against Lohfink, "Der junge Jeremia," 355, n. 21, who follows G.

parallels in Deut 32:10, "He [Yahweh] found him [Israel] in a desert land," and Hos 9:10, "Like grapes in the wilderness, I found Israel" (compare Hos 12:5b). "Find" is thus to be seen as a verb of election.[71]

The participle "encamped" (חֹנֶה), or something like it, is the only plausible candidate for the curious "grace" (חֵן), as Volz suggested, and nun-he might well have been misconstrued in G as mem.[72] Now is one to understand the colon as "he found (me) encamped in the wilderness," with the object understood?—for the syntax compare 2 Kgs 19:8, "he found the king of Assyria fighting." Or should one reconstruct a suffix here, "he found me" (מְצָאַנִי), which would have dropped out by haplography because of the nun in *חֹנֶה?—could מְצָאַנִי have given rise to G εὗρον = מְצָאתִי? Should one construe the first-person singular ("to me") as feminine (compare the feminine singulars in vv 3b–5a), so that the participle should be חֹנָה (or even חֹנִיָה, compare בוֹכִיָה, Lam 1:16)?—in which case one would have a repeated nun-yod. These notions are too speculative; it is best to stay close to the text as is.

I would propose, for "sword" (חֶרֶב) at the end of the next colon, the vocalization "Horeb" (חֹרֵב). The word makes an admirable parallel to "in the wilderness," with double-duty preposition. The end of the strophe is preoccupied with "mountains": there are the "mountains of Samaria" and the "mountain of Ephraim," and finally "Zion," so that the mountain of Horeb makes a good beginning with that theme. In 1 Kings 8 the Deuteronomic historian describes how the ark of the covenant, in which the two tables of the law had been placed at Horeb (v 9), was carried from the city of David which is Zion (v 1 there), and Deuteronomy mentions "Horeb" nine times—one notes, for example, Deut 18:16, part of a passage crucial to Jrm in his call (see on 1:7, 9). But if the word is to be vocalized חֹרֵב and be parallel to "in the wilderness" before, this vocalization is open to a second meaning, "sword-wielder, slayer": the verb is found in 50:21, 27. And that second meaning prepares for the following colon, since "repose" suggests the absence of

any military threat. Thus if the word is correctly restored here, it is an instance of what Cyrus Gordon has called "Janus-parallelism" (for a possible previous instance see 17:1).[73]

The use of the singular "people" followed by a plural construct chain (עַם שְׂרִידֵי) is striking, but Judg 3:18 (הָעָם נֹשְׂאֵי הַמִּנְחָה) is a good parallel.

The infinitive absolute הָלוֹךְ is surely a wrong form of that verb; Volz revocalizes it to הֹלֵךְ to match the participle חֹנֶה. But if Yahweh is the subject of "appear" and "find," then one must look for the same subject here, so I propose הוֹלִיךְ "he brought" (compare the hip'il participle of that verb in 2:6 and the imperfect in 31:9). Now the hip'il לְהַרְגִּיעוֹ can carry its normal causative meaning, and one need not assume the necessity to emend the text or struggle with it (compare Rudolph, Bright).

So understood, the four cola summarize the *Heilsgeschichte* from the wilderness into Canaan; it is closely analogous to 2:6–7, which by the proposal of the present study took shape in its own early recension at the same period in the prophet's life.

■ **31:3b** For the parallelism between "love" (אַהֲבָה) and "kindness" (חֶסֶד) see 2:2: there the words appear to refer to both Yahweh's love for Israel and Israel's love for Yahweh; in the present passage they refer specifically to Yahweh's love for Israel. The cognate accusative expression with "love" ("an eternal love I have loved you") here is unique in the OT for this verb; and it may further be noted that the use of the verb and cognate noun to refer to Yahweh's love is far less common than its use for human love.[74] One has then a striking phrase using a verb used more for human love, and reinforced by the cognate accusative, and then reinforced still more by "eternal" (עוֹלָם). When that term is not used for a description of punishment ("eternal reproach," 23:40 and the like), it is used of Yahweh's decree (5:22) or his paths

---

71 See Wolff, *Hosea*, 164.
72 Compare Joseph Reider, "Etymological Studies in Biblical Hebrew," *VT* 4 (1954) 277.
73 For the literature on the phenomenon see 17:1–4, n. 7.
74 For the verb, 24 instances out of 138; for the noun, 4 instances out of 52.

(6:16); nowhere else is it used of his love. For "that is how" for עַל־כֵּן see 5:27. The expression "prolong kindness" (מָשַׁךְ חֶסֶד) is found twice in the Psalms (Pss 36:11; 109:12), and its opposite "prolong anger" (מָשַׁךְ אַף) is found in Ps 85:6, where the parallel "will you be angry with us for ever?" is reminiscent of the similar question in Jer 3:5. The verb מָשַׁךְ means "carry off, drag," therefore "protract, prolong." The verb-object structure of the parallels in the Psalms indicates that the suffix meaning "you" on מְשַׁכְתִּיךְ must be taken as a dative,[75] against G, S, and T, and against the traditional translations, which have taken חֶסֶד as an adverbial accusative (KJV: "with lovingkindness have I drawn thee"). It follows that the suffix on אֲהַבְתִּיךְ must likewise be construed as a dative. Both are datives of advantage, analogous to לְךָ in 2:2.[76]

■ **31:4–5** The thrice-repeated "again" (עוֹד) is a striking rhetorical effect. The collocation of two stems of the same verb, "I shall build you so that you may be built" (אֶבְנֵךְ וְנִבְנֵית), is a favorite device of Jrm (compare v 18 below, and 11:18; 17:14; 20:7; 30:16): the second verb is scarcely coordinate but must be understood as a subordinate verb of purpose, as in the parallels cited. "Again" reinforces the nuance of "rebuild" which the verb carries, as in 30:18. For "maiden Israel" (בְּתוּלַת יִשְׂרָאֵל) compare the same expression in 18:13; for an analogous vocative, see "my poor people" (בַּת־עַמִּי) in 6:26.

The denotation of the third colon of v 4 is not clear. G takes "your timbrels" as the object of the verb (though it translates a singular), "again you shall take your timbrel," perhaps simply a reminiscence of Exod 15:20; V, S, and T all assume "your timbrels" is an adverbial accusative, "you shall be adorned with timbrels." And recent translations have tended to follow either of these options, NAB and NJV following G (NJV: "again you shall take up your timbrels") and RSV following the other Versions ("again you shall adorn yourself with timbrels"). The difficulty, of course, is that timbrels (or "tambourines," see below) are not ornamentation; NEB therefore shades

the matter by rendering "again you shall adorn yourself with jingles," and JB paraphrases "adorned once more, and with your tambourines." The verb עדה in the lexica is identified as qal in all its occurrences and defined as "adorn oneself with," with the accusative of the ornament. But in Ezek 16:11 the text reads וָאֶעְדֵּךְ עֶדִי: the verb here has two accusatives (or a dative suffix and cognate accusative) and must mean "and I adorned you with ornaments." It is thus the suggestion of BDB and Franz Zorell, noted as a possibility by KB (but not by HALAT), that the verb in that passage is hip'il, not qal, and should be vocalized וָאַעְדֵּךְ. If the hip'il exists (or if the qal carries this meaning) then I propose that this is the form of the verb here (and the vocalization for a hip'il here will be identical to the qal): the colon will thus mean "again you shall adorn your timbrels"—Israel, personified as a woman, is told the time has come to redecorate her timbrels to prepare to dance once more. The OT indicates that the timbrel was (primarily, if not exclusively) a woman's instrument, so that decorations on such an instrument are altogether likely; Ezek 28:13 seems to describe ornamental timbrels, but unfortunately the text is obscure. The timbrel was associated with dancing (beyond the present passage, see Exod 15:20; Judg 11:34; 1 Sam 18:6; Ps 149:3); it was "beaten" (compare the verb in 1 Sam 21:14 G), and the G translation τύμπανον suggests then a small hand-drum or a membrane stretched on a frame (German Rahmentrommel), whether or not there were metal jingles attached (our tambourine) to increase the tone. Many representations of such timbrels have survived.[77] By the present proposal there is therefore no necessity to posit a derived meaning for the noun in question, "bangles" or "jingles."[78]

"Dance" (מָחוֹל) is related to the verb "whirl" (חוּל, 23:19). The same noun is found in Ps 149:3, and the equivalent noun מְחֹלָה is found in Judg 11:34 and 1 Sam 18:6.[79] The presence here of "go forth" and "merrymakers" suggests a close association with the diction of

75   GKC, sec. 117x.

76   For this analysis see Dahood, *Psalms I*, 223, against André Feuillet, "Note sur la traduction de Jér. xxxi 3c," *VT* 12 (1962) 122–24.

77   See the bas-relief at Zinjirli in *ANEP*, 63, fig. 199, or in Hans Peter Rüger, "Musikinstrumente," *Biblisches Reallexikon* (ed. Kurt Galling; HAT, Erste Reihe, 1; Tübingen: Mohr [Siebeck], 1977) 235–36, and the

carving on a tomb wall in Sakkarah, Egypt, in *ANEP*, 66, fig. 211; for discussion see the article of Rüger already cited, which offers citations to further illustrations, and Eric Werner, "Musical instruments," *IDB* 3:474.

78   The suggestion is made in Herbert G. May, "Ezekiel, Exegesis," *IB* 6:220; compare the translation of the present passage in *NEB*, already cited.

30:19, a passage with cultic overtones (see there), and those cultic concerns will be reinforced in the present passage by v 6 (Ps 149:3 is another appropriate parallel). But two other sets of associations lie close at hand. The first is the traditional celebration by women of the victory of their warriors (so Exod 15:20; Judg 11:34; 1 Sam 18:6): here "maiden Israel" will celebrate victories once more. The second is the exodus from Egypt itself (once more Exod 15:20): if Yahweh could bring Israel out of Egypt, then he will do a similar action for his people once more: this association is prepared for by the exodus imagery in vv 2–3a. This nuance is particularly apposite for the recension to the south, whose audience would be the exiles of Judah sent to Babylon (compare the use of exodus imagery by Deutero-Isaiah, Isa 51:9–11 and often); but it is not inappropriate for the recension to the north, whose hearers would be those who had suffered under Assyrian oppression.

"Build" and "plant" are the two positive verbs of Jrm's call (1:10; compare 18:9; 24:6; 29:5, 28). Planting vineyards, like building houses, is an occupation that presumes a stable future under the blessing of Yahweh (Deut 20:5–6; Isa 65:21–22; compare Deut 28:30; Amos 5:11). The "mountain(s) of Samaria" are mentioned otherwise only in Amos 3:9; 4:1; 6:1—the plural in 3:9 and the singular in the other two passages. But G has the singular in all three of these passages, probably correctly;[80] the phrase here is thus striking, parallel to "mount Ephraim" in v 6 (and "Horeb" in v 2, if that revocalization is correct). Samaria is on a hill (1 Kgs 16:24) but is surrounded by four higher hills.[81] Hills, less appropriate for cereal crops, were ideal for vines (Isa 5:1; Amos 9:13). By this promise the whole hilly region will be replanted with vines.

The last three words of v 5 in *M* are a textual puzzle: they read "planters (shall) have planted and enjoyed" (נָטְעוּ נֹטְעִים וְחִלֵּלוּ). The Versions differ rather widely. *G* reflects two words, "plant and praise" (plural imperatives). *V* paraphrases, "the planters shall plant and until the time comes they shall not gather (the vintage)." Both *S* and *T* read three words and construe the verbs as imperatives: *S*, "plant a planting and sing" (feminine singular imperatives); *T*, "plant, you planters, and enjoy."

Duhm, convinced of the necessity of finding qinah meter, saw the colon as what was left of a bicolon, and found the verb for the second colon in *G*: "the planters shall plant and enjoy, and praise Yahweh" (וְהִלְלוּ אֶת־יהוה), and Giesebrecht followed him in this. More recently commentators have omitted the three words as a gloss paraphrasing Deut 28:30 (so Cornill, Volz, Rudolph; so also Lohfink).[82]

As to the text and the Versions, *M* and *T* have read the last word as חלל pi'el "profane" in the special sense of "put to common use"; by this understanding the words refer to Deut 28:30. *G* and *S* have read the last word as הלל pi'el "praise," and the occurrence of that root in Judg 9:27 in the context of gathering the vintage suggests that it is a plausible reading. There is uncertainty whether the verbs are to be construed as perfect (*M, V*) or imperative (*G, S, T*) and whether the second word is to be vocalized as "planters" (נֹטְעִים: *M, V, T*) or "planting" (נֹטְעִים? or singular נֶטַע: *S*). The vocative assumed for "planters" in *T* is forced, and the feminine singular imperatives assumed in *S* are doubtless a secondary accommodation to the second singular feminine address in the rest of vv 4–5.

A tricolon is likely (compare 30:15b, 20, 21a); one does not need the speculation of Duhm's two bicola to see a place for the words. On the other hand, the hypothesis that the words are a gloss is an attractive one, given the connection with Deut 28:30. It is the resemblance of וחללו (whatever the vocalization) to בְּמָחוֹל in v 4 that suggests that a genuine poetic line lies here. But three occurrences of the root נטע are too many: the evidence in *G* of two words in the colon is persuasive. Now "build" and "plant" are correlatives (see above), so that if "build" appears in v 4 in the qal (active) and in the nip'al (passive), then the verb "plant" here in the qal may be followed by the nip'al: נָטְעוּ may be revocalized נִטְּעוּ "they [the vineyards] are planted." This suggests in turn that וְחִלֵּלוּ (pi'el, active) should be revocalized to וְחֻלְּלוּ or וְחֻלְּלוּ (pu'al, passive). Then when the passives were revocalized as active verbs, a plural subject became

---

79   For Egyptian depictions of dancers see *ANEP*, 65–66, figs. 208–211, and see the discussion in G. Henton Davies, "Dancing," *IDB* 1:760–61, with bibliography.

80   Wolff, *Joel and Amos*, 190.
81   Ibid.
82   Lohfink, "Der junge Jeremia," 354, n. 17.

necessary, and "planters" (נֹטְעִים) was supplied, perhaps influenced by "watchmen" (נֹצְרִים) in the first colon of v 6. (Luther shows a fine instinct in offering an indefinite subject: *Du sollst wiederum Weinberge pflanzen an den Bergen Samarias; pflanzen wird man sie und ihre Früchte geniessen.*) So understood, the phrase reverses the curse enunciated in Deut 28:30 and Amos 5:11.

■ **31:6** The general thrust of this verse is clear, but comment is necessary on the "watchmen" (נֹצְרִים). The word occurs in 4:16, and the present study suggests that in that passage the word carries a double meaning, both "watchmen" and "shouters" (see there). This double meaning is appropriate here also: "watchmen" guard a vineyard (Isa 27:3), yet the context here is one of cultic shouting ("merrymakers," v 4; "will call," v 6).[83]

"There is a day": this word is in balance with "long ago" in the first colon of the strophe (v 3a). "Have called": the perfect appears to reflect the perfects in the last colon of v 5 (see above). Current translations favor "there shall be a day when watchmen will call" (*RSV*), but the particle of existence יֵשׁ and the perfect verb that follows suggest that the future event is an accomplished certainty (the prophetic perfect).[84] For "Mount Ephraim" see 4:15; here it is simply a poetic parallel to "mountains of Samaria" in v 5. The last two cola embody a pilgrim cry (see Form): compare the ironic use of "arise, let us go up [to Jerusalem]" by the enemy besieging the city (6:4–5).

In the recension to the north vv 2–6 are completed by v 9b (see there, and see Preliminary Observations).

■ **31:7–9a** The parallel of "sing" (רנן) and "shout" (צהל) is found in the Isaianic tradition beginning with Deutero-Isaiah (Isa 54:1; later 12:6; 24:14) but is not otherwise cited in earlier material. Jrm used צהל for "neigh" in 5:8 and 13:27, so it is conceivable that he stimulated the association of the two verbs and that Deutero-Isaiah adopted it from him. The use of צהל for "neigh" suggests a wider reach than "shout" for that verb; and רנן is used not only of joy (often) but once of distress (Lam 2:19), so that "sing" may suggest too disciplined a sound: KB suggests "cry shrilly, yell" (*gellen*) for the basic meaning. Different cultures stylize their expressions of emotion differently.

The parallel for "Jacob" here is "the chief of the nations" (רֹאשׁ הַגּוֹיִם); this is the only instance of רֹאשׁ in this meaning in the OT, but it is reminiscent of the phrase רֵאשִׁית הַגּוֹיִם in Amos 6:1 for the leadership in Samaria (and Zion, if that reference is not a gloss). That reference in Amos is ironic, a contemptuous description of the complacent ruling class, but here there is no trace of irony, except for the larger historical irony that the "fewest of all peoples" (Deut 7:7) should become the chief of the nations in Yahweh's great action to come. And is there assonance between "chief" (רֹאשׁ) and "remnant" (שְׁאֵרִית)?

The tumble of imperatives here is reminiscent of 4:5; breathlessly the hearers are to shout the news of Yahweh's deliverance of his people. (The form of text in *M*, petition rather than affirmation—"O Yahweh, save your people!"—is understandable, given the pressures of the postexilic period, but surely wrong.)

For the parallel "land of the north" and "ends of the earth" see 6:22: there those regions were the home of the foe, but now they are the places from which the exiles will return. The listing of "the blind and the lame, those pregnant and those in labor together" is a reversal of the listing in 6:21 (on this see Preliminary Observations): here are those who are handicapped, who hinder the easy migration of people. It is the only occurrence of "blind" (עִוֵּר) and "lame" (פִּסֵּחַ) in the book. To current perceptions "blind" and "deaf" are appropriate parallels, and one finds this in the OT (Lev 19:14), but the present parallel is found as well (Job 29:15). The point, of course, is that such people must be helped to walk and cannot fight (1 Sam 5:6, 8). In the later Isaiah tradition there is a fourfold parallelism of "blind," "deaf," "lame," and "dumb" (Isa 35:5–6), which interweaves the pairs. The words "pregnant" and "in labor" are often associated (Isa 7:14) but not elsewhere as parallels (Mark 13:17 and parallels have "those pregnant" and "those nursing"). A "great company" (קָהָל גָּדוֹל) may be a congregation for worship (1 Kgs 8:65) or an army coming for battle (Ezek 38:15): but this "great company," typified by the handicapped and women hindered by pregnancy and childbirth, is not fit to fight or bring terror to the world (compare the "great nation" [גּוֹי גָּדוֹל] that is the enemy

83   On this suggestion see Lohfink, "Der junge Jeremia," 356, n. 22, with bibliography.
84   GKC, sec. 106n.

from the north in 6:22). It is they whom Yahweh will bring home.

Most commentators revocalize הֵנָּה ("hither") at the end of v 8 to הִנֵּה (literally "behold!") and place it at the beginning of v 9; but this is an unnecessary correction—הֵנָּה occurs in a similar context in 50:5.

Verse 9 in *M* opens with "with weeping they shall come, and with supplications I shall lead them": "weeping" and "supplications" are found in 3:21. As both Jerome and Qimḥi note in their commentaries, this "weeping" is joyous; Qimḥi cites Gen 29:11 as a parallel. But "supplications" is hardly right, and *G*, which reads "consolations," is surely correct (the word appears also in 16:7).

"Brooks of water" (נַחֲלֵי מַיִם) is found only otherwise in Deut 8:7 and 10:7: the latter passage is in the midst of a specific geographical notice, but the former introduces a glowing idealistic description of Canaan;[85] one must assume therefore that Jrm intended the phrase here to be shorthand for the lovely land to which they would return. The "straight path" (דֶּרֶךְ יָשָׁר) is surely reminiscent of the "straight path" (דֶּרֶךְ יְשָׁרָה) in Ps 107:7 by which Yahweh led his people, till they reached a city to dwell in, a description of the exodus: the first seven verses of that psalm match the mood of the present passage, so that one must conclude that Jrm has combined phrasing from both Deuteronomy and Psalm 107 to set forth the new exodus. For "stumble" see 6:21.

■ **31:9b** In the first recension these two cola form the conclusion to vv 2–6 (see Preliminary Observations). They are a striking variation of the covenant formula, reinforcing v 1 (see Form) and preparing for vv 18–20, especially v 20. The immediate stimulus for the image of "father/son" here is doubtless Deuteronomy 32; given the resemblance of "found (him) in the wilderness" in v 2 to Deut 32:10, it is appropriate that "father" here is reminiscent of Deut 32:6b, in which Israel is addressed: "Is not he your father, your creator?" Israel is called Yahweh's "first-born" (בְּכוֹר) in Exod 4:22, and Israel/Ephraim is called Yahweh's "son" in Hos 11:1–3. In the present context what is the nuance of "first-born"? Hos 11:1–3 and Exod 4:22 are open to the possibility that Israel is Yahweh's only son. On the other hand Deut

32:6–9 suggests that Israel is preeminent among the nations (compare Jer 31:7), so that that understanding is primary for the recension of the present material for the south, and perhaps for the recension for the north as well. But the text of *G* for 2 Sam 19:44, followed by most commentators and translations, suggests that there were those among the northern tribes who could call themselves "first-born" over against Judah (so explicitly 1 Chr 5:1–2, and compare Ezek 16:46; 23:4), and this nuance would be appropriate to the passage in the recension to the north.

■ **31:10–11** For "coastlands" see 2:10; the unmodified term is used often in Deutero- and Trito-Isaiah for the far nations of the earth: for the association of the word with the root "far" see Isa 49:1.

The verb "scatter" (זרה pi'el) is a favorite in the Book of Ezekiel for Yahweh's scattering of the people, and it is found also in Lev 26:33, part of the end of that book evidently added in the context of the exile.[86] For "gather" (קבץ pi'el) see 23:3; indeed the last colon of v 10 shares diction with 23:1–4.

For the parallelism of "ransom" (פדה) and "redeem" (גאל) see Preliminary Observations: the phraseology here is reminiscent of Isa 51:10–11. These verbs play an important role in OT theology.[87] And the phrase "from the hand of one stronger than he" is reminiscent of Ps 35:10, "Yahweh . . . who rescues the weak from one stronger than he."

■ **31:12–13** For "sing" (רנן) see v 7. Its parallel here, "be radiant" (נהר II), does not otherwise occur in Jer, but it is used in Isa 60:5 of Jerusalem in a context very much like the present one. "Height" (מָרוֹם) refers to heaven in 17:12 and 25:30; here it is used of Zion. The parallel "bounty of Yahweh" is at first sight puzzling; it occurs elsewhere in the book of the bounty of agricultural produce (2:7) and carries that implication in v 14. How does it function as a parallel to Zion? In Ps 128:5 "bounty of Jerusalem" is parallel to Zion: clearly then one has here to do with the ideology of Zion, by which the prosperity of Jerusalem is tied in to the glory of the temple on Zion; and the metaphorical semantic field of v

---

85   Compare Weinfeld, *Deuteronomy*, 172.

86   Noth, *Leviticus*, 199–200.

87   Robert C. Dentan, "Redeem, redeemer, redemp-
tion," *IDB* 4:22, with bibliography; Elliger, *Deutero-jesaja*, 150, with bibliography.

12b, that the inhabitants of the city and the land shall be prosperous and joyful, points in the same direction. But a glossator wished to press "bounty" into a more concrete form of specific agricultural produce: the triad "grain, wine and oil" is exactly the sequence of Hos 2:10, and "flock" and "herd" are a conventional parallel (5:17; and, in a gloss, 3:24). The simile "watered garden" (גַּן רָוֶה) is found in a similar context in Isa 58:11. In Deutero-Isaiah the wilderness of the homeland would be turned into the garden of Yahweh (Isa 51:3), but in this postexilic material such images shift easily into the prosperity of individuals: here it is the נֶפֶשׁ of returning Israel, their "life" as spirit and appetite, which will be like a watered garden, so that they will never "languish" again—the verb (דאב) means "become faint (from hunger)": compare v 25.

"Virgin" occurs in the book in listings only otherwise in 51:22; elsewhere it occurs in a simile (2:32) or in personifications like "virgin Israel" (vv 4, 21). The parallel in 51:22, "young man" (בָּחוּר) occurs also here (and in Deut 32:25 and elsewhere), and the parallelism between "young men" and "elders" is common (Lam 5:14; Joel 3:1). For "dance" see v 4; for "rejoice" (שמח) see 20:15. The restored verb "be merry" (חדד) does not otherwise occur in Jer but does in Exod 18:9.

The word "gladness" in the third colon (שָׂשׂוֹן) is often a correlative of the noun שִׂמְחָה (for example, 15:16), the related verb of which is found in the first colon ("rejoice") and (in the causative stem) in the last colon ("give them joy"); in this way the verse is strongly united within itself. For "mourning" (אֵבֶל) see 6:26; for "sorrow" (יָגוֹן) see 8:18. Yahweh will transform despair into joy.

■ **31:14** Translations have not in general caught the concrete imagery of this bicolon, which is difficult to translate concisely: *RSV* has "I will feast the soul of the priests with abundance, and my people shall be satisfied with my goodness"; *NJV* has "I will give the priests their fill of fatness, and My people shall enjoy My full bounty." Beyond the obvious pairing of "the priests" and "my people," the operative parallel here is that between the assuaging of thirst and the assuaging of hunger. The verb רוה pi'el means "drench, water abundantly"—

compare the "watered" (רָוֶה) garden in v 12; שבע means "eat one's fill" (compare the hip'il stem in 5:7). But the נֶפֶשׁ ("appetite, craving," compare again v 12) of the priests is to be drenched this time not with water but with "fatness" (דָּשֶׁן), a term that may be used either of olive oil (Judg 9:9) or of animal fat (the word is used of the fatty ashes of animal offerings, Lev 4:12), and fatness occurs associated with "eat one's fill" (שבע, Ps 63:6), so that to be "drenched with fatness" is a rich blessing indeed (the same association is found in Ps 36:9). A parallelism similar to "fatness" and "bounty" (טוב) occurs in Ps 65:12, where the second noun is טוֹבָה. It is a verse that comes out of a context of poverty and hunger.

■ **31:15** The interpretation of the first colon is disputed, and there are interlocking uncertainties. (1) Is there a reference to "Ramah" in the colon, or is the noun simply a common noun, "height"? (2) If "Ramah," is this a reference to Rachel's tomb? (3) If this is a reference to Rachel's tomb, how is the passage to be squared with references elsewhere to Rachel's tomb other than at Ramah?

The traditional translation is "A voice in Ramah is heard . . . Rachel bewailing her children." By this understanding Rachel is haunting her tomb in Ramah, weeping for her lost children; the tomb in question is thus placed in Ramah of Benjamin (Josh 18:25; 1 Kgs 15:17, 21–22), the present-day *er-rām* (Atlas of Israel grid 172–140) nine kilometers north of Jerusalem (compare Josephus *Ant.* 8.12.3). Lohfink suggests, in fact, that the pilgrims from Ephraim on their way to Jerusalem (v 6) come through Ramah and hear Rachel weeping.[88]

But there are difficulties. Except in the present passage (if so understood) and Neh 11:33, the village of Ramah always carries the definite article: the vocalization here then should be בָּרָמָה rather than בְּרָמָה—not an insuperable difficulty, of course, but worth noting (Rudolph revocalizes the noun). *G* and *S* translate with the place name, "Ramah," but *V* and *T* translate with "height." It is noteworthy that Matt 2:17–18 follows *G*, so that Jerome perforce uses *in Rama* in Matt 2:18 but *in excelso* in Jer 31:15, and he discusses the question at length in his commentary: he insists that Rachel's tomb is near Bethlehem (see below). It may also be stated negatively

---

88   Lohfink, "Der junge Jeremia," 361–62.

that there is no passage in the OT (beyond the disputed present one) in which Rachel's tomb is said to be "in Ramah": the tradition in 1 Sam 10:2 is simply that her tomb is in Benjamin. The Genesis tradition (Gen 35:19–20; compare 48:7) offers its own share of difficulties: Rachel is said to be buried "on the way to Ephrath(ah)," and both passages add the gloss "that is, Bethlehem" (most commentators attribute 35:19–20 to E, but Claus Westermann assigns it to J; 48:7 is evidently a supplementary verse not attributable to any of the primary sources).[89] It is generally agreed that the gloss is misguided,[90] but at the same time it is also not certain where the location of Ephrath(ah) is to be placed: Ps 132:6 parallels it with "the fields of Jaar," which may well be Kiriath-jearim (so most). Matitiahu Tsevat in a recent study concludes that Rachel's tomb is to be located in the vicinity of Kiriath-jearim.[91] The data are substantial enough to bring the traditional understanding of the present colon into grave question.

There are two other considerations in clarifying the present passage, both mentioned by Tsevat. (1) There is in the passage no wording that implies a tomb; Rachel need not be conceived as weeping at her grave. (2) There is a close parallel between this passage and 3:21: there the expression equivalent to בְּרָמָה is עַל־שְׁפָיִם, here translated "on the caravan-tracks." The parallel does not insist that the word here be a common noun but at least suggests it. On balance the translation "on the height" is indicated.

For "height" (רָמָה) see 1 Sam 22:6. Rachel's bewailing her childlessness on the height is reminiscent of Jephthah's daughter bewailing her virginity on the mountains (Judg 11:37–38); and compare further 9:9 and 22:20. For "may be heard" see 3:21. For "lamenting" (נְהִי) see 9:9. For "bitter" (here the abstract noun תַּמְרוּרִים) see 6:26; the noun here is linked by word-play to its homonym "guideposts" in v 21.

Though according to the Genesis accounts Rachel is the mother of Joseph (and thus the grandmother of Ephraim and Manasseh) and of Benjamin (Gen 30:23–24; 35:16–18; 41:51–52), at issue here is Ephraim (vv 18, 20), the tribe that exemplifies the northern kingdom (v 16). These are her children for whom she is weeping,

at least in the setting of the recension to the north. But in the recension to the south Benjamin may also be in the mind of the prophet (compare 6:1).

Something is wrong with the text at the end of the verse. In spite of Volz's judgment that the end of the verse displays Jrm's great art, כִּי אֵינֶנּוּ cannot stand alone as a colon;[92] one notes further that the only other instance in Jrm's poetry in which כִּי plus a single word ends a colon is 4:13, where the full colon is אוֹי לָנוּ כִּי שֻׁדָּדְנוּ. The repetition of "for her children" (עַל־בָּנֶיהָ) is also suspect (one notes that both G and S omit one occurrence of the phrase), and one expects "she refuses to be consoled" to be the full colon (compare other cola where "refuse" is completed by an infinitive—3:3; 5:3; 8:5; 15:18).

Both these considerations point toward the possibility that the second occurrence of "for her children" embodies the remains of a lost first part of the last colon of the verse. Since other passages in Jrm's poetry that mention "a voice" (קוֹל), lamentation, or the like, embody a quotation (3:21–23; 4:8, 20–21, 31, and others), one expects a quotation in the last colon.[93] If this is the case, then there is the possibility that just before כִּי stood בָּנַי "my children." The he, now the suffix on בָּנֶיהָ, may be construed as the interrogative הֲ with כִּי: an exact parallel may be found in 2 Sam 9:1, "Is there still anyone left of the house of Saul?" (הֲכִי יֶשׁ־עוֹד אֲשֶׁר נוֹתַר לְבֵית שָׁאוּל). The עַל preceding may either be a secondary effort to patch up a misunderstood text or, more likely, the remains of עֻלַי "my sucklings" (Isa 49:15; 65:20): the spelling עלי might have been misunderstood as the archaic spelling of עַל. Indeed Isa 49:15 might well be considered a variation on the present text. So understood, the two cola become even more a poignant expression of desolation; Volz remarks, "The whole pain felt by the prophet because of the fraternal tribes which had been carried off and because of the land which had been devastated

---

89 For Gen 35:19–20 see Westermann, *Genesis II*, 675; for Gen 48:7 see Westermann, *Genesis III*, 208–9.

90 Westermann, *Genesis II*, 668, 676.

91 Matitiahu Tsevat, "Rachel's tomb," *IDBSup*, 724–25.

92 O'Connor, *Structure*, 75.

93 So also Trible, *Rhetoric*, 40.

is embodied for him in the image of the lamenting matriarch."[94]

For further evidence (though indirect) that the analysis in two cola of Rachel's lament is correct, see the analysis of vv 15–17 in Preliminary Observations.

There is uneasiness whether the singular suffix on אֵינֶנּוּ is correct: there is a similar expression in Gen 31:2, 5, where the M אֵינֶנּוּ is replaced by אֵינָם in the Samaritan text, and some commentators emend the text here (Condamin, and recently Raphael Weiss[95]); אֵינָם appears in a similar context in 10:20. On the other hand כֻּלּוֹ or כֻּלֹּה appears for "each one" in 6:13 and 15:10, where one might expect כֻּלָּם; it is better therefore to retain the text.[96]

■ **31:16–17** The two poetic cola of v 16a exactly match the pattern of 2:25a. Here Yahweh reassures Rachel: for similar phraseology see Ps 116:8.

As they stand, vv 16b–17 are closely parallel. The general message is clear: Rachel's children will return to their own borders from the land of the enemy. But either the specific nuance of some of the words needs explication or the text is in disarray, because there is no subject expressed for "shall return" (וְשָׁבוּ) in v 16 to match the subject "(your) children" with the repetition of that verb in v 17. "Future" (אַחֲרִית, v 17) implies "posterity" in Ps 109:13, and probably in Ps 37:37, 38 as well (though Dahood argues strongly for the meaning "future life" in these passages).[97] If this is the nuance here, the parallelism argues strongly that פְּעֻלָּה in v 16, translated here "effort," would likewise imply "children" or "posterity," and indeed that noun in Isa 40:10 (*RSV*: "his recompense is before him") implies "his people."[98] Such an implication for the noun would supply the missing subject for "shall return." But all this is rather remote: in Isa 40:10 the "reward" and "recompense" of Yahweh is his effort and the reward of that effort is winning his people back from the enemy; but here Rachel has not won her children back by her own effort—her "effort" is her work of rearing her children (so Rudolph). The textual

solution of Volz therefore commends itself: to shift the last colon of v 16 to a position at the end of v 17. It is to be noted that an expression with "to" (לְ) may precede one with "from" (מִן): see 3:23a. The solution is to be preferred to one that excises phrases as glosses (Cornill and Giesebrecht, differently), though G is shorter in v 17. One could imagine the colon falling out by haplography of וְשָׁבוּ and then being replaced at the wrong spot.

The repetition of "there is" (יֵשׁ) is the positive contradiction of the negative "is there not?" (אֵין־) in v 15. The use of "reward" (שָׂכָר) already implies the existence of children: doubtless behind the present verse lies the psalmist's verse, "Lo, sons are a heritage from Yahweh, the fruit of the womb a reward" (Ps 127:3). For "effort" see above. "Hope" (תִּקְוָה) appears with "future" (אַחֲרִית) in M of 29:11, but the former word is there either a gloss or evidence of a conflate text.

"Children" must be understood from the second singular suffix on "your effort" and "your future": it is "your children" who return (compare the occurrences in v 15). "Border" of course implies "territory" (so often, thus Deut 19:8), particularly where it is parallel with "land of the enemy."

The question arises of the reference here to "children" returning "to their own border from the land of the enemy": Rudolph says that the reference is neither to the Israelites who remained in the northern kingdom nor to the reincorporation of the northern kingdom into the southern.[99] But surely one cannot press the poetry too literally. If this sequence was part of the recension to the north (see Preliminary Observations), then the reference in that recension is surely to the inhabitants of the erstwhile northern kingdom, whether they were allowed to remain in Samaria or whether they were exiled to the east (2 Kgs 17:6): in either event they were in "the land of the enemy," territory controlled by Assyria. Yahweh will bring the children home, whether it is those exiled to the east, or those in Samaria who will find themselves within the borders of an enlarged southern kingdom by

94 Volz, p. 293: "Der ganze Schmerz, den der Prophet über die weggeführten Bruderstämme und über das verwüstete Land empfand, verkörpert sich ihm in dem Bild der klagenden Ahnfrau."

95 Raphael Weiss, "On Ligatures in the Hebrew Bible (נו=ם)," *JBL* 82 (1963) 191.

96 König, *Syntax*, sec. 348u; GKC, sec. 145m.

97 See the comments in Dahood, *Psalms I* and *III* on the

respective passages.

98 See conveniently Elliger, *Deuterojesaja*, 37.

99 Rudolph, p. 197.

the program of Josiah: it is all the word of Yahweh (compare on 30:20). But obviously the words become even more appropriate in the recension to the south, for those who find themselves exiled in Babylon.

■ **31:18-19** These two verses bring Yahweh's report of Ephraim's repentance and quote Ephraim's word—so much is clear. But there are several questions of detail that render interpretation difficult.

If the first word of v 18 is an infinitive absolute, as it is now vocalized, then the first four words of the verse make up a single colon (so Volz), or even a prose rubric unrelated to the cola that follow; the words cannot be analyzed as two cola of poetry as Rudolph and Bright have it, for verb and object cannot be separated into two cola.[100] And if the infinitive absolute is correct, that the verbal expression must mean something like "I do hear (Ephraim rocking with grief)," the expression would suggest that there has been a previous denial that Ephraim would repent. But the previous denial in the context of the sequence of poetry is rather that Ephraim still exists (v 15). And as for the possibility that the clause is a prose rubric, it is clear that the participle modifying "Ephraim," namely "rocking with grief" (מִתְנוֹדֵד), is hardly the stuff of prose. All these difficulties are obviated if one follows *G*, vocalizing the infinitive absolute as a cognate accusative, שָׁמֵעַ (which appears as a cognate accusative in 50:43), or possibly reading שְׁמוּעָה (which appears as a cognate accusative in 49:14). Now the four words may be construed as two cola, matching the length of the following four cola.

The participle מִתְנוֹדֵד modifying "Ephraim" is evidently intended to carry a double meaning. *G* and *S* translate "lamenting"; *V*, however, translates "wandering"; and *T* paraphrases with both meanings ("The house of Israel is heard and revealed before me, for they weep and lament because they are exiled"). It should be added that Jerome in his commentary also records both meanings. The qal stem of נוד may mean both "wander" (4:1) and "grieve" (15:5). The hitpolel stem, which occurs here, is found in two other passages in the OT—in 48:27, where it denotes a gesture of mockery or disdain (*RSV*: "wagged your head"); and in Isa 24:20, where it denotes the motion of an earthquake (*RSV*:

"sways"). The use of this stem suggests motion to and fro (compare the hitpa'el of הלך). Thus "wander to and fro" is appropriate for the fate of Ephraim in captivity; and the use of "return" (שׁוב), understood in a spatial sense (v 18b), and the use of "captivity" (v 19, if that reconstruction is correct) encourage that meaning. But the meaning of the verb in 48:27 and Isa 24:20 suggests that what is denoted here is a stylized oscillation of the head or body in grief or dismay. But this motion is inaudible!—so such motion of the one grieving must have involved moaning or sobbing as well. And words!—a quotation follows.

The third and fifth cola of the verse each consist of a pair of verbs in related stems, the first of each pair being a second-person singular transitive verb with first-person singular object ("you" [Yahweh] do something to "me"), the second being a correlative first-person singular intransitive verb ("I" undergo the action), but the relation between the transitive verbs and the correlative intransitive ones is not identical, for the first pair is a perfect verb followed by a waw-consecutive imperfect, thus consecutive narration, while the second pair is an imperative followed by a cohortative, presumably simultaneous actions. The pairings of the related stems invite the hearer to ponder the relationship of meaning between those related stems, pi'el and nip'al in the first pair, hip'il and qal in the second, and in particular to ponder the relationship between Yahweh's initiative with Ephraim and Ephraim's initiative, a matter not easy to state with precision.

The verb in the third colon (יסר) is found in the pi'el in 2:19 and in the nip'al in 6:8; for the range of meanings see 2:19. The best meaning here is "punish," though it must be understood that the punishment is with a view to correction (note the fourth colon, "like a calf untrained"). But simply to repeat the verb in the passive voice (*RSV*: "thou hast chastened me, and I was chastened") is not enough (see above). The nip'al is reflexive as well as passive, and in particular the agent of a passive action is rarely expressed,[101] a circumstance suggesting that the subject of a nip'al verb has more initiative than a passive translation would imply;[102] thus the translation suggested here, "you punished me, and I took the

---

100 O'Connor, *Structure*, passim, notably 67–78.
101 Compare GKC, sec. 121f.
102 See ibid., 51c.

punishment" (so *JB*: "you have disciplined me, I accepted the discipline"). (Rudolph compares 17:14a, but those expressions, while linking active and "passive" expressions, are not wholly comparable, since they are imperatives rather than narrative past: the verbs in the fifth colon of the present verse are of course imperatives, but they are causative and simple correlates, not active and "passive" ones.)

"Like a calf untrained" is a phrase based on two in Hosea. That prophet had said that originally Ephraim was a "trained heifer" (וְאֶפְרַיִם עֶגְלָה מְלֻמָּדָה, Hos 10:11), but that "like a stubborn cow, Israel is stubborn" (כְּפָרָה סֹרֵרָה סָרַר יִשְׂרָאֵל, Hos 4:16), where "cow" (פָּרָה) is a word-play on "Ephraim" (אֶפְרַיִם). Now Jrm moves out from Hos 10:11 in a different direction: the sex of the animal is changed and the verb negated: Ephraim is "like a calf untrained" (כְּעֵגֶל לֹא לֻמָּד). The verb לֻמָּד is normally construed as a pu'al perfect, the predicate of a relative clause without אֲשֶׁר (so BDB), but given the parallel with Hos 10:11, it is more likely to be a participle without mem:[103] it is noteworthy that *G* presumes a perfect verb, while *V*, *S*, and *T* presume a participle. The assumption of the image is that the calf is "trained" for the yoke (so *T* explicitly here); for a parallel rejection of the yoke see 2:20.

That the hip'il and the qal of "return" (שׁוב) are not to be considered identical actions is indicated not only by the considerations already discussed, but more particularly by the diction of 15:19a (see there). Given the context of "return" in v 17 and the implication of restored relationship in v 20, one can only imagine within the ambiguities of this expression what the possibilities are—for example, "bring me back" (from exile), "and let me come back" (in loyalty to you).

For "for you are Yahweh my God" compare 3:22, "for you are Yahweh our God."

Verse 19a brings several uncertainties of text and meaning. *M* reads, "For after I (re)turned, I was sorry, and after I was known [or recognized], I slapped my thigh." The expressions "I was sorry" and "I slapped my thigh" are understandable: they are parallel phrases indicating repentance. But "after X" and "after Y": what are these? One expects expressions for wrongdoing or

for Yahweh's chastisement of Ephraim.

It is easier to begin with the second expression (הִוָּדְעִי). As it stands, it is a nip'al infinitive of ידע, but the ordinary range of meanings hardly fits ("I was made known, discovered"; conceivably "I was introduced," Ruth 3:3). Generally the expression here is translated "after I was instructed," and in the lexica this meaning is entered, for the nip'al, for this passage only (BDB, *HALAT*). But such a meaning suits the hop'al rather than the nip'al, and the consonantal text is likely to represent a hop'al, though the hop'al infinitive is so rare that one is doubtful about the vocalization (הוּדְעִי or הוֹדְעִי). The rare occurrences of the hop'al of this verb are used only of inanimate subjects (something "is made known"), but this stem of the verb occurs in post-biblical Hebrew in exactly this meaning ("become informed, conscious").[104]

As for the first expression, traditional translations have gone a variety of ways. *KJV* assumes another hop'al in intention ("surely after that I was turned . . ."), and *V* paraphrases in the same direction ("for after you brought me back," *postquam enim convertisti me*). *RSV* takes the meaning "turned away" ("for after I had turned away I repented"), and *JB* is similar; but this shift of meaning is unlikely, given the context. Other recent translations are frankly periphrastic. *G* is probably the clue, reading שִׁבְיִ for שׁוּבִי, "after my captivity," given the context of vv 16–17 and the implication of "you punished me" in v 18 (Rudolph accepts this reading). The noun appears in the recension to the south (30:10, 16).

But there is a further problem, for which Rudolph has also supplied a solution. The cola in this sequence are all short (two or three words), and the structure suggests a missing word for a full second colon. Rudolph has suggested that שַׁבְתִּי has fallen out by haplography before נִחַמְתִּי: "For after my captivity I was sorry once more."[105] Though Rudolph does not cite it, indirect reinforcement of the suggestion comes from 18:4–10. There in v 4 וְשָׁב denotes "again" before a coordinate verb, and in vv 8 and 10 there וְנִחַמְתִּי occurs; in v 4 the subject is the potter (who represents Yahweh), and in vv 8 and 10 the subject is Yahweh. The diction of that sequence is similar to the diction here and at least suggests the plausibility of Rudolph's restoration.

103 Compare ibid., 52s: for both alternatives see *HALAT*.
104 See Marcus Jastrow, *A Dictionary of the Targumim, The Talmud Babli and Yershalmi, and the Midrashic Literature* (New York: Putnam, 1903) 565a.
105 For the idiom see GKC, sec. 120g.

The two terms with "after" then expand on "you punished me" in v 18.

For "be sorry" (נחם nip'al) with Israel as subject compare 8:6. The phrase "slap one's thigh," an expression of remorse or sorrow, is found also in Ezek 21:17, and Rudolph adds two citations from Homer.[106]

The verb "be humiliated" (כלם nip'al) may mean "blush" (see the discussion on 3:3); in any event the diction here suggests that it is a more intense or profound state that "be ashamed" (thus "even," גַּם); for this particle with these verbs compare 2:36 and 6:15. (One notes Calvin's comment: "The particle shews that the Prophet enhances the greatness of the sorrow and shame when he says, *I was ashamed and even confounded.*")

For "bear disgrace" see 15:15. The phrase "disgrace of one's youth" is found in the context of forgiveness in Isa 54:4.

■ **31:20** Now comes Yahweh's reply. Do the parallel questions in the first two cola imply a positive or negative answer? Normally it would take the presence of negatives in such questions to imply a positive answer, but there are several examples of such questions implying a positive answer without a negative (Gen 27:36).[107] Adriaan van Selms comes to another conclusion: he suggests that such questions, when followed by the conjunction כִּי (as here), imply an unreality to the questions, but that they are motivated by the reality of what is expressed in the כִּי clause: by this reading the cola imply, "Is Ephraim my dear son?—of course not, but he could just as well be, given the fact that every time I speak of him. . . ."[108] Of course v 9b has affirmed a father-son relationship, but van Selms still may have a point: the operative words may be "dear" and "endearing."

The adjective "dear" (יַקִּיר) occurs only here in the OT, but cognates appear in 15:19 and 20:5. The noun translated "darling" (שַׁעֲשֻׁעִים) appears only here in Jer; one suspects that the prophet intends a reminiscence of the phrase "pleasant planting" (נְטַע שַׁעֲשֻׁעִים), a description of the men of Judah in Isa 5:7, and perhaps of Dame Wisdom as the "delight of God" (Prov 8:30).

The last four cola need careful scrutiny. The traditional translation has understood the expression with מִדֵּי (usually rendered "as often as") in the third colon as

subordinate to the fourth colon, and the expression עַל־כֵּן as "therefore." There is uncertainty, however, whether the expression דבר pi'el + בְּ here means "speak about" or "speak against," since it can mean either: *V* elects the former, followed by Duhm, Cornill, Volz, Weiser, and Bright; the latter is chosen by Giesebrecht and most recent translations. But Rudolph remarks that "speak about him" is too trite, and "speak against him" is too weak for the judgment that has overtaken Ephraim;[109] he therefore ingeniously emends to הִנָּכְרִי "(as often as) I make myself a stranger (to him)." But the emendation does not commend itself; in 20:8 Jrm follows מִדֵּי with a (finite) form of דבר pi'el, and 48:27 is evidently a secondary reflection of vv 18–20: there מִדֵּי is followed by what is evidently an infinitive of דבר pi'el with suffix (see Text there), followed by בּוֹ, followed by נוד hitpalel (as in v 18 of the present passage). An understanding of the cola must be sought in another direction.

I propose that מִדֵּי governs both the third and fourth cola (reinforced in the fourth colon by עוֹד) and is subordinate to the parallel fifth and sixth cola introduced by עַל־כֵּן, and that one may translate מִדֵּי as "every time" and עַל־כֵּן as "that is when." An almost exact parallel may be found in 1 Sam 1:7: the only difference is the occurrence of כֵּן instead of עַל־כֵּן. That verse, I submit, must be translated: "So he [Elkanah] would do year after year; every time [מִדֵּי] she [Hannah] went up to the house of Yahweh, that was when [כֵּן] she [Peninnah] would provoke her [Hannah]—she [Hannah] would weep and not eat." The word כֵּן frequently is part of temporal expressions: there is the frequent אַחֲרֵי־כֵן "afterward" and the combination עַד־כֵּן "until then" (Neh 2:16). It should also be pointed out that עַל־כֵּן sometimes introduces verb expressions virtually equivalent to what occurs just before עַל־כֵּן (see 5:27; 31:3; Isa 57:10), so that "therefore" or "that is why" is not appropriate, but "that is how" or the like is.

If this analysis is correct, then דבר pi'el + בְּ and זכר are parallel (though זכר may express more intensity than דבר does: see below). There is no reason why the ambiguity in דבר בְּ ("speak against" and "speak about," see above) cannot be Jrm's intention: clearly the context implies Yahweh's judgment (v 19), and זכר "remember" can be

---

106 *Iliad* 16.125, *Odyssey* 13.198.

107 See BDB, 210a, sec. 1c.

108 Adriaan van Selms, "Motivated Interrogative

Sentences in Biblical Hebrew," *Semitics* 2 (1971/72) 148–49.

109 Rudolph, p. 196.

for a person's advantage (see 2:2) or disadvantage (see Deut 25:17). Both verbs therefore may carry ambiguity: Yahweh's attitude toward Ephraim may remain ambivalent in these two cola. Now the verb זכר may mean "mention" (23:36, and see the discussion on 20:9), so the contrast may be between "speaking extensively" and "mentioning in passing," but the contrast between "my very heart trembles" and "show compassion," explored below, suggests that the contrast here is simply that between outward "speaking" and inward "remembering."

What is the nuance of the adverb עוֹד with "remember"? If "remember" parallels "speak of," then it doubtless reinforces "every time"—the translation "again" fits. And what is the nuance of the infinitive absolutes in the fourth and sixth cola? In spite of the fact that the fourth colon is (by the present analysis) part of the protasis and the sixth part of the apodosis, it is clear that they are to be seen together. If the infinitive absolute with a finite verb serves to reverse a previous denial (compare 22:10), the translation "in fact" works here. The verb רחם pi'el, though usually translated "have compassion on," appears in contexts that imply "show compassion on" (30:18, and see further 6:23; Deut 13:18; 30:3); that is, it moves beyond emotion (the import of "my very heart trembles," see below) to action. This progression implies a corresponding progress between דבר בְּ and זכר in the previous two cola, and indeed a progression from outer speaking to inner remembering (see above), so that the reference is chiastic: outer, inner; inner, outer.

The expression הָמוּ מֵעַי is noteworthy. The subject מֵעַי (literally "my bowels") occurs of Jrm's inner turmoil (4:19), and the verb המה occurs in that verse with the subject "my heart." The same double expression is found in Isa 16:11, part of a passage doubtless dependent on Jrm,[110] and in Cant 5:4. In the latter passage the maiden speaks, it would seem, of the sexual advance of her lover;[111] the context then suggests erotic emotion,[112] so that the organs in question are not the bowels but the womb (Gen 25:23).[113] Given this parallel Trible has

proposed that the present passage offers female imagery for God;[114] if that is not explicit here, it is surely implicit, especially given the verb in the last colon, רחם pi'el, whose cognate noun רֶחֶם means "womb" (1:5).

The emotion of Yahweh over Ephraim is then profound and overwhelming: every time he speaks or even thinks of Ephraim he is overpowered by his affection, so that he cannot help showing compassion (רחם) on him.

■ **31:21–22** This last strophe of the recension to the north is a counterfoil to the first one (30:5–7). There the theme was mockery of the male (זָכָר, v 6) for acting like a female in the demoralization of battle. Here the reference is to the female (נְקֵבָה, v 22) who has taken on the role of the male: this is not simply in the controverted last colon of v 22 but throughout the whole of the two verses, as will become clear. The address is feminine singular, to the personified "virgin Israel" (v 21), and the opening feminine singular imperative must have come to the ears of the hearers, without warning, as a thunderclap: "Set up for yourself stone cairns!" (for the meaning of the noun see below). Such a command to a single woman, and to a "virgin" at that, thus normally to be protected and watched over, to make pile after pile of stones, would have been grotesque. (A passing thought: a "virgin of Israel" might well have had a different experience with piles of stones: see Deut 22:13–21!) The matter of a woman doing men's work is stressed here because it is not simply the last colon of v 22 that is startling: the whole passage is startling.

If the last colon of v 22 has attracted much attention, at least its text may be made to yield sense as it stands. But there appears to be something wrong with the text in the last colon of v 21.

The text of the last half-verse is all but universally accepted: "Return, virgin Israel, return to these your cities" (only Giesebrecht of the major commentators in this century has attempted to emend the text: see below). If אֵלֶּה "these" is correct, then an article is missing; the grammars discuss the phenomenon,[115] but many of the

---

110 Wildberger, *Jesaja*, 629.

111 Marvin H. Pope, *Song of Songs* (AB 7C; Garden City, NY: Doubleday, 1977) 517–21.

112 Ibid., 519.

113 See further BDB, 589a, (3).

114 Trible, *Rhetoric*, 44–45; compare "God, nature of," 368a.

115 See König, *Syntax*, sec. 334y; GKC, sec. 126y.

parallels adduced likewise represent dubious texts. It is to be noted that two articles are present in the second colon of v 22. But beyond the missing article is the simple fact that "these" adds nothing to the colon, and that there is no other demonstrative in the vicinity for a parallel (one notes the diction in the refrain of 5:9, 29; 9:8, where two demonstratives are in parallelism). G in the present text read πενθοῦσα, a feminine participle, "bewailing," which reflects (not אֲבֵלָה, as Rudolph assumes in *BHK* and *BHS*, but) the same consonantal text, אלה (for the verb אלה see Joel 1:8); that meaning does not fit the context, but G at least senses the need for a feminine substantive here. Charles François Houbigant (1753) emended to עֹלָה "ascending" (feminine); Giesebrecht emended to אַלְלַי "woe" as an introduction to v 22. These attempts are unsatisfactory but at least betray the awareness of a problem. The other alternative has been to delete the word (Volz), but G is against it. The context leads one to expect a word connoting "joyful" or "triumphant": compare the similar pattern in Isa 51:11a.

There is no emendation that occurs to me that employs the existing consonant sequence, nor the existing consonant sequence with the addition of a single consonant. The only proposal I can make is a bold one, and that is to read בֹּעֲלָה "with mastery," the feminine participle of בעל "be master, enter into marriage." There are several intersecting considerations that point toward this proposal, some fairly substantial and some less substantial; I shall present the more substantial considerations first.

It would fit the proposal I make for the trajectory of the whole passage, by which the female undertakes the male role, not only sexually (the last colon of v 22, for which see below) but also in other ways, as has been anticipated by the remarks on the first colon of v 21. If the metaphor of the verses is of the giddy girl in the wilderness ("dillydally" in Bright's translation of the operative word in the first colon of v 22), then the proposal expresses an effective contrast.

"Virgin" (בְּתוּלַת) Israel is being addressed. Now one must conclude that there was a firm association in the mind of the Israelite between "virgin" (בְּתוּלָה) and "married woman" (בְּעוּלָה): both the assonance and the semantic transition made the association inevitable. One sees it in Isa 62:4 (בְּעוּלָה) and 62:5 (בְּתוּלָה and the verb בעל "marry"), and in Deut 22:22 (בְּעוּלַת) and 22:23

(בְּתוּלָה). Given בְּתוּלַת in the preceding colon, then, I submit that the active participle בֹּעֲלָה (instead of the passive participle בְּעוּלָה) is appropriate.

The only other occurrence of "virgin Israel" in this recension (31:4) likewise hints of sexuality and the sex role appropriate for women in the culture: thus "you shall be built, virgin Israel" is to be compared with the expression of Sarai and Rachel (especially the latter, compare v 15) in allowing a concubine to produce children for her: "I shall be built up from her" (Gen 16:2; 30:3). Then virgin Israel is bidden to take up timbrel and dance, an activity of women to greet the victorious warriors (1 Sam 18:6). A word here defining the sexual role of virgin Israel is therefore appropriate (in this case an innovating role).

Now there are two less substantial but still suggestive considerations. The first is that in similar diction in 3:14 (part of a passage sharing a setting similar to that of the present one, a word to the north) שׁוּבוּ בָנִים שׁוֹבָבִים "return, turnable children" is followed by an occurrence of the verb בעל. There, it is true, it is Yahweh who is the "master," not virgin Israel, but it is at least an indication that this verb is at home in the context.

Finally the same verb בעל occurs once more in v 32, part of the "new covenant" passage (again with Yahweh as subject). If a form of the verb occurs in the present passage, then vv 31–34 may be linked to the present verses by that catchword as well as by the feminine adjective "new" (חֲדָשָׁה, vv 22, 31).

The four cola of v 21 make up two bicola, each of which shows tight parallelism, but the two bicola are closely linked to each other as well.

The words "roadmarkers" (צִיֻּנִים) and "signposts" (תַּמְרוּרִים) are both rare words: the former appears otherwise only in 2 Kgs 23:17 and Ezek 39:15, and the latter is unique here to the OT. Both words function here to close off the cycle of the redaction to the north, תַּמְרוּרִים by echoing its homonym "bitter(ness)" in v 15, and צִיֻּנִים doubtless echoing "Zion" (צִיּוֹן) in v 6, given the fact that "virgin Israel" appears in vv 4 and 21 (see above).

"Roadmarkers" must have set up a set of resonances in the hearer that one can trace only in part. The occurrence in Ezekiel 39 is subsequent to its use here, but one must reckon with its use in 2 Kgs 23:17: there Josiah, after he destroyed the altar at Bethel and burned the bones from tombs there, then asked, "What is this monument?"—מָה הַצִּיּוּן הַלָּז, using a rare word for "this." It was the tomb of the "man of God" who figured in 1 Kings 13. This noun then must have been used by Jrm with the thought in mind of Josiah and his program for political reunion in Jerusalem and cultic reunion on "Zion." (One notes that G did not recognize the word here and simply transliterated it, σιωνιμ, and some MSS. of G read "Zion," σιων.) It is something "built" (Ezek 39:15), which may mark a tomb; the Semitic cognates indicate that it means "stone cairn."

As for "signposts" (תַּמְרוּרִים), Giesebrecht doubted the existence of the word and emended to תָּמֹרִים "columns" (following the hint of G). But there is no reason to doubt the word—it seems to be a *qatlūl* formation[116] related to תָּמָר "palm tree" and תִּימֹרָה "column," so that "signposts" is the appropriate translation.

It has already been affirmed that piling up stone cairns is men's work, but so is erecting signposts; the underlying message is, "Do not be a passive victim—take charge, take responsibility for yourself": one notes "for yourself" (לָךְ) twice. (Compare the contrasting mood of contempt in Yahweh's address to the besieged Jerusalem in 10:17–18.)

The phrase "set one's mind on" (שִׁית לֵב לְ) may mean nothing more than "put one's attention to," but in several passages it connotes more specifically "inspect" (Prov 27:23; Job 7:17). A particularly apt parallel is Ps 48:13–14; the phrase in question occurs there in v 14, but both verses are part of a call to a cultic procession in Jerusalem, and the commands there suggest the systematic task of inspecting the city ("number her towers"). A "highway" (מְסִלָּה) is not simply a road with heavy traffic but is a road that must be "built up" (Isa 62:10; compare 57:14, and negatively Jer 18:15). So even though the colon here might be taken to be little more than "keep in mind the highway" (so *NJV*), the phrase could well imply "inspect the highway," which again is normally taken to be men's work. (Question: Does Ps 84:6, part of a Zion psalm, lie in the background here?—"Blessed are those whose strength is in you, in whose heart are the highways.")

The fourth colon reinforces the third and specifies the road, the one "you went on," and this verb of motion sets the stage for the command "return" in the last two cola (for correlative "go" [הלך] and "return" [שוב] see 3:1; 22:10).

In the repeated command "return" the personified "virgin Israel" is told to come back home. The plural "your cities" is curious, given what one assumes is Jrm's concern for Zion (at least in v 6, and by implication with the word-play on "Zion" in the first colon of v 21). Of course, in the recension to the south the reference is clear, given the repeated reference to Judah's cities (for example, 2:28), but what is the implication in the recension to the north? Even then it is doubtless the cities of Judah: Jerusalem had her "daughter cities" (thus 19:15), and this reference, too, like others, bespeaks Jrm's concern for political reunion between north and south.

For the proposed emendation of the last word in v 21 to "with mastery" see above. If such a startling reading is correct, it is no more surprising than the remainder of the strophe.

For "how long?" in an impatient question see 4:14. The verb חמק hitpaʿel appears only here in the OT (the qal stem occurs in Cant 5:6, but the context there does not help overmuch in clarifying its meaning); the Arabic *ḥamiqa/ḥamuqa* means "be stupid, silly," and the suggestion of motion to and fro which the hitpaʿel stem often has (compare the discussion on נוד hitpolel in v 18) renders the translation of Bright ("how long dillydally?") an inspired one: the context suggests irresolution (Qimḥi).

The adjective descriptive of the "daughter," שׁוֹבֵבָה, also raises questions. The parallel phrase in 49:4 offers no help, since the adjective there appears to be a textual error; the adjective occurs again in Mic 2:4, but there again the text is uncertain. The fact that the phrase בָּנִים שׁוֹבָבִים occurs in 3:14 and 22 in a context and setting close to the present one, and that the masculine singular שׁוֹבָב occurs in Isa 57:17 in a context similar to the present one, suggests that the word here could well be vocalized שׁוֹבֵבָה (so Rudolph), or at least that the meaning here is not significantly different from that of שׁוֹבָב. On the other hand, Jrm may intend here a polel

116 Bauer-Leander, sec. 61sδ.

participle without mem, given the possibility of a pu'al participle without mem in v 18 (see there) and given the assonance with the polel תְּסוֹבֵב in the last colon: BDB suggests this possibility.[117] The traditional translation "apostate," that is, "turning away," cannot be far wrong (see the discussion on 3:14).

This is the only occurrence of "create" (ברא) in Jer, and (assuming the last two cola in v 22 are authentic) one of the handful of occurrences in preexilic OT material.[118] It is therefore an expression that merits close attention. Jrm deals with themes of creation elsewhere (notably in 4:23–26, and in 10:12–13 if that passage is authentic to him). The themes of both "new" and "create" are characteristic of Deutero-Isaiah, though the terms do not appear together in Isaiah 40—55 (note Isa 43:19; 48:7), and the setting of Exod 34:10, where there is a similar motif, is also not far from that of Deutero-Isaiah.[119] The only other occurrence of "new" in Jer (other than "New Gate," 26:10; 36:10) is that of the "new covenant," v 31. Yahweh thus states his innovativeness with "virgin Israel"—it will be a new beginning analogous to that in Genesis 1.

Now the last colon. "A female" (נְקֵבָה) is here a counterpoise to "a male" (זָכָר) in 30:6; in both passages "a hero" (גֶּבֶר) occurs. The verb סבב polel occurs in eleven other passages in the OT: it means either "go around" ("I go around your altar," Ps 26:6) or "make the rounds" (of the city), used of watchmen or the like (Ps 55:11; 59:7 = 15; Cant 3:2), or else "surround, encircle, enfold" (twice of Yahweh surrounding the worshiper, Ps 32:7, 10; once of Yahweh surrounding Jacob like an eagle over its young, Deut 32:10; once of the worshiping people surrounding Yahweh, Ps 7:8; twice of flood waters surrounding the speaker, Jonah 2:4, 6).

The Versions all diverge on the rendering of this colon, beginning with G and the Greek revisions subsequent to it. Roman Catholic exegesis till modern times has been dominated by Jerome's view that the clause refers to the Virgin enfolding Christ in her womb. It

would serve no purpose here to survey various suggestions.[120]

I propose the intersection of two meanings here, one in the forefront and one in the background. The first is sexual: "a female shall encompass a hero" suggests that the female shall be the initiator in sexual relations. This meaning is suggested by the meaning of the verb, especially given the parallel in Deut 32:10 (compare other reminiscences of that poem in Jrm's early oracles, thus 2:31); it is suggested by the parallel in 30:6, where the male is mocked for acting as if he is female; and it is suggested by the implication of the earlier cola of the present strophe, which offers other images in which the female is bidden to take on a male role.[121]

The second is "surround" in the military sense; "return" might well suggest military prowess, and the taunt in 30:6 suggests lack of military prowess. This is Calvin's view and is not unlikely; if the warriors had been taunted as turning into women (30:6), then those "women" will ultimately be victorious.

It is also possible, but less likely, that there is in the verb a connotation of "transform." That nuance is not recorded for the polel stem but is for the pi'el (2 Sam 14:20) and may be implied in the background of the expression מִסָּבִיב in the set phrase "terror on every side."[122]

Jrm here indicates two convictions: first, that the situation is far worse than people could imagine, so that Yahweh must move all the way back to Genesis 1 to make it right; and second, that Yahweh will make it right even so. The reassignment of sexual roles is innovative past all conventional belief, but it is not inconceivable to Yahweh. (One may also add that it is no more inconceivable than the assumption behind the notion of a new covenant, vv 31–34, for which see there.)

■ 31:23 It is difficult to know whether to take this verse in unity with vv 24–25 or to view it as a separate fragment (see Preliminary Observations). The verse in its message

---

117 BDB, 1000a.

118 Compare the treatment of Karl-Heinz Bernhardt, "בָּרָא," *TDOT* 2:245.

119 Brevard S. Childs, *The Book of Exodus, A Critical, Exegetical Commentary* (Philadelphia: Westminster, 1974) 613.

120 See, for example, Condamin, pp. 227–28.

121 For this interpretation see William L. Holladay, "Jer.

xxxi 22b reconsidered: 'The Woman Encompasses the Man,'" *VT* 16 (1966) 236–39; and further Trible, *Rhetoric*, 47–50, and "God, nature of," 368a, and Lohfink, "Der junge Jeremia," 355–56 and n. 41.

122 See Holladay, "Jer 20:1–6," 314.

of shift of speech pattern resembles 16:14–15 = 23:7–8. For "restore their fortunes" see 29:14. The little poem invokes God's blessing on Zion, the "holy hill" (הַר הַקֹּדֶשׁ), a phrase that occurs twenty-three times in the prophets (notably six times in Isaiah 40—66) and Psalms.[123] The parallel phrase "righteous home" (נְוֵה־צֶדֶק) appears only here with this meaning (but the same phrase appears in 50:7 as a designation for Yahweh himself). The noun נָוֶה alone or in another construct phrase (for example, נְוֵה קָדְשׁ, Exod 15:13) is frequently used to designate the land of Canaan or Yahweh's sanctuary within that land (compare 10:25). The translation given here is plausible, but the meaning of both צֶדֶק and קֹדֶשׁ might be somewhat different: one might translate the second colon as "legitimate home"[124] and the third colon as "hill of the sanctuary" (compare Ps 134:2).

■ **31:24–25** "In it" in v 24 refers to "the land" (feminine in Hebrew); "Judah and all its cities" is best taken as a gloss to explain "in it" (see Text) rather than as the subject of "shall dwell" as *RSV* and *NAB* have it: "farmhands and those who journey with flocks" is the true subject of the verb. For "farmhands" (אִכָּרִים) see the discussion in 14:4; in that passage they were described as suffering from the drought. The expression "those who journey with flocks" is unique. If "farmhands" suggests the lowest social group working on the land, does this phrase suggest in parallel fashion the shepherd boys actually out with the flocks of sheep and goats in contrast to those who own the flocks? It is possible; in this case the meaning of the passage seems to be that the humblest folk of all will find a secure living on the land; and this nuance is reinforced by v 25.

For "slake the thirst" in v 25 see v 14. The word "every" (כָּל־) in the second colon appears to do double duty for the first colon as well.[125] This is the only occurrence in Jer of "faint one" (עֲיֵפָה, adjective), but the related verb appears in 4:31 ("ebbs away"). For "weary one" (דָּאֲבָה) see v 12; conceivably this verb should be vocalized as an adjective (דְּאֵבָה: so a suggestion of Rudolph).

■ **31:26** Bright's comment suggests both the difficulty and some of the solutions proposed for this verse: "The verse seems to be a marginal comment, but its meaning is obscure. Some see it as the ejaculation of one who, as it were, awakes refreshed from a beautiful dream; others see the dejection of one who awakes from a beautiful dream to confront the hard realities. Still others (cf. Rudolph, Weiser), translating, 'For this reason (it is said), "I awoke . . . ,"' believe it to be a citation, perhaps of a well-known song. I confess that I am baffled."[126]

Form-critically the verse seems to be a fragment of a vision report (see Form), and the diction is close to that in Zechariah 1—8, notably that in Zech 4:1–2: "The angel . . . waked me like a man that is wakened out of his sleep. And he said to me, 'What do you see?'" (see Preliminary Observations). One may assume then that a visionary who has communicated either vv 23–25 or vv 24–25 thus closes his account, but it is curious that there is no correlative opening to the vision. On the other hand, perhaps "Thus Yahweh of hosts, the God of Israel, has said" (v 23) is sufficient opening.

For "be pleasant" (ערב) compare 6:20, where the verb is in a very different context.

■ **31:27–28** These two verses serve to close the scroll of hope destined for the south that opens with 30:1–3 (see Preliminary Observations, Form: some details of Jrm's style, and comparison with passages elsewhere, are given in those discussions). "House of Israel and house of Judah" suggests the way material directed originally to the north is now adapted for the south: both entities alike will share in the good days to come (compare the same phrase for the sin of both north and south in 11:10). Yahweh promises to sow the metaphorical "seed" (offspring) of both human beings and animals in the land. The phraseology is unparalleled in the OT, but the thought of Yahweh's re-sowing the land must go back to Hos 2:25, where the reference is a word-play on "Jezreel"; the words "I will make for them a covenant on that day with the beasts of the field, the birds of the air, and the creeping things of the ground" (Hos 2:20) must have encouraged Jrm's formulation here. Nebuchadrezzar had jurisdiction over both man and beast (27:5); now a time will come when both will be restored to the land.

Verse 28 plays on words of chapter 1: "watch over" (שקד) is reminiscent of 1:12, and the four original verbs "uproot," "demolish," "build," and "plant" recall 1:10.[127]

123 BDB, 871b.

124 Compare Dahood, *Psalms III*, 117–18.

125 Helmer Ringgren, "The omitting of *kol* in Hebrew parallelism," *VT* 32 (1982) 101.

126 Bright, pp. 282–83.

127 For the expansion of the text with further verbs see

Here is the explicit statement that Yahweh's words of judgment are replaced by words of restoration.

■ **31:29–30** For the evidence that this passage is secondary to Ezekiel 18 see Preliminary Observations. For the announcement of a change in speech form, and for the suggestion that the passage here is intended as a (priestly?) mitigation of the unlimited salvation suggested by vv 31–34 see Form. The old proverb is likewise found in Ezek 18:2.

The meaning of the Hebrew verb describing the state of the children's teeth (קהה qal) is uncertain. (That uncertainty is masked by the traditional English translation "are set on edge": that translation, which is already found in Wyclif in the fourteenth century, is itself of uncertain meaning, as the *Oxford English Dictionary* notes.)[128] G translates by a verb referring to bloody gums, as from scurvy (ἠμωδίασαν), V by "become numb" (*obstipuerunt*). This qal stem of the Hebrew verb appears only here and in Ezek 18:2, and the pi'el stem means "become blunt" (of iron, Eccl 10:10). Is it assumed that the children's teeth decay, or ache, or become numb? In any event, the metaphorical reach of the proverb is clear from v 30: "everyone shall die for his (own) sin," so much so that T paraphrases the proverb itself: "The parents have sinned, and the children are punished."[129]

The passage, and Ezekiel 18, figure largely in discussions of the OT view of individual and corporate responsibility.[130] One may conclude that these passages do not negate the OT sense of corporate responsibility, but they moderate it in the direction of the accountability of the individual for his or her actions before God.

■ **31:31–34** Significant features of the interpretation of this passage have already been given in Preliminary Observations: (1) the passage is authentic to Jrm and offers themes and phrases characteristic of his expression elsewhere; (2) the likeness to Deuteronomic diction, notably in the first half, is deliberate, since the setting proposed is the recitation of the Deuteronomic law during the feast of booths (tabernacles) in the autumn of

587, after the destruction of Jerusalem; and (3) the passage structurally breaks in two, a prose section (vv 31–33aα) and a poetic section (vv 33aβ–34), each chiastic in form—the first section centering on the old covenant, the second on the new.

The passage must have been shocking in Jrm's day and thereafter; after all, the passage implies that Yahweh will draw up a fresh contract without the defects of the old, implying in turn that he could improve on the old one, that he had learned something from the failure of the old (compare the theological implication of "What did your fathers find wrong with me?" 2:5). Is the affirmation of Deutero-Isaiah, "The word of our God will stand for ever" (Isa 40:8), intended as a reassurance against these implications? On the other hand, the idea had been prepared for by Hosea's word about a fresh covenant to be given by Yahweh (Hos 2:20), and it is likewise true that the crisis of the fall of Jerusalem and exile was so severe that the word "new" figures largely in the hopeful words of the prophets of the exile ("Get yourselves a new heart and a new spirit!" Ezek 18:31; compare Ezek 11:19; Ezek 36:26; "behold, the former things have come to pass, and new things I now declare," Isa 42:9).

■ **31:31–33aα** For "house of Israel" and "house of Judah" compare v 27. This passage closely resembles 11:10b, "the house of Israel and the house of Judah have broken my covenant which I made with their fathers"; see there. "The day I brought them out of the land of Egypt" is found in 7:22, and similar expressions are widespread; but "take (them) by the hand" is unique in the OT with the exodus expression.

Verse 32b offers unusual syntax: the half-verse begins with the conjunction אֲשֶׁר, which can only be parallel with אֲשֶׁר in the first half-verse; both subordinate clauses thus modify "the covenant" at the head of the verse, yet the second אֲשֶׁר is reinforced by a resumptive "my covenant" that participates in the contrast expressed by the subject pronouns "they" and "I." That contrast gives a nuance that *RSV* has not caught ("my covenant which

Holladay, "Prototype," 363–64.

128 *The Oxford English Dictionary*, "E," 40a.

129 For discussion of the nature of the proverb see William McKane, *Proverbs A New Approach* (Philadelphia: Westminster, 1970) 29–30; Carole R. Fontaine, *Traditional Sayings in the Old Testament* (Bible and Literature Series 5; Sheffield: Almond, 1982) 246–48.

130 See, beyond the items in the bibliography, von Rad, *OT Theology 2*, 266–67; Walther Eichrodt, *Theology 2 of the Old Testament* (Philadelphia: Westminster, 1967) 435–37; Theodorus C. Vriezen, *An Outline of Old Testament Theology* (Newton, MA: Branford, 1970) 382–87.

they broke, though I was their husband"). "That covenant of mine" seems to be the best way in English to do justice to the second אֲשֶׁר (so also *JB*). The effect of the emphatic subject pronouns emerges only when the meaning of the verb בעל (here "be master") is clarified. In the other instance of the verb in Jer (3:14, where it is likewise accompanied by a subject pronoun), the clause is a reassuring clarification: the implication there is "Return to me (rather than staying with the fertility god *ba'al*), for I am your (real) master (*ba'al*)." Here, on the other hand, the issue would seem to be not that Yahweh rather than Baal is master of Israel, but rather that Yahweh is the senior partner in the covenant, while Israel (or, more specifically, the "fathers") can only be the junior partner. In 14:21 it is implied that Yahweh might be breaking the covenant; here ironically Jrm perceives Yahweh to be saying that it was the fathers that did the breaking, even though Yahweh had set the terms of the covenant. The verb here then does not mean "I had to show them who was master" (*JB*, similarly *NAB*): it does not express a contrasting action but an ironically contrasting state.

Question: If the linking of "house of Israel" and "house of Judah" suggests the rejoining of north and south, then is the occurrence only of "house of Israel" in v 33 a suggestion of a new total unity (compare Ezek 37:15–19), or is it simply rhetorical abbreviation? ■ **31:33aβ–34** "I shall put my law within them, and on their heart shall write it" is commonly understood as Yahweh's move to plant his law within the interior intentionality of the people, so that obedience becomes natural. This is certainly a strong emphasis in the passage (see below), but both "within them" (literally "in their interior") and "on their heart" appear to be ambiguous, given Jrm's diction. Thus "interior" (קֶרֶב) is used by Jrm of the city (6:1, where the Benjaminites are to flee from the "midst" of Jerusalem; 6:6, where there is nothing but extortion in her "midst"), and "heart" is used in parallelism with "altars" (17:1, where the sin of Judah is engraved upon the tablet of the "heart," and on the horns of their altars). "Interior" and "heart" then both suggest the city within the land and the temple within the city (compare Pss 46:5–6 and 55:11–12 for similar diction). The priestly covenant formula, too ("I shall be to them God, and they shall be to me a people"), has associations for Jrm with the temple: it is cited in the

context of sarcastic words about sacrifice (7:21–23; 11:4 + 15). One may conclude that "within them" and "on their heart" suggest a renewal of worship in the temple.

The other direction of meaning is the one commonly understood: Yahweh's law will be written in the interior intentionality of the people. It is to be stressed that "heart," like "interior," is singular in Hebrew: it is the corporate will and intention of the people that is at stake. Two contrasts are in the background: one is the sin of Judah that is written, engraved on the tablet of their heart (17:1); the other, of course, is the law of Yahweh written on tablets of stone (Deut 5:22 and often). The difficulty with the old covenant, then, is that it was written exteriorly and allowed for insincere obedience (compare 12:2b) or for outright rebellion on the part of the people. Yahweh's new action will bring about a new situation wherein the people will obey freely and gladly, and rebellion will be a thing of the past. (The passage offers no solution to the riddle of how the new situation will reconcile human freedom with the new exercise of God's sovereignty in injecting his law into the heart of the people: the NT sets forth its own fresh clues on the question, as Mark 14:36 and parallels, Rom 7:21–25, and many other passages witness.)

For the covenantal formula "I shall be to them God, and they shall be to me a people," see 7:23.

The implication for Jrm of v 34a ("no longer shall they teach one another or each other, saying, 'Know Yahweh!'") is double. The Deuteronomic law lays upon the Israelite the obligation to teach the divine words to his children (Deut 11:19); instead what has happened is that the people have deceived their brother and neighbor and taught their tongue to speak lies, refusing to "know Yahweh" (Jer 9:4–5). If the law is external, teaching is a necessity; now that Yahweh will make his law internal, teaching will be a thing of the past. For "know Yahweh" see 2:8; but it should be pointed out that the phrase, with an imperative, as a summary of covenant obligation, is unique in the OT (the closest parallel is "in all your ways know him," Prov 3:6).

One could take "from the least of them to the greatest" to mean either "from young to old" or "from the lowest class to the aristocracy." The phrase appears in 6:13 in the context of a listing of the population from children to aged (6:11), and the implication of "teaching" in Deuteronomy is that of teaching one's children (see above). On the other hand, the context of a similar contrast in 5:4–5 (where the word "great" is identical, but "poor" appears instead of "least") is that of social class (one notes that that passage deals with "knowing the way of Yahweh"). Doubtless both nuances are intended; and behind it all is the memory of King Jehoiakim, the "greatest" in the kingdom, burning the scroll Jrm has dictated (36:20–31).

The citation of 5:4–5 is relevant likewise for "forgive" (סלח), since the only previous occurrences of this verb in Jer are in 5:1 and 7. What Yahweh yearned to do before, he will now be able to do. And "remember their sin" has a double resonance in earlier words of Jrm: at the beginning Yahweh "remembered" the people's primal loyalty (2:2), but during the period of the drought it is said that Yahweh will "remember" their iniquity and punish their sin (14:10). "Remember" implies taking action (see on 2:2), so that Yahweh's promise to remember their sin no more is one more way to express the reassurance that there will never be an impediment again to the free relationship between Yahweh and his people.

■ **31:35–37** This passage argues from the permanence and scale of the cosmos to the permanence of the covenant; its setting appears to be the time of Nehemiah—for both these matters see Preliminary Observations. For the hymnic form in v 35, and the "if . . . then" structure offering a contrary-to-fact (or unlikely) condition to affirm the contrary, see Form. Little more need be said on these verses. The triad of "sun," "moon," and "stars" is an obvious convention, as is their association with the day and the night (compare Ps 136:8–9, and, with euphemisms, Gen 1:16). The addition of the "sea" here seems surprising, and since "who stirs up the sea so that its waves roar, Yahweh of hosts is his name" is a duplication of part of Isa 51:15, one would be tempted to think of v 35b as a secondary addition; but Psalm 148 moves from "sun," "moon," and "stars" in v 3 there to the "waters above the heavens" in v 4, and the same word "statute" (חֹק) appears in regard to them in v 6, so the association of ideas is doubtless sound here. (Compare

Jrm's own use of Yahweh's establishment of a "statute" for the sea, and of the phrase "waves roar" in 5:22.)
■ **31:38–40** The setting for this passage, like vv 35–37, is doubtless in the time of Nehemiah: see Preliminary Observations.

Conceivably the phrase in v 38 could mean "the city shall be rebuilt *by* Yahweh";[131] Yahweh is the agent of "sowing" in v 27. On the other hand, the phrase "holy to Yahweh" in v 40 suggests that "the city shall be rebuilt *for* Yahweh" is the nuance here. It is preferable to take the phrase as ambiguous (so Rudolph) than to insist that "by Yahweh" is impossible, as Volz does.[132]

Though specific commentaries give specific answers to the location of the geographical landmarks mentioned here, there is as yet no general agreement on the extent of Jerusalem in Nehemiah's day.[133] Thus there are three different plans—those of Michael Avi-Yonah, Jan J. Simons, and L. Hugues Vincent—in the location of the Tower of Hananel and the Corner Gate.[134] Myers offers a convenient full discussion of the topography of Jerusalem in this period.[135]

The Tower of Hananel is mentioned also in Neh 3:1 and 12:39, and in Zech 14:10. It must have been along the north wall of the city.[136] The Corner Gate is also mentioned in 2 Kgs 14:13 (= 2 Chr 25:23) and 2 Chr 26:9; it was evidently on the west or northwest side of the city.[137] The wording of v 38 then refers to the rebuilding of the northwest portion of the city wall.

"Gareb Hill" and "Goah" are otherwise unknown; the sequence of landmarks in these verses suggests a movement counterclockwise around the city, so that Gareb Hill would be on the southwest and Goah on the southeast, but this is only what may be deduced from the passage itself.[138] It may be added that Giesebrecht suggests reading the rather puzzling "opposite it" (נֶגְדּוֹ) as "southwards" (נֶגְבָּה, see *BHK*, *BHS*); if that suggestion is sound (and compare "eastwards" in v 40), then the location of Gareb Hill on the southwest is reinforced.

131 For this use of לְ see König, *Syntax*, sec. 103.
132 Volz, p. 284.
133 See conveniently Ruth Amiran and Yael Israeli, "Jerusalem," *IDBSup*, 475b.
134 These three plans are displayed in Burrows, "Jerusalem," 854.
135 Jacob M. Myers, *Ezra, Nehemiah* (AB 14; Garden City, NY: Doubleday, 1965) 112–19.
136 Ibid., 113, compare Millar Burrows, "Jerusalem," *IDB* 2:853a; see specifically Georges A. Barrois, "Hananel, Tower of," *IDB* 2:520.
137 Burrows, "Jerusalem," 850a, and Gray, *Kings*, 609, both assume northwest, following Jan J. Simons; Michael Avi-Yonah assumes west, compare Myers, *Ezra, Nehemiah*, 118.
138 See Burrows, "Jerusalem," 853a.

It is at least clear that the difficult first part of v 40 refers to the area around the Kidron Valley on the southeast of the city. The word שְׁדֵמוֹת (qere': here "terraces") is difficult. It appears (in singular or plural) beyond the present passage in Deut 32:32; 2 Kgs 23:4; Isa 16:8; Hab 3:17 (Isa 37:27 is dubious); and in two Ugaritic passages, Ug. 2.1.43 and 23.10. The proposal has been made to analyze the word as "field(s) of Mōt," that is, of the Canaanite god of death (see on Jer 9:20).[139] If that explanation is correct, then the Hebrew phrase might suggest a location where sacrifice to Baal or Mot was carried on, a connotation that would fit the present passage, or it might even suggest "cemetery" (so Bright). The difficulty with this explanation is that "field" in Hebrew is spelled with a שׂ (śin), not a שׁ (šin); if correct, one would have to assume a borrowing from another dialect. On the other hand, several of the instances of the word show a parallelism or close association with "vine": of the Ugaritic passages, 2.1.43 is fragmentary, but 23.10 clearly offers the word in a context where vines grow, and of the OT passages, three (Deut 32:32; Isa 16:8; Hab 3:17) have associations with "vine"—in Hab 3:17 the word is associated with "fig-tree," "vine," and "olive-tree"; and 2 Kgs 23:4 associates the word with Kidron. And of the OT passages only 2 Kgs 23:4 and Deut 32:32 associate the word with pagan ways (beyond the possibility of pagan associations in the present passage). The best solution is to posit the meaning "terrace(s)."[140] Terraces are found everywhere in Palestine for vineyards (and fig-trees and olive-trees), and terraces were doubtless in the Kidron Valley in ancient times as they are today.[141] In later times the word evidently ceased to be understood: the renderings in the Versions are simply guesses and vary in the several passages where the word occurs; Jerome discusses the

word in detail in his commentary. The words preceding "and all the terraces" in the verse, missing in *G*, are thus variant readings or glosses (see Text). The "corpses" (פְּגָרִים) would be those offered in pagan sacrifice, and "ashes" (דֶּשֶׁן) refers to the fatty ashes (compare its occurrence meaning "fatness," in v 14) of victims; the words then really make up a hendiadys. "The whole valley" by this understanding would be the Valley of Ben-Hinnom; see the discussion on 2:23 and 7:30–34. The brook Kidron is on the east of Jerusalem.[142]

The "Horse Gate" was evidently on the east wall of the city, at the northern end of the Kidron Valley, but whether it was directly east of the southeast corner of the temple area, where Avi-Yonah places it, or further south, as Vincent has it, is uncertain.[143] The only other reference to it is Neh 3:28.

Thus the whole outline of the city of Jerusalem at this period encloses an area that will become "holy" to Yahweh (compare the use of that phrase to designate the people Israel, 2:3); compare a similar proclamation in Ezek 45:1.

The promise that the city shall not be "uprooted" or "overthrown" is a late use of two of the verbs that appear in (the last stage of the text of) 1:10; for the thought compare (the reconstructed text of) 18:14b.

Aim

These two chapters are the end result of a process of compilation of words of hope for the community; it began with Jrm's early words of appeal to the north to return, words that he himself expanded with words of hope to the south in the time of the last agony of the kingdom of Judah and that were compiled in a new scroll. This scroll received a notable addendum that was genuine to the prophet, that of the word on the new

139 For the Ugaritic word see Joseph Aistleitner, *Wörterbuch der ugaritischen Sprache* (4th ed.; Berlin: Akademie, 1974), 2586; for the Hebrew word see Manfred R. Lehmann, "A New Interpretation of the Term שדמות," *VT* 3 (1953) 361–71, and José S. Croatto and J. Alberto Soggin, "Die Bedeutung von שדמות im Alten Testament," *ZAW* 74 (1962) 44–50.

140 So now John C. L. Gibson, *Canaanite Myths and Legends* (Edinburgh: Clark, 1978) 158b, for Ugaritic; for Hebrew: KB, 950b; and see further on Isa 16:8 in Wildberger, *Jesaja*, 627.

141 For the archeological evidence, and this meaning of

שְׁדֵמוֹת, see Lawrence E. Stager, "The Archaeology of the East Slope of Jerusalem and the Terraces of the Kidron," *JNES* 41 (1982) 117–18, 121; for a photograph of the terraces today see Kathleen M. Kenyon, *Jerusalem, Excavating 3000 Years of History* (New York: McGraw-Hill, 1967) plate 6 (following p. 32).

142 See Georges A. Barrois, "Kidron, brook," *IDB* 3:10–11.

143 Compare the two diagrams in Burrows, "Jerusalem," 854.

covenant (31:31–34), and then further additions later in the sixth and fifth centuries.

This fresh scroll of hope shares a characteristic with the earlier second dictated scroll of the prophet (36:28, 32): both are the product of the prophet's own redaction of his earlier material—the second scroll reinterpreted words of warning into words announcing the irrevocability of Yahweh's punishment (see chapter 36), and the present scroll reinterpreted words to the north into words to the south (in particular, 30:10–11 reshapes 30:5–7, and 30:16–17 reshapes 30:12–15).

But if words of warning can be reinterpreted as words of Yahweh's irrevocable punishment, words of irrevocable punishment cannot be reinterpreted as words of hope. That is to say, there is no way in which the second scroll could have undergone a further redaction to express hope for the future; such hope must be embodied in a fresh set of utterances. Thus even though the new covenant passage was an addendum to the scroll of hope, its message, that Yahweh will put all the past behind and make a fresh start with his people, was already foreshadowed by the preparation of a fresh scroll.

Theologically the shape of both the OT and the NT suggests that if judgment is God's penultimate word, then God's ultimate word is hope, comfort, restoration. Historically Jrm may well have taken his cue from Hosea in this regard,[144] and in the context of the fall of Jerusalem his scroll of hope gave prophetic circles the warrant to overlay Yahweh's judgments by words of hope (Ezekiel 33—39; Isaiah 40—66; Amos 9:11–15, and the

like). Indeed the specific motifs of "building" and "planting" found in this scroll were gratefully echoed in later material (Ezek 28:26; 36:36; Isa 65:21; Amos 9:14).

The people are personified as Yahweh's son in 31:9b, and the compassion of Yahweh for that son, set forth in 31:20, is unforgettable. This kind of portrayal may have its background in Hos 11:1–4, 8–9 (Jerome in his commentary on Jer alludes to Hosea 11 in his remarks on the present passage). The context of chapter 31 collocates diction of both fatherhood (v 9b) and motherhood (v 15), with the result that the diction of v 20 (like that of Hosea 11) may imply maternal love as much as paternal love. This depiction perhaps prepares the way for the expression in Deutero-Isaiah, "Can a woman forget her sucking child, that she should have no compassion on the son of her womb? Even these may forget, yet I will not forget you" (Isa 49:15). And the resemblance of 31:20 to Jesus' parable of the prodigal son (Luke 15:11–32) has often been noted.[145]

And if the new covenant passage (31:31–34) has for Christians a crucial importance (so Heb 8:8–12; 10:16–17), it is anticipated by Hos 2:18–25 and helped to shape Ezek 36:26[146] and doubtless encouraged Deutero-Isaiah's stress on Yahweh's bringing of "new things" (Isa 42:9) and "a new thing" (Isa 43:19).[147]

Yet even Jrm's words called out for supplementation —in the details of feasting in time to come (31:10–14), in the reassurance that Yahweh's love for Israel is as secure as the cosmos (31:35–37), and in the specific landmarks in Jerusalem to be rebuilt and reconsecrated (31:38–40).

---

144 Hos 2:18–25; 3:1–5; 14:2–9; see Wolff, *Hosea*, for the settings of these passages.

145 George A. Smith, *Jeremiah, Being the Baird Lecture for 1922* (4th ed.; Garden City, NY: Doubleday, Doran, 1929) 303; Volz, p. 295; David L. Bartlett, "Jeremiah 31:15–20 (Exposition)," *Int* 32 (1978) 77.

146 Zimmerli, *Ezekiel 2*, 249; von Rad, *OT Theology 2*, 235, 270–71.

147 See von Rad, *OT Theology 2*, 271.

Jeremiah Buys a Field

Bibliography

On 32:1–44:

Wang, Martin Cheng-Chang
   "Jeremiah's Message of Hope in Prophetic Symbolic Action—The 'Deed of Purchase' in Jer. 32,"
   South East Asia Journal of Theology 14/2 (1972/73)
   13–20.

On Baruch, and the Bulla of Baruch:

Avigad, Nahman
   "Baruch the Scribe and Jerahmeel the King's Son,"
   IEJ 28 (1978) 52–56.
Avigad, Nahman
   *Hebrew Bullae from the Time of Jeremiah, Remnants
   from a Burnt Archive* (Jerusalem: Israel Exploration
   Society, 1986) n. 9, pp. 28–29.
Avigad, Nahman
   "Jerahmeel & Baruch, King's Son and Scribe," *BA*
   42 (1979) 114–18.
Herr, Larry G.
   "Paleography and the Identification of Seal
   Owners," *BASOR* 239 (Summer 1980) 67–70.
Muilenburg, James
   "Baruch the Scribe," *Proclamation and Presence, Old
   Testament Essays in Honour of Gwynne Henton Davies*
   (ed. John I. Durham and J. Roy Porter; Richmond:
   Knox, 1970) 215–38.

On 32:1–15:

Begg, Christopher T.
   "Yahweh's 'Visitation' of Zedekiah (Jer 32,5),"
   ETL 63 (1987) 113–17.
Chang, Peter M.
   "Jeremiah's Hope in Action—An Exposition of
   Jeremiah 32:1–15," *East Asia Journal of Theology* 2
   (1984) 244–50.
Fischer, Leopold
   "Die Urkunden in Jer. 32,11–14 nach den Aus-
   grabungen und dem Talmud," *ZAW* 30 (1910)
   136–42.
Migsch, Herbert
   *Gottes Wort über das Ende Jerusalems, Eine literar-,
   stil- und gattungskritische Untersuchung des Berichtes
   Jeremia 34,1–7; 32,2–5; 37,3—38,28* (Öster-
   reichische Biblische Studien 2; Klosterneuburg:
   Österreichisches Katholisches Bibelwerk, 1981).
Peters, John P.
   "Notes on Some Difficult Passages in the Old
   Testament," *JBL* 11 (1892) 43.
Stade, Bernhard
   "Miscellen, 8: Jer. 32,11–14," *ZAW* 5 (1885) 175–
   78.

On 32:26–44:

Keukens, Karlheinz H.
   "Zur Übersetzung von Jer 32,33b," *Biblische Notizen*
   16 (1981) 18–19.
Weippert
   Prosareden, 209–27.

32

1   The word which came to Jeremiah from
    Yahweh in the tenth year[a] of Zedekiah, king
    of Judah: [it was the eighteenth year of
    Nebuchadrezzar.][b] [2/ At that time the army
    of the king of Babylon was besieging Jeru-
    salem, and Jeremiah {the prophet}[b] was
    confined in the court of the guard which was
    in the house of the king {of Judah,}[c] 3/
    where [d]《 King Zedekiah 》 {*M*: Zedekiah king
    of Judah}[d] had confined him, saying, "Why
    are you prophesying, 'Thus Yahweh has
    said, I am going to give this city into the
    hand of the king of Babylon, and he shall
    capture it, 4/ and Zedekiah {king of Judah}[e]
    shall not escape from the hand of the
    Chaldeans but really be given into the hand
    of the king of Babylon, and shall speak to
    him face to face and see him [f]eye to eye,[f] 5/
    and (to) Babylon he shall take Zedekiah and
    there he shall stay {until I attend to him,
    oracle of Yahweh; no matter how much you
    fight against the Chaldeans, you shall not
    succeed'}[g]?"] [a] 6/ [And Jeremiah said,][a] The
    word of Yahweh came to me, saying, 7/
    "Hanamel, the son of Shallum your uncle, is
    going to come to you, saying, 'Buy for your-
    self my field which is at Anathoth, for the
    right of redemption by purchase is yours';
    《 buy (it) for yourself." 》[a] 8/ And Hanamel,
    son of my uncle, came to me [according to
    the word of Yahweh][b] in the court of the
    guard and said to me, "Please buy my field
    [which is at Anathoth][c] which is in the land
    of Benjamin, for the right of possession is
    yours [and the redemption is yours:][d]

Text

1a   For the double reading, qere' בְּשָּׁנָה, ketib בִּשְׁנַת,
   see GKC, sec. 134p (compare 28:1).

b   This synchronism is a later expansion: see Structure, Form, Setting, and Interpretation.

2–5a   Verses 2–5 are a digression to explain the
   circumstances; see Structure, Form, Setting.

b   Omit with *G* (compare 28:5 and many other such
   passages); see Janzen, pp. 69–70.

c   Omit with *G* (compare note b); see Janzen, pp.
   69–70.

d—d   Read "King Zedekiah" with *G* (compare 21:1;
   34:8, and often).

e   Omit with *G*; compare the simple "Zedekiah" in v
   5.

f—f   The Hebrew idiom is "and his eyes with his eyes,"
   and so read with the qere'; the ketib has omitted the
   second yod in the second term.

g   Omit with *G*; in its use of "attend to" this expansion resembles that in 27:22. See Janzen, p. 104.

6a   Omit with *G* and *S*.

7–8a   Insert the divine command from v 8a to the end
   of v 7 (compare v 25). The words are missing in *G*.
   See further Structure, Form, Setting.

b   Omit with *G*.

c   In *G* these words appear after "which is in the
   land of Benjamin." Janzen, p. 133, believes that
   "which is at Anathoth" is original and "which is in
   the land of Benjamin" is a gloss, but why would one
   need a gloss here when "Anathoth" has already
   appeared in v 7? I would suggest instead that the
   wording here is deliberately varied and either that
   the bracketed words are inserted as a gloss before
   (*M*) or after (*G*) the original phrase, or that both *M*
   and *G* offer a conflate text with different order of
   the variants. It should also be noted that "land of
   Benjamin" prepares the way for that phrase in v 44,
   and that "which was at Anathoth" is also to be
   omitted in v 9.

d   For the *M* reading וּלְךָ הַגְּאֻלָּה *G* has καὶ σὺ
   πρεσβύτερος "and you are older," which is evidently
   a periphrasis for a reading וּלְךָ הַגְּדֻלָּה "and to you is
   the greatness" (that is, of age) (so Hitzig, Cornill).
   The words look suspiciously like a conflate text,
   given "the right of redemption" in v 7. The question
   devolves to some degree on how מִשְׁפַּט הַיְרֻשָּׁה is
   translated; if it is "the right of inheritance" (with
   most commentators) then there was doubtless a
   technical difference between that right and the duty
   of redemption, but if it is "the right of possession,"
   then one may take it as a synonym (see Interpre-

[. . . ."]ᵃ And I knew that this was the word of Yahweh.

9   So I bought the field from Hanamel, son of my uncle, [which was at Anathoth,]ᵃ and I weighed out for him [the silver,]ᵇ seventeen shekels of silver: 10/ I wrote up (the purchase) in the deed and sealed (it) and had witnesses witness and weighed the silver in scales. 11/ And I took the deed of purchase, (both) the sealed (part) [the commandment and the ordinances]ᵃ and the public (part), 12/ and I gave ᵃ(it) [M: the deed/deed of purchase]ᵃ to Baruch, son of Neriah, son of Mahseiah, in the presence of Hanamel ᵇson ofᵇ my uncle, and of the witnesses signingᶜ in the deed of purchase, andᵈ of [all]ᵉ the Jews sitting in the court of the guard. 13/ And I commanded Baruch in their presence, saying, 14/ Thus Yahweh of hosts, [the God of Israel,]ᵃ has said: Take [these deeds,]ᵇ this deed of purchase, [both]ᶜ the sealed (part) and the [M: this]ᵈ public [deed]ᵉ and ᶠ⟨put⟩ (it) [M: put them]ᶠ in an earthen vessel, so that ᵍ⟨it may remain⟩ [M: they may remain]ᵍ a long time. 15/ For thus Yahweh [of hosts, the God of Israel,]ᵃ has said: [Houses and]ᵇ fields [and vineyards]ᵇ shall again be bought in this land!

16   And I prayed to Yahweh after I had given the deed of purchase to Baruch son of Neriah: 17/ Ah Lord Yahweh, look, it is you who have made the heavens and the earth by your great power and your outstretched arm; nothing is too hard for you; [18/ showing love to the thousandth generation but paying back the iniquity of the fathers into the lap of their children after them, God great and mighty, Yahweh {of hosts is his name,}ᵇ 19/ great in counsel and mighty in deed, whose eyes are open to all the ways of humankind, to give to each according to his ways {and according to the fruit of his doings,}ᶜ 20/ who have set signs and wonders in the land of Egypt, to this day both in Israel and among mankind (in general), and made yourself a name as at

tation). The fact that the text anterior to *M* was misread in *G* (after the phraseology of v 7) might well suggest a half-legible interlineation or marginal addition.

9a   Omit with *G*; the words belong with "field" and are awkward here (Janzen, p. 49).

b   Omit with *G* (a dittography from v 10?—Janzen, p. 49).

11a   These words are omitted in *G* and make no sense in the context. John P. Peters, "Notes on some Difficult Passages in the Old Testament," *JBL* 11 (1892) 43, suggests that they are a gloss to explain אֶת־הֶחָתוּם, given the fact that חָתוּם in Isa 8:16 is followed by תּוֹרָה. See further Interpretation.

12a—a   Hebrew idiom does not demand a pronoun object here (see Gen 3:6); compare *G* of v 14. I propose either that the text had no object and that *G* supplied one ("it") or else that *G* reflects an original pronoun here. The *M* noun or noun phrase is heavy in the context and thus dubious. The nouns in *M* are thus all secondary and, being ungrammatical as they stand, represent a conflate text (הַסֵּפֶר and סֵפֶר הַמִּקְנָה): see Janzen, p. 16. The qere' of the Oriental recension omits the article with סֵפֶר, but whether this represents a correction or a trace of the original alternative reading is impossible to say.

b—b   So some MSS., *G*, and *S* (compare *V*); *M* omits the word.

c   For הַכֹּתְבִים many MSS., *V*, *S*, and *T* have הַכְּתֻבִים "signed." Either reading is possible.

d   So read with many MSS., *G*, *V*, and *S*; *M* omits.

e   Omit with *G* (see Janzen, pp. 65–67, esp. 66).

14a   Omit with *G* (compare Janzen, pp. 84–86).

b   Omit with *G*; this is an expansionist gloss by someone who either assumed two documents or else was careless about the nature of the document being drawn up (Janzen, p. 15).

c   *M* has "and" here, which may be construed with the following "and" as "both . . . and" (so Rudolph). But *G* omits the word, and it should be omitted as a late expansion (compare its omission in v 11).

d   Omit with *G*.

e   Omit with *G*; the construction in any case is ungrammatical (Janzen, p. 15).

f—f   Read וְנָתַתָּ with *G* (compare v 12, note a—a). *M* "put them" is an expansion in the line of the plural "these deeds" (see note b).

g—g   Read יַעֲמֹד with *G*; the *M* plural "they may remain" (יַעַמְדוּ) is an expansion consistent with the verb in the previous clause.

15a   Omit with *G* (compare v 14, note a).

b   The sequence in *G* is "fields and houses and vineyards"; the instability of the sequence and the fact that v 44 mentions only "fields" suggests that "houses" and "vineyards" are a later addition. See further Structure, Form, Setting.

18–20a   Omit vv 18–20, conventional language of congregational prayer; for a discussion and a justification for the retention of all v 17 see Structure, Form, Setting.

this day,]ª 21/ and you brought your people Israel out of the land of Egypt with signs and wonders, with mighty hand and outstretched arm, and with great terror, 22/ and you gave them this land which you swore to their fathers [to give them,]ª a land flowing with milk and honey, 23/ and they came in and took possession of it, but did not obey your voice, nor walk in your law,ª and nothing of what you commanded them to do did they do, and you made all this evil befall them. 24/ Look: the siege-mounds have come to the city to capture it, and the city has been given into the hand of the Chaldeans who are fighting against it in the face of sword and famine [and pestilence:]ª so that what you have spoken has come true, as you see for yourself! 25/ Then you for your part have said to me, [Lord Yahweh,]ª Buy for yourself the field with silver, and have witnesses witness—and the city has been given into the hand of the Chaldeans!

26   And the word of Yahweh came 《to me》ª saying, 27/ Behold, I am Yahweh, God of all flesh: is anything too hard for me? [28/ Therefore, thus Yahweh has said, ᵇthis city 《shall indeed be given》 {M: I am going to give this city}ᵇ into the hand of {the Chaldeans and into the hand of Nebuchadrezzar}ᶜ the king of Babylon, and he shall capture it. 29/ And the Chaldeans who are fighting against this city shall come in and set this city on fire and burn {it and}ᵈ the houses on whose roofs they sacrifice to Baal and pour out drink-offerings to other gods to vex me. 30/ For the children of Israel and the children of Judah have indeed been doing evil from their youth; {for the children of Israel are indeed vexing me in the deeds of their hands, oracle of Yahweh;}ᵉ 31/ for my anger and wrath have been aroused by this city from the day they built it until today, to remove it from my presence, 32/ because of all the evil of the children of Israel and the children of Judah which they have done to offend me, they, their kings, their officials, their priests and their prophets, {both}ᶠ the men of Judah and the inhabitants of Jerusalem. 33/ And they turned to me their back and not their face: to think I taught them early and constantly, but they are not listening, to take correction! 34/ And they set up their abominations in the house which is called by my name, to defile it, 35/ and they built high places to Baal which are in the Valley of Ben-Hinnom, to deliver up their sons and daughters as an offering by fire to Molech, something which I did not command them, nor did it come to my mind, to do this abomination, so as to make Judah sin.ᵍ] ª 36/ So now [therefore]ª thus ᵇ〈I shall say〉 [M: Yahweh God of Israel has said]ᵇ to the [M this]ᶜ city which 《you are saying》ᵈ has been given into the hand of the

b   Omit with G: see Janzen, p. 79.

c   Omit with G, a gloss from 17:10: see Janzen, p. 49.

22a   Omit with G, a gloss from 11:5: see Janzen, p. 49.

23a   The qere', many MSS., V, S, and T read "your law"; the ketib and G read "your laws." The plural is rare in the OT and not otherwise cited in Jer.

24a   Omit with G: it is likely that M has expanded the first two words by the addition of the third. See the discussion in Janzen, p. 43–44, 205 n. 19.

25a   The vocative is probably to be omitted with G; compare a similar vocative omitted in G in 38:9. See Janzen, p. 82.

26a   So read with G (compare v 16); M "to Jeremiah." Compare 35:12; 36:1.

28–35a   Omit vv 28–35 as a secondary addition (like vv 38–40); see Structure, Form, Setting.

b—b   For M הִנְנִי נֹתֵן אֶת־הָעִיר הַזֹּאת G reads Δοθεῖσα παραδοθήσεται ἡ πόλις αὕτη. The same contrast is found in 34:2, and the form of text in G is found in M for 38:3 (הִנָּתֹן תִּנָּתֵן הָעִיר הַזֹּאת). The text of G is to be preferred here and in 34:2 (so also Duhm and Cornill).

c   Omit with G: see Janzen, p. 72.

d   For M וּשְׂרָפוּהָ וְאֵת read וְשָׂרְפוּ אֵת with G: the rhetoric is smoother.

e   Omit with G: the text of M is doubtless conflate; see Janzen, p. 16.

f   Omit with G.

g   The ketib has omitted the final 'alep by haplography.

36a   Omit with G and S.

b—b   Revocalize M אָמַר as אֹמַר: by this emendation "Yahweh God of Israel" is judged to be a secondary addition (so also v 42). See Structure, Form, Setting.

c   Omit הַזֹּאת with G (so also v 43); it is an addition from vv 28, 29, and 31 (so Janzen, p. 49).

d   Read the pronoun and participle in the singular (אַתָּה אֹמֵר) with G for the plurals in M (so also v 43); compare 33:10, where G reads a plural.

king of Babylon with sword, famine and pestilence: 37/ I am going to gather them from all the land[s]ᵃ where I have driven them in my anger and wrath and great rage, and I shall bring them back to this place and shall settle them securely; [38/ and they shall be to me a people, and I shall be to them God. 39/ And I shall give them one heart and one way to fear me all the days, for good for them and their children after them. 40/ And I shall make with them an everlasting covenant, from whom I shall not turn away, {to do good to them,}ᵇ and my fear I shall put in their heart, so as not to turn aside from me.]ᵃ 41/ And I will rejoice over them, to do them good, and I shall plant them in this land in truth with all my heart and with all my soul. 42/ For thus ᵃ⟨I shall say⟩ [M: Yahweh has said,]ᵃ Just as I have brought in upon this people all this great evil, so I am bringing in upon them all the good which I am speaking over them. 43/ So the field shall be bought in the [M: this]ᵃ land, which ⟪you are saying⟫ᵇ is a desolation, without man or beast: [it has been given into the hand of the Chaldeans.]ᶜ 44/ Fields with silver they shall buy, and they shall sign with a deed and seal and make witnesses witness in the land of Benjamin and the region of Jerusalem and the cities of Judah [and the cities of the hill country and the cities of the Shephelah and the cities of the Negeb,]ᵃ for I shall restore their fortunes, [oracle of Yahweh.]ᵇ

37a   Read the singular with G instead of the M plural "lands," a generalizing alteration.

38–40a   Omit as a secondary addition (compare vv 28–35); see Structure, Form, Setting.

b   Omit with G, an intrusion from v 41: see Janzen, p. 29.

42a—a   Revocalize M אָמַר as אֹמַר: by this emendation "Yahweh" is to be judged a secondary addition (so also v 36). See Structure, Form, Setting.

43a   Omit הַזֹּאת with G (as in v 36); it is an addition from vv 28, 29, and 31 (Janzen, p. 29).

b   Read the pronoun and participle in the singular with G (see v 36).

c   This clause is used elsewhere to refer to the city, not the land; it lacks a conjunction and is out of place here (so Volz). See further Structure, Form, Setting.

44a   Omit; the phrases break the rhetorical pattern (see Structure, Form, Setting).

b   Omit with G.

Structure, Form, Setting

For placement of this chapter within chapters 26—36 see Introduction, sec. 22.

The chapter falls easily into three sections: the narrative of Jrm's purchase of a family field in Anathoth (vv 1–15), his prayer to Yahweh (vv 16–25), and Yahweh's response (vv 26–44).

The passage presents many difficulties in text and literary history, in some of which form-critical issues play a part; the chapter is obviously a crucial one in affirming Jrm's proclamation of future hope, and the chapter has had a complicated history of expansions. Some of these are clear in a comparison between the (shorter) G text and the (longer) M text, but not all. Other difficulties originate in the technical language of vv 10–14.

The word of hope is secure and uncontested in the authentic portions of chapters 30—31. Here, by contrast, Jrm expresses dismay at the shift of Yahweh's will from irrevocable judgment to hope for the future (vv 17, 24–25). It is altogether likely, then, that the event of the purchase of the field is precisely the catalyst that brought the prophet to proclaim a future hope; it is therefore crucial to follow Jrm's train of thought insofar as that is possible. It is not always easy to do this, since it is clear that Jrm was surprised that hope should be proclaimed, and later tradents were anxious to affirm at all costs that hope be proclaimed. Thus one curious problem that emerges is why Jrm should wait until *after* the proclamation of the divine word of hope, v 15, before he expressed his dismay to Yahweh, vv 17ff. Again, if Yahweh's ironic question in v 27, "Is anything too hard for me?" is authentic to Jrm's perception, as all commentators agree it is, then it surely matches Jrm's affirmation, "Nothing is too hard for you" in v 17: the only expression resembling it in the OT is the source for both, Gen 18:14, "Is anything too hard for Yahweh?" (Volz, Rudolph, and Bright reject this part of v 17 as secondary, but I shall argue below that all of v 17 is authentic.) But if both phrases are authentic, then they are in essential agreement; so the question arises, why should Jrm express dismay?—why pray to Yahweh at all? It is clear that one must proceed with care.

If the event of the purchase of the field was crucial for a shift in Jrm's perception of Yahweh's will for the people, then the substance both of Jrm's prayer and of Yahweh's response will deal with the immediate circumstance. It follows then that material of a more general nature within vv 16–44 is to be viewed with suspicion.

It is best to begin, then, with vv 16–44. It will be convenient to deal first with vv 26–44. All commentators conclude that vv 26–27 are original. Thus the phrase "God of all flesh" in v 27 is not conventional: it is unique in this form in the OT, doubtless a more concise version of a phrase found twice in P, "God of the spirits of all flesh" (Num 16:22; 27:16). Jrm may well have had access to the tradition embodied in P (see on 4:23–28; 20:1–6), and he certainly used the phrase "all flesh" elsewhere (25:31; compare 12:12). And the question "Is anything too hard for me?" (v 27) has already been touched on. One wonders: Is the assonance of כָּל־בָּשָׂר "all flesh" and כָּל־דָּבָר "anything" deliberate? It is safe to affirm that vv 26–27 are authentic.

Commentators differ on vv 28–29: Volz accepts the two verses as genuine, Rudolph and Weiser accept vv 28–29a as genuine and v 29b as the beginning of a late expansion, and Bright judges vv 28–29 to be part of that late expansion that continues in v 30 and beyond (see below). There are several considerations. (1) The third-person messenger formula at the beginning of v 28 is odd; similar formulas at the beginning of vv 36 and 42 will have another solution (see below), but that formula here, I propose, is part of a secondary expansion. (2) The diction of vv 28–29 matches that of Jrm elsewhere, a datum which could mean either that it is authentic or that it is a secondary expansion. Substantively the problem between Jrm and Yahweh is that Jrm has been preaching irrevocable judgment on the people and is puzzled that Yahweh should suddenly communicate hope; words of doom from Yahweh are therefore not germane to the issue. I therefore follow Bright and view vv 28–29 as part of a late addition.

There is agreement among commentators that vv 30–35 are unauthentic: the passage is a pastiche from genuine parenetic material elsewhere, notably 19:13 and 7:30–31, and from genuine poetry (for v 33a see 2:27) (thus see Volz, Rudolph, Bright).

Verses 36–44 embody the word of hope, introduced by "so now" (וְעַתָּה); this is an appropriate expression to follow vv 26–27. But commentators again disagree on the extent of genuine material in these verses: Volz holds that "so now" is authentic but that what follows through "thus Yahweh has said" in v 42 is secondary, and that the rest of v 42 and all of vv 43–44 are authentic; Rudolph believes that only vv 42–44 are authentic; Bright takes all of vv 36–44 as authentic.

The place to begin is with the participial phrase "you are saying" in vv 36 and 43. *G* reads the second-person singular, *M* the second-person plural. If the phrase is genuine, the plural hardly makes sense as an address to Jrm: the issue is not Jrm and those with him, but Jrm alone who continues to preach doom; thus if genuine, the form of the phrase in *M* must represent a generalization for the exilic community—the phraseology is found elsewhere in the book only in 33:10, imitative of v 43 here. The implication is that Yahweh is contradicting the steady message of Jrm. If both participial phrases are genuine, then one has a frame for Yahweh's response: "the city which, you are saying, has been given into the hand . . ." (v 36) and "the land which, you are saying, is a desolation . . ." (v 43). Tentatively, then, one may judge the words after the messenger formula in v 36 to be authentic.

But what about the third-person messenger formula here (and in v 42)? The issue is what Jrm is saying (vv 36 and 43) and what Jrm accuses Yahweh of having said (v 25). The solution that seems plausible is that the original text of v 36 (and v 42) read "Thus shall I say" (כֹּה אֹמַר), a unique phrase in the OT. Here is the contrast between what Jrm is now saying (vv 36 and 43) and what Yahweh will say from now on. If this is the original reading, then in a consonantal text it would inevitably have been expanded to read כֹּה אָמַר יהוה "Thus Yahweh has said": compare the textual issue in Isa 40:6, where וָאֹמַר "and I said" (so *G*) was revocalized וְאָמַר "and he said" with the curious simple וְ.

In v 37 there are three noteworthy idioms. The triplet "in my wrath, anger and great rage" appears in the genuine 21:5 and in Deut 29:27, a late passage.[1] The

---

1   Mayes, *Deuteronomy*, 366–67.

word-play on "I shall bring them back" (וַהֲשִׁבֹתִים) and "I shall settle them" (וְהֹשַׁבְתִּים) is striking—this is the only occurrence of the hip'il stem of ישב in Jer; one recalls the similar play on the imperative plurals of the qal stems of ישב and שוב in 25:5. Finally, the expression "securely" (לָבֶטַח) is found in 23:6, likewise with "dwell," ישב. This verse gives every evidence of being genuine.

Verses 38–40 are more difficult to assess. Verse 38 embodies the covenant formula; it is found in this form in authentic passages (7:23; 11:4; 24:7; 31:33) and in variants as well (31:1, 9); obviously it could be authentic here. Verses 39–40 continue reassuring covenantal formulations; in particular the phrase "everlasting covenant" (בְּרִית עוֹלָם) is widely scattered in the OT—in P (Gen 7:16), in Ezek 16:60, in Isa 55:3, in Ps 105:10.[2] Since v 41 continues the verbs expressing the action of Yahweh in restoring the exiles on the land, verbs which were last heard in v 37, I suggest that vv 38–40 are a later insertion offering language a bit softer than that of the "new covenant" passage. It may be significant that Zech 8:8 offers diction that is much like the movement here from v 37 to v 38.

Verse 41 is authentic. Specifically the use of "with all my heart and with all my soul" in reference to Yahweh is unique in the OT,[3] and the phrase "rejoice to do them good" is found only here in Jer, and outside the book only in Deut 28:63 and 30:9, two late passages.[4] Finally, vv 42–44 are authentic, less short textual expansions (so all commentators: see above).

To summarize: in vv 26–44 the original material is made up of vv 26–27, 36–37, and 41–44; vv 28–35 and 38–40 are secondary. What emerges then, given the reading "thus I shall say" at the beginning of vv 36 and 42, is a striking response from Yahweh in which he speaks of "the city" (v 36) and "the land" (v 43), and contrasts what Jrm has been saying about them with what he is about to say about them.

With regard to Jrm's prayer to Yahweh (vv 16–25) there is general agreement that vv 24–25 are authentic:

they are heavy with specifics of the prophet's bafflement. But with regard to vv 17–23 commentators differ. Volz, Rudolph, and Bright excise v 17 beginning with "look, it is you," through v 23, arguing that such general liturgical material (reminiscent of Neh 9:6–37) is inappropriate here; Weiser, on the other hand, argues for authenticity, pointing out that Jrm was the son of a priest and could be expected to know the tradition.[5]

The question, however, is not whether Jrm could have used such phrases but whether they are appropriate here. And the judgment already offered on vv 26–44 is relevant: what is here judged authentic is diction dealing with the buying of the field and the return of the people to repopulate the land. Jrm is dismayed, as the phrase "Ah, Lord Yahweh" indicates (see above). It is the specific issue of the reversal of Yahweh's word that is at issue.

There is evidence that all of v 17 is genuine, not simply the words of dismay at the beginning. The only parallel in the OT for creation "by your/his great power and your/his outstretched arm" is 27:5, part of Jrm's word to the pagan kings (and compare the similar 10:12). And "Nothing is too hard for you" surely matches "Is anything too hard for me?" in v 27 (compare the remarks above; for the shift of meaning between the two expressions see below). So reconstructed, Jrm's prayer is organized about "look" (הִנֵּה, vv 17, 24 twice) and subject pronouns (vv 17, 25).

There is a contrast in the character of vv 18–20 and vv 21–23. Verses 21–23 are closely modeled on Deuteronomy and reflect language Jrm has used elsewhere (thus for vv 21–22 compare Deut 26:8–9, and for vv 22–23 compare 11:4–5; for the details see Interpretation). Verse 23b, with its unique hip'il stem of קרא II "befall," leads directly into v 24.

On the other hand, vv 18–20 reflect a variety of parallels in the OT, not Deuteronomy specifically. Thus v 18 is close to Exod 34:7 and Isa 65:6–7; v 19, though unique in phraseology, reflects wisdom motifs; the verb

2   For a complete listing see BDB, 762b, "d."
3   Weinfeld, *Deuteronomy*, 334, #9; compare Weippert, *Prosareden*, 23, n. 108.
4   Von Rad, *Deuteronomy*, 176, 183–84; Mayes, *Deuteronomy*, 349, 367–68.
5   Weiser, pp. 296–97. For bibliography for and against authenticity see Berridge, 115, n. 10.

"set" (שׂים) with "signs" and "wonders" in v 20 is found otherwise only in Pss 78:43 and 105:27. Verse 20 tries awkwardly to generalize the specifics of the language of the deliverance of Israel from Egypt ("signs and wonders") to the world in general ("to this day," "both in Israel and among mankind"), whereas vv 21–23 detail strictly the specifics of Israel's story. One notes further that "signs" and "wonders" are duplicated in vv 20 and 21, awkward if the two verses had a common origin. The conclusion to which the data point is that vv 18–20 are secondary, and vv 21–23 authentic, to the prayer. (It may be added that "outstretched arm" in vv 17 and 21 is not a duplication: in v 17 it describes the power of God in creation, in v 21 it describes the power of God in bringing Israel out of Egypt.)

If the analysis thus far is correct, Yahweh's response matches Jrm's prayer closely, not only in the parallel of the descriptions of Yahweh's sovereignty over all creation (vv 17, 27) and the associated parallel of "Nothing is too hard for you" and "Is anything too hard for me?" (for which see further below) but also in Yahweh's quotation in v 36 of Jrm's statement in v 24.

The general flow of thought from Jrm's prayer to Yahweh's response is now clear. There is tension in Jrm's mind between the field in Anathoth which has just been purchased and the city which is under siege; that contrast between a country field and the capital city reinforces the tension between judgment and hope. The contrast is clear in v 25, and the connection is made in Yahweh's response—the population of "the city" (v 36) will be brought back (v 37) and planted in "this land" (v 41), and therefore "the field is to be bought" (v 43: for this understanding of v 43 see Interpretation). The matching of "city" and "land" in Yahweh's response is made plain by Yahweh's second quotation of Jrm's words (v 43), a quotation that is *not* to be found in the prophet's prayer —instead, the words are a combination of Jrm's declaration that the land will be a desolation (several instances, notably 4:27) and that the land will be without man or beast (36:29). Jrm perceives Yahweh to be making the connection between the siege of the city and the relevance of the land. And the unity between field, city, and land is, I suggest, subtly achieved by the mention in v 44

of "the land of Benjamin" (the location of the field at Anathoth), "the region around Jerusalem" (the city under siege), and "the cities of Judah" (the land).

If this analysis is sound, it has a bearing on two sequences within vv 26–44 which, I suggest, are secondary. The first is v 43bβ, "it has been given into the hand of the Chaldeans." Volz excises this clause as an expansion from v 36; he points out that it is descriptive of the city, not the land, and further that it is not connected by a conjunction. I concur. The second is v 44aβ, "and (in) the cities of the hill country and (in) the cities of the Shephelah and (in) the cities of the Negeb." Volz points out acutely that these three phrases are really appositional with "the cities of Judah," though he does not propose excising them. I would so propose and point out two other bits of evidence. (1) The first three geographical phrases are each introduced by a different designation—"land," "region," and "cities"—whereas the last three simply repeat "cities"; rhetorically then the last three are not parallel to the first three. (2) The last three (which I propose to excise) occur in the same order before the three that (I propose) are original in 33:16, a circumstance suggesting that the three in dispute are a "floating" expansion.

One other textual problem, namely in v 25, needs scrutiny in the light of the whole chapter. Where M in v 25aβ has "Buy for yourself the field with silver and have witnesses witness," G has a longer text, "Buy for yourself the field with silver; and I wrote a deed and sealed (it) and had witnesses witness." Since an analogous sequence of verbs is found in vv 9–10a and v 44, the question arises whether M is defective or G expansionist at this point. Janzen argues[6] that G is expansionist, a view in agreement with Bright. It is difficult to decide the question, so it is safer to stay with Bright.

Within vv 1–15 there are several textual-literary problems. The first is v 1b, the synchronism with Nebuchadrezzar, which G includes. There are two other such

---

6   Janzen, p. 64.

synchronisms in the book, 25:1 and 52:12, and in both of these *G* omits the synchronism; tentatively then one may conclude that all three are later additions to the text. (It may be added that all three give an identical chronological difficulty; on this see Interpretation.)

The second is the literary history of v 1a, of the long digression in vv 2–5, and of the resumptive introduction in v 6. The body of the chapter is a first-person narrative (vv 8–13, 16, 25); in the divergence between *M* and *G* in vv 6 and 26, therefore (v 6: *M* "to me," *G* "to Jeremiah"; v 26: *M* "to Jeremiah," *G* "to me"), the first-person readings are correct. Verse 1 is thus an editorial superscription imposed on the narrative that begins in v 6: the nearest parallels in the book are 1:1–2 + 4, and 18:1 + 5 (compare 3), and in both those passages the third-person introductory words are clearly a later addition. Given those parallels, the material in vv 2–5 is clearly secondary, an appendix (Volz, Bright); it adapts for third-person diction ("Zedekiah shall not escape," v 4) the second-person diction of 34:2–3 ("you shall not escape," 34:3). These verses must have been added as guidance to the reader when the material of the chapter was placed in its present position after chapters 30—31; but the awkwardness of vv 2–5 and the distance it produces between vv 1 and 6 make it clear that it is not from the same hand as v 1. As for the opening words of v 6, one cannot determine whether they are from the same hand as that which produced vv 2–5 or whether they are from still another hand to smooth over the transition from v 5 to v 6.

There are two more issues emerging from vv 7–8. The first is both form-critical and textual. Form-critically there is a divine word of prediction in vv 6–7 followed by Jrm's narrative in v 8 that the word of prediction came true, but the sequence is as it stands only *implicitly* a divine command to perform a symbolic act. It is clear from the circumstances that the act is intended to carry a message (thus v 15), but there is no divine command (compare 13:1 and 19:1, both of which have the command to "buy"). Yet v 25 quotes such a divine command. Is there one missing? The little phrase at the end of v 8a, "buy (it) for yourself," is missing in *G*, and it is clearly extraneous to v 8. But it is an ideal divine command if it were inserted at the end of v 7. It is plausible to imagine a copyist omitting the phrase either inadvertently or intentionally, given the synonymous "please buy" earlier

in the verse, under the assumption that the phrase was still part of Hanamel's speech. Then in the proto-Masoretic text tradition it was either reinserted at the wrong spot or was a marginal addition subsequently reinserted at the wrong spot.

The second issue in vv 7–8 is a stylistic one. The quotation in v 8 is longer than the parallel quotation in v 7. The fact that "which was at Anathoth" in v 9 is undoubtedly secondary raises the question whether the same phrase in v 8 is not also secondary alongside "which is in the land of Benjamin" (compare the contrasting order of the phrases in *M* and *G* here), an effort to make the wording of v 8 conform to that of v 7. And one is impelled to see "and the redemption is yours" in v 8 as secondary: the deformation of that phrase in *G* (after the same words in v 7) suggests that it may have begun as a half-legible interlineation. One may conclude that the narrator (Jrm? Baruch?) wished deliberately to vary the diction in the second quotation, either for stylistic variety or because Jrm's cousin really did use slightly different language than that for which Jrm was prepared. Does this consideration lead then to the conclusion that the last clause of v 8 implies, "I knew it was the word of Yahweh, even though the wording of Hanamel's speech was not quite the same"?

There are two more textual-literary questions, both in vv 14–15. The first has form-critical consequences, and that is the messenger formula at the beginning of v 14. Volz, Rudolph, and Bright all excise it on the assumption that v 15 contains the divine word but that v 14 contains Jrm's own command. But the immediate issue on Jrm's mind is the puzzle that Yahweh should command him to buy the field (v 25); it is the details of the purchase rather than the wider consequence expressed in v 15 that concern the prophet (compare v 16). As I shall try to demonstrate, the operative word of v 14 is evidently "a long time," and this is part of an expression which must indeed be understood as a divine word. The double divine word, v 14 and v 15, will become a clue for the solution of one of the questions with which this discussion began, namely, why Jrm should wait to express his dismay with Yahweh until after his purchase of the field (see below). The messenger formula belongs at the beginning of v 14 as well as at the beginning of v 15.

The second question is the status of the words "houses" and "vineyards" in v 15. The variant order of the three members of the compound subject in *G* (see Text) suggests that the two words were added secondarily. It is "fields" that are mentioned in Yahweh's response in v 44, not "houses" and "vineyards": those were evidently added to bring chapter 32 into conformity with chapters 30—31.

As for a *specific setting* for the chapter, the event of the purchase of the field must have taken place in the course of the summer of 588 (see Interpretation on v 1), and the authentic portions of the chapter must have been recorded soon after. As for the secondary additions, there is no way to date any of them with precision: one may suspect that "houses" and "vineyards" were added early in the compilation process, perhaps by Baruch (compare above), but most of the additions in the chapter are expansionist imitations of diction found elsewhere in the book. The only distinctive phraseology is that of vv 18–20, liturgical language comparable with that in Neh 9:6–37 (see above), but it need not be dated so late as Nehemiah's time—it is traditional diction.

With regard to *form-criticism* of the chapter, little more need be said. Verses 6–7 are a divine word of both prediction and (with the restoration of "buy [it] for yourself" at the end of v 7) command to perform a symbolic act. Verses 8–12 embody the narrative of the sequence of events that parallel the divine word; all this is in the first person. The first-person narrative continues in v 13, quoting an extension of the divine command (v 14): what Yahweh commands becomes implicitly what Jrm commands Baruch. Verse 15 is a fresh divine word, a proclamation of salvation (*Heilsankündigung*). (For the relation between vv 14 and 15 see the historical reconstruction below.) The balance of the chapter continues the first-person narrative: Jrm cites his own prayer to Yahweh (vv 17 + 21–25) and Yahweh's response (vv 27 + 36–37 + 41–44). His prayer opens with the words of dismay "Ah, Lord Yahweh" and continues in v 17 with hymnic phrases. He continues (vv 21–23) with traditional phrases drawn from the recitation of Yahweh's salvific acts preserved in Deuteronomy and from the announcement of Israel's breaking of the covenant (compare 11:4–8). He continues by reporting the details of the siege of the city, which are obvious to Yahweh (v 24), and repeats to Yahweh the divine command, which seems so incongruous. Yahweh's response begins with a self-description (*Selbstbeschreibung*) (v 27) and continues (if the

textual reconstruction offered here is correct) with a surprising first-person variation on the messenger formula, "Thus I shall say" (vv 36, 42), and with a proclamation of salvation to the city (vv 36–37, 41–42), closing with a reaffirmation of the validity of the command to Jrm (v 43) and a generalization of that reaffirmation in a final proclamation of salvation (v 44).

Now one can deal with one of the questions with which this discussion began, namely: Why should Jrm express his dismay to Yahweh after he has obeyed his command and uttered the proclamation of salvation (vv 15, 16)? Jrm's objection is understandable: he has been preaching the irrevocability of Yahweh's punishment since December 601 (36:31), and now suddenly there comes a hopeful word from Yahweh (v 15). But given the sequence of 1:4–10 (Yahweh's call, Jrm's objection, Yahweh's reassurance, and finally the implicit acceptance by Jrm of the call), one would have expected here that Jrm would object before he obeys Yahweh's command. Any number of explanations might be proposed: the narrative is (1) form-critically stylized; or (2) evidence of Jrm's dogged obedience to Yahweh's sovereign word, no matter how puzzling; or (3) evidence of Jrm's conviction that Yahweh can change his intention "suddenly" (18:7, 9); or (4) some combination of these. Nevertheless the mode of presentation is surprising.

Duhm assumed that all of vv 16–44 is redactional. If this were true, it would solve the problem, but it is not acceptable (see above).

I propose that the clue is in the double messenger formula, at the beginning of both v 14 and v 15; I have already affirmed that that formula is authentic in v 14 (see above). It turns out that there is a tissue of shared vocabulary between this symbolic act and two other symbolic acts of Jrm, both involving purchases, that of the linen loincloth (13:1–11) and that of the earthen flask (19:1–15). There is not only the verb "buy" (קָנָה, 13:1, 2, 4; 19:1; 32:7, 8, 9, 25, 44). Jrm took an "earthen" (חֶרֶשׂ) flask (19:1), also called a "vessel" (כְּלִי, 19:11), and smashed it as a symbol of the destruction of Jerusalem, whereas here he has the deed of purchase preserved in an earthen vessel (v 14). Jrm had purchased a loincloth and under divine compulsion hidden it at Parah, and then after "a long time" (יָמִים רַבִּים, 13:6) he had gone back and found it spoiled; this act was symbolic of the pride of Judah, to be spoiled by the stay in Babylon. Here the deed of purchase is to be preserved for "a long time" (v 14), clearly a reference to the Babylonian exile (compare "[a] long [time]" [אֶרְכָּה], 29:28). One may imagine Jrm then preoccupied with the homely details of the purchase and the normal preservation of the deed as a surprising symbol of the integrity of Yahweh's purpose for the future (thus v 14) without at the moment his expecting the divine word of v 15.

Can one discern Jrm's expectations in that event previous to the divine word of v 15? I may venture a guess. There is evidence that the opposition from Jrm's family described in 12:6 and hinted at in 15:10 arose at the same time as opposition from the optimistic prophets in the summer of 594 (compare 28:1–17; 29:24–32; and Setting for the Confessions). If 20:13 was Jrm's response to the death of Hananiah, as is here proposed, and further if 20:14–18 is evidence that opposition from his family persisted after the death of Hananiah, as is plausible, then that opposition, continuing after the summer of 594, was not only a source of personal grief to Jrm but also a continued challenge to his prophetic vocation—in short, it was a theological problem. One could imagine then that the opportunity to effect the redemption of his cousin's field was a sign from Yahweh that not all the members of the "house of his father" (12:6) would continue to deal treacherously with him. If Yahweh had warned him of family opposition, Yahweh now has brought him news of modest reconciliation. It is therefore a divine word that Jrm could purchase a field and that the record of that purchase could be public knowledge "for a long time." (Is this the significance of the specification of both the sealed part and the public part of the deed in vv 11 and 14?) If Jrm was vindicated before the optimistic prophets by the death of Hananiah (so the purpose of the words of 28:17), then he is now vindicated before his family. But one could then imagine Jrm, carried along by the logic of the symbolic acts, becoming aware that Yahweh means to communicate a word to the people regarding their future as well: that if the loincloth was spoiled and the earthen vessel smashed, the deed to this property would on the contrary be preserved. And in this new understanding there comes the second divine word, that in v 15. But it is a word that Jrm will then need to have clarified: in the light of all you have said and done, Yahweh, what is the meaning of this shift in your will?

To surmise Jrm's train of thought to this degree is to press beyond what can confidently be known, and yet it is enticing to try to take one more step: to discern the meaning of the parallel between Jrm's words to Yahweh, "Nothing is too hard for you" (v 17), and Yahweh's counter-question, "Is anything too hard for me?" (v 27)—because on the face of it Jrm's words would cover his objection to Yahweh's shift in purpose.

The immediately preceding expression in Jrm's prayer is an affirmation that Yahweh is creator by his great power and outstretched arm (v 17a). The earlier instance when he made that affirmation was in the word to the pagan kings (27:5), and it was in the context of Yahweh's rule over all creation, a rule implying his giving total power to Nebuchadrezzar. Since the genuine portion of Jrm's prayer continues this line of thinking (v 24), that Yahweh has indeed given Jerusalem into the hand of Babylon, one must understand "Nothing is too hard for you," at least on the surface, to imply no limit to Yahweh's power, indeed perhaps "Nothing is too inconceivable for you," even the destruction of Jerusalem. On a deeper level, of course, Jrm opens his mind to the possibility that the affirmation may imply Yahweh's shift of purpose expressed in v 15, but it is evidently not a shift that he wishes for the moment to accept. In a kind of self-mockery, however, Jrm by his very affirmation leaves himself open to Yahweh's ironic counter-question in v 27 and to Yahweh's affirmation that "the field is to be bought" (v 43: for this rendering see Interpretation there) because in the future "fields shall be bought" (v 44).

Interpretation

■ 1 The tenth year of Zedekiah, assuming a spring new year, extended from March/April 588 to March/April 587. The purchase took place in the court of the guard where Jrm was confined (the witnesses were drawn from the group there, v 12). Though the narrative does not specify that Hanamel came from Anathoth (he might have been a refugee within the city), the impression left by the narrative is at least that there was communication between Anathoth and Jerusalem, an impression which in turn suggests that the event took place at the time the Egyptian army had forced the Babylonians temporarily to pull back from Jerusalem in the course of their siege (37:5). That event probably took place in the summer of

588.[7] (If the rather cryptic wording of 37:11–12 has reference to the purchase of the field, the suggestion is reinforced: see on that passage.)

The synchronism in v 1b gives the same chronological difficulty as that in 25:1 (and that in 52:12); Nebuchadrezzar's eighteenth year extended from March/April 587 to March/April 586. That matter is discussed in more detail, and a suggestion offered for the source of the error, in the discussion on 25:1 (which see).

For the repetition of שָׁנָה, "year," in the Hebrew expression with compound numbers see GKC, sec. 134o.

■ **2** The verb "confine" (כלא, here and in v 3) is a general word for "restrain"; the phrase "house of confinement" (בֵּית הַכֶּלֶא) means "prison" (37:4), but "imprison" (*NEB*, *NAB*) here gives the wrong connotation. The "court of the guard" was in the palace, and at least on a similar occasion (37:21) Jrm was confined there in honorable circumstances, a kind of "protective custody." At least he had more freedom than when he was put into the cistern there (38:6).

■ **3** "Why are you prophesying . . . ?": there is no parallel in the book for this formulation of a challenge to Jrm's prophesying.

■ **4** "Face to face" is literally "his mouth with his mouth," and "eye to eye" is "his eyes to his eyes." The pairing of the two clauses is found otherwise only in 34:3, the source of the present passage; but "mouth to mouth" is found, with another preposition and without personal suffixes, in Num 12:8. Given the fate that ultimately befell Zedekiah (39:5–7), the reference to "mouth" and "eyes" is ironic.

■ **5** "Stay" in Hebrew is literally "be" (היה). The verb does have this nuance elsewhere,[8] but it is striking phraseology here; *G* has "remain" (καθιεῖται) and *G*[A] has "die" (ἀποθανεῖται), which is what one might expect (compare 20:6). "No matter how much you fight" is literally "when you shall fight"; the second-person verbs are here plural.

■ **6–7** The word "uncle" (דּוֹד) is specifically "father's brother" (thus the Versions). The name Hanamel is not found for any other person in the OT, but Shallum is a common name. Robert Wilson speculates that Jrm's Uncle Shallum may have been identical with the husband of Huldah the prophetess (2 Kgs 22:14),[9] but even though the chronology is appropriate, one has the impression from 2 Kings that that Shallum was a member of a Jerusalem family, and the impression from the present passage that this Shallum was a member of Jrm's clan in Benjamin.

"Buy" (קנה) has a wide connotation, "acquire" (often by barter or purchase). Without standardized coinage, purchase was accomplished by barter (Hos 3:2) or by weighing silver (v 9).

The "right of redemption" (מִשְׁפַּט הַגְּאֻלָּה) is set forth in Lev 25:25–32; it is as much an "obligation" as a right. If a piece of land is sold out of the family because of economic pressure (Lev 25:25), or if the land is in danger of being sold (so evidently the situation here with Hanamel), then since property should stay in the family,[10] the next of kin has an obligation to buy it back. The law is the background for the role of Boaz in the Book of Ruth.[11] There is no way to determine Hanamel's circumstances, whether he had fallen into debt, or whether he despaired of the future and was selling out, or both.[12]

There is also no way to determine the way the "word of Yahweh" came to Jrm; Johannes Lindblom remarks, "Jeremiah's foreknowledge that he would be called on by his kinsman Hanamel (xxxii. 6f.) was a sort of presentiment such as we have all experienced."[13]

For the restoration of "Buy (it) for yourself" see Text, and see Structure, Form, Setting.

■ **8** For the possibility that the narrator here intends a modest shift in wording between the quotation here and that in v 7 see Text, and see Structure, Form, Setting.

The phrase "right of possession" (מִשְׁפַּט הַיְרֻשָּׁה) is sometimes assumed to mean "right of inheritance" (*KJV*,

7   See in detail Bustenay Oded, "Judah and the Exile," *Israelite and Judaean History* (ed. John H. Hayes and J. Maxwell Miller; Philadelphia: Westminster, 1977) 473.

8   BDB, 226b, III, 2.

9   Wilson, *Prophecy and Society*, 223.

10 De Vaux, *Ancient Israel*, 166.

11 For bibliography see Robert C. Dentan, "Redeem, redeemer, redemption," *IDB* 4:21–22, with bibliography; Helmer Ringgren, "גָּאַל," *TDOT* 2:350–55, esp. 352, and bibliography; and commentaries on Lev 25:25–34 and Ruth.

12 So the speculations of Thompson, p. 588.

13 Lindblom, *Prophecy*, 200.

JB) or "right of succession" (*NJV*). The verb ירש means "come into possession" (by taking property over from others, either by conquest or by inheritance). It is possible that inheritance rights are at issue here: one assumes that Hanamel had no sons, or he would not have approached Jrm to buy the field. (Compare Bright's remark: "We know too little about Jeremiah's family connection, and about the operation of property and inheritance laws at the time, to say whether in this case Jeremiah was actually the next of kin, as vs. 8 might imply, or whether these rights and privileges had devolved upon him because others closer of kin had refused to exercise them.")[14] But the interpretation here is that there is no legal distinction intended between "possession" and "redemption," simply a variation in wording; if this is the case, then it is fruitless to pursue a distinction.

RSV and *NJV* translate v 8b "then I knew that this was the word . . . ," and *JB* has "I knew then." This understanding is based on the match between the wording of v 7 and v 8a. The present text of v 8a does match, but the proposal of the present study of variation of wording between the two quotations (see Structure, Form, Setting) renders so interpretive a translation questionable. Even with the variation of wording assumed here the meaning of v 8b may be "then I knew," but if so, it implies "in spite of verbal variation" as much as "because of matching of diction."

■ **9** The average weight of the Israelite shekel, according to the handbooks, is 11.424 grams,[15] so that it is a matter of a little less than 200 grams of silver, something less than a half pound. Since neither the size of Hanamel's field nor the purchasing power of silver at the time is known, there is no way to determine whether the price was normal, high, or low; conceivably the amount communicated some nuance at the time that is lost on later generations—for example if the amount paid was generous for the piece of land.

■ **10–14** These verses offer the most detailed description of the process of transfer of property to be found in the OT. Some of the terms are technical, however, and not everything is as clear as one could wish.

■ **10** The first clause is literally "and I wrote in the document [that is, the deed]." There must be a nuance here that is not patent; Jrm dictated his material (36:4, 32), so that, his scribe Baruch nearby (v 12), it is unlikely he would write out the deed himself. It is possible that it means "drafted orally for (eventual) writing" (*JB*: "drew up the deed"). It is not likely that it means "signed the deed" (*RSV*, *NEB*): surely the personal validation betokened by a "signature" is the seal (second clause). One possibility is that the verb stem is not qal but hip'il (וָאֶכְתֹּב rather than וָאֶכְתֹּב): the hip'il is not cited in the OT but occurs in postbiblical Hebrew in the meaning "cause to be written."[16]

The "sealing" (חתם) evidently both closed the document (v 11) and attested Jrm's subscription to the transaction (compare the use of witnesses in the next clause). The seals in use during the late monarchy in Israel and Judah were stamp seals (rather than cylinder seals).[17] Many of them were inscribed with the name of the owner:[18] compare the discovery of the seal impression of Baruch (see on v 12). But there is no information on the nature of Jrm's seal.

Jrm got witnesses for the transaction.[19] Then he weighed out the silver on scales.[20]

Some commentators have been puzzled that the mention of witnesses comes after the sealing of the document; the suggestion has been made that the clauses are simply topical, not strictly chronological (Naegelsbach, Rudolph), but the evidence of deeds from Elephantine and the Judean desert (see below on v 11) indicates that the witnesses signed the outside of the sealed section of the deed.

■ **11** The deed (הַסֵּפֶר, literally "the document," v 10) is now more specifically called "the deed of purchase" (סֵפֶר הַמִּקְנָה, literally "the document of acquisition"), and is further specified as "both the sealed and the public [or revealed]." Does one have to do here with two objects or

---

14 Bright, p. 239.

15 Georges A. Barrois, "Chronology, Metrology, etc.," *IB* 1:156; Ovid R. Sellers, "Shekel," *IDB* 4:317.

16 Jastrow, p. 679a.

17 For specimens see Olga Tufnell, "Seals and scarabs," *IDB* 4:256–57, nos. 18–29; *ANEP*, 85, nos. 276–78.

18 For these see now Herr, *Scripts*.

19 Compare Moshe Greenberg, "Witness," *IDB* 4:864,

or Cornelis van Leeuwen, "עֵד, Zeuge," *Theologisches Handwörterbuch zum Alten Testament* (ed. Ernst Jennis and Claus Westermann; Munich: Kaiser, 1971–), II, col. 211.

20 For pictures and description of ancient balances see Ovid R. Sellers, "Balances," *IDB* 1:342–43; fig. 14 there = *ANEP*, 210, #639; see also *ANEP*, 40, #133.

one? *M* in v 14 has a plural ("these deeds" and "them," though one could make a case for a singular meaning for הַסְּפָרִים—compare Isa 37:14). Older commentators (thus Calvin, Naegelsbach) assumed two objects, "to have a second copy in case the first is lost" (Naegelsbach). But it became clear to commentators, beginning with Hitzig, that the plural phrase in v 14 is a gloss[21] and that ancient archeological material suggests a single object (a Babylonian clay tablet with a clay "envelope" inscribed thereon with a copy of the document).[22] And recent discoveries of deeds at Elephantine from the fifth century b.c.e. and in the Judean desert from the end of the first century or the beginning of the second century c.e., written on papyrus, make the terminology of this verse clear.[23]

The procedure was as follows. On a single sheet (in the present instance, whether of parchment or of papyrus we do not know) the text was written twice, on the upper half and the lower half, with a small gap between the lines of the one and the other. Then the upper half was rolled up, perhaps folded as well, and then sealed, perhaps having been tied (the Judean desert deeds were tied with two-ply thread), and the witnesses' names were written on the outside of the sealed section. The unsealed section was then loosely rolled but available. As Bright observes, "Thus the sealed copy protected the document from fraudulent alteration, while the open copy was available for ready reference."[24]

The phrase here translated "the command and the ordinances" is puzzling. The phrase is omitted in *G*, a circumstance suggesting either that it is a clarifying gloss or else that *G* omitted words that the translator did not understand.[25] The words may be technical terms. In the case of the deeds in the Judean desert, "occasionally, though rarely, the wording of the interior was not absolutely identical with that of the exterior, but gave only an abstract of the subject matter."[26] It is possible that this phrase, a further description of the sealed copy, may indicate that stipulations were detailed in that copy which were not specified in the open copy: the words might mean "the contract and conditions" or the like. But since both words have general import, seeming to imply nothing more than "Torah" would, the present study follows with some hesitation the suggestion of John Peters, that the words are a gloss based on Isa 8:16:[27] since in that passage the word חָתוּם (or חָתוֹם?—see *BHS*) is followed by תוֹרָה, Peters suggests הַמִּצְוָה וְהַחֻקִּים was added here after הֶחָתוּם.

■ **12** Jrm gave the deed to Baruch for safekeeping: this is the first mention of Jrm's scribe in the book. Chronologically he enters the story first in the narrative of the dictation of the first scroll in 605 (36:4). Normally he is called "Baruch the son of Neriah"; this is the only instance in the book where his grandfather's name is given as well. Since Baruch's brother Seraiah was part of a delegation from Zedekiah to Babylon (51:59), one may surmise that the two were members of a family prominent at the royal court. Baruch is specifically called "the scribe" in *M* of 36:26, 32 (the word is omitted in *G*), and it is striking that a bulla (stamp-seal impression) has turned up recently (it is now in the Israel Museum) inscribed לברכיהו בן נריהו הספר "belonging to Berechiah son of Neriah the scribe" in formal-cursive Hebrew of the seventh century[28] (a photograph of the bulla appears on the endpapers of the present volume). There is no doubt that the owner of the seal was none other than Jrm's scribe: "Neriah" is a name not otherwise attested in the OT for anyone but the father of Baruch and of Seraiah. The evidence, then, is that "Baruch" here is a shortened form of the name (literally "blessed" for

---

21 So already Bernhard Stade, "Miscellen, 8: Jer. 32,11–14," *ZAW* 5 (1885) 175–78.

22 See Giesebrecht, p. 177.

23 For Elephantine see Bezalel Porten, *Archives from Elephantine, The Life of An Ancient Jewish Military Colony* (Berkeley/Los Angeles: University of California, 1968) 197–99; for the Judean desert see Yigael Yadin, "Expedition D—The Cave of the Letters," *IEJ* 12 (1962) 236–38, and fig. 48B; and finally compare the wording of *m. B. Bat.* 10:1, and compare further *ANEP*, 82, fig. 265.

24 Bright, p. 238.

25 Janzen, p. 16.

26 Yadin, "Expedition D," 237.

27 John P. Peters, "Notes on Some Difficult Passages in the Old Testament," *JBL* 11 (1892) 43.

28 See bibliography, and in addition Yigal Shiloh and David Tarler, "Bullae from the City of David: A Hoard of Seal Impressions from the Israelite Period," *BA* 49 (1986) 204.

"blessed of Yah[weh]"); compare the number of bearers of the name "Berechiah" in the OT.[29] Baruch was doubtless trained in a scribal school.[30]

Since he went into hiding with Jrm in the events of 601 (36:19, 26), and since he would accompany Jrm in their final exile to Egypt (43:6), one wonders whether he was sharing at this time Jrm's confinement in the court of the guard.

Conceivably "the Jews sitting in the court of the guard" was originally intended as an apposition to "the witnesses signing in the deed of purchase," and "and" was added secondarily; but it is safer to take them as an additional group. "Sitting" (הַיֹּשְׁבִים) reminds one of Ruth 4:4, a description of the witnesses to that sale of property, so the expression may be a conventional description of the context of transfer of land.

■ 14 The messenger formula at the beginning of the verse is not to be excised (against Volz, Rudolph, Bright); the command to Baruch is a divine word (for a discussion of the question see Structure, Form, Setting, and compare the following remark on the infinitive absolute).

The infinitive absolute לָקוֹחַ ("take") functions as an emphatic imperative (compare הָלוֹךְ in 2:2 and often); this usage is found particularly when Yahweh is the speaker.[31]

The question whether the words "the sealed (part) and the public" are original to the verse is difficult. G has "the public" but not "the sealed." It is safer to assume that the tradition in G has been compressed or shortened by haplography than to assume that the whole phrase is secondary.[32]

Baruch is to deposit the document in an earthen vessel. The preservation of the Qumran scrolls of Cave I in pottery storage jars is a splendid archeological parallel.[33] Those scrolls were preserved in their storage jars for a far "longer time" than Jrm presumably had in mind for his property deed!

■ 15 The second divine word is a generalizing one: one field suggests fields, plural. It is an astonishing statement

(compare vv 16–25) and a turning point in Jrm's message; for an exploration of these matters, and of the addition of "houses" and "vineyards" here, see Structure, Form, Setting.

■ 16–17, 21–25 "And I prayed": the only other instance in the book in which Jrm is recorded as praying (by the occurrence of this verb) is 42:4, a prayer in response to the request for guidance from the group proposing to go down to Egypt. The present passage is the only occurrence of the verb in Jrm in which he prays for his own guidance. For the mind-set of Jrm at this time compare Structure, Form, Setting.

"Ah, Lord Yahweh": these words of dismay are found in three other passages—1:6; 4:10; 14:13—all reflections of crises for Jrm: his call (1:6), and then the circumstance in which the optimistic prophets claim to have the truth (4:10; 14:13), a period dated in the present study to December 601 or early 600.

For Jrm's affirmation of the power of Yahweh in creation (v 17) see Structure, Form, Setting: the diction is close to the word to the pagan kings in 27:5.

Verses 21–22 replicate the phraseology of the old credo in Deut 26:8–9 with appropriate shifts of person (Deuteronomy: "Yahweh brought us out . . ."; the present passage: "you brought Israel out . . .").[34]

"Came in and took possession" (v 23) is a repeated combination in Deuteronomy (Deut 1:8; 4:1, 5); for the theology compare the treatment in this study of 2:7. "Did not obey your voice": a convention in Jer, both in poetry (3:13) and prose (7:28). "Walk in your law": compare 26:4. "Made all this evil befall them": this expression is found only here in the OT: the hip'il stem of קרא II "befall" is found only here—the reference is of course to the siege of the city.

The diction of the beginning of v 24 is odd: the "siege-mounds" are personified. G has attempted to soften the phrase by translating "The multitude has come . . . ," but it is doubtful that this is a clue to a superior text; Rudolph ingeniously suggests that the G reading (ὄχλος)

29   Harvey H. Guthrie, Jr., "Berechiah," IDB 1:385.
30   For a solid reconstruction of Baruch's training as a scribe see Muilenburg, "Baruch"; for a general survey of the known events of his life see James M. Ward, "Baruch," IDB 1:361.
31   GKC, sec. 113bb; Joüon, Gramm., sec. 123u.
32   So also Janzen, p. 15, who discusses thoroughly the textual questions of the verse.
33   See for example Frank M. Cross, "The Dead Sea Scrolls," IB 12:645b, and the illustration in IB 12 after p. 628, fig. 12; and Otto Betz, "Dead Sea Scrolls," IDB 1:790a.
34   For a discussion of the confession in Deuteronomy see von Rad, Old Testament Theology 1, 122–23, and compare 297–98; for the phraseology here compare the treatment of 11:4–5.

is a corruption of ὁ χοῦς, "dust."[35]

"The city has been given" (vv 24, 25) is of course proleptic, a prophetic perfect (compare Volz): the city will inevitably fall.

"What you have spoken has come true" is syntactically coordinate with the preceding clauses but is intended as a summarizing statement. The bold words "as you can see for yourself," literally "and here you are, seeing," are omitted by G, doubtless because they are too anthropomorphic.[36] The rhetoric continues to be bold in v 25: the verse begins with the emphatic subject pronoun and ends with a repetition of "the city has been given . . . ." Jrm wants clarity and consistency from Yahweh: "You have decreed the destruction of the city, and then you turn around and say, Buy the field!"

G in v 25 has a longer text, "Buy for yourself the field with silver, and I wrote a deed, and sealed (it), and had witnesses witness"; the expansion is doubtless secondary, from v 10.[37]

■ 18–20 The phrase "showing love to the thousandth generation" (v 18) is found identically in Exod 20:6 and Deut 5:10, and with variation of wording in Exod 34:7 and Deut 7:9. Translations have been uncertain whether to translate "to thousands" or "to the thousandth generation"; in favor of the latter rendering is the implied contrast with "the third and fourth generation" in Exod 20:5 and Deut 5:9 and the explicit language of Deut 7:9.[38] For "show love" (אשה חסד) compare 9:23 and the more extended discussion of חֶסֶד in 2:2: the emphasis here is on Yahweh's unconditional love, which is eternal.[39]

"Paying back the iniquity of the fathers into the lap of their children after them"; there is a similar phrase in Exod 34:7, but the wording here ("lap") is close to that of Isa 65:6–7. There it is part of a pronouncement of sentence (Strafankündigung);[40] here it functions as part of hymnic affirmation as the corresponding phrase in Exod 34:7 does. The collocation of expressions of Yahweh's love and judgment here is severe, more so than in Exod 34:7, where it is softened somewhat by the interposition of "yet not declaring the guilty guiltless" (NAB).

"God great and mighty" (הָאֵל הַגָּדוֹל הַגִּבּוֹר): the phrase appears in Deut 10:17 and Neh 9:32; similar diction is found in Dan 9:4; Neh 1:5, and elsewhere. This epithetic phrase for Yahweh has its roots far back in the liturgical tradition of Israel—indeed it is doubtless pre-Israelite,[41] revived here at a late period.

Verse 19, "great in counsel and mighty in deed" (גְּדֹל הָעֵצָה וְרַב הָעֲלִילִיָּה): there is no exact parallel for this phrase elsewhere in the OT. One has the impression that behind it lies the diction of Exod 34:6, "slow to anger and abounding in covenant love and faithfulness" (אֶרֶךְ אַפַּיִם וְרַב־חֶסֶד וֶאֱמֶת), but a closer parallel might be Ps 147:5, "great is our Lord, and abundant in power" (גָּדוֹל אֲדוֹנֵינוּ וְרַב־כֹּחַ). The parallel of גָּדוֹל and רַב is found in 50:41, and its existence suggests that רַב, normally rendered "numerous" or the like, must be extended to mean "wondrous" as well.[42] The word עֲלִילִיָּה for "deed" appears nowhere else in the OT. The normal form is עֲלִילָה, to which Duhm emends the word here, but most would assume the word simply to be carrying the suffix -iyyâ like פְּלִילִיָּה in Isa 28:7.[43]

"Whose eyes are open to all the ways of humankind": again this phrase lacks a parallel in the rest of the OT, though the general notion is a convention of wisdom (Prov 5:21; Job 34:21). "To give to each according to his ways": the phrase is found in 17:10—"ways" reflects here its occurrence in the phrase just preceding.

Verse 20, "who have set signs and wonders in the land of Egypt": the verb "set" (שׂים) is not common with "signs and wonders"—elsewhere only in Pss 78:43 and 105:27. The parallel of "signs" and "wonders" is common (see v 21), especially in Deuteronomy to describe the deliverance of Israel from Egypt (Deut 26:8 once more). The effort here is to take the specific words of Israel's salvation history and adapt them for more universal application: "humankind" in v 19, and "to this day" and "both in Israel and among mankind" in the present verse

35   See BHK and BHS.

36   Rudolph, p. 211.

37   Janzen, p. 64.

38   Compare Childs, Exodus, 388.

39   See the analysis of Exod 34:7 in David N. Freedman, "God Compassionate and Gracious," Western Watch 6 (1955) 17.

40   Westermann, Isaiah 40—66, 402.

41   See G. Ernest Wright, "Deuteronomy, Introduction and Exegesis," IB 2:401; Frank M. Cross, "אל," TDOT 1:257–58.

42   Adele Berlin, "On the Meaning of rb," JBL 100 (1981) 91–92.

43   Rudolph, p. 210; KB followed Duhm, but HALAT follows Rudolph.

(compare Structure, Form, Setting). The closing of the verse, "and made yourself a name as at this day," is duplicated in Neh 9:10 and Dan 9:15, in both of which the context is again the deliverance from Egypt.

■ **27** Jrm has addressed Yahweh (v 17), so that Yahweh's self-asseveration here is surprising (compare "I am Yahweh" in 17:10, expressed in another crisis in the prophet's life). The expression "God of all flesh" is unique in this form in the OT (see Structure, Form, Setting); it is an affirmation that stretches Jrm's understanding of the sovereignty of God to the utmost (compare the use by Deutero-Isaiah of the same diction, Isa 49:26, and indeed 40:5, 6). For the question "Is anything too hard for me?" and its evident assonance of "anything" (כָּל־דָּבָר) and "all flesh" (כָּל־בָּשָׂר) see Structure, Form, Setting.

■ **28–35** See below, after vv 41–44.

■ **36–37** If the textual reconstruction "thus I shall say" here and in v 42 is correct, it would be a unique variation of the messenger formula, a self-imposed affirmation of what Yahweh will say in time to come (for justification see further Structure, Form, Setting).

The citation in v 36 is a paraphrase of v 24. The verb "gather" in v 37 is found in an analogous line of poetry, 31:8; "where I have driven them" paraphrases the hopeful expression in 30:11, and the phrase in turn entered into other passages as a gloss (23:8; 24:9; 27:10, 15; 29:14, 18). For "in anger, wrath and great rage" see 21:5 (without personal suffixes). For the word-play in "bring them back" and "settle them" see Structure, Form, Setting. For "securely" (לָבֶטַח) compare 23:6. The affirmation in v 37 is the fount out of which all the other prose affirmations of restoration come.

■ **38–40** See below, after vv 41–44 and 28–35.

■ **41** The phrase "rejoice to do them good" is found only here in Jer, and in two late passages in Deuteronomy (see Structure, Form, Setting); indeed it is the only occurrence of "rejoice" (שׂוֹשׂ) in the book, a verb found often in Trito-Isaiah, both of Yahweh (Isa 62:5; 65:19) and of the people over Yahweh (Isa 61:10). "Plant" of course reflects that verb in Jrm's call (1:10) and elsewhere. "With all my heart and with all my soul" is unique here of Yahweh (see Structure, Form, Setting). All these aston-

ishing turns of phrase suggest the marvel by which Jrm perceives Yahweh to be liberated to speak of the restoration of his people.

■ **42** For the emendation "thus I shall say" compare v 36. The structure of "just as" (כַּאֲשֶׁר) and "so" (כֵּן) is identical to that in 31:28, and the thought is the same (see there). "Bring evil upon" is a convention of the book (4:6; 6:19, and often), but the phrase "bring good (upon)" is unique here to the book. The parallel with Josh 23:15 is striking: the latter is evidently dependent upon the present passage.[44]

■ **43** All four Versions translate "the field" (הַשָּׂדֶה) as a plural, and the commentators either assume that a plural is meant (Rudolph speculates that the he is dittographic), or else that the singular is "collective" (again Rudolph)—Freedman states that the singular here means "a rural district as distinct from urban settlements."[45] Giesebrecht notes that the singular would suggest the specific field that Jrm bought at Anathoth, but he then rejects this reading in favor of an emendation based on G ("fields shall again be bought"). To the contrary, M makes a contrast between "the field"—Jrm's specific field—in this verse and "fields" in general in v 44. Yahweh is here validating the symbolic action that Jrm has undertaken.

If the citation of Jrm's words in v 36 represents a paraphrase of v 24, the citation in this verse is not a paraphrase of anything in vv 16–25. The closest expression in poetry is perhaps 4:23–28: "desolation" (שְׁמָמָה) occurs in 4:27, and the pairing of "man" and "bird" in 4:25 (one notes that "beasts" and "birds" are paired in a passage from the same period, 12:4). But the word "desolation" occurs often elsewhere in the book, and pairing of "man" and "beast" is a convention of the prose (7:20 and elsewhere).

■ **44** The diction of the first part of the verse is reminiscent of v 10. M has "they shall buy," a qal verb, whereas vv 15 and 43 offer nip'al verbs: these precedents led V here to vocalize the verb as a nip'al, יִקָּנוּ, thus "fields with silver shall be bought." But the verb in M is followed by a series of infinitive absolutes: the syntax suggests an identity of subjects for all the verbs, and therefore M should be retained. The use of the infinitive absolute in a

---

44 Weippert, *Prosareden*, 206–8.
45 Freedman, p. 224.

series after a finite verb is found not only in the OT[46] but also in inscriptional material of the period.[47]

For "in the land of Benjamin and the region of Jerusalem and the cities of Judah" see Structure, Form, Setting, and for the individual phrases see 17:26; for "I shall restore their fortunes" see 29:14.

■ **28–29** These two verses are a pastiche of diction found elsewhere: for v 28 compare v 24 and 21:10; for v 29a compare 21:10 and 14, and for v 29b see 19:13.

■ **30–31** These two verses offer distinctive phraseology. Thus the form of the word "youth" in v 30a (נְעֻרֹת) is unique in the OT, a by-form of the normal נְעֻרִים.[48] The reinforcement of the participle in v 30a ("doing evil") by the perfect "have been" is not common, but compare 26:18; here it indicates durative action up to the present.[49] The participle is here reinforced by "indeed" (אַךְ), as is a corresponding participle in v 30b.

The idiom in v 31b, literally, "for on my anger and on my wrath has been for me this city," is unique, though something like it appears in 52:3; the general meaning is clear, though the precise nuance is not.[50]

"From the day they built it until today," a reference to the founding of the city of Jerusalem and its steady wickedness, appears to be unique both phraseologically and thematically. Thus the idiom וְעַד + לְמָן appears elsewhere designating a span of time within a given human life (2 Sam 19:25) and appears in Jer 7:25 of the exodus from Egypt (compare Deut 9:7), but nowhere else of the founding of Jerusalem (one notes its occurrence in Deut 4:32, a late addition, of God's creation of man); and I find no reference elsewhere to the time when Jerusalem was built, though the idea of Jerusalem as a locus of wickedness is common elsewhere (thus 6:7 and Ezek 24:6, 9).

The phrase "remove it from my presence" (הֲסִירָהּ מֵעַל פָּנַי) is reminiscent of 2 Kgs 23:37, a product of the exilic redactor of Kings.

■ **32** Verse 32aα is similar to 11:17, itself a late gloss (see there); the listing of "they, their kings, their officials, their priests and their prophets" reflects the same kind of listing as in the late 8:1 and in the gloss in 2:26; and "the men of Judah and the inhabitants of Jerusalem" is a convention not only of Jrm himself (11:2, 9) but of late material as well (17:25).

■ **33** "Turn their back and not their face": compare 7:24. The rendering "to think I taught" renders the independent infinitive absolute (compare 3:1; 4:18; 8:15; 22:14–15). For "early and constantly" see 7:13; for "take correction" see 2:30 and 7:28.

■ **34–35** These verses reflect, with few changes of wording, 7:30–31: see there. Verse 35 contains the divine designation "Molech." The problem this term presents is a complex one.[51] It has traditionally been assumed that the M form מֹלֶךְ is a deformation of מֶלֶךְ "king," understood as a divine designation, by the vowels of בֹּשֶׁת "shame."[52] Then in 1935 Eissfeldt proposed (from Punic evidence) that the vocalization is genuine (originally *molk*) as the designation not of a divinity but a type of offering.[53] Recently, however, George Heider has reviewed all the relevant evidence and concluded that the original vocalization was probably a participle, מֹלֵךְ, "Ruler,"[54] that the Punic designation of a type of offer-

---

46 See GKC, sec. 113z.

47 For example, the Yavneh-Yam inscription, lines 5 and 6–7: see Frank M. Cross, "Epigraphic Notes on Hebrew Documents of the Eighth–Sixth Centuries B.C.E.: II. The Murabbaʿât Papyrus and the Letter Found Near Yabneh-yam," *BASOR* 165 (February 1962) 42–45, esp. 44, n. 43; compare 4Q Samᵃ, col. 10, lines 6–7: see Frank M. Cross, "The Ammonite Oppression of the Tribes of Gad and Reuben: Missing Verses from 1 Samuel 11 Found in 4QSamuelᵃ," *The Hebrew and Greek Texts of Samuel* (ed. Emanuel Tov; 1980 Proceedings, International Organization for Septuagint and Cognate Studies, Vienna, 1980; Jerusalem: Academon, 1980) 108.

48 Compare אֱמוּנִים seven times in the OT, אֱמוּנוֹת once: see Joüon, *Gramm.*, sec. 136g.

49 See GKC, sec. 116r.

50 Compare Bright, p. 296.

51 For recent bibliography of the question see *HALAT*, 560b.

52 Compare Richard W. Corney, "Ishbosheth," *IDB* 2:747a.

53 Otto Eissfeldt, *Molk als Opferbegriff im Punischen und Hebräischen und das Ende des Gottes Moloch* (Halle [Saale]: Niemeyer, 1935).

54 George C. Heider, *The Cult of Molek, A Reassessment* (JSOT Supplement Series 43; University of Sheffield, 1985) 401.

ing is an inner Punic (or Phoenician-Punic) development,[55] and that "the cult of Molek was Canaanite in origin, well-established by the time of Ahaz, and was practiced at least in Jerusalem until the fall of the city in 587/6 B.C.E., with the exception of the reign of Josiah and possibly of Hezekiah."[56] In any event, the question of the original meaning of the term is hardly relevant to the immediate context here: the assumption of the author is simply the designation of a pagan deity associated with child sacrifice.

■ **38** For the covenantal formula see 7:23.

■ **39** For *M* "one heart and one way" *G* has "another way and another heart" and *S* "a new heart and a new spirit." The phrase in *S* is that of Ezek 18:31. One can imagine a graphic confusion in Hebrew between "one" (אחד) and "another" (אחר) and in Syriac between "one" (*ḥd*) and "new" (*ḥdt*). All of these readings are equally plausible; it is best, then, to stay with *M*. The phrase "for good for them" is not easy to parallel: in general of course it reverses "for evil for you" (7:6) and the like and is thus a word of hope for the future.

■ **40** The expression "everlasting covenant" (בְּרִית עוֹלָם) occurs eighteen times in the OT. Eight of them are in P,[57] beginning with Gen 9:16, where the rainbow is the sign of the "everlasting covenant" God makes with all flesh. It appears in 2 Sam 23:5 (part of the "last words of David"), where God makes with David and his house an "everlasting covenant": it is not possible to date that passage, but in any case it is an expression of the Davidic covenant (based on 2 Sam 7:11–16) rather than the covenant with Israel. Ps 105:10 (quoted in 1 Chr 16:17)

is equally difficult to date. Perhaps the key passage is Isa 55:3, which appears to build on 2 Sam 23:5, universalizing for Israel the provisions of the Davidic covenant.[58] The present context ("my fear I shall put in their heart") looks like a reformulation of the new covenant passage (31:31–34) in terms less controversial by recourse to a phrase which became common coin in the exilic and early postexilic period (P; and, beyond those citations already named, Jer 50:5; Isa 24:5; 61:8; Ezek 16:60; 37:26, all late).

Aim

The chapter narrates a turning-point in Jrm's life and mode of proclamation: suddenly, in the midst of the fulfillment of the disaster the inevitability of which the prophet has been proclaiming for thirteen years, good news is revealed to him. He is dismayed: why should God shift ground? The prophet Jonah is portrayed as responding in anger to God's grace to the hated Ninevites (Jonah 4). But God's sovereign decisions again and again leave human expectations in disarray. The title of C. S. Lewis's autobiography, *Surprised by Joy*,[59] touches the same motif from the Christian perspective. And so the way is opened, by Jrm's gesture of solidarity with his family's patrimony, for God to speak a word of restoration to his people, a word that emerged in the ensuing months in the new scroll of hope (the core of chapters 30—31), a word that would sustain the people in the dark years to come.

55   Ibid.
56   Ibid., 405.
57   Westermann, *Genesis* 1:635.
58   See Westermann, *Isaiah 40—66*, 283–84.
59   C. S. Lewis, *Surprised by Joy* (New York: Harcourt, Brace, 1956).

God Will Rebuild
the Houses of Jerusalem

Bibliography

Wambacq, Bernard N.
"Jérémie 33,4–5," *Bib* 54 (1973) 67–68.

33

1 And the word of Yahweh came to Jeremiah a
second time, when he was again confined in
the court of the guard, as follows: 2/ Thus
Yahweh has said, [a]⟨who makes⟩ ⟪whatever
is,⟫ who shapes ⟪whatever is to come,⟫[a] to
establish it—Yahweh is his name: 3/ Call to
me and I shall answer you, so that I may tell
you great and inaccessible[a] things which
you do not know. 4/ For thus Yahweh [God
of Israel][a] has said concerning the houses of
this city and houses of the kings of Judah,
demolished for merlons and for ⟪crenels⟫[b]
5/ [coming][a] to fight with[b] the Chaldeans,
and to fill them with human corpses [whom
I have struck down in my anger and wrath
and from whom I hid my face {from this
city}[d] because of all their evil:][c] 6/ I am
going to bring ⟪to them⟫[a] recovery and
⟨have (them) healed⟩;[b] [I shall heal them][c]

Text

2a—a The text of *M* is impossible: "who makes it,
Yahweh, who shapes it," offering an object suffix
with the first participle and an attached object pronoun with the second. *G* reads the first half differently, "who makes the earth," and that reading is
followed by Duhm, Cornill, Condamin, and Bright;
but the content of v 3 is against the specificity of
"the earth." I follow all the commentators in
rejecting the suffix in עֹשָׂהּ, reading עֹשֶׂה (so *G*). And
I follow the brilliant suggestion of Rudolph to read
אוֹתָיה, the feminine singular participle of אתה
"come," for the object pronoun אוֹתָהּ; the feminine
plural participle occurs in Isa 41:23; 44:7; 45:11.
Parallelism suggests another feminine singular
participle in place of the *M* reading יהוה: I therefore
suggest הוֹיָה: the form appears in Exod 9:3; this is
preferable to the finite verb suggested by Rudolph,
וְהָיָה.

3a For בְּצֻרוֹת a few MSS., the Oriental ketib, and *T*
read נְצֻרוֹת "secret." Since בְּצֻרוֹת ordinarily means
"fortified" (Isa 2:15) and the meaning "inaccessible"
is not found elsewhere, the reading "secret" is
doubtless a secondary correction.

4a Omit with *G*; compare Janzen, pp. 75–86.

b Reading הַחֲרַכִּים with Volz (compare Cant 2:9) for
M הֶחָרֶב "the sword." It is to be noted that *G* reads a
plural word here, "ramparts." One can surmise that
kap was first misread as bet, and then the word was
"corrected" from plural to singular. For a full
discussion see Interpretation.

5a Omit with *G*; the word was inserted on the pattern of 32:24 when הַסֹּלְלוֹת was understood not as
"merlons" but as "(Chaldean) siege-mounds."

b For אֵת some MSS. read אֶל; either preposition is
possible.

c The original section of the passage refers to the
houses of Jerusalem; these two אֲשֶׁר clauses assume
judgment on those who have died. See further
Structure, Form, Setting, and Interpretation.

d *G* omits; this is a further gloss.

6a For *M* לָהּ "to it" (feminine, the city) read לָהֶם with
G[A] and *T* (so all commentators): compare the plural
references of the rest of the verse.

b Revocalizing *M* מַרְפֵּא "healing" as the pi'el participle מְרַפֵּא, parallel with the earlier participle;
compare 1 Kgs 18:30, where the pi'el verb is used of
repairing an altar.

c The expression "I shall heal them" is evidently a
variant reading in a conflate text: the expression
occurs in *G* after "show to them."

and I shall uncover for them fragrance,[d] [《 trustworthy peace, 》][e] 7/ [and I shall restore the fortunes of Judah and Israel,][a] and I shall (re)build them as before 8/ and shall purify them [from all their iniquity by which they sinned against me, and shall forgive all their iniquities by which they sinned against me and rebelled against me; 9/ and it shall be for me a joyful name, a praise and honor for all the nations of the earth, who shall hear all the good which I am doing to them, and they shall fear and tremble over all the good which I am doing to it.][a]

10   Thus Yahweh has said, Again there shall be heard in this place [about which you are saying, It is a waste, without man and {without}[b] beast, in the cities of Judah and in the deserted streets of Jerusalem, without man and {without inhabitant and without}[c] beast,][a] 11/ the voice of joy and the voice of gladness, the voice of the bridegroom and the voice of the bride, [the voice of those saying, "Give thanks to Yahweh of hosts, for Yahweh is good, for his loyalty is for ever," bringing thank-offerings to the house of Yahweh,][a] for I shall restore the fortunes of the land as before, [Yahweh has said.][b]

[12   Thus Yahweh {of hosts}[b] has said, Again there shall be in this place which is a waste, {without man or beast,}[c] and in all its cities, pasturage of shepherds resting their flocks; 13/ in the cities of the hill country and the cities of the Shephelah and the cities of the Negeb and in the land of Benjamin and the region of Jerusalem and the cities of Judah flocks shall again pass under the hands of the one who counts them, Yahweh has said.][a]

d   The vocalization should perhaps not be עֲתֶרֶת but עֲתֶרֶת; for the translation see Interpretation.

e   Reading the expression as either a hendiadys or a construct phrase: it is evidently a gloss borrowed from 14:13 to explain the difficult word preceding.

7a   Generalizing expansion; the passage is concerned with "houses."

8–9a   More generalizing expansions.

10a   Omit the bracketed material: it separates the subject (v 11a) from the verb and offers the same diction as that in 32:36 and 43 as modified in the text tradition of M; see Structure, Form, Setting.

b   Omit with G; see Janzen, p. 49.

c   Omit with G; see Janzen, pp. 49–50.

11a   The bracketed material comes out of the milieu of the postexilic period: see Structure, Form, Setting.

b   This expression duplicates the messenger formula at the beginning of v 10.

12–13a   These verses attempt to parallel vv 10–11; the negative word again is "waste," but this time the positive word is not the voices of joy but the presence of flocks. This is not an interest of Jrm's but reflects the interest of 31:24 (compare 31:12): see further Structure, Form, Setting.

b   Omit with G.

c   Omit with G; this gloss is from v 10 (see Janzen, p. 50).

Structure, Form, Setting

Chapter 33 breaks into two halves. The second half, vv 14–26, is lacking in G, the longest such passage in the book; it therefore needs separate treatment. The first half, vv 1–13, appears to break into three sections, vv 1–9, 10–11, and 12–13; vv 1–9 seem to offer some form-critical unity (see below), whereas vv 10–11 and 12–13 seem to supplement vv 1–9. The chapter begins with introductory words (v 1) that link the material that follows to chapter 32, but it is unclear how much material is understood to be "governed" by those introductory words, and it is unclear whether v 1 is added secondarily to what follows. However, in contrast to chapter 32, some material of which has been widely taken as authentic (see there), the material in 33:1–13 has been viewed with more suspicion: Duhm, Cornill, and Volz reject it outright; Rudolph, on the other hand, and Bright, too, evidently, accept all three sections.

A first inspection of vv 4–9 suggest that words concerning the houses of the city (v 4) have been adapted to refer to the city in general and its inhabitants (vv 5aβ–9: compare Rudolph). It is also clear that the text of vv 4b–5aα is damaged. Given the problem posed by a damaged text and by a suspicion of expansions to the original wording, one must proceed with great care. But the evidence, examined below, is that the core of the passage is authentic to Jrm: the use of "purify" in v 8, the datum that the passage expresses a reversal of the judgment in 19:13, the use of technical terms for battlements in v 4b, and the evident irony in the first of those terms all point to authenticity.

The easiest entry into the complex of difficulties is the first verb in v 8, וְטִהַרְתִּים, "and I shall purify them." This is the only occurrence of טהר pi'el in the book: it is not therefore the convention of a glossator. The antonym of "purify" is "defile" (root טמא): significantly that root occurs in 19:13 (in the present study read as מְטֻמְאִים: see there) as the predicate of "the houses of Jerusalem and the houses of the kings of Judah": there is no other comparable passage in the book. I propose, then, that the present passage is a reversal of the declaration of judgment in 19:13: the houses of the city having been defiled (in the present instance by serving for the disposition of corpses during the siege, v 5), they will be purified. The remainder of v 8 will then be a generalizing gloss.

The judgment of 19:13 is in the context of the breaking of the flask (19:10); the houses in the present passage have been "demolished" (v 4). The reversal then affirms that the houses will be rebuilt: one is confident that the verb of v 7b is original to the passage, and one can read, "And I shall (re)build them as before and shall purify them" (vv 7b–8a).

Given these data, it is clear that the passage, focusing on houses to be rebuilt, is a companion to chapter 32, which focuses on fields to be planted (see Introduction, sec. 22).

I accept the reconstruction of Volz for v 4b (see Text), but I read the two noun phrases as "for merlons and for crenels" (see Interpretation). Some of the houses, having been built on the walls of the city, are being demolished to construct battlements and also to dispose of the corpses which accumulate within the city, since access to tombs outside the city walls is denied the defenders (v 5: see further Interpretation). If the translation "merlons" for סֹלְלוֹת, literally "mounds," is correct, and if the setting for this passage is some weeks or months after that for chapter 32 (see below), then the use of that noun here is highly ironic: the "siege-mounds" (סֹלְלוֹת) of the Chaldeans have moved up to the city, and the response of the city is simply to construct "(little) mounds" in emergency battlements. It is no wonder that the irony was lost on later interpreters who read the word here as a reference to the Chaldean siege-mounds.

The word עֲתֶרֶת in v 6b is a puzzle. The usual translation "abundance" (*RSV*, *NAB*, *NJV*) assumes the word is an Aramaism, cognate with the Hebrew root עשר. But this is dubious; the word עֲתַר, evidently the construct of a noun עָתָר, occurs in Ezek 8:11 with the meaning "fragrance" (of incense): I suggest that the word here in v 6 is a feminine by-form of that word, in the semantic field of incense and purification (compare the vocabulary of the law for the day of atonement in Leviticus 16), the

expression then indicating that Yahweh will reverse the stench of corpses. It is still the "houses" that are at issue: Yahweh will "uncover a fragrance with respect to them."

There is no reason to doubt the thrust of v 6a: it is the reversal of 8:22 (see Interpretation). By this understanding vv 6–8a offer four clauses concerning the actions by which Yahweh will restore the houses of the city, a proclamation of salvation (*Heilsankündigung*).

By contrast the remainder of the material in vv 4–9 is vague and refers not to "houses" but more generally to the city or the people—the judgment on the dead (v 5: see in detail Interpretation), "restore the fortunes of Judah and Israel" (v 7a), "from all their iniquity by which they sinned against me, and I shall forgive their iniquities by which they sinned against me and rebelled against me" (v 8b), and the description of the new identity of the city (feminine singular) in v 9.

Verse 3 attracts attention: it is a divine invitation or summons (compare the wording of Isa 55:6), but a summons to Jrm personally. It suggests that Jrm has been troubled and has called on Yahweh for guidance (compare the wording of Ps 102:2–3). In the summons Yahweh promises to tell Jrm "inaccessible things," really "fortified things." Since the material in v 4 and beyond deal with fortifications for the siege, one infers that Jrm has been dismayed about the destruction of houses for the purpose of strengthening the fortifications of the city, so Yahweh promises to tell him what has theretofore been "fortified," that is, inaccessible in the divine plan.

Verse 2, if the text is here rightly understood, adds to the messenger formula hymnic phrases describing Yahweh's sovereignty over all creation reminiscent of 32:17 and 27. Such phrases are necessary to the discourse of chapter 32 but are unessential to the messenger formula. At the same time the phrases are unusual enough here to commend themselves as original: that is, Jrm is reaching out to Yahweh as creator, since he is convinced the covenant is dead (compare the remarks on 4:23–28). These considerations suggest that the introductory words in v 1 are likely to be dependable, likely to be integral to the passage from the beginning (against Rudolph and Weippert,[1] who believe that vv 1–3 are a secondary bridge between chapters 32 and 33).

If the setting for the purchase of the field (chapter 32) is the summer of 588, then the setting of the genuine portions of vv 1–9 that commends itself is a time following that purchase (v 1: "a second time"), after the Egyptian army had withdrawn from Jerusalem and the Babylonians had tightened the siege, when the defenders of the city began to resort to desperate measures (v 4). The expression עוֹדֶנּוּ in v 1 is ambiguous: it is normally translated "while he was still (confined)" (*RSV, JB, NEB, NAB, NJV*); but it could equally well mean "while he was again (confined)." If one understands the sequence of events correctly, Jrm had been confined in the court of the guard (32:2), was evidently released (37:4, 12), was subsequently imprisoned in a dungeon (37:15–16), and then was transferred by the king to the court of the guard (37:21). This second stay at the court of the guard was at a time of short rations (again 37:21). The situation of the city was by that time desperate: the setting is likely to be the winter or spring of 587.

There is no way to determine the time when the expansions (vv 7a, 8b, 9) were added.

Verses 10–11 are another proclamation of salvation (*Heilsankündigung*); the core of the passage is a reversal of 7:34. Since the genuine portions of vv 1–9 reverse 8:22 and 19:13 (see above), there is no reason to doubt that Jrm understood Yahweh to reverse 7:34 as well. But the words in v 10 that are bracketed in the present study, which intervene between verb and subject, are clearly of the same sort as the modification in *M* of 32:36 and 43, and they can safely be called secondary. The additional words after "the voice of the bride" are more difficult to judge. On the one hand the words are striking enough that they might be an innovation of Jrm (compare the diction of 30:19). On the other hand, the run-on style of those words suggests a secondary addition, a midrash on 30:19; the phraseology reminiscent of Ps 136:1 suggests that we are here in the orbit of the concerns of the second temple. But the phrase "restore the fortunes of the land" (שׁוּב שְׁבוּת הָאָרֶץ) is unique to the book here, and there is no reason why it cannot be original.

The question then arises whether the introductory words (v 1) "govern" vv 10–11 as well. There is no way to be sure, but it would seem doubtful: the original core of vv 1–9 is full of the specifics of the siege, whereas the original diction here has no specific tie with that setting. One has the impression that a genuine word from Jrm was lodged here with the more specific proclamation of salvation, whether before or after its expansion would be impossible to say. Nor is it possible to offer a precise setting other than the general period after Jrm bought the field and was moved to offer such proclamations of salvation.

Verses 12–13 do not reverse anything. They are a third proclamation of salvation in this chapter, with imagery similar to that of 31:23–25 (end of the sixth century or beginning of the fifth?).

Interpretation

■ **1** For the implication of "the second time" and for the translation "again" see Structure, Form, Setting; for "court of the guard" see 32:2.

■ **2** For the justification of the reading of the text in these striking descriptions of Yahweh see Text. Both "make" (עשׂה) and "shape" (יצר) are verbs for creation in Genesis, the former in the P narrative of Gen 1:1—2:4a (eleven instances), the latter in the J narrative in Gen 2:7, 8, 19. (For another possible linking of those two narratives in Jrm's expression see 4:23–26.) For Jrm's frame of mind in depicting Yahweh as creator see the remarks in Structure, Form, Setting on a parallel between this verse and 32:17 and 27.

■ **3** The verb in v 3b is a cohortative introduced by וְ, a sequence expressing purpose ("so that I may tell you").[2] The participle בְּצֻרוֹת normally means "fortified"; its implication here, "inaccessible things," is unique in the OT (hence the confusion generating the variant reading נְצֻרוֹת "hidden": see Text), and one may suspect the word is used because of Jrm's concern expressed in v 4 for the fortifications of the city (see Structure, Form, Setting).

■ **4–5** The text of these two verses is very uncertain. For the details of the reconstruction offered here, see Text; the crucial reconstruction, in v 4b, is that of Volz.

For the parallel of "houses of this city and the houses of the kings of Judah" compare 19:13. "Demolish" (נתץ)

---

1   Helga Weippert, *Schöpfer des Himmels und der Erde* (SBS 102; Stuttgart: Katholisches Bibelwerk, 1981) 73.

2   Joüon, *Gramm.*, sec. 116a–b, d.

is one of the four original verbs in 1:10, in Jrm's call; it immediately raises the question in Jrm's mind whether "(re)building," its antonym, is a possibility (compare v 7).

Verse 4b contains two nouns crucial to the understanding of the passage; significantly G translates with two terms concerned with defense installations: "for palisades and ramparts" (εἰς χάρακας καὶ προμαχῶνας). The meaning of סֹלְלָה is a "mound"; the verb סלל means "pile up" (50:26). The noun elsewhere in the OT signifies a siege-mound (thus 6:6; 32:24), and, especially given the propinquity of 32:24, it is understandable that the word should early be so understood here, with the resultant confusion that the word here refers to Chaldean siege works (compare Structure, Form, Setting). Volz has rightly understood the word to refer to a defense installation, but his translation, "bulwarks," is, I propose, erroneous, as I shall show below. He emends the parallel word to חֲרַכִּים, a word that appears in Cant 2:9 in the meaning "lattice (window)" and that he translates here as "gaps"; the emendation is correct, I submit. But to what, precisely, do these two terms refer? "Bulwarks" is too general a word, and what would the "gaps" be? The reference cannot be to "towers" and the intervening walls between the towers; "towers" would surely be מִגְדָּלִים (Ps 48:13). I propose that what is meant here is the saw-tooth profile of both towers and the intervening wall-line between the towers which is a notable feature of defense-walls from the Bronze Age onward. Yigael Yadin writes, "[The crenelated parapet] looked from a distance like a row of teeth with gaps between them. The teeth are known as caps or merlons. The gaps are called embrasures or crenels. The defending soldier would fire his weapon through the embrasure and find protection from enemy missiles by dodging behind the merlon."[3] Depictions of merlons of the period show them to be slightly rounded on their sides, precisely like small "mounds," and the bases of the crenels are either extremely narrow or missing altogether;[4] this shape is contrived to give maximum protection to the defenders.

(For the irony implied in the use of this term for "mounds" see Structure, Form, Setting.) The houses of the city are thus being demolished to create the battlements "to fight against the Chaldeans" (v 5): houses were often built into the structure of city walls (compare the house of Rahab in Josh 2:15)—this must particularly have been the case with the eastern wall of Jerusalem on the flank of the Kidron Valley.[5]

The other purpose of demolishing houses was to dispose of corpses within the city as the siege progressed, since the cemeteries of Jerusalem lay outside the city walls[6] beyond the reach of the defenders. The expression "human corpses" (פִּגְרֵי הָאָדָם) is curious, since there is no contrast implied with animal corpses here; it evidently simply underlines the horror of the necessity of the disposal of the dead of the city during the siege along with the consequent permanent defilement of the houses (compare Num 19:11–22).

The judgmental secondary words at the end of v 5 appear to be adapted from 21:5–6 and Deut 31:17, itself part of a late addition to Deuteronomy.[7]

■ **6** For "recovery" (literally "new flesh") see 8:22. For the translation "fragrance" for the difficult word עֲתֶרֶת see Structure, Form, Setting.

■ **8** For "purify" see Structure, Form, Setting.

■ **9** The phrase "name, praise and honor" is imitative of 13:11; it is also found in a late addition to Deuteronomy, Deut 26:19.[8] The trembling of the nations is a theme found also in Isa 64:1.

■ **10–11** These verses are a reversal of 7:34: see Structure, Form, Setting.

The word "waste" in v 10 (חָרֵב) is found in the book only here and in v 12; it is reminiscent of its use in Hag 1:4, 9.

For a discussion of the bracketed words after "the voice of the bride" see Structure, Form, Setting.

■ **12–13** For "waste" in v 12 see above, on vv 10–11. The phraseology of "pasturage of shepherds resting their flocks" and "flocks shall pass under the hands of the one

3 Yigael Yadin, *The Art of Warfare in Biblical Lands* (New York: McGraw-Hill, 1963) 20.

4 See the illustrations in ibid., 20, 21, 158–59, and compare the Assyrian depiction of Lachish in ibid., 434.

5 For an archeological description of the walls of Jerusalem at this period see Kathleen M. Kenyon, *Digging up Jerusalem* (New York: Praeger, 1974)

167–69.

6 Compare Reed, "Burial," 475b, and Ruth Amiran and Yael Israeli, "Jerusalem," *IDBSup*, 476b–77a.

7 Mayes, *Deuteronomy*, 376.

8 Ibid., 338.

who counts them" is unique in the OT but is surely foreign to Jrm's concern (for the setting compare Structure, Form, Setting). For the individual phrases of the geographical listing see 17:26.

Aim

The core of the passage reflects the dismay Jrm experiences in seeing the houses of Jerusalem being demolished and becoming steadily more defiled as the siege grinds to its end; into this bleak world comes a word of restoration from Yahweh, who creates all things and holds the future in his hand. This specific word about the houses of the city was expanded in the years thereafter to include the whole city, the whole people, the whole land.

A Future for Levitical Priests
and Davidic Kingship

Bibliography

Baldwin, Joyce G.
"Ṣemaḥ as a Technical Term in the Prophets," *VT*
16 (1964) 93–97.

Grothe, Jonathan F.
"An Argument for the Textual Genuineness of
Jeremiah 33:14–26 (Massoretic Text)," *Concordia
Journal* 7 (1981) 188–91.

Lipiński, Edouard
"Etudes sur des textes 'messianiques' de l'Ancien
Testament," *Semitica* 20 (1970) 41–57.

Snaith, Norman H.
"Jeremiah xxxiii 18," *VT* 21 (1971) 620–22.

Vawter, Bruce
"Levitical Messianism and the New Testament,"
The Bible in Current Catholic Thought (ed. John L.
McKenzie; New York: Herder, 1962) 83–99.

33

14 The days are surely coming, oracle of Yahweh, when I shall perform the good word which I have spoken about[a] the house of Israel and the house of Judah: 15/ In those days and in that time I shall make a scion [a]of righteousness[a, b] spring forth for David, and he shall do justice and righteousness in the land. 16/ In those days Judah shall be rescued and Jerusalem shall dwell securely; and this is [a] the name[a] [b]it shall be called[b]: *Yahweh-ṣidqēnû.*

17 For thus Yahweh has said, No one sitting on the throne of the house of Israel shall be cut off for David, 18/ nor shall any Levitical priests be cut off before me, who offer burnt offerings, burn cereal offerings, and make sacrifices, for all time.

19 And the word of Yahweh came to Jeremiah as follows: 20/ Thus Yahweh has said, if my covenant ⟪can be broken⟫[a] with the day and my covenant with the night, [b]so that[b] day[c] and night are not in their time, 21/ (then) also my covenant will be broken with David my servant, that the have no son reigning on his throne, and with the Levites, the priests, my ministers. 22/ As the hosts of heaven cannot be counted, nor the sand of the sea be measured, so shall I increase the offspring of David my servant, and the Levites [a]who minister to me.[a]

23 And the word of Yahweh came to Jeremiah as follows: 24/ Have you not seen what these people have spoken?—"The two tribes which he has chosen, he has rejected"; my people they have disdained, so they are no longer a nation before me. 25/ Thus Yahweh has said, If [a]⟪I did⟫ not ⟪create⟫[a] day[b] and night, statutes of heaven and earth I did not set, 26/ then the offspring of Jacob and of David my servant I will reject from

Text

14a *M* reads אֶל instead of the expected עַל (see the parallel): *T* reads עַל in both cases (*S* omits "the house of Israel"). The reading of *M* is evidently due to carelessness.

15a—a A few MSS., and *G*[O, L], and *θ'*, read צַדִּיק instead of the *M* reading צְדָקָה, thus "a rightful scion" (compare 23:5).

b Many MSS. add "and a king shall reign and be successful," as in 23:5.

16a—a *M* omits a form of "name," but a few MSS. and *S* include it (compare 23:6); it should presumably be שְׁמָה (compare note b—b).

b—b *M* has a pronoun implying a feminine referent, but a few MSS. and *V* and *S* offer a masculine referent.

20a *M* reads a second-person plural hip'il here, "you can break (my covenant)," awkward after the singular implied in v 19. Since v 21 offers a hop'al, and *G*[L], *V*, and *T* imply a passive in the present verse, it is better to read תֻּפַּר here.

b—b *M* reads וּלְבִלְתִּי, but the copula is hardly correct; omit with *θ'*, *V*, and *S*.

c Should one read יוֹם for *M* יוֹמָם (so Rudolph; see BDB, 401b), or is this simply careless Hebrew? Compare v 25, note b.

22a—a The text here is bizarre: there is no parallel elsewhere for a plural construct followed by an object pronoun (compare GKC, sec. 116g, Joüon, *Gramm.*, secs. 121k, note 1, and 129m). One should undoubtedly read מְשָׁרְתַי, as in v 21.

25a—a Read with Duhm, Cornill, and Rudolph בָּרָאתִי for *M* בְּרִיתִי "my covenant"; a verb is needed after אִם־לֹא.

b One would expect to read יוֹם for *M* יוֹמָם (see v 20, note c).

taking any of his offspring as rulers[a] over the offspring of Abraham, Isaac and Jacob, for [b]I shall restore[b] their fortunes and shall show compassion on them.

26a For the plural מֹשְׁלִים one expects a singular מֹשֵׁל (compare vv 17 and 18), and $G^{O, L}$, θ', and S read a singular.

b—b The qere' and many MSS. read אָשִׁיב, and the ketib reads אָשׁוּב; the same situation prevails in 49:39, and evidently both the qal and the hip'il are acceptable with this idiom (see Holladay, Šûbh, 111).

Structure, Form, Setting, Interpretation

This passage, as is well known, is the longest passage of the book that is missing in G. This fact alone should not absolutely exclude its authenticity—G might have suffered a large haplography; but it does raise a grave suspicion regarding its authenticity and should be laid alongside other data, namely the Hebrew style, the anthological nature of the passage, and the themes it sets forth.

The Hebrew style is careless and inelegant (compare the remarks on 3:6–11 in Setting and Interpretation there): it is difficult to know in some instances whether one has to do with carelessness of textual transmission, carelessness of style, or both. Giesebrecht notes problems with the Hebrew of v 20, but there is more. Not all of the following are necessarily indications of late Hebrew, but several of them must be. (1) There are readings that are probably a matter of textual carelessness (see in each instance the notes in Text): in v 14 אֶל is parallel with עַל; a word designating "name" is missing in v 16; there is the strange expression מְשָׁרְתֵי אֹתִי in v 22; the word בְּרִיתִי is evidently a textual error in v 25. (2) There are readings that are either textual errors or careless idiom (see again the notes in Text): the second person plural verb "you can break" in v 20, given the address to Jrm implied in v 19, and the passive verb in v 21; the use of יוֹמָם for יוֹם in vv 20b and 25 (compare יוֹם in v 20a, and compare the curious expression בְּיוֹמָם in Neh 9:19); the use of the plural מֹשְׁלִים in v 26 when one would expect a singular (compare the phraseology of vv 17 and 18). In addition there is a shift of personal reference to Yahweh and to the people from v 24a to v 24b, a shift that leads Duhm, Cornill, and Condamin to correct the personal suffixes in v 24b. Other solutions to the problem are possible: translations assume that the quotation ends with v 24a; Duhm suggests that v 24b may be a secondary addition. But the implication of parallelism between the two halves of the verse leaves a puzzling situation. (3) The "Levitical priests" are called הַכֹּהֲנִים הַלְוִיִּם in v 18, הַלְוִיִּם הַכֹּהֲנִים in v

21, and simply הַלְוִיִּם in v 22. (4) The use of קטר hip'il with מִנְחָה (v 18) is striking; the usual verbs for "offer" with this noun are קרב hip'il, בוא hip'il, and עלה hip'il. There is no other instance of this verb with מִנְחָה except in 2 Kgs 16:13 and 15, where מִנְחָה is the second noun of a compound object along with עֹלָה. (5) The suffixed construct noun בְּרִיתִי twice in v 20 and once in v 25 is strange,[1] but the same phenomenon (with the same noun) occurs in Lev 26:42, so that this may be an exilic or postexilic priestly idiom.[2] (6) The use of גַּם to introduce an apodosis (vv 21, 26) is not common. There is one early instance, Gen 13:16 (J), and three other late passages, Jer 31:36, 37, and Zech 8:6, beside the two instances under discussion. The idiom of Gen 13:16 may have been imitated in late passages. (7) The conjunction אֲשֶׁר for כַּאֲשֶׁר (v 22) seems to occur otherwise only in Isa 54:9.[3] (8) The usage of the preposition אֶל with משׁל (v 26) is unique.

The passage draws on existing passages but adapts them for a fresh purpose. Thus 23:5–6 is the source for vv 15–16 of the present passage: the earlier passage speaks of a name for the new king (see there), whereas v 16 in the present passage (if the text is sound) speaks rather of a new name for Jerusalem. Verse 14 of the present passage appears to derive its key expression ("perform the good word") from 29:10, but it is to be noted that in 29:10 ("perform my good word") "good" is missing from G and is doubtless secondary (see there). This datum suggests that the present passage was drafted at the same time that "good" was inserted in 29:10. The phrase "no one shall be cut off for X" (לֹא יִכָּרֵת אִישׁ לְ) in vv 17 and 18 appears in Deuteronomistic passages in promises for the Davidic dynasty (1 Kgs 2:4; 8:25 = 2 Chr 6:16; 1 Kgs 9:5 = 2 Chr 7:18),[4] but it is here expanded to refer not only to the Davidic king but to the Levitical priests as well; it appears in Jer only otherwise in 35:19, in reference to Jehonadab the son of Rechab. And 31:35–37 is the model for both vv 19–22 and 23–26: the earlier passage argues from the constancy of the

1   See GKC, sec. 128d, and Joüon, Gramm., sec. 129a, n. 2.
2   For Lev 26:40–45 see Eissfeldt, Introduction, 237–38.
3   BDB, 83b.
4   Weinfeld, Deuteronomy, 355, #8.

sun, moon, and stars and of the heavens and the earth to God's covenantal tie with Israel; vv 19–22 argue from the unbreakableness of God's covenant with day and night to the unbreakableness of his covenant with the Davidic king and the Levitical priests, and vv 23–26 use a double negative to argue from the covenant of day and night to God's fidelity to Israel and to David. Both 31:37 and vv 24 and 26 here use the verb "reject" (מאס); nevertheless it is clear that the two sections of the present passage expand and reinforce the words of the model in 31:35–37. All these data suggest a late setting for the passage.

The content of the passage likewise points to a setting in the postexilic period. Thus the curious beginning of Yahweh's word to the prophet, "Have you not seen?" (הֲלוֹא רָאִיתָ, v 24), is reminiscent of the opening of Yahweh's word to the prophet in 3:6, "Have you seen?" (הֲרָאִיתָ), part of a passage dated in the present study to the Persian period. The renaming of the city of Jerusalem (v 16) is reminiscent of that theme in Trito-Isaiah (Isa 62:4).

But the most substantial datum for establishing a setting is the pairing of "Levitical priests" with the Davidic king (vv 17–18, 21–22). Now the expression הַכֹּהֲנִים הַלְוִיִּם is translated "Levitical priests" in v 18, but it is to be noted that the double expression can equally be rendered "priests, Levites," that the two words are reversed in v 21 ("Levites, priests"), and that "Levites" appears without "priests" in v 22 (see above on the nature of Hebrew style in the passage). The double expression in question appears elsewhere in the OT as well (see below); its meaning, however, is complicated by the existence of the more common expression using the same two substantives but linked by "and"—"priests and Levites"—particularly in Chronicles. Thus Roland de Vaux, in a discussion of "Levites," offers a discussion of both "Levite-priests" and "priests and Levites."[5] Indeed there is the possibility of textual confusion between the two expressions, as Isa 66:21 illustrates. Thus the expression in the present passage raises complicated historical questions about priests and about Levites as well as about the use of the phrase in question.

It is best to begin by listing the occurrences of the double phrase. It occurs, so far as one can discern, almost entirely in the exilic and postexilic period: the only occurrence that may be preexilic is Deut 17:9.[6] The other four occurrences in Deuteronomy (17:18; 18:1; 24:8; 27:9) are either suspected of being part of late passages or are almost surely late;[7] one might add the analogous phrase "the priests the sons of Levi," Deut 31:9, likewise late.[8] Then there are two occurrences in Joshua, 3:3 and 8:33, both part of the Deuteronomistic redaction,[9] and two in 2 Chronicles, 23:18 and 30:27. Finally, there are two occurrences in Ezekiel, 43:19 and 44:15. Those two passages offer their own complications, but it may be said that Ezek 43:19 appears to be a late harmonization[10] and that in any event there is Versional evidence in that verse for the reading "priests and Levites";[11] and that Ezek 44:15 occurs in a passage stemming from the postexilic period that radically separates priests and Levites,[12] so that the word "Levitical" in that passage may need special explanation.

In the preexilic period the Levites had supplied priests for all the sanctuaries,[13] but the reform of Josiah reinforced the claims of the Zadokite priesthood in Jerusalem over against the claims of the Levitical priests outside the central sanctuary.[14] The program of Deuteronomy is intended to guarantee the economic support of Levites who had priestly status outside Jerusalem;[15] the implication of Deuteronomy is that the category "Levites" has equal status with the category "priests."[16] As already noted, the program reflected in Ezek 44:6–31 reflects the demotion of Levites to subpriestly rank; this is the situation reflected in the P code and the period of the second temple.[17] Hanson sees the prophetic program of Trito-Isaiah as a plea of the Levitical community in process of becoming disenfranchised by the Zadokite

5 De Vaux, *Ancient Israel*, 362–64, 364–66.
6 Mayes, *Deuteronomy*, 268–69.
7 Ibid., 273, 274, 324, 343, respectively.
8 Ibid., 374.
9 J. Alberto Soggin, *Joshua* (Philadelphia: Westminster, 1972) 55, 241.
10 Zimmerli, *Ezekiel 2*, 551.
11 *S* and some traditions of *V*.

12 Zimmerli, *Ezekiel 2*, 452–64, esp. 463; and his bibliography, 446–47.
13 See the careful discussion in ibid., 456–57.
14 Hanson, *Dawn of Apocalyptic*, 222–23.
15 De Vaux, *Ancient Israel*, 362–64.
16 Compare Weinfeld, *Deuteronomy*, 228.
17 Raymond Abba, "Priests and Levites," *IDB* 3:883–86.

priesthood,[18] and he sees Zechariah 10—14 as a later set of apocalytic visions offered by that submerged community, who drew on material from the classical prophets, particularly from the royal ideology.[19] If that analysis is sound, then the message of the present passage, which offers a double vision, of the legitimacy of the Levitical priesthood and of the legitimacy of the Davidic king, fits the period of Zechariah 10—14.

Indeed the insistence on God's covenant with the Levitical priests is a concern reflected in Mal 1:6—2:9 and 3:1–5, and the linking of David and the Levitical priests is perhaps reflected in Zech 12:12–13 as well ("family of the house of David," "family of the house of Levi").[20] Malachi is to be dated to about 450,[21] and Zechariah 12 can be dated in the same period.[22]

Now the date for the present passage must be later than that for 31:35–37 (the middle of the fifth century, in the conclusion of the present study): that passage is present in *G*, whereas the present passage is lacking in *G*, and the present passage appears to use 31:35–37 for a model (see above). A date toward the end of the fifth century, therefore, cannot be far wrong.

The mention of "Jeremiah" twice (vv 19, 23) is probably the effort of the anonymous framer of the passage to gain legitimation by the use of the name of the prophet; but it may be noted in passing that the name "Jeremiah" was current at the time of Ezra and Nehemiah (Neh 10:2; 12:34), so that it is not altogether out of the question to envisage a namesake of the original prophet as the author of the passage.

The catchword link between the passage and vv 1–13 is evidently "restore one's fortunes" (שוב שבות), v 26 and v 11 (the occurrence in v 7 is evidently secondary: see there); see Introduction, sec. 22.

The passage breaks into four subsections marked in each case by introductory words (vv 14–16, 17–18, 19–22, 23–26): vv 19 and 23 are identical, and v 20 in addition has "thus Yahweh has said," which is also at the head of v 17. But the third-person references to Jrm in

vv 19 and 23, and the lack of anything similar in vv 14 and 17, suggest either careless drafting or the existence of several previously unrelated sequences.

Form-critically the sections are all proclamations of salvation (*Heilsankündigungen*). Verse 15, like 23:5–6, is the announcement of a royal savior, but v 16 shifts to the promise of a new name for the city (again if the text is sound). Both vv 19–22 and 23–26 are parallel divine guarantees of the stability of Yahweh's covenant by reference to the stability of the cosmos, couched as contrary-to-fact conditions (vv 20–21, 25–26): as already noted, these passages are modeled (in form as well as in content) on 31:35–37. Verse 24 is a divine acknowledgment of what the prophet has experienced (compare Ezek 37:11); vv 25–26 is the divine response.

Little more need be said about particular expressions in the passage. The stress in vv 20–26 is on "my [Yahweh's] covenant" (vv 20, 21, 25). The model passage (31:35–37) does not use "covenant"; the expressions in this passage are reminiscent of the covenant with Noah (Gen 9:9–17 [P]; compare Isa 54:10). The phrase "David my servant" appears in the book only here (vv 21, 22, 26); it is a convention of the D tradition and later material shaped by that tradition.[23] The phraseology of "the hosts of heaven cannot be counted, nor the sand of the sea be measured" is reminiscent of the phrases of Gen 13:16 and 22:17 (J).

Scholars differ in their identification of the "two tribes" in v 24a: the foregoing would suggest the descendants of Levi and the descendants of David (so Volz), and the use of "tribe" (מִשְׁפָּחָה) with "house of David" and "house of Levi" in Zech 12:12–13 would reinforce this identification. On the other hand the equation with "my people" in v 24b and the reference to the offspring of the patriarchs in v 26 suggests that the phrase refers rather to Israel and Judah (so Cornill, Rudolph); but one should note the suggestion of Duhm that v 24b is a secondary addition (see the discussion above on the shift of personal reference between v 24a and 24b). Israel and Judah are

18   Hanson, *Dawn of Apocalyptic*, 95–96.
19   Ibid., 280–380; see notably 351–52.
20   See in detail Vawter, "Levitical Messianism," 83–88.
21   Eissfeldt, *Introduction*, 442–43; William Neil, "Malachi," *IDB* 3:228–32.
22   Hanson, *Dawn of Apocalyptic*, 368; Paul D. Hanson, "Zechariah, Book of," *IDBSup*, 983.
23   For a full list of passages see BDB, 188a, lines 8–11; compare the listing for the phrase "for the sake of David my/his servant" in Weinfeld, *Deuteronomy*, 354, #1.

not otherwise called "the two tribes" (v 24), but the expression (with "two") is reminiscent of the designations of Israel and Judah in Isa 8:14; Ezek 35:10; 37:15–19.

Aim

Hope for the future here takes on a partisan form (see Structure, Form, Setting, Interpretation): it is not only the assurance of a future Davidic king that sustains this section of the community but also the affirmation of the future status of the Levitical priests as well. This hope continued to carry weight in the ensuing centuries: it entered into the perspective of Sir 45:15, 23–26, which exalts the covenant with Aaron over the covenant with David; into that of the Testaments of the Twelve Patriarchs, which assume two Messiahs, from Judah and from Levi; and into that of the Qumran community, which likewise expected two Messiahs, of Aaron and of Israel.[24] It evidently had a part to play in NT thinking as well: a priestly figure, John the Baptist, recorded as a descendant of Aaron on both his father's and his mother's side (Luke 1:5), is brought into conjunction with the Davidic Messiah Jesus.[25]

---

24 See in general Vawter, "Levitical Messianism," 84–94; for the Testaments of the Twelve Patriarchs see Howard C. Kee, "Testaments of the Twelve Patriarchs," *The Old Testament Pseudepigrapha* 1 (ed. James H. Charlesworth; Garden City, NY: Doubleday, 1983) 779, and in more detail H. Dixon Slingerland, "The Levitical Hallmark within the Testaments of the Twelve Patriarchs," *JBL* 103

(1984) 531–37; and for Qumran see the bibliography in Joseph A. Fitzmyer, *The Dead Sea Scrolls, Major Publications and Tools for Study* (SBLSBS 8; Missoula, MT: Scholars, 1975) 114–18.

25 For a discussion of the theme in the NT see Vawter, "Levitical Messianism," 997–99.

The Fate of Zedekiah

Bibliography

On chapters 34—38:

Martens, Elmer A.
  "Narrative Parallelism and Message in Jeremiah 34—38," *Early Jewish and Christian Exegesis, Studies in Memory of William Hugh Brownlee* (ed. Craig A. Evans and William F. Stinespring; Atlanta: Scholars, 1987) 33–49.

On 34:1–7:

Lipiński, Edouard
  "Prose ou poésie en Jér. xxxiv 1–7?" *VT* 24 (1974) 112–13.

Migsch
  Das Ende Jerusalems.

34

1 The word which came to Jeremiah from Yahweh [when Nebuchadrezzar king of Babylon and all his army and all ᵇthe kingdoms of 《 the earth, 》 {*M*: the land of the authority of his hand, and all the peoples}ᵇ were fighting against Jerusalem and against all her cities,]ᵃ as follows: 2/ [Thus Yahweh {God of Israel}ᵇ has said:]ᵃ Go [and say]ᶜ to Zedekiah king of Judah and say to him, Thus Yahweh has said: I am going to give this city into the hand of the king of Babylon, 《 and he will capture it 》ᵈ [and he will burn it with fire;]ᵉ 3/ as for you, you will not escape from his hand—rather you shall be captured and given into his hand; and your eyes will see the eyes of the king of Babylon, ᵃand his mouth will speak with your mouth,ᵃ [and to Babylon you shall go.]ᵇ 4/ Only heed the word of Yahweh, O 〉Zedekiah,〈ᵃ king of Judah: [Thus Yahweh has

Text

1a This chronological notice breaks the continuity and appears to be secondary (so Giesebrecht), adapted from the diction of v 7 (compare 32:2–5).

b—b The present text of *M*, "the kingdoms of the land of the authority of his hand," is conflate. *G* reads "the land of his authority." "Kingdom" (מַמְלָכָה) and "authority" (מֶמְשָׁלָה) are synonyms: in Isa 39:2 *M* reads מֶמְשַׁלְתּוֹ, 1Q Isaᵃ reads ממלכתו. One assumes that the original reading of *M* was "the kingdoms of the earth" (two MSS. read the article with "earth") and that after the variant readings were added הָאָרֶץ was accommodated to אֶרֶץ. See Janzen, pp. 16, 197, n. 30.

2a The formula is mechanical here and is doubtless secondary (so Volz): compare 35:1–2.

b Secondary expansion, omitted by *G*.

c Omit with *G*.

d *G* adds καὶ συλλήμψεται αὐτήν = וּלְכָדָהּ. Opinion differs: Janzen, p. 65, believes the expression is secondary in *G*, but I follow Rudolph in assuming that the expression dropped out of *M* by haplography (compare 32:3), given the sequence מלכבבל just before it.

e Omit this phrase with Rudolph as a *vaticinium ex eventu* (39:8), given the phrasing of 38:17–18; compare the text of 37:8, 10. See Structure and Form.

3a—a This phrase is lacking in *G* and may be secondary in *M* (so the suggestion of Janzen, p. 50); but 32:4 offers a similar double expression in *G* as well as *M*, so that *G* is likely to be defective here.

b Omit the phrase as a *vaticinium ex eventu* (39:7); it contradicts the implication of the first clause of v 5 as here reconstructed.

4a One may suspect that "Zedekiah" is secondary here (compare 22:2) from v 2 (and v 6); a vocative

said {concerning you,}[c]] [b] [d]you shall not die by the sword,[d] 5/ in peace 《in Jerusalem》[a] you shall die; and as (spices) were burned for your fathers [b]⟨who reigned⟩ [earlier, who were][b] before you, so they shall burn (spices) for you and shall lament "Alas, lord!" for you: for a promise I myself have spoken, oracle of Yahweh.

6 So Jeremiah the prophet spoke to Zedekiah king of Judah all these words [in Jerusalem][a] 7/ while the army of the king of Babylon was fighting against Jerusalem and against [all][a] the cities of Judah which remained: Lachish and Azekah, for they were the ones which were left of the fortified cities of Judah.

with an appositive is possible (Zech 3:8) but is not common.

b   When the imperative of v 4a was misunderstood as "hear the word of Yahweh" (see Structure and Form), it was easy to add the rubric "thus Yahweh has said" (so Rudolph; compare 2:4–5; 7:2–3; 17:20–21; 19:3; 29:20–21; 42:15; 44:24–25).

c   Omit with G; it is a later extension of the rubric (so Rudolph; see b).

d   These words are omitted by G, but are evidently to be retained, given the contrastive parallelism with the first clause of v 5a (so also Rudolph). They may have dropped out by haplography (תָּמוּת).

5–6a   "In Jerusalem" evidently dropped out in v 5 and was later wrongly reinserted at the end of v 6 (so Rudolph): or was it deliberately displaced when the prediction did not come true (39:7)? See Interpretation.

b—b   For הַמְּלָכִים "kings" read הַמֹּלְכִים "reigning" with G; 22:11 is a model for the use of the participle of this verb. M may offer a conflate text; it is to be noted that G πρότερον renders both לְפָנִים and רִאשׁוֹן (Hatch-Redpath, 1230b, c). Once the participle was misconstrued as "kings," the phraseology of M becomes plausible (compare the diction of 11:10).

7a   G omits: the word is contradicted by the context (compare Janzen, p. 66).

Structure and Form

Verses 1–7 make up a unit of their own, a word through Jrm to Zedekiah; v 8 is parallel with v 1, introducing another word given to Jrm, this time not to Zedekiah but about him. For the placement of this unit here see Introduction, sec. 22.

Verses 1–5 are the report of Yahweh's command to the prophet to deliver a divine word to the king; vv 6–7 are the report of the execution of that command.

Form-critically the divine word does not fit any standard category. It concerns both the city in general (v 2) and the king personally (vv 3–5); and the word to the king is evidently both a judgment speech (v 3) and at the same time a contingent prophecy of (moderate) salvation (*Heilsweissagung*):[1] if the king responds to the exhortation to heed the word (v 4a), then there is an implied promise that he will die peacefully (vv 4b–5). The situation is complicated still further by the fact that the text was evidently later expanded at several points to conform

with the actual fate of both the city and Zedekiah. Thus the end of v 3 indicates that Zedekiah will go to Babylon, whereas v 5 at least implies that the king will die like his fathers in Jerusalem.

It is best to begin with the expression "in Jerusalem," which makes no sense at the end of v 6; where else, one might ask, would Jrm speak to Zedekiah except in Jerusalem? I therefore accept Rudolph's suggestion that the expression is displaced from a position after "in peace" at the beginning of v 5; haplography of the sequence שׁלם would explain its loss in v 5, but the fact that Zedekiah did not die in Jerusalem (39:7; 52:11) may have played a part in its displacement.

Verses 4–5 thus attract attention as offering material most contrastive with the ultimate turn of events.

The general message that Jrm was giving Zedekiah in the siege of Jerusalem was that if he surrendered, he would live, but if he did not surrender, he would die: the choice is implied in 21:8–9 and is explicit in 38:17–18. It

---

1   March, "Prophecy," 162.

is best then to see a similar choice implied in vv 4–5: the striking particle אַךְ before שְׁמַע דְּבַר־יהוה, and the position of that clause within vv 2–5, suggests that the clause means "heed the word of Yahweh" rather than simply "hear the word of Yahweh"; the clause will then be an implied protasis, and vv 4b–5 will be the implied apodosis (so Rudolph; but his suggestion of inserting וְ before לֹא in the last clause of v 4 is not necessary—see Ps 139:18a). The urgency of the choice is underlined by the curious expression at the end of v 5; it is not "for I have spoken the word" (*RSV*)—the Hebrew is literally "a word"—but "a promise I have spoken" (so Duhm). The contingent good news, though unlikely, is guaranteed by Yahweh.

Verses 2–5 divide into two sections, a shorter one pertaining to the city (v 2) and a longer one pertaining to the king himself (vv 3–5: note the emphatic וְאַתָּה, "as for you," v 3); but the sequence is united by the fact that both the city and the king will be given into the "hand" of the king of Babylon, and both will be "captured" (if that verb is correctly restored at the end of v 2). Then the longer section, pertaining to the king, is itself divided into the moderate bad news, "you will be captured" (v 3), and the moderate good news, "If you heed the word of Yahweh, you will not die violently."

Given this shape to the passage, the clauses at the end of v 2 and at the end of v 3 must be secondary (so also Rudolph): "and he will burn it with fire" contradicts the word of Jrm to Zedekiah in 38:17, and "to Babylon you shall go" contradicts the promise of vv 4–5; but both reflect the events recorded in 39:7–8.

Setting

A chain of probabilities produces a similar setting for the word in 21:1–7 and for the present word (see below). But the two passages offer contrastive predictions for the mode of Zedekiah's death—21:7 states that he will die violently, whereas the present word is that if he heeds the word of Yahweh he will die peacefully. It is therefore important to set forth the evidence as carefully as possible and see what might be made of the contradiction. Indeed the contradiction leads one to examine the chronological sequence of 21:1–7, the present passage,

37:3–10, 17–21, and 38:14–28, each of which in some way sets forth Jrm's word to Zedekiah.

It is convenient to begin with 37:3–10, 17–21, and 38:14–28. It is explicitly stated in 37:3–10 that the encounter took place at the time of the Egyptian invasion, when the Babylonian army had temporarily retired (37:5); this was probably in the late spring or early summer of 588. Since the material in chapters 37—44 forms a continuous narrative, it is to be assumed that 37:3–10, 17–21, and 38:14–28 are in chronological order. In 34:8–22, the reenslavement of the manumitted slaves was the result of the Egyptian invasion (vv 21–22). The setting of the present passage was evidently some time before that for vv 8–22: the wording of v 7 suggests the original Babylonian offensive (compare v 22 and 37:8), in which all the outlying cities of Judah except Lachish and Azekah were captured (v 7).[2] And if the reconstruction of the text of the present passage is sound, it is a nuanced word to Zedekiah, offering both bad news and, if the king chooses soundly, moderate good news as well (compare Structure and Form); in contrast, the word to Zedekiah in 21:1–7 offers no choice to the king. Since there is an analogous expression of choice in 38:17–18, one must conclude that the present passage embodies a fresh revelation to Jrm beyond that in 21:1–7. But there is no way to arrive at a close absolute date for the event narrated here; one must be content to affirm that it would have taken place in the late winter or early spring of 588 (see Interpretation on v 1).

Interpretation

■ 1 Though the wording of the present text of *M* suggests that the chronological note is secondary, there is no reason to doubt its accuracy. The day when Nebuchadrezzar began the siege is named (52:4 = 2 Kgs 25:1); by the chronology adopted in the present study the siege began by January 588.[3] For the time of the event narrated here see Setting.

"Kingdoms of the earth" here suggests the vassals of Babylon (compare the implication of 27:8), contingents of which were evidently part of the besieging army (compare the wording of 1:15 and 25:9).

---

2   Compare Bright, *History*, 329–30.
3   Ibid.

■ **3** The expressions with "eyes" and "mouth" are an implied threat: Bright translates "you will be made to confront him face to face and answer to him personally"; compare 32:4.

■ **5** Zedekiah hardly died "in peace" (39:5–7); for the implied condition see Structure and Form.

The Hebrew text simply says "were burned" and "burn," without an explicit statement of what is burned; but the phraseology of 2 Chr 16:14 and 21:19 makes it clear that it is spices that were burned. For the lament "Ah lord!" see 22:18.

■ **7** Lachish is the present-day *tall ad-duwayr* (Atlas of Israel grid 135–108): the identification is secure from literary, geographical, and archeological data.[4] Azekah is to be identified with *tall zakariyā* (Atlas of Israel grid 144–123).[5] They are cities of the Shephelah, between the Philistine plain and the mountains of Judah. As is well known, the Lachish ostraca date from this Babylonian campaign, and Ostracon 4 offers a dramatic

sidelight on this verse; the closing sentence of that message to the military commander at Lachish reads, "And let (my lord) know that we are watching for the signals of Lachish, according to all the indications which my lord has given, for we cannot see Azekah."[6] It is possible that Azekah was not visible from the location of the writer, but it is more likely that by the time the message was written, Azekah had fallen.[7]

Aim

Zedekiah is not strong (compare 38:19). Could he trust that Jrm speaks for Yahweh, and could he thereby trust Yahweh? Could he resolve to surrender his city?

---

4   See conveniently Richard W. Hamilton, "Lachish," *IDB* 3:53–57.

5   Victor R. Gold, "Azekah," *IDB* 1:326; Denis Baly, *The Geography of the Bible* (New York: Harper, 1974) 142.

6   Lachish 4.10–13; see *ANET*, 322.

7   Bright, *History*, 330, and n. 58 there.

**Breach of Faith
Concerning Slavery**

Bibliography

Baltzer, Klaus
The Covenant Formulary in Old Testament, Jewish, and Early Christian Writings (Philadelphia: Fortress, 1971) 54–56.

Cardellini, Innocenzo
Die biblischen "Sklaven"-Gesetze im Lichte des keilschriftlichen Sklavenrechts: Ein Beitrag zur Tradition, Überlieferung und Redaktion der alttestamentlichen Rechtstexte (BBB 55; Bonn: Hanstein, 1981), esp. 312–23.

David, Martin
"The Manumission of Slaves Under Zedekiah (A Contribution to the Laws About Hebrew Slaves)," *OTS* 5 (1948) 63–79.

Hasel, Gerhard F.
"The Meaning of the Animal Rite in Genesis 15," *JSOT* 19 (1981) 61–78.

Kapelrud, Arvid S.
"The Interpretation of Jeremiah 34,18ff.," *JSOT* 22 (1982) 138–40.

Kessler, Martin
"The Law of Manumission in Jer 34," *BZ* NF 15 (1971) 105–8.

Lemke, Niels P.
"The 'Hebrew Slave,' Comments on the Slave Law Ex. xxi 2–11," *VT* 25 (1975) 129–44.

Lewy, Julius
"The Biblical Institution of *dᵉrôr* in the Light of Akkadian Documents," *Eretz-Israel* 5 (1958) 21*–31*.

Miller, Patrick D.
"Sin and Judgment in Jeremiah 34:17–19," *JBL* 103 (1984) 611–13.

Sarna, Nahum M.
"Zedekiah's Emancipation of Slaves and the Sabbatical Year," *Orient and Occident, Essays presented to Cyrus H. Gordon on the Occasion of His Sixty-Fifth Birthday* (ed. Harry A. Hoffner; AOAT 22; Neukirchen: Neukirchener, 1973) 143–49.

Schedl, Claus
"Zur logotechnischen Struktur von Jeremia 34,18," *BZ* 26 (1982) 249–51.

Weippert
Prosareden, 86–106, 148–91.

34

8 The word which came to Jeremiah from Yahweh after King Zedekiah had made a covenant with [all]ᵃ the people [who were in Jerusalem]ᵇ to proclaim [to them]ᶜ liberty, 9/ that each should send out his male Hebrew slave and each his female Hebrew slave free, so that none should enslave (any) of them, (namely) his Jewish brother. 10/

Text

8a Omit with *G*; compare Janzen, p. 65.
b   Omit with *G*; see Janzen, p. 50.
c   Omit with *G* and *S*; see Janzen, p. 50.

Then all the officials and all the people
ᵃ《reneged》 [M: heeded]ᵃ who had entered
the covenant, each to send out his male
slave and each his female slave [free, so as
not to enslave them again, and they heeded,
and they sent (them) out; 11/ and they
reneged after that, and brought back the
male slaves and the female slaves which
they had sent out free]ᵇ ᶜand subjugated
themᶜ as male slaves and female slaves. 12/
And the word of Yahweh came to Jeremiah
[from Yahweh]ᵃ as follows: 13/ Thus Yahweh [God of Israel]ᵃ has said: I myself made
a covenant with your fathers on the day I
brought them from the land of Egypt, from
the house of slavery, as follows: 14/ "After
sevenᵃ years ᵇyou shall send outᵇ each his
Hebrew brother who shall sell himself to
you; he will serve you six years, and (then)
you shall send him out [from you]ᶜ free." But
they [your fathers]ᵈ did not listen to me or
turn their ear to me. 15/ You [yourselves]ᵃ
turned and did what was right in my eyes by
proclaiming liberty each to his fellow, and
you made a covenant before me in the house
which bears my name. 16/ But then you
turned and profaned my name and took back
each his male slave and each his female
slave whom you had sent out free according
to their desire, [and you subjugated them to
become]ᵃ for yourselves male slaves and
female slaves.

17   Therefore thus Yahweh has said: You yourselves have not obeyed me in proclaiming
liberty [each to his brother and]ᵃ each to his
fellow; I am going to proclaim to you liberty,
oracle of Yahweh—to the sword andᵇ to
pestilence and to famine, and I shall make
you a terrorᶜ to all the kingdoms of the
earth. 18/ And I shall make the men breaking my covenant, who have not performed
[the words of]ᵃ the covenant which they
made before me, (into) the calf which they
cut in two and between the parts of which
they passed— 19/ the officials of Judah,
[and the officials of Jerusalem,]ᵃ the
eunuchs and the priests and [all]ᵇ ᶜ《the
people》 [M: the people of the land,]ᶜ [who

10–11a—a   Read וְיָשׁוּבוּ with G for M וַיִּשְׁמְעוּ. I accept
the analysis of Janzen, pp. 50–51, that in vv 10–11
the shorter text of G is to be accepted (so also
Cornill and Duhm); Rudolph's suggestion that G is
haplographic is to be rejected. There is evidence
elsewhere for a confusion between these two verbs.
Thus in 12:17 M reads שׁמע and G reads שׁוב; and in
Isa 37:9b M reads שׁמע, G evidently reads שׁוב,
1QIsaᵃ has a conflate text (שׁמע + שׁוב), and the
parallel in 2 Kgs 19:9 reads שׁוב.

b   Omit with G; once the first verb in v 10 was misread,
the text was expanded with material from v 16 to
smooth the narrative (see a—a).

c—c   Read the verb as a qal with the qere' (compare v
16); the ketib reads a hip'il.

12a   Omit with G, S, and some editions of T; the
phrase has crept in from v 8 and similar expressions.
See Janzen, p. 51.

13a   Omit with G; compare Janzen, pp. 75–76.

14a   G reads "six," a reading preferred by RSV. But the
phraseology of M here is that of Deut 15:1 and is
undoubtedly correct; the wording of Deut 15:12
and Exod 21:2 indicate that "in the seventh year" is
meant (see further Interpretation). G evidently took
the Hebrew wording "at the end of" too literally and
"corrected" the text.

b—b   I suspect that G rightly preserves a second singular here (which would reflect תְּשַׁלַּח). The second
plural תְּשַׁלְּחוּ would then be an error continuing the
plural diction of v 13 ("your fathers"). By this
understanding all of v 14a then would consistently
offer a second singular, evidently an indication of a
citation (see further Interpretation). The second
plural returns in v 15 (and in the gloss in v 14b).

c   Omit with G; M has expanded the text from Deut
15:12 and 13 (see Janzen, p. 51).

d   Omit with G; the clarification is introduced from v
13. See Janzen, p. 51.

15a   Omit with G; a position after the verb is odd for
an emphatic subject pronoun. G reads all of the
second plural verbs in this verse as third plurals; for
such a shift of person, the antecedent text of G must
have lacked the pronoun (see Janzen, p. 51).

16a   Omit with G; the expansion is suggested by v 11
(see Janzen, p. 51).

17a   Omit with G and S. It is possible that the archetype of those two Versions suffered haplography,
but given the phraseology of v 15, it is more likely
that M has expanded the formula under the influence of 23:35 and 31:34; Deut 15:2 may also offer a
secondarily expanded text.

b   Read "and" with many MSS., with G, S, and some
MSS. of T; M lacks "and."

c   See 15:4, Text.

18a   Omit with G; see Janzen, p. 51.

19a   Omit with G.

b   Omit with G: the same situation prevails in v 8.

c—c   Read וְהָעָם with G (compare vv 8, 10); "the people

pass between the parts of the calf.]^d 20/
And I will give them into the hand of their
enemies [and into the hand of those seeking
their life,]^a and their corpses shall become
food for the birds of the heavens and the
beasts of the earth. 21/ And Zedekiah king
of Judah and his officials I shall give into the
hand of their enemies [and into the hand of
those who seek their lives;]^a and [into the
hand of]^b the army of the king of Babylon,
which has withdrawn from you, 22/ I am
going to command, oracle of Yahweh, and I
shall bring them back to this city, and they
shall fight against it and capture it and burn
it with fire, and the cities of Judah I shall
make a desolation, without inhabitant.

of the land" is out of place here (see Janzen, p. 204
n. 5).

d   Omit with G.
20a Omit with G: the situation is discussed in Janzen,
     p. 42, (e'). Note the similar expansion in 19:9.
21a Omit with G: see v 20.
b   Omit with G; I follow Giesebrecht is construing
     "army" as the object of "command" at the beginning
     of v 22. M then represents a misconstrual of "army"
     as parallel with "their enemies." See the discussion in
     Janzen, p. 42, (f').

Preliminary Observations and Setting

This passage has been attributed by many commentators
to a Deuteronomistic editor.[1] But Weippert has demonstrated that the diction of the passage is appropriate to
Jeremianic tradition and that its resemblance to the
diction of Deuteronomy is a result of its subject matter.[2]
Many of the stereotypical phrases in the passage have
already been dealt with in the present study; for example, the triad "sword," "famine," "pestilence" (v 17)
appears in 14:12: see 14:1—15:9, Setting.

The passage has attracted much attention: it describes
the carrying out of a specific law on an occasion that can
be dated within fairly narrow limits (and of course the
subsequent breaking of that law). It therefore offers
precious evidence of how such a statute was carried out
in practice, but at the same time it raises many questions
of detail.

The citation of the law of the release of Hebrew slaves
in v 14 paraphrases Deut 15:1 and 12, particularly in the
phrases "after seven years" and "you shall send him out
free" (שלח pi'el + חׇפְשִׁי); comparable laws are found in
Exod 21:2 and Lev 25:40–41. But these laws all differ
from each other in specific phraseology. Thus the present passage (vv 8, 15, 17) speaks of קׇרׇא דְרוֹר "proclaiming liberty"; this is the phrase found in Lev 25:10,
on which Lev 25:40 is dependent, but it is not the phrase
in Deut 15:1: that verse speaks instead of עׇשׇה שְׁמִטׇּה
"making a release." In Deuteronomy the "release" is to be
proclaimed at the end of a seven-year period (the sabbatical year: compare the similar wording in Exodus),
whereas in Leviticus the "liberty" is to be in a jubilee

year, which is at the end of a fifty-year period. Furthermore the release of slaves is associated in some way with
the requirements to leave the land fallow every seven
years (Lev 25:2–7) and to forgive debts every seven years
(Lev 25:8–55; Deut 15:1–11). It is thus evident not only
that the laws recorded variously in Exodus 21, Leviticus
25, and Deuteronomy 15 have undergone a complicated
evolution but also that the specific application of the law
referred to in the present passage of Jer uses phraseology
that does not reflect directly any single extant formulation of the law. One wonders, then, whether the
avoidance in the present passage of the phrase of Deuteronomy 15 ("make a release") is deliberate or whether the
writer is simply using a synonymous phrase.

A related problem is the meaning of מִקֵּץ in v 14 (and
its parallel in Deut 15:1): the expression seems literally to
mean "at the end of," suggesting that the slave works for
seven years and is then released. But Exod 21:2 and Deut
15:12 suggest that the slave works six years and is
released at the beginning of the seventh (thus the G
reading in v 14). How is this matter to be solved? Meir
Wallenstein suggests on the basis of phrases in the
Qumran documents[3] that the expression here means "at
the beginning of," thus "at the beginning of the seventh
year."

There is a second major issue. Zedekiah's proclamation of liberty is referred to as his כׇּרׇת בְּרִית, "making
a covenant," with the people (v 8), and again as the people's "making a covenant" before Yahweh (v 15); in v 18
this covenant is actually equated with the covenant that
Yahweh made with the ancestors (v 13). And Yahweh's

---

1   See for example Rudolph, pp. 222–23.
2   Weippert, *Prosareden*, 86–106.
3   Meir Wallenstein, "Some Lexical Material in the

Judean Scrolls," *VT* 4 (1954) 213.

punishment of those who broke the covenant (v 18) makes reference to the procedure of a covenant ceremony described otherwise only in Gen 15:9–21 (though in Genesis it is a heifer [עֶגְלָה], here a [bull-]calf [עֵגֶל] which is slaughtered). The verse may imply that the procedure of Genesis 15 was carried out by Zedekiah. Whether it was or not, the vocabulary of covenant making suggests that Zedekiah was not simply administering a law in the normal course of events but rather that he sponsored something exceptional. What, precisely, did Zedekiah do, under what circumstances, and how was it understood? Verse 14 suggests that the law had been ignored for a long period of time; one wonders, then, was the emancipation an exceptional occasion in being carried out at all, or because it was not proclaimed at the normal time of a sabbatical year, or because the Babylonian siege was under way, or in all of these ways?

Attempts have been made, one should note, to affirm that Zedekiah's declaration of emancipation took place during a sabbatical year: Nahum Sarna dates a sabbatical year to 588/587,[4] and Innocenzo Cardellini dates a sabbatical year to 590/589.[5]

Verses 21 and 22 indicate the context of the events referred to in this passage: the slaveholders had taken their slaves back at the time when the Egyptian army had made its approach to Jerusalem and the Babylonian army had withdrawn its siege. Thus one is led to assume that Zedekiah had proclaimed the emancipation of slaves at the time the Babylonian army was first besieging Jerusalem. Commentators point out that the motives for this emancipation were doubtless mixed: the city could enlarge its complement of defenders, slaveholders would have fewer mouths to feed—and one could gain favor with Yahweh as well.[6] The Babylonians began their siege in January 588 (39:1); the city fell in July 587 (39:2). Some time during that period the Egyptian army approached Jerusalem and the Babylonian army withdrew (37:11). Though the date of the Egyptian advance is not

given, it was doubtless in the spring or summer of 588:[7] spring and summer were the normal time for military ventures, and the spring or summer of 587 is too late, given the record of famine in the city when it fell (2 Kgs 25:3; compare Jer 37:21). One must therefore assume that Zedekiah proclaimed the emancipation of the slaves sometime after January 588, and that the slaveholders took back their slaves sometime in the course of the summer of that year. By the assumptions of the present study (see Introduction, sec. 28) the law of Deuteronomy would be read in September/October 587, the feast of booths in a "year of release," that is, a sabbatical year (Deut 31:10). One must conclude, then, that Zedekiah's proclamation of emancipation was not connected (in either season or year) with the feast of booths in a sabbatical year. One could speculate whether it took place during the feast of weeks in 588. That feast, which would fall in late May or June, became associated with covenant renewal at least in the postexilic period[8] and perhaps earlier. One notes the tradition recorded in 2 Chr 15:10–14, that King Asa (end of the tenth century) entered into a covenant on the feast of weeks: it is perhaps significant that the phrase "enter into the covenant" (בוא בַבְּרִית) is found only in v 10 of the present passage and in 2 Chr 15:12, of Asa's covenant. One could then imagine that the emancipation of Jewish slaves was promulgated in a covenant ceremony at the feast of weeks in the late spring of 588.

Structure and Form

For the position of this unit here see Introduction, sec. 22.

The passage is an extended judgment oracle on the leaders of Jerusalem, though the oracle proper begins only in v 12.

The syntax and the form of vv 8–11 are odd—these four verses are an extended title for vv 12–22: "the word which came to Jeremiah from Yahweh after King Zedekiah had made a covenant with the people." That title is

4   Nahum Sarna, "Zedekiah's Emancipation of Slaves and the Sabbatical Year," *Orient and Occident, Essays Presented to Cyrus H. Gordon on the Occasion of His Sixty-fifth Birthday* (ed. Harry A. Hoffner; AOAT 22; Neukirchen: Neukirchener, 1973) 149.

5   Innocenzo Cardellini, *Die biblischen "Sklaven"-Gesetze im Lichte des keilschfiftlichen Sklavenrechts: Ein Beitrag zur Tradition, Überlieferung und Redaktion der alttesta-*

mentlichen Rechtstexte (BBB 55; Bonn: Hanstein, 1981) 322; see the further literature in his n. 50.

6   So Rudolph, p. 223, and Bright, p. 223, but other commentators make much the same point.

7   Bright, p. 223; Bright, *History*, 330.

8   Kraus, *Worship*, 59–61.

followed in the rest of vv 8–9 by dependent infinitive phrases giving the purpose of the covenant; but verses 10–11 (shorter in the original text) offer a narrative of the subsequent action of the covenanters with finite verbs: those verbs are logically parallel to "after King Zedekiah had made a covenant" in v 8, as if v 10 were to begin "and after all the officials and all the people had reneged." The four verses then are form-critically equivalent to the introductory words in 7:1; 11:1; 18:1; 21:1; 30:1; 32:1; and 34:1.

Verse 12 offers a fresh introductory phrase in the third person (compare 29:30 and 32:26). The messenger formula (v 13a) introduces an address by Yahweh in the second-person plural, an address to an assemblage in Jerusalem. The address begins with a recital of past events in two parts, the events in the past, at the time of "your fathers" (vv 13b–14) and the events of recent months (vv 15–16). Yahweh recalls that he made a covenant with the fathers (v 13b), one of the stipulations of which was the liberation of Hebrew slaves every seven years (v 14a), but that the fathers did not obey the covenant (v 14b). In recent months, however, his audience determined to obey the stipulation (v 15), only to decide once more to disobey (v 16). Verses 14b and 16 thus emerge as the accusation on which Yahweh's judgment is based. Verse 17a offers a reiterated messenger formula and a recapitulation of the accusation; vv 17b–22 embody the announcement of judgment, an announcement that seems to be divided into three sections (vv 17b, 18–19, 20–22) on the basis of three links that express "let the punishment fit the crime"— "proclaim liberty"; עבר; שוב hip'il (for all of which see Interpretation, vv 17–22).

Interpretation

The expression "proclaim liberty" (קְרָא דְּרוֹר) is found, beyond vv 9, 15, and 17, in Lev 25:10 and Isa 61:1, and the noun (in the phrase "year of liberty") is found additionally in Ezek 46:17. The references in Lev 25:10 and in Ezek 46:17 are to the jubilee year; the proclamation of liberty to captives in Isa 61:1 is part of the task of the prophet. The noun is evidently cognate with the Akkadian *durâru* "move about, run away, be at large, be(come) free."[9]

The phrase is reinforced in vv 9, 14, 16 by its synonym "send out free" (חָפְשִׁי + pi'el שלח), which also appears in the same context in Deut 15:12, 13, and 18, and in addition in Isa 58:6 ("let the oppressed go free") and Job 39:5 ("let the wild ass go free").

The slaves in question had sold themselves into slavery for debt[10] (hence the translation favored in v 14, "shall sell himself": see there). Such people had an ambiguous position in the legal system: in Leviticus the practice is forbidden (Lev 25:42–43, 46), but since selling oneself to a fellow Israelite did occur, he is to be treated like a paid worker or a sojourner (Lev 25:39–43); and the evil of the practice is indicated in the present passage by the phrase "so that none should enslave any . . . Jewish brother" (v 9). On the other hand, Exodus 21:2 deals with the "Hebrew" male slave, and Deut 15:12 deals with the "Hebrew" man or woman who "is sold to you," who is specifically identified in that text as "your brother." All three legal traditions make provision for the release of such slaves after a period of time, though the details differ (see Preliminary Observations and Setting).[11]

The term for male slave in the passage is עֶבֶד, that for female slave is שִׁפְחָה. Beyond this passage the two terms are correlative in thirteen passages,[12] but none of those is a legal text; the place of שִׁפְחָה is normally taken by אָמָה (seventeen times in Exodus, Leviticus, and Deuteronomy). The word for the male refers to a variety of status of servant or slave (see 2:14), and the word for the female refers to a concubine (Gen 32:23) as well as to a servant or slave (Ps 123:2); it is the context here that determines the meaning "slave." As already indicated, these terms are not matched in any existing law: indeed Exod 21:2 refers only to male slaves (compare Exod 21:7).

9   Julius Lewy, "The Biblical Institution of *dᵉrôr* in the Light of the Akkadian Documents," *Eretz-Israel* 5 (1958) 21*–31*.

10   See for example Isaac Mendelsohn, "Slavery in the OT," *IDB* 4:384–85; de Vaux, *Ancient Israel*, 83.

11   See in more detail de Vaux, *Ancient Israel*, 82–83.

12   Gen 12:16; 20:14; 24:35; 30:43; 32:6; Deut 28:68; 1 Sam 8:16; 2 Kgs 5:26; Isa 14:2; Joel 3:2; Eccl 2:7; Esth 7:4; 2 Chr 28:10.

The passage further specifies both male slave and female slave as "Hebrew" (masculine עִבְרִי, feminine עִבְרִיָּה); the antecedent Exod 21:2 uses the adjective with (male) slave alone, and Deut 15:12 uses the masculine and feminine forms as nouns to refer to "a Hebrew man" and "a Hebrew woman." The prebiblical history of the term "Hebrew" is complex;[13] if the term in the Covenant Code (specifically, in Exod 21:2) carried some archaic nuance of "one belonging to the outcast group,"[14] in Deut 15:12 it is understood to refer to a fellow Israelite,[15] as the parallel "your brother" indicates, and that understanding is reinforced in the present passage (v 9) by the expression "his Jewish brother."

■ **8** For the historical context in which Zedekiah sponsored a covenant between the slaveholders and Yahweh see Preliminary Observations and Setting.

■ **10–11** The form of שׁוב restored at the beginning of v 10 (or its occurrence in v 11a, here bracketed) means "change one's mind"; a similar instance is found in 2 Kgs 24:1, where Jehoiakim turned from being a vassal of Nebuchadrezzar to rebellion against him.

For "enter the covenant" see Preliminary Observations and Setting.

The verb "subjugate" (כבשׁ) is a strong verb; it is used of "raping" a woman (Esth 7:8), and it is one of the words occurring in Gen 1:28 ("subdue [the earth]").

■ **13** "From the land of Egypt, from the house of slavery": this is the only occurrence of the second of these phrases in Jer. It is a traditional expression, perhaps originating in prophetic circles, found both in Exod 13:3, 14; 20:2, and six times in Deuteronomy.[16]

■ **14** For the translation "after seven years" for שָׁנִים מִקֵּץ שֶׁבַע, and for the source of the paraphrase of the law in Deut 15:1 and 12, see Preliminary Observations and Setting.

The forms of address in vv 13–17 are in general second-person plural; thus the shift to singular in (at least most of) v 14a is curious (for the form of the first verb in v 14a see Text). The shift is doubtless intentional; there are similar shifts within Deuteronomy,[17] though not within Deut 15:1 or 12. It has been suggested that one function of the shifts of number in Deuteronomy was to mark citations of earlier material,[18] and the shift here may have the same function.

It should be noted that יִמָּכֵר (both in the present verse and the antecedent Deut 15:12) may mean either "shall be sold" (G, V; Condamin; RSV, NJV) or "shall sell himself" (Cornill, Giesebrecht, Volz, Rudolph, Bright, Thompson; JB, NEB, NAB, NJV footnote).

There is uncertainty how to group the clauses in v 14a: the Masoretic punctuation suggests "who shall sell himself to you and serve you six years; (then) you shall send him out" (so Giesebrecht, Thompson, and RSV and NEB), but G, V (and most recent commentators, notably Rudolph and Bright, and JB and NAB) group the clauses as given here.

For "they did not listen . . . or turn their ear" see 7:24.

■ **15–16** The two occurrences of שׁוב qal at the beginning of each verse of course signify opposite movements, to good in v 15 and to evil in v 16; compare the use of the same verb (here translated "reneged") in v 10. The parallel of the two opposite movements is surely deliberate, a specific instance of the people's shifting loyalty which is implied with this verb in 4:1 and 8:4–5 (see there).[19] The parallelism of these two occurrences of שׁוב qal is reinforced by the addition of the hip'il stem of the verb in v 16: "you turned . . . and you made to return" your slaves.

"In the house which bears my name" underlines the solemnity and seriousness of what Zedekiah and the

13 For bibliographies see Michael C. Astour, "Habiru," *IDBSup*, 382–85; *HALAT*, 739a.

14 Childs, *Exodus*, 468.

15 Mayes, *Deuteronomy*, 250.

16 See the discussion in Masséo Caloz, "Exod xiii 3–16 et son rapport au Deutéronome," *RB* 75 (1968) 5–62, esp. 37.

17 There is a substantial literature on the matter; see Georges Minette de Tillesse, "Sections 'tu' et sections 'vous' dans le Deutéronome," *VT* 12 (1962) 29–87, and the bibliography cited in his n. 1; Christopher T. Begg, "The Literary Criticism of Deut 4,1–40,

Contributions to a Continuing Discussion," *ETL* 56 (1980) 12–23.

18 See Begg, "Literary Criticism of Deut 4,1–40, 28–45.

19 See further the discussion in Holladay, *Šûbh*, 1–2.

slaveholders agreed to do (compare Preliminary Observations and Setting). So when they broke the covenant they "profaned" Yahweh's "name": this verb (חלל pi'el) appears in Jer with the object "land" (16:13) but only here with the object "name" (of Yahweh). The combination is an idiom in the Holiness Code (six times) and in Ezekiel (five times),[20] occurring also in Amos 2:7 and Mal 1:12. The occurrence in Amos is almost certainly a gloss,[21] so that its use in the present passage may well be its earliest appearance.[22] There is no reason to doubt its authenticity here, and Jrm's use of a priestly expression points up the awesome wrong of the people's conduct; they have profaned, polluted Yahweh's very identity. "It is then an intolerable profanation of God's name whenever it is falsely appealed to; and thus perjury is allied with sacrilege" (Calvin).

The expression "according to their desire" (לְנַפְשָׁם) reminds the hearer of the wishes of the slaves themselves, something one might have forgotten in all the decision making of the slaveholders; for the meaning compare the same nuance of נֶפֶשׁ in Deut 21:14, and for the sentiment compare the implication of "Jewish brother" in v 9. The expressions closing v 16 are awkward in English and probably in Hebrew: the gloss in *M* may be an attempt to clarify the meaning. But the diction seems deliberately to collocate the sequence of expressions with the preposition לְ "for": each of you took back your male slave and your female slave whom you had liberated "for their desire, for yourselves, for male slaves and female slaves."

■ **17–22** The punishment fits the crime: if the slaveowners have not obeyed in "proclaiming liberty," then Yahweh will "proclaim liberty" to them—to the sword, pestilence, and famine; and again those who break (literally "pass over," עבר) Yahweh's covenant he will treat like those who "pass through" (the same verb, עבר) the halves of the sacrificial animal.[23] And there is a possible third parallel: if the slaveholders have "brought back" their slaves (v 16), then Yahweh will "bring back" the army of Babylon to the city (v 22)—in both cases שוב hip'il.

■ **17** The triad "sword," "famine," and "pestilence" recurs often in Jer (see on 14:12), but the occurrence in v 17 is the only one in which "famine" and "pestilence" are reversed (compare 21:7, where the order is "pestilence," "sword," and "famine").[24]

■ **18** This verse continues the announcement of punishment, but the relationship between v 18b (beginning הָעֵגֶל, "the calf") and v 18a is not clear, and the Versions and commentators have solved the question variously. *G* does not integrate "the calf" with v 18a, and what follows the noun is a dubious paraphrase; the other Versions simply replicate *M*, and their rendering leaves v 18b an anacoluthon. Sebastian Schmidt (1706) lists two possibilities. One is to construe הָעֵגֶל as if בָּעֵגֶל, "by the calf"; by this understanding v 18b modifies "the covenant which they made before me," and this is evidently the basis for the rendering of *KJV*, "the covenant that they made before me, when they cut the calf in twain" (so also Calvin). The other possibility is to construe הָעֵגֶל as if כָּעֵגֶל "like the calf"; by this understanding v 18b modifies "and I shall make the men." This is the rendering of Luther. Duhm, Cornill, and Giesebrecht try to solve the problem by deleting phrases in vv 18–20 (Cornill suggests jumping from "And I shall make the men breaking my covenant" in v 18 to "into the hands of their enemies" in v 20). But this suggestion destroys the play on עבר already noted. Volz and Rudolph accept Luther's interpretation but go on actually to emend הָעֵגֶל to כָּעֵגֶל (and so *RSV*, *JB*, *NEB*, *NAB*, and *NJV*); there is, however, no textual warrant for this. I would take the text as it stands; נתן (the opening verb in v 18) may take two accusatives in the meaning "make something into something"—Isa 3:4 is an instance in which Yahweh likewise announces a punishment. The difficulty in the present passage is the distance of "the calf" from the verb, but I suggest that this is the construction nevertheless. By this understanding the men who broke the covenant will become the sacrificial animal and will be cut in two.

The words "the calf which they cut in two and between

20   Lev 18:21; 19:12; 20:3; 21:6; 22:2, 32; Ezek 20:39; 36:20, 21, 22, 23.

21   Wolff, *Joel and Amos*, 133–34.

22   Sheldon H. Blank, "Isaiah 52:5 and the Profanation of the Name," *HUCA* 25 (1954) 6–7.

23   Patrick D. Miller, "Sin and Judgment in Jeremiah 34:17–19," *JBL* 103 (1984) 611–13.

24   Weippert, *Prosareden*, 168.

the parts of which they passed" immediately recall the narrative of Yahweh's covenant with Abram in Gen 15:9–11, 17–21 (though, as noted in Preliminary Observations and Setting, in Genesis the animal is a heifer, עֶגְלָה, rather than a calf). Two related questions emerge. Who is the subject of "cut in two" and "passed"? And is this a description of the procedure in the ratification of Zedekiah's covenant, or does the diction simply refer to Yahweh's covenant with Abram?

The verb translated "make" with "covenant" here (and in vv 8, 13, and 15, and in 11:10 and 31:31–33 and 40) is כרת, literally "cut." There has been much discussion of the relation between this idiom, which is so common in the OT, and the ceremony described in Genesis 15; one may surmise that there is a connection between them but that the relationship is more complicated than a simple equation.[25] But it is striking that such a ceremony is not referred to in the ratification of the Mosaic covenant; one hears instead of the sprinkling of blood and of a covenant meal (Exod 24:6–8, 9–11); nor (beyond Genesis 15 and the present passage) is such a ceremony referred to elsewhere in the OT. All this is an argument from silence, but no prophet says anything like "Remember the calf through whose parts you passed." The impression given by the narrative in Gen 15:9–21 is of a rite remembered from early times, archaic by the time it was fixed in the tradition; if this is the case, the idiom כרת בְּרִית will simply be a technical term.[26] On the other hand, it is just as striking that there is specific reference to such a ceremony in one of the Aramaic inscriptions of Sefire (north Syria, eighth century): "[Just as] this calf is cut in two, so may Matî'el be cut in two, and may his nobles be cut in two."[27] Given the pattern of the biblical and extrabiblical evidence, one may tentatively conclude that such a ceremony was not part of the ratification of Zedekiah's covenant and that Jrm is making reference to the old tradition of the covenant between Yahweh and Abram, doubtless with an eye on non-Israelite practice as well. It would then follow that one cannot use the present passage (as Volz and Thompson do) as evidence for such a procedure in the ratification of Zedekiah's covenant. The subject of "cut in two" and "passed" will then be indefinite and not "the men."

■ **20** For the diction see 7:33.

■ **21** For the phrase עלה מֵעַל in the meaning "withdraw from" see 21:2.

Aim

What motives led the slaveholders to agree to the covenant, to agree to give the slaves their freedom? Were they idealistic, or prudent, or fearful, or glad to have fewer mouths to feed? And then what motives led them to change their minds and take their erstwhile slaves back? Were they fickle, or selfish, or cynical? Whatever their array of motives, they broke their promise to Yahweh, and his anger blazes forth.

---

25 Literature on the question is full. See in general the literature on covenant cited in 11:1–17, and further the literature cited in *HALAT*, 476b. Note particularly Martin Noth, "Old Testament Covenant-making in the Light of a Text from Mari," *The Laws in the Pentateuch and Other Studies* (Philadelphia: Fortress, 1967) 108–17; Moshe Weinfeld, "בְּרִית," *TDOT* 2:259–60, 262–63.

26 George E. Mendenhall, "Covenant," *IDB* 1:715–16; Hans-Joachim Kraus, *Worship in Israel* (Richmond: Knox, 1966) 119–20.

27 Sefire 1.A.40: Joseph A. Fitzmyer, *The Aramaic Documents of Sefire* (BibOr 19; Rome: Pontifical Biblical Institute, 1967) 14, 15, 56–57.

The Example of the Rechabites

Bibliography

Abramsky, Samuel
"בית הרכבים — גיניאלוגיה וצביון חברתי" ("The House of Rechab—Genealogy and Social Character"), *Eretz-Israel* 8 (1967) 255–65, English summary 76*.

Cummings, John T.
"The House of the Sons of the Prophets and the Tents of the Rechabites," *Studia Biblica 1978, I. Papers on Old Testament and Related Themes, Sixth International Congress on Biblical Studies* (ed. E. A. Livingstone; JSOT Supplement Series 11; Sheffield: JSOT Press, 1979) 119–26.

Frick, Frank S.
"Rechabites," *IDBSup*, 726–28.

Frick, Frank S.
"The Rechabites Reconsidered," *JBL* 90 (1971) 279–87.

Keukens, Karlheinz H.
"Die rekabitischen Haussklaven in Jeremia 35," *BZ* NF 27 (1983) 228–35.

Levenson, Jon D.
"On the Promise of the Rechabites," *CBQ* 38 (1976) 508–14.

Pope, Marvin H.
"Rechab," *IDB* 4:14–16.

Weippert
Prosareden, 121–48.

35

1 The word which came to Jeremiah from Yahweh in the days of Jehoiakim [son of Josiah]ᵃ king of Judah, as follows: 2/ Go to the house of the Rechabites [and you shall speak with them]ᵃ and you shall bring them into the house of Yahweh, to one of the chambers; and you shall give them wine to drink. 3/ So I took Jaazaniah son of Jeremiah,ᵃ son of Habazziniah,ᵇ and his brothers, and [all]ᶜ his sons, and the whole house of the Rechabites, 4/ and I brought them into the house of Yahweh, to the chamber of the ᵃsons of Hananᵃ son of Igdaliahᵇ the man of God, which was next to the chamber of the officials above the chamber of Maaseiah the son of Shallum,

Text

1a   Omit with *G*; compare Janzen, pp. 69–71.

2a   Omit with *G*.

3a   So *M*, but the Versions curiously diverge: *G* Ιερεμιν = ?; *S 'mry'* = אֲמַרְיָהוּ Amariah. Did *M* err because of the closeness of "Jeremiah" in v 1, or did the Versions for some reason go astray?

b   The name is otherwise unattested. The *G* Χαβασιν suggests that the antecedent form lacked יָה; the *V Absanias* and *S ḥabṣānyā'* suggest that the antecedent was vocalized חַבְצַנְיָה, but the formation is odd.

c   Omit with *G* (compare Janzen, pp. 65–67).

4a—a   It is conceivable that בניחנן should be divided בֶּן יְחָנָן "son of Johanan": one MS. of *M* and some traditions of *G* and *T* do read "son of," and *G*ᴮ reads ιωναν; this is Volz's reading—he says it is more likely that the chamber would belong to one person, a prophet. But if "sons of" implies "disciples of" (compare v 5), then the chamber was perhaps a meeting place; it is better to stay with *M*.

b   Both *G* and *S* read גְּדַלְיָהוּ "Gedaliah." The form in

the keeper of the threshold; 5/ and I put
a《 before them》 [*M*: before the sons of the
house of the Rechabites]a b《 a drinking-bowl》
[*M*: drinking-bowls full]b of wine and cups,
and I said [to them,]c "Drink some wine." 6/
But they said, "We must not drink wine, for
it was Jonadab son of Rechab, our father,
who commanded us, 'You shall not drink
wine, neither you nor your children for ever;
7/ no house shall you build, nor seed shall
you sow, nor vineyard shall you)plant or(a
have, but in tents shall you dwell all your
days, so that you may live many days on [the
surface of]b the ground where you sojourn.'
8/ And we obeyed the voice of Jehonadab
[son of Rechab]a our father [in all that he
commanded us,]b not to drink wine all our
days, we, our wives, our sons and our
daughters, 9/ and not to build houses to live
in; we do not have vineyard or field or seed,
10/ and have lived in tents: we have obeyed
and done everything which Jonadab our
father commanded us. 11/ But when Nebuchadrezzar [king of Babylon]a came up
against b the land, we said, 'Come, let us go
into Jerusalem, away from the army of the—
Chaldeans and away from the army of the
Arameans,'c so we have lived d《 there》 [*M*:
in Jerusalem."]d

12 Then the word of Yahweh came a《 to me》 [*M*:
to Jeremiah]a as follows: 13/ Thus Yahweh
[of hosts, the God of Israel]a has said: Go
and say to the men of Judah and the inhabitants of Jerusalem, Will you not take a
lesson, to listen to my words? oracle of
Yahweh. 14/ The words of Jehonadab son
of Rechab, which he commanded his children, have been upheld, not to drink wine:
they have not drunk (it) [to this day, for they
have obeyed the commandment of their
father;]a but I have spoken to you early and
constantly, and you have not obeyed me.
15/ And I sent to you my servants the
prophets [early and constantly,]a saying,
Just turn, each from his evil way, and make
good your doings, and do not walk after
other gods to serve them, and live on the
ground which I have given to you and to
your fathers; but you did not turn your ear
nor listen to me. 16/ The children of Jehonadab son of Rechab upheld the commandment of their father [which he commanded
them;]a but this people has not obeyed me.
17/ Therefore thus Yahweh [God of hosts,
the God of Israel]a has said: I am going to
bring on Judah and on [all]b the inhabitants
of Jerusalem all the evil which I have spoken against them, [because I have spoken to
them but they have not listened, and I have
called to them but they have not
answered.]c 18/ And a[to the house of the
Rechabites Jeremiah said,] thus Yahweh [of
hosts, God of Israel] has said, because 《 the
children of Jehonadab, the son of Rechab,
have obeyed the commandments of their

M (יְגַדְלְיָהוּ) is not an implausible formation, but the
name is otherwise unattested, while "Gedaliah" is a
name known elsewhere.

5a—a   Read with *G*; the pronoun has been expanded to
the corresponding name in *M* (see Janzen, p. 74,
[n]).

b—b   Read the singular with *G*, a more plausible reading than *M*.

c   Omit with *G*.

7a   *G* lacks לֹא תִּשְׁמְעוּ; one can imagine either that *G* is
deficient by haplography (two occurrences of לֹא) or
that *M* has expanded the text, but the wording of v
9 suggests that the wording of *G* is original and that
M has expanded the text. See Janzen, p. 51.

b   Omit with *G*.

8a   Omit with *G* (compare Janzen, p. 150).

b   Omit with *G*; *M* has expanded from vv 10 and 14
(see Janzen, p. 51).

11a   Omit with *G* (compare Janzen, p. 140).

b   *M* reads אֶל, but some MSS. read עַל.

c   For אֲרָם *G* reads "Assyrians" (אַשּׁוּר) and *S* reads
"Edom" (אֱדֹם). *M* is probably correct (compare 2 Kgs
24:2).

d—d   Read with *G*; *M* has expanded שָׁם to the corresponding name (Janzen, p. 74, [o]).

12a—a   The reading of *G* is to be preferred (Cornill); it
continues the first-person narrative of vv 3–5 and is
also preferable on form-critical grounds (see Structure, Form, Setting).

13a   Omit with *G* (compare Janzen, pp. 75–76).

14a   Omit with *G*; the expansion is from vv 8, 10, and
16. For the words "to this day" in a gloss compare
25:18. See Janzen, pp. 50–51.

15a   Omit with *G*, a gloss from 25:4; see Janzen, p. 52.

16a   Omit with *G*; see Janzen, p. 52.

17a   Omit with *G* (compare v 13).

b   Omit with *G* (compare v 3).

c   Omit with *G*; the gloss is from 7:13 (see Janzen, p.
52).

18–19a—a   Read *G*; *M* has both expanded the diction
and recast the verses as an address to the Rechabites; see the discussion in Janzen, pp. 105–6.

father ⟫ [*M*: you have obeyed the command of Jehonadab your father,] [and kept all his commandments,] ⟪ to do ⟫ [*M*: and done] as [*M*: according to all] their father commanded them, 19/ [therefore thus Yahweh of hosts, the God of Israel has said,]ᵃ no one (belonging) to Jonadab son of Rechab standing before me shall be cut off all the days.

Structure, Form, Setting

For the position of this chapter see Introduction, sec. 22.

This chapter has been judged by many commentators to be of Deuteronomistic origin (one notices the diction of v 15 especially),[1] but Weippert has demonstrated that the phrases of the chapter are at home with Jrm.[2] Many of these phrases have already been dealt with in the present study: for example, for "turn, each from his evil way, and make good your doings" (v 15) appears in 18:11: see 18:1–12, Setting.

The setting for the incident is indicated by v 11. Jehoiakim died in December 598, near the time Nebuchadrezzar began the siege of Jerusalem. Before the siege began, Nebuchadrezzar had dispatched bands of Chaldeans, Arameans, Ammonites, and Moabites to harass Judah (2 Kgs 24:2): this must have been in 599 or early in 598. It was in the context of these raids that the Rechabites evidently moved to Jerusalem. The incident recounted here will then have taken place in the course of 599 or 598.

The passage has been taken to be the report of a symbolic action[3] (compare 13:1–12aα; 19:1—20:6; 27:2–11; 32:1–15). The diction, however, closely resembles that of 18:1–12, the report of a symbolic event: both passages begin with the introductory words הַדָּבָר אֲשֶׁר־הָיָה אֶל־יִרְמְיָהוּ מֵאֵת יהוה לֵאמֹר, and both passages subsequently shift to first-person narrative in the report of the execution of the first command (18:3; vv 3–5 here) and in the introduction to a subsequent word from Yahweh (18:5; v 12 here [in *G*, see Text]). But it must be pointed out that the event does not really symbolize anything: it is an action entered into as an example; one thinks of exemplary events in the Gospels, such as that of the widow's mite (Mark 12:41–44) or that of the woman who poured ointment on Jesus' feet (Mark 14:3–9).

The passage easily breaks into two sections: (1) the first command and its consequences, an action with the Rechabites (vv 1–11); and (2) the speech to the men of Judah and the inhabitants of Jerusalem (vv 12–19).

After the introductory words (v 1) there is the first command of Yahweh to tempt the Rechabites to break a commandment of their order (v 2), followed by the report not only of the execution of the command (vv 3–5) but also of the consequence: a speech by the Rechabites (vv 6–11) affirming their present and past adherence to the commandments of Jehonadab their founder and explaining their seeming breaking of the rule on living in a house as a temporary measure during the military emergency (vv 6–11).

Verse 12 introduces a second command from Yahweh to set forth the meaning of the symbolic act (vv 12–19). The speech begins with a word of reproach to the audience (v 13b) and continues with an oracle which, strikingly, is one of both judgment and salvation—judgment on the general population and salvation on the Rechabites. The reason for the contrasting proclamation is set forth in vv 14–16: there is a commendation of the fidelity of the Rechabites (vv 14a, 16a) and a contrasting accusation leveled at the general population for their infidelity (vv 14b–15, 16b). There follows the consequent announcement of judgment on the general population (v 17) and of salvation on the Rechabites (vv 18–19). The arrangement of the antecedent reasons, and of the consequent judgment or salvation, is thus in general chiastic.[4]

Interpretation

■ **2–19** Many questions cluster around the nature and the history of the Rechabites, who are described only here in the OT. The only further information available is the mention of Jehonadab son of Rechab, the founder of the order, in 2 Kgs 10:15–23 in the narrative of Jehu's massacre of the Baal worshipers in Samaria, and the citing of "the house of Rechab" in 1 Chr 2:55 as one of the subgroups of Kenites. In addition we know that the order continued its existence into the postexilic period.[5]

The terminology for those connected with the group in this chapter is not self-evident. For the proper name

---

1   See, for example, Rudolph, p. 225.
2   Weippert, *Prosareden*, 121–48.
3   Thompson, p. 73. For bibliography on symbolic actions see 13:1–12aα.
4   Janzen, p. 106.
5   *m. Taʿan.* 4.5; for further references to rabbinic

"Rechab" (רֵכָב) see below. The plural form הָרֵכָבִים in vv 2 and 3 (and in the gloss of *M* in v 18) is evidently a gentilic adjective, translated here "Rechabites"; the singular would be רֵכָבִי. The phrase "house of the Rechabites" in v 3 (and in the glosses of *M*: "sons of the house of the Rechabites" in v 5 and "house of the Rechabites" in v 18) is evidently the equivalent of "house of Rechab" in 1 Chr 2:55 and is evidently a kinship term, but "house of the Rechabites" in v 2 is evidently a reference to their dwelling (so, probably, the distinction in *G* between οἶκος, v 2, and οἰκία, v 3). "Son of Rechab" occurs in vv 6, 14, and 16 (and the gloss of *M* in v 8) and in 2 Kgs 10:15–23; the expression appears at first glance to be the patronymic of J(eh)onadab, but given the data already offered, the expression could as well suggest not a father-son relationship but descent from a distant ancestor (conceivably the one mentioned in 2 Sam 4:2–9), or from an eponymous ancestor, or simply membership in a guild. The scattered data are enticing but not conclusive. Thus since the root רכב means "ride" and מֶרְכָּבָה means "chariot," it has been suggested that "son of Rechab" originally meant "charioteer" or "chariot-maker"; and since the Rechabites are recorded as a subgroup of the Kenites (1 Chr 2:55), and since the Kenites are suspected of being originally a clan of smiths, the Rechabites, too, may have been a subgroup specializing in making chariots and weaponry, perhaps in the northern Arabah.[6]

Two further questions emerge. First, there seems to be no significance to the shift of spelling of J(eh)onadab's name: the short form in vv 6, 10, and 19; the long form in vv 8, 14, 16, and 18. Second, if the general location of the Rechabites was in the Arabah, what was Jehonadab doing in the north during Jehu's purge?

The vows enjoined by Jehonadab, to abstain from wine, from living in houses, and from engaging in viticulture or agriculture (vv 8–9), have widely been thought to represent the persistence of the nomadic ideal as a testimony over against the corruptions of agriculture and city life.[7] But the OT does not idealize the nomadic period (compare 2:6). If, however, the Rechabites were a clan of smiths, then their vows might have another function. Thus abstaining from wine might aid in keeping the secrets of metallurgy within the clan; the nature of their work would prevent them from having a permanent home or engaging in agriculture—they would need to leave a given locality once the supply of ore was exhausted.[8] In any event, the stress in the present passage is not on the content of these vows but rather on the fact that the Rechabites were faithful to them.

■ **3** One assumes that this Jaazaniah was the head of the Rechabite group with whom Jeremiah dealt. The name was a common one at the time.[9] His father Jeremiah was not of course the prophet: that name was also a common one (see 1:1). The name of his grandfather is otherwise unattested and may have been transmitted wrongly (see Text). "House" in this verse implies "household" (see Structure, Form, Setting); for the question whether women were included in the group, see the remarks in vv 6–11.

■ **4** "Man of God" is a designation for prophet.[10] The appositional phrase would most naturally refer to Hanan. If the sons of Hanan had designated quarters in the temple, then they were doubtless guild prophets, part of the temple personnel.[11] It must be stressed that "sons of" here may mean "members of the guild of" (see Structure, Form, Setting for the similar problem with "son of Rechab").

material see Samuel Abramsky, "בית־הריכבים — גיניאלוגיה וצביון חברתי" ("The House of Rechab—Genealogy and Social Character"), *Eretz-Israel* 8 (1967) 76*.

6   For the data suggesting these lines of speculation see Frank S. Frick, "Rechabites," *IDBSup* 716–17, and further idem, "The Rechabites Reconsidered," 285–87; on the Kenites see George M. Landes, "Kenites," *IDB* 3:6.

7   For a survey of the literature on the "nomadic ideal," see Frick, "The Rechabites Reconsidered," 279–81.

8   Ibid., 284–85; compare the mention of "itinerant

smiths" in Robert J. Forbes, "Extracting, Smelting, and Alloying," *A History of Technology* I (ed. Charles Singer, E. J. Holmyard, and A. R. Hall; Oxford: Oxford University, 1954) 579.

9   James M. Ward, "Jaazaniah," *IDB* 2:777.
10   Johnson, *Cultic Prophet*, 53, n. 1.
11   Ibid., 62; Lindblom, *Prophecy*, 208.

The specific location is like many such specifics in biblical material, of little help to the modern reader.

"Keeper of the threshold" is the title of a particular priest. In 52:24 (= 2 Kgs 25:18) three keepers of the threshold are mentioned, presumably titular guards for the three principal gates of the temple (compare Ezek 40:6, 20, 24).[12]

■ **5** If the reading of the singular גָּבִיעַ (here translated "drinking-bowl") is correct, then it is evidently a large vessel from which individual cups are filled, but it is difficult to identify the word with any given pottery form from the period. James L. Kelso identifies it with a "pitcher,"[13] but Baumgartner defines it here as a "drinking-bowl."[14] The word appears only otherwise in Gen 44:2–17, of Joseph's silver vessel; and in Exod 25:31–34 and 37:17–20, and with a derivative denotation in the description of the lampstand in the temple, a lampstand with multiple branches: each lamp rests on a "cup" in the shape of an almond blossom (Exod 25:33, 34).[15] One assumes then that the vessel in question has the shape either of a chalice or of a shallow bowl.[16]

A כּוֹס is an individual drinking cup (compare 16:7).

■ **6–11** The Rechabites quote Jehonadab (vv 6bβ–7), but then in their affirmation that they have obeyed him (vv 8–10) they expand on his words. Thus "you" and "your children" in v 6 become "we, our wives, our sons and our daughters" in v 8; and "house," "seed," and "vineyard" in v 7 become "houses," "vineyard," "field," and "seed" in v 9. These expansions raise the question what effect is intended. "Field" is certainly implied by Jehonadab's command, though one may suspect that one function at least of the word is to place the present passage in congruence with chapters 30—31 and chapter 32 (compare the text note of 32:15, and see Introduction, sec. 22). But Jehonadab has said בָּנִים (v 6), which may be either "sons" or "children." Is the command to be understood to include females, or are the Rechabites to be understood as extending Jehonadab's command to indicate their willingness to be faithful beyond his

intention? One could hardly imagine the wives of Rechabites being allowed access to wine when it is forbidden their husbands. One must therefore understand בָּנִים in v 6 to mean "children," not "sons" only; so also in v 16 and in the reconstructed text of v 18. But one assumes that the words "his brothers" and "his sons" in v 3 do imply males only, not "his siblings" and "his children"; surely if women had been included in the group, they would have been mentioned explicitly (compare the diction in 44:7, 9, 15, 19, 20, 24, 25); so also in the gloss of M in v 5.

■ **7** The phrase "the ground where you sojourn" (הָאֲדָמָה אֲשֶׁר אַתֶּם גָּרִים שָׁם) is striking: it appears to be an ironic variant of traditional expressions like "[Canaan,] the land in which they [the patriarchs] dwelt as sojourners" (Exod 6:4, P), "you were sojourners in the land of Egypt" (Lev 19:34, H), and above all "the land into which you enter to possess it" and the like (Deut 4:5, compare Jer 32:23).[17] The patriarchs had been sojourners in the land of Canaan; the Israelites had been sojourners in Egypt and were then given the land of Canaan for their own possession. The Rechabites, on the other hand, continued to be sojourners on the land.

■ **13–19** If the setting proposed for the encounter with the Rechabites is sound (see Structure, Form, Setting), Jrm is by this time convinced that repentance is an impossibility for the people (v 17; compare Introduction, sec. 32). It follows that "Will you not take a lesson, to listen to my words?" (v 13) is not an invitation to the people to change their ways but a challenge to hear the announcement of their doom: "a lesson" implies "chastisement." See the difference between your infidelity and the fidelity of the Rechabites!

For the phrases of vv 14b–15, 17 see 7:3–9, 25; 18:11.

For the expression "shall be cut off for" (v 19) see the discussion in 33:14–26 (on 33:17, 18).

Aim

One is either faithful or unfaithful, obedient or disobe-

---

12   G. Henton Davies, "Threshold," *IDB* 4:636.

13   James L. Kelso, "Pottery," *IDB* 3:851b.

14   *HALAT*, 166a.

15   For literature on the lampstand see Childs, *Exodus*, 524, on v 31.

16   For such pottery of the period see Amiran, *Ancient Pottery of the Holy Land* (New Brunswick, NJ: Rutgers University, 1970) plate 68.

17   For variations of this phrase, and citations, see Weinfeld, *Deuteronomy*, 342, #2 (compare #3).

dient. The Rechabites may have had to move into Jerusalem temporarily, but they will not break their vow and touch wine. How great a contrast with the general population of Jerusalem, which has not taken heed of Yahweh's word! The Rechabites will survive, but the people in general will face doom.

**The King Burns
Jeremiah's Scroll**

Bibliography

On Chapters 36—45:
Abrego, José María
    Jeremías 36—45, El Final del Reino (Valencia:
    Institución San Jerónimo, 1983).
Abrego, José María
    "El Texto Hebreo Estructurado de Jeremías 36—
    45," *Cuadernos Bíblicos* 8 (Valencia: Institución San
    Jerónimo, 1983) 1–49.

On Chapters 36—44:
Rietzschel
    Urrolle, 95–110.

On 36:1–32:
**Discernment of the Contents of the Dictated
    Scrolls from the Data of Chapter 36:**
Baumann, Arnulf
    "Urrolle und Fasttag: Zur Rekonstruktion der
    Urrolle des Jeremiabuches nach den Angaben in
    Jer 36," *ZAW* 80 (1968) 350–73.
Hicks, R. Lansing
    "*Delet* and *meḡillāh*, A Fresh Approach to Jeremiah
    xxxvi," *VT* 33 (1983) 46–66.
Robinson, Theodore H.
    "Baruch's Roll," *ZAW* 42 [NF 1] (1924) 209–21.

On Baruch, and the bulla of Baruch:
See bibliography in 32:1–44.

**On the chapter in general, or details of the
    chapter:**
Fohrer, Georg
    "Prophetie und Magie," *ZAW* 78 (1966) 45–46.
Galling, Kurt
    "Die Halle des Schreibers," *PJ* 27 (1931) 51–57.
Isbell, Charles D.
    "II Kings 22:3—23:24 and Jeremiah 36: A Stylistic
    Comparison," *JSOT* 8 (1978) 33–45.
Kessler, Martin
    "Form-Critical Suggestions on Jer 36," *CBQ* 28
    (1966) 389–401.
Kessler, Martin
    "The Significance of Jer 36," *ZAW* 81 (1969) 381–
    83.
Lemaire, André
    "Note sur le titre *bn hmlk* dans l'ancien Israël," *Sem*
    29 (1979) 59–65.
Lohfink
    "Kurzgeschichte."
William McKane
    Prophets and Wise Men (SBT 44; Naperville, IL:
    Allenson, 1965) 118–22.
Nielsen, Eduard
    Oral Tradition (SBT 11; Chicago: Allenson, 1954)
    64–79.

Stade, Bernhard
    "Streiflichter auf die Entstehung der jetzigen
    Gestalt der alttestamentlichen Prophetenschriften,
    2) Weshalb diktiert Jeremia seine Weissagungen
    Baruch? Jer. 36,4," *ZAW* 23 (1903) 157–61.

Wanke
    Baruchschrift, 59–74.

36

1   **In the fourth year of Jehoiakim son of Josiah, king of Judah, ⟨the word of Yahweh⟩ came to Jeremiah [*M*: this word came to Jeremiah from Yahweh; *G*: the word of Yahweh came to me]ᵃ as follows: 2/ Take for yourself a document-scroll and write on it all the words which I have spoken to you concerning Israelᵃ and Judah and all the nations, from the day I (first) spoke to you, from the days of Josiah to this day. 3/ Perhaps the house of Judah will hear all the evil which I am planning to do to them, so that they may turn each from his evil way and I can forgive their iniquity and their sin.**

4   **So Jeremiah called Baruch son of Neriah, and he [*M*: Baruch]ᵃ wrote at the dictation of Jeremiah all the words of Yahweh which he had spoken to him, on a document-scroll. 5/ And Jeremiah commanded Baruch as follows: "I am restricted: I cannot enter the house of Yahweh. 6/ So you shall go yourself and read ᵃin ⟨this⟩ scroll [*M*: in the scroll (on) which you have written at my dictation the words of Yahweh]ᵃ in the hearing of [all]ᵇ the people (in) the house of Yahweh on a day of fasting, and also in the ears of all Judah who come in from their cities shall read them. 7/ Perhaps their plea will fall before Yahweh, and they may turn each from his evil way, for great is the anger and wrath which Yahweh has spoken to this people." 8/ And Baruch [son of Neriah]ᵃ did according to everything which Jeremiah [the prophet]ᵇ commanded him, to read in the document the words of Yahweh (in) the house of Yahweh.**

9   **And in the ᵃ⟨eighth⟩ [*M*: fifth]ᵃ year of Jehoiakim [son of Josiah king of Judah,]ᵇ in the ninth month, all the people called a fast before Yahweh in Jerusalem, [and all the people who were entering from the cities of Judah into Jerusalem.]ᶜ 10/ And Baruch read in the document the words of Jeremiah (in) the house of Yahweh, in the chamber of Gemariah son of Shaphan the scribe, in the upper court (at) the entrance of the new gate of the house of Yahweh, in the ears of [all]ᵃ the people.**

11   **And Micaiah son of Gemariah son of Shaphan heard all the words of Yahweh from the document; 12/ and he went down to the house of the king, to the chamber of the scribe, and sitting there were all the officials, Elishama the scribe, and Delaiah son of Shemaiah,ᵃ and Elnathanᵇ son of**

Text

1a—a   The *M* reading "this word . . . from Yahweh" is found also in 26:1, and there *G* reads as *M* does; in the present passage, however, *G* reads a shorter text, "the word of Yahweh," a circumstance that suggests that *M* has expanded an original text. But if "the word of Yahweh" is original, then there must have been either "to Jeremiah" (so *M*) or "to me" (so *G*). The narrative continues in the third person (v 4), so that "to Jeremiah" must be correct; the reading in *G* offers the same contrast between first and third person as that found in 35:12.

2a   *G* reads "Jerusalem," a reading preferred by Duhm, Cornill, Giesebrecht, Condamin, and Rudolph; Volz and Bright prefer *M*. By the assumptions of the present study Jrm began his career addressing words to the northern kingdom (see on 1:4–19 and 2:1—4:4).

4a   Omit with *G* (compare Janzen, p. 148).

6a—a   Read with *G*. *M* offers a gloss from v 4; see Janzen, pp. 74, 106.

b   Omit with *G*; compare Janzen, pp. 65–67.

8a   Omit with *G*; compare Janzen, p. 149.

b   Omit with *G* (compare Janzen, p. 146).

9a—a   For *M* הַחֲמִשִׁית read with *G* הַשְּׁמִנִית. For the choice of this reading see Interpretation.

b   *G* reads simply "King Jehoiakim"; both designations of "king" are doubtless glosses (compare Janzen, p. 143).

c   In place of the bracketed words *G* has "and the house of Judah." Giesebrecht and Rudolph assume that *G* has shortened *M*; on the other hand, Duhm points out that the contemporaneous listing in *M* here clashes with the sequential command of v 6, so that *M* here is suspect. Both sequences seem awkward in their context; the sequence in *M* appears to be a gloss from v 6, and the shorter sequence in *G* appears to be a gloss from v 3. See the discussion in Janzen, p. 107.

10a   Omit with *G*; see v 6, note b.

12a   For שְׁמַעְיָהוּ *G* has Σελεμίας = שְׁלֶמְיָהוּ "Shelemiah"; this reading may be corrupted because of the occurrence of "Shelemiah" in v 14.

Achbor, and Gemariah son of Shaphan, and Zedekiah son of Hananiah, and all the (other) officials. 13/ And Micaiah told them all the words which he had heard when Baruch read in the document in the ears of the people.

14 And all the officials sent to Baruch[a] Jehudi son of Nethaniah son of Shelemiah son of Cushi, saying, "The scroll in which you have read in the ears of the people, take it in your hand and come." So Baruch [son of Neriah][a] took the scroll [in his hand][b] and went in to them. 15/ And they said to him, "Now ⟨read it again⟩[a] in our ears"; and Baruch read (it) [in their ears.][b] 16/ And when they heard all the words, they turned in alarm to each other and said [to Baruch,][a] "We must certainly tell the king all these words." 17/ Then they asked Baruch, "Now tell us, how did you write all these words? At his dictation?" 18/ And Baruch said [to them,][a] "Yes; he would recite to me all these words, while I was writing (them) in the document, with ink." 19/ And they [M: the officials][a] said to Baruch, "Go, hide, you and Jeremiah, and let no one know where you (both) are."

20 And they went in to the king, to the courtyard, but the scroll they had stored in the chamber of Elishama [the scribe:][a] they told in the ears of the king all [b]the words.[b] 21/ So the king sent Jehudi to get the scroll, and he got it from the chamber of Elishama [the scribe,][a] and Jehudi read it in the ears of the king and in the ears of all the officials standing above the king. 22/ Now the king was sitting in the winter house [in the ninth month][a] and [b]⟨the fire of⟩[b] a brazier before him [burning].[b] 23/ And as[a] Jehudi read[a] three or four columns, he would tear it with the scribe's knife and would throw (it) into the fire in the brazier, until the whole scroll was consumed in the fire in the brazier. 24/ But they were not alarmed, nor did they tear their garments, neither the king nor [any of][a] his servants listening to all these words. 25/ [a] Elnathan and ⟨Gedaliah had⟩ also ⟨urged the king to burn the scroll, but⟩ De-

b For וֶאֶלְנָתָן G has Ιωναθαν = יְהוֹנָתָן "Jonathan," but G has "Elnathan" in v 25. Semantically the names are equivalent, and the same man could have been called either (compare "Eliakim" and "Jehoiakim," 2 Kgs 23:34).

14a At the first occurrence in the verse of "Baruch," G adds "son of Neriah," which M lacks; at the second occurrence M has "son of Neriah," which G lacks. Since "Baruch" has already occurred in v 13 without patronymic, the patronymic here would seem to be a gloss that entered the tradition (from the margin?) at different points. See Janzen, p. 73.

b Omit with G, an expansion from v 14a; see Janzen, p. 52.

15a Vocalizing M שֵׁב, "Sit down (and read it)" as שֻׁב with G, a', s', and T, literally "Return (and read it)"; so Volz. There would be no reason for him to sit in the presence of the officials (compare "all the officials standing" in v 21, and "the king was sitting" in v 22). He had read the scroll the first time to the people in the temple area (v 10).

b Omit with G, an expansion from v 15. See Janzen, p. 52.

16a Omit with G; the officials speak to each other in this verse, and to Baruch in v 17 (note the word order there); so also Duhm, Cornill, Giesebrecht, Volz, Rudolph. See Janzen, p. 52.

18a Omit with G.

19a Omit with G.

20a Omit with G; compare Janzen, p. 152.

b—b Many MSS., some traditions of G, S, and Codex Reuchlianus of T adds הָאֵלֶּה, thus "these words." It is a possible reading but not a necessary one.

21a Omit with G (see v 20, note a).

22a Omit with G, a gloss from v 9; see Janzen, p. 52.

b—b G, S, and T read אֵשׁ before הָאָח; M seems to have omitted it by haplography with אֶת־ (compare the wording of v 23). G and T omit "burning," which is probably a gloss added after "fire" dropped out.

23a For M בִּקְרוֹא the Oriental ketib reads כְּקְרוֹא; the difference of meaning is imperceptible.

24a Omit with G.

25a—a M reads literally, "Elnathan and Delaiah and Gemariah also urged the king not to burn the scroll, but he did not listen to them." G offers several interesting readings. G[A] has, "And Elnathan and Gedeliah and Gemariah urged the king not to burn the scroll," without v 25b, but in addition G[B, S*] omit both "and Gemariah" and "not." There are the following considerations. (1) The use of the subject "the king" in v 26a suggests strongly that v 25b is a gloss. (2) The use of גַּם at the beginning of v 25a is dubious if a contrast is intended. (3) Elnathan headed the posse that brought Uriah back from Egypt eight years before (26:22–23); he is likely then to be opposed to Jrm's word. If G is correct that "Gedaliah" originally stood in the verse, and if that Gedaliah was the son of Pashhur, then he too would be opposed to Jrm's word (see 38:1–6).

laiah and Gemariah urged him not to burn the scroll; [he did not listen to them.]ᵃ 26/ Then the king commanded Jerahmeel the king's son and Seraiah son of Azriel and Shelemiah the son of Abdeel to arrest Baruch [the scribe]ᵃ and Jeremiah [the prophet,]ᵃ ᵇ《but they hid》 [*M*: but Yahweh hid them.]ᵇ

27 And the word of Yahweh came to Jeremiah after the king had burned the scroll, ᵃthe wordsᵃ which Baruch had written at the dictation of Jeremiah, as follows: 28/ Again, get yourself another scroll and write [on it]ᵃ all the former words which were on the [first]ᵇ scroll which Jehoiakim [king of Judah]ᶜ burned. 29/ And ᵃto Jehoiakim [king of Judah]ᵃ you shall say: Thus Yahweh has said, You are the one who burned this scroll, saying, Why have you written on it, The king of Babylon really will come in and destroy this land and remove from it man and beast? 30/ Therefore thus Yahweh has said concerning Jehoiakim king of Judah: He shall not have anyone sitting on the throne of David, and his corpse shall be thrown out to the heat by day and the frost by night; 31/ and I shall punish him and his offspring and his servants [for their iniquity,]ᵃ and I shall bring in upon them and upon the inhabitants of Jerusalem and upon the men of Judah all the evil which I have spoken against them but they would not hear.

32 ᵃ《Then Baruch》 got another scroll [*M*: Then Jeremiah got another scroll and gave it to Baruch son of Neriah the scribe]ᵃ and he wrote on it at the dictation of Jeremiah all the words of the document which Jehoiakim [king of Judah]ᵇ had burned [with fire;]ᵇ and still he added to them many words like these.

There is no information about the point of view of Delaiah. Gemariah was evidently a supporter of Jrm (compare v 10); one notes the conduct of his brother Ahikam eight years earlier (26:24). Now given the readings without the negative in *G*, I propose that the text has suffered haplography between "Gedaliah" and "Delaiah," and that the verse originally set forth the contrasting advice of two pairs of officials (compare the suggestion of Duhm). Verse 25b will then have been added after the haplography had arisen.

26a Omit both designations with *G* (compare Janzen, pp. 146, 149).

b—b Read וַיִּסָּתֵרוּ with *G* (compare v 19); *M* reads וַיַּסְתִּרֵם יהוה. So Volz (compare Rudolph).

27a—a *G* reads "all the words"! It is possible that *M* has omitted "all" by haplography.

28a Omit with *G*.

b Omit with *G*.

c Omit; the situation is the same as in v 9: see note b there.

29a—a *G* omits "to Jehoiakim king of Judah"; Janzen therefore suggests that the expression in *M* is secondary from v 30 (pp. 52, 72). But some identification of the addressee is necessary; Rudolph tentatively suggests that *G* omits by haplography. I assume that there was both haplography in *G* and the addition of "king of Judah" in *M* (compare v 28, note c).

31a Omit with *G* (compare the diction of 11:22).

32a—a Read with *G*. It is easy to imagine how *M* might have expanded the text in order to bring it into conformity with v 28; it would be difficult to imagine any purpose served by a secondary shortening in *G* that shifts the responsibility to Baruch. So Duhm and Cornill, against Giesebrecht, Volz, and Rudolph; see Janzen, pp. 72, 107.

b Omit with *G* both expressions, which occur side by side in *M*. For the designation of Jehoiakim see Janzen, p. 144. It is noteworthy that "burn" occurs five times in the present chapter, but only here does it occur in *M* with "with fire"; see Janzen, p. 52.

Preliminary Observations and Setting

This chapter has attracted great attention, in that it allows one to see the process by which oral tradition becomes written text.[1] Indeed it is natural to see in Jrm's scrolls the genesis of the Book of Jer, and much effort has been expended in using the chapter for clues by which to reconstruct the contents of the original scroll(s).

It therefore becomes particularly important to inquire as to the authenticity of the narrative. Mowinckel assigned the chapter to his "Source B" (biographical material);[2] those who favor the hypothesis of large-scale Deuteronomistic editing see evidence of such activity in the chapter.[3] But the presumed Deuteronomistic phrases in the chapter are clearly part of Jrm's diction.[4] Since

---

1 Eduard Nielsen, *Oral Tradition* (SBT 11; Chicago: Alec R. Allenson, 1954) 64–79.

2 Mowinckel, *Komposition*, 24.

3 Nicholson, *Jer. 26—52*, 104.

4 See Weippert, *Prosareden*, 140–48 for the expressions in vv 3 and 7.

Baruch took part in the events narrated, one may presume that it is composed by him.[5]

The datum of v 1 indicates that the first scroll was dictated sometime between March/April 605 and February/March 604; v 9 indicates that the initial reading of the scroll was either in November/December 604 (the reading of *M*) or November/December 601 (the reading of *G*): the present study follows *G* (see Interpretation of v 9). There is no way to know, of course, when Baruch might have drafted this memoir, but it is clear that it is associated with chapter 26 (see Structure).

Structure and Form

It is widely assumed that this chapter opens the narrative section of the book that continues through chapter 44[6] or chapter 45.[7] But the resemblance of chapter 36 is with chapter 26: in both Jrm is threatened (26:8; 36:26) after the hope is expressed for repentance ("perhaps they will hear" and "turn," 26:3; 36:3). Chapter 26 offers a narrative of Jrm's quintessential call for repentance; the present chapter narrates the event that signaled the end of any hope for repentance (see Introduction, secs. 22, 30, 32). It is better, then, to see the chapter, in the present form of the book, closing the sequence that begins with chapter 26 (for the process by which the two chapters became separated see further Introduction, sec. 22).

Like chapter 26 this chapter is a unit of prophetic biography, a confrontation between Jrm and Jehoiakim. It falls into three sections:[8] vv 1–8, the commission to dictate a scroll; vv 9–26, the three readings of the scroll; and vv 27–32, the conclusion.

After the initial indication of time (v 1a) the commission falls into two sections, Yahweh's commission to Jrm (vv 1b–4) and Jrm's commission to Baruch (vv 5–8). These are quite parallel: introduction (vv 1b, 5a); commission proper (vv 2, 5b–6); reason for the commission ("perhaps . . . ," vv 3, 7), and the execution of the commission (vv 4, 8). This parallelism is in some tension with the division by the setuma sign between vv 3 and 4 in *M* (so the paragraph division in the translation here offered).

After a second indication of time (v 9) the narrative sets forth three readings of the scroll. The first is found in vv 10–14: there is the reading (v 10), the reaction to the reading consisting of the report to others (vv 11–13) and the consequent reaction to that report, the fetching of the scroll (v 14). The narratives of the second and third readings have the same elements, but the two subsections are interwoven. For the second reading there is the reading proper (v 15), the reaction to the reading consisting of a report to others (vv 16–18, 20), the reaction to that report, the fetching of the scroll (v 21a), and then, in addition, a warning to Jrm and Baruch (v 19). For the third reading there is the reading proper (vv 21b–22), followed by two reactions, the destruction of the scroll (v 23) and the attempt to fetch Jrm and Baruch (v 26a), and in addition the consequence of the warning to them (v 26b).

The conclusion (vv 27–32) reflects the elements of the commission in vv 1–4: an indication of time and an introduction of the word of Yahweh (v 27), the commission to Jrm (v 28), and the execution of the commission (v 32). This section is enlarged by a judgment oracle addressed to Jehoiakim: the commission to Jrm and the messenger formula (v 29a); the accusation (v 29b) identifying the king as the one who burned the scroll and quoting the question of the king which implies that the king holds Jrm to be a false prophet; and the announcement of punishment (vv 30–31).

Interpretation

■ **1–32** The narrator of this chapter has precedents in mind: that of the finding of the scroll in Josiah's time (2 Kgs 22—23),[9] and that of Moses, who has to duplicate the tablets of the Ten Commandments after the first tablets were broken (Exod 34:1).[10] But surely behind the

5   So, typically, Rudolph, p. 229; Bright, p. 182.
6   Thus Rietzschel, *Urrolle*, 95–110.
7   Thus Rudolph, p. 1, and recently José María Abrego, "El Texto Hebreo Estructurado de Jeremías 36—45," *Cuadernos Bíblicos* 8 (Valencia: Institución San Jerónimo, 1983) 1–49.
8   For the outline see Wanke, *Baruchschrift*, 71.
9   Martin Kessler, "Form-Critical Suggestions on Jer

36," *CBQ* 28 (1966) 396; Charles D. Isbell, "II Kings 22:3—23:24 and Jeremiah 36: A Stylistic Comparison," *JSOT* 8 (1978) 33–45.
10 Luis Alonso Schökel, "Jeremías como anti-Moisés," *De la Tôrah au Messie, Mélanges Henri Cazelles* (Ed. M. Carrez, J. Doré, and P. Grelot; Paris: Desclée, 1981) 252.

intention of the narrator is that of Jrm himself, who understood himself to be the prophet like Moses (see on 1:4–19) and who had in mind the precedent of the Deuteronomic scroll, understood to be the words of Moses.

■ **1–8** The commission to dictate a scroll falls sometime within the span of a year (v 1), April 605 to March 604 (see Preliminary Observations and Setting), without further designation. One would of course like to understand the circumstances. The fact that Jrm is restricted from going into the temple area (v 5) is a clue but not a definitive one. The fact, however, that the Battle of Carchemish took place in May or June 605, a circumstance that left Jehoiakim a vassal to the losing side, suggests that Jrm's words about the foe from the north might have brought him fresh opposition (see further Introduction, sec. 30). Jrm intends that Baruch read the scroll on a "fast day" (v 6). There is no information in the OT with regard to regular fast-days in the preexilic period:[11] the fast mentioned in v 9 was evidently a special occasion (see on that verse). But if Jrm intended a fixed fast-day, it is likely to have been the Day of Atonement.[12] One could then imagine Jrm, already *persona non grata* because of his words regarding the foe from the north, preparing a scroll in the late summer of 605 with the intention that it be read by Baruch on the occasion of the Day of Atonement in the early autumn of that year.

■ **2** "Document-scroll" is an attempt to render the curious expression מְגִלַּת־סֵפֶר, literally "scroll of a document," both here and in v 4; in both instances G has the same expression. One can only assume that it means "a scroll suitable for a document" or the like. Further reference in the chapter is either to "the scroll" (vv 4, 14 twice, 20, 21, 25, 27, 28 twice, 29, 32) or to "the document" (vv 8, 10, 11, 13, 18, 32); there seems to be no pattern for the choice of terms.

For "Israel" G has "Jerusalem," and several commentators favor that reading (see Text). The present study proposes that Jrm addressed early words to the north "from the days of Josiah," but words to the north would not be a concern to the Jewish community in Alexandria that produced G, and given the standard parallelism of "Jerusalem" and "Judah" it is an understandable reading.

■ **3** For "perhaps they will hear" and "turn" compare 26:3. At this point Yahweh's plans are only plans, and if the people repent, then Yahweh will forgive.

■ **4** Chronologically this is the entrance of Baruch into the story of Jrm; see 32:12.

■ **5** Volz suggests shifting v 9 to a position before v 5; in this way the gathering of people in Jerusalem is brought into the context of Jrm's restriction on going to the temple. This relocation has been followed by many (so *JB, NAB*). But such a shift brings difficulties in its train—how could the present sequence of wording have arisen?[13]—and the chronological problem becomes severe if the date given by G is followed, as is done in the present study. The present order of verses offers satisfactory structure (see Structure and Form).

"Restricted" is a rendering of עָצוּר, which is ambiguous. It may imply "imprisoned," or at least "in custody" (33:1); it may simply mean "prevented [from doing something]," as in Gen 16:2; or it may mean "I am in hiding" (1 Chr 12:1; compare 1 Sam 23:19). The present passage may mean "I am in custody: I cannot go to the temple," "I am barred from going to the temple," or "I am in hiding, so that I cannot go to the temple"; there is no way to settle the matter. There is no way to know why he would have been restricted; conceivably it was for delivering 4:5–8, 13–18, 29–31, and 6:1–8, material which could well have angered the authorities enough to bar him from the temple area at that time. At any rate here is the motive for writing the prophecies down: Jrm cannot deliver them personally.

■ **6** For "day of fasting" see above, vv 1–8.

■ **7** For the phraseology see v 3.

■ **9–11** The present study follows Lohfink[14] in preferring the reading of G, "eighth," rather than that of M, "fifth." (The defense of this choice, offered in "A Chronology of Jeremiah's Career," in *Jeremiah 1*, is repeated here.) There are two reasons for the choice.

(1) The two words resemble each other to some degree (see Text), so that one is likely to be a "correction" of the other. "Eighth," however, is the *lectio difficilior*; "fifth" would seem a natural word to follow on

11 Harvey H. Guthrie, Jr., "Fast, Fasting," *IDB* 2:242.

12 Kraus, *Worship*, 68–70; compare J. Coert Rylaarsdam, "Atonement, Day of," *IDB* 1:314.

13 See Rudolph, p. 232, and the discussion by Nielsen, *Oral Tradition*, 72.

14 Lohfink, "Kurzgeschichte," 324–28.

"fourth" (v 1), but "eighth" is more difficult to explain as an error.

(2) Jehoiakim's act of burning the scroll (v 23) is more plausibly understood in the historical context of November/December 601 than in the context of November/December 604. In November/December 604, the Babylonian army had marched west to the Mediterranean Sea and south along the Palestinian coastal plain, sacking the Philistine city of Ashkelon.[15] This event clearly threatened Judah, and a scroll that included words of warning about Yahweh's sending a foe from the north would hardly have been burned even by so insensitive a king as Jehoiakim. But in November/December 601, the Babylonian army, by then fighting in the Egyptian delta, was dealt a defeat by the Egyptian forces and withdrew to Babylon.[16] If the defeat suggested that Babylon was nothing but a "paper tiger," then one has a possible motive for the king's burning of the scroll (see further on v 23).

It is true, it has been proposed (for example, by Malamat) that the reading "fifth" is correct, that indeed the fast in the ninth month of the fifth year was called precisely because of the military emergency signaled by the sack of Ashkelon.[17] But again, why would the king burn the scroll if the scroll contained such warnings? If, on the other hand, the date in 601 is correct, the fast cannot have been called because of a military emergency; the present study accepts Rudolph's suggestion that the fast was called because of the great drought reflected in 14:1—15:9:[18] indeed Rudolph cites a passage from the Mishna, "If the first of Chislev [= November/December] was come and no rain had fallen, the court enjoins on the congregation three days of fasting."[19] The association of the narrative of the king's burning the scroll and the drought is reinforced by the parallel of 14:16 in the sequence on the drought (14:1—15:9) and v 30 here, "shall be thrown out" (the imperfect of היה plus the hop'al participle of שלך), found only in these two passages in the OT.

Of course if the reading "eighth" is correct, then the lapse of time between the dictation and presumed first use of the scroll and the incident now narrated, a lapse of more than four years, is curious. But it has already been shown that v 9 opens a new section of the narrative (see Structure and Form). The incidents of the chapter are chosen for their appropriateness; one does not expect a full account of the vicissitudes of the scroll. One could imagine any number of circumstances that would bring about the events described here. For example, it is possible that in 605 Jrm was only temporarily unwelcome at the temple area and that in the autumn of 604 the authorities, alarmed by the Babylonian march southward along the coast, were more ready to hear Jrm personally, and the scroll was laid aside. But if the setting proposed in the present study for 8:4–13 is correct (September/October 601), such a prophecy, by November/December of that year, the time of the present narrative, might well have rendered Jrm once more unwelcome in the temple area (see further below). On the other hand, it is possible that Jrm might have continued to be unwelcome in the temple area after 605 and the scroll might have been read regularly but outside the orbit of responsible officials. Obviously there is no way to know. One must conclude, however, that Baruch read the scroll at this juncture because Jrm could not be present personally (compare vv 5–6).

The contents of the scroll were designated "the words of Yahweh" in v 8, they are designated as "the words of Jeremiah" in v 10, and then once more as "the words of Yahweh" in v 11; there is no obvious implication of these shifts.

It may be only a coincidence, if (as the present study proposes) the setting of 8:4–13 is September/October 601, a passage that speaks of the "lie of the scribes" (8:8), that it was in the chamber of a scribe in the temple area that Jrm's scroll was read two months later; but again it may not be a coincidence. The reading took place in the chamber of Gemariah son of Shaphan the scribe, though

---

15   The Babylonian reference is British Museum #21946, obverse, line 18: see Wiseman, *Chronicles*, 68, 69, and see further Bright, *History*, 326.

16   The Babylonian reference is British Museum #21946, reverse, line 7: see Wiseman, *Chronicles*, 70, 71, and see further Bright, *History*, 327.

17   Malamat, "Twilight of Judah," 130.

18   Rudolph, p. 233.

19   *m. Ta'an.* 1:5.

evidently Gemariah himself was not present (compare v 12); his son Micaiah was present (v 11), along with others (v 10).

It is appropriate at this point to raise the question: Was Baruch already known in scribal circles in Jerusalem? It is altogether likely that he was: he must have been trained in a scribal school alongside scribes who at this point in the narrative formed the circle of the king's councilors. Certainly one has the impression here that Baruch had access to these circles. Thus in v 10 there is no indication that Baruch had been summoned to the chamber of Gemariah the scribe (compare v 14): one has the impression that Baruch had direct access to the chamber.[20] The affirmative answer to the question has consequences for an understanding of vv 17–18 (see below). But there is no way to know whether Baruch was bold or timid, whether Micaiah's reaction to the reading was panic or anger, indeed whether Micaiah was reluctant or eager to report the words of the scroll to higher authority. (Compare the discussion of the motive of the officials in wishing to report the matter to the king, v 16 below.) Since Gemariah was the brother of Ahikam, who had protected Jrm on a previous occasion (26:24), and the brother of Gedaliah who will guard him on a future occasion (39:14), one could guess that Gemariah and his son might be sympathetic to Jrm, but more cannot be said.[21] What is clear is that Baruch and the scroll are being moved from one audience to the next; the existence of the scroll is a phenomenon that can no longer be ignored by the officials.

In recent excavations of Jerusalem, in the context of the last decade or two before the fall of the city, a bulla (stamp-seal impression) has come to light bearing the inscription "לגמריהו (ב)ן שפן "(belonging) to Gemariah [so]n of Shaphan";[22] there is no doubt that the bulla is a relic of the Gemariah son of Shaphan mentioned here (compare the bulla of Baruch described in Interpretation on 32:12, and the bulla of Jerahmeel the king's son described below, v 26).

The identity of "the people" in v 10 is not self-evident; compare the discussion on "all the people" in Interpretation, 26:7–19.

Micaiah son of Gemariah is mentioned only in v 11 and in v 13.

■ **12–13** Micaiah went down from the temple area to the palace to report the existence of Jrm's scroll (compare "went up," 26:10). The "chamber of the scribe" is mentioned only here; from the narrative one gathers that it served as a meeting-room for the king's councilors (Luther translates it "chancery"). One may note in passing that although Elishama is named here as a scribe, there is no way to know whether the "chamber of Elishama" (vv 20, 21) is the same as the "chamber of the scribe" or another.

Among the officials sitting in the chamber, to whom Micaiah reported, five are named. Elishama is mentioned only here (and in vv 20 and 21). It is conceivable that this Elishama is identical with the Elishama who was the grandfather of the assassin of Gedaliah (41:1; so the suggestion of Naegelsbach), in which case he is a member of the royal family. Delaiah is mentioned only here and in v 25. Elnathan the son of Achbor had been in charge of the posse sent to fetch Uriah the prophet from Egypt (26:22); it is likely that he was father-in-law of the king (2 Kgs 24:8; see the discussion on 26:20–24). He is mentioned again in v 25. For Gemariah see above on v 10; he is mentioned again in v 25. Zedekiah the son of Hananiah is mentioned only here.

It is noteworthy that Achbor and Shaphan had participated in the validation of the scroll discovered in the temple in Josiah's time (2 Kgs 22:12, 14); the narrator means to underline the parallels between that incident and the present one (see vv 1–32).

■ **14** Jehudi son of Nethaniah appears here and in vv 21

20   Muilenburg, "Baruch," 227–28.
21   See the survey of the family in James M. Ward, "Shaphan," *IDB* 4:307–8.
22   Yigal Shiloh, "Excavations at the City of David, I, 1978–82, Interim Report of the First Five Seasons," *Qedem* 19 (1984) 19–20, and plate 35/3; "A Hoard of Hebrew Bullae from the City of David" [English title], *Eretz-Israel* 18 (1985) 83; plate 10/1; English summary, 68*; Shiloh and Tarler, "Bullae," esp. 204–5.

and 23. The listing of three patronymics, back to his great-grandfather, is strange, but there is no need with Cornill and Rudolph to emend the text to two messengers, Jehudi son of Nethaniah and Shelemiah son of Cushi. Both Jehudi's name ("the Judahite") and that of his great-grandfather ("the Cushite") are gentilics, leading to the suspicion that the name Jehudi marks the naturalization of a foreigner (Duhm, Giesebrecht).[23] The narrative indicates that he serves as an adjutant in the group of councilors; he is sent to summon Baruch to bring the scroll.

■ **15** Again Baruch may already have been known to some or all of the officials present (compare v 10 and vv 17–19).

For "read it again" instead of "sit down and read it" see Text. Baruch would stand in the presence of the seated councilors (compare v 12), just as the councilors would stand (v 21) in the presence of the seated king (v 22). The command implies, "Read it a second time, this time in our hearing." Baruch obeys.

■ **16** "They turned in alarm to each other": the text is harsh, literally, "They trembled, each to the other." Accordingly Volz, Rudolph, and Bright wish to transfer "and they said" to a position before "each to the other." This would smooth the narrative, but G reflects the same word order as does M. Furthermore the verb פחד is followed by אֶל in Hos 3:5 as well, so the idiom appears to be acceptable. (It also appears in Mic 7:17, but there the prepositional phrase seems to be a gloss.)

The officials feel impelled to tell the king, not to get Baruch and Jrm into trouble (v 19 suggests that the officials wish to protect them), but because the issue of the truth or falsity of the words is of the highest importance.

■ **17–19** A choice must be made in text tradition here. G omits "at his dictation" at the end of v 17, and G and S read "Jeremiah" as the subject of the verb in v 18a. It is clear that "at his dictation" (here translated simply "yes") is the crucial portion of Baruch's answer in v 18; if the Masoretic punctuation of "all these words" (conjunctive accent on "these") at the end of v 17 is correct, then "at his dictation" in v 17 is almost surely a gloss (so Duhm, Cornill, Giesebrecht, Volz, Condamin, Rudolph, and

Bright).[24] Furthermore the name "Jeremiah" seems to be necessary in v 18a (so Duhm, Cornill, Giesebrecht, Volz, Rudolph, Bright). But if Baruch's association with Jrm is already known, then "at his dictation" at the end of v 17 may be a second question: Bright suggests, if that is the case, that an interrogative he has dropped out before מִפִּיו (compare also Naegelsbach). And the reading without "Jeremiah" is surely the *lectio difficilior*. It would therefore seem preferable to follow M here and see G as a secondary reconception of the interchange without the assumption that both the officials and Baruch could speak of "him" without identifying him. (It should be noted that the officials would in any case have heard the name "Jeremiah" in the course of Baruch's reading of the scroll: for example, in 1:11.) By this understanding, Baruch answers the two questions in reverse order.

Verse 18 begins, literally, with "at his dictation": this is the device for answering "yes."

The officials do not deal with the question whether Jrm is a true prophet; their question stays with the legitimacy of the scroll. Is it what it purports to be? "How did you come to write the words? Was it really at his dictation?" But Baruch's answer is curious; he answers in the flattest, most literal way: "Yes, he would dictate the words to me, and I would write them down, with ink." Pray how else would he write them down, except with ink? (It may be noted in passing that G omits "with ink," but that omission is doubtless secondary; either the translator did not know the word [דְּיוֹ, a *hapax legomenon*], or else he may have felt the same difficulty here discussed.) One almost has the impression Baruch is mocking his questioners, or else that he is playing the "good soldier Schweik,"[25] answering naively in order not to become involved more deeply than he is already, but these may be modern perceptions. In any event, the officials support Baruch (and Jrm) by urging both to go into hiding.

The imperfect verb יִקְרָא in v 18 is frequentative ("would recite"); compare the frequentative verbs in v 23.

As to the nature of ink: black ink varied in its composition. The Egyptians used a carbon ink, soot (lampblack) mixed in a gum solution;[26] but the ink of the Lachish

23 So also James M. Ward, "Jehudi," *IDB* 2:819.
24 So also Janzen, p. 52.
25 Jaroslav Hasek, *The Good Soldier Schweik* (Garden City,

NY: Doubleday, Doran, 1930).
26 Robert J. Forbes, "Chemical, Culinary, and Cosmetic Arts," *A History of Technology* I (ed. Charles Singer, E.

letters was a mixture of carbon ink and iron ink, the iron perhaps derived from oak-galls.[27]

■ **20–26** Baruch and Jrm must have heard the details of these events from an eyewitness; there was evidently more than one person present who was sympathetic to Jrm (see on v 25).

■ **20** The "chamber of the scribe" (v 12) may have been situated on the outside of the palace; now the officials went into the courtyard of the palace to report the matter to the king himself. The scroll itself, however, they left behind for safekeeping. The chamber of Elishama is not necessarily identical with the "chamber of the scribe" (compare v 12).

■ **21** Jehudi continues to do the errands (see v 14): he fetches the scroll so it can be read in full in the presence of the king.

■ **22** The "winter house" in this instance was certainly not a separate dwelling, but "winter quarters," a room or series of rooms that could be expected to retain the heat.[28]

Though current translations agree on "brazier" for אָח, it could well have been a fixed hearth rather than a portable firepan; G translates ἐσχάρα, which can be either a hearth or a brazier; V translates arula ("little altar," that is, as if for sacrifice); S and T simply render "fire." The king's winter quarters might well have had some permanent installation for a fire.

■ **23** Both the imperfect יִקְרָעֶהָ and the waw-consecutive perfect וְהַשְׁלֵךְ are frequentative ("would tear," "would throw"); compare the frequentative in v 18.

The word translated "columns" (דְּלָתוֹת) is literally "doors." There seems no doubt that the term is used for a column of writing; the word "door" in this meaning may originally have referred to a "writing-board," specimens of which have turned up in the ancient Near East—for example, sixteen writing-boards made of ivory at Nimrud. The word also appears in Lachish Letter 4, where it may literally mean "writing-board."[29] In any event, one must understand that every so often a portion of the scroll would be thrown into the fire.

It has become an assumption in this century that it is the king who tore sections of the scroll and threw them in the fire (so Duhm, Condamin, Rudolph, Bright; so *RSV, JB, NEB, NAB, NJV*); Bright remarks, "It was, of course, the king who destroyed the scroll, not Yehudi."[30] To the contrary, as the text stands, "Jehudi" is the subject of the verbs. Of course it is the king who is responsible for destroying the scroll (vv 25, 29); but the king would hardly have wielded the scribe's knife himself—that is the task of an underling. The king would have given the orders, or simply nodded in Jehudi's direction. (Compare the implication of the diction in v 29: Yahweh accuses Jehoiakim of being the one who really burned the scroll.)

The verb "tear" (קרע) is noteworthy; a contrast is implied in "tearing" the scroll rather than "tearing" one's garments (v 24).

The word here for "knife" (תַּעַר) in Isa 7:20 means a "razor"; the "scribe's knife" is evidently a penknife.[31]

The fact that the scroll could be burned suggests strongly that it was of papyrus, not leather, which would have burned with difficulty and caused a stench.[32]

Why would the king have seen to the destruction of the scroll? Of course one cannot minimize the element of irrationality that may motivate those in authority when they are challenged. Nevertheless it is worth attempting

J. Holmyard, and A. R. Hall; Oxford: Oxford University, 1954) 245; Ronald J. Williams, "Writing and Writing Materials," *IDB* 4:919.

27   Alkin Lewis, "Report on the Lachish Letters, With Remarks Upon the Use of Iron Inks in Antiquity," and "Tests Upon the Ink of the Letters," *Lachish I, The Lachish Letters* (ed. Harry Torczner; London: Oxford University, 1938) 188–93, 194–95, esp. 195.

28   Compare the remarks on Amos 3:15 in William R. Harper, *A Critical and Exegetical Commentary on Amos and Hosea* (ICC; New York: Scribner's, 1905) 78; see more generally Shalom M. Paul, "Amos iii 15—

Winter and Summer Mansions," *VT* 28 (1978) 358–59.

29   R. Lansing Hicks, "*delet* and *mᵉgillāh*, A Fresh Approach to Jeremiah xxxvi," *VT* 33 (1983) 49–53.

30   Bright, p. 180.

31   Ronald J. Williams, "Penknife," *IDB* 3:711.

32   Menahem Haran, "Scribal Workmanship in the Biblical Period—Scrolls and Writing Implements," *Tarbiz* 50 (1980/81) 65–87; see the English summary by Frederick E. Greenspahn in *Old Testament Abstracts* 6 (1983) 217.

to discern what moved the king to his action. The only indication is the question in v 29 attributed to the king, "Why have you written on it, The king of Babylon will indeed come in and destroy this land and remove from it man and beast?" It is further said that neither the king nor his servants were in dread (v 24), as at least some of his advisors had been in the previous reading of the scroll (v 16), and that there were those who urged him not to destroy the scroll (as well as those, evidently, who did urge him to destroy it: see on v 25). Duhm remarks that the king acts like a critic, destroying what does not please him![33] Volz and Rudolph assume that the king is frivolous, not taking the scroll seriously, though Cornill points out that the king, having heard a few columns of the scroll, did not burn the whole scroll all at once but did hear it through. This much can be said: on a previous occasion Jrm has pronounced Yahweh's judgment on Jehoiakim (22:13–19), a judgment that must have become known to the king; the king must at the very least have been unfriendly toward Jrm. It is possible, if the king suspected Jrm was a true prophet, that he wanted to rid the land of the power of the prophet's words.[34] On the other hand, if the king is struck by the contrast between Jrm's description of the foe from the north and the setback dealt the Babylonian forces that same month, then he might well have judged the words to be worthless,[35] or even destroyed the words of the false prophet in anticipation of destroying the false prophet himself (v 26; compare Deut 18:20). But none of this may have been conscious to the king: he may simply have done what he felt impelled to do (compare the remarks below on the lack of specificity in v 29 as to the subject of "have written"). The narrative, in any case, sets the action forth as the king's blasphemous destruction of the words of Yahweh. Calvin puts the whole matter in perspective. "Now as to the king, we see in him as in a glass how monstrous is their blindness who are the slaves of Satan. Surely the king, when God so thundered in his ears, ought to have been terrified. He could not indeed treat the word with ridicule, but he became enraged, and acted violently like a rabid wild beast, and vented his rage against the roll itself! If he thought Jeremiah to have been the author, why did he not disregard him as a man

of no authority in public affairs? for Jeremiah could not have lessened his character as a king. There is then no doubt but that he perceived, though unwillingly, that he had to do with God; why then did he become thus enraged? what could he hope to gain by such madness towards God? But this, as I have said, was that dreadful blindness which is found in all the reprobate, whose minds the devil has fascinated; for on the one hand they perceive, willing or unwilling, that God is present, and that they are in a manner summoned to his tribunal; and on the other, as though they were forgetful of God, they rage madly against him."

■ 24 Neither the king nor his servants were "alarmed" (פחד); this is in contrast to the officials who were in alarm on the occasion of an earlier reading (v 16). Nor did they "tear" (קרע) their clothes, as King Josiah had done when the Deuteronomic scroll was read to him (2 Kgs 22:11): instead, the king saw to it that the scroll itself was torn (v 23: see above, on vv 1–32).

The king's "servants" are evidently another group than the "officials" who had come in to the presence of the king and were standing in his presence (vv 20–21; so Thompson); the word perhaps refers to those named in v 26.

■ 25 The existence of a text of *G* without "not," and the presence of וְגַם (normally "also") at the beginning of the verse suggests strongly that the text originally offered a contrast between those who urged the king to burn the scroll and those who urged the opposite (against Giesebrecht, who insists that וְגַם is adversative); for a justification of the reconstruction offered here see Text. By the reconstruction, the king's officials are divided: Elnathan urges him to burn the scroll (compare 26:22–23), and Gedaliah likewise (compare 38:4); at the same time Delaiah and Gemariah urge the opposite. The verb פגע hip'il, translated here "urge," means "intervene" (see on 15:11).

■ 26 Jerahmeel the king's son is named only here. A bulla (stamp-seal impression) has come to light from Jerusalem in the last few decades of the monarchy bearing the inscription לירחמאל בן המלך "(belonging) to Jerahmeel the king's son."[36]

Opinion has differed whether "king's son" is to be

---

33 Duhm, p. 294.
34 Sheldon H. Blank, *Jeremiah, Man and Prophet* (Cincinnati: Hebrew Union College, 1961) 28–29.

35 See n. 14.
36 Nahman Avigad, "Baruch the Scribe and Jerahmeel the King's Son"; "Jerahmeel & Baruch"; *Hebrew*

taken literally or whether it is the designation of an office. In favor of the latter is the fact that both Joash (1 Kgs 22:26) and Malchiah (Jer 38:6), who bear the title, seem to have had a police function, as Jerahmeel did;[37] furthermore it has been urged that Jehoiakim is too young to have had an adult son,[38] but this contention is based on the date of 604 for the burning of the scroll. In 601 Jehoiakim is thirty-three years old (2 Kgs 23:36). Jehoiachin was born in 616 (2 Kgs 24:8); Jerahmeel, if he were the son of the king, might have been born soon thereafter and be fourteen or fifteen years old in 601. André Lemaire, after surveying the biblical and extra-biblical evidence, likewise concludes that "the king's son" is to be taken literally,[39] but a recent study suggests that the term was current in Egyptian chronicles as a title for a functionary in the court, so that the same idiom may have been current in Judah.[40]

The Seraiah and Shelemiah mentioned here are otherwise unknown.

These three (who may be the king's servants mentioned in v 24: see there) the king dispatches to arrest Baruch and Jeremiah; but the two remain in hiding.

■ **27–28** A report would have come quickly to Jrm that the king had burned the scroll; Jrm is then bidden to dictate a duplicate. The narrator doubtless has the precedent of Moses in mind (Exod 34:1): on this see vv 1–32.

■ **29** Yahweh accuses Jehoiakim of being the one who burned the scroll: this is one slight indication that it was Jehudi who did the actual burning (see on v 23).

It is a pretty problem who the subject of "you have written" (כָּתַבְתָּ) is understood to be—Yahweh, Jrm, or Baruch; the narrator would appear to have left the matter intentionally open.

The king knew the identity of the foe from the north! The king's citation of the contents of the scroll is a summary: no phraseology akin to this is to be found in passages preserved for us. In particular there is no occurrence elsewhere in Jer of the infinitive absolute together with a finite form of בוא "come in": the combi-

nation here suggests that Yahweh is insisting against denials that the king of Babylon really will come in after all (compare 5:12 and 14:15). It is noteworthy that the king says nothing about the drought, but this silence is doubtless due to the fact that the scroll, dictated four years previously, has not been expanded since that time (compare the discussion of "Group B" oracles in 4:5—10:25, Preliminary Observations; see on v 32 below).

■ **30** The judgment on the king is that he shall have no successor, and that his corpse shall not receive proper burial. The former judgment is repeated for Jehoiachin (22:30), since obviously it was not fulfilled in the literal sense in Jehoiakim's case. The latter judgment is a variation on 22:18–19; it offers the same kind of peri-phrastic expression found in 14:16, וְנִבְלָתוֹ תִּהְיֶה מֻשְׁלֶכֶת: the phrase really means "his corpse shall remain lying."[41]

■ **31** Here, almost inadvertently, is the indication that Yahweh is now going to bring to bear upon the whole nation the destruction that had up to then been voiced only as warning (vv 3, 7); on this matter see Introduction, sec. 32. If the king could not heed the words of the scroll, then there is no hope for the nation (compare 5:4–5). The phrase "men of Judah and inhabitants of Jerusalem" appears eight times in Jer: 4:3, 4; 11:2, 9; 17:25; 18:11; 32:32; 35:13. This is the sole occurrence with the elements in reverse order. Is a stylistic purpose served here?—that one moves from the king to his family, to his courtiers, to the rest of Jerusalem, to the surrounding countryside?

■ **32** The narrator evidently has in mind the second pair of stone tablets that Moses used (Exod 34:1: see on vv 1–32). Jrm's second scroll contained not only the contents of the first scroll but also oracles that came to him in the

---

Bullae from the Time of Jeremiah, Remnants from a Burnt Archive (Jerusalem: Israel Exploration Society, 1986) no. 8, p. 27; Shiloh and Tarler, "Bullae," 204; Larry G. Herr, "Paleography and the Identification of Seal Owners," *BASOR* 239 (Summer 1980) 67–70.

37 Avigad, "Jerahmeel & Baruch," 117.
38 Bruce T. Dahlberg, "Jerahmeel," *IDB* 2:822.
39 Lemaire, "*bn hmlk.*"

40 Manfred Görg, "Zum Titel *BN HMLK* ('Königs-sohn')," *Biblische Notizen* 29 (1985) 7–11.
41 Joüon, *Gramm.*, sec. 121e.

period since the dictation of the first scroll (see especially 2:1—4:4, Preliminary Observations, and 4:5—10:25, Preliminary Observations).

Aim

The word of God had not in those years become flesh, but it had been deposited in written form, and that written deposit, at that moment, was despised and rejected by men and was destroyed. But the written deposit was not the word, it bore witness to the word. And because "the word of our God will stand for ever" (Isa 40:8), the written deposit could be reproduced, and was—with increase. The king could not doom the word: the word doomed the king, and with him his people.

**The Final Months
of Jeremiah's Career**

Bibliography

On Chapters 37—44:

Ackroyd, Peter R.
"Historians and Prophets: Jeremiah and the Fall of
Jerusalem," *SEÅ* 35 (1968) 37–54.

Kremers, Heinz
"Leidensgemeinschaft mit Gott im Alten Testament," *EvT* 13 (1953) 122–40.

Pohlmann, Karl-Friedrich
*Studien zum Jeremiabuch, Ein Beitrag zur Frage nach
der Entstehung des Jeremiabuches* (FRLANT 118;
Gottingen: Vandenhoeck & Ruprecht, 1978) 48–
225.

On 37:1—43:13:

Lohfink
"Kurzgeschichte."

Seitz, Christopher R.
"The Crisis of Interpretation Over the Meaning
and Purpose of the Exile," *VT* 35 (1985) 78–97.

Wanke
Baruchschrift, 91–133, 155–56.

On 37:1—39:18:

Reymond, Philippe
"Un aspect de la liberté dans l'Ancien Testament
d'après Jérémie 37—38, 39.15–18," *VCaro* 14
(1960) 39–48.

On 37:1—38:28:

Migsch
Das Ende Jerusalems.

On 37:1–21:

Hoffmeier, James K.
"A New Insight on Pharaoh Apries from Herodotus, Diodorus and Jeremiah 46:17," *Journal of the
Society for the Study of Egyptian Antiquities* 11 (1981)
165-70.

Jong, Stephan de
"Hizkia en Zedekia, Over de verhouding van 2
Kon. 18:17—19:37/Jes. 36—37 tot Jer. 37:1–
10," *Amsterdamse Cahiers voor Exegese en Bijbelse
Theologie* 5 (ed. Karel A. Deurloo; Kampen: Kok,
1984) 135–46.

Pohlmann
Studien, 49–69.

Reventlow
Liturgie, 143–49.

Wanke
Baruchschrift, 95–102.

On 38:1-28:

Budde, Karl
"Ein althebräisches Klagelied," *ZAW* 3 (1883) 299–306.

Görg, Manfred
"Jeremia zwischen Ost und West (Jer 38,1–6), Zur Krisensituation in Jerusalem am Vorabend des Babylonischen Exils," *Künder des Wortes: Beiträge zur Theologie der Propheten; Josef Schreiner zum 60. Geburtstag* (ed. Lothar Rupper, Peter Weimar, and Erich Zenger; Würzburg: Echter, 1982) 121–36.

Lemaire
"bn hmlk."

Long, Burke O.
"Reports of Visions Among the Prophets," *JBL* 95 (1976) 355.

Pohlmann
Studien, 69–93.

On 38:28b–40:12:

Eissfeldt, Otto
"Baruchs Anteil an Jeremia 38,28b—40,6," *OrAnt* 4 (1965) 31–34 = *Kleine Schriften IV* (Tübingen: Mohr [Siebeck], 1968) 176–80.

Wanke
Untersuchungen, 102–16.

On 39:1–40:6:

Bewer, Julius A.
"Nergalsharezer Samgar in Jer. 39:3," *AJSL* 42 (1925/26) 130.

Deist, Ferdinand E.
"The Punishment of the Disobedient Zedekiah," *Journal of Northwest Semitic Languages* 1 (1971) 71–72.

Diringer, David
"Seals and Seal Impressions," *Lachish III, The Iron Age* (ed. Olga Tufnell; London: Oxford University, 1953) 347–48.

Feigin, Samuel I.
"The Babylonian Officials in Jeremiah 39 3, 13," *JBL* 45 (1926) 149–55.

Paton, Lewis B.
"The Meaning of the Expression 'Between the Two Walls,'" *JBL* 25 (1906) 1–13.

Pohlmann
Studien, 93–107.

Power, Edmond
"Jer. 39,3. 13 novo textu cuneato elucidatus et confirmatus," *Bib* 7 (1926) 229–30.

Unger, Eckhard
"Namen im Hofstaate Nebukadnezars II," *TLZ* 50 (1925), cols. 481–86.

de Vaux, Roland
"Le sceau de Godolias, maître du Palais," *RB* 45 (1936) 96–102.

On 40:7–41:18:

Ammassari, Antonio
"Un precedente biblico del terrorismo," *BeO* 20 (1978) 241–44.

Pohlmann
Studien, 108–22.

On 40:7–16:

Herr, Larry G.
"Is the Spelling of 'Baalis' in Jeremiah 40:14 a Mutilation?" *AUSS* 23 (1985) 187–91.

Herr, Larry G.
"The Servant of Baalis," *BA* 48 (1985) 169–72.

On 41:1–18:

Boehmer, Julius
"Silo, 2. Zu Jer 41,5," *ZAW* 29 (1909) 145–46.

On 41:16–43:7:

Wanke
Baruchschrift, 116–33.

On 42:1–22:

Berridge
pp. 202–8.

Pohlmann
Studien, 123–45.

Reventlow
Liturgie, 143–49.

On 43:1–13:

Boer, Pieter A. H. de
"Some Remarks Concerning and Suggested by Jeremiah 43:1–7," *Translating & Understanding the Old Testament, Essays in Honor of Herbert Gordon May* (ed. Harry Thomas Frank and William L. Reed; Nashville: Abingdon, 1970) 71–79.

Gall, August G. E. K. von
"Jeremias 43,12 und das Zeitwort עטה," *ZAW* 24 (1904) 105–21.

Lemke
"Nebuchadrezzar."

Pohlmann
Studien, 145–66.

On 44:1–30:

Pohlmann
Studien, 166–82.

Smith, Morton
"The Veracity of Ezekiel, the Sins of Manasseh and Jeremiah 44 18," *ZAW* 87 (1975) 11–16.

[*Note:* On "queen of heaven" in vv 17–19 see bibliography on 7:16–20.]

1 [King]a Zedekiah son of Josiah reigned instead
of Coniah son of Jehoiakim, whom
Nebuchadrezzar [king of Babylon]b
appointed to reign in [the land of]c Judah.
2/ But neither he nor his servants nor the
people of the land obeyed the words of
Yahweh which he spoke by means of Jeremiah [the prophet.]a

3 King Zedekiah sent Jehucal son of Shelemiah,
and Zephaniah the son of Maaseiah the
priest, to Jeremiah [the prophet,]a saying:
"Please pray on our behalf to Yahweh [our
God."]b 4/ Jeremiah was (still) going in and
out aamong the people,a and they had not
(yet) put him in prison.b 5/ Meanwhile the
army of Pharaoh had come out of Egypt, and
the Chaldeans [who were besieging
Jerusalem]a heard news of them and took
themselves away from Jerusalem.

6 Then the word of Yahweh came to Jeremiah
[the prophet]a saying: 7/ Thus Yahweh [God
of Israel]a has said, This is what the two of
you shall say to the king of Judah who sent
you to me to inquire of me: The army of
Pharaoh, which has come out to you to help,
is going to return to his own land [Egypt.]b
8/ And the Chaldeans shall return and fight
against this city and capture it [and burn it
with fire.]a 9/ 《For》a thus Yahweh has said,
Do not deceive yourselves, saying, "The
Chaldeans will indeed go away from us," for
they will not go away. 10/ [For]a (even) if
you have struck down the whole army of
Chaldeans who are fighting with you and
there remain [among them]b (only) some
wounded, each in his tent, they shall rise up
and 《capture》c this city [with fire.]c

11 Now when the army of the Chaldeans had
taken themselves away from Jerusalem,
from the presence of the army of Pharaoh,
12/ Jeremiah went out from Jerusalem to
go (to)a the land of Benjamin, b《to take》〈a
share (of property)〉b from there in the midst
of the people, 13/ but when he was at the
Benjamin Gate, an officer of the guard there
named Irijaha son of Shelemiah son of
Hananiah arrested Jeremiah [the prophet,]b
saying, "You are deserting to the Chaldeans!" 14/ He [M: Jeremiah]a said, "It is
false, I am not deserting to the Chaldeans,"
but he did not listen to him; Irijahb seized
Jeremiah and brought him in to the officials.
15/ And the officials became furious at
Jeremiah, beating him and putting him [in
jail]a in the house of Jonathan the scribe, for
it had been made a prison. 16/ 《So》a Jeremiah 《was put》a in the cistern house, in the
cells, and he [M: Jeremiah]b stayed there
many days.

Text

37:1a Omit with G; see Janzen, pp. 142, 155.

b Omit with G; compare Janzen, p. 140.

c Omit with G; compare 31:23.

2a Omit with G; see Janzen, p. 146.

3a Omit with G (compare 2a).

b Omit with G; see Janzen, pp. 80, 81. For "our
God" S reads "your God."

4a—a M בְּתוֹךְ הָעָם, G "through the midst of the city" =
בְּתוֹךְ הָעִיר; the readings are equally plausible.

b The spelling of the word is uncertain: ketib כליא,
qere' כְּלוּא (so also 52:31).

5a Omit with G; M has filled out the text from 21:4,
9 (compare Janzen, p. 52).

6a Omit with G (compare 2a).

7a Omit with G; compare Janzen, p. 75.

b M "his land Egypt" is odd. G reads "to the land of
Egypt," though GL reads "to his land"; S reads "to
his land, to Egypt," and T "to their land, to Egypt."
It would appear that M reflects a conflate text, "to
his land" and "to Egypt." See Janzen, p. 22.

8a Omit with Rudolph as a *vaticinium ex eventu*: see
38:3. Compare Text on 34:2.

9a Read כִּי with G; the word evidently dropped out
in M by haplography with כה, was noted in the
margin, and was reinserted wrongly at the beginning of v 10 (see there).

10a The conjunction כִּי belongs at the beginning of v
9 (so G); see there.

b Omit with G.

c With Rudolph read "capture" instead of "burn
with fire" (see v 8).

12a M lacks a preposition, but a fragment from the
Cairo Geniza has לְ, and a few MSS. have אֶל.

b—b Reading לָקַחַת חֵלֶק; I propose that a haplography
arose because of the repetition of consonants. See
Interpretation.

13a For this name G has "Zeruiah" (compare 2 Sam
2:18) and S has "Neriah" (compare 36:4).

b Omit with G (compare v 2).

14a Omit with G; M has added the clarifying subject.

b See 13a.

15a Omit with G; while G may have suffered haplography (two occurrences of בֵּית), it is more likely that
M offers a conflate text. See Janzen, p. 22 (compare
118).

16a The M reading, כִּי בָא, "For he [Jeremiah]
entered," is odd; G reads, "And Jeremiah went," and
S "And they threw Jeremiah." For the conjunction
and verb I propose to read וַיֻּבָא, the hop'al; the qal
stem ("entered") is far too bland for the narrative.
Waw and kap would easily be confused in the Old
Aramaic script (see Frank M. Cross, "The Development of the Jewish Scripts," *The Bible and the Ancient
Near East* [ed. G. Ernest Wright; New York: Doubleday, 1961] 137). It is likely that Prov 7:22 also
contains a qal of בוא which must be read as a hop'al.

b Omit with G (compare v 14); compare Janzen, p.
147.

Then [King][a] Zedekiah sent and brought him, and the king asked him in his house secretly and said, "Is there a word from Yahweh?" And he [*M*: Jeremiah][b] said, "Yes." [c] ⟪And the king said, "How is it?"⟫ And he said,[c] "Into the hand of the king of Babylon you will be given." 18/ Then Jeremiah said to the king [Zedekiah,][a] "What wrong have I done to you or to your servants or to this people that [b]you should put[b] me into prison? 19/ And where[a] are your prophets who prophesied to you, saying, 'The king of Babylon will not come against you and against this land'? 20/ And now please hear, my lord king, please let my plea fall before you: do not send me back to the house of Jonathan the scribe, that I might not die there." 21/ So the king [Zedekiah][a] commanded, and they committed him [*M*: Jeremiah][b] to the court of the guard, and they gave him a slab of bread each day from the bakers' street, until all the bread of the city was used up; and Jeremiah stayed in the court of the guard.

Now Shephatiah son of Mattan, Gedaliah son of Pashhur, Jucal son of Shelemiah, and Pashhur son of Malchiah heard the words which Jeremiah was speaking to the people, as follows: 2/ Thus Yahweh has said, He who stays in this city shall die by sword ⟪and⟫[a] famine [and pestilence;][a] he who goes out to the Chaldeans [b]shall live:[b] he shall at least have his life and shall live. 3/ ⟪For⟫[a] thus Yahweh has said: This city will really be given into the hand of the army of the king of Babylon and he will capture it. 4/ And they [*M* the officials][a] said to the king, "This man ought to be put to death, inasmuch as he is weakening the hands of the soldiers who are left in this city, and the hands of all the people, in speaking to them in words like these; for this man is not seeking welfare for this people, but evil." 5/ The king [Zedekiah][a] said, "Here he is—he is in your hand"; for the king ⟨was not able⟩[b] (to do) anything ⟪against them.⟫[c] 6/ So they took Jeremiah and threw him into the cistern of Malchiah the king's son, who was in the court of the guard, [and they let [b]⟪him⟫ {*M*: Jeremiah}[b] down by ropes;][a] now there was no water in the cistern, only mud, and he [*M*: Jeremiah][c] sank into the mud.

7/ Ebed-melech the Ethiopian, [a eunuch,][a] who was in the king's house, heard that they had put Jeremiah in the cistern; the king was sitting in the Benjamin Gate. 8/ So he [*M*: Ebed-melech][a] left the king's house and spoke to the king as follows: 9/ ["My lord king,][a] [b] ⟪you have done wrong in

17a   Omit with *G*; compare Janzen, p. 142.
b   Omit with *G*; compare Janzen, p. 147.
c   Omit with *G*; the verb appears to be dittographic.
c—c   Restore these words, וַיֹּאמֶר הַמֶּלֶךְ אֵיךְ יֵשׁ, with *S*. *M* omits the words, leaving the now illogical fourth occurrence of "said" in the verse; *G* omits the fourth occurrence of "said." *M* is evidently defective by haplography; *G* either "corrected" the text by omitting the second "and he said" or is defective by a longer haplography.
18a   Omit with *G*; compare Janzen, p. 142.
b—b   *M* wrongly reads a second-person plural here; read the second singular with *G* and *V*. The diction shifts to the second-person plural in v 19.
19a   Read the qere' וְאַיֵּה; the ketib erroneously reads וְאַיּוֹ "and where is he?"
21a   Omit with *G*; compare Janzen, p. 142.
b   Omit with *G*; compare Janzen, p. 147.
38:2a   Read with *G* "by sword and famine" instead of *M* "by sword, famine and pestilence." The situation is identical with that in 21:9: see there, and see the discussion in Janzen, pp. 43–44 and 205, n. 19.
b—b   The reading of the ketib, יִחְיֶה, is preferable to the qere' וְחָיָה, but both are possible (so identically 21:9).
3a   Insert כִּי with *G*. Without it the bare messenger formula is odd: compare the beginning of v 2. Rudolph solves the problem by deleting v 2 as an insertion from 21:9, but this is arbitrary.
4a   Omit with *G*.
5a   Omit with *G*; compare Janzen, p. 142.
b   Vocalizing the participle יָכוֹל (compare the *G* imperfect ἠδύνατο) for the *M* imperfect יוּכַל; so Arnold B. Ehrlich and Rudolph.
c   Read אֹתָם (or אֶתָם) with *G*, which understands the quotation to close with "in your hands"; *M* understands the quotation to continue to the end of the verse, reading, "For the king is unable to do anything against you." But the third person use of "the king" in his own mouth is odd, to say nothing of the admission of weakness. So Duhm, Cornill, Giesebrecht, Condamin.
6a   The verbs שׁלך hip'il "throw" and שׁלח pi'el "let down" are hardly sequential actions: yod-kap and ḥet resemble each other in the script of the fifth and fourth centuries (Janzen, p. 52), and the text is evidently conflate. "With ropes" is lacking in *G*, which has instead "into the cistern": both text traditions evidently filled out the clause in different ways. See Janzen, p. 207, n. 38.
b—b   "Jeremiah" is a further addition in *M*; compare Janzen, p. 147.
c   Omit with *G*; compare Janzen, p. 147.
7a   Omit with *G*; the gloss explains "who was in the king's house" (compare 2 Kgs 20:18). See Janzen, p. 73.
8a   Omit with *G*; compare Janzen, p. 152.
9a   The bracketed words are omitted by *G*. Since *G* renders them in 37:20, and since there appears to be no reason for *G* to omit them here, they are

what you did, (to try) to kill this man》 [M: these men have done wrong in all they have done to Jeremiah the prophet in throwing (him) into the cistern, 〈 that he might die 〉c on the spot]b in the presence of hunger, for there is no more bread in the city." 10/ So the king commanded Ebed-melech [the Ethiopian]a as follows: Take with you from here 《 three 》b men and bring c《 him 》 [M Jeremiah the prophet]c up from the cistern before he dies." 11/ So Ebed-melech took the men [with him]a and went (to) the house of the king, to 《 the wardrobe 》b cof the storeroom,c and he got from there clothing-scrapsd and rags, 《 and he threw them down 》e to Jeremiah in the cistern [by ropes.]f 12/ Then he [M: Ebed-melech the Ethiopian]a said [to Jeremiah,]b "《 These 》c put [M: Just put the clothing-scraps and rags under your armpits]c under the ropes." And Jeremiah did so. 13/ And they drew a《 him 》 [M: Jeremiah]a out with the ropes and lifted him up from the cistern; and Jeremiah stayed in the court of the guard.

14 The king [Zedekiah]a sent and brought him [M: Jeremiah the prophet]b to himself at the third entrance of the house of Yahweh, and the king said c《 to him 》 [M: to Jeremiah,]c "I have something to ask you; do not hide anything from me." 15/ And Jeremiah said a《 to the king 》 [M: to Zedekiah,]a "If I tell you, you will kill me, will you not? and if I advise you, you will not listen to me." 16/ So the king [Zedekiah]a swore b《 to him 》 [M: to Jeremiah]b [secretly,]c saying, "By the life of Yahweh who has given this life of ours, I shall neither kill you nor put you into the hand of these men [who seek your life."]d 17/ Then Jeremiah said a《 to him 》 [M: to Zedekiah,]a "Thus Yahweh [God of hosts, the God of Israel]b has said, If you will only surrender to the officials of the king of Babylon, then your life will be saved, and this city will not be burned with fire, and you and your household will live. 18/ But if you do not surrender [to the officials of the king of Babylon,]a then this city will be given into the hand of the Chaldeans, and they will burn it with fire, and you yourself will not escape [from their hand.]b 19/ Then the king [Zedekiah]a said to Jeremiah, "I am anxious about the Jews who have deserted to the Chaldeans, that I might be given into their hand and they mistreat me." 20/ But Jeremiah said, "That will not happen. Just obey the voice of Yahweh in what I speak to you, so that it may go well for you and your life be saved. 21/ But if you are determined not to surrender, this is what Yahweh has shown me— 22/ a vision of all the women remaining in the house of the king of Judah being led out to the officials of the king of Babylon and saying,

'They've led you off and overcome you,
   your fine friends;

probably secondary; the original text would have omitted them to underline the boldness of Ebed-melech's approach to the king (compare "spoke" in v 8).

b—b Read G. Given the contrast here between G and M, there is no way to derive one from the other. G is clearly the harsher text: one assumes therefore that M has softened the words of the courtier to the king. "This man" evidently suggested "these men"; "Jeremiah the prophet" is a typical expansion of M; "throwing him into the cistern" is derived from v 6. The text antecedent to G would be הֲרֵעֹתָ אֶת־אֲשֶׁר עָשִׂיתָ לְהָמִית הָאִישׁ הַזֶּה.

c   Revocalizing M וַיָּמָת "and he died" to וְיָמֻת.

10a   Omit with G; compare Janzen, p. 152.

b   Read שְׁלֹשָׁה with one MS. for M שְׁלֹשִׁים "thirty": so Hitzig, Duhm, Cornill, Giesebrecht, Volz, Condamin, Rudolph, Bright. One would expect the singular אִישׁ with "thirty." And certainly the task would demand only the smaller number.

c—c Read with G; compare Janzen, p. 147.

11a   Omit with G; it is an addition from v 10 (compare Janzen, p. 52).

b   Reading מֶלְתַּחַת (compare 2 Kgs 10:22) with Ehrlich, Volz, Condamin, Rudolph, Bright for M תַּחַת "under."

c   One wonders whether "storeroom," omitted in G, is a gloss on the word "wardrobe."

d   Ketib בְּלוֹיֵ סְחָבוֹת, read qere' בְּלוֹיֵ הַסְּחָבוֹת.

e   Read with G וַיַּשְׁלִיכֵם for M וַיִּשְׁלְחֵם; compare the remarks on v 6, note a (Janzen, p. 52).

f   Omit with G; again compare v 6, and see Janzen, 52.

12a   Omit with G; compare Janzen, p. 152.

b   Omit with G; compare Janzen, p. 147.

c   Insert הָאֵלֶּה with G; M clarifies with a gloss which includes material from v 11 (see Janzen, p. 53). So also Duhm, Cornill.

13a—a Omit with G; compare Janzen, p. 147.

14a   Omit with G; compare Janzen, p. 142.

b   Omit with G; compare Janzen, p. 147.

c—c Omit with G; compare Janzen, p. 147.

15a—a Read with G; compare Janzen, p. 142.

16a   Omit with G; compare Janzen, p. 142.

b   Read with G; compare Janzen, p. 147.

c   Omit with G. This is a gloss from 37:17; see Janzen, p. 53.

d   Omit with G; see Janzen, pp. 41, 42.

17a—a Read with G; compare Janzen, p. 142.

b   Omit with G; compare Janzen, pp. 75, 76.

18a   Omit with G, an expansion from v 17 (see Janzen, p. 53).

b   Omit with G, a gloss from 34:3 (see Janzen, p. 53).

19a   Omit with G.

⟨they got⟩ᵃ your foot ⟨stuck⟩ᵃ in the mud
and drew back,'
23/ and [all]ᵃ your wives and your children
⟨being led out⟩ᵇ to the Chaldeans, and you
yourself not escaping [from their hand,]ᶜ for
by the hand of the king of Babylon you shall
be seized and this city ᵈshall be burnedᵈ with
fire." 24/ Then ᵃ⟨ the king ⟩ [M: Zedekiah]ᵃ
said ᵇ⟨ to him ⟩ [M: to Jeremiah,]ᵇ "Let no one
know of these words or you will die: 25/ if
the officials hear that I have spoken with
you and they come and say to you, 'Just tell
us what you spoke to the king—do not
conceal it from us or we will kill you; and
what did the king speak to you?' 26/ then
you shall say to them, 'I was presenting my
plea before the king not to send me back to
the house of Jonathan to die there.'"

27 Then all the officials came to Jeremiah and
they questioned him, but he answered them
with words like these, as the king ᵃhad
commanded him,ᵃ so they stopped
questioning him, for the matter had not
been overheard.
ᵃ 39:15 But to Jeremiah there came the
word of Yahweh [while he was restricted]ᵇ
in the court of the guard, as follows, 16/ Go
and say to Ebed-melech the Ethiopian as
follows, Thus Yahweh [of hosts,]ᶜ God of
Israel, has said, I am going to bringᵈ my
words upon this city for evil and not for
good; [and they shall happen before you on
that day.]ᵉ 17/ But I will save you on that
day, oracle of Yahweh; and you shall not be
given into the hand of the men whose
presence you fear; 18/ for I really will rescue
you, and you shall not fall by the sword; you
shall at least have your life, for you have
trusted in me, oracle of Yahweh.ᵃ

28 So Jeremiah stayed in the court of the guard
until the day Jerusalem was captured.

39

1 ᵃAnd it happenedᵃ [as Jerusalem was taken]ᵇ
in the ninth year of Zedekiah king of Judah,
in the tenth month: Nebuchadrezzar king of
Babylon came, and all his army, against
Jerusalem, and they besieged it; 2/ in the
eleventh year of Zedekiah, in the fourth
month, on the ninth day of the month, the
city was breached.

3 ⟨ And when Jerusalem was taken, ⟩ᵃ all the
officials of the king of Babylon came in and
sat at the Middle Gate: Nergalsharezer ⟨ the
official of Sin-magir the Rab-mag,
Nebushazban ⟩ᵇ the Rab-saris, [. . . .]ᵇ and all

22a Vocalize a hipʿil הֻמְבְּעוּ with G and V for M hopʿal
הָמְבְּעוּ "[your feet] are stuck"; so also Duhm, Cornill,
Giesebrecht, Volz.

23a Omit with G; compare Janzen, pp. 65–67.

b Vocalizing with V and T a hopʿal participle מוּצָאִים
(compare v 22) for M hipʿil; this is preferable to a
participle without subject (on which see GKC, sec.
144i). For אֶת־ with a passive see Joüon, *Gramm.*, sec.
128b.

c Omit with G; see v 18, note b.

d—d Vocalize תִּשָּׂרֵף with a few MSS., G, S, and T; M
reads a qal, thus "and you shall burn this city," and V
reads "and he shall burn this city."

24a—a Read with G; compare Janzen, p. 142.

b—b Read with G; compare Janzen, p. 147.

27a—a Read with some MSS., G, V, S צִוָּהוּ for M צִוָּה.

39:15–18a—a These verses fit poorly after 39:14. Volz
and others who accept their present position believe
they are there because the prophecy to Ebed-melech
was fulfilled at that time. But the secondary words in
v 15 suggest a clarifying gloss after a displacement.
Other commentators believe the natural position of
the verses is after 38:13, the narrative of Ebed-
melech's rescue of Jrm (Condamin, Thompson).
Bright places the verses after 38:28a. The difficulty
is that 39:15 begins with the emphatic וְאֶל־יִרְמְיָהוּ
"but to Jeremiah," suggesting that the clause immediately preceding 39:15–18 (in its original position)
had another subject than "Jeremiah" (see Wanke,
Baruchschrift, 111). The natural position is then after
38:27, after Jrm's colloquy with Zedekiah; there is
then a nice play on דָּבָר between 38:27 and 39:15.
One can assume that the verses were originally
omitted by haplography: "in the court of the guard"
occurs in both 39:15 and 38:28; the verses were
then reinserted after "from the court of the guard"
in 39:14.

b Omit with G; the words were added in M to
clarify the situation after 39:15–18 was dislocated.

c Omit with G; compare Janzen, pp. 162–70.

d The ketib has omitted an 'alep because of the
following 'alep (just as in 19:15); read qere' מֵבִיא.

e Omit with G; the phrase "on that day" is unlikely
in both vv 16b and 17a. Cornill suggests it is a
dittography from v 17 (compare Rudolph).

28a—a The expression וְהָיָה appears in a few MSS. as
וַיְהִי (but compare 37:11); either one or the other is
preferable before 39:1 (compare 52:4).

b These words are either dittographic from v 28a,
or else they need to be inserted at the beginning of
39:3 (so Bright).

39:3a See 38:28b.

b M has evidently mangled the Babylonian names
and titles here: it reads Nergalsharezer, Samgar-
nebo, Sarsechim, Rabsaris, Nergalsharezer, Rabmag
(*KJV*). The words may be divided differently (compare G, V), but G, for example, is not substantially
different from M; the corruptions in the text must
have started early. The reconstruction here, reflect-

the rest of the officials of the king of Babylon. [4/ And when Zedekiah {king of Judah}[b] saw them, and all the soldiers, they fled and went out at night from the city by way of the king's garden through the gate between the two walls, [c]and they went out[c] on the road to the Arabah. 5/ But the army of the Chaldeans pursued them and overtook Zedekiah in the plains of Jericho, [d]and all his army was scattered from him,[d] and they took him and brought him up to {Nebuchadrezzar}[e] the king of Babylon at Riblah, in the land of Hamath; and he passed judgment upon him. 6/ And the king of Babylon slaughtered the sons of Zedekiah at Riblah before his eyes, and all the nobles of Judah the king of Babylon slaughtered; 7/ and the eyes of Zedekiah he blinded, and he bound him in shackles to take him to Babylon.

8 And the house of the king and the house of《Yahweh and the houses of》[f] the people the Chaldeans burned with fire, and the walls of Jerusalem they demolished. 9/ And the rest of the people who remained in the city, and those who had deserted to him, and the rest of《the artisans》[g] were exiled to Babylon by Nebuzaradan the provost marshal. 10/ And from the city the poor who had nothing Nebuzaradan the provost marshal left in the land of Judah, and he gave them vineyards and fields that day.][a]

11 And [Nebuchadrezzar][a] the king of Babylon commanded through[b] Nebuzaradan the provost mashal concerning Jeremiah as follows, 12/ "Take him and look after him; do not do any harm to him, but[a] whatever he says to you, do with him." 13/ So Nebuzaradan the provost marshal [and Nebushazban the Rab-saris and Nergal-sharezer the Rab-mag,][a] and [all][a] the chiefs of the king of Babylon sent 14/ and took Jeremiah from the court of the guard and gave him to Gedaliah son of Ahikam son of Shaphan, to let him go out《and come in,》[a] and he stayed in the midst of the people. 15–18 . . . .][a]

40

1 The word which came to Jeremiah from Yahweh after Nebuzaradan the provost marshal let him go [《when he took him》][a] from Ramah, [. . . .][a] [while he was bound][b] in manacles[c] in the midst of [all][d] the exiles

ing the wording of v 13, is that of Rudolph and Bright. Thus there is evidently one Nergalsharezer, the Babylonian form of which would be Nergal-šarri-uṣur, probably identical with the one of that name who succeeded to the Babylonian throne in 560. For further details concerning the names and titles see Interpretation.

4–10a   The textual problem of vv 4–13 is severe; all these verses, until the verb "sent" in v 13, are missing in G. It is clear that vv 4–10 are secondary: they do not deal with Jrm, and they are drawn from 52:7–11, 13–16 (see Janzen, p. 118). For v 13 see below.

b   Though the witness of G is missing here (see note a), the bracketed words are surely an expansion (compare 32:4).

c—c   Read וַיֵּצְאוּ with some MSS., θ', V, and S for M וַיֵּצֵא "and he went out."

d—d   A few MSS. and S add these words, which are also found in 52:8 and 2 Kgs 25:5; they are missing in M.

e   Though the witness of G is missing here (see note a), the name is probably an expansion (compare the diction of v 3, and compare 29:3, 21).

f   M reads "house of the people," evidently by haplography. S reads the entire compound object as "house of the king and houses of the people," whether by a different haplography or by a secondary correction. Compare 52:13 and 2 Kgs 25:9.

g   M reads "the people who remained," dittography from the beginning of the verse; read הָאָמוֹן with 52:15.

11a   Although the witness of G is missing, the name is probably secondary here (compare v 5, note e).

b   Also M reads בְּיַד, the word is missing in s', V, and S.

c   Read with many MSS. and the qere' כִּי; ketib reads כִּי אִם.

13a   The bracketed material has arisen as a notation correcting the corrupt text in v 3; these senior officers are not needed to fetch Jrm. The notation may have been attracted here because of the names beginning with "Nebu-." In the meantime G has suffered a haplography from v 3 until "sent" in this verse, again because of the similarity of names with "Nebu-" (compare Janzen, p. 118).

14a   M reads "[to bring him out] to the house," which gives little sense. I follow Rudolph in reading וְלַהֲבִאוֹ (compare 37:4). It is to be noted that G omits "to the house."

15–18a   These verses have been restored to their place after 38:27: see the discussion there.

40:1a   Though the words בְּקַחְתּוֹ אֹתוֹ appear in G as well as M, they are evidently a misplaced variant of "after he let him go" in a conflate text.

b   Omit with G; clarifying gloss.

c   Qere' בָּאזִקִים; read ketib בָּאזִקִּים.

d   Omit with G; compare Janzen, pp. 65–67.

of [Jerusalem and]^e Judah being deported to Babylon 《 . . . .:》^f 2ab*a*/ [. . . .]^a 2b*βγ*/ "It is Yahweh 《 your God 》^b who has spoken this evil against this place, 3/ [and he brought in]^a and Yahweh did ^b as he had spoken,^b for you have sinned ^c《 against him 》 [*M*: against Yahweh]^c and not obeyed his voice; [and there has come this thing."]^e ^d

2ab*a* ^cThen the provost marshal got ^d《 him 》 [*M* to Jeremiah]^d and said to him,^c 4/ ["So now,]^a look, I have released you today from the manacles^b which are on your hands.^c If it is good in your eyes to come with me to Babylon, come, and I will look after you, but if it is bad [in your eyes to come with me to Babylon,]^d [do not;]^e [see, all the land is before you; where 《 it is good 》^g and proper in your eyes to go, go;]^f 5/ [and]^a 《 run off 》^b and return to Gedaliah son of Ahikam son of Shaphan, whom the king of Babylon

e   Omit with *G*; this expansion is from 29:1, 4, 20 (see Janzen, p. 53).

f   It is possible that one or more phrases may have dropped out by haplography; for example, "Speak to the exiles who are being deported to Babylon and say to them, Thus Yahweh has said."

2a   The bracketed words are misplaced here—they belong before v 4 (see there v 2, note c—c): vv 2b*βγ*–3 contain the oracle introduced in v 1. The divine judgment can hardly be on the lips of Nebuzaradan (Volz).

b   For אֱלֹהֶיךָ read אֱלֹהֵיכֶם (Volz): the references in the second-person plural in v 3 indicate that Jrm is addressing the group being deported. The plural was changed to singular in this instance after the words at the beginning of v 2 were inserted.

3a   This verb is evidently a variant of "and (Yahweh) did" in a conflate text. See Janzen, p. 22.

b—b   Though these words are omitted in *G*, they are rhetorically necessary; *G* has evidently suffered haplography, perhaps between כַּאֲשֶׁר and כִּי (compare Janzen, p. 22).

c—c   Read *G*; *M* has filled out the name under the influence of 44:23 (Janzen, p. 53).

d   This clause is evidently a variant of "and Yahweh did as he had spoken" (see Janzen, p. 22).

e   Ketib lacks the definite article on דָּבָר; read qere' with article. But see Godfrey R. Driver, "Jeremiah xl 3," *VT* 1 (1951) 244–45.

2c—c   Verse 2ab*a* belongs here, introducing the speech of Nebuzaradan to Jrm. If there are missing words at the end of v 1 (see there, note f), then the displacement of v 2ab*a* may be related to that error.

d—d   *M* "to Jeremiah" is impossible; the expression may have originated as a gloss on אֵלָיו "to him" and been inserted here erroneously. Read "him" with *G*.

4a   Omit with *G*; compare the same omission in 42:15, note a.

b   See v 1, note c.

c   *M* "hand"; read with many MSS., *G*, *V*, and *S* "hands."

d   *G* omits not only these words but what follows in the rest of the verse as well. The words here bracketed seem rhetorically unnecessary and dittographic; compare the phraseology of Zech 11:12.

e   Omit with *G*. If "run off" is correct in v 5 (see note b there), then the present word and the conjunction "and" with "run off" are unnecessary; I suggest they are a variant of "run off" in a conflate text.

f   Omit with *G* (compare note d); the words are evidently a variant of the phraseology of v 5a*β*.

g   Read אֶל־הַטּוֹב; the phrase is perhaps a variant of אֶל־הַיָּשָׁר.

5a   See v 4, note e.

b   The text of *M* is untranslatable: וְעוֹדֶנּוּ לֹא־יָשׁוּב, "and he will still not return." *G* strikingly has ἀπότρεχε, "run off," at this point, a reading which fits the context. I therefore suggest that the text

appointed over 《the land》[c] of Judah, and stay with him in the midst of the people; where it is proper in your eyes to go, go." And the provost marshal gave him [provisions and][d] goods[e] and sent him away. 6/ So he [*M*: Jeremiah][a] went to Gedaliah [son of Ahikam][b] at Mizpah, and he stayed [with him][c] in the midst of the people who were left in the land.

7 All the officers of the army units who were in the open country, and their men, heard that the king of Babylon had appointed Gedaliah [son of Ahikam][a] over the land and had committed to him men and women [and children and some poor people,][b] from those who were not deported to Babylon. 8/ So they came to Gedaliah at Mizpah: Ishmael son of Nethaniah, and Johanan [and Jonathan][a] son[s][b] of Kareah, and Seraiah son of Tanhumeth, [c]and the sons of Ephai[c] the Netophathite, and Jezaniah[d] son of the Maacathite, they and their men. 9/ Gedaliah [son of Ahikam son of Shaphan][a] swore to them and to their men, as follows: "Do not be afraid of[b] 《the servants of》[c] the Chaldeans; remain in the land and serve the king of Babylon, and let it go well with you. 10/ As for me, look, I am staying in Mizpah to stand before the Chaldeans, who keep coming in on us; as for you, gather wine and fruit and oil and put it in your vessels, and stay in 《the cities》[a] which you have seized." 11/ And all the Jews who were in Moab and among the Ammonites and in Edom and 《every (other) land》[a] also heard that the king of Babylon had left a remnant for Judah and that he had appointed over them Gedaliah son of Ahikam [son of Shaphan,][b] 12/ [so all the Jews returned from all the places where they had been scattered,][a] and they came [to the land of Judah][b] to Gedaliah at Mizpah, and they gathered wine and fruit in great abundance.

13 Now Johanan son of Kareah and all the officers of the army units who were in the open country came to Gedaliah at Mizpah 14/ and said to him, "You know, do you not, that Baalis king of the Ammonites has sent[a] Ishmael [son of Nethaniah][b] to take your

originally read רוצה; reš might be misread as 'ayin in the early Aramaic script, and ṣade as dalet, and he as nun-waw, especially if for the whole word there was damage on the lower edge of the line. Since "running" is associated with the work of a prophet (compare 12:5 and 23:21), the word would make nice irony in Jrm's case. The words לֹא־יָשׁוּב are a puzzle. Johann D. Michaelis suggested that they are a misreading of לֹא־יָשִׁיב, "he does not answer," and that is a possibility, once the text is assumed to have read וְעוֹדֶנּוּ, but they are probably no more than a dittography of the following וְשָׁבָה.

c   So read with *G*; *M* "the cities of." Compare v 7.

d   Omit with *G*; the words appear to be a variant in a conflate text.

e   *G* δῶρα "gifts" is plural; *M* מַשְׂאֵת is singular, but conceivably could be vocalized as a plural מַשְׂאֹת.

6a   Omit with *G*; compare Janzen, p. 147.

b   Omit with *G*; compare Janzen, p. 149.

c   Omit with *G*, a gloss from v 4 (Janzen, p. 53).

7a   Omit with *G* and 2 Kgs 25:23; compare Janzen, p. 149.

b   Omit with *G*; "children" and "poor people" did not appear in the tradition out of which *G* came, since *G* "their wives, whom" renders וּנְשֵׁיהֶם אֲשֶׁר, a misdividing of וְנָשִׁים מֵאֲשֶׁר (see Janzen, p. 53).

8a   Omit with a few MSS., *G*, and the Codex Reuchlinianus of *T*, and with 2 Kgs 25:23; *M* is a conflate text (see Janzen, p. 17).

b   Read the singular with many MSS., *G*, and many MSS. of *T*, and with 2 Kgs 25:23; the plural is an adaptation to the conflate text (see note a).

c—c   The parallel in 2 Kgs 25:23 omits these words, thus reading "Seraiah son of Tanhumeth the Netophathite." There is no way to decide between these readings; indeed there is uncertainty about "Ephai" itself (עֵיפַי), which is the reading of the qere', *S*, and *T*; the ketib, *G*, and *V* read "Ophai" (עוֹפַי).

d   The spelling "Jezaniah" (יְזַנְיָהוּ) is a shortened form of "Jaazaniah" (יַאֲזַנְיָהוּ), the spelling in the parallel 2 Kgs 25:23 and in the Jaazaniah seal (see Interpretation, 40:6).

9a   Omit with *G* and 2 Kgs 25:24; compare Janzen, p. 149.

b   *G* presupposes מִפְּנֵי from *M* מֵ.

c   Read עָבְדֵי with *G* and 2 Kgs 25:24 for *M* עֲבוֹד.

10a   Read with *G* הֶעָרִים; *M* עָרֵיכֶם "your cities."

11a   Read singular אֶרֶץ with *G*; *M* plural "all (other) lands." See Janzen, p. 208, n. 43.

b   Omit with *G*; compare Janzen, p. 149.

12a   Omit with *G*; this stereotypical clause does not fit the description of those who temporarily took refuge in the hills when danger struck and who filtered back once the fighting was over (Janzen, p. 53).

b   Omit with *G*.

14a   *G* adds πρὸς σέ; it is possible that *M* has erroneously omitted אֵלֶיךָ.

b   Omit with *G*; compare Janzen, p. 151.

life?" but Gedaliah [son of Ahikam]c did not believe them. 15/ Then Johanan [son of Kareah]a said to Gedaliah secretly at Mizpah as follows: "Just let me go and kill Ishmael [son of Nethaniah]b and no one will know; why should he take your life and all Judah, which has gathered around you, be scattered, and the remnant of Judah perish?" 16/ But Gedaliah [son of Ahikam]a said to Johanan [son of Kareah,]b c"Do not doc such a thing, for what you are saying about Ishmael is a lie."

1 Now in the seventh month Ishmael son of Nethaniah son of Elishama, of the royal family, [and chiefs of the king,]a came, and ten men with him, to Gedaliah [son of Ahikam]b at Mizpah, and they ate bread there together [at Mizpah.]c 2/ And Ishmael [son of Nethaniah]a rose up, and the ten men who were with him, and they struck down Gedaliah [son of Ahikam son of Shaphan]b [with the sword, and he killed him,]c [whom the king of Babylon had appointed over the land,]d 3/ and [all]a the Jews who were with him [with Gedaliah]b at Mizpah, and the Chaldeans who were found there, [the soldiers, Ishmael killed.]c

4 And on the day after the killing of Gedaliah, while no one knew of it, 5/ men came from Shechem and Shiloh and Samaria, eighty men, their beards shaved and their clothes torn, and gashing themselves, with cereal offerings and incense in their hands, to bring to the house of Yahweh. 6/ Ishmael [son of Nethaniah]a went out to meet them [from Mizpah,]b weepingc as he went; and [when he encountered them,]d he said to them, come in to Gedaliah [son of Ahikam.]e 7/ When they came to the middle of the city, he [Ishmael son of Nethaniah]a slaughtered them ⟪ and threw them ⟫b into [the middle of]c the cistern, [he and the men with him.]d 8/ But ten men were found aamong thema and they said to Ishmael, "Do not kill us; for we have stores in the field—wheat and barley and oil and honey"; so he desisted and did not kill them among their brothers. 9/ Now the cistern into which Ishmael had thrown all [the corpses of the men]a whom he had killed ⟪ was a great cistern ⟫b which King Asa had made against Baasha king of Israel—this was the one which Ishmael [son of Nethaniah]c filled with slain. 10/ Then Ishmael atook captivea all the remnant of the

---

c   Omit with *G*; compare Janzen, p. 149.

15a   Omit with *G*; Janzen, p. 150, has recorded the data wrongly.

b   Omit with *G*; compare Janzen, p. 151.

16a   Omit with *G*; compare Janzen, p. 149.

b   Omit with *G*; compare Janzen, p. 150.

c—c   Ketib אַל־תַּעַשׂ, qere' אַל־תַּעֲשֵׂה. The meanings are identical; for the unusual qere' see GKC, sec. 75hh.

41:1a   Omit with *G* and 2 Kgs 25:25; see Janzen, pp. 199–200, n. 59.

b   Omit with *G*; compare Janzen, p. 149.

c   Omit with *G*; see Janzen, p. 53.

2a   Omit with *G*; compare Janzen, p. 151.

b   Omit with *G* and 2 Kgs 25:25; compare Janzen, p. 149.

c   Omit with *G*. It is to be noted that 2 Kgs 25:25 reads "and he died" (וַיָּמָת). "Struck down" (וַיַּכּוּ) implies "killed" (compare 40:15), but "and he died" in 2 Kgs 25:25 appears to be a gloss making the matter clearer, and *M* in the present passage appears to expand the text even further.

d   Though this clause is present in *G* as well as *M*, it is missing in 2 Kgs 25:25 and interrupts the listing of those killed; omit as a gloss from 40:5, 7, 11.

3a   Although both *G* and *M* have "all," it is missing in 2 Kgs 25:25; it is to be noted that the second occurrence of "all" (with "the Chaldeans") is present in *G* but not in *M*! The word is an expansion in both instances (compare Janzen, pp. 65–67).

b   Omit with *G* and 2 Kgs 25:25; it is an expansionist gloss (see Janzen, p. 17).

c   Omit with *G* and 2 Kgs 25:25; compare Janzen, p. 24.

6a   Omit with *G*; compare Janzen, p. 151.

b   Omit with *G*; the expression appears to be a gloss (compare v 1, note c).

c   For the participle וּבֹכֶה some MSS. read the infinitive absolute וּבָכֹה; for the grammatical situation see GKC, sec. 113u. The meaning is clear in either case.

d   Omit with *G*; the words may be a gloss or a variant in a conflate text.

e   Omit with *G*; compare Janzen, p. 149.

7a   Omit with *G*; Janzen, p. 151, wrongly states that "Ishmael" but not "son of Nethaniah" appears in *G*, whereas neither expression appears.

b   Supply וַיַּשְׁלִיכֵם with *G*V, C', and *S*; compare v 9.

c   Omit with *G*; it is dittographic from the previous occurrence (see Janzen, p. 53).

8a—a   For בָּם *G* has "there" = שָׁם; either reading is possible.

9a   Omit with *G*; explanatory gloss.

b   *M* בְּיַד־גְּדַלְיָהוּ "by the hand of Gedaliah" cannot be right; read *G* בּוֹר גָּדוֹל with Giesebrecht, Duhm, Cornill, Volz, Condamin, Rudolph, Bright.

c   Omit with *G*; compare Janzen, p. 151.

10a—a   For וַיִּשְׁבְּ *G* reads "took them back" = וַיָּשֶׁב; this is a possible vocalization, given 40:14. But the vocalization of *M* is a less common verb (and com-

people who were in Mizpah, and[b] the daughters of the king [and all the people who remained in Mizpah][c] whom [Nebuzaradan][d] the provost marshal had committed to Gedaliah son of Ahikam; [Ishmael son of Nethaniah took them captive][e] and he went to cross to the Ammonites.

11 Johanan son of Kareah and all the officers of the army units who were with him heard of all the evil which Ishmael [son of Nethaniah][a] had done, 12/ and they took all 《their men》[a] and went to fight [b]《with him》 [*M*: with Ishmael son of Nethaniah,][b] and they found him at the great pool which is at Gibeon. 13/ And when all the people who were with Ishmael saw Johanan [son of Kareah][a] and [all][b] the officers of the army units who were with him, [they rejoiced,][c] 14/ [and all the people whom Ishmael had taken captive from Mizpah turned around;][a] they returned [and went][b] to Johanan [son of Kareah.][c] 15/ But Ishmael [son of Kareah][a] escaped with eight men [from the presence of Johanan,][b] and he went off to the Ammonites. 16/ And Johanan [son of Kareah][a] and all the officers of the army units who were with him took all [the remnant of][b] the people whom Ishmael [son of Nethaniah][c] 《had taken captive》[d] from Mizpah [after he had killed Gedaliah son of Ahikam,][e] [f]〈warriors〉 [men of war][f] and women and children and eunuchs, whom he brought back from Gibeon. 17/ And they went and stayed at Geruth Chimham[a] near Bethlehem, in order to go [to enter][b] Egypt, 18/ from the presence of the Chaldeans, for they were afraid of them, for Ishmael [son of Nethaniah][a] had struck down Gedaliah [son of Ahikam,][b] whom the king of Babylon had appointed over the land.

42

1 Now all the officers of the army units, and Johanan [son of Kareah,][a] and 《Azariah》[b] son of Hoshaiah,[c] and all the people from small to great, came near 2/ and said to Jeremiah 〉the prophet,〈[a] "Please let our

pare the doublets in vv 10b and 14). Compare also, however, v 16, note d!

b   Read ן with many MSS. and *G*; the ן evidently was attached wrongly to the following bracketed words (see note c); see Janzen, p. 17.

c   These words are clearly a variant in a conflate text; see Janzen, p. 17.

d   Omit with *G*; compare Janzen, p. 151.

e   Omit with *G*; the verb is a repetition from v 10a, and the name is an expansion (see Janzen, p. 53).

11a   Omit with *G*; compare Janzen, p. 151.

12a   *M* reads הָאֲנָשִׁים "the men"; read אַנְשֵׁיהֶם with *G*.

b—b   Read with *G*; the name is an expansion in *M* (compare Janzen, p. 151).

13a   Omit with *G*; compare Janzen, p. 150.

b   Omit with *G*; compare Janzen, pp. 65–67.

c   This expression and the bracketed material in v 14, note a, are omitted in *G*. Conceivably *G* might be defective by haplography, but the material in v 14, note a, is evidently the original form of v 16; and the expression "they rejoiced" appears to be a clarifying gloss. See Janzen, pp. 22–24, 53–54.

14a   See v 13, note c.

b   Omit with *G*.

c   Omit with *G*; compare Janzen, p. 150.

15a   Omit with *G*; compare Janzen, p. 150.

b   Omit with *G*; see Janzen, pp. 23, 199, n. 55.

16a   Omit with *G*; compare Janzen, p. 150.

b   Omit; the bracketed material in v 14, which omits "the remnant of," is probably the original form of v 16 (see v 14, note c, and Janzen, p. 23).

c   Omit with *G*; compare Janzen, p. 151.

d   Reading שָׁבָה אֹתָם for *M* הֵשִׁיב מֵאֵת "whom he had brought back from Ishmael . . . ." It appears that the bracketed material in v 14 (note a) is a correction of the phrase here: see Janzen, pp. 23–24. This correction was already suggested by Hitzig, and is accepted by Duhm, Cornill, Volz, Condamin, and Rudolph.

e   Omit with *G*; it is evidently a secondary expansion from vv 2 and 18 (see Janzen, p. 23).

f—f   *M* has vocalized the first word as גְּבָרִים "men"; but the gloss suggests that it should have been vocalized as גֻּבְּרִים; see the discussion in Janzen, pp. 24–25.

17a   Read with many MSS. and qere' כִּמְהָם (compare 2 Sam 19:38–40); ketib כמוהם is inexplicable.

b   Omit with *G*; a gloss or variant, perhaps from 42:17 (see Janzen, p. 54).

18a   Omit with *G*; compare Janzen, p. 151.

b   Omit with *G*; compare Janzen, p. 150.

42:1a   Omit with *G*; compare Janzen, p. 150.

b   *H* reads יְזַנְיָה "Jezaniah"; read with *G* Aζαρίας = עֲזַרְיָה "Azariah," given that name with the same father in 43:2.

c   The name is so given, הוֹשַׁעְיָה, both here and in 43:2, but *G* in both instances gives Μαασαίας = מַעֲשֵׂיָה (compare 37:3). There is no way to decide between the readings.

2a   Though both *M* and *G* include "the prophet," it is omitted in *S*, and the word is therefore likely to be

plea fall in your presence, and pray [b]on our behalf[b] to Yahweh your God [on behalf of [all][c] this remnant][b]—for we are left but a few out of many, as your eyes see— 3/ let Yahweh your God tell us the way we should go and what we should do." 4/ Jeremiah [the prophet][a] said to them, "Very well: I am going to pray to Yahweh your God in words like yours, and whatever Yahweh answers you I will tell you: I will not withhold a thing." 5/ They in their turn said to Jeremiah, "May Yahweh be a true and faithful witness against us if we do not do according to everything which Yahweh [your God][a] sends you for us; 6/ whether good or bad, the voice of Yahweh our God to whom we[a] are sending you we shall obey, so that it may go well with us; for we will obey the voice of Yahweh our God."

7 At the end of ten days the word of Yahweh came to Jeremiah. 8/ So he summoned Johanan [son of Kareah][a] and [all][b] the officers of the army units [who were with him][c] and all the people from small to great. 9/ And he said to them, "Thus Yahweh [God of Israel][a] has said, [to whom you have sent me to lay down your plea in his presence:][a] 10/ If you [a]go back and[a] stay in this land, then I shall build you up and not overthrow, and plant you and not uproot; for I shall have retracted the disaster which I have done to you. 11/ Do not be afraid of the king of Babylon, as you have been: do not be afraid of him, oracle of Yahweh, for I am with you to rescue you and save you from his hand. 12/ I have granted you mercy, that he may have mercy on you and bring you back to your soil. 13/ But if you keep saying, 'We will not stay in this land,' thus disobeying the voice of Yahweh [your God,][a] 14/ [saying, 'No!'][a] rather to the land of Egypt we will go, where we will neither see battle nor hear the sound of the trumpet nor famine for bread, and there we will stay,' 15/ [so now][a] therefore hear the word of Yahweh, [remnant of Judah:][b] Thus Yahweh [of hosts, the God of Israel,][c] has said: If you do set your faces [to go][d] to Egypt and go in to settle there, 16/ then the sword which you fear shall overtake you in [the land of][a] Egypt, and the famine of which you are anxious shall [there][b] cling to you in Egypt, and there you shall die. 17/ And all the men who have set their faces [to go][a] to Egypt to settle there shall die by the sword «and»[b] by famine [and by pestilence;][c] and none of them shall be a survivor or fugitive from the evil which I am bringing in upon them."[d]

43

1 Now when Jeremiah had finished speaking to [all][a] the people all the words of Yahweh

secondary (compare Janzen, p. 147).

b—b   *G* omits "on our behalf" and *S* omits "on behalf of all this remnant"; *M* is clearly conflate (see Janzen, p. 17). The bracketed phrase is evidently the secondary one, given the following clause.

c   *G* omits "all," which is therefore likely to be added still later than the material in square brackets.

4a   Omit with *G*; compare Janzen, p. 147.

5a   Omit with *G*; compare Janzen, p. 81.

6a   The qere' is the normal אֲנַחְנוּ; the ketib is the postbiblical Hebrew form אָנוּ. This is the only occurrence of the form in biblical Hebrew.

8a   Omit with *G*; compare Janzen, p. 150.

b   Omit with *G*; compare Janzen, pp. 65–67.

c   Omit with *G*; the gloss is from 41:11, 16 (see Janzen, p. 54).

9a   Omit the two bracketed sequences with *G*; "God of Israel" is a typical expansion of *M* (compare Janzen, pp. 80–81); the rest is an expansion from vv 2, 6, and 20 (see Janzen, p. 54).

10a—a   Given the finite verb (יֵשֵׁב), *G*, *V*, and *T* read the infinitive absolute of that verb, יָשׁוֹב, for *M* שׁוֹב (the infinitive absolute of שׁוּב); the commentators (Duhm, Giesebrecht, Cornill, Volz, Condamin, Rudolph, Bright) assume that the Versions are correct. But שׁוֹב is the *lectio difficilior*, and I suggest that it is possible to have a combination of an infinitive absolute of one verb and a finite form of a like-sounding verb (see 8:13; 48:9; compare König, *Syntax*, sec. 219 d, and see Interpretation).

13a   Omit with *G*; compare Janzen, p. 80.

14a   Omit with *G*; the expression is a reinforcement of v 13 to clarify the meaning "rather" of כִּי.

15a   Omit with *G*; compare 40:4, note 4.

b   Omit with *G*; the gloss is from v 19 (see Janzen, p. 54).

c   Omit with *G*; compare Janzen, pp. 76–78.

d   Omit with *G*; compare 41:17, note b, and see Janzen, p. 54.

16a   Omit with *G*.

b   Omit with *G*; the word looks like a variant of "in Egypt," or dittographic from the last clause.

17a   Omit with *G*; compare v 15, and see Janzen, p. 54.

b   So read with *G*: compare note c.

c   Omit the last noun in the series with *G*; see the discussion in Janzen, pp. 44, 205, n. 19.

d   For v 18 see below, after v 21. Verse 18 was wrongly inserted here: after the shift of position of 43:1–3, 42:18 was shifted either deliberately or accidentally to its present position after vv 15–17: v 15 has a matching introduction and messenger formula. The verse implies that the decision by Johanan and his followers has already been made ("when you go to Egypt": compare notes on vv 19–21, 18, 22a—a); form-critically the verse is appropriate before v 22. See further Preliminary Observations, and Form and Structure.

43:1a   Omit with *G*; compare Janzen, pp. 65–67.

[their God]b which Yahweh [their God]c had sent him for them, all these words, 2/ Azariah son of Hoshaiaha and Johanan son of Kareah and all the (other) [insolent and]b 《obstinate》c men said to Jeremiah 《as follows,》d ["You are speaking]e a lie! Yahweh [. . . .]f did not send you 《to us》f to say, 'You shall not go into Egypt to settle there,' 3/ but Baruch son of Neriah is inciting you against us, so as to put us into the hand of the Chaldeans to kill us or to exile us to Babylon."

42:19 a 《But Jeremiah said to them,》b "Yahweh 《did》c speak to you, remnant of Judah: do not go into Egypt. You do know dthat I have warned you todayd 20/ that eyou have led astraye at the cost of your lives, for it is you who sent me [to Yahweh your God,]f saying, 'Pray on our behalf to Yahweh [our God,]g and according to everything

b   Omit with G; compare Janzen, p. 81.

c   Omit with G; אֱלֹהֵיהֶם here may be a variant of אֲלֵיהֶם "to them" in a conflate text: see Janzen, pp. 17, 81.

2a   See 42:1, note c.

b   The word is omitted in G and does not belong here; it may well be a misreading of an early gloss on הָאֲנָשִׁים in 42:17, where G has a plus, καὶ πάντες οἱ ἀλλογενεῖς = וְכָל־הַזָּרִים. The word could originally have been placed in the margin between two columns; see Janzen, pp. 65, 133, 233, n. 23.

c   M אֹמְרִים (without article!) is hardly right; read with Giesebrecht, Cornill, Rudolph, and Bright הָאֹמְרִים.

d   Insert with G לֵאמֹר (compare the following inner quotation).

e   Omit with G; the words are a clarifying gloss: compare the diction of 37:14.

f   אֱלֹהֵינוּ is a miscopying of אֵלֵינוּ (so read with G). Note that the diction of the officers to Jrm has been "Yahweh your God" (42:2).

42:19–21, 18, 22a—a   The material through 42:17 is Jrm's initial presentation of the word from Yahweh. Verses 19–22 (and v 18—see above) assume that the officers have rejected the word. In 43:1–3 they overtly reject it. In particular in 43:2 the officers deny that Yahweh sent Jrm; in 42:21 Jrm affirms that Yahweh sent him. Commentators who accept the present order of verses must assume that Jrm has "read" the faces and gestures of the officers between 42:18 and 19, and that then the officers make their objection verbal in 43:1–3 (Thompson, p. 667; compare Bright, p. 256). But this is too subtle: the order of 42:19–22 and 43:1–3 must be reversed (so Volz, Rudolph, Bright). I propose that there was haplography between עֲלֵיהֶם at the end of v 17 and a reconstructed עֲלֵיהֶם (or אֲלֵיהֶם) in the first clause of v 19, now missing (see note b), that the material of 43:1–3 was later inserted after the verses containing the divine words (compare 43:1), thus after 42:22.

b   Volz, Rudolph, and Bright suggest introductory words: I propose וַיֹּאמֶר יִרְמְיָהוּ עֲלֵיהֶם (or אֲלֵיהֶם); compare note a—a.

c   Supply an infinitive absolute, דַּבֵּר, which has dropped out by haplography: Jrm is contradicting the officers. Compare the following infinitive absolute יָדֹעַ.

d—d   These words are omitted by G, but probably by haplography, given the likeness of כי העידתי in v 19 to כי התעתים in v 20 (so Janzen, p. 118); the words do not sound like a gloss.

e—e   The Hebrew phrase has a verb followed by בְּנַפְשׁוֹתֵיכֶם. The ketib of the verb, התעתים, is not comprehensible; read the qere', הִתְעֵיתֶם, from תעה hip'il. For the meaning see Interpretation.

f   Omit with G; expansion from vv 2–4 (see Janzen, p. 54).

g   Omit with G; see Janzen, p. 80.

Yahweh [our God]^h says [thus tell us,]ⁱ we will do.' 21/ [And I told you today,]^j but you have not obeyed the voice of Yahweh [your God]^k [and for all]^l who sent me to you. 18/ ^m For thus Yahweh [of hosts, the God of Israel,]ⁿ has said: Just as my wrath [and my anger]^o has been poured out on the inhabitants of Jerusalem, so my wrath will be poured out upon you when you go to Egypt; and you shall be a curse and a desolation, an object of contempt and a reproach, and you will not see this place again.^m 22/ So now [you do know that]^p by sword 《 and 》^q by famine [and by pestilence]^r you shall die in the place where you wish to go to settle."^a

4 But Johanan [son of Kareah]^a and all the officers of the army units and all the people did not obey the voice of Yahweh, to stay in the land of Judah. 5/ So Johanan [son of Kareah]^a and all the officers of the army units took all the remnant of Judah who had returned [from all the nations where they had been scattered]^b to settle^c in the land of 《 Egypt 》^c — 6/ 〈 the warriors, 〉^a women, children, the daughters of the king, and every person whom Nebuzaradan [the provost marshal]^b had put with Gedaliah son of Ahikam [son of Shaphan,]^c and Jeremiah the prophet and Baruch son of Neriah; 7/ and they went to [the land of]^a Egypt, for they did not obey the voice of Yahweh, and they went to [as far as]^b Tahpanhes.

8 Then the word of Yahweh came to Jeremiah in Tahpanhes, as follows: 9/ Take in your hand large stones and hide them in the clay pavement (?) [in the brick-terrace (?)]^a which is at the entrance of the house of Pharaoh in Tahpanhes, in the eyes of Jewish people; 10/ and you shall say to them, Thus Yahweh [of hosts, the God of Israel]^a has said: I am going to send and fetch Nebuchadrezzar king of Babylon [my servant,]^b 《 and he shall set 》^c his throne above

h   Omit with G; see Janzen, p. 81.

i   Omit with G; expansion from v 3 (see Janzen, p. 54).

j   Omit with G; the material is repeated from v 20 (see Janzen, p. 54).

k   Omit with G; see Janzen, p. 80.

l   Omit with G; the expression is imitative of v 20, so that M would have to mean something like "in all that he sent me to you (to tell)." G is clearly superior; see Janzen, p. 67.

m—m See v 17, note d above.

n   Omit with G; compare Janzen, pp. 76–78.

o   Omit with G; the word spoils the symmetry with v 18b. See Janzen, p. 54.

p   Omit with G, material from v 19; see Janzen, p. 54.

q   So read with G: compare note n.

r   Omit with G; see Janzen, p. 205, n. 19.

43:4a Omit with 4QJer^b (Janzen, p. 182) and G; compare Janzen, p. 150.

5a   Omit with 4QJer^b (Janzen, p. 182) and G; compare Janzen, p. 150.

b   Omit with G; see Janzen, p. 54, and compare 40:12, note a. Though 4QJer^b has a lacuna at this point, the gap can be filled with the text of G, not the text of M: see Janzen, pp. 182–83.

c—c The textual question is complicated. M reads בְּאֶרֶץ יְהוּדָה "in the land of Judah"; G reads "in the land" = בָּאֶרֶץ. In 4QJer^b the tail of the ṣade of בארץ is visible, followed by a lacuna; the final mem of מצרים is clearly visible. The verb גור is always associated with Egypt (42:15, 17; 43:2; 42:22); the verb associated with staying in Judah is ישׁב (42:10, 13). It is best then to stay with the indication of 4QJer^b; see Janzen, pp. 182–83.

6a   Vocalize with G הַגְּבֹרִים; see 41:16, note f—f.

b   Omit with 4QJer^b (Janzen, pp. 182–83) and G; compare Janzen, p. 151.

c   Omit with 4QJer^b (Janzen, pp. 182–83) and G; compare Janzen, p. 150.

7a   Omit with G, though 4QJer^b agrees with M: see Janzen, pp. 182–83.

b   Omit with G and, evidently, 4QJer^b: see Janzen, pp. 182–83.

9a   בְּמֶלְבֵּן is evidently a doublet or gloss of בַּמַּלֵּט; both words (and the following אֲשֶׁר) are omitted in G, probably by haplography. There may be more that is wrong with the text; Janzen suggests that 4QJer^b (which has a lacuna at this point) may have read, ". . . in the clay pavement, in the terrace which is at the gate of the house of Pharaoh which is at the entrance of Tahpanhes" (for "gate" compare some MSS. of G). But this is not necessarily the most original text. For a discussion see Janzen, pp. 29, 183–84.

10a   Omit with G; compare Janzen, pp. 80–81.

b   Omit with G; this is evidently a gloss from 27:6; for a full discussion see Janzen, pp. 54–57, and also 107.

these stones which I have hidden, and he shall spread ᵈhis canopyᵈ over them. 11/ ᵃHe shall comeᵃ and strike the land of Egypt: those (marked) for death, to death, and those (marked) for exile, to exile, [and those (marked) for the sword, to the sword.]ᵇ 13/ ⟪And he will shatter the obelisks of the house of the Sun⟫ᵃ [which is in the land of Egypt,]ᵇ 12/ ⟪and he shall set⟫ᵃ fire to the houses of ᵇ⟪their gods⟫ [M: the gods of Egypt,]ᵇ and he shall burn them and take them captive, and he shall delouse the land of Egypt as a shepherd delouses his garment, and he shall go out in safety. 13/ [. . . ,]ᵃ [and ᵈ⟪their houses⟫ {M: the houses of the gods of Egypt}ᵈ he will burn with fire.]ᶜ

44

1/ The word which came to Jeremiah for all the Jews dwelling in the land of Egypt, those living in Migdol and in Tahpanhes [and in Memphis]ᵃ and in the land of Pathros, as follows: 2/ Thus Yahweh [of hosts]ᵃ the God of Israel has said: You yourselves have seen all the evil which I have brought in upon Jerusalem and upon [all]ᵇ the cities of Judah, and there they are, a ruin [this day]ᶜ without any inhabitant in them, 3/ because of their evil which they have done to offend me, to go to make sacrifices [to serve]ᵃ to other gods, whom ᵇthey did not know, [they, you and your fathers.]ᵇ 4/ So I sent to you [all]ᵃ my servants the prophets, early and constantly, as follows: Do not commit this abominable thing which I hate! 5/ But they did not obey or incline their ear to turn from their evil, so as not to make sacrifices to other gods. 6/ So my wrath and my anger were poured out and burned the cities of Judah and the streets of Jerusalem, and they became a ruin andᵃ a desolation as at this day.

7/ So now thus Yahweh [God]ᵃ of hosts [God of Israel]ᵃ has said, Why are you doing a great evil against yourselves, to cut off for yourselves man and woman, child and nursling from the midst of Judah, so as to leave yourselves no remnant 8/ to offend me by the worksᵃ of your hands, to make sacrifices to other gods in the land of Egypt, where you came to settle, so as to cut yourselves off and to become an object of contempt and a reproach in [all]ᵇ the nations of the earth? 9/ Have you forgotten the evils of your fathers and the evils of the kings of Judah [and the evils of his wives]ᵃ [⟨and your evil⟩]ᵇ and the

c   Read with G and S וְשָׂם אֶת־; M וְשַׂמְתִּי "and I shall set." The third person matches וְנָתַן in v 10b (and compare 1:15). So Duhm, Giesebrecht, Cornill, Volz, Rudolph, and Bright. But, as Bright points out, M is not impossible.

d—d   Ketib שַׁפְרוּרוֹ, qere' שַׁפְרִירוֹ. The word is a *hapax legomenon.*

11a—a   Read qere' וּבָא; the ketib might perhaps be read וּבָאָהּ "and he shall come in upon it" (Rudolph), but it is to be rejected.

b   "Death" here cannot imply "pestilence," as in 15:2, a matter over which Nebuchadrezzar has no control; "sword" therefore appears to be a secondary expansion from 15:2 (so Rudolph).

13a   Verse 12 clearly closes the speech. I propose (with Volz) that v 13a dropped out of the text at an early stage, doubtless by haplography; it was subsequently restored wrongly after v 12 (Cornill sees the problem and brackets all of v 13 as secondary; Volz moves v 13a, but wrongly, I believe, to a position between v 12a and v 12b). See further Preliminary Observations and Interpretation.

b   Omit, a clarifying gloss; G has a similar gloss ("those in On"). See Janzen, p. 133, and see Interpretation.

12a   Read וְהִצִּית with G, S, and V; M וְהִצַּתִּי "and I shall set."

b   So read with G; M is an expansion with the proper name (see Janzen, p. 74).

13c   Verse 13b is evidently an expansion, using material from v 12, to round off v 13a when it was displaced (so Volz; compare v 13, note a, before v 12).

d—d   So read with G; M is an expansion with the proper name (see Janzen, p. 74).

44:1a   Omit with G. The addition is probably from 2:16 and 46:14; see Janzen, p. 57.

2a   Omit with G; compare Janzen, p. 78.

b   Omit with G; compare Janzen, pp. 65–67.

c   Omit with G; the addition is perhaps from v 6 (compare Janzen, p. 57).

3a   Omit with G; the expansion is from 16:13.

b—b   G οὐκ ἔγνωτε = לֹא יְדַעְתֶּם is evidently a variant of M לֹא יָדְעוּם; S presupposes לֹא יְדָעוּם הֵמָּה וַאֲבֹתֵיהֶם; M conflates that expansion and the second-person reference indicated in the type of text reflected in G. See Janzen, pp. 17–18.

4a   Omit with G; see v 2, note b.

6a   So read with some MSS. and with G, V, and S; M omits "and."

7a   Omit expansions with G; compare Janzen, pp. 76–78 (and 157, item i).

8a   Many MSS. and S read "work."

b   Omit with G; compare v 2, note b.

9a   Omit with G. Some Greek recensional texts read נְשֵׁיהֶם "their wives"; the expression in M evidently arose out of a text tradition that had read מֶלֶךְ יְהוּדָה "king of Judah" by haplography. For the emergence of an expression with "wives" compare note c. See

evils of 《 your officials 》[c] which they did in the land of Judah and in the streets of Jerusalem? 10/ They have shown no contrition to this day, [and they did not fear][a] and they did not walk [in my law and][b] in my statutes which I set [c][before you and] before 《 their fathers. 》[c]

11   Therefore thus Yahweh [of hosts, God of Israel][a] has said: I am going to set my face [against you for evil,][b] to cut off all [Judah,][c] 12/ [and I shall take][a] the remnant [of Judah][b] who (are) [have set their face to go into the land of Egypt to settle there, and they shall be consumed][c] in [the land of][d] Egypt, and they shall fall by sword, and[e] by famine they shall be consumed, from small to great, [by sword and famine they shall die,][f] and they shall become [a curse,][g] a desolation, an object of contempt and a reproach. 13/ And I shall deal with those who dwell in [the land of][a] Egypt as I have dealt with Jerusalem, with sword 《 and 》[b] with famine [and with pestilence.][c] 14/ And there shall be no fugitive or survivor of the remnant of Judah 《 who dwell 》[a] [there][b] in the land of Egypt [and][c] to return to the land of Judah, where they desire to return [to settle,][d] for they shall not return [except (as) fugitives.][e]

15   But Jeremiah was answered by all the men who knew that their wives were offering sacrifices to other gods, and by all the women [who were standing (there),][a] a

Janzen, p. 19.

b   Omit with G. The other occurrences of the word "evil" in the context are plural and written *plene*; M vocalizes the present expression as a plural, רָעֹתְכֶם, but the defective spelling is dubious. Its original vocalization is therefore probably רָעַתְכֶם, and one must assume that it stems from a text tradition in which the other occurrences of the word "evil" were likewise singular. See Janzen, p. 18.

c   Read שָׂרֵיכֶם with G; M has נְשֵׁיכֶם "your wives" (as does G as a plus). It is evidently an early misreading: see Janzen, pp. 18–19.

10a   Omit with G; the expression is probably a variant or gloss on לֹא דִכְּאוּ. See Janzen, p. 25.

b   Omit with G; the expression is from v 23. See Janzen, p. 57.

c—c   G correctly reads "before their fathers." M has shifted to "your fathers" because of the diction of v 9 and elsewhere, and has added "you and," given the diction of 7:14 and 23:39. See Janzen, p. 58.

11a   Omit with G; compare Janzen, pp. 76–78.

b   Omit with G; the expansion is evidently from 21:10. See Janzen, p. 58.

c   Omit with G; compare v 27. See Janzen, p. 58.

12a   Omit with G; the verb is a secondary addition after a distinction arose between "all Judah" and "the remnant." S reads "and I shall break" = וְשָׁבַרְתִּי. See Janzen, p. 58.

b   Omit with G; the addition is from vv 14, 28, etc. See Janzen, p. 58.

c   Omit with G; the addition is from 42:19, 22. Jrm's audience is already in Egypt. See Janzen, p. 58.

d   Omit with G; see Janzen, p. 58.

e   So read with many MSS. and with G, V, and S; M omits "and."

f   Omit with G and S; the bracketed words are evidently a doublet, originating with a miscopying of יתמו as ימתו. See Janzen, pp. 19, 58.

g   Omit with G; see Janzen, p. 58.

13a   Omit with G; see v 12, note d.

b   So read with G, V, and S; M omits. Compare note c.

c   Omit with G; see Janzen, p. 205, n. 19.

14a   Read הַבָּאִים לָגוּר or הַגָּרִים or הַיֹּשְׁבִים with G for M. See Janzen, p. 58.

b   Omit with G; see Janzen, p. 58.

c   Omit with G; so Rudolph.

d   Omit with G and S; see Janzen, p. 25.

e   Although the expression is present in both M and G, it is an early gloss from v 28, since it contradicts v 14a (so Volz, Rudolph, so also Alonso Schökel, "Jeremías como anti-Moisés," 250); the diction of 22:27 is very close and ends with לֹא יָשׁוּבוּ.

15a   Though these bracketed words are in both G and M, I would suggest they are an early expansion; Jrm is answered by the men in vv 15–18 and by the women in v 19. Compare the presumed expansions in v 20.

large company, ⟩and all the people who were living in the land of Egypt ⟪ and ⟫ᶜ at Pathros,⟨ ᵇ as follows: 16/ "The word which you have spoken to us in the name of Yahweh— we are not listening to you; 17/ instead we shall do every word that comes forth from our mouth, to offer sacrifices ᵃto the queen ofᵃ heaven and to offer her drink offerings, just as we and our fathers, our kings and our officials did in the cities of Judah and the streets of Jerusalem; and we ate enough bread, and we were well off, and evil we did not see. 18/ But since we stopped offering sacrifices ᵃto the queen ofᵃ heaven ⟩and offering drink-offerings to her,⟨ ᵇ we have lacked everything, and by sword and by famine we have been consumed." 19/ ⟪And all the women answered and said,⟫ᵃ "When we were sacrificing ᵇto the queen ofᵇ heaven and offering drink-offerings to her, was it against the will of our husbands that we made for her cakes [⟨to make her image⟩]ᶜ ⟩and offered drink-offerings to her?⟨ ᵈ

20 Then Jeremiah said ⟩to all the people,⟨ ᵃ to the menᵇ ⟩and women, and all the people⟨ ᵃ who were answering him anything, as follows: 21/ "Has not the sacrificing which you did in the cities of Judah and in the streets of Jerusalem, you and your fathers, your kings and your officials, and the people of the land, [. . .]ᵃ been remembered by Yahweh, and has it not come to his mind? 22/ And Yahweh can no longer bear the sight of the evil of your doings, the sight of the abominations which you have done, and your land has become a waste and a desolation and an object of contempt, [without an inhabitant]ᵃ as at this day. 23/ Because you have offered sacrifices and sinned against Yahweh, and in his law and his statutes and his testimonies you have not walked, that is why this evil has befallen you, [as at this day."]ᵃ

24 And Jeremiah said [to {all}ᵇ the people and]ᵃ to [all]ᶜ the women, "Hear the word of

b   Though these words are in both *M* and *G*, they are probably a gloss, given "a large company," which appears to be a summarizing phrase; it is doubtful that all the Jews in Egypt were present (so Volz, Rudolph, Bright).

c   Insert with *S*; one assumes "Egypt" is Lower Egypt and that "Pathros" is Upper Egypt (so Volz, Rudolph).

17a—a   Many MSS. read לִמְלָאכֶת "to the service of," and the vocalization of *M*, לִמְלֶכֶת, suggests the same euphemistic distortion; vocalize לְמַלְכַּת. See 7:18.

18a—a   See v 17, note a—a.

b   *G* omits these words. Janzen, p. 118, assumes haplography in *G*, but it is just as likely that the phrase was originally lacking over against v 17. That is to say, the rhetoric becomes compressed: compare v 19, and v 20, note d.

19a   So read with *S*; *M* has only "and." It is clear that the women speak ("our husbands"). *S* offers a text that is parallel to v 15 and does not appear to be a gloss. *M* is defective by haplography. It is a difficult question whether to reconstruct the texts with feminine plural or masculine plural verbs: one might argue for feminine because *S* here offers feminine verbs, but then in 1 Kgs 11:3b *M* has a masculine plural verb with a feminine subject, and *S* there has a feminine verb. Masculine verbs would make a haplography with waw likely. Compare Janzen, p. 133.

b—b   See v 17, note a.

c   Vocalize לְהַעֲצִבָה (compare GKC, sec. 58g); but omit with *G* and *S*. The form is probably secondary, perhaps having originated as a gloss לְעַצְבָּה (compare σ' [Syro-Hexapla] τῷ γλυπτῷ αὐτῆς). See Janzen, p. 108.

d   Though both *M* and *G* have the phrase, I would suggest that it is an early expansion.

20a   Though both these bracketed sequences are in both *G* and *M*, some or all portions appear to be expansions (note "all the people" twice). If Jrm replies to the women in vv 24–25, then he responds to the men here. These expansions are comparable to those in v 15.

b   *G* reads "warriors," thus vocalizing גִּבֹּרִים.

21a   The Hebrew inverted active voice in v 20aba has been rendered by a passive (see Interpretation); the object pronoun here, אֹתָם, should be omitted with *G* (but it should in any case be אֹתָה, feminine: compare וַתֵּעָלֶה).

22a   Omit with *G*, an addition from v 2; see Janzen, p. 58.

23a   Omit with *G*, an addition from vv 6 and 22; see Janzen, p. 58.

24a   Though the bracketed words are in both *M* and *G*, they are to be omitted as a gloss from vv 15 and 20, since v 25 is addressed to the women (וַתְּדַבֵּרְנָה); so Volz, Rudolph. See Janzen, p. 133.

b   A secondary addition, lacking in *G*.

Yahweh, [all Judah who are in the land of Egypt:]ᵈ 25/ Thus Yahweh [of hosts]ᵃ the God of Israel has said, [as follows:]ᵇ 《You women,》ᶜ you have both spoken with your mouth and with your hands have fulfilled (it), saying, 'We really will perform our vows which we have vowed, to offer sacrifices ᵈto the queen ofᵈ heaven and to offer her drink-offerings!' Do ⟨confirm⟩ᵉ your vows and do perform (them) [your vows!"]ᶠ

26 Therefore hear the word of Yahweh, all Judah dwelling in the land of Egypt: Look, I have sworn by my great name, Yahweh has said, that my name will no more be invoked in the mouth of ᵃall [M: every man of]ᵃ Judah who says, "By the life of [the Lord]ᵇ Yahweh," in all the land of Egypt. 27/ I am going to watch over you for evil and not for good, and ᵃall [M: every man of]ᵃ Judah who is in the land of Egypt shall be consumed by sword and famine until they are completely gone. 28/ [And the fugitives of the sword shall return {from the land of Egypt}ᵇ to the land of Judah few in number,]ᵃ and [all]ᶜ the remnant of Judah who entered the land of Egypt to settle there shall know whose word shall stand, [mine or theirs.]ᵈ 29/ And this is the sign to you, [oracle of Yahweh,]ᵃ that I am taking care of you for evil in this place, so that you may know that my words will indeed stand over you for evil. 30/ Thus Yahweh has said, I am going to give ⟩Pharaoh⟨ ᵃ Hophra king of Egypt into the hands of his enemies and into the hand of those seeking his life, just as I have given Zedekiah king of Judah into the hand of Nebuchadrezzar king of Babylon, his enemy and one who seeks his life.

c   Omit with *G*; compare Janzen, pp. 65–67.
d   Omit with *G*, an expansion from v 26; see Janzen, p. 58.
25a Omit with *G*; compare Janzen, pp. 76–78.
b   Omit with *G* and *S*.
c   Read with *G* אַתֶּנָה הַנָּשִׁים for *M* אַתֶּם וּנְשֵׁיכֶם "You [masculine] and your wives"; so Duhm, Cornill, Giesebrecht, Volz, Rudolph, Bright. The verb that follows is feminine.
d—d See v 17, note a—a.
e   The verb is doubtless to be vocalized תְּקִימֶנָה or (if the yod is secondary) תְּקֵמְנָה; see GKC, sec. 72k.
f   Omit with *G*; the expresssion is secondary from the previous clause. See Janzen, p. 58.
26a—a Omit אִישׁ with *G*; compare "all Judah" earlier in the verse.
b   Omit אֲדֹנָי with *G*; see Janzen, p. 81.
27a—a Omit אִישׁ with *G*; compare v 26, note a—a.
28a Although this half verse is found in both *G* and *M*, it must be bracketed as a mitigating expansion (so Duhm, Volz; so also Alonso Schökel, "Jeremías como anti-Moisés," 250), contradicting both v 27 and the implication of v 28b; compare a similar mitigation at the end of v 14.
b   Omit with *G*.
c   Omit with *G*.
d   Omit with *G*, a clarifying expansion.
29a Omit with *G*.
30a Perhaps omit with *G*, though Janzen, p. 118, suggests that *G* is deficient by haplography.

Preliminary Observations

Chapters 37—44 offer a sustained narrative of Jrm's last months (see Form and Structure).

Passages in which Jrm Appears Not to Be Central. Within these eight chapters are two sections in which Jrm appears not to be the central character. The first of these is the narrative of the fall of Jerusalem in 39:1–10. Of these verses, however, vv 4–10 are missing in *G* and are derived secondarily from 52:7–11, 13–16 (see Text, and see 52:1–34, Structure, Form, Setting). What remains, vv 1–3, necessarily introduces the Babylonian officers; it is the provost marshal Nebuzaradan who deals with Jrm in vv 11–14.

The second such section, 40:7—41:18, centers on Johanan and the other "officers of the army units"; within this section is the narrative of Ishmael's assassination of Gedaliah and his slaughter of the pilgrims from the north. But this material is necessary for the narrative. It

is not simply that Johanan needs to be introduced, because Jrm and Baruch are among the refugees in the group led by Johanan going down to Egypt (43:4–7): Jrm himself has been moved about as the various military forces engage each other. Thus Jrm was entrusted to Gedaliah (40:6); he must have been among the people whom Ishmael took hostage after the latter assassinated Gedaliah and slaughtered the pilgrims: when Johanan caught up with Ishmael at Gibeon, the people who had been with Ishmael gladly "returned to Johanan" (41:14), and Johanan "brought them back from Gibeon," presumably to Mizpah (41:16), from which they set off to the region of Bethlehem (41:17)—and at this point Jrm surfaces again among the group (42:1–2).

And not only was Jrm there all the time; so, evidently, was Baruch: by implication Baruch is present when the group stops near Bethlehem (43:3), and he is specifically named as part of the group in 43:6. Is one to assume that he was with Jrm all the time? Baruch certainly had access to Jrm when he was confined in the court of the guard during the previous year (32:12), and it is thus probable that he stayed with Jrm all through the events narrated in these chapters.

Text Dislocations. Within these eight chapters there are evidently several dislocations of text; it is convenient to discuss these here, although the restoration of each of them is discussed in the text notes.

Thus (to begin with the one most commonly recognized) it is necessary to insert 42:19–22 between 43:3 and 4 (so also Volz, Rudolph, and Bright): 42:19–22 assumes that the officers have already rejected Yahweh's word, but only in 43:1–3 do they overtly reject it. But the situation is more complicated: 42:18 likewise assumes that the officers have rejected Yahweh's word (בְּבֹאֲכֶם מִצְרַיִם, "when you go to Egypt"): contrast the phrasing of vv 15 and 17. I therefore propose that v 18 originally stood before v 22, with which it forms a form-critical unity: v 18 states the intervention of Yahweh, and v 22 the results of the intervention (compare Mic 2:3 and 4).[1] In this way vv 18 + 22 summarize the rhetoric of vv 15–17. I assume that at an early point in the transmission of the text it suffered haplography between עֲלֵיהֶם at the end of v 17 and עֲלֵיהֶם (or its synonym אֲלֵיהֶם) in the first clause of v 19, thus omitting the narrative of the officers' speech in 43:1–3. The first clause of v 19 was permanently lost; the first three verses of chapter 43 were restored but in the wrong position after Jrm's speech ending in 42:22, inasmuch as the loss of the first clause of v 19 prevented a recognition of the additional exchange between the officers and Jrm: the scribe simply followed the clue of "when Jeremiah had finished speaking" in 43:1. Subsequently v 18 was shifted to its present position, either inadvertently or deliberately: a scribe may have been convinced that the sequence beginning in v 19 is simply to contain Jrm's words and that the divine word of v 18 belongs with the rest of the divine words of vv 9–17.

The narrative in 39:11–14 describes the orders given by the Babylonian provost marshal regarding the care of Jrm, and this is followed curiously by the word to Jrm regarding the fate of Ebed-melech (39:15–18), who was last heard of pulling Jrm out of the muddy cistern in 38:7–13: clearly 39:15–18 fits poorly in the context. Cornill discusses the matter and suggests that the passage might well be shifted to a position after either 38:13 or 38:28a, but he finally follows Duhm in assuming the passage is redactional. Volz assumes it is in its present position because chronologically this is when the word was fulfilled, not when it was delivered. Bright does shift it to a position after 38:28a. The difficulty with that solution, however, is that the word-order of 39:15 (emphasis on "Jeremiah") suggests a shift of subject, and a position after 38:28a would not offer such a shift. But a position after 38:27 does offer a shift of subject: the subject of v 27 is "all the officials," and a placement there would allow a nice play on "word" in 38:27 and 39:15 (in 38:27, "matter"). In this way the word regarding Ebed-melech rounds off the section on Zedekiah's third inquiry to Jrm and the prophet's rescue from the muddy cistern before the closing word in 38:28a ("Jeremiah stayed").

In 40:1 a word from Yahweh to Jrm is announced but is missing, and then in vv 2–3 the Babylonian provost marshal, in an unlikely sequence, addresses Jrm with a word from Yahweh, in the second-person singular in v 2 and in the plural in v 3. The commentators deal with the matter in various ways: thus Volz assumes two parallel damaged texts interwoven together in vv 1–3, and Rudolph suggests an elaborate reconstruction. The solution I propose is the working-out of a query of Bright's: "In vs. 1a an oracle is introduced, but never given (Is there a misplaced relic of it in vss. 2–3?)."[2] I propose that v 2abα is misplaced: that v 2bβγ–3 is "the word which came to Jeremiah from Yahweh" referred to in v 1, that that word is directed to the people—thus the second-person plural reference in v 3—and that the second singular reference in v 2bβ is an erroneous secondary shift after the text was misarranged. It is possible that some words are missing from the end of v 1 as well, and that the misplacing of v 2abα is related to the loss of those words.

At the end of chapter 43 there is a problem. Verse 12 there clearly rounds off the divine speech: one notes that "and he shall come" (וּבָא) at the beginning of v 11 is

1   Claus Westermann, *Basic Forms of Prophetic Speech* (Philadelphia: Westminster, 1967) 170–71, 174–75.

2   Bright, p. 244.

closed off by "and he shall go out" (וְיָצָא) at the end of v 12, to say nothing of the climactic simile about the shepherd "delousing" his cloak. Cornill solved the problem by bracketing v 13 as a secondary addition, but the vivid rhetoric of v 13a does not sound like an editorial expansion. Volz rightly saw v 13a as displaced, but he wrongly (in my estimation) placed it between v 12a and v 12b. My own solution is to restore it before v 12. In that way the rhetoric moves from "house" of a god (singular) in v 13a to "houses" of the gods (plural) in v 12a, and then the pillaging of all of Egypt in v 12b. A haplography, by which a copyist's eye jumped from שבילשבי at the end of v 11 past ביתשמש at the end of (the unexpanded text of) v 13a, may have been responsible. Verse 13a would then subsequently have been reintroduced into the text at the wrong spot, after v 12, and additional explanatory material (v 13b), adapted from v 12a, would have been added to round off the rhetoric.

Form and Structure

There have been scattered passages of prophetic biography in the book up to this point (19:1—20:6; 26:1–24; 28:1–17; 29:29–32), but the present passage, chapters 37—44, offers a sustained narrative of events at the end of the prophet's life, from a time during the second siege of Jerusalem just before the Egyptians forced the Babylonians temporarily to withdraw, presumably in the spring or early summer of 588, until he and Baruch were forced to migrate with other refugees to Egypt, probably in the winter of 587/586: a period thus of roughly a year and a half. It is then an example par excellence of prophetic biography.[3]

Customarily, chapter 45 has been included in this unit,[4] but it is clear that both form-critically and chronologically that chapter is separate from what precedes (see there).

The proposal has been made that chapter 38 is a duplicate account of the incident recorded in 37:11–21: it was argued by Skinner[5] and is considered by Bright

and Thompson.[6] Thus in both accounts he is brought before the pro-Egyptian courtiers, in both he is charged with treason, and in both he is confined in a place related to a cistern. But the differences in detail between the two accounts are considerable, and the analysis given here of structure and setting rules out the suggestion.

Wanke, basing his analysis on a dissertation of Kremers, divides 37:1—43:7 (after the introductory 37:1–10) into ten sections: 37:11–16; 37:17–21; 38:1–6; 38:7–13; 38:14–28a; 38:28b—40:6; 40:13–41:2; 41:4–9; 41:10–15; and 41:16—43:7.[7] In his analysis each of the sections has an introduction, naming the persons in the situation, followed by the main body—which usually consists of a conversation or address, often with consequences—and then a closing observation. This analysis is suggestive but not altogether satisfactory; thus there is no reason to divide 38:1–13 in two—even though there is a shift from the courtiers' action with Jrm to Ebedmelech's action with Jrm, nevertheless the narrative of vv 7–13 is a continuation of that of vv 1–6. Furthermore, Wanke has not taken account of all the dislocations of text that evidently exist (see above, Preliminary Observations). The question of the structure of the passage therefore needs a fresh examination.

Wanke points out correctly that the clauses containing the verb וַיֵּשֶׁב "and he stayed" with subject "Jeremiah" (37:16b, 21b; 38:13b, 28a; 39:14b; 40:6b) mark the end of six of the sections within this narrative.[8] Given this sixfold repetition, it is then attractive to see a balance between the narrative that occurs just before the unit ending in 37:16b, namely 37:3–10, and the narrative afterward, 40:7—42:17 + 43:1–3 + 42:19–21 + 18 + 22: in the former sequence Zedekiah asks Jrm to "pray on our behalf to Yahweh" (37:3), and in the latter sequence Johanan and the rest of the "officers of the army units" ask Jrm to "pray on our behalf to Yahweh" (42:2; compare 42:20): these are the only occurrences of this phraseology in the eight chapters. The opening and closing sections would thus form an inclusio.

---

3   Koch, *Growth*, 203–205; March, "Prophecy," 174–75; and, in detail, Wanke, *Baruchschrift*, 91–133.
4   Koch, *Growth*, 203; March, "Prophecy," 174.
5   Skinner, pp. 258–60.
6   Bright, pp. 232–34; Thompson, pp. 636–37.
7   Wanke, *Baruchschrift*, 94–95.
8   Ibid., 92.

What follows in 43:4—44:30 narrates Jrm's migration to Egypt; structurally it is an appendix.

The material of 37:1—43:3 thus narrates Jrm's final span of time in Jerusalem. Each of the eight sections, the six in the center ("and he stayed") and the two that enclose them ("pray on our behalf"), narrates a single scene. A scene may depict actions done to Jrm by his adversaries or protectors, a word from Yahweh to Jrm relevant to the one(s) in dialogue with him, a word from Jrm himself to the one(s) in dialogue with him, or some combination of these. Preceding the eight scenes there is an introduction (37:1–2). There then follows:

(1) Zedekiah's first inquiry of Jrm,[9] through the mediation of courtiers, that Jrm pray for the nation; the word of Yahweh to Jrm in answer to Zedekiah (37:3–10).

(2) Jrm's attempt to go to the land of Benjamin; his conversation with the sentry; his imprisonment (37:11–16).

(3) Zedekiah's second, direct inquiry of Jrm, and the prophet's deliverance of Yahweh's word to the king; the king's transfer of Jrm to the court of the guard (37:17–21).

(4) The courtiers' successful pressure on the king to give Jrm over to them; his removal to the muddy cistern; his rescue by Ebed-melech and return to the court of the guard (38:1–13).

(5) Zedekiah's third inquiry of Jrm, and the prophet's deliverance of Yahweh's word to the king; a vision of the humiliation of the women of the palace if the king disregards Yahweh's word; the courtiers' subsequent questioning of the prophet; a word to Jrm from Yahweh regarding Ebed-melech (38:14–27 + 39:15–18 + 38:28a).

(6) An introduction narrating the fall of Jerusalem (38:28b + 39:1–3); Nebuchadrezzar's command to Nebuzaradan to protect Jrm (39:11–14).

(7) The word from Yahweh to Jrm for his fellow prisoners; the word of Nebuzaradan to Jrm; Jrm's choice to stay with Gedaliah (40:1, 2bβγ–3, 2abα, 4–6).

(8) An introduction narrating the activities of Johanan and his fellow officers, their protection of refugees, Ishmael's assassination of Gedaliah and his slaughter of the pilgrims from the north (40:7—41:18); the request by Johanan and those with him that Jrm pray for them; the word of response from Yahweh; the dispute between Johanan and those with him on the one hand and Jrm on the other about the validity of Yahweh's word (42:1–17 + 43:1–3 + 42:19–21, 18, 22).

The appendix begins with an introduction, the migration to Egypt of Johanan, the other officers, and the people in their care, in particular Jrm and Baruch (43:4–7). There follow three sections, in each of which Jrm offers Yahweh's word: (1) the symbolic action and word at Tahpanhes (43:8–13); (2) the word to the Jews in Egypt on the worship of the queen of heaven (44:1–14), their responses (44:15–19), and Jrm's responses to them (44:20–25); and (3) Jrm's last words of divine judgment (44:26–30). One has the impression that there is symmetry among these sections: The first and the last both deal with the coming defeat by Nebuchadrezzar of the Pharaoh of Egypt (43:10–13 and 44:30), and the central section is of course the most elaborate.

The introduction (37:1–2) consists of a historical notice about Zedekiah (v 1) followed by a judgment on him (v 2). These two verses resemble similar sequences within the Book of Kings, and they may well be redactional, to relate chapters 37—44 to the rest of Jer.

The first section (vv 3–10) begins with a description of the delegation from Zedekiah to Jrm to ask him to intercede for the nation (vv 3–5), but the bulk of the section (vv 6–10) records the divine word to Jrm for the emissaries, an announcement of the city's coming calamity: even if only wounded Babylonians were left, they would prevail (for this rhetorical flourish compare 2 Sam 5:6). No report is recorded of Jrm's delivering the word to them (compare 29:30–32 and often).

The second section (vv 11–16) narrates the sentry Irijah's arrest of Jrm when he attempted to go north to the land of Benjamin—he is accused of deserting to the Babylonians, though he denies it—and his subsequent imprisonment.

The third section (vv 17–21) narrates the first direct conversation between Zedekiah and Jrm; the king asks for a word from Yahweh, and Jrm offers it, an announcement of the king's coming misfortune. Then Jrm takes the initiative, first posing to the king a reproachful

---

9   "First" inquiry, that is, in the present narrative sequence: the incident in 37:3–10 was evidently preceded by the material recorded in 21:1–7 and 34:1–7 (see Setting on 34:1–7).

question—the prophet has been wrongfully imprisoned, and he asks, "What wrong have I done to you?" (v 18; compare Gen 20:9), and follows this with another rhetorical question, "Where are your optimistic prophets?" (v 19; compare 2:28). Finally (v 20) he pleads that he not be sent back to prison, and the king accordingly allows him to stay in the court of the guard.

The fourth section (38:1–13) describes the maneuver by which the courtiers put pressure on the king to give Jrm over to their power—they accuse Jrm of lowering the morale of the soldiers—and have him lowered into a muddy cistern (vv 1–6). Thereupon a courtier, Ebed-melech, confronts the king with his act, either by accusing the courtiers of wrongdoing (M), or, more likely, by accusing the king directly of wrongdoing (G), and the king gives orders for him to have Jrm pulled out of the cistern and returned to the court of the guard (vv 7–13).

In the fifth section (38:14–27 + 39:15–18 + 38:28a) the king summons Jrm once more; the king wishes reassurance (ultimately from Yahweh) about his fate, but Jrm wishes reassurance from the king about his own fate, since the king is unable to accept the word from Yahweh. Jrm announces the word from Yahweh, this time not as an announcement of the coming calamity on the city (see 37:8) but as a choice offered the king, alternative scenarios for both the king and the city (38:17–18), each couched in the form of protasis-apodosis ("if/then"). This form, a presentation of contrastive choices, is evidently a variation of the presentation of the covenant condition, a part of the old covenantal formulation: compare "I am setting before you the way of life and the way of death" (Deut 30:15 and 19; for a transitional example see Jer 21:8–10).[10] The king thereupon admits he is frightened of being mistreated by deserters, and Jrm reiterates the word from Yahweh and then reinforces it with another, a vision of the humiliation of the harem and an audition of their lament (which is also a taunt-song—see Interpretation). In all this Jrm is really offering a summons to repentance.[11] Finally the king instructs Jrm how to answer the officials if they question him about his conversation with the king (vv 14–26). This long section is completed by the notice that the officials do indeed question Jrm and that Jrm answers

them as the king had instructed him (v 27); by the record of a divine word to Jrm for Ebed-melech (39:15–18)—and again, as in 37:6–10, there is no notice to the delivery of this word; and by a closing notice (38:28a).

After an introduction giving details of the fall of Jerusalem (38:28b + 39:1–3 [4–10]), the sixth section describes the Babylonian provost marshal's entrusting of Jrm to Gedaliah the governor (vv 11–14).

The seventh section (40:1, 2bβγ–3, 2bα, 4–6), as here reconstructed, consists first of a report of a divine word to Jrm for his fellow captives, a word of instruction giving the reason for the calamity that has taken place; here, as before, there is no report of the delivery of that word (compare 37:6–10; 39:15–18). This is followed by the word of the Babylonian officer Nebuzaradan to Jrm, giving him his freedom and offering him a choice of where to go. The passage closes with the statement of Jrm's decision to remain with the people in Judah.

The eighth section begins with a long historical introduction (40:7—41:18) narrating the activities of Johanan and other officers before they consulted Jrm. This introduction consists of five scenes. (a) The officers of army units, among whom are Ishmael and Johanan, and their followers, come to Gedaliah the governor. Gedaliah urges them to remain in the land and serve Babylon (40:7–12). (b) Johanan tries to tell Gedaliah that Ishmael, sponsored by the Ammonites, intends to assassinate him, but Gedaliah does not believe him (40:13–16). (c) Ishmael and his men come to Gedaliah and assassinate him and his retainers during a meal (41:1–3). (d) Ishmael proceeds to kill seventy of eighty pilgrims from the north and takes captive the people in Mizpah who had been under the protection of Gedaliah (41:4–10). (e) Johanan pursues Ishmael, who slips back to the Ammonites; Johanan takes over the protection of those who had been held by Ishmael, and the group settles near Bethlehem, intending to migrate to Egypt to be out of the way of the Babylonians (41:11–18). One might propose some symmetry among these five scenes: The third (central) scene narrates the (climactic) assassination of Gedaliah, and the first and last indicate the relation between Johanan and Ishmael, parallel in the first and in opposition in the last.

---

10 This analysis is preferable to the suggestion that this formulation switches from a prophecy of salvation to a prophecy of disaster (as set forth in Koch,

Growth, 215).

11 Thomas M. Raitt, "The Prophetic Summons to Repentance," *ZAW* 83 (1971) 39–40.

This long introduction leads into the eighth section proper (42:1–17 + 43:1–3 + 42:19–21, 18, 22), in which Johanan, his fellow officers, and followers come to Jrm to ask him to intercede for them and gain guidance where to go. This scene, as already noted, is a balance to the first section, in which Zedekiah had asked Jrm to intercede for the nation. Jrm agrees to their request for intercession and guidance, and Johanan and his followers in turn agree to abide by the divine word, whatever it is (42:1–6). Ten days later, according to the narrative, the divine word comes to Jrm, but here, in contrast to what one has in earlier chapters, the content is not given without a report to deliverance, but to the contrary the content is given in the report of its deliverance, to Johanan and his followers (42:7–17).

After the messenger formula (v 9), that word (vv 10–17) consists of the presentation of contrastive choices, for which see above on 38:17–18. But the form has become more elaborate here than in that earlier passage: the contrastive choices are both expanded beyond the immediate "if/then" clauses, especially the negative choice in vv 13–17. Indeed, v 15, with its renewed introduction and messenger formula, strikes one at first as a secondary expansion, but since part of the apodosis of the positive choice (v 10aβ), in its use of the four original verbs of 1:10, mentions the negative as well as the positive consequence, one must simply assume that the primary text offers rhetorical elaboration. After the presentation of the positive choice proper (v 10) there is an oracle of salvation (*Heilsorakel*—for this form compare Isa 43:1–4), beginning (v 11) with the reassurance formula ("do not be afraid . . .") and the support formula ("for I am with you . . .")—for these see on 1:8—and continuing (v 12) with a statement of divine intervention.[12] The elaborate protasis in the presentation of the negative choice (vv 13–14) consists mostly of a citation of the (as yet) hypothetical words of Johanan and his followers. Verse 15 curiously renews the introduction and messenger formula (see above) and paraphrases the protasis. Verses 16–17 offer the apodosis of the negative choice.

In 43:1–3 the officers reject the genuineness of the divine word Jrm has proclaimed and accuse Baruch as the instigator of the trouble. There is no way, of course, to know whether the officers are sincere in their challenge or are simply indulging in rhetoric because they have already made their decision to go to Egypt.

In 42:19–21 Jrm replies, contradicting the officers' accusation that the divine word is spurious and reminding them that he is following out their request for divine guidance, only to see them reject it. Then in vv 18 + 22 (assuming the text is here correctly restored) he reiterates the apodosis of the negative half of the divine word: the officers have already made up their minds, so the word is an announcement of judgment, the intervention of Yahweh in v 18 and the results of the intervention in v 22.[13]

The appendix (43:4—44:30) begins (43:4–7) with a narrative of the migration to Tahpanhes, in Egypt, of Johanan and his officers, the people in his care, and in particular Jrm and Baruch. Verses 8–13 are a report of Yahweh's command to Jrm in Tahpanhes to perform a symbolic act (v 9: for such symbolic acts see 13:1–11) and to speak an associated divine word, an announcement of judgment (vv 10–13): Nebuchadrezzar will extend his power over Egypt. There is no report of the execution of the command, either to perform the act or to speak the word.

In 44:1–14 there is another report of a divine word that came to Jrm in Egypt; again there is no report of its delivery, but the response of the audience in vv 15–19 indicates that one must understand vv 1–14 to imply its delivery.

Verses 2–6 review the evidence of the past disobedience of the nation and her consequent destruction by Yahweh. To some degree these verses are arranged chiastically. Thus vv 2 and 6 speak of Yahweh's destruction of Jerusalem and Judah, which the hearers themselves have seen, vv 3 and 5 speak both specifically and generally of the disobedience of the nation that brought on the destruction, and v 4 is a recollection of Yahweh's effort to communicate with the people (compare 7:25).

Verses 7–10 begin with accusatory questions (compare 6:20); these rhetorical questions could be taken theoretically as a kind of appeal for repentance, but actually the verses are Yahweh's accusation: the second question

---

12 For a discussion of the oracle of salvation see March, "Prophecy," 163, and Westermann, *Isaiah 40—66*, 11–13; for a discussion of vv 10–12 here see

Berridge, pp. 202–207.

13 See n. 1.

moves back once more to the negative example of earlier folk in Judah and Jerusalem, an example confirmed by the condemnation of v 10.

Verses 11–14 are the pronouncement of judgment, the divine intervention in vv 11–13 and the result of the intervention in v 14.

Verses 15–19 are the report of the answer of Jrm's hearers, that of the men in vv 16–18 and of the women in v 19. The men reject the word of Yahweh and affirm their loyalty to the queen of heaven, arguing likewise from the evidence of history (vv 17–18); the women defend themselves by suggesting that the actions had the approval of their husbands (v 19).

Jrm's response falls into two parts (vv 20–23, 24–25); evidently the first part is directed to the men and the second part to the women. To the men he reiterates his argument from history; to the women he simply tells them sarcastically to continue in their ways (compare the sarcasm of 7:21).

The final sequence (vv 26–30) may be unrelated to the interchange in vv 1–25; it is likewise an announcement of judgment, Yahweh's own oath that his name will no longer be invoked by Jews in Egypt (v 26) and the reiteration that nothing but disaster lies ahead—Nebuchadrezzar will take over control of Egypt.

Setting

These chapters are the largest bulk of what Mowinckel called "Source B," the biographical material of the book. Critical discussion on the origin of this material is conveniently summarized by Thompson.[14] Most commentators have affirmed the traditional attribution of these chapters to Baruch: Duhm,[15] Volz,[16] Eissfeldt,[17] Rudolph,[18] and Bright ("it is entirely likely that it was Baruch").[19] With this view Kremers agrees.[20] But there have been dissenting voices. Thus Mowinckel ruled out Baruch, concluding that the author was a scribe, probably in Egypt, working some time in the century after Jrm's death.[21] Herbert G. May proposed an anonymous

biographer who lived in the fifth century,[22] but no other critic has accepted this proposal. Wanke rejects Baruch's authorship because, he suggests, if Baruch had written it, one must assume it arose in Egypt, but in that case Baruch would surely have rounded it off with an account of Jrm's further experience in Egypt.[23] And recently Nicholson has rejected Baruch's authorship, suggesting instead a "circle of traditionists."[24]

It is a commonplace of the commentators to state that these chapters do not represent a "biography" in the modern sense; what they offer is a sequence of incidents from the last months of Jrm's career in which the prophet is confronted by various persons or groups. But the sequence is not random: if the analysis of the structure of this section of the book offered here is sound, it suggests that these chapters emerged in two stages, 37:1—43:7 and 43:8—44:30, and that each stage was conceived as a totality.

The incidents narrated in these chapters are full of striking and realistic details; in particular Jrm is not painted as a hero, nor are his opponents depicted as villains. Thus there is the pathos of Jrm's words to Zedekiah in 37:18 and 20 (compare 38:15) and the king's surprising admission of weakness in 38:19 (compare v 5). There are the homely details of Ebed-melech's rescue of Jrm (38:11–13). There are the vicissitudes of Jrm's situation in the confusing days immediately after the fall of Jerusalem (39:11–14; 40:1–6). There is in 44:1–23 the argument of the *Heilsgeschichte* of Yahweh and the counter-argument of the *Heilsgeschichte* of Astarte. All this suggests not "traditionists" but an eyewitness account, or at least access to Jrm's own testimony; in short, Baruch. One can imagine him devising 37:1—43:7 in the days just after the group arrived in Tahpanhes, and then 43:8—44:30 some time thereafter.

It should be noted that chapter 44 is particularly heavy with the repeated phrases that some commentators have associated with Deuteronomistic editing; but the present study sees no reason to deny the material to Jrm. Thus

14 Thompson, pp. 38–43.
15 Duhm, p. xvi.
16 Volz, p. xlvi.
17 Eissfeldt, *Introduction*, 354.
18 Rudolph, pp. xv–xvi.
19 Bright, lxvii.
20 Heinz Kremers, "Leidensgemeinschaft mit Gott im Alten Testament," *EvT* 13 (1953) 123.

21 Mowinckel, *Komposition*, 30.
22 Herbert G. May, "Towards an Objective Approach to the Book of Jeremiah: The Biographer," *JBL* 61 (1942) 139–55.
23 Wanke, *Baruchschrift*, 146.
24 Nicholson, *Preaching*, 18.

44:2–6 appears to be a variation of Huldah's prophecy, 2 Kgs 22:16–17 (see the remarks on 1:17–19, and n. 76 there).

The question why one has no notice of Jrm's death is of course insoluble; one can only conclude that Baruch predeceased Jrm, leaving these memoirs as they were when the scribe last enlarged them.

There are no firm data for a specific date for the material. The present study assumes that Gedaliah was assassinated in September/October 587 (see Interpretation on 41:1), and that not too many months elapsed before Jrm and Baruch went to Egypt. One can guess therefore that 37:1—43:7 was written early in 586 and 43:8—44:30 not too long thereafter.

Interpretation

■ **37:3** Zephaniah is mentioned in 21:1 and 29:25; the name of Jehucal is rendered as Jucal in 38:1. These are the only other passages where these courtiers are cited. Through them Zedekiah makes an overture to the controversial prophet Jrm; one wonders what lies behind the contrast between the use of intermediaries in this first instance and the direct conversations narrated in vv 17–20 and 38:14–26. Thompson suggests that the king "seems to have lacked the courage for a more open approach,"[25] but precedent or protocol may have lain behind his use of emissaries; his later, direct conversations were out of sight of the courtiers. Zedekiah asks Jrm to pray for the nation; for the verb "pray" (פלל hitpa'el) see 7:16. One assumes that the narrator had in mind the precedent of Hezekiah's request that Isaiah pray for the remnant of the people (2 Kgs 19:4 = Isa 37:4). For the question of Zedekiah's motivation see 21:1–7, especially Aim there.

■ **37:4** For Jrm's imprisonment see vv 15–16. The term for "prison," בֵּית הַכְּלִיא (qere') or בֵּית הַכְּלוּא (ketib), appears only here and in 52:31 (of Jehoiachin in Babylon), but it appears to be a variant of the commoner בֵּית הַכֶּלֶא (vv 15, 18). It must be stressed that imprisonment was not a legal punishment in Israel until the Persian period, so that prison (literally "house of confinement") was a simply place of detention, under guard, until clarification of a case.[26] Note that v 15 describes the conversion of a residence into a prison.

■ **37:5** This verse and the following verses (vv 7, 11) are the most direct evidence for the attempt by Egyptian forces to drive the Babylonian army away from its siege of Jerusalem, an attempt that doubtless took place in the spring or summer of 588 (see Introduction, sec. 35);[27] compare the discussion in 34:8–22. The Pharaoh was Hophra (Apries: see 44:30); it was the beginning of his reign.[28] It is likely that 46:14–24 was delivered at this time (see there). The verb עלה nip'al here and in v 11 means "withdraw (from)"; the translation here, "take themselves away," is an attempt to render what may be the reflexive connotation of the stem.

■ **37:12** Jrm's purpose in leaving Jerusalem has been much discussed, for the verbal phrase in question (לַחֲלֹק מִשָּׁם) is not clear: the verb is the only instance of the hip'il stem of חלק in the OT, and the preposition "from" in the second word ("from there") is curious. The qal stem means "share," and the related noun חֵלֶק means "portion"—some have thought the verb to be a denominative. The rendering of G may be simply a guess, τοῦ ἀγοράσαι ἐκεῖθεν, literally "to buy from there," presumably meaning "to do business from there"; the Lucianic recension then added the object "bread," assuming that Jrm was seeking provisions for the siege. The three revisions of G (α', s' and θ') stay with the meaning "share," and render "receive a share (from) there," using the middle or passive of μερίζειν. V translates ut . . . divideret ibi possessionem, "to divide a possession there," S "to divide there a portion," and T "to divide an inheritance which he had there." There is another interpretation, which originates with Qimḥi, that the verb means "divide oneself," that is, "separate oneself" (so Calvin, and so *KJV*), "escape from there," that is, to avoid capture. This interpretation at least makes sense out of the expression "from there," but it is no longer current. Luther, in the meantime, connected the expression with the incident of Jrm's buying of the field (chapter 32), rendering "to take possession of his field" (*seinen Acker in Besitz zu nehmen*), and most commentators have deemed the connection at least probable (Giesebrecht, Volz, Rudolph, Bright).

25   Thompson, p. 631.
26   Moshe Greenberg, "Prison," *IDB* 3:891–92.
27   See Bright, *History*, 330.
28   John A. Wilson, "Hophra," *IDB* 2:643–44; and see now Hoffmeier, "Apries," 165.

The vocalization of the verb as לַחֲלֹק, a hip'il infinitive of חלק, "share," is dubious: one must assume a syncope for לְהַחֲלִיק; the last vowel is written defectively, and there is no other instance of the hip'il of this verb. I propose that the text read לָקַחַת חֵלֶק and that there has been haplography because of similar consonants. It is to be noted that the noun חֵלֶק "share" is the object of the verb לקח in Gen 14:24. Cornill points out that G translates לקח by ἀγοράζειν in Neh 10:32, so that G may have read לקח in the present text, but that datum may be a coincidence: if G so renders לקח, there is no trace there of חלק, which must surely be read. The expression מִשָּׁם "from there" is still odd; conceivably the object of the verb was חֶלְקָה "a piece of land," and the he was misread as a mem—one would then read "to take a piece of land there."

In any event a connection with the narrative of the purchase of the field (chapter 32) seems assured: the chronological data, so far as one can tell, mesh (see Setting, and see Structure, Form, Setting on chapter 32).

Related to the meaning of the verb phrase is the connotation of בְּתוֹךְ הָעָם, literally, "among the people": there is the strong suspicion among many commentators that the implication is "among his people, within his family" (Duhm, Volz, Rudolph, Bright; *HALAT* likewise suggests the meaning[29]). The suggestion is plausible if Jrm's intention is to go to Anathoth to settle the matter of the field he had bought from Hanamel. The difficulty, however, is that the noun has the article, not a possessive suffix (compare Job 18:19). Furthermore, the same phrase appears in 39:14 and 40:6, and presumably all three occurrences carry the same connotation: or is it conceivable that in 39:14 and 40:6, where Jrm is in the care of Gedaliah, the phrase likewise means "(stayed) with his kinsmen"?

■ **37:13–14** The phrase בַּעַל פְּקִדֻת appears only here. It denotes someone more than a "sentry" (*RSV, JB*): the man, after all, is named, with patronymic. "Officer of the guard" or even "commander of the guard" (*HALAT*) is the meaning required.

The verb תפש appears twice: clearly the meaning shifts slightly, "detained" in v 13 and "took into custody" in v 14.

"Desert" is the connotation here of נפל, literally "fall" (so the gloss in 21:9).

■ **37:15–16** Verse 15 begins, as one would expect, with the narrative tense, the waw consecutive with the imperfect ("became furious"). The following two verbs, with simple waw and the perfect, denote actions expressed by the previous verb (compare Exod 18:25–26);[30] hence the translation here with participles. For "prison" see v 4. For the emendation of כִּי בָא to וַיָּבֹא see Text. Alternatively one could construe the כִּי of *M* as a reinforcing conjunction: "Indeed Jeremiah went (not only to Jonathan's house but) into the cistern house"; this is the analysis of Bright. It is unclear whether "cistern house" (בֵּית הַבּוֹר) is a separate house or a cistern used for a prison (so Exod 12:29), and it is likewise unclear whether the second expression, "in the cells" (וְאֶל־הַחֲנֻיוֹת) is intended as a hendiadys (Bright: "in one of the vaults of the cistern house"; similarly Rudolph), or is intensive ("indeed in the cells," so Volz). The word חֲנֻיוֹת is the plural of חָנוּת "vault"; this is the only occurrence of the word in the OT. It appears in postbiblical Hebrew for a "shop": merchants in the Near East use the successive vaults in the bazaar for their stalls or shops (on this see Volz). One has the impression, then, that Jrm was confined to an underground dungeon in which he might have died (Thompson): compare vv 18, 20.

■ **37:17** This time Zedekiah consults Jrm directly, but secretly, doubtless out of fear of his courtiers (compare 38:24–25). The king continues to hope that Yahweh has changed his mind. But Jrm's word to the king is the same word he has heard before.

■ **37:18–20** For the pathos of Jrm's personal word to the king see Structure and Form, and Setting. The prophet appeals to the king's sense of justice (Rudolph): his prophecies had continued to be sound, and he had been put into prison while the optimistic prophets were presumably free (Thompson).

■ **37:21** The king accedes to Jrm's plea and commits him to the court of the guard (for which see 32:2).

The translation "loaf" for כִּכָּר (*RSV, JB, NEB, NAB, NJV*) is misleading to a North American or European: the word means literally "disk," and refers to the round unit of bread similar to the present-day Near Eastern

---

29 *HALAT*, 792a.
30 Joüon, *Gramm.*, sec. 119v.

"pita" bread. There is of course no way to determine the standard diameter or thickness of such a unit of bread, but the impression of the passage is that this is a ration for a time of famine (compare 1 Sam 2:36).

■ **38:1–27** For the proposal, here rejected, that this chapter offers a duplicate account of the incident already narrated in 37:11–21, see Form and Structure.

■ **38:1–5** Shephatiah and Gedaliah are mentioned only here; "Jucal" is a variant spelling for Jehucal, mentioned in 37:3; Passhur is mentioned in 21:1. All four are pro-Egyptian courtiers who wish to kill Jrm. "Go out" (v 2) connotes surrender (see 21:9); for the idiom translated "shall at least have his life" see likewise 21:9. The nip'al infinitive absolute, reinforcing the finite verb in v 3 ("will really be given") appears otherwise only in the editorial expansion in 32:4, there of Zedekiah, who will likewise be given into the hand of the king of Babylon. Jrm had asked the king that he not be put to death, and the king had agreed (37:20–21); now the courtiers ask the king to allow Jrm to be put to death, and the king, powerless against his courtiers, again agrees.

The expression "weaken the hands" (v 4: רפה pi'el + יָדַיִם) of course connotes "discourage, lower the morale of"; it occurs otherwise in the OT only in Ezra 4:4, but it has turned up in one of the Lachish ostraca:[31] it was thus current in the military vocabulary of the time.

Jrm was put into a cistern belonging to Malchiah (v 6), who is identified as "the king's son, who was in the court of the guard"; the designation "the king's son" offers the same difficulty as it does for Jerahmeel in 36:26 (see there). If the datum in 2 Kgs 24:18 is correct, Zedekiah would be thirty years old at this time. If Malchiah was Zedekiah's son, he could be approximately fifteen years old, own a cistern and function as a guard; but, on the other hand, "king's son" may simply mean "of the royal family." If he is Zedekiah's son, he is certainly not the father of Pashhur (38:1)![32]

The courtiers "throw" Jrm (so the verb שלך hip'il) into the cistern. It is to be borne in mind that the cross section of most domestic cisterns was shaped like a bottle, with a small opening in the top, often covered by a stone;[33] if this was the shape of Malchiah's cistern, it would be impossible for Jrm to climb out. Whether the gloss in *M*, "and they let him down by ropes," is correct or only an attempt to soften the violence of the verb "throw" is impossible to say: they may really have thrown him into the mud (טיט). That word denotes wet mud, tossed up by the sea (Isa 57:20); it occurs several times in the phrase "mud of the streets" (for example, Mic 7:10). It would be difficult for Jrm to find a footing, and he would not survive too long.

■ **38:7–13** Jrm is rescued by an Ethiopian palace servant named Ebed-melech. For "Ethiopian" see 13:23. His name means simply "servant [or slave] of the king." No one else in the OT carries this name: it sounds like the kind of ad hoc name given to a slave whose original name no one could pronounce; no patronymic is given. Whether his identification as a "eunuch" in the gloss is correct one cannot know; for "eunuch" see 29:2. The text identifies him simply as "in the palace." It is now a virtually anonymous foreigner, rather than a native, who acts to save Jrm's life (compare the judgment in 39:18b). Is he, as his name implies, a personal servant of the king? He is certainly acquainted personally with the king, and he uses this personal acquaintance with astonishing boldness: he goes out deliberately to confront the king and, what is more, to confront him at the gate, the place of public assembly. His boldness (v 9) is particularly striking when one accepts the text of *G* to be the original: *M* has then added the polite vocative "my lord king" (the equivalent of "your majesty") and has shifted "you have done wrong" to "these men have done wrong." Ebed-melech, a foreign servant, accuses the king far more directly than Nathan the prophet did when he accused David in the Bathsheba episode (2 Sam 12:1–12). And as astonishing as the servant's boldness is the king's lack of anger, indeed his positive response. He knows the difference between right and wrong; he is simply weak.

---

31   Lachish 6.6. See *ANET*, 322b, and for the Hebrew text see conveniently John C. L. Gibson, *Textbook of Syrian Semitic Inscriptions* (Oxford: Clarendon, 1971) 1:45.

32   Compare Bruce T. Dahlberg, "Malchijah," *IDB* 3:232b, #3.

33   Richard W. Hamilton, "Water-works," *IDB* 4:813a.

The king gives Ebed-melech orders to save Jrm. The servant knows his way about the palace; he goes to a storeroom and gets some clothing-scraps and rags (these two expressions are found only here in the OT and are hardly to be distinguished). He goes out with his men and throws the clothing-scraps and rags down to Jrm, who can then protect himself when he is pulled up by ropes. The expression אַצִּלוֹת יָדָיִם, literally, "joints of the hands," is usually understood here as "armpits," but אַצִּיל means "elbow" in postbiblical Hebrew, and "elbows" may be correct.

After his rescue Jrm is returned to the court of the guard (compare 37:21); if the narrative is not a duplicate of that in chapter 37, then it is not clear how Jrm in the court of the guard is secure from the persecution of the pro-Egyptian officials; one must assume that he is put under friendly guard, or that word has gone out that he is to be under the king's protection.

■ **38:14–16** Zedekiah sends for Jrm at the third entrance of the temple. The location is unknown; Bright suggests that it might have been the king's private entrance, perhaps an entrance leading directly from the palace— this conversation, in contrast to that between the king and Ebed-melech, is certainly private (see v 27b). The king speaks to Jrm even more strangely than before, as if he is the petitioner of the prophet: "I have something to ask you." Jrm's reaction is curious: "If I tell you, you will kill me, will you not?" He knows without hearing it, of course, what the king wants to know—What is the word from Yahweh? (compare 37:17)—and he knows the king will reject it. But does he not recognize that the king, weak as he is, is still his protector against the pro-Egyptian courtiers? Or is he so overwrought by the horror of the muddy cistern that he is unable to react appropriately? The king continues his approach as petitioner, reassuring Jrm, swearing to protect him.

■ **38:17–18** Jrm reiterates the word from Yahweh.

■ **38:19** The king then opens out his heart to Jrm even more: he cannot face the possibility of surrender because he is anxious about ill treatment from those who have surrendered previously. The king has status now, but if he surrenders he is just one more refugee, stripped of his prerogatives (compare 22:30), open to the gibes of the earlier deserters, who may well be opportunists (Calvin), who are now pro-Babylonian and who could view the king as an enemy prisoner of war (compare Rudolph), who could at the very least resent the king's holding out as long as he does (Thompson).

■ **38:22–23** Jrm's vision and audition is of the women of the palace being led away to captivity, singing a lament to the king. Among the women are those of the harem and those of previous kings (so Rudolph). They sing a short song which is in the so-called dirge (qinah) meter.[34] Commentators argue whether it is a lament (as Duhm and Rudolph insist) or a taunt-song (so Giesebrecht, Volz). Clearly it is not a true lament (for which see 9:18); it is addressed to the king—"Your intimates have left you in the lurch!" Outwardly a lament, inwardly it is a taunt-song; for the combination one may compare Isa 14:4b–21.[35] The king has dreaded the prospect of surrender, since he fears mistreatment at the hand of deserters, but according to the word from Yahweh this fear is an empty one; on the other hand, the alternative now looms before him of being taunted by his own women (compare Volz).

The first verb of the poem, סות hip'il, means "lead astray" (Johanan and his fellow officers accuse Baruch of leading Jrm astray, 43:3). The diction of the first two cola resembles that in 20:10, a passage in one of Jrm's confessions (יכל, "overcome"; אַנְשֵׁי שְׁלֹמֶךָ, here "your fine friends," literally, "men of your peace"), and that of the third colon is clearly an ironic comment on Jrm's experience in the muddy cistern (though the word for "mud" is different, here בֹּץ, in v 6 טִיט). And the phrase סוג nip'al + אָחוֹר is a standard phrase for "withdraw, draw back" from military and psychological pressure. The vision is closed off by a depiction of the king's children as well as his wives being led off to captivity, and the king as well.

■ **38:24–27** The king then admits that their conversation must be kept from the pro-Egyptian courtiers or the prophet will be killed; he devises a cover story Jrm is to use if the courtiers begin to press him on any conversation with the king. They do question him, but the cover story protects him.

■ **39:1–14** See below, after 39:15–18.

■ **39:15–18** It is a touching postscript to the narrative of Ebed-melech's rescue of Jrm (38:7–13) that Jrm should

---

34 See conveniently Norman K. Gottwald, "Poetry, Hebrew," *IDB* 3:834.

35 Wildberger, *Jesaja*, 539–41.

have perceived a word from Yahweh with regard to his rescuer, that even in the midst of the coming catastrophe of the fall of the city, Yahweh will keep Ebed-melech from harm: the servant will escape with his life, because he trusted in Yahweh in circumstances when no citizen of Judah could be found to trust in him. For the idiom here translated "you shall at least have your life" see 21:9.

■ **39:1–10** Verses 1–2, 4–10 are a duplicate or adaptation of 52:4–16 = 2 Kgs 25:1–12.

■ **39:1–2** In the chronology adopted here, the siege began in December 589/January 588, and the city fell in June/July, 587.

■ **39:3** The one verse that does not appear in chapter 52 and 2 Kings 25 is this one, with its exotic Babylonian names and titles (they are reproduced in the gloss in v 13).

The Middle Gate is mentioned only here in the OT, and there is no way to locate it with certainty. One assumes that the Babylonian army entered Jerusalem from the north, where the city is not surrounded by ravines,[36] so that it is altogether likely that the Middle Gate is on the north side of the city (Duhm). Lewis B. Paton, Simons, and Millar Burrows suggest identifying it with the Fish Gate (Zeph 1:10; 2 Chr 33:14) in the north wall (Neh 3:3).[37] The difficulty has been that until recently there was no archeological evidence for the location of the north wall in the monarchical period.[38] Nahman Avigad has now published, however, the discovery of remains of a northern wall from that period, notably of a gate structure located in the present-day Jewish Quarter (הרובע היהודי) 340 meters west-southwest of the highest point of the Temple Mount, 45 meters south of the Street of the Chain (רחוב השלשלת) and 40 meters east of Jewish Quarter Street (Jews Street, רחוב היהודים.) This gate was evidently in the middle of the northern wall at that period. Just outside the gate (that is, to the north) was found evidence of battle—arrowheads, charred wood, ashes, and soot. Avigad proposes the identification of this gate with the Middle Gate in the present verse, and the evidence of battle with the final siege of Jerusalem in 587.[39]

The Babylonian officers sat at the gate to assert and enforce their new authority over the city (see on 1:15).

"Nergalsharezer" is the Akkadian *Nergal-šar-uṣur*, meaning "May [the god] Nergal protect the king." This officer is likely to be identical with the one of that name (also rendered Neriglissar) who ruled Babylon from 560 to 556; according to Berosus he was a son-in-law of Nebuchadrezzar.[40] The Hebrew "Samgar" must be revocalized to Sammagir, equivalent to the Akkadian "Sin-magir." That is the name of a Babylonian city or district; a Babylonian prism lists the names of officials of Nebuchadrezzar, among whom is "Nergal-šar-uṣur, man of Sin-magir."[41] The insertion of שַׂר, "official of," before "Sin-magir" is the suggestion of Rudolph and Bright, given שַׂר־אֶצֶר before רַב־מָג in v 13. "Rab-mag" (Akkadian *rab mugi*) is the designation of a court official of the Babylonian king; *rab* means "chief," but the meaning of the second element is unknown.[42] "Nebushazban" represents the Akkadian *Nabū-šuzibanni*, "May [the god] Nabu save me." The term Rab-saris is, like Rab-mag, a title, the Akkadian *rab-ša-rēši*, "chief who [stands at] the head," that is, chief attendant. Though the Hebrew סָרִים (*sārîs*), "eunuch," is derived from the second part of the Akkadian expression, evidently as a euphemism for "eunuch," Rudolph points out that the expression here should not be translated "chief eunuch": the title in Akkadian was a military or diplomatic one.[43]

36 So Paton, "'Two Walls,'" 3.

37 Ibid.; Jan J. Simons, *Jerusalem in the Old Testament* (Leiden: Brill, 1952) 276; Burrows, "Jerusalem," 853b, and the map, p. 854.

38 For the view that the Fish Gate is located at the present-day Damascus Gate see Paton, "'Two Walls,'" 4, and compare Michael Avi-Yonah, "The Walls of Nehemiah—A Minimalist View," *IEJ* 4 (1954) 242; for the view that the Fish Gate was located at a similar position in a wall located inside the present-day Turkish Wall see Jan J. Simons, *Jerusalem in the Old Testament* (Leiden: Brill, 1952) 443.

39 Nahman Avigad, *Discovering Jerusalem* (Nashville and New York: Nelson, 1983) 50–59.

40 A. Leo Oppenheim, "Nergal-sharezer," *IDB* 3:537; compare "Assyria and Babylonia," *IDB* 1:270b.

41 Istanbul Museum 7834: see conveniently *ANET*, 307b–308a; the phrase appears in column 4, line 22. The prism is published by Eckhard Unger, "Namen im Hofstaate Nebukadnezars II," *TLZ* 50 (1925) columns 481–86.

42 See A. Leo Oppenheim, "Rab-mag," *IDB* 4:3b; *HALAT*, 515.

43 Rudolph, p. 245; so also *HALAT*, 727a.

■ **39:4-10** Although these verses are secondarily inserted here, and commentary is available in studies of 2 Kings, an account of the material is appropriate here.

■ **39:4** If the Babylonian officers sat at a gate on the north side of the city (see on v 3), Zedekiah and his followers slipped out through a gate on the south side. Neh 3:15 locates the "king's garden" adjacent to the Pool of Shelah: these are located near the junction of the Tyropoeon Valley and Kidron Valley.[44] There is evidence for orchards and gardens watered by the Kidron, which must have been a royal estate.[45] There is the mention of a reservoir in that part of Jerusalem "between the two walls" in Isa 22:11. There is no way to locate the spot with precision, but it is to be noted that in 2 Chr 32:5 it is stated that Hezekiah repaired an existing wall, "and outside he built another wall; and he strengthened the Millo in the city of David," a location again in the same part of Jerusalem; these may then be the two walls referred to.[46] Burrows suggests that the gate here mentioned was Nehemiah's Dung Gate (Neh 2:13; 3:13–14; 12:31).[47] The road taken by Zedekiah and his followers to the plains of Jericho doubtless was that called the "ascent of Adummim" (Josh 15:7; 18:17), the present-day *ṭal'at ad-damm*, Atlas of Israel grid 184–135.[48] For "Arabah" see 2:6. One assumes that Zedekiah was doubtless trying to cross the Jordan, perhaps to gain the protection of the Ammonite king (compare 40:14; 41:15).[49]

■ **39:5** The "plains of Jericho" (עַרְבוֹת יְרֵחוֹ) is a set phrase: the first word is the plural of "Arabah," and refers to the semi-desert plains south of Jericho beyond the reach of irrigation.[50] Zedekiah, his family, and his retainers were captured here (compare v 6) and taken north to Nebuchadrezzar's headquarters at Riblah in north Syria. Riblah is the modern *rabla*, situated on the Orontes

River south of Lake Homs: it is on the present-day highway from Baalbek to Homs, eighteen kilometers northeast of the present Lebanon-Syria border. Riblah had been the Pharaoh's headquarters in 609 (2 Kgs 23:33).[51] Hamath is the modern Syrian city of Hama (Arabic *ḥamāt*); it was the center of a kingdom in the Assyrian period,[52] hence the phrasing here. For the expression "pass judgment upon him," literally, "speak judgments with him," see 1:16. "Pass judgment" implies "pronounce sentence" as well; the sentence was cruel (vv 6–7).

■ **39:6-7** The verb שׁחט, "slaughter," mostly occurs with animals as object: the princes and other nobles were summarily executed. The chiasmus and repetition of v 6 is curious. The sentence is centered on Zedekiah's eyes—his sons and his nobility were slaughtered "before his eyes," and then his eyes were blinded; the narrative may well have in mind the prediction addressed to Zedekiah recorded in 34:3, "Your eyes will see the eyes of the king of Babylon, and his mouth will speak with your mouth." The word "shackles" is the dual of "bronze," as in English one might say "double irons"; the dual doubtless refers to shackles on both hands and feet: an Assyrian bas-relief reproduced in *ANEP*, no. 10, clearly shows Egyptian prisoners in such double shackles.[53]

■ **39:8-10** According to 2 Kgs 25:8 it was a month after the city fell that Nebuzaradan gave the orders to burn the palace (and the temple!) and private houses and to demolish the walls of the city. "Nebuzaradan" represents the Akkadian *Nabū-zēr-iddin*, "[The god] Nabū has given offspring." His title is given as רַב־טַבָּחִים, which means, literally, "chief of the butchers (or cooks)." It is striking that an officer with this name is listed among Nebucha-drezzar's officers on the same prism referred to in the

44   See conveniently the discussions in Georges A. Barrois, "Shelah, Pool of," *IDB* 4:319–20; Burrows, "Jerusalem," 855a; Myers, *Ezra, Nehemiah*, 114.

45   Georges A. Barrois, "Kidron, brook," *IDB* 3:10b.

46   As a suggestion, Burrows, "Jerusalem," 853b; with more conviction, Wildberger, *Jesaja*, 824.

47   Burrows, "Jerusalem," 853b.

48   Victor R. Gold, "Adummim," *IDB* 1:51; Martin Noth, *The Old Testament World* (Philadelphia: Fortress, 1966) 90; Baly, *Geography*, 185–86, Soggin, *Joshua*, 173.

49   Compare Yohanan Aharoni, *The Land of the Bible, A*

Historical Geography (Philadelphia: Westminster, 1967) 353.

50   Gray, *Kings*, 765.

51   See Alfred O. Haldar, "Riblah," *IDB* 4:78.

52   Alfred O. Haldar, "Hamath," *IDB* 4:516.

53   The detail is shown more clearly, and in color, in Yadin, *Warfare*, 462.

discussion of Nergalsharezer (v 3), and there this Nabū-zēr-iddin is given the same title in Akkadian, *rab nuḥtim-mu*, "chief cook."[54] It is likely that this reference is to the same officer, and one must understand that the title is archaic and that in this period it is the designation of a high Babylonian officer; "provost marshal"[55] corresponds well enough to Nebuzaradan's responsibility. He exiles the leading citizens to Babylon (one sees them later in Ramah, manacled and awaiting orders to move out, 40:1). Included among the exiles are artisans (if the text, emended from 52:15, is correct). Eleven years before, after the first fall of Jerusalem, Nebuchadrezzar had exiled many artisans (2 Kgs 24:14, where different terms are used); now, evidently, more are rounded up. At the same time he redistributes some land for the peasants, doubtless both as an economic necessity and as a measure of pacification. But Calvin, at least, offers no sentimentalizing of the proletariat: he describes the envy of the landowners who are being led away, "for they saw that needy and worthless men dwelt in that land from which they had been banished" (compare the remarks on "the needy," 5:28aβb).

■ **39:11–12** According to the narrative, Nebuchadrezzar had given orders to Nebuzaradan to protect Jrm. One might think that the Babylonian king would hardly bother himself with a prophet in Judah: Bright remarks, "We may suppose that this was actually a general order that all friends of Babylon were to be treated well, and that Nebuzaradan, having on his arrival made inquiry as to who these were, found Jeremiah's name high on the list."[56] Perhaps; but Calvin nicely cites a parallel, the concern evinced by the Roman general Marcellus for the mathematician Archimedes in the siege of Syracuse in 212 B.C.E. (a concern which in that instance was unavailing). One must remember that the population of Jerusalem was not high at that period—perhaps twenty thousand in Josiah's time.[57] Those who had deserted to the Babylonians before the city fell (38:19) would have been pressed by the authorities for intelligence;[58] Jrm

must have been known to the deserters as one who appeared to be pro-Babylonian (38:4).

■ **39:13–14** According to these verses, Nebuzaradan releases Jrm from the court of the guard and entrusts him to Gedaliah, who would be appointed governor (40:5). The verses appear to contradict 40:1, which states that Nebuzaradan finds Jrm among a group of manacled refugees at Ramah. Commentators have thought that vv 13–14 and 40:1 are part of alternative accounts (Bright, Thompson), but they go on to suggest another possibility, that Jrm was released into the general population (v 14), was rearrested by some zealous Babylonian official, and then was found again by Nebuzaradan at Ramah:[59] one may note the contrast between "gave him to Gedaliah" in v 14 and "return to Gedaliah" in 40:5.

This is the first mention of the governor Gedaliah (who of course is a different figure than the Gedaliah mentioned in 38:1). The grandfather of the governor, Shaphan, had been secretary and financial officer to Josiah in the incident of the finding of the Deuteronomic scroll in the temple in 622 (2 Kgs 22:1–10), and his father, Ahikam, joined Shaphan in the delegation to Huldah to verify that scroll. Later, in 609, after Jrm's trial in connection with the temple sermon, his father, Ahikam, helped shelter Jrm from being executed (26:24). Gedaliah was then a member of a family that had long been a part of the court. A bulla (clay stamp-seal impression) was discovered at Lachish which reads *lgdlyhw (')šr 'l hbyt*, "(Belonging) to Gedaliah, who is over the house":[60] the title of the owner then corresponds to "major domo" (compare 1 Kgs 4:4 and elsewhere); it is altogether possible that the seal belonged to the governor Gedaliah. One assumes that his outlook was moderate,[61] but obviously there is no way to know why he had not fled with Zedekiah or how he felt at being chosen by the Babylonians to be governor (40:5).

■ **39:15–18** See above, after 38:27.

■ **40:1** Ramah in Benjamin (modern *ar-rām*) is located nine kilometers north of Jerusalem (Atlas of Israel grid

54 Compare n. 41. For the reference see *ANET*, 307b; in the prism it is found in column 3, line 36.

55 This is the rendering in Montgomery, *Kings*, 562.

56 Bright, p. 245.

57 See 9:11–15, n. 11.

58 Thompson, p. 648, and n. 2 there.

59 Bright, pp. 245–46.

60 Roland de Vaux, "Le sceau de Godolias, maître du Palais," *RB* 45 (1936) 96–102.

61 Montgomery, *Kings*, 565; Gray, *Kings*, 771.

172–140).[62] It was evidently a staging area for those to be exiled to Babylon; so much of Jerusalem had been burned that the capital of the province would be located at Mizpah (compare v 6). The exiles are manacled (compare v 4, "which are on your hands"). Jrm is caught up in this group and needs to be released (compare 39:11–14).

■ **40:2b$\beta\gamma$–3** If the text is correctly rearranged, these verses give the content of a divine word that came to Jrm (v 1), a word addressed to the exiles. The emphasis is on the identity of the one responsible for the disaster that has overtaken them: it is Yahweh.

■ **40:2ab$a$, 4–5** Nebuzaradan frees Jrm and gives him a choice of where to go; he may either go to Babylon with the guarantee of good treatment or stay in Judah under the protection of Gedaliah. (Verse 4b, that seems to offer a third option, simply to go free, is evidently secondary.) Nebuzaradan gives Jrm rations and sends him off.

■ **40:6** Jrm chooses to put himself under the protection of Gedaliah at Mizpah.

"Mizpah" (מִצְפָּה) means "observation point, watchtower"; there are several sites with that name, but the one in the present narrative is the Mizpah in Benjamin. In the present passage (40:6—41:16) it always occurs with the definite article, thus "the watchtower."

The location of this Mizpah is not settled. Traditionally the name has been attached to Nebi Samwil (*an-nabi ṣamwīl*), eight kilometers northwest of Jerusalem (Atlas of Israel grid 167–137).[63] But as a consequence of the excavations of Tell en-Naṣbeh beginning in 1926–27, a strong argument has been offered in favor of the identification of that site with Mizpah, and most current handbooks assume that the identification is secure.[64] That site (*tall an-naṣba*) lies twelve kilometers north of Jerusalem (Atlas of Israel grid 170–143). But Nabi Samwil is on a high point (elevation 895 meters) above the surrounding plain—it is 151 meters above Jerusalem (measured at the present-day Dome of the Rock) and so gives an unblocked view in every direction, something that Tell en-Naṣbeh does not afford; and an unblocked view would seem a necessity for a "watchtower."[65]

One datum that strengthens the proposal of Tell en-Naṣbeh is the discovery on that site of a seal with the inscription "(belonging) to Jaazaniah servant of the king," with letter forms of the seventh century:[66] there is a "Jaazaniah" mentioned in connection with Gedaliah at Mizpah (2 Kgs 25:23 = "Jezaniah" in Jer 40:8). Attempts have been made to establish a linguistic identity between the Hebrew *miṣpâ* and the Arabic *naṣbā*,[67] but even though this equivalence has been accepted by some,[68] it remains less than convincing. Unfortunately, Nebi Samwil has not yet been excavated, so the question at the present time is still open; the arguments for and against the two sites are judiciously presented by Muilenburg.[69]

I would propose, however, that the movements of the military forces recorded in chapter 41 make plausible Nebi Samwil as the site of Mizpah and make Tell en-Naṣbeh altogether implausible, and since one's understanding of that chapter depends on an understanding of those movements, it is appropriate to discuss the matter here.

The day after Ishmael assassinated Gedaliah he went

---

62 William H. Morton, "Ramah," *IDB* 4:8.
63 See for example Cornill.
64 See for example Denis Baly and A. Douglas Tushingham, *Atlas of the Biblical World* (New York: World Publishing, 1971), 190b; Herbert G. May, ed., *Oxford Bible Atlas* (London/New York: Oxford University, 1974) 95, 135b. Commentaries are more cautious; both Bright and Thompson call the identification with Tell en-Naṣbeh "probable."
65 So the report of Prescott H. Williams, Jr., in "Archaeological Newsletter" of the American Schools of Oriental Research, Jerusalem and Baghdad, #4, March 1, 1965, p. 5, and so the opinion of Bruce T. Dahlberg (by personal correspondence).
66 For illustrations see *IDB* 2:777, and *ANEP*, 85, figure 277. The seal is published in Chester C. McCown, "Inscribed Material Including Coins," *Tell en-Naṣbeh*

(ed. Chester C. McCown; Berkeley: Pacific School of Religion; New Haven: American Schools of Oriental Research, 1947) 1:163.
67 James Muilenburg, "The Literary Sources Bearing on the Question of Identification," *Tell en-Naṣbeh* (ed. McCown) 1:43–44.
68 Aharoni, *Land of the Bible*, 111.
69 James Muilenburg, "Mizpah," *IDB* 3:407–8, and in more detail "Survey of the Literature on Tell en-Naṣbeh" and "The Literary Sources Bearing on the Question of Identification" *Tell en-Naṣbeh* (ed. McCown) 1:13–44.

out to meet the eighty pilgrims from the north (41:5–6). It follows that Ishmael or his guards could see the approach of the pilgrims from a distance: it was autumn, before the rainy season, and such a procession would have raised a great cloud of dust, especially if, as is altogether likely, it included pack animals. From Nebi Samwil the view is clear to the north for several kilometers, but the view to the north from Tell en-Naṣbeh is blocked by the Ramallah-Bira ridge.[70] After Ishmael slaughtered the pilgrims, he took (as hostages, or as knowledgeable witnesses) the people from Mizpah who had been entrusted to Gedaliah and set out to cross the Jordan to reach the Ammonites (41:10). He was overtaken at Gibeon by Johanan, who wanted to avenge Ishmael's crimes, especially the assassination of Gedaliah (41:11–12). Now the road out of Gibeon toward which he was going was undoubtedly that from Bethel to Ai to Michmash, then, following the ridge north of the Wadi Qilt, to Jericho.[71] If Ishmael indeed wished to move across the Jordan to the Ammonites, and if Mizpah were Tell en-Naṣbeh, then it makes no sense to go to Gibeon. (The map on page 178 of Baly, *Geography*, where Mizpah is located at Tell en-Naṣbeh, makes the matter clear.) Similarly after Johanan collected the hostages at Gibeon, he "brought them back from Gibeon" (41:16), presumably to Mizpah. His aim at this point was to get clear of the Babylonians, who he feared would take vengeance on one and all for the assassination of Gedaliah (compare 40:15); he therefore moved quickly to the area of Bethlehem, intending to take his group to Egypt (41:17–18). Tell en-Naṣbeh is north of Gibeon: Johanan would hardly want to take the hostages north and then quickly head south again. These considerations, it seems to me, effectively rule out Tell en-Naṣbeh as the site of Mizpah. (Rudolph alludes to the same problem.)[72]

A contributing consideration is a simple one: Nebi Samwil is visible from every part of Jerusalem, it is the defensible strong point accessible to Jerusalem, and it would therefore commend itself as a replacement for Jerusalem as the capital of the Babylonian province.

■ **40:7–8** The "officers of the army units who were in the open country" are commanders of forces outside Jerusalem who had been scattered during the siege (compare 52:8b): in the terrain of Judah there are plenty of places to hide (Bright, Thompson). After it becomes known that Gedaliah had been appointed governor and put in charge of that portion of the population that is not to be deported, these military officers and their men gather around Gedaliah, whom they undoubtedly know personally (see the remarks on Gedaliah in the discussion of 39:13–14, and compare vv 13–14 below), to assess the situation. Johanan becomes the leader and spokesman for the group (40:13–16; 41:11; 42:8; 43:4–5). Ishmael is specified in 41:1 as being a member of the royal family. The remainder of the officers named here are not mentioned again in the narrative; indeed "the sons of Ephai" may be textually erroneous (see Text). Netophah is a site near Bethlehem, probably ḥirbat badd fālūḥ, five kilometers southeast of Bethlehem (Atlas of Israel grid 172–121).[73] For a possible connection of Jezaniah (= Jaazaniah, 2 Kgs 25:23) with the Jaazaniah seal see above on v 6. The term "Maacathite" refers to someone from Maacah, an Aramean kingdom immediately southwest of Mount Hermon, west of Bashan.[74]

■ **40:9–10** Gedaliah swears an oath: he will "stand before the Chaldeans," that is, as the servant of the Babylonians and their deputy; on the other hand, he will represent the Jewish population to the Babylonian authorities and will guarantee the safety of the Jewish military men who have come before him: he presses them to demobilize and get the harvest in and in general to settle in the cities at their disposal. Of course he is caught and has little freedom; nevertheless his oath implies a covenant under Yahweh with his hearers[75] and, as Calvin points out, makes all the more execrable Ishmael's later assassination of him.

■ **40:11–12** This word goes out to Jews who had sought sanctuary across the Jordan that not everyone is to be

---

70 Bruce T. Dahlberg, in the Newsletter of the American Schools of Oriental Research, 1964–65, #4, p. 5.

71 Smith, *Historical Geography*, 180, and in less detail, Aharoni, *Land of the Bible*, 56, and Baly, *Geography*, 99. For the location of the Wadi Qilt see the map in Baly, *Geography*, 178.

72 Rudolph, p. 253.

73 See conveniently William H. Morton, "Netophah,"

IDB 3:541, and in detail Konrad Kob, "Noch einmal Netopha," *ZDPV* 94 (1978) 119–34.

74 Benjamin Mazar, "Geshur and Maacah," *JBL* 80 (1961), 16–28; Baly, *Geography*, 213–15.

75 For the oath see Pedersen, III/IV, 449–50.

exiled to Babylon and that someone in whom they can have confidence has been named governor, so they begin to return to the land and to reap the harvest as well.

■ **40:13–16** Johanan and other military officers come again to Gedaliah with word of a plot: Ishmael, one of the officers who had been a witness to Gedaliah's oath, is planning, with the sponsorship of the Ammonite king, to assassinate Gedaliah—but Gedaliah does not believe the report. Johanan then has a private conversation with Gedaliah and offers to kill Ishmael, convinced that if Ishmael succeeds it would mean chaos for the country; Gedaliah for his part, still convinced the report is untrue, urges him not to.

Whether Ishmael was determined to carry on a resistance movement or had simply planned revenge on a "traitor" is impossible to say. Was the fact that he was a member of the royal family a factor in his decision?—was he jealous because a non-Davidite was in authority and he was not?—it is to be noted that the king's daughters were among those entrusted to Gedaliah (41:10). In any event the ideology of the Davidic monarchy must have been an insistent one for many.

The Ammonite king's name is given as "Baalis" (בַּעֲלִים, v 14), a curious spelling. The name is clarified by a bulla (stamp-seal impression) discovered in 1984 at Tell el-'Umeiri, thirteen kilometers southwest of Amman (thus in Ammonite territory); the inscription on the bulla reads *lmlkm'wr 'bd b'lyš'*, "(Belonging) to Milcom'ûr servant of Ba'alyiš'a" (though the vocalization of the names cannot be altogether certain). The script suggests a dating around 600 B.C.E. The bulla offers the first Ammonite proper name compounded with "Milcom," the principal Ammonite deity (compare 49:1) and, what is relevant here, give us the Ammonite spelling of the king in question. The Hebrew consonantal text could be vocalized *ba'lyis*, and this may be how the Jewish ear heard the Ammonite pronunciation of the king's name.[76]

■ **41:1–3** The assassination of Gedaliah occurred in the "seventh month," but the year is not given; the most natural conclusion is that it is the same year as the fall of Jerusalem, therefore September/October 587 (so Volz, Condamin, Rudolph). Some commentators are not so sure, pointing out that the narrative of 40:7–16 describes many events, such as the return of Jews from abroad; it might then be a subsequent year (Bright, Thompson). Hyatt proposes that the third deportation by the Babylonians, in 582 (52:30), was a response to the assassination of Gedaliah; by this proposal Gedaliah would have served as governor for about five years.[77] But I assume that the "seventh month" is in the same year; the seventh month is the month for the feast of booths, doubtless the goal of the pilgrims from the north (v 5). According to the chronology of the present study, the feast of booths in 587 was the occasion for a reading of the law of Deuteronomy (see Introduction, sec. 36, and compare the Setting for 31:31–34), all the more reason for pilgrims to come to Jerusalem from the north.

Ishmael was a member of the royal family (literally "from royal offspring"): his father and grandfather are not further identified, but this is not surprising if one assumes that the kings were polygamous.

Ishmael came with ten soldiers, and they were received by Gedaliah at a meal. If Gedaliah's oath implies a covenant (see above on 40:9–10), a shared meal does as well: a host is bound to entertain and protect his guest (compare Gen 19:1–3; Judg 19:15), and by the same token the guest is under the benevolent protection of his host.[78] Further, they are not strangers to each other (40:8); they had doubtless known each other for years. They are roughly peers in social status, Gedaliah the governor, Ishmael the officer of royal lineage: "together" suggests parity. Ishmael's assassination of Gedaliah is therefore the basest treachery, and thereafter the Jews observed an annual fast to recall the event (Zech 7:5; 8:19)[79]—it was observed on the third day of Tishri.[80] (For a discussion of the possible motive that led Ishmael to his act see above on 40:13–16.) And it is not only

76 Larry G. Herr, "The Servant of Baalis," *BA* 48 (1985) 169–72.

77 Hyatt, p. 1084.

78 Vernon H. Kooy, "Hospitality," *IDB* 2:654.

79 Petersen, *Haggai and Zechariah 1–8*, 285.

80 Jacob Milgrom, "Fasting and Fast Days, in the Bible," *EncJud* 6:1191a.

Gedaliah whom Ishmael and his entourage kill but also Gedaliah's Jewish retainers and the Babylonians who happen to be there; no one escapes (compare v 4). One has the impression that Ishmael and his soldiers thus made a clean sweep of whatever stronghold there was at Mizpah ("no one knew of it," v 4): is a stronghold suggested by the expression "middle of the city" (תּוֹךְ־הָעִיר, v 7)? But there were still folk in the locality dependent on the protection of those in charge (v 10).

■ 41:4–9 Ishmael or his guards must have seen from a distance the dust cloud of the approach of the pilgrims from the north (see the discussion on the location of Mizpah, 40:6).

The pilgrims are evidently on their way to Jerusalem for the feast of booths; it is the seventh month (v 1). They are doubtless those loyal to Josiah's program of cultic reunion between north and south (see Introduction, sec. 36, and 30:1—31:40, Preliminary Observations, Structure, Setting). If the chronology proposed in the present study is correct, this is a year when the law of Deuteronomy would be recited once more: all the more reason for pilgrims to make their journey.

The pilgrims come, literally, "shaved of beard and torn of clothes . . ."; both participles are passive (pu'al and qal passive, respectively), and both are rightly translated by G and V with perfect passive participles—thus the translation of the RSV, "with their beards shaved and their clothes torn" (and so similarly other recent translations). But the third participle, וּמִתְגֹּדְדִים, is a hitpa'el participle that calls for the translation "and gashing themselves": both G and V offer present participles here. The scene is a lurid one. Their conduct is appropriate for mourning (48:37): these customs, though forbidden by the law (Lev 19:27; 21:5; Deut 14:1), must have been common nevertheless.[81] Here the mourning is for the fall of Jerusalem, more specifically for the destruction of the temple.

The pilgrims come prepared to sacrifice at the temple site. One may ask whether they are prepared to offer animal sacrifice at the temple or simply nonanimal sacrifice: the text says, "מִנְחָה and incense were in their hand." There are three other occurrences of מִנְחָה in Jer, two of which are late (17:26; 33:18); in the remaining one, 14:12, the word surely implies nonanimal sacrifice (see there). Related is the question whether animal sacrifice was still possible at the temple; Martin Noth assumes it was not,[82] but Rudolph leaves the question open.[83]

Ishmael's conduct, the text implies, is utterly insincere; one assumes, then, that it is a ruse that he has prepared. Seeing the procession from a distance, does he jump to the conclusion that the word about the assassination of Gedaliah has got out and that this is a military force coming to retaliate? As he approaches the procession he must surmise that these are northerners. His weeping simulates the pilgrims' mourning, and he welcomes them in the name of Gedaliah. One assumes that they would have turned aside in any event to pay their respects to the governor and to learn the present situation in Jerusalem; but now Ishmael takes the initiative in escorting them into Mizpah. When it is clear that he intends to kill them all, ten are able to avoid their fate by bribery (v 8), but the other seventy are slaughtered and their corpses thrown into a cistern.

What is Ishmael's motive in this mass murder? Weiser raises the question and suggests that Ishmael is enraged that northerners would participate in Jerusalem cultic celebrations, gestures acceptable to folk like Jrm and (presumably) Gedaliah.[84] But it may simply be that Ishmael does not like northerners. Or robbery may play a part. Or it may be that Ishmael is simply embarked upon an orgy of violence: Calvin remarks, "Thus wicked men become hardened; for even if they dread at first to murder innocent men, when once they begin the work, they rush on to the commission of numberless murders." The ten who buy their lives have goods "in the field" (v 8), but it is unclear what the phrase means. Have they brought the goods along for trading purposes on their

---

81 See the discussion in Mayes, *Deuteronomy*, 238–39.

82 Martin Noth, "The Jerusalem Catastrophe of 587 B.C., and Its Significance for Israel," *The Laws in the Pentateuch and Other Studies* (Philadelphia: Fortress, 1966) 264.

83 Rudolph, p. 253.

84 Weiser, pp. 356–57; so also Masao Sekine, "Davidsbund und Sinaibund bei Jeremia," *VT* 9

(1959) 56–57.

pilgrimage, loaded on pack animals, left at the roadside in the care of servants; or are these goods that are stored at home in the north, so that their families would have to provide them as ransom (Bright's suggestion)?

The cistern at Mizpah into which the corpses of the seventy pilgrims were thrown is identified as one that King Asa of Judah had dug when he was preparing defenses against King Baasha of Israel (compare 1 Kgs 15:16–22, esp. v 22 there).

■ **41:10** The Babylonians had entrusted not only Jrm to the protection of Gedaliah (40:5–6) but others as well, described in v 16 as "warriors and women and children and eunuchs." Here in the present verse the "daughters of the king" are mentioned as part of the group (so also in 43:6). One thinks of the fate of the "sons of the king" (39:6 = 52:10; 2 Kgs 25:7); it is surprising, given Jrm's vision of the captivity of the wives of the king (38:22–23), that royal daughters were left behind, but of course there is no information on the circumstance of Zedekiah's retreat from Jerusalem. It is equally surprising, one might add, that the Babylonians did not take these daughters captive but saw to their safety in Judah. (Are the eunuchs mentioned in v 16 present to protect the princesses?—this is Rudolph's suggestion.[85]) Ishmael takes the whole group captive, whether as hostages or as dangerous witnesses to the bloodbath he has just undertaken is impossible to say; and he starts off with them toward the Ammonites (for the route he intended to take see the discussion on 40:6).

■ **41:11–16** Johanan now moves in to try to do what he had proposed doing while Gedaliah was still alive (40:15), to kill Ishmael. He and his troops catch up with Ishmael's party at Gibeon (for which see 28:1) by the great pool there: the pool has been excavated in our day, by James Pritchard.[86] It is the place where the forces of David and Ishbaal had encountered each other centuries earlier (2 Sam 2:12–17); doubtless Ishmael's party had encamped there.

The people whom Ishmael had taken captive rejoice at their rescue by Johanan's forces. But Ishmael escapes to the Ammonites, along with eight of his men. Since there were ten men with him on the day he assassinated Gedaliah (v 1), he has lost two along the way. Johanan "brings back" from Gibeon Ishmael's captives, this time described as "warriors, women, children and eunuchs": it is presumably to Mizpah that they are brought back (see once more the analysis of their route in the discussion of 40:6). For the suggestion that the eunuchs may have had responsibility to protect the princesses, see above on v 10.

■ **41:17–18** They move out quickly toward Egypt, fearing the reprisals of the Babylonians, and stop at Geruth Chimham near Bethlehem. The precise location of this stopping place is not known. The word "geruth" (גֵּרוּת) is a place where גֵּרִים, resident aliens, may stay (for the word גֵּר see 7:6); it is then probably a caravansary or khan, but the word appears only in this single place-name here. There is a Chimham mentioned in 2 Sam 19:37–40; that narrative hints that he is a son of Barzillai (v 38 there). The sons of Barzillai were later granted a royal pension (1 Kgs 2:7), and it has been supposed that Chimham was given a grant of land near Bethlehem where the khan was built,[87] but the data are insufficient for certainty.

■ **42:1–6** The name "Jezaniah," the son of Hoshaiah in v 1, is corrected to "Azariah" on the basis of *G* and of the name given in 43:2, presumably of the same man; there is a Jezaniah mentioned in 40:8, but he is identified there as "son of the Maacathite."

Johanan and his fellow officers come to ask Jrm to pray to Yahweh for guidance, "the way we should go and what we should do." But behind the narrative of the simple request lie many innuendoes that are not easy to sort out. Thus Volz points out the shift of possessive references to God in the interchange: the group asks Jrm to pray to "Yahweh your [second-person singular] God" (vv 2–3); Jrm in his turn assures the group that he will pray to "Yahweh your [second-person plural] God" (v 4); the group then agrees to obey the voice of "Yahweh our God" (v 6). These shifts are not accidental; each side is making points. The group says in effect to Jrm, "Deal with Yahweh: that is your specialty." Jrm says to the group, "I shall deal with Yahweh, but it is you who are obligated by the transaction." The group senses that Jrm has made his point, so it says, in effect, "We accept our obligation." (It is to be noted that Isaiah in speaking to

---

85   Rudolph, p. 252.
86   See conveniently James Pritchard, "Gibeon," *IDB* 2:392–93, with illustration; and in more detail *Gibeon, Where the Sun Stood Still* (Princeton: Princeton University, 1962) 64–70.
87   Edward R. Dalglish, "Chimham," *IDB* 1:561.

Ahaz uses "your God" and "my God" in the same sort of way, Isa 7:10, 13;[88] and see further Exod 32:7, 11.) Furthermore, as Thompson points out, the folk who speak to Jrm go out of their way (vv 5–6) to emphasize how they will follow the word of Yahweh: Yahweh is not only a "witness" to their promise but a "true and faithful witness"; they say they will do the will of Yahweh, and they say twice that they will obey the voice of Yahweh, and they add, "whether (it is) good or bad." This is rhetorical overkill! One wonders, Are those who speak this way among the folk who will later admit to worshiping other gods, especially the queen of heaven (44:17)?

But Johanan and his fellow officers have already decided to go to Egypt (41:17), and so (by the hint in the [corrected] text of 43:5) have those Jews who rallied around Gedaliah; why then would they suddenly come to consult Jrm? And when, after a ten-day wait, the word does come from Yahweh and it is negative, they reject it as a scheme of Baruch's to have them killed or sent into exile (43:1–3): the narrator calls them "obstinate men" (43:2). (One is reminded of the king of Israel who was persuaded to consult Micaiah ben Imlah but hated him because his word was always negative: 1 Kgs 22:8, 18.) Calvin accuses them of being dissembling, stupid, or hypocritical. This they may be, but the tone they offer suggests desperation—"we are left but a few out of many."

One clue may be that it is not only the officers and those who voluntarily rallied around Gedaliah but also "all the people from small to great," who are involved in the interchange with Jrm: one wonders, does the use of this phrase suggest that those folk whom Nebuzaradan had put in the care of Gedaliah are beginning to murmur? Those princesses, for example (41:10; 43:5)—are they suddenly uneasy about being moved out of Judah?! There could well be dissension among those who are not part of the military forces.

Jrm for his part is well aware that Johanan and his fellow officers have determined on their course (see the analysis below of the rhetoric of vv 8–17). Furthermore, as Rudolph points out, Jrm has been convinced for years that Yahweh's will is to be found in surrendering to the will of Nebuchadrezzar (27:6; compare 43:8–13). Given

that both Johanan and his group on the one hand and Jrm on the other have predetermined convictions, why does Jrm not simply repeat his perception of Yahweh's word? One must assume that he is aware of whatever dissension there is within the group, and in any event he has been asked specifically to pray to Yahweh for the welfare of the group. So he agrees to seek the word of Yahweh and to report it to them.

■ **42:7** And he waits ten days for Yahweh's word! This is remarkable, given the emotions within the group; the question must have been posed to him more than once during those ten days that had once been posed by Zedekiah to Jrm, "Is there a word from Yahweh?" (37:17). The length of time offers just a hint of the process by which a prophet seeks the will of Yahweh (compare 28:11–12).[89]

■ **42:8–17** If the officers and "all the people from small to great" who have inquired for the word of Yahweh have emphasized by repetition that they will obey that word (vv 5–6), the word of Yahweh that Jrm mediates likewise offers emphasis by repetition (see Form and Structure on this section). Furthermore, the phrasing of that word acknowledges that the folk in the group have already made their decision as to what they wish to do. Thus both the positive and negative alternatives are expressed by a protasis ("if"-clause) and an apodosis ("then"-clause); the protasis of the positive alternative (v 10aα) is correlative with two parallel protases in the negative alternative (vv 13–14, 15b).

The protasis in v 13, with a participial phrase, must be understood to mean, "But if you keep saying" (see on 2:26–27): the rendering of current translations, "But if you say," would reflect וְאִם־תֹּאמְרוּ (compare Exod 21:5; Prov 1:11). The protasis in v 15 is synonymous: "If you do set your faces to Egypt" is the equivalent of "If you are determined to go to Egypt" (so *JB*, *NAB*; Bright: "If you have really made up your minds to go to Egypt"). Both protases thus reflect the decision that has already been made.

The protasis in v 10, by contrast, implies a change of

---

88   Wildberger, *Jesaja*, 288; William L. Holladay, *Isaiah, Scroll of a Prophetic Heritage* (Grand Rapids: Eerdmans, 1978) 69.

89   Skinner, pp. 336–37.

mind, and that is why I believe that the text of *M* is preferable to that of the Versions (see Text): the curious forms offered in the first colon of 8:13 (and its antecedent Zeph 1:2) and the second colon of 48:9 suggest that it is possible to have an infinitive absolute of one verb and a finite form of a second verb related by word-play (see the discussion of 8:13). If *M* is correct here, then, v 10 will mean something like "If you change your mind and stay in this land. . . ." That conclusion is reinforced by the close resemblance of v 10 to 18:7–8. Though the group "is left but a few out of many" (v 2), nevertheless if they reverse their plans, Yahweh will treat them like one of the nations in the scheme presented in 18:1–12: if a nation that he has uprooted and demolished makes a decision and "turns" from its evil, Yahweh will suddenly build them up and plant them, and he will retract the disaster which he has done (שׁוּב in the present passage corresponds to וְשָׁב in 18:8). Thus the verbal expression in v 10b, כִּי נִחַמְתִּי אֶל־, cannot mean "for I repent of" (*RSV*), "for I regret" (*JB, NJV*), or "for I am sorry for"; as in 18:7–8 the change on Yahweh's part is dependent on the change on the part of the people. In the present instance Yahweh cannot call back the fall of Jerusalem, but he can shift the fortunes of the people from evil to good.

The clauses of vv 11–12 continue to imply the protasis of v 10: if they change their mind and stay in Judah, then they need not fear Nebuchadrezzar, as they have feared him (41:18): Yahweh, who has set him over the whole world (27:6), controls the king's hand and exercises his mercy through the king. But if they persist in going to Egypt, then they will need to fear Nebuchadrezzar (v 16).

The double protasis of the negative alternative is baroque in its length, extending from v 13 through v 15; the second, parallel protasis (v 15) is preceded by a fresh messenger formula (for all this see Form). For "if you keep saying" (v 13) see above. The hypothetical quotation in vv 13–14 begins and ends with the verb נֵשֵׁב "we will stay": "We will not stay in this land," "There (in the land of Egypt) we will stay." The great fears are war and famine; if they persist in their decision to go to Egypt, it will be because they are convinced that once in Egypt they will be away from both.

The apodosis of the negative alternative finally comes in vv 16–17, and it cites both fears with slightly different wording: if they choose to go to Egypt, war and famine will overtake them there.

■ **42:19–21, 18, 22** For these verses see below, after 43:1–3.

■ **43:1–3** For these verses in this sequence see Text, Preliminary Observations.

For a discussion of what may have lain behind the "obstinate" reaction of the people, see above on 42:1–6. The mind of the group is already made up, and they reject the word that Jrm shares with them. But they dare not admit it is a word from Yahweh; to them it is a "lie." To a degree they misquote the word of Yahweh, making the protasis of the negative alternative into a permanent prohibition (with לֹא and the imperfect): "Yahweh did not send you to us to say, 'You shall not go into Egypt'" (v 2). Indeed they are right, Yahweh has not permanently prohibited them from going into Egypt. (For another example of distortion by the omission of a protasis see 26:9.) But they do not accuse Jrm of lying to them; instead, it is Baruch whom they accuse of having put the words in Jrm's mouth in order to entrap them into suffering Babylonian reprisals. Baruch is portrayed in chapters 32 and 36 simply as a scribe doing the bidding of Jrm; only in chapter 45 is there a glimpse of the scribe's own reactions. The accusation of Jrm's opponents here offers at least a hint that Baruch has an independent point of view. If Baruch is the narrator of chapters 37—44, as is commonly believed, then the attempt to blame him for the word delivered by Jrm must have offered him sardonic amusement.

■ **42:19–21, 18, 22** For this order of verses see Text, Preliminary Observations.

If the reconstruction of the text offered here is correct, Jrm contradicts the word of his opponents: the word he has delivered is indeed a word from Yahweh, and they do indeed know that Jrm has warned them today. And if his opponents have paraphrased the word, Jrm paraphrases it somewhat in their fashion but softens it to the immediate prohibition (with אַל־ and the imperfect): "Do not go to Egypt."

"Remnant of Judah" is construed by all recent translations as a vocative spoken by Jrm, but what is "Do not go to Egypt"? Is it to be understood as cited by Jrm as Yahweh's word or as Jrm's own word? The commentators are unanimous in taking the words as a citation of Yahweh's word (Duhm, Cornill, Giesebrecht, Volz,

Condamin, Rudolph; Bright with a paraphrase), and so have several recent translations (*RSV*, *JB*, and *NEB*); but *NAB* and *NJV* assume it to be Jrm's word. Obviously either is possible, but I opt for the second alternative, since form-critically vv 19–21 are all words of Jrm. This interpretation is particularly appropriate if the words "that I have warned you today" are original (see Text).

The first verb phrase in v 20, הִתְעֵיתֶם בְּנַפְשׁוֹתֵיכֶם, has caused difficulty. The verb (reading the qere'), תעה hip'il, normally means "mislead, lead (someone) astray"; the difficulty is that there is no object, or else the object must (oddly) be found in the object of בְּ. *G* translates ἐπονηρεύσασθε ἐν ψυχαῖς ὑμῶν, "You have done wrong in your souls," thus reading the verb as הֲרֵעֹתֶם, and Duhm, Cornill, and Condamin follow that reading; but Volz rightly rejects it as simply a paraphrase of the puzzling Hebrew reading. *V* translates "You have deceived your own souls" (*decepistis animas vestras*), and this paraphrase has been followed by Giesebrecht, Volz, and KB, and by *NEB*. *NJV* understands "deceive" but takes the prepositional phrase more literally: "You were deceitful at heart." Several commentators and translations have (rightly, I believe) understood the בְּ as a בְּ of price, "at the cost of your lives" (compare the same expression, with the same meaning, in 17:21). *NAB*, surprisingly, supplies "me" as an object of the verb: "At the cost of your lives you have deceived me"! But all of these commentators and translations translate the hip'il as if it were a qal: thus *RSV*, "You have gone astray at the cost of your lives," and so similarly BDB. Rudolph, Bright, and *JB* follow this interpretation but paraphrase; Bright: "You are making a fatal mistake," and so the others similarly.

But although there are instances in which the meaning of a hip'il is identical with the meaning of the corresponding qal, I submit that one should take the use of the hip'il seriously. There are other instances where this verb in the hip'il, carrying the meaning "mislead, lead astray," has no object (Isa 3:12; 9:15; perhaps Hos 4:12); in these passages the implicit object is assumed from the context, and I propose that one has the same situation here. In that case Jrm is addressing the leaders of the group, saying, "You have led astray the whole group at the cost of your lives."

Jrm's reply continues (v 20) with a clause containing an emphatic subject pronoun: "It is you who sent me"—that is to say, it was your idea in the first place. He continues by quoting their own words back to them: "Pray on our behalf to Yahweh, and according to everything Yahweh says, we will do." And then (v 21) he accuses them of breaking their promise: "But you have not obeyed the voice of Yahweh, who sent me to you."

He closes with a final divine word (vv 18 + 22): Yahweh will treat the group going into Egypt exactly as he has treated Jerusalem: the phraseology is similar to that found in 29:18.

■ **43:4–7** The group migrates to Egypt. The passage reviews, beyond the officers who are its leaders, the varied composition of the group: those Jews who had been scattered in the course of the final siege of Jerusalem and who subsequently rallied around Gedaliah (40:11–12); dependents; those whom Nebuzaradan had specifically assigned to the care of Gedaliah, notably the princesses (41:10); and finally Jrm and Baruch. The group settles for the moment at Tahpanhes at the eastern edge of the Nile Delta (for the location see 2:16); there is doubtless a colony of Jews already there (compare the general term "Jewish people" in v 9).

■ **43:9** In a symbolic action Jrm buries several large stones in front of the governmental building (so one must understand "the house of Pharaoh") in Tahpanhes. The noun מֶלֶט, here translated "clay pavement," is a *hapax legomenon* in the OT and is of uncertain meaning. It seems to have been rare enough to call forth a gloss or variant reading, מַלְבֵּן, which itself has given difficulty; *G* omits both expressions. One guess reflected in the Versions is that the first noun, מֶלֶט, is either to be read as לָט, "secrecy," or to be a mem-preformative derivative from that noun; hence some revisions of *G* (Origen: οἱ λοιποί) read the expression as "in secret"; so evidently *V*, which reads "in the vault." But "in secret" cannot be right: Jrm wishes to do his symbolic action in the open. *T* simply paraphrases. *S*, on the other hand, is evidently on the right track in rendering the word by its cognate *mĕlāṭā*, which also translates the Hebrew חֹמֶר, "clay," in the meaning "mortar" in Gen 11:3; there is likewise an Arabic cognate *milāṭ*, "mortar." "Clay-pavement" is then a good guess.

The noun that occurs in the gloss or variant, מַלְבֵּן, occurs in 2 Sam 12:31 qere' and Nah 3:14 in the meaning "brick-mold"; only here does it have another meaning related to "bricks"—the revisions of *G* are content to leave it a vague adjective, "related to bricks"; *V* takes the expression to mean "under the brick wall." "Brick-terrace" is evidently intended.

The expression בַּמֶּלֶט, "in the clay pavement," was evidently in Jrm's mind in assonance with "and hide them" (וּטְמַנְתָּם). This verb (טמן) has occurred once before in a symbolic action, when Jrm is told to hide his linen loin-cloth, 13:4–7; both actions signify the power of Babylon. Why does he bury large stones? The obvious answer is that while the linen loincloth soon decayed, the stones will remain, and some time may elapse before Nebuchadrezzar arrives. But more substantially, the clay pavement is doubtless an unsatisfactory platform for Nebuchadrezzar's throne: stones constitute the secure foundation that is needed (compare Calvin).

■ **43:10–11** Yahweh has control over the world, and he will bring Nebuchadrezzar even to this spot; the king will set up his throne over the stones (for the expansion "my servant" see 27:6). The scene envisages the king's imposition of sovereignty and judgment over subject peoples (compare the discussion on 1:15). There is no escape for those who had hoped to get out of the way of Babylonian power: Nebuchadrezzar will bring destruction to those in Egypt. For the expression "those for death, to death, and those for exile, to exile," compare 15:2b.

■ **43:13a** For the restoration of v 13a before v 12 see Preliminary Observations.

"Obelisks" is literally "pillars." "House of the Sun" is a translation of the Hebrew "beth-shemesh." This Hebrew expression normally designates a place-name, one of several cities in Palestine; in this one passage, however, an Egyptian locality is obviously intended. Most have taken the locality to be the Egyptian city translated "Heliopolis" in *G* (so *RSV*); the normal name in the OT for this city is On (אֹן, Gen 41:45: compare the gloss in *G* in the present passage, noted in Text note b), a rendering of the Egyptian *'iwnw*. The site of this city is at present a suburb on the northeast side of Cairo. Since in ancient times the city was an important cult center,[90] and since the Egyptian obelisk, originally a symbol of Atum-Re, the sun-god, originated here,[91] one is led to the conclusion that Jrm is using the Hebrew translation "house of the Sun" here to call attention to the pagan worship of the city. On the other hand, Jrm may be gesturing at a temple of Atum-Re in Tahpanhes. One is therefore left uncertain whether to translate the designation with the name "Beth-shemesh" (*NEB*), with "Heliopolis" (*RSV*), or with a rendering like "temple of the sun [or Sun]" (*JB*, *NAB*, *NJV*).

■ **43:12** Nebuchadrezzar will burn the temples of Egypt and will take (the images of) its gods back to Babylon—there is a description of such an action in Isa 46:1–2, and Assyrian royal inscriptions frequently mention the practice.[92]

The simile in v 12b evidently involves a witty double meaning, inasmuch as there are two homonymous verbs עטה. The first, meaning "wrap oneself with" (a garment), cognate with the Arabic *ǧaṭā*, is reflected in *V*, *S*, and *T* (so *KJV*): "He shall enwrap himself with Egypt as a shepherd wraps himself with his garment." The second, first isolated by August G. E. K. von Gall,[93] means "delouse" (so all recent commentaries and translations with the exception of *NJV*); it is cognate with the Arabic *'aṭā* (base stem) "grasp," (fourth stem) "give." One is tempted to hear the simile in the first meaning, but the occurrence of "a shepherd" (which under other circumstances would suggest "a ruler"—see 2:8!), followed by "his garment," leads one to hear the second, far more inelegant meaning. Nebuchadrezzar will "delouse" the whole land of Egypt, that is, pillage it; so much for the riches of Egypt! And then he will get away scot-free. Since the last encounter of Nebuchadrezzar with the Egyptians in the Nile Delta, in December 600, resulted in his defeat, this prophecy is a striking one; but as it happens, he did invade Egypt in 568.[94]

■ **44:1** What now follows (vv 1–14) is a general word from Yahweh for all Jews living in Egypt, not only those in Tahpanhes (compare 43:7, 9) but also those living in

90 See Thomas O. Lambdin, "Heliopolis," *IDB* 2:579–80.

91 Thomas O. Lambdin, "Obelisk," *IDB* 3:581–82.

92 For example, Sargon II against Ashdod, *ANET*, 286a; Esarhaddon against the Arabs, *ANET*, 291b. For the belief system behind the practice see A. Leo Oppenheim, *Ancient Mesopotamia, Portrait of a Dead Civilization* (Chicago: University of Chicago, 1964)

183–98, esp. 184.

93 So first August G. E. K. von Gall, "Jeremias 43,12 und das Zeitwort עטה," *ZAW* 24 (1904) 105–21.

94 Bright, *History*, 352; see the fragmentary text in *ANET*, 308b.

Migdol, a location that is evidently also in northern Egypt (see below), and those living in Pathros, a designation for Upper Egypt (that is, south of the Delta).

"Migdol" is a Northwest Semitic word meaning "tower" or "fortress": the word was borrowed in Egyptian both as a common noun and as a proper noun. The Migdol of Jrm has until recently been identified with *tall al-ḥayr*, 30° 59' N, 32° 28' E, but a recent Israeli survey has determined that the location of this Migdol is about one kilometer north of *tall al-ḥayr*, at a site designated T. 21; its location is 31° 0' N., 32° 28' E, roughly forty kilometers east-northeast of Tahpanhes. The central feature of the site is a square fortified structure two hundred meters on a side; pottery from the site include Saite pottery from the sixth century and Syro-Palestinian (or Phoenician) and Greek ware from the same period. By contrast, the earliest remains from *tall el-ḥayr* date from the Persian period (fifth century).[95]

Pathros, as already stated, is a designation for upper (southern) Egypt: the Hebrew word פַּתְרוֹס is a rendering of the Egyptian *p'-t'-rsy*, "the Southern Land."[96]

No indication is given how much time has passed since the word and action narrated in 43:8–13, nor where Jrm and his group are at the moment. Indeed, it is difficult to envisage the implication of this verse: on the one hand, it suggests a message to be delivered to all the Jews in Egypt, as if it were a kind of general epistle; but, on the other hand, data in the remainder of the chapter (vv 15, 19, 20) indicate that what one has here is (at least in the first instance) an address to an assemblage, and it is implausible to imagine all the Jews living in Egypt gathering for such an occasion. If Migdol is on the road to Tahpanhes, perhaps one should envisage Jews who were refugees in Migdol attaching themselves to the group in which Jrm found himself and moving with them to Tahpanhes; and if some length of time had passed since the action and word reported in 43:8–13, then perhaps word had gone out to Jews in the south of the presence of Jrm in Egypt, so that again they may have drifted into the group to be addressed by the prophet. The phraseology would then imply "The word which came to Jeremiah for the Jews (assembled), all of whom dwell in Egypt, whether in Migdol or in Tahpanhes or in the south."

■ **44:2–10** The passage plays on the various connotations of "evil": Yahweh has brought all the evil (that is, disaster) on the inhabitants of Jerusalem and Judah (v 2) because of the evil that the inhabitants have done to offend him (v 3). So now why are those in Jrm's hearing continuing to do evil to hurt themselves (v 7)?

■ **44:2–6** If the description of Jrm's audience is here correctly understood (v 1), one cannot take v 2 with strict literalness: not all of his audience necessarily witnessed the fall of Jerusalem and its consequences, but some of them certainly had. Again, though one cannot take literally the statement that Jerusalem and the cities of Judah are utterly without inhabitant, it is clear that the state of the decimated population was desperate (compare Lamentations 4).

The rhetoric of these verses closely resembles that of Huldah's prophecy, 2 Kgs 22:16–17 (see Setting); Jrm is moved to say that the disaster that Huldah prophesied has now fallen upon Judah. For "ruin" (חָרְבָּה) see 7:34; for "without any inhabitant" compare 2:6, 15; for "offend me" see 7:18; for "make sacrifices to other gods" see 1:16; for "I sent to you my servants the prophets, early and constantly" see 7:25; for "commit abomination" see 7:10; for "listen or incline (turn) their ear" see 7:24; for "pour out my anger and my wrath" see 7:20.

■ **44:7–10** The evil, particularly the pagan worship, committed by the inhabitants of Judah and Jerusalem (vv 2–6) should be a cautionary example to the group that has settled in Egypt; instead they have shown no contrition, they have cut themselves off from the land of Judah, and they continue to worship pagan gods in Egypt. As a result they too will be punished. The participial phrase "Why are you doing a great evil?" (v 7) suggests "Why do you continue to do a great evil?" "For yourselves" (לָכֶם) after "cut off" is a dative of disadvantage (GKC, sec. 119s), reflecting the earlier "against yourselves" (אֶל־נַפְשֹׁתֵכֶם, for which see the discussion on 26:19); "cut off man and woman, child and nursling from the midst of Judah" is reminiscent of "cut off the child(ren) from the streets, the youth from the squares" (9:20). Verse 8 reflects the diction of v 3, and v 9 to a lesser degree the diction of v 2. "They have shown no

95   Eliezer D. Oren, "Migdol: A New Fortress on the
       Edge of the Eastern Nile Delta," *BASOR* 256 (Fall
       1984) 7–44; for the earlier identification see Thomas

       O. Lambdin, "Migdol," *IDB* 3:377, or Aharoni, *Land
       of the Bible*, 43–44.
96   Thomas O. Lambdin, "Pathros," *IDB* 3:676.

contrition" translates לֹא דֻכָּאוּ; this verb (דכא pu'al) appears only here in Jer and means "be crushed."

For "so now" see 7:13. For "my statutes which I set before their fathers" compare "my law which I set before you," 9:12 and 26:4.

■ **44:11–14** Though all these chapters exhibit text expansions, the expansions are particularly lavish in this section.

Yahweh will deal with the remnant in Egypt as he has dealt with Jerusalem; the words of 42:17 and 18 + 22 are here reinforced. The diction is very strong: "they shall fall by sword, and by famine they shall be consumed" (compare 14:15)—those who hoped to escape sword and famine by going to Egypt (42:14) will in no way escape them. There will be no refugees (the last expression of v 14 is a gloss: see Text; and compare 42:17).

■ **44:15–19** First the men in the company answer Jrm. Though the men were aware that their wives had been offering pagan sacrifices (v 15), they make the same choice themselves (v 17); for "the queen of heaven" (vv 17, 18, 19) and for the cakes baked for her (v 19) see 7:18. This sentiment is a far cry from that expressed in 42:5–6; whether it is the same group, and they have changed their minds (43:2!), or whether the original group is now greatly expanded (44:1?) by folk with pagan sentiments is impossible to say. They are portrayed not only as loyal to Astarte but as arguing for her on the basis of *Heilsgeschichte*: when they worshiped her they had plenty to eat, but when they stopped worshiping her, presumably at the time of Josiah's reform, they suffered (vv 17–18). Here is a firm rejection of that Deuteronomic reform! And the women (v 19) reinforce their husbands' word: of course we have worshiped Astarte, but we have done so with our husbands' approval.

■ **44:20–23** Jrm replies to the men. He cannot refute their *Heilsgeschichte* except with his own (compare his inability on the spot to outdo Hananiah's optimistic divine word, 28:11b). The word-order of v 21abα, however, gives evidence of high emotion: the sequence הֲלֹא plus אֵת־ and the object is found in Jer otherwise only in 23:24, and in both passages the present study translates with a passive voice. Yahweh could not stand the sight of the pagan sacrifices that they offered, and he is responsible for the

disaster that has overtaken them. Jrm continues to ring the changes on phrases he has already spoken: thus "they [the fathers] did not walk in my statutes" in v 10 becomes "in his law and his statutes and his testimonies you did not walk" here in v 23.

■ **44:24–25** Jrm does not try to argue with the women; instead he simply affirms that what they have vowed to do they have done, and then he tells them to go ahead and do it, a sarcastic word reminiscent of that in 7:21.

■ **44:26–30** Jrm offers a summary word from Yahweh: it is addressed to "all Judah living in the land of Egypt" (compare v 1). If the Jews in Egypt persist in their devotion to pagan gods, then Yahweh swears that his name will no longer be invoked in Egypt. In a sense this is tautological; but behind the tautology lies Yahweh's reversal of Israel's *Heilsgeschichte*: he had revealed to Israel his name in Egypt (Exod 3:14), and in the theology of Deuteronomy Yahweh's name is virtually a hypostasis of his saving presence.[97] The Jews in Egypt have reversed *Heilsgeschichte* by moving from Canaan back into Egypt again; so Yahweh erases his name from the lips of his people, and Jrm once more finds himself an anti-Moses figure[98] (compare 7:16–20). For the oath-phrase "by the life of Yahweh" see 4:2.

The verb "watch" (שֹׁקֵד, v 27) is that used in 1:12; Jrm has rounded off the scroll of hope with this verb in a positive sense (31:28), but now the word is utterly pessimistic once more. For the phrase "for evil and not for good" compare 39:16.

Verse 28a is a mitigating expansion (see Text): Yahweh's word is that everyone will die (v 27), and it is to be Yahweh's word against that of the Jews in Egypt (v 28b)! (In order to salvage the half-verse, Rudolph is impelled to begin the sentence with the adversative "however" [*jedoch*], but there is no sign of a shift in viewpoint in the Hebrew text.)

The guarantee that Yahweh's word will stand is that Hophra, Pharaoh of Egypt, will be given into the hands of his enemies just as Zedekiah was (vv 29–30). This Pharaoh, whom Herodotus called Apries, carries the Egyptian name *w'ḥ-ib-r'*, "the heart of (the sun-god) Re endures." He began his reign in 589/588 (compare 37:5) and ruled until 569, when he lost power to his general

---

97   Von Rad, *Studies in Deuteronomy*, 37–44.

98   Alonso Schökel, "Jeremías como anti-Moisés," 248–49.

Amasis;[99] see further 46:17. Jrm doubtless had Nebuchadrezzar in mind (compare 43:10–13), but the prophecy is so shaped that Hophra's ultimate fate conforms to it.

Aim

Jerusalem is under siege and then falls, and what follows is chaos. And what befalls Jrm in that chaos is here narrated in detail.

On the one hand, he is kept moving here and there, caught up in the swirl of events: The palace officials falsely accuse him of desertion and put him in prison, then the king releases him to the court of the guard, then the officials throw him into a muddy cistern, then again the king agrees to have him pulled out and reassigned to the court of the guard, where he stays until the city falls; he finds himself shackled along with other citizens waiting to be deported, when he is suddenly released by the Babylonian provost marshal; he is entrusted to the governor in Mizpah, but when the governor is assassinated, he finds himself along with others captured as a hostage by the assassin Ishmael, who intends to take the group across the Jordan to the Ammonites, but then the hostages are suddenly rescued in Gibeon by Johanan, taken back to Mizpah and then quickly moved on to Bethlehem; eventually he is moved down to Egypt along with the others, and there we finally lose sight of him.

In a curious way it is a passion narrative. Von Rad writes,

Jeremiah's sufferings are described with a grim realism, and the picture is unrelieved by any divine word of comfort or any miracle. The narrator has nothing to say about any guiding hand of God; no ravens feed the prophet in his hunger, no angel stops the lion's mouth. In his abandonment to his enemies Jeremiah is completely powerless—neither by his words nor his sufferings does he make any impression on them. What is particularly sad is the absence of any good or promising issue. This was an unusual thing for an ancient writer to do, for antiquity felt a deep need to see harmony restored before the end. Jeremiah's path disappears in misery, and this without any dramatic

accompaniments. It would be completely wrong to assume that the story was intended to glorify Jeremiah and his endurance. To the man who described these events neither the suffering itself nor the manner in which it was borne had any positive value, and least of all a heroic value: he sees no halo of any kind round the prophet's head.[100]

On the other hand, in all the changes of fortune that he undergoes in this last period of his life, Jrm is portrayed as an active spokesman for the word of Yahweh. In his comment on 37:17–21 Duhm takes note of the curious way in which Jrm the prisoner is freer than the king who seeks him out.

This scene is just as moving as it is historically interesting: on the one hand is the prophet, disfigured by mistreatment, the prison atmosphere and privations, but firm in his predictions, without any invective against his persecutors, without defiance, exaggeration or fanaticism, simple, physically mild and humble; on the other hand is the king, who obviously against his own will had been led by his officials into the war adventure, anxiously watching the lips of the martyr for a favorable word for himself, whispering secretly with the man whom his officials had imprisoned for treason, weak, a poor creature but not evil, a king but much more bound than the prisoner who stands before him.[101]

This paradox of Jrm, a victim yet curiously free, is the same paradox manifest in the narrative of Jesus' passion. Günther Bornkamm remarks,

Gethsemane is the place where Jesus is arrested by the band of his opponents under the leadership of Judas—a scene which, according to the description of the Gospels, finds Jesus prepared and the disciples unprepared. As elsewhere in the story of the Passion, the picture presented by the account is not one of Jesus and his followers on the one side, his enemies on the other. Rather it shows Jesus alone, and on the other side his enemies, led by one of the Twelve, and all

---

99 For references see n. 28.
100 Von Rad, *Old Testament Theology 2*, 207–8.
101 Duhm, p. 301; the translation is taken from

Hyatt, p. 1072.

around the disturbed band of his disciples, only one of whom tries, suddenly and helplessly, to intervene.[102]

Jrm is free by his steady proclamation of Yahweh's word, not only to Zedekiah but to Ebed-melech, to his fellow citizens in shackles (if the text of 40:1–3 is correctly reconstructed), to Johanan and the others in his group in Bethlehem, to his group and any others who are listening in Egypt. It is a word that cuts across all the human expectations of those around him. "Surrender to Babylon and live!" "Stay in Judah: there is no safety in Egypt!" And in no single instance does Jrm have any reassurance that anyone is listening: no one but Baruch, who writes it all down. That his words will be translated into Greek in Egypt two and a half centuries later, that his words will be meditated upon by the Qumran community in the wilderness of Judea five centuries later, that his words will become part of the Scripture of the peoples of the covenant and be pondered from one end of the world to the other—all this is completely beyond his ken. Surely "God chose what is foolish in the world to shame the wise, God chose what is weak in the world to shame the strong, God chose what is low and despised in the world, even things that are not, to bring to nothing things that are, so that no human being might boast in the presence of God" (1 Cor 1:27–29).

---

102 Günther Bornkamm, *Jesus of Nazareth* (New York: Harper, 1960) 162–63.

Bibliography

Boer, Pieter A. H. de
"Jeremiah 45, Verse 5," *Symbolae Biblicae et Mesopotamicae Francisco Mario Theodoro de Liagre Böhl Dedicatae* (ed. Martinus A. Beek et al.; Leiden: Brill, 1973) 31–37.

Graupner, Axel
"Jeremia 45 als 'Schlusswort' des Jeremiabuches," *Altes Testament und christliche Verkündigung, Festschrift für Antonius H. J. Gunneweg zum 65. Geburtstag* (ed. Manfred Oeming and Axel Graupner; Stuttgart: Kohlhammer, 1987) 287–308.

Selms, Adriaan van
"Telescoped discussion as a literary device in Jeremiah," *VT* 26 (1976) 99–112.

Taylor, Marion Ann
"Jeremiah 45: The Problem of Placement," *JSOT* 37 (1987) 79–98.

Wanke
Baruchschrift, 133–36, 140–43.

Weiser, Artur
"Das Gotteswort für Baruch Jer. 45 und die sogenannte Baruchbiographie," *Theologie als Glaubenswagnis: Festschrift für Karl Heim zum 80. Geburtstag* (Hamburg: Furche, 1954) 35–46 = *Glaube und Geschichte im Alten Testament und andere ausgewählte Schriften* (Göttingen: Vandenhoeck & Ruprecht, 1961) 321–29.

45

1 The word which Jeremiah the prophet spoke to Baruch son of Neriah when he wrote these words in a document from the dictation of Jeremiah in the fourth year of Jehoiakim son of Josiah king of Judah: 2/ Thus Yahweh [God of Israel]ᵃ has said to you, Baruch: 3/ You have said, "Woe is me, that Yahweh has added torment to my pain; I am tired of my groaning, and rest I have not found!" 4/ Thus you shall say to him, Thus Yahweh has said, Look, what I have built I am overthrowing, and what I have planted I am uprooting [that is, the whole land.]ᵃ 5/ And you seek great things for your own self!—do not; for I am going to bring evil on all flesh, oracle of Yahweh—but I shall at least give you your life in ᵃany placeᵃ you may go.

Text

2a   Omit with *G*; compare Janzen, p. 78.

4a   Omit with *G* (so Duhm, Giesebrecht, Cornill, Condamin, Bright); see Janzen, p. 134 (though his citation of the gloss is erroneous).

5a—a   Read פָּל־מָקוֹם with *G* for *M* "all the places" (compare 1 Sam 30:31, where the plural כָּל־הַמְּקֹמוֹת is rendered by a plural with article in *G*). The expansion to the plural in *M* may be due to the same kind of activity represented in the glosses in 24:9; 29:14; 40:12.

Structure, Form, Setting

This short chapter stands by itself, Yahweh's reply to a lament of Baruch's similar to one of Jrm's confessions. Because it is the only point in the book at which one hears the voice of Baruch, it is difficult to discern the circumstances in which the word was delivered and the part it plays in the literary history of the book. Hyatt sums up the situation of earlier scholarship:

The actual date of the oracle has been debated by scholars. Some (e.g., Cornill, Volz, Rudolph, Peake) accept the date in vs. 1 as correct, and believe that its present position is due to the modesty of Baruch rather than to chronological considerations. They point to vs. 4 as indicating that the destruction of Judah lies in the future. Others (e.g., Giesebrecht, Duhm, Skinner, Erbt) reject the date in vs. 1, and believe that the position of the oracle and the nature of its contents favor placing it after the fall of Jerusalem, near the end of Jeremiah's life. Skinner says that it sounds like a farewell oracle or even a deathbed charge from the prophet to Baruch.[1] According to Wilhelm Erbt, (*Jeremia und seine Zeit* [Göttingen: Vandenhoeck & Ruprecht, 1902], pp. 83–86), these were the final words of the prophet to his companion and scribe before he sent Baruch to the exiles in Babylonia to continue to be his witness.[2]

Hyatt then offers his own view:

It should be recognized that, though this oracle is basically authentic, it has come to us through the Deuteronomic editor (so Mowinckel, though not Rudolph). His phraseology is evident especially in vss. 4, 5*b*. The contents of the oracle do seem to be more appropriate to the end of Jeremiah's life, after he and Baruch had undergone much suffering, than to the time of the writing of the scroll of ch. 36; the date in vs. 1 is from the Deuteronomic editor, who is respon-

sible for a similar date in 25:1.[3]

But there is no reason to doubt the authenticity of the oracle as it stands. The Deuteronomic phraseology to which Hyatt refers in v 4 is the series of four verbs that reflect the diction of 1:10. But surely these verbs have a specific application here, just as they do in 18:7–9; 24:6; 31:28; 42:10 as well: they are not evidence of Deuteronomistic diction.[4] And what the presumed Deuteronomistic phraseology is in v 5b is not apparent.

The notion that the date in v 1 is wrong, that the oracle is to be placed at the end of the prophet's life (see above), is at first sight attractive: the closing words of v 5 suggest that Baruch and Jrm are parting. But against it are two considerations. First, the destruction of the normal order of life is announced as if it were news, not a confirmation of what has taken place. Second, and more crucially, it is hard to imagine the motive for the drafting of the specific date given in v 1 if it were invented. The most economical view is that the passage is what it says it is.

The chapter is analogous to a colophon in a manuscript—an inscription at the end of a manuscript giving details of its production. Rom 16:22 offers a partial parallel in the NT: "I Tertius, the writer of this letter, greet you in the Lord." (Unfortunately it is letters rather than longer documents that have survived from antiquity, so parallels are not precise; Gordon Bahr has collected examples of "subscriptions" in letters and records of antiquity.[5]) That is to say, at some point in Baruch's preparation of a scroll for Jrm he allowed himself the freedom to append the oracle that he himself received through Jrm.

To what was the addition appended? Given the fact that the date in v 1 is the year when the first scroll was dictated (36:1–2), one might assume that it was appended to the first scroll, then to the second scroll, then to any subsequent enlargements of the second scroll: indeed the expression "these words" in v 1 might imply

---

1   Skinner, p. 346.
2   Hyatt, 1101–1102.
3   Ibid., 1102.
4   So also Weippert, *Prosareden*, 193–202.
5   Gordon J. Bahr, "The Subscriptions in the Pauline Letters," *JBL* 87 (1968) 27–41; and for the possible mention of a scribe or secretary in one of the letters from Muraba'at see Pardee, "Epistolography," 341.

that the chapter was originally appended to the first scroll. And if any given scroll began with Jrm's call, then this closing oracle, with the four verbs in v 4 matching those in 1:10, would have made a pleasing inclusio. But the identity of the date of this oracle with the date of the writing the first scroll need not guarantee that the oracle was actually written at the end of the first scroll. Thus it is suggested in the present study that the first set of Jrm's confessions took shape in 600 but that these confessions, and more, were not added to the growing corpus of written material until 594. The same situation may then prevail with Baruch's oracle: Rietzschel suggests that chapter 45 may have stood originally after 20:18 (יָגוֹן, "hardship," in 20:18 and 45:3).[6] If the present chapter was the last item in any given form of Jrm's scroll, then it would have been added finally after the narrative material in chapters 37—44; but it is not appropriate to view chapter 45 as forming a unit with chapters 37—44 (see on this 37:1—44:30, Form and Structure). (It is to be noted that the present study assumes that the original placement of the foreign nations oracles, chapters 46—51, was as G has them, in the middle of chapter 25: see the essay on 46:1—51:58.)

What might be the nature of the crisis that led Baruch to his lament and to the oracle in response to that lament? There is of course no way to know; all one can do is work out a chain of probabilities.

The earliest association of Baruch with Jrm is recorded in the same year, the fourth year of Jehoiakim, 605/604 (36:1), when Jrm summoned Baruch to write a scroll at his dictation, because he was restricted from entering the temple (36:4–5). As pointed out in Interpretation on 36:1–8, the dictation of the scroll is likely to have been after news of the Battle of Carchemish had reached Judah: Jehoiakim was thereupon a vassal to the losing side, and Jrm's words about a foe from the north might have brought him fresh opposition. The association of Baruch with Jrm lasted for another twenty years, and the shared emotion evident in the words of the present chapter suggests that Baruch's association with Jrm was not simply professional: he had cast his lot with Jrm and with the divine word mediated through Jrm. As a scribe he had surely been trained in a scribal school and

would be well known to the officials of the palace and temple (see on 36:9–11), and by his association with Jrm he would incur the scorn of those officials who had been harassing Jrm: later, after Jehoiakim burned the scroll, the king commanded the arrest of both Baruch and Jrm (36:26).

And beyond the personal opposition that Baruch must have suffered, one suspects that he was overcome by the words he was writing down at the dictation of Jrm, words portraying the disaster that was looming over Judah (4:29; 6:4–5); one notes once more the phrase "these words" in v 1.[7] The words of 18:1–11 are relevant at this point: in that passage, too, the words of construction and destruction from 1:10 are used. As the hope that the nation would repent receded more and more, Baruch must have heard the word of the possibility of Yahweh's sudden shift from blessing to disaster in his plan for a given nation (18:9–10) as a word about Yahweh's plan for Judah. No wonder he sought a word of reassurance from Yahweh.

Form-critically the chapter is the record of a divine word to Baruch delivered by Jrm. But the situation is complicated: as van Selms has pointed out, the verses telescope the record of a sequence of discourses. (1) Baruch shares his lament with Jrm; (2) Jrm shares Baruch's lament with Yahweh in prayer; (3) Jrm perceives Yahweh's answer to Baruch; (4) Jrm shares that answer with Baruch.[8] Yahweh's answer addresses Baruch directly and begins with a quotation of Baruch's lament (v 3); it then shifts to address Jrm, commanding him to pass on Yahweh's answer (v 4aα). Though the result is that the personal references are mixed, there is no reason to delete v 4aα as Cornill, Giesebrecht, Volz, Condamin, Rudolph, and Bright do.

One has then: notice of the speaker (Jrm), the addressee (Baruch), and the circumstance (all in v 1); the messenger formula for a divine word, specifying the addressee (v 2); and the oracle proper (vv 3–5). Yahweh first cites Baruch's original lament (v 3), a lament that Baruch originally addressed not to Yahweh ("Yahweh" is referred to in the third person) but, presumably, to Jrm (compare Jrm's "woe is me" addressed at least formally to his mother, 15:10). Verse 4 begins by Yahweh's address

6   Rietzschel, *Urrolle*, 128.

7   Compare the overelaborated reconstruction in Adriaan van Selms, "Telescoped discussion as a literary device in Jeremiah," *VT* 26 (1976) 101–3.

8   Ibid., 103.

to Jrm to speak Yahweh's answer (see above), and by the messenger formula. The divine answer proper is a mixture of an announcement of judgment and of consolation. The announcement of judgment (vv 4a, 5a) is intended, it is implied, for the nation, or indeed, it is stated explicitly, for "all flesh," referred to in the third person (v 5a); the word of consolation is addressed to Baruch (v 5b). Since the announcement of judgment, intended for the rest of the world, is addressed to Baruch, Wanke calls it an "admonition" (*Mahnung*).[9] A parallel mixture of forms may be found in Isa 7:10–17: there the judgment speech (v 17) is intended for the king, and the salvation speech (vv 14–16) is intended for those who believe.[10] The admonition in v 4a is really a matter of information: Yahweh indicates to Baruch what he is going to do with the rest of the world. The admonition in v 5a begins with an ironic exclamation (or question, see Interpretation) addressed to Baruch, followed immediately by its corresponding prohibition; Yahweh then reverts to what he intends to do with the rest of the world. And even the consolation is modest, with a bitter edge to it (see Interpretation).

Interpretation

■ **3** For "woe is me!" see 4:13 and 31; and for the translation "that" for the following conjunction כִּי see again 4:13. For יָגוֹן, "torment," see 8:18; for מַכְאֹב, "pain," see 30:12–15. The assonance is nice of יָגַעְתִּי, "I am tired," with יָגוֹן, "torment," and of מְנוּחָה, "rest," with אַנְחָתִי, "my groaning."

■ **4** It is an insoluble question whether the occurrences of אֲשֶׁר refer to persons or things—"those whom I have built up I am overturning, and those whom I have planted I am uprooting" (so *G*, *V*) or "what I have built up I am overturning, and what I have planted I am uprooting" (so Luther, Calvin, *KJV*, and all recent commentaries and translations); the Hebrew text covers both, and Cornill nicely covers both: "My own building I myself must destroy, and my own planting I myself must uproot."[11] Cornill points out that *G* remarkably appends the emphatic subject pronoun ἐγώ to all four verbs (and, it may be added: *V* adds the corresponding pronoun *ego* to the two verbs of destruction; the verbs of destruction

in Hebrew are participles, and with the participles in Hebrew the subject pronouns are necessary, but both *G* and *V* render those participles by finite verbs, so that in those Versions the subject pronouns are emphatic). Cornill suggests, rightly I believe, that this is the intention of the Hebrew: that Yahweh himself is moved to destroy his own work.

■ **5** The emphatic pronoun אַתָּה evidently reinforces the suffix of לְךָ (GKC, sec. 135g). Recent commentators and translations have assumed that the first clause is a question without the interrogative particle הֲ (so, for example, GKC, sec. 150a; Rudolph). But it is also possible that a ה has dropped out after אַתָּה. On the other hand, it is equally possible to read the clause as an ironic exclamation: "So, in the light of my determination to destroy my own work, you have great ambitions for your own self!" (compare Gen 18:12b, which again can be either a question or an ironic exclamation).[12]

"Great things" (גְּדֹלוֹת) suggests God's mighty deeds (Deut 10:21; Ps 71:19). At one point the psalmist says he does not occupy himself with "great things" (Ps 131:1). The implication in the present passage, then, is not only that Baruch has had hopes for "rest" and security, but, with gentle irony, that he is overreaching himself, seeking for what is too great: *JB* translates, "And here you are asking for special treatment!"

"All flesh" here implies "all humankind": see the discussion in 12:12.

The expression "but I shall at least give you your life," וְנָתַתִּי לְךָ אֶת־נַפְשְׁךָ לְשָׁלָל, literally "and I shall give you your life as booty," is a variation on the expression "he shall at least have his life" discussed in 21:9 (see there) and found also in 38:2 and 39:18: here, as in those other passages, it is ironic and bittersweet. But it is a promise, a promise parallel to the one Jrm would deliver to Ebed-melech at the time of the final collapse of Jerusalem (39:15–18).[13]

The phrase "in any place you may go" is an ominous hint that Baruch may have to undergo exile.

Aim

Almost by accident there is tossed up before us the vignette of Jrm's ministry to an individual. Normally it is

9   Wanke, *Baruchschrift*, 135.
10   Westermann, *Basic Forms*, 186–87.
11   *Meinen eigenen Bau muss ich selbst zerstören und meine*

eigene Pflanzung muss ich selbst ausreissen.
12   König, *Syntax*, sec. 353b.
13   Artur Weiser, "Das Gotteswort für Baruch Jer. 45

a whole nation that the prophet addresses, or a group within a nation; when the prophet addresses an individual, it is usually an official—a king (Zedekiah, in chapters 37—38) or a priest (Pashhur, 20:1–6), and the word has to do with official policy; and when the prophet addresses someone who is not an official, the word is usually unsought (Ebed-melech, 39:15–18). Here, by contrast, Baruch seeks (to use the current term) spiritual direction, and Jrm gives it. The existence of the passage reminds us of the range of religious transactions that the OT does not happen to record.

Calvin judges Baruch harshly for his egotism: "Baruch has been thus far severely reproved, as he deserved, on account of his self-indulgence." But this is not fair: it is human nature that each person should consider himself or herself special. After all, Baruch had joined himself to Jrm and believed in the validity of the word Jrm proclaimed on behalf of Yahweh: why then, given a theology of rewards and punishments, should he not expect "great things for himself," or at least "rest" (v 3) and security? Jrm would have to struggle with the same issues with Yahweh: "Why has my pain become endless, my wound incurable, refusing to be healed?" (15:18).

It is not a fair world, Baruch: but at least you will have your life.

---

und die so genante Baruchbiographie," in *Theologie als Glaubenswagnis: Festschrift für Karl Heim zum 80. Geburtstag* (Hamburg: Furchte, 1954) 35 = *Glaube und Geschichte im Alten Testament und andere ausgewählte Schriften* (Göttingen: Vandenhoeck & Ruprecht, 1961), 321.

**The Oracles against
Foreign Nations (46:1—51:58)**

Bibliography

Asurmendi Ruiz, Jesús M.
"Jeremías y las naciones," *Simposio bíblico español
(Salamanca, 1982)* (ed. N. Fernandez Marcos, J.
Trebolle Barrera, J Fernandez Vallina; Madrid:
Universidad Complutense, 1984) 325–43.

Bardtke, Hans
"Jeremia der Fremdvölkerprophet," *ZAW* 53
(1935) 209–39; 54 (1936) 240–62.

Cassuto, Umberto
"The Prophecies of Jeremiah concerning the
Gentiles," translated from the Italian text of 1916–
17, *Biblical and Oriental Studies, I: Bible* (Jerusalem:
Hebrew University, 1973) 178–226.

Fohrer, Georg
"Vollmacht über Völker und Königreiche, Beob-
achtungen zu den prophetischen Fremdvölker-
sprüchen anhand von Jer 46—51," *Wort, Lied und
Gottespruch, II, Beiträge zu Psalmen und Propheten,
Festschrift für Joseph Ziegler* (ed. Josef Schreiner;
Forschung zur Bibel 2; Würzburg: Echter, 1972)
145–53 = *Studien zu alttestamentlichen Texten und
Themen (1966–72)* (BZAW 155; Berlin/New York:
de Gruyter, 1981) 44–52.

Höffken, Peter
"Zu den Heilszusätzen in der Völkerorakelsammlung des Jeremiabuches," *VT* 27 (1977) 398–
412.

Jong, Cornelis de
*De Volken bij Jeremia, Hun Plaats in zijn Prediking en
in het Boek Jeremia* (Kampen, 1978).

Michaud, Henri
"La Vocation du 'prophète des nations,'" *Maqqél
Shâqqédh, La Branche d'Amandier, Hommage à
Wilhelm Vischer* (Montpellier: Causse, Graille,
Castelnau, 1960) 157–64.

Rietzschel
Urrolle, 25–90.

Schwally, Friedrich
"Die Reden des Buches Jeremia gegen die Heiden,
XXV. XLVI—LI," *ZAW* 8 (1888) 177–217.

General Remarks

These six chapters of oracles against foreign nations
make up a distinct collection within the book, with their
own superscription (46:1). These oracles are found in *G*
after 25:14, and in a different order, so that the chapter
numeration of the book after that point differs in *M* and
G (on this matter see further below, *Placement and Order
of the Oracles*).

Several earlier critical scholars denied the authenticity
of all of the oracles—so Schwally,[1] Duhm, and Volz.
Giesebrecht did admit the authenticity of the core of the
oracle against the Philistines (47:2 and parts of vv 3–5)
and against Edom (49:7–8, 10–11). On the other hand,
Cornill defended the authenticity of much of the mate-

1   Friedrich Schwally, "Die Reden des Buches Jeremia
     gegen die Heiden. XXV. XLVI—LI," *ZAW* 8 (1888)
     177–217.

rial in these chapters, and as one might expect, Condamin did as well. More recently Hans Bardtke[2] and Eissfeldt[3] have defended the core of chapters 46—49 as authentic, and Rudolph and Bright have defended the authenticity of some of the material in all six chapters.

Much of the argumentation about the authenticity of these oracles has been a priori, dealing with the historical circumstance of this or that nation about which Jrm might or might not have delivered oracles. And there is justification for separating chapters 46—49 from chapters 50—51: The material against Babylon has its own literary history, given the narrative in 51:59–64. But I shall not review any of this argumentation here, because I think it better to examine the oracles one by one in the hope that their authenticity and their settings may thereupon be determined. Indeed this essay might more logically come after a consideration of the oracles themselves. Before the discussion *Placement and Order of the Oracles*, therefore, I shall confine myself to one observation on the nature of this material and summarize my findings in regard to authenticity.

My observation is the impression one gains, as one works through these oracles, of their variety. I do not have in mind the variety of nations, though that is obviously basic, but the variety of tone, form, and approach that these oracles display. The oracles against Moab are a veritable gazetteer of place-names. Most of the oracles in these chapters have a tone of mockery—understandably, since these nations are about to fall; but not the oracle against Philistia, whose words simply depict the sad downfall of a people. Most of the oracles are filled with the particularities of the people, their customs (49:28–33), the names of their gods (46:15; 48:7; 49:1; 50:2), their wisdom (49:7) or their wine (48:11), but not the oracle against Elam: in that sequence the only subject of the verbs is Yahweh, acting beyond the far horizon. And not only is a variety of forms used but also there is no standard sequence of forms for the oracles (compare on this 50:1—51:58, *Preliminary Observations*). These oracles are in no way standardized.

And the conclusion of the present study is that the material is by and large authentic to Jrm. Of course there are additions, a half-verse or a full verse or three or four verses, that betray the hand of editors. But the basic material gives every evidence of the diction and the outlook of Jrm in the course of his career, beginning with oracles delivered in the context of the battle of Carchemish in 605 (46:3–12; perhaps 48:1–4, 6–9, 11–12; and perhaps 49:3–5) and ending with the second oracle to Egypt (46:13–24) in the months just before Jerusalem fell in 587.

Placement and Order of the Oracles. As already noted, the text traditions of *M* and *G* differ both in the placement of this collection of oracles, and in the order of the oracles within the collection: *G* places the material of chapters 46—51 after 25:14 (though, as it happens, 25:14 itself is omitted in *G*), and the oracles appear in the following order: against Elam (*G*: the balance of chapter 25 through 26:1); against Egypt (*G*: 26:2–28); against Babylon (*G*: 27:1—28:58); against Philistia (*G*: 29:1–7); against Edom (*G*: 29:8–23); against the Ammonites (*G*: 30:1–5); against Kedar (*G*: 30:6–11); against Damascus (*G*: 30:12–16); and against Moab (*G*: 31:1–44). Bright and Thompson believe that the contrasting positions of the collection within the book and the contrasting orders of the oracles within the collection indicate that, as Bright says, "They were for some time transmitted independently of the remainder of the book, perhaps being added to it only after the textual traditions underlying MT and LXX, respectively, had diverged."[4] But I believe that more precision is possible.

G associates the oracles with (*M*) 25:15–29, a sequence listing various nations that will drink the cup of wrath, and this placement in the book is undoubtedly the original one:[5] the fact that 25:15–29 is where it is suggests that the oracles against foreign nations were moved secondarily in the tradition that gave rise to *M*. It could be maintained that Baruch added the collection at a particular time late in Jrm's career as an appendix to 1:1—25:14.

However, the sequence of individual oracles in *M* seems to be the original order, an order that in the main is both chronological and geographical (compare in general the sequence of nations listed in 25:19–26). Thus there is no reason to question the date in the superscription of the first oracle against Egypt (605—see

2   Bardtke, "Fremdvölkerprophet."

3   Eissfeldt, *Introduction*, 362–64.

4   Bright, p. 307; so similarly Thompson, p. 686.

5   Rudolph, p. 265; Rietzschel, *Urrolle*, 43–46, 93; Janzen, p. 115.

46:2); the second (later) oracle against Egypt (46:13–24) will then have been associated with it. The oracle against Philistia (chapter 47) also may have been delivered in 605—it was certainly no later than 604. I suggest that the material against Moab (chapter 48) was delivered in three successive settings, the earliest being 605. Then associated with Moab is material against two other Transjordanian peoples: the core of the oracle against Ammon (49:1–6) may be dated to 600 or thereabouts, and the oracle against Edom (49:7–22) is perhaps to be dated to 594. The remainder of chapter 49 contains oracles against people more distant from Judah— Damascus (49:23–27), the Arab tribes (49:28–33), and Elam, on the far horizon (49:34–39). The material against Babylon (chapters 50—51) must have taken shape late in Jrm's career, and in any case would understandably be put last, since Jrm had been convinced that Nebuchadrezzar's yoke would be imposed on the whole world (27:4–7), and the downfall of Babylon would be accomplished much later. And even if it is argued that the oracles against Babylon had not originally been last, there would be great pressure to place them last in the second century B.C.E. when "Babylon" would have been heard as the Seleucid Empire (compare the Book of Daniel, and see below): this empire will be the last to fall (so also Rietzschel).[6] The shift in the text tradition antecedent to *M* to place all the oracles against foreign nations at the end of the Book of Jer was doubtless part of such an impulse.

On the other hand, the individual order of the oracles in *G* has evidently been shifted (against Janzen, who holds that the order in *G* is original).[7] Most remarkable is that Elam should head the list: historical Elam is at the farthest remove from the world of Judah (see the treatment on 49:34–39), and the placement of Elam at the head of the sequence attracts attention. Earlier commentators had assumed that *G* understood Elam to be the Persian Empire and placed the three world empires first—Persia, Egypt, and Babylon.[8] But, as Rietzschel points out, this can hardly be: when *G* was translated, it distinguished "the kings of Elam" and "the kings of the Medes" (*M* 25:25) as "the kings of Elam" and "the kings of Persians" (*G* 32:11).[9] Rietzschel suggests that Elam was highlighted as representing the Parthian Empire;[10] this suggestion was accepted as an alternative view by Rudolph[11] and is, I believe, correct. The Parthians had claimed independence from the Seleucids in the middle of the third century B.C.E. Then when Antiochus IV Epiphanes (175–163) came to power he found himself threatened by the Parthians, among others. Bright observes, "Internally unstable, its heterogeneous population without real unity, it was threatened on every side. Its eastern provinces were increasingly menaced by the Parthians, while to the south it faced an unfriendly Egypt, whose king, Ptolemy VI Philometor (181–146), was ready to renew claim to Palestine and Phoenicia."[12] This point in history offers an appropriate setting for the reordering of the oracles in *G*: Elam (the Parthian Empire), Egypt (the Ptolemaic Empire), Babylon (the Seleucid Empire). Rietzschel suggests that the rest of the nations are ordered geographically: Philistia (the west), Edom (the south), Ammon and "Kedar" (the east), and Damascus (the north). Moab does not fit the pattern, but he accepts Rudolph's suggestion that the longest is placed at the end, and since Babylon is no longer at the end, Moab is instead.[13]

It is likely then that the turmoil of the Maccabean revolt is the setting both for the reordering of the oracles in *G* and the shift of the oracles to the end of the book in the text tradition behind *M*.

---

6   Rietzschel, *Urrolle*, 85.
7   Janzen, pp. 115–16.
8   Cornill, p. 439; Weiser, p. 381.
9   Rietzschel, *Urrolle*, 82.
10 Ibid., 83–84.
11 Rudolph, p. 266.
12 Bright, *History*, 419.
13 Rietzschel, *Urrolle*, 83; Rudolph, p. 266.

Egypt Has Stumbled
and Fallen

Bibliography

On 46:1–28:
Eissfeldt, Otto
"Jeremias Drohorakel gegen Ägypten und gegen
Babel," *Verbannung und Heimkehr, Beiträge zur
Geschichte und Theologie Israels im 6. und 5. Jahr-
hundert v. Chr., Wilhelm Rudolph zum 70. Geburtstage*
(Tübingen: Mohr [Siebeck], 1961) 31–37 = *Kleine
Schriften* 4 (Tübingen: Mohr [Siebeck], 1968) 32–
38.
Snaith, John G.
"Literary Criticism and Historical Investigation in
Jeremiah Chapter XLVI," *JSS* 16 (1971) 15–32.

On 46:1–12:
Christensen, Duane L.
*Transformations of the War Oracle in Old Testament
Poetry* (HDR 3; Missoula, MT: Scholars, 1975)
215–21.
Condamin, Albert
"Transpositions accidentelles (1): Jér 46,3–12," *RB*
12 (1903) 419–21.
Everson, A. Joseph
"The Days of Yahweh," *JBL* 93 (1974) 333–34.
Green, Alberto R.
"The Chronology of the Last Days of Judah: Two
Apparent Discrepancies," *JBL* 101 (1982) 67–73.
Jong, Cornelis de
"Deux oracles contre les Nations, reflets de la
politique étrangère de Joaqim," *Le Livre de Jérémie,
Le prophète et son milieu, les oracles et leur transmission*
(ed. Pierre-Maurice Bogaert; BETL 54; Leuven:
Leuven University, 1981) 369–79.
Zenner, Johann Konrad
"Ein Beispiel 'kolumnenweiser Verschreibung,'"
BZ 3 (1905) 122–27.

46

1   [This has come as the word of Yahweh to
Jeremiah the prophet concerning the nations.]ᵃ

2   For Egypt; concerning the army of Pharaoh
Neco king of Egypt, who was on the river
Euphrates at Carchemish, whom Nebuchad-
rezzar king of Babylon defeated in the fourth
year of Jehoiakim [son of Josiah]ᵃ king of
Judah:

3   Ready with buckler and shield,
      and advance for battle!

4   Harness the horses,
      and mount the steeds!
    Form up with helmets,
      《uncover》ᵃ lances,
        put on coat of mail!

5   Why [have I seen (it),]ᵃ are they panic-
      stricken,

Text

1a   This verse is missing in *G*; it is a general title
added at some point as a heading for chapters 46—
51. Compare 25:13, note c. See the discussion in
Janzen, pp. 112–14.

2a   Omit with *G*; compare Janzen, pp. 69–75, 144.

4a   For מִרְקוּ, "polish," read הָרִקוּ, "uncover, draw"
(ריק hip'il) with Rudolph (the emendation is derived
from Ehrlich, *Randglossen*, 352–53, who proposed
the perfect הֵרִיקוּ); compare Ps 35:3, and see further
Interpretation. The letters he and mem would be
easy to confuse in the early Aramaic script (see
Cross, "Scripts," 137).

5a   Omit with *G* (against Janzen, pp. 108–109); there
is no other first-person singular reference in the
poem. The verb is evidently inserted on the analogy

drawing back?
Their warriors are beaten down,
    headlong have fled,
       have not turned back terror [all
         around!][b]
            oracle of Yahweh.

6   **The swift cannot flee,**
       nor the warrior escape:
    in the north on the bank of the [river][a]
       Euphrates
       they have stumbled and fallen.

7   **Who is this who rises like the Nile,**
       like the rivers whose waters are con-
       vulsed?

8   **[Egypt rises like the Nile,**
       like rivers whose waters are convulsed!][a]
    He said, ⟨"Let me arise,⟩[b]
       let me cover the earth,
          let me destroy [a city and][c] **its inhabi-**
          tants!"

9   **Advance, O horses,**
       and run wild, O chariots,
    [a]**《 go forth, 》 O warriors,**[a]
       Cush and Put, who grasp the buckler,
       men of Lud, [who grasp][b] **who draw the**
       bow!

10 **[That day (belongs) to {the Lord}**[b] **Yahweh {of**
       hosts,}[b]
    a day of retribution to gain redress from his
       foes:][a]
    a sword shall devour and be sated,
       and drink its fill from their blood,
    for a sacrifice (belongs) to [the Lord][b]
       Yahweh [of hosts,][b]
    in the land of the north
       by the river Euphrates.

11 **Go up to Gilead,**
       and obtain balm,
       poor virgin Egypt!
    In vain [a]**you multiply**[a] **remedies,**
       new skin none for you.

12 **Nations have heard of your shame,**
       of your outcry the earth is full;
    for warrior on warrior has stumbled,
       together both have fallen.

of 30:6, a passage that is form-critically parallel. See further Interpretation.

b   Omit: gloss from 6:25; 20:3, 10; 49:29. In 6:25 the phrase is parallel with a nominal clause, and in 20:10 and 49:29 it is a quotation. The verb phrase לֹא הִפְנוּ cannot stand alone in a colon. See further Setting.

6a   Omit with *G*, an addition from v 2; see Janzen, p. 58.

8a   For the bracketed sequence *G* reads only "The waters of Egypt rise like a river." The repetition is not in keeping with the concise style (and sudden transitions: see Snaith, "Jeremiah XLVI," 22–23); omit entirely as an unnecessary gloss (so Cornill, Volz, Rudolph). The gloss may have simply begun as "Egypt," then been expanded first to the form in *G* and then to that of *M*.

b   The verb אַעֲלֶה is vocalized as a hip'il, but surely a qal is intended (אֶעֱלֶה): so the Versions and translations; compare Condamin.

c   Omit with *G*, an expression added from 8:16 (so also Cornill); see Janzen, p. 59.

9a—a   Read וּצְאוּ with *G*; if one reads *M* וְיֵצְאוּ, the colon would mean "and let the warriors go forth" or "so that the warriors may go forth." Either *G* or *M* is possible, but the parallelism favors *G*.

b   Dittographic; so Cornill, Rudolph, Bright, and so *JB*, *NAB*. Volz suggests reading וְנַפְתּוּחִים "and the Naphtuhim" (Gen 10:13; 1 Chr 1:11). This is ingenious but unconvincing; it is not necessary to have two ethnic groups in the second colon.

10a   These words break with the style of the poem, making the meaning of the battle explicit; the sequence is similar to Isa 34:8 (Volz).

b   Omit these epithets with *G*; since in the first colon *G* reads "to the Lord our God," the text of *G* itself seems to have undergone expansion (see Janzen, pp. 79, 81, 216 n. 23).

11a—a   Qere' הִרְבֵּית, ketib הרביתי: this is the archaic spelling (compare 2:19, 20, 33).

Structure

For the ordering of the oracles against Egypt in the array of oracles against foreign nations, see the general article above.

Verses 2–12 make up the first oracle against Egypt; chronologically it is prior, being dated in 605 (vv 13–24 are to be dated in 589/588 or thereafter, given the pun on the name of Hophra in v 17). Each of the oracles has a superscription (vv 2, 13); the poetry of vv 3–12 gives every evidence of unity.

The poem is dominated by short cola of two or three accented words[1] and by sequences of a bicolon plus a tricolon (see below).

The poem offers sudden transitions,[2] so that some earlier critics were impelled to rearrange the verses in a more "logical" order;[3] but to the contrary, these very shifts help to generate excitement.

The poem falls into two halves, vv 3–8 and 9–12; I suggest later (see Form) that vv 3–8 are addressed to the Babylonians and vv 9–12 to the Egyptians. Each half begins with a series of masculine plural imperatives: the two occurrences of עֲלוּ (vv 4, 9) help to bind the two

---

1   Two or three "units" in the terminology of Michael P. O'Connor: see his *Structure*, 314.

2   Snaith, "Jeremiah XLVI," 22–23.

3   Albert Condamin, "Transpositions accidentelles (1): Jér 46,3–12," *RB* 12 (1903) 419–21; Johann Konrad Zenner, "Ein Beispiel 'kolumnenweiser Verschrei-

halves together, not the least because both play with ambiguity (see Interpretation); and they are reinforced by the first-person singular (implied) cohortative אֶעֱלֶה in v 8 and the feminine singular imperative עֲלִי in v 11. The two parts are also bound together by the two occurrences of "Euphrates" (vv 6, 10) and by the verbs "stumble" and "fall" in association with "warrior" (גִּבּוֹר, vv 6, 12), and more subtly by the contrast between the boastfulness of Egypt, personified in the masculine singular, who will "cover the earth" (v 8), and the outcry of Egypt, personified in the feminine singular, which "fills the earth" (v 12).

The first part begins with imperatives that are battle orders (vv 3–4) and ends with a quotation that offers three cohortatives (two of them implied: see Interpretation) (v 8b). Verse 5 and 7 open with the interrogatives "why?" (מַדּוּעַ) and "who?" (מִי), respectively. Verse 5 and its continuation in v 6 offer both "warrior" (גִּבּוֹר) and "flee" (נוס) twice, and v 7 continues in v 8b with an indirect answer to "who?" with the quotation from that personage.

Within the second part (vv 9–12) the masculine plural imperatives in v 9 are paralleled by the feminine singular imperatives in v 11 (one notes again עֲלוּ in v 9 and עֲלִי in v 11). But whereas the imperatives in vv 3–4 were transparent battle orders, those in v 9 are ambiguous; they may be understood either as parallel battle orders or as mocking orders enjoining panic (see Interpretation), and those in v 11 can be taken only as mockery. It is in vv 10 and 11 that the principal personages are introduced explicitly, Yahweh in v 10 and Egypt in v 11.

Verses 3–4 are analyzed as a bicolon and two tricola; vv 5–6, by contrast, consist of a bicolon, a tricolon, and two bicola, and vv 7–8 are a bicolon and a tricolon. Verse 9 is a bicolon followed by a tricolon, as is v 10 as well (if "in the land of the north by the river Euphrates" is taken as two cola). Verse 11, by contrast, appears to be a tricolon followed by a bicolon (the vocative "poor virgin Egypt" being taken as the closing of a tricolon), and v 12 closes the poem with two bicola.

Form

After the superscription (v 2), the poem proper (vv 3–12) is a mocking song, taunting Egypt for its lack of prowess in the battle at Carchemish (for mockery in general in these oracles see Form in Oracles against Foreign Nations). The mockery is achieved by sudden transitions (see Structure); by ambiguity in vv 4 and 9 (see Interpretation), in which the commands shift from a summons to battle (vv 3–4) to what may be a summons to battle but which can equally well be a summons to flight (v 9) to a summons to seek medical help (v 11); by ironic rhetorical questions (vv 5, 7); by the contrast between the cited boastful words of Egypt personified as a conquering king (v 8) and the affirmation of the wailing of Egypt personified as a virgin (v 11); and by the emphatic "in vain" in v 11 as a judgment on all the efforts of Egypt. Tension is achieved in the poem by leaving much unsaid: if the Nile rises (v 7), it also falls; and the identity of the one mocked is only hinted at (the references to horses in vv 4 and 9 and to the battle at the Euphrates in vv 6 and 10, the simile of the rising and falling of the Nile in vv 7 and 8) until the explicit words of v 11 ("poor virgin Egypt").

Who speaks? It is not clear (the one occurrence of a first-person singular verb, v 5, is evidently unoriginal—see Text and Interpretation). The poem begins (vv 3–4) with seven imperatives making up a summons to battle (compare 6:4–6),[4] specifically calling for the preparation of weapons and equipment, so that ostensibly the speaker is a commander, evidently a Babylonian one (see below), but the tone of mockery that emerges suggests either Yahweh (in spite of a third-person reference to Yahweh in v 10), Jrm, or even a bystander.[5] (Compare the discussion on the form of 4:5–6.)

bung,'" *BZ* 3 (1905) 122–27; Bardtke, "Fremdvölker-prophet," *ZAW* 53 (1935) 230; Condamin, pp. 296–301.

4   Robert Bach, *Die Aufforderungen zur Flucht und zum kampf im alttestamentlichen Prophetenspruch* (WMANT 9; Neukirchen: Neukirchener, 1962) 51, 63.

5   Ibid., 67.

Who is being addressed? In v 9 it is implicitly Egypt, and in vv 11–12 it is explicitly so. But I would suggest that Babylon is addressed in vv 3–4, and by implication in vv 5–8: one notes that it is "they" and "their warriors" in v 5 that are panicked and beaten down, not "you." Furthermore, if the battle orders in v 4aα are to cavalry, and if Egypt lacked cavalry (see Interpretation), then one is moved to hear the orders as being addressed to Babylon.

Verse 5 suddenly asks the ironic question, "Why have the warriors fled?" (compare the question in 30:6), and v 6 continues with more details of the debacle.

Verse 7 raises the parallel ironic question, "Who is this who behaves like the Nile?" and continues by citing the boastful words of him who is mocked (compare Isa 14:13–14; 37:24–25; Ezek 27:3; 28:2).[6] Verse 9 reverts to military commands, but this time they may be not words of summons to battle but a summons to flight (see Interpretation).[7] Verse 10aα is evidently a secondary explanation; v 10aβb is an explicit announcement of judgment (compare Isa 31:8), closing with the explanation that the debacle is a sacrifice to Yahweh (the diction is imitated in Isa 34:6). In v 11 the speaker mockingly urges Egypt to get medical help: the incurable wound is a traditional curse.[8] Verse 12a affirms that the humiliation of Egypt will be known by all, and v 12b recapitulates v 6b.

Setting

Only earlier critics who rejected the authenticity of all the oracles against foreign nations (see the general article Oracles against Foreign Nations) have rejected the authenticity of this oracle; Hyatt states, "This oracle has greater claim to authenticity than any other in the collection,"[9] and Bright says, "The poem seems unquestionably to come from Jeremiah himself and is, for vividness and poetic quality, unexcelled by anything in the book."[10]

Jrm evidently reacted to the battle of Carchemish by proclaiming 4:5–8, 13–18, 29–31, and 6:1–8 over Judah (see Setting on those passages), and it is altogether plausible to envisage his proclaiming the present passage over Egypt at the same time.

A major difficulty, given the conclusions of the present study, is the occurrence of the phrase "terror all around" in v 5: if that phrase was devised by Jrm originally as a new name for Pashhur (20:1–6); if that incident of renaming took place in the context of the smashing of the flask (chapter 19); and if that smashing of the flask was a public gesture symbolizing the inevitability of punishment, dated here to December 601, then the occurrence of the phrase in the present passage is an anomaly. I hope that the solution proposed here, that מִסָּבִיב "all around" is an early gloss, is not ad hoc: for indications that the full phrase is out of place here see Text.

One may thus take the datum of v 2 as the setting: the battle took place in May or June of 605, so that a date for this poem in the summer of 605 is undoubtedly correct.

Of course Jrm's expectations in uttering the oracle were undoubtedly mixed: the mockery of Egypt would not only disgrace Egypt but would also disgrace those officials in Judah who had been counting on Egypt as a counterpoise to Babylonia.

The vocabulary of the passage is that of Jrm. Particularly noteworthy is v 11a, where "balm" and "Gilead" are used in phraseology distinct from that in 8:22: the two nouns occur otherwise in the OT in the context of seeking relief from pain only in 51:8. (And it may be added that v 11 shares vocabulary with 30:13 as well.) Equally noteworthy is the verb גָעַשׁ hitpa'el or hitpo'el "be convulsed," which occurs with "waters" in v 7 and with that noun restored in 5:22; such a subject and this verb do not appear otherwise in the OT.

Interpretation

■ 1 For the peculiar syntax of this introduction see 1:2 and 14:1.

6   See Hans Walter Wolff, "Das Zitat im Propheten-spruch," *Gesammelte Studien zum Alten Testament* (TBü 22; Munich: Kaiser, 1973) 83–85; Otto Eissfeldt, *Der Maschal im Alten Testament* (Giessen: Töpelmann 1913) 66.

7   Compare Bach, *Flucht*, 15–20.

8   Hillers, *Treaty-Curses*, 64–66.

9   Hyatt, p. 1105.

10   Bright, p. 308.

■ **2** Pharaoh Neco (II) ruled Egypt from 610/609 to 594. In 609 he marched north through Palestine; King Josiah was killed trying to prevent his progress. Neco continued to Carchemish on the River Euphrates in Syria and consolidated his position west of the river; the site of Carchemish is northeast of Aleppo, near the present-day Syrian village of Jerablus (36° 50' N, 38° 0' E) on the Turkish frontier; the ruins are on the Turkish side of the border. Having fortified the city, Neco threatened the power of Babylon, and in 605 the Babylonian king Nabopolassar sent his son Nebuchadrezzar north; the latter inflicted a crushing defeat on Neco. It is this battle that is celebrated in the present passage. Though Nebuchadrezzar was not yet "king of Babylon," he would become so a few months after the battle, his father having died.[11] For פְּרָת "Euphrates" compare the discussion in 13:1–12aα.

■ **3** In the context of battle the verb ערך means "arrange" or "prepare" soldiers or weapons; its passive participle occurs in a battle context in 6:23. The two nouns מָגֵן and צִנָּה refer to two kinds of shields, a small one (the buckler) held in the left hand to protect the head, and a large one, the full body shield.[12] (Neither *G* nor *V* reflect the difference.) The relative size of the two is secured by 1 Kgs 10:16–17 and the parallel 2 Chr 9:15–16: in that narrative it is said that Solomon made each צִנָּה of six hundred shekels of gold, and made each מָגֵן of three minas of gold (1 Kings) or three hundred shekels of gold (2 Chr); whether the mina is fifty shekels or sixty,[13] the מָגֵן is smaller than the צִנָּה, and thus the translation "buckler and shield" is correct.[14]

■ **4** The noun in the second colon, פָּרָשִׁים, covers two homonyms: (1) a synonym for "horses" (singular *pārāš*, theoretical plural *pĕrāšîm*, actual plural perhaps attracted to the form of the second homonym); (2) "horsemen" (singular **parrāš* > *pārāš*, plural **parrāšîm* > *pārāšîm*: for that meaning see 4:29).[15] The verb is likewise open to several meanings: עָלָה can mean "go up" into battle, "mount" (one's horse or chariot), or of horses, "rear." Syntactically the noun can be taken either as a complement or as a vocative. Robert Bach lays out three possible meanings: (1) "mount your steeds," (2) "mount, O horsemen," and (3) "rear up, O horses,"[16] and Rudolph notes the first two;[17] both conclude correctly that the parallelism favors the first meaning. It must be noted, however, that the similar nouns in the battle orders of v 9 are vocatives (see there), so the possibility of multiple meanings here helps to generate the diction there.

These first two cola then suggest orders to cavalry. Cavalry as well as chariotry were employed in warfare in this period. Assyria certainly had cavalry (2 Kgs 18:23, and one notes the many depictions in Assyrian bas-reliefs),[18] and thus the Babylonians; but the Egyptians did not. The phraseology in Isa 31:1 suggests that the Egyptians boasted in their chariotry,[19] but the skills and equipment necessary for cavalry evidently came from the steppes of Asia into Mesopotamia, and from there into Europe.[20] These battle orders are thus ironic, reminding the hearer of this lack in the Egyptian forces (compare

11   John A. Wilson, "Neco," *IDB* 3:530–31; Cyrus H. Gordon, "Carchemish," *IDB* 1:536; Bright, *History*, 326.

12   For depictions see Yadin, *Warfare*, 13–14.

13   Ovid R. Sellers, "Weights and measures," *IDB* 4:832–33.

14   See Gray, *Kings*, 265; W. Stewart McCullough, "Buckler," *IDB* 1:472–73.

15   Zorell, pp. 671–72, has two entries; *HALAT*, 919, discusses the two meanings under a single entry. See in detail Sigmund Mowinckel, "Drive and/or Ride in O.T.," *VT* 12 (1962) 289–95.

16   Bach, *Flucht*, 51, n. 1.

17   Rudolph, p. 266.

18   Yadin, *Warfare*, 297; for illustration see conveniently John Alexander Thompson, "Camel," *IDB* 1:491, and in more detail, Yadin, *Warfare*, 380–85.

19   Wildberger, *Jesaja*, 1226, 1230.

20   Adolf Erman, *Life in Ancient Egypt* (London: Macmillan, 1894, rep. New York: Dover, 1971) 492–93, 546; Barbara Mertz, *Red Land, Black Land, Daily Life in Ancient Egypt* (New York: Dodd, Mead, 1978) 144; Edward M. Jope, "Vehicles and Harness," *A History of Technology* (ed. Charles Singer et al.; New York/London: Oxford University, 1956) 2:555–56.

the mockery of the Assyrian commander to those in Jerusalem in regard to their depending on Egypt for chariots and horsemen, 2 Kgs 18:23–24).

The translation "form up" for יצב hitpa'el is an approximation: the verb elsewhere means "station oneself" (compare v 14), "present oneself" (for example, before God: Josh 24:1).[21] The כּוֹבַע is a helmet; it was probably made of leather for soldiers, and doubtless consisted of a cap with a long flap to cover the cheek and ears.[22]

The verb in M in the next colon, מרק, means "polish, burnish," not "whet" (Bright) or "sharpen" (JB). Conceivably the troops might be commanded to polish their lances to frighten the enemy, but as Rudolph remarks,[23] when forming up for battle it is too late to polish one's lance. The emendation of Rudolph, suggested by Ehrlich, then commends itself, to read "uncover, draw" (ריק hip'il): this verb appears in exactly this context in Ps 35:3. The רֹמַח is a lance, a spear with a long shaft, evidently used for thrusting rather than hurling;[24] an Egyptian model from the Middle Kingdom (2050–1800) shows soldiers with shield and lance, and the lance appears to be about the length of a soldier's height or a trifle longer[25] (compare the description of the כִּידוֹן, "spear," in 6:23).

The word סִרְיוֹן is "scale-armor," a coat of mail,[26] small pieces of metal joined together like fish scales.[27] Depictions of Assyrian scale-armor show a shirt reaching down simply to the waist.[28]

■ 5 The text of M has רָאִיתִי, "I have seen," after מַדּוּעַ "why?" so that one would have to read the first colon as "Why have I seen (it)?" and the second as "They are panicked." G omits the verb; one would then read the first colon as "Why are they panicked?" The occurrence of the same pair of words in 30:6, part of another mocking song, is an argument in favor of the reading of the verb; but in the present passage, in contrast to 30:6, the verb does not take an object and really does not add strength to the poem, which is extremely concise. The fact that G omits it suggests that it is a secondary addition.

The adjective חַתִּים "panicked" is related to the verb חתת, for which see 1:17. For סוג nip'al + אָחוֹר "draw back" see 38:22.

The verb יֻכַּתּוּ is כתת hop'al (or passive qal), "be beaten down, beaten to pieces": the same stem is used of idol-images (Mic 1:7) and the city gate (Isa 24:12).

The noun מָנוֹס appears to be a cognate accusative, thus "they have fled a fleeing" (so BDB; the present study notes the possibility of another cognate accusative with a verb of motion, 3:12), but some references suggest it is a substitution for an infinitive absolute (Zorell; HALAT; compare GKC, sec. 117q). The translation here, "headlong," is that of JB and NAB; Bright uses "pell-mell." But conceivably the noun carries the meaning it does elsewhere, "refuge," thus "they have fled (for) safety."

If the text is correctly reconstructed here, I suggest that the use of the hip'il stem be taken into account, that is, that the verb here may be transitive, and מָגוֹר, "terror," its object. The soldiers then were not able to turn terror away. For מָגוֹר "terror" see 20:3–6.

This verse offers marvelous assonance: the repeated ā-ô sequence (מָגוֹר, מָנוֹס, אָחוֹר), the sequence of doubled consonants (יֻכַּתּוּ, גִּבּוֹרֵיהֶם, חַתִּים, הֵמָּה—the second and fourth are particularly close with ḥatt- and -katt-) and the sequence n-s (מָנוֹס נָסוּ, נְסוּגִים).

■ 6 The two jussives in the first half of the verse do not mean "let him not," but "he cannot," as Luther already recognized.[29] JB uses superlatives for the subjects of the verbs: "The fastest cannot escape, nor the bravest save himself."

■ 7 Behind the question "Who rises like the Nile?" is the awareness that the Nile also sinks, as the antecedent passage Amos 8:8 affirms. And not only does the Nile itself rise, but Pharaoh Neco has "ascended" with his army to the upper Euphrates (one notes the same verb in that context in 2 Kgs 23:29); but again, having "ascended" to the Euphrates, he will descend to his own

21   Walter J. Harrelson, "Worship in Early Israel," BR 3 (1958) 4–5.
22   John W. Wevers, "Helmet," IDB 2:580; Yadin, Warfare, 15, with illustration; for further illustrations see ANEP, numbers 160 and 174.
23   Rudolph, p. 266.
24   John W. Wevers, "Weapons and implements of war," IDB 4:824.

25   ANEP, number 180.
26   HALAT, 726–27, with bibliography.
27   ANEP, number 161.
28   Yadin, Warfare, 418–19.
29   See König, Syntax, sec. 186c; GKC, sec. 107p; Joüon, Gramm., sec. 114k.

territory once more. (And the verb will be used in a still more universal sense in the Egyptian boast cited in v 8b.)

The plural "rivers" (נְהָרוֹת), given the parallel with the Nile, may be the canals of Egypt (compare Exod 7:19), but the verb "are convulsed" and the cosmic boast of v 8b suggest the underground rivers (Pss 24:2; 74:15). For "are convulsed" (געשׁ hitpa'el) compare 5:22. The lack of concord between the plural "rivers" and the singular suffix on "waters" is curious, but the original text may be מָיִם (compare v 8a).

■ **8** For the bracketing of v 8a see Text.

Given the cohortative אֹבִידָה in the last colon, the previous two verbs must likewise be construed as cohortatives: lamed-he verbs have no separate cohortative forms (GKC, sec. 75l).

"Arise," "cover the earth": the metaphorical Euphrates is portrayed by Isaiah in a similar vein (Isa 8:7–8), and there too "arise" (עלה) is used. Of course the Nile does cover the dry land every year. But given the context, is there an ironic reminder here of the waters that "covered" the Egyptian chariots at the exodus (Exod 14:28; 15:5, 10)?

The first vowel in אֹבִידָה "let me destroy" is odd (GKC, sec. 68i).

■ **9** Here the Egyptians are addressed (see Form). The first colon is a clever variation on the first two cola of v 4: there עֲלוּ הַפָּרָשִׁים was determined to mean "mount the steeds"; here the phrase is עֲלוּ הַסּוּסִים, which by the analogy of that colon would be taken to mean "mount the horses." But the verb in the second colon of the present verse is intransitive, so that the noun that follows it must be a vocative; therefore the noun "horses" in the first colon must likewise be vocative. All three verbs in v 9a are ambiguous: עלה may mean "go up, advance" into battle, or "rear up"; הלל hitpo'el could presumably mean "rage into battle" as well as "run wild"; "go out" (יצא) may mean "go forth to battle" (the normal implication) or "escape the disaster" (compare 11:11). The pessimistic meanings are prominent, given the tone of the whole

poem. Thus the major participants in the battle are addressed, the horses, the chariotry, and the warriors.

For "Cush," the area of what is today southern Sudan, see the discussion of כּוּשִׁי "Ethiopian" in 13:23. "Put" is a geographical term that cannot be located with precision. However, G and V here, as often, translate "Libyans," and the associations of the term, both in the OT and in Persian and Babylonian texts, are with Libya; and identification with Punt, in Somaliland (so Rudolph and Bright), is to be rejected.[30] "Lud" can only be Lydia in Asia Minor; Lydian mercenaries were present in Egypt ever since their king Gyges sent military aid to Pharaoh Psammetichus late in the first half of the seventh century.[31] Thus all three of these regions represent contingents in the Egyptian army. "Who grasp the buckler" and "who draw the bow" are simple references to infantry.[32]

■ **10** For the secondary addition in v 10aα see Text: it resembles Isa 34:8, a verse which is part of a passage best dated at the end of the sixth century.[33] For the image of the sword "devouring" as a metaphor for Yahweh's punishment see 2:30. For the parallel of שׂבע, "be sated," and רוה, "drink one's fill," see 31:14. The metaphor of a "sacrifice" (זֶבַח) for the punishment of a nation on the day of Yahweh is found, previous to Jrm, in Zeph 1:7.

■ **11** G went astray in the syntax here, understanding "Gilead" as a vocative parallel to the vocatives in v 9— "Go up, O Gilead, and get balsam for the virgin daughter of Egypt"! For the balm in Gilead see 8:22. One notes early evidence for the export of balm from Gilead to Egypt in Gen 37:25.

"Poor virgin Egypt" is literally "virgin daughter Egypt": this personification combines both "daughter" (compare 4:11) and "virgin" (compare 31:4). The double appellation probably did not exist before Jrm's time: it occurs both in Isa 23:12, in reference to Sidon (evidently not authentic to Isaiah but to be dated to the time of Esarhaddon),[34] and in Jer 14:17, in reference to "my people," but in both passages G lacks "virgin." However it

---

30   Thomas O. Lambdin, "Put," *IDB* 3:971.

31   Machteld J. Mellink, "Lud, Ludim," *IDB* 3:178–79.

32   Compare the Egyptian models, *ANEP*, numbers 179, 180.

33   Wildberger, *Jesaja*, 1341.

34   Ibid., 865. Wildberger cautiously proposes that the double appellation is correct in the passage: ibid., 858.

occurs in Lam 1:15 with Judah and in Lam 2:13 with Zion, and then in Isa 47:1 with Babylon.

For the association of "remedies" (רְפֻאוֹת) with "new skin" (תְּעָלָה) see 30:13.

■ 12 Given both the verb שׁמע, "hear (of)," in the first colon and the noun צְוָחָה, "outcry," in the second colon, one expects קוֹלֵךְ, "your voice," in the first colon, not what is in *M*, קְלוֹנֵךְ, "your shame"; so it is not surprising that *G* does read "your voice," but that is surely the *lectio facilior*. For קָלוֹן, "shame," see 13:26, where the word is used in a sexual sense; for צְוָחָה, "outcry," see 14:2. "Warrior on warrior" (גִּבּוֹר־בְּגִבּוֹר) is an example of the form X-preposition-X, for which see 9:2, 5 (on this see 9:1–8, Structure and Form). "Stumble" (כשׁל) and "together" (יַחְדָּו) are associated in 6:21 as well.

Aim

Judah had been a vassal of Egypt, but suddenly (18:7) that day was over; by Yahweh's plan it was Babylon that loomed over the horizon. There were always those in Judah who hoped for support from Egypt against the pressure of the Mesopotamian power (Isa 30:1–5; 31:1–3; compare Jer 37:5), but that hope would now be in vain. Poor pathetic Egypt! By Yahweh's act the bows of the mighty are broken, but the feeble put on strength (1 Sam 2:4): it is a crucial lesson for the people of God to remember.

Egypt Will Go into Exile

Bibliography

Christensen
  Transformations, 218–21.
Condamin, Albert
  "Notes d'exégèse de l'Ancien Testament, III. Le boeuf Apis restitué dans Jér. 46,15," *RSR* 7 (1917) 98–100.
Girard, L. Saint-Paul
  "La colère de la Colombe (note sur Jérémie 25,38 et 46,16; 50,15)," *RB* 40 (1931) 92–93.
Hoffmeier
  "Apries."

46

13 [The word]ᵃ what [*M*: that]ᵃ Yahweh spoke
  to Jeremiah [the prophet]ᵇ in regard to
  the coming of [Nebuchadrezzar]ᶜ the
  king of Babylon to strike down the
  land of Egypt:

14 Declare [in Egypt and announce]ᵃ in Migdol,
  and announce in Memphis [and in Tahpanhes,]ᵇ
  say, "Form up
    and stand ready,
      for a sword has devoured those around
        you."

15 Why ⟨is Apis fleeing?⟩ᵃ
  ᵇYour stalwart oneᵇ has not stood fast,
    for Yahweh thrust him out.

16 ᵃ⟨Has⟩ ⟪Rahab⟫ ⟨been great?⟩ᵃ
  ⟨he has stumbled,⟩ᵇ yes, fallen!—
  ⟪and they said⟫ᶜ to each other, [. . .]ᶜ
    "Up,ᵈ let us return to our people,
      and to the land of our birth,
        from the presence of the sword of ⟨the
          oppressor!⟩ᵉ

Text

13a Omit הַדָּבָר with *G* (compare *G* in 25:2).
b   Omit with *G*; compare Janzen, p. 148.
c   Omit with *G*; compare Janzen, p. 141.
14a Omit with *G* (so Duhm, Giesebrecht, Cornill, Condamin, Rudolph, Bright).
b   Omit with *G* (so Duhm, Giesebrecht, Cornill, Volz, Condamin, Rudolph, Bright), an addition from 44:1.
15a Revocalize *M* נִסְחַף, "he was swept away," as נָס חַף with *G*; see further Interpretation.
b—b It is a temptation to read *M* אַבִּירֶיךָ, "your stalwart one," as אַבְרֵךְ, evidently an Egyptian word (Gen 41:43); see further Interpretation.
16a—a *M* is clearly wrong: the first part of the verse reads, "He increased one stumbling; also each fell to his neighbor. . . ." The verbs כשל and נפל must make up a colon of their own (compare v 6bβ). I follow the suggestion of Rudolph to see "Rahab" in the first colon, a nickname for Egypt; but Rudolph reads the colon as רַהַב הָרַב, "Rahab the great," words which cannot stand as a colon of their own. The simplest solution is to leave the consonants of the verb intact, vocalizing הָרְבָה and inserting רַהַב, which will have dropped out by haplography. The he interrogative will then mark a question parallel to the one at the beginning of v 15.
b   Revocalize *M* כּוֹשֵׁל to כָּשַׁל with *G* (so all commentators).
c   Replacing וַיֹּאמְרוּ before אִישׁ אֶל־רֵעֵהוּ (so all commentators).
d   For קוּמָה (singular) the Oriental qere' has the more logical קוּמוּ (plural). The same pattern evidently occurs in Judg 18:9: see George F. Moore, *A Critical and Exegetical Commentary on Judges* (ICC; Edinburgh: Clark, 1895) 393. Given the probability that the plural imperative is to be read at the beginning of v 17, the plural is preferable here. See further Form.
e   Revocalizing הַיּוֹנָה. One assumes that Rahab (Egypt) is the oppressor, and it is referred to in the masculine singular. See further Interpretation.

⟨Call⟩[a] ⟨the name of⟩[b] Pharaoh [king of Egypt][c]
'Loudmouth missed his chance'!"

18 By my life,
oracle of [the king,][a]
Yahweh ⟩of hosts⟨[a] [is his name,][a]
《he shall be bypassed》[b] like Tabor among the mountains,
and like Carmel into the sea ⟨he shall be brought.⟩[c]

19 Baggage for exile prepare for yourself,
poor enthroned Egypt!—
for Memphis shall become a desolation
and shall be burned, without inhabitant.

20 A splendid[a] heifer is Egypt:
horseflies[b] from the north are coming
[c]upon her![c]

21 Even her mercenaries in her midst are like fatted calves:
yes, even they have turned and fled,
not one has stood fast,
for the day of their calamity has come upon them,
the time of their punishment.

22 Her voice 《like bronze》[a] goes forth,
for in a swarm they come,
and with axes they enter upon her,
like those felling trees.

23 [a]They have cut down[a] her forest,
oracle of Yahweh,
《like》[b] exploring 《hoppers,》[b]
for they are more than locusts
and are without number.

24 Poor Egypt has stood ashamed,
has been given into the hand of the people of the north.

25 {Yahweh of hosts, God of Israel, has said,}[b] I am going to punish Amon of Thebes, and Pharaoh, {and Egypt, and her gods, and her kings, and Pharaoh,}[c] and those who trust in him. {26/ And I shall give them into the hand of those who seek their life and into the hand of Nebuchadrezzar king of Babylon and into the hand of his servants; and after that she shall dwell as in days of old, oracle of Yahweh.}[d] [a]

27 [And you, do not fear, my servant Jacob,
and do not be dismayed, Israel,
for I am going to save you from afar,
your offspring from the land of their captivity;
Jacob shall return and rest,
be relaxed with none to frighten him.

28 You, do not fear, my servant Jacob,
oracle of Yahweh,
for I am with you;
for I shall make an end of all the nations
where I have driven you,
but of you I will not make an end,
and I will chastise you moderately,
though I certainly will not leave you unpunished.][a]

17a Vocalize קְרָאוּ with *G* and *V* (so all commentators). *M* "they called" would be odd without a connective.

b Vocalize שֵׁם with *G* and *V* (so all commentators); *M* "there."

c Though both *G* and *M* have these words, they are surely an early gloss; omit (so also Rudolph, Bright).

18a *G* reads simply "says the Lord God"; at least "the king" and "is his name" are additions, and perhaps "of hosts" as well (see Janzen, pp. 79, 216, n. 22).

b A verb is missing; I propose הֶעֱבַר: it would be a variant on הֶעֱבִיר in v 17 and would be in assonance with כְּתָבוֹר which follows—indeed the double sequence bet + reš would be a plausible occasion for haplography. See Preliminary Observations and Structure.

c Vocalizing יָבֹא (or יוּבָא) for *M* יָבוֹא; compare 37:16 and Prov 7:22, where the same revocalization seems necessary.

20a Read with many MSS. יָפֶה-פִיָה; *M* יְפֵה-פִיָה.

b Collective (see Interpretation).

c—c Read with many MSS. (and *G*, *V*) בָהּ for *M* בָא.

22a Following *V*, either read נְחֹשֶׁת, or perhaps assume a Hebrew by-form נָחֻשׁ homonymous with the *M* reading נָחָשׁ, "snake" (compare Aramaic נְחָשׁ, "bronze," and, perhaps, the proper name עִיר נָחָשׁ, 1 Chr 4:12: see Victor R. Gold, "Irnahash," *IDB* 2:725).

23a—a Construe *M* כָּרְתוּ as perfect qal rather than as pi'el imperative.

b The text of *M*, כִּי לֹא יֵחָקֵר, cannot be right, since it is not a full colon, having only one "unit" (O'Connor, *Structure*, 315); read כִּי-לָֽק חֵקֶר. For כִּי-לָֽק compare 51:14, and for the parallel between יֶלֶק and אַרְבֶּה see Nah 3:15b.

25–26a These two verses are in prose and are a later addendum to vv 13–24 (so Volz, Rudolph, Bright ["probably of later date," p. 308]). Rudolph points out that v 25 is a commentary on v 24a, and v 26a on v 24b.

b Omit with *G* (so also Cornill).

c Omit with *G* (so also Cornill, against Janzen, p. 118, who believes *G* is deficient by haplography). Rudolph omits only the second "Pharaoh," and in *BHS* he suggests, like Janzen, that *G* is deficient by haplography.

d *G* omits; the entire verse is a late addition. The first half of the verse is similar to 44:30, and the second half is the kind of mitigation found also in 49:6. Compare Janzen, pp. 41–43.

27–28a These verses are virtually identical with 30:10–11; they appear to belong in the context of chapter 30 and not here—though it is to be noted that these verses are missing in that chapter in *G* (that is, *G* 37:10–11 are missing), and they are present here in *G*. There are both verbal differences and spelling differences between the two texts. Verbal differences: 30:10, after יַעֲקֹב has נְאֻם-יהוה, and the words are missing in 46:27; in 46:28 the first words are אַתָּה אַל-תִּירָא עַבְדִּי יַעֲקֹב נְאֻם-יהוה, and these words

are missing in 30:11; in 30:11 נְאֻם־יהוה appears after
כִּי־אִתְּךָ אֲנִי, and these words are missing in 46:28;
30:11 has הֲפִצוֹתִיךָ שָּׁם, and 46:28 has הִדַּחְתִּיךָ שָׁמָּה;
30:11 has אַךְ אֹתְךָ, and 46:28 has וְאֹתְךָ. Spelling
differences: 30:10 מוֹשִׁיעֲךָ, 46:27 מוֹשִׁיעֲךָ; 30:10b
יַעֲקֹב, 46:27b יַעֲקֹב.

Preliminary Observations and Structure

There is no reason to doubt that after the introduction in
v 13 vv 14–24 make up a single poem: there is repeated
material that helps to bind the material together. Thus
Apis (v 15) is the bull-god: he "flees" (נוס) and "has not
stood fast" (לֹא עָמָד); Egypt's mercenaries (v 21) are "like
fatted calves," they "have fled" (נוס) and "have not stood
fast" (לֹא עָמְדוּ); and both of these sequences are followed
by a כִּי-clause of explanation. The figure of the bull-god
and the fatted calves is expanded by the metaphor of
Egypt as a splendid heifer (v 20), and the occurrences of
the verb "stand fast" (עמד) are enriched by the assonantal
variant הַמּוֹעֵד in v 14. In addition there are the two
occurrences of בַּת־מִצְרַיִם in vv 19 and 24 (here "poor
Egypt"). And it is equally clear that vv 25–26 and 27–28
are material added later.

Nevertheless, it is not easy to sense the shape and
movement of the poem, not only because of the shifts of
its rhetoric but also because at crucial points the text has
suffered damage. Verse 17 offers an unexpected play on
the name of Pharaoh, and v 18 brings an oath by Yahweh followed by an opaque comparison; Volz omits both
verses as the words of a later reader, but this solution is
inadmissible.

An understanding of v 18b is crucial. *T* assumed that
the subject of the verb (יָבוֹא in *M*, "come" or "come in") is
"his destruction," and this interpretation is reflected in
Calvin (so *NJV*: "So shall this come to pass," with the
notation "Meaning of Heb. uncertain"). More recently
commentators have assumed that the subject is personal,
Nebuchadrezzar or Babylon (*RSV*: "Like Tabor among
the mountains, and like Carmel by the sea, shall one
come"). Bright expresses the usual understanding of the
force of the comparison: "The last bicolon . . . describes
Babylon's irresistible might as towering over Egypt like a
lofty mountain peak. Though neither Tabor (on the
north of the Plain of Esdraelon) nor Carmel (by the sea,
behind Haifa) are especially tall, they give that impression because of their isolated positions and sheer

slopes."[1] This understanding of the half-verse goes back
at least to Luther: "That one shall march in as high as
Tabor is among the mountains and as Carmel is at the
sea";[2] compare *NEB*.

Now it is true that Babylon is represented in the
metaphor of the horseflies (singular in Hebrew, but, as I
propose, collective—see Interpretation) from the north
in v 20 and by "they" in vv 22–23, and is finally identified
as the "people of the north" in v 24, but it is gratuitous to
assume that Babylon is the subject of "come" in v 18. I
suggest that בַּיָּם (*RSV*, "by the sea") does not modify
"Carmel" but rather the verb, so that it must be understood as "go into the sea" or the like. It is Pharaoh and
his chariots that "went into the sea" in Exod 15:19, and I
suggest that it is Egypt and its chariots that are understood here. Carmel then may be understood as plunging
into the sea (perhaps Ps 46:3 lies in the back of the
thought).

But Tabor is not among the mountains, nor "going in"
among the mountains, as Carmel "goes into" the sea;
Tabor, as a matter of fact, is an isolated peak far from
other mountains.[3] If the comparison of Tabor likewise
refers to Egypt, then it is the isolation of Tabor that may
be the point of the comparison: one thinks of Isa 1:8,
"And poor Zion is left like a booth in a vineyard, like a
lodge in a cucumber field"—in both phrases the prepositions are כְּ and בְּ, as in the present passage. These
considerations suggest in turn that a verb has dropped
out at the beginning of the "Tabor" colon: "come," at the
end of the "Carmel" colon, is in any event in a position
curiously deferred. It must be a verb that reflects the
isolation of Tabor, and it must be a verb that could have
dropped out by haplography. I suggest a stem of עבר:
that verb has already occurred in the play on Pharaoh's
name in v 17, and the sequence bet-reš would then occur
in both the verb and the end of "Tabor." The verb I
propose then is יֵעָבֵר, literally "he shall be made to pass
by": the translation given here, "he shall be bypassed," is
not strictly speaking the same meaning but is smoother

---

1   Bright, p. 306.
2   "Jener wird daherziehen so hoch, wie der Berg
    Thabor unter den Bergen ist und wie der Karmel am

Meer ist."
3   See the photograph in Gus W. Van Beek, "Tabor,
    Mount," *IDB* 4:509.

English. Thus: "He shall be bypassed like Tabor among the mountains." And if a passive verb is correct here, then it is appropriate to read "come" as a passive, thus יָבָא, "he shall be brought" (compare the same emendation in 37:16). By this understanding Egypt, or the Pharaoh, shall be isolated and then plunged into the sea like the Pharaoh of old. This interpretation gains slightly in plausibility in that it moves smoothly from one of the meanings proposed here for the taunting name given to the Pharaoh in v 17 (see on this Interpretation for both vv 17 and 18).

The poem appears to break in two between vv 18 and 19 on the basis of gender reference. Egypt is addressed in the masculine singular in v 14b, and those second-person forms become third-person in vv 15–18—the name "Apis" reconstructed in v 15, the name "Rahab" perhaps to be restored in v 16, Pharaoh in v 17, and various third-person masculine pronouns in vv 15–18. (Rudolph is therefore in error to construe the masculine singular imperatives in v 14 as infinitive absolutes and to revocalize "those around you" with a feminine singular suffix.) By contrast Egypt is addressed as בַּת־מִצְרַיִם in v 19, thus feminine singular, and those second-person forms become third-person in vv 20–24. This analysis is preferable to that of Condamin and Rudolph, who divide the poem into two strophes, vv 14–19 and 20–24: Rudolph bases his division on the number of cola,[4] and Condamin, inserting v 25 between vv 21 and 22, believes that vv 14–19 deal with the invasion of Lower Egypt (Memphis), and vv 20–21, 25, 22–24 deal with the invasion of Upper Egypt (No-Amon).[5] Thus instead of an inclusio formed by vv 14 and 19 (Condamin), v 19 is parallel to v 14 in beginning the second half of the poem (commands addressed to Egypt, two occurrences of "Memphis").

Verses 15 and 21 likewise appear to be analogous verses in the two halves of the poem: both offer "flee" (נום) and "not stand fast" (לֹא עמד) followed by a כִּי-clause describing Yahweh's punishment. But there seem to be no other parallels between the two halves. Nor are there discernible symmetries in the sequence of groups of cola, or in the placement of כִּי-clauses; one can only point out that the number of cola introduced by כִּי increases as the poem proceeds: one colon in vv 14 and 15, two cola in vv 18, 19, and 21 (there twice!), and three cola in v 22, before reverting to two cola in v 23.

If the first colon of v 16 is correctly reconstructed, vv 15 and 16 open with parallel questions.

Verse 14 consists of a bicolon and a tricolon; the tricolon offers close parallelism in the first two cola and a כִּי-clause to close it off. Verse 15 is a tricolon, again with parallelism in the first two cola and a כִּי-clause to close it off. Verse 16, if the first colon is correctly reconstructed, consists of a bicolon and a tetracolon. Verse 17 can only be a bicolon, but not one with close parallelism. Verse 18 is doubtless a tricolon: the second and third cola are closely parallel, and the oath-form must serve as the first colon (compare Isa 49:18b). Verse 19 consists of two bicola; for the resemblances to v 14 see above. Verse 20 is a bicolon whose parallelism depends on the parataxis of the two metaphors. Verse 21 consists of a tricolon and a bicolon; again the first colon stands apart from the parallelism of the remaining two pairs of cola; for the resemblances to v 15 see above. Semantically vv 22 and 23 are close. Verse 22 is a tetracolon: the first colon stands apart from the כִּי-clauses, but the first two cola share the verb הלך; the second and third cola are in close parallelism, and the fourth colon extends the third with a simile. Verse 23a, if the text is correctly reconstructed, is a bicolon that develops the image of the last two cola of v 22, and v 23b, another bicolon, develops the simile of the second colon of v 23a. Finally v 24 is a closing bicolon.

Much of vv 25–26 is lacking in *G*; the verses are a midrash on the poem—v 25 on v 21 ("punish") and v 26 on v 24 ("into the hand").

Verses 27–28 duplicate 30:10–11; they are integrated into chapter 30 and are not here (for their structure therefore see there). The circumstance that *G* preserves the verses here and not in chapter 30 is explained by the order of the chapters in *G*: there the oracles against foreign nations precede chapter 30, and the duplication was omitted on its second occurrence.

Form

The poem of vv 14–24 is a judgment oracle against Egypt characterized by irony and mockery.

---

4   Rudolph, p. 271.
5   Condamin, pp. 302, 304.

The imperatives "declare," "announce," and "say" in v 14 are in the second-person plural; they are addressed to messengers or heralds, who are to fan out through Egypt to urge preparation for war (compare 4:5–6).[6] The battle orders to be given by the heralds, "form up" and "stand ready," are curiously in the second-person masculine singular; what battle orders are given to a single soldier? There is surely irony here (compare the commands to road-builders addressed to a single female, 31:21). The commands are of course addressed to Egypt personified as a man, but the identity of the personification is not made clear: v 15 mentions "Apis," v 16 "Rahab" (if the text is correctly reconstructed), and v 17 "Pharaoh," but inasmuch as the verb "flee," associated with Apis (v 15), and the verbs "stumble" and "fall," evidently assocated with Rahab (v 16), are elsewhere associated (v 6), it is clear that the reference of the personification shifts casually. There is another aspect to the irony: if the setting proposed for this poem is correct (the incursion of the Egyptian forces in 588 to relieve the Babylonian siege of Jerusalem: see Setting), the address to Egypt in Migdol and Memphis is an address to the home front, far from the present battle: not only will the Babylonians defeat Egypt in Judah but also they will press the battle back to Egypt proper. The battle commands are followed by the reason they have been uttered (the כִּי-clause, v 14bβ): the battle is going badly in the neighborhood.

Verse 15 opens with a rhetorical question, mocking Apis, the god of Memphis manifested as a bull: why is the god running away from battle? It is bad enough when gods are shipped away (43:12), but when they themselves run away, the lands they protect are truly helpless! The mocking would be reinforced if "your stalwart one" were revocalized as אַבְרֵךְ, evidently an Egyptian word (see Text and Interpretation), a word under other circumstances used to clear the way for an official chariot (Gen 41:43). There follows a brief report: Apis "has not stood fast." And again (v 15bβ) the reason for the flight of the god is made clear: it is at Yahweh's initiative.

If the text is correctly reconstructed, v 16 opens with a rhetorical question parallel to that which opens v 15, this time mocking Rahab, the personification of Egypt,

particularly of the Nile, which rises (and now falls!): compare v 8. There is again a brief report, "He has stumbled, yes fallen." The second part of the verse cites the words of the Egyptians in the context of their defeat, urging retreat (for the call to retreat compare 1 Kgs 22:36, and for an analogous call to attack compare 6:5). Does the singular "up!" suggest that there are only two soldiers, one speaking to the other, or does a similar sequence in Judg 18:9 suggest that the singular is idiomatic in this context?—see Text. There is even a hint that the speakers may be mercenaries: mercenaries are referred to in the earlier poem against Egypt (v 9), and the quotation "let us return to our people and to the land of our birth" may suggest non-Egyptians (one notes that 50:16b, with similar wording, refers to non-Babylonians). See further Interpretation.

Verse 17 offers a mocking change of name for the Pharaoh, evidently Hophra (see Setting and Interpretation): for such a change of name see 7:30–34 and 20:1–6. One is reminded of the mocking appellation of Rahab in Isa 30:7. If it is mercenary soldiers who speak at the end of v 16, do they continue their speech in this verse? It seems altogether likely: the mocking twisting of Pharaoh's name is certainly appropriate in their speech.

In v 18 Yahweh swears an oath that Egypt will be destroyed (at least this seems to be the point of the double simile: see Preliminary Observations).

Verse 19a resembles a battle-call, but it is a call to prepare to march out along with other prisoners of war (compare 10:17): the adjective "enthroned" is a taunt (compare both 10:17 and 21:13). The occasion for the call (v 19b) is the destruction of the great city Memphis.

Verse 20 is very similar to 6:2–3; that passage offers a description of lovely Zion and a description of her attackers, the two descriptions being laid side by side in ironic parataxis. So here: there is no irony here in the metaphor of the "heifer," which is an admirable beast; the irony is in the paratactic collocation with the horseflies (for the plural see Interpretation) that are landing on her.

The metaphor of the heifer leads to the simile in v 21: her mercenaries are like fatted calves. Again there is no irony in the simile as such, but fatted calves are raised for

---

6   For literature see 4:5–31, n. 4.

slaughter (see Interpretation). There follows another brief report: the mercenaries "have turned and fled," have not "stood fast"; likened to fatted calves, they have fled like the bull-god Apis. The כִּי-clause, like those in vv 14, 15, and 19, gives the reason for the debacle.

If "like bronze" is a correct restoration in v 22, the metaphors of v 20 continue in the report of Egypt's distress: the heifer lows as the horseflies attack her "with axes." This metaphor leads to the simile of the timbermen (the last colon of v 22) and to "her forest" (v 23), presumably a metaphor for her pride (see Interpretation), and to the comparison of the Babylonians to locusts in their number.

Verse 24 offers a summary, reporting the shame of Egypt when she is delivered into the power of Babylon.

Verses 25–26 are a divine announcement of judgment against Egypt; vv 27–28 are an oracle of salvation to Judah (for an analysis see on 30:10–11).

Setting

The poem is commonly accepted as authentic to Jrm. One may point particularly to v 19a; the phraseology there is close to that of 10:17. If the point of v 17 is a play on Hophra's name (see below), then that too argues in favor of authenticity.

It was originally Heinrich Ewald,[7] and then Cornill and Duhm, who proposed that the taunt in v 17 is a play on the name of Pharaoh Hophra (for the details see Interpretation); the proposal, however, has not won general acceptance (in favor of it: Eissfeldt,[8] Thompson, Hoffmeier;[9] judging it possible: Volz, Condamin; doubting it: Hyatt; against it: Rudolph; recognizing the existence of a pun, but not mentioning Cornill's suggestion: Bright).

Rudolph assigns to the poem the same setting as that for vv 3–12, that is, the year 605. But this is arbitrary: the locale of vv 3–12 was the Euphrates (vv 6, 10); here, by contrast, Babylon is represented as coming from the north to attack Egypt (vv 20, 24) in the same way as she is represented in attacking Judah (4:6 and often).

The mention of Tabor and Carmel likewise suggest a Palestinian locale for the poem. The incursion of Hophra's army into Palestine in the spring or early summer of 588 was an occasion for Jrm to insist that Babylon would prevail (37:7), and that incursion thus offers a fitting setting for the poem. There is therefore no reason to doubt that the pun in v 17 refers to Hophra.

There is no way to date the addition of that portion of v 25 found in G: it is tempting to suggest the invasion by Nebuchadrezzar of Egypt in 570, but of that invasion we have no details.[10] The material in vv 25–26 not found in G will have been added still later.

The setting of vv 27–28 = 30:10–11 will be not long after that proposed here for vv 14–24, so that it is understandable that the passage would be added as a counterpoise.

Interpretation

■ 14 For "Migdol" see 44:1; for "Memphis" see 2:16; for "form up" see v 4. "Stand ready" (כון hip'il with ל and a reflexive suffix) is found otherwise only in Ezek 38:7. For a possible ironic use of the singular imperatives here see Form. The address is to Egypt at home ("Migdol" and "Memphis"). "Those around you" suggests "those in your neighborhood" (NAB: "your neighbors"): if the setting proposed here is correct, those on the home front are being told that their forces in Judah have been defeated.

■ 15 The reconstruction of "Apis" here is accepted by most commentators and translations (exceptions: Volz, Rudolph, NJV). Apis (חַף) reflects the Egyptian ḥp; he was the bull-god, worshiped in Memphis from earliest times as a general god of fertility.[11] For the irony expressed by the image of the fleeing of the god see Form.

The word following "flee" in M is אַבִּירֶיךָ, construed as "your stalwart (bull)" in a plural of majesty. The noun occurs in 8:16; 47:3; 50:11 as a synonym for "stallions" (see there); it occurs several times with the implied meaning "bulls" (for example, Isa 34:7; Ps 22:17) and so fits here admirably. But it is tempting to ponder the possibility that the expression here should be revocalized as the exclamation "Abrek!" shouted before Joseph's chariot, Gen 41:43: the consonants match, and one can easily imagine the two yods to be secondary. Of course the vowels in "Abrek!" are not secure, nor is the (Egyptian?) word secure behind the Hebrew expression (see below), so it is even conceivable that Jrm intended a pun

7   Heinrich Ewald, *Die Propheten des Alten Bundes* (Stuttgart: Krabbe, 1841) 2:200.
8   Eissfeldt, "Drohorakel."
9   Hoffmeier, "Apries," 167–68.
10 Bright, *History*, 352; *ANET*, 308.
11 Thomas O. Lambdin, "Apis," *IDB* 1:157.

here on "your stalwart one." As for "Abrek," there is no consensus on whatever Egyptian expression may be represented by the Hebrew word.[12] Perhaps the most favored is that first suggested by Wilhelm Spiegelberg in 1903, 'b.-r.k "attention," literally "give your heart."[13] An alternative suggesion is ibrk, imperative, "do obeisance."[14] But if the word does occur in the present passage, the context favors a meaning like "Watch out!" more than "Do obeisance!"

"Thrust out" (הדף) is used in Ezek 34:11 of cattle "shoving": here Yahweh is stronger than the bull-god in a shoving match.

■ **16** Any reconstruction of the first colon must be tentative. I propose a he interrogative to match the question in v 15 (compare the two questions in vv 5 and 7). I further accept the suggestion of Rudolph that "Rahab" was originally in the colon; but whereas he proposes that הִרְבָּה is to be read רָהַב הָרַב, "Rahab the great," I retain the four consonants present, vocalizing הָרְבָה, and propose that רַהַב fell out after the verb by haplography.

"Rahab" makes a nice parallel to "Apis" in v 15. This name appears in several passages in the OT, sometimes to denote a primordial sea monster defeated by Yahweh (Job 9:13), sometimes as a symbol for Egypt (Isa 30:7); that is to say, the myth was historicized when Yahweh's primordial combat with the sea was identified with Yahweh's defeat of the Egyptians at the sea (compare Isa 51:9–10).[15] If the verb is רָבָה, it is a verb used in the flood narrative for the increase of the waters (Gen 7:17, 18). The passage will then be a taunt: Rahab, the sea monster, has been great, as the primordial waters were great at the time of the flood, and as the Nile is great at flood time (compare v 7); but Yahweh is victor.

The reference of "they" is not immediately clear: if the setting proposed for the passage is correct, it is the Egyptian soldiers fighting in Judah who speak, indeed perhaps just two mercenaries, urging each other to flee for home (on this see Form).

The last colon offers the first of two occurrences of a puzzling phrase that M transmits as מִפְּנֵי חֶרֶב הַיּוֹנָה; the other occurrence is 50:16 (see also there). Translations, beginning with the Versions, have treated both occurrences identically. The Versions differ from each other in their renderings: G renders "from the presence of the Greek sword," as if הַיּוֹנָה were יְוָנָה; V reflects a possible rendering of M, "from the presence of the sword of the dove"; S and T are similar, S offering "from the presence of the sword of the weakener" (mdwy, 'ap'el participle masculine singular of dwy, "become weak"), and T "from the presence of the sword of the enemy." Commentators and translations in the modern period have understood the second and third words of the phrase in either of two ways. Most have understood הַיּוֹנָה as a feminine participle modifying חֶרֶב "sword," even though the participle carries the article and "sword" does not[16] (so Giesebrecht, Cornill, Volz, Condamin, Rudolph, Bright; so KJV, JB, NEB, NJV, NAB: for example, Bright, "dreadful sword"; JB, "destroying sword"). Luther and RSV, however, understand the words as a construct phrase (RSV: "sword of the oppressor").

Clearly, taking the expression as a construct phrase is preferable. The present passage and the passage in chapter 50 that offers the other occurrence of the expression evidently have settings within a year of each other (see Setting on the present passage, and see 50:1—51:58, Structure, Form, Setting, *The Structure of 50:1—51:58; A Possible Setting for the Material in 50:1—51:58*). Therefore, in interpretation both passages have to be examined together. I propose that the two occurrences offer variant vocalizations. As already noted, the speakers in the last portion of the present verse are underlings, perhaps mercenaries, fighting in Judah (see Form); the appeal to flee is thus to abandon the ranks of the army. In 50:16, by contrast, the speakers are subject peoples in Babylon; the immediate context is not combat but lack of food. I propose then that in the present passage חֶרֶב, "sword," is correct, but that in 50:16 the word is to be

---

12 Westermann, *Genesis* 3:99.

13 So Thomas O. Lambdin, "Egyptian Loan Words in the Old Testament," *JAOS* 73 (1953) 146; so also Speiser, *Genesis*, 314; Bruce Vawter, *On Genesis, A New Reading* (Garden City, NY: Doubleday, 1977) 415.

14 Jozef Vergote, *Joseph en Egypte: Genèse chap. 37—50, à la lumière des études Egyptologiques récentes* (Louvain:

Publications universitaires, 1959) 135–41.

15 The mythological background is still not altogether clarified: see Wildberger, *Jesaja*, 1164, and compare Theodor H. Gaster, "Rahab," *IDB* 4:6, and Marvin H. Pope, *Job* (AB 15; Garden City, NY: Doubleday, 1973) 71.

16 See the discussions in König, *Syntax*, sec. 334p; GKC, sec. 126w.

vocalized חֹרֶב, "devastation, drought" (compare the shift from the repeated חֶרֶב, "sword," in 50:35–37 to חֹרֶב, "drought" in 50:38). If "Rahab" is correctly restored in the present verse, the oppressor is construed as masculine: the participle must therefore be הַיּוֹנֶה. In 50:16, by contrast, the oppressor is Babylon, construed as feminine: the participle there must therefore be הַיּוֹנָה. (For another instance of variant vocalizations of the same consonant sequence see 7:3 and 7.)

■ **17** Here is a taunt: Pharaoh is to receive a new name, šā'ôn he'ĕbîr hammô'ēd. The suggestion, made by several scholars, that the verb he'ĕbîr is a play on the name of the Pharaoh, Hophra, is accepted here (see Setting for the variety of opinion on the matter). Hophra's name in Egyptian, as noted in the discussion of 44:26–30, is w'h-ib-r'. A difficulty in the presumed pun is the contrast between the Egyptian ḥ, reproduced in the Hebrew spelling of his name with ḥ (חָפְרַע), and the h in the pun, but this may not be insuperable.[17]

The taunting name of the Pharaoh can be understood in several ways. The first is the understanding ordinarily given, rendered in the translation here by "Loudmouth missed his chance." The noun שָׁאוֹן, literally "din, uproar," here "loudmouth," is used more than once of the roaring of waves (Isa 17:12; Ps 65:8); the word here may then not only refer to Hophra's boasting but to the water of Egypt, defeated by Yahweh. The noun מוֹעֵד is an appointment, an appointed time (8:7); by this understanding, then, the Pharaoh is a boaster who has let the opportune time slip by. Hoffmeier suggests that Jrm is here calling attention to a convention of Egyptian wisdom, by which the loud, boisterous man is impetuous and uncontrollable and hence a fool, the very contrast to the Egyptian ideal, the wise and pious man.[18] But there is an altogether different possibility in the name: the second noun, הַמּוֹעֵד, can be read as the participle of the verb מעד: "he who is unsteady, who wobbles" (compare Ps 26:1; Job 12:5). This meaning of the word is particularly appropriate if it is intended to reflect to any degree the sounds of עמד (vv 15, 21): Egypt has not "stood fast." Further the first noun of the name, שָׁאוֹן, "din," is often used of the din of battle (for example, 25:31; Isa 13:4). And the verb עבר hip'il may mean "cause to pass away."

What one has then is "The roar (of battle) does away with the wobbler." But there is still another possibility for the noun שָׁאוֹן: there is a homonym, recorded only once in the OT, meaning "desolation, waste" (Ps 40:3), evidently a description of the underworld;[19] the name then can be taken to mean "Desolation does away with the wobbler." He is already under the jurisdiction of Sheol.

The way of understanding the name as "Din/desolation makes the wobbler pass away" paves the way for the first simile in v 18, which, by the emended text suggested here, is to be understood as "he shall be made to pass by like Tabor among the mountains" (see Preliminary Observations and Structure, and see below on v 18).

It is appropriate to quote Hoffmeier.

When we examine the extant historical evidence . . . , particularly the character sketch by Herodotus, we see an impetuous monarch struggling to secure his position in Egypt and abroad. He made two serious mistakes. The Syro-Palestinian campaign served only to raise the ire of Nebuchadrezzer [sic], and secondly his dispatching of troops to Libya was ill-timed and of no practical advantage to Egypt because the Chaldeans were still Egypt's enemies. His follies cost him the throne and the civil war that took place severely weakened Egypt, leaving Amasis, the usurper, vulnerable to Babylonian attack.[20]

It would appear, then, that if it was to Hophra that Jrm applied the mocking name, the name caught his character in several respects.

■ **18** The same oath form is found in 22:24.

The discussion in Preliminary Observations and Structure affirms that, given the present text, the point of the comparisons with Tabor and Carmel is not evident (so also Rudolph);[21] but at the same time one needs clarity in this verse in order to move through the remainder of the poem with any confidence. That discussion offers my tentative solution and the reasoning behind it: to insert יֵעָבֵר, literally "he shall be made to pass by," here translated "he shall be bypassed," before "like Tabor," and perhaps to revocalize the last word of the verse, יָבוֹא "he shall come," to יָבָא, "he shall be brought." By this

17   Hoffmeier, "Apries," 167–68.
18   Ibid., 168.
19   Kraus, *Psalmen*, 307; Dahood, *Psalms I*, 245.

20   Hoffmeier, "Apries," 168.
21   Rudolph, p. 270: "Man vermisst den Vergleichungs-spunkt."

understanding then the Pharaoh's venture in Judah is doomed.

Mount Tabor is an isolated peak at the eastern end of the Valley of Jezreel[22] (Atlas of Israel grid 188–233) with an elevation of 588 meters.[23] Mount Carmel juts out into the Mediterranean Sea just to the west of the present-day port of Haifa; there is today a Carmelite monastery at the northwestern end of the mountain at an elevation of 150 meters. The mountain extends to the southeast, reaching an elevation of 528 meters at its highest point 13 kilometers away.[24]

■ 19 There is a complicated relation between v 19a and 10:17: both mock a nation personified as a young woman to get ready for exile, by implication Judah in 10:17, Egypt here (compare Form). Here the address is to יוֹשֶׁבֶת בַּת־מִצְרַיִם, literally "O seated daughter Egypt," here translated "poor enthroned Egypt", and in 10:17 the address, astonishingly, is יֹשֶׁבֶת בַּמָּצוֹר, literally "O seated one under siege," translated in the present study "(you who are) enthroned under siege." The phrases are so close as to reinforce the suspicion, put forth in Interpretation on 10:17, that בַּמָּצוֹר (or בְּמָצוֹר) is to be heard as "in Egypt" as well as "under siege." If the settings proposed for the two passages are correct, 598 for 10:17–25 and 588 for the present passage, then the present half-verse is a creative variation on 10:17.

The phrase כְּלֵי גוֹלָה may be construed not only as "baggage of exile" but also as "baggage of one [feminine] going into exile" (participle of גלה). The phrase is found three times in Ezekiel 12 (vv 3, 4, and 7 there—has he borrowed the phrase from Jrm?), and there גוֹלָה must be the noun "exile," but the presence of the participle יוֹשֶׁבֶת in the present passage suggests the possibility that גוֹלָה may be heard as a participle: in that case "one going into exile" is in ironic contrast to "one sitting (or enthroned)."

The noun כְּלִי covers weapons, tools, pottery, and other gear of various sorts, but there will be no room in "gear for exile" for any large utensils, and certainly the occasion for weapons is past; therefore the alliterative

phrase כְּלֵי גוֹלָה is marked with pathos (see the rhetoric of Ezek 12:4). Assyrian bas-reliefs of captive women and children being led off from Lachish are vivid evidence that one carried a minimum in one's sack.[25]

For יוֹשֶׁבֶת "enthroned" compare 21:13; for בַּת־מִצְרַיִם (here "poor Egypt") compare v 11.

Verse 19b offers diction close to that of 2:15b; in particular the second verb is identical ("shall be burned," יצת nip'al, for which see there).

■ 20 Given the address to Egypt as a female, the image shifts to that of a heifer (compare the heifer for Ephraim in Hos 10:11). One may suspect that the shift of image (and the description in v 21 of mercenaries as "fatted calves") is prepared for by the mention of the bull-god Apis in v 15. The adjective modifying "heifer" is to be read as יְפֵה־פִיָּה, a reduplicated form signifying "very lovely."[26]

For the irony implied by the parataxis of the second colon see Form. The identity of the insect קֶרֶץ is uncertain; the noun occurs only here. The Versions offer guesswork, though a' and s' translate ἐγκεντρίζων "one who stings," and V renders stimulator "one who goads." The early moderns, beginning with Cocceius, resorting to the Arabic qaraṣa "bite, sting" (as of a flea), translated "gadfly" (that is, any of various flies that annoy livestock). In this century other suggestions have been made, notably that of Friedrich S. Bodenheimer, adopted by KB and HALAT, namely "mosquito,"[27] but Rudolph reaffirms the meaning "gadfly." Wendell Frerichs rightly points out that the context suggests a more formidable foe than the mosquito[28] (and see below). Though technically the "gadfly" is a more general term and applicable here to the insects that prey on cattle, I have adopted the translation "horsefly" as more familiar to readers in the United States (so also NAB).

But the imagery of v 22 ("with axes they enter upon her"), suggests not one horsefly but a swarm, that is, that the Hebrew word is a collective (it is to be noted that אַרְבֶּה, "locusts," in v 23b is a collective, and so is יֶלֶק

22 Van Beek, "Tabor."
23 So in David H. K. Amiran and others, eds., Atlas of Israel (Jerusalem: Survey of Israel, 1970), and in May, Oxford Bible Atlas, 49 (= 1,929 feet), against Van Beek, "Tabor," 508, who gives the elevation as 1,843 feet.
24 See in general Gus W. Van Beek, "Carmel, Mount," IDB 1:538; for the elevation of the monastery see

Israel, The Nagel Travel Guide Series (Geneva/ Paris/Munich: Nagel, 1965) 205, and for the elevation of the highest point see Atlas of Israel (n. 23).
25 See Yadin, Warfare, 433; compare ANEP, number 167.
26 GKC, sec. 84[b] n.
27 KB, 857; HALAT, 1071.
28 Wendell W. Frerichs, "Gadfly," IDB 2:336.

"hoppers," proposed in v 23a). The heifer is delectable, and the swarm of horseflies settles on her and bites her, leaving her frantic!—thus the metaphor of the Babylonian attack on Egypt.

■ 21 The image of Egypt as a heifer (v 20) leads to the simile of her mercenaries as fatted calves. Of course fatted calves are fattened for slaughter.[29] What is the implication of the repeated "even" (גַּם)?—that the foreigners in her midst, who are presumably less dependent on Egyptian dainties and are better fighters, are no less destined for destruction? For the Egyptian use of mercenaries see the discussion of the Lydians in v 9.

For "day of their calamity" see 18:17; for "time of their punishment" compare 6:15 and 10:15.

■ 22 M reads "her voice like the snake goes forth": clearly something is amiss. All the Versions are periphrastic to some degree: G offers "their voice is as of a hissing snake"; V "her voice shall sound as of bronze"; S "the noise of the army is like a creeping serpent"; T "the noise of their clash of weapons is like creeping serpents." Condamin and Bright are uneasy at the repeated verb of motion, יֵלֵךְ and יֵלְכוּ, in adjoining cola, and so they adopt the reading of G, שֹׁרֵק, "hissing." The problem is not only that a hiss is hardly a sound of distress (compare the diction of v 12) but also that the snake would hardly be a simile for Egypt, but rather for her enemy. Rudolph emends כְּנָחָשׁ יֵלֵךְ to כְּנֶחֱם יֹלְדָה "like the moaning of one giving birth"; the simile is good (compare 4:31), but the text is not close to what has been transmitted. I suggest that one go with the reading of V, "bronze": that is, Jerome either read נְחֹשֶׁת or understood נָחָשׁ as "bronze" (see Text). The lowing of a heifer in distress may certainly be compared to the sound of a bronze gong. There is archeological evidence for bronze musical instruments—bronze cymbals excavated from Hazor from the fourteenth or thirteenth century,[30] a bronze bell excavated from Megiddo from the tenth or ninth century.[31] By this understanding the verbs, though in form identical, deal ironically with opposite motions: the voice of

the heifer "proceeds" out into the world because they, the attackers, "proceed" to attack her. The attackers come בְּחַיִל, literally "in strength"; but חַיִל is also used for an army (Exod 15:4). I propose that the image is still that of the horseflies attacking the heifer (v 20): "they enter upon her with axes" is then a metaphor for the stinging insects. "In a swarm" is therefore not an inappropriate rendering for בְּחַיִל.

Timber-cutting was of course commonplace in the ancient Near East; ANEP reproduces a wall painting of an Egyptian cutting down a tree with an ax,[32] and John Pairman Brown has gathered a whole series of texts dealing with the deforestation of Lebanon.[33]

■ 23 In the first colon, "They have cut down her forest," the simile of the end of v 22 (horseflies like woodsmen) has become a metaphor; now, one wonders, what is meant here by "her forest"? There is a similar passage in Isa 10:33–34: there Yahweh himself will cut down the lofty trees of the forest. That passage offers its own difficulties of interpretation, but it is clear that the "forest" in that passage refers to the pride of Yahweh's enemy, either that of Assyria or perhaps that of the leaders in Jerusalem who are opposed to Yahweh's will (compare vv 18–19 in that chapter).[34] It may be significant that Isa 10:34 mentions Lebanon, and that Egypt for her part imported timber from Lebanon whenever possible.[35] Conceivably also the trees of the forest represent soldiers:[36] compare the figure of Deut 20:19. In Jer the only comparable passage is 21:14: there "her forest" evidently refers to the palace and temple in Jerusalem, paneled in wood. One must conclude that "her forest" in the present passage represents the pride of Egypt, perhaps her public buildings in which wood is used, and perhaps the multitude of her army as well.

In the second colon, however, I suggest that something is wrong; it reads כִּי לֹא יֵחָקֵר. This expression has been construed in either of two ways: (1) "which cannot be counted" (V, so Volz and Rudolph)—but this translation ignores the כִּי; or (2) "for it cannot be penetrated"

29   W. Stewart McCullough, "Calf," IDB 1:488.
30   Hazor I (ed. Yigael Yadin et al.; Jerusalem: Hebrew University, 1958), plate CLXII.
31   Robert S. Lamon and Geoffrey M. Shipton, Megiddo I (Chicago: University of Chicago, 1939) plate 77.
32   ANEP, plate 91.
33   John Pairman Brown, The Lebanon and Phoenicia, Ancient Texts Illustrating Their Physical Geography and

Native Industries, Volume 1, The Physical Setting and the Forest (Beirut: American University, 1969) 175–212.
34   Wildberger, Jesaja, 433.
35   Compare John A. Wilson, The Culture of Ancient Egypt (Chicago: University of Chicago, 1951) 183.
36   So BDB, 420b, on this passage.

(Bright: "since it is impenetrable")—but such a train of thought, given "for" or "since," is puzzling. Other translations use "though" instead of "for" or "since" (*RSV*: "though it is impenetrable," and similarly *NAB*; *NJV*: "though it cannot be measured"), but one questions whether כִּי can sustain this meaning. *NEB* translates "and it flaunts itself no more," but this is periphrastic and again ignores the כִּי.

I propose that the כִּי is wrong, and that the colon begins with כְּיֶלֶק, "like hopping (locusts)": the third colon reads כִּי רַבּוּ מֵאַרְבֶּה, "for they are more than locusts"; the two words for locust are likewise in parallelism in Nah 3:15b and Ps 105:34. The verb in the second colon, חקר, means "explore, spy out"; the qal participle, חֹקֵר, would fit the context admirably. By this reconstruction the 'alep and yod of *M* will be an early misreading of qop. Locusts swarm and move into everything; they "explore" and pry into every hole and corner.

Wolff offers a full discussion of the various words for "locust": according to him, the word suggested for the second colon, יֶלֶק, "probably designates the youngest locust, just hatched from the egg, with wing structures still invisible," and the word in the third colon, אַרְבֶּה, "refers to the fully developed, winged migrant locust. . . ."[37] The innumerability of locusts is a commonplace (Judg 6:5; 7:12; again Nah 3:15b; Ps 105:34).

■ **24** For "poor Egypt" see v 11; for a discussion of בושׁ

hip'il see 2:26. The verse summarizes the oracle: in humiliation Egypt is delivered into the power of Babylon.

■ **25** Amon, or Amon-Re, was the imperial god of Egypt; his chief center of worship was at the temple of Karnak in Thebes.[38] Thebes (Hebrew נֹא, representing the Egyptian *niwt* "the city") was the chief city of Upper (southern) Egypt (25° 42′ N, 32° 37′ E) from the time of the Middle Kingdom (about 2000 B.C.E.) until the Assyrians' invasion under Ashurbanipal.[39] The time of Jrm and the half-century after him was the period of the twenty-sixth Dynasty (663–525), also known as the Saitic period, when the center of Egyptian government was at Sais in the west central Delta,[40] but the temple of Karnak, and Thebes in general, continued to be preeminent in this period.[41]

■ **27–28** See 30:10–11.

Aim

Hope springs eternal, and in spite of Egypt's setback in 605 (vv 3–12) there were those in Judah who hoped in 588 that Egypt could rescue them from Nebuchadrezzar (37:7). Alas, Egypt is a fat heifer, about to be attacked by a swarm of horseflies. Egypt, like the rest of the world (27:5–6), will be given into the hand of the people of the north (v 24).

37   Wolff, *Joel and Amos*, 27; see the whole excursus, "The Designations for the Locusts," ibid., 27–28.
38   Wilson, *The Culture of Ancient Egypt*, 126; compare "Amon," *IDB* 1:115.
39   Thomas O. Lambdin, "Thebes," *IDB* 4:615–17.
40   John A. Wilson, "Egypt," *IDB* 2:54b; Alan H. Gardiner, *Egypt of the Pharaohs* (New York: Oxford University, 1966) 362.
41   Compare Gardiner, *Egypt of the Pharaohs*, 360.

Philistia Will Be Washed Away

Bibliography

Christensen
Transformations, 211–15.

Katzenstein, H. Jacob
"'Before Pharaoh conquered Gaza' (Jeremiah xlvii 1)," *VT* 33 (1983) 249–51.

Kutsch, Ernst
"'. . . denn Jahwe vernichtet die Philister': Erwägungen zu Jer 47,1–7," *Die Botschaft und die Boten: Festschrift für Hans Walter Wolff zum 70. Geburtstag* (ed. Jörg Jeremias and Lothar Perlitt; Neukirchen: Neukirchener, 1981) 253–67.

Malamat, Abraham
"The Historical Setting of Two Biblical Prophecies on the Nations," *IEJ* 1 (1950–51) 154–59 = *Israel Exploration Journal Reader* (New York: Ktav, 1981) 1:45–50.

Quinn, Jerome D.
"Alcaeus 48 (B 16) and the Fall of Ascalon (604 B.C.)," *BASOR* 164 (December 1961) 19–20.

47

1 [This has come as the word of Yahweh to Jeremiah the prophet][a] concerning the Philistines [before Pharaoh struck Gaza:][a] 2/ Thus Yahweh has said:
  Look, waters are coming up from the north,
    to become an overflowing stream,
      to overflow the land and what fills it,
        a city and its inhabitants;
    humanity shall cry out and wail,
      every inhabitant of the land.
3 From the noise of pounding of his stallions' hoofs,
    from the shaking from his chariots,
      the din of his wheels,
    parents have not turned back for children,
      from slackness of hands,
4 because of the day that is coming,
    to devastate all the Philistines,
      [a]⟨to be cut off⟩ by Tyre and Sidon,[a]
    every surviving helper,
      for Yahweh is devastating [the Philistines,][b] the remnant of
        [c]《the coasts》[of Caphtor.][c]
5 Baldness has come upon Gaza,
    Ashkelon has become silent,
      the remnant of 《the Anakim.》[a]
  How long [b]will you cut back and forth,[b]

Text

1a   Omit both sequences with *G* (compare 46:1); see Janzen, pp. 112–14.

4a—a   Vocalizing the verb as the nipʿal infinitive לְהִכָּרֵת with *V*, and construing the preposition לְ before "Tyre" and "Sidon" as introducing the agent (GKC, sec. 121f; Joüon, *Gramm.*, sec. 132f), in place of *M* "to cut off [hipʿil] for Tyre and Sidon." *G* renders "and I shall obliterate [ἀφανίζω] Tyre and Sidon"; *V* "Tyre and Sidon shall be scattered"; *S* and *T* = *M*. The focus of the poem continues to be on the fate of the Philistines rather than on that of Tyre and Sidon (compare Rudolph, 272).

b   Omit with *G*, a gloss from v 4a (so Janzen, p. 59). Janzen also points out that 2Q Jer seems to support *G* (Janzen, p. 210, n. 67).

c—c   Reading אִיִּים with *G* for *M* אִי (so also Janzen, pp. 59, 74). Compare the diction of v 5.

5a   Reading עֲנָקִים with *G* (compare Josh 11:22) for *M* "their valley"; so Duhm, Giesebrecht, Volz, Condamin, Rudolph.

b—b   This verb is a central problem for the poem. As it stands, it is גדד hitpoʿel; this verb has elsewhere the meaning "slash oneself" (5:7; 16:6; 41:5; Deut 14:1; 1 Kgs 18:28; Mic 4:14 is obscure). Given the association of slashing oneself with making oneself bald in mourning rites (16:6; Deut 14:1), it is no wonder that *M* has associated the present colon with "baldness has come upon Gaza" in the verse. Yet the parallelism of the two "how long" questions suggests that the colon is to be associated with "sword." With hesitation, therefore, I propose the meaning "cut

6   [. . .]ᵃ O sword of Yahweh,
                     how long will you be without rest?
                Withdraw toᵇ your sheath,
                     retreat and be silent!

7   How ᵃ《 can it be at rest 》ᵃ
                     when Yahweh has given it a command?
                Against Ashkelon and the shore of the sea,
                     there he has appointed it.

back and forth" on the analogy of הלך hitpaʿel "walk back and forth" and נוד hitpolel "rock back and forth" (see 31:18 and the discussion there). There are at least two other possibilities, either one involving a slight emendation of the text. One is to read the verb as a piʿel, תְּגַדְּדִי; such a form might be implied by *G* and *V*, which read κόψεις and *concideris*, respectively. The piʿel stem is attested in postbiblical Hebrew (see Jastrow *sub voce*). It is clear in any event that *G* and *V* understand the subject of the second-person verb to be expressed by the vocative "sword" rather than by "remnant." There is a second possibility, to my mind less likely: 2Q Jer appears to read תתגורדי (Maurice Baillet, Jozef T. Milik, and Roland de Vaux, *Les ʼPetites Grottesʼ de Qumrân* (DJD 3; Oxford: Clarendon, 1962) 65, 66 ["lecture certaine"], Planche XIII, 8). This verb (גרר hitpoʿel) evidently appears in 30:23 as a variant of חול hitpolel (23:19), thus to mean "whirl, roar, rush" or the like; this reading is accepted by Christensen, *Transformations*, 212–13. See further Interpretation.

6a   Deleting הוֹי "alas" with *G* (compare *V*): the word is evidently a secondary attempt to find meaning for "sword" after the preceding colon was attached to "remnant" (see 5b—b).

b   Reading with many MSS. אֶל; *M*, by a copyist's error, reads אַל.

7a   Reading the third-person תִּשְׁקֹם with *G*, *V*, and *S* for *M* תִּשְׁקְטִי "can you be at rest" (so all commentators). The copyist slipped because of the correct תִּשְׁקְטִי in v 6.

Structure

This oracle is set apart from what precedes and what follows not only by the superscription in v 1 but by references to Philistines in vv 4–7. It is noteworthy that there are no such references in vv 2–3, but it is not plausible to divide the poem: v 4 is syntactically dependent on v 3.

The poem appears to break into two unequal sections, vv 2–5a (the destruction of Philistia) and vv 5b–7 (the sword of Yahweh). The two sections are united not only by "Yahweh" (v 4, vv 6 and 7) but more particularly by "coasts" (v 4) and "shore" (v 7), perhaps by "waters" (v 2) and "the sea" (v 7), and, in a nice touch, "(Ashkelon) is silent [from the effects of war]" (דמה nipʿal, v 5) and "(O sword,) be silent [that is, stop killing]" (דמם qal, v 6).

Verse 2 is made up of a tetracolon and a bicolon in close parallelism ("overflow" in the second and third cola, "inhabitant[s]" in the fourth and sixth). Verse 3 appears to be made up of five cola, a tricolon and a bicolon. The prepositional phrases in the tricolon balance the second half of the bicolon ("from"); the first half of the bicolon is thus the center ("parents have not turned back for

children"). (It should be noted that one may take the second and third cola as a single colon with internal parallelism, as Rudolph does.) Verse 4 continues the syntax of v 3 and can only be a pentacolon, the first four cola closely parallel like the tetracolon in v 2 (one notes the parallel infinitives in the second and third cola), the last colon a כִּי-clause introducing Yahweh, a clause that, however, repeats "destroy" (שדד) from the second colon of the verse. (The text of *M* offers the possibility of construing the כִּי-clause as two cola, but the repetition of "is destroying the Philistines" in the fifth colon after "to destroy all the Philistines" in the second is dubious.) Verse 5a is a tricolon, vv 5b–6a (as reconstructed here) are another tricolon with the two "how long?" clauses (עַד־אָנָה, מָתַי עַד־) surrounding the vocative. Verse 6b is a simple bicolon, imperatives to the sword that reflect the diction of v 6a. Verse 7 finally is made up of two bicola: the first colon picks up the verb of the second colon of v 6, and the second and fourth cola of the verse are parallel.

Form

This poem is a judgment oracle against Philistia, but its form is unusual: it does not begin with battle orders (compare 46:3–4, 14) or references to the gods or nations or cities in question (compare the oracles against the Philistines in Isa 14:28–32; Amos 1:6–8; Zeph 2:4–7; and oracles against other nations in 48:1; 49:1, 7, 23). Instead it begins starkly (v 2a) with the announcement of punishment coming from the north in the form of a flood, a traditional curse[1] (compare Isa 8:7). This punishment comes against a land that is unnamed until v 4; furthermore neither the speaker nor the audience is named (there are no first-person forms in the poem, and the only second-person forms involve the apostrophe to the sword, vv 5b–6), nor is the king named whose war chariots mediate the punishment (the anonymous "his" in v 3). This nonspecific tone communicates distance and a kind of cosmic totality, a tone reinforced by the word הָאָדָם, "humanity," in v 2b (compare the distance and totality expressed in Zeph 1:2–3, though there the speaker is clearly Yahweh). The sound of battle (v 3a) is evidently the sound of holy war; it elicits the traditional response from the victims of holy war, that of lamentation (v 2b; compare 4:8) and paralysis (v 3b; compare 6:24 and the literature cited there), a paralysis so overwhelming as to inhibit the basic instinct of parent to protect child.

The poem turns specific in v 4. The first colon refers to "the day" that is coming, clearly the day of Yahweh (last colon);[2] it is the Philistines who are being isolated and destroyed. Yet having finally named the Philistines, the poet immediately retreats to name their erstwhile Phoenician allies Tyre and Sidon (see Setting and Interpretation) and to parallel the Philistines by the impersonal "remnant of the coasts": what lies behind this delay in naming the Philistine cities? Whatever the cause, the hesitation is overcome in v 5a when one finally hears diction appropriate to this form—the naming of cities of the realm (compare Isaiah 15, and note particularly

"baldness" there in v 2), cities that manifest lamentation and paralysis. Yet even in that verse it is noteworthy that Gaza and Ashkelon are not portrayed as doing anything: it is not that "every head in Gaza is shaved bald" (compare 48:37), but that "baldness has come upon Gaza" (see further Interpretation).

If the analysis of the present study is correct, v 5b is to be associated with v 6, a sudden apostrophe to the sword of Yahweh (compare the apostrophe to Death and Sheol in Hos 13:14). Verses 5b–6a offer parallel rhetorical questions ("how long?"). Verse 6b mimics battle orders: one may note אסף nip'al in battle orders in 4:5 and 8:14 and דמם in 8:14, and one may note further the format of a bicolon consisting of an imperative phrase paralleled by two parallel imperatives in 4:5–6a and 5:1. But these battle orders, addressed to the sword of Yahweh, are to cease and desist, and they are ironic in that they are only hypothetical, being annulled by the rhetorical question of v 7a. The poem closes with the summary of v 7b.

Setting

Nebuchadrezzar destroyed Ashkelon in 604 (see below); there is no evidence for any Philistine independence thereafter[3]—it is particularly to be noted that there was no representative from Philistia at the Jerusalem conference of 594 (27:3), since by then the Philistine cities had been for some time Babylonian provinces.[4] There is thus no occasion for an oracle against Philistia after Jrm's lifetime. And there is no reason to question the authenticity of this oracle to Jrm: its form is unconventional (see Form), and its phraseology is not imitative—the one duplication ("land and what fills it, a city and its inhabitants," v 2, see 8:16) appears simply to be Jrm's own reuse of a bicolon.

But given insufficient internal evidence for the historical setting of the oracle and insufficient data from external history as well, its setting has been controverted. The text of v 1 in *M* indicates a setting, but the Pharaoh in question is unnamed, and in any case the event is other-

---

1   Hillers, *Treaty-Curses*, 70–71.
2   For literature on the day of Yahweh see Ernst S. Jenni, "Day of the Lord," *IDB* 1:784–85; A. Joseph Everson, "Day of the Lord," *IDBSup,* 209–10, and bibliography in both articles; and von Rad, *OT Theology 2,* 119–25.
3   Jonas C. Greenfield, "Philistines," *IDB* 3:795.
4   Malamat, "Twilight of Judah," 135.

wise undocumented. Thus Pharaoh Psamtik (Psammetichus) I might have struck Gaza at some time toward the end of his reign (he died in 610): according to Herodotus[5] Psammetichus captured Ashdod after a long siege, and he doubtless took the more southerly cities of Ashkelon and Gaza as well.[6] Or Pharaoh Neco (II) might have struck Gaza on his way to the north just before the battle of Megiddo in the spring of 609 or sometime thereafter, since Palestine was under Egyptian vassalage until 605: again Herodotus records[7] that Neco, after the battle at Magdolon (probably Megiddo), conquered the city of Kadytis (usually identified with Gaza).[8] Or Neco might have struck Gaza as an aftermath of the defeat of the Babylonian army in the Egyptian Delta in December 601. But in any case the datum from v 1 is evidently secondary (so also Rudolph and Bright).

Verse 4 evidently implies that at the time of the delivery of the oracle Tyre and Sidon were allies of Philistia, but this detail does not give help. One wonders also: Does the fact that only Gaza and Ashkelon are mentioned suggest that what remained to the Philistines at the time of the oracle was simply a narrow coastal strip?—and could this not be the implication of "the remnant of the coasts" in v 4 and "Ashkelon and the shore of the sea" in v 7?

Abraham Malamat is convinced that vv 2–3 describe the Scythians, who, as he interprets the evidence of Herodotus, invaded the coast of Palestine in the spring of 609 and conquered Gaza in September of that year.[9] But Richard Vaggione has refuted the proposal that the Scythians invaded Palestine,[10] and in any event v 3 describes chariotry, while the Scythians fought on horseback.

Chariotry from the north (v 2) immediately suggests the Babylonians; the metaphor of waters from the north

fits the Babylonians in 46:6–8, and there is no reason to find another identification here. Since one now has the Babylonian Chronicle with a notice of Nebuchadrezzar's sack of Ashkelon in December 604,[11] one could suggest that a date for the oracle in the autumn of that year is best (so also Rudolph, Bright). But if the collection of oracles against foreign nations began with a chronological sequence, if the first oracle against Egypt (46:3–12) was delivered at the time of the battle of Carchemish (605), and if the first sequence of material against Moab was also delivered at the time of Carchemish (many ifs!), then one could propose that setting for this oracle as well: in the light of Carchemish Jrm would then be proclaiming the defeat of Egypt, Philistia, and Moab by Babylon.

Interpretation

■ 1 The Philistines had settled on the southern coastal strip of Palestine at the end of the thirteenth century, centering in their pentapolis of Gath, Ekron, Ashdod, Ashkelon, and Gaza. Since we have as yet no Philistine documents, our knowledge of their history is confined to notices in the texts of other peoples and to their material remains; and archeological investigation of the Philistines has become intensive only in recent years.[12]

The site of Philistine Gaza is disputed. In 1930–34 Sir Flinders Petrie excavated *tall al-'ajjūl* (Atlas of Israel grid 093–097) on the assumption that it was Gaza, but that tell is now identified with either Beth-eglaim or Sharuhen; the presence of present-day Gaza over what is presumably the old site prevents extensive digging.[13]

For the difficulty of identifying the event referred to in the clause "before Pharaoh struck Gaza" see Setting.
■ 2 The verb שׁטף, "overflow," is curiously used with "horse" in 8:6 (see there); with the waters of a river it

---

5   *Hist.* 2.157.

6   Ernst Vogt, "Die neubabylonische Chronik über die Schlacht bei Karkemisch und die Einnahme von Jerusalem," *Volume du Congrès, Strasbourg, 1956* (VTSup 4; Leiden: Brill, 1957) 77.

7   *Hist.* 2.159.

8   Bright, p. 311. Vogt "Die neubabylonische Chronik," 77 n. 4, believes that Herodotus was wrong on this point.

9   Abraham Malamat, "The Historical Setting of Two Biblical Prophecies on the Nations," *IEJ* 1 (1950–51) 154–59 = *Israel Exploration Journal Reader* (New

York: Ktav, 1981) 45–50.

10 Richard P. Vaggione, "Over All Asia? The Extent of the Scythian Domination in Herodotus," *JBL* 92 (1973) 523–30; idem, "Scythians," *IDBSup*, 797–98.

11 The Babylonian reference is British Museum no. 21946, obverse, line 18: see Wiseman, *Chronicles*, 68, 69, and see further Bright, *History*, 326.

12 See Jonas C. Greenfield, "Philistines," *IDB* 3:791–95, and "Philistines," *IDBSup*, 666–67, and bibliography in both these articles.

13 William F. Stinespring, "Gaza," *IDB* 2:358, and "Beth-eglaim," *IDB* 1:389. For recent excavation in

occurs in Isa 8:8 and 28:17 to refer metaphorically to Assyria. Here, correspondingly, it refers to Babylon (see Setting, and see further 46:6–8). For "land and what fills it, a city and its inhabitants," see 8:16. For the curious use of אָדָם, "humanity," for the victims of the metaphorical flood see Form. For the parallel "cry out" (זעק) and "wail" (ילל hip'il) compare 25:34.

■ **3** For the parallel of horses' hoofs and chariot wheels compare Isa 5:28. The chariot wheels in late Assyrian bas-reliefs approach in height that of a man,[14] and the quaking of the earth under the pounding of horses' hoofs and chariot wheels strikes terror in a population (compare the remarks on 4:13). There is irony in the contrast between the power of the "hoofs" of the "awesome ones" (אַבִּירִים), the word used here for stallions, and the "slackness" of the "hands" of the people (for a cognate expression see 6:24). The people's paralysis is manifest in inconceivably unnatural behavior—the abandonment by parents of their children: I am aware of no parallel for this description, though Jrm describes the doe abandoning her young in the field in time of drought (14:5).

■ **4** What is coming is the day of Yahweh (on which see Form). And finally one hears the identity of the victims of this disaster—"all the Philistines" (for the delay in identification see again Form). Question: Is the word "to devastate" (לָשְׁדוֹד) a near miss on "to Ashdod" (לְאַשְׁדּוֹד), a city not mentioned here? (Compare Condamin and Rudolph, who wish to insert "Ashdod" in v 5 before "the remnant of the Anakim.")

The verb with "Tyre and Sidon" is puzzling; *M* reads literally "to cut off for Tyre and Sidon every survivor that helps." But the focus should hardly turn to these Phoenician cities in a poem about Philistia. I propose therefore that the verb be vocalized as a nip'al (passive): the two cola will then signify "so that they [the Philistines] will be cut off by every potential ally, including Tyre and Sidon." There is no other evidence of such an alliance (compare Setting), but it is not unlikely; it is

perhaps worth noting that Amos 1:9–10, an oracle against Tyre, offers the same accusation as that in Amos 1:6–8, a parallel oracle against Philistia: most commentators have taken the oracle against Tyre as a later imitation, but one might equally propose that both states conspired in the same atrocity.[15] (It may be added also that Ps 83:3 pairs Philistia and the inhabitants of Tyre.)

For "the coasts" (אִיִּים, reconstructed here) see 2:10–11. "Caphtor" is now securely identified with Crete.[16]

■ **5** For Gaza see v 1. The expression "baldness has come upon Gaza" is altogether curious: the reference is to the custom of shaving one's head bald as a sign of lamentation (on this see 16:6). But other references to the custom either use a stem of the verb קרח "shave bald," or if the noun "baldness" (קָרְחָה) occurs as the subject, as it does here, it is in a nominal clause ("[on] every head is baldness," 48:37, so Isa 15:2; Ezek 7:18; compare Isa 3:24). In the present passage, on the other hand, the impression given is that "baldness" comes over Gaza like a blight, as if the people in question have nothing to do with it (for this impression of passivity see further Form).

Ashkelon is the only one of the traditional Philistine cities that is directly on the seacoast.[17] The verb נִדְמְתָה is the nip'al stem of דמה. Traditionally this stem has been translated "be destroyed" (so BDB, Zorell). But recently it has become clear that several if not all of the citations should be translated "become silent": *HALAT* cites two homonymous verbs (דמה II and III, respectively), but it is not at all clear that דמה nip'al can ever mean "be destroyed";[18] *V* translates "become silent" here (*conticuit*).

There is no warrant to insert Ashdod at the beginning of the third colon, as Condamin and Rudolph do (so also *JB*). And the third colon of the verse ("remnant of the Anakim") is not to be construed as a vocative, as Condamin, Rudolph, and Bright and current translations (*RSV, JB, NEB, NAB, NJV*) have it—there are no other vocatives addressed to the Philistines in the poem; rather the phrase is in parallel with the first two cola (see Structure). "Anakim" (a reading restored from *G*) refers to a

Gaza see "Gaza," *IDBSup*, 353, and Vogel and Holtzclaw, *Bibliography II*, 29–30.

14   See Yadin, *Warfare*, 452.

15   For the view that Amos 1:9–10 is original, and for bibliography for both sides of the question, see Shalom M. Paul, "Amos 1:3—2:3: A Concatenous Literary Pattern," *JBL* 90 (1971) 397–403.

16   Jonas C. Greenfield, "Philistines," *IDBSup*, 666.

17   For the history and excavations of the city see William F. Stinespring, "Ashkelon," *IDB* 1:252–54, and further Vogel, *Bibliography I*, and Vogel and Holtzclaw, *Bibliography II*, 12.

18   See Wildberger, *Jesaja*, 232–33, for a discussion of the occurrence in Isa 6:5, with bibliography.

pre-Israelite population in Palestine, represented as a fearsomely tall people; the tradition in Josh 11:21–22 is that Joshua exterminated them except for a small remnant in Gaza, Gath, and Ashdod.[19]

For the association of the last colon of the verse with "sword of Yahweh" in v 6 see Structure. Since the verb of that colon, גדד hitpoʻel, elsewhere means "slash oneself," a sign of mourning associated with shaving one's head bald (compare 16:6), it is natural that translations and commentaries would have accepted that meaning here (*RSV*: "O remnant of the Anakim, how long will you slash yourselves?"). But the Versions and the structure of the poem suggest a different meaning, whether one may posit the meaning "cut back and forth," as proposed here, or whether the text must be slightly emended to mean "cut off" or the like (for these alternatives see Text). However, if this understanding is correct, it still remains true that the occurrence of the verb here is prepared for by "baldness" and its association in the first colon of the verse: in this way the apostrophe to the sword of Yahweh is linked to the affirmations about Gaza and Ashkelon. See further v 6.

■ 6 For "sword of Yahweh" compare 12:12; for the striking vocative to that sword, see the remarks in Form.

The expression "how long" in the second colon of the verse is not the common עַד־מָתַי (literally "up to when?"), which occurs in the parallel final colon of v 5 (and in 4:14, 21; 12:4; 23:26; 31:22), but rather עַד־אָנָה, literally "up to whither?" (this is the only occurrence of the expression in Jer).[20] For שקט, "be at rest," see 30:10.

"Withdraw" is not a common nuance of אסף nipʻal, but

Isa 60:20 offers another instance. The noun תַּעַר means both "razor" or "knife" (36:23) and (as here) "sheath." The verb רגע nipʻal here evidently means "retreat."[21] Its companion דמם, "be silent," has occurred in 8:14; this verb (here וְדֹמִּי) is doubtless intended to be heard in assonance with נִדְמְתָה (דמה nipʻal), used of Ashkelon, in v 5.

■ 7 The verb in the first colon is picked up from that of the second colon of v 6. For the suggestion that "Ashkelon and the shore of the sea" implies that Philistia at the time of the oracle consisted only of a narrow coastal strip, see Setting. These are the only occurrences in Jer of חוֹף, "shore," and יעד, "appoint."

Aim

It is doubtful if Jrm or most of his fellow Judahites had ever seen a Philistine. The Philistines in the best of times were distant from the ken of those who would hear the oracle; now, in the worst of times, they recede almost to the vanishing point, as if viewed through the wrong end of a telescope. The traditional enemy of Israel was by now reduced to a small enclave on the coast, so diminished as no longer even to merit contempt (compare Ps 60:10 = 108:10), only a brief image of pathetic demoralization (v 3b). Cut off from any help (v 4), Philistia can only await its doom, to be swept away by the flood of history.

---

19 R. F. Schnell, "Anak," *IDB* 1:123–24.
20 There are twelve other occurrences in the OT: see BDB, 33a.

21 Lienhard Delekat, "Zum hebräischen Wörterbuch," *VT* 16 (1964) 59, and more generally 56–66.

Moab Will Be Brought Down

Bibliography

Clark, David J.
"Wine on the lees (Zeph 1.12 and Jer 48.11)," *BT* 32 (1981) 241–43.

Couroyer, Bernard
"Corne et arc," *RB* 73 (1966) 510–21.

Eissfeldt, Otto
"Der Gott Bethel," *ARW* 28 (1930) 1–30, esp. 10–12 = *Kleine Schriften I* (Tübingen: Mohr [Siebeck], 1962) 206–33, esp. 214–16.

Irwin, William A.
"An Ancient Biblical Text," *AJSL* 48 (1931/32) 184–93.

Kegler, Jürgen
"Das Leid des Nachbarvolkes, Beobachtungen zu den Fremdvölkersprüchen Jeremias," *Werden und Wirken des Alten Testaments, Festschrift für Claus Westermann zum 70. Geburtstag* (ed. Rainer Albertz et al.; Göttingen: Vandenhoeck & Ruprecht: Neukirchen: Neukirchener, 1980) 271–87.

Kuschke, Arnulf
"Jeremia 48,1–8. Zugleich ein Beitrag zur historischen Topographie Moabs," *Verbannung und Heimkehr, Beiträge zur Geschichte und Theologie Israels im 6. und 5. Jahrhundert v. Chr., Wilhelm Rudolph zum 60. Geburtstage* (ed. Arnulf Kuschke; Tübingen: Mohr [Siebeck], 1961) 181–96.

Moran, William L.
"Ugaritic ṣiṣûma and Hebrew ṣîṣ (Eccles 43,19; Jer 48,9)," *Bib* 39 (1958) 69–71.

48

1 For Moab. Thus Yahweh [of hosts, God of Israel][a] has said:

Alas for Nebo, oh, it is ruined!
  Kiriathaim [has stood ashamed,][b] is captured,
the Citadel has stood ashamed, is terrified,
  2 the renown of Moab is no more.
In Heshbon they planned evil against her:
  "Come, let us end her as a nation!"
Madmen, too: you shall weep,
  pursued by the sword.
3 The sound of a cry from Horonaim,
  "Ruin and great collapse!"
4 "Moab is broken!"—
  [a]they have made (their) cry heard ⟨to Zoar.⟩[a]
[5 Yes, (at) the ascent of Luhith[b] [c]⟪weeping⟫ shall go up ⟪in it;⟫[c]

Text

1a Omit with *G*; compare Janzen, p. 78.

b Omit with *G*; the word is evidently dittographic from v 1b (see Janzen, p. 59).

4a—a Vocalizing the last word of the colon with *G* as צֲעִרֶה for *M* (qere') צְעִירֶיהָ "her young ones," by which reading the colon must be translated "her young ones let a cry be heard" (so Volz, Condamin, Rudolph, Bright; so *RSV, JB, NEB, NAB*). The ketib צעוריה cannot be explained: the same qere'/ketib variation is found in 14:3.

5a This verse duplicates with a few variations Isa 15:5b. Inasmuch as Isa 15:5a is to some degree duplicated in v 34a of the present chapter and Isa 15:6 in v 34b, it is likely that an omission in v 34 was written in the margin and erroneously incorporated into the previous column: see Structure, Form, Setting. Rudolph likewise omits the verse, and Volz omits v 5a.

b The qere' reads הַלְּחִית (and Isa 15:5 הַלּוּחִית); the ketib reads הלחות.

c *M* reads "with weeping weeping shall go up"; Isa

yes, at the descent of Horonaim {. . .}[d] the
cry of destruction [e]they shall hear.[e]] [a]

6   Flee, escape for 《 your lives, 》[a]
         [b]and let them be[b] ⟨ like a juniper ⟩[c] in the
            wilderness!

7   For because of your trust [a][in your works
            and] in your treasures,[a]
         you too shall be captured,
      and Chemosh[b] 《 shall be taken off 》[c] into
            exile,
         his priests and his officials together. [d]

8   A devastator will come into every city,
         and no city shall escape;
      the Valley shall perish,
         the Plateau shall be wiped out,
            [as Yahweh has said.][a]

9   Give a salt-field[a] to Moab,
         for [b]《 in ruins 》 she shall go out,[b]

15:5 reads "with weeping one (?) shall go up in it." I
accept the reading "in it" for *M* "weeping"; it is likely
that בְכִי is a dittography from the following כִּי (so
Condamin, Rudolph, Bright). On the other hand,
the wording of the last colon suggests that "weeping" is here the subject of the verb, so the preposition בְּ with "weeping" is wrong at the beginning of
the colon (is it misplaced from the beginning of
מַעֲלֵה—compare בְּמוֹרַד in the parallel).

d   Omit צָרֵי "distresses of (?)" or "foes of (?)" with *G*
         and Isa 15:5.

e—e   Isa 15:5 offers a *lectio difficilior* here, יְעֹרְרוּ; unfor-
         tunately the form gives difficulty. *HALAT* assumes it
         must be read יְעַרְעֲרוּ, a pilpel of עוּר, thus "they stir
         up." One wonders whether the reading in the
         present passage is a flat substitution for a puzzling
         text.

6a   Read נַפְשֹׁתֵיכֶם (plural noun, plural possessor) with
         G and *V* for *M* נַפְשְׁכֶם (singular noun, plural posses-
         sor). Note that there are instances in which נַפְשְׁכֶם is
         rendered by ἡ ψυχὴ ὑμῶν (Isa 55:2, 3). See note b—
         b.

b—b   There is no need to emend this verb (third-person
         plural feminine) if "your lives" in the first colon is
         read as a plural with *G*.

c   For *M* "like Aroer" (כַּעֲרוֹעֵר) read כְּעַרְעָר; it should
         be noted that *V* and *a'* read עַרוֹעֵר as "tamarisk."

7a—a   *G* here reads simply "in your stronghold," and
         because the colon in *M* is overloaded, most com-
         mentators accept *G*, reading a plural (so Duhm,
         Cornill, Volz, Rudolph, Bright; so *RSV, JB*). But
         "trust in her treasures" appears in 49:4, so that "in
         your treasures" is a likely reading. The reading "in
         your works and" will then represent a conflate text
         with an unsatisfactory alternative reading, and the *G*
         reading, evidently בְּמְצָדֹתָךְ, will be a misreading of
         בְּאוֹצְרֹתַיִךְ. Compare Janzen, pp. 19–20.

b   Read with many MSS. and qere' כְּמוֹשׁ; ketib כְּמִישׁ
         is a copyist's error.

c   For *M* וְיָצָא, "shall go out," read יוּצָא (hop'al): this
         passive would give better parallelism with the nip'al
         (passive) תִּלָּכְדִי in the previous colon; compare the
         revocalizations to passive verbs in v 15.

d   Ketib יַחַד is a less frequent alternate for the
         common יַחְדָּו; the qere' יַחְדָּיו is found in 46:12, 21;
         49:3.

8a   There is no parallel for such a sequence in Jer,
         and it adds nothing to the discourse; the אֲשֶׁר looks
         like a dittography from הַמִּישֹׁר and is omitted by
         Rudolph; I follow Volz in omitting the whole clause.

9a   Ugaritic *ṣṣ* means "salt mine, salt field," and this
         meaning for צִיץ fits the context here (so also Bright;
         compare *NEB* margin). It is better than the usual
         emendation to צִיּוּן, "tombstone," on the basis of *G*
         σημεῖα, "signs," accepted by Volz, Rudolph; *HALAT*;
         JB, NAB. The translation "wings" (Cornill, Con-
         damin; *RSV, NJV*) is an erroneous assumption from
         the Aramaic צִיץ.

b—b   *S* reads נָצֹה תִצֶּה, "she shall surely be in ruins," and

and her cities shall become a desolation,
   without inhabitant in them.
[10/ Cursed be he who does the work of
      Yahweh lazily, ⟩and cursed be⟨[b] he
      who restrains his sword from blood.][a]

11 Moab has been relaxed from his youth,
      he has been resting on his lees;
[and][a] he has not been poured from vessel
      to vessel,
   and into exile has not gone,
that is why his flavor has remained as it
      was,
   and his bouquet undeveloped;

12 [therefore the days are surely coming,
      oracle of Yahweh:][a]
   I shall send to him decanters to decant
      him,
and his vessels they shall empty,
   ⟪and his jars⟫[b] they shall smash.
[13/ And Moab shall be ashamed of Che-
      mosh just as the house of Israel was
      ashamed of Bethel their trust.][a]

14 How can you say, "We are warriors
      and men fit for battle!"?

15 Moab is destroyed,
   ⟪and his cities are carried off,⟫[a]
      his choicest young men ⟨shall be brought
         down⟩[b] to slaughter,
      [oracle of the King, Yahweh of hosts is
         his name.][c]

16 The calamity of Moab is near to coming,
      and his disaster is hurrying greatly.

17 Grieve for him, all you his neighbors,
      and all you who know his name;
   say, "How the victorious scepter is broken,
      the glorious staff!"

18 Descend from glory [a]and sit[a] ⟪in dung,⟫[b]

so evidently does *G*; this reading is accepted by Volz,
Rudolph, and Bright, and by *JB*, *NEB*, and *NAB*.
But it is possible that the second verb is here
correctly preserved with תֵּצֵא: יצא, "go out," may
suggest surrender. One notes elsewhere the seeming
mixture of verb roots in the infinitive absolute–finite
verb combination (8:13 and 42:10).

10a   A comment in prose (so also Volz, Condamin,
Rudolph, Bright).

b   *G* omits וְאָרוּר; it is likely to be a clarifying expansion.

11a   Omit with *G* (compare Rudolph).

12a   These words spoil the concision of the poem and
suggest a postponement of the destruction of Moab
(so Cornill, Rudolph; compare Volz). If לָכֵן, "therefore," belongs to the original layer of material, then
the verb וְשִׁלַּחְתִּי has been altered from אֶשְׁלָח.

b   So read with *G* for *M* "their jars."

13a   Prose comment (so Volz, Rudolph, Bright). It may
have originally been a comment on v 39 ("shame")
and wrongly inserted in the previous column of text
(compare the remarks on v 5, and see Structure,
Form, Setting).

15a   The text of v 15aα is disturbed: *M* reads literally
"Moab is ruined, (against?) her cities he has come
up." The usual solution, adopted by Volz, Rudolph,
and Bright, and by *RSV*, *JB*, *NEB*, and *NAB*, is to
revocalize שֻׁדַּד to שֹׁדֵד in conformity with the third
colon of v 18, thus reading "the destroyer of Moab
and her cities has come up." But שֻׁדַּד מוֹאָב is correct
in v 20b. Furthermore in v 18 "the destroyer" is the
subject of the following colon as well, whereas in the
present verse "the destroyer" is not matched by what
follows. It is clear that Jrm can play with his diction,
so that it would be like him to offer שֻׁדַּד מוֹאָב here
and in v 20 and שֹׁדֵד מוֹאָב in v 18. Janzen, p. 59,
assumes, since *G* omits עָלָה here, that the word is
dittographic from v 18; but this will not do—there
is evidently a play on עלה, "go up," and ירד, "go
down," in this half-verse, so that *G* must simply have
omitted a verb it could not construe. Since the suffix
of עָרֶיהָ, "her cities," is wrong (compare the masculine reference in the next colon, as well as in vv 11–
12), I propose reading עָרָיו הֹעַלוּ, a passive parallel to
the passive of שֻׁדַּד.

b   Vocalizing *M* יֻרְדוּ as יָרְדוּ; this passive is then in
parallel with the previous two, and one may compare also the passive in the similar phrase יוּבַל
לַטֶּבוֹחַ, 11:19.

c   Omit with *G*; so Volz, Rudolph; Janzen, p. 79;
Bright, "probably." The phrase is imported from
46:18.

18a—a   Read with many MSS., the Versions and qere'
וּשְׁבִי; ketib ישׁבי is a copyist's error.

b   Read בָּצָא or בָּצָאה for *M* בַּצָּמָא, "in thirst," with
Cornill, Volz, Rudolph, Bright (so also *JB*). The text
of *M* does not give good contrast, nor does the
revocalization to בַּצָּמָא (compare Isa 44:3) "in arid
land" (Condamin; so also *RSV*, *NEB*). *S* reads "in

poor enthroned Dibon!—
for the devastator of Moab has come up
    against you,
has ruined your fortifications.

19   On the road stand and watch,
    O enthroned Aroer;
ask the man fleeing and the woman escap-
    ing,
say, "What has happened?"

20   "Moab has stood ashamed, yes terrified,"[a]
    [b]wail and cry out;[b]
    "Tell it at the Arnon,
    'Moab is destroyed!'"

[21   And judgment has come upon the land of the
    plateau, on Holon, on Jahzah, on
    Mephaath,[b] 22/ on Dibon, on Nebo, on
    Beth-diblathaim, 23/ on Kiriathaim, on
    Beth-gamul, on Beth-meon, 24/ on Kerioth,
    on Bozrah, and on all the cities of the land of
    Moab, far and near.][a]

25   "'The horn of Moab is cut off,
    and his arm is broken!'"
                  [oracle of Yahweh.][a]

[26   Make him drunk, for against Yahweh he has
    set himself up; and Moab will overflow with
    his vomit, and he too shall become a
    laughingstock. 27/ Surely for you Israel has
    been ⟨a laughingstock, has he not?⟩[b] Surely
    [c]he has never been found[c] among thieves,
    has he? Yet whenever ⟨you have spoken⟩[d] of
    him you have wagged your head!][a]

28   Leave the cities,
    and make the rocks your home,
        inhabitants of Moab,
and be like the dove who nests
    in the walls of the yawning gorge!
    [29 We have heard of the pride of Moab—
very proud!—his height, and his pride, and
his arrogance, and his haughtiness of heart.

30   I myself know, ⟨oracle of Yahweh,⟩[b] his
        insolence;
    his bragging is false,
        false what [c]they do.[c]

31   On this account over Moab I shall wail,
    and for Moab, all of it, I shall cry out,
    [d]for the men of[d] Kir-heres[e] [f]I shall
        moan.[f]

32   ⟨Fountain of⟩[g] Jazer, I weep for you,
    《vine of》[h] Sibmah:
    your shoots extended to the sea,
        as far as Jazer[i] they reached;
    on your fruit and on your vintage[j]
        the devastator[k] has fallen.

33   Gladness and rejoicing have been taken
        away ⟨from the orchard-land and⟩[l]
    from the land of Moab,

---

contempt," but whether that is a euphemistic translation of the emendation suggested here or simply a
guess on the basis of context would be difficult to
say. Bright suggests that the mem was probably
added to soften an offensive text (compare the
remarks on the possibility of a censored text in
17:1–4, and n. 21 there).

20a–a   The feminine form חַתָּה is odd after הֹבִישׁ, and
Rudolph corrects it to חַת. But given the feminine
imperatives in the second colon (see b—b), it is
better to read הֹבִישָׁה. Compare the last colon of v 1.

b—b   MSS. and Versions divide as to whether to read
these imperatives as masculine plural (qere') or
feminine singular (ketib): one finds feminine singular imperatives in v 19 and a masculine plural
imperative in v 20b (see 6:25 for the identical issue).
I suspect that the feminine singular forms are
correct, but there is no way to be sure: see the form-
critical analysis in Structure, Form, Setting, *Structure
and Form of the Authentic Material.*

21–24a   This prose listing interrupts the poem: so Volz,
Rudolph, Bright.

b   Read qere', *V, S, T* מֵיפַעַת; ketib and *G* read
מוֹפָעַת.

25a   Omit with *G*.

26–27a   A prose addition (so Rudolph, Bright).

b—b   Vocalizing הֲשְׂחֹק (he interrogative) for *M* הַשְׂחֹק
(noun with article); compare König, *Syntax*, sec.
353i, and so Volz and Rudolph.

c—c   Reading the masculine verb נִמְצָא with the qere'
instead of the feminine נִמְצָאָה.

d   For דְּבָרֶיךָ (or the reading of a few MSS., דְּבָרֶךָ)
read דַּבֶּרְךָ (so, evidently, s' [Syro-hexapla]).

29–33a   This material is also found, with some variation,
in Isa 16:6–10 and is surely secondary here (so also
Rudolph).

b   Omit with *G*.

c—c   *G* "he does."

d—d   Isa 16:7 reads לַאֲשִׁישֵׁי, "for the raisin-cakes of": *M*
here is a milder reading.

e   For Kir-heres (קִיר־חֶרֶשׂ) Isa 16:7 has Kir-hareseth
(קִיר־חֲרָשֶׂת).

f—f   So read with one MS. and the Oriental qere'; *M*
"he will moan."

g   Vocalizing מַבֻּךְ for *M* מִבְּכִי, "more than the
weeping of," following a suggestion of George M.
Landes, "The Fountain at Jazer," *BASOR* 144
(December 1956) 30–37, and Menahem Mansoor,
"The Thanksgiving Hymns and the Massoretic Text
(Part II)," *RevQ* 3 (1961/62) 394; so Rudolph,
Bright, Thompson.

h   Reading גֶּפֶן with *G* and Isa 16:8; *M* הַגֶּפֶן, "vine"
(thus making "Sibmah" an appositive).

i   *M* has יָם before "Jazer": omit with two MSS. and
with Isa 16:8; so the commentaries, and so *RSV, JB,
NEB, NAB.*

j   Isa 16:9 reads קְצִירֵךְ "your (grain) harvest."

k   Isa 16:9 reads הֵידָד "war-cry."

l   Omit with *G* (so Duhm, Volz; so also Janzen, p.
59).

the wine from the wine presses 《 has
    ceased; 》[m]
《 the treader does not tread,
    the shout is not shouted. 》] [a]

[34   Heshbon 《 and 》[b] Elealeh 《 cry out, 》[c]
    as far as Jahaz they utter their voice,
       from Zoar to Horonaim, {Eglath-
          shelishiyah,}[d]
        indeed the waters of Nimrim too have
          become desolate.][a]

[35   And I shall bring an end to Moab,
                    oracle of Yahweh,
   who offers 《 a burnt offering on 》[b] a high
       place,
    who burns to his gods.][a]

[36   On this account [b]my heart wails for Moab
    like flutes,
   and my heart wails for the men of Kir-heres
    like flutes;[b]
       on this account the savings[c] they gained
        have perished.

37   For on[d] every head is baldness,
    and every beard is shaved,[e]
   on all the hands are gashes,
    and on all[f] loins is sackcloth.

38   On all the roofs of Moab and in her squares,
    all of it is mourning;][a]
   for I have broken Moab
    like a vessel no one cares for,
                  [oracle of Yahweh.][g]

39   How terrified he is ⟨ in wailing!
    and ⟩[a] how Moab has turned his back in
    shame!
   So Moab shall become a laughingstock
    and a fright to all his neighbors.
   40/ For thus Yahweh has said,
   [see, like an eagle he soars,
    and spreads his wings over Moab.][a]

41   The cities have been captured,
    and the strongholds seized,
   [and the heart of the warriors of Moab
   shall be on that day like the heart of a
   woman in labor.][a]

m   For הִשְׁבַּתִּי, "I have stopped," read הָשְׁבַּת (so
Rudolph): the first-person diction appears to cease
with v 32. The verb הִשְׁבַּתִּי appears in Isa 16:10,
and there G suggests likewise reading הָשְׁבַּת (so
Wildberger, *Jesaja*, 594).

n   M is in confusion; literally "one shall not tread
(with) a shout, a shout not a shout" (compare *KJV*).
The first clause may be read with Isa 16:10, לֹא־יִדְרֹךְ
הַדֹּרֵךְ; parallelism then suggests that the root is
repeated in subject and verb in the second clause, so
that one may reconstruct a denominative verb יְהֵדַד
or יְהוֹדַד (so Rudolph; compare Bright).

34a   Material in this verse is also found in Isa 15:4 and
6 and is surely secondary here (so also Rudolph).

b   Read וְ with Isa 15:4 for M עַד "as far as" (so
Rudolph, Bright; so *RSV*).

c   Read וַתִּזְעַק with Isa 15:4 for M מִזַּעֲקַת, "and from
the cry of [Heshbon]" (so Rudolph, Bright; so *RSV*).

d   This place-name appears in Isa 15:5 to be a gloss
on Zoar (Wildberger, *Jesaja*, 591), and it appears to
be equally a gloss here.

35a   This verse is redactional and is perhaps prose
(compare 33:18); so also Rudolph.

b   Insert עָלָה עַל־הַ with T. G reads the colon as הָעֹלֶה
עַל־בָּמָה. The text of M evidently suffered double
haplography; so Rudolph (Bright: "perhaps").

36–38a   Much of this material is found also, with some
variation, in Isa 15:6 and 2b–3, and it is surely
secondary here (so also Rudolph).

b—b   Isa 16:11: "My bowels wail for Moab like a lyre,
and my inwards for Kir-heres." One suspects that
the text of the first colon in Jer has suffered dittography from the second colon and perhaps an
expansion ("the men of") in the second colon, and
conversely that the text of Isaiah has suffered
haplography.

c   The vocalization should probably be יִתְרַת with
some MSS. rather than M יִתְרַת (so Rudolph).

d   Read עַל with a few MSS.; Isa 15:2 has בְּ; M here
omits a preposition.

e   So M here and in Isa 15:2; but some MSS. here
read גָּרְעָה, "cut off," and many MSS. in Isa 15:2
likewise read גְּרוּעָה.

f   So read with the Cairo Geniza, with many MSS.,
with G and V; M omits כָּל־.

g   Omit with G.

39a   Volz and Rudolph wish to excise this word (and
compare Bright), but the Versions include it. I
propose reading הֵילֵל וְ: the verb is then construed
as an adverbial infinitive absolute parallel with בּוֹשׁ
in the next colon.

40–41a   Omit both sequences with G (so also Duhm,
Giesebrecht, Rudolph): they are taken from 49:22.
Both 48:24 and 49:22 mention "Bozrah." Janzen, p.
59, suggests that the phrases were perhaps a gloss on
Bozrah in v 24 and were taken into the wrong
column of a manuscript, with appropriate change of
names.

42	Moab shall be wiped out as a people, for against Yahweh he has set himself up.

43	Terror and pit and trap are against you,
	    enthroned Moab!
	                [oracle of Yahweh;]ᵃ

44	ᵇhe who fleesᵇ ᶜfrom the presence ofᶜ the
	    terror shall fall into the pit,
	and he who gets out fromᵈ the pit shall be
	    caught in the trap,

45a	《 in the shadow of Heshbon they have
	    stopped exhausted [those flee-
	    ing,]ᶠ 》 ᵉ

44	for I shall bring ⟨a curse⟩ᵍ on Moab,
	    the year of their punishment,
	              [oracle of Yahweh;]ᵃ

45	[. . . .]ᵉ
	[for a fire ⁱhas gone forthⁱ from Heshbon,
	    andʲ a flame ᵏfrom the house ofᵏ of Sihon;
	    and it has consumed the forehead of
	    Moab,
	    ˡand the skull ofˡ the children of up-
	    roar.ᵐ

46	Woe to you, Moab,
	    ⁿthe people of Chemosh have perished,ⁿ
	for your sons have been taken captive,
	    your daughters into captivity.]ʰ
	[47/ But I shall restore the fortunes of
	Moab in time to come, oracle of Yahweh.
	Thus far is the judgment of Moab.]ᵃ

43–46a This phrase is omitted in both vv 43 and 44 in *G*; both occurrences are thus secondary.

b—b Read with qere' הַנָּם; the ketib הנים is a scribal error.

c—c For מִפְּנֵי *S* reads with Isa 24:18 מִקּוֹל "from the sound of."

d For ־מִן some MSS. and *S* and *T* read with Isa 24:18 מִתּוֹךְ "from the midst of."

e Verse 45a is omitted not only by *G* but by *S* as well. Yet (in contrast to vv 45b–46) the colon is not borrowed from another passage but appears to be original. It fits admirably after v 44a; I propose that it accidentally dropped out by haplography between כפה at the end of v 44a and מכה at the end of v 45a (kap and pe resemble each other closely in the early Aramaic script: see Cross, "Scripts," 137): this is the stage of *G* and *S*. Subsequently it was restored in the wrong order. See further Structure, Form, Setting, *Possible Authentic Material in Verses 29–47*.

f If v 45a is misplaced (see note e) then this word is probably to be omitted as a gloss; the word order is odd, and the proposed haplography causing the omission and subsequent misplacement of the colon is more plausible without the word.

g For אֵלֶיהָ, "to her," *G* and *S* read אֵלֶּה, "these (things)"; I propose to read those consonants as אָלָה (compare 2:34; 4:12; 5:25; 14:22); it is to be noted that both 11:23 and 23:12 read רְעָה in the pattern of the phrase under discussion.

h Verses 45b–46 are omitted in *G* and are secondary here: v 45bα is taken from Num 21:28a, v 45bβ from Num 24:17bβ, and v 46 from Num 21:29 (compare Janzen, p. 59).

i—i Read with many MSS. and Num 21:28 יָצְאָה; *M* יָצָא.

j Num 21:28 omits "and."

k—k Read with a few MSS. מִבֵּית; *M* reads מִבֵּין "from among." Num 21:18 reads מִקִּרְיַת "from the city of."

l—l For וְקָדְקֹד a few MSS. and Num 24:17 read וְקַרְקַר. If the latter is a genuine reading (and the verb occurs twice in reminiscences of the Numbers passage in Qumran documents), its meaning is disputed; perhaps read וְקַרְקַר, "and he will beat down" (Godfrey R. Driver, "Myths of Qumran," ALUOS 6 [1966–68] 45, assuming a cognate with Arabic *qāra*, "fell"; so also *HALAT*, 1071b).

m For שָׁאוֹן Num 24:17 reads שֵׁת, a reading interpreted in various ways: as the proper name "Seth" (Gen 4:25), or as the equivalent of שְׁאֵת, "desolation" (?: Lam 3:47), or to be read as the equivalent of שְׂאֵת "defiance"; see the commentaries.

n—n Num 21:29 offers a second-person verb, doubtless a preferable reading: "You have perished, O people of Chemosh."

47a This verse likewise is omitted in *G* and consists of two late additions: the first half resembles Ezek 29:14aα (with "Moab" substituted for "Egypt"), and the second half is an editorial note. Compare Janzen, p. 59.

Structure, Form, Setting

Preliminary Remarks. This long chapter is devoted solely to Moab: it has not only an editorial superscription (v 1) but a subscription (v 47b). Roughly the first half consists of material found only here, whereas the second half contains many duplications or reminiscences of material about Moab found elsewhere, strikingly in the case of vv 29–38, much of which is also to be found within Isaiah 15—16, but also in the case of vv 43–46, which contain phrases found also in Isa 24:17–18; Num 24:17; 21:28–29. An analysis of the literary history of the chapter is thus a prime consideration. This analysis, however, is complicated by a whole series of difficulties. Thus the variations between the duplicated material in this chapter and in Isaiah 15—16 seem sometimes to be the result of the misreading or carelessness of copyists (v 32: "on your fruit and on your vintage [בְצִירֵךְ] the destroyer [שֹׁדֵד] has fallen"; Isa 16:9: "on your fruit and on your grain harvest [קְצִירֵךְ] the shout [הֵידָד] has fallen"), sometimes a result simply of free variation (v 34a: "they utter their voice [נָתְנוּ קוֹלָם]"; Isa 15:4: "their voice is heard [נִשְׁמַע קוֹלָם]"). And the text of G offers further variation in these duplicated texts as well as in the unduplicated ones. Again, the material in Jer 48 that overlaps Isaiah 15—16 is not in the sequence found in Isaiah, and the duplicated material is interspersed with phrases not found elsewhere. To take a simple example, in v 29 one has "we have heard of the pride of Moab," but the diction shifts in v 30 to the singular, "I myself know, oracle of Yahweh, his insolence." Now the material beginning with "we have heard of the pride of Moab" is duplicated in Isa 16:6, but the words "I myself know, oracle of Yahweh" are not duplicated—the duplication begins again with "his insolence"; furthermore the phrase "oracle of Yahweh" is missing in G for v 30, so the question becomes: Is there is a significant form-critical shift in v 30, or did an adapter carelessly add "I myself know," a gloss that necessitated the clarification "oracle of Yahweh" by still another glossator? Finally, the literary

history of Isaiah 15—16 is itself tangled: it is not self-evident that the material in Isaiah that duplicates material in the Jer chapter is in every instance antecedent to the duplications in the Jer chapter (see below, specifically *Verses 29–47* and *Authentic Material in Verses 29–47*).

The impression of adaptation and redaction produces uncertainty whether a given sequence should be displayed as poetry or as prose (for example, v 38). And it produces form-critical uncertainty as well: what form, after all, should one expect in one or more oracles against Moab, when the material here offers such a confusing array of both unduplicated material and material developed out of bits and pieces of Isaiah 15—16 and 24 and Numbers 21 and 24?

Nevertheless, after secondary material in the chapter has been bracketed, the authentic material turns out to manifest structure and shape, a series of sections comparable to those in chapter 2 or 4:5–31.

Secondary Material within Verses 1–28. As already noted, the large-scale duplications with Isaiah 15—16 and other material begin with v 29. It is therefore appropriate to deal first with the material in vv 1–28.

Here there is only one duplication: v 5 duplicates Isa 15:5b. Curiously enough, portions of Isa 15:4 and the end of v 5a are found in the present chapter in v 34a (the rest of Isa 15:5a is missing in the present chapter) and Isa 15:6a is found in the present chapter in v 34b; in other words, the sequence of Isa 15:4–6a is parallel to the present chapter, v 34a + 5 + 34b. It would be too much to insist that v 5 breaks the continuity between vv 4 and 6, but it certainly does not aid their continuity. The most plausible solution is that v 5 represents an omission written in the margin and incorporated by error into the preceding column of text.[1]

There are four sequences that are probably in prose and in any case intrude upon the continuity of the text: vv 10, 13, 21–24, and 26–27. Verse 10 is probably in prose, and in any event the curse, with its mention of Yahweh in the third person, comes out of context; it is

---

1   It may be noted, for what it is worth, that 1QIs^a, in Isaiah 40—55, offers between 19 and 32 verses per column, with an average of 26: see *Scrolls from Qumrân Cave I, The Great Isaiah Scroll, The Order of the Community, The* Pesher *to Habakkuk* (ed. Frank M. Cross et al.; Jerusalem: The Albright Institute of Archaeological Research and The Shrine of the Book, 1972) 80–105. Further, 2Q13, fragment 9, overlaps two columns and offers Jer 48:7 adjoining 48:27: see Maurice Baillet, Jozef T. Milik, and Roland de Vaux, *Les 'Petite Grottes' de Qumrân* (DJD 3; Oxford: Clarendon, 1962) 64 and Planche XIII.

rightly bracketed by most commentators. Similarly to be bracketed is v 13 with its comparison of Moab with the house of Israel: I would propose that this marginal note was originally a response to v 39 and, like v 5, was inserted by error in the previous column of text (see above). Verses 21–24 are an obvious prose listing. And again vv 26–27 appear to be a patchwork, perhaps two separate additions. As for v 26, "for against Yahweh he set himself up" is found in v 42, and "he shall become a laughingstock" in v 39; the theme of a drunken man in his vomit is found in Isa 19:14. In v 27 there is a sudden shift to second-person singular address, and the syntax appears to be colloquial (see Interpretation); form-critically the theme of reciprocity in treatment (Moab has treated Israel as a laughingstock) comes on unexpectedly (compare the mention of Israel in v 13). Volz, Rudolph, and Bright in most details concur with these judgments.

The Authenticity of the Primary Material within Verses 1–28. What remains in vv 1–28 may lay claim to be authentic to Jrm: there are many turns of phrase that appear to be distinctive to him, and they are used here in fresh ways. Thus הוֹי אֶל־נְבוֹ כִּי שֻׁדָּדָה, "Alas for Nebo, how ruined it is!" in v 1 resembles אוֹי לָנוּ כִּי שֻׁדָּדְנוּ, "Woe to us, oh, we are ruined!" in 4:13; there is no other passage in the OT that resembles these sequences so closely. The phrase שֶׁבֶר גָּדוֹל, "great destruction," (v 3) is found otherwise in 4:6; 6:1; 14:17; 50:22; 51:54; and Zeph 1:10. "And let them be like a juniper in the wilderness" (v 6, וְתִהְיֶינָה כַּעֲרָעָר בַּמִּדְבָּר, if the first noun is correctly vocalized) resembles "he shall be like a juniper in the desert" (וְהָיָה כְּעַרְעָר בָּעֲרָבָה) in 17:6; the noun עַרְעָר does not otherwise appear in the OT. "And her cities shall become a desolation, without inhabitant in them" (v 9) is a variation on "they have made his land a desolation, his cities have been burned, without inhabitant" in 2:15, "to make your land a desolation—your cities shall be in ruins, without inhabitant" in 4:7, and "every city is deserted, without inhabitant in them" in 4:29. The parallelism in v 11 of שאן pa'lal, "be relaxed," and שקט, "rest," is found otherwise only in 30:10. The phraseology of "decanters to decant" in v 12 is paralleled by "fishermen . . . and they shall fish" and "hunters . . . and they shall hunt" in 16:16. The phrase "How can you say, 'We are X'?" in v 14 is found also in 8:8 (compare 2:23). Verse 18a, "descend from glory and sit in dung (?), poor enthroned Dibon," is similar to the word to the king and

queen-mother in 13:18, "take a lower seat, for there comes down from your heads your splendid crown," as well as 10:17, "gather up from the land your bundle, you who are enthroned under siege," and the parallel of עלה, "come up," and שחת pi'el, "destroy," is found also in 5:10; and in a more general way the rhetoric of v 18, with "enthroned" (יֹשֶׁבֶת) and "come up against you," resembles that of 21:13, with "enthroned" (יֹשֶׁבֶת) and "who can come down against us, who can enter our habitations?" "On the road stand and watch" (אֶל־דֶּרֶךְ עִמְדִי וְצַפִּי) in v 19 is parallel to "stand on the roads and look" (עִמְדוּ עַל־דְּרָכִים וּרְאוּ) in 6:16. One may add that the phraseology of v 28a ("leave the cities and make the rocks your home") resembles 4:29. These turns of phrase are distinctive to Jrm, and their shape in the present material is not a slavish imitation but fresh usage.

Verses 29–47. As already recorded in the Text notes, there is a literary relation between vv 29–33 + 35–36a and Isa 16:6–12, between v 34 and Isa 15:4–6, between 36b and Isa 15:7, between vv 37–38a and Isa 15:2–3, between 43–44a and Isa 24:17–18a, and between vv 45b–46 on the one hand and Num 24:17 and 21:28–29 on the other. The parallels are laid out in adjoining columns in Wildberger, *Jesaja,* 607–609 (though in the case of vv 29–37 the material is displayed in the order in which it appears in Isaiah 15—16 rather than in the order of the text in the present chapter); in this way both the shared and nonshared material may be seen. In addition to these parallels in vv 29–46, vv 40aβb, 41b, and 45–47 are lacking in G (and vv 40aβb and 41b are duplicates of 49:22 with "and spread his wings against Bozrah" omitted and "Moab" substituted for "Edom").

With regard to the material duplicated in Isaiah 15—16 three conclusions may be made. (1) None of this shared material has any of the characteristics of Jrm's poetry (compare the listing of phrases in the treatment of vv 1–28 above). (2) Structurally and form-critically the material in Isaiah 15—16 has shape, whereas the material in Jer is a conglomerate of literary reminiscences; the material in Isaiah 15—16 is therefore prior to that in

Jer.[2] (3) The borrowing from Isaiah was not done by Jrm himself: not only was he able to produce material on the Moabites himself but also the *variations* in Jer in the shared material with Isaiah 15—16 bear no stamp of his usage.

Wildberger, after careful analysis, tentatively assigns at least Isa 15:1b–8 and perhaps 16:1, 3–5, 8–11 (12?) as well to the second half of the eighth century, therefore conceivably to the prophet Isaiah: an Assyrian letter from that period mentions a raid on Moab by the people of the land of Gidir; but the history of Moab is far too poorly known to allow a confident dating.[3]

Authentic Material within Verses 29–47. One's attention is first drawn to vv 38b–40aα, 41a, and 42, material present in *G* and not duplicated elsewhere. The most striking phrase in these verses is that in v 39a, "How Moab has turned his back in shame!" (אֵיךְ הִפְנָה־עֹרֶף מוֹאָב בּוֹשׁ): פנה qal or hip'il (the two stems in this instance seem to be nearly or entirely synonymous) with object עֹרֶף is found in Jer only in 2:27 and the secondary imitation in 32:33; outside of Jer it is found only in Josh 7:12. In 2:27 the Israelites "have turned their back to me [Yahweh] and not their face" in deliberate apostasy; in the present instance, 48:39, "Moab has turned his back" in the shame of military defeat. But this striking phrase is a strong indicator of the diction of Jrm. One may also note in passing that אֵיךְ "how!" is common in Jrm's diction and is rare in other prophetic material.[4] The distinctive diction of v 39a is reinforced by that of v 39b, "So Moab shall become a laughingstock and a fright to all his neighbors." "Become a laughingstock" (היה לִשְׂחֹק) is found in the OT only otherwise in Jer 20:7 and 48:26 (for that verse see above, *Secondary Material within Verses 1–28*). "Become a fright" (היה לִמְחִתָּה) is found in the OT only otherwise in Jer 17:17 (there translated "become a terror"). In 20:7 Jrm complains of having become a laughingstock to those who persecute him, and in 17:17 he asks Yahweh not to become a terror to him. In the present instance Moab is to become a source of derision and fright to

neighboring peoples: in short, in this instance too diction found elsewhere in Jrm's authentic words is used here in a fresh way.

Verse 38b reads "for I have broken Moab like a vessel no one cares for." The idiom "vessel no one cares for" (כְּלִי אֵין־חֵפֶץ בּוֹ) is found in the OT only otherwise in 22:28 and Hos 8:8 (in the latter passage likewise with "like" [כְּ]). In 22:28 it is Jehoiachin who is to be treated as a discarded piece of pottery, "a vessel no one cares for"; in Hos 8:8 it is Israel that is among the nations like a discarded piece of pottery. Although the phrase here in v 38b does not have to stem from Jrm—anyone is free to use the phrase in Hosea—Jrm used the same verb "break" (שׁבר qal) in the episode of the breaking of the flask (19:10, 11), an act symbolic of the breaking of the nation; and in the first part of the present chapter, in what is presumably authentic material, the verb appears three times in the nip'al (passive), vv 4, 17, 25. It is therefore altogether likely that this half-verse too is authentic to the prophet.

Verse 40aα is simply "For thus Yahweh has said." Verses 41a and 42 offer little that is distinctive, but one may note: (1) that v 41a is arranged in a chiasmus; (2) that the nip'al וְנִשְׁמַד in v 42a follows well after the two nip'al verbs in v 41a (נִתְפְּשָׂה and נִלְכָּדָה); (3) that the form וְנִשְׁמַד appears also in v 8, presumably an authentic passage, and שׁמד nip'al does not appear otherwise in Jer; and (4) that the expression מֵעָם in v 42, literally "from (being) a people," is analogous to מִגּוֹי, literally "from (being) a nation," in v 2, likewise presumably an authentic passage. These observations all suggest authenticity and lead to the conclusion that vv 38b–40aα, 41a, and 42 make up material authentic to Jrm in the chapter.

Another sort of problem emerges with vv 43–44, duplicated in Isa 24:17–18. The verses in Isaiah are part of the Isaiah Apocalypse (chapters 24—27), dated well into the postexilic period: Wildberger gives a date between 500 and 400.[5] In these chapters are many duplications or reminiscences of phrases found elsewhere

---

2 Wildberger, *Jesaja*, 605.

3 Ibid., 603–11, esp. 606, 611; see further 597 for the raid of the Gidir.

4 See Solomon Mandelkern, *Veteris Testamenti Concordantiae Hebraicae atque Chaldaicae* (rep. Graz: Akademische Druck- und Verlagsanstalt, 1955) 42d–43a.

5 Wildberger, *Jesaja*, 911.

in prophetic material, and Isa 24:13–23 is particularly heavy with such duplications—from elsewhere in Isaiah, from Jer, from Hosea, Amos, and Micah.[6] The question then arises whether vv 43–44 in the present chapter are not authentic to Jrm, borrowed much later for use in the Isaiah Apocalypse. The triple word-play of פַּחַד וָפַחַת וָפָח "terror and pit and trap" in v 43 and the subsequent phrases in v 44 using these three nouns are not comparable to anything in the authentic material of Jrm, but they are obviously worthy of him (for the word-play see further Interpretation). The phrase שְׁנַת פְּקֻדָּתָם, "the year of their visitation," is found in the OT only otherwise in 11:23 and 23:12, and the synonymous phrase עֵת פְּקֻדָּתָם, "time of their visitation," occurs in five other passages in Jer[7] but not outside the book. And if the restoration of "curse" in v 44 is correct, this usage too occurs several times in Jrm's oracles (see Text).

Still a different problem is presented by v 45a. This half-verse is missing in both G and S, and it has therefore been presumed to be secondary. But in contrast to vv 45–46, it does not duplicate anything in Numbers or elsewhere, nor does its diction appear to be modeled on phraseology elsewhere. It fits admirably in the context of vv 43–44a, and therefore I suggest that it is original but misplaced (see Text): "the year of their visitation" elsewhere closes off a poetic unit (11:23; 23:12).

One may conclude that vv 38b–40aα, 41a, 42–44a + 45a + 44b make up authentic Jrm material.

Structure and Form of the Authentic Material. As already noted, the material of this chapter offers form-critical uncertainty, and this is just as true after the secondary material is bracketed.

One may be tolerably certain that the sequence begins with three sections, each of which displays structural and form-critical integrity. In the first two sections (vv 1–4, vv 6–9) the speaker is unidentified.

The first section (vv 1–4) consists of six bicola. This section is heavy with place-names, some with word-play, thus "Heshbon" (חֶשְׁבּוֹן) and "planned" (חָשְׁבוּ), "Madmen"

(מַדְמֵן), and "you shall weep" (תִּדֹּמִי). These verses are comparable to Mic 1:10–15 in such use of place-names: both poems have the form of a lament over the "death" of communities, an adaptation of the funeral dirge at the death of an individual: in such a dirge there is word-play on the name of the deceased (compare 2 Sam 1:19–27; 3:33–34).[8] The poem begins with the interjection הוֹי, "alas!" associated with the dirge (see 22:18, and the discussion in 22:13–19, Form), and continues with the lament כִּי שֻׁדָּדָה, "oh, it is ruined!" for which compare 4:13, כִּי שֻׁדָּדְנוּ, "oh, we are ruined!." In v 2aγ one hears the cry of Moab's enemy urging the destruction of the nation, for which compare 6:4a, 5; and in v 3b one hears the cry of the Moabite population exclaiming over their ruin, for which compare the cries in 4:20 (following the interpretation of the present study). This section speaks of Moab or its cities in the third-person singular feminine, but a city is once addressed directly (second-person singular feminine, v 2b) and once there seems to be a reference to Moab in the third-person plural (v 4b). Since Moab is mentioned twice (vv 2a, 4a), there may be an attempt here to mention both cities in the north (vv 1–2) and Horonaim in the south (v 3; for the possible location of Horonaim see Interpretation). The passage in general offers a static depiction of the ruin of Moab. Is there is mood of taunting here in the depiction, as there seems to be in Mic 1:10–15?[9] Perhaps; does "has stood ashamed," v 1b, communicate this? And it is possible that a reference to "dung-heap" stands behind the mention of "Madmen" in v 2 (see Interpretation). But if there is taunting here (on which compare further the discussion below on v 18, and the subsection *The Tone of the Chapter*), it is subdued: there is no talk of a city being stripped naked (Mic 1:11). The depiction is sober.

The second section is vv 6–9, again a sequence of bicola, this time seven of them. These verses are bracketed by second-person plural imperatives (three addressed to the Moabites in v 6, one evidently addressed to the enemy in v 9b); yet the plural address to

---

6   Ibid., 910.

7   8:12; 10:15; 46:21; 50:27; 51:18.

8   For the dirge in general see Eissfeldt, *Introduction*, 94–98; for word-play in the dirges in 2 Samuel see William L. Holladay, "Form and word-play in David's lament over Saul and Jonathan," *VT* 20 (1970) 153–89; for the poem in Micah see Wolff, *Micha*, 17–18; Mays, *Micah*, 54; Hillers, *Micah*, 24–30.

9   Hillers, *Micah*, 28.

the Moabites shifts, puzzlingly, to the feminine singular in v 7a ("you, too": who is being addressed?). Verse 6 is a summons to flee: for this compare 4:5–6a (see 4:5–31, Form, on those verses, and note 5 there). Verse 7 (and perhaps v 8) offer the reason for the summons to flee, introduced by כִּי (compare vv 28 + 38b: there too the reason, v 38b, appears to follow the summons to flee, v 28). The reason is essentially religious, a trust in "your treasures" (idols?: compare 46:25), so that the god Chemosh and his priests will go into exile. Verse 8 offers a depiction of Moab's ruin such as one has heard in vv 1–4; but it is noteworthy that it contradicts the summons to flee in v 6 ("no city shall escape"). Verse 9a is evidently a summons to the enemy to make Moab a salt-field (see Interpretation), followed by the reason or, perhaps better, the concomitant circumstances (with כִּי).

The third section is made up of vv 11–12, which consists of three bicola and a closing tricolon. Here, suddenly, Yahweh speaks (v 12, "I shall send"): the verses are a judgment oracle, giving the reason for the judgment (v 11) and the consequent announcement of Yahweh's action (v 12). The verses are not only united form-critically but in subject matter: they play on the metaphor of Moab as wine.

These three sections appear to be discrete; from v 14 onward, however, it becomes more difficult to locate boundaries in structure. But when one notices that place-names recur in vv 18–20 ("Dibon," "Aroer," "the Arnon") and v 28 is a summons to flee, one can suggest that there is a repetition of structure in the latter part of the sequence.

If v 18 begins a section parallel to vv 1–4, vv 14–17 emerge as the fourth discrete section. And indeed v 14a begins with "How can you say" and v 17b with the imperative "say," nicely bracketing this section (compare the same device in 2:20–25: "and you said" in v 20, "how can you say" in v 23a, and "but you said" in v 25b; for this see 2:1—4:4, Structure). The structure is evidently a bicolon (v 14), a tricolon (v 15), followed by three bicola (vv 16–17). No speaker is identified, though the rhetoric of disputation in v 14 implies that the speaker is Yahweh (see below). The address in v 14, in the second-person plural, is to the Moabite soldiers; this is balanced by the plural imperative in v 17 addressed to Moab's neighbors (there is a parallel to the pattern of second-person references in vv 6 and 9, in v 6 to the Moabites and in v 9 to

the enemy). Verse 14 is the rhetoric of disputation, quoting one's adversary; this rhetoric is appropriate in legal speech (compare both 2:23 and 8:8 for this form). Verses 15 and 16 continue the depictions of Moab's ruin such as one has heard in vv 1–4 and 8. Verse 17 is a call to lamentation: in 4:8 that form is a call for the community to lament over its own ruin (see there)—and so it is below, in v 20; but here the call is slightly different—it is a call to one group of people to lament over the ruin of another people. This call includes the words of the lament (so also 4:8b, according to the suggestion of the present study).

Verse 18 begins a fifth section, parallel to the first (vv 1–4) in the use of place-names (see above). This section evidently includes not only vv 18–20 but v 25 as well: one notes (1) that v 28, the beginning of further authentic material, begins with a summons to flee as v 6 does (see above), and (2) that the first section offers נִשְׁבְּרָה מוֹאָב, "Moab is broken," near its close (v 4), and v 25 offers "the bow of Moab is cut off, and his arm is broken [נִשְׁבָּרָה]," evidently to close off the section. If that is the case, then the section has four bicola (vv 18–19) followed by what may well be a hexacolon (vv 20 + 25), or at least a tetracolon (v 20) plus a bicolon (v 25)—the decision depends upon whether v 25 is construed as a quotation alongside "Moab is destroyed!" in v 20 (see below). There is no identification of the speaker(s) of the imperatives "descend," "ask," and "say" in vv 18–19; for a possible identity of the speaker(s) in vv 20 and 25 see below. As already affirmed, place-names characterize this section as they do the first section, but whereas in that section only one place was addressed with second-person forms (Madmen, v 2), here several of them are addressed with vocatives and imperatives. In v 18a Dibon is told to get down from her throne and sit in humiliation—"in the dung," if the text is rightly reconstructed. Is this call to humiliation a taunt?—compare the same question raised with regard to vv 1–4. Such rhetoric is indeed a taunt in Isa 47:1; in Ezek 26:15–18, however, it functions in a description of lamentation. It would be easy to assume that the tone in the present passage is one of taunting (perhaps reinforced by "has stood ashamed" in v 20): 21:13 is a comparable verse, sharing as it does some phraseology with v 18 here, and there the tone would seem to be one of contempt (see above, *The Authenticity of the Primary Material within Verses 1–28*). On the other

hand the tone here may be closer to humiliation and
lament, given further phrases in v 20 like "wail and cry
out" (compare the rhetoric of 13:18, which resembles the
present verse to some degree). Verse 18b gives the
reason for the call to humiliation (introduced by כִּי). The
imperatives in v 19 are battle orders (compare 6:16),
orders to a scout or messenger. But these orders are in
the context of defeat: "Ask the refugee what has happened"! Verse 20 brings difficulties in the nature of the
quotation(s) (see the punctuation here). "Wail and cry
out" would appear to be parallel with "say" in v 19; in this
case the feminine singulars are correct (see Text). I
propose that "Moab has stood ashamed, yes terrified" is
the content of the wail (compare the probability of
similar quotation before "wail" in 51:8). But the imperative "tell it [at the Arnon]" is masculine plural, allowing
the conclusion that "tell" begins a quotation completing
"cry out." It must be said, however, that there are two
other possibilities. (1) "Moab has stood ashamed, yes
terrified" might be the (complete) answer from the
refugees, and in the translation the closing quotation
marks would then be followed by a semicolon; "wail"
(feminine singular) would then point not backward but
forward (with "cry out") to the following quotation,
"Tell. . . ." Or (2) "Moab has stood ashamed, yes terrified" might begin the answer of the refugees that continues with "wail and cry out, tell it . . ." (all parallel
masculine plurals). There is no way to be sure. The כִּי
that marks the last colon of v 20, I suggest, introduces a
subquotation, completing "tell it at the Arnon" (for this
use of כִּי, notably in laments, compare 4:8, 13). What one
has in this verse then is a sense of the echoing of lamentation within the Arnon gorge announcing the ruin of
Moab (compare the description of the gorge of the
Arnon in Interpretation, vv 19–20). Verse 25 belongs
with vv 18–20 (see above), and the rhetoric suggests it is
a continuation of the last colon of v 20, thus the conclusion of the subquotation.

Verse 28, like v 6, is a summons to flee and thus begins
a sixth section. Verse 6 is followed in v 7 by the reason
for the summons to flee introduced by כִּי, and v 38b,
which in the foregoing analysis is the next authentic
material, appears to offer a parallel reason for the summons to flee introduced by כִּי.

It is not easy to establish firm boundaries for the
sections in the final verses of the authentic material,
because form-critical parallels with the early sections of
the chapter are no longer discernible. We remind ourselves that the authentic material beyond vv 28 and 38b
consists of 39 (40aα), 41a, 42, 43, and 44a + 45a + 44b.
With hesitation I suggest that a fresh section begins with
v 39: the twofold exclamatory אֵיךְ "how!" appears to open
fresh material. And likewise v 43 opens fresh material:
"terror and pit and trap" has not been prepared for by
anything before. By this analysis v 38b closes with a כִּי
clause and v 42 with another: both כִּי clauses deal with
Yahweh's action, directly in the first person in v 38b and
indirectly in v 42 by reference to Moab's setting himself
up against Yahweh. If this analysis is sound, vv 28 + 38b
will make up a short sixth section, vv 39–40aα, 41a, and
42 a seventh section, and vv 43–44a + 45a + 44b an
eighth. The eighth section will then close (v 44b) in the
same way as does the sixth (v 38b), with a כִּי clause
announcing in the first person Yahweh's judgment on
Moab. On this matter see further below, *Plausible Settings
for the Authentic Material.*

The sixth section, vv 28 + 38b, will then consist of a
tricolon followed by two bicola. As already noted, v 28 is
a summons to flee; the call to "be like a dove" in v 28b is
comparable in the OT only to the call to "be like he-
goats" in 50:8. Verse 38b offers the reason for the
summons: it is Yahweh who smashes Moab.

The seventh section, vv 39, 41a, 42, consists of four
bicola (excluding from consideration v 40aα, which
stands outside the poetic structure). The double אֵיךְ
"how!" in v 39a is characteristic of laments: the half-verse
then offers lamenting exclamations from bystanders over
the ruin of Moab; v 39b is a prediction of the contempt
with which Moab's neighbors will hold her. Verses 41–
42a are a depiction of the ruin of Moab much like that
already heard earlier in the chapter (for example, v 8),
and v 42b states the reason for the ruin, comparable to
the assessment of Moab in v 11.

The final section, vv 43–44a + 45a + 44b, will then
consist of a bicolon (v 43), a tricolon (vv 44a + 45a), and
a bicolon (v 44b). Verse 43, "Terror and pit and trap are
against you, enthroned Moab!" is an affirmation of the
encounter of Moab with a triple danger; as such it is
comparable to the formula of encounter in 21:13,
literally "Behold I am against you, (who are) enthroned
over the valley." Verses 44a + 45a explicate the affirmation of v 43 with a depiction of the multiple entrapment

of any refugee, and v 44b closes the section (and the authentic material on Moab) with an affirmation by Yahweh that it is he who will destroy Moab.

Structure and Form of the Secondary Material. Much of the secondary material extends the depictions of Moab's ruin already found in the authentic material. Verse 5, an adaptation of Isa 15:5b, is a bicolon, a depiction of the ruin of Moab, comparable to v 3. Verse 10 is a curse formula (compare 17:5). Verse 13 may be a bicolon: it describes the shame of Moab in comparison to the shame of Israel (for similar rhetoric see 2:36b). Verses 21–24 are of course a listing of Moabite place-names on which judgment has come; there is no discernible order to this sequence of localities. Verses 26–27 are a curious sequence of prose. Thus v 26 begins with the command to make Moab drunk as a punishment (compare 25:15: see the treatment in Structure, Form, Setting and in Interpretation on that verse). It continues with a כִּי clause reminiscent of v 42b (see above, on the authentic material). And it concludes with a further depiction of Moab's discomfiture (and compare v 39b). Then v 27 suddenly moves to accusation against Moab, addressed in second-person singular masculine; the verse, it is implied, is spoken by Israel, but Israel is referred to in the third person. The syntax of the verse gives evidence of being colloquial and argumentative (see Interpretation on the verse).

Verses 29–38a comprise the sequence of material borrowed from Isaiah 15—16. Verses 29–30 are an adaptation of Isa 16:6. Verse 29 as it stands can be nothing but prose; it is an affirmation by Moab's neighbors (primarily Israel, no doubt), speaking in the first-person plural, of their knowledge of Moab's pride. Verse 30 may be analyzed as a tricolon; in contrast to Isa 16:6, the diction here shifts to the first-person singular with the implication that the speaker who affirms his knowledge of Moab's pride is now Yahweh—and that implication is made explicit by the later addition of "oracle of Yahweh." (Curiously *G* accommodates v 29 ["I have heard"] to v 30 ["I have known"].) The rhetoric of these verses is similar to that of Zeph 2:8, and it is evidently intended as invective.[10] Verses 31–32 may be analyzed as a tricolon (v 31) and three bicola (v 32). These verses

have adapted phrases of Isa 16:7–9, but in such a way as to shift the form-critical categories. As for the material in Isaiah 16, after the seeming invective in v 6, v 7 is evidently a threat of divine judgment ("on this account let Moab wail": compare Zeph 2:9–10 after 2:8),[11] while vv 8–11 shift the form (and perhaps these verses originate from a different hand):[12] they are a lament, mixing a depiction of the ruin of Moab, referred to in the third person (vv 8, 9b, 10) with an affirmation in the first-person singular that the speaker weeps (vv 9a, 11)—that speaker is unidentified but is presumably the poet.[13] But in the adaptation in Jer 48 the affirmation of weeping is found not only in v 32 (parallel to Isa 16:9a) but in v 31 as well ("on this account over Moab I shall wail"), transforming the threat of divine judgment into antecedent phrases in the affirmation of weeping. This shift has the curious consequence of bringing the affirmation of weeping (first-person singular) in v 31 directly after the affirmation of the knowledge of Moab's pride in v 30 (first-person singular), presumably spoken by Yahweh (see above); but the precritical commentators recognized a disjunction here and assumed that the speaker in v 31 has shifted to Jrm (see Calvin, Naegelsbach). It must be stressed, however, that by the transformation all the cola of vv 31–32aα have become a dirge. And there is a further shift: v 32 addresses localities in Moab in the second-person singular feminine instead of referring to them in the third person as Isa 16:8–9 does. The remainder of v 32, an adaptation of Isa 16:8b–9, and v 33, two bicola that are an adaptation of Isa 16:10, continue the depiction of the ruin of Moab. Verse 34 is best analyzed as a tetracolon (the כִּי is deictic: see Interpretation). The first three cola of the verse adapt Isa 15:4–5a; the words depict the lamentation of cities of Moab, comparable to v 3. The last colon adapts Isa 15:6a, further description of the desolation of Moab. Verse 35 is perhaps triggered by Isa 16:12, itself doubtless a prosaic addition;[14] both it and the version here in v 35 (which may be analyzed as a tricolon) are testimony against pagan worship, here couched as Yahweh's judgment, set forth in the first person. Verse 36, curiously, combines the diction of two scraps from Isaiah, both beginning with עַל־כֵּן, namely, 16:11 and 15:7a: one may construe this verse as a tri-

---

10 Wildberger, *Jesaja*, 624.
11 Ibid.
12 Ibid., 601–02.

13 Ibid., 626, 628.
14 Ibid., 603, 629–30.

colon. Both expressions with עַל־כֵּן, "on this account,"
offer substantiations of the desolation declared here,
both the emotion of the speaker (v 36a; compare vv 31–
32a) and the depiction of the ruin of Moab (v 36b): but
the verse is not overly coherent. Verses 37–38a, finally,
are an adaptation of Isa 15:2bβ–3: there are three bicola
in this sequence. Like their antecedent in Isaiah, these
cola are a lament in the form of a depiction of lamentation.[15]

Both vv 40aβb and 41b are taken from 49:22. The
former is a bicolon. Its context here does not allow one
to discern whether it is a description of Yahweh or the
enemy: the verb ראה, "soar," is used of Yahweh in Ps
18:11, and Yahweh is compared to an eagle with outspread wings in Deut 32:11; on the other hand Deut
28:49 takes the image of the present passage and applies
it to the enemy from afar, and Ezek 17:3–5, 7–8 offers
the image of two eagles, evidently representing Babylon
and Egypt. The analysis of 49:22a offered in the present
study suggests that it is closely tied with 49:10b–11: it
describes (not the compassionate neighbor but) the
neighbor who comes to impose his sovereignty, that is,
Babylon. Doubtless then its reuse here carries the same
implication.

Verse 41b appears to be prose, a declaration of the
panic of Moabite soldiers on the day of defeat (compare
4:9; 30:5–7).

Verses 45b–46 are an adaptation from sections of
Numbers 21 and 24: v 45bα from Num 21:28a, v 45bβ
from Num 24:17bβ, and v 46 from Num 21:29. But
these adaptations are wrested out of the contexts and
implications of the original sayings: Num 21:28–29 are
part of an old ballad that recalled the prowess of King
Sihon in spreading military destruction from his seat at
Heshbon,[16] and Num 24:17 is part of one of Balaam's
oracles predicting a military deliverer from Israel who
will crush Moab; the phrases are now woven together to
depict the destruction of Moab by the current enemy,
presumably Babylon. For example, Num 21:29 understands Moab to have "given" his sons and daughters to
Sihon and thus into captivity; v 46 here sees Moab's sons
and daughters "taken" into captivity by Babylon. On the
other hand both Num 21:29 and v 46 are form-critically

identical, a "woe"-saying.

Verse 47a is a divine proclamation of salvation to
Moab (compare 30:3); this word is comparable to that for
Ammon (49:6) and Elam (49:39), and less closely to that
for Egypt (46:26b). At least in the case of Moab and
Ammon these words may be linked with the Deuteronomic program for the restitution of the territory of the
ideal Israel (Joshua 22).[17]

And v 47b is a rubric closing off the chapter.

Plausible Settings for the Authentic Material. Three
considerations combine to suggest that there is more
than one poem here—that is, that Jrm delivered more
than one oracle against Moab and that the oracles are
collected here.

First there is the sheer length of the authentic material. The first oracle against Egypt (46:3–12) contains
forty cola, the second (46:14–24) thirty-nine cola; the
oracle against Philistia (47:2–7) contains twenty-eight
cola. The material in the present chapter deemed to be
authentic comprises eighty-two cola. There is no reason
why such an oracle has to be limited to a particular
length, but the extent of the authentic material preserved here against Moab is striking.

Second, there are only three occurrences of first-
person singular verbs spoken by Yahweh in the sequence:
v 12 ("therefore I shall send to him decanters to decant
him"), v 38 ("for I have broken Moab"), and v 44b ("for I
shall bring a curse on Moab"). These verses, I propose,
close off three poems on Moab. Tentatively, then, the
first poem would comprise the first three sections already
isolated, namely, vv 1–4, 6–9, 11–12; the second poem
would comprise the fourth through the sixth sections,
namely, vv 14–17, 18–20 + 25, 28 + 38b; and the third
poem would comprise the seventh and eighth sections,
namely, vv 39–40aα + 41a + 42, 43–44a + 45a + 44b. In
this scheme the first poem would comprise thirty-five
cola, the second poem thirty-three cola, and the third
poem fifteen cola. It is to be noted that because the first
and fifth sections of the authentic material are form-
critically parallel, and the second and sixth sections
likewise, the first and second of the poems proposed here
share form-critical categories.

The third consideration is afforded by the dates

---

15 Ibid., 611.

16 Martin Noth, *Numbers* (Philadelphia: Westminster,
1968) 165.

17 Peter Höffken, "Zu den Heilszusätzen in der
Völkerorakelsammlung des Jeremiabuches," *VT* 27
(1977) 402.

proposed in the present study for parallel passages that contain the phrases validating the authenticity of the material in the present chapter. Before a discussion of this matter, however, it is appropriate to look at the points at which Moab impinged on Judah during Jrm's career.

There are two points during Jrm's career in which Moab touched on affairs in Judah. The first was in 599 or early in 598 when Moab was one of the client states of Babylon sent to harass Judah (2 Kgs 24:2): for the date see the discussion in 35:1–19, Structure, Form, Setting, with respect to 35:11. The second is the representation of Moab in the conference called by Zedekiah in the spring or early summer of 594 (27:3): for the date see 27:1–22, Setting.

Now it is striking that when the three poems already proposed are laid out and the parallel passages elsewhere in Jrm's poetry are recorded alongside them together with the dates suggested in the present study for those parallel passages, the dates cluster in such a way as to suggest settings for the three poems on Moab in 605, 599/598, and 594, respectively. (For these parallel passages see above, *The Authenticity of the Primary Material within Verses 1–28* and *Authentic Material within Verses 29–47*.)

Specifically, for the first proposed poem one has four parallels to material in 605—v 1 (compare 4:13), v 3 (compare 4:6; 6:1), v 9 (compare 2:15; 4:7, 29), and v 12 (16:16); two parallels to material in 601/600—v 3 (compare 14:17) and v 6 (compare 17:6); and one parallel to material in 587—v 11 (compare 30:10). For the second proposed poem one has one parallel to material in 605—v 28 (compare 4:29); three parallels to material in 601/600—v 14 (compare 8:8), v 18 (compare 5:10), and v 19 (compare 6:16); and three parallels to material in 598/597—v 18a (compare 10:17; 13:18), v 18aβb (compare 21:13), and v 38b (compare 22:28). For the third proposed poem one has one parallel to 601/600—v 44b (compare 11:23; 23:12), and two or three parallels to material in 594—v 39a (compare 2:27) and v 39b (compare 17:17; 20:7). These comparisons suggest shifts in Jrm's diction as the years passed and make altogether plausible the dates already suggested.

I propose therefore that the first poem, vv 1–4, 6–9, and 11–12, was delivered in 605, in the context of the battle of Carchemish, when Jrm perceived Nebuchadrezzar to be capable of defeating other states besides Judah; that the second poem, vv 14–20, 25, 28, 38b, was delivered in 599 or 598, when Nebuchadrezzar sent Moab along with other Transjordanian states to harass Judah; and that the third poem, vv 39–40aα, 41a, 42–44a, 45a, 44b, was delivered in 594 at the time of the Jerusalem conference.

Possible Settings for the Secondary Material. Here one moves into *terra incognita.* Moab was still a nation after the fall of Jerusalem (40:11). If one may believe Josephus, Nebuchadrezzar attacked Moab and Ammon in 582 and defeated them;[18] by this time Jrm had presumably died (see 37:1—44:30, Setting). In this context, or soon thereafter, in the absence of Jrm himself, an editor might well have expanded the prophet's material on Moab from relevant material in Isaiah (thus vv 29–34, 36–38a of the present chapter). Indeed if the date for vv 38b–40aα, 41a, 42–44a + 45a + 44b is 594 (see above, *Plausible Settings for the Authentic Material*), and if the blocs of material in the chapter were added in rough chronological order, then a date early in the exile for vv 29–34, 36–38a is certainly indicated.

There is no way to determine settings for vv 5, 10, 13, 21–24, 26–27, and 35, verses that offer glosses and expansions of various sorts. But it is clear that last of all vv 45b–47 were added: the verses are missing in *G* and were therefore added at a time after the two textual traditions diverged. It is likely that they are added by three different hands: vv 45b–46, v 47a, and v 47b.

The Tone of the Chapter. Some further account must now be given of what, for want of a better word, one may call the "tone" of the chapter, specifically whether there is any note of taunting or mocking in the chapter. The question was raised above (see *Structure and Form of the Authentic Material*) in the discussion of the form of vv 1–4 and of v 18 (and see further Interpretation on "Madmen" in v 2). It is of course difficult to establish the emotional tone of such poems as these, delivered so long ago, but one may at least compare the rhetoric with similar material elsewhere.

---

18   *Ant.* 10.9.7.

Mockery is found in many oracles against foreign nations, notably against Assyria in Nahum (see especially Nah 2:6; 3:6, 8, 13, 15b–19), against Babylon in Deutero-Isaiah (see especially Isa 46:1, and a great deal of chapter 47), and against Egypt in Jer (46:7–8, 15, 16–17). Typical in such mockery is the affirmation of the powerlessness of foreign gods (Isa 46:1–2; Jer 46:15) or kings (Jer 46:17), the quoting of the boastful words of the nation (Isa 47:7, 8, 10; Jer 46:8) and the prediction that the nation will be stripped (Nah 3:5; Isa 47:3).

In the material of this chapter authentic to Jrm it is said that the god Chemosh will go into exile (v 7), but there is no mockery of him as there is of Apis (46:15) or of Bel and Nebo (Isa 46:1–2). The king of Moab is not mentioned. The Moabite soldiers are quoted once, "We are warriors and men fit for battle!" but this is hardly a boast like that of Babylon, "I shall be mistress for ever" (Isa 47:7), simply an affirmation that the soldiers are convinced they can fulfill their task. Moab is confident, even relaxed (v 11). There is no mention here of the nation being stripped; she is humiliated, true (v 18), but then so is any nation suffering defeat. Only once in the authentic material is Moab described as a laughingstock (v 39). One hears of her humiliation (vv 1, 20, 39), one hears much crying and mourning, wailing and weeping (vv 3, 4, 20, 39), one sees streams of bewildered refugees (vv 19, 28, 44–45). Only once does Jrm affirm that Moab has set himself up against Yahweh (v 42), but there is no extensive description of Yahweh's anger, simply affirmations at the end of each poem of his action to destroy (vv 12, 38b, 44b). One may conclude that Jrm depicted the tragedy of Moab's ruin but offered little if any mockery over her plight.

Curiously enough the secondary material does not add appreciably to the tone of mockery. Some notes are highlighted: the pride of Moab (vv 29, 30) and his setting himself up against Yahweh (v 26), Moab's sense of shame regarding Chemosh (v 13), his becoming a laughingstock (v 26), his former mockery of Israel (v 27); but mostly Jrm's poems are simply extended by more descriptions of mourning and desolation. Was there a sense of kinship between Judah and Moab that prevented those in the exilic and postexilic periods from mocking Moab?

Interpretation

■ 1 Moab designates the high plateau immediately to the east of the Dead Sea, and its people, whose history is known only in part.[19]

Nebo is here not the mountain (Deut 32:49; 34:1) but the city associated with it. This city is most likely to be identified with *ḫirbat al-muḥayyaṭ*[20] about five kilometers northwest of Medeba (Atlas of Israel grid 220–129). Kiriathaim has usually been identified with *ḫirbat al-qurayyāt*[21] about twenty-two kilometers south-southwest of Medeba (Atlas of Israel grid 215–105), doubtless on the basis of the likeness of names. But the oldest potsherds that Nelson Glueck found at that site were Nabatean,[22] and Eusebius states that Kiriathaim lies ten Roman miles [thus roughly fourteen kilometers] west of Medeba; this suggests the site identified by Arnulf Kuschke, namely, *ḫirbat al-qurayya*[23] (Atlas of Israel grid 221–125). If this identification is correct, the sites of the two cities named here are near each other, roughly eleven kilometers apart.

The expression הַמִּשְׂגָּב is here translated "the Citadel"; it is not known whether the word functions here as a common noun, as it does elsewhere, or as a proper noun (so Zorell, so *NJV* margin): BDB offers both possibilities. Volz emends the text to הַפִּסְגָּה "(Mount) Pisgah," which is ingenious but unconvincing. The common noun is

---

19 For general surveys see Edward D. Grohman, "Moab," *IDB* 3:409–19; A. H. Van Zyl, *The Moabites* (Leiden: Brill, 1960). For a recent survey of archeology of the area see James R. Kautz, "Tracking the Ancient Moabites," *BA* 44 (1981) 27–35, and James A. Sauer, "Transjordan in the Bronze and Iron Ages: A Critique of Glueck's Synthesis," *BASOR* 263 (August 1986) 1–26, esp. 16.

20 Edward D. Grohman, "Nebo," *IDB* 3:528b; Rudolph, p. 287; Arnulf Kuschke, "Jeremia 48,1–8. Zugleich ein Beitrag zur historischen Topographie Moabs," *Verbannung und Heimkehr, Beiträge zur Geschichte und*

Theologie Israels im 6. und 5. Jahrhundert v. Chr., Wilhelm Rudolph zum 60. Geburtstage (ed. Arnulf Kuschke; Tübingen: Mohr [Siebeck], 1961) 188.

21 Edward D. Grohman, "Kiriathaim," *IDB* 3:37.

22 Nelson Glueck, *Explorations in Eastern Palestine, III* (AASOR 18–19; New Haven, CT: American School of Oriental Research, 1939) 131.

23 Kuschke, "Jeremia 48,1–8," 192–93; so now also Rudolph, p. 287.

assumed to be masculine, and therefore Rudolph emends the associated feminine verbs here to masculine ones; but it is probably better to stay with the text at hand and argue that the presence of feminine verbs suggests that the subject is a city (so Zorell), like the others in this section. But it is impossible to be sure.

■ **2** The name of Heshbon still survives in the modern ḥisbān (Atlas of Israel grid 226–134); this site has been extensively excavated and deposits of the Iron Age brought to light.[24]

The idiom with מִן, "from (being)"—here "from (being) a nation"—is rare but occurs in poetry (see also v 42).

The text here indicates a city called "Madmen," but this name occurs only here, and the text raises questions. G, V, and S read not a place-name but an infinitive absolute, thus דָּמוֹם, and this reading is adopted by Kuschke.[25] But one surely expects a place-name here. Given the form of the place-name (מַדְמֵן), commentators refer to Isa 25:10b, "Moab shall be trodden down in his place, as straw is trodden down in a מַדְמֵנָה": clearly in that passage the word means "dung-pit," a cognate of דֹּמֶן, "dung." Was there then a Moabite city named "Madmen," with which name the writer in Isa 25:10b played?[26] On the other hand perhaps "Madmen" is itself a distortion of a Moabite city; or the text may here be the victim of dittography of mem, so that it should read דִּמֹן, "Dimon," as in Isa 15:9.[27] There is evidence that "Dimon" is an alternative of "Dibon": Jerome wrote, "Down to our day this village is called either 'Dimon' or 'Dibon.'"[28] And one notes the probability that "Dibon" in v 18 is associated with a word for "dung" (see there). Tentatively, then, one may assume that Jrm is using either "Madmen" or "Dimon" for the sake of word-play with the following verb תִּדֹּמִי, and that the implication of

"dung-pit" hangs in the background. If "Dibon" is being referred to, it is the modern ḏībān (Atlas of Israel grid 224–101): see further below, v 18.

The verb תִּדֹּמִי is normally understood as "you shall be silent," but there is a second verb דמם meaning "weep" (see the discussion on 8:14); though a double meaning may be intended here, the meaning "weep" is surely foremost.

For the word-plays in this verse see Structure, Form, Setting, *Structure and Form of the Authentic Material*.

■ **3–4** The location of Horonaim is disputed. The context of Isa 15:5, the use of "descent" with Horonaim in v 5 of the present chapter, and other evidence suggest a location in the southwest part of Moab, below the highest part of the plateau. A. H. van Zyl suggests ḥirbat aḏ-ḏubāb about five kilometers west-northwest of Majrā[29] (Atlas of Israel grid 211–050); Willi Schottroff suggests ḥirbat al-maydān,[30] which is west of the village of kaṭrabbā, on top of the highest hill in the vicinity[31] (Atlas of Israel grid 208–061). Recently, however, Udo Worschech and Ernest Knauf have suggested ed-dayr, three kilometers northwest of Rākin (Atlas of Israel grid 215–072): they propose that Horonaim lies under the ruins of a Hasmonean fortress there.[32]

"Zoar" is doubtless a correct reading in v 4 (compare Isa 15:5), but again the location is uncertain; it is one of the "cities of the valley" (Gen 13:12). Most assume a location at or near aṣ-ṣāfī[33] (Atlas of Israel grid 195–048). The verses here then suggest that the cry from Horonaim comes down off the Moabite plateau all the way to the Dead Sea.

■ **5** With Horonaim this verse associates Luhith, a city whose location is likewise unknown; but "ascent" suggests a city standing above a nearby road. Van Zyl has suggested ḥirbat madīnat er-ra's[34] about two kilometers west-

24 See Siegfried H. Horn, "Heshbon," *IDBSup* 410–11.
25 Kuschke, "Jeremia 48,1–8," 185.
26 So the suggestion of Wildberger, *Jesaja*, 970–71.
27 Compare Edward D. Grohman, "Dimon," *IDB* 1:843; Van Zyl, *Moabites*, 80, and nn. 4 and 5.
28 *Usque hodie indifferenter et Dimon et Dibon hoc oppidulum dicitur*, cited in Rudolph, p. 274.
29 Van Zyl, *Moabites*, 64–65; Glueck, *Explorations, III*, 86.
30 Willi Schottroff, "Horonaim, Nimrim, Luhith und der Westrand des 'Landes Ataroth,' Ein Beitrag zur historischen Topographie des Landes Moab," *ZDPV*

82 (1966) 207; Wildberger, *Jesaja*, 616.
31 Glueck, *Explorations, III*, 94–95.
32 Udo Worschech and Ernst A. Knauf, "Dimon und Horonaim," *Biblische Notizen* 31 (1986) 80–95.
33 J. Penrose Harland, "Zoar," *IDB* 4:962; Rudolph, p. 287.
34 Van Zyl, *Moabites*, 64–65.

southwest of Khanzīra[35] (Atlas of Israel grid 205–051), and Schottroff has suggested *ḫirbat ad-dubāb*,[36] which has been van Zyl's suggestion for Horonaim (see above, vv 3–4). But recently Siegfried Mittmann has argued persuasively for *kaṭrabbā*[37] (Atlas of Israel grid 209–061). There is a Roman road still evident that goes from *ḡawr 'isāl* (Atlas of Israel grid 202–066), near the Dead Sea, along the south flank of the *wādī 'isāl* (*wādī sulaymān*) and up to *kaṭrabbā*; this road would then mark the "ascent of Luhith." And there is other evidence: a Nabatean inscription found at Medeba records the burial of an officer who was commander of a Nabatean camp near Luhith, and there are ruins of a Nabatean fort at *tall al-maydān* (Atlas of Israel grid 208–060) west of *kaṭrabbā*.

■ **6** If the emendation accepted here is sound, it is not particularly good news: the juniper does survive in the wilderness, but normally only as a low shrub (see 17:6). For the lives of refugees to be so stunted is hardly to be living at all.

■ **7** The address shifts from second-person plural (v 6) to second-person singular feminine here. Who is being addressed as "you, too"? One assumes Moab as a whole.

If "in your treasures" is a correct reading, the expression refers to all kind of supplies, not only gold, silver, and the like, but also weapons as well (compare the diction of 50:25).

Chemosh is the god of the Moabites; a deity by the same name is already known in the Ugaritic texts (*kmṯ*),[38] and the Moabites are called the "people of Chemosh" in Num 21:29. Inasmuch as in the inscription of the Moabite king Mesha the god Chemosh is compounded with Ashtar, the god of the planet Venus, one may suppose that Chemosh is the manifestation of (or is identified with) this astral deity.[39]

The linking of "priests" and "officials" is found in a similar context in 49:3; there is no way to determine whether these "officials" are civil or religious functionaries.

■ **8** "The Valley" (הָעֵמֶק) and "the Plateau" (הַמִּישֹׁר) occur in Joshua 13 as designations of specific regions in what was in Jrm's time Moabite territory, and these terms appear to carry those specific references here (so also Rudolph). "The Valley" refers to the Jordan rift valley north of the Dead Sea (see Josh 13:27), here doubtless the eastern side only; "the Plateau" (see Josh 13:15–17) refers to the region north of the Arnon as far as the latitude of Heshbon.

■ **9** The establishment of the meaning "salt-field" for צִיץ on the basis of Ugaritic evidence now seems assured.[40] The colon would then mean "make Moab a salt-field (by sowing it with salt)"; for this idea compare Judg 9:45. Is the propinquity of Moab to the salt-pans at the southern edge of the Dead Sea part of the flow of thought here?

The second colon gives difficulty as well: see Text.

■ **11–12** Moab, among other districts, produced wine,[41] perhaps notable wine: compare Isa 16:8–10, reflected in the present chapter in vv 32–33. Curiously, a stamp evidently used for wine-jar seals turned up many years ago offering the text of v 11, perhaps from the early Christian centuries, but unfortunately its provenience is unknown.[42] With this background Jrm develops the

---

35 Glueck, *Explorations, III*, 86.

36 Schottroff, "Horonaim," 207.

37 S. Mittmann, "The Ascent of Luhith," *Studies in the History of Archaeology of Jordan I* (ed. A. Hadidi; Amman: Department of Antiquities, 1982) 175–80.

38 UG5 7.36; 10.1.5.

39 The reference in the Mesha inscription is line 17; see Ronald J. Williams, "Moabite Stone," *IDB* 3:420, or Walter Beyerlin, *Near Eastern Texts Relating to the Old Testament* (Philadelphia: Westminster, 1978) 236–40. For the Moabite text see conveniently Van Zyl, *Moabites*, 203. For Chemosh in general see John Gray, "Chemosh," *IDB* 1:556, and in more detail, Van Zyl, *Moabites*, 195–202.

40 The evidence is in Ugaritic glosses on Akkadian texts found at Ugarit: 2096 and 2097, passim. The meaning was first suggested by William L. Moran,

"Ugaritic *ṣiṣūma* and Hebrew *ṣîṣ* (Eccles 43,19; Jer 48,9)," *Bib* 39 (1958) 69–71. Rudolph calls it "interesting" and wonders whether it will prevail. *HALAT* lists it, 959, but calls it questionable. Bright and Thompson accept it.

41 See James F. Ross, "Wine," *IDB* 4:850a.

42 William A. Irwin, "An Ancient Biblical Text," *AJSL* 48 (1931/32) 184–93.

metaphor of Moab as wine, but wine which is "resting on his lees," that is, allowed to remain with its dregs without having been strained. The customary procedure, after the wine had been pressed, was to leave it in skins for forty days to continue fermenting, after which time it was poured into another jar or skin, thus straining out the dregs.[43] The image of "resting on the lees" was doubtless proverbial for complacency (compare Zeph 1:12): "into exile [Moab] has not gone."

But v 11b is puzzling: the wording, literally "that is why his flavor remains in him, and his scent is unchanged," sounds as if the wine of Moab is being praised (*NJV*: "therefore his fine flavor has remained and his bouquet is unspoiled"). But the half verse is part of the reason for Yahweh's judgment: the wine is therefore being disparaged.[44] Moffatt has caught this nuance and has managed to render the verse in rhyme as well: "Moab from the first has lain at ease, never known exile afar, lain like wine left on the lees, never poured from jar to jar, that tastes the same as ever, and its scent mellows never."

Yahweh now intervenes to send decanters. "Decanters" and "decant" are literally "tilters" and "tilt"; it is the same verb as that in 2:20, used there of the whore who "sprawls." The decanters (v 12), representing the enemy, evidently the Babylonians, will not only pour the wine to other vessels, a figure for exile (v 11), but also will smash the (old) jars. All the former serenity, all the former identity of Moab will be gone.

■ 13 To this judgment someone has added a remark about Moab's becoming ashamed of (or because of) Chemosh. One wonders what triggered this addition; is it possible that the lees on which Moab had settled were perceived to represent Chemosh?[45]

"Bethel" here implies the designation of a deity in Israel, devotion to whom was illegitimate. A god by this name is attested outside Israel: he is mentioned as a Syrian god in a treaty between Esarhaddon of Assyria and Ba'al of Tyre (seventh century); his name figures as a divine element in personal names in neo-Babylonian texts (sixth century: the names are evidently of both non-Babylonian and Babylonian persons) and as a divine element in Jewish names at Elephantine (fifth century).[46] Suggestions have been made of other occurrences of this divine name in the OT, such as Gen 35:7,[47] but none has been generally convincing. The deity would originally have have been the deification of a temple ("beth") of the god El; and the fact that there was a sanctuary city in Israel named "Bethel" with patriarchal traditions meant that worship of the god Bethel could be syncretized with a normative Yahwistic cult. Nevertheless this verse suggests that someone affirmed such a syncretism to be illegitimate.

■ 15 "Be brought down" with "to slaughter" suggests dead bodies prostrate on the ground.

■ 16 For "calamity" (אֵיד) see 18:17.

■ 17 The nuance of "victory" for עֹז rather than the usual meaning "strength" was proposed by William F. Albright for Ps 68:29[48] and adopted by Dahood for several passages (Pss 21:2; 29:11; 68:36; 89:18; 110:2);[49] in particular the phrase in the present passage, מַטֵּה עֹז, occurs also in Ps 110:2, and the rendering "victorious scepter" here makes a good inclusio with the words of the soldiers in v 14.

■ 18 Dibon has retained its name, the modern *dībān*, twenty-one kilometers east of the Dead Sea and five kilometers north of the Arnon (Atlas of Israel grid 224–101). It is the site where the inscription of King Mesha was discovered, and it was evidently his capital. The site was excavated in the 1950s; there are wadis around it,[50]

43   Clark, "Wine on the lees," 241; James F. Ross, "Lees," *IDB* 3:108.

44   Clark, "Wine on the lees," 242–43.

45   Compare ibid., 243.

46   Otto Eissfeldt, "Der Gott Bethel," *ARW* 28 (1930) 1–30 = *Kleine Schriften I* (Tübingen: Mohr [Siebeck], 1962) 206–33; J. Philip Hyatt, "Bethel (deity)," *IDB* 1:390–91; the evidence, with citations, is gathered in his "The Deity Bethel and the Old Testament," *JAOS* 59 (1939) 81–98. For the Elephantine material see for example Arthur E. Cowley, *Aramaic Papyri of the Fifth Century B.C.* (Oxford: Clarendon, 1923) 55–56

(number 18, line 4), and further xviii.

47   See the citations to Hyatt's articles in n. 46, and see further *HALAT*, 121a, and the literature cited there. For Gen 35:7 see Westermann, *Genesis* 2:672.

48   William F. Albright, "A Catalogue of Early Hebrew Lyric Poems (Psalm LXVIII)," *HUCA* 23 (1950/51) part 1, 31.

49   Dahood, *Psalms I*, 131, 180; *Psalms II*, 152, 315; *Psalms III*, 115.

50   Chester C. McCown, "Dibon," *IDB* 1:840–41. For a complete bibliography of the excavations see Vogel, *Bibliography I*, 26–27; Vogel and Holtzclaw, *Bibli-*

so that "descend" and "come up" can be understood literally as well as figuratively. For "enthroned," implying royal prerogatives, see 10:17.

■ **19** The name of Aroer, again, is preserved in the modern *'arā'ir*, five kilometers to the southeast of Dibon (Atlas of Israel grid 228–097); the ancient mound is just west of the modern village. The site was excavated in the 1960s.[51] The city stands just north of the deep gorge of the River Arnon (the modern *wādī al-mawjib*).[52]

■ **20** For a discussion of the quotations see Structure, Form, Setting, *Structure and Form of the Authentic Material*.

■ **21** For "Plateau" see v 8.

"Holon" is mentioned only here, and its site is unknown.

"Jahzah," an alternative form of "Jahaz" (v 34; Num 21:23 and elsewhere), is mentioned in the Mesha inscription.[53] De Vaux proposed *hirbat libb* on the main road between Dibon and Medeba (Atlas of Israel grid 222–113) for its location,[54] and this site is still a plausible candidate. Rudolph points out not only that Eusebius locates the city between Medeba and Dibon but also that Mesha associates the city with Dibon,[55] so that he suggests *hirbat iskandar* (Atlas of Israel grid 224–106) for the site.[56] Edward Grohman lists three suggestions, *jalūl* five and a half kilometers east of Medeba (Atlas of Israel grid 231–125), *hirbat et-taym* one and a half kilometers southwest of Medeba (Atlas of Israel grid 224–124), and *umm al-walīd* twelve kilometers southeast of Medeba (Atlas of Israel grid 236–117).[57] The John Peterson survey suggests *hirbat al-madayyina* (Atlas of Israel grid 236–111),[58] and Andrew Dearman has recently reinforced

this suggestion.[59] The location is thus very much still an open question.

Mephaath is also not securely identified, but opinion favors *tall aj-jāwa*, ten kilometers south of Amman (Atlas of Israel grid 238–141).[60]

■ **22** For Dibon see v 18; for Nebo see v 1.

Beth-diblathaim is mentioned in the Mesha inscription,[61] but it is mentioned only here in the OT (unless it is identical with Almon-diblathaim, Num 33:46–47). Some authorities have suggested *hirbat ad-dalaylāt aš-šarqiyya* four kilometers northeast of *hirbat al-libb* (Atlas of Israel grid 226–115).[62]

■ **23** For Kiriathaim see v 1.

Beth-gamul is evidently *hirbat al-jumayl* about twelve kilometers east of Dibon (Atlas of Israel grid 235–099).[63]

Beth-meon is also called Baal-meon (Num 32:38) and Beth-baal-meon (Josh 13:17); the Mesha inscription mentions "Baal-meon" and "Beth-baal-meon."[64] The name is preserved in the modern *mā'īn* (Atlas of Israel grid 219–120).[65]

■ **24** "Kerioth" occurs in Amos 2:2—the implication there is that it was the capital in Amos's day; the name also occurs in the Mesha inscription.[66] It has been identified with *hirbat al-qurayyāt* (Atlas of Israel grid 215–105), but,

ography II, 26.

51 See William H. Morton, "Aroer," *IDB* 1:230–31; Nelson Glueck, "Explorations in Eastern Palestine, I," AASOR 14 (1933/34) (Philadelphia: American Schools of Oriental Research, 1934) 49–50; William G. Dever, "Aroer," *IDBSup* 55. For a complete bibliography of the excavations see Vogel, *Bibliography I*, 10; Vogel and Holtzclaw, *Bibliography II*, 11.

52 See Edward D. Grohman, "Arnon," *IDB* 1:230, and the picture there.

53 Lines 19, 20; see the references in n. 39.

54 Roland De Vaux, "Notes d'histoire et de topographie transjordaniennes," *Vivre et Penser* 1 [= *RB* 50] (1941) 20.

55 Lines 20–21; see the references in n. 39.

56 Rudolph, p. 285; see further Glueck, *Explorations III*, 127–29.

57 Edward D. Grohman, "Jahaz," *IDB* 2:788.

58 Boling and Wright, *Joshua*, 494.

59 J. Andrew Dearman, "The Location of Jahaz," *ZDPV* 100 (1984) 122–26.

60 Edward D. Grohman, "Mephaath," *IDB* 3:350; Boling and Wright, *Joshua*, 494; compare Rudolph, p. 287.

61 Line 30; see the references in n. 39.

62 Van Zyl, *Moabites*, 86; Rudolph, p. 285; compare Edward D. Grohman, "Almon-diblathaim," *IDB* 1:86.

63 Edward D. Grohman, "Beth-gamul," *IDB* 1:393; Rudolph, p. 285.

64 Lines 7 and 31 respectively; for the references see n. 39.

65 Edward D. Grohman, "Baal-meon," *IDB* 1:332; Rudolph, p. 285.

66 Line 13; for the references see n. 39.

as already affirmed in the discussion of Kiriathaim in v 1, surface exploration has indicated that this site was not occupied at this period. Therefore Kuschke suggests *ḥirbat qurayyāt ʿalayyān* (Atlas of Israel grid 233–105);[67] in this he is followed by Rudolph.[68]

The "Bozrah" here is to be distinguished from the Edomite capital (49:13). The city here is perhaps to be identified with Bezer (Josh 20:8; 21:36), but the location of Bezer itself is not secure; the suggestion usually accepted is *umm al-ʿamad* fourteen kilometers northeast of Medeba[69] (Atlas of Israel grid 235–132).

■ 25 "Horn" is a well-known metaphor for strength (Pss 18:3; 75:5). But Bernard Couroyer has made the suggestion[70] that "horn" here connotes a bow: he offers instances from Egyptian, Greek, and Latin literature of "horn" in the meaning of "bow," and he suggests that the reason is one of the materials of a composite bow is horn.[71] One notes "I will break the bow of Elam" (49:35) and "I will break the bow of Israel" (Hos 1:5); this understanding of the present passage is therefore plausible.

■ 26–27 The addition here, with its call to make Moab drunk because of her mocking of Israel, is reminiscent of the word to Edom in Lam 4:21–22 that she shall become drunk and be paid back for her taking advantage of Israel. In v 26 the writer takes the judgment mediated by Jrm that Moab has set himself up against Yahweh (v 42) and makes it more vivid and immediate! But here it is the mockery of Israel that is the substance of the arrogance against Yahweh, whereas in v 42 the expression connotes for Jrm something deeper.[72] (For the possibility of an alternative translation, "for Yahweh he has calumniated," see v 42.)

For "become a laughingstock" compare 20:7.

■ 26 The meaning of the verb translated "overflow" (ספק) has been disputed. There appears to be no justification for "wallow," the translation of *KJV* and *RSV*. The verb is normally transitive, meaning "slap" (one's thigh), "clap" (one's hands); Bright assumes, therefore, that it means here "slap one's thigh" (in disgust) or the like. BDB and

Zorell, assuming that the verb betokens a sudden loud noise, suggest "splash." But recently Godfrey Driver has suggested "overflow," citing evidence from Aramaic and Syriac (particularly the Syriac *spq* paʿel "vomit")[73] (thus *NEB*), and Rudolph has accepted this; this seems to be the best solution.

■ 27 The syntax of the verse is not obvious. The expression אִם לוֹא often introduces an oath (compare 15:11); here it evidently carries a reduced value, hence "surely." But then one is faced with a dilemma. Either (1) the following ־אִם is correlative with the initial אִם לוֹא and thus to be translated "surely not," or else (2) the ה which follows אִם לוֹא is to be construed as the interrogative ה, and the following ־אִם is thereupon a correlative interrogative. All translators and commentators assume (2), that is, that one has a double question, but in doing so they tend to ignore the opening אִם לוֹא. For example, van Selms discusses this sequence as a pair of rhetorical questions, translating, "Was not Israel a derision to you? Was he found among thieves, that whenever you spoke of him you wagged your head?" But he goes on to say, "We will not discuss the first clause; וְאִם לֹא is rather difficult to account for."[74] At this point one may offer two conclusions. First, if the clauses are questions, they are rhetorical questions, and therefore there is little difference between "Surely for you Israel has been a laughingstock" and "Has Israel not been for you a laughingstock?" Second, the level of the language is colloquial and argumentative, and therefore there may easily be a blending of asseverative statements ("surely," "surely not") and rhetorical questions; this is the solution adopted here. But then there is a further problem: most commentators and translations take the second half of the verse, the כִּי clause, to be dependent on the ־אִם clause only: "Was he found among thieves, that whenever you spoke of him you wagged your head?" (*RSV*). But surely the wagging of the head here is connected as much with treating Israel as a laughingstock as with his being hypothetically caught stealing; it is better, then, to

67 Arnulf Kuschke, "Das Deutsche Evangelische Institut für Altertumswissenschaft des Heiligen Landes, Lehrkursus 1959," *ZDPV* 76 (1960) 23.
68 Rudolph, p. 287.
69 Ibid., p. 285; Boling and Wright, *Joshua*, 475, 494.
70 Bernard Couroyer, "Corne et arc," *RB* 73 (1966) 510–21.
71 For the construction of the composite bow see Yadin,

Warfare, 7.
72 Rudolph, p. 281.
73 Godfrey R. Driver, "Difficult Words in the Hebrew Prophets," *Studies in Old Testament Prophecy, Presented to Theodore H. Robinson* (ed. Harold H. Rowley; Edinburgh: Clark, 1950) 61–62.
74 Van Selms, "Motivated Interrogative Sentences," 146.

take the כִּי clause as a contradiction of the spurious logic in Moab's action, analogous to כִּי meaning "but rather."

Moab did mock Israel—at least that is the testimony of Zeph 2:8, 10.

For "be found among thieves" see 2:26. For מִדֵּי "whenever" see 20:8. "You have wagged your head" is the rendering of *RSV* for נוד hitpolel; this verb appears in 31:18 in a context of grief or dismay and denotes a stylized oscillation of the head or body (the hip'il stem of the verb, with "head," appears in a context of mockery in 18:16.)

■ **28** The call to flee the cities to make the rocks one's home is reminiscent of 4:29. If the call to nest like the dove in the walls of the gorge is a reference to territory like the gorge of the Arnon, then it is a call to do the implausible.[75] This is the only mention of the "dove" (יוֹנָה) in Jer. "In the walls of the yawning gorge" is literally "in the sides of the mouth of the pit" ("pit" in the sense of "chasm").

■ **29-30** These verses are an elaboration of Isa 16:6: the last half of that verse reads "his arrogance and his pride and his insolence, his bragging is false." For the shift from "we have heard" in v 29 to "I know" in v 30 see Structure, Form, Setting, *Structure and Form of the Secondary Material.* Divine judgment on nations for their pride is a convention among the prophets (on Moab and Ammon, see Zeph 2:10; on Judah see Jer 13:9);[76] one wonders, however, whether in this instance it is not only Moab's complacency but also her geographical elevation on the Moabite plateau that is at issue here.

■ **31** This verse is an adaptation of Isa 16:7, which reads, "On this account let Moab wail, let everyone wail for Moab; for the raisin-cakes of Kir-hareseth you (?) shall moan, utterly broken." The adapter here has continued his use of first-person singular verbs (compare v 30); thereby the word כֻּלֹּה, "everyone" in Isaiah, has become "all of it" here. The mysterious "raisin-cakes" has become the conventional "men," and in one or two other details the text has been smoothed over.

The city mentioned here is called "Kir-hareseth" not only in Isa 16:7 but also in 2 Kgs 3:25 (Kir-haraseth in the latter passage is doubtless a pausal form); it is called Kir-heres not only here but in v 36 and in Isa 16:11 (and Kir-hares in the last-named passage is again doubtless a pausal form). The element "Kir" (קִיר) evidently reflects one of two homonyms, or one of two distinct meanings of a single lexeme: "city," a word that does not appear in the OT outside of proper names but does appear in Moabite, occurring three times in the Mesha inscription;[77] and "wall." Thus the meaning of the first element is doubtless "city," though G, being unaware of the meaning "city," uses "wall" when it translates the name. Even though there is uncertainty in the OT regarding the shape of the second element, it was doubtless heard in Hebrew as "city (or wall) of potsherds [חֶרֶשׂ]." But the rendering of G in Isa 16:7, Δεσεθ, and the translation of G in Isa 16:11, τεῖχος ὃ ἐνεκαίνισας, "wall which you have renewed," suggests that the name was originally קִיר חָדָשׁ Kir-hadash "new city," and that the present Kir-heres (and the like), "city (or wall) of potsherds," was a mocking deformation.[78] There is evidently a "Kir-moab" or "Kir of Moab" mentioned in Isa 15:1 (*NEB*, though the syntax in the verse offers uncertainty—see *RSV*); this is evidently a designation of the capital city of Moab, generally identified with Kerak:[79] and Kir-heres is again assumed to be identical with Kir-moab and identified with Kerak, though there is no way to be sure.[80]

■ **32-33** This verse is a shortened adaptation of Isa 16:8–9, specifically of vv 9aα + 8b + 9b there.

If the reading "fountain" is correct, it is an ironic collocation, for weeping hardly reproduces a fountain (for the image compare 8:23).

The location of Jazer is uncertain. It was an important site; it was evidently an Ammonite border city (Num 21:24 G) and was designated a Levitical city (Josh 21:39). Eusebius and Jerome locate a place named Azer or Iazer ten Roman miles (i.e., fourteen kilometers) west of

75   See the reference in n. 52 to a picture of the Arnon gorge.

76   Wildberger, *Jesaja*, 625.

77   Lines 11, 12, and 24; see the references in n. 39.

78   Edward D. Grohman, "Kir-hareseth," *IDB* 3:36; Wildberger, *Jesaja*, 625–26; Van Zyl, *Moabites*, 70–71.

79   Wildberger, *Jesaja*, 611; Van Zyl, *Moabites*, 70–71.

80   Edward D. Grohman, "Kir-hareseth," *IDB* 3:36; Rudolph, p. 287; Wildberger, *Jesaja*, 626; Van Zyl, *Moabites*, 70–71.

Rabbah of the Ammonites (that is, the present-day Amman: see 49:2). The suggestion cited by Simon Cohen, *kom yājūz*,[81] is doubtful; it is north of Amman (Atlas of Israel grid 236–161), and John Peterson's survey found there only a smattering of Iron II and Persian potsherds.[82] By the same token the proposal in Boling and Wright, *ḥirbat jazzir*, 3.8 kilometers south of eṣ-Ṣalt[83] (Atlas of Israel grid 219–157), would seem to be too far north to be included in Moabite territory; and it may be added that the seeming identity of the names is superficial and linguistically dubious.[84] Since the middle of the nineteenth century an identification with *ḥirbat eṣ-ṣār* was assumed, ten kilometers west of Amman (Atlas of Israel grid 228–151), but this site is too close to Amman (the datum of Eusebius and Jerome cited above).[85] There are two leading candidates. One, suggested by Rolf Rendtorff, is *tall 'arayma*, about five kilometers northwest of Nā'ūr[86] (Atlas of Israel grid 225–146); this site is accepted by Wildberger and provisionally by Rudolph.[87]

The other, proposed by George Landes, is *ḥirbat es-sīrah*[88] (Atlas of Israel grid 227–152); this site is about the right distance from Amman, and it is near a good spring ("fountain of Jazer" in the present verse). But the question must remain open.

The location of Sibmah is likewise uncertain; general opinion favors *ḥirbat (qurn) al-qibš* about five kilometers east-northeast of Mount Nebo[89] (Atlas of Israel grid 225–132).

The vine of Sibmah reaches from Jazer in the north to the "sea" in the west: it is the Dead Sea that is meant.[90]

For the references to vines and wine-making in these verses see on vv 11–12.

■ **34** This verse is an adaptation of Isa 15:4a*a*, plus two place-names from v 5, plus v 6a; the quality of the poetry is not thereby improved.

For Heshbon see v 2.

Elealeh is the present-day *al-'āl* three kilometers north-northeast of Heshbon[91] (Atlas of Israel grid 228–136).

For Jahaz see Jahzah, v 21; for Zoar see v 4; for Horonaim see v 3.

Eglath-shelishiyah is a mystery. In Isa 15:5 the name appears after Zoar without syntactic marker, as if it is a gloss, and in the present passage it is again without a syntactic marker as if a gloss, but here it appears after Horonaim instead. Wildberger wonders if the gloss did not begin in the present passage, to be taken later into the Isaiah passage,[92] but there is really no way to determine whether it was intended to refer to Horonaim or Zoar.[93] The expression means "third Eglath [or Egla],"[94] conceivably "third heifer." This curious appellation may be partially explained by the discovery of a place-name *'gltyn* (Eglathain, with Aramaic dual ending, corresponding to Hebrew Eglathaim), mentioned several times in documents discovered at Naḥal Ḥever (*wādī ḥabra*) southwest of 'En Gedi; the name is evidently of a place located in the region of the southeast coast of the Dead Sea. That name would mean "double Eglath," lending plausibility to the name under consideration, "third Eglath,"[95] but until the discovery of new data the expression must leave us no wiser.

The כִּי that introduces v 34b must be taken as deictic

---

81   Simon Cohen, "Jazer," *IDB* 2:806.
82   Boling and Wright, *Joshua*, 344.
83   Ibid.
84   Landes, "Jazer," 35.
85   Ibid., 31.
86   Rolf Rendtorff, "Zur Lage von Jaser," *ZDPV* 76 (1960) 124–35.
87   Wildberger, *Jesaja*, 627; Rudolph, p. 286.
88   Landes, "Jazer."
89   Edward D. Grohman, "Sibmah," *IDB* 4:342; Van Zyl, *Moabites*, 91; Boling and Wright, *Joshua*, 342. For the location of the site see Nelson Glueck, *Explorations in Eastern Palestine, II*, AASOR 15 (1934–35) (New Haven, CT: American Schools of Oriental Research, 1935) 111. Note that while Wildberger, *Jesaja*, 627, also favors this identification, he gives an erroneous location for it between *ḥirbat al-muḥayyaṭ* and Medeba

(see also his 610).
90   Wildberger, *Jesaja*, 628.
91   Edward D. Grohman, "Elealeh," *IDB* 2:75; Wildberger, *Jesaja*, 613; Rudolph, p. 284.
92   Wildberger, *Jesaja*, 591.
93   Schottroff, "Horonaim," 186.
94   For the peculiar syntax, without articles, see König, *Syntax*, sec. 337r; for the unusual form of the feminine ordinal see GKC, sec. 98b, and Jöuon, *Gramm.*, sec. 101b.
95   For one example see conveniently Yigael Yadin, "More on the Letters of Bar Kochba," *BA* 24 (1961) 94; for all the references see Schottroff, "Horonaim," 186.

("indeed"), since that is the function of the conjunction in the antecedent Isa 15:6a.[96]

Though the likeness of names might suggest that "the waters of Nimrim" be identified with *wādī nimrīn*, that wadi empties into the Jordan about thirteen kilometers north of the Dead Sea, just north of the present-day Allenby Bridge (Atlas of Israel grid 201–143), and if the passage refers to locations in the southern area of Moab (compare the discussion of Horonaim above on vv 3–4), then a more likely candidate is *wādī* [or *sayl*] *en-numayra* (= *wādī ḥudayra*, Atlas of Israel grid 205–057).[97]

■ **35** This verse appears to be a marginal note of contempt for the paganism of Moab (see Text), perhaps triggered by Isa 16:12, which also mentions Moab's activity "upon the high place" (see above, Structure, Form, Setting, *Structure and Form of the Secondary Material*). For "high place" see 7:31. "His gods" could as well be translated "his god" (that is, Chemosh, v 7).

■ **36–38a** Verse 36a is a copy of Isa 16:11 (though each text appears in different respects to have suffered damage: see Text, b—b), and v 36b is an adaptation of Isa 15:7; and as with v 34, the sequence is not overly coherent. Verses 37–38a are an adaptation of Isa 15:2bβ–3.

■ **36** Curiously enough the antecedent colon in Isa 16:11 has not "flute" but "lyre." As to the identity of the instrument here translated "flute" (חָלִיל), opinion differs whether to understand it as "flute" or "clarinet." The translations of the Versions give no help: *G αὐλός* is either, while *V tibia* is a pipe or flute (and *S* and *T* use "lyre" found in Isa 16:11!). The root חלל means "pierce, bore." Beyond the occurrence here the noun appears in 1 Sam 10:5; 1 Kgs 1:40; Isa 5:12; 30:29; and Sir 40:21. It was used in joyous contexts (all the citations except the present one) as well as that of mourning. None of these data help identify the instrument; one must simply say that at present German scholars prefer "flute,"[98] whereas American scholars maintain the word means "clarinet."[99]

For Kir-heres see v 31.

■ **37** For the various signs of mourning see 4:8; 16:6; 41:5.

■ **38a** In 19:13 there is mention of "roofs" as a place of cultic observance, and that may be the implication here; or it may be that the mention of both "roofs" and "squares" simply implies the ubiquity of lamentation.

■ **38b** For the implication of "vessel no one cares for" see 22:28.

■ **39** For the possibility of an adverbial infinitive absolute unrelated to the associated finite verb compare v 9 and the parallel passages in Text note b—b there; the phenomenon evidently occurs twice here in parallel cola.

"Become a laughingstock" has already occurred in vv 26 and 27; for a discussion of the phrase see 20:7. For "become a fright" (היה לְמְחַתָּה) see 17:17. For the use of "neighbors" see v 17.

■ **40** This verse evidently describes the enemy attacking Moab (see Structure, Form, Setting, *Structure and Form of the Secondary Material*). The verb דאה means "soar," as of an eagle (Deut 32:11), as its cognate does in Ugaritic;[100] it does not imply "swoop,"[101] except as swooping is potential in the flight of a bird of prey. And it should be pointed out that נֶשֶׁר may mean "vulture" as well as "eagle."[102]

■ **41** The noun מְצָד means a place difficult of access,[103] thus a "stronghold," particularly a mountain fastness (the place-name Masada is a related word).

■ **42** For the idiom with מִן, "from (being) [a people]," compare v 2.

Dahood suggests that the phrase in the second colon, גדל hip'il + עַל, means not "set oneself up against" but "calumniate";[104] given the existence of a root גדל II "twist" as well as גדל I "be(come) great," this is an interesting possibility. But given the likelihood that יוֹשֵׁב מוֹאָב

96   Wildberger, *Jesaja*, 615.
97   Edward D. Grohman, "Nimrim, The waters of," *IDB* 3:551; Rudolph, p. 287; Wildberger, *Jesaja*, 615–16.
98   *HALAT*, 305; Wildberger, *Jesaja*, 186.
99   Eric Werner, "Musical instruments," *IDB* 3:472; P. Kyle McCarter, *I Samuel* (AB 8; Garden City, NY: Doubleday, 1980) 182.
100 For example, Ug. 16.5.48, 16.6.6; 19.3.120 and

often in that sequence.
101 As *HALAT* maintains.
102 See, for example, *HALAT* with bibliography, and see also Wolff, *Hosea*, 137.
103 *HALAT*, 587; Wildberger, *Jesaja*, 1296.
104 Dahood, *Psalms I*, 216, and compare 73.

means "enthroned Moab" in v 43 (see below), it is safer to stay with "set oneself up."

■ **43–44** Verse 43 begins with a spectacular triple word-play, *pahad wāpahat wāpāh*; these nouns are etymologically unrelated. Though the third noun is more accurately "snare" than "trap," it seems worth trying to find three words in English translation that communicate some of the assonance. The first noun, פַּחַד, is related to a root meaning "tremble, be in terror." The second noun, פַּחַת, has already appeared in v 28 (translated there "gorge"). And פַּח, as already noted, is a snare or net for catching birds (see on 18:22, and note 7 there).

The phrase יוֹשֵׁב מוֹאָב is universally understood to be "inhabitant of Moab," and the quick sketches of refugees that follow fit that interpretation. But I suggest that more prominent is the possibility of translating "enthroned Moab" (compare v 18): the image is explored in 21:13, and there, too, it is part of the formula of encounter (and compare further 10:17). It has just been stated that Moab has set himself up against Yahweh (v 42, part of the same poem: see Structure, Form, Setting, *Plausible Settings for the Authentic Material*); if Moab has arrogated to himself a position which is only to be Yahweh's, then "enthroned Moab" is an appropriate expression.

■ **45b–46** Verse 45bα is an adaptation of Num 21:28a, v 45bβ of Num 24:17bβ, and v 46 of Num 21:29; for the shift of viewpoint in this material between Numbers and Jer see in general Structure, Form, Setting, *Structure and Form of the Secondary Material*.

For Heshbon see v 2. Sihon was remembered by the Israelites as a "king of the Amorites" (Num 21:21) who ruled from Heshbon at the time of their passage through Transjordan; in the tradition he is linked with Og king of Bashan (Num 21:33)—these were the two kings who opposed the Israelites' passage through their realms, whom Yahweh defeated (Deut 1:4; Ps 135:11; and often).[105]

Num 24:17 says "has crushed the forehead of Moab," whereas the present text, linking the material with Num 21:28a, where the subject is "fire, flame," reads "has consumed the forehead of Moab." Num 24:17 thus implies the use of a club to crush the skull of personified Moab;[106] one wonders whether here, however, "fore-

head" and "skull" have not shifted to represent here the king, the "head" of his people (compare that possibility for קָדְקֹד, "skull," in 2:16)—though see Text, note l—l.

For Chemosh see v 7.

■ **47** For "restore the fortunes" (שׁוּב שְׁבוּת) see 29:14.

Aim

Jrm's oracles against Moab find their place in the years of his proclamation along with those against Philistia, Ammon, Edom, and the rest: the Babylonians, by his understanding, were moving across the Near East in universal hegemony, and the era of these small states was at an end.

Yet one must raise the issue of the reason for the extent of this material. There may be little taunting of Moab in the chapter (see Structure, Form, Setting, *The Tone of the Chapter*), but still the words on the ruin of Moab go on and on: on the ruin of Moab's sister-nation the Ammonites Jrm uttered only one oracle of five verses (49:1–5), but by the reckoning of the present study, he uttered three on the ruin of the Moabites, and then these three were in turn expanded to double the length by secondary material borrowed from Isaiah and elsewhere. The bulk devoted to Babylon in chapters 50—51 one can understand: ultimately the question of the destiny of Babylon was a burning question for Jrm and for his hearers, and for Jews in the decades that followed. But why Moab? One might assume some occasions of harassment that the Jews underwent at the hands of the Moabites during the exilic period about which we know nothing: the Edomites evidently harassed them (Lam 4:21–22; Obadiah), and the Moabites might have done the same. But it may be simply a matter of geography (compare the remarks in Interpretation on vv 29–30). Was it perhaps the sheer impression of height that Moab offered to those who viewed it from Jericho or from the eastern edge of the Judean hills, the awareness of the precipitous walls of the Arnon gorge and the heights to the south, which rise above twelve hundred meters? Denis Baly writes, "Anyone who stands upon the eastern edge of the Judean hills sees the ground drop away in front of him in a succession of tumbled yellow slopes and the clouds dissolve into nothing above his head, as the air

---

105 Robert F. Johnson, "Sihon," *IDB* 4:351.
106 Martin Noth, *Numbers* (Philadelphia: Westminster, 1968) 171.

starts its tumultuous descent into the rift. Twenty-five miles or so to the east is an almost unbroken wall of rock, dwarfed by the distance, but still tremendous. . . ."[107] (Parts of the plateau of Edom are even higher but are too far to the south to be seen from this vantage point.) Enthroned Dibon was told to "descend from glory" (v 18). Jrm affirmed that Moab had "set himself up against Yahweh" (v 42), and that affirmation was later repeated by a redactor (v 26). Whether the Moabites really did boast from their elevation (vv 29–30) or whether Judah simply assumed they did, it is clear that when Judah thought about other nations Moab loomed high.

Jrm insisted that Moab and Judah would suffer the same fate at the hands of the Babylonians. But this parity in destruction attracted more words to describe the destruction of Moab. It is easy to be preoccupied with the ruin of a rival people, most especially if one's own people have likewise undergone ruin.

---

107 Baly, *Geography*, 210, compare 230–31; see further George A. Smith, *Historical Geography of the Holy Land* (London: Hodder & Stoughton, 1931; rep. Collins, 1966) 380.

Rabbah Will be Destroyed, and the Ammonites Dispossessed

Bibliography

Christensen, Duane L.
"'Terror on Every Side' in Jeremiah," *JBL* 92
(1973) 498–501.
Christensen
Transformations, 224–27.
North, Francis S.
"The Oracle Against the Ammonites in Jeremiah
49 1–6," *JBL* 65 (1946) 37–43.

49

1 For the Ammonites. Thus Yahweh has said:
Has Israel no sons?
  Has he no heir?
    Why then has ⟨Milcom⟩[a] dispossessed
    Gad,[b]
      and his people settled in its cities?

2 [Therefore the time is surely coming, oracle
of Yahweh,][a]
so I shall let the blast of battle be heard
  against [b]《 Rabbah 》[of the Ammonites,][b]
    and it will become a desolate ruin,
      her daughter-villages will burn with fire,
      and Israel shall dispossess his dispos-
      sessors, [Yahweh has said.][c]

3 Wail, O Heshbon,
  "Oh, ⟨this heap is ruined!"⟩[a]
Cry out, daughters of Rabbah,
  gird on sackcloth and lament,
    and run to and fro among the sheep-
    folds,
for ⟨Milcom⟩[b] into exile shall go,
  his priests and officials together.

4 Why do you boast 《 of your ebbing
  strength, 》[a]
《 complacent 》[b] daughter?
[c]She trusts in her treasures,[c] saying,[d]
  "Who will come against me?"

5 I am going to bring upon you terror [oracle of
{the Lord}[b] Yahweh {of hosts}[b]][a] from
every side,
  and you shall be scattered, each headlong,
  with none to gather [c]the refugee.[c]

Text

1a   Reading מַלְכָּם with *G*, *V*, and *S* for *M* מַלְכָּם "their
king."

b   *G* reads "Gilead" (גִּלְעָד).

2a   These words spoil the concision of the poem and
suggest a postponement of the destruction of the
Ammonites (so Cornill, Rudolph); compare 48:12,
note a. If לָכֵן, "therefore," belongs to the original
layer of material, then the verb וְהִשְׁמַעְתִּי has been
altered from אַשְׁמִיעַ.

b—b   Read רַבָּה with *G* for *M* רַבַּת בְּנֵי עַמּוֹן: note that
Ραββαθ in *G* reproduces רַבָּה not only in v 3 but in
1 Sam 11:1 as well.

c   Omit with *G*.

3a   Read שֻׁדְּדָה הָעִי for *M* שֻׁדַּד עַי, "Ai is destroyed."
The reference here cannot be to the city of Ai near
Bethel but is likely to be the generic noun behind
the name of that city.

b   See v 1, note a.

4a   *G* reads simply בָּעֲמָקִים. *M* is evidently a conflate
text (so Janzen, p. 20). Volz and Rudolph read
simply בְּעִמְקֵךְ; I propose בְּעִמְקֵךְ הַזָּב, assuming a
double meaning in the expression (see Interpretation). Kap-he might easily have been misread as
yod-mem in the early Aramaic script (see Cross,
"Scripts," 137).

b   Reading with Duhm, Cornill, Rudolph הַשַּׁאֲנַנָּה.
The misreading of הַבַּת הַשּׁוֹבֵבָה was made under the
influence of 31:22; "turnable daughter" does not fit
the context (see Cornill).

c—c   Literally "trusting in her treasures"; *V* reads more
logically "trusting in your treasures," but this may
represent not a better text but a secondary correction for consistency.

d   Inserting הָאֹמְרָה with a few MSS. and with *G*, *V*, *S*,
and *T*; *M* omits the word, evidently by haplography.

5a   This phrase interrupts the colon; it should either
be deleted (Rudolph) or moved to the end of the
colon (compare Bright).

b   These phrases are lacking in *G* and were added
even later.

c—c   This word is missing in *G* and is not necessary for

[6/ And afterward I shall restore the fortunes of the Ammonites, oracle of Yahweh.][a]

the colon (compare 9:21bβ), but נדד does not otherwise appear in Jer and seems to be in assonance with ונדחתם; if it were a gloss one would expect אֶת־הַגּוֹ or the like (compare 48:19, 44).

6a   Omit with *G* (compare 48:47).

Structure, Form, Setting

Verses 1–6 make up the material on the Ammonites. Of these, v 6 is clearly an addition, comparable to 48:47a. The rest of the material gives evidence of being genuine to Jrm (see below).

It is convenient to begin with form-criticism. Verse 1aβb is in the form of a threefold question: on this see the treatment of 2:14. The questions are rhetorical, presumably posed by Yahweh (compare v 2): Why has an illegitimate god (Milcom) dispossessed Israel from land Yahweh has apportioned to her? The rhetorical effect of the questions is thus an accusation. This accusation is followed in v 2 by Yahweh's announcement of judgment. Verse 3a is a summons to lament, for which see 4:8a; v 3b offers the reason for the summons (see the similar 48:7b). Verse 4 is a rhetorical question addressed to the Ammonites personified as a woman: the question implies an accusation ("you have boasted, have trusted"). This accusation is then followed by Yahweh's announcement of judgment (v 5). In short, there are two brief judgment oracles, each with form-critical integrity, vv 1aβb–2 and vv 3–5.

And both units share diction with authentic poetry of Jrm's (for the details see below). But v 2b immediately offers a problem: Rudolph excises it as late because it expresses "a dream of later Judaism," and indeed it appears to contradict the message of Jrm that Yahweh has given "all these lands" into the hands of Nebuchadnezzar (27:6). On the other hand, the phrase "shall dispossess his dispossessors" is reminiscent of "all who eat of you shall be eaten" and "all those looting you I shall give for loot" in 30:16, and furthermore the use of "Israel" and "dispossess" in v 2b balances the mention of "Israel" and "dispossess" in v 1. The present study assigns 30:16–17 to the recension to the south in the "Book of Comfort," dated between the summer of 588 and the summer of 587; at that time Jrm was proclaiming an eventual restoration of Israel to its territory, and that is a message congruent with the one in vv 1–2. As a matter

of fact, one wonders whether the Ammonite sponsorship of Ishmael, the assassin of Gedaliah (40:14; 41:15), dated here to the late summer of 587, was not the occasion for these verses.

If vv 1aβb–2 are to be dated to 588/587, vv 3–5 must be earlier. Thus vv 3b–4 resemble 48:7; v 4 resembles 21:13, dated in the present study tentatively to the time just before the siege of 598, and v 5a appears to be a variation of the expression *māgôr-missābîb* (see 20:1–6),[1] dated in the present study to 600. There were raids on Judah a year or two before the siege of 598, in which the Ammonites participated (2 Kgs 24:2), and that occasion would be a plausible one for vv 3–5.

It remains to list parallels to authentic material of Jrm's beyond the parallel between v 2b and 30:16–17 already discussed. For the threefold question form (הֲ, מַדּוּעַ, אִם־) in v 1 compare 2:14, 31; 8:4–5, 19, 22; 14:19; 22:28. For "blast of battle" (תְּרוּעַת מִלְחָמָה) see 4:19; there are no other instances of this phrase in the OT. The resemblances of v 3aβ to 4:8, of v 3b to 48:7b, and of v 4 to 48:7a have already been noted. For הִנְנִי מֵבִיא with עַל or אֶל and a word for disaster see 5:15; 6:19; 11:11; and 19:3.

Verse 1aβb may be analyzed as a tetracolon (compare 2:31aβb); v 2, excluding "therefore the time is surely coming, oracle of Yahweh" and "of the Ammonites," would likewise seem to be a tetracolon: the second and third cola are closely parallel, and the fourth colon serves as an inclusio with v 1b, as already noted. Verse 3a begins with a bicolon (the imperative to Heshbon, and the כִּי clause that follows) and it continues with a tricolon (the three clauses with feminine plural imperatives); v 3b is a bicolon—the closing כִּי clause. Verse 4 could be taken either as two bicola or a tetracolon: "boast" and "trust" are closely parallel, but the diction shifts (at least as the text now stands) from the second person in v 4a to the third person in v 4b. Verse 5 (without the added phrases) is a tricolon.

---

1   Christensen, "Terror," 498–501.

Interpretation

■ **1–2** For "Ammonites" (literally "children of Ammon") see 9:25. The traditional territory of the Ammonites was centered around their capital, Rabbah (present-day Amman), and the valley of the River Jabbok; they attempted repeatedly to extend their holdings north and south from that area, but their territory was never so clearly defined as those of Moab and Edom were.[2]

The participle translated "heir" in v 1 and "dispossessor" in v 2 and the finite verb "dispossess" in vv 1 and 2 are all forms of the verb ירשׁ qal, which essentially means "take over property," whether by inheritance or conquest. The participle is translated "new owner" in 8:10a\alpha (see the discussion of the verb there). The questions in v 1 and the divine word in v 2 are dependent on the words of Jephthah to the Ammonite king in Judg 11:24: there he says, "Will you not possess [ירשׁ qal] what Chemosh your god gives you to possess [ירשׁ hip'il]? And all that Yahweh our God has dispossessed [literally 'given to possess,' ירשׁ hip'il] before us, we will possess [ירשׁ qal]." The implication here is that that division has not been honored more recently.

That speech also suggests an identity between Milcom, the god of the Ammonites, and Chemosh, the god of the Moabites; for the latter god see 48:7. Milcom is called "the abomination of [or 'god of,' so S] the Ammonites" in 1 Kgs 11:5 in reference to Solomon's introducing his cult into Jerusalem (and "Molech" in 1 Kgs 11:7 is evidently a scribal error for "Milcom"), and so similarly in 2 Kgs 23:13 in reference to Josiah's abolition of the cult.[3] The name "Milcom" is related both to the word "king" (melek) and to the name "Molech"; for the latter see 32:35. The relationship among these three words is a tangled tale. M in the present passage reads "their king," whereas "Milcom" is the reading of the Versions: a similar issue is presented by Amos 1:15, where M reads "their king" and some Lucianic MSS. of G, and a' and s' and V read "Milcom."[4] It is likely that "Milcom" is a deformation of the name of the god, or rather of his title "king."[5]

Though the reading "Gilead" of G instead of "Gad" is a plausible one (the territories overlap), "Gad" is preferable in being one of the sons of Jacob-Israel. The territory of Gad is outlined in Num 32:34–36 and Josh 13:25–27: essentially from Heshbon northward to a point somewhat to the north of the River Jabbok. Two data should be noted. First, Jrm mentions Heshbon as belonging to both Moab and Ammon (48:2, 33–34; 49:3; compare Josh 13:26–27). Second, Mesha, king of Moab, mentions Gad in his inscription as having lived in the region of Ataroth:[6] that city, the modern ḥirbat 'aṭarūz (Atlas of Israel grid 214–109), is far to the south of Heshbon. That is to say, the territory in which a given group of people held sway did not always correspond to the boundaries set forth for them.

Rabbah is the present-day Amman.[7]

For "ruin" (תֵּל) see 30:18.

"Daughter-villages" is literally simply "daughters": the reference is to villages dependent on a city.[8]

The verb תִּצַּתְנָה, "will burn," is יצת qal; the occurrence of that verb in 2:15 qere' is the nip'al stem: see 2:15, Text note a—a, for the variations of verb in parallel contexts.

■ **3** For "wail," "gird yourself with sackcloth," and "lament" see 4:8. For Heshbon see 48:2.

The word here translated "this heap," הָעַי, normally "Ai" (so RSV, NEB, NJV), is puzzling, since "the" Ai is near Bethel, and no Ai east of the Jordan is known. Volz emended the verb and noun to שֻׁדַּד עָלָה following 48:18, and that emendation is adopted by Rudolph (and so also JB and NAB). But there is no indication in the text or the Versions that anything is amiss; one must conclude either that there is another Ai about which we otherwise know nothing (the name after all means "ruin"), or else that the word is a common noun, perhaps with variant vocalization (see Text).

Are the "daughters of Rabbah" understood to be women (compare 2 Sam 1:24) or "daughter-villages" of Rabbah (compare v 2)?—it could be either.

2   George M. Landes, "Ammon, Ammonites," *IDB* 1:110; Baly, *Geography*, 226–27. For recent archeological data on Ammonite sites during this period see Sauer, "Transjordan," 16, with full bibliography.

3   For these texts see Noth, *Könige*, 241; Gray, *Kings*, 276–78.

4   See Wolff, *Joel and Amos*, 131–32.

5   John Gray, "Molech, Moloch," *IDB* 3:422–23;

Kings, 276–77.

6   Lines 10–11: see the references in 48:1–47, n. 38.

7   George M. Landes, "Rabbah," *IDB* 4:1–3.

8   See conveniently C. Umhau Wolf, "Village," *IDB* 4:784, and further Frank S. Frick, *The City in Ancient Israel* (SBLDS 36; Missoula, MT: Scholars, 1977) 57, and n. 203.

The last phrase of v 3a, וְהִתְשׁוֹטַטְנָה בַּגְּדֵרוֹת, is puzzling. *G* omitted it, perhaps simply because the translator did not understand it. The polel stem of the verb שׁוּט appears in 5:1, where the present study translates it "search": it means "range" or "roam." This is the only occurrence in the OT of the hitpolel stem: one suspects that it refers to oscillating or repetitive movement associated with lamentation. The noun גְּדֵרָה denotes a stone pen for sheep; Num 32:36 refers to such sheepfolds in the territory of Gad (compare Num 32:16). So what does the phrase imply?—moving back and forth from one sheepfold to another in a vain effort to seek safety? The phrase is odd enough that Duhm proposed emending בַּגְּדֵרוֹת to בִּגְדֻרוֹת, "with gashes" (compare 48:37), and this emendation is accepted by Giesebrecht, Volz, and Rudolph (and so *JB*, *NEB*, and *NAB*); but it is preferable to stay with *M*.

For v 3b compare 48:7b.

■ **4** For הלל hitpaʿel, "boast"; see 4:2. The noun עֵמֶק normally means "valley," and "your flowing valley" (in the text proposed) is a plausible phrase: it might well refer to the valley of the Jabbok. On the other hand the noun sometimes carries the meaning "strength" (see 21:13, and notes 4 and 5 there), and the verb זוב may mean not "flow" but "ebb away" (Lam 4:9). There is thus the possibility of a nice double meaning here.

The phrase הַבַּת הַשּׁוֹבֵבָה occurs in 31:22 (translated there "turnable daughter"), but that expression, appropriate there, is inappropriate here—for in what way could Rabbah be considered disobedient or faithless? I therefore accept the emendation to הַבַּת הַשַּׁאֲנַנָּה, "com-

placent daughter" (the phraseology of Isa 32:9 is close to that in the present verse).

For "treasures" see 48:7. For "Who can come in against me?" compare again 21:13.

■ **5** For פַּחַד, "terror," see 48:43; פַּחַד, along with מִכָּל־ סְבִיבָיִךְ, "from every side," is evidently a variation of *māgôr-missābîb* in 20:1–6 and elsewhere (see Structure, Form, Setting, and n. 1).

The shift from second-person feminine singular in v 5a to second-person plural in v 5b is curious, but the meaning of the verb phrase ("you shall be scattered") makes the shift plausible. Though the expression אִישׁ לְפָנָיו (literally "each before him") is not at first clear, there is a parallel in Amos 4:3, וּפְרָצִים תֵּצֶאנָה אִשָּׁה נֶגְדָּהּ, "Through the breaches you shall go out, each (woman) (straight) ahead of her"; the image is of the break-up of the community—Bright translates "you'll be driven in headlong flight" and remarks, "i.e., *sauve qui peut!*"

■ **6** See 48:47a.

Aim

These two little units seem to be little more than an extension of the words to Moab. Rabbah will fall, doubtless to Nebuchadnezzar, as the other little states of the area are destined to fall. The only surprise here is Jrm's last word, that Israel shall dispossess the Ammonites as they had dispossessed him: in that way Yahweh's dream will be fulfilled, "I gave you a lovely land, the most glorious inheritance of the nations" (3:19).

Edom Will Fall

Bibliography

Bekel, Heinrich
"Ein vorexilisches Orakel über Edom in der Klageliederstrophe—die gemeinsame Quelle von Obadja 1–9 und Jeremiah 49,7–22," *TSK* 80 (1907) 315–43.

Kselman, John S.
"A Note on Jer 49,20 and Zeph 2,6–7," *CBQ* 32 (1970) 579–81.

Ogden, Graham S.
"Prophetic Oracles Against Foreign Nations and Psalms of Communal Lament: The Relationship of Psalm 137 to Jeremiah 49:7–22 and Obadiah," *JSOT* 24 (1982) 89–97.

49

7 For Edom. Thus Yahweh [of hosts][a] has said:
 [b]Wisdom in Teman is no more,[b]
   counsel has perished from the perceptive,
   their wisdom has turned rank.

8 Flee, [a]turn back,[a] make your dwelling in the depths,
   inhabitants of Dedan,
 for the calamity of Esau I have brought upon him,
   the time when I punish him.

9 [If grape-harvesters have come upon you,
   they would not leave gleanings;
 if thieves, by night,
   [b]they would destroy[b] what suits them.][a]

10 Indeed I myself have stripped Esau bare,
   I have uncovered his hiding-places,
   ⟨and to conceal himself⟩[a] he is not able.
 Destroyed is ⟪the arm of his brothers,⟫[b]
   ⟪and there is no neighbor of his⟫[c] (to say,)[d]

Text

7a Omit with *G*.

b—b Omit the interrogative הֲ with *G* and *S*; so also Cornill. For the phraseology see 48:2aα. I suggest that the he was originally dittographic after יהוה. For a discussion of the question see Structure, Form, Setting.

8a—a The vocalization of *M* is הָפְנוּ, the hoph'al stem, meaning perhaps "be turned back," but the vocalization הַפְנוּ, the hiph'il stem, is preferable (compare 46:5, 21; 47:3; 49:24); this is the suggestion of Rudolph.

9a This is a variation of Obad 5b + a; omit with Rudolph.

b—b The perfect verb here is puzzling: perhaps יַשְׁחִיתוּ should be read.

10a Following *G* and *V*, vocalize וְנֶחְבָּא = נֶחְבֹּה, nip'al infinitive absolute of חבא, with Duhm, Giesebrecht, Cornill, Volz, Rudolph; one may assume that when the infinitive comes before יכל it may be the infinitive absolute (compare v 23). *M* appears to vocalize the word as a perfect, but the construction is then more difficult.

b The exegesis of vv 10b–11 is tangled. *G* reads here ὤλοντο ἐπίχειρα ἀδελφοῦ αὐτοῦ; I suggest that this presupposes שֻׁדַּד זְרוֹעַ אָחִיו, though I prefer the vocalization of *M* for the last word, אֶחָיו. *G* ἐπίχειρον renders זְרוֹעַ twice (27:5 = *G* 34:5; 48:25 = *G* 31:25); for the diction see 48:25.

c *G* reads καὶ γείτονος αὐτοῦ καὶ οὐκ ἔστιν, which presupposes וּשְׁכֵנוֹ וְאֵנֶנּוּ. I understand the syntax differently but read with *G* the singular "and his neighbor" and omit the following ו as dittographic or otherwise secondary.

d *s'* adds here ὃς ἐρεῖ, a reading that moves Rudolph and Bright to emend וְאֵינֶנּוּ to וְאֵין אֹמֵר. But surely such a Hebrew text would produce καὶ οὐκ ἔσται ὁ

11 "Leave your orphans,
　　I will keep them alive,
　　　　and your widows can depend on me."
　　[12/ For thus Yahweh has said, Look, if
　　those who do not deserve to drink the cup
　　still have to drink it, shall you be the one to
　　be exempt? No, you will not! {—for drink it
　　you must.}[b] 13/ For by myself I have sworn,
　　oracle of Yahweh, that Bozrah shall become
　　a desolation, a reproach, {a devastation}[c]
　　and an object of contempt, and all her cities
　　shall become everlasting ruins.][a]

14 [News I have heard from Yahweh,
　　and an envoy among the nations [b]has
　　　　been sent:[b]
　　"Gather yourselves and come against her,
　　　　and rise up for battle!"

15 For[c] you see, I have made you least among
　　　　the nations,
　　　　despised [d]by mankind.[d]

16 [e]Your "horror"[e] ⟨ has deceived you,⟩[f]
　　the arrogance of your heart,
　　(you) who live[g] in the clefts of Sela,
　　　　who hold[g] the height of the hill:
　　though[h] you make your nest as high as the
　　　　eagle's,
　　　　from there I will bring you down,
　　　　　　　　　　　　oracle of Yahweh.][a]

17 [Edom shall become a desolation; everyone
　　passing by her shall {be horrified and}[b] hiss
　　{at all her blows.}[b]] [a]
　　18/ Like the overthrow of Sodom and
　　Gomorrah and her neighbors,
　　　　　　　　　[a]Yahweh has said,[a]
　　no one shall live there,
　　　　and no human being shall sojourn in her.

19 See, like a lion (that) comes up
　　from the thicket of the Jordan to the
　　　　perennial pasture,
　　indeed I shall suddenly ⟪ chase her suck-
　　　　lings, ⟫[a]
　　⟨ and the choicest of her rams ⟩[b] I will single
　　　　out.
　　For who is like me?
　　　　and who can summon me?
　　　　　　and what shepherd can stand before
　　　　　　　　me?

20 Therefore hear the counsel of Yahweh that
　　　　he has counseled against Edom,
　　and his plans that he has planned against
　　　　　　the inhabitants of Teman:
　　surely the shepherd boys shall drag them
　　　　off,
　　　　surely their pasture shall horrify ⟨ their
　　　　　　sucklings. ⟩[a]

21 At the sound of their fall the earth quakes;
　　a cry at the Red Sea is heard [her voice.][a]

22 See, like an eagle he [rises and][a] soars
　　and spreads his wings over Bozrah,
　　and the heart of the warriors of Edom shall
　　　　be [on that day][b]
　　like the heart of a woman in labor.

εἰπών (compare 9:21; 46:27 = G 26:27); I suggest
that the reading of s' is an explanatory insertion
rather than a clue to the original text. See further
Interpretation.

12–13a　Omit this prose sequence with Volz and Ru-
　　dolph; v 12 is reminiscent of 25:28–29, and v 13
　　imitates such passages as 7:34; 19:8; 22:5; 25:9.

b　　Omit with G.

c　　Omit with G; so also Janzen, pp. 25, 59.

14–16a　These verses are a variation of Obad 1–4; omit
　　with Rudolph.

b—b　M offers שָׁלוּחַ, qal passive participle, "is (one)
　　sent"; the reading of Obad 1, שֻׁלַּח, pu'al perfect, is
　　preferable, given the perfect in the first colon. G
　　reads "he [Yahweh] has sent," שָׁלַח.

c　　Obad 2 omits כִּי, perhaps rightly.

d—d　Obad 2 reads here אַתָּה מְאֹד "you (are) greatly."
　　As to the present reading, there was evidently a god
　　"Edom": one wonders then whether the vocalization
　　here was not originally בֶּאֱדֹם, "by (the god) Edom,"
　　rather than בָּאָדָם "by mankind" (so Duhm; compare
　　note e—e, and see further Interpretation).

e—e　The noun תִּפְלֶצֶת is a *hapax legomenon*; I suggest
　　that the noun may well be מִפְלֶצֶת with suffix (com-
　　pare 1 Kgs 15:13). The mem may have been mis-
　　read as a taw in the early Aramaic script: see Cross,
　　Scripts, 137. See further Interpretation.

f　　Read with Ehrlich (*Randglossen*, 361) and Rudolph
　　הִשִּׁיאַתְךָ: the feminine verb is necessary with the
　　subject. Compare Obad 3.

g　　Two instances of the so-called ḥireq compaginis:
　　see GKC sec. 90k, l; Joüon *Gramm.*, sec. 93n. Obad
　　3 offers the same text for the first of the two cola.

h　　Obad 4 has אִם־, "if," for כִּי.

17a　This is a prose addition (compare 19:8); so Cor-
　　nill, Rudolph.

b　　These words are missing in G and are later
　　expansions (compare 19:8); see Janzen, pp. 59–60.

18a—a　Surprisingly G here has εἶπε κύριος παντοκράτωρ
　　= אָמַר יהוה צְבָאוֹת; 50:40 has נְאֻם יהוה.

19a　This sequence needs emendation, but I think not
　　so drastic an emendation as Rudolph proposes. I
　　suggest reading אָרִיצָה עָלֶיהָ. The verb would be
　　cohortative, parallel with אַרְגִּיעָה; the he would be
　　misread as nun-waw, producing the text of M. When
　　that false object suffix was established, "her suck-
　　lings" (compare note e) was misread as "against her,"
　　and the מִן was added to ease the diction.

b　　Read וּמִבְחַר אֵילֶיהָ with Cornill, Rudolph, and
　　Bright; M reads, "And who is chosen (whom?) I may
　　appoint (?) over her?" See further Interpretation.

20a　Read עֲלֵיהֶם (compare v 19) with John S. Kselman,
　　"A Note on Jer 49,20 and Zeph 2,6–7," *CBQ* 32
　　(1970), 579–80.

21a　This gloss is omitted by G and 50:46.

22a　Omit with G and 48:40 (compare Janzen, p. 25).

b　　The phrase overloads the colon; omit with Ru-
　　dolph.

Structure, Form, Setting

This section, on Edom, extends through v 22. Four verses (vv 9, 14–16) are closely related to Obad 1–5; three other verses (vv 12–13, 17) are prose, offering variations on material found elsewhere in Jer. None of these seven verses exhibits any of the diction of Jrm's poetry, and with Cornill and Rudolph I bracket them as secondary. Verse 12 is noteworthy—it is a rhetorical flourish in which Edom is compared unfavorably with Israel: Rudolph remarks that the contention that the Jews suffered unjustly flies in the face of everything Jrm says elsewhere, that what one has here is a distorted understanding of election.[1]

Four more verses (vv 18–21) are virtually identical with 50:40 + 44–46: Cornill and Rudolph judge these verses as well to be secondary, but evidence in chapter 50 indicates to the contrary that they are secondary there and original here (see 50:1—51:58, Structure, Form, Setting, *Authentic and Unauthentic Material in 50:2—51:19*). Nine verses, then—7aβ–8, 10–11, 18–22—appear to reflect Jrm's diction, and they form a form-critical unity.

In regard to Jrm's diction, there are in the course of these verses three particulars that belong specifically to Jrm. (1) The summons to flight (v 8) appears to be confined almost exclusively to Jrm (beyond the present instance: 48:6, 28; 49:30; 50:8; 51:6, 45; compare 6:1; outside of Jer: Zech 2:10–11).[2] (2) Similarly the association of "flee" (נום) with "turn back" (פנה hip'il) is confined to Jrm; beyond v 8 (where the verb is probably to be vocalized as a hip'il: see Text, note a—a): 46:5, 21; 47:3; 49:24. (3) "The time when I punish him" or the like (עֵת plus a form of פקד, v 8) is not found outside Jrm (beyond the present instance: 6:15; 10:15; 50:27; 51:18; further, with "year" instead of "time": 11:23; 23:12; 48:44; outside Jer, with "day(s)": Isa 10:3; Hos 9:7). Beyond these data it may be noted (4) that the diction of v 19b is similar to that in 10:6–7, part of a passage cautiously accepted in the present study as authentic, and (5) that the phrasing of v 20a is close to that in 49:30b, part of a passage accepted here as authentic (see there). Finally there are other expressions that are characteristic of Jrm's diction without being exclusively his: "make

your dwelling in the depths" (הֶעְמִיקוּ לָשֶׁבֶת, v 8, compare "take a lower seat," הִשְׁפִּילוּ שֵׁבוּ, 13:18); "is destroyed" (שֻׁדַּד, v 10, compare 10:20; 48:15, 20; outside of Jer, Isa 15:1; 23:1, 14; Joel 1:10; Zech 11:3).

In regard to form-criticism, *M* of v 7aβ offers a rhetorical question, "Is there no more wisdom in Teman?" Since 49:1aβ begins with rhetorical questions, this diction seems altogether plausible. But there are no further interrogative particles in the verse: one must either assume that the second and third cola are affirmations (so evidently *V* and *T*), or one must assume that the interrogative particle הֲ governs all three cola (so the commentators and translations in general). Since 48:2aα also offers אֵין עוֹד with a completion for the colon analogous to that in the present instance, it is better to follow Cornill and delete הֲ as dittographic (see Text, note b—b). By this reading the verse depicts the breakdown of Edom, known for its wisdom (Obad 8: see further Interpretation); form-critically it is comparable to 48:2aα, as already affirmed. Verse 8a is a summons to flee (for which see 4:5, and more immediately 48:6); for the possibility that it is addressed not to the Edomites but to Dedanite traders from Arabia see Interpretation. Verse 8b is the reason for the summons to flee, introduced by כִּי, in which Yahweh speaks in the first person (compare 48:38b); this reason is essentially an announcement of judgment. For the inserted v 9 see below, on the parallels with Obadiah. The double form of v 8b, the reason for the summons and the announcement of judgment, is repeated or continued in vv 10–11 (one notes the renewed כִּי at the beginning of v 10, which seems to be parallel to that at the beginning of v 8b). Indeed v 10 seems to parallel v 8 in other respects as well—"depths" (v 8) and "hiding-places" (v 10); the repetition of "Esau." Verse 10b offers difficulties in text and exegesis, but in any event it continues the declaration of judgment. Verse 11 has puzzled commentators; Duhm, Cornill, and Giesebrecht assumed that Yahweh promises to take care of the orphans and widows of Edom, whereas Volz and Condamin reject the verse as secondary, having nothing to do with what has preceded it. But I concur with Rudolph and Bright that the verse offers the hypothetical reassuring words of the nonexistent neighbor (I only

---

1 Rudolph, p. 291.
2 Bach, *Flucht*, 15–21.

reject their reconstructed text at the end of v 10).

Verses 12–13 are a later insertion: in v 12 Edom is directly addressed and compared to Israel, and v 13 is of course a divine oath. For the inserted vv 14–16 see below, on the parallels with Obadiah. Verse 17, another insertion, is an announcement of judgment, embodying the traditional curse of the shuddering of passers-by over a desolation (compare 18:16).[3] Verse 18 resumes the announcement of judgment from v 11: this verse too is a traditional curse, the comparison to the destruction of Sodom and Gomorrah.[4] Verse 19aα offers a divine self-comparison—Yahweh compares himself to a lion (so also Hos 13:7), and consequently in v 19aβ Edom is compared to sheep: this simile continues through v 20. Verse 19b is a kind of summons or challenge of Yahweh to his opposition (in this case, Edom) in which he proclaims his own incomparability;[5] for such rhetorical questions compare Isa 44:7. In v 20 the diction changes—Yahweh is referred to in the third person. Verse 20a is a summons (spoken by whom, one wonders: divine heralds?) to receive instruction (*Lehreöffnungsformel*), for which compare Isa 1:10 and Hos 5:1;[6] the instruction (v 20b) is in the form of a divine oath (or at least asseveration) that judgment will come upon Edom (compare 15:11). Verse 21 resumes the declaration of judgment. In the context the third-person masculine reference in v 22 can only be to Yahweh; the diction then resumes that of v 20a, a final affirmation by the speakers (divine heralds?) of the work of Yahweh in judgment. The two halves of v 22 then each offer a simile: the first half is a description of Yahweh, and the second half a description of the demoralization of the defenders (for the theme of warriors reacting like women in labor see Form on 30:6). Do the two similes in v 22 balance the one in v 19a?

Verse 7 is a tricolon, v 8 is two bicola, v 10 is a tricolon followed by a bicolon, and v 11 is a tricolon. Verse 18 is a tricolon, v 19 is two bicola and a tricolon, v 20 is two bicola, v 21 is a bicolon, and v 22 is two bicola. There is no evident patterning of structure within the oracle.

There is no way to find a secure setting for this little poem. Edom is not recorded as having been involved in the raids on Judah of 599 or 598 (2 Kgs 24:2); Edom appears in the record only as a participant in the Jerusalem conference of 594 (27:3). The resemblance between v 8b and 48:44b (the latter half-verse a part of a poem tentatively dated in the present study to 594) is as good an indication as any to suggest a date for this poem to 594 as well, but clearly there can be no certainty with so short a unit.[7]

The four verses that overlap Obadiah (vv 9, 14–16) demand an explanation: how did this material find its way into both books? Given the amount of secondary material in chapters 46—51, one might assume that the verses are original in Obadiah and secondary here, but actually opinion has been divided: (1) Obadiah is original, Jer is secondary; (2) Jer is original, Obadiah is secondary; (3) both are dependent on an older third text.[8]

After examining the differences between the texts, Wolff concludes that both Jer 49:9, 14–16 and Obad 1–5 are dependent on the same orally transmitted text; that Obad 1–4 is a self-enclosed messenger speech, and so is Jer 49:14–16 (both are rounded off with נְאֻם יהוה); that form-critically Obad 5 begins a fresh word on Edom, and correspondingly Jer 49:9 is separated from 49:14–16 (and one notes the oral character of the two texts in the fact that in Obad 5 the apodoses are rhetorical questions while in Jer 49:9 they are declarative).[9] Wolff finds the most plausible setting for Obad 1–14 + 15b in the circle of cult prophets in Jerusalem between 594 and 587.[10]

If the analysis offered above for the present passage is correct, that v 18 is linked with vv 10b–11, then Jrm himself did not insert a version of Obad 1–4 between vv 11 and 18: the insertion manifests none of the diction of Jrm. By the same token one may conclude that Jrm did not insert v 9 between vv 8 and 10: v 9 breaks the link between "the depths" and "Esau" in v 8 and "Esau" and "hiding-places" in v 10. But since the insertions were on

3   Hillers, *Treaty-Curses*, 76–77.
4   Ibid., 74–76.
5   See on 10:1–16 and in particular n. 16 there.
6   Wolff, *Hosea*, 96.
7   Compare the remarks in Hans Walter Wolff, *Obadja und Jona* (BKAT 14/3; Neukirchen: Neukirchener, 1977) 24–25.
8   For literature see ibid., 12 (sec. 8); for the three

        views see p. 20.
9   Ibid., 21–22.
10   Ibid., 25.

the basis of an oral version of the material, they were not late, as one could conclude if it were a matter of the insertion of a written text. Jewish anger at Edom was high in the years just after 587 (Lam 4:21–22). If a date just before 582 is appropriate for the duplication of verses of Isaiah 15—16 in Jer 48:29–34, 36–38a (see 48:1–47, Structure, Form, Setting, *Possible Settings for the Secondary Material*), then an analogous insertion of anti-Edom material from oral tradition in that same period is certainly likely. By the year 582 Jrm had presumably died (see 37:1—44:30, Setting), and tradents would have felt free to expand Jrm's material on Edom.

Verse 9 is made up of two bicola, two parallel conditional sentences (the two halves of the verse are reversed from the order in Obad 5, and as already mentioned, the apodoses here are declarative, rather than being rhetorical questions, as they are in Obad 5). Wolff suggests that they are sayings about Edom previously known;[11] they affirm indirectly that when the enemy comes, nothing will be left.

Verses 14–16 are a unity (see above) consisting of six bicola; they are an audition report of Yahweh's summons to the nations to attack Edom.[12] Verse 14b is the quotation of a second messenger, delivering Yahweh's summons; for the diction compare 6:4a, 5. Verses 15–16 continue Yahweh's speech: now he is addressing Edom directly. Verses 15–16 are an affirmation that judgment will be rendered: v 16aα and v 16bα imply accusations against Edom of haughtiness and pride, but these accusations are enveloped in the divine judgment.

Interpretation

■ **7** The northern boundary of Edom was the Brook Zered (*wādī al-ḥasā*, Atlas of Israel grid 215–045). The southern boundary is ordinarily given as the scarp of *naqb al-*

aštar (Atlas of Israel grid 195–933),[13] but there were evidently periods when Edomite territory reached much further south.[14] The history of Edom can be discerned only from non-Edomite literary data (particularly the OT) and from archeology.[15]

For the reading of v 7aβ without the interrogative he, see not only Text, note b–b, but also Structure, Form, Setting.

On the assumption that Teman was a city, Glueck identified it as the modern *ṭawīlān*, northeast of the present village of *al-jī*, near Petra (Atlas of Israel grid 197–971).[16] But given the fact that Bozrah is a city (see on v 13), the wording of Amos 1:12 and 2:2 suggests that Teman is instead the region in which Bozrah is to be found,[17] that is, the northern half of Edom, north of the Punon (Feinan) Embayment (Atlas of Israel grid 195–005).[18] (It should be pointed out, however, that there are authorities who declare that Teman refers to southern Edom, doubtless because of a derivation of the name from יָמִין, "right hand = south."[19] But one may raise the question of the reference point from which Teman is reckoned to be south.)

For wisdom in general see the remarks on 9:22–23.

Edom was famed for its wisdom: this reputation is affirmed not only in the present verse but also in Obad 8. Suggestions have been made for two centuries that the Book of Job is Edomite in origin, but there is no consensus on the matter. The same can be said for a possible Edomite origin for Prov 30:1–4 and 31:1–8.[20] Baly attributes the wisdom of the Edomites to their experience in trading with caravans from Arabia and other distant parts,[21] but of course there is no way to substantiate this.

For "counsel" (עֵצָה) compare 18:18. The word מִבָּנִים may be understood in two ways. It may be taken as "from

11   Ibid., 22.
12   Ibid., 20.
13   Simon Cohen, "Edom," *IDB* 2:24; Baly, *Geography*, 233–35.
14   Crystal-Margaret Bennett, "Edom," *IDBSup* 251.
15   For a recent survey of the archeology of Edom in this period see Sauer, "Transjordan," 16, with full bibliography.
16   Nelson Glueck, *The Other Side of the Jordan* (Cambridge, MA: American Schools of Oriental Research, 1970) 29–32; compare Victor R. Gold, "Teman," *IDB* 4:533.

17   See Roland de Vaux, "Téman, Ville ou Région d'Édom?" *RB* 76 (1969) 379–85.
18   Baly, *Geography*, 235.
19   de Vaux, "Téman, Ville ou Région d'Édom?" 385; Bennett, "Edom," 252.
20   The most thorough survey of Edomite wisdom is Robert H. Pfeiffer, "Edomitic Wisdom," *ZAW* 44 (1926) 13–25, though much of that study is speculative in present-day perspective; see the balanced remarks in Otto Plöger, *Sprüche Salomos* (BKAT 17; Neukirchen: Neukirchener, 1984) xxviii–xxix. For a possible Edomite origin for Job see briefly Marvin H.

(the) sons," that is, given the context, "from the pupils" (compare the diction of Prov 4:1; 5:7; 7:24; 8:32); this is the understanding of *V*, *T*, and Rashi (indeed the Talmud understood this phrase as referring to the children of Israel).[22] Or it may be taken as "from the perceptive," the plural participle of בִין; this is the understanding of *G*, *S*, and Qimḥi. One must assume that pupils in Israel were subjected to endless moralistic injunctions employing this word-play, "sons"/"perceptive"—Prov 4:1 offers just a hint of it; so one assumes the word-play was deliberate on Jrm's part. For the verb בין see 9:11.

It is curious to see "wisdom" (חָכְמָה) repeated in the third colon—one might have expected a further synonym, but all the Versions repeat the word. The verb נִסְרְחָה, סרח nipʿal, occurs only here in the OT, but it occurs in postbiblical Hebrew, and there is no question of its meaning, "become rank, decay."

■ **8** Dedan is a city in northwest Arabia, probably the present-day *al-ʿulā*, 26° 38′ N, 37° 57′ E (see on 25:23). It does not appear that Edom ever extended its territory so far to the southeast,[23] so the question arises, What is the significance of the reference here? Was there a colony of Dedanite traders residing in Edom?[24]—one thinks of the reference to Benjaminites in Jerusalem in 6:1. Or is the address to Dedanites in Dedan, or in caravans on their way to Edom? The clue may lie in the phraseology of the first colon, to which we now turn.

The expression הֶעְמִיקוּ לָשֶׁבֶת, literally "make deep to dwell (or to sit)," may be understood in several ways. (1) It may be taken as "take a low seat," that is, sit on the ground in humiliation; this is the implication of similar diction regarding Moab in 48:18, and regarding the king and queen mother of Judah in 13:18. It is the understanding of *G* and of *NJV*. (2) It may be taken as "move your dwellings down from the heights of Edom"; this is the implication of v 16, which is similar to Obad 3–4. If there were a colony of Dedanites living in Edom, this interpretation would suggest "go back home." (3) It may be taken as "find hiding places"—so the implication of v

10. This is the interpretation of most commentators and translations (Giesebrecht, Cornill, Volz, Condamin, Rudolph, Bright; *JB*, *NEB*, *NAB*). But there is a further possibility. An earlier use of the parallel of "flee" and "turn back" (46:21) was used of mercenaries in the service of Egypt, told to return to their country. I suggest then that (4) the expression is to be heard as an address to Dedanite caravans on their way up to the heights of Edom: "remain down in the lower elevations." Denis Baly writes,

> Perched upon their majestic heights, the Edomites could not hope to get their wealth by farming nor maintain the huge Moabite herds of fat-tailed sheep, and were therefore taught by the stern land in which they lived to find their fortune in trade. Their riches came from the export of copper and from the lumbering caravans of the south, laden with the luxury products of southern Arabia, toiling wearily up from the hot deserts of the Wadi Hasma onto the heights of Edom, where the cultivated land stretched out a long arm into the wilderness to greet them.[25]

(The location of Wadi Hasma is Atlas of Israel grid 195–897; its elevation is approximately eight hundred meters, whereas much of Edom lies above fifteen hundred meters.)

Esau, the twin brother of Jacob (Gen 25:25), was always associated with Edom (the pun on "red," *ʾadmônî*, in that verse of Genesis, and explicitly in Gen 25:30);[26] Jrm plays on the name of Jacob in 9:3.

■ **9** For the general meaning of this verse see Structure, Form, Setting. For the image of the grape-gatherer and gleanings compare 6:9. When the enemy finishes with Edom there will be no gleanings left. The noun דַּי means "sufficiency"; דַּיָּם, here "what suits them," is literally "their sufficiency," thus "what they need," then "what they want."

Pope, "Job, Book of," *IDB* 2:912, and for Job and for the passages in Proverbs see Robert B. Y. Scott, *Proverbs, Ecclesiastes* (AB 18; Garden City, NY: Doubleday, 1965) xlii and n. 36 there.

21   Baly, *Geography*, 237.
22   *b. Ḥag.* 5b.
23   This is disputed; see Rudolph, p. 290, n. 1.
24   See the suggestion of Simon Cohen, "Dedan," *IDB*

1:812.
25   Baly, *Geography*, 237.
26   On the connection see conveniently Cohen, "Edom," 26; for further bibliography see Westermann, *Genesis*, 2:501, 508; and see Genesis 36 and the bibliography on that chapter in ibid., 680.

■ **10–11** For חשׂף, "strip bare," see 13:26. Curiously Obad 6 has חפשׂ nip'al, "be searched out": Jrm's word appears to be more violent. For מִסְתָּרִים, "hiding-places," see 23:24. Esau has no protection.

Verses 10b–11 are difficult. I accept the interpretation of Rudolph and Bright, that v 11 is the quotation of the hypothetical helpful neighbor (see Text, notes c and d, and Structure, Form, Setting; and see further below). The first colon of v 10b reads in *M*, "destroyed is his offspring and his brothers," a reading which gives at least superficial sense. But זֶרַע ("offspring") does not otherwise occur in chapters 46—51 (except in 46:27, an understandable exception), and "offspring" and "brothers" is a curious parallel. The reading of *G*, "destroyed is the arm of his brother," therefore commends itself: for זְרֹעַ "arm" see 48:25. If "his brother" (singular) is correct, one would assume a reference to Jacob/Israel (compare Amos 1:11); but the parallel "neighbor(s)" tells against this assumption, and if v 11 is the voice of the neighbor(s), it does not appear to be a likely word from Israel. It is difficult then to choose between singular and plural for "brother" and "neighbor" (in *G* both are singular, in *M* both plural): I have assumed that if "brother(s)" does not refer to Jacob/Israel, the plural "brothers" is preferable, but that the parallel with a negative is "neighbor," singular. Now if vv 10–11 are to be heard closely with v 8, "brothers" and "neighbor" may refer to the Dedanites, potential allies to come to the aid of Edom. By this understanding vv 10b–11 speak not of the wiping out of Edom but of the elimination of any protection from allies.

The lack of a marker like "to say" before v 11 is surprising, but 20:10 offers similar diction: there only the word "defamation" suggests the following quotation.

The verb חיה pi'el in v 11 is literally "make to live"; English idiom demands something like "I will take care of them" (Thompson) or "I will rear them" (*NJV*).

The verb with "widows" appears to be a second-person plural masculine, impossible in the context; it is a mixed form, with the *t*-prefix of the third-person feminine and the *û* suffix of the plural (masculine): see GKC, sec. 47k.

■ **12** For the image of drinking the cup see 25:15. The idiomatic diction of this verse closely resembles that of 25:29 (which see): though there is no formal interrogative particle, the phrase לֹא תִנָּקֶה, just after the 'atnaḥ, is a response to an implied question, and the question in turn depends upon an implied protasis (literally, "Look, there are those who do not have [= have not received] the judgment to drink the cup and they do drink it (nevertheless), and you are the one to go unpunished even so?").

■ **13** Bozrah had been the chief city of Edom (Amos 1:12). It is the modern *buṣayrā* (Atlas of Israel grid 208–016) and has been the site of excavations in recent years.[27] For the phraseology of this verse see 7:34; 19:8.

■ **14–16** For the parallels with Obad 1–4 see Text, and Structure, Form, Setting. The nations gather to defeat Edom.

"News I have heard" in v 14 repeats the root שׁמע, "hear." For שְׁמוּעָה, "news, rumor," see the discussion in 10:22. The word for "envoy," צִיר, appears only here in Jer; since in Prov 13:17 it is in close parallel with the common מַלְאָךְ, "messenger," it is not to be distinguished in meaning from the latter.

"Least" (קָטֹן, literally "small") in v 15 as a designation for Edom is reminiscent of that designation for Jacob in Amos 7:2, 5. "Despised by mankind" (בָּזוּי בָּאָדָם) is reminiscent of Ps 22:7, "scorned by men and despised by the people" (חֶרְפַּת אָדָם וּבְזוּי עָם). But given the probable implication of the first word in v 16, that is, the idolatrous object of Edomite worship (see below), one wonders whether "by mankind" should not rather be בָּאֱדֹם, "by (the god) Edom": there evidently was a god "Edom" (compare the proper name Obed-edom, literally "servant of Edom").[28]

The equivalent in Obad 3 of the first two cola of v 16 is one colon, "the insolence of your heart has deceived you," so that the noun translated "your 'horror'"

27 See conveniently Victor R. Gold, "Bozrah," *IDB* 1:459–60; J. Basil Hennessy, "Bozrah (in Edom)," *IDBSup* 119; Bennett, "Edom," 252. For full bibliography see Vogel, *Bibliography I*, 22, and Vogel and Holtzclaw, *Bibliography II*, 20.

28 See the entries in the lexica for אֱדֹם, "Edom," and see recently Mitchell Dahood, "Hebrew-Ugaritic Lexicography I," *Bib* 44 (1963) 292.

(תִּפְלַצְתֶּךָ, presumably תִּפְלֶצֶת) is not in Obadiah—indeed it occurs only here in the OT and does not occur in postbiblical Hebrew, so that there has been doubt about the soundness of the text. The Versions evidently simply guessed the meaning of the noun: G ἡ παιγνία σου, "your play, sport"; V arrogantia tua, "your arrogance"; S 'awlāk, "your iniquity"; T טַפְשׁוּתָךְ, "your folly." The root פלץ means "shake, shudder," so that the translation "horror" cannot be far off. But one wonders whether תִּפְלַצְתֶּךָ is not a miscopying of מִפְלַצְתֶּךָ (see Text, note d—d): in 1 Kgs 15:13 (and the parallel in 2 Chr 15:16) that noun is used for some kind of idolatrous image.[29] Thus whether the noun in the present passage begins with mem or taw, the suspicion that the expression here refers to Edom's god is strong enough to warrant the use of quotation marks around "horror" (so Bright). But there may also be a second meaning here, a subjective genitive, "the horror you arouse" (so the interpretation of Volz).

The presumptuous spirit of Edom is her complacency, the unwarranted self-confidence she has in her high defensive installations:[30] all that will tumble down.

"Sela" (הַסֶּלַע) is literally "the crag." There is no way to determine whether the reference here is to Sela, the Edomite city (2 Kgs 14:7), or whether it is a common noun, "the crag." If the city is meant, the identification with Umm el-Bayyarah near Petra[31] must be abandoned; the city is rather to be identified with the present-day as-sil'[32] (Atlas of Israel grid 205–020). For a different use of the image of the bird's nest high in the cliffs see Cant 2:14.

■ 17 The diction is similar to that in v 13; for the significance of "hissing" see 18:16.

■ 18 The noun מַהְפֵּכָה, "overthrow," like the related verb הפך (see 20:16), is used repeatedly for the destruction of Sodom and Gomorrah (beyond the present passage: 50:40; Deut 29:22; Isa 13:19; Amos 4:11). Though some scholars attribute to the prophet Amos the passage in which Amos 4:11 appears,[33] Wolff finds its setting in Josiah's time;[34] we then may have to do here with a

cliché of the late seventh and the sixth centuries. The addition "and her neighbors," which also occurs in 50:40, evidently refers to Admah and Zeboiim (Deut 29:22).

■ 19–20 There are several questions of text and interpretation that conspire to bring uncertainty to any understanding of these two verses. In the fourth colon of v 19 RSV has "and I will appoint over her whomever I choose" (similarly JB, NAB, NJV). There are two issues here. First, it is unlikely in the extreme that the first מִי should introduce a relative interrogative clause ("whomever I choose") whereas the following three מִי clauses should introduce independent interrogative clauses; second, this colon (and the parallel in 50:44) would be the only passage in the OT in which פקד qal with אֶל means "appoint over" (one notes that BDB says that the אֶל stands for עַל). The clue comes in v 20: there Rudolph, following Schwally, emends יִסְחָבוּם, "shall drag them off," to יִסָּחְבוּ, the nip'al, and so RSV, JB, NEB, and NAB, under the assumption that the subject of the verb is הַצֹּאן צְעִירֵי, understood as "the little ones of the flock." But Rashi and Luther correctly saw that צְעִירֵי הַצֹּאן means "the shepherd boys"; so Cornill and Volz, and so NJV (compare 14:3, where צְעִירֵיהֶם is translated "their menials"). It is the shepherd boys that "drag off" something, presumably corpses. This conclusion leads to the light emendation in v 19 proposed by Cornill and Rudolph, discussed by Bright, to read וּמִבְחַר אֵילֶיהָ, "and the choicest of her rams." It is to rams that Edom is compared, not the smallest of the flock. Now, it appears, the verb פקד is ironic: it often occurs in the meaning of "attend to, tend (sheep)" (see 23:2), but a lion "attends" to sheep only to pick out which ones he will devour. Having arrived at this point, however, one must nevertheless affirm that even though these two verses are heavy with the image of the lion chasing the sheep (beyond the phrases already dealt with: "pasture" and "shepherd" in v 19), nevertheless the image need not be concerned with sheep at all, but human beings, pursued by Yahweh. Thus "pasture" (נָוֶה) is a poetic term for

29   See Noth, Könige, 324; Gray, Kings, 349–50.
30   Wolff, Obadja und Jona, 29–30.
31   Simon Cohen, "Sela," IDB 4:262.
32   Anson F. Rainey, "Sela (of Edom)," IDBSup 800; Bennett, "Edom," 252.
33   See, for example, Victor Maag, Text, Wortschatz und Begriffswelt des Buches Amos (Leiden: Brill, 1951) 23–24; James L. Mays, Amos (Philadelphia: Westminster,

1969) 77–78.
34   Wolff, Joel and Amos, 217–18.

habitation (see 25:30); though "sucklings" (עוֹלְלִים), reconstructed in both verses, can refer to animals, it may equally well refer to human infants (Isa 49:15); אֵילִים, translated "rams," may equally well mean the "leaders" of their people (אֵילֵי מוֹאָב, Exod 15:15, "the leaders of Moab"); and "shepherd," of course, likewise may refer to rulers (2:8).

For "thicket of the Jordan" see 12:5. For "perennial pasture" (נְוֵה אֵיתָן) compare "perennial nation" (גּוֹי אֵיתָן), 5:15. For Teman see v 7.

■ 21 For "the earth quakes" see 8:16 and compare 4:24.

It is not appropriate here to undertake a full treatment of the meaning of *yām-sûp* in the OT, whether "the Red Sea" or (in the interpretation since the end of the nineteenth century) "the Sea of Reeds" in the Egyptian Delta,

but it is clear that in the present passage the intention is "the Red Sea" rather than (as Duhm, Giesebrecht, Cornill, Volz, Rudolph, Bright, *JB*, and *NJV* have it) "the Sea of Reeds."[35]

■ 22 For the eagle as a simile for the enemy see Structure, Form, Setting. For Bozrah see v 13.

Aim

For Jrm Edom did not loom large: it was simply one participant in the conference in Jerusalem called by Zedekiah in 594. But in the years after Jrm had left the scene Edom, by her actions against Jerusalem, became the focus of Judah's hatred (Ps 137:7; Lam 4:21–22). Esau had been Jacob's twin brother—how terrible when one twin turns against the other!

---

35 See recent treatments of this question by Norman H. Snaith, "יַם־סוּף: The Sea of Reeds: The Red Sea," *VT* 15 (1965) 395–98; Bernard F. Batto, "The Reed Sea: *Requiescat in Pace,*" *JBL* 102 (1983) 27–35; Magnus Ottosson, "סוּף," *TWAT* 5, column 796.

49

**The Aramean Cities Will Panic
and Be Deserted**

23   For Damascus.
    Hamath and Arpad are ashamed,
      for bad news they have heard,
    they waver 《like the sea》[a] (in) anxiety,
      [b](that) cannot rest.[b]

24   Damascus has lost heart,
      she has turned to flee,
        [a]panic has gripped her,[a]
    [misery and pangs have seized her like a
      woman in labor.][b]

25   How deserted[a] is [not][b] the city of renown,[c]
    the town of 《exultation!》[d]

26   Therefore her youth shall fall in her squares,
      and all her warriors shall lie silent [on that
      day,][a]
           oracle of Yahweh [of hosts.][b]

[27   And I shall set fire to the wall of Damascus,
      and it shall devour the strongholds of Ben-
      hadad.][a]

Text

23a   For בְּיָם, "at (or in) the sea," read כַּיָּם; compare the diction of Isa 57:20.

b—b   Perhaps one should read יוּכָלוּ, "they can(not rest)."

24a—a   The vocalization of *M*, without a mappiq in the final he of the verb, implies "she has seized panic," but *G*, *V*, and *T* read "panic has seized her," and this is the reading implied by the parallel diction in 6:24 and 8:21; therefore read or understand הֶחֱזִיקָה (GKC, sec. 58g).

b   Omit with *G*; the clause is reminiscent of 6:24; 13:21; and Isa 13:8.

25a   The vocalization of *M* is as a pu'al (or passive qal) perfect; but a vocalization of עֲזֻבָה (qal passive participle, compare 4:29) is possible.

b   Delete the negative with *V*; Rudolph believes it to be the marginal note of someone who was convinced the description of Damascus should apply only to Jerusalem ("Zum Text des Jeremia," *ZAW* 48 [1930] 285).

c   The qere' reads תְּהִלַּת: this may be an attempt to offer a parallel תְּהִלָּתִי to מְשׂוֹשִׂי in the next colon (compare note c): see GKC, sec. 80g.

d   *M* reads מְשׂוֹשִׂי, presumably "my exultation," but α', ς', θ', *V*, *S*, and *T* omit the suffix.

26a   *G* omits; a later insertion.

b   *G* omits; a later expansion.

27a   This verse is modeled on Amos 1:4, 14 and is a later insertion here (so also Rudolph).

Structure, Form, Setting

In this passage v 27 is clearly a later addition on the model of the divine words of judgment (with the first-personal singular verb) in Amos 1:4 and 14. And v 24b, missing in *G*, is a short addition modeled on 6:24 and Isa 13:8. (Rudolph's omission of v 26 is to be rejected: the verse is secondary in 50:30—see there.) This leaves vv 23–24a, 25–26: two bicola (v 23), a tricolon (v 24a), and two bicola (vv 25–26), eleven cola in all. Verses 23–24a are a depiction of the demoralization and desolation of the Syrian cities Hamath and Arpad (v 23) and Damascus (v 24a). Verse 25 is an exclamatory lament over Damascus—it may even be intended as a quotation of the inhabitants (compare 9:18; 48:17). Verse 26 is the announcement of judgment, introduced by "therefore"

(לָכֵן).

It would be bold indeed to propose a setting for so short a passage. Most commentators reject it as late (Cornill, Volz, Rudolph, Bright). Bright states, "Although it may be in good part because of the incompleteness of our knowledge, it is impossible to relate this prophecy to any known event during Jeremiah's lifetime."[1] Rudolph lists five reasons to deny the passage to Jrm. (1) The terror of Hamath and Arpad depends on the fall of Damascus, so that the enemy cannot come from the north, as in the genuine oracles. (2) Damascus is lacking in the list of peoples in chapter 25. (3) The geographical plan of 46:1—49:33 is disturbed by a Damascus oracle. (4) The passage lacks any religious thrust. (5) The fate of Damascus, in comparison with that

---

1   Bright, p. 337.

of other foreign nations, is mild: there is no destruction of the city, simply its abandonment.[2] Some of these observations are sound but may cut the other way.

One may say that most of the vocabulary argues neither for or against authenticity to Jrm. Thus the use of "be ashamed" (בוש) in v 23 is typical of Jrm (2:36; 14:3, 4; 15:9; 48:39; and other passages) but is by no means confined to him. Verse 26a associates "youth" with "squares," as does 9:20, but again the diction may be imitative. On the other hand, the phraseology of v 25 (אֵיכָה/אֵיךְ + passive verb + construct phrase subject, followed by parallel construct phrase subject) is identical with that of 48:17b, and there is no phraseology like this elsewhere in the prophets. This resemblance in itself is to me convincing in arguing for authenticity to Jrm.

The Syrians (Arameans) were among those whose contingents harassed Judah in raids sponsored by Nebuchadrezzar in 599 or 598 (2 Kgs 24:2). And it is noteworthy that the parallel of v 25, namely 48:17b, is part of the oracle against Moab that is dated in the present study to that occasion (see there).

The various Aramean states lost their independence to Assyria toward the end of the eighth century.[3] When Assyria collapsed, these cities doubtless regained their independence until the sway of Nebuchadrezzar was established over the west after the battle of Carchemish in 605.[4] There is no mention in the present passage of states that boast of their power, only cities—Hamath, Arpad, Damascus—suggesting (as Rudolph has noted) that they are not really independent. But they were an identifiable contingent in the attacks on Judah instigated by Nebuchadrezzar in 599/598 and thereby appear to have merited a brief word from Jrm.

Interpretation

■ **23** Damascus was the center of the Arameans in OT times as it has been the capital since of various Syrian states.[5] For Hamath see 39:5. Arpad is about thirty kilometers north of Aleppo, the present-day *tall rif'at*,

36° 29′ N, 37° 5′ E; the site has recently been excavated.[6]

For "be ashamed" (בוש) see 2:26. For the combination of שמע and שְׁמוּעָה see v 14, and for the noun see 10:22.

Volz has suggested an emendation of the third colon that is adopted by Rudolph and (with hesitation) by Bright, to read נָמוֹג לְבָּם מִדְּאָגָה, "their heart wavers in anxiety." This is logical but seems unnecessarily far from *M*: the diction of Isa 57:20 suggests the reading proposed here (see Text, note a). This is the only occurrence of מוג nip'al in Jer: it means "totter" (of the earth, Ps 75:4), "surge" (of a crowd, back and forth, 1 Sam 14:16). Though the noun דְּאָגָה occurs only here in the book, the related verb דאג, "be anxious," occurs in 17:8.

The meaning of the hip'il stem of שקט, "rest," is scarcely to be distinguished from that of the qal stem, for which see 30:10. For the use of the infinitive absolute before יכל, "be able," compare v 10 and Text note a—a there.

■ **24** For רפה, "lose heart," see 6:24 (translated there "fall slack").

The noun רֶטֶט appears only here in the OT, but the cognate Aramaic verb רטט, "tremble," is a guarantee of the meaning.

For the diction of v 24b see 6:24; 13:21.

■ **25** For the curious negative (לֹא) before the verb see Text. The description of the city here employs diction ordinarily heard in reference to Zion and Jerusalem (Ps 48:2–3)—and such vocabulary would be used in that context even more in visions elaborated in the decades after Jrm (Isa 60:15, 18; 62:7; Zeph 3:19, 20). There was surely irony therefore in Jrm's mind as he applied these words to Damascus.

■ **26** For the phrasing of v 26a see 6:11; 9:20; for דמם, "lie silent," in v 26b see 25:37.

■ **27** For "set fire to" (יצת hip'il + אֵשׁ) see 11:16.

Ben-hadad was the name of at least two rulers in Damascus, one who ruled about 880 BCE (1 Kgs 15:18), and one who ruled about 790 (2 Kgs 13:3, 24); in

---

2   Rudolph, p. 293.

3   See conveniently Bright, *History*, 275, 276, and Raymond A. Bowman, "Arameans," *IDB* 1:193; compare 2 Kgs 18:34; and see in detail the annals of Tiglath-pileser III, *ANET*, 282–88.

4   See again Bowman, "Arameans," 193, and further Bright, *History*, 326–27.

5   See Alfred O. Haldar, "Damascus," *IDB* 1:757–58.

6   Arvid S. Kapelrud, "Arpad," *IDB* 1:231; Michael C. Astour, "Arpad," *IDBSup* 55–56.

addition there may have been a third by that name who ruled after 870, and even a fourth who ruled about 845.[7] The controversy is not directly relevant to the present passage, since the name was used to refer to the royal house in general, like "house of Omri" in Assyrian annals to refer to the northern kingdom of Israel, and the name here is simply a designation of the ruling house in Damascus.

independent of Babylon, but Judah could still identify them among the bands of raiders sent against them. Who instigated those raiders? It was Babylon, of course. But the Arameans' willingness to move at the behest of Babylon would not save them: there is bad news ahead, and their cities will shudder in fear.

Aim

The Aramean cities might no longer have been

---

7   For detailed discussion see conveniently Raymond A. Bowman, "Ben-hadad," *IDB* 1:381–82; Haldar, "Damascus," 758; Robert M. Talbert, "Ben-hadad," *IDBSup* 95; Wolff, *Joel and Amos*, 155–56.

**Both Nomadic and Sedentary Arabs
Will Be Defeated**

Bibliography
Christensen
Transformations, 208–11
Dumbrell, William J.
"Jer 49.28–33; An Oracle Against a Proud Desert
Power," *AJBA* 2:1 (1972) 99–109

49

28 For Kedar and the kingdoms of settled folk
   which Nebuchadrezzar king of Babylon
   struck down. Thus Yahweh has said:
   Arise, attack Kedar,
      and devastate the children of the east!

29 Their tents and their sheep they shall take,
      their curtains and all their goods,
   and their camels—they shall lift for them,
      and they shall cry over them,
         "Terror on every side!"

30 Flee, bemoan[a] greatly,
      get down to the dwelling of [inhabitants
         of][b] settled folk,
                              [oracle of Yahweh,][c]

   for he [{Nebuchadrezzar} the king of
         Babylon][d] has counseled against you a
            counsel
      and planned [e]against them[e] a plan.

31 Arise, attack a nation at ease,
      dwelling securely,
                              [oracle of Yahweh,][a]

   he has neither doors nor bar:
      they dwell (in) isolation.

32 Their camels shall become loot,
      and the commotion of their cattle booty;
   I shall scatter them to every wind,
      (those who are) shaven at the temple,
      and 《 to all the kings of the Arabs 》[a]
   I shall bring their calamity,
                              oracle of Yahweh.

33 [Hazor shall become a lair of jackals,
      a desolation forever;
   no one shall live there,
      and no human being shall sojourn in her.][a]

30a   נָדוּ is omitted by *G*, and Janzen judges it to be a
      variant of נָסוּ (so Janzen, p. 25). But the length of
      colon is more satisfactory with it, and the word
      appears to carry a double meaning: see Structure
      and Form, and see Interpretation.

b   The word overloads the colon; it is a gloss from v
      8 inserted after חָצוֹר was understood to be a city
      (compare v 33).

c   Omit with *G*.

d   *G* reads "the king of Babylon" and *M* has not only
      "the king of Babylon" but "Nebuchadrezzar"; both
      units are glosses (see Structure and Form).

e—e   The ketib reads עֲלֵיהֶם, "against them"; the qere'
      עֲלֵיכֶם, "against you," accommodates the expression
      to the previous "against them." *G, V,* and *T* read
      both expressions "against you," whereas *S* has
      revocalized the verbs at the beginning of the verse
      and reads both expressions as "against them." The
      ketib is the *lectio difficilior* and should be retained
      (against other commentators and translations): see
      Structure and Form.

31a   Omit with *G*.

32a   For *M* מִכָּל־עֲבָרָיו, "from all his sides" (Versions
      "from all their sides"), I suggest לְכָל־מַלְכֵי־עֲרָב:
      compare the sequence in 25:24. I have suggested a
      metathesis of עבר for ערב in 5:28 as well. See
      further Interpretation.

33a   Omit as a later expansion (so also Rudolph): חָצוֹר
      is misunderstood as a city; v 33a is adapted from
      9:10, and v 33b is identical with v 18. See further
      Structure and Form.

Structure and Form

This is a baffling text. As is often the case, one has here a
poem that suggests the cutting edge of irony, but the
implications of the phrases are nearly lost in the additions
and interpretations of later times. There are three
clusters of questions to be dealt with: (1) the meaning of
חָצוֹר; (2) the ambiguity of v 29; and (3) the general shape
of the poem and the meaning of v 30.

   (1) The most basic question is that of the meaning of
חָצוֹר (conventionally rendered by the transliteration

"Hazor," vv 28, 30, 33). Verse 33 implies that Hazor is a
city, but no city of that name has been located in north
Arabia. Since the expression נְאֻם־יהוה closes v 32 and
since v 33a is an adaptation of 9:10 and v 33b an adaptation of 49:18b, Rudolph brackets the verse as a secondary addition—rightly, I believe; the poem that remains,
vv 28b–32, breaks exactly into two parallel halves, each
with ten cola (see below). The necessity that Hazor be
understood as a city may then be laid aside.

   The cognate noun חָצֵר is evidently the product of two

different Semitic roots that have fallen together in Hebrew: one means "enclosure, court," the Arabic cognate being ḥaẓīra; the other means "settlement, village," the Arabic cognate being ḥaḍara, "be present, settle, dwell."[1] Given the similarity in the meanings of these two roots, there is an obvious possibility of semantic confusion when the two roots fall together in Hebrew. In its rendering of חָצוֹר in this passage G assumes the meaning of the first root (ἡ αὐλή), but it is clear that the term instead reflects the second root—it is a reference to the settled population as opposed to nomads. Thus Edward Lane quotes the Arabic dictionary Táj el-'Aroos in its extended definition of ḥāḍir: "Any people that have alighted and taken up their abode by a constant source of water, and do not remove from it in winter nor in summer, whether they have alighted and taken up their abode in towns or villages, and cultivated land, and houses of clay, or pitched their tents by the water, and remained there, and sustained their beasts with the water and herbage around them."[2] The Hebrew חָצוֹר then refers to Arabs who had settled by water sources, particularly at oases, and it thus stands in opposition to the nomads or Bedouin,[3] who are referred to here by the term "Kedar" (on this see Interpretation, v 28).

(2) The second question involves the possibility of ambiguity in all four cola of v 29. Verse 28b is evidently a summons to the enemy to attack Kedar (see below). But then v 29a reads, "Their tents and their sheep they shall take, their curtains and all their gear." What is going on here?—does it mean that the enemy will take the possessions of the Kedarites (so all commentators and translations), or does it mean that the Kedarites will take their own possessions away for safekeeping? That is, are there two third-person plural references or only one? The ambiguity continues in the third colon, literally "and their camels they lift for them." Is one to understand that the enemy troops "lift for themselves" (that is, carry off) the Kedarites' camels (so again all commentators and translations, in consistency with the first alternative for v 29a), or do the Kedarite camels themselves "lift" burdens and people for their masters? That is to say, is v 29 the depiction of a raid by the enemy on the Kedarites (so the implication of both v 28 and v 32aα), or is v 29 the

depiction of the migration of the Kedarites to avoid a raid (so the implication of v 30)? Obviously it could be either, and one cannot avoid the conclusion that the ambiguity is intended. And the ambiguities continue in the last colon of the verse: clearly those who shout "Terror on every side!" over the Kedarites can be either the enemy or the Kedarites themselves. And if it is the Kedarites themselves, then the expression עֲלֵיהֶם may mean not "over them(selves)" but "on them," that is, "on their camels": this understanding is appropriate if הָעְמִיקוּ in v 30 is heard as "get down from your camels" (see below). Finally, it is argued in the present study that the expression מָגוֹר מִסָּבִיב—translated here "Terror on every side!"—is actually ambiguous (see Interpretation on 20:3–6). That analysis proposes that the noun מָגוֹר in this phrase means not only "terror" but "enmity" and "sojourning." Now the meanings "terror" and "enmity" would fit the depiction of a raid, but "sojourning" would fit a migration to avoid a raid. That analysis also proposes that "on every side" carries not only a spatial meaning but a notional one, "māgôr from every point of view," and that possibility is again plausible for the ambiguity of the verse in the present passage.

(3) The third set of questions that must be addressed is the general shape of the poem and specifically the text and meaning of v 30. One must take account of the following matters.

(a) There are two sections of the poem: the first colon of each (v 28bα, v 31aα) begins קוּמוּ עֲלוּ אֶל־, the third colon of each (v 29aα, v 31bα) contains two parallel nouns ("their tents and their flocks"; "gates and bars"), and the fifth colon of each (v 29aγ, v 32aα) mentions "their camels." This parity is so striking that Rudolph brackets vv 28b–29 as secondary; this excision is in error, but the question still remains of the meaning and function of the parity.

(b) In v 30b the first colon offers "against you" (עֲלֵיכֶם) and the parallel second colon offers (in the ketib) "against them" (עֲלֵיהֶם), a reading evoking the qere' "against you" (עֲלֵיכֶם). G, V, and T read the second person in both instances, and S reads the third person in both instances (but takes the verbs at the beginning of v 30a as third-

1   Harry M. Orlinsky, "'Ḥāṣēr' in the Old Testament," *JAOS* 59 (1939) 22–37; but see the caution expressed in Vinzenz Hamp, "חָצֵר," *TDOT* 5:131.

2   Edward W. Lane, *An Arabic-English Lexicon* (London/ Edinburgh: Williams & Norgate, 1863–93) 590b.

3   Rudolph, p. 294.

person perfects to correspond). The occurrence of an identical prepositional expression in the second colon is poetically redundant, so that the second occurrence is omitted by Volz and Rudolph; but the tradition in *M* ketib, by which there is a shift of personal reference, attracts attention as the *lectio difficilior*. Is Jrm affirming something both about "you" and about "them"?

(c) There is a problem with the expression הֶעְמִיקוּ לָשֶׁבֶת יֹשְׁבֵי חָצוֹר in v 30a. The expression הֶעְמִיקוּ לָשֶׁבֶת occurs in v 8, followed by the vocative יֹשְׁבֵי דְדָן, "inhabitants of Dedan." Rudolph excises הֶעְמִיקוּ לָשֶׁבֶת in the present passage as a gloss from v 8. This seems arbitrary, however: at least the verb הֶעְמִיקוּ is likely to play a part in the irony of the poem. But if that verb is original here, one immediately wonders what its nuance is. In v 8 the present study has been able to locate an ironic connotation—an address to the caravaneers of Dedan to go back down to their desert land, for the heights of Edom will be destroyed. But it is not immediately clear how the settled Arabs (if that is what "inhabitants of Hazor" means here) are to "go down deep." One can always assume the expression means "hide, take cover" or the like, but given the wit seemingly present in v 8, one expects more. The clue, I suggest, fits in with the shift from "against you" to "against them" already noted in (2) above. The address in v 30 is to Kedar, that is, to the Bedouin, whereas the third-person reference is to sedentary Arabs: one is thus pressed to understand "inhabitants of Hazor" not as a vocative but as a third-person reference. I propose, in other words, that v 30a means something like "flee, wander widely, get down (from your camels) to the dwelling of sedentary Arabs": one recalls the word "alight" in the definition cited above for the Arabic *ḥāḍir*—and it goes without saying that such an "alighting" is utter humiliation for proud Bedouin. If this is the meaning of that expression, then the previous נֻדוּ may carry a double meaning, not only "wander," in parallel with "flee," but also "bemoan (your fate)" (compare 48:17), in anticipation of the following phrase. And one may go on to suggest that יֹשְׁבֵי is superfluous, a gloss from v 8 inserted at a time when חָצוֹר was taken to be a city, as it also was in v 33.

(d) The last portion of the second half of the poem

offers the only first-person singular verbs, clearly spoken by Yahweh (v 32aβb); it is possible that the form-critical equivalent in the first half is the two third-person verbs in v 30b. In that half-verse the word "Nebuchadrezzar" is lacking in *G* and is therefore a later gloss, but one can go on to suggest that "the king of Babylon" is itself an earlier gloss:[4] in the similar 50:45 (= 49:18) the subject of the verbs is Yahweh. The two halves of the poem thus will be in exact parity: vv 28b–30 and vv 31–32 each have ten cola, the first half concerning the nomads and the second half concerning the settled Arabs. The characteristics offered for each group do not tell against this analysis: the first group has tents, flocks, curtains, household goods, camels that will be pillaged (v 29); the second group does not need doors or a bar, but their camels and cattle too will be pillaged (vv 31–32aα).

By this analysis then the first half of the poem (vv 28b–30) concerns the nomads. In v 28b, a bicolon, the enemy (identified at least in the superscription as the army of Nebuchadrezzar) is summoned to attack. Verse 29, two bicola, is ambiguous; it is a depiction either of the raid that will annihilate the nomads or of their carrying off their own goods for safekeeping (see [2] above). In v 30a, a bicolon, the nomads are suddenly addressed directly. (Question: Does v 30 embody another quotation parallel with "Terror on every side!"?) They are summoned to flee and told to take on a sedentary existence in the permanent encampments and villages. Verse 30b, again a bicolon, gives the reason for the summons (with כִּי): Yahweh has a plan both for the nomads and for the sedentary Arabs. But a surprise comes in the second half of the poem, vv 31–32, because that half is concerned for the sedentary Arabs: v 31, two bicola, offers an identical summons to the enemy to attack them as well, a complacent people who need neither doors nor a bar in their settlements. Verse 32aα, a bicolon, is a depiction of the raids that will annihilate them, and v 32aβb, two bicola, by the first-person singular verbs, renders that depiction part of Yahweh's declaration of judgment. The fact that nomads are told to seek shelter with sedentary Arabs and then the declaration is heard that the latter will be destroyed as well is reminiscent of 8:14, where the summons to flee to the walled cities is ironic—people will

---

4   So William J. Dumbrell, "Jer 49.28–33: An Oracle Against a Proud Desert Power," *AJBA* 2:1 (1972) 103, and Christensen, *Transformations*, 209.

only die there. And one recalls another poem with two parallel halves, 17:5–8.

Setting

If the foregoing analysis is correct, there is a strong presumption that the poem is authentic to Jrm: it shares the irony and surprise of other poems authentic to him. But beyond this general impression there is diction attributable to him. Thus the use of "terror on every side" is found in a similar context in 6:25; it is practically a watchword of Jrm's[5] (compare 20:10). The summons to flee is almost exclusively a mark of Jrm (see vv 7–22, Structure, Form, Setting). The expression הֶעְמִיקוּ לָשֶׁבֶת (here "get down to the dwelling") is found only otherwise in v 8. It may be added that the parallel of "tents" and "curtains" (v 29) is also found in 4:20 and 10:20; though it occurs outside Jer in two other passages in the prophets (Isa 54:2 and Hab 3:7), the parallel is at least appropriate to Jrm.

The Babylonian Chronicle relates that in the sixth year of Nebuchadrezzar in the month of Kislev (November/December 599) his army, "scouring the desert, took much plunder from the Arabs, their possessions, animals and gods."[6] There is no way to establish that that was the occasion for this oracle, but the parallel passages reflecting Jrm's diction (see above) are in the present study dated in this period: 4:20 and 6:25 perhaps early in 600; 10:20 just before December 598; and 49:8 in 594. The superscription may be editorial, but it is likely to be correct.

A setting for v 33 is impossible to determine: one could hazard a guess it is in the postexilic period when the knowledge of the meaning of חָצוֹר had faded.

Interpretation

■ **28** It was stated in the comment on 2:10 that "Kedar" refers to an Arab tribe in northern Arabia, and this is true so far as it goes. OT references have them living in both courtyards (Isa 42:11) and tents (Ps 120:5). The group is mentioned in Assyrian annals.[7] But authorities have concluded that the term here is a general designation for nomads or semi-nomads,[8] and the depiction of the group in v 29 reinforces that conclusion (see further Structure and Form). For "settled folk" as a translation for חָצוֹר see Structure and Form: that translation makes the reading "kingdoms" in *M* plausible: if the term does not designate a city "Hazor," then the reading "queen" in *G* (compare Duhm) is uncalled for.

For the imperative form שָׁדְדוּ see GKC, sec. 67cc. "Children of the east" (בְּנֵי קֶדֶם) is a very general term for peoples living to the east of the Israelites; the term has no exactitude but is used here for poetic parallelism, and *qedem*, "east," makes a good assonance with *qēdār*, "Kedar."[9]

■ **29** For the ambiguity of the whole verse see Structure and Form, (2).

"Tents" and "curtains" are of course the dwellings of nomads. It may be noted that the Arabic cognate of אֹהֶל, "tent," is *ahl*, "family, kinsfolk," suggesting the extended family:[10] when "their tents" is linked with "their sheep," then, one thinks not only of the shelter afforded by the tents but of all who live within that shelter (compare the possibility of a similar implication in Judg 6:5).[11] There is a relief surviving from Ashurbanipal's palace showing Assyrian infantry sacking and burning Arab tents.[12]

The domestication of the camel, evidently near the end of the second millennium BCE, made Arab nomadism possible.[13]

For "terror on every side" see the first occurrence, 6:25; 20:3–6 (for the implicit ambiguity of the expression); 20:10 (for the phrase as a watchword of Jrm's); and Structure and Form (2) above (for the possible ambiguity in the present passage).

■ **30** The verb נֻדוּ may mean "wander (aimlessly)" (see 4:1), and that is the meaning suggested by "flee"; but it may also mean "bemoan" (see 15:5; 48:17), and that meaning is at least a possibility, given the implication of "get down to the dwelling of settled folk" (see Structure

5 Christensen, *Transformations*, 210–11.
6 Wiseman, *Chronicles*, 72, 73: the reference is British Museum 21946, reverse, lines 9–10.
7 See conveniently *ANET*, 298–300 (spelled there Qedar).
8 Zimmerli, *Ezekiel 2*, 68; Wildberger, *Jesaja*, 802.
9 Simon Cohen, "East, the people of the," *IDB* 2:4; Zimmerli, *Ezekiel 2*, 13–14.

10 De Vaux, *Ancient Israel*, 7.
11 So J. Alberto Soggin, *Judges* (Philadelphia: Westminster, 1981) 109.
12 See Yadin, *Warfare*, 451.
13 John Alexander Thompson, "Camel," *IDB* 1:490–91.

and Form [3c], and see below). The use of the word here has something in common with the phenomenon of so-called Janus parallelism.[14]

For the implication of humiliation involved in the expression "get down to the dwelling of settled folk" see Structure and Form (3c).

■ **31** This is the only occurrence in Jer of the adjective שָׁלֵיו (or שָׁלֵו), "at ease," but for the verb שׁלה, "be at ease, have peace and quiet," see 12:1. For the phrase "dwell securely" see 23:6.

The pairing of "doors" and "bar" implies the gate of a walled city (Deut 3:5; Sir 49:13). "Doors" is a dual, דְּלָתַיִם. As Yadin explains,

Since the entrance [of the city gate] had to be wide enough to allow the passage of chariots, double doors were required. This meant, however, that the barrier was weakest at its center, along the line where the two doors met. To strengthen it against an attempted enemy breakthrough, it was fitted with huge bolts. These usually took the form of a heavy beam which ran right across the back of the double doors, and was held in position by sockets in both doorposts. One of these sockets was a very deep recess into which the beam would be moved to allow the doors to be opened. The other socket was just deep enough to hold the other end of the beam after the doors were closed.[15]

But the settlements of the sedentary Arabs, whether permanent encampments of tents or clusters of clay-brick houses, were not cities with defense walls. These Arabs dwelt "in isolation"—the noun בָּדָד occurs also in 15:17 (there translated "alone"); here "isolation" implies "independence, freedom from attack" (Deut 33:28; Mic 7:14). The sedentary Arabs live in the complacent confidence they are secure.

■ **32** Now the Arabs' camels are clearly to become loot, and their cattle too. "Cattle" (מִקְנֶה) appears in Jer only otherwise in 9:9; the word covers not only sheep and goats (צֹאן, v 29) but bovines as well (see Gen 26:14). The noun הָמוֹן means both the steady noise of a crowd, the confusion that a crowd manifests, and the large numbers of people in a crowd (3:23); here "commotion" will have to do—one hears the bellowing of the animals as they are driven off in a new direction by the raiders.

For זרה pi'el, "scatter," see 31:10–11. "To every wind" of course means "in every direction": רוּחַ (here "wind") is used for the four sides of the temple area in Ezek 42:16–20.

For the phrase קְצוּצֵי פֵאָה, translated here "shaven at the temple," see the discussion in 9:24–25. Is there a rhetorical effect here in that פֵּאָה, like רוּחַ, is used for the "side" (of a building) as well as the side of the face (see Ezek 41:12)?

The text of M in the last two cola gives good sense and parallelism, with the exception of the possessive suffix on "side"—"and from every side I shall bring their calamity"; "side" offers parallelism with רוּחַ and פֵּאָה (see above). Nevertheless I would suggest reading "to all the kings of the Arabs I shall bring their calamity." Two data suggest the plausibility of this emendation: the sequence in 25:24 is likely to be a reflection of the diction here; and the phrase "kingdoms of Hazor" in v 28 suggests the possibility of the word "kings" here. And given the ambiguity of the poem, one has the sense that a proper noun is appropriate at the end of the poem; but that impression cannot carry too much weight.

■ **33** The term חָצוֹר has here become the name of a city: hence the translation adopted here. For the description in v 33a see 9:10.

Aim

If this poem is understood correctly, it is a summons to the destroyer to attack the nomadic Arabs, followed by a summons to them to flee for safety to the settlements of their sedentary brothers, followed then by a summons to the destroyer to attack the sedentary Arabs as well. Neither group of Arabs will survive.

Jrm's word to foreign nations is not limited to Judah's immediate neighbors but reaches far beyond.

---

14 See 17:1–4, n. 7.
15 Yadin, *Warfare*, 22.

49

34 ᵃThis has come as the word of Yahweh to Jeremiah the prophet about Elamᵃ [in the accession year of Zedekiah king of Judah, as follows:]ᵇ 35/ Thus Yahweh [of hosts]ᵃ has said:

I am going to break the bow of Elam,
the mainstay of their might.

36 And I shall bring upon Elam four winds
from the four sides of heaven,
[and I shall scatter them to all these winds,
and there shall be no nation where the
outcasts of Elamᵇ shall not come.]ᵃ

37 I shall panic ᵃthem [M: Elam]ᵃ before their
enemies,
[and before]ᵇ those who seek their lives,
and I shall bring upon them evil,
my hot anger,
[oracle of Yahweh;]ᶜ
[and I shall send after them the sword until I
have destroyed them.]ᵈ

38 And I shall place my throne in Elam,
and I shall destroy from there 《kings》ᵃ
[and officials,]ᵃ
[oracle of Yahweh.]ᵇ

39 [But it will happen in time to come that ᵇI shall
restore the fortunes ofᵇ Elam,
oracle of Yahweh.]ᵃ

Text

34a—a *G* is altogether different, ἃ ἐπροφήτευσεν Ιερεμίας ἐπὶ τὰ ἔθνη τὰ Αιλαμ, suggesting an antecedent אֲשֶׁר הִנָּבֵא יִרְמְיָהוּ אֶל־הַגּוֹיִם עֵילָם. Perhaps a very simple superscription like אֶל־עֵילָם, "for Elam," was expanded in different ways in the two traditions.

b   This sequence is missing in *G*.

35a   Omit with *G*.

36a   This prose expansion is secondary (so Rudolph, and with hesitation, Bright): "these winds" is not poetic diction, nor is הַגּוֹי אֲשֶׁר (compare the poetic diction of 5:15).

b   The ketib עוֹלָם is evidently a copyist's error for עֵילָם (so qere').

37a   Reading the suffix ם (or the pronoun אֹתָם) with *G* (compare Bright).

b   Omit with *G*; see Janzen, pp. 41, 42.

c   Omit with *G*.

d   This sequence is taken from 9:15b and must be secondary here (Rudolph).

38a   *G* and *M* both read "king and officials"; but *V* and *S* read "kings and officials," and *T* reads "king and ruler." Given the phrase "kings of Elam" in 25:25, one suspects that "kings" alone stood here, and that "king and officials" is a substitution derived from 4:9 and the like.

b   Omit with *G*.

39a   The oracle of salvation is a late addition (compare 48:47).

b   The ketib אָשׁוּב אֶת־שְׁבִית is curious, and the qere' אָשִׁיב אֶת־שְׁבוּת normalizes the phrase (compare v 6). On the other hand, the same qere'/ketib pattern for the verb is found in 33:26 (see there) and Joel 4:1, and for the noun in 29:14 (see there) and Ezek 16:53; Job 42:10. It is likely that the idiom allowed either the qal or the hip'il stem for the verb, and that there was a noun שְׁבִית as well as שְׁבוּת; on this see Holladay, *Šûbh*, 110–12.

Structure, Form, Setting

There are two overriding characteristics of this passage. The first is that all the verbs are first-person singular, so that the speaker is Yahweh (one notes "I shall bring four winds" in v 36); there are no imperatives to the Elamites (compare v 30) or their enemy (compare vv 28b, 31a), no third-person verbs describing actions of the Elamites taken or about to be taken. The second is that there are no specifics given: no names of cities (compare vv 2, 8, 23, and often), no names of gods (compare 48:7; 49:1), no names of the royal house (compare v 27), no characteristics of the life of the Elamites (compare vv 29, 31–32aα). The prophet cannot envision a single concrete detail of the Elamites: the name "Elam" evidently stands at the remotest edge of the prophet's knowledge. Given then the lack of specificities with respect to Elam, it is Yahweh alone who acts upon that nation. The sense of uncanniness is increased by two details. There is the mention of the "four winds from the four sides of heaven" (v 36): the four winds have their origin close to

God (compare Ps 135:7).[1] And then there is the statement that Yahweh himself will place his throne in Elam (v 38): besides the present passage there are nine other references to Yahweh's throne in the OT,[2] but these nine speak of his throne in cosmic terms, for example, "your throne endures to all generations" (Lam 5:19). The statement in the present passage is unique, and it is comparable in Jer only to the divine word that Nebuchadrezzar will place his throne on the stones in Tahpanhes (43:10, on which see below).

The oracle is then entirely an announcement of divine judgment. It contains five bicola; the second, third, and fourth bicola each open with a waw-consecutive perfect verb (the verb in the second and fourth bicola being identical, וְהֵבֵאתִי), whereas the first bicolon opens with the appropriate opening for an announcement of judgment, הִנְנִי and a participle, and both cola of the final bicolon open with a waw-consecutive perfect verb, forming a climax.

Is the oracle authentic to Jrm? It is difficult in such a short passage to prove or disprove distinctive vocabulary, particularly when divine announcements of judgment use conventional phrases. Nevertheless, there are some suggestive details. Thus the only other occurrence in the prophets of שׂים with the object "throne" (כִּסֵּא) is in Jer 43:10: in the midst of narrative there is a quotation of a divine word—Nebuchadrezzar will "set his throne" on the stones in Tahpanhes (see above). Again חתת hip'il, "panic," followed by לִפְנֵי, "before," occurs in the prophets only otherwise in 1:17. Further the phrase רֵאשִׁית גְּבוּרָתָם, "mainstay of their might," curiously resembles רֵאשִׁית תְּבוּאָתֹה, "the first-fruits of his harvest," in 2:3: there is no phrase with רֵאשִׁית of such comparable shape elsewhere in the prophets. And one might also cite "the horn of Moab is cut off, and his arm is broken" (48:25) as a parallel for "I am going to break the bow of Elam" in v 35; occurrences of "break" (שׁבר) with the object "bow" appear in the prophets only otherwise in Hos 1:5; 2:20. And the phrases of v 37 are found several times elsewhere in authentic material; thus "enemies" (אֹיְבִים) paralleled by "those who seek one's life" (נֶפֶשׁ מְבַקְשֵׁי): 19:7; 21:7; 44:30; "bring evil on" (בוא hip'il + רָעָה עַל־): 4:6; 6:19; 11:11; 19:3, 15; 23:12; 35:17;

36:31; 44:2; 45:5; "hot anger (of Yahweh)" (חֲרוֹן אַף): 4:8, 26; 25:37, 38. One may conclude that the passage is authentic to Jrm.

Elam was a nation centering in the southwestern part of what is present-day Iran, with its capital at Susa. It fell under Assyrian control about 645. After the collapse of Assyria in 612, it became a protectorate of the Medes, who centered in the northwestern part of what is present-day Iran, and Elam continued to be so until it came under Persian rule in 550.[3] That is to say, though it continued its national identity in Jrm's time, that identity was simply as a vassal state to one great power or another; as noted in the comment on 25:25, damaged lines in the Babylonian Chronicle may refer to a campaign of Nebuchadrezzar against Elam in 596/595, but one cannot be sure.[4] If there was such a campaign, it might afford a setting for the present passage. The datum "in the accession year of Zedekiah" (thus early in 597) in v 34 is lacking in G and therefore likely to be a late addition to the text, but for all we know it may be based on a correct tradition. On the other hand 594 may have been the setting: compare the discussion of Jrm's "cosmicizing" of Amos 1:2 in 25:30–38, assigned to that year in the present study, and see below on the motive for an oracle against Elam.

But the question still remains, Why would Jrm be impelled to frame an oracle against Elam, a nation with whom Judah had no dealings whatever? I have three suggestions that may not be mutually exclusive. The first is that the name עֵילָם, "Elam," resembles עוֹלָם, "extreme of time" (one notes the miswriting of עֵילָם as עוֹלָם in the ketib at the end of v 36); it is conceivable, therefore, that the sound of the name then may have encouraged Jrm to see Elam as a place at the end of the world: one thinks of the association of "far away" and "long ago" in the description of the foe from the north in 5:15. Second, there was a real king of Elam about whom Jrm doubtless would have heard, from the narrative preserved in Gen 14:1–17: Chedorlaomer, defeated by Abram/Abraham and his forces; and since Jrm evidently made use on other occasions of traditions about Abraham (compare the remarks on 10:23–25 and 20:3–6), this narrative may have encouraged him to speak of Elam, on the edge

1   For a discussion of the four winds see Zimmerli, *Ezekiel 2*, 261, 566.

2   1 Kgs 22:19 = 2 Chr 18:18; Isa 66:1; Ezek 43:7; Ps 9:8; 89:15; 93:2; 97:2; Lam 5:19.

3   Mark J. Dresden, "Elam," *IDB* 2:70–71.

4   See 25:15–29, n. 20.

of the known world. Finally, Jrm had been appointed "a prophet to the nations" (1:5), and at a point in his career he proclaimed that the yoke of Nebuchadrezzar was to be universal, that "all nations shall serve him" (27:7); it would therefore be appropriate for him to name the most distant nation to symbolize that universality.

Verse 39 is a divine proclamation of salvation, added like the comparable passages in 48:47a and 49:6. But given the distance of Elam from Judah, it is difficult to discern any motivation for this addition except an affirmation of ultimate universalism, an affirmation that must stem from a time well into the Persian period.[5]

Interpretation

■ **34** For Elam see 25:25. For "accession year of" (רֵאשִׁית מַלְכוּת) see the phrase רֵאשִׁית מַמְלְכוּת in 26:1. By the reckoning of the present study this would refer to the few weeks before the new year of March/April, 597.

■ **35** To "break the bow" of Elam is to destroy her military power (compare Hos 1:4–5).[6] The noun רֵאשִׁית means "first-fruits" in 2:3; here it suggests "first" or "best"—*JB* uses "source," whereas "mainstay" is the rendering of *RSV*, *NAB*, *NJV*, and Bright.

■ **36** For the "four winds from the four sides of heaven" see Structure, Form, Setting. For "scatter to all these winds" compare v 32. This is the only occurrence in Jer of the noun נִדָּח, "outcast," but the verb נדח, "scatter,"

both in the hip'il stem and in the nip'al (passive), occurs frequently: see 30:17. The phraseology of the last clause is close to an expansion in 43:5.

■ **37** The verb וְהַחְתַּתִּי, "and I shall panic them," is חתת hip'il (see 1:17); for the uncontracted form (instead of וַהֲחִתּוֹתִי*) see GKC, sec. 67aa. The diction of this verse uses phrases common in Jer: for the details see Structure, Form, Setting.

■ **38** For the unique notion of Yahweh's placing his throne in Elam see the discussion at two points in Structure, Form, Setting; it suggests Yahweh's final sovereignty and judgment on Elam (compare the analysis of this phrase in 1:15, and the bibliography in n. 70 there). For "destroy" (אבד hip'il, really "put to death") see 1:10.

■ **39** For the phrase "restore the fortunes" (שׁוּב שְׁבוּת) see 29:14. For the function of this verse see Structure, Form, Setting.

Aim

There is no limit to Yahweh's sovereignty. Jrm had heard Yahweh say, "Am I a God nearby and not a God far off? Can anyone hide in some hole without being seen by me? Are not heaven and earth filled by me?" (23:23). Yahweh's hand is not shortened (Isa 59:1) and reaches even to Elam.

---

5   Compare Wildberger's dating of Isa 19:18–23 in the Persian period: Wildberger, *Jesaja*, 734, 740, 744.

6   Robert Bach, "'. . . Der Bogen zerbricht, Spiesse zerschlägt und Wagen mit Feuer Verbrennt,'" *Probleme biblischer Theologie, Gerhard von Rad zum 70. Geburtstag* (ed. Hans Walter Wolff; Munich: Kaiser, 1971) 13–14; Nahum M. Waldman, "The Breaking of the Bow," *JQR* 69 (1978/79) 82–83.

Babylon Too Will Fall

Bibliography

On 50:1—51:58:

Aitken, Kenneth T.
"The Oracles Against Babylon in Jeremiah 50—
51: Structures and Perspectives," *Tyndale Bulletin*
35 (1984) 25–63.

Ammassari, Antonio
"Le profezie di Geremia contro Babilonia (Ger 50
e 51)," *La Religione dei Patriarchi* (Rome: Città
Nuova Editrice, 1976) 149–91.

Budde, Karl
"Über die Kapitel l und li des Buches Jeremia,"
Jahrbücher für deutsche Theologie 23 (1878) 428–70,
529–62.

Eissfeldt
"Drohorakel."

Kessler, Martin
"Rhetoric in Jeremiah 50 and 51," *Semitics* 3 (1973)
18–35.

Robinson, Theodore H.
"The Structure of Jeremiah l, li," *JTS* 19
(1917/18) 251–65.

Smelik, Klaas A. D.
"De functie van Jeremia 50 en 51 binnen het boek
Jeremia," *Nederlands Theologisch Tijdschrift* 41
(1987) 265–78.

On 50:1–46:

Emerton, John A.
"A Problem in the Hebrew Text of Jeremiah vi. 23
and l. 42," *JTS* NS 23 (1972) 106–13.

Girard, L. Saint-Paul
"La colère de la Colombe (note sur Jérémie 25,38
et 46,16; 50,16)," *RB* 40 (1931) 92–93.

On 51:1–58:

Dahood, Mitchell
"The Integrity of Jeremiah 51,1," *Bib* 53 (1972)
542.

Dimant, Devorah
"Jeremiah 51:55—Versions and Semantics," *Textus*
8 (1973) 93–99.

Hartberger, Birgit
*"An den Wassern von Babylon . . .": Psalm 137 auf dem
Hintergrund von Jeremia 51, der biblischen Edom-
Traditionen und babylonischer Originalquellen* (BBB
63; Frankfurt/Bonn: Hanstein, 1986) 16–133.

McKane, William
"Poison, trial by ordeal and the cup of wrath," *VT*
30 (1980) 474–92.

Reimer, David J.
"A Problem in the Hebrew Text of Jeremiah x 13,
li 16," *VT* 38 (1988) 348–54.

Wiklander, Bertil
"The Context and Meaning of NHR 'L in Jer. 51:44," *SEÅ* 43 (1978) 40–64.

50

1   [a]The word that Yahweh spoke[a] against Babylon [against[c] the land of the Chaldeans by
means of Jeremiah the prophet:][b]

2   Declare among the nations and announce,
[and raise a signal, announce,][a]
    do not conceal (it), say,
Babylon has been captured,
    [b]Bel is ashamed,
      Marduk[c] is panicked,
    [her idols are ashamed,
      her godlets are panicked.][b]

3   For there has gone up against her a people
    from the north,
      he it is who shall make her land a desola-
      tion,
      and there shall be no inhabitant in her,
      from man to beast [they have fled,
      have gone.][a]

4   [In those days and at that time, {oracle of
    Yahweh,}][b] [a]
the children of Israel shall come, [they and
    the children of Judah together,][c]
    walking and weeping they shall go,
      Yahweh their God they shall seek;

5   (for) Zion they shall ask,
    the way hither is before them,
[a]《 and they shall come 》 and join themselves[a]
    to Yahweh:
    the everlasting covenant will never be
      forgotten.

6   Perishing sheep were[a] my people,
    their shepherds led them astray,
      (to) mountains [b]they turned them away,[b]
      from mountain to hill they went,
      they forgot their fold.

7   All who found them ate them,
    and their enemies said, "We are not
      guilty,"
inasmuch as they sinned against Yahweh,
    righteous home,
    hope of their fathers.[a]

8   《 Oh! 》[a] wander from the midst of Babylon,
    and from the land of the Chaldeans [b]go
    out,[b]
      and be like he-goats before the flock.

Text

50:1a—a   *G* reads "The word of Yahweh that he spoke"
(דְּבַר יהוה אֲשֶׁר דִּבֶּר); either reading may be original.

b   The bracketed words are an expansion missing in
G; so Janzen, pp. 60, 112–14, against Rudolph and
Bright, who maintain that *G* is a shortened version.

c   Many MSS. and *V*, *S*, and *T* read "and against."

2a   The bracketed words are missing in *G*; "raise a
signal" is an expansion from 4:6, and "announce" is
dittographic.

b—b   The bracketed words are not in *G* and represent
an extension of the original words in a conflate text.
G evidently originally read בֵּל חַת as בָּל חָת, "not
panicked," thus ἡ ἀπτόητος, "fearless," and guessed
at a meaning for מרדך (ἡ τρυφερά, "luxurious"); the
present text of *G* thus represents a conflate text,
corrected to *M*. See Janzen, p. 20.

c   Though the Akkadian vocalization is *marduk*, the
vocalization in *M* is מְרֹדָךְ (compare *KJV* "Mero-
dach"). It has been speculated that the vowels of אֲדֹנָי
were given to this name (Rudolph cites Felix Perles,
Babylonisch-jüdische Glossen [Berlin: Peyser, 1905] 7,
but I have been unable to verify this reference).

3a   Omit with *G*; an expansion from 9:9 (Janzen, p.
60).

4a   These words add nothing to the poem; compare v
20.

b   Omit with *G*, though it is to be noted that 4QJer[b]
here sides with *M* (Janzen, p. 184).

c   These words are superfluous: "Israel" here refers
to the whole community, not the northern kingdom
(Rudolph).

5a—a   Read with *G* וּבָאוּ וְנִלְווּ (so Duhm, Giesebrecht; so
NEB, *NJV*). *M* בֹּאוּ, "come" (imperative), demands
that the following verb be וְנִלְוֶה, "and let us join our-
selves," understanding a quotation (so Cornill, Volz,
Condamin, Rudolph; so Luther, *KJV*, *RSV*, *JB*,
NAB). Bright leaves both options open.

6a   Ketib singular הָיָה, qere' plural הָיוּ; given the
singular צֹאן (collective) and the singular עַמִּי, and the
plural adjective אֹבְדוֹת, either will do.

b—b   Reading qere' שׁוֹבְבוּם (so also *G*, *V*), שׁוּב polel;
ketib שׁוֹבְבִים is an adjective modifying הָרִים: "(to)
faithless (mountains)."

7a   See 8a.

8a   *M* יהוה, "Yahweh," does not belong at the end of v
7 (compare 17:13); the word is omitted by *G*. It is
likely that it is a relic of הוֹי (or even of הוֹי הוֹי),
which dropped out at the beginning of v 8 (so Volz,
Rudolph, Bright); compare Zech 2:10.

b   There are two interlocking problems here. The

9   For I am going to arouse [and bring up]ᵃ
          against Babylon ᵇa great company [*M*:
          a company of great nations,]ᵇ
       from the land of the north 《they will form
          up》ᶜ against her,
       from there she will be captured;
     their arrows are like (those of) a 〈bereav-
          ing〉ᵈ warrior,
       he shall not return empty-handed.
10   And Chaldea shall become loot,
       and all those looting her shall be sated,
                                    [oracle of Yahweh.]ᵃ
11   Though ᵃyou rejoice,ᵃ though ᵇ ᵃyou exult,ᵃ
       plunderers of my possession,
     though ᵃyou friskᵃ 《like calves at pasture》ᶜ
       ᵃand neighᵃ like stallions,
12   your mother is greatly shamed,
       she who bore you abashed:
     〈look: she is〉ᵃ the last of the nations,
       a wilderness, a drought and waste.
13   Because of the fury of Yahweh she shall not
          be inhabited,
       and she shall become a desolation, all of
          her,
     everyone passing by Babylon will be horri-
          fied
       and will hiss at all her blows.
14   Form up against Babylon (all) around,
       all (you) who draw the bow,
          shootᵃ at her,
       do not spare any arrow,
     [for against Yahweh she has sinned.]ᵇ
15   Shout against her [(all) around,]ᵃ

first is that the ketib reads יָצְאוּ, "they have gone
out," or יֵצְאוּ, "they will go out," a reading that does
not fit the context, whereas the qere' reads צְאוּ
(imperative pausal); the qere' is the reading followed
by *V*, *S*, and *T*, and *G* reads וּצְאוּ. The second is that
there is uncertainty where the third colon begins:
Volz and Rudolph end the second colon at "the
Chaldeans," reading "go out and be" at the beginning of the third colon, as seems to be indicated by
G.

9a   Omit with *G* (so Rudolph); *M* conflates synony-
       mous variants—for מַעֲלֶה see 33:6 (Janzen, p. 20).

b—b   *G* reads "companies of nations" (קְהָלֵי גוֹיִם),
       whereas *M* reads קְהַל־גּוֹיִם גְּדֹלִים. Janzen assumes
       that גְּדֹלִים is a gloss (p. 60), but the situation is
       probably more complicated than that. See Inter-
       pretation.

c   The reading of *M*, וְעָרְכוּ, and the Masoretic
       punctuation assume that "from the land of the
       north" is taken with what precedes; but "from there"
       suggests that "from the land of the north" begins the
       parallel colon. Read יַעַרְכוּ, matching the imperfect
       of תִּלָּכֵד (so Rudolph).

d   The Masoretic punctuation of this word is מַשְׁכִּיל,
       the hip'il participle of שׁכל, "be bereft of one's child
       or children." The hip'il is cited only once otherwise,
       Hos 9:14, of a "miscarrying" womb. If the connec-
       tion with this root is intended, then, it is likely to be
       the pi'el participle מְשַׁכֵּל: the pi'el does mean "make
       someone childless" and occurs in 15:7. The reading
       with šin is followed by many MSS., by α', and by *V*
       and *T*; the reading מַשְׂכִּיל, "successful," is offered by
       some MSS. and followed by *G*, s', and *S*. One
       suspects that the reading with šin is the *lectio dif-
       ficilior*.

10a   Omit with *G*.

11a—a All four of these verbs have a ketib in the
       feminine singular and a qere' in the masculine
       plural. The plural שֹׁסֵי "plunderers of" indicates that
       the qere' is correct (and compare the plural suffixes
       in v 12).

b   Many MSS., *S*, and the codex Reuchlinianus of *T*
       read וְכִי, "and though," here (and this reading is also
       implied by *G*).

c   Read כְּעֵגֶל בַּדֶּשֶׁא with *G* or כְּעֶגְלֵי בַדֶּשֶׁא, "like a
       calf in the grass," with *V*; *M* כְּעֶגְלָה דָשָׁה, "like a
       threshing heifer."

12a   *M* has הִנֵּה, literally "look," a word omitted in *G*.
       Rudolph suggests reading הִיא to make a nominal
       clause; but I would propose to vocalize the conso-
       nants as הִנָּה (a form that one might expect, though
       it is otherwise unattested). The suggestion may gain
       slightly with the occurrence of כָּלָה in v 13.

14a   *M* reads יִדְרוּ (ידה qal), whereas a few MSS. read יְרוּ
       (ירה qal); both verbs have a virtually identical
       meaning.

b   Omit with *G* and *S* (so Giesebrecht, Cornill, Volz,
       Rudolph, Bright).

15a   Omit with *G*; the word is dittographic from v 14.

> [b]her hand ⟨has been offered,⟩[b]
> [c]her towers[c] have fallen,
>   her walls have been destroyed;
> [for that is the retribution of Yahweh,][d]
> gain satisfaction against her,
>   as she has done, do to her!

16 [a]Cut off[a] the sower from Babylon,
>   and him who wields the sickle at time of
>   harvest;
> from the presence of ⟨the devastation of⟩[b]
>   her who oppresses
>   let each return to his own people,
>   and let each flee to his own land.

17 A stray ewe-lamb is Israel,
>   lions have chased (her).
> [The first one devoured him—the king of
> Assyria, and this, the last one, gnawed his
> bones—{Nebuchadrezzar}[b] the king of
> Babylon. 18/ Therefore thus Yahweh {of
> hosts, God of Israel}[c] has said: I am going to
> punish the king of Babylon and his land as I
> punished the king of Assyria.][a]

19 But I shall bring back Israel to his pasture,
>   and he shall graze Carmel [and Bashan,][a]
> and on Mount Ephraim and Gilead
>   he shall eat his fill.

20 [In those days and at that time, {oracle of
> Yahweh,}[b]][a]
>   the guilt of Israel will be sought for, but
>   there is none,
>   and the sins of Judah, but they will not be
>   found,
>   for I shall forgive those I have spared.

21 [a]⟨Go up (against) the land of⟩ Merathaim,[a]
>   go up against her,
> and against the inhabitants of Pekod,
>   ⟪pursue⟫[b] ⟪after them!⟫[c]
> Slay and devote to destruction [. . . ,][c]
>   oracle of Yahweh,
>   and do all I have commanded you.

22 The sound of battle in the land,
>   and great collapse!

23 How cut down and broken is the sledge-
>   hammer of all the earth,
>   how Babylon has become a desolation
>   among the nations!

24 ⟨You set a snare⟩[a] for yourself and then
>   were captured,
>   [Babylon,][b] but you yourself did not know;
> you were found and then seized,
>   because you challenged Yahweh.

25 Yahweh has opened his storehouse,
>   and brought forth the weapons of his fury,
> for there is [M: this is][a] work for the Lord
>   Yahweh [of hosts][a]
>   in the land of the Chaldeans.

b—b Reading נְתָנָה יָדָהּ for M נָתְנָה יָדָהּ, "she has offered
her hand." M is an acceptable reading, but because
the next two cola have "her X" as subject (compare
the rendering of G, "her hands are weakened"), the
revocalization to a niphʿal (passive) is appropriate.

c—c Read the qere' אֶשְׁוִיֹתֶיהָ; the ketib אשׁויתיה is
unintelligible, a copyist's error.

d Though this clause is conceivably original as a
summary appraisal (see Form), it is unlikely to be,
given the rhetoric of the rest of vv 14–16. It is
perhaps a gloss modeled on 51:6. Duhm and Cornill
retain the כִּי clause and excise "gain satisfaction
against her"!

16a—a The qal כָּרְתוּ is possible (11:19), but the hipʿil
הַכְרִתוּ is suggested by Rudolph as more idiomatic;
the he could have dropped out by haplography.

b Vocalizing חֹרֶב; see Interpretation, and compare
46:16.

17–18a This is a prose addition (so Rudolph).

b Omit with G.

c Omit with G.

19a Omit with G: the fact that the fourth colon of the
verse has two words suggests that only two words
are original here.

20a These words add nothing to the poem; compare v
4.

b Omit with G.

21a—a M reads "On the land, Merathaim," but one
needs a verb. S reads "go up [plural] against a
stubborn land," a reading at least implying the verb
עֲלוּ in first position. The simplest solution is to
revocalize to עֲלֵה אֶרֶץ (so Rudolph, Bright).

b, c The present position of אַחֲרֵיהֶם (after "devote to
destruction") makes little sense, and G omits the
word. In the meantime there is at least the possibility that a two-word colon dropped out after
"Pekod." I propose then (with Rudolph) to reconstruct that colon as רְדֹף אַחֲרֵיהֶם. These words would
have dropped out by haplography (פְּקוֹד has a pe,
like *רְדֹף; אַחֲרֵיהֶם has ḥet-reš like חָרֵם and וַהַחֲרֵם)
and אַחֲרֵיהֶם restored at the wrong point.

24a The verb יָקֹשְׁתִּי is vocalized as a first person
singular, and this is possible; but the remainder of
the verbs in the verse are second-person singular
feminine, and it is altogether likely that this verb is
the archaic second singular feminine and therefore
to be vocalized as יָקֹשְׁתִּי (see 2:19, 20, 33); see
further Structure, Form, Setting, 50:22–34. So
Cornill, Rudolph, Bright; so NEB, NAB.

b The placement of this vocative is wrong: a vocative made up of a construct chain may fill the second
colon (46:19; 48:18, and often), but a single word
normally occurs as the second element in a colon
(49:3). This vocative has either fallen out after לָךְ
and has been replaced wrongly, or more probably is
to be omitted as a gloss (so Duhm, Giesebrecht,
Cornill, Volz; so JB).

25a Omit הִיא and צְבָאוֹת with G (so Duhm, Cornill,
Rudolph, Bright); for the latter word see also
Janzen, pp. 79, 81.

26	Come in to her ^afrom every side,^a
	  open her granaries,
	pile her up 《in》^b heaps and devote her to
	   destruction,
	  let her have no remnant;

27	Slay all her bulls,
	  let them go down to slaughter;
	alas for them!
	  for their day has come,
	    the time of their punishment.

26 Come in to her ^afrom every side,^a
  open her granaries,
pile her up 《in》^b heaps and devote her to
   destruction,
  let her have no remnant;

27 Slay all her bulls,
  let them go down to slaughter;
alas for them!
  for their day has come,
    the time of their punishment.

28 The sound of those in flight and fugitives
    from the land of Babylon,
  to tell to Zion the retribution of Yahweh
    [our God,]^a
  [retribution for his temple.]^b

29 Summon against Babylon 〈archers,〉^a
  those who draw the bow,
encamp against her (all) around,
  let there be ^bto her^b no escape,
recompense her according to her deed,
  [according to everything she has done, do to
    her,]^c
  for against Yahweh she has been arro-
    gant,
  [against the holy one of Israel.]^d

30 [Therefore her youth shall fall in her
    squares,
  and all her warriors shall perish {on that
    day,}^b
                    oracle of Yahweh.]^a

31 I declare myself against you, Sir Arrogance,
    oracle of [the Lord]^a Yahweh [of hosts,]^a
  for your day has come,
    the time ^bwhen I punish you.^b

32 Sir Arrogance will stumble and fall,
    with none to set him up,
  and I shall set fire to his cities,
    and it shall consume all ^ahis surround-
      ings.^a

33 Thus Yahweh [of hosts]^a has said:
Oppressed are the children of Israel,
    and the children of Judah together;
all who take them captive have held them
    fast,
  they refuse to let them go.

34 ^aBut their redeemer^a is strong,
    Yahweh of hosts is his name,
he will indeed^b pursue their case,
  so as to 〈give rest〉^c to all the earth,
    〈and shake〉^c the inhabitants of Babylon.

35 A sword on Chaldea,
                    [oracle of Yahweh,]^a
  and on the inhabitants of Babylon,
    and on her officials and her wise men!

36 A sword on 《her diviners,》^a that they may
    prove foolish,
  a sword on her warriors, that they may be
    panicked!

37 A sword [on his horses and on his chariots
    and]^a on [all]^b the rabble [who are]^c in
    her midst, that they may become
    women!
  A sword on her treasuries, that they may be
    plundered!

38 A drought on her waters, that they may dry
    up!

394

26a—a The meaning of מִקֵּץ is uncertain. "From every side" is the meaning of מִקָּצֶה (Gen 19:4, compare Jer 51:31); the present text may have omitted a he, or else מִקֵּץ may carry this meaning here.

b For כְּמוֹ read בְּמוֹ with V (so Rudolph, and so evidently Bright).

28a Omit as an expansion: אֱלֹהֵינוּ does not fit the diction (compare Volz), and in 37:3 and 42:20 it is an expansion omitted by G (see Janzen, pp. 80–81).

b Omit with G (so Rudolph; so Janzen, p. 60).

29a Vocalizing רֹבִים for M רַבִּים, "many."

b—b Read לָהּ with many MSS., the Versions, and qere'; ketib omits the expression.

c These words, with the addition of the prosaic כָּל־, are an expansion from v 15; the two cola of v 15b are expressed here by "recompense her according to her deed."

d "Holy one of Israel" does not otherwise appear in Jer, but is a stock phrase in Isaiah; it is surely a late gloss here. For a synonymous כִּי-clause as the last colon of a verse see v 24.

30a This verse duplicates 49:26 and interrupts the continuity here (v 29, זָדָה; vv 31 and 32, זָדוֹן).

b This is a later addition, lacking in G.

31a Omit both expressions with G.

b—b For פְּקַדְתִּיךְ a few MSS. and the Versions read פְּקֻדָּתֶךָ, "of your punishment."

32a—a For סְבִיבֹתָיו a few MSS. read סְבִיבָיו, as is M for 21:14. The meaning is unaffected.

33a Omit with G.

34a—a Read וְגָאַלָם with G (so also Rudolph).

b For an infinitive absolute one would expect רוֹב, רִיב being the infinitive construct. Perhaps it is a slip of the pen. See GKC, sec. 73d.

c Rather than the two perfect verbs, vocalize as infinitives, הַרְגִּיעַ and הַרְגִּיז (so Rudolph in BHS); or assume irregular infinitives (GKC, sec. 53l).

35a A later addition, omitted in G.

36a Read בַּדֶּיהָ in consistency with the other nouns in the poem (Rudolph). It may be surmised that a he was misread as mem, and the article added later. But some scholars believe בָּרֶיהָ should be read: see Interpretation.

37a These two terms are later additions from 51:21, given their suffixes: "horses" and "chariots" do not "become women" (so also Volz, Rudolph, Bright).

b Omit with G.

c The אֲשֶׁר is probably a prose addition.

for it is a land of idols,
and with terrors ᵃthey run wild.ᵃ

39 [Therefore goblins shall live with ghouls,
and ostriches shall live in her;
she shall continue uninhabited without end,
⟨she shall not dwell for ever and ever,⟩ᵇ

40 like God's overthrow of Sodom and
Gomorrah and her neighbors,
oracle of Yahweh,
no one shall live there,
and no human being shall sojourn in
her.]ᵃ

41 [See, a people is coming from the north,
and a great nation ⟨and many kings⟩ᵇ are
aroused from the extremes of the
earth;

42 bow and spear they grip,
they are cruel and show no mercy,
their sound roars like the sea,
and on horses they ride,
drawn up for battle like footsoldiers
against you, fair Babylon!

43 The king of Babylon has heard a rumor of
them,
and his hands have fallen slack,
misery has gripped him,
writhing like a woman in labor.]ᵃ

44 [See, like a lion (that) comes up
from the thicket of the Jordan to the
perennial pasture,
indeed I shall suddenly ⟪chase her sucklings,⟫ᵇ
⟨and the choicest of her rams⟩ᶜ I will single
out.
For who is like me?
and who can summon me?
and what shepherd can stand before
me?

45 Therefore hear the counsel of Yahweh that
he has counseled against Babylon,
and his plans that he has planned against
ᵈthe land ofᵈ the Chaldeans:
surely the shepherd boys shall drag them
off,
surely the pasture shall horrify ⟨their
sucklings.⟩ᵉ

46 At the shout "Babylon is seized!"
the earth quakes;
and a cry among the nations is heard.]ᵃ

51

1 Thus Yahweh has said:
I am going to arouse [against Babylon and]ᵃ
against [the inhabitants of]ᵇ ⟪Chal-
dea⟫ᶜ a destructive wind,

38a—a For יִתְהֹלָלוּ two MSS. and the Versions read
יִתְהַלְלוּ, "they boast (in terrors)."

39–40a These two verses are a rearrangement of
material in Isa 13:19–22 and Jer 49:18 (it is to be
noted that Isa 13:19b resembles Jer 49:18a), and
one must judge the two verses here to be an addition to vv 35–38 (see Structure, Form, Setting,
50:33–45; see further Janzen, pp. 60–61).

b This colon is missing in *G* and is identical with Isa
13:20aβ. Its use here is triggered by the likeness of
v 39bβ with Isa 13:20aα. Conceivably the colon was
added along with the previous three cola, so that *G*
is defective by haplography, but the solution here is
preferable: it explains the triple use of ישׁב in the
first three cola of v 39.

41–43a This material is taken from 6:22–24. In the
first two verses "fair Zion" has been shifted to "fair
Babylon," and in the last verse the first-person plural
has been shifted to third-person singular with "the
king of Babylon" the subject; other changes are
minimal. See Structure, Form, Setting, *Preliminary
Observations*, and *Authentic and Unauthentic Material in
50:2—51:19*.

b This expansion is not in 6:22: it was either added
at the time these verses were adapted for use here
or else added later.

44–46a These verses are a secondary adaptation of
49:19–21. Aside from the presence or absence of
matres lectionis and the secondary addition of קוֹלָה at
the end of 49:21, an addition that consequently
produces the nonpausal form נִשְׁמָע, the contrasts are
follows: 49:19 אֲרִיצֵם, 50:44 qere' אֲרִיצֵם; 49:20
אֶרֶץ כַּשְׂדִּים, 50:45 אֱדוֹם; יֹשְׁבֵי תֵימָן 49:20, 50:45 בָּבֶל;
נִתְּפְשָׂה 49:20, 50:46 נִמְלָם; נָוֶה 49:21, 50:45 נָוֵה;
וּזְעָקָה בַּגּוֹיִם 49:21 צַעֲקָה בְּיַם־סוּף 50:46 בְּכֹל. See the
discussion in Structure, Form, Setting, *Authentic and
Unauthentic Material in 50:2—51:19*.

b See 49:19, note a. Here the he of the reconstructed אֲרִיצָה was misread as mem.

c See 49:19, note b.

d—d For אֶרֶץ some MSS. and *G* read יֹשְׁבֵי, "the
inhabitants of," as does 49:20.

e See 49:20, note a.

51:1a These words are secondary (so also Volz and
Rudolph). There are two considerations. (1) The
colon is limited to five "units" (that is, words—see
O'Connor, *Structure*, 75), and the pattern is that of
6:22; 50:9. (2) If "to Babylon" is original in the
second colon, it is likely to be secondary here, given
the parallel of "Babylon" and "Chaldea" elsewhere in
these chapters (compare vv 24, 35).

b יֹשְׁבֵי is metrically superfluous (compare note a).

c *M* reads לֵב קָמָי, an "athbash" cipher for כַּשְׂדִּים
"Chaldea(ns)": compare 25:25, Text note c, and see
Bleddyn J. Roberts, "Athbash," *IDB* 1:306–307.
Since *G* has "Chaldea" here, not a transliteration of
the cipher, and since *G* is not likely to have been
able to interpret the cipher, the cipher was doubtless
a late, secondary development (so also Janzen, p.

⟨and I shall send⟩[a] to Babylon ⟨win-
nowers⟩[b] and they shall winnow
her,
  so that they lay waste her land,
for they have closed in around her
  on the day of disaster.

3 Let ⟨not⟩[a] [b]⟨her bowman⟩ [. . .] draw [. . .][b]
his bow,
  and let him ⟨not⟩[a] raise himself up in his
  coat of mail,
do not spare her youths,
  devote her whole army to destruction.

4 The slain shall fall in the land of the Chaldeans,
  and the wounded in her streets,

5b [a] for their land is full of guilt [against the
holy one of Israel,][b, a]

5a but Israel is not widowed [nor Judah][c] of
his God [Yahweh of hosts.][d]

6 Flee from the midst of Babylon,
  and escape, each for his life,
  do not perish in her punishment,
for it is a time of retribution for Yahweh,
  it is the requital (with which) he recom-
  penses her.

7 Babylon is a golden cup [in the hand of
Yahweh,][a]
  making all the earth drunken,
  from her wine the nations drank,
  that is why they [*M*: the nations][b]
  went mad.

8 "Suddenly Babylon has fallen and is
broken!"
  wail over her,
obtain balm for her pain,
  perhaps she shall be healed!

9 "We treated Babylon, but she was untreatable;
  [a]abandon her[a] and let us go ⟩each to his
  land,⟨[b]
for her judgment has touched the heavens
  and is exalted to the clouds.

10 Yahweh has brought forth ⟨our righteousness:⟩[a]

230, n. 3): there is another secondary athbash in v
41.

2a *M* reads וְשִׁלַּחְתִּי, "and I shall send away." A
parallel elsewhere in this pattern reads the qal
(16:16), and I therefore propose that the verb
should be vocalized וְשָׁלַחְתִּי.

b For זָרִים, "strangers," read זֹרִים with α', σ', and *V*.

3a To both the verb יִדְרֹךְ and the verb יִתְעַל *M*
prefixes אֶל־ "(un)to," an expression that makes no
sense in these two instances. *G* omits the expression
in both cases; some MS. traditions of *G* read אֵלֶיהָ,
"unto her," that is, "against her"; some MSS. and *V*,
S, and *T* read אַל־, thus "let not the bowman [so the
subject in *M*] draw his bow," "let him not draw
himself up in his armor." If the bowman is attacking
Babylon, then a negative is wrong (so *G*); if the
bowman is Babylonian, then a negative is called for
(so *V*, *S*, and *T*). I argue that "the bowman" must be
read as "her bowman" and so is Babylonian (see note
b—b, and see in detail Interpretation). In this case
the reading אַל־ is an effort to annul the negations.

b—b The ketib repeats the verb יִדְרֹךְ; the qere' omits
the repetition, as do many MSS. and the Versions.
The context demands "her bowman," דֹּרְכָהּ (see
Interpretation). The present text of *M* has suffered
dittography.

5a—a I place v 5b before v 5a with Cornill, Condamin,
Rudolph: "guilt" refers to Babylon (compare "her
iniquity" in v 6). If v 5b were to come after v 5a,
and "their land" refers to Israel, then the clause
must be translated "though their land was filled with
guilt" or the like (Bright; *KJV*). If v 5b was originally
before v 5a, one assumes that v 5b was omitted by
haplography with כִּי and subsequently replaced in
the wrong position.

b I excise this expression, which is part of the
vocabulary of Isaiah (compare 50:29, note d). It may
be pointed out that in 23:10aα אֶרֶץ and מָלְאָה
likewise appear in a colon of three units.

c I excise "and Judah": "his God" suggests a singular
subject (and compare 50:4).

d These designations are doubtless expansions.

7a Delete with Duhm, Giesebrecht, Cornill, Rudolph;
the passage is a description of the downfall of
Babylon ("requital," v 6), so a punishment by
Yahweh is not at issue. The phrase is derived from
25:15. For a similar colon see 12:8bβ.

b Omit with *G*.

9a It is possible that the verb was originally נַעַזְבֶנָּה or
נַעַזְבָהּ, "let us abandon her," as *G*, *V*, and *S* read it:
compare the diction of 9:1. On the other hand, v
10bα has an imperative followed by a cohortative,
perhaps parallel to the sequence here.

b These words add little to the colon and are
unlikely if vv 9–10 are a quotation of Israel (see
Form). They are likely to be an expansion from
50:16; Volz omits them, and Cornill suggests it, or
at least suggests omitting אִישׁ and reading אַרְצֵנוּ.

10a Read with *S* צִדְקָתֵנוּ; *M* reads the plural צִדְקֹתֵינוּ,

come, 〈let us tell it〉[b] in Zion,
  the deed of Yahweh our God."

11 Sharpen the arrows,
  fill the quivers,
[Yahweh has aroused the spirit of 〈the king of〉[b] the Medes, for against Babylon is his decision, to destroy it: that is the retribution of Yahweh, the retribution of his temple.][a]

12 Against the walls of Babylon raise a signal,
  strengthen the watch,
    set up sentries,
      prepare those in ambush,
        for Yahweh has both decided and done (it),
      [what he has spoken against the inhabitants of Babylon.][a]

13 [a]You who dwell[a] by many waters,
  great in treasures,
  your end has come,
    the extent of your share.

14 [Yahweh of hosts has sworn by himself,][a]
for 《 surely 》[b] [c]I have filled you[c] with people like locusts,
  and they shall utter against you a shout.

15 [《 Yahweh 》[b] is the maker of the earth by his power,
    the establisher of the world by his wisdom,
      and by his understanding he stretched out the heavens.

16 《 At his voice is poured out 》[c] an uproar of waters in the heavens,
  [d]and he has made[d] mists [d]rise[d] from the ends of [e]the earth,[e]
    lightning-bolts for the rain he has made,
    and has brought forth the wind from his storehouses.

17 Every person is too stupid to know,
  every smith is put to shame by (his) idol,
    for his (molten) image is falsehood,
      there is no breath in them.

18 They are a nothing,
  a work of mockery,
    at the time of their punishment they shall perish.

19 Not like these is the portion of Jacob,
  for he forms everything,
    and [f]Israel is[f] the tribe of his possession,
    Yahweh [g]of hosts[g] is his name.][a]

20 You are a mace to me,
  〈a weapon of〉[a] war:
and I shall smash with you nations,
  and I shall destroy with you kingdoms,

21 and I shall smash with you horse and his rider,
  and I shall smash with you chariot and 〈its charioteer,〉[a]

22 and I shall smash with you husband and wife,
  and I shall smash with you elder and youngster,
    and I shall smash with you youth and maiden,

23 and I shall smash with you shepherd and his flock,

whereas *G* reads צִדְקָתוֹ, "his righteousness."

b Vocalize וּנְסַפְּרָה, to include the object within the colon.

11a This prose section is secondary: v 11aα leads directly into v 12; so also Volz, Rudolph, Bright. For v 11aβ compare Isa 13:17; for v 11b see 50:15, 28.

b Read מֶלֶךְ with *G* and *S*; *M* "the kings of."

12a Prosaic gloss.

13a—a The qere'/ketib contrast is similar to that in 10:17 and 22:23. The ketib is the archaic perfect second-person singular feminine, שָׁכַנְתִּי, "you have dwelt" (compare 2:19); the qere' should be read, a feminine singular participle, vocalized here שֹׁכַנְתְּ, but this may itself be a mixed form between the perfect and a participle שֹׁכֶנֶת: see GKC, sec. 90n.

14a These words are a gloss taken from Amos 6:8: כִּי־אִם־ by itself introduces an oath (so also Volz).

b I accept the suggestion to read אִם־לֹא (compare Rudolph): the sequence כִּיאִמְלֹאמִלֵּת would have become deficient by haplography. For an interpretation without inserting לֹא see GKC, sec. 163d.

c—c It is tempting to suggest reading מֻלֵּאתִי, the archaic second-person singular feminine, "you have been filled" (for the archaic form compare the ketib in v 13), and to assume that when the form was reconstrued as a first-person singular (pi'el) the suffix was added on the verb (so a suggestion of Rudolph). This suggestion is more plausible if the first clause of the verse was added secondarily (see note a).

15—19a This passage reproduces 10:12–16 and is secondary here.

b See 10:12, note a.

c See 10:13, note a.

d—d For וַיַּעֲלֶה in 10:13 the present passage has וַיַּעַל; the meaning is unaffected.

e—e The present passage follows the ketib in 10:13: see note b—b there.

f—f So read with 10:16 and with many MSS., *V*, and *T*; *M* lacks יִשְׂרָאֵל. Compare 10:16, note a—a.

g—g *G* omits the expression; compare 10:16, note b—b.

20a Vocalize כְּלִי with Duhm, Giesebrecht, Condamin, Rudolph; *M* כְּלֵי, "weapons of."

21a Vocalize וְרַכָּבוֹ with Duhm, Cornill, Volz, Rudolph, Bright; *M* וְרֹכְבוֹ, "and its rider."

and I shall smash with you farmer and his
    team,
and I shall smash with you governors
    and prefects.

24 And I shall recompense Babylon
and all the inhabitants of Chaldea
    [for all their evil that they have done on
    Zion before you, oracle of Yahweh.]ᵃ

25 I declare myself against you, Mount of
《 (Sesame-)oil, 》ᵃ
    [oracle of Yahweh,]ᵇ
[the destroyer of all the earth,]ᶜ
and I shall stretch out my hand against
    you and roll (the wheel) over you
    [down the rocks,]ᵈ
and I shall make you a Mount of Burnt
    Bricks.

26 They shall not take from you a stone for a
    corner,
nor a stone for a foundation,
    for you shall be ⟨a desolation⟩ᵃ for ever,
        oracle of Yahweh.

27 Raise a signal in the land,
sound the trumpet among the nations,
prepare nations against her,
summon against her kingdoms,
[Ararat, Minni and Ashkenaz,]ᵃ
appoint against her a marshal,
bring up horses like bristling
    locusts.

28 [Prepare nations against her, ⟨the king of⟩ᵇ the
Medes 《 and of the whole earth 》ᶜ and 《 his
governors 》ᵈ and all 《 his prefects 》ᵈ {M: and
all the land of}ᶜ {his authority.}ᵉ] ᵃ

29 The earth will quake and writhe,
for ᵃthe plan ofᵃ Yahweh has arisen
    against Babylon,
to make the land of Babylon a deso-
    lation,
without inhabitant.

30 The warriors of Babylon have stopped
    fighting,
they sit in (their) strongholds,
their strength is dried up,
they have become women;
her dwellings ⟨are burned,⟩ᵃ
her bars are broken.

31 Runner runs to meet runner,
courier to meet courier,
to tell the king of Babylon

32 that his city is captured from every side,
and the fords have been seized,
her marsh-reeds they have burned with
    fire,
and the soldiers are terrified.

33 For thus Yahweh [of hosts, the God of
    Israel]ᵃ has said:
Fair Babylon is like a threshing-floor (at) the
    time of ⟨her treading:⟩ᵇ
in a little while [the time of]ᶜ (her) harvest
    ᶜwill have comeᶜ to her.

34 ["Nebuchadrezzar]ᵃ the king of Babylon

24a Volz deletes the whole verse as a secondary
addition; but the verb וְשִׁלַּמְתִּי and what immediately
follows it closes the poem just as חֶרֶב does in 50:38
after the series of occurrences of חֶרֶב in 50:35–37.
The remainder of the verse is a prose addition: the
shift of address from masculine singular in vv 20–23
to masculine plural is dubious.

25a For M הַמַּשְׁחִית, "Destruction" (or "the Destroyer")
read הַמִּשְׁחָה, "Oil" or "Anointing"; הַר הַמִּשְׁחָה was a
name given to the Mount of Olives, displaced to
"Mount of Destruction" (see the commentaries on
2 Kgs 23:13). The name is here applied to Babylon
(see further Interpretation).

b Omit with G.

c This is an addition to explain the reference of
הַמַּשְׁחִית; Volz and Rudolph also delete the phrase
(see further Interpretation).

d A glossator evidently understood וְגִלְגַּלְתִּיךָ to
mean "and I shall roll you down (the crags)";
Rudolph likewise deletes the phrase (see further
Interpretation).

26a Read שְׁמָמַת with G, V, S, T; M reads שְׁמָמוֹת,
"desolations."

27a The names of these nations break the poetic unity
(compare vv 11, 28); so also Volz, Rudolph.

28a The verse begins with a dittograph from v 27 and
continues with a gloss derived in part from the end
of v 23. The last phrase may have been added still
later. So also Volz, Rudolph, and Bright.

b Read מֶלֶךְ with G and S; M "the kings of." Compare v 11, note b.

c Read "and of all the earth" after "the Medes" with
G; in the text tradition antecedent to M the phrase
evidently fell out and was restored in the wrong
position. See Janzen, p. 62.

d Reading masculine suffixes in these expressions
with G and S for the feminine ones in M; M evidently shifted them to refer to "the earth/land"
when that phrase was wrongly reinserted.

e Omit with G, a late addition: see Janzen, p. 62.

29a—a Read מַחְשֶׁבֶת with some MSS., G, V, and S; M
מַחְשְׁבוֹת, "the plans of." Because of this plural
subject the Oriental qere' reads the verb as the
plural קָמוּ.

30a For the hip'il הִצִּיתוּ, "they have burned," read
with G, V, and T the hop'al הֻצְּתוּ. The reading of M
necessitates a dubious change of subject. Giesebrecht and Cornill likewise suggest the revocalization to the
hop'al but hesitate because that stem of יצת is
otherwise unattested. Duhm emends to the nip'al
נִצְּתוּ, but it is better to preserve the he.

33a Omit with G.

b Vocalizing הַדְרִיכָהּ, infinitive construct; M (at the
time) "(when) one has trodden her," perfect.

c Omit "the time of" with G and S (the word is an
expansion from 50:16); thus read the verb וּבָא for M
וּבָאָה.

34a Omit this name, which overloads the line (so
Cornill, Volz, Condamin, Rudolph).

[. . .]b chas discomfited me,c
chas set mec an empty vessel,
《 has eaten me, 》b,c chas swallowed mec
like a monster,
has filled his belly ⟨ with my deli-
cacies,⟩d [⟨ has driven me
out."⟩]e, c

35 "The violence 《 and destruction 》a done to
me be upon Babylon,"
let enthroned Zion say,
and "my blood be upon the inhabitants
of Chaldea,"
let Jerusalem say.

36 Therefore thus Yahweh has said:
I am going to pursue your case,
and I shall bring your retribution,
and I shall dry up her sea,
and make her source run dry,

37 and Babylon shall become [stone-heaps, a
lair of jackals,]a a desolation [and a
hissing,]b
without inhabitant.

38 ⟨ They shall be quick⟩a like lions [they shall
roar,]b
⟨ they are aroused⟩c like lionesses' cubs.d

39 When they are hot I shall set out their feast,
and I shall make them drunk so that 《 they
faint, 》a

40 《 I shall bring them down like lambs for the
slaughter,
like rams with he-goats, 》b

(39) and they shall sleep an everlasting sleep
and not wake up,
oracle of Yahweh.
[40 . . .]b

41 How the renown of all the earth ["She-
shach"]a is captured and seized,
how Babylon has become a desolation
among the nations!

42 The sea has come up against Babylon,
she is covered with the tumult of its
waves.

43 Her cities have become [a desolation,]a a
land of drought and waste,
[a land]b there does not dwell in them
⟨any⟨c man,
nor does a human being cross in them.

44 And I shall punish Bel in Babylon,
and I shall make him disgorge what he
swallowed from his mouth;
no longer shall the nations stream to
him,
even the wall of Babylon has fallen!

45 [Go out from her midst, my people,
and escape, each for his life,
from the fierce anger of Yahweh.]a

46 [And beware of being faint-hearted or fearful
at the rumors heard in the land, and
《 when 》b a rumor comesb in one year and

b Move the verb "has eaten me" to the third colon
with Cornill; having dropped out, the verb was
evidently reinserted before the wrong companion.

c—c The ketib of all five verbs reads the first-person
plural suffix ("us"); read with a few MSS., the qere',
and the Versions אֲכָלַנִי, etc.

d For M מַעֲדָנָי, "with my pleasures," read מַעֲדָנָי.

e This verb is evidently a gloss (see Interpretation);
probably read with G the common נדח hip'il, "has
driven me out" (הִדִּיחַנִי), rather than M "has washed
me away" (דוח hip'il).

35a Read וְשׁוֹדִי (compare G, who reads this lexeme but
reads the plurals of both nouns); for the pairing of
חָמָס and שֹׁד see 6:7; 20:8; Ezek 45:9; Isa 60:18;
Amos 3:10; Hab 1:3. M "and my flesh" does not fit
the context.

37a Omit with G; the words are an expansion from
9:10 (see Janzen, p. 63).

b Omit with G; the word is an expansion from
18:16; 19:8; and elsewhere (see Janzen, p. 63).

38a Read יַחְדוּ חדד qal imperfect: compare Hab 1:8);
יַחְדָּו, "together," is dubious as first unit in a colon,
where a verb suggests itself.

b Omit with G; the verb was inserted after נערו was
understood as "growl" (see note c) and יחדו was
understood as "together" (see note a).

c Read נֵעֹרוּ עור nip'al: compare 6:22) with G. The
meaning "growl" for נער would appear only here in
the OT.

d Perhaps read גּוּרֵי with a few MSS.; M גּוֹרֵי carries
the same meaning.

39–40a Read יֵעָלָפוּ with G and V (compare S, T; so
Duhm, Giesebrecht, Cornill, Volz, Rudolph). M
יַעֲלֹזוּ, "they rejoice," makes little sense here, though
the interpretation "they become happy (= tipsy)" has
been suggested (so Bright).

b Insert v 40 within v 39 after "so that they faint"
with Rudolph; the sequence makes little sense after
"and not wake up, oracle of Yahweh."

41a M שֵׁשַׁךְ is an "athbash" cipher for בָּבֶל, "Babylon"
(see Roberts, "Athbash"); it is, however, secondary
here and should be omitted with G (see Janzen, p.
230, n. 3).

43a Omit with G; this is an expansion from vv 37, 41
(so Janzen, p. 63).

b Omit with G and S; בָּהֵן refers to "her cities."

c A few MSS. omit כָּל-; it is possible that it is
secondary.

45a The diction of this verse is conventional and to be
judged secondary: the first colon is modeled on Isa
52:11, the second is also found in v 6, and the last
colon is found in 12:13. Though the last colon is
possible in the mouth of Yahweh, it is unlikely here.

46a This verse is prose and to be judged secondary.
The independent clause with פֶּן- is unique in Jer,
and its tone of reassurance suggests a time when bad
news continues to come year after year. See further
Interpretation.

b The masculine וּבָא does not fit the feminine

	another rumor in the next year: "Violence in the land!" or "Ruler against ruler!"][a]
47	[Therefore the time is surely coming, and I shall punish the idols of Babylon, and all her land shall be shamed, and all her slain shall fall in her midst.
48	And heaven and earth and everything in them shall sing over Babylon, for from the north [b]devastators shall come[b] to her, oracle of Yahweh.][a]
49	Babylon 《 shall fall, 》[a] O slain of Israel, as because of Babylon there have fallen the slain of all the earth!
50	Fugitives 〈from her sword, go,〉[a] do not stand still! Remember Yahweh from afar, and let Jerusalem come to your mind:
51	"We are shamed, for we have heard disgrace, dishonor has covered our face, for strangers have come against [a] 《 our sanctuary 》 [M: the sanctuaries of the house of Yahweh."][a]
52	Therefore the time is surely coming, oracle of Yahweh, that I shall punish her idols, and in all her land the slain will groan;
53	though Babylon should go up to the heavens, and though she should put her strong height out of reach, from me devastators shall come upon her, oracle of Yahweh.
54	The sound of a cry from Babylon, and great collapse from the land of Chaldea!—
55	for Yahweh is devastating Babylon, and will wipe out from her a great noise: their waves will roar like many waters, the uproar of their noise 〈is raised;〉[a]
56	[for a devastator has come {against her,}[b] against Babylon,][a] her warriors shall be captured, [c]《 their bow 》〈is shattered,〉[c] for Yahweh is a God of requitals, he shall indeed recompense.
57	[And I shall make drunk her officials, her wise men, her governors and her prefects and her warriors, and they shall sleep an everlasting sleep and not wake up, oracle of the King, Yahweh of hosts is his name.][a]
58	Thus Yahweh [of hosts][a] has said: The broad wall[b] of Babylon shall indeed be demolished, and her high gates shall be burned with fire; "The peoples toil for naught, and the nations 《 wear themselves out 》[c] for fire."

subject; König, *Syntax*, sec. 413g, suggests reading וּבְבֹא, the infinitive, and Giesebrecht and Rudolph follow him in this.

47–48a   These verses are a less convincing doublet of vv 52–53 in a conflate text: compare Janzen, p. 119, and see Structure, Form, Setting, *Authentic and Unauthentic Material in 51:25–58*.

b—b   Read יָבֹאוּ instead of *M* יָבוֹא, and שׁוֹדְדִים instead of *M* הַשּׁוֹדְדִים: so v 53. Volz notes that there are MSS. that read the noun without article here; perhaps the he was repeated by dittography. As to the verb, the reading יָבוֹא is sometimes marked with sebir (a notation analogous to qere': see Christian D. Ginsburg, *Introduction to the Massoretico-Critical Edition of the Hebrew Bible* [London: Trinitarian Bible Society, 1897; rep. New York: Ktav, 1966] 187–96) for יָבֹאוּ, and so also the reading of a few MSS.

49a   For לִנְפֹּל read תִּפֹּל. The syntax of *M*, with ל and the infinitive construct, would be appropriate to late Hebrew (parallels: Esth 7:8; 2 Chr 11:20; 12:12; see Joüon, *Gramm.*, sec. 154d). See further Interpretation.

50a   The form הִלְכוּ is dubious; read מֵחַרְבָּה לְכוּ with Volz and Rudolph (compare Bright).

51a—a   *V* and *S* read "sanctuary" in the singular (and compare *T*); *G* reads "our sanctuaries." Given פָּנֵינוּ in the previous colon, given the fact that the plural of מִקְדָּשׁ does not appear in Jer, and given the occurrence of מִקְדָּשֵׁנוּ in 17:12, the most economical solution is the one proposed.

55a   Vocalize נֹתֵן, participle: it will then be symmetrical in chiastic form with שֹׁדֵד.

56a   This sequence is evidently a variant of or a gloss on v 55aα (so Rudolph).

b   This word is omitted by *G* and *S*; *M* is conflate (see Janzen, p. 20).

c—c   Read חִתְּתָה קַשְׁתָּם with *G* and *V*. In *M* the noun is קַשְּׁתוֹתָם, "their bows"; the verb is חִתְּתָה, pi'el feminine singular (or plural?—see Bauer-Leander, secs. 42o', 58p'), but the pi'el, which is securely cited only once otherwise (Job 7:14), is there transitive, whereas the context here demands an intransitive (but compare GKC, sec. 52k). The simplest solution is to read the noun as singular (so the alternative suggestion of Rudolph) and then to vocalize the verb as a qal feminine singular.

57a   This is a prose addition: the listing comes from 50:35 and 51:23 and v 57b comes from v 39 (so also Volz, Rudolph).

58a   Omit with *G*.

b   Read with many MSS., *G*, and *V* חוֹמַת for *M* חֹמוֹת, "walls of." The adjective is feminine singular; *M* could conceivably be construed as "the walls of broad Babylon," but the verb is singular as well, and the parallel "her high gates" suggests that "broad" modifies "wall." *M* is thus doubtless a slip of the pen.

c—c   Read יִיעָפוּ with *G*, θ', and *S*, and with Hab 2:13; *M* וְיָעֵפוּ, "and they shall wear themselves out."

Structure, Form, Setting

Preliminary Observations. These 104 verses represent (except for chapters 37—44, which total 166 verses) the longest unified sequence of material in the book; but whereas chapters 37—44 are a sequential narrative, the present chapters offer what appears to be utterance after utterance over Babylon. It is clear that whatever original stratum of material lies here has been supplemented and expanded by later hands. For example, in chapter 50 verses 17b–18 are hardly poetry, and the matching of Assyria with Babylon is distracting and surely secondary. Yet one hardly knows where to begin in isolating that original stratum: what is one looking for?—and does it manifest any structure, or is it simply "one thing after another"?

These chapters have been treated in a variety of ways by commentators. Earlier commentators (Duhm, Giese-brecht, Cornill) regarded the sequence as a single oracle, this in spite of repetitions of themes and phraseology. Condamin set forth three full poems (50:2–20; 50:21–46; 51:1–37), and a fourth (51:38–58) that is in some disorder;[1] Volz analyzes the series of poems mostly into strophes in groups of three lines;[2] neither Rudolph nor Bright sees any coherent structure,[3] offering a series of short sections for convenience only (Rudolph, fifteen; Bright, eight). Earlier commentators (Duhm, Giese-brecht, Cornill, Volz) rejected the possibility that any of this material is authentic. Condamin argues that the chapters are genuine, but without dealing with specific passages in great detail.[4] Rudolph rejects any authen-ticity;[5] Bright says cautiously that the majority of the poems are probably anonymous.[6] Their basic arguments rest on whether Jrm can have written this material, given his view that Babylon would fall after seventy years (29:10), and on whether these chapters could have been sunk in the Euphrates in the fourth year of Zedekiah, 594 (51:59–64).[7] Conclusions argued from style and vocabulary have taken second place to these a priori considerations.

It may be useful at this point to offer two examples of what needs to be done. The first part of 50:9 offers material similar to that in 6:22: both have הִנֵּה, but in 50:9 the hip'il of עור occurs in the first colon ("I am arousing"), whereas in 6:22 the nip'al of עור occurs in the second colon ("is aroused"); in 50:9 the object of "arouse" is in the reconstructed text "a great company" (*M*: "a company of great nations"—see the discussion in Inter-pretation), whereas in 6:22 the subject of "is aroused" is "a great nation"; contrariwise "from the land of the north" appears in the first colon in 6:22 and in the second colon in 50:9; furthermore the second colon in 50:9 has "they will form up" (ערך), whereas the same verb appears in 6:23 but in the passive participle. One may go on to examine the second half of 50:9, that "bereave" appears in 15:7 (שכל in both passages, pi'el in 15:7 and probably in 50:9 as well) and that שׁוּב רֵיקָם, "return empty(-handed)," appears in 14:3. On the other hand 50:41–43 is a virtual reproduction of 6:22–24: aside from minor verbal differences 6:22–24 has simply been taken over, with "fair Zion" in 6:23 replaced by "fair Babylon" in 50:42 and the first-person plural forms in 6:24 replaced by "the king of Babylon" and third-person singular masculine forms in 50:43. The contrast in treatment of the raw material of 6:22–24 in the two passages is extreme and leads to the conclusion that 50:9 is part of material genuine to Jrm, whereas 50:41–43 is secondary.

By data to be offered below, it appears that about eighty-two verses or portions of verses are genuine to Jrm. Nothing elsewhere in the book suggests that these eighty-two verses can be one single oracle—such a se-quence is far too long; the material undoubtedly em-bodies several oracles. And if there are several oracles, one assumes that there is some ordering structure to the present sequence.

Though there is no way to determine a setting for these oracles at the beginning of one's investigation, it is clear that one cannot presume an extended span of time

1   Condamin, p. 351.
2   Volz, p. 423.
3   Compare Rudolph, p. 297; Bright, p. 359.
4   Condamin, pp. 354–57.
5   Rudolph, pp. 297–98.
6   Bright, p. 359.
7   See particularly Rudolph, pp. 297–98.

for that setting within which any shift of diction might be detectable: this in contrast to the seventeen-year interval suggested in the present study between the two oracles against Egypt, 46:3–12 and 46:14–24, or the similar span for the proposed three oracles against Moab in chapter 48.

By the same token there appears to be no way to separate the oracles on the basis of a likeness of presumed beginnings or endings. A likeness of presumed beginnings has appeared to work for the material in 4:5–6:30: it is proposed in the present study that bursts of imperatives begin each unit (see 4:5—10:25, Preliminary Observations). There are bursts of such commands in the present chapters (50:2–3, 8, 14–16, 21, 26–27, 29; 51:3, 6, 8, 11–12, 27, and 50), and for chapter 50 at least one might propose beginnings at 50:2, 14, and 26, but such demarcations become arbitrary in chapter 51. Again, one might propose that first-person singular announcements of judgment by Yahweh might mark endings: these are found in 50:9, 19–20, 31–32; 51:1–2, 14, 20–23, 25–26, 39–40, 44, and 53. One might also propose endings in 50:9, 20, and 32, but if the next such first-person sequence, 51:1–2, marks an ending, 51:3 would mark a new beginning, and this is hardly possible, since it gives no immediate antecedent for "her youths" in that verse. Indeed the discrete foreign nations oracles in chapters 46—49 offer a variety of beginnings and endings: as for beginnings, one finds battle orders (46:3; 49:28), a summons to announce (46:14), הִנֵּה followed by a depiction of the coming judgment (47:2), a "woe" oracle (48:1), a mocking rhetorical question (49:1), a mocking depiction of demoralization (49:23), and an announcement of judgment by Yahweh (49:35). And as for endings, one does indeed find first-person announcements of judgment (49:5, 27, 38), but one also finds assurances (by divine heralds?) regarding Yahweh's judgment in the third person (49:20), depictions of the coming judgment (46:12, 24; 49:26) and an apostrophe to Yahweh's sword (47:6–7). Given such variety, there is no way by an a priori determination of form-critical categories to determine the boundaries.

How then to proceed? I see no way to avoid the necessity of working simultaneously with issues of diction, form, and structure, moving from what is plausible to what may be derived from those plausibilities.

Once the unauthentic material is isolated and laid aside, a form-critical analysis of most of the authentic material will be clear: a summons to heralds (50:2), battle orders to the enemies of Babylon (50:14), descriptions of Israel (50:6), mockery addressed to Babylon (50:11), depictions of the ruin of Babylon (50:3), and the like. But one sequence is form-critically puzzling (51:20–24), and the solution to the puzzle will help make clear the general approach of all of 50:2—51:58. Therefore I shall separate unauthentic from authentic material in 50:2—51:19, then deal with 51:20–24 in detail, and then complete the separation of unauthentic from authentic material in 51:25–58.

Authentic and Unauthentic Material in 50:2—51:19. A great deal of the material in 50:1—51:58 is, by the analysis of the present study, authentic to Jrm; the first task is to offer the evidence, tedious though it is.

The diction of 50:2–3 strikes one as appropriate to Jrm: v 2 offers commands to heralds (compare 4:5; 46:13) to proclaim the news of the collapse of Babylon; v 3 offers a כִּי clause giving the basis for these commands, the divine judgment through the coming of a people from the north to destroy Babylon. These verses do not mechanically adapt material from elsewhere but offer a fresh use of phraseology. Thus v 2 resembles 4:16; the mockery of gods is found in 48:7 and (by the reconstruction of the present study) 46:15; the "people from the north" is a constant feature of Jrm's diction as a designation of Babylon itself (most closely, 6:22) and, if it designates Babylon's enemy, its application here carries irony; "make her land a desolation" is found in 2:15, and "no inhabitant in her" is found in a variety of expressions beginning in 2:6.

Verses 4–7 shift the scene—these verses are a prophecy of salvation (*Heilsweissagung*) for Israel[8] in which the promise comes first (vv 4–5) followed by the indication of the situation in the immediate past (vv 6–7). One might assume that these verses are material unrelated to vv 2–3, either a separate oracle parallel with vv 2–3 or a later supplement to vv 2–3: thus Volz brackets all of vv 4–7 as secondary. Against this assumption two observations

---

8   March, "Prophecy," 162.

must be made. First, vv 4–7 (except for the bracketed words in v 4) appear to be authentic to Jrm. Thus "walking and weeping they shall go" (v 4) resembles "with weeping they shall come" in 31:9 in a similar context of the homecoming of Israel. "From mountain to hill" (v 6) resembles 3:23a. And the diction of כָּל־מוֹצְאֵיהֶם אֲכָלוּם, "all who found them ate them" (v 7), is reminiscent of two other passages of Jrm: the first is 2:3, כָּל־אֹכְלָיו יֶאְשָׁמוּ, "All who ate of him were held guilty," particularly when one notes that the following colon here in v 7 reads אָמְרוּ לֹא נֶאְשָׁם, "They have said, 'We are not guilty'"; the second is 30:16, כָּל־אֹכְלַיִךְ יֵאָכֵלוּ, "All who eat of you shall be eaten." (For further observations on these parallels to v 7 see Interpretation.) The date assigned for both 30:16 and 31:9, two of the parallels cited for vv 4–7, is 588–587: the parallels will be discussed again below, *Setting*. The second observation to be made about the authenticity of vv 4–7 is that in vv 14–16 one has a series of battle commands to the enemies of Babylon analogous to the commands to the heralds in v 2 followed in vv 17–20 (less the bracketed material in vv 17b–18) by analogous words about the return of Israel: one notes, for example, "a perishing flock were my people" in v 6 and "a lonely ewe-lamb is Israel" in v 17. Verses 4–7, then, are likely to continue authentic material; and this likelihood is increased if the "people from the north" (v 3) is an ironic designation for Israel (for this identification see below, *51:20–24*).

Evidence has already been offered that 50:9 offers diction appropriate to Jrm (see above, *Preliminary Observations*). In v 10 "Chaldea shall become loot" resembles "Why then has he [Israel] become a victim?" in 2:14 and is even closer to the diction of 49:32, and שבע, "be sated," occurs in a similar context in 46:10.

The parallelism of שמח, "rejoice," and עלז, "exult," in 50:11 is reminiscent of the association of the two roots in 15:16 and 17 (the association is found otherwise only in Zeph 3:14); צהל, "neigh," is found in 5:8. The association of "be ashamed" (בוש) and "be abashed" (חפר) with "bear (a child)" (ילד) in v 12 is likewise found in 15:9, and the association of "wilderness, drought and waste" in v 12 is reminiscent of 2:6. The curious use of לֹא תֵשֵׁב, "[she] is not/shall not be inhabited," in v 13 is also found in 17:6; שְׁמָמָה, "desolation," is a favorite word of Jrm's; and "everyone passing shall be horrified" and "hiss at all her blows" are found in 19:8.

The battle orders of 50:14–16 are like those found elsewhere in the oracles against foreign nations: thus for "form up" (ערך, v 14) compare 46:3. And one notes the resemblance between v 16b and 46:16b.

The sequence 50:17–20 comes on unexpectedly just as vv 4–7 do, and again Volz deletes the verses as secondary (see above). But if diction and form suggest that vv 4–7 are authentic, the same considerations obtain for these verses. And one notes that v 19 resembles 23:3, dated in the present study to 588, and אֶסְלַח, "I shall forgive," in v 20 is reminiscent of 31:34, again dated here to 587.

Battle orders resume in 50:21; the word-plays evident in "Merathaim" and "Pekod" suggest Jrm's diction. The expression "sound of battle" (קוֹל מִלְחָמָה) in v 22 is a recombination of "sound of the trumpet . . . . the blast of battle" in 4:19; the phrase is found otherwise only in Exod 32:17. The expression "great collapse" (שֶׁבֶר גָּדוֹל) is found four times otherwise (4:6; 6:1; 14:17; 48:3). Verse 23a closely resembles 48:17; the expression "become a desolation" (הָיָה לְשַׁמָּה) in v 23b is found in previous oracles against foreign nations (46:19; 48:9) and elsewhere (25:38). In v 24 the sequence "X + וְגַם + Y," where X and Y are verbs of the same person and number, which occurs in this verse twice, is reminiscent of the same sequence in 31:19, and the expression וְגַם־נִלְכַּדְתְּ, "and then were captured," is reminiscent of גַם־אַתְּ תִּלָּכֵדִי, "you too shall be captured," in 48:7.

The diction of 50:25 is not close to that of material elsewhere, but there is some resemblance to 10:10, a resemblance that suggests authenticity to Jrm if 10:1–16 itself is authentic (see there). Again vv 26–27a brings battle commands. "Devote to destruction" (v 26) has already appeared in v 21, and "have no remnant" (negative + הָיָה שְׁאֵרִית לְ) appears in 11:23 and not otherwise in the OT; "go down to slaughter" (ירד לַטֶּבַח, v 27a) has appeared in 48:15. "The time of their punishment" (עֵת פְּקֻדָּתָם, v 27b) appears in 8:12; 10:15; and 46:21, and there are variants, such as "year of their punishment" (11:23) and "the time when I punish you" just ahead in 50:31. Volz omits all of v 28 as the addition of a pious glossator, but, as already noted, he omits vv 4–7 and 17–20 as well: he is understandably suspicious of "our God" in the context, but I propose that it is an early expansion. The linking of the plural participle of נוס ("those in flight") with a synonym is comparable to the linking of the singular participle of נוס with a synonym in

48:19; and Jrm appeals to the "retribution" (נְקָמָה) of Yahweh in his confessions (11:20 = 20:12).

The diction of 50:29a closely resembles that of v 14a; the verb זוד does not appear otherwise in Jer, but the related noun זָדוֹן, "arrogance" (vv 31, 32), has appeared in 49:16. As the text note states, v 30 duplicates 49:26 and appears to interrupt the continuity between vv 29 and 31–32; I therefore take it to be a secondary addition. The formula of encounter (v 31a) occurs elsewhere (21:13). For "the time when I punish you" (v 31b) compare "the time when I punish him" (49:8). "Stumble" and "fall" (v 32a) are paired elsewhere (46:6, 12, and 16); the pattern אֵין + לְ and suffix + participle occurs elsewhere (14:19, and with different word order, 30:17; 49:1); for v 32b see 21:14b and 49:27 (it is a pattern dependent on Amos 1:14), and for the next-to-last colon of the verse see also 43:12.

The verb "oppress" (עשׁק, 50:33) is used by Jrm elsewhere (7:6; 21:12), and the related noun "oppression" (עשׁק as well (6:6; 22:17). He uses "refuse" (מאן pi'el) followed by לְ and an infinitive construct again and again (3:3; 5:3 [twice]; 8:5; 11:10; 13:10; 15:18; 25:28; 31:15; 38:21), and it is an expression that occurs only twice in the rest of the prophetic literature (Hos 11:5; Zech 7:11); it is further to be noted that the expression here, "refuse to let them go," is one used in the narrative of the exodus from Egypt (Exod 4:23; 7:14, 27; 9:2—all J or JE).

On first hearing 50:34 would seem to offer late diction: the use of גאל, "redeemer," is common in Isaiah 40—66, and "give rest to all the earth" sounds a bit like Isa 14:7. But the word-play between הַרְגִּיעַ, "give rest," and הִרְגִּיז, "shake," suggests strongly that the verse is authentic to Jrm.

Verses 35–38a raise the question whether such a sequence, based on repetition, is appropriate to Jrm (and the question is raised by 51:20–23 as well). But such repetition is found in 4:23–26 and 5:17, both part of passages judged authentic. One notes further the shift from חֶרֶב in vv 35–37 to חֹרֶב in v 38 (a shift that was subtler in Jrm's pronunciation, from ḥarb to ḥorb), a shift missed in G^{O, L} and S: M is surely the lectio difficilior here and correct. Given the fact that both 4:23–26 and 5:17 offer symmetry of structure in their repetition, one may raise the question whether these four verses offer some kind of symmetry. Verse 35 has "sword" once in the context of a tricolon that lists the general population and its leaders. In vv 36–37a "her diviners" moves out from "her wise men" at the end of v 35, but here "sword" occurs three times in a tricolon, not only for "her diviners" but also for "her warriors" and "the rabble in her midst"—the last two forming a pair. Verses 37b–38a are a bicolon, first "sword" and then "drought," each of them directed to an impersonal target ("her treasuries," "her waters"). One may go on to note that the verb יאל nip'al, "prove foolish" (v 36), occurs in 5:4, and חתת, "be panicked," appears frequently (the qal beginning in 8:9). The theme of warriors becoming women (v 37) is set forth in different vocabulary in 30:6. Verse 38b is an unexpected turn: Rudolph deletes it, saying that an accusation of idolatry is irrelevant to the rest of the poem, but "idols" (פְּסִילִים) occurs in 8:19, and הלל hitpo'el, here "run wild," occurs in 25:16 and 46:9; it is better then to retain it and try to follow the train of thought.

The eight verses 50:39–46 make up three sequences that are near-duplicates of material elsewhere: vv 39–40 adapt material in Isa 13:19–22 and Jer 49:18; vv 41–43 are almost identical with 6:22–24, with the referents shifted; and vv 44–46 are almost identical with 49:19–21, again with the referents shifted.

It is convenient to deal with vv 41–43 and vv 44–46 first. As for vv 41–43 and 6:22–24, one may say: (1) The setting proposed in the present study for 6:22–24 is 600, whereas if 50:41–43 is authentic here, any plausible setting for the verses would surely be later; but (2) the wording of vv 41–43 is so close to that of 6:22–24 that one is justified in judging vv 41–43 a secondary adaptation by an editor (see the discussion above, *Preliminary Observations*). As for vv 44–46 and 49:19–21, the question is more difficult to solve; Cornill and Rudolph assume that these verses are original here and secondary in 49:18–21 (see Structure, Form, Setting on that passage). One may say: (1) There is the same kind of relation between these verses and 49:19–21 as between vv 41–43 and 6:22–24—verbal identity except for the change of referents (see Text note a for both vv 41–43 and vv 44–46); and (2) the reference to "the Jordan" in v 44 and 49:19 is more appropriate to a word against Edom than to a word against Babylon, and the expression "the Red Sea" (49:21) is more specific than "among the nations" (v 46). One may then conclude that vv 44–46 were adapted secondarily from 49:19–21. It is altogether probable, then, that vv 39–40 are likewise an adaptation, the mention of "idols" and "terrors" in v 38 triggering the use of "goblins" and "ghouls" (or whatever these words mean: see Interpretation) in v 39. Wildberger dates Isaiah 13 to the end of the Babylonian Empire,[9] and one may therefore presume that all three sequences were added early in the Persian period.

Material appropriate to Jrm resumes in 51:1. "I am going to arouse" (מֵעִיר + הִנֵּה אָנֹכִי or הִנְנִי) occurs in 50:9 as well. "Winnowers and they shall winnow her" in v 2 is a phrase like "fishermen, and they shall fish them out . . . hunters, and they shall hunt them out" in 16:16. The verb בקק, "lay waste," is found in 19:7; the phrase הָיוּ עָלֶיהָ מִסָּבִיב, "they have closed in around her," is found in 4:17 as well.

In 51:3 the words of the third colon are reminiscent of 13:14; חרם hip'il, "devote to destruction," has already occurred in 50:21 and 27. Verse 4 is similar to 14:18. For "land is full" (v 5b) compare 23:10. And the colon of v 6 is similar to diction in 50:29.

The verb הלל hitpo'el in 51:7 (here "go mad") has occurred in 46:9 and 50:38; the עַל־כֵּן phrase ("that is why") in the last colon of the verse is comparable to the diction of the last colon of 12:8. "Suddenly," which begins v 8, is a favorite word of Jrm's in laments (4:20; 6:26; 18:22; compare 15:8); the diction of the verse in general is comparable to that in 30:15. The use of רפא, "heal, treat" (qal and pi'el), and of the passive of the verb (nip'al), is common in Jrm—the diction of the first colon of v 9 is reminiscent of that in 6:14 and 17:14; and the phraseology of the second colon of that verse is reminiscent of that in 9:1. And the diction of v 10b is reminiscent of that in 31:6b.

The first two cola of 51:11, battle orders, offer no likeness to vocabulary elsewhere; such battle orders, however, are not alien to authentic material in these chapters. But the prose sequence in the rest of the verse interrupts the flow and is clearly a later addition. "Raise a signal" (v 12) recalls 4:6 and 6:1. "Decide" (זמם) appears only here in v 12 and in 4:28 in Jer, and nowhere else in the prophets except for three stereotyped passages in Zechariah (Zech 1:6; 8:14, 15). The noun בֶּצַע, "cut,

profit," (v 13) occurs in 6:13 (= 8:10) and 22:17. The association in v 14 of הֵידָד, "shout," with ענה (literally "answer") is found also in 25:30.

The following five verses, 51:15–19, reproduce 10:12–16 without variation. The issue of idolatry does not loom large in these chapters, and the passage must be judged secondary here.

51:20–24. These five verses are repetitive as 50:35–38 is, and their cola are arranged chiastically (see below). But beyond the question of authenticity the sequence presents a major puzzle: Who is addressed? The answer to this question has consequences not only for an understanding of the sequence itself but for the understanding of all of 50:2—51:58, and it is therefore appropriate at this point not only to deal with the question of authenticity but also with the larger question of the whole intent of the sequence.

It is convenient to deal with vv 20–23 first. Clearly these verses make up a unity. The question whether such repetition is appropriate to Jrm has already been answered in the affirmative with respect to 50:35–38 above and may be reaffirmed here. And it may further be observed that the objects of the verb are arranged chiastically in groups of three (vv 20a–21, v 22, v 23). Thus "nations" and "kingdoms," synonymous plurals in the political sphere, parallel "governors and prefects." "Horse and his rider" and "chariot and its charioteer" (figures from war, in which the person comes second in each pair) parallel "shepherd and his flock," "farmer and his team" (figures from peace, in which the person comes first in each pair). And "husband and wife" parallel "youth and maiden" (masculine and feminine in each case), and these two pairs surround "elder and youngster."[10] There is no reason to deny these verses to Jrm.

But how far does the sequence continue? In vv 20–23 the identity of the one addressed, in the masculine singular, is not stated, for there is no vocative. There is a series of six repetitions of וְנִפַּצְתִּי בְךָ, "and I shall smash with you," in vv 20bα, 21–23, as well as the parallel וְהִשְׁחַתִּי בְךָ, "and I shall destroy with you," in v 20bβ. Form-critically these verses identify the one addressed, or designate the one addressed, as Yahweh's instrument for punishment, but again, one does not hear who it is who is

9   Wildberger, *Jesaja*, 510.
10   Jack R. Lundbom, *Jeremiah, A Study in Ancient Hebrew Rhetoric* (SBLDS 18; Missoula, MT: Scholars, 1975) 91–92.

addressed. Verse 24 opens with a verb that appears to be parallel to those in vv 20b–23, namely וְשִׁלַּמְתִּי, "and I shall recompense," but this verb lacks בָךְ, the verb instead being completed with לְבָבֶל, "[to] Babylon," and its parallel "and all the inhabitants of Chaldea." The address in (the latter part of) that verse is masculine plural, and the verse appears to be a salvation oracle addressed to Israel. Verse 25 begins with a formula of encounter: once more the one addressed is masculine singular, but at this point there is a vocative, here emended and translated "Mount of Sesame-oil" (see Interpretation). Verse 25b is an announcement of judgment, extended in v 26 by a depiction of ruin. Though the vocative is a figure of speech, there is no reason to take it as anything but a figure for Babylon. If the emendation "Mount of Sesame-oil" is correct, the seeming verbal tie in M between vv 20–24 and vv 25–26 disappears, namely, that between the finite verb "destroy" (שׁחת hip'il) in v 20 and the participial form מַשְׁחִית, "destroyer," occurring in the initial vocative (with "Mount") of v 25. Thus one cannot use vv 25–26 to interpret vv 20–23. The question then of the authenticity of v 24 and its connection, if any, to vv 20–23, is dependent on an understanding of the nature of vv 20–23.

Commentators have gone in a variety of directions in dealing with the problems raised by vv 20–23. Most have assumed that it is Babylon that is addressed (so Calvin, and in the past century so Duhm, Giesebrecht, Cornill, Volz, Condamin, Rudolph, Bright); after all, Babylon is "the sledgehammer of all the earth" (50:23). A few scholars have suggested an alternative (for example, Naegelsbach, who suggested it is an enemy of Babylon), but current interpretation assumes the identification with Babylon.

Now since v 24 as it stands is surely addressed to Israel, commentators who assume that Babylon is addressed in vv 20–23 deal with the question of connection between vv 20–23 in a variety of ways. Thus Volz deletes v 24 as a secondary addition. Rudolph associates v 24 with vv 25–26 rather than with vv 20–23, but at the same time he affirms that Israel is addressed in v 24 and Babylon in vv 25–26.

Several observations need to be made. (1) It may be a small matter, but a different word is used for "sledge-hammer" in 50:23 (פַּטִּישׁ) than is used for "mace" in

51:20 (מַפֵּץ). (2) If Babylon is addressed, why is the address not in the feminine singular, like that in vv 13–14 (which, if vv 15–19 are a secondary addition, originally adjoined vv 20–23)? (3) The rhetoric of 50:23 is different from that in vv 20–23 here: In 50:23 one has a mocking lament of Babylon as "the sledgehammer of all the earth," now in ruins—the tone there is "How are the mighty fallen!"; and indeed in that verse, as it happens, the sledgehammer is specifically identified as Babylon. But not only is there no identification of the mace in the present verses, there is no tone of "How are the mighty fallen!" either. One could say that v 24 brings the great reversal, but if so, that reversal is signaled with curious subtlety. One assumes that the waw-consecutive perfects in vv 20–23 here express action still to come; and if Yahweh is still to smash everything in sight through Babylon, then one would expect a reversal in v 24 to begin with something like לָכֵן, "therefore," or עַל־כֵּן, "that is why" (compare the move from 30:12–15 to 16–17). But no; one has simply a verb at the beginning of v 24 that appears to be parallel, וְשִׁלַּמְתִּי. (4) How, after all, does one understand vv 20–23 to function within 50:2—51:58? If it is Babylon that is addressed, why the necessity to reiterate Yahweh's use of her to destroy everything in sight? This is not news (compare again the rhetoric of 50:23). One can always assume that a prophetic word that in another context had depicted Yahweh's action of judgment through Babylon is now incorporated into surrounding material to communicate her ruin, but as it now stands it is a strange way to do it. One has to conclude that the mace in vv 20–23 is not Babylon.

Who, then? One can exclude the suggestion of Naegelsbach, of an unidentified enemy of Babylon: Later Deutero-Isaiah will perceive God to speak in the third person of one from the east (Isa 41:2) or north (Isa 41:25), but when he addresses him directly (Isa 45:2–5) his name, Cyrus, is given (Isa 44:28; 45:1). Such an anonymous addressee would have been of no interest to listeners in Jerusalem. It certainly cannot be Yahweh; Yahweh is the speaker. There remain only two options, Jrm himself or Israel.

Jrm is elsewhere given a destructive call (1:10; 5:14b; compare the similes for Yahweh's word in 23:29); but there is no other instance in 50:2—51:58 in which Jrm is addressed, and there is no form-critical clue in the present context that would make this identification likely.

The other option is Israel. As it ultimately turned out, Cyrus conquered Babylon and then allowed subject peoples, including Israel, to return: Israel played no military part in her own liberation. But even so, Deutero-Isaiah could envision Israel as a threshing-sledge to thresh mountains and hills (Isa 41:15: were these the ziggurats of Babylon?—see Interpretation below on v 25). So Jrm in his day could have envisioned a great reversal in which Israel emerged as the devastator of Babylon. Such a great reversal is suggested by the movement from 50:6, "a perishing flock were my people," to 50:8, "be like rams before the flock"; it is also suggested by the imagery of 31:21–22, in which Jerusalem, portrayed as a vulnerable woman, is commanded to undertake tasks ordinarily done by men (see Interpretation on that passage). The mastery of Israel over Babylon is suggested by the words of Israel in 51:9, "We treated Babylon, but she was untreatable"—the speakers continue, "Come, let us tell it in Zion, the deed of Yahweh our God" (51:10). If this identification is valid, it opens the possibility that some of the battle commands in 50:2—51:58, offered in the second person plural, are directed not to the enemies of Babylon in general but more specifically to Israel. That may be particularly the case when the rhetoric moves from battle orders to a concern for Israel; thus, beyond the movement from 50:6 to 8, one notes the transition from 50:3 to 4, the transition from 50:16 to 17, the specificity of 50:21 that it is Yahweh who commands those addressed to do the battle task, the transition from 50:27 to 28, the reverse transition from 50:33 to 35–38 (is Israel the sword? one now wonders), and the transition from 51:3–4 to 5a. Indeed could the "people from the north" in 50:3 be an ironic reference to Israel, who came from the north (-west) into exile? That would be a great reversal indeed! If the identification of Israel as the mace in 51:20–23 is valid, the inner logic of the material of 50:2—51:58 becomes far more cogent.

But v 24 is still a problem. I suggest that the verb that begins the verse, וְשִׁלַּמְתִּי, belongs with the series of verbs in vv 20–23: the shift from the repeated וְנִפַּצְתִּי to וְשִׁלַּמְתִּי may be analogous to the shift from the repeated חֶרֶב in

50:35–37 to חֹרֶב in 50:38. The phrase "inhabitants of Chaldea" occurs elsewhere (51:35), and "Babylon" and "Chaldea" are appropriate parallels (50:8–9). But the last part of the verse is clearly secondary prose, and the shift from the second-person singular in vv 20–23 to the second-person plural in this part of the verse is a mark of its secondary nature.

Authentic and Unauthentic Material in 51:25–58. Like 50:31, 51:25 offers the formula of encounter, and there is no reason to doubt its basic authenticity. A detailed discussion of the meaning of v 25 must be saved until Interpretation: by the analysis there the verse has a couple of explanatory glosses but otherwise is an ironic expression of judgment on Babylon that cannot be otherwise than authentic to Jrm; the same may be said for v 26, which closes the sequence.

The diction of 51:27 and 29 is similar to that in 4:5–7, and the diction of v 27 is likewise similar to that found in 6:4 and 50:29. Verse 28 is a secondary prose expansion of phrases found in vv 23 and 27; v 11 likewise offers a prose passage mentioning the Medes. The diction of v 30 is not the same as that in 30:6, but the motif of warriors turned to women is the same. The repetition of nouns within a colon in v 31 is reminiscent of that in 9:5. None of the rest of the diction in vv 32–33 strikes one as alien to Jrm; though "fair Zion" (בַּת־צִיּוֹן) in 6:23 was transformed by a later editor into "fair Babylon" (בַּת־בָּבֶל) in 50:42, this is not to say that Jrm cannot have used the phrase himself here in 51:33—indeed its use here may have encouraged the adaptation in 50:41–43.

Though much of the diction in 51:34–44 strikes out in fresh directions, none of it is alien to that of Jrm. And even here there are reminiscences of phrasing elsewhere. Thus the use of the cognate accusative of רִיב in v 36 is reminiscent of the cognate accusative of דִּין in 5:28, and the phraseology of v 37 occurs elsewhere frequently. And most notable in v 43 there is a nice variation on the vocabulary found in 2:6: the terms are rearranged, and the context of Babylon of course brings an ironic reuse of that diction.

The material from 51:45 to 53 offers problems for literary criticism. Verses 44b–49a are missing in *G*, but evidently by haplography (from ‫גַּם־‬ in v 44b to ‫גַּם־‬ in v 49b);[11] if vv 47–48 were not present in the text antecedent to G before that text suffered the haplography (on those two verses see below), then of course v 49b would have been closer to v 44b than is the case in M. Verses 45–49 appear to have entered the text antecedent to M in various ways. Thus v 45 is conventional diction in comparison with the other verses in 50:2—51:58 that are a summons to flee (50:8; 51:6, 50); as Text note a indicates, the verse embodies material drawn from elsewhere. Verse 46 is in prose and is a reassurance to a community that continues year by year to hear bad news. Verses 47–48 offer a peculiar parallel to vv 52–53: material that is identical (or virtually identical) alternates with material that is altogether different; the two sequences evidently represent a conflate text.[12] It is possible therefore that two or three lines of a left-hand or right-hand portion of the column in question had broken off, perhaps at the top or bottom of the scroll, and the missing portion was imaginatively reconstructed. Of the two texts, vv 52–53 strike one as authentic; the diction of v 48a, of the heavens and earth singing for joy, is not otherwise found in Jer but is similar to diction in Deutero-Isaiah (Isa 52:9; 55:12; compare further Ps 96:11–13). Verses 45–48, then, for various reasons, are to be judged secondary.

The diction of 51:49–53 is appropriate to Jrm. Thus the phrase "the slain of Israel" in v 49 is reminiscent of "the slain of my fair people" in 8:23. "Remember Yahweh from afar [‫מֵרָחוֹק‬]" is reminiscent of "long ago [‫מֵרָחוֹק‬] Yahweh appeared to him" in 31:3a. And the wording of v 51 is close to that of 3:25, although the contexts are very different. The first colon of v 53 is reminiscent of similar phraseology in Amos 9:2b.

And finally vv 54–58 likewise appear to be genuine to Jrm. For v 54 see 50:22. Verse 55 resembles 5:22 and 6:23. The verb ‫יצת‬, "be burned," is a favorite with Jrm, but the only other occurrence in Jer of the qal stem is found in 49:2. And the last two cola of v 58 are evidently a citation of Hab 2:13 (see Interpretation): Jrm elsewhere closes a sequence with citations of Scripture known to him (compare 4:3–4 and 10:23–25).

Form of the Authentic Material. Before turning to the

question of the demarcation of the units within this sequence, one needs to analyze the material form-critically.

At the beginning, in 50:2, one hears commands to heralds (compare 4:5; 46:13) to proclaim the news of the collapse of Babylon. Verse 3 offers a ‫כִּי‬ clause giving the basis for these commands, the divine judgment through the coming of a people from the north to destroy Babylon; the question was raised above (see *51:20–24*) whether the people from the north is not Israel. If so, the shift to vv 4–7 is appropriate: the verses are a prophecy of salvation (*Heilsweissagung*) for Israel in which the promise comes first (vv 4–5) followed by the indication of the situation in the immediate past (vv 6–7).

In 50:8 plural imperatives are resumed: the verse is a summons to flee. Again there is the hint that Israel is specifically being addressed, not simply the general population of Babylon: "be like rams before the flock" appears to pick up "perishing sheep were my people" in v 6. Verses 9–10 are the first occasion in the sequence for a first-person singular announcement by Yahweh of divine judgment; otherwise the verses are analogous to v 3, in form (a ‫כִּי‬ clause stating the divine judgment), in phraseology ("a people from the north"), and in personal reference (in both v 3 and vv 9–10 Babylon is referred to in the third-person singular feminine). Thus if the "people from the north" in v 3 is to be identified with Israel, then it is Israel about whom Yahweh speaks in v 9.

On first hearing the first colon of 50:11, with its somewhat ambiguous repeated ‫כִּי‬, suggests a summons to rejoice (compare Lam 4:21), but (again like Lam 4:21) it is ironic: the Babylonians who are addressed are given a depiction of the humiliation and desolation of their nation (vv 12–13): in v 13 they are told that it is because of the fury of Yahweh that the land will be depopulated.

Plural imperatives resume in 50:14–16a, battle commands addressed to the enemies of Babylon. The second, third, and fourth cola of v 15 shift to a depiction of the surrender and desolation of Babylon, and v 16b shifts from commands addressed to the enemies of Babylon to imperfects regarding the subject peoples of Babylon, not a summons to flee but an indirect command to flee (if the verbs are construed to be jussives) or a depiction of

---

11 Janzen, p. 119.
12 Compare again ibid., 119.

fleeing (if the verbs are construed as simple imperfects). And again, as with v 8, it may be Israel that is addressed here.

Like 50:4–7, vv 17a, 19–20 are a prophecy of salvation; but in contrast to those earlier verses this section offers two first-person singular verbs of Yahweh's action, "I shall bring back Israel to his pasture" (v 19) and "I shall forgive those I have spared" (v 20).

Imperatives recur in 50:21, battle orders addressed to the enemy of Babylon, but in contrast to those in vv 14–16 these verbs are masculine singular. Is it Israel that is addressed? If so, Israel is here commanded to attack Babylonian localities; and the possibility is increased when one hears that the localities are to be "devoted to destruction" and that the addressee is to "do all I have commanded you." Verse 22 offers a representation of battle sounds, and v 23 is a mocking lament over Babylon. Verse 24 is mockery addressed to Babylon affirming her collapse (particularly if the opening verb is second-person singular feminine—see Text, note a), and the last colon of that verse offers in a כִּי clause the reason for Babylon's collapse—she challenged Yahweh.

Verse 25a is an announcement of Yahweh's judgment on Babylon (in the third person), and in v 25b a כִּי clause summarizes the situation (compare the summary appraisal, for which see 4:18; 10:19b).

Plural imperatives return in 50:26–27a, commands to the enemies of Babylon to destroy. Verse 27b is an "alas" cry, either a sincere lament or a mocking one, followed by the כִּי clause giving the justification for the "alas" cry; compare 48:1 for the form. Verse 28 picks up v 22 once more ("the sound of"), the representation of battle sounds, but this time it is hinted that it is the sound of Israel moving back to Jerusalem. Verse 29 offers in the first five cola more battle commands to the enemies of Babylon; the verse closes in its last colon with a כִּי clause parallel to that in the last colon of v 24. Verses 31–32 bring a first-person singular word from Yahweh, a formula of encounter (compare 21:13) in v 31a, a כִּי clause in v 31b announcing the destruction of Babylon, and an expansion in v 32 of that announcement.

In 50:33–34 one finds a prophecy of salvation (*Heilsweissagung*—compare vv 4–7): v 33 gives the indication of the situation, the captivity of Israel in Babylon; v 34a is a hymnic affirmation (compare 10:16), a characterization of Yahweh as the one bringing about deliverance;

and v 34b is the prediction of salvation proper.

The repetitive sequence in 50:35–38a is a series of imprecations (like the English "a plague upon . . .") that function in a way analogous to a series of "woe" oracles like Isa 5:20–22. In their reversal of normal status, one or two of the imprecations use traditional curses (the warriors become women: see Form on 30:6, and see 51:50). Verse 38b is a כִּי clause offering the reason for the imprecations: Babylon is a land of idols.

In 51:1–2 one hears an announcement of divine judgment (in the first person); v 2b is a כִּי clause giving the basis for the judgment.

There is uncertainty whether the "bowman" in 51:3 is an enemy of Babylon or a Babylonian; evidence offered in Interpretation suggests that it is "her bowman," Babylon's bowman. The cola of v 3a must then be read with "not"; they are jussives, expressing the wish that Babylonian archers turn weak. And v 3b offers battle commands to the enemies of Babylon. Verse 4 moves to a brief depiction of the ruin of Babylon; v 5b (introduced by כִּי) is a judgment on Babylon, v 5a (again with כִּי) is an explanatory contrast, depicting the current situation with respect to Yahweh and Israel. Verse 6a is a summons to flee: it appears to be addressed to the Babylonians, but the context suggests that it is the subject peoples within Babylon, doubtless particularly Israel, inasmuch as v 6b (with כִּי) offers the reason for the summons—it is Yahweh's retribution (compare the diction of v 10).

In 51:7a is a metaphor for Babylon, an announcement of her identity, analogous to that for Israel in 2:3 (compare v 20 below); v 7b extends the metaphor in reviewing the events of the recent past (compare, for example, 2:5–8); the last colon (with עַל־כֵּן) offers an explanation (compare 5:27b–28aα). I suggest that the first colon of v 8 is a quotation. It is true that those commentators and translations that mark vv 9–10 as a quotation (Volz and Rudolph, *NAB*) do not mark this colon so. But פִּתְאֹם, "suddenly," at the beginning of a colon marks a quoted lament twice otherwise (4:20; 6:26), and the imperative "wail" suggests a quotation (compare 4:8 and perhaps 48:20). If the first colon is a quotation, the second colon is a call to lament, ironic in the context (compare the irony of v 8bγ, "Perhaps she shall be healed!"). Verses 9–10 are certainly a quotation, and the speakers are Israel (compare v 10b); if the addressees in v 8b are likewise Israel, as is likely, then Israel is called to lament over

Babylon—indeed she is not only called to lament but to function as a healer treating Babylon (v 8bβ). Verse 9aα is on the face of it a report of the healers, but in the light of v 10 it must be heard as testimony within the community. Verse 9aβ resumes the summons to flee (v 6a), and v 9b (the כִּי clause), like v 6b, gives the basis for the summons. Verse 10a, like v 9a, is a testimony within the community, so that v 10b is an invitation to share the testimony with those in Jerusalem.

Like 51:3, vv 11–12 offers battle orders—indeed v 11 begins with "sharpen the arrows," whereas v 3 begins with "let not her bowman draw his bow." The כִּי clause (v 12b) is an affirmation of Yahweh's determined effectiveness (compare Lam 2:17). Verses 13–14 are an address to Babylon, personified as a woman: in v 13 she is mocked, or at least the contrast between her former glory and her present ruin is affirmed, and in v 14 Yahweh affirms his judgment on Babylon by oath, or at least by asseveration.

It has already been stated that 51:20–24 identifies the one addressed, or designates the one addressed, as Yahweh's instrument for punishment, and that the one addressed is Israel (see above, *51:20–24*); Yahweh promises that that punishment will come on Babylon.

Like 50:31, 51:25a brings a formula of encounter: the one addressed is a figure for Babylon (for the emendation "Mount of Sesame-oil" see Interpretation). Verse 25b is an announcement of judgment, extended in v 26 by a depiction of ruin.

Again in 51:27 one hears battle orders to the enemies of Babylon. Verses 29–32 are a long depiction of the demoralization of her fighters and in general of her ruin; for the motif of the warriors turned to women (v 30a), a traditional curse form, see the discussion on 30:5–7 in 30:1—31:40, Form, *The Northern Recension: 30:5–7*. Verse 33aβ could be taken as a continuation of that depiction, but v 33b is an indication of divine judgment (though without a direct mention of Yahweh either in the first or third person).

The words of 51:34 are spoken by Jerusalem, parallel to the two quotations in v 35; v 35 offers parallel jussives, indirect commands that these words be announced in Jerusalem (compare Isa 40:9): these are a description of Israel's suffering at the hand of Babylon (v 34) and petitions for retribution (v 35). Verse 36a is Yahweh's assurance of his retributive justice; this assurance is reinforced by his announcement of divine judgment on Babylon in vv 36b–37. Verse 38 appears to be a description of the Babylonians in their power, but in the context of vv 39–40, an announcement of divine judgment, v 38 is evidently ironic. Verse 41, like 50:23, is a mocking lament; vv 42–43 are a depiction of the ruin of Babylon, and v 44 is a divine announcement of judgment.

In 51:49 there is a reassurance to Israel, virtually a fragment of an oracle of salvation. Verse 50a is a summons to flee, and v 50b is a command to remember Yahweh and Jerusalem, to be aware once more of the covenant bond. Verse 51 is a quotation of those in exile from Jerusalem, an affirmation of dismay. Verse 52 is a divine announcement of judgment on Babylon, reinforced by the assurances in v 53.

Like 50:22 and 28, 51:54 is a representation of battle sounds; v 55, with כִּי, gives the explanation of the battle sounds—Yahweh's action. Verse 56a is an assurance of Babylon's ruin, reinforced in v 56b by the assurance of Yahweh's retributive justice (compare v 36a). Verse 58a is an announcement of judgment on Babylon, reinforced in v 58b by a citation from Hab 2:13 (see Interpretation), a description of futility.

Form of the Unauthentic Material. For completeness' sake one must record the form of various expansions. In chapter 50, v 17b is a kind of midrashic instruction, identifying the two "lions" that have chased Israel as Assyria and Babylon; v 18 is announcement of divine judgment on Babylon. Verse 30, like its antecedent 49:26, is an announcement of judgment. Verses 39–40 are an announcement of judgment in the form of the traditional curse on the land as the dwelling-place of animals (or demons) (compare 9:9–10),[13] destroyed like Sodom and Gomorrah (for which see 49:18). And both vv 41–43 and 44–46 extend the announcement of judgment: for the form in detail see, respectively, 6:22–24 and 49:19–21.

In chapter 51 verse 11aβb is a midrashic explanation applying the oracle to the king of the Medes. Verses 15–19, a portion of 10:1–16, offers hymnic sequences

---

13   See Hillers, *Treaty-Curses*, 44–54, esp. 53.

devoted to Yahweh (vv 15–16, 19) enclosing the mockery of idols and their worshipers (vv 17–18): for the details see 10:1–16. Verse 28 picks up the phrase "prepare nations against her" in v 27 and specifies the Medes as the nation in question (compare v 11aβb). Verse 45 is a summons to flee; v 46 is evidently a warning not to become demoralized by rumors of bad news, thus a kind of reassurance (on the syntax of the first clause see Interpretation). Verse 47 largely duplicates v 52, a divine announcement of judgment; v 48a is an affirmation that heaven and earth join in a hymn of rejoicing over the fall of Babylon (compare Isa 55:12; Ps 96:11–13). And v 57 is a divine announcement of judgment.

Identification of the Units. The authentic material offers a kaleidoscope of forms, and the sequence of forms offers no guide to a division into units (compare the remarks in *Preliminary Observations*). Bright is refreshingly frank in his approach:

> The section [50:1—51:58] consists of a series of shorter poems, with a few prose expansions, which have been drawn together in such a way that it is frequently difficult to tell where one poem leaves off and another begins. Although the material has been broken down in the translation by the use of subheadings in the hope that the reader will not find himself too confused, it must be admitted that the analysis adopted is largely one of convenience; others just as satisfactory could doubtless be proposed.[14]

Though a division must be tentative, it may be possible to gain somewhat greater certainty.

As one begins in chapter 50 one datum looms large, the parallel between v 17 ("a stray ewe-lamb is Israel") and v 6 ("perishing sheep were my people"). If that parallel is significant, one can lay the neighborhood of these two verses side by side and try to locate the boundary between them. The natural boundary will then be between vv 13 and 14: v 14 will begin with battle orders like 46:3 and 49:28, and v 13 will end with phraseology like that of Zeph 2:15.[15] Rudolph groups vv 2–7 and vv 8–20; conceivably one would wish to see units in vv 2–7 and 8–13, each section beginning with plural imperatives, but this would separate "perishing sheep were my people" (v 6) from "be like rams before the flock" (v 8). It is better to isolate vv 2–13 as the first unit, with four sections: (1) vv 2–3, the battle for Babylon; (2) vv 4–7, the return of Israel, the perishing people; (3) vv 8–10, the command to leave Babylon, the ruined nation; (4) vv 11–13, mockery of Babylon, and the closing declaration. In this unit the second and fourth sections are matched: there is in the second a mention of "Israel" (v 4) and in the fourth an allusion to her ("my possession," v 11), and there is in both the second and the fourth sections a mention of "Yahweh" (v 7, "sinned against Yahweh," and v 13, "because of the fury of Yahweh"). And the unit offers a chiasmus of "be ashamed" (בוש), vv 2 and 12.

If v 17 matches v 6 (see above), there are other parities as well between the unit beginning in v 14 and vv 2–13. Thus the opening section (vv 14–16) in general matches vv 2–3, the battle for Babylon, and a second section (vv 17a, 19–20) matches vv 4–7, the return of Israel. If v 8 hinted that the addressee is Israel ("be like rams before the flock," compare v 6), then so does v 21 ("do all I have commanded you"). And v 24 addresses Babylon mockingly as vv 11–12 do. Verses 21–23 then make up the third section of this unit as vv 8–10 make up the third section of the first unit.

There is a problem whether the unit ends with v 24 or with v 25. Verse 25 has "Yahweh . . . has brought forth the weapons of his fury [זַעְמוֹ]," and one might think that this phrase is parallel to "because of the fury [קֶצֶף] of Yahweh" in v 13: in this case v 25 would end the unit. But if so, "to her" in the first colon of v 26 would lack an antecedent. It is therefore preferable to close the second unit with v 24 and begin the third unit in v 25. This division underlines the nice play on the two occurrences of "open" (פתח), "Yahweh has opened his storehouse" in v 25 and the command to "open her granaries" in v 26. The second unit thus closes with v 24.

If the third unit begins in 50:25, and if v 26 is united with v 25 by the verb "open" (פתח, see above), v 27 continues the imperatives of v 26. Verse 28 shifts the focus to Israel and mentions "Zion," as v 5 does after the battle scenes of vv 2–3. If there is any match between the present unit and the first or second unit, one may assume

---

14 Bright, p. 359.

15 That verse is accounted the end of the poem in which it stands by all commentators: see for example

Eissfeldt, *Introduction*, 423; Arvid S. Kapelrud, *The Message of the Prophet Zephaniah* (Oslo: Universitetsforlaget, 1975) 33.

that the battle orders in v 29 continue the unit after the allusion to Israel in v 28 just as the battle orders in v 21 continue the second unit after the allusions to Israel in vv 17a, 19–20. Verses 31–32 (with זָדוֹן, "Arrogance") continue v 29 (זָדָה, "has been arrogant"). I propose that the unit ends with v 32: if v 31 offers the formula of encounter, it is comparable to 21:13, and the last colon of 21:14 is almost identical with the last colon of v 32 here. Furthermore, the form of the second colon of v 32, אֵין with a participle, also closes other oracles (9:21; 21:12). One wonders then whether the shift in the use of "open" from v 25 to v 26 is balanced by the move from "has been arrogant" in v 29 to "Arrogance" in vv 31–32.

The fourth unit then begins with 50:33. If there is any parity in length, then vv 33–34 can hardly make up a full unit. One is thus led to include the repetitive sequence of vv 35–38 in the unit. Following v 38 is a long sequence of secondary material (vv 39–46). One might imagine the unit continuing with 51:1 and beyond. First of all, it is clear that 51:2 cannot close the unit: The interpretation of 51:3 precludes that possibility. Specifically, 51:3a turns out to be a mocking wish that Babylonian bowmen be weak (see Interpretation); "bowman" in the first clause is thus parallel with "her youths" and "her whole army" in v 3b, and the text is therefore likely to have been "her bowman." In that case, v 3 cannot begin a fresh unit, because the antecedent of the possessive suffix would be missing (compare the similar argument above that 50:26 cannot begin a unit). If 51:3b has battle orders, so does v 6: they can hardly be separated. But v 7 really begins something new, the description of Babylon as a cup. The question then arises, Do 50:33–38 + 51:1–6 make up one unit or two? I propose that 50:33–38 is a unit of its own, the fourth of the series; it offers a contrast between the "children of Israel" and the "children of Judah" (v 33) and "Yahweh of hosts" (v 34) with the "idols" and "terrors" with which the Chaldeans run wild (v 38). It is not a strong argument for the location of the end of a unit to see secondary material added after it, but it is at least conceivable that the material was expanded by those who were aware where a unit ends.

The fifth unit of the series will then be 51:1–6, comparable in length to the fourth, 50:33–38. One senses that there is a balance between "the day of disaster" in v 2 and "the time of retribution for Yahweh" in v 6. Whether there is a sensed parallel between Yahweh's

sending "winnowers" at the beginning of this unit (51:2) and Yahweh's opening his "storehouse" at the beginning of the third unit (50:25) would be difficult to say.

The sixth unit will then begin with 51:7. The diction of v 7 continues with the quotations of Israel in vv 8–10. It is appropriate not to cut off the unit at v 10 but to continue with the battle orders in vv 11aα–12, just as the battle orders of 50:21 continue the second unit. In this way the mocking address to Babylon in vv 13–14 will close the oracle just as v 7, the description of Babylon, opened it, and the reference to "gold" in v 7 will be balanced by the reference to "treasures" in v 13. Verse 20 obviously begins something new, and the secondary material (vv 15–19) will again have been added at the end of a unit (compare the remarks on 50:39–46 above). The sixth unit will therefore be made up of 51:7–14.

The seventh unit will then begin with 51:20. The repetitious sequence will continue through the authentic phrases of v 24. The question then arises whether the formula of encounter and its closing in vv 25–26 are to be included in the unit. It has already been argued that it is Israel who is addressed in vv 20–24 (see 51:20–24), but it is Babylon that is addressed in vv 25–26: can these be heard together? I propose that they can. For one thing, the formula of encounter in 50:31 introduces the close of that unit. One looks then for some verbal link between the two portions of the sequence; that link may be supplied by נָפוּץ "(lest) we be scattered" in Gen 11:4 in the narrative of the Tower of Babel and the repeated וְנִפַּצְתִּי in vv 20–23 here: v 25 evidently depends on a recollection of the narrative of the Tower of Babel (on this see Interpretation). The unit will thus end with v 26.

The eighth unit then begins with 51:27. The diction of battle continues without interruption through v 32. And if כִּי is correct at the beginning of v 33, it cannot begin a unit. Verse 34 moves rhetorically in a fresh direction, and "swallow" (בלע) in v 34 surely is picked up in some fashion by "what is swallowed" (בֶּלַע) in v 44. In short, v 33 closes the eighth unit.

The ninth unit thus opens with 51:34, and the quotation begun in that verse continues in the quotations of v 35. Verses 36–37 begin with לָכֵן, "therefore," and therefore continue the discourse. Verse 38 moves in a fresh direction, but it is analogous to 50:17 within the second unit, 50:14–24, the comparison of Babylon to lions, and this material continues through vv 39–40. If the parallel with the pattern of the second unit continues here, then, the "how!" of v 41 is analogous to the "how!" of 50:23 (in both cases אֵיךְ). The phraseology of v 41 continues through v 44. Verses 45–48 are secondary additions, and it is altogether likely that this unit closes with v 44: in that case the unit will be bracketed by the two occurrences of the root "swallow" (vv 34, 44), as already noted.

The tenth unit thus begins with 51:49: there is obviously a verbal link ("fall") between v 49 and v 44, but v 49 can hardly be a smooth continuation of v 44. If text of the first colon of v 49 is correctly understood, Israel is addressed, and that address continues in vv 50–51; and vv 52–53 begin with לָכֵן, "therefore," and thus continue the discourse (compare vv 36–37). The question then arises whether this unit ends with v 53, with a final unit covering vv 54–58, or whether the tenth unit reaches from vv 49 to 58. One can certainly conceive the rhetoric moving from v 53 to v 54. There is furthermore a verbal link between v 53 ("destroyers") and v 55 ("has destroyed"), but this link admittedly could be taken as a link between two adjoining units rather than as a link within a single unit. Given the question of the length of respective shorter units or of one longer one, and given the symmetry of these units to be discussed below, it is better to take vv 49–58 as a single unit.

Structure within and among the Units. The foregoing analysis has yielded ten units; the repetitive sequences are found in the fourth (the "sword") and in the seventh (the "mace"), and therefore by this analysis are placed symmetrically with each other. I will admit that, given the uncertainties of the analysis of structure, I prefer a number like ten and an arrangement in which the two repetitive sequences are symmetrically placed, but I have attempted to set forth the data without predetermining the issue, and I must say that this analysis is by far the most plausible that I have been able to devise.

The analysis of the internal structure of the first unit (50:2–13) has already been set forth (see above, *Identification of the Units*): four sections (vv 2–3, vv 4–7, vv 8–10, and vv 11–13). Verses 2–3 are a bicolon, a tricolon, and a tetracolon. Verses 4–7 are a tricolon, two bicola, a pentacolon, a bicolon, and a tricolon: is v 7 then a balance to v 2?—and similarly is v 3 in rough parity with v 6? Verses 8–10 consist of two tricola and two bicola. Verses 11–13 are a series of six bicola.

An analysis of the internal structure of the second unit (50:14–24) has likewise already been given (see above, *Identification of the Units*): four sections, each analogous to the corresponding sections of the first unit—the battle for Babylon (vv 14–16), the return of Israel (vv 17a, 19–20), the ruin of Babylon (vv 21–23), and the mockery of Babylon (v 24). Verses 14–16 consist of two tetracola, two bicola, and a tricolon; vv 17a + 19–20 of three bicola and a tricolon; vv 21–23 of five bicola; and v 24 of two bicola; the long series of bicola in vv 21–24 thus correspond to a similar series in vv 10–13.

The third unit (50:25–32) seems to fall into three sections (in the form A-B-A'): a short opening, Yahweh's work (v 25); a long central section, the battle for Babylon (vv 26–29); and a short closing, Yahweh's challenge to Babylon (vv 31–32). Verse 25 consists of two bicola; vv 26–29 of three bicola, a tricolon, and four bicola; and vv 31–32 of one tricolon and two bicola.

The fourth unit (50:33–38) consists of two sections: the oppressed children of Israel and their redeemer (vv 33–34); and the sword (vv 35–38). Verses 33–34, after the opening messenger formula, consists of three bicola and a tricolon; vv 35–38 of two tricola and two bicola: There is a certain symmetry here.

The fifth unit (51:1–6) would appear to fall into three short sections, Yahweh's judgment (vv 1–2), the weakness of Babylon (vv 3–5), and the summons to flee (v 6). Verses 1–2, after the messenger formula, consist of a tricolon and a bicolon; vv 3–4 + 5b + 5a of four bicola; and v 6 of a tricolon and a bicolon. Structurally, then, v 6 balances vv 1–2.

It would appear that in the sixth unit (51:7–14) v 7, the description of Babylon as a golden cup, balances vv 13–14, the mocking address to Babylon. In that case the two central sections will be vv 8–10, the report of Israel the healer, and vv 11–12, battle orders. Verse 7 consists of a tetracolon, vv 8–10 of four bicola and a tricolon, vv 11–12 of a bicolon and what can only be a pentacolon, v 13 of a tetracolon, and v 14 of a bicolon.

The seventh unit (51:20–26) obviously divides into two sections: vv 20–24, the mace; and vv 25–26, the challenge to the "Mount of Sesame-oil." Verses 20–24 consist of three bicola, two tricola, and a bicolon; vv 25–26 of two tricola.

The eighth unit (51:27–33) appears to divide into three sections: v 27, battle orders; vv 29–32, the ruin of

Babylon; and v 33, the assurance of Yahweh's judgment. Verse 27 can only be a hexacolon; vv 29–32 are two tetracola, a bicolon, a tricolon, and a closing tetracolon; and v 33, after the messenger formula, is a simple bicolon.

The ninth unit (51:34–44) would appear to divide into four sections: vv 34–35, the words of Jerusalem; vv 36–37, Yahweh's promised retribution; vv 38–39aα + 40 + 39aβb, Babylon the guest at Yahweh's feast; and vv 41–44, Yahweh's punishment of Babylon. These four sections are closely allied: the first and last in the use of the root בלע, "swallow" (vv 34, 44); the first and third in the image of the feast; and the second and fourth in the use of "sea" (vv 36, 42) and images of drought (vv 36, 43). Verses 34–35 consist of two tetracola; vv 36–37, after the messenger formula, of a tetracolon and a bicolon; vv 38–39aα + 40 + 39aβb of two bicola and a tricolon; and vv 41–44 of two bicola, a tricolon, and a tetracolon.

Finally, the tenth unit (51:49–58) appears to break into two sections: vv 49–53, an address to Israel, ending with Yahweh's first-person announcement of judgment; and vv 54–56 + 58. Both sections are matched in their content, depictions of the ruin of Babylon. Verses 49–53 consist of a bicolon followed remarkably by four tricola; vv 54–56 + 58 of seven bicola, excluding the messenger formula at the beginning of v 58.

These ten units are generally comparable in length. The total number of cola of the successive units (not counting the occasional messenger formulas) are as follows: (1) 50:2–13: *48*; (2) 50:14–24: *38*; (3) 50:25–32: *28*; (4) 50:33–38: *19*; (5) 51:1–6: *18*; (6) 51:7–14: *28*; (7) 51:20–26: *20*; (8) 51:27–33: *25*; (9) 51:34–44: *32*; (10) 51:49–58: *28*.

One might propose a pattern in length wherein the first three and the last three are the longest and the middle four are short, short, long, and short, respectively—in general the series might be an example on a large scale of what I have elsewhere called "skewed chiasmus";[16] but such an analysis is obviously far from exact.

The symmetry of the "sword" sequence and the "mace" sequence in the fourth and seventh units, respec-

tively, is noteworthy (see above), but beyond the obvious parallel in structure between the first and second units (see again above), there are no obvious symmetries among the units. There are observations that might be made—for example, that the quotations of Israel are confined to the sixth unit (51:8–10), the ninth (51:34–35), and the tenth (51:51), or again that the occurrences of "be ashamed" (בוש) are confined to the first unit (50:2, 12) and the tenth (51:51), but such data may not really be significant; given the form-critical variety and the unit of content, it is hard to see any overall pattern.

Setting. Nothing in this inquiry argues against a setting for all the units of authentic material within a relatively short space of time (see *Preliminary Observations*). That is to say, the diction that Jrm had used to portray the advent of the foe from the north against Jerusalem was now used to indicate a great reversal, by which Babylon would herself be subjected to her own foe from the north, by implication Israel (50:3); so the sense of that reversal may have stimulated the whole array of oracles within a short period of time. The dearth of obvious structural patterns among the units may suggest that the present order of the units is chronological, or roughly so.

There are two sorts of data that suggest a setting. The first is the narrative in 51:59–64, that in 594 Baruch's brother took with him to Babylon a document with "all these words," "all the evil that should come upon Babylon": the wording is enough like 30:2 to suggest a substantial number of oracles. The summary of Yahweh's words against Babylon in 51:62 reflect two passages in 50:2—51:58: "not to be any inhabitant in it, from man to beast" reflects 50:3, and "it shall be a desolation for ever" reflects 51:26. The spread of these two passages at least suggests the possibility that the whole collection before us was sent to Babylon in 594 and therefore had taken shape in Jrm's mind during the months of that year. He had sent a letter to the Jewish exiles in Babylon, evidently in 594; the occasion of a visit by Baruch's brother to Babylon may have stimulated these present oracles.

Again, there are a couple of links with material elsewhere that may be dated on other grounds: there is notably the link between 50:4 ("walking and weeping

---

16   Holladay, "Recovery," 431–33.

they shall go") and 31:9a ("with weeping they shall come"), part of a passage dated tentatively in the present study to the time after the summer of 588; and there is the contrast between "an everlasting covenant will not be forgotten" (50:5) and the "new covenant" passage (31:31–34), dated in the present study to the autumn of 587. Such links, however, reinforce only slightly the setting already suggested.

Many of the unauthentic additions doubtless antedate the fall of Babylon (50:17b–18; 51:11aβb, the gloss in v 27, vv 28, 46), but given that "Babylon" was used in later centuries for other empires, it is not always possible to be certain.

Interpretation

■ **50:2** For the imperative verbs here compare those in 4:5.

Bel is the title, and Marduk is the name, of the state-god of Babylon: *bel* is the Akkadian form of the Northwest Semitic *ba'al* (on Baal see 2:8). He was conceived as a storm-god and creator.[17]

The two nouns עֲצַבִּים and גִּלּוּלִים, in the secondary addition at the end of the verse, occur only here in Jer. The first, עָצָב, is a general word for "idol"; the related verb עצב means "shape" (Job 10:8). The parallel גִּלּוּל (here "godlet"), a favorite word in Ezekiel, evidently suggests "dung-pellet" (גָּלָל, Zeph 1:17). Both words carry a tone of contempt.[18]

■ **50:3** Though there is no exact parallel for "nation from the north" (גּוֹי מִצָּפוֹן) elsewhere in Jer, there are of course similar phrases (4:6; 5:15; 6:1—and, in the present sequence, v 9). Since references to the foe from the north in chapters 4—6 are understood in the present study to refer to Babylon, the question becomes crucial here what the expression means in the present context. Of course by the time of the advent of Cyrus the reference could be to him (compare Isa 41:25, and compare the secondary addition in Jer 51:11aβ), but Jrm could hardly have had the Medes specifically in mind. He

might have used the expression as a general term for a powerful enemy (see Excursus: The Problem of the Identity of the Foe from the North, after 1:16; so Thompson for the present instance; and *M* in v 9 here suggests this). But there is another possibility, and that is that the "people from the north" here is the exiles of Israel, who could be said to have come to Babylon along the Euphrates from the north: evidence has already been given for the identity of the "mace" in 51:20 as Israel (see Structure, Form, Setting, *50:20–24*). If this identification is possible, it is certainly not explicit in this unit; the expression would lead hearers to wonder who it could be: who in the world could make Babylon a desolation? But if the identification is plausible, it makes the transition to v 4 smoother. (For the identification of the enemy of Babylon in v 9 see there.)

■ **50:4–5** For "walking and weeping they shall go" compare 31:9. "Seek Yahweh" (בקשׁ pi'el + יהוה) is not otherwise found in Jer, but the phrase is found in earlier prophets (Hos 3:5; 5:6; Zeph 1:6; 2:3)—indeed the phrasing here may be a reflection of Hos 3:5. It suggests approaching the deity through the cult (compare Hos 2:9), and that implication is reinforced by "for Zion they shall ask" in v 5. For "ask" in association with "way" compare 6:16; for the return to Zion compare 31:6. This is the only ocurrence of the verb "join oneself" (לוה nip'al) in Jer. In Gen 29:34 this verb functions in word-play on the name of "Levi" at his birth: is there here an echo of that word-play, with its suggestion of the renewal of the cult?

The phrase "everlasting covenant" (בְּרִית עוֹלָם) stands in contrast to the implication of 31:31–34; one can only conclude that this unit is to be dated appreciably earlier than 31:31–34 (see 30:1—31:40, Preliminary Observations, Structure, Setting, *"Sour Grapes" [31:29–30] and the New Covenant [31:31–34]*, and see on the present passage Structure, Form, Setting, *Setting*). On the other hand, in the "new covenant" passage Yahweh promises that he will remember their sin no more, and in this

17   See John Gray, "Bel," *IDB* 1:376, and "Marduk," *IDB* 3:263, with bibliography. The latter article offers a depiction of Marduk on lapis lazuli from the ninth century; it is also reproduced in *ANEP*, 177, figure 523.

18   Christopher R. North, "The Essence of Idolatry," *Von Ugarit nach Qumran, Beiträge zur alttestamentlichen und altorientalischen Forschung Otto Eissfeldt zum 1.*

September 1957 dargebracht (ed. Johannes Hempel and Leonhard Rost; BZAW 77; Berlin: Töpelmann, 1958) 154–55.

respect "remember" is analogous to "not be forgotten" here. One more parallel to "the everlasting covenant will never be forgotten" is to be noted, and that is in 20:11, כְּלִמַּת עוֹלָם לֹא תִשָּׁכֵחַ, "The everlasting disgrace will never be forgotten": in both expressions it is assumed that it is Yahweh who will not forget, though the agent is left unstated in both expressions.

■ **50:6** The first word of the verse, צֹאן ("flock"), echoes the first word of v 5, צִיּוֹן ("Zion"). The diction of the first colon, "Perishing sheep were my people" (צֹאן אֹבְדוֹת הָיָה עַמִּי), is strongly reminiscent of Deut 26:5, "A perishing Aramean is my father" (אֲרַמִּי אֹבֵד אָבִי). The parallel underlines the addition of the perfect verb here, "were"; there will be a change soon. For the use of "sheep" for Israel see 23:1. For the plural adjective with the collective צֹאן compare Gen 30:43.

For "lead astray" (תעה hip'il) compare 23:13; for the indictment of Israel's "shepherds" see 23:1–4. It is possible that "mountain" and "hill" here suggest the place of fertility cult worship (see the discussion of 2:20; and compare the diction of 3:23). This is the only occurrence of רֵבֶץ, "fold," in Jer: It denotes a place where animals may "lie" (רבץ).

■ **50:7** The first colon, כָּל־מוֹצְאֵיהֶם אֲכָלוּם, "All who found them ate them," is a variant of the third colon of 2:3, כָּל־אֹכְלָיו יֶאְשָׁמוּ, "All who ate of him were held guilty," and of the first colon of 30:16, כָּל־אֹכְלַיִךְ יֵאָכֵלוּ, "All who eat of you shall be eaten." In both 30:16 and the present verse it is the Babylonians who "eat" Israel.

And it is "their enemies," the Babylonians, who claim they are not guilty; this claim is comparable to Israel's claim in 2:23, "I have not sinned." Is the quotation complete with "we are not guilty," or does it continue? Volz and Rudolph restrict the quotation to "we are not guilty," but Bright, along with current translations (*RSV, JB, NEB, NAB, NJV*), extends the quotation to the end of the verse. The subject of "they sinned against Yahweh . . . hope of their fathers" is clearly Israel. The other occurrence of תַּחַת אֲשֶׁר (here "inasmuch as") in the book is 29:19; there, in a similar context, Yahweh speaks judgment against Israel; this suggests that it is Yahweh who speaks here, not the Babylonians. Furthermore 30:15, on which 30:16 is built (which resembles the first colon of the present verse), offers a judgment on Israel's sin spoken by Yahweh. It is better then to confine the quotation to "We are not guilty" and to understand that

the Babylonians ate Israel and said what they did because Israel had sinned against Yahweh. The verb "be guilty" itself, אשם, means "be held guilty" as well (see the discussion in 2:3).

For "righteous home" (נְוֵה־צֶדֶק) see 31:23. For מִקְוֵה, "hope of," see 14:8.

■ **50:8** If הוֹי or הוֹי הוֹי is correctly restored at the beginning of the verse, it is little more than a call for attention, in much the way it functions in Isa 55:1. The imperative נֻדוּ means "wander (aimlessly)," and it is possible that it is a miscopying of נֻסוּ, "flee" (so the sequence in 51:6). But the two verbs are associated elsewhere (49:30), and refugees do not always have a firm goal, so the word may be correct here. The expression "be like he-goats before the flock" is of course linked to v 6: the diction implies an address to Israel to manifest strong leadership (like the implication of 31:21–22: see there). The עַתּוּד normally refers to the mature he-goat, though in Gen 31:10, 12 it appears to refer to the ram as well.

■ **50:9** The text offered by both *G* and *M* describe the enemy of Babylon as a coalition of nations (see Text), a description suggesting a different identity for that enemy than the one proposed for v 3, namely Israel. But it is noteworthy that in 31:8 returning Israel is called קָהָל גָּדוֹל, "a great company"; and since 31:8 also contains a phrase close to a phrase in v 4 here, "walking and weeping they shall go," the way is open to understand the original reference here likewise to be to Israel: I propose to read "a great company" here. This reconstruction gains slightly in plausibility when it is noticed that in 6:22 the text reads "a great nation" (גּוֹי גָּדוֹל), and 6:22–23 offers diction of which the present verse is a variation (see Structure, Form, Setting, *Preliminary Observations*). If this reconstruction is sound, then both *G* and *M* will represent different expansions of the text: it is possible that גָּדוֹל was misread as גּוֹיִם. The diction used by Jrm continues (as in v 3) to vary that used to describe the attack by the foe from the north against Judah: thus "arouse" (עור hip'il) is comparable to the use of the nip'al stem of that verb in 6:22, and for "form up" (ערך) compare 6:23. If, then, Israel is that "great company," the great reversal continues.

For "bereave" compare Text and see 15:7; "return empty" is reminiscent of 14:3. (It appears that these last two cola are a deliberate reminiscence of the opening and closing sections of 14:1—15:9.)

■ **50:10** For the phrase "become loot" compare 49:32; "all those looting her" (כָּל־שֹׁלְלֶיהָ) is reminiscent of "all those plundering you" (כָּל־בֹּזְזַיִךְ) in 30:16. "Be sated" (שׂבע) means of course "eat one's fill": for the connection between "eat" and "plunder" see 31:16.

■ **50:11** The inhabitants of Babylon are addressed. The three occurrences of כִּי here are concessive ("though"),[19] at least by implication; *NAB* translates them "yes," and *JB* paraphrases to indicate irony ("Rejoice, if you like!"). "Rejoice" and "exult" refer to Babylon's victories (for "exult," עלז, compare 15:17). For "despoil" (שׁסה) compare 30:16. "My possession" (נַחֲלָתִי) refers both to the land given to Israel (2:7) and to the people Israel (10:16): see the discussion on 12:7.

The verb פּושׁ is used both here and in Mal 3:20 of the behavior of calves let out to pasture. For אַבִּירִים in the meaning "stallions" see 47:3.

■ **50:12** "Your mother" is Babylon personified (compare the personifications in Hos 2:4 and Isa 50:1). For "be greatly shamed" compare 20:11 (there "be utterly discredited"). The designation "last of the nations" (אַחֲרִית גֹויִם) for Babylon is the opposite of "first of the nations" (רֵאשִׁית הַגֹּויִם) in Amos 6:1 (compare the discussion in Interpretation for Jer 2:3 on that expression in Amos). For the vocabulary of the last colon see 2:6. The primary meaning here is that Babylon will become a literal wilderness (compare v 13a), but the fact that "your mother" resembles Hos 2:4 suggests that Babylon will become a metaphorical wilderness as well, as Yahweh threatened to make Israel in Hos 2:5.

■ **50:13** For "fury" (קֶצֶף) see 10:10. For ישׁב in the meaning "be inhabited" see 17:5–6. For "become a desolation" see 4:27; for "everyone passing will be horrified" and "hiss" see 18:16; "hiss at all her blows" occurs first in 19:8.

■ **50:14–16** The imperatives in these verses are directed to the enemies of Babylon: if foremost in the attention is Israel (compare the discussion on v 9), then here, too, Israel is the primary addressee (note ערך, "form up,"

here as well as in v 9).

■ **50:14** For "who draw the bow" see 46:9. "Shoot" (ידה) occurs only here in the qal stem in the OT, though the pi'el occurs elsewhere, and the meaning is not in doubt. The verb "spare" (חמל) has occurred earlier in the book (see 13:14), but this is its first occurrence as a transitive verb; this use recurs in 51:3.

■ **50:15** This is the only occurrence of רוע hip'il, "shout," in Jer; though it is used in a variety of contexts, here it is clearly a war-cry. "Offer [נתן] one's hand" means "submit, surrender" (so Lam 5:6). The noun אָשְׁיָה, "tower," occurs only here in the OT, but its Akkadian cognate assures its meaning.[20] For "destroy" (הרס) see 1:10. For "retribution" (נְקָמָה) see 11:20; for the related "gain satisfaction" (נקם nip'al) see 15:15. The closing colon is a perfect expression of the reversal of the position of Babylon and Israel.

■ **50:16** Though it is the hip'il stem of כרת that is more common with persons (9:20—see Text on the present passage), the qal does occur in that sense (11:19). Sowing and reaping are obvious correlatives (Ps 126:5). For "wield" (תפשׂ) see 2:8 (there "handle"). The sickle (מַגָּל) was doubtless similar in shape to modern sickles: The cutting edge of earlier ones consisted of flints arranged on a haft; later sickles were made of iron.[21]

This verse offers the second occurrence of a puzzling phrase that *M* transmits as מִפְּנֵי חֶרֶב הַיֹּונָה; the other occurrence is 46:16. Translations, beginning with the Versions, have treated both occurrences identically: for these renderings see 46:16.

The two passages evidently have a setting in the last part of Jrm's career (see 46:13–28, Setting, and see on the present passage Structure, Form, Setting, *Setting*). Therefore in interpretation both passages have to be examined together. As with 46:16, I assume that the last two words of the expression form a construct phrase (see there). I further propose that the two occurrences offer

---

19 Joüon, *Gramm.*, sec. 171b.

20 See Harold R. (Chaim) Cohen, *Biblical Hapax Legomena in the Light of Akkadian and Ugaritic* (SBLDS 37; Missoula, MT: Scholars, 1978) 46–47.

21 For an Egyptian wall-painting portraying reaping see *ANEP*, figure 91. For sickle flints see "Sickle," *IDB* 4:343, with photograph; for iron sickles see Barrois, *Manuel*, 313, figure 115; and for both sickle flints

and iron sickles see Kurt Galling, "Sichel," in *Biblisches Reallexikon* (Tübingen: Mohr [Siebeck], 1977) 293, figure 77.

variant vocalizations. In the last part of 46:16 the speakers are underlings in the Egyptian army, perhaps mercenaries, fighting in Judah (see Form and Interpretation there); the appeal to flee in that passage is to abandon the ranks of the army. Here, by contrast, the speakers are subject peoples in Babylon; the immediate context is not combat but lack of food. I propose then that חֶרֶב, "sword," is correct in 46:16 but that the word is to be vocalized חֹרֶב, "devastation, drought," here (compare the shift from the repeated חֶרֶב, "sword," in vv 35–37 to חֹרֶב, "drought," in v 38). In 46:16 the oppressing power is evidently Rahab (if the text is correctly emended), construed as masculine: the participle there must therefore be הַיּוֹנֶה. Here, by contrast, the oppressor is Babylon, construed as feminine (v 15b): the participle here must therefore be הַיּוֹנָה. (For another instance of variant vocalizations of the same consonant sequence see 7:3 and 7.)

For the last two cola compare again 46:16. The verbs may also be translated "each will return" and "each will flee," but the association of these verbs with the imperatives in vv 14–16a, and the existence of the cohortative "let us return" in the analogous 46:16, makes the assumption of jussives here preferable.

■ **50:17a** The first colon is similar to the first colon of v 6. But whereas צֹאן (v 6) is a collective term for sheep and goats, שֶׂה evidently denotes an individual sheep,[22] usually a female, as here; some authorities assume it is a juvenile, but not all.[23] This is the only occurrence of the word in Jer. The participle פְּזוּרָה means literally "scattered"; Israel was scattered in the exile, but it is better to stay with the diction of the personification of a single ewe-lamb that has strayed from her pasture. It is ironic that one ewe-lamb should be chased by many lions! For "chase" (נדח hip'il) see 23:2.

■ **50:17b–18** The lion is a simile or metaphor for both Assyria (Isa 5:29) and Babylon (4:7), so that a later midrash on the "lions" becomes plausible.

■ **50:19** For the first colon compare 23:3; but here, in contrast to 23:2 and 4, the subject of רעה is not the shepherds but the sheep. For Carmel see 46:18; for Bashan see 22:20; for Mount Ephraim see 4:15; for Gilead see 8:22. These areas are famous for lush pasture (Mic 7:14).

■ **50:20** For the parallel of עָוֹן, the offense and the consequent "guilt" (2:22), and חַטָּאת, "sins," in a passage declaring the opposite of the affirmation of the present verse, see 30:15; that verse is reversed by 30:16–17 (see there), and the diction of the present verse (with "sin" and "forgive") is similar to that in 31:34b.

■ **50:21** The imperatives in this verse are masculine singular, in contrast with the masculine plural imperatives in vv 14–16a. The addressee is evidently Israel: so particularly the expression "do all I have commanded you" (on the identification see Structure, Form, Setting, *Form of the Authentic Material*).

"Merathaim" and "Pekod" are Babylonian names representing Babylon. They are names with which Jrm can offer word-play: *mĕrātayim* would mean "double rebellion" in Hebrew, derived from the root מרה, "be rebellious"; *pĕqôd* would mean "punishment" (פקד). But "Merathaim" is evidently a reference to *(nār) marratu*, "bitter river," either the Persian Gulf or a lagoon area near the mouth of the Tigris and Euphrates, or both;[24] "Peqod" refers to the *puqūdu*, one of the Aramean tribes in southeastern Babylonia (compare Ezek 23:23).[25] There is no obvious answer to the question why מְרָתַיִם should be dual: one thinks of the dual form of מִצְרַיִם, "Egypt" (so Rudolph), and one thinks too of the "double crime" (שְׁתַּיִם רָעוֹת) of which Israel was accused (2:13), but the precise point is lost on us.

This is the first occurrence of חרב, "slay," in Jer (but compare 31:2). For "devote to destruction" (חרם hip'il) see 25:9.

■ **50:22** Surprisingly there is no exact parallel in Jer for the expression קוֹל מִלְחָמָה, "the sound of battle" (it also occurs in Exod 32:17), but Jrm has used קוֹל, "the sound of," in a variety of phrases connected with battle, begin-

---

22 Zorell, p. 794b.
23 Not specifically juvenile: BDB, Zorell; specifically juvenile: KB; B. Davie Napier, "Lamb," *IDB* 3:58. Commentators and translations also differ.
24 For references see *AHR*, 612b.
25 See Manfred Dietrich, *Die Aramäer Südbabyloniens in der Sargonidenzeit (700–648)* (AOAT 7; Neukirchen: Neukirchener, 1970) 5–6; Zimmerli, *Ezekiel 1*, 488,

n. 29, gives additional references.

ning in 4:19. "Great collapse" (שֶׁבֶר גָּדוֹל) is found first in 4:6.

■ **50:23** This verse is a mocking lament (see Structure, Form, Setting, *Form of the authentic material*). For . . . אֵיךְ וַיִּשָּׁבֵר compare אֵיכָה נִשְׁבַּר (48:17). Babylon is the "sledgehammer" (פַּטִּישׁ) of all the earth: for this word see 23:29.

■ **50:24** The mockery of v 23 continues. For the reading of the first verb as second-person singular feminine see Text. This is the only occurrence of יקשׁ, "set a snare," in Jer, but the derived noun יָקוֹשׁ, "fowler," is found in 5:26. "For yourself" is ambiguous—the ethical dative may be of either advantage or disadvantage (GKC, sec. 119s). The phrase suggests that Babylon set a snare for her advantage, and it turned out to be a disadvantage. It is hard to avoid the conclusion that when Jrm said יָקֹשְׁתִּי לָךְ וְגַם־נִלְכַּדְתְּ he had in mind the pattern of 31:19, בֹּשְׁתִּי, וְגַם־נִכְלַמְתִּי, "I was ashamed, even humiliated," in spite of the contrast of word choice; even closer to וְגַם־נִלְכַּדְתְּ is גַּם־אַתְּ תִּלָּכֵדִי (48:7).

This is the only occurrence in Jer of גרה hitpaʿel, "challenge": it means "provoke a fight."

■ **50:25** Yahweh has a "storehouse" (אוֹצָר) for rain, hail, or snow (see 10:13); this is the only occurrence of the word in the Hebrew Scriptures for Yahweh's storehouse of weapons, though it occurs in Sir 39:30. Yahweh has the work of battle to do with the Babylonians!

■ **50:26–27** The commands in these verses are to the enemies of Babylon; the diction of v 28 suggests that they are directed specifically to Israel. They are analogous to the commands in v 16: there the commands were to bar the process of sowing and reaping, while here they are to destroy food supplies. One assumes a movement of thought from "storehouse" in v 25 to "granaries" in v 26. This is the only occurrence of "granary" (מַאֲבֻס) in the OT, but the connection with אבם, "fatten (on grain)," and with אֵבוּס, "feeding-trough," makes the meaning secure.

The function of the suffix in סָלּוּהָ is unclear: it is probably accusative, "pile her up," metonymy for "pile up her substance" (so the implication of the following verb, וְהַחֲרִימוּהָ, and compare the diction of 5:17a), but it could be taken as dative as well, "pile up (her supplies) to her disadvantage," given the existence of לָהּ at the end of v

26 (compare the remark on the dative in v 24). For "devote to destruction" in v 26 and "slay" in v 27 compare v 21. For "slay all her bulls" G has "dry up all her fruits," a translation implying a homonymous חרב and כָּל־פְּרִיהָ, and the Syro-Hexapla implies that aʾ read the same. This is plausible for the colon itself but does not fit what follows!

This is the only occurrence in Jer of פַּר. There has been uncertainty whether to understand the word as "bull" in general or specifically "young bull"; a recent study has indicated that the word refers to a bull-calf between the ages of four months and a year, approximately.[26] The bulls here may be literal bulls (meat alongside of grain in v 26), but since "bulls" are used also of personal and national enemies (Ps 22:13; Ezek 39:18), one assumes that the reference here may equally be to the Babylonians themselves. For "go down" with "to slaughter" compare 48:15.

■ **50:28** The exiles from Israel will return to Zion (compare v 5). For "retribution of Yahweh" see 11:20, and compare v 15b.

■ **50:29** The reconstructed word "archers," רֹבִים, singular רֹבֶה, occurs in Gen 21:20. "Escape" (פְּלֵטָה) picks up "fugitives" (פְּלֵטִים) in v 28: those fugitives were presumably exiles from Israel, whereas here there is to be no escape for Babylon. For "Recompense her according to her deed," compare v 15, "As she has done, do to her."

This is the only occurrence in Jer of the verb זיד/זוד, "be arrogant"; the other occurrence of the qal stem is in Exod 18:11, unfortunately in an obscure text. The noun derivative, however, has appeared in 49:16 (see there), and appears in vv 31–32: the verb covers "be insolent, presumptuous" and the like.

■ **50:30** See 49:26.

■ **50:31–32** In the formula of encounter Babylon is given the cover name of זָדוֹן, "Arrogance": Babylon personifies arrogance. Verse 31b is a variation on v 27b. "Stumble and fall" in v 32 is found elsewhere (46:6, 12, 16). The pattern of "with none to [restore]" is found with other verbs (4:4; 9:21). Verse 32b is a variation on 21:14; both follow the pattern of Amos 1:14a.

■ **50:33** "Oppress" (עשׁק) is used by Jrm for the oppression of the poor by the rich (7:6; 21:12; compare עֹשֶׁק,

26   René Péter, "פר et שׁור, Note de lexicographie hébraïque," *VT* 25 (1975) 486–96.

"oppression," 6:6; 22:17); now it is the oppression of Israel by Babylon. The verb "refuse" (מאן pi'el) is common in Jrm, but with "to let go" (שלח pi'el) the phrase specifically recollects the exodus tradition (Exod 4:23; 7:14, 27; 9:2—all J[27]). Babylon thus takes on the role of Pharaoh of old.

■ **50:34** If Babylon "has held (Israel) fast" (הֶחֱזִיקוּ, v 33), Israel's redeemer is "strong" (חָזָק). For "redeemer" see on 31:10–11.[28] For the cognate accusative phrase with ריב compare the similar cognate accusative phrase with דין in 5:28; 22:16; 30:13. The word-play between הַרְגִּיעַ, "give rest," and הִרְגִּיז, "shake," is typical of Jrm (compare Structure, Form, Setting, *Authentic and Unauthentic Material in 50:2—51:19*). "Give rest" occurs also in 31:2.

■ **50:35–38** For this sequence see Structure, Form, Setting, *Form of the Authentic Material*.

Beyond the question of a feminine suffix on the word "diviners" (v 36), which is surely necessary, the noun itself is uncertain. It is given as בַּדִּים, and there is one other occurrence of this word where the meaning "diviners" fits (Isa 44:25). There is clear attestation for בַּדִּים in the meaning "bragging" or "braggarts" (48:30), and since in the convention of the mockery of pagan religion pagan diviners could always be called "braggarts" or "liars," it is difficult to insist on the meaning "diviners." On the other hand the existence of the Akkadian word *bārû*, "diviner," suggests the possibility of reading בָּרִים in both the present passage and Isa 44:25. But *HALAT* records an Amorite word *baddum* for a functionary, so it is possible that בַּדִּים is correct here after all, and that Jrm intends a pun on "liars," given "her wise men" just previous.[29]

For "rabble" (v 37) see the discussion on 25:20. For the curse of warriors become women see Form on 30:6.

"Drought" is surely correct in v 38, though S has "sword"; Rudolph argues for the latter reading, suggesting that "sword" has the extended meaning of "war," and that the reference is not to the Tigris and Euphrates but to irrigation canals. But "drought" is the *lectio difficilior*. (See further Structure, Form, Setting, *50:33–45*.)

For "idols" see 8:19. This is the only occurrence of אֵימָה, "terror," in Jer, and the only occurrence in the OT of the noun in the meaning "idol": whether the implication here is "a shape that inspires dread in its devotees" (the implication of *HALAT*) or "a dreadful thing (from the point of view of the Yahwist)" (so BDB) is uncertain—perhaps both. For הלל hitpo'el, "run wild," see 25:16 (and compare 46:9).

■ **50:39–40** It is uncertain whether the nouns translated here "goblins" and "ghouls" (צִיִּים and אִיִּים) refer to wild animals (*RSV*: "wild beasts" and "hyenas") or demons (the rendering here is that of Bright). One thing is certain: that the words are chosen for their rhyme (like תֹהוּ וָבֹהוּ in 4:23 and Gen 1:2)—one notes the altogether different denotation of the same words in Ps 72:9, 10. Cornill, and Rudolph following him, translates the words in the present passage *Fuchs und Luchs*, literally "fox and lynx." Both are evidently adjectival forms; the first refers to one who lives in the צִיָּה, the land of arid wastes (see 2:6), the second evidently refers to one who lives in the אִיִּים, the coastlands and islands, thus the far reaches (2:10). The Versions are of no help, offering various animals or mythic creatures. Thus G understands the clause differently ("Idols shall live in the islands"). V reads "Dragons shall live with fig fauns," "fauns" denoting the rural deities associated with Pan, and the attribute "fig" perhaps referring to their rank luxuriance. S has only one noun, "Sirens shall dwell in it." T has "Desert beasts [or, according to others, monkeys] shall join with cats." Charles C. Torrey insists persuasively that the words refer to various demons.[30] Julius Wellhausen offers many observations on the association of demons and wild animals in the surviving pagan beliefs of the Arabs: "Zoology is demonology as well"; "Ostriches and foxes are the animals that demons prefer to ride"; "Simeon Stylites drove out demons and wild animals at the same time as paganism from the landscape of Lebanon."[31]

27 Martin Noth, *Exodus* (Philadelphia: Westminster, 1962) 34, 70; Childs, *Exodus*, 94, 131.

28 See further n. 87 in the discussion of 31:10–11.

29 See further Elliger, *Deuterojesaja*, 453–54.

30 Charles C. Torrey, *The Second Isaiah, A New Interpretation* (New York: Scribner, 1928) 289–91.

31 Julius Wellhausen, *Reste arabischen Heidentums* (Berlin: Reimer, 1897) 151, 152, 152, n. 2.

Given the association of wild animals and demons as expressions of the uncanny, there is no way to determine the meaning of these nouns with precision;[32] it may be noted that Wildberger, for Isa 13:21–22, translates them as "demons" and "wild dogs," respectively.[33]

This is the only occurrence in Jer of the expression בְּנוֹת יַעֲנָה, "ostriches": these birds were proverbial inhabitants of deserted places (Isa 13:21).[34]

■ **50:41–43** These verses are an adaptation of 6:22–24: for the details of wording see there, and for the identity of the "people coming from the north" in the present passage see v 3.

■ **50:44–46** These verses are an adaptation of 49:19–21: for the details of wording see there.

■ **51:1–2** For "arouse" (עור hip'il) see 50:9.

Jrm must have had 4:11 in mind when he associated a "destructive wind" with "winnow"; for this wind see the description of the hot wind in 4:11 (and compare further the desert wind, 13:24, and the east wind, 18:17). For "winnowing" as a symbol of judgment see 15:7. "Lay waste" is בקק polel: this is the only occurrence of this stem of the verb in the OT, but the qal stem occurs in 19:7. For "close in around her" (הָיָה עָלֶיהָ מִסָּבִיב) see 4:17.

■ **51:3** The interpretation of this verse is difficult: if the occurrences of אַל in each of the first two cola are to be read as jussive negatives, then the "bowman" represents the Babylonian army; if there are no negatives, then the "bowman" represents the enemy of Babylon. One can argue either way. In favor of the latter alternative, that the "bowman" is the enemy of Babylon, one may assume that if the cola of the verse are addressed to the enemy (so certainly the last two cola), then all the verbs of the verse express actions under the control, so to speak, of the enemy of Babylon (so Cornill, Volz, Condamin; so Bright, with hesitation). On the other hand, one could see two jussive negatives in the first two cola completed by a third jussive negative in the third colon. And one must reckon with the connotation of the verb עלה (יִתְעַל hitpa'el), which occurs only here in the OT; it surely must mean "raise oneself up," or "try to raise oneself up," but in that case is a curious verb here: why not use לבש, "put on (a coat of mail)," as in 46:4?—indeed Rudolph

actually emends the present text with לבש. I can only conclude that the verb is used to mock the Babylonian bowmen, too weak to pull themselves up to a standing position with the weight of their armor: if such armor is rightly described in the discussion of 46:4 (see Interpretation there), the weight should not be excessive! By this interpretation the "bowman" will stand in parallel with "her youths" and "her whole army." And under the assumption that this verse continues a unit begun in v 1, I emend "the bowman" to "her bowman" (see Text, note b—b): the parallel will then be even closer.

The phrase "do not spare [חמל] any arrow" has occurred in 50:14; here the verb takes as object not the weapon but the victim: "Do not spare her youths." For "devote to destruction" compare 50:21 and 26, and see 25:9.

■ **51:4** "The slain" (חֲלָלִים) is literally "those pierced" (on the word see 8:23); the word here may thus refer to those who are mortally wounded rather than those who are dead. The parallel דקר, מְדֻקָּרִים pu'al is synonymous, but the context of the other occurrence of this word in Jer, 37:10, necessitates the meaning "wounded."

■ **51:5** For the rearrangement of v 5b before v 5a see Text, note a—a.

This is the only occurrence in the book of אָשָׁם, "guilt," but the related verb אשם, "be guilty, be held guilty," occurs in a similar context in 50:7—there the Babylonians insist they are not guilty (for the meaning of the verb see 2:3).

The operative word in v 5a, אַלְמָן, is the masculine form of אַלְמָנָה, "widow," either a noun "widower" or an adjective "widowed." The implication is that Yahweh is the husband of Israel and has not deserted her: if the use of "guilt" in v 5b recalls 2:3, the image of Yahweh as the husband of Israel recalls 2:2.

■ **51:6** The diction of the first two cola closely resembles that of the first colon of 48:6.

The intent of the third colon is not clear, because the nuance of עָוֹן here, and of the verb, דמם nip'al, is not clear. Given אָשָׁם, "guilt," in v 5b, one assumes that עָוֹן carries its normal meaning "iniquity"; the phrase may then mean "Do not grow silent [or perish, or weep: see 8:14] in her iniquity," that is, "Do not become paralyzed,

32 See further Pedersen, I/II, 455, and the bibliography in Theodor H. Gaster, "Demon, demonology" *IDB* 1:824, sec. 21.

33 Wildberger, *Jesaja*, 501, 504; see the discussion in 523.

34 W. Stewart McCullough, "Ostrich," *IDB* 3:611–12.

or fall dead, under Babylon's oppression of you." But עָוֹן may mean "punishment (for one's iniquity)" as well, and the fact that the following colon refers to the "retribution" of Yahweh suggests that "punishment" is the meaning here—thus, "Do not perish in her punishment," that is, flee the city before Yahweh's punishment comes upon her.

"Retribution" occurs frequently (see 11:20); its parallel גְּמוּל, "requital," appears in the book only here, but its accompanying verb "recompense" (שלם pi'el) has occurred in 50:29.

■ **51:7** For the image of the cup from which the guests are forced to drink and from which they become drunken see the discussion on 25:15. Babylon is a "cup of gold," presumably because she is "great in treasures" (v 13). It is evidently a glossator who has explained that she is a cup "in the hand of Yahweh": one might compare the metaphor of Coniah, the signet ring on Yahweh's right hand (22:24). Not only is "Babylon" feminine, but so is the noun כּוֹס, "cup" (Lam 4:21); therefore the participle מְשַׁכֶּרֶת, "making drunken," may modify either noun, and "her wine" may as well be "its wine." For הלל hitpo'el, "go mad," see 25:16.

■ **51:8** For the evidence that the first colon is a quotation see Structure, Form, Setting, *Form of the Authentic Material*. For צֳרִי, "balm," see 8:22; "obtain balm" is found likewise in 46:11, there a recommendation for healing Egypt.

■ **51:9** For רפא pi'el meaning "treat" rather than "heal" see 6:14; for the potential meaning of the nip'al participle ("[un]treatable") see 3:21.

"Touch" means "reach to": the punishment (and thus the guilt) of Babylon is piled up so high it reaches the heavens (compare the same use of נגע, "touch," in Mic 1:9 in the context of an unhealable wound). One wonders whether the expression is not a cliché; Thompson suggests it is proverbial. But it may indicate that the judgment reaches to the top of the Babylonian ziggurats (compare v 53) or even to the Babylonian gods;[35] that

impression is reinforced by the last colon, "and is exalted to the clouds," since "is exalted" (נשא nip'al) is used of Yahweh's servant (Isa 52:13) and of Yahweh himself (Isa 57:15). This is the only occurrence of שַׁחַק, "cloud," in the book: the word originally meant "dust cloud."

■ **51:10** "Bring forth (our righteousness)" means "exhibit" it; the same verb, with the object צֶדֶק, occurs in Ps 37:6. "Our righteousness" (צִדְקֹתֵנוּ) here implies "our vindication" (so *RSV*, *NJV*); it is not really "our innocence" (so *NEB*) but "our integrity" (*JB*). That is to say, Yahweh has restored Israel to himself by generous justice; compare the explanation of Zorell: "From the benevolent justice of God flow generous gifts that are given to the just."[36]

■ **51:11** "Sharpen" (ברר hip'il) occurs only here in the book.

The meaning of שְׁלָטִים (here "quivers") has been uncertain. Beyond the present passage the word occurs six times in the OT: 2 Sam 8:7 = 1 Chr 18:7; 2 Kgs 11:10 = 2 Chr 23:9; Ezek 27:11; Cant 4:4. In the present passage *G* renders φαρέτρας, and *V faretras*, thus "quivers" (and this is also the rendering of *G* and *V* for Ezek 27:11 and of *s'* for 2 Sam 8:7); the translation of *S* and *T* in the present passage is simply the cognate of the word. Rashi interprets the word here by "quivers," Qimḥi by "shields"; the meaning "shields" won out in Luther and *KJV* and in the commentaries. If "shields" is correct, then the verb "fill" here must be understood either as "gather" (so Qimḥi) or as "fill out," that is, "make ready" or "take up" (the last is the rendering of *RSV*). But Rykle Borger has recently published a thorough study of the word[37] and concludes that "quivers" is correct, and this translation has been accepted by *JB*, *NEB*, *NAB*, and *NJV*; "fill" can now be taken in its normal meaning. There are, however, several details that remain obscure. The word occurs in Akkadian (*šalṭu*), presumably with the same or similar meaning, but it is evidently an Aramaic loanword into Akkadian. Again, there is another Hebrew word that clearly means quiver, אַשְׁפָּה (5:16), a word occurring with this meaning in Ugaritic as well ('*utpt*), and the

---

35 So the suggestion of Philippe Reymond, *L'eau, sa vie, sa signification dans l'Ancien Testament* (VTSup 6; Leiden: Brill, 1958) 30.

36 "*Ex benevola iustitia Dei fluunt larga dona quae iustis dantur*," Zorell, p. 684a.

37 Rykle Borger, "Die Waffenträger des Königs Darius, Ein Beitrag zur alttestamentlichen Exegese und zur semitischen Lexikographie," *VT* 22 (1972) 385–98.

Akkadian cognate *išpatu* is the normal word for quiver. Borger suggests that the word originally meant "bow-case" (this meaning would fit the occurrence in 2 Sam 8:7);[38] the word then may have shifted to cover "quiver" as well, perhaps of a different style.

For the Medes see 25:25–26. The Median Empire loomed large until the middle of the sixth century, when it was incorporated into the Persian Empire under Cyrus; the anticipated Median attack on Babylon therefore never materialized (compare Isa 13:17–19).[39]

■ **51:12** Again the enemies of Babylon are told to take military steps for the coming battle. For "raise a signal" see 4:6. "Strengthen the watch": this is the only occurrence in the book of "(the) watch" (מִשְׁמָר)—the word covers a variety of meanings connected with guarding and custody. The following phrase, with the cognate שֹׁמְרִים (here "sentries"), would seem to be indistinguishable from it, but doubtless some special meaning is intended: Bright translates "set up the road blocks," suggesting that these are to prevent sorties from the city. On the other hand, "prepare those in ambush" suggests that the enemy can take advantage of sorties from the city in order to rush the gates (Bright, Thompson).

■ **51:13** שָׁכַן, "dwell," is really a synonym for the more common יָשַׁב "live," but if there is a difference, שָׁכַן suggests a temporary stay: if that nuance is perceived here, it is an ironic word indeed for Babylon. "Many waters" originally referred to the mythological underground ocean, the source of the streams that fertilize the earth.[40] The expression is used of the Euphrates in Isa 8:7; here it suggests not only the Euphrates and the many Babylonian irrigation canals but the cosmic pretensions of Babylon as well.

It is a nice touch to place רַבַּת, "great (in)," after מַיִם רַבִּים, "many waters." "Treasures" may equally well be "storehouses" (see the remark on 48:7).

"Your end has come" is reminiscent of Amos 8:2, "The end has come upon my people Israel": "end" not only refers to the time-span of Babylon but is a word for annihilation.[41]

The phrase translated "the extent of your share" is literally "the cubit of your cut." The first word, אַמָּה, "cubit," means "measure, extent" only in the present passage. The second word, בֶּצַע, is, however, evidently ambiguous, and the translation given is an attempt to cover both meanings. The first is to take the word as the noun "(your) profit," the meaning of the noun in 6:13: the implication is that Babylon has become great in treasures by taking her cut, but that now she has received all she will ever get (so Luther; so *KJV*, "the measure of thy covetousness," and *JB*, "the finish of your pillaging"; so BDB). The second is to take the word either as the noun in the meaning of "(your) breaking off," that is, "(your) end of life" (so Zorell), or more commonly, as the infinitive construct of the verb בצע, "cutting you off," that is, "cutting off the threads of your life" (so *RSV*, "the thread of your life is cut," and so *NAB*, "the term at which you shall be cut off"; so *HALAT*; so Rudolph, Bright). It is to be noted that a suffixed infinitive construct may have *i* in the first syllable (GKC, sec. 61b). The pi'el stem of בצע appears with this meaning in Isa 38:12, "He cuts me off from the loom," so that the qal stem might carry the meaning as well. Given "treasures" in the second colon and "end" in the third, it is likely that both meanings are present.

■ **51:14** Yahweh's threat to Babylon is a terrible one. Babylon had been a huge city: in the Chaldean period it covered a thousand hectares (2,500 acres),[42] and it therefore had an immense population. Yet Yahweh will fill it with the enemy, human beings (אָדָם) as numerous as locusts. The word for "locusts," יֶלֶק, is the designation for the first developmental stage of the insect.[43] For the destructiveness of locusts see the remarks on 5:16.

For "shout" (הֵידָד) see 25:30.

■ **51:15–19** See on 10:12–16.

■ **51:20–24** The noun מַפֵּץ, "mace," occurs only in v 20 in the OT, though the noun is probably to be restored in Prov 25:18. In both the present passage and Prov 25:18

---

38   P. Kyle McCarter, *II Samuel* (AB 9; Garden City, NY: Doubleday, 1984) 250.

39   Mark J. Dresden, "Media," *IDB* 3:320.

40   Herbert G. May, "Some Cosmic Connotations of *mayim rabbîm*, 'Many Waters,'" *JBL* 74 (1955) 9–21.

41   See the remarks on Ezek 7:2 in Zimmerli, *Ezekiel 1*, 203–204.

42   Oppenheim, *Ancient Mesopotamia*, 140.

43   Wolff, *Joel and Amos*, 27–28.

it is clear that the noun refers to a weapon, and the expression כְּלִי מַפָּץ in Ezek 9:2 is synonymous. Though Babylon is called a "sledgehammer" in 50:23, that is another word, פַּטִּישׁ. The verb נפץ, to which the present noun is related, means "shatter, smash" in both the qal and pi'el stems—the qal passive participle occurs in 22:28 (see there), and it is the pi'el verb that occurs nine times in the present passage. The noun must therefore mean "war club," "maul," "mace."[44]

For the identification of the addressee as Israel in exile, and for the scheme of listing in these verses, see Structure, Form, Setting, *51:20–24*. Given the sort of pairings one has here, it is clear that the contrast of זָקֵן וָנַעַר is one of age (here "elder and youngster"), though נַעַר is not at all precise in its age range: it is translated "youth" in 1:6–7. On the other hand, the contrast here of בָּחוּר וּבְתוּלָה is, like "husband and wife," one of sex (here "youth and maiden"): the reference is evidently to unmarried adolescents: for בָּחוּר see 6:11, whereas בְּתוּלָה is normally "virgin" (as in 2:32). For a discussion of אִכָּר, "farmer," see 14:4. This is the only occurrence in Jer of צֶמֶד, "team"; the word applies to any plowing team, but normally of oxen. "Governors and prefects" translates two terms (פַּחוֹת וּסְגָנִים) that are loanwords from Akkadian designating ranks of officials: פֶּחָה is the Akkadian *bêl pīḥati* or *bêl pāḥati*, "lord of a district"; סָגָן (or סֶגֶן) is the Akkadian *šaknu* "appointed."[45] In the OT the two words form a pair and occur frequently in passages from this period onward, not only for officials of the Assyrians (Ezek 23:6), Babylonians (the present passage), and Medes (v 28) but also for the leadership of the postexilic Jewish community as well. The terms are without exact designation, though the Aramaic cognate of סָגָן sometimes designates an official with judicial functions.[46]

The first part of v 24 is evidently the climax of the poem (see Structure, Form, Setting, *51:20–24*); "recompense" (שלם pi'el) has already occurred in 50:29 and 51:6. The bracketed additional words are reminiscent of the words added in 50:29.

■ **51:25** This verse offers severe difficulty in interpretation. The text of *M* reads, "Behold, I am against you, O Mountain of the Destroyer [or, of Destruction], oracle of Yahweh, the one destroying the whole earth; I will stretch out my hand against you, and roll you down from the rocks, and make you a mountain of burning." *G* omits "oracle of Yahweh," reads הַר הַמַּשְׁחִית as if הָהָר הַמָּשְׁחָת, "the ruined mountain," reads "on the rocks" instead of "from the rocks," and interprets "mountain of burning" as "burned mountain." The other Versions offer no significant variations from *M*.

The verse makes a kind of sense: clearly Yahweh will destroy Babylon, depicted here in various metaphorical ways. But what, really, does it mean to roll a mountain down from the rocks? And what is a "mountain of burning"? Commentators have long thought of a volcano, which is a "mountain of burning" and sends portions of itself down from the top (so Michaelis, Naegelsbach, Condamin); but Duhm rightly doubts a reference to a volcano here. Certainly vulcanism is not a characteristic of Mesopotamia. And the interpretations of this verse are not really internally coherent: one has the impression that something specific is being said in this verse which has passed us by.

Rudolph is correct to bracket "the one destroying the whole earth"; the phrase adds nothing to the context and appears to be a clarifying gloss to explain the preceding הַמַּשְׁחִית. He further brackets "from the rocks" as a nonsensical addition, since one cannot roll a mountain from the rocks. Thus far I believe he is correct. But he explains וְגִלְגַּלְתִּיךָ as a denominative from גַּל, "heap of stones," thus "and I shall make you a heap of stones," an interpretation I believe to be wrong.

One recent theory is that "Mount of the Destroyer" refers to the mountain of the god Nergal, known in Palestine as Molech or Chemosh, and perhaps worshiped on the Mount of Olives;[47] it would then be appropriate to call Babylon "Mount of Nergal," with the implication that she herself will be destroyed.

---

44 John W. Wevers, "Weapons and implements of war," *IDB* 4:824; and see in more detail Yadin, *Warfare*, 11, with illustrations.

45 For bibliography on the two terms see Zimmerli, *Ezekiel 1*, 485, n. 18, and see recently Thierry Petit, "L'évolution sémantique des termes hébreux et araméens *phh* et *sgn* et accadiens *pāhatu* et *šaknu*," *JBL* 107 (1988), 53–67.

46 *DISO*, 190.

47 John B. Curtis, "Corruption, Mount of," *IDBSup* 186–87.

But I propose another solution. There are two clues from parallel passages. The first is the occurrence of שְׂרֵפָה, "burning," in Gen 11:3, in the narrative of the Tower of Babel, where the word means "burnt bricks": Jrm here appears to make reference to that narrative and the tower made of burnt bricks.

The second clue is the fact that in 2 Kgs 23:13 הַר הַמַּשְׁחִית likewise appears: there it is a reference to the Mount of Olives (so, rightly, *T* there); in the Mishna the Mount of Olives is called הַר הַמִּשְׁחָה (*m. Roš Haš.* 2:4), literally "Mount of Anointing," that is, "Mount of Oil" (in Zech 14:4 the Mount of Olives is called הַר הַזֵּתִים). Commentators thus note that the phrase in 2 Kgs 23:13 is deformed into "Mount of the Destroyer."[48] Montgomery suggests that the deformation was made in 2 Kgs 23:13 to conform to the word of Jer 7:32 that the Valley of Kidron would be called the Valley of Slaughter,[49] but the matter is probably more complicated than that (see below); after all, it was the valley below the Mount of Olives that was the locality of forbidden practices, not the mount itself. One might propose that הַמַּשְׁחִית is original in the present passage and subsequently modified in 2 Kgs 23:13 under the influence of the present passage. After all, Babylon is indeed a destroyer, as the bracketed phrase affirms. But then why does הַמַּשְׁחִית carry the article?—if in the metaphor Babylon is the mountain, the article is unnecessary. This line of thinking suggests then that as a matter of fact the phrase in the present passage has something to do with a deformation of "Mount of Olives."

With regard to the Mount of Olives, one might hazard the guess that the Babylonian army, in besieging Jerusalem the second time, cut down the olive trees; after all, "they built siegeworks against it [Jerusalem] round about" (2 Kgs 25:1). Josephus, in recounting the siege of Jerusalem by Titus in the year 70, describes how the Roman army leveled the hedges and cut down all the fruit-trees nearer to the city than Scopus, and again describes the desolation of the city afterward, when all the trees of the suburbs had been cut down.[50] It is altogether likely, therefore, that the cynical joke was passed around in Jerusalem that the Mount of Olives was now הַר הַמִּשְׁחָה no more, but הַר הַמַּשְׁחִית, "Mount of Destruction," and that the joke stuck.

But one may hazard a further guess: that during the first siege some Babylonian officer had looked at the "Mount of Oil" opposite Jerusalem and had mocked it, saying, "That's no 'Mount of Oil,' that's a perfectly ordinary mountain with a few olive trees on it. Now in Babylon I could show you a real 'Mount of Oil,' heaps and heaps of sesame seeds," and that that word had reached the ears of Jrm. Jrm perceived Yahweh to be judging Babylon for her haughtiness and insolence: the earlier formula of encounter (50:31) says so. Thus I propose that a boast about the Babylonian sesame crop lay at the basis of the present formula of encounter.

The sesame crop was the source of oil in Mesopotamia at every period.[51] In two letters of Hammurabi to Sin-idinnam, a royal official in Larsa, there are references to sesame seeds in transactions.[52] And after Jrm's time Herodotus states, "[The Babylonians] use no oil except what they make from sesame."[53] In the Talmud the judgment is recorded of R. Tarfon that one should light the sabbath lamp only with olive oil, to which R. Johanan b. Nuri asks, "What shall the Babylonians [that is, the Jews in Babylon] then do who have only sesame oil?"[54]

This suggestion may gain plausibility by an understanding of the verb וְגִלְגַּלְתִּיךָ. This verb is likely to be a denominative from גַּלְגַּל, "wheel" (or גִּלְגָּל, Isa 28:28). The production of olive oil was done in two stages. The olives were first crushed, and then the pulp was pressed. An installation for olive oil production dating to the seventh century BCE has recently been excavated at Tel Miqne (Atlas of Israel grid 136–133, evidently the Philistine Ekron): there the olives were first crushed in a basin, evidently with a roller; then the pulp, stacked in baskets, was pressed under a heavy beam weighted like a lever.[55] In an olive oil installation found at Tirat-Yehuda

---

48 Gray, *Kings*, 737–38: "probably a parody"; see further Montgomery, *Kings*, 533, 540.

49 Montgomery, *Kings*, 540.

50 *J. W.* 5.3.2; 6.1.1.

51 Oppenheim, *Ancient Mesopotamia*, 44, 86, 313.

52 Leonard W. King, *The Letters and Inscriptions of Hammurabi* (London: Luzac, 1900) 3:45–47 (British Museum 23130); 54–55 (British Museum 12855).

53 Herodotus *Hist.* 1.193.

54 *b. Šabb.* 26a.

55 Seymour Gitin, "The Rise and Fall of Ekron of the Philistines: Urban Growth and Decline in the Iron II Period," *BA* 50 (1987) 208–9; see especially the reconstruction, 208.

(Atlas of Israel grid 143–158) from the second century BCE the olives were crushed by an actual crushing wheel: the olives were placed in a waist-high circular trough in which the wheel rolled—one end of the axle of the wheel fitted into a rotating vertical shaft, whereas the other end of the axle was turned by a man walking in a circle outside the trough.[56] Then again in the second stage the soft mash was pressed under a heavy weight. It is thus likely that Jrm had an olive roller or crushing-wheel in mind in the present instance. The mechanism of actual sesame seed presses in Babylon is hardly at issue here, though they could well have taken the same pattern. An "oil factory" at Pumbeditha is mentioned in the Talmud, with oil in barrels:[57] doubtless this was a central oil-pressing installation.

If the foregoing analysis is sound, it is highly ironic for Jrm to address Babylon by the same phrase used for the Mount of Olives east of Jerusalem: he offered on another occasion a formula of encounter against Zion (21:13); now he offers a formula of encounter against another mountain, another "Mount of Oil" far away—just as he had evidently hidden a linen loincloth at Parah, just northeast of Jerusalem, as a symbol for the Euphrates (13:1–11). And the designation of Babylon as a "mountain" suggests the ziggurats at her center: Jrm would not only have had the story of the Tower of Babel in Gen 11:1–9 in mind, but reports he had heard of the ziggurats in Babylon in his day.[58] Whether the ziggurat represented the cosmic mountain or not,[59] the designation of the ziggurat as a "mountain" is an obvious one and appropriate for Babylon. Indeed it has been plausibly suggested that in the lines in Deutero-Isaiah, "Behold, I will make of you a threshing sledge, . . . you shall thresh the mountains and crush them, and you shall make the hills like chaff" (Isa 41:15), the "mountains" and "hills" refer to the ziggurats of Babylon.[60]

The scenario that I propose, therefore, is as follows. (1) The reading in both 2 Kgs 23:13 and the present verse was originally הַר הַמִּשְׁחָה, "Mount of (Sesame-)oil."

(2) After 587 the text of 2 Kgs 23:13 was changed to "Mount of Destruction" because of the destruction of the olive trees at the time of the siege of Jerusalem (the name הַר הַזֵּתִים, "Mount of Olives," in Zech 14:4 would then represent a subsequent renaming of the place). (3) An editor of the Jeremiah material, encountering in the present passage "Mount of Oil," the old name of the Mount of Olives, and convinced it "made no sense," corrected the text to the current name of the Mount of Olives, namely, "Mount of Destruction," and added the gloss that Babylon herself is the "Destroyer of all the earth."

Of course oil is for "burning" in lamps: this, then, is a final fate for oil, whether extracted from olives or from sesame seeds. But הַר שְׂרֵפָה, "Mount of Burning," has a more specific implication in reference to Babylon, as already noted: שְׂרֵפָה means "burnt bricks" in the narrative of the Tower of Babel, Gen 11:3. The normal bricks used for building in Mesopotamia were sun-dried, but for special purposes they were baked in a kiln (that is, terracotta); kiln-dried bricks were used particularly in the façades of ziggurats.[61] Such is evidently the reference in Gen 11:3. And although there is no notice in that narrative of any destruction of the Tower of Babel, it is a symbol of the pride of humankind standing under the judgment of God, and "they left off building the city" (Gen 11:8). The phrase הַר שְׂרֵפָה then suggests not only a ziggurat made of kiln-dried bricks but also a huge heap of tiles, utterly dead.

■ **51:26** If no one takes from the heap any stone for a new corner or foundation, then Babylon will not be rebuilt. This word is the opposite of the word of Isaiah that speaks of the cornerstone or foundation stone by which Zion will be built (Isa 28:16): one wonders if Jrm had that passage in mind.[62]

■ **51:27** These battle orders resemble the phraseology of 4:5–6 and, within the oracles against Babylon, v 12. "Prepare" is literally "consecrate": for this usage see 6:4.

The gloss mentions three peoples who were centered

---

56 For illustrations see Ruth Hestrin and Zeev Yeivin, "Oil from the Presses of Tirat-Yahuda," *BA* 40 (1977) 30; Barrois, *Manuel*, 324.

57 *b. B. Qam.* 27b.

58 See Thorkild Jacobsen, "Babel," *IDB* 1:334; "Babylon (OT)," *IDB* 1:336, 337.

59 H. W. F. Saggs, *The Greatness That Was Babylon* (New York: Hawthorn, 1962; rep. Mentor, 1968) 53.

60 E. John Hamlin, "The Meaning of 'Mountains and Hills' in Isa. 41:14–16," *JNES* 13 (1954) 185–90.

61 Seton Lloyd, "Building in Brick and Stone," *A History of Technology* (ed. Charles Singer, E. J. Holmyard, and A. R. Hall; Oxford: Oxford University, 1954) 1:460–62, 467.

62 For general remarks on cornerstones and foundation stones see Edwin M. Good, "Cornerstone," *IDB*

to the north of Mesopotamia. Ararat is the Assyrian *Urarṭu*, a people centering around Lake Van in what is now eastern Turkey; their language was evidently related to Hurrian. Urartu was a political power from the ninth century to the early sixth.[63] The Minni were the Manneans, Assyrian *Mannay*; this people was centered just south of Lake Urmia in what is now northwest Iran, and they were a political power from the ninth to the seventh century.[64] Ashkenaz are to be identified with the Assyrian *Ašguzay* (or *Iškuzay*), applied to the people later known as the Scythians, a people speaking an Indo-Iranian dialect; they ranged from what is now southern Russia through the Caucasus and into the Near East.[65] By the sixth century all three peoples were subject to the Medes (compare v 28). Since the Median empire, under Astyages, was defeated by the Persians under Cyrus the Great in the middle of the sixth century, one must assume that this gloss, and v 28, were added before that time.

The noun מִפְסָר ("marshal") occurs only here and in Nah 3:17; it seems to be a loan-word from Akkadian *ṭupšarru*, "tablet-writer," and refers to a rank of officer. For יֶלֶק, "locust," see v 14. The adjective סָמָר, "bristling," appears only here in the OT, and its meaning is not altogether certain: the Versions scatter (*G*: "a multitude"; *V*: "prickly"; *S* omits; *T*: "made [red or] yellow"). The medieval Jewish commentators offer an equal variety: "bristling" is the definition of Rashi, who compares the verb סמר pi'el in Job 4:15, "bristle" (of hair), and so *KJV* "rough," whereas Qimḥi suggests "fluttering," and so Luther.

■ **51:28** For the Medes see v 11, and 25:25–26; for "governors" and "prefects" see v 23.

■ **51:29** "Quake" occurs with "earth" elsewhere in Jer (8:16; 10:10; 49:21), but this is the only occurrence of חול/חיל qal, "writhe, tremble," with this subject—it does, however, occur in Pss 96:9; 97:4; 114:7. For the association of "earth quakes" and "plan of Yahweh" compare 49:20–21.

■ **51:30** For מְצָד, "stronghold," see 48:41. This is the only occurrence of נשת, "dry up," in the metaphorical sense: The other occurrences (Isa 19:5; 41:17) are concrete. For the motif of warriors becoming women see 50:37 and, in detail, 30:5–7. For בְּרִיחַ, "bar," see 49:31.

■ **51:31** "Runner" (רָץ) and "courier" (מַגִּיד, literally "announcer") are of course parallels: the news comes from every direction. Compare the description of the demoralization of the king of Babylon in 50:43. It is worth recording the extent of fortifications in Babylon: two defense walls, the inner one about six and a half meters in thickness, the outer one over three meters in thickness, outside of which was a water-filled defensive ditch;[66] see further v 44.

■ **51:32** There is no doubt of the meaning of מַעְבָּרוֹת, "fords"; these fords would be either of the Euphrates itself or of various irrigation canals. But the meaning here of the parallel noun אֲגַמִּים has been in doubt. The noun (or a homonym) occurs several times in the meaning of "(reed) pool" (for example, Exod 7:19): the Arabic cognate *ajama* means "marshy jungle, canebrake,"[67] and it may be that the Hebrew word implies "marsh" as much as "pool." But because the verb in the present passage is "burn," the suggestion has been made since Ibn Janāḥ in the eleventh century that the word here is cognate with the Arabic *ujum*, "fortress," and this rendering has been revived in the present century (so Condamin, Rudolph; so Zorell and *HALAT*; and so *RSV*, *JB*, *NEB*, *NAB*).[68] But this interpretation is unnecessary; outside the walls of Babylon "for further security a system of artificial lakes and flooded areas was established to the N and the E,"[69] and "in low-lying regions, cane grows in the numerous swamps."[70] Setting fire to the reeds would have cut off escape from the city and expelled refugees hiding there (Bright).

This is the only occurrence in Jer of בהל nip'al "be terrified"; the verb later takes on the meaning "be in

1:700, and Ovid R. Sellers, "Foundation," *IDB* 2:322; for further bibliography, especially in regard to cornerstones and foundation stones in Babylon, see Wildberger, *Jesaja*, 1077.

63 Machteld J. Mellink, "Ararat," *IDB* 1:194–95.

64 Ignace J. Gelb, "Minni," *IDB* 3:392.

65 Machteld J. Mellink, "Ashkenaz," *IDB* 1:254; A. Leo Oppenheim, "Scythians," *IDB* 4:252.

66 Thorkild Jacobsen, "Babylon, (OT)," *IDB* 1:335–36, with illustrations.

67 See Lothar Kopf, "Arabische Etymologien und Parallelen zum Bibelwörterbuch," *VT* 8 (1958) 163–64.

68 For bibliography see *HALAT*, 10b.

69 Jacobsen, "Babylon," 336.

70 Oppenheim, *Ancient Mesopotamia*, 42.

haste" (Eccl 8:3), and that meaning would be appropriate here as well.

■ **51:33** Though דרך, "tread," is used of judgment (Mic 5:4–5, and so the revocalization suggested in this study for 4:11), here the point of the comparison is not that Babylon will be trampled down, but rather that when a threshing-floor is trodden down it is a sure sign of the harvest, that is, judgment. With regard to the preparation of the threshing-floor Gustaf Dalman quotes the Spanish Latin author Columella:

> The threshing-floor, too, if it is of earth, to be satisfactorily prepared for threshing should first be scraped, then dug thoroughly, with an admixture of chaff and oil lees which have not been salted, and moistened; for such treatment protects the grain from the ravages of mice and ants. Then, after being smoothed down, it should be packed hard with rammers or with a millstone, and, again strewn with chaff, it should be tramped down and left in this condition to be dried by the sun.[71]

There is no evidence that such elaborate preparations were made in the Near East, but at least the threshing-floor needed to be moistened and then tamped down or trampled to make it clean and smooth before threshing.[72] For "harvest" (קציר) as an expression of judgment compare the gloss in Hos 6:11.

■ **51:34** Even after "Nebuchadrezzar" is omitted as a gloss with several commentators, the text of this verse is unsatisfactory. The second verb in the first colon, המם, has an established meaning, "confuse, discomfit," and it is hard to see any meaning in "he has confused me," or the like, directly after "he has eaten me." Volz emends הֲמָמַנִי to הֲרָמַנִי, "he has destroyed me" (compare 8:14), that is, "he has devoured me," which is ingenious. Given "empty vessel" in the second colon, Rudolph proposes to identify the verb with the Arabic *hamma* "suck dry," and so *NEB*. The difficulty is that this is not really a meaning of the Arabic *hamma*, which, like its Hebrew cognate, essentially means "disquiet." It is cited meaning "liquefy (suet)," "exhaust (milk from a camel),"[73] but not "suck dry." I accept the solution of Cornill: he points out that

"he has eaten me" really goes closely with "he has swallowed me" in the third colon, and he therefore proposes that "he has eaten me" rightly belongs at that point—that the verb fell out of the text and was reinserted at the wrong point. The last verb of the verse, whether understood as the common "has driven me out" or as "has washed me away" (in reference to the empty vessel), is evidently a gloss (so also Cornill, Condamin, Rudolph): without a copula it comes on strangely at the end of the verse. Each of the four cola in the resulting verse will then have three units.

The meaning of the verbs in the first two cola is not immediately clear. The basic meaning of יצג hip'il in the second colon is "set (up), place" (rather like שים). One may therefore understand the suffix of the verb as dative: the meaning will then be "he has set for me an empty dish," suggesting the action of a cruel or insulting host—this figure is picked up in v 39 in the description of Yahweh's feast for the Babylonians. And indeed the verb in the first colon, המם, may mean "put (an enemy) to confusion" (for example, Exod 14:24). But the contrast between the first half of the verse and the second is that between "empty" and "fill": the king of Babylon has filled his belly, whereas the dish is empty, suggesting in turn that the empty dish itself is a metaphor for Israel, and indeed יצג hip'il may take two accusatives, as שים can, in the meaning of "make someone/something into something" (for יצג hip'il in this meaning, though without the second accusative, see Hos 2:5, "lest . . . I make her as the day she was born"). Here, then, the colon may mean, "He made me (into) an empty dish." It is to be noted that, as the vocalization stands, the phrase is literally "vessel of emptiness" (ריק) is a noun: the adjective "empty" would be ריק); thus given the broad meaning of כלי, "vessel," the meaning here is similar to "worthless vessel (or thing)" applied to Jehoiachin (22:28). And there is another possible meaning for the verb in the first colon: as well as "put to confusion" it may mean "disperse," as it does in Pss 18:15 and 114:6, given the parallel פוץ hip'il in both those passages.[74] And "disperse" is an appropriate meaning, given the events surrounding the Babylonian exile.

The תנין is the primordial sea-monster. In the Ugaritic texts the creature with the name *tnn* is another desig-

---

71 Columella, *De Re Rustica* 2.19.

72 Compare *m. Makš.* 3.5, and see further Gustaf Dalman, *Arbeit und Sitte in Palästina* (Gütersloh:

Bertelsmann, 1928–39) 3:72.

73 Georg W. Freytag, *Lexicon Arabico-Latinum* (Halle: Schwetschke, 1830–37) 4:406.

nation for Yamm, "Sea," or Nahar, "Stream," thought to have seven heads[75] (compare Rev 12:3); the mythical creature appears occasionally in the OT (for example, Isa 27:1; Ps 74:13; Job 7:12).[76]

For the vocalization of מְלָא (instead of מָלֵא) see GKC, sec. 75oo. This is the only occurrence of כָּרֵשׂ (or כְּרֵשׂ) "belly" in the OT, but its occurrence in cognate languages guarantees its meaning.

■ **51:35** The possessive suffixes on "violence" and "destruction" are objective genitives (GKC, sec. 135m); for these two nouns see 6:7.

Zion/Jerusalem uses an expression from sacral law ("the blood of A be upon B," compare Lev 20:9, 11–13, 27) to insist that Babylon undergo sufferings like theirs.[77] The participle יֹשֶׁבֶת is poised between "enthroned" (so the translation here: see the discussion on 21:13) and "inhabitant [feminine] of," given the occurrence of יֹשְׁבֵי, "inhabitants of," in the following colon.

■ **51:36** The cognate accusative phrase "pursue one's case" has already occurred in 50:34; the parallel cognate accusative phrase "bring one's retribution" occurs only here in the OT. For "vindication" (נְקָמָה) see 11:20.

The reference to "her sea" is evidently manifold, as is the reference to "many waters" in v 13. It is not only the Euphrates and irrigation canals, not only artificial lakes constructed for the defense of Babylon (for which see v 32). The sea, symbolized as the monster in v 34, represents chaos; there is irony in that whereas in the Babylonian myth Bel is the conqueror of the chaotic waters,[78] here it is Yahweh who is the ultimate conqueror over those waters (for references to this cosmic battle see 5:22 and n. 9 there): compare Rev 21:1, "and the sea was no more."[79] Again, though "her source" may refer to the source of the Euphrates (so *HALAT*), the phrase here, paralleling "her sea," doubtless refers to the source of

Babylonia's vigor (compare Hos 13:15: so BDB), or indeed to a mythic fountain (compare Yahweh as the "spring of running water," 2:13). But there will be more irony in v 42, where it is said that Babylon will be swallowed up by the sea (see there).

■ **51:37** For the phrasing of this verse compare 2:15.

■ **51:38–40** These verses offer the scene of Yahweh's banquet at which the guests, like lions, are eager and alert for the food and drink but will drink the cup of wrath (25:27–29) and fall.

■ **51:38** The first word, given its position, is hardly "together" but surely a verb; the verb I propose, הדד qal, occurs in Hab 1:8 and means "be quick, sharp." The meaning "growl" for נער is cited only for this passage, and the verb is surely to be read as עור nip'al with *G*.

■ **51:39–40** "Be hot" (חמם) is used figuratively for the passions in Hos 7:7 as well. If the guests have been comparable to lions, once drunk they are like lambs. The noun כַּר ("lamb," v 40) probably refers to a half-grown ram in contrast to the full-grown ram (אַיִל).[80] For עַתּוּד, "he-goat," see 50:8.

■ **51:41** In 48:2 "the renown of [תְּהִלַּת] Moab" refers to Moab's reputation, but here "the renown of all the earth" is not the reputation of Babylon but of course Babylon herself (compare תְּהִלָּה for Israel and Judah in 13:11).

■ **51:42** This verse stands in ironic contrast to "I shall dry up her sea" in v 36. Here the sea is hardly the Euphrates or local canals or lakes (see v 36), nor the Persian Gulf, but is the primeval sea as a metaphor for the enemies of Babylon (compare 46:7; 47:2). The noun הָמוֹן, "tumult," implies both abundance and loud roaring (see 3:23), but this is the only occurrence of הֲמוֹן גַּלִּים: it looks like a compression of "the roaring of their waves, the tumult of their peoples" in Ps 65:8 (compare Isa 17:12).

---

74 So the translation of Dahood, *Psalms I*, 102, and *Psalms III*, 327.

75 Ug. 3.3.35–39. For a Mesopotamian cylinder-seal depicting a fiery seven-headed dragon see *ANEP*, 221, figure 691.

76 For a brief discussion see Theodor H. Gaster, "Cosmogony," *IDB* 1:706a; for a more extended discussion, with bibliography, see Wildberger, *Jesaja*, 1001–1006.

77 See Pedersen, *Israel*, I/II, 420, and n. 2; Noth, *Leviticus*, 149–50; Hans Walter Wolff, *Anthropology of the Old Testament* (Philadelphia: Westminster, 1974)

62; and see recently Jean-Marc Babut, "Que son sang soit sur sa tête!" *VT* 36 (1986) 474–79.

78 Gray, "Bel."

79 There are several parallels in intertestamental literature: *T. Levi* 4:1; *As. Mos.* 10:6; *Sib. Or.* 5:159, 447; 8:236.

80 So *HALAT*; see also B. Davie Napier, "Lamb," *IDB* 3:58.

■ **51:43** For the diction see 2:6.

■ **51:44** For Bel see 50:2. "I shall make him disgorge what he swallowed from his mouth" is a reference to "[the king of Babylon] has swallowed me like a monster" in v 34; "what he swallowed" is a noun in Hebrew (בֶּלַע) and refers of course to Israel. The reference to what Bel has swallowed reminds one of the story of Bel in the additions to the Book of Daniel, of the god who was fed by his devotees but who, it turned out, could not eat, and it is possible that that story of Bel is not a reflex of the present passage in Jer but that the present passage itself reflects some mythic material lying behind that story.[81] And the mention here of the falling of the wall of Babylon may have reference to the names of the defense walls of Babylon, the inner wall being called Imgur-Enlil, the outer Nimitti-Enlil: Bel assumed the role of the Sumerian god Enlil.[82] Though there is doubtless a connection between "no longer shall the nations stream to him" and "all the nations shall stream to [the mountain of the house of Yahweh]" in Isa 2:2, it is not possible to determine the direction of borrowing, given the lack of consensus on the date of Isa 2:2–5.[83] *NJV* assumes that נהר here is not "stream" but the homonym "gaze with joy" (see 31:12), but though that meaning might fit Isa 2:2, it hardly fits here, where it is a matter of vassal kings, traders, captive peoples.

■ **51:46** For שְׁמוּעָה, "rumor," see the discussion in 10:22. There was extreme instability in the last few decades of the Babylonian Empire,[84] doubtless the background for this verse. The syntax is peculiar: the verse begins with וּפֶן, literally "and lest." The matter is dealt with in Joüon, *Gramm.*, sec. 168g, n. 3: it is evidently a negative optative clause, "And be sure not to. . . ."

■ **51:47–48** For the origin of these two verses see the discussion in Structure, Form, Setting, *Authentic and Unauthentic Material in 51:25–58*; for the expressions common with vv 52–53 see on those verses. One wonders, given the pattern of Isa 52:9, whether at the beginning of v 48 one should not read רַנּוּ, imperative, thus

"Sing over Babylon, heaven and earth and everything in them." For destroyers "from the north" compare 50:41.

■ **51:49** If לִנְפֹּל is correct in the first colon, then it is more natural to understand or supply לְ before חַלְלֵי, which might have dropped out by haplography, thus reading "Babylon must fall for the slain of Israel" (so Cornill, Volz, Condamin, Rudolph, Bright; so *RSV*). But given the vocative in v 50, it is more natural to understand a vocative here (so Duhm, Giesebrecht, and at least the suggestion of Cornill and Condamin), and since this use of the independent infinitive construct with לְ appears to be late (see Text), it is better to restore a finite verb here. For "slain" see 8:23, and for "fall" with this noun see v 4. The notion that Babylon will suffer as she made others to suffer is found also in v 35.

■ **51:50** The text of the first colon may need more remedy than offered here: given "remember from" at the beginning of the second colon, one wonders whether the first word is not also an imperative, פַּלְּטוּ, "escape," or פַּלְּטוּם, "get them to safety."

Israel in exile is bidden to remember Yahweh once more, to reestablish the covenantal bond with him in the context of the temple in Jerusalem: "remember" suggests active involvement (see 2:2), and "from afar" may suggest "from long ago" as well (compare Isa 22:11).

■ **51:51** In response the people give voice to their humiliation and bewilderment at the seeming weakness of Yahweh: strangers have dishonored his very temple.

■ **51:52** In v 44 one heard that Yahweh will punish Bel; now this has been generalized to "her idols" (for which see 8:19).

"Slain" (חָלָל) is literally "pierced," and so can mean both "seriously wounded" and "slain": though "groan" does not fit "slain," it seems better to be consistent with the rendering in v 47 and elsewhere.

■ **51:53** The first two cola are reminiscent of the story of the Tower of Babel in Gen 11:1–9. In that story the top of the tower was to be in the heavens (Gen 11:4), and Yahweh's judgment on its builders was that "nothing that

---

81   See the discussion in Carey A. Moore, *Daniel, Esther, and Jeremiah: The Additions* (AB 44; Garden City, NY: Doubleday, 1977) 121–25.

82   Jacobsen, "Babylon," 335–36; Gray, "Bel"; for literature on the suggestion see Rudolph, p. 313.

83   Wildberger, *Jesaja*, 80, believes the passage to be authentic to Isaiah, while other scholars date it in the postexilic period. For a recent survey of literature on

the question see Otto Kaiser, *Isaiah 1–12* (Philadelphia: Westminster, 1983), 52, n. 14.

84   See Bright, *History*, 351–54.

they may presume to do will be out of their reach [בצר nip'al]" (Gen 11:6);[85] here though Babylon should go up to the heavens, and though she should put out of reach (בצר pi'el) her strong height, Yahweh will bring about her destruction. The impression of the excavators of Babylon is of extensive building and rebuilding by Nebuchadrezzar of the fortifications and public buildings of Babylon;[86] but whether the "strong height" here refers to ziggurats, palaces, or fortifications, it will be brought down. The plural שֹׁדְדִים, "devastators," perhaps suggests that more than one enemy will bring Babylon down (compare the singular participle in 48:8, 18, 32).

■ **51:54–55** Volz and Rudolph assume that the "waves" in v 55b belong to Babylon and therefore that v 55b must concessive: they therefore emend "their waves" to "her waves" (they retain "their noise" in the next colon, assuming that the reference is to the noise of the waves). This is also the understanding of *JB*, *NAB*, and by implication, *NJV*. To the contrary, the roaring of the waves is the action of the enemy against Babylon, as in v 42. Ironically, then, the "sound" or "noise" (קוֹל) of Babylon (vv 54–55a) is drowned out by the "noise" of the waves (v 55b). This irony is reinforced by "great": Babylon's noise has been great (v 55a), but then so will her collapse be great (v 54); and it is reinforced by the phrase "many waters" (v 55b), which in v 13 referred to the waterworks of Babylon but here refers to the waves of Babylon's enemy.

■ **51:56** "Bow" represents military power (so 49:35). For v 56b compare v 6b.

■ **51:58** The first verb expression mixes stems, the infinitive absolute being pilpel and the finite verb hitpalpel (compare GKC, sec. 113w). These stems of the verb are unique here, and it is possible that an intended nuance of meaning is unrecoverable. "High gates": it is estimated that the entry of the Ishtar gate was nine meters high; it was flanked on each side by a massive square tower.[87]

Verse 58b is duplicated in Hab 2:13, and this duplication is explained variously. Thus William H. Ward assumed that Hab 2:13 was borrowed from the present passage;[88] Condamin suggests that both passages have borrowed from a common source, and Thompson shares this view, calling the two cola "a popular saying."[89] The problem is complicated by the fact that the earlier critical view of both passages is that they are late. Eissfeldt[90] and Elliger[91] both suggest that the Habakkuk passage is part of a woe against the Chaldeans. There is no way, of course, to demonstrate that the passage in Habakkuk did not use a proverb or cite some previous source, but the cola appear to be integrated into the discourse of Habakkuk in a way that they are not in the present passage. That is to say, it would be a crowning irony for Jrm to quote a word of Habakkuk originally intended for the Babylonians: They shall suffer the same fate as they have imposed on the rest of the earth (compare the beginning of this unit, v 49). Jrm has closed other discourses with citations (4:3–4; 10:23–25). The ultimate result of people's toil is destruction.

Aim

For Jrm and for his fellow citizens the ultimate fate of Babylon was *the* issue of those days. Jrm could tell the exiles in Babylon to settle down and pray for the welfare of that empire (29:7), but his commission to build and to plant (1:10) would be for nought unless the ultimate question of the fall of Babylon could be dealt with.

And so, though it will be a long time (29:28), Babylon will fall! Not only will she fall by Yahweh's hand, but her fall will be Yahweh's recompense for what Babylon has done to other nations, notably to Israel. This sense that the punishment should fit the crime suggests that Israel will have a crucial role to play in that fall.

And this reassurance has helped later generations look to the fall of the Babylon of their day: "Fallen, fallen is Babylon the great, she who made all nations drink the wine of her impure passion" (Rev 14:8).

85   Speiser, *Genesis*, 74.
86   Leonard W. King, *A History of Babylon from the Foundation of the Monarchy to the Persian Conquest* (London: Chatto & Windus, 1915) 24–27, 58, 280.
87   Jacobsen, "Babylon," 336: see figures 9 and 10 on pp. 336–37.
88   William H. Ward, *A Critical and Exegetical Commentary on Habakkuk* (ICC; New York: Scribner's, 1911) 16.
89   Thompson, p. 769.
90   Eissfeldt, *Introduction*, 419–20.
91   Karl Elliger, *Das Buch der zwölf Kleinen Propheten* (ATD 25; Göttingen: Vandenhoeck & Ruprecht, 1975) 2:46.

Jeremiah Sends Word to Babylon of Her Destruction

Bibliography

Avigad, Nahman

‏"חותמו של שריהו בן נריהו,"‏ *Eretz-Israel* 14 (1978) 86–87.

Gosse, Bernard

"La malédiction contre Babylone de Jérémie 51,59–64 et les rédactions du livre de Jérémie," *ZAW* 98 (1986) 383–99.

Wanke

Baruchschrift, 136–43.

51

59 The word that 《 Yahweh 》[a] commanded Jeremiah the prophet 《 to say to 》[a] Seraiah son of Neriah son of Mahseiah when he went 《 from 》[a] Zedekiah king of Judah to Babylon in the fourth year of his reign: Seraiah was the officer of 〈 tribute. 〉[b] 60/ Jeremiah wrote[a] all the evil that would come on Babylon in one document, all these words written about Babylon. 61/ And Jeremiah said to Seraiah, "When you enter Babylon, then you shall see and read all these words, 62/ and you shall say, 'Yahweh, it is you who have spoken against this place, to cut it off, so that there not be in it any inhabitant, from man to beast, for 〈 a desolation 〉[a] for ever it shall be.' 63/ And when you finish reading this document, you shall tie to it a stone and throw it into the middle of the Euphrates, 64/ and you shall say, 'Thus Babylon will sink and not rise in the face of the evil that I am bringing upon her.'" ["And wear themselves out": thus far the words of Jeremiah.][a]

Text

59a Reading the longer text of *G*: inserting יהוה אֶת after צִוָּה, inserting לֵאמֹר after הַנָּבִיא, reading אֶל־ for אֶת־ before שְׂרָיָה, and reading מֵאֵת for אֶת־ before צִדְקִיָּהוּ. For the reading of *M* and for a discussion of the preference for *G* see Preliminary Observations.

b Reading with *G* and *T* מִנְחָה (note that the Greek plural δῶρα renders the Hebrew singular in the meaning "tribute"—see Judg 3:15, 17, 18; 2 Chr 17:11; 26:8); *M* מְנוּחָה has been taken (in combination with שַׂר) to mean "quartermaster." See further Preliminary Observations, Interpretation.

60a Since Jrm otherwise employed a scribe (36:4), either "wrote" here means "caused to write" (compare 36:2 and the like), or one should revocalize the qal וַיִּכְתֹּב to the hip'il וַיַּכְתֵּב: the hip'il of this verb occurs in postbiblical Hebrew (compare the discussion in Interpretation of 32:10).

62a Reading שְׁמָמָה with *G, V, S, T*; *M* reads שְׁמָמוֹת "desolations" (compare v 26, note a).

64a *G* lacks the bracketed words; "and wear themselves out" is the last word of v 58.

Preliminary Observations

In v 59 *G* has a longer text than *M*, with three short plusses: *M* reads, "The word that Jeremiah the prophet commanded Seraiah son of Neriah son of Mahseiah when he went with Zedekiah king of Judah to Babylon . . . ," and *V* is identical; *G* reads, "The word that Yahweh commanded Jeremiah the prophet to say to Seraiah son of Neriah son of Mahseiah when he went from Zedekiah king of Judah to Babylon. . . ." This contrast raises two questions. The first is a historical one: Did Zedekiah make a journey to Babylon in 594, as *M* indicates, a journey otherwise unattested? The question is obviously an old one: *T* reads in part, "when he [Seraiah] went in the delegation of Zedekiah," a rendering that leaves the historical question unresolved, whereas *S* follows *M* until it reads "when he [Zedekiah] went to Babylon in the *eleventh* year of his reign": both these readings appear to be secondary adaptations. The second question is a form-critical one: Do we have here a report of a command of Yahweh to Jrm to extend the divine word to Babylon, or do we have a report of Jrm's own command to extend the divine word to Babylon? Both these questions need to be dealt with here, because I propose that the text questions are related.

The commentators all prefer *M* in this verse. A few note the reading "Yahweh" in *G*; Duhm simply says that the reading of *M* is doubtless more natural. Several commentators note that with the *G* reading "from Zedekiah" there is no journey by Zedekiah to Babylon in 594, but they go on to accept the reading of *M* (Duhm, Giesebrecht, Volz, Bright).

A general consideration is that plusses in *G* over *M* in the book are unusual enough to demand a reason: *G* is not in the habit of adding midrashic material to solve problems.

As to the historical question, commentators assume that if Zedekiah did make the journey to Babylon in 594, it was doubtless to pay tribute and to make his peace with Nebuchadrezzar after the collapse of discussions on a possible revolt earlier in the year (see chapter 27). But if Zedekiah did make a journey to Babylon in 594, the diction of the present verse is an unlikely way to say it: One might expect "when Zedekiah king of Judah went with his servants to meet the king of Babylon" or "when Zedekiah brought him with him to meet the king of Babylon." The narrative of 2 Kgs 16:10a is somewhat analogous: There the focus of interest is the altar, just as the focus of interest in the present verse is Seraiah; that half-verse reads, "When King Ahaz went to Damascus to meet Tiglath-pileser king of Assyria, he saw the altar that was at Damascus." A journey from Jerusalem to Damascus is one of perhaps 250 kilometers, but a journey to Babylon is five times as far; a royal visit to the king of Babylon would be a major event, not to be buried in a preposition. Calvin has no doubt about the matter: "But what the Jews say, that Zedekiah went to Babylon, is wholly groundless; and we know that Sederola [*Sēder 'Ôlām*, a historical work], whence they have taken this, is full of all kinds of fables and trifles; and on such a point as this, sacred history would not have been silent, for it was a thing of great moment." It is better to conclude that Seraiah was sent to pay tribute to Nebuchadrezzar: this is evidently the meaning of v 59b (see further Interpretation).

As to the form-critical question, whether one has here the report of a divine command to Jrm to extend the divine word to Babylon or simply a report of Jrm's command to extend that word to Babylon, again one may answer in favor of *G*. The expected subject of צִוָּה in the book is Yahweh (compare 13:5); it is a matter here of a symbolic action (compare Form), and it would be natural to phrase it as a command from Yahweh.

In the Hebrew text reconstructed as an antecedent of *G*, then, one reads: הדבר אשר צוה יהוה את ירמיהו הנביא לאמר אל שריה בן נריה בן מחסיה בלכתו מאת צדקיהו. The inclusive distance from יהוה to אל לאמר is twenty-three consonants, and from שריה to the mem of מאת is twenty-three consonants. One could imagine, then, a text with approximately twenty-three consonants to a column in which this sequence begins the top of the column (perhaps the last column of the scroll?), broken at both the right and the left ends of the first two lines; such a damaged text could then be the antecedent to *M*.

Structure

These five verses are associated with 50:1—51:58: One assumes that the authentic material in that collection was the contents of the document sent by Jrm to Babylon. Indeed the present study might well have dealt with these verses in the context of the discussion of 50:1—51:58; it is considered separately here because 50:1—51:58, indeed all of 46:1—51:58, is oracular material, without associated narrative.

Form

The text reconstructed from *G* for v 59 makes the passage a report of Yahweh's command to Jrm to see that Seraiah does a symbolic action in Babylon (for the form according to *M* see Preliminary Observations). Verse 59a refers to the divine command implied by the report without setting it forth in detail; v 59b is an explanatory note. Verses 60–64 are a report of Jrm's execution of the command. Verse 60 reports Jrm's action of writing the requisite words in a document, and vv 61–64 report his series of instructions to Seraiah: the latter is to read the words of the document in Babylon (v 61), he is to add to that reading a prayer to Yahweh affirming a summary of Yahweh's words concerning Babylon (v 62), he is to tie the document with a stone and throw it into the Euphrates (v 63) and to say an accompanying predictive word over Babylon (v 64a): for the phrasing of the word, beginning with כָּכָה, "thus," compare 28:11, and for the theology of symbolic actions see the excursus, "The Theology of Symbolic Actions," in 13:1–12aα. There is no report of Seraiah's carrying out Jrm's instructions.

Setting

There is no reason to question the historical data here: The event took place in the fourth year of Zedekiah (594/593) (see further discussion in Interpretation on v 59).

Interpretation

■ 59 Seraiah was the brother of Jrm's scribe Baruch (compare 32:12), so inasmuch as he is being sent to Babylon, he is the natural person to carry out Jrm's commission. The phrase denoting his office (v 59b) and its meaning have been uncertain. M reads שַׂר מְנוּחָה, an office not otherwise attested—it would seem to mean literally "official of the resting-place," that is, of the bivouac or billeting (so also S), therefore "quartermaster" (so the recent translations). But this office would be military and as such would not really make sense in the context (why would a quartermaster be going to Babylon?). V reads "chief of prophecy"; this understanding derives from a postbiblical understanding of "resting-place" as "inspiration," an interpretation based on Isa 11:2, "And the spirit of Yahweh shall rest [וְנָחָה] upon him."[1] Certainly this interpretation has a plausibility in the context! But it is striking that both G and T agree in reading "chief of tribute": the noun מִנְחָה means "tribute" in several other passages (see 2 Kgs 17:3, 4; Hos 10:6). This is an appropriate office for a courtier; if tribute was paid yearly, one need not think of a delegation for a special historical circumstance. There is no way, of course, to determine whether Seraiah went along with Elasah son of Shaphan and Gemariah son of Hilkiah (29:3: see there).

It is striking that a bulla (stamp-seal impression) has turned up recently inscribed לשריהו נריהו, "(belonging) to Seraiah (son of) Neriah";[2] this bulla joins the bullae of Baruch (see 32:11), of Gemariah son of Shaphan (see

36:9–11), and of Jerahmeel the king's son (see 36:26), all persons mentioned in Jer.

■ 60 "Document" (סֵפֶר) is likewise used in 30:2 for what doubtless included most of chapters 30 and 31 and perhaps more. The phrase "one document" here is curious: it may imply "a single document in spite of the length of the material." The summary in v 62 suggests that all of the authentic material in 50:1—51:58 was included (see Structure, and see further 50:1—51:58, Structure, Form, Setting, *Setting*).

■ 61 The implication of "see and read" is uncertain. It is commonly taken to mean "see that you read," that is, "be sure to read" (so Cornill, Condamin, Rudolph, Bright; so *RSV*, *JB*, *NAB*, *NJV*). Volz thinks it implies "avail yourself of the right time and place and read." But it is most likely to be simply as *NEB* has it, "look at this, read it all." Seraiah will not have examined the document before his arrival; and "reading" in this period is always reading aloud.

■ 62 For "Yahweh" G has Κύριε κύριε; "Yahweh, Yahweh" does not occur in M anywhere in Jer. Does G here represent אֲדֹנָי יהוה, "Lord Yahweh"? That combination is original after the interjection אֲהָהּ in 1:6; 4:10; 14:13; 32:17 (though in these passages G renders differently); either "Lord Yahweh" or "Yahweh, Yahweh" might be correct here.

For "so that there not be in it any inhabitant, from man to beast" see 50:3; for "for a desolation for ever it shall be" see 51:26.

■ 63–64 The symbolic action signals the end of Babylon; she will drop without a trace. Using a stone to sink the document suggests that the document was of papyrus, for leather would sink;[3] compare the remarks on 36:23. For פְּרָת, "Euphrates," compare the discussion in 13:1–12aα.

Aim

Yahweh entrusted his word and his action to Jrm, and Jrm in turn entrusted that word and action to the

1 *Num. R.* 10.5: see Jastrow, p. 798b.

2 Nahman Avigad, "חותמו של שריהו בן נריהו," *Eretz-Israel* 14 (1978) 86–87 and figure 3; see also Shiloh and Tarler, "Bullae," 204.

3 Menahem Haran, "More on Scrolls in the Biblical Period: A Fifth Proof," *Tarbiz* 52 (1982/83) 643–44; English summary by Frederick E. Greenspahn in *Old Testament Abstracts* 7 (1984) 118.

brother of his scribe to deliver in Babylon, as on another occasion he entrusted the divine word to messengers going to Babylon (29:1–13). As it happened, Jewish tradition later perceived Yahweh's word and action to continue to be manifest in Babylon, through the medium of Ezekiel and Deutero-Isaiah.

A Historical Appendix

Bibliography

Green, Alberto R.
"The Chronology of the Last Days of Judah: Two Apparent Discrepancies," *JBL* 101 (1982) 63–67.

52

1 Zedekiah was twenty-one years of age when he began to reign, and he reigned eleven years in Jerusalem; and the name of his mother was Hamital,[a] daughter of Jeremiah from Libnah. 2/ And he did evil in the eyes of Yahweh according to everything that Jehoiakim had done; 3/ indeed what was done in Jerusalem [a]and Judah[a] so aroused the anger of Yahweh that [b]he flung them away[b] from his presence.

And Zedekiah rebelled against the king of Babylon, 4/ and in the ninth year of his reign, in the tenth month, on the tenth day of the month Nebuchadrezzar king of Babylon came, he and all his army, against Jerusalem, and they encamped against it and built siege-works around it. 5/ So the city came under siege until the eleventh year of King Zedekiah. 6/ In the fourth month, on the ninth day of the month, the famine became so severe in the city that there was no bread for the people of the land. 7/ And the city fell, 《 and the king saw, 》[a] and all the soldiers, 《 and 》[b] they fled and went out of the city at night by way of the gate between the two walls that is at the king's garden, while the Chaldeans were all around the city, and they went on the road to the Arabah. 8/ But the army of the Chaldeans pursued the king and overtook Zedekiah in the plains of Jericho, and all his army was scattered from him. 9/ And they seized the king and brought him up to the king of Babylon at Riblah [in the land of Hamath,][a] and he passed judgment upon him. 10/ And the king of Babylon slaughtered the sons of Zedekiah before his eyes, and all the officials of Judah he slaughtered at Riblah; 11/ and the eyes of Zedekiah he blinded, and he bound him in shackles, and the king of Babylon took him to Babylon, and he put him in the house of 《 milling 》[a] until the day of his death.

12 In the fifth month, on the tenth[a] day of the month [it was the nineteenth year of King Nebuchadrezzar, king of Babylon][b] Nebuzaradan the provost marshal, [c]〈 an attendant 〉 before[c] the king of Babylon, came into Jerusalem. 13/ And he burned the house of Yahweh, and the house of the king,

Text

1a The reading may be either חֲמוּטַל or חֲמִיטַל, probably the former. The first is that of the ketib and *G* and *V*, whereas the second is that of the qere' and *T*; *S* reads it *ḥamṭûl*. This distribution of readings is found identically in 2 Kgs 24:18; in 2 Kgs 23:31 *M* reads חֲמוּטַל without ketib/qere' contrast, but many MSS. read חֲמִיטַל, and *G* and *V* do likewise. See further Interpretation.

3a—a Many MSS. and 2 Kgs 24:20 read "and in Judah."

b—b *M* reads הִשְׁלִיכוֹ אוֹתָם, as does 2 Kgs 24:20, where one would expect הַשְׁלִיכוֹ אוֹתָם; see GKC sec. 53l.

7a Restoring וַיַּרְא הַמֶּלֶךְ or the like, compare 39:4; so Rudolph, Bright, compare Volz.

b For יִבְרְחוּ read וַיִּבְרְחוּ with 39:4.

9a These words are lacking in *G* and in 2 Kgs 25:6; they are inserted from 39:5.

11a Reading *G* μυλῶνος (הַפַּחֲנָה or the like?) as the *lectio difficilior*; *M* has evidently corrected the text to הַפְּקֻדֹּת, "punishments." See Interpretation.

12a 2 Kgs 25:8 reads "seventh."

b This gloss is missing in *G*, though found in 2 Kgs 25:8. For the chronological difficulty see Interpretation.

c—c For *M* עָמַד לִפְנֵי, literally "(who) stood before," vocalize עֹמֵד לִפְנֵי, literally "standing before"—*G*, with a perfect participle, suggests the Hebrew participle here. The reading of 2 Kgs 25:8 is עֶבֶד, "servant of," which is equivalent.

and all the houses of Jerusalem, [and every ᵇ《large》 houseᵇ he burned]ᵃ with fire. 14/ And allᵃ the walls around Jerusalem [all]ᵇ the army of the Chaldeans demolished who were with the provost marshal. 15/ [ᵇAnd some of the poor ofᵇ the people]ᵃ and the rest of the people who remained in the city, and those who had deserted to the king of Babylon, and the rest of the artisans were exiled by Nebuzaradan the provost marshal. 16/ ᵇBut some of the poor ofᵇ the land Nebuzaradan the provost marshal left for vinedressers and plowmen.

17 And the bronze pillars inᵃ the house of Yahweh, and the stands, and the bronze sea in the house of Yahweh, the Chaldeans broke up, and they carried allᵇ their bronze to Babylon; 18/ and the pots, and the shovels, 《and the meat-forks,》ᵃ [and the (blood-)basins,]ᵃ and the ladles, and all the (other) implements of bronze used in the service, they took; 19/ [and the bowls,]ᵃ and the firepans, and the (blood-)basins, [and the pots, and the lampstands, and the ladles, and the libation-cups,]ᵃ whatever (was of) gold the provost marshal took (as) gold, and whatever (was of) silver, (as) silver. 20/ And (as for) the two pillars, the oneᵃ sea, [and the twelve bronze bulls that were under 《the

13a   Though these words are present in *G* they appear to be an early variant in a conflate text (so also Rudolph).

b—b   For *M* בֵּית הַגָּדוֹל, "house of the notable person (?)," read גָּדוֹל with *G*, *V*, and 2 Kgs 25:9.

14a   "All" is not present in 39:8 and 2 Kgs 25:10.

b   Omit with *G*.

15–16a   This phrase, partially dittographic from v 16, is the less plausible variant in a conflate text (Janzen, pp. 19–20, and so all the commentators); it is not found in 39:9 or 2 Kgs 25:11.

b   This phrase, in both verses, is spelled וּמִדַּלּוֹת; in 2 Kgs 25:11–12 the text reads וּמִדַּלַּת. The noun דַּלָּה is understood as a collective, "poor people," so a plural is puzzling. Was a plural vocalization the attempt of someone to understand the expression as "the poor women," feminine plural of דַּל?

17a   Read with a few MSS. and *G*, *V*, and *T* בְּ (compare the following phrase); *M* לְ "(which) belong to." The first phrase in 2 Kgs 25:13 omits the preposition; the second phrase has בְּ.

b   "All" is not in 2 Kgs 25:13.

18–19a   The lists of objects at the beginning of each of these two verses offer an almost insoluble textual problem, since *M* differs from *G* in both verses, and *M* and *G* offer two further texts in 2 Kgs 25:14. In v 18 *M* has five objects (pots, shovels, snuffers, blood-basins, ladles); *G* appears to have been damaged, offering three objects (a garland, ιαμιν [evidently a transliteration for יָעִים, "shovels"], meat-forks); 2 Kgs 25:14 *M* has four objects (pots, shovels, snuffers, ladles); 2 Kgs 25:14 *G* has a different four (pots, ιαμιν, meat-forks, ladles). I propose that there has been confusion among three words, מִזְרָקוֹת, "blood-basins," מְזַמְּרוֹת, "snuffers," and מִזְלָגוֹת, "meat-forks": Exod 27:3 lists "blood-basins" and "meat-forks" among bronze implements, 1 Kgs 7:40 lists "blood-basins" in a list of (presumably) bronze implements, and 1 Kgs 7:50 lists "snuffers" and "blood-basins" in a list of gold implements. Given this overlapping of items in texts elsewhere, there is great opportunity for confusion here. Since 2 Kgs 25:14 has "snuffers" in *M* and "blood-basins" in *G*, and since both terms appear in *M* for v 18 here, I propose that these two items are evidence of a conflate text, and since *G* in v 18 here has "blood-basins" and "meat-forks," evidently also a conflate text, though a different one, I propose that "meat-forks" is the *lectio difficillima* of the three and is correct. As for v 19, the parallel 2 Kgs 25:15 has only two items, identical in *M* and *G*, "firepans" and "blood-basins." These items are the second and third of the seven items in *M* for v 19. In this verse *G* offers six items; some of the six are to be explained as repetitions from v 18 in the text antecedent to *M*, others as textual variants of the original two. Compare the expansion in v 20, and see further Interpretation.

20a   For *M* אֶחָד 2 Kgs 25:16 reads more correctly הָאֶחָד.

sea,》c] b and the 《ten》d stands of bronze that King Solomon made for the house of Yahweh, there was no weighing ºtheir bronze, [(of) all these implements.]º 21/ ªAs for the pillars:ª eighteenb cubits (was) ºthe height ofº one pillar, ªand its circumference twelve cubits, and its thickness was four fingers—(it was) hollow.ª 22/ And a capital (was) upon it, of bronze, and the height of one capital was fiveª cubits; and filigree and pomegranates (were) around the top of the capital, all of bronze; and like these (it was) for the second pillar, 《filigree》b and pome- granates, 《eight to a cubit for the twelve cubits,》b 23/ and (so) there were ninety-six pomegranates, 《and (in addition) four pome- granates, one for each (?)》ª direction; all the pomegranates were a hundred, around the filigree.

24 And the provost marshal took [Seraiah]ª the chief priest, and [Zephaniah]ª the second priest, and three keepers of the threshold, 25/ and [from the city he took]ª one eunuch who was in command of the soldiers, and sevenb men from the royal privy council who were found in the city, and the scribe of [the commander of]c the army who mustered the people of the land, and sixty men of the people of the land found in the midst of the city. 26/ Nebuzaradan the provost marshal took them and brought them to the king of Babylon at Riblah. 27/ And the king of Babylon struck them down [and killed them]ª at Riblah, in the land of Hamath. 》And Judah went into exile from its soil.《 b [28/ This is (the number of) the people whom Nebuchadrezzar exiled: in the seventh year, three thousand twenty-three Jews; 29/ in the eighteenth year of Nebu- chadrezzar, from Jerusalem eight hundred thirty-two persons; 30/ in the twenty-third year of Nebuchadrezzar, Nebuzaradan the provost marshal exiled, of Jews, seven hundred forty-five persons; all the persons (were) four thousand six hundred.]ª

31 And in the thirty-seventh year of the captivity of Jehoiachin, king of Judah, in the twelfth month, on the twenty-fifthª day of the month, Evil-merodach, king of Babylon, in the year 《he became king,》b he lifted up the head of Jehoiachin king of Judah, and he brought him out of prison.c 32/ And he spoke kindly to him and gave him his seat above the seat of ªthe kingsª who were with him in Babylon. 33/ So he changed his prison clothes and ate bread before him regularly all the days of his life. 34/ And as for his allowance, a regular allowance was given him from the king of Babylon, his daily due, until the day of his death, [all the days of his life.]ª

b   This phrase is not in 2 Kgs 25:16 and does not belong in the listing; see Interpretation.

c   Insert הַיָּם with G; the word evidently dropped out by haplography.

d   Given the other numbers in this verse, restore אֲשֶׁר עֶשֶׂר, which dropped out by haplography with אֲשֶׁר (so Cornill, Rudolph, Bright).

e—e   G reads "their bronze," whereas 2 Kgs 25:16 reads "the bronze of all these implements." M has a conflate text.

21a–a   These words are lacking in 2 Kgs 25:17.

b   G here reads "thirty-five," as does 2 Chr 3:15; 2 Kgs 25:17 (in both M and G) reads "eighteen." "Thirty-five" may have been the result of the abbreviation יח being miswritten as לה. See further Curtis and Madsen, *Chronicles*, 328.

c—c   The ketib reads the absolute קוֹמָה; read the construct with the qere' and 2 Kgs 25:17.

22a   2 Kgs 25:17 reads "three"; 1 Kgs 7:16 reads "five."

b   M is defective; "with the filigree" is found in 2 Kgs 25:17, "eight" and "to a cubit for the twelve cubits" are found in G.

23a   This is Volz's hypothetical reconstruction of a damaged text. There were evidently ninety-six pomegranates in one series, plus an extra four, and רוּחָה, evidently "to a direction," suggests that each of those four faced a compass point. See further Interpretation.

24a   Both names are missing in G; there seems to be no reason for G to omit them, so they are evidently secondary. "Zephaniah" is easily supplied from 21:1; 29:25, 29; 37:3; "Seraiah" would have been avail- able to scribes who wished to expand the text. See Janzen, p. 71.

25a   These words are lacking in G.

b   2 Kgs 25:19 reads "five."

25c   Omit with G.

27a   Omit with G.

b   These words are lacking in G, though they are present in 2 Kgs 25:21 (in contrast to the situation in vv 28–30). They appear to round off the pre- ceding narrative, and they may have been inadver- tently omitted in G (haplography of ἐν γῇ Αιμαθ and τῆς γῆς αὐτοῦ?).

28–30a   These verses are lacking in G and 2 Kgs 25 and are secondary here; see Janzen, p. 122.

31a   G reads "twenty-fourth"; 2 Kgs 25:27 reads "twenty-seventh."

b   Read with G and 2 Kgs 25:27 מָלְכוֹ; M reads "(in the year of) his kingship."

c   The spelling of this word is uncertain: ketib כליא, qere' כְּלוּא (so also 37:4).

32a—a   Ketib omits the article; read the noun with the article with a few MSS., the qere', G, and 2 Kgs 25:28.

34a   This is the less likely reading in a conflate text: "until the day of his death" is lacking in a few MSS. and in 2 Kgs 25:30, and the bracketed words are lacking in G. See Janzen, p. 21.

Structure, Form, Setting

This chapter does not deal with Jrm the prophet. Except for vv 28–30, the chapter is a duplication of 2 Kgs 24:18—25:30, with some plusses and minuses of text, the most prominent being vv 10–11, which expand 2 Kgs 25:7, and vv 21–23, which expand 2 Kgs 25:17.[1] Verses 28–30 are not duplicated in 2 Kings 25; these verses are a register of the number of persons deported in the three successive deportations to Babylon drawn from a separate source.

It must be stressed that by the conclusions of the present study the order of chapters in *G* is the original one (see 46:1—51:58, General Remarks, *Placement and Order of the Oracles*): Thus the contents of the present chapter must be understood as having come directly after what appears in *M* as 37:1—44:30 + 45:1–5.

The direction of borrowing was from 2 Kings to the present chapter. This direction of borrowing is indicated not only by the plusses in Jer (there would be no reason for 2 Kings to abbreviate Jer) but also by the fact that Isaiah 1—39 closes in a similar fashion, with relevant material borrowed from 2 Kings (in that instance Isa 36:1—39:8 borrows 2 Kgs 18:13—20:19). It is to be noted that 2 Kings 19—20 mentions Isaiah, whereas (as already noted) 2 Kings 24—25 does not mention Jrm. That is to say, there was immediate relevance to the narrative about the prophet in question in the borrowing from 2 Kings 19—20, whereas it was the simply the pattern of closing a prophetic scroll with narrative from 2 Kings about the historical events of the period that was followed in the present instance.

The other duplication should be mentioned here: 39:4–10 is missing in *G* and is evidently secondarily derived from material in vv 7–16 of the present chapter. The relation among these texts suggests a period when editors or copyists felt free to add material. For example, 2 Kgs 25:7 reads, "And the sons of Zedekiah he (?) slaughtered before his eyes; and the eyes of Zedekiah he blinded, and he bound him in shackles and brought him to Babylon." Jer 52:10–11bα reads, "And the king of Babylon slaughtered the sons of Zedekiah before his eyes, and all the officials of Judah he slaughtered at Riblah; and the eyes of Zedekiah he blinded, and he bound him in shackles, and the king of Babylon took him to Babylon." Jer 39:6–7 reads, "And the king of Babylon slaughtered the sons of Zedekiah at Riblah before his eyes, and all the nobles of Judah the king of Babylon slaughtered, and the eyes of Zedekiah he blinded, and he bound him in shackles to take him to Babylon." And 52:11 adds a final clause not in either of the other two texts, "and he put him in the house of the mill until the day of his death."

One must assume then that an editor added this chapter at some point after Jehoiachin's death; the year of his release from captivity (v 31) would be 562, when he would be fifty-three years old (2 Kgs 24:8), so the origin of the chapter would be in the last decade or two of the exile.

As already indicated, the material taken from 2 Kings is historical narrative, whereas vv 28–30 are a summary evidently drawn from a contemporary compilation;[2] for vv 28–30 see further Interpretation. As it stands, the chapter falls into seven sections: (1) introduction to Zedekiah's reign, vv 1–3; (2) the siege and fall of Jerusalem, and the fate of Zedekiah, vv 4–11; (3) the fate of the houses and people in Jerusalem, vv 12–16; (4) the temple furnishings of bronze, gold, and silver taken as booty, vv 17–23; (5) the courtiers taken captive to Riblah, vv 24–27; (6) the summary of those taken in the three deportations, vv 28–30; and (7) the rehabilitation of Jehoiachin, vv 31–34. There are no discernible rhetorical features that mark this chapter as a self-defined unit.

Interpretation

As already noted, this chapter (except for vv 28–30) is taken with small variations from 2 Kgs 24:18—25:30. It would serve no useful purpose to offer a full-scale

---

1   For a convenient survey of the sources for the narrative in 2 Kings and the parallels in Jer 52 see Gray, *Kings*, 751–54, 773.

2   For a brief discussion of the relation between historical writing and historical documents see Jay A. Wilcoxen, "Narrative," *Old Testament Form Criticism* (ed. John H. Hayes; San Antonio: Trinity University, 1974) 74–75.

commentary appropriate to that section of 2 Kings; the reader can obtain basic material on the events during and just after the fall of Jerusalem in recent commentaries on that book.[3] There, too, the reader can find a discussion of problems that emerge from the texts, such as the age of Zedekiah at the beginning of his reign (v 1) over against the data in 1 Chr 3:15.[4] The reader is further reminded that for the sake of continuity in the present study the treatment of 37:1—44:30 has already offered details in the interpretation of 39:4–10 that duplicate vv 7–16 here. The verse-by-verse discussion that follows thus concentrates on more recent information or conclusions that supplement or correct material generally found in the commentaries and reference books (thus the location of Libnah, v 1), on those additions in the text of the present chapter not found in Kings (thus the "house of milling" in v 11, and vv 28–30), and on textual variations within the present chapter (thus the various implements in vv 18–19). It is also to be noted that many of the terms pertaining to the temple appurtenances appearing in vv 17–23 (borrowed, with variations, from 2 Kgs 25:13–17) are already discussed in commentaries dealing with 1 Kings 7.[5]

■ **1** There is no way to determine whether the name of Zedekiah's mother was *ḥămûṭal* (the qere') or *ḥămîṭal* (the ketib): see Text. The etymology of the name is likely to be "my father-in-law [*ḥāmî*, that is, the (divine) father of my husband] is shelter [Aramaic *ṭal*]"; if so, the form with *î* is probably correct.[6] Her father, Jeremiah, is the third person by that name to be mentioned in the book (compare 35:3).

Libnah was an important city in the Shephelah. Though it has long been identified with *tall eṣ-ṣāfî* (Atlas of Israel grid 135–123),[7] recent evidence excludes that site as a candidate;[8] the preferred site is now to the south, *tall burnat* (Atlas of Israel grid 138–116).[9]

■ **3** The meaning of the first half of the verse is not at all clear. It reads literally, "For on [or concerning, or because of] the anger of Yahweh it [impersonal feminine] was in Jerusalem and Judah until [or up to] his flinging them from his presence." Does this mean that Yahweh's anger caused things to be bad in Jerusalem and Judah, or did Jerusalem and Judah cause Yahweh's anger? Given the analogous idiom in 32:31 (see the discussion there), I assume that the latter is correct (so also Rudolph, Bright, and so also *NEB*, *NJV*, *NAB*, against Giesebrecht, Cornill, Volz, Condamin, and *JB*); see the discussion in Naegelsbach, Rudolph, and Bright.

■ **4–6** See 39:1–2. The precise meaning of דָּיֵק in v 4 (here "siege-works") is not altogether certain; it appears here and twice in Ezekiel with "build" (Ezek 4:2; 17:17), and in Ezek 4:2 the phrase appears alongside of "throw up a siege-mound" (see Jer 6:6; compare 32:24), so that it is evidently a specific artificial construction,[10] probably a "rampart."[11]

The famine in the city became severe (compare 37:21). The phrase "the people of the land" in v 6 evidently simply means "the general population" (as in 37:2; so Rudolph, who, however, also cites contrary opinion). It must be borne in mind, however, that there must have been many refugees from the countryside within Jerusalem at that time (compare v 25).

■ **7–11bα** See 39:4–7.

■ **11bβ** A detail not in either 39:7 or 2 Kgs 25:7 is the last clause, "And he [Nebuchadrezzar] put him [Zedekiah] in the house of X until the day of his death." *M* here reads "house of punishments" (בֵּית הַפְּקֻדֹּת), a phrase otherwise unattested; *G*, however, offers the striking reading "house of milling" (οἰκίαν μυλῶνος), that is, a place where prisoners are punished by being put to grinding. These

3   For 2 Kgs 24:18—25:30 see particularly Montgomery, *Kings*, 559–69; Gray, *Kings*, 762–75; and now Mordechai Cogan and Hayim Tadmor, *II Kings* (AB 11; New York: Doubleday, 1988) 315–30.

4   On this particular question Rudolph, 318, believes that "twenty-one" is too low; for possible solutions see Curtis and Madsen, *Chronicles*, 100, and Jacob M. Myers, *I Chronicles* (AB 12; Garden City, NY: Doubleday, 1965) 20.

5   For 1 Kings 7 see not only Montgomery, *Kings*, 160–84, and Gray, *Kings*, 176–204, but also Noth, *Könige*, 130–67.

6   So Gray, p. 749. The suggestion by Montgomery, *Kings*, 551, that the name is Arabic is less likely.

7   May, *Oxford Bible Atlas*, 133c, and maps; compare Richard W. Corney, "Libnah," *IDB* 3:123.

8   Anson F. Rainey, "Libnah (City)," *IDBSup* 546.

9   Boling and Wright, *Joshua*, 386; Nancy L. Lapp, "Libnah," *Harper's Bible Dictionary* (ed. Paul J. Achtemeier; San Francisco: Harper & Row, 1985) 560; compare Richard W. Corney, "Libnah," *IDB* 3:123.

10 Zimmerli, *Ezekiel 1*, 162.

11 Cooke, *Ezekiel*, 50.

readings are so far apart (see Text) that one must be a deliberate substitution for the other. Kurt Galling assumes that the rendering in *G* is that of a translator who had been in such a place,[12] but recently K. van der Toorn has published evidence that for two millennia prisoners of war in Mesopotamia, often blinded, were put into workhouses grinding grain, not only to gain work from them but to humiliate them, since grinding is women's work; one is reminded of the fate of Samson in Judg 16:21.[13] The phrase "passing through the rivers" in Isa 43:2 suggests the dangers incurred by the exiles between Jerusalem and Babylon, and the same phrase in Isa 47:2 suggests that a like danger will threaten Babylon; then is the mocking command to Babylon in the same verse, Isa 47:2, to "take the millstones and grind meal," a reflex of what happened to Zedekiah?

It is of interest in this regard that a room has recently been excavated at Ebla with sixteen grindstones arranged around the perimeter;[14] that room may not have been such a workhouse for prisoners, but it at least allows us to see one such large-scale installation. I assume then (against Galling) that this specific punishment was Zedekiah's fate, and that the reading was later generalized to that of *M* when the custom was no longer self-evident.

■ **12** A month after the fall of the city Nebuzaradan entered it to supervise its destruction. For Nebuzaradan see 39:8–10. "Nineteenth year" in the gloss, which likewise occurs in 2 Kgs 25:8, appears to be a mistake for "eighteenth year," if Jerusalem fell in July, 587 (so v 5 and by implication v 29).[15]

■ **13–15** See 39:8–9.

■ **16** The יֹגְבִים, "plowmen," were evidently workmen engaged on highly organized state-managed terraced estates producing export-quality produce, such as wine and oil.[16]

■ **17** Compare 2 Kgs 25:13. For details on the bronze pillars, the stands, and the "sea," see commentaries on 1 Kgs 7:15–37 and general reference works.[17]

■ **18** The implements in this verse are those of bronze. For סִיר "(cooking-)pot" see 1:13.

The second noun in the verse, יָעִים, appears only in the plural (the singular may be יָע or יָעֶה). They are evidently "shovels" for scraping away coals and ashes: the related verb יעה occurs in Isa 28:17 meaning "sweep away."[18]

The third noun in *M*, מְזַמְּרוֹת, singular evidently מְזַמֶּרֶת, is related to the verb זמר, "prune": it is evidently an instrument to trim wicks—the traditional translation is "snuffers."[19] But evidence is given in Text for emending the word here to מִזְלָגוֹת: the singular of that word, מִזְלֵג, appears in 1 Sam 2:13–14 as a (three-tined) meat-fork.

The fourth noun in *M* I take to be a secondary addition: מִזְרָקוֹת (singular מִזְרָק) are evidently bowls or basins used to dash sacrificial blood on the altar (זרק, 2 Kgs 16:13); the word is used of wine-basins in Amos 6:6.

The fifth noun, כַּפּוֹת, is the plural of כַּף "palm (of the hand)." The word suggests a smaller pan or ladle, perhaps for incense; in postbiblical Hebrew the word was used, among other things, for a mason's trowel.[20]

■ **19** The implements in this verse are understood to be of gold or silver. By the analysis in the Text notes, only two items were in the original text, the other five having been added secondarily. Beyond the purely textual data, one may note that Nebuchadrezzar is not likely to have left many gold or silver implements in the temple from his earlier victory in 598 (compare 2 Kgs 24:13).

The first noun in *M*, סִפִּים, singular סַף, here bracketed, is another sort of vessel—"bowl" will have to do.

The next two nouns are taken as original to the text.

12 Kurt Galling, "Datum und Sinn der graeco-koptischen Mühlenostraka im Lichte neuer Belege aus Jerusalem," *ZDPV* 82 (1966) 48.

13 K. van der Toorn, "Judges xvi 21 in the Light of the Akkadian Sources," *VT* 36 (1986) 248–53.

14 For a photograph see Lorenzo Viganò and Dennis Pardee, "Literary Sources for the History of Palestine and Syria, the Ebla Tablets," *BA* 47 (1984) 9.

15 For a recent discussion of the problem see Ernst Kutsch, *Die chronologischen Daten des Ezechielbuches* (OBO 62; Freiburg, Switzerland: Universitätsverlag; Göttingen: Vandenhoeck & Ruprecht, 1985) 10–32.

16 J. N. Graham, "'Vinedressers and Plowmen,' 2 Kings 25:12 and Jeremiah 52:16," *BA* 47 (1984) 55–58.

17 See n. 5; and see further conveniently Georges A. Barrois, "Pillar," *IDB* 3:815–16; Joseph L. Mihelic, "Sea, molten," *IDB* 4:253.

18 Joseph L. Mihelic, "Shovel," *IDB* 4:340.

19 Joseph L. Mihelic, "Snuffers," *IDB* 4:394.

20 Jastrow, p. 657a.

The first one, מַחְתָּה, here "firepan," is related to the verb חתה that occurs in Isa 30:14, "take (coals) out (of a fire), rake."[21] For the second, "blood-basins," see v 18.

The remaining nouns are here bracketed as secondary. For "pots," a repetition from v 18, see 1:13. The מְנוֹרָה, "lampstand," is a device for raising or displaying a lamp (נֵר, 25:10).[22] For "ladles" see v 18. The מְנַקִּיּוֹת (singular evidently מְנַקִּית) are mysterious. In postbiblical Hebrew the word is given as "tubes";[23] Rashi, drawing on the Talmud, explains them as "frames" for displaying the bread of the presence. On the other hand *G* and *V* translate with κυάθους, "wine-cups": they may have been libation-cups (so the translation here).

The nuance of the idiomatic phraseology in v 19aβ, אֲשֶׁר זָהָב זָהָב וַאֲשֶׁר־כֶּסֶף כָּסֶף, is not clear. König[24] explained such an idiom as distributive, "whatever was of gold or silver," and this is the understanding of Rudolph and Bright, and so *JB*, *NEB*, *NAB*, *NJV*: Bright translates "both the ones that were of gold and the ones that were of silver." The suggestion of GKC is to be rejected, that the Hebrew repetition implies superfine gold and silver.[25] But the resemblance to the idiom in 15:2 suggests that the provost marshal took them away for the gold and silver content: Joüon suggests "all the gold there was, and all the silver there was."[26] It seems best then to stay with a translation that resembles that for 15:2 (so also *RSV*).

■ **20** For the items in general see the references in v 17. The phrase "the twelve bronze bulls that were under the sea" does not belong: as commentators have pointed out, these bronze bulls were part of the tribute that had been sent by King Ahaz to the king of Assyria.

■ **21** A cubit, the distance from the elbow to the tip of the middle finger, is roughly a half-meter; by this description, then, the pillars were roughly 9 meters or 30 feet high. The phrase "its circumference twelve cubits" is literally "and a cord of twelve cubits would encircle it." The data regarding the circumference and the thickness of the pillars are not found in 2 Kgs 25:17; the datum

regarding the circumference, however, is found in 1 Kgs 7:15, and that regarding the thickness is found in *G* of 1 Kgs 7:15 (*G* 7:3), though not in *M*. A circumference of 12 cubits means a diameter of roughly 1.9 meters, well over 6 feet, not a slim pillar. "Four fingers" would be about 7.4 centimeters or 3 inches.

■ **22** The discrepancy in the texts on the height of the capital, "three" or "five" cubits, may have arisen if the numbers had been written with numeral values of single letters; 3 cubits would seem to be a more likely measure for a pillar of 18 cubits, but both Montgomery and Gray affirm that "five" is correct,[27] perhaps simply because it is the majority reading. Would "five" be the appropriate height of a capital on a pillar of 35 cubits, and "three" the appropriate height for one of 18 cubits (compare v 21)?

"Filigree" is the translation of *JB* for שְׂבָכָה, a word for "lattice" (2 Kgs 1:2): some kind of "network" (*RSV*, *NEB*, *NAB*) or "meshwork" (*NJV*) is indicated.

Decoration representing pomegranates was common: there was such decoration on the fringe of the robe of the ephod (Exod 28:33), and there is a bronze laver-stand from Ras Shamra with pomegranate pendants.[28]

The restored text of v 22b is a guess; though the expansions here may be glosses, it is clear that the text of *M* has suffered loss (see the notes of Rudolph and Bright).

■ **23** The restored text of this verse is likewise a guess, but the difference between ninety-six and one hundred pomegranates, and the occurrence of the curious word רוּחָה, seemingly "to a wind," suggests that there were four further pomegranates, one facing each compass point.

■ **24** The chief priest Seraiah mentioned here is not of course to be identified with the military officer in 40:8, nor with the brother of Baruch in 51:59, 61. This priest is listed in 1 Chr 6:14 as the grandson of Hilkiah, who was high priest when the Deuteronomic scroll was discovered in the temple (2 Kgs 22:4).

For "keeper of the threshold" see 35:4.

---

21 Joseph L. Mihelic, "Firepan," *IDB* 2:270.
22 Lawrence E. Toombs, "Lampstand," *IDB* 3:64–66.
23 Jastrow, p. 802b.
24 König, *Syntax*, sec. 85.
25 GKC, sec. 123e.
26 Joüon, *Gramm.*, sec. 135e.
27 Montgomery, *Kings*, 568; Gray, *Kings*, 768.
28 *ANEP*, figure 588.

■ **25** For "eunuch" see 29:2. "Who was in command of the soldiers" is literally "who was overseer over the soldiers"; there is no way to determine whether פָּקִיד, "overseer," is a specific rank or whether it is a general term (compare 20:1).

"Royal privy council" is literally "those seeing the face of the king" (compare Esth 1:14).

The "scribe of the army who mustered the people of the land" must have been in charge of conscription lists. For the "people of the land" see 1:17–19; the context here, leading citizens, suggests heads of families of country gentry who had sought shelter in Jerusalem.

■ **28–30** In this summary "Jews" (יְהוּדִים) and "persons" (נֶפֶשׁ) are used interchangeably. The first deportation was in 598, after the first fall of Jerusalem; the second was in 587, after the second fall; and the third was in 582. There is no way to determine whether the totals given for the number of deportees are for adult males only, and thus whether accompanying women and children would have swelled the numbers, or whether the totals are for men, women, and children; נֶפֶשׁ, "persons," would imply the latter. There is a discrepancy between the number of deportees in 598 given in 2 Kgs 24:14 and 16 on the one hand ("ten thousand" or again as "eight thousand") and here ("three thousand twenty-three"), a discrepancy that has been explained in various ways. Montgomery has suggested[29] that the larger figures are approximations for the number of men, women, and children, whereas the smaller number given here, three thousand twenty-three, is for adult males only; Malamat proposes two deportations at that time, the smaller number immediately upon the surrender of Jerusalem and a larger number, consisting of armorers and sappers, some weeks later.[30] But the number in v 30 offers a grand total of all deportations, so that the most likely solution is that the higher numbers in 2 Kgs 24:14 and 16 are from later redactors, who might have been impelled to exaggerate, and that the numbers here, with their specificity, are from a contemporary compilation.

The "eighteenth year of Nebuchadrezzar" (v 29) conflicts with the "nineteenth year of King Nebuchadrezzar" in v 12: see there.

There is no way to learn the occasion for the third deportation, in 582. As noted in the discussion of 41:1–3, Hyatt has proposed that it was in response to the assassination of Gedaliah, if that event did not take place in the autumn of 587 but perhaps four years later, but I prefer to date the assassination of Gedaliah to the autumn of 587.

■ **31–34** "Evil-merodach" is the Akkadian *Amīl-Marduk*, "man of Marduk" (for the name of the god see 50:2), the son and successor of Nebuchadrezzar; he ruled for only two years (562–560), being succeeded by his brother-in-law Nergal-šar-uṣur (for whom compare 39:3). He pardoned Jehoiachin, brought him out of prison, and gave him daily rations and a seat of honor. For "lift up the head" as an expression of pardon compare Gen 40:13. One wonders who the other exiled kings were who are mentioned in v 32!

The verbs in v 33 are perfects with the simple וְ. The second verb could be understood as the equivalent of a repetitive imperfect, but the first is evidently an Aramaism (so Rudolph). One is left uncertain whose life is referred to in "all the days of his life" (v 33), and since Evil-merodach died after only two years' reign, one wonders what became of Jehoiachin if the implication is "all the days of the Evil-merodach's life" (as Cornill and Rudolph hold), if the Jewish king outlived the Babylonian one; "until the day of his death" (v 34) may be ambiguous as well, though the phrase would more likely be heard as "until the day of Jehoiachin's death."

The "regular allowance" (אֲרֻחָה) in v 34 is dramatized by the existence of Babylonian texts listing rations for Jehoiachin and his sons.[31]

Aim

The addition of this chapter to the words and events associated with Jrm can hardly be attributed only to the analogy with Isaiah 36—39 or to an antiquarian interest (compare Structure, Form, Setting): the immediate fate of Jerusalem is covered at least to some degree by 39:4–10. But it is not easy to discern what lies behind the addition of this appendix; one can only speculate.

It has already been noted that we lack any notice of

---

29   Montgomery, *Kings*, 556.
30   Malamat, "Twilight of Judah," 134.
31   *ANET*, 308b.

the death of Jrm (see 37:1—44:30, Setting). It may be then that we have in compensation a narrative of the "death" of Jerusalem, of the death of Zedekiah, and of the ultimate death of Jehoiachin.

Furthermore the "death" of Jerusalem and the death of Zedekiah were the burden of Jrm's message to the king (38:17–18), and it may be that an editor wished to turn from the chaos of Jrm's stay in Egypt narrated in 43:8—44:30 and from Baruch's lament in 45:1–5 to stress the working out of the word of Yahweh: The book begins with the announcement of the coming of that word in the thirteenth year of Josiah; so this appendix reminds the reader of the working out of that word in the extinction of kingship in Judah.

Finally, there are royal motifs in the wording of Jrm's call (see 1:4–19, Form). Now that the community can no longer rally around its kingship or its temple, its identity must be found in the presence of the prophetic word.

Bibliography
Indices

This bibliography is intended not to be complete, but to be useful. To that end, studies published before 1918 are cited only if they appear to continue to contribute to current scholarship. General studies on the prophets of the OT, or on the phenomenon of prophetism, are included only if they contain significant sections on Jeremiah. Material intended for the instruction of youth or adults in the church, when it seems merely reflective of the state of scholarly discussion at the time of publication, is not included, nor are sermons, meditations, or essays on spirituality; material of these sorts is included only if the author has demonstrated scholarship in other studies, or if such material becomes part of the discussion (see Section 6, Summary Presentations of the Book of Jeremiah and of the Prophet Jeremiah). Most of the studies cited are in English, French, or German, but studies in Latin, Italian, Spanish, Dutch, and Afrikaans are occasionally included, particularly if the contents are striking. Since I cannot read the Scandinavian languages or Modern Hebrew, studies in these and other languages have had to be excluded.

The citations are given in full (rather than being referred to by short titles).

It is important to remember that beyond the bibliographies cited in Section 1, many of the other studies cited here offer bibliographies of their own, particularly the commentaries in Section 2b.

1. Bibliographies and Surveys

a. Bibliographies

Fohrer, Georg
"The Book of Jeremiah—Some Recent Studies," *JSOT* 28 (1984) 47–59.
Idem
"Neuere Literatur zur alttestamentlichen Prophetie," *TRu* NF 19 (1951) 277–346, esp. 305–308 [on literature from 1932–39].
Idem
"Neuere Literatur zur alttestamentlichen Prophetie," *TRu* NF 20 (1952) 193–271, 295–361, esp. 242–49 [on literature from 1940–50].
Idem
"Zehn Jahr Literatur zur alttestamentlichen Prophetie (1951–60)," *TRu* NF (1962) 1–75, 235–97, 301–74, esp. 250–61.
Idem
"Neue Literatur zur alttestamentlichen Prophetie (1961–70)," *TRu* NF 45 (1980) 109–21.

b. Surveys of Trends in Jeremiah Studies; Encyclopedia Articles with Bibliographies

Bonnard, Pierre-E.
"Jérémie (prophète), Le livre et la personnalité," *Dictionnaire de Spiritualité* 8 (1974), columns 877–89.
Clamer, Albert
"Jérémie," *DTC* 8 (1924) columns 842–86.
Claudel, Paul
"Note complémentaire sur Jérémie," *DTC, Table Générales* II, columns 2492–97.
Crenshaw, James L.
"A Living Tradition, The Book of Jeremiah in Current Research," *Int* 37 (1983) 117–29.
Eissfeldt, Otto
"The Prophetic Literature," *The Old Testament and Modern Study, A Generation of Discovery and Research, Essays by Members of the Society for Old Testament Study* (ed. Harold H. Rowley; Oxford: Clarendon, 1951) 131–32, 151–53.
Gelin, Albert
"Jérémie," *DBSup* 4 (1948) columns 857–89.
Gressmann, Hugo
"Neue Hilfsmittel zum Verständnis Jeremias," *ZAW* 43 (1925) 138–47.
Herrmann, Siegfried
"Forschung am Jeremiabuch, Probleme und Tendenzen ihrer neueren Entwicklung," *TLZ* 102 (1977) columns 481–90.
Idem
"Jeremia/Jeremiabuch," *Theologische Realenzyklopädie*, 16 (ed. Gerhard Müller; 1907) 568–86.
Holladay, William L.
"Jeremiah the prophet," *IDBSup* (1976) 470–72.
Jobling, David K.
"The Quest of the Historical Jeremiah: Hermeneutical Implications of Recent Literature," *USQR* 34 (1978–79) 3–12; rep. *A Prophet to the Nations, Essays in Jeremiah Studies* (ed. Leo G. Perdue and Brian W. Kovacs; Winona Lake, IN: Eisenbrauns, 1984) 285–97.
Kieser, O.
"Das Jeremiabuch im Licht der Neuesten Kritik," *TSK* 78 (1905) 479–520.
Lipinski, Edward [= Edouard Lipiński]
"Jeremiah, In the Bible," *EncJud* 9, columns 1345–59; 1361.
Muilenburg, James
"Jeremiah the prophet," *IDB* (1962) 2:823–35.

Schmidt, Nathaniel

"Jeremiah," *Encyclopedia Biblica* (ed. Thomas K. Cheyne et al.; 1901), columns 2366–72; "Jeremiah (Book)," op. cit., columns 2372–95.

Vogt, Ernst

"Jeremiasliteratur," *Bib* 35 (1954) 357–65.

Wildberger, Hans

"Jeremia," *RGG* III (1959), columns 581–84.

Idem

"Jeremiabuch," *RGG* III (1959), columns 584–90.

2. Commentaries

a. Through the Nineteenth Century

Calvin, John

Commentaries on the Book of the Prophet Jeremiah and the Lamentations (Calvin Translation Society, 1850–55; rep. Grand Rapids: Eerdmans, 1950).

Hitzig, Ferdinand

Der Prophet Jeremia erklärt (Kurzgefasstes exegetisches Handbuch zum Alten Testament; Leipzig: Hirzel, 1866).

Jerome

(S.) Hieronymi Presbyteri in Hieremiam Prophetam, Libri Sex (ed. Siegfried Reiter; CChr, Series Latina 74; Turnhout: Brepols, 1960).

Michaelis, Johann D.

Observationes Philologicae et Criticae in Jeremiae Vaticinia et Threnos (Göttingen: Vandenhoeck & Ruprecht, 1793).

Naegelsbach, C. W. Eduard

The Book of the Prophet Jeremiah, Theologically and Homiletically Expounded (New York: Scribner's, 1886).

Qimḥi, David

See דדק in מקראות גדולות (Warsaw, 1874–77; rep. New York: Pardes, 1951).

Rashi (Rabbi Solomon ben Isaac)

See רשי in מקראות גדולות (Warsaw, 1874–77; rep. New York: Pardes, 1951), and further Johann Friedrich Breithaupt, ed., *R. Salomonis Jarchi,* רשי *Dicti, Commentarius Hebraicus, in Prophetas Maiores et Minores* (Gotha: Schall, 1713) 3:326–472.

Schmidt, Sebastian

Commentarii in Librum Prophetiarum Jeremiae (Frankfurt am Main, 1706).

b. Critical Commentaries in the Twentieth Century

Bright, John

Jeremiah (AB 21; Garden City, NY: Doubleday, 1965).

Carroll, Robert P.

Jeremiah (Old Testament Library; Philadelphia: Westminster, 1986).

Condamin, Albert

Le Livre de Jérémie (EBib: Paris, Gabalda, 1936).

Cornill, Carl H.

Das Buch Jeremia (Leipzig: Tauchnitz, 1905).

Duhm, Bernhard

Das Buch Jeremia (Kurzer Hand-Commentar zum Alten Testament; Tübingen/Leipzig: Mohr [Siebeck], 1901).

Elliott-Binns, Leonard E.

The Book of the Prophet Jeremiah (Westminster Commentaries; London: Methuen, 1919).

Giesebrecht, Friedrich

Das Buch Jeremia (HKAT 3,2; Göttingen: Vandenhoeck & Ruprecht, 1907).

Hyatt, J. Philip,

"Introduction and Exegesis, Jeremiah," *IB* 5 (1956) 775–1142.

McKane, William

A Critical and Exegetical Commentary on Jeremiah, 1 (ICC; Edinburgh: Clark, 1986).

Nicholson, Ernest W.

The Book of the Prophet Jeremiah (The Cambridge Bible Commentary on the New English Bible; Cambridge: Cambridge University, 1973, 1975).

Nötscher, Friedrich

Das Buch Jeremias (Die Heilige Schrift des Alten Testaments 7, 2; Bonn: Hanstein, 1934).

Rudolph, Wilhelm

Jeremia (HAT 12; Tübingen: Mohr [Siebeck], 1968).

Schreiner, Josef

Jeremia 1—25,14; Jeremia 25,15—52,34 (Die Neue Echter Bibel, Kommentar zum Alten Testament mit der Einheitsübersetzung; Würzburg: Echter, 1981, 1984).

Thompson, John Arthur

The Book of Jeremiah (NICOT; Grand Rapids: Eerdmans, 1980).

Volz, Paul

Der Prophet Jeremia (KAT 10; Leipzig: Deichert, 1928).

Weiser, Artur

Das Buch Jeremia (ATD 20/21; Göttingen: Vandenhoeck & Ruprecht, 1969).

c. Commentaries in the Jewish Tradition

Freedman, Harry, *Jeremiah* (Soncino Books of the Bible; London: Soncino, 1949).

Rosenberg, Abraham J., ed.

מקראות גדולות, *Jeremiah, A New English Translation, Translation of Text, Rashi and Commentary by Rabbi A. J. Rosenberg* (New York: Judaica, 1985).

3. Collections of Essays and Studies on Jeremiah

Bogaert, Pierre-Maurice, ed.

Le Livre de Jérémie, le prophète et son milieu, les oracles et leur transmission (BETL 54; Leuven: Leuven University, 1981).

Perdue, Leo G., and Brian W. Kovacs, eds.

A Prophet to the Nations, Essays in Jeremiah Studies (Winona Lake, IN: Eisenbrauns, 1984).

4. Texts and Versions

a. Editions
(1) Hebrew Text
(a) Masoretic Text
Rudolph, Wilhelm, ed.
> *Liber Jeremiae* (Biblia Hebraica Stuttgartensia 8; Stuttgart: Württembergische Bibelanstalt, 1970) = Karl Elliger and Wilhelm Rudolph, eds., *Biblia Hebraica Stuttgartensia* (Stuttgart: Deutsche Bibelstiftung, 1977) 780–895.

(b) Qumran Fragments
Baillet, Maurice, Jozef T. Milik, and Roland de Vaux
> *Les 'Petites Grottes' de Qumrân* (DJD 3; Oxford: Clarendon, 1962) 62–69.

Janzen, J. Gerald
> *Studies in the Text of Jeremiah* (HSM 6; Cambridge: Harvard University, 1973) 173–84.

(2) Septuagint
Field, Frederick, ed.
> *Origenis Hexaplorum quae Supersunt, Sive Veterum Interpretum Graecorum in Totum V. T. Fragmenta II* (Oxford: Oxford University, 1875) 573–740, and "Auctarium ad Origenis Hexapla," 36–54.

Ziegler, Joseph, ed.
> *Ieremias, Baruch, Threni, Epistula Ieremiae* (Septuaginta, Vetus Testamentum Graecum 15; Göttingen: Vandenhoeck & Ruprecht, 1957).

(3) Vulgate
Fischer, Bonifatius, et al., eds.
> *Biblia Sacra Iuxta Vulgatam Versionem* (Stuttgart: Württembergische Bibelanstalt, 1969) 1166–1248.
> *Liber Hieremiae et Lamentationes ex Interpretatione Sancti Hieronymi* (Biblia Sacra Iuxta Latinam Vulgatam Versionem, 14; Rome: Vatican, 1972).

(4) Peshiṭta
[*Note:* There is at the moment no critical edition of the Peshiṭta of Jeremiah; such an edition has been completed by Donald M. Walter, forthcoming as *The Old Testament in Syriac, According to the Peshiṭta Version*, III/2 (Leiden: Brill). Until its appearance, the standard text is:]

Ceriani, Antonio M., ed.
> *Translatio Syra Pescitto Veteris Testamenti ex Codice Ambrosiano Sec. fere VI* (Milano: Pogliani, 1876–83) 323–56.

See further: ktb' qdyš' (Urmia: 1852; rep. London: Trinitarian Bible Society, 1954) 421–57.

Note: A Latin translation of the Peshiṭta is to be found in: Walton, Brian, ed.
> *Biblia Sacra Polyglotta* (London: Roycroft, 1657) III.2, 177–371.

(5) Targum Jonathan
> *The Aramaic Bible (The Targums)*, 12 (ed. C. T. Robert Hayward; Wilmington, DE: Glazier, 1987) [includes introduction, bibliography, English translation, and notes].

Sperber, Alexander, *The Bible in Aramaic, Based on Old Manuscripts and Printed Texts*, III (Leiden: Brill, 1962) 133–263

b. Concordances and Other Aids
Andersen, Francis I., and A. Dean Forbes, eds.
> *A Linguistic Concordance of Jeremiah* (The Computer Bible 14, 14A; Wooster, OH: Biblical Research Associates, 1978).

Rudolph, Wilhelm
> *Hebräisches Wörterbuch zu Jeremia* (Einzelwörterbücher zum Alten Testament 3; Berlin: Töpelmann, 1927).

c. Studies
(1) *G* Alone; Comparisons of *M* and *G*
Bogaert, Pierre-Maurice
> "De Baruch à Jérémie, Les deux rédactions conservées du livre de Jérémie," *Le livre de Jérémie, le prophète et son milieu, les oracles et leur transmission* (ed. Pierre-Maurice Bogaert; BETL 54; Leuven: Leuven University, 1981) 168–73.

Brock, Sebastian P., Charles T. Fritsch, and Sidney Jellicoe
> *A Classified Bibliography of the Septuagint* (Leiden: Brill, 1973) 139–40.

Janzen, J. Gerald
> "Double Readings in the Text of Jeremiah," *HTR* 60 (1967) 433–47.

Idem
> *Studies in the Text of Jeremiah* (HSM 6; Cambridge: Harvard University, 1973).

Köhler, Ludwig
> "Beobachtungen am hebräischen und griechischen Text von Jeremia Kap. 1—9," *ZAW* 29 (1909) 1–39.

Rudolph, Wilhelm
> "Zum Text des Jeremia," *ZAW* 48 (1930) 272–86.

Soderlund, Sven
> *The Greek Text of Jeremiah, A Revised Hypothesis* (JSOT Supplement Series 47; Sheffield: JSOT, 1985).

Stulman, Louis
> *The Other Text of Jeremiah, A Reconstruction of the Hebrew Text Underlying the Greek Version of the Prose Sections of Jeremiah With English Translation* (Lanham, MD/New York/London: University Press of America, 1985).

Idem
> "Some Theological and Lexical Differences Between the Old Greek and the MT of the Jeremiah Prose Discourses," *Hebrew Studies* 25 (1984) 18–23.

Talmon, Shemaryahu, and Emanuel Tov
> "A Commentary on the Text of Jeremiah, 1. The LXX of Jer. 1:1–7," *Textus* 9 (1981) 1–15.

Thackeray, H. St. John
> "The Greek Translators of Jeremiah," *JTS* 4 (1902/03) 245–66.

Tov, Emanuel

"L'incidence de la critique textuelle sur la critique littéraire dans le livre de Jérémie," *RB* 79 (1972) 189–99.

Idem

The Septuagint Translation of Jeremiah and Baruch, A Discussion of an Early Revision of the LXX of Jeremiah 29—52 and Baruch 1:1—3:8 (HSM 8; Missoula, MT: Scholars, 1976).

Idem

"Some Aspects of the Textual and Literary History of the Book of Jeremiah," *Le Livre de Jérémie, le prophète et son milieu, les oracles et leur transmission* (ed. Pierre-Maurice Bogaert; BETL 54; Leuven: Leuven University, 1981) 145–67.

Wells, Roy D., Jr.

"Indications of Late Reinterpretation of the Jeremianic Tradition from the LXX of Jer 21 1—23 8," *ZAW* 96 (1984) 405–20.

Yerkes, Royden K.

"The Lucianic Version of the Old Testament as Illustrated from Jeremiah 1—3," *JBL* 37 (1918) 163–92.

Ziegler, Joseph

Beiträge zur Ieremias-Septuaginta (Nachrichten der Akademie der Wissenschaften in Göttingen I. Philologisch-historische Klasse, Jahrgang 1958), 45–235 = (Mitteilungen des Septuaginta-Unternehmens 6; Göttingen: Vandenhoeck & Ruprecht, 1958).

Idem

"Die Septuaginta Hieronymi im Buch des Propheten Jeremias," *Colligere Fragmenta, Festschrift A. Dold* (Beuron: 1952) 13–24 = *Sylloge, Gesammelte Aufsätze zur Septuaginta* (Mitteilungen des Septuaginta-Unternehmens 10; Göttingen: Vandenhoeck & Ruprecht, 1971) 345–56.

(2) Other Versions

Kedar-Kopfstein, Benjamin

"Textual Gleanings from the Vulgate to Jeremiah," *Textus* 7 (1969) 36–58.

Schäfers, Joseph

Die äthiopische Übersetzung des Propheten Jeremias (Freiburg im Breisgau: Kreysing, 1912).

Sperber, Alexander

The Bible in Aramaic, Based on Old Manuscripts and Printed Texts, IV-B, *The Targum and the Hebrew Bible* (Leiden: Brill, 1973) 324–34.

5. Philological Studies, Systematic Suggestions for Fresh Readings

Driver, Godfrey R.

"Linguistic and Textual Problems; Jeremiah," *JQR* 28 (1937/38) 97–129.

Ehrlich, Arnold B.

Randglossen zur hebräischen Bibel 4 (Leipzig: Hinrichs, 1912).

Volz, Paul

Studien zum Text des Jeremia (Beiträge zur Wissenschaft vom Alten Testament 25; Leipzig: Hinrichs, 1920).

6. Summary Presentations of the Book of Jeremiah and of the Prophet Jeremiah

a. Within Introductions or General Treatments of the Prophets

Blenkinsopp, Joseph

A History of Prophecy in Israel, From the Settlement in the Land to the Hellenistic Period (Philadelphia: Westminster, 1983) 153–69, 172–76.

Childs, Brevard S.

Introduction to the Old Testament as Scripture (Philadelphia: Fortress, 1979) 339–54.

Eissfeldt, Otto

The Old Testament, An Introduction (Oxford: Blackwell, 1965) 346–65.

Hanson, Paul D.

The People Called, The Growth of Community in the Bible (San Francisco: Harper, 1986) 198–208.

Heschel, Abraham J.

The Prophets (New York/Evanston: Harper, 1962) 103–39.

von Rad, Gerhard

Old Testament Theology 2 (New York: Harper, 1965) 191–219.

Sellin, Ernst, and Georg Fohrer

Introduction to the Old Testament (New York/Nashville: Abingdon, 1968) 388–402.

b. Independent Works

Blank, Sheldon H.

Jeremiah, Man and Prophet (Cincinnati: Hebrew Union College, 1961).

Brueggemann, Walter

"The Book of Jeremiah, Portrait of the Prophet," *Int* 37 (1983) 130–45.

Calkins, Raymond

Jeremiah the Prophet (New York: Macmillan, 1930).

Carroll, Robert P.

From Chaos to Covenant, Prophecy in the Book of Jeremiah (New York: Crossroad, 1981).

Füglister, Notker

"Ganz von Gott in Dienst genommen: Jeremias," *Wort und Botschaft, Eine theologische und kritische Einführung in die Probleme des Alten Testaments* (ed. Josef Schreiner; Würzburg: Echter, 1967) 178–95.

Gordon, T. Crouther

The Rebel Prophet, Studies in the Personality of Jeremiah (New York/London: Harper, 1932).

Holladay, William L.

Jeremiah, Spokesman Out of Time (New York: Pilgrim, 1974).

Honeycutt, Roy L.

"Jeremiah, the Prophet and the Book," *RevExp* 78 (1981) 303–18.

Kraus, Hans-Joachim
  Prophetie in der Krisis, Studien zu Texten aus dem Buche Jeremia (BibS[N] 43; Neukirchen-Vluyn: Erziehungsverein, 1964).
Ridouard, André
  Jérémie, L'épreuve de la foi (Paris: Cerf, 1983).
Skinner, John
  Prophecy and Religion, Studies in the Life of Jeremiah (Cambridge: Cambridge University, 1922).
Steinmann, Jean
  Le Prophète Jérémie, Sa vie, son oeuvre et son temps (LD 9; Paris: Cerf, 1952).
Welch, Adam C.
  Jeremiah: His Time and His Work (London: Oxford University, 1928; rep. Westport, CT: Greenwood, 1980).
Westermann, Claus
  Jeremia (Stuttgart: Calwer, 1967).

7. Redaction History of the Book of Jeremiah

a. General Considerations; Attempts to Reconstruct the Original Scroll(s)

Baumann, Arnulf
  "Urrolle und Fasttag, Zur Rekonstruktion der Urrolle des Jeremiabuches nach den Angaben in Jer 36," *ZAW* 80 (1968) 350–73.
Bogaert, Pierre-Maurice
  "La tradition des oracles et du livre de Jérémie, des origines au moyen âge, Essai de synthèse," *RTL* 8 (1977) 305–28.
Bright, John
  "The Prophetic Reminiscence: Its Place and Function in the Book of Jeremiah," *Biblical Essays, Proceedings of the Ninth Meeting of "Die Ou-Testamentiese Werkgemeenskap in Suid-Afrika," Held at the University of Stellenbosch 26th–29th July 1966* (Potchefstroom: Pro Rege, 1966) 11–30.
Hobbs, Trevor R.
  "Some Remarks on the Composition and Structure of the Book of Jeremiah," *CBQ* 34 (1972) 257–75; rep. *A Prophet to the Nations, Essays in Jeremiah Studies* (ed. Leo G. Perdue and Brian W. Kovacs; Winona Lake, IN: Eisenbrauns, 1984) 175–91.
Holladay, William L.
  The Architecture of Jeremiah 1—20 (Lewisburg, PA: Bucknell University, 1976).
Hölscher, Gustav
  Die Profeten, Untersuchungen zur Religionsgeschichte Israels (Leipzig: Hinrichs, 1914) 379–405.
Marx, Alfred
  "A propos des doublets du livre de Jérémie: Réflexions sur la formation d'un livre prophétique," *Prophecy, Essays Presented to Georg Fohrer on His Sixty-fifth Birthday, 6 September 1980* (ed. John A. Emerton; BZAW 150; Berlin/New York: de Gruyter, 1980) 106–20.
May, Herbert G.
  "Jeremiah's Biographer," *JBR* 10 (1942) 195–201.

Idem
  "Towards an Objective Approach to the Book of Jeremiah: The Biographer," *JBL* 61 (1942) 139–55.
Mowinckel, Sigmund
  Zur Komposition des Buches Jeremia (Kristiania [= Oslo]: Dybwad, 1914).
Overholt, Thomas W.
  "Remarks on the Continuity of the Jeremiah Tradition," *JBL* 91 (1972) 457–62.
Podechard, Emmanuel
  "Le livre de Jérémie: Structure et formation," *RB* 37 (1928) 181–97.
Rietzschel, Claus
  Das Problem der Urrolle, Ein Beitrag zur Redaktionsgeschichte des Jeremiabuches (Gütersloh: Gütersloher [Gerd Mohn], 1966).
Robinson, Theodore H.
  "Baruch's Roll," *ZAW* 42 (1924) 209–21.
Tov, Emmanuel
  "The Literary History of the Book of Jeremiah in the Light of its Textual History," *Empirical Models for Biblical Criticism* (ed. Jeffrey H. Tigay; Philadelphia: University of Pennsylvania, 1985) 211–37.

b. The Prose Speeches; Relation of the Prose Speeches to Poetry; Relation of the Book of Jeremiah to Deuteronomy

Brekelmans, Christianus
  "Some Considerations on the Prose Sermons in the Book of Jeremiah," *Bijdragen* 34 (1973) 204–11.
Bright, John
  "The Date of the Prose Sermons of Jeremiah," *JBL* 70 (1951) 15–35; rep. *A Prophet to the Nations, Essays in Jeremiah Studies* (ed. Leo G. Perdue and Brian W. Kovacs; Winona Lake, IN: Eisenbrauns, 1984) 193–212.
Cazelles, Henri
  "Jérémie et le Deutéronome," *RSR* 38 (1951) 5–36 = "Jeremiah and Deuteronomy," *A Prophet to the Nations, Essays in Jeremiah Studies* (ed. Leo G. Perdue and Brian W. Kovacs; Winona Lake, IN: Eisenbrauns, 1984) 89–111.
Davidson, Robert
  "Orthodoxy and the Prophetic Word, A Study in the Relationship between Jeremiah and Deuteronomy," *VT* 14 (1964) 407–16.
Granild, Sigurd
  "Jeremia und das Deuteronomium," *ST* 16 (1962) 135–54.
Holladay, William L.
  "A Fresh Look at 'Source B' and 'Source C' in Jeremiah," *VT* 25 (1975) 392–96, 402–12; rep. *A Prophet to the Nations, Essays in Jeremiah Studies* (ed. Leo G. Perdue and Brian W. Kovacs; Winona Lake, IN: Eisenbrauns, 1984) 213–14, 220–28.
Idem
  "Prototype and Copies: A New Approach to the

Poetry-Prose Problem in the Book of Jeremiah,"
JBL 79 (1960) 351–67.

Hölscher, Gustav

*Die Profeten, Untersuchungen zur Religionsgeschichte
Israels* (Leipzig: Hinrichs, 1914) 382–84, n. 2.

Holt, Else K.

"Jeremiah's Temple Sermon and the Deuteronomists: An Investigation of the Redactional Relationship Between Jeremiah 7 and 26," *JSOT* 36
(1986) 73–87.

Hyatt, J. Philip

"The Deuteronomic Edition of Jeremiah," *Vander-
bilt Studies in the Humanities* 1 (Nashville: Vander-
bilt University, 1951) 71–95; rep. *A Prophet to the
Nations, Essays in Jeremiah Studies* (ed. Leo G.
Perdue and Brian W. Kovacs; Winona Lake, IN:
Eisenbrauns, 1984) 247–67.

Idem

"Jeremiah and Deuteronomy," *JNES* 1 (1942)
156–73; rep. *A Prophet to the Nations, Essays in
Jeremiah Studies* (ed. Leo G. Perdue and Brian W.
Kovacs; Winona Lake, IN: Eisenbrauns, 1984)
113–27.

McKane, William

"Relations Between Poetry and Prose in the Book
of Jeremiah with Special Reference to Jeremiah iii
6–11 and xii 14–17," *Congress Volume, Vienna, 1980*
(ed. John A. Emerton; VTSup 32; Leiden: Brill,
1981) 220–37; rep. *A Prophet to the Nations, Essays
in Jeremiah Studies* (ed. Leo G. Perdue and Brian
W. Kovacs; Winona Lake, IN: Eisenbrauns, 1984)
269–84.

Nicholson, Ernest W.

*Preaching to the Exiles, A Study of the Prose Tradition
in the Book of Jeremiah* (Oxford: Blackwell, 1970).

Robinson, Theodore H.

"Baruch's Roll," *ZAW* 42 (1924) 209–21.

Rowley, Harold H.

"The Prophet Jeremiah and the Book of Deuteronomy," *Studies in Old Testament Prophecy, Presented
to Theodore H. Robinson by the Society for Old Testament Study on His Sixty-fifth Birthday, August 9th,
1946* (ed. Harold H. Rowley; Edinburgh: Clark,
1950; rep. 1957) 157–74 = *From Moses to Qumran,
Studies in the Old Testament* (New York: Association,
1963) 185–208.

Stulman, Louis

*The Prose Sermons of the Book of Jeremiah, A Rede-
scription of the Correspondences with the Deuteronomistic Literature in the Light of Recent Text-critical
Research* (SBLDS 83; Atlanta: Scholars, 1986).

Sturdy, John V. M.

"The Authorship of the 'Prose Sermons' of
Jeremiah," *Prophecy, Essays Presented to Georg Fohrer
on His Sixty-fifth Birthday, 6 September 1980* (ed. John
A. Emerton; BZAW 150; Berlin/New York: de
Gruyter, 1980) 143–50.

Thiel, Winfried

Die deuteronomistische Redaktion von Jer 1—25
(WMANT 41; Neukirchen: Neukirchener, 1973).

Idem

Die deuteronomistische Redaktion von Jer 26—45
(WMANT 52; Neukirchen-Vluyn: Neukirchener,
1973)

Weinfeld, Moshe

Deuteronomy and the Deuteronomic School (Oxford:
Clarendon, 1972) esp. 27–32, 138–46, 359–61.

Weippert, Helga

"Der Beitrag ausserbiblischer Prophetentexte zum
Verständnis der Prosareden des Jeremiabuches,"
*Le Livre de Jérémie, le prophète et son milieu, les oracles
et leur transmission* (ed. Pierre-Maurice Bogaert;
BETL 54; Leuven: Leuven University, 1981) 83–
104.

Idem

Die Prosareden des Jeremiabuches (BZAW 132;
Berlin: de Gruyter, 1973).

c. The Narrative Material; the Man Baruch

Augustin, F.

"Baruch und das Buch Jeremia," *ZAW* 67 (1955)
50–56.

Holladay, William L.

"A Fresh Look at 'Source B' and 'Source C' in
Jeremiah," *VT* 25 (1975) 394–402; rep. *A Prophet
to the Nations, Essays in Jeremiah Studies* (ed. Leo G.
Perdue and Brian W. Kovacs; Winona Lake, IN:
Eisenbrauns, 1984) 213–20.

Lundbom, Jack R.

"Baruch, Seraiah, and Expanded Colophons in the
Book of Jeremiah," *JSOT* 36 (1986) 89–114.

Muilenburg, James

"Baruch the Scribe," *Proclamation and Presence, Old
Testament Essays in Honour of Gwynne Henton Davies*
(ed. John I. Durham and J. Roy Porter; Richmond,
VA: John Knox, 1970) 215–38; rep. *A Prophet to
the Nations, Essays in Jeremiah Studies* (ed. Leo G.
Perdue and Brian W. Kovacs; Winona Lake, IN:
Eisenbrauns, 1984) 229–45.

Wanke, Gunther

Untersuchungen zur sogenannten Baruchschrift
(BZAW 122; Berlin: de Gruyter, 1971).

8. Form Criticism and Rhetorical Criticism in the Book of Jeremiah

a. Form Criticism

[*Note: See also* Section 12, The Forms of the Utterances of Jeremiah.]

Berridge, John M.

*Prophet, People, and the Word of Yahweh, An Examina-
tion of Form and Content in the Proclamation of the
Prophet Jeremiah* (Basel Studies of Theology 4;
Zurich: EVZ, 1970).

Eissfeldt, Otto

"Unheils- und Heilsweissagungen Jeremias als

Vergeltung für ihm erwiesene Weh- und Wohl-
taten," *Wissenschaftliche Zeitschrift der Martin-Luther-
Universität Halle-Wittenburg, Gesellschafts- und
Sprachwissenschtliche Reihe* 14 (1965) 181–86 =
Kleine Schriften 4 (Tübingen: Mohr [Siebeck],
1968) 181–92.

Reventlow, Henning Graf von
Liturgie und prophetisches Ich bei Jeremia (Gütersloh:
Gütersloher, 1963).

b. Rhetorical Criticism

[*Note: See also* Section 16 a, The Rhetoric of
Jeremiah.]

Lundbom, Jack R.
Jeremiah, A Study in Ancient Hebrew Rhetoric (SBLDS
18; Missoula, MT: Scholars, 1975).

9. The Message of the Book of Jeremiah

[*Note: See also* Section 15, Theology, Ethics, Message
of the Prophet Jeremiah.]

a. Specific Themes

Ackroyd, Peter R.
"Aspects of the Jeremiah Tradition," *Indian
Journal of Theology* 20 (1971) 1–12.

Idem
Exile and Restoration (Philadelphia: Westminster,
1968) 50–61.

Auld, A. Graeme
"Prophets and Prophecy in Jeremiah and Kings,"
ZAW 96 (1984) 66–82.

Brueggemann, Walter
"Israel's Sense of Place in Jeremiah," *Rhetorical
Criticism, Essays in Honor of James Muilenburg* (ed.
Jared J. Jackson and Martin Kessler; Pittsburgh
Theological Monograph Series 1; Pittsburgh:
Pickwick, 1974) 149–65.

Hyatt, J. Philip
"Torah in the Book of Jeremiah," *JBL* 60 (1941)
381–96.

Orlinsky, Harry M.
"Nationalism–Universalism in the Book of
Jeremiah," *Understanding the Sacred Text, Essays in
Honor of Morton S. Enslin on the Hebrew Bible and
Christian Beginnings* (ed. John Reumann; Valley
Forge, PA: Judson, 1972) 61–83 = *Essays in
Biblical Culture and Bible Translation* (New York:
Ktav, 1974) 117–43.

Overholt, Thomas W.
"King Nebuchadnezzar in the Jeremiah Tradition," *CBQ* 30 (1968) 39–48.

Idem
*The Threat of Falsehood, A Study in the Theology of the
Book of Jeremiah* (SBT Second Series 16; London:
SCM, 1970).

Penna, Angelo
"L'esodo nella storia della salvezza (Es., Deut., Is.,
Ger., Sap.)," *RivB* 15 (1967) 337–56.

Idem
"Il Messianismo nel libro di Geremia," *Il Messian-
ismo, Atti della XVIII Settimana Biblica* (Brescia:
Paideia, 1966) 135–78.

Raitt, Thomas M.
*A Theology of Exile, Judgment / Deliverance in Jeremiah
and Ezekiel* (Philadelphia: Fortress, 1977).

Schreiner, Josef
"'Prophet für die Völker' in der Sicht des Jeremia-
buches," *Ortskirche, Weltkirche, Festgabe für Julius
Döpfner* (ed. Heinz Fleckenstein et al.; Würzburg:
Echter, 1973) 15–31.

Wang, Martin Cheng-Chang
"Jeremiah and the Covenant Traditions," *South
East Asia Journal of Theology* 14 (1972) 3–13.

Weippert, Helga
*Schöpfer des Himmels und der Erde, Ein Beitrag zur
Theologie des Jeremiabuches* (SBS 102; Stuttgart:
Katholisches Bibelwerk, 1981).

Welten, Peter
"Leiden und Leidenserfahrung im Buch Jeremia,"
ZTK 74 (1977) 123–50.

Williams, Prescott H., Jr.
"Living Toward the Acts of the Savior-Judge: A
Study of Eschatology in the Book of Jeremiah,"
Austin Seminary Bulletin, Faculty Edition 94/4
(November, 1978) 13–39.

Wisser, Laurent
"La création dans le livre de Jérémie," *La Création
dans l'Orient Ancien* (ed. Louis Derousseaux; LD
127; Paris: Cerf, 1987) 241–60.

b. Specific Expressions

Baumgärtel, Friedrich
"Zu den Gottesnamen in der Büchern Jeremia und
Ezechiel," *Verbannung und Heimkehr: Beiträge zur
Geschichte und Theologie Israels im 6. und 5. Jahrhundert v. Chr., Wilhelm Rudolph zum 70. Geburtstage*
(ed. Arnulf Kuschke; Tübingen: Mohr [Siebeck],
1961) 1–29.

Fensham, F. Charles
"Nebukadrezzar in the Book of Jeremiah," *Journal
of Northwest Semitic Languages* 10 (1982) 53–65.

Rendtorff, Rolf
"Zum Gebrauch der Formel *ne'um Jahweh* im
Jeremiabuch," *ZAW* 66 (1954) 27–37.

10. The Mutual Interaction of the Events of 609–538 and the Book of Jeremiah; Struggle over the Meaning of the Exile; Effect of the Book of Jeremiah on Those in Exile; Material in Jeremiah Understood as the Product of Later Generations

Ackroyd, Peter R.
*Exile and Restoration, A Study of Hebrew Thought of
the Sixth Century BC* (London: SCM, 1968).

Carroll, Robert P.
*From Chaos to Covenant, Prophecy in the Book of
Jeremiah* (New York: Crossroad, 1981).

Patterson, Robert M.
"Reinterpretation in the Book of Jeremiah," *JSOT* 28 (1984) 37–46.

Schenker, Adrian
"Nebukadnezzars Metamorphose vom Unter-jocher zum Gottesknecht, Das Bild Nebukad-nezzars und einige mit ihm zusammenhängende Unterschiede in den beiden Jeremia-Rezensionen," *RB* 89 (1982) 498–527.

Seitz, Christopher R.
Theology in Conflict: Reactions to the Exile in the Book of Jeremiah (BZAW 176; Berlin: de Gruyter, 1989).

Stulman, Louis
"Some Theological and Lexical Differences Between the Old Greek and the MT of the Jeremiah Prose Discourses," *Hebrew Studies* 25 (1984) 18–23.

Weinfeld, Moshe
"Jeremiah and the Spiritual Metamorphosis of Israel," *ZAW* 88 (1976) 17–55.

Wells, Roy D., Jr.
"Indications of Late Reinterpretation of the Jeremianic Tradition from the LXX of Jer 21 1—23 8," *ZAW* 96 (1984) 405–20.

11. The Prophet Jeremiah and the Historical Events of His Day; Reconstructions of the Career of Jeremiah; Settings of His Oracles, Early or Late

Gunneweg, Antonius H. J.
"Heil im Gericht, Zur Interpretation von Jeremias später Verkündigung," *Traditio—Krisis—Renovatio aus theologischer Sicht, Festschrift Winfried Zeller zum 65. Geburtstag* (ed. Berndt Jaspert and Rudolf Mohr; Marburg: Elwert, 1976) 1–9 = *Sola Scriptura, Beiträge zu Exegese und Hermeneutik des Alten Testaments* (Göttingen: Vandenhoeck & Ruprecht, 1983) 107–15.

Hertzberg, Hans W.
"Jeremia und das Nordreich Israel," *TLZ* 77 (1952) columns 595–602.

Horst, Friedrich
"Die Anfänge des Propheten Jeremia," *ZAW* 41 (1923) 94–153.

Hyatt, J. Philip
"The Beginning of Jeremiah's Prophecy," *ZAW* 78 (1966) 204–14; rep. *A Prophet to the Nations, Essays in Jeremiah Studies* (ed. Leo G. Perdue and Brian W. Kovacs; Winona Lake, IN: Eisenbrauns, 1984) 63–72.

Levin, Christoph
"Noch einmal: die Anfänge des Propheten Jeremia," *VT* 31 (1981) 428–40.

Moreno, Antonio
"Jeremías, La política en la vida de un profeta," *Teología y Vida* 12 (1971) 187–208.

Rost, Leonhard
"Jeremias Stellungnahme zur Aussenpolitik der Könige Josia und Jojakim," *Christentum und Wissenschaft* 5 (1929) 69–78.

Rowley, Harold H.
"The Early Prophecies of Jeremiah in Their Setting," *BJRL* 45 (1962/63) 198–234 = *Men of God, Studies in Old Testament History and Prophecy* (London/New York: Nelson, 1963) 133–68; rep. *A Prophet to the Nations, Essays in Jeremiah Studies* (ed. Leo G. Perdue and Brian W. Kovacs; Winona Lake, IN: Eisenbrauns, 1984) 33–61.

Rowton, M. B.
"Jeremiah and the Death of Josiah," *JNES* 10 (1951) 128–30.

Scharbert, Josef
"Jeremia und die Reform des Joschija," *Le livre de Jérémie, le prophète et son milieu, les oracles et leur transmission* (ed. Pierre-Maurice Bogaert; BETL 54; Leuven: Leuven University, 1981) 40–57.

Telcs, George
"Jeremiah and Nebuchadnezzar, King of Justice," *CJT* 15 (1969) 122–30.

Vogt, Ernst
"I tempi di Geremia secondo nuovi documenti," *La Civiltà Cattolica* 108/2 (1957) 28–36.

Idem
"La caduta di Gerusalemme secondo nuovi documenti," *La Civiltà Cattolica* 108/2 (1957) 267–78.

Whitley, Charles F.
"Carchemish and Jeremiah," *ZAW* 80 (1968) 38–49; rep. *A Prophet to the Nations, Essays in Jeremiah Studies* (ed. Leo G. Perdue and Brian Kovacs; Winona Lake, IN: Eisenbrauns, 1984) 163–73.

Idem
"The Date of Jeremiah's Call," *VT* 14 (1964) 467–83, rep. *A Prophet to the Nations, Essays in Jeremiah Studies* (ed. Leo G. Perdue and Brian Kovacs; Winona Lake, IN: Eisenbrauns, 1984) 73–87.

12. The Forms of the Words of the Prophet Jeremiah (Form Criticism)

Berridge, John M.
Prophet, People, and the Word of Yahweh, An Examination of Form and Content in the Proclamation of the Prophet Jeremiah (Basel Studies of Theology 4; Zurich: EVZ, 1970).

Cummins, Patrick
"Jeremias Orator," *CBQ* 11 (1949), 191–201.

Wildberger, Hans
Jahwewort und prophetische Rede bei Jeremia (Zurich: Zwingli, 1942).

13. Sociological Studies

[*Note: See also* Section 18, The Person of Jeremiah.]

a. Status, Role, Vocation of the Prophet Jeremiah; Process of Revelation

[*Note:* The bibliography on prophetic call narratives, and on Jeremiah's call, and on prophetic visions in *Jeremiah 1*, 18–19, is not repeated here.]

Alonso Schökel, Luis
"Jeremías como anti-Moisés," *De la Tôrah au Messie, Mélanges Henri Cazelles* (ed. M. Carrez, et al.; Paris: Desclée, 1981) 245–54.

Arnold, Patrick M.
"Jeremiah and Black Elk," *TBT* 23 (1985) 182–85.

Berquist, Jon L.
"Prophetic Legitimation in Jeremiah," *VT* 39 (1989) [forthcoming].

Devescovi, Urbano
"La vocazione di Geremia alla missione profetica," *BeO* 3 (1961) 6–21.

Eissfeldt, Otto
"Voraussage-Empfang, Offenbarungsgewissheit und Gebetskraft-Erfahrung bei Jeremia," *NovT* 5 (1962) 77–81.

Goldman, M. D.
"Was Jeremiah Married?" *AusBR* 2 (1952) 42–47.

Kelso, Alexander P.
"The Religious Consciousness of Jeremiah," *AJSL* 41 (1924/25) 233–42.

Long, Burke O.
"Social Dimensions of Prophetic Conflict," *Semeia* 21: *Anthropological Perspectives on Old Testament Prophecy* (ed. Robert C. Culley and Thomas W. Overholt; Chico, CA: Scholars, 1982) 31–53.

Meek, Theophile J.
"Was Jeremiah a Priest?" *Expositor*, 8th series, 25 (1923) 215–22.

Overholt, Thomas W.
"Jeremiah and the Nature of the Prophetic Process," *Scripture in History & Theology, Essays in Honor of J. Coert Rylaarsdam* (ed. Arthur L. Merril and Thomas W. Overholt; Pittsburgh Theological Monograph Series 17; Pittsburgh: Pickwick, 1977) 129–50.

Pilch, John J.
"Jeremiah and Symbolism," *TBT* 19 (1981) 105–11.

Reventlow, Henning Graf von
Liturgie und prophetisches Ich bei Jeremia (Gütersloh: Gütersloher, 1963).

Seierstad, Ivar P.
Die Offenbarungserlebnisse der Propheten Amos, Jesaja und Jeremia, Eine Untersuchung der Erlebnisvorgänge under besonderer Berücksichtigung ihrer religiössittlichen Art und Auswirkung (Oslo: Dybwad, 1946).

Vogt, Ernst
"Vocatio Jeremiae," *VD* 42 (1964) 241–51.

Wilson, Robert R.
Prophecy and Society in Ancient Israel (Philadelphia: Fortress, 1980) 231–51.

Zimmerli, Walther
"Visionary Experience in Jeremiah," *Israel's Prophetic Tradition: Essays in Honour of Peter R. Ackroyd* (ed. Richard J. Coggins, Anthony Phillips, and Michael A. Knibb; Cambridge: Cambridge University, 1982) 95–118.

b. Jeremiah and the False Prophets

[*Note:* For bibliography before 1975 see the bibliography in James L. Crenshaw, "Prophecy, false," *IDBSup* 702; that bibliography is not duplicated here.]

Carroll, Robert P.
"A Non-Cogent Argument in Jeremiah's Oracles against the Prophets," *ST* 30 (1976) 43–51.

Meyer, Ivo
Jeremia und die falschen Propheten (Göttingen: Vandenhoeck & Ruprecht, 1977).

Sisson, Jonathan Paige
"Jeremiah and the Jerusalem Conception of Peace," *JBL* 105 (1986) 429–42.

Wilson, Robert R.
Sociological Approaches to the Old Testament (Guides to Biblical Scholarship; Philadelphia: Fortress, 1984) 67–80.

14. Sources of the Message and Self-Understanding of the Prophet Jeremiah; His Use of His Heritage

a. In General

Holladay, William L.
"The Background of Jeremiah's Self-Understanding: Moses, Samuel and Psalm 22," *JBL* 83 (1964) 153–64; rep. *A Prophet to the Nations, Essays in Jeremiah Studies* (ed. Leo G. Perdue and Brian W. Kovacs; Winona Lake, IN: Eisenbrauns, 1984) 313–24.

Idem
"Jeremiah and Moses, Further Observations," *JBL* 85 (1966) 17–27.

b. Covenant Traditions

Wang, Martin Cheng-Chang
"Jeremiah and the Covenant Traditions," *South East Asia Journal of Theology* 14 (1972) 3–13.

c. The Prophetic Tradition in General

Biggs, C. R.
"Prophets and Traditions: The Relationship between Jeremiah and the Traditions of Northern Israel," *AusBR* 20 (1972) 1–15.

Macholz, Georg Christian
"Jeremia in her Kontinuität der Prophetie," *Probleme biblischer Theologie, Gerhard von Rad zum 70. Geburtstag* (ed. Hans Walter Wolff; Munich: Kaiser, 1971) 306–34.

d. The Tradition of Amos

Berridge, John M.
"Jeremia und die Prophetie des Amos," *TZ* 35 (1979) 321–41.

e. The Tradition of Hosea

Adinolfi, Marco
"Appunti sul simbolismo sponsale in Osea e Geremia," *Euntes Docete* 25 (1972) 126–38.

Deissler, Alfons
"Das 'Echo' der Hosea-Verkündigung im Jeremia-buch," *Künder des Wortes, Beiträge zur Theologie der Propheten, Josef Schreiner zum 60. Geburtstag* (ed. Lothar Ruppert, Peter Weimar, and Erich Zenger; Würzburg: Echter, 1982) 61–75.

Gross, Karl
"Hoseas Einfluss auf Jeremias Anschauungen," *NKZ* 42 (1931) 241–56, 327–43.

Lindars, Barnabas
"Rachel Weeping for Her Children, Jeremiah 31, 15–22," *JSOT* 12 (1979) 47–62.

f. The Wisdom Tradition

Gilbert, Maurice
"Jérémie en conflit avec les sages?" *Le Livre de Jérémie, le prophète et son milieu, les oracles et leur transmission* (ed. Pierre-Maurice Bogaert; BETL 54; Leuven: Leuven University, 1981) 105–18.

Hobbs, Trevor R.
"Some Proverbial Reflections in the Book of Jeremiah," *ZAW* 91 (1979) 62–72.

Lindblom, Johannes
"Wisdom in the Old Testament Prophets," *Wisdom in Israel and in the Ancient Near East, Presented to Professor Harold Henry Rowley by the Society for Old Testament Study in Association with the Editorial Board of Vetus Testamentum in Celebration of His Sixty-fifth Birthday, 24 March 1965* (ed. Martin Noth and D. Winton Thomas; VTSup 3; Leiden: Brill, 1955) 192–204.

McKane, William
Prophets and Wise Men (SBT 44; Naperville, IL: Allenson, 1965), esp. "Jeremiah and Pre-exilic Legal Piety," 102–12.

Whybray, Roger N.
The Intellectual Tradition in the Old Testament (BZAW 135; Berlin: de Gruyter, 1974) 21–31.

g. The Legal Tradition

Smith, Eustace J.
"The Decalogue in the Preaching of Jeremias," *CBQ* 4 (1942) 197–209.

15. Theology, Ethics, Message of the Prophet Jeremiah

[*Note: See also* Section 9, The Message of the Book of Jeremiah.]

a. The Theology Affirmed by Jeremiah

Küchler, Friedrich
"Jahwe und sein Volk nach Jeremia," *ZAW* 28 (1908) 81–109.

Plotkin, Albert
The Religion of Jeremiah (New York: Bloch, 1974).

b. Ethics of Jeremiah

Knight, Douglas A.
"Jeremiah and the Dimensions of the Moral Life," *The Divine Helmsman, Studies on God's Control of Human Events, Presented to Lou H. Silberman* (ed. James L. Crenshaw and Samuel Sandmel; New York: Ktav, 1980) 87–105.

Wisser, Laurent
Jérémie, Critique de la vie sociale, Justice sociale et connaissance de Dieu dans le livre de Jérémie (Le monde de la Bible; Geneva: Labor et Fides, 1982).

c. Specific Themes in the Message of Jeremiah

Caballero, José María
"La restauración de Israel según el profeta Jeremías (Análisis y ambientación de los textos)," *Burgense* 13 (1972) 9–67.

Fournel, A., and P. Rémy
"Le sens du péché dans Jérémie," *BVC* 2 (1954/55) #5, 34–46.

Gross, Heinrich
"Umkehr im Alten Testament, In der Sicht der Propheten Jeremia und Ezechiel," *Zeichen des Glaubens, Studien zu Taufe und Firmung Balthasar Fischer zum 60. Geburtstag* (ed. Hansjörg auf der Maur and Bruno Kleinheyer; Einsiedeln: Benziger; and Freiburg: Herder, 1972) 19–28.

Holladay, William L.
The Root Šûbh in the Old Testament, With Particular Reference to Its Usages in Covenantal Contexts (Leiden: Brill, 1958) 1–2, 128–39, 149–54.

López de las Heras, L.
"Los animales en la visión religiosa de Jeremías," *Studium* 16 (1976) 217–44.

Muilenburg, James
"The Terminology of Adversity in Jeremiah," *Translating and Understanding the Old Testament, Essays in Honor of Herbert Gordon May* (ed. Harry T. Frank and William L. Reed; New York/Nashville: Abingdon, 1970) 42–68.

Raitt, Thomas M.
"Jeremiah's Deliverance Message to Judah," *Rhetorical Criticism, Essays in Honor of James Muilenburg* (ed. Jared J. Jackson and Martin Kessler; Pittsburgh Theological Monograph Series 1; Pittsburgh: Pickwick, 1974) 166–85.

Rost, Leonhard
"Jeremias Stellungnahme zur Aussenpolitik der Könige Josia und Jojakim," *Christentum und Wissenschaft* 5 (1929) 69–78.

Sekine, Masao
"Davidsbund und Sinaibund bei Jeremia," *VT* 9 (1959) 47–57.

Uffenheimer, Benyamin
"The Historical Outlook of Jeremiah," *Immanuel* (Jerusalem) 4 (1974) 9–17.

Unterman, Jeremiah
   From Repentance to Redemption, Jeremiah's Thought in Transition (JSOT Supplement Series 54; Sheffield: JSOT, 1987).

16. Jeremiah's Use of Words

a. The Rhetoric of Jeremiah; Style, Irony, Poetry

Brueggemann, Walter A.
   "Jeremiah's Use of Rhetorical Questions," *JBL* 92 (1973) 358–74.
Dorn, Louis
   "The Unexpected as a Speech Device: Shifts of Thematic Expectancy in Jeremiah," *BT* 37 (1986) 216–22.
Holladay, William L.
   "The Recovery of Poetic Passages of Jeremiah," *JBL* 85 (1966) 401–35.
Idem
   "Style, Irony and Authenticity in Jeremiah," *JBL* 81 (1962) 44–54.
Keller, Bernard
   "Le langage de Jérémie," *ETR* 53 (1978) 360–65.
Lundbom, Jack R.
   Jeremiah, A Study in Ancient Hebrew Rhetoric (SBLDS 18; Missoula, MT: Scholars, 1975).
Selms, Adriaan van
   "'Whate'er my God ordains is right'—A Figure of Style in the Book of Jeremiah," *Semitics* 5 (1977) 1–8.

b. Pronunciation of Hebrew in Jeremiah's Day

Harris, Zellig S.
   "Linguistic Structure of Hebrew," *JAOS* 61 (1941) 143–67.

17. Audience Reaction and Alleged Audience Reaction to Jeremiah

Horwitz, William J.
   "Audience Reaction to Jeremiah," *CBQ* 32 (1970) 555–64.
Overholt, Thomas W.
   "Jeremiah 2 and the Problem of 'Audience Reaction,'" *CBQ* 41 (1979) 262–73.
Willis, John I.
   "Dialogue between Prophet and Audience as a Rhetorical Device in the Book of Jeremiah," *JSOT* 33 (1985) 3–25.

18. Person of Jeremiah; Aspects of His Personality; His Originality

[*Note: See also* Section 13, Sociological Studies.]
Balentine, Samuel E.
   "Jeremiah, Prophet of Prayer," *RevExp* 78 (1981) 331–44.

Clements, Ronald E.
   "Jeremiah, Prophet of Hope," *RevExp* 78 (1981) 345–63.
Eldridge, Victor J.
   "Jeremiah, Prophet of Judgment," *RevExp* 78 (1981) 319–30.
Jean, F.-Charles
   "De l'originalité de Jérémie," *RSPT* 8 (1914) 423–38.
Marböck, Johannes
   "Jeremia: Unter der Last des Wortes," *BLit* 50 (1977) 85–95.

19. Jeremiah as Intercessor; Jeremiah's Sympathy with His People

[*Note:* The bibliography for 7:16–20 in *Jeremiah 1*, 250–51, is not duplicated here.]
Krinetzki, Leo
   "Jeremia als Beter," *BK* 16 (1961) 74–80.
Langer, Birgit
   "Vom Leiden Gottes nach Jeremia," *BLit* 58 (1985) 3–8.
Stoop, François
   "L'amour d'un prophète pour son peuple," *VCaro* 24 (1970) #95, 10–22.

20. Experience of Jeremiah; His Suffering, Doubt, and Isolation

[*Note:* The bibliography for Jeremiah's "Confessions," *Jeremiah 1*, 357–58, is not duplicated here; and *see further* the bibliography on the Confessions in the Additional Bibliography Pertaining to *Jeremiah 1* below.]
Moore, Michael S.
   "Jeremiah's Progressive Paradox," *RB* 93 (1986) 386–414.
Reedy, Gerard
   "Jeremiah and the Absurdity of the Prophet," *TBT* 7 (1969) #40, 2781–87.
Robinson, H. Wheeler
   The Cross of Jeremiah (London: SCM, 1925) = *The Cross in the Old Testament* (London: SCM, 1955, and Philadelphia: Westminster, 1956) 115–92.
Zimmerli, Walther
   "Frucht der Anfechtung des Propheten," *Die Botschaft und die Boten, Festschrift für Hans Walter Wolff zum 70. Geburtstag* (ed. Jörg Jeremias and Lothar Perlitt; Neukirchen-Vluyn: Neukirchener, 1981) 131–46 = "The Fruit of the Tribulation of the Prophet," *A Prophet to the Nations, Essays in Jeremiah Studies* (ed. Leo G. Perdue and Brian W. Kovacs; Winona Lake, IN: Eisenbrauns, 1984) 349–65.
Idem
   "Jeremia, der leidtragende Verkünder," *Internationale Katholische Zeitschrift "Communio"* 4 (1975) 97–111.

21. Influence of the Prophet Jeremiah on Later Portions of the Old Testament

a. Ezekiel

Carley, Keith W.
Ezekiel among the Prophets (SBT, Second Series, 31; Naperville, IL: Allenson, 1975) 51–57.

Lust, Johan
"'Gathering and Return' in Jeremiah and Ezekiel," *Le livre de Jérémie, le prophète et son milieu, les oracles et leur transmission* (ed. Pierre-Maurice Bogaert; BETL 54; Leuven: Leuven University, 1981) 119–42.

Miller, John W.
Das Verhältnis Jeremias und Hesekiels sprachlich und theologisch untersucht (Assen: Van Gorcum, 1955).

Raitt, Thomas M.
A Theology of Exile, Judgment / Deliverance in Jeremiah and Ezekiel (Philadelphia: Fortress, 1977).

Unterman, Jeremiah
The Relationship of Repentance to Redemption in Jeremiah (JSOT Supplement Series 54; Sheffield: JSOT, 1987) 167–70.

Vieweger, Dieter
Die Spezifik der Berufungsberichte Jeremias und Ezechiels im Umfeld ähnlicher Einheiten des Alten Testaments (Beiträge zur Erforschung des Alten Testaments und des Antiken Judentums; Frankfurt am Main/Bern/New York: Lang, 1986).

Zimmerli, Walther
Ezekiel 1 (Hermeneia; Philadelphia: Fortress, 1979) 44–46.

b. Job

Habel, Norman C.
The Book of Job, A Commentary (Philadelphia: Westminster, 1985) 41.

Holladay, William L.
"Jeremiah's Lawsuit with God," *Int* 17 (1963) 285–86.

Terrien, Samuel
"Job, Introduction," *IB* 3:888–89.

c. Deutero-Isaiah

Farley, Fred A.
"Jeremiah and 'The Suffering Servant of Jehovah' in Deutero-Isaiah," *ExpTim* 38 (1926/27) 521–24.

Unterman, Jeremiah
The Relationship of Repentance to Redemption in Jeremiah (JSOT Supplement Series 54; Sheffield: JSOT, 1987) 171–75.

d. Later Prophetic Material

Christensen, Duane L.
Transformations of the War Oracle in Old Testament Prophecy (HDR 3; Missoula, MT: Scholars, 1975) passim.

Dommershausen, Werner
"Der 'Spross' als Messias-Vorstellung bei Jeremia und Sacharja," *TQ* 148 (1968) 321–41.

Petersen, David L.
Late Israelite Prophecy: Studies in Deutero-Prophetic Literature and in Chronicles (SBLMS 23; Missoula, MT: Scholars, 1977) passim.

22. Influence of the Prophet Jeremiah on Early Judaism, Early Christianity, and Islam

a. In General

Steck, Odil Hannes
Israel und das gewaltsame Geschick der Propheten, Untersuchungen zur Überlieferung des deuteronomistischen Geschichtsbildes im Alten Testament, Spätjudentum und Urchristentum (WMANT 23; Neukirchen: Neukirchener, 1967) esp. 72–74, 137–39.

Wolff, Christian
Jeremia im Frühjudentum und Urchristentum (TU 118; Berlin: Akademie, 1976).

b. Early Judaism

Neher, André
"Jérémie le pharisien, Un exemple d'interprétation typologique juive de la Bible," *Maqqél shâqédh, La branche d'amandier, Hommage à Wilhelm Vischer* (Montpellier: Causse, Graille, Castelnau, 1960) 171–76.

Rothkoff, Aaron
"Jeremiah, In the Aggadah," *EncJud* 9, columns 1359–60; 1361.

Wieder, Arnold A.
"Josiah and Jeremiah: Their Relationship according to Aggadic Sources," *Texts and Responses, Studies Presented to Nahum N. Glatzer on the Occasion of His Seventieth Birthday by His Students* (ed. Michael A. Fishbane and Paul R. Flohr; Leiden: Brill, 1975) 60–72.

c. Jesus; the New Testament

Boekhoven, Henry J.
"The Influence of Jeremiah upon New Testament Literature," *Reformed Review* 14/1 (September, 1960) 37–43.

Carmignac, Jean
"Pourquois Jérémie est-il mentionné en Matthieu 16,14?" *Tradition und Glaube, Das frühe Christentum in seiner Umwelt, Festgabe für Karl Georg Kuhn zum 65. Geburtstag* (ed. Gert Jeremias, Heinz-Wolfgang Kuhn, and Hartmut Stegemann; Göttingen: Vandenhoeck & Ruprecht, 1971) 283–98.

Dahlberg, Bruce T.
"The Typological Use of Jeremiah 1:4–19 in Matthew 16:13–23," *JBL* 94 (1975) 73–80.

Dequeker, Luc
"Het Nieuwe Verbond bij Jeremia, bij Paulus en in de Brief aan de Hebreën," *Bijdragen* 33 (1972) 234–61; English Summary 260–61.

Groenewald, Evert P.
"Jer 14:8–9 en Emmaüs," *Nederduitse Gereformeerde Teologiese Tydskrif* 13 (1972) 77–82.

Schreiner, Josef

"Jeremia 9,22–23 als Hintergrund des paulini-
schen 'Sich-Rühmens,'" *Neues Testament und Kirche,
Für Rudolf Schnackenburg* (ed. Joachim Gnilka;
Freiburg/Basel/Vienna: Herder, 1974) 530–42.

Williamson, H. A.

"Jeremiah and Jesus," *ExpTim* 34 (1922/23) 535–
38; 35 (1923/24) 39–42.

d. The Church Fathers

Kannengiesser, Charles

"L'interprétation de Jérémie dans la tradition
alexandrine," *Studia Patristica* 12 (TU 115; Berlin:
Akademie, 1975) 317–20.

Idem

"Jérémie, Chez les Pères de l'Église," *Dictionnaire de
Spiritualité* 8 (1974) columns 889–901, with
bibliography.

Idem

"Le recours au livre de Jérémie chez Athanase
d'Alexandrie," *Epektasis, Mélanges patristiques offerts
au Cardinal Jean Daniélou* (ed. Jacques Fontaine
and Charles Kannengiesser; Paris: Cerf, 1972)
317–25.

e. Islam

Hirschberg, Haïm Z'ew

"Jeremiah, In Islam," *EncJud* 9, columns 1360,
1361.

23. Modes of Interpretation of the Book of Jeremiah

Herrmann, Siegfried

"Die Bewältigung der Krise Israels, Bemerkungen
zur Interpretation des Buches Jeremia," *Beiträge
zur alttestamentlichen Theologie, Festschrift für Walther
Zimmerli zum 70. Geburtstag* (ed. Herbert Donner,
Robert Hanhart, and Rudolf Smend; Göttingen:
Vandenhoeck & Ruprecht, 1977) 164–78 =
"Overcoming the Israelite Crisis, Remarks on the
Interpretation of the Book of Jeremiah," *A Prophet
to the Nations, Essays in Jeremiah Studies* (ed. Leo G.
Perdue and Brian Kovacs; Winona Lake, IN:
Eisenbrauns, 1984) 299–311.

Holladay, William L.

"Jeremiah in Judah's Eyes and Ours, Musings on
Some Issues in Old Testament Hermeneutics,"
ANQ 13 (1972/73) 115–32.

Polk, Timothy

*The Prophetic Persona, Jeremiah and the Language of
the Self* (JSOT Supplement Series 32; Sheffield:
University of Sheffield, 1984).

Additional Bibliography Pertaining to
Jeremiah 1 (either omitted or appearing after
preparation of that volume)

Chapters 1–25, Poetic Analysis

Cloete, W. T. Woldemar

*Versification and Syntax in Jeremiah 2—25: Syntactical
Constraints in Hebrew Colometry* (SBLDS; forthcoming).

Chapter 1

Conrad, Edgar W.

*Fear Not Warrior, A Study of 'al tîrā' Pericopes in the
Hebrew Scriptures* (Brown Judaic Studies 75; Chico,
CA: Scholars, 1985).

García López, Félix

"Election-vocation d'Israël et de Jérémie: Deutéronome vii et Jérémie i," *VT* 35 (1985) 1–12.

Herrmann, Siegfried

"Die Bewältigung der Krise Israels, Bemerkungen
zur Interpretation des Buches Jeremia," *Beiträge
zur alttestamentlichen Theologie, Festschrift für Walther
Zimmerli zum 70. Geburtstag* (ed. Herbert Donner,
Robert Hanhart, and Rudolf Smend; Göttingen:
Vandenhoeck & Ruprecht, 1977) 164–78.

Idem

"Die Herkunft der 'ehernen Mauer,' Eine Miszelle
zu Jeremia 1,18 und 15,20," *Altes Testament und
christliche Verkündigung, Festschrift für Antonius H. J.
Gunneweg zum 65. Geburtstag* (ed. Manfred Oeming
and Axel Graupner; Stuttgart: Kohlhammer,
1987) 344–52.

Kreuzer, Siegfried

"Zur Bedeutung und Etymologie von *hištaḥawāh/
yšthwy*," *VT* 35 (1985) 39–60.

Lewin, Ellen Davis, "Arguing for Authority, A
Rhetorical Study of Jeremiah 1.4–19 and 20.7–
18," *JSOT* 32 (1985) 105–19.

March, W. Eugene

"Jeremiah 1: Commission and Assurance," *Austin
Seminary Bulletin* 86 (1970/71) 5–38.

Vieweger, Dieter

*Die Spezifik der Berufungsberichte Jeremias und
Ezechiels im Umfeld ähnlicher Einheiten des Alten
Testament* (Beiträge zur Erforschung des Alten
Testaments und des Antiken Judentums; Frank-
furt am Main/Bern/New York: Lang, 1986).

Chapters 2—6

Patterson, Robert M.

"Repentance or Judgment: The Construction and
Purpose of Jeremiah 2—6," *ExpTim* 96 (1985)
199–203.

Chapter 2

Daniels, Dwight R.

"Is There a 'Prophetic Lawsuit' Genre?" *ZAW* 99
(1987) 339–60, esp. 343–45.

Neef, Heinz-Dieter

"Gottes Treue und Israels Untreue, Aufbau und
Einheit von Jeremia 2,2–13," *ZAW* 99 (1987) 37–
58.

Olyan, Saul M.

"The Cultic Confessions of Jer 2,27a," *ZAW* 99
(1987) 254–59.

Chapter 3

Kaufmann, Stephen A.

"Rhetoric, Redaction and Message in Jeremiah,"
Judaic Perspectives on Ancient Israel (ed. Jacob

Neusner, Baruch Levine, and Ernest S. Frerichs; Philadelphia: Fortress, 1987) 63–74.

Chapter 4
Kaiser, Barbara Bakke
   "Poet as 'Female Impersonator': The Image of Daughter Zion as Speaker in Biblical Poems of Suffering," *JR* 67 (1987) 164–82, esp. 166–74.

Chapter 5
Carroll, Robert P.
   "Theodicy and Community: The Text and Subtext of Jeremiah v 1–6," *Prophets, Worship and Theodicy, Studies in Prophetism, Biblical Theology and Structural and Rhetorical Analysis and on the Place of Music in Worship* (OTS 23; Leiden: Brill, 1984) 19–38.

Chapter 7
Holt, Else K.
   "Jeremiah's Temple Sermon and the Deuteronomists: An Investigation of the Redactional Relationship Between Jeremiah 7 and 26," *JSOT* 36 (1986) 73–87.

Chapter 8
Moore, Michael S.
   "Jeremiah's Progressive Paradox," *RB* 93 (1986) 386–414.

Chapter 9
Smith, Mark S.
   "Jeremiah ix 9—A Divine Lament," *VT* 37 (1987) 97–99.

Chapter 10
Clendenen, E. Ray
   "Discourse Strategies in Jeremiah 10:1–16," *JBL* 106 (1987) 401–8.
Reimer, David J.
   "A Problem in the Hebrew Text of Jeremiah x 13, li 16," *VT* 38 (1988) 348–54.
Ziderman, Irving
   "First Identification of Authentic *Těkēlet*," *BASOR* 265 (February 1987) 25–33.

The Confessions
Baumgartner, Walter
   Jeremiah's Poems of Lament (Historic Texts and Interpreters 7; Sheffield: Almond, 1988) [tr. of *Die Klagegedichte des Jeremia* (BZAW 32; Giessen: Töpelmann, 1917].
Diamond, A. R.
   The Confessions of Jeremiah in Context, Scenes of Prophetic Drama (*JSOT* Supplement Series 45; Sheffield: JSOT, 1987).
Gunneweg, Antonius H. J.
   "Konfession oder Interpretation im Jeremiabuch," *ZTK* 67 (1970) 395–416 = *Sola Scriptura, Beiträge zu Exegese und Hermeneutik des Alten Testaments* (Göttingen: Vandenhoeck & Ruprecht, 1983) 61–82.
Hermisson, Hans-Jürgen
   "Jahwes und Jeremias Rechtsstreit, Zum Thema der Konfessionen Jeremias," *Altes Testament und christliche Verkündigung, Festschrift für Antonius H. J. Gunneweg zum 65. Geburtstag* (ed. Manfred Oeming and Axel Graupner; Stuttgart: Kohlhammer, 1987) 309–43.
Herrmann, Siegfried
   "Die Herkunft der 'ehernen Mauer,' Eine Miszelle zu Jeremia 1,18 und 15,20," *Altes Testament und christliche Verkündigung, Festschrift für Antonius H. J. Gunneweg zum 65. Geburtstag* (ed. Manfred Oeming and Axel Graupner; Stuttgart: Kohlhammer, 1987) 344–52.
Lundbom, Jack R.
   "The Double Curse in Jeremiah 20:14–18," *JBL* 104 (1985) 589–600.
Mottu, Henry
   Les 'Confessions' de Jérémie: Une protestation contre la souffrance (Le monde de la Bible; Genève: Labor et Fides, 1985).
O'Connor, Kathleen M.
   The Confessions of Jeremiah: Their Interpretation and Role in Chapters 1—25 (SBLDS 94; Atlanta: Scholars, 1988).
Polk, Timothy
   The Prophetic Persona, Jeremiah and the Language of the Self (JSOT Supplement Series 32; Sheffield: JSOT, 1984).
Roberts, J. J. M.
   "Does God Lie? Divine Deceit as a Theological Problem in Israelite Prophetic Literature," *Congress Volume, Jerusalem, 1986* (VTSup 40; ed. John A. Emerton; Leiden: Brill, 1988), 211–20, esp. 217–18.
Soggin, J. Alberto
   "Geremia, la persona ed il ministero," *Protestantesimo* 19 (1964) 78–84.

Chapter 12
Seybold, Klaus
   "Der 'Löwe' von Jeremia xii 8, Bemerkungen zu einem prophetischen Gedicht," *VT* 36 (1986) 93–104.

Chapter 17
Seybold, Klaus
   "Das 'Rebhuhn' von Jeremia 17,11, Erwägungen zu einem prophetischen Gleichnis," *Bib* 68 (1987) 57–73.

Chapter 18
Fretheim, Terence E.
   "The Repentance of God: A Study of Jeremiah 18:7–10," *Hebrew Annual Review* 11 (1988) 81–92.

Chapters 21–25
Seitz, Christopher
   "The Crisis of Interpretation over the Meaning and Purpose of the Exile, A Redactional Study of Jeremiah xxi—xliii," *VT* 35 (1985) 78–97.

Chapter 25
Grabbe, Lester L.
   "'The End of the Desolations of Jerusalem': From Jeremiah's 70 Years to Daniel's 70 Weeks of Years," *Early Jewish and Christian Exegesis, Studies in Memory of William Hugh Brownlee* (ed. Craig A.

Evans and William F. Stinespring; Atlanta: Scholars, 1987) 67–72.

Laberge, Léo
"Jérémie 25,1–14: Dieu et Juda ou Jérémie et tous les peuples," *ScEs* 36 (1984) 45–66.

Indices for Jeremiah 1 and 2

The index of passages is complete, with certain exceptions. Subdivisions of a verse are disregarded: 5:7a is cited as if 5:7. Further the index does not include citations of verses included within the relevant Interpretation section: citations of 5:7b or 5:8 are not recorded in the Interpretation of 5:7b–8, but a citation to 5:7a there is recorded (as simple 5:7, as noted above). By the same token all individual verses or groups of verses subsumed within the larger discussions in Preliminary Observations, Structure, Form, and Setting are disregarded: references within Structure on 5:1–9 to vv 1–9, v 1 and the like are not recorded. To put it positively: references are complete to individual verses and groups of verses *outside their primary discussion*.

The index of authors is likewise complete, with the exceptions noted below. In the alphabetical listing all diacritical marks, including umlauts, are disregarded. Because I have consulted the commentary of Naegelsbach in its American edition, the listing is C. W. Eduard Naegelsbach rather than Karl Wilhelm Eduard Nägelsbach. Premodern commentators are listed under their common designation (Jerome rather than Hieronymus, Rashi rather than Solomon ben Isaac, but [David] Qimḥi rather than Redak). When there is difference of judgment as to the alphabetical listing of an author's surname, the Library of Congress decision is followed. Thus Georges Minette de Tillesse is listed under "M," although the annual index in *VT* lists him under "T"; similarly A. H. Van Zyl is listed under "V," although *VT* lists him under "Z". Readers are reminded that Americans with surnames of Continental origin containing prefixes list their names under the prefix (Gus W. Van Beek under "V"), while Europeans disregard prefixes (Roland de Vaux under "V," Gerhard von Rad under "R," P. A. H. de Boer under "B" and A. S. van der Woude under "W"); likewise that double Spanish surnames are listed

under the father's name (Luis Alonso Schökel under "A"). If an author has changed his or her name and both names occur in publications, the primary listing is the more recent name, with a cross reference at the former name (see Barrois, Borger and Cogan). Standard reference works referred to by abbreviations are *not* cited: there are no citations to BDB or GKC. This policy leads to a certain amount of inconsistency. If there are no citations to BDB, there are to Zorell's lexicon; if there are no citations to GKC, there are to Joüon's grammar and to König's *Syntax*. If there are no references to James Pritchard at citations to *ANET* or *ANEP*, there are references under "Pritchard" to his publications on Gibeon. Biblical translations in general are not listed (*RSV*, *JB*), but personal translations are listed (Luther, Moffatt).

The index of subjects is selective. There are no entries to Jeremiah, or to Yahweh; there are no entries to Israel or Judah or Jerusalem. There are no entries to Nebuchadrezzar. There are, however, entries for Assyria, and for Babylon (but not for references within chapters 50—52), for Egypt (but not for references within chapter 46), and for Philistia (but not for chapter 47). There are no entries to geographical names that are dealt with in the first occurrence in Jer: a concordance is sufficient to locate the discussion (thus the discussion of Mizpah is found at 40:6). There are entries for the various kings of Israel and Judah, and to Gedaliah; there are entries for prophets such as Elijah and Huldah, but not to prophets where books exist under their names (such as Isaiah or Amos). There are entries for various grammatical features discussed in some detail in the present study, for example: cognate accusative, dative suffix, infinitive absolute; and for various rhetorical effects, for example: ambiguity, assonance and word-play, irony, mockery, and rhetorical question. But form-critical categories are not listed. There are no listings for various ancient languages.

1. Passages

a / Old Testament and Deutero-Canonical Books

■ Genesis

1:1—2:25	I.148
1:1—2:4	II.224
1:1–31	II.86, 195
1:2–3	II.36
1:2	I.39, 148, 163, 165, 625, 626; II.36, 420
1:3–5	I.165
1:3	I.148, 163; II.36
1:7	II.36
1:14–16	II.166
1:14	I.330, 332
1:16	II.199
1:22	I.544; II.138, 141
1:26	I.482; II.36, 172
1:27–28	I.469
1:28	I.544, 640; II.36, 138, 241
1:29	I.285; II.117
1:31	I.167
2:4	II.36
2:5	I.148, 163, 378, 488; II.36
2:7	I.336, 515; II.36, 224
2:8	I.336, 515; II.36, 224
2:13	I.96
2:17	II.105
2:18—3:21	II.36
2:19	I.305, 336; II.36, 224
2:21–24	I.469
2:24	I.397
3:1	II.108
3:6	II.204
3:13	I.155
3:16	I.610
4:1	I.33
4:3	I.399
4:5–6	I.119
4:10	I.343
4:14	I.127
4:15	I.56
4:18	I.498
4:25	II.345
5:24	I.186
6:5	I.495; II.37

464

38:18	I.605	4:12	I.151	15:5	II.38, 321
40:5	I.652	4:13	I.34	15:8	I.524
40:8	I.643	4:14–17	I.30	15:9	I.409
40:9	I.643	4:15	I.36	15:10	II.38, 321
40:13	II.177, 443	4:21	I.177	15:13	II.196
40:14	I.378	4:22	I.122; II.185	15:15	I.532; II.378
40:23	I.554	4:23	II.38, 404, 420	15:19	II.38, 325
41:43	II.323, 327, 328	5:1	I.439; II.38	15:20	II.38, 181, 182
41:45	II.302	5:3	I.435	15:21	I.16
41:51–52	II.187	5:7–12	I.644	16:14	I.293
42:22	I.240, 247	5:12	I.415	16:20	I.53
42:34	I.437	5:23	I.555; II.38	17:4	I.359
43:7	I.403	6:1–30	I.30	17:15	I.619
43:11	I.37, 294	6:2–13	I.27	18:9	II.186
43:23	II.138	6:4	II.248	18:11	II.419
43:28	I.217	6:12	I.28, 29; II.38	18:14	II.177
44:2–17	II.248	6:28	I.27	18:25–26	II.288
44:4	I.342, 530	6:30	I.28, 29; II.38	19:3–6	I.239, 352
44:31	I.293	7:1–29	I.30	19:5–6	I.451
48:4	I.544	7:1–5	I.27, 30	19:5	I.261, 262
48:7	II.187	7:1	I.33	19:6	I.397
48:20	II.139	7:2	I.29, 34	20:1–17	I.244, 261; II.39
48:21	I.279	7:14	II.38, 404, 420	20:2	II.241
49:3	II.140	7:16	I.440; II.38	20:3	I.42, 92, 243
49:5	I.200	7:18	I.53	20:5	I.42, 97, 182; II.217
49:7	I.411	7:19	I.433; II.321, 427		
49:10	I.487; II.38	7:26	I.440; II.38	20:6	I.83, 92; II.217
49:17	II.92	7:27	II.38, 404, 420	20:7	I.128, 245
49:22	I.69–70	8:3	I.350	20:10	I.510
49:26	I.95	8:13	I.256	20:12	I.88, 243
49:27	I.179	8:14	I.256	20:13	I.244
50:20	I.658	8:16	I.440; II.38	20:14	I.117
■ Exodus		8:17	I.350	20:15	I.244
2:1–25	I.28; II.38	9:1	I.440; II.38	20:24	I.261, 268
2:14	I.124	9:2	II.38, 404, 420	20:25	I.486
2:19	I.34; II.38	9:3	II.221	21:2	II.237, 238, 240, 241
3:1—4:17	I.27	9:13	I.440; II.38		
3:1–22	I.30	9:19	I.153, 205	21:5	II.299
3:1–9	I.27	10:3	I.440; II.38	21:7	II.240
3:1	I.304	12:4	I.224	21:8–10	I.412, 417; II.39
3:3	I.214	12:29	II.288	21:8–9	I.417
3:4	I.214	12:37	I.379	21:8	I.123, 417; II.39
3:8	I.29	12:38	I.674	21:9	II.39
3:10–12	I.27; II.38	13:1–2	I.268	21:10	I.417
3:10	I.27	13:3	II.241	21:15	I.651
3:11	I.27, 28, 307	13:5	I.350	21:16	I.651
3:12	I.25, 27, 29, 30, 31, 35, 97; II.38	13:14	II.241	21:17	I.651
		14:24	II.428	22:1	I.56, 103, 110; II.39
3:14	II.38, 304	14:28	II.321		
3:16	II.180	14:31	I.333	22:3	I.92
4:1–31	I.30	15:1–21	II.38	22:15	I.552, 553; II.39
4:1–19	I.31	15:1–18	I.328; II.54	22:20–21	II.59
4:6	I.462	15:1	I.16	22:20	I.243, 580, 582
4:10	I.28, 29, 34; II.38	15:4–10	I.526	22:21	I.243
4:11–12	I.30	15:4	II.332	22:22	I.425

473

474

477

480

2:23–25	I.109; II.79		526, 541, 637,	2:37	I.57, 110, 132,
2:23–24	I.114, 280		638, 678; II.4, 47,		151, 170
2:23	I.65, 66, 74, 77,		56, 194, 284	3:1–4:4	I.117, 464
	89, 96, 102, 103,	2:29–37	I.3, 413; II.19, 20	3:1–25	I.58, 127; II.156
	104, 108, 109,	2:29–32	I.108; II.18	3:1–5	I.57, 58, 72, 98,
	110, 113, 119,	2:29	I.111, 119, 131,		117, 119; II.20, 45
	123, 131, 149,		220, 375	3:1–2	I.2, 3, 23, 67, 114,
	169, 178, 181,	2:30–31	II.54, 56		120, 628; II.19, 27
	240, 241, 243,	2:30	I.50, 96, 153, 170,	3:1	I.66, 72, 75, 85,
	268, 275, 276,		177, 179, 233,		115, 116, 117,
	277, 279, 281,		263, 388, 438,		118, 119, 122,
	308, 330, 413,		524; II.54, 175,		123, 131, 160,
	417, 577, 578;		219, 321		173, 244, 292,
	II.71, 78, 139,	2:31	I.87, 107, 124,		300, 369, 417,
	200, 347, 350, 416		131, 266, 434,		427, 464, 595,
2:24–25	I.131		438, 451, 461,		602, 627, 631,
2:24	I.99, 108, 109,		462, 464, 609,		652; II.15, 53, 56,
	156, 167, 180,		611, 639; II.45,		57, 75, 78, 194,
	280, 432, 434,		54, 195, 367		219
	550, 557, 635;	2:32	I.66, 83, 91, 107,	3:2–3	I.6; II.78
	II.46, 75, 78		123, 131, 170,	3:2	I.72, 116, 123,
2:25	I.101, 103, 104,		265, 413, 416,		131, 156, 199,
	108, 109, 110,		469, 522, 524,		388, 413, 416,
	120, 131, 149,		643; II.55, 56, 77,		432; II.18
	170, 191, 206,		87, 186, 424	3:3	I.177, 197, 211,
	413, 417, 517;	2:33–37	I.478; II.18, 29		217, 439; II.18,
	II.45, 55, 56, 71,	2:33–36	I.83		20, 77, 187, 191,
	88, 139, 188, 350	2:33	I.51, 52, 58, 66,		404
2:26–28	I.6, 131, 260, 276,		109, 110, 111,	3:4–5	I.2, 3, 23, 65, 67,
	330, 505; II.18,		116, 123, 131,		76, 120, 121;
	20, 21		142, 170, 230,		II.19, 27
2:26–27	II.88, 299		241, 329, 413,	3:4	I.23, 25, 52, 58,
2:26	I.23, 61, 65, 77,		415; II.154, 316,		72, 121, 122, 126,
	105, 111, 115,		393		131, 142, 173,
	198, 217, 256,	2:34	I.97, 99, 103, 106,		372, 579, 601;
	276, 283, 313,		110, 141, 171,		II.18, 139, 154
	389, 404, 436,		193, 198, 243,	3:5	I.xii, 51, 52, 56,
	484, 506, 672,		414, 439, 523,		86, 119, 142, 193,
	678; II.39, 219,		540, 558, 597,		279, 412, 461;
	333, 361, 380		627, 628; II.39,		II.88, 128, 154,
2:27–28	I.157, 326, 328,		107, 143, 345		182
	354, 438, 578;	2:35	I.126, 131, 154,	3:6–11	I.118; II.15, 18,
	II.55, 56, 65		368, 535, 549,		24, 82, 228
2:27	I.54, 72, 103, 105,		567, 577, 635,	3:6	I.xii; II.57, 229
	108, 116, 208,		676, 680; II.71	3:7	I.58, 122
	260, 262, 276,	2:36–37	I.131, 411, 413,	3:8–9	I.628
	441, 487, 505,		416; II.42, 80	3:8	I.58, 180, 245,
	517, 522, 526;	2:36	I.3, 66, 93, 100,		300, 627; II.140
	II.55, 56, 139,		103, 115, 123,	3:9	I.245, 264, 416,
	207, 348, 354		131, 240, 243,		530, 628; II.177
2:28	I.72, 86, 105, 107,		389, 442, 503,	3:10	I.659
	245, 254, 260,		545, 601, 603;	3:11	I.630, 632
	276, 237, 354,		II.26, 46, 191,	3:12–4:2	I.66
	413, 442, 456,		352, 380	3:12–15	I.3, 32, 514; II.20
	474, 521, 524,			3:12–14	I.72; II.16, 88

	225, 303, 304, 305, 323, 343, 386, 387, 520, 521, 525, 577, 584, 679, 681; II.10, 78, 106, 172, 347, 354, 418		519, 523, 627; II.17, 143, 345	4:19–21	I.137, 160, 163, 164, 172, 285, 290, 533, 625; II.167
4:13–18		I.3, 24, 132, 134, 135, 136, 146, 172, 204, 205, 209; II.17, 18, 19, 29, 80, 255, 318	4:19–20	I.146, 292, 340; II.17
4:8	I.66, 110, 130, 132, 133, 137, 146, 147, 149, 152, 153, 157, 166, 219, 220, 226, 265, 304, 305, 311, 312, 437, 587, 601, 625, 635, 681; II.17, 75, 90, 187, 336, 350, 351, 363, 367, 368, 388, 409	4:13	I.43, 126, 134, 146, 154, 157, 158, 162, 168, 171, 204, 207, 224, 226, 289, 290, 292, 311, 312, 313, 342, 437, 450; II.17, 18, 51, 53, 74, 88, 171, 187, 310, 338, 347, 349, 351, 354	4:19	I.66, 126, 145, 146, 160, 161, 162, 163, 171, 173, 177, 196, 197, 208, 460, 562, 565, 625; II.17, 77, 192, 367, 403, 419
				4:20–21	II.187
		4:14	I.3, 4, 67, 132, 134, 146, 158, 160, 170, 172, 204, 205, 207, 209, 222, 226, 302, 406, 486, 495, 619; II.16, 17, 48, 59, 69, 74, 79, 165, 194, 339	4:20	I.66, 133, 136, 149, 153, 157, 161, 163, 185, 226, 339, 340, 342, 514, 516, 532; II.75, 82, 83, 171, 176, 349, 385, 405, 409
4:9–12	I.5, 135, 146, 172, 429; II.17, 18, 20, 30				
4:9–10	I.146, 428; II.17			4:21	I.126, 153, 161, 164, 214, 294, 625; II.339
4:9	I.45, 54, 86, 103, 140, 143, 146, 156, 161, 166, 263, 271, 681; II.17, 49, 59, 105, 173, 353, 387			4:22	I.xii, 56, 92, 109, 137, 149, 162, 172, 195, 196, 229, 241, 281, 299, 300, 301, 318, 329, 343, 388, 402, 415; II.70, 75, 77, 165
		4:15–17	I.146		
		4:15–16	I.289, 292		
4:10	I.5, 34, 124, 135, 141, 146, 156, 160, 216, 217, 222, 273, 292, 329, 396, 397, 426, 435, 517, 528, 531, 552, 634, 635; II.17, 43, 73, 75, 79, 138, 141, 216, 434	4:15	I.66, 137, 146, 159, 163, 290, 441; II.26, 75, 171, 184, 418	
		4:16–17	I.204, 388	4:23–28	I.146, 164, 256, 285, 315, 378, 428; II.207, 218, 223
		4:16	I.66, 159, 188, 356, 413, 663, 668; II.26, 75, 173, 176, 184, 402		
		4:17	I.134, 146, 159, 160, 206, 386, 388, 523, 659; II.47, 405, 421	4:23–26	I.6, 165, 172, 437, 544, 634; II.36, 47, 78, 195, 224, 404
4:11–12	I.5, 43, 135, 146, 198, 416, 428, 519; II.47				
4:11	I.59, 113, 114, 146, 154, 171, 187, 217, 273, 293, 300, 301, 388, 396, 397, 441, 526, 634, 636; II.17, 51, 152, 170, 321, 421, 428	4:18	I.96, 113, 137, 161, 182, 241, 244, 288, 290, 292, 372, 413, 487, 494, 496, 595, 601, 631; II.75, 83, 84, 219, 409	4:23	I.91, 165, 166, 167, 168, 261, 525; II.36, 420
				4:24–25	II.79
				4:24	I.164, 166, 292, 379; II.52, 378
		4:19–28	I.6, 135, 146, 172, 429; II.17, 18, 20, 30	4:25–26	I.146
4:12	I.22, 40, 56, 146, 161, 172, 193, 387, 414, 439,			4:25	I.166, 167, 281, 305; II.36, 218
		4:19–22	I.146, 428	4:26	I.51, 87, 146, 154, 167, 168, 302, 303, 384, 389,

23:32	I.577, 643, 645; II.82
23:33–40	I.649–50
23:33	I.190, 266, 652; II.82, 84
23:34–40	I.81, 190, 652, 655; II.24
23:34–38	I.xii
23:34	I.182, 647, 651
23:35	I.648, 652, 667; II.237
23:36	I.333, 414, 554, 648; II.192
23:37	I.651
23:38	I.187, 648, 652
23:39	I.266; II.278
23:40	I.284, 624, 654; II.181
24:1–10	I.31, 233; II.22, 32, 47, 80, 135, 137, 142
24:1–3	I.396
24:1	I.242, 355, 605; II.128, 132, 138
24:3	I.31; II.142
24:4–7	II.135
24:5–7	II.139
24:5	I.655, 659; II.128, 143
24:6	I.21; II.45, 163, 169, 183, 308
24:7	I.81, 118; II.15, 59, 165, 208
24:8–10	II.135
24:8	I.619, 655, 658; II.136, 142
24:9	I.421, 452, 622, 655; II.62, 104, 134, 142, 143, 218, 307
24:10	I.652, 655; II.121, 122, 142
25:1–14	I.581, 670; II.19
25:1–13	II.14, 20, 21, 23
25:1–11	II.2, 11
25:1–7	I.238; II.18, 19, 20, 29
25:1	I.662, 663; II.7, 210, 213, 308
25:2	II.323
25:3–5	I.662
25:4	I.258, 262; II.104, 134, 245
25:5–7	I.237
25:5	I.237, 241, 243, 516, 581, 622, 652; II.15, 23, 80, 89, 208
25:6	I.663, 676
25:7	I.662
25:8	I.238
25:9	I.22, 523, 581, 652, 659, 663, 672; II.8, 88, 115, 125, 234, 371, 418, 421
25:10	I.270, 469; II.19, 95, 177, 442
25:11	I.159, 581, 659, 663, 669, 672; II.89, 90, 125, 139, 141, 173
25:12	I.652, 663, 681; II.115, 121
25:13	I.350, 354; II.1, 5, 12, 23, 140, 315
25:14	I.585, 595, 663; II.121, 312, 313
25:15–38	I.662, 664, 665, 679; II.5, 14
25:15–29	I.541, 679; II.5, 313
25:15–17	I.402, 675; II.24
25:15	I.35, 404, 674; II.40, 352, 376, 394, 422
25:16	I.674, 675; II.404, 420, 422
25:17	I.404, 541, 674
25:18–21	I.671
25:18	I.452, 523, 581, 659, 660, 675; II.245
25:19–26	II.313, 379
25:19	I.674
25:20–22	II.120
25:20	II.420
25:21–22	I.671
25:21	I.670
25:23	I.319; II.375
25:24	I.674; II.382, 386
25:25–26	II.423, 427
25:25	II.7, 387, 388, 389, 394
25:26	I.310; II.7
25:27–29	I.402; II.24, 429
25:27	I.278, 674
25:28–29	II.371
25:28	I.404; II.404
25:29	I.245, 674, 679; II.376
25:30–38	II.24, 388
25:30–37	I.384, 385
25:30	I.385, 579, 672, 680, 681; II.44, 185, 378, 405, 423
25:31	I.374, 385, 388, 680, 681; II.46, 207, 330
25:32	I.224
25:33	I.29, 310, 384, 388, 680
25:34–36	I.680
25:34	I.226, 680, 681; II.179, 338
25:35	I.677
25:36–37	I.385
25:36	I.343, 681
25:37	I.291, 384, 678; II.380, 388
25:38	I.153; II.388, 403
26:1—45:5	II.5
26:1—36:32	II.24, 126, 137, 206
26:1—35:19	II.14, 23
26:1—29:32	II.2, 11
26:1–24	I.239, 266, 375, 536, 537, 538, 539, 582; II.4, 11, 13, 16, 23, 254, 282
26:1–6	II.11
26:1–4	II.81
26:1–2	I.226
26:1	I.3, 240, 537, 668; II.26, 28, 112, 115, 117, 124, 251, 389
26:2–3	I.239
26:2	I.3, 235, 241; II.105
26:3	I.134, 571, 666; II.15, 23, 89, 107, 108, 254, 255
26:4	I.237, 240, 306, 307, 666; II.65, 100, 103, 105, 107, 216, 304
26:5	I.238, 262, 665, 666, 667
26:6	I.16, 81, 236, 237, 238, 240, 247, 659, 666; II.28,

28:17	I.8, 361, 551; II.4, 9, 20, 33, 125	29:24–25	II.7, 9, 134, 136, 146	30:11	I.6, 26, 67, 144, 167, 183, 190, 308, 622; II.39, 89, 173, 218, 325
29:1–32	II.11, 13, 23, 147, 156	29:24	II.136, 137		
		29:25	I.570; II.22, 136, 140, 145, 287, 438	30:12–15	I.2; II.27, 48, 173, 176, 310, 406
29:1–23	I.7, 330; II.22, 32, 80, 81, 145, 146	29:26	I.381, 472, 542; II.109, 141, 145	30:12	I.208, 342, 495
29:1–13	II.435	29:27	I.371; II.146	30:13	I.199, 342 318, 322, 420
29:1	II.114, 132, 270	29:28	I.666; II.23, 71, 80, 136, 147, 161, 183, 212, 431	30:14–15	II.171
29:2	I.409, 654, 657; II.128, 134, 289, 443			30:14	I.170, 179, 197, 602; II.176
29:3	II.32, 114, 132, 134, 269, 434	29:29–32	II.282	30:15	I.126, 179, 195, 197, 208, 289, 414, 439, 495; II.44, 49, 75, 150, 151, 183, 405, 416, 418
		29:29	II.114, 140, 145, 147, 438		
29:4–23	I.657	29:30–32	II.283		
29:4	II.270	29:30	II.136, 240		
29:5	II.23, 88, 146, 147, 161, 183	29:31	II.23, 129, 136, 137, 145, 146		
29:6	I.344; II.37, 178	29:32	I.182; II.136	30:16–17	I.9; II.34, 367, 406, 418
29:7	I.10, 252, 391; II.35, 141, 142, 431	30:1—33:13	II.22		
		30:1—31:40	I.2, 24, 32, 37, 63, 514, 617; II.11, 12, 16, 47, 135, 147, 206, 211, 220, 248	30:16	I.390, 531, 602; II.40, 182, 190, 367, 403, 417
29:8	II.113				
29:9	I.375; II.23, 133, 134			30:17	I.233; II.389, 404
29:10	I.663, 665; II.89, 115, 133, 146, 147, 228, 401	30:1–24	II.10	30:18–21	I.2; II.27, 72, 79, 171, 172, 179
		30:1–3	I.15, 253; II.22		
		30:1	I.241; II.240	30:18	I.463; II.22, 142, 172, 180, 182, 192, 368
29:11	I.658; II.188	30:2–4	I.9; II.34		
29:12–14	II.141, 176	30:2	II.414, 434		
29:13	I.81, 118; II.59	30:3	I.617, 652; II.136, 142, 147, 353	30:19	I.144, 344, 459; II.183, 224
29:14	I.622; II.22, 46, 136, 146, 171, 196, 218, 219, 307, 364, 387, 389	30:4	I.15; II.22	30:20	I.182, 549; II.152, 155, 183, 189
		30:5–7	I.2, 220; II.22, 27, 173, 174, 180, 192, 353, 410, 427	30:21	II.62, 75, 152, 179, 183
29:15	II.143				
29:16–20	I.657; II.141	30:5	I.66; II.52	30:22	I.659
29:16	I.238; II.133	30:6–7	II.52	30:23	I.130, 633; II.335
29:17	I.201, 657, 660; II.134	30:6	I.98, 417, 498; II.44, 192, 195, 316, 318, 320, 373, 404, 407, 409, 420	30:24	I.110, 633
				31:1–40	I.80
29:18	I.421, 523, 622, 659, 660, 663; II.62, 90, 91, 92, 133, 218, 301			31:1	I.2, 23, 63, 659; II.22, 27, 152, 155, 176, 179, 185, 208
		30:7	I.67, 323, 454, 619; II.150		
29:19	I.262, 665, 666; II.416	30:8–9	II.24	31:2–9	II.22
		30:8	I.97, 191, 595	31:2–6	I.2; II.27, 179
29:20–21	II.233	30:10–21	II.22	31:2–3	II.46, 183
29:20	II.270	30:10–11	I.9, 29, 326; II.7, 34, 87, 172, 324, 326, 328, 333	31:2	II.54, 56, 76, 183, 185, 418, 420
29:21–22	II.146				
29:21	I.375; II.114, 132, 134, 269			31:3–4	II.180
29:22	II.90, 134, 143	30:10	I.40, 44, 67, 619; II.50, 150, 172, 190, 324, 325, 339, 347, 354, 380	31:3	I.83; II.75, 78, 171, 177, 180, 184, 191, 408
29:23	I.555				
29:24–32	I.7, 282; II.22, 32, 81, 84, 135, 137, 212			31:4–6	II.79, 177
				31:4–5	II.44, 180

32:32	I.667; II.261	34:1–5	I.656	35:15	I.262, 516, 652, 665, 666; II.9, 15
32:33	I.107, 253, 595, 665, 666; II.348	34:1	I.571; II.240	35:16	II.245, 248
32:34	I.245, 675	34:2–3	II.210	35:17	I.236, 238, 258, 356; II.388
32:35	I.264; II.368	34:2	I.81; II.205, 232, 265	35:18–19	II.7
32:36	I.273; II.206, 218, 222, 224	34:3–5	I.570	35:18	II.248
32:37	I.569, 572; II.63, 133	34:3	II.210, 213, 267, 292	35:19	II.228
32:38–40	II.86, 205	34:4	II.128	36:1—45:5	II.2, 23
32:38	I.659	34:5	I.592, 598; II.23, 233	36:1—44:30	II.11, 14
32:39	I.658	34:6	II.232	36:1—37:2	II.11
32:40	II.15, 59	34:7	II.232	36:1–32	I.15, 24, 78, 369, 458; II.2, 12, 13, 14, 16, 23, 103, 106, 162, 257, 260, 261, 300, 308
32:41	I.81, 118; II.13, 63, 206	34:8–22	II.2, 11, 23, 234, 287		
32:42	I.273; II.40, 205, 218	34:8	II.78, 203, 233, 237, 243	36:1–8	I.3; II.16, 255, 309
32:43	II.205, 218, 222, 224	34:9	I.404, 595	36:1–4	II.13
32:44	I.510; II.22, 203, 204, 218	34:10	I.595; II.78, 237, 241	36:1–2	I.370; II.308
33:1–26	II.224	34:11	II.237	36:1	I.4, 32, 133, 152, 226, 428, 664, 667; II.16, 23, 205, 256, 309
33:1–13	II.23, 230	34:13	I.353; II.78, 237, 243		
33:1–11	II.22	34:14	I.404, 665, 666	36:2–8	II.171
33:1	II.255	34:15	I.245, 675; II.15, 78, 237, 243	36:2–3	I.63, 133, 537; II.101
33:2	II.36	34:16	II.15, 237	36:2	I.63, 117, 666; II.16, 432
33:3	II.221	34:17	I.404, 421, 588, 660; II.62	36:3	I.3, 134, 514, 581, 666, 667; II.15, 16, 23, 89, 104, 106, 251, 255, 261
33:4	II.43, 224	34:18	I.588; II.78		
33:5	II.34	34:19	I.23, 45		
33:6	I.420; II.23, 392	34:20	II.62, 238	36:4–5	II.309
33:7	II.34, 80, 225, 230	34:21–22	II.234	36:4	II.16, 214, 215, 251, 255, 265, 432
33:10–11	II.225	34:21	I.619		
33:10	II.205, 207, 222	34:22	II.234, 238	36:5–6	II.256
33:11	I.270, 508; II.177, 222, 230	35:1–19	II.2, 11, 23, 31, 92	36:5	I.3, 226, 369, 370; II.29, 161
33:12	I.680; II.225	35:1–2	II.232	36:6–15	I.370
33:13	I.510	35:1	II.244	36:6–7	I.63
33:14–26	II.1, 8, 166, 248	35:2	I.81	36:6	I.63, 80, 427, 434; II.7, 29, 251
33:15–16	I.616	35:3–5	II.245	36:7	I.3, 666; II.15, 16, 23, 89, 106, 261
33:15	I.617	35:3	I.15; II.245, 248, 440		
33:16	I.619; II.53, 209	35:4	II.442	36:8	II.255, 256
33:17	II.228, 248	35:5	II.89, 244, 248	36:9–31	I.581
33:18	II.228, 248, 297, 344	35:7	I.310; II.23	36:9–26	I.176, 213
33:19	II.227	35:8	II.245	36:9–11	II.16, 29, 309, 434
33:20–21	II.166	35:9	II.245	36:9	I.4, 5, 66, 369, 427, 428, 434, 673; II.16, 18, 26, 29, 105, 252, 255
33:20	I.351; II.166, 227	35:10	II.245		
33:21	I.415; II.227	35:11	I.391, 555; II.354		
33:22	I.416	35:12	II.205, 251		
33:24	I.222; II.129	35:13	I.81, 107; II.245, 261		
33:25–26	II.166			36:10–32	II.81
33:25	II.166, 227	35:14	I.236, 665, 666; II.245	36:10–19	I.369
33:26	I.415; II.387			36:10–11	I.135
34:1–7	I.569, 570; II.2, 11, 23, 283				

507

511

12:3	II.429
13:9–10	II.95
14:8	II.431
14:10	I.673
16:19	I.673
17:4	I.673
18:1–24	II.95
18:2	II.95
18:3	II.95
18:4	II.95
18:6	I.673
18:8	I.440
18:21	II.95
18:22–23	II.95
18:22	I.668
21:1	II.429
21:5	I.415
22:18–19	II.104

d / Mesopotamian Texts

Gilgamesh
2.216	I.254
3.2.8	I.541

Enuma Êliš
4.139–40	I.196

Code of Hammurabi
25	II.143
110	II.143
157	II.143

Letters of Hammurabi
British Museum 12855
54–55	II.425

British Museum 23130
45–47	II.425

Rassam Cylinder
6.70–76	I.272
9.68–72	I.585

Istanbul Museum 7834
3.36	II.293
4.22	II.291

British Museum 21946
(Babylonian Chronicle)
obv. 11	I.668
obv. 18	II.256, 337
rev. 7	II.256
rev. 9–10	II.385
rev. 10	I.675
rev. 12	I.605
rev. 17	I.675
rev. 20	I.675
rev. 21–22	I.7; II.118

British Museum 98396
	II.169

e / Ugaritic Texts

2.1.37	I.333
2.1.43	II.200
3.3.25	I.354
3.3.35–39	II.429
4.1.39	I.87
4.5.123–27	I.314
4.8.9	I.503
4.8.11	I.443
5.5.10	I.628
5.6.11–14	I.409
5.8.8	I.407
5.8.9	I.407
5.8.12	I.407
5.8.19	I.407
14.12	I.618
14.76	I.541
14.80	I.541
14.147–48	I.313
14.295	I.313
15.1.17	I.600
16.1.25–26	I.291
16.1.26–28	I.294
16.5.48	II.363
16.6.6	II.363
16.6.49–50	I.243
17.2.14	I.564
17.5.8	I.243
17.6.45	I.578
18.4.20	I.626
18.4.21	I.626
18.4.31	I.626
18.4.32	I.626
19.1.32	I.626
19.3.120	II.363
23:10	II.200
23.33	I.488
23.34	I.488
23.35	I.488
24.33–34	I.597
35.50	I.541
49.5.5–6	I.59
49.6.34–35	I.59
1001.1.3	I.374
2048	I.331
2053	I.331
2096, 2097	II.357
UG5 7.36	II.357
10.1.5	II.357

f / Hebrew Non-literary Texts

Lachish Letters
2	II.138
4.3	II.259
4.10–13	II.235
4.10	I.205
6.6	II.289

Yavneh-Yam
1–14	II.158
5	II.219
6–7	II.219
14	I.433

papMur 42
42	II.139

g / Phoenician Inscriptions

Karatepe
A 1.3	I.597

Ešmun'azar
1–2	I.14
12	I.600

KAI, I, #16
1	I.618

KAI, I, #43
11	I.618

h / Deir 'Alla Inscriptions

1, comb. 1	II.121

i / Mesha Inscription (Moabite Stone)

7	II.359
10–11	II.368
11	II.361
12	II.361
13	II.359
17	II.357
19	II.359
20–21	II.359
20	II.359
24	II.361
30	II.359
31	II.359

j / Aramaic Non-literary Texts

Kilamuwa = Zinjirli
1.10–11	I.597

Irenaeus
    Adv. Haer.
      5.30.2   II.92
Augustine
    In epistolam Joannis ad Parthos
      7.8   I.163

p / Medieval Works

Thomas Aquinas
    Summa Theologica
      II.ii.162.5–8   I.400

q / English Literary Works

Shakespeare
    Ant. and Cleo.
      2.2.236   I.487
    Hamlet
      1.3.75–76   I.452
    Merch. Ven.
      1.3   I.344

2. Authors

Aalders, Gerhard C.
I.477

Abba, Raymond
II.229

Aberbach, D.
I.273, 275

Abrabanel, Isaac
I.6, 459, 520; II.107

Abramsky, Samuel
II.244, 246–47

Abrego, José María
II.250, 254

Ackerman, James S.
I.132

Ackroyd, Peter R.
I.321, 324, 618, 661;
II.80, 263, 453

Adinolfi, Marco
II.456

Aharoni, Yohanan
I.205, 396, 409, 487, 541,
594; II.292, 294

Aḥituv, S.
I.542

Ahlström, Gösta
I.300

Ahuis, Ferdinand
I.357

Aisleitner, Joseph
I.408; II.200

Aitchison, Leslie
I.227, 231

Aitken, Kenneth T.
II.390

Alberz, Rainer
I.47

Albright, William F.
I.16, 43, 89, 97, 267, 328,
333, 437, 519, 523; II.54,
358

Allen, Leslie C.
I.483

Alonso Schökel, Luis
I.5, 10, 19, 253, 440, 489,
497, 501; II.77, 254, 278,
280, 304, 455

Alt, Albrecht
I.16, 244; II.61

Althann, Robert
I.129, 139, 504; II.75

Altschuler, Jehiel H. ben
David
I.108, 255, 543

Amiran, David H. K.
II.331

Amiran, Ruth
I.39, 539; II.199, 225,
248

Ammassari, Antonio
II.264, 390

Andersen, Francis I.
II.449

Anderson, Bernhard W.
I.15, 272; II.149, 157

Andreasen, Niels-Erik A.
I.409, 508, 509

Andrew, Maurice E.
I.244, 245, 321

Arnold, Patrick M.
II.455

Astour, Michael C.
I.334 II.241, 380

Asurmendi Ruiz, Jesús M.
II.312

Audet, Jean-Paul
I.270

Augustin, F.
II.452

Auld, A. Graeme
II.453

Avigad, Naḥman
I.282; II.202, 260, 261,
291, 432, 434

Avishur, Yitshak
I.294

Avi-Yonah, Michael
II.199, 200, 291

Baab, Otto J.
I.122, 245

Babut, Jean-Marc
II.429

Bach, Robert
I.19, 132, 149, 150;
II.317, 318, 319, 372, 389

Bahr, Gordon J.
II.308

Bailey, Kenneth E.
I.48, 100, 101, 566

Baillet, Maurice
II.335, 346, 449

Baldwin, Joyce G.
I.616, 618; II.227

Balentine, Samuel E.
I.250; II.457

Balla, Emil
I.393

Baltzer, Klaus
I.18, 26, 30, 76, 353–54;
II.236

Baly, Denis
I.84, 87, 93, 114, 139,
156, 179, 186, 268, 293,
294, 335, 396, 492, 510,
523, 602, 636; II.235,
292, 294, 295, 364–65,
368, 374, 375

Bardtke, Hans
I.670, 677; II.66, 313,
316–17

Barnes, W. Emery
I.508

Barnett, Richard D.
I.115, 170, 314, 595

Barrick, W. Boyd
I.267, 510

Barrois, Augustin-Georges:
see Barrois, Georges A.

Barrois, Georges A.
I.92, 103, 198, 228, 268;
II.120, 123, 199, 200,
214, 292, 417, 426, 441

Barstad, Hans M.
I.466

Bartlett, David L.
II.149, 201

Barton, George W.
I.432

Batto, Bernard F.
II.378

Bauer, Hans
I.60, 114, 116, 122, 229,
284, 288, 334, 479;
II.151, 194, 400

Baumann, Arnulf
I.167; II.250, 451

Baumann, Eberhard
I.393

Baumgärtel, Friedrich
II.453

Baumgartner, Walter
I.128, 203, 269, 280, 324,
357, 372, 457, 500, 501,
548, 549, 554; II.64, 248,
460

Beck, Harrell F.
I.222

Beer, Georg
I.140

Begg, Christopher T.
II.202, 241

Begrich, Joachim
I.31, 259; II.103, 173

Behler, Gebhard-Maria
I.357, 445, 462

Behm, Johannes
I.168; II.95

Bekel, Heinrich
II.370

Ben-Dor, Immanuel
I.668

Ben-Dov, Meir
I.541

Bennett, Crystal-Margaret
II.374, 376, 377

Bentzen, Aage
I.358, 422; II.1

Bergman, A.
I.16

Bergman, Jan
II.121

Berlin, Adele
II.131, 141, 217

Bernhardt, Karl-Heinz
II.195

Berquist, Jon L.
II.73, 455

Berridge, John M.
I.3, 13, 19, 20, 27, 28, 29,
31, 32, 34, 35, 38, 44, 49,
75, 79, 88, 94, 139, 140,
150, 151, 153, 154, 155,
156, 158, 161, 164, 166,
173, 202, 205, 207, 210,
213, 218, 220, 226, 273,
276, 277, 278, 280, 287,
289, 296, 338, 344, 357,
359, 361, 362, 368, 376,
419, 420, 424, 426, 427,
436, 441, 445, 450, 457,
458, 460, 500, 501, 506,
547, 548, 552, 553, 554,
570. 572, 573, 607, 608,
611, 624, 625, 654; II.25,
44, 45, 58, 61, 64, 66,
148, 208, 264, 285, 452,
454, 456

Bertholet, Alfred
I.399

Bertram, Georg
I.107

Betz, Otto
II.216

Beuken, W. A. M.
I.418, 422, 427

485, 492, 500, 501, 502,
503, 505, 519, 520, 523,
524, 525, 532, 541, 553,
560, 578, 583, 591, 592,
597, 600, 603, 608, 626,
628, 635, 644, 673; II.66,
68, 69, 70, 75, 131, 148,
151, 162, 172, 174, 175,
176, 178, 179, 182, 188,
196, 330, 358, 363, 376,
390, 428

Daiches, Samuel
I.600

Dalglish, Edward R.
I.16; II.298

Dalman, Gustaf
I.268, 356; II.428

Daniels, Dwight R.
II.459

David, Martin
II.236

Davidson, Robert
I.321, 489; II.53, 451

Davies, G. Henton
I.267; II.183, 248

Davies, Paul E.
I.107

Davis, Paul R.
I.207

Day, John
I.234, 248

Dearman, J. Andrew
II.359

Deissler, Alfons
II.45, 456

Deist, Ferdinand E.
I.321, 322, 331; II.264

Delcor, Matthis
I.250

Delekat, Lienhard
II.339

Dentan, Robert C.
II.174, 185, 213

Dequeker, Luc
II.458

De Roche, Michael
I.47, 48, 163, 273, 284,
285, 670, 672

De Rossi, Giovanni B.
I.52, 60, 112, 143, 173,
251, 348, 446

Dever, William G.
I.491; II.359

Devescovi, Urbano
II.149, 455

De Vries, Simon J.
I.1, 353; II.103, 126

Diamond, A. R. Pete
II.7, 460

Dietrich, Ernst L.
I.142

Dietrich, Manfred
II.418

Dijkstra, Meindert
II.145

Di Lella, Alexander A.
I.96

Dimant, Devorah
II.390

Diringer, David
II.264

Dommershausen, Werner
II.458

Dorn, Louis
II.457

Dresden, Mark J.
I.675; II.388, 423

Driver, Godfrey R.
I.221, 226, 227, 280, 302,
338, 362, 381, 396, 519,
575, 651, 657, 681; II.99,
100, 180, 270, 345, 360,
450

Driver, Samuel R.
I.207, 322, 341, 347, 355,
380, 615, 631; II.85

Duhm, Bernhard
I.14, 39, 43, 51, 53, 54,
56, 58, 59, 62, 80, 83,
102, 103, 106, 107, 113,
114, 116, 117, 122, 125,
126, 130, 140, 142, 144,
146, 155, 159, 169, 171,
177, 181, 187, 211, 228,
229, 236, 237, 247, 266,
269, 274, 278, 281, 282,
284, 292, 296, 297, 298,
303, 315, 324, 339, 348,
349, 363, 381, 384, 385,
390, 403, 405, 421, 423,
431, 437, 440, 447, 449,
453, 454, 458, 464, 478,
483, 495, 498, 504, 506,
508, 514, 520, 524, 527,
528, 534, 536, 549, 561,
569, 580, 581, 582, 591,
593, 596, 602, 607, 608,
617, 622, 626, 627, 637,
641, 643, 648, 649, 654,
655, 662, 663, 664, 674;

II.11, 12, 13, 14, 50, 105,
132, 135, 141, 150, 152,
153, 156, 163, 164, 183,
191, 205, 211, 217, 221,
222, 227, 228, 230, 234,
237, 242, 251, 252, 253,
258, 259, 260, 266, 267,
268, 272, 273, 274, 277,
280, 281, 286, 288, 290,
291, 300, 301, 305, 307,
308, 312, 323, 328, 334,
341, 343, 344, 366, 369,
370, 371, 372, 378, 385,
391, 393, 396, 397, 398,
399, 400, 401, 406, 424,
430, 433, 448

Duhon, Kathrene
I.429

Dumbrell, William J.
II.382, 384

Dus, Jan
I.241

Edelstein, Gershon
I.186

Efros, Israel
I.140

Ehrlich, Arnold B.
I.115, 145, 197, 215, 553,
651, 652, 678; II.101,
113, 266, 267, 315, 320,
371, 450

Ehrman, Albert
I.362

Eichhorn, Johann G.
I.214

Eichrodt, Walther
I.164, 168, 197, 223, 234,
353, 415, 471, 533, 571,
640; II.197

Eissfeldt, Otto
I.28, 43, 150, 256, 265,
267, 312, 328, 349, 350,
361, 422, 466, 479, 489,
492, 538, 541, 558, 573,
642; II.14, 40, 54, 66,
137, 219, 228, 230, 264,
286, 313, 315, 318, 328,
340, 349, 358, 390, 411,
431, 447, 450, 452, 455

Eldridge, Victor J.
II.457

Elliger, Karl
I.44, 113, 284, 328, 343,

433; II.52, 173, 185, 188,
420, 431

Elliott-Binns, Leonard E.
I.403; II.1, 448

Emerton, John A.
I.192, 218, 225, 383;
II.390

Eppstein, Victor
I.140, 164

Erbt, Wilhelm
II.308

Erlandsson, Seth
I.123

Erman, Adolf
II.319

Eusebius
II.355, 359, 361, 362

Everson, A. Joseph
I.164; II.315, 336

Ewald, Heinrich
I.54, 214, 246; II.328

Fabry, Heinz-Josef
I.555; II.93

Fackenheim, Emil L.
II.148

Farley, Fred A.
II.458

al-Fāsī, David ben-
Abraham
I.379, 395

Feigin, Samuel I.
II.264

Fensham, Frank Charles
I.153, 492; II.453

Feuillet, André
II.149, 182

Fichtner, Johannes
I.334

Field, Frederick
II.8, 449

Finkelstein, Israel
I.248

Fischer, Bonifatius
II.449

Fischer, Leopold
II.202

Fishbane, Michael A.
I.48, 112, 122, 140, 508,
547, 661, 664; II.53, 57

Fitzmyer, Joseph A.
I.xiv, 255, 542; II.142,
231, 243

Fleming, Daniel E.
II.104

Floss, Johannes Peter
I.97
Fohrer, Georg
I.234, 393, 394, 395, 418;
II.14, 19, 54, 56, 61, 148,
250, 312, 447, 450
Fontaine, Carole R.
I.317, 642; II.197
Forbes, A. Dean
II.449
Forbes, Robert J.
I.99, 227, 230, 231, 232,
353, 596; II.247, 258
Forshey, Harold O.
I.88, 385
Fournel, A.
II.456
Fowler, Mervyn D.
I.267
Fox, Michael V.
I.48, 82, 382
Frankena, R.
I.179
Frankfort, Henri
I.443
Freedman, David N.
I.107, 123, 158, 288, 563,
616; II.41, 54, 116, 217
Freedman, Harry
I.207, 251, 430, 463, 515;
II.107, 218, 448
Freifelder, F.
II.9
Frerichs, Wendell W.
II.331
Fretheim, Terence E.
II.460
Freytag, Georg W.
I.626; II.428
Frick, Frank S.
I.44; II.244, 247, 368
Friedman, Richard E.
I.162, 466
Fritsch, Charles T.
II.449
Frost, Stanley Brice
I.10, 469; II.35
Füglister, Notker
II.450
Funk, Robert W.
I.232, 668

Gailey, James H., Jr.
I.139

Gale, Noël H.
I.228
Gall, August G. E. K. von
II.264, 302
Galling, Kurt
I.294, 487, 572; II.120,
250, 417, 441
García López, Félix
II.459
García-Moreno, Antonio
I.18
Gardiner, Alan H.
II.333
Garner, Gordon
I.248
Gaster, Theodor H.
I.192, 194, 196, 503;
II.329, 421, 429
Gataker, Thomas
I.431
Gaudefroy-Demombynes,
Maurice
II.128
Gehman, Henry S.
I.647, 650
Gelb, Ignace J.
II.427
Gelin, Albert
II.447
Gemser, Berend
I.47, 73, 75, 86, 90, 96,
199, 413, 452
Gerlach, Monica
II.148
Gerstenberger, Erhard
I.445; II.169
Gese, Hartmut
I.431
Gesenius, Wilhelm
I.626
Gevirtz, Stanley
I.287, 294, 644
Gibson, John C. L.
I.334; II.121, 200, 289
Giesebrecht, Friedrich
I.22, 39, 51, 54, 56, 58,
61, 85, 100, 101, 106,
113, 114, 116, 123, 126,
130, 140, 142, 144, 155,
177, 181, 210, 214, 218,
222, 230, 236, 237, 247,
249, 274, 278, 281, 283,
284, 292, 293, 297, 298,
299, 303, 305, 309, 315,
318, 322, 323, 326, 336,

338, 339, 342, 348, 349,
363, 378, 381, 401, 403,
421, 422, 431, 433, 436,
440, 446, 447, 458, 463,
483, 492, 498, 504, 506,
510, 515, 520, 525, 527,
528, 531, 536, 549, 560,
565, 569, 570, 605, 607,
617, 622, 626, 627, 631,
638, 641, 651, 662, 663,
664; II.3, 13, 26, 102,
116, 131, 132, 135, 163,
183, 188, 191, 192, 193,
194, 199, 215, 218, 228,
232, 238, 241, 242, 251,
252, 253, 258, 260, 266,
267, 268, 272, 274, 275,
277, 280, 287, 290, 300,
301, 307, 308, 309, 312,
323, 329, 334, 344, 369,
370, 372, 375, 378, 391,
392, 393, 396, 397, 399,
399, 400, 401, 406, 430,
433, 440, 448
Gilbert, Maurice
II.456
Gilula, M.
I.19
Ginsberg, Harold Louis
I.313, 314
Ginsburg, Christian D.
I.50, 57; II.400
Girard, L. Saint-Paul
I.677; II.323, 390
Gitin, Seymour
II.425
Glück, J. J.
I.86
Glueck, Nelson
I.48; II.355, 356, 357,
359, 362, 374
Gold, Victor R.
II.235, 292, 324, 374, 376
Goldbaum, Frederick J.,
I.124
Goldenberg, Robert
II.124
Goldman, M. D.
I.466, 469; II.455
Goldstein, Jonathan A.
II.91
Good, Edwin M.
I.150, 403, 487; II.76,
139, 426

Goodspeed, Edgar J.
I.430
Gordis, Robert
I.8, 454, 519
Gordon, Cyrus H.
I.331, 333, 408, 437, 486;
II.181, 319
Gordon, R. P.
I.251
Gordon, T. Crouther
II.123, 450
Görg, Manfred
I.29, 235, 542; II.261,
264
Gosse, Bernard
II.432
Gottwald, Norman K.
I.132, 247; II.290
Gouders, Klaus
I.18, 19
Goulder, Michael D.
II.94
Gowan, Donald E.
I.188
Grabbe, Lester L.
II.90, 460
Graesser, Carl F.
I.103
Graetz, Heinrich
I.181
Graf, Karl H.
I.228, 255, 333, 403, 500,
510, 598; II.160, 177
Graham, J. N.
II.441
Granild, Sigurd
I.345; II.451
Grant, Elihu
I.15
Graupner, Axel
II.307
Gray, George B.
I.631
Gray, John
I.42, 57, 89, 130, 249,
250, 255, 267, 271, 335,
350, 440, 540, 585, 588,
594, 619, 659; II.41, 57,
62, 63, 64, 122, 123, 158,
199, 292, 293, 319, 357,
368, 377, 415, 425, 430,
439, 440, 442
Green, Alberto R.
II.315, 436

Greenberg, Moshe
I.128; II.82, 107, 214, 287

Greenfield, Jonas C.
I.90, 334; II.142, 336, 337, 338

Greenspahn, Frederick E.
II.434

Gressmann, Hugo
I.268, 404; II.447

Grimm, Karl
I.37

Groenewald, Evert P.
II.458

Grohman, Edward D.
II.355, 356, 359, 361, 362, 363

Grol, H. W. M. van
I.418, 422, 427

Groom, Nigel St. J.
I.222

Gross, Heinrich
II.456

Gross, Karl
II.456

Grossberg, Daniel
I.88

Grothe, Jonathan F.
II.227

Grotius, Hugo
I.542

Guilbert, Pierre
II.93

Guillaume, Alfred
I.20, 38, 261, 363; II.71

Gundry, Robert H.
II.94

Gunkel, Hermann
I.450, 628; II.170

Gunn, David M.
I.547, 549, 552

Gunneweg, Antonius H. J.
I.19, 45; II.131, 454, 460

Guthrie, Harvey H., Jr.
II.216, 255

Habel, Norman C.
I.18, 27, 403; II.86, 458

Hadey, Jean
I.234; II.99

Haldar, Alfred O.
I.83; II.292, 380, 381

Halpern, Baruch
I.241

Hamilton, Richard W.
I.15, 291; II.235, 289

Hamlin, E. John
II.426

Hamp, Vinzenz
II.383

Hanson, Paul D.
I.74, 164, 488, 649; II.88, 144, 229, 230, 450

Haran, Menaḥem
I.16, 49, 163, 241, 267; II.259, 434

Harden, Donald
I.333

Hare, Douglas R. A.
II.92

Har-El, Menashe
I.380

Harland, J. Penrose
II.356

Harper, William R.
I.91, 92; II.259

Harrelson, Walter J.
I.89; II.320

Harrington, Daniel J.
II.92

Harris, Scott L.
I.20

Harris, Zellig S.
I.164, 208, 593; II.457

Harrison, Roland K.
I.294

Hartberger, Birgit
II.390

Hartman, Geoffrey
I.547

Hartman, Louis F.
I.96

Harvey, Julien
I.47, 357; II.149

Hasek, Jaroslav
II.258

Hasel, Gerhard F.
II.236

Hatch, Edwin
I.258; II.233

Hauret, Charles
I.504

Hayward, C. T. Robert
II.10, 449

Healey, John F.
I.159

Heider, George C.
II.219, 220

Held, Moshe
I.44, 505

Hennessey, J. Basil
II.376

Henry, Marie-Louise
I.18

Herdner, Andrée
I.xii

Hermisson, Hans-Jürgen
I.408, 604; II.460

Herntrich, Volkmar
II.82

Herr, Larry G.
I.15, 541; II.109, 202, 214, 264, 296

Herrmann, Johannes
I.235, 242, 607, 609, 610

Herrmann, Siegfried
I.514; II.12, 447, 459, 460

Herrmann, Wolfram
I.639

Hertzberg, Hans W.
I.82, 250, 370; II.149, 454

Heschel, Abraham J.
I.137, 305, 389; II.450

Hestrin, Ruth
II.426

Hicks, R. Lansing
II.250, 259

Hidal, Sten
II.54

Hillers, Delbert R.
I.76, 95, 171, 179, 216, 220, 270, 292, 317, 426, 440, 468, 530, 541, 594; II.44, 84, 101, 149, 167, 318, 336, 349, 373, 410

Hirschberg, Haïm Z'ew
II.459

Hirschberg, Harris H.
I.255

Hitzig, Ferdinand
I.363, 374, 378, 396, 403, 422, 431, 446, 453, 455; II.105, 203, 215, 267, 273, 448

Hobbs, Trevor R.
I.48, 77, 205; II.57, 451, 456

Hoenig, Sidney B.
I.333

Höffken, Peter
II.312, 353

Hoffmann, Y.
I.48, 55, 106, 107

Hoffmeier, James K.
II.263, 287, 323, 328, 330

Hoffner, Harry A. §§25 I.85

Hoftijzer, Jacob
I.417, 440; II.121

Holladay, Catherine
I.460

Holladay, William L.
I.xi, 1, 3, 5, 6, 13, 19, 21, 25, 33, 44, 45, 46, 48, 56, 75, 78, 80, 84, 98, 100, 101, 117, 122, 127, 133, 139, 140, 141, 143, 163, 164, 713, 174, 185, 192, 195, 200, 202, 210, 216, 218, 222, 225, 227, 239, 252, 256, 276, 278, 287, 293, 304, 315, 316, 326, 332, 339, 358, 359, 362, 367, 371, 372, 376, 405, 418, 440, 442, 446, 449, 453, 458, 463, 466, 468, 477, 481, 483, 489, 490, 496, 516, 522, 523, 534, 536, 538, 543, 544, 547, 548, 549, 558, 562, 563, 613, 626, 632, 641, 642, 658; II.1, 9, 13, 15, 19, 27, 36, 37, 41, 43, 45, 46, 48, 57, 65, 66, 76, 82, 85, 86, 88, 89, 92, 93, 94, 103, 131, 142, 149, 164, 195, 196, 228, 241, 299, 349, 387, 414, 447, 450, 451, 452, 455, 456, 457, 458, 459

Holman, Jan
I.640

Holm-Nielsen, Svend
I.247, 248

Hölscher, Gustav
I.151; II.53, 451, 452

Holt, Else K.
II.99, 452, 460

Holtzclaw, Brooks
II.109, 338, 358, 359, 376

Honeycutt, Roy L.
II.450

Honeyman, A. M.
I.402, 492, 534, 590, 605

Hopper, Stanley R.
I.496; II.123

Kieser, O.
II.447
Kilian, Rudolf
I.18
King, Leonard W.
II.425, 431
Kislev, Mordechai
I.186
Kissane, Edward J.
I.322
Kittel, Gerhard
I.120
Kittel, Rudolf
I.325, 489
Kjaer, Hans
I.248
Klein, Ralph W.
I.613
Klijn, A. F. J.
II.91
Klopfenstein, Martin A.
I.103, 115, 275, 300
Knauf, Ernest
II.356
Knibb, Michael A.
II.110
Knight, Douglas A.
II.456
Knox, Ronald
I.162, 163, 430
Kob, Konrad
II.295
Koch, Klaus
I.30, 162, 220; II.102,
124, 282, 284
Köhler, Ludwig
I.48, 280, 294, 387, 397,
459, 469, 591; II.449
König, Eduard
I.108, 161, 195, 196, 213,
257, 314, 323, 405, 415,
445, 515, 542, 553, 561,
571, 605, 638; II.104,
122, 127, 128, 129, 143,
147, 171, 188, 192, 199,
274, 310, 320, 329, 343,
362, 400, 442
Kooij, G. van der
II.121
Kooy, Vernon H.
I.171; II.296
Kopf, Lothar
II.427
Kovacs, Brian W.
II.448

Kraft, Robert A.
II.91
Kramer, Samuel N.
I.28, 404; II.169
Krapf, Thomas
I.243
Krašovec, Jože
I.321, 326
Kraus, Hans-Joachim
I.18, 30, 84, 129, 223,
264, 371, 377, 379, 427,
433, 434, 489, 578, 584,
635; II.65, 66, 67, 68, 69,
70, 84, 239, 243, 255,
330, 451
Kremers, Heinz
II.13, 263, 282, 286
Kreuzer, Siegfried
II.459
Krinetzki, Leo
II.457
Kselman, John S.
I.88; II.177, 370, 371
Küchler, Friedrich
II.456
Kuenen, Abraham
I.536, 537; II.101
Kugel, James L.
I.xii, 86, 94
Kumaki, F. Kenro
I.140, 162, 338, 342
Kümmel, Werner Georg
II.94
Kuschke, Arnulf
II.340, 355, 356, 360
Kutsch, Ernst
I.316, 345, 548; II.334,
441

Laberge, Léo
II.461
Labuschagne, C. J.
I.112, 321, 328
Lackey, E. Dent
I.117
Lambdin, Thomas O.
I.94, 95, 415; II.302, 303,
321, 328, 329, 333
Lamon, Robert S.
II.332
Lamparter, Helmut
I.357
Lande, Irene
I.277

Landes, George M.
I.320; II.247, 343, 362,
367
Lane, Edward W.
I.460, 626; II.383
Lang, Bernhard
II.111
Langer, Birgit
II.457
Lapp, Nancy L.
II.440
Lasch, Richard
I.525
Lattey, Cuthbert
I.483
Lauha, Aarre
I.20, 43, 432
Laurentin, André
I.76
Leander, Pontus
I.60, 114, 116, 122, 229,
284, 288, 334, 479;
II.151, 194, 400
Leclercq, J.
I.357
Le Déaut, Roger
I.49
Lederman, Zvi
I.248
Leeuwen, Cornelis van
II.214
Lehmann, Manfred R.
II.200
Lemaire, André
II.250, 261, 264
Lemke, Werner E.
I.639, 661, 662; II.111,
112, 115, 149, 236, 264
Lempp, Walter
II.149
Leslie, Elmer A.
I.313
Levenson, Jon D.
I.547, 555; II.244
Levey, Samson H.
I.620
Lévi, Israel
I.387, 495, 644
Levin, Christoph
II.149, 454
Levine, Baruch A.
I.241
Levitan, Isidor S.
I.140

Levy, Abraham J.
I.345
Lewin, Ellen Davis
II.459
Lewis, Alkin
II.259
Lewis, C. S.
II.220
Lewy, Julius
I.668; II.236, 240
Liedke, Gerhard
II.105
Limburg, James
I.47, 73, 90
Lindars, Barnabas
II.149, 456
Lindblom, Johannes
I.20, 31, 38, 84, 107, 140,
150, 163, 167, 273, 282,
340, 353, 399, 489, 625,
643, 657, 673; II.71, 78,
123, 129, 213, 247, 456
Lipiński, Edouard
I.616, 617, 633, 634, 636;
II.149, 227, 232, 447
Lisowsky, Gerhard
I.520
Lloyd, Seton
II.426
Loewenclau, Ilse von
I.48, 106
Lohfink, Norbert
I.2, 4, 63, 427, 487; II.27,
57, 58, 61, 62, 63, 99,
148, 156, 157, 158, 171,
180, 183, 184, 186, 195,
250, 255, 263
Löhr, Max
II.85
Long, Burke O.
I.19, 31, 48, 76, 151, 190,
306, 401, 413, 426, 474,
585, 647, 649, 654, 656;
II.168, 264, 455
López de las Heras, L.
II.456
Loretz, Oswald
I.13, 227, 287, 466, 519;
II.104
Lovelace, Marc H.
I.128
Lowth, Robert
I.403
Luckenbill, Daniel D.
I.28, 181, 661, 669

Puukko, Antti F.
  I.345

Qimḥi, David
  I.15, 16, 40, 41, 59, 108,
  113, 117, 160, 180, 198,
  226, 247, 261, 263, 269,
  273, 276, 278, 281, 286,
  290, 292, 381, 432, 440,
  461, 497, 498, 520, 543,
  554, 556, 571, 588, 610,
  626, 637, 645, 650, 651;
  II.146, 185, 194, 287,
  375, 422, 427, 448
Qimḥi, Joseph
  I.16
Quell, Gottfried
  I.345
Quinn, Jerome D.
  II.334

Rabin, Chaim
  I.139, 159
Rad, Gerhard von
  I.88, 121, 155, 195, 223,
  246, 269, 289, 293, 317,
  336, 353, 357, 399, 426,
  440, 497, 530, 541, 547,
  553, 554, 573, 623, 640,
  659; II.45, 57, 61, 62, 63,
  167, 168, 197, 201, 208,
  216, 304, 305, 336, 450
Rainey, Anson F.
  II.377, 440
Raitt, Thomas M.
  I.48, 74, 654; II.284, 453,
  456, 458
Ramsey, George W.
  I.47, 73, 374
Rashi
  I.59, 100, 101, 102, 113,
  117, 122, 180, 201, 226,
  247, 261, 266, 278, 280,
  285, 288, 296, 381, 387,
  398, 415, 429, 440, 446,
  454, 461, 498, 515, 539,
  543, 554, 556, 561, 571,
  574, 610, 626, 645, 651,
  674; II.142, 144, 375,
  377, 422, 427, 442, 448
Rast, Walter E.
  I.250
Ratschow, Carl H.
  I.32

Redpath, Henry A.
  I.258; II.233
Reed, William L.
  I.104, 154, 293, 436, 487,
  598; II.225
Reedy, Gerard
  II.457
Reider, Joseph
  II.181
Reifenberg, Adolf
  I.541
Reimer, David J.
  II.390, 460
Renaud, Bernard
  I.13; II.150
Rendsburg, Gary
  I.471, 486
Rendtorff, Rolf
  I.35, 119; II.362, 453
Renfrew, Jane M.
  I.389
Reventlow, Henning Graf
  von
  I.19, 20, 31, 139, 150,
  234, 287, 289, 338, 358,
  359, 362, 418, 422, 426,
  445, 454, 457, 458, 460,
  500, 501, 567, 654; II.2,
  100, 111, 263, 264, 453,
  455
Reymond, Philippe
  I.257, 492; II.263, 422
Rhodes, Arnold B.
  I.250
Riaud, Jean
  II.91
Richardson, H. Neil
  I.99, 159, 415, 441, 668
Richter, Wolfgang
  I.19
Ridgeway, William
  I.486
Ridouard, André
  II.1, 72, 451
Riemann, Paul A.
  I.345
Riesener, Ingrid
  I.97
Rietzschel, Claus
  I.13, 133, 661, 664; II.14,
  16, 99, 137, 250, 254,
  309, 312, 313, 314, 451
Ringgren, Helmer
  I.117, 122, 334, 469, 603,
  673; II.196, 213

Roach, Corwin C.
  I.587
Robert, André
  I.345
Roberts, Bleddyn J.
  I.671, 675; II.6, 8, 9, 395,
  399
Roberts, Jimmy J. M.
  I.460; II.67, 460
Robertson, David A.
  II.54, 66
Robinson, H. Wheeler
  II.73, 457
Robinson, Stephen E.
  II.91
Robinson, Theodore H.
  I.139, 227, 352; II.12, 14,
  250, 390, 451, 452
Rose, Ashley S.
  II.168
Rosemüller, E. F. C.
  I.381
Rosenberg, Abraham J.
  II.448
Ross, James F.
  I.19, 30; II.357, 358
Rost, Leonhard
  II.454, 456
Roth, Wolfgang M. W.
  I.120; II.143
Rothkoff, Aaron
  II.458
Rothstein, Johann W.
  I.192, 247
Rowley, Harold H.
  I.261, 345, 362; II.452,
  454
Rowton, M. B.
  II.454
Rubinger, Naphtali J.
  II.131
Rudolph, Wilhelm
  I.4, 5, 8, 14, 15, 17, 21,
  22, 35, 43, 44, 49, 50, 51,
  53, 54, 55, 56, 57, 58, 59,
  61, 62, 63, 64, 65, 69, 70,
  71, 73, 78, 79, 80, 81, 84,
  85, 88, 93, 94, 96, 101,
  102, 104, 105, 106, 107,
  108, 112, 113, 114, 123,
  124, 125, 126, 129, 133,
  137, 140, 141, 142, 143,
  144, 145, 146, 147, 148,
  149, 150, 151, 152, 154,
  155, 156, 158, 159, 160,

161, 162, 166, 167, 168,
174, 177, 178, 180, 181,
183, 184, 185, 186, 187,
188, 190, 191, 192, 193,
194, 196, 197, 200, 201,
202, 203, 204, 205, 206,
207, 208, 210, 211, 212,
213, 214, 215, 218, 219,
220, 221, 222, 225, 226,
228, 229, 230, 235, 236,
237, 239, 240, 247, 255,
257, 258, 260, 261, 264,
268, 269, 274, 275, 276,
278, 279, 281, 282, 283,
284, 285, 288, 289, 290,
291, 292, 293, 294, 296,
297, 298, 299, 300, 303,
304, 307, 309, 310, 311,
312, 313, 314, 315, 317,
318, 319, 320, 322, 323,
324, 329, 331, 332, 335,
338, 339, 340, 342, 343,
347, 348, 349, 350, 353,
354, 355, 356, 363, 364,
368, 370, 371, 372, 376,
378, 381, 383, 384, 386,
387, 390, 391, 394, 398,
401, 403, 405, 409, 410,
411, 412, 414, 417, 420,
422, 424, 425, 427, 431,
433, 434, 435, 436, 437,
438, 441, 442, 446, 447,
448, 449, 453, 454, 455,
458, 461, 462, 463, 467,
468, 470, 474, 477, 478,
479, 480, 483, 489, 492,
494, 497, 498, 500, 504,
505, 506, 508, 509, 510,
512, 514, 515, 519, 520,
522, 523, 525, 527, 528,
531, 534, 535, 536, 537,
539, 542, 544, 549, 554,
555, 556, 561, 564, 565,
568, 569, 570, 571, 573,
575, 576, 577, 580, 586,
587, 588, 590, 591, 592,
593, 596, 600, 602, 603,
604, 605, 607, 608, 613,
617, 619, 622, 625, 626,
627, 631, 632, 635, 638,
639, 641, 642, 643, 647,
648, 651, 654, 655, 657,
659, 662, 663, 664, 665,
666, 669, 670, 671, 672,
674, 678, 680, 681; II.2,

Vogt, Ernst
I.13, 18, 39, 335, 661;
II.142, 337, 448, 454, 455
Volz, Paul
I.21, 22, 39, 43, 50, 51,
54, 55, 58, 59, 61, 62, 63,
64, 65, 79, 85, 88, 96,
100, 104, 106, 113, 115,
116, 123, 124, 125, 126,
140, 142, 144, 145, 146,
150, 154, 155, 156, 158,
161, 164, 166, 168, 169,
177, 179, 181, 183, 184,
185, 186, 187, 188, 191,
194, 202, 203, 210, 211,
212, 213, 216, 220, 221,
228, 230, 235, 236, 237,
247, 249, 254, 255, 256,
260, 273, 276, 278, 279,
281, 282, 283, 284, 285,
288, 290, 292, 293, 294,
296, 297, 298, 299, 300,
303, 304, 309, 310, 311,
313, 314, 315, 317, 318,
320, 322, 324, 335, 338,
339, 341, 346, 347, 348,
349, 353, 354, 355, 356,
363, 364, 376, 378, 379,
381, 383, 384, 386, 390,
391, 397, 401, 402, 403,
404, 411, 412, 414, 416,
420, 422, 423, 431, 436,
437, 440, 441, 442, 446,
447, 448, 453, 454, 461,
463, 467, 468, 470, 477,
478, 480, 483, 484, 485,
489, 494, 498, 504, 506,
510, 512, 515, 517, 520,
521, 522, 523, 527, 528,
535, 536, 537, 539, 542,
545, 548, 549, 561, 565,
569, 571, 574, 576, 577,
580, 587, 588, 591, 596,
605, 607, 611, 613, 614,
615, 617, 622, 626, 627,
635, 638, 641, 643, 645,
647, 648, 652, 654, 655,
659, 660, 663, 665; II.4,
17, 19, 102, 103, 105,
123, 124, 132, 133, 134,
135, 136, 137, 150, 151,
152, 153, 154, 155, 157,
158, 162, 163, 167, 171,
174, 175, 179, 180, 181,
183, 187, 188, 189, 191,

193, 199, 206, 207, 208,
209, 210, 216, 217, 221,
222, 223, 224, 225, 230,
232, 241, 242, 243, 244,
251, 252, 253, 255, 258,
260, 267, 268, 270, 273,
274, 275, 277, 278, 279,
280, 281, 282, 286, 287,
288, 290, 296, 298, 300,
301, 308, 309, 312, 316,
323, 324, 325, 328, 329,
332, 334, 340, 341, 342,
343, 344, 346, 355, 366,
368, 369, 370, 371, 372,
375, 376, 378, 379, 380,
384, 391, 392, 393, 394,
395, 396, 397, 398, 399,
400, 401, 402, 403, 406,
409, 416, 421, 428, 430,
433, 434, 436, 438, 440,
448, 450
Vööbus, Arthur
II.9
Vriezen, Theodorus C.
I.376; II.197

Wächter, Ludwig
I.534
Wagner, Siegfried
I.82
Waldman, Nahum M.
II.389
Walker, Norman
I.647
Wallenstein, Meir
I.560; II.238
Walter, Donald M.
II.449
Walton, Brian
I.430; II.449
Wambacq, Bernard N.
I.321; II.140, 221
Wang, Martin Cheng-chang
I.358; II.202, 453, 455
Wanke, Gunther
I.512, 534, 536, 537, 569;
II.13, 100, 102, 103, 105,
111, 117, 126, 131, 146,
251, 254, 263, 264, 268,
282, 286, 307, 310, 432,
452
Ward, James M.
II.110, 140, 216, 247,
257, 258

Ward, William H.
II.431
Watson, Wilfred G. E.
I.48, 68, 636
Weiger, Josef
II.1
Weil, Hermann M.
I.647
Weinfeld, Moshe
I.49, 118, 240, 246, 249,
251, 257, 261, 262, 264,
267, 345, 353, 384, 386,
397, 426, 476, 536, 541,
572, 573, 580, 621, 622,
652, 675; II.12, 53, 59,
85, 89, 104, 119, 150,
171, 185, 208, 228, 229,
230, 243, 248, 452, 454
Weippert, Helga
I.19, 199, 234, 235, 240,
243, 246, 256, 270, 415,
418, 424, 434, 440, 442,
512, 514, 517, 523, 567,
569, 570, 642, 643; II.4,
13, 40, 55, 58, 63, 74,
112, 118, 119, 142, 150,
203, 208, 218, 224, 236,
238, 242, 244, 246, 253,
308, 452, 453
Weiser, Artur
I.59, 106, 123, 140, 144,
275, 349, 390, 402, 406,
422, 443, 458, 480, 497,
498, 500, 506, 514, 568,
578, 598, 622, 664, 668;
II.14, 21, 102, 106, 108,
191, 196, 207, 208, 297,
307, 310, 314, 448
Weisman, Ze'eb
I.215
Weiss, Raphael
II.188
Welch, Adam C.
II.131, 451
Wellhausen, Julius
I.167, 281, 454; II.420
Wells, Roy D., Jr.
II.450, 454
Welten, Peter
I.358; II.453
Werblowsky, R. J. Zwi
I.641, 644, 645
Wernberg-Moller, Preben
I.343, 505, 647

Werner, Eric
II.182, 363
Wertime, Theodore A.
I.227
Westbrook, Raymond
II.57
Westermann, Claus
I.19, 30, 73, 74, 82, 89,
96, 165, 167, 183, 185,
307, 328, 333, 334, 342,
343, 385, 427, 437, 522,
538, 581, 587, 594, 604,
613, 626, 675; II.138,
146, 166, 173, 187, 217,
220, 281, 285, 310, 329,
358, 375, 451
Wevers, John W.
II.320, 424
Whitley, Charles F.
I.235, 661; II.454
Whybray, Roger N.
I.273, 282, 283; II.456
Wickwire, Chester L.
I.170, 595
Widengren, Geo
I.255, 669
Wieder, Arnold A.
II.458
Wiéner, Claude
I.48
Wiklander, Bertil
II.391
Wilcoxen, Jay A.
I.234; II.439
Wildberger, Hans
I.32, 74, 92, 109, 130,
150, 223, 269, 271, 280,
281, 302, 333, 398, 415,
416, 441, 447, 459, 575,
590, 619, 665, 675; II.19,
89, 147, 162, 166, 170,
174, 192, 200, 290, 292,
299, 319, 321, 329, 332,
337, 344, 348, 349, 352,
353, 356, 361, 362, 363,
385, 389, 405, 421, 426,
429, 430, 448, 454
Wilhelmi, Gerhard
I.346
Wilke, Fritz
I.43
Williams, Prescott H., Jr.
I.48; II.294, 453
Williams, Ronald J.
I.282; II.259, 357

In the design of the visual aspects of *Hermeneia*, consideration has been given to relating the form to the content by symbolic means.

The letters of the logotype *Hermeneia* are a fusion of forms alluding simultaneously to Hebrew (dotted vowel markings) and Greek (geometric round shapes) letter forms. In their modern treatment they remind us of the electronic age as well, the vantage point from which this investigation of the past begins.

The Lion of Judah used as visual identification for the series is based on the Seal of Shema. The version for *Hermeneia* is again a fusion of Hebrew calligraphic forms, especially the legs of the lion, and Greek elements characterized by the geometric. In the sequence of arcs, which can be understood as scroll-like images, the first is the lion's mouth. It is reasserted and accelerated in the whorl and returns in the aggressively arched tail: tradition is passed from one age to the next, rediscovered and re-formed.

"Who is worthy to open the scroll and break its seals. . . ."

Then one of the elders said to me

"weep not; lo, the Lion of the tribe of David,
the Root of David, has conquered,
so that he can open the scroll and
its seven seals."

Rev. 5:2, 5

To celebrate the signal achievement in biblical scholarship which *Hermeneia* represents, the entire series will by its color constitute a signal on the theologian's bookshelf: the Old Testament will be bound in yellow and the New Testament in red, traceable to a commonly used color coding for synagogue and church in medieval painting; in pure color terms, varying degrees of intensity of the warm segment of the color spectrum. The colors interpenetrate when the binding color for the Old Testament is used to imprint volumes from the New and vice versa.

Wherever possible, a photograph of the oldest extant manuscript, or a historically significant document pertaining to the biblical sources, will be displayed on the end papers of each volume to give a feel for the tangible reality and beauty of the source material.

The title-page motifs are expressive derivations from the *Hermeneia* logotype, repeated seven times to form a matrix and debossed on the cover of each volume. These sifted-out elements will be seen to be in their exact positions within the parent matrix. These motifs and their expressional character are noted on the following page.

Horizontal markings at gradated levels on the spine will assist in grouping the volumes according to these conventional categories.

The type has been set with unjustified right margins so as to preserve the internal consistency of word spacing. This is a major factor in both legibility and aesthetic quality; the resultant uneven line endings are only slight impairments to legibility by comparison. In this respect the type resembles the handwritten manuscripts where the quality of the calligraphic writing is dependent on establishing and holding to integral spacing patterns.

All of the type faces in common use today have been designed between A.D. 1500 and the present. For the biblical text a face was chosen which does not arbitrarily date the text, but rather one which is uncompromisingly modern and unembellished so that its feel is of the universal. The type style is Univers 65 by Adrian Frutiger.

The expository texts and footnotes are set in Baskerville, chosen for its compatibility with the many brief Greek and Hebrew insertions. The double-column format and the shorter line length facilitate speed reading and the wide margins to the left of footnotes provide for the scholar's own notations.

Kenneth Hiebert

542

Category of biblical writing,
key symbolic characteristic,
and volumes so identified.

1
Law
(boundaries described)
  Genesis
  Exodus
  Leviticus
  Numbers
  Deuteronomy

2
History
(trek through time and space)
  Joshua
  Judges
  Ruth
  1 Samuel
  2 Samuel
  1 Kings
  2 Kings
  1 Chronicles
  2 Chronicles
  Ezra
  Nehemiah
  Esther

3
Poetry
(lyric emotional expression)
  Job
  Psalms
  Proverbs
  Ecclesiastes
  Song of Songs

4
Prophets
(inspired seers)
  Isaiah
  Jeremiah
  Lamentations
  Ezekiel
  Daniel
  Hosea
  Joel
  Amos
  Obadiah
  Jonah
  Micah
  Nahum
  Habakkuk
  Zephaniah
  Haggai
  Zechariah
  Malachi

5
New Testament Narrative
(focus on One)
  Matthew
  Mark
  Luke
  John
  Acts

6
Epistles
(directed instruction)
  Romans
  1 Corinthians
  2 Corinthians
  Galatians
  Ephesians
  Philippians
  Colossians
  1 Thessalonians
  2 Thessalonians
  1 Timothy
  2 Timothy
  Titus
  Philemon
  Hebrews
  James
  1 Peter
  2 Peter
  1 John
  2 John
  3 John
  Jude

7
Apocalypse
(vision of the future)
  Revelation

8
Extracanonical Writings
(peripheral records)